P R O G R A M M I N G
WINDOWS™

PROGRAMMING
WINDOWS™

Microsoft
PRESS
®

Charles Petzold

PUBLISHED BY
Microsoft Press
A Division of Microsoft Corporation
One Microsoft Way
Redmond, Washington 98052-6399

Library of Congress Cataloging-in-Publication Data

Petzold, Charles, 1953–
   Programming Windows : the Microsoft guide to writing applications
for Windows 3 / Charles Petzold. -- 2nd ed.
      p.   cm.
   ISBN 1-55615-264-7
   1. IBM Personal computer--Programming. 2. Microsoft Windows
(Computer programs) I. Title.
QA76.8.I2594P474   1990
005.4'3--dc20   90-35467
                                      CIP

Printed and bound in the United States of America.

4 5 6 7 8 9 MLML 4 3 2 1

Distributed to the book trade in Canada by General Publishing Company, Ltd.

Distributed to the book trade outside the United States and Canada by Penguin Books Ltd.

Penguin Books Ltd., Harmondsworth, Middlesex, England
Penguin Books Australia Ltd., Ringwood, Victoria, Australia
Penguin Books N.Z. Ltd., 182-190 Wairau Road, Auckland 10, New Zealand

British Cataloging-in-Publication Data available

Project Editor: Jack Litewka
Technical Editor: Wm. Jeff Carey
Acquisitions Editor: Dean Holmes

Contents

Preface

When I began writing the first edition of PROGRAMMING WINDOWS in the early spring of 1987, Microsoft Windows 1.0 had been released for about a year and a half, a beta-test version of Windows 2.0 was just becoming available, and Windows 3.0 could only be regarded as a far-fetched dream. At that time, the eventual success of Windows in the personal computer marketplace was more a matter of faith than a certain-to-come reality.

With the release of Windows 3, more people than ever are interested in this operating environment. Windows 3 runs Windows programs in Intel 80286–compatible protected mode, giving Windows and Windows programs access to 16 megabytes of memory. This exciting enhancement to Windows—coupled with the many Windows applications released over the past few years—has made Windows 3 an important piece of systems software released for IBM-compatible personal computers. Windows is the graphical interface that many computer users will first encounter.

Since the publication of the first edition of PROGRAMMING WINDOWS in early 1988, many programmers have told me that the book has been useful in helping them learn how to write applications for Windows. Nothing could make me happier.

It was my intention with the first edition of PROGRAMMING WINDOWS to show the basics of writing programs for Windows using the C programming language. A book like this cannot delve into the complexities of a full-fledged application program, of course, but it can show how to handle all the various components of a Windows program. It is up to the application programmer to merge these components into a coherent whole.

In this second edition of PROGRAMMING WINDOWS, I have updated the text where necessary, updated the code listings for a more modern style of C programming, tightened the early chapters (where I felt I had been more theoretical than practical), and added two new chapters—one on Dynamic Data Exchange (DDE) and one on the Multiple Document Interface (MDI). Interestingly enough, the Windows application program interface has been fairly stable over the years and very few changes had to be made to the sample programs.

Windows has a reputation for being easy for users but tough for programmers. Often, aspiring Windows programmers face a steep learning curve, and they want to see lots of programming examples. To satisfy that desire, this book contains more than 50 complete programs. Many of them are short and stripped down to clearly illustrate various Windows programming techniques. Others are a bit longer to show how everything fits together. Several of the programs are useful utilities. Others are tools for exploring Windows.

What I don't do in this book is teach you how to use Windows. If you have no experience using the environment, now is the time to install it and play with it for awhile. Windows is very easy to learn.

Nor will I teach you how to program in C. Before you even think about programming for Windows, you should have a good working knowledge of programming in C for a more conventional environment such as MS-DOS. If your C is a little rusty, you may want to spend some time becoming better acquainted with the topics of structures and pointers.

A good familiarity with the segmented architecture of the Intel 8086 family of micro-processors will also help. If you know how 80286 addressing works (in both real mode and protected mode) and the difference between near and far pointers and functions, you're in good shape. If you don't, I've included some explanations along the way.

To compile the programs in this book and to write your own programs for Windows, you need the following software packages:

- Microsoft Windows 3

- Microsoft Windows Software Development Kit 3

- Microsoft C Professional Development System (aka Microsoft C 6)

If you haven't yet installed Microsoft C 6, you should know that the programs in the book require only the small-model MS-DOS libraries using the math emulator. You may be able to use a C compiler other than Microsoft's if the compiler is suitable for compiling Windows programs. Most other C compilers can't be used for this purpose.

To run Windows and the Windows Software Development Kit, you need the follow-ing hardware:

- An IBM personal computer (or compatible) based on the Intel 80286 or 80386 microprocessor with a hard disk and 640 KB of memory running MS-DOS 3.1 or later. An 80386-based machine with a couple megabytes of extended memory is ideal.

- A graphics display and video board, preferably compatible with the IBM VGA (Video Graphics Array) or better.

- A mouse. Although a mouse is generally optional for most Windows programs, some of the programs in this book require one.

Sometimes readers of computer books are curious about the author's own system. When I was writing the first edition of PROGRAMMING WINDOWS, I used an IBM PC/AT Model 339 (8 MHz) with two 30-megabyte (MB) hard disks, 512 KB of memory on the sys-tem board, and a 1.5 MB Intel Above Board PS/AT. The system included a Microsoft mouse, an IBM 256-KB Enhanced Graphics Adapter (EGA), and a NEC MultiSync monitor. I wrote the book using WordStar 3.3 and printed everything on an IBM 5152 Graphics Printer.

For the second edition, I used a 20-MHz IBM PS/2 Model 70 with a 120-MB hard disk, 6 MB of memory, an IBM 8514/A graphics board (although I generally ran Windows in VGA mode), a NEC MultiSync 4D monitor, and a Microsoft mouse. I used Microsoft Word for revising the book chapters, printing on a NEC SilentWriter LC-890 PostScript printer. (Word for Windows was not available until I was well into the revision.)

A book such as this could not have come about without help and encouragement from some very special people. I offer my heartfelt thanks with a handshake or hug (as appropriate) to the following people:

- To everyone at Microsoft involved in Windows 3, for creating a system with fascinating depth and seemingly endless things to learn.

- To all the Windows 3 developers who reviewed my chapters and offered comments and suggestions: Clark Cyr, David D'Souza, and particularly David Weise.

- To the MS Online System Support people in the Windows SDK group who reviewed galleys of the entire book: Much gratitude to Todd Cole, who volunteered his group and coordinated the effort; special thanks to John Hagerson, Mike Thurlkill, Dennis Crain, David Long, Ed Mills, Steve Molstad, Richard Herrmann, Dan Boone, and Kyle J. Sparks; thanks also to Jeff Stone, Dan Quigley, Steve Thompson, Larry Israel, Teresa Posakony, Neil Sandlin, Curt Palmer, David Flenniken, Charles E. Kindel Jr., and Doug Laundry.

- To everyone at Microsoft Press who has been involved in the first and second editions of PROGRAMMING WINDOWS, for behind-the-scenes work that makes all the difference in the world.

- To my friends and editors at *PC Magazine* and *Microsoft Systems Journal* for their help and encouragement over the years.

- To the readers of the first edition of PROGRAMMING WINDOWS who wanted to see a second edition. It's here and it's yours!

- To my family, who thought I was crazy when I quit my job to write full time: to my Mom, my brother Steve and his wife Bernie and Christopher and Michelle, my sister Sue and her husband Rich and Erika and another one on the way. You're right. I was crazy.

- To my friend Karen. Words cannot express....

- To my friends at the "DH" (and especially Devon and Leslie) for enjoyable company and interesting conversation that has nothing whatsoever to do with computers. Completing this book gets me closer to writing that novel!

- And most of all, as always, to Jan, who was as happy as I was when I called her and said, "I finally finished the chapter on DDE."

Charles Petzold
July 29, 1990

Special Offer

Companion Disks for
PROGRAMMING WINDOWS, 2nd ed.

Microsoft Press has created a set of timesaving Companion Disks for PROGRAMMING WINDOWS that include the more than 50 complete Windows programs provided in this book. Available in either 5 ¼-inch format (1.2-MB disk) or 3 ½-inch format (720-KB two-disk set), the Companion Disks contain both the source code and executable (EXE) files for all the book's programs. These include many useful utilities that let you explore and understand Windows' use of the keyboard, mouse, memory, graphics, color, and fonts. These Companion Disks are a valuable ready-to-use resource for Windows programmers. Order your set today!

Domestic Ordering Information:
To order, use the special reply card bound in the back of the book. If the card has already been used, please send $29.95, plus sales tax in the following states if applicable: AZ, CA, CO, CT, DC, FL, GA, ID, IL, IN, KY, ME, MD, MA, MI, MN, MO, NE, NV, NJ, NY, NC, OH, SC, TN, TX, VA, and WA. *Microsoft reserves the right to correct tax rates and/or collect the sales tax assessed by additional states as required by law, without notice.* Please add $5.50 per disk set for domestic postage and handling charges. Mail your order to: Microsoft Press, Attn: Companion Disk Offer, 21919 20th Ave SE, Box 3011, Bothell, WA 98041-3011. Specify 5 ¼-inch or 3 ½-inch format. Payment must be in U.S. funds. You may pay by check or money order (payable to Microsoft Press) or by American Express, VISA, or MasterCard; please include both your credit card number and the expiration date. Allow 2 – 3 weeks for delivery.

Foreign Ordering Information (except within the U.K.; see below):
Follow procedures for domestic ordering and add $6.00 per disk set for foreign postage and handling.

U.K. Ordering Information:
Send your order in writing along with £27.95 (includes VAT) to: Microsoft Press, 27 Wrights Lane, London W8 5TZ. You may pay by check or money order (payable to Microsoft Press) or by American Express, VISA, MasterCard, or Diners Club; please include both your credit card number and the expiration date. Specify 5 ¼-inch or 3 ½-inch format.

Microsoft Press Companion Disk Guarantee
If a disk is defective, a replacement disk will be sent. Please send the defective disk along with your packing slip (or copy) to: Microsoft Press, Consumer Sales, One Microsoft Way, Redmond, WA 98052-6399.

If you have questions or comments about the files on the disk, you can contact the author through MCI mail (CPETZOLD or 143-6815).

The Companion Disks for PROGRAMMING WINDOWS, 2nd ed.,
are available only from Microsoft Press.

SECTION I
GETTING STARTED

Chapter 1

Hello, Windows

Since its introduction in November 1985, Microsoft Windows has emerged as the most popular graphical user interface environment for MS-DOS. Several million copies of Windows have been shipped, and hundreds of Windows applications are currently available.

For the user, Windows provides a multitasking graphical-based windowing environment that runs programs especially designed for Windows. Such programs include Microsoft Excel (spreadsheet and business graphics), Microsoft Word for Windows (word processing), Aldus's PageMaker (desktop publishing), Samna's Ami (word processing), Micrografx's Designer (drawing), IBM's Current (a personal information manager), Asymetrix's ToolBook (a software construction kit), and many others. Programs written for Windows have a consistent appearance and command structure, and are thus often easier to learn and use than conventional MS-DOS programs. Users can easily switch among different Windows programs and exchange data between them. Windows also provides an easy-to-use icon-based Program Manager for running programs as well as a File Manager and Print Manager for file maintenance and printer-queue management.

Although Windows exists primarily to run applications especially written for the environment, Windows can also run many programs written for MS-DOS. Of course, these programs cannot take advantage of many Windows features, but in some cases they can be windowed and multitasked alongside Windows programs.

For the program developer, Windows provides a wealth of built-in routines that allow the use of menus, dialog boxes, scroll bars, and other components of a friendly user interface. Windows also contains an extensive graphics programming language that includes the use of formatted text in a variety of fonts. Programmers can treat the keyboard, mouse, video display, printer, system timer, and RS-232 communication ports in a device-independent manner. Windows programs run the same on a variety of hardware configurations.

The "look and feel" of Windows also shows up in the OS/2 Presentation Manager. OS/2 is the protected mode operating system developed by International Business Machines Corporation (IBM) and Microsoft Corporation as a successor to MS-DOS; the graphical user interface under OS/2 is called the Presentation Manager. While the application program interfaces of Windows and the OS/2 Presentation Manager are not the same, they have many similarities and common structural elements.

A BRIEF HISTORY OF WINDOWS

Windows was announced by Microsoft Corporation in November 1983 and released two years later in November 1985. Over the next two years, Windows 1.01 (the first released version) was followed by several updates to support the international market and to provide drivers for additional video displays and printers.

Windows 2.0 was released in November 1987. This version incorporated several changes to the user interface to make it consistent with the forthcoming OS/2 Presentation Manager (released in October 1988). The most significant of these changes involved the use of overlapping windows rather than the "tiled" windows found in the earlier versions of Windows. Windows 2.0 also included enhancements to the keyboard and mouse interface, particularly for menus and dialog boxes.

Windows/386 (released shortly after Windows 2.0) used the Virtual-86 mode of the 386 microprocessor to window and multitask many DOS programs that directly access hardware. For symmetry, Windows 2.1 was renamed Windows/286.

Windows 3—the subject of this book—was introduced in a spectacular product announcement on May 22, 1990. The earlier Windows/286 and Windows/386 versions have been merged into one product with this release. The big change in Windows 3 is the support of the protected mode operation of Intel's 80286 and 80386 microprocessors. This gives Windows and Windows applications access to up to 16 megabytes of memory. The Windows "shell" programs (the Program Manager, Task Manager, and File Manager) have been completely revamped.

THE USER'S PERSPECTIVE

Windows provides considerable advantages to both users and programmers over the conventional MS-DOS environment. The benefits to users and the benefits to program developers are really quite similar, because the job of a program developer is to give users what they need and want. Windows makes this possible.

The Graphical User Interface (GUI)

Windows is a graphical user interface (GUI), sometimes also called a "visual interface" or "graphical windowing environment." The concepts behind this type of user interface date from the mid-1970s, with the pioneering work done at the Xerox Palo Alto Research Center (PARC) for machines such as the Alto and the Star and for environments such as Smalltalk.

The work done at Xerox PARC was brought into the mainstream and popularized by Apple Computer, Inc., first in the ill-fated Lisa and then a year later in the much more successful Macintosh, introduced in January 1984. The Apple Macintosh remains a significant challenger to IBM's dominance in the personal-computer business market. It is not so much the hardware of the Macintosh but its operating system that makes the machine so appealing to users. The Mac is simply easier to use and learn than an IBM PC running MS-DOS.

Since the introduction of the Macintosh, graphical user interfaces have bloomed like wildflowers throughout the personal-computer industry and the not-so-personal computer industry as well. For IBM-compatibles running MS-DOS, there is Windows. For IBM-compatibles running OS/2, there is the Presentation Manager. For the Commodore Amiga, there is Intuition. For the Atari, there is GEM. For machines running UNIX, there is the X-Window system. For Sun Microsystems workstations, there is NeWS. For the NeXT, there is NextStep.

It is obvious that the graphical user interface is now (in the words of Microsoft's Charles Simonyi) the single most important "grand consensus" of the personal-computer industry. Although the various graphical environments differ in details, they have similar characteristics.

GUI Concepts and Rationale

All graphical user interfaces make use of graphics on a bitmapped video display. Graphics provides better utilization of screen real estate, a visually rich environment for conveying information, and the possibility of a WYSIWYG (what you see is what you get) video display of graphics and formatted text prepared for a printed document.

In earlier days, the video display was used solely to echo text that the user typed using the keyboard. In a graphical user interface, the video display itself becomes a source of user input. The video display shows various graphical objects in the form of icons and input devices such as buttons and scroll bars. Using the keyboard (or, more directly, a pointing device such as a mouse), the user can directly manipulate these objects on the screen. Graphics objects can be dragged, buttons can be pushed, and scroll bars can be scrolled.

The interaction between the user and a program thus becomes more intimate. Rather than the one-way cycle of information from the keyboard to the program to the video display, the user directly interacts with the objects on the display.

The Consistent User Interface

Users no longer expect to spend long periods of time learning how to use the computer or mastering a new program. Windows helps because all Windows programs have the same fundamental look and feel. The program occupies a window—a rectangular area on the screen. It is identified by a caption bar. Most program functions are initiated through the program's menu. Figure 1-1 shows a typical Windows program (in this case Write, the word processor included in Windows) with the various window components labeled.

Some menu items invoke dialog boxes, in which the user enters additional information. One dialog box found in almost every large Windows program opens a file. (See Figure 1-2.) This dialog box looks the same (or very similar) in many different Windows programs, and it is almost always invoked from the same menu option.

Once you know how to use one Windows program, you're in a good position to easily learn another. The menus and dialog boxes allow a user to experiment with a new program and explore its features. Most Windows programs have both a keyboard interface and a mouse interface. Although most functions of Windows programs can be controlled through the keyboard, using the mouse is often easier for many chores.

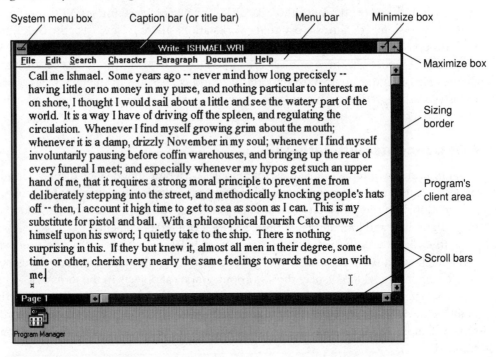

Figure 1-1. *WRITE, a typical Windows program.*

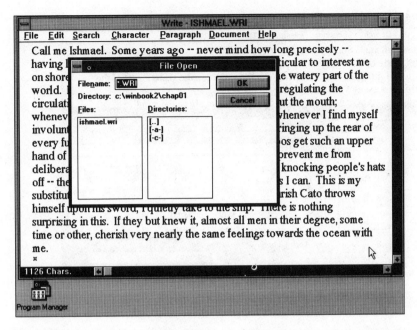

Figure 1-2. *A dialog box to open a file.*

From the programmer's perspective, the consistent user interface results from using the routines built into Windows for constructing menus and dialog boxes. All menus have the same keyboard and mouse interface because Windows, rather than the application program, handles this job.

The Multitasking Advantage

Although some people continue to question whether multitasking is really necessary on a single-user computer, users definitely are ready for multitasking and can benefit from it. The popularity of MS-DOS RAM-resident programs such as Sidekick proves it. Although popups are not, strictly speaking, multitasking programs, they do allow fast context switching. This involves many of the same concepts as multitasking.

Under Windows, every program in effect becomes a RAM-resident popup. Several Windows programs can be displayed and running at the same time. Each program occupies a rectangular window on the screen, as shown in Figure 1-3 on the following page. The user can move the windows around on the screen, change their size, switch between different programs, and transfer data from one program to another. Because this display looks something like a desktop (in the days before the desk became dominated by the computer itself, of course), Windows is sometimes said to use a "desktop metaphor" for the display of multiple programs.

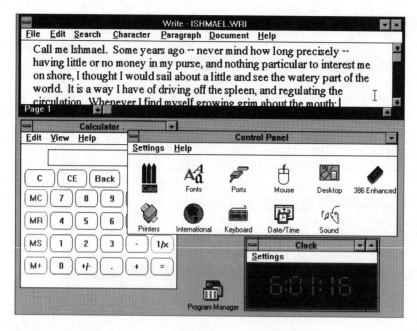

Figure 1-3. *Several programs running under Windows.*

Memory Management

An operating system cannot implement multitasking without doing something about memory management. As new programs are started up and old ones terminate, memory can become fragmented. The system must be able to consolidate free memory space. This requires the system to move blocks of code and data in memory.

Even Windows 1, running on an 8088 microprocessor, was able to perform this type of memory management. Under real mode, this can only be regarded as an astonishing feat of software engineering. Programs running under Windows can overcommit memory; a program can contain more code than can fit into memory at any one time. Windows can discard code from memory and later reload the code from the program's .EXE file. A user can run several copies (called "instances") of a program; all these instances share the same code in memory. Programs running in Windows can share routines located in other .EXE files called "dynamic link libraries." Windows includes a mechanism to link the program with the routines in the dynamic link libraries at run time. Windows itself is a set of dynamic link libraries.

Thus, even in Windows 1, the 640-KB memory limit of the PC's architecture was effectively stretched without requiring any additional memory. But Microsoft didn't stop there: Windows 2 gave the Windows applications access to expanded memory (EMS), and Windows 3 runs in protected mode to give Windows applications access to up to 16 megabytes (MB) of extended memory.

The Device-Independent Graphics Interface

Windows is a graphical interface, and Windows programs can make full use of graphics and formatted text on both the video display and the printer. A graphical interface is not only more attractive in appearance, but it can also impart a high level of information to the user, as you can see in Figure 1-4.

Programs written for Windows do not directly access the hardware of graphics display devices such as the screen and printer. Instead, Windows includes a graphics programming language (called the Graphics Device Interface, or GDI) that allows the easy display of graphics and formatted text. Windows virtualizes display hardware. A program written for Windows will run with any video board or any printer for which a Windows device driver is available. The program does not need to determine what type of device is attached to the system.

Putting a device-independent graphics interface on the IBM PC was not an easy job for the developers of Windows. The PC design was based on the principle of open architecture. Third-party hardware manufacturers were encouraged to develop peripherals for the PC and have done so in great number. Although several standards have emerged, conventional MS-DOS programs for the PC must individually support many different hardware configurations. For example, it is fairly common for an MS-DOS word-processing program to be sold with one or two disks of small files, each one supporting a particular printer.

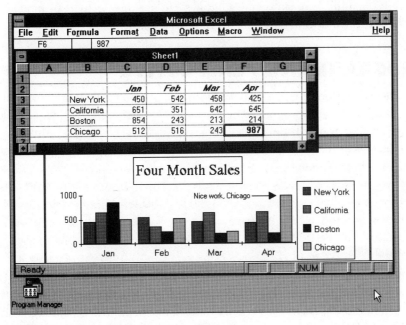

Figure 1-4. *Microsoft Excel running under Windows.*

Windows programs do not require these drivers because the support is part of Windows. This benefits users because most Windows programs require very little in the way of installation. Everything a program needs can be included in the program's single .EXE file. The user can often copy the .EXE file to the fixed disk, load Windows, and go.

MS-DOS Applications

Although Windows primarily exists to run new programs specifically designed for the environment, Windows can also run many non-Windows MS-DOS programs. The Windows User's Guide refers to these as "standard applications," but many Windows programmers call them "old applications" or "old apps."

These MS-DOS programs can be divided into two broad categories: Well-behaved applications (or "good old apps") are those that use the MS-DOS and PC ROM BIOS (basic input/output system) software interrupts to read the keyboard and write to the video display. These programs can generally run in a window.

"Bad apps" are those that write directly to the video display, use graphics, or take control of the hardware keyboard interrupt. The term "bad" here refers not to the quality of the program—many of the best programs written for the PC are bad apps when it comes to Windows—but to the way in which the program uses the hardware of the PC. When running on a 286-based machine, there is simply no way Windows can allow such a program to be windowed or multitasked. However, Windows can use the "virtual 86" mode of the 386 microprocessor to window and multitask even bad applications.

THE PROGRAMMER'S PERSPECTIVE

Windows has the reputation of being easy for users but difficult for programmers. If you have no prior experience with programming for a graphical user interface, you should be warned right now that you will encounter some very strange concepts. Almost every programmer who begins writing code for Windows must go through some mental reorientation to assimilate these concepts.

If at first you find Windows programming to be difficult, awkward, bizarrely convoluted, and filled with alien concepts, rest assured that this is a normal reaction. You are not alone.

Windows and MS-DOS

You start up Windows as if it were a normal application program running under MS-DOS. But as Windows loads, it becomes almost a full-fledged operating system. It's not quite an operating system because it runs on top of MS-DOS. While Windows is running, it shares responsibility with MS-DOS for managing the hardware resources of the computer. Basically, MS-DOS continues to manage the file system, while Windows does everything else. Windows commands the video display, keyboard, mouse, printer, and serial ports and is responsible for memory management, program execution, and scheduling.

Windows is strong where MS-DOS is weak, and weak where MS-DOS is adequate. Windows includes almost no support of file I/O, which is one of the most essential chores of a minimal operating system such as MS-DOS. This leads to some amusing—or not so amusing—consequences. It is easier in a Windows program to create a disk-based metafile containing a complex series of graphics drawing commands than to create a simple ASCII text file. The former is a Windows job; the latter requires that the program use MS-DOS.

The Windows Commitment

Programming for Windows is an all-or-nothing proposition. For example, you cannot write an MS-DOS application—even a well-behaved one—and use Windows only for some graphics. If you want to use any part of Windows, you must make the commitment to write a full-fledged Windows program.

The reason for this will become more obvious as you learn about the structure of a Windows program. Everything in Windows is interconnected. If you want to draw some graphics on the video display, you need something called a "handle to a device context." To get that, you need a "handle to a window." To get that, you must create a window and be prepared to receive "messages" to the window. To receive and process messages, you need a "window procedure." And at that point you're writing a Windows program. You can't fly unless you leave the ground.

The Function Calls

Windows 3 supports over 550 function calls that applications can use. It is highly unlikely that you will ever memorize the syntax to all these calls. Most Windows programmers keep the Windows Programmer's Reference manual within easy reach.

Each of the Windows functions has a descriptive name written in mixed uppercase and lowercase letters, such as *CreateWindow*. This function (as you might guess) creates a window for your program. Another example: the function *IsClipboardFormatAvailable* determines whether the clipboard is holding data of a particular format.

All the Windows functions are declared in a header file named WINDOWS.H, included in the Windows Software Development Kit. WINDOWS.H is an important part of the Windows documentation. You might want to print a copy or use a file browser for quick reference.

You use these Windows functions in your Windows program the same way you use C library functions such as *strlen*. However, there are some differences between the Windows functions and the standard C library functions.

Windows functions are always declared as *far pascal* functions. These are two keywords that Microsoft has added to its version of C. The *far* keyword indicates that the

Windows function is in a different code segment than the program's code. (You'll see the reason for this shortly.)

The *pascal* keyword indicates that the function's calling sequence is different than the normal C calling sequence. Normally, the C compiler generates code that pushes parameters on the stack from right to left beginning with the last parameter. The code calling the function is responsible for adjusting the stack pointer after the function returns. With the *pascal* calling sequence, the parameters are pushed on the stack from left to right and the called function cleans up the stack. The *pascal* calling sequence is used in Windows because it is more efficient.

With one oddball exception, any pointer passed to a Windows function must be a *far* pointer. This is something you normally don't have to worry about because the compiler will extend short pointers to long pointers based on the function template in WINDOWS.H.

Dynamic Linking

If you've been working with MS-DOS programming for awhile, you might guess that a Windows program interfaces with Windows through a software interrupt such as the MS-DOS Interrupt 0x21. You might guess that the linker adds bindings to your Windows programs that convert the Windows function calls into this software interrupt. But you would be wrong. A Windows program interfaces to Windows through a process called "dynamic linking."

Like MS-DOS programs, Windows executables have the filename extension .EXE. However, this is not the same .EXE format that is used in MS-DOS. Instead, Windows programs use a .EXE format called the New Executable file format, similar to that used in OS/2. Whenever a Windows program calls a Windows function, the C compiler generates assembly-language code for a far call. A table in the .EXE file identifies the function being called using a dynamic link library name and either a name or a number (called the ordinal number) of the function in that library.

Windows itself consists largely of three dynamic link libraries, called KERNEL (responsible for memory management, loading and executing programs, and scheduling), USER (the user interface and windowing), and GDI (the graphics). These libraries contain the code and data for the Windows functions. You can find these three dynamic link libraries in the SYSTEM subdirectory of your Windows directory.

When a Windows program is loaded into memory, the far calls in the program are resolved to point to the entry of the function in the dynamic link library, which is also loaded into memory. This is why all Windows functions must be defined as *far*: The code in the dynamic link libraries is not in the same segment as the program's code. Also, pointers passed in Windows functions must also be defined as *far* to avoid confusion with the dynamic link library's own code and data segments.

Generally, you don't have to worry about the use of far calls and far pointers because the functions are declared as far functions with far pointers in WINDOWS.H: The C compiler will perform the necessary address translations for you.

When you link a Windows program to produce an executable, you must link with a special "import library" provided with the Windows Software Development Kit. This import library contains the dynamic link library names and ordinal numbers of all the Windows functions. LINK uses this information to construct the table in the .EXE file that Windows uses to resolve calls to Windows functions when loading the program.

Object-Oriented Programming

When programming for Windows, you're really engaged in a type of object-oriented programming. This is most evident in the object you'll be working with most in Windows—the object that gives Windows its name, the object that will soon seem to take on anthropomorphic characteristics, the object that may even show up in your dreams, the object known as the "window."

Windows are rectangular objects on the screen. A window receives user input from the keyboard or mouse and displays graphical output on its surface.

An application window usually contains the program's title bar, menu, sizing border, and perhaps some scroll bars. Dialog boxes are additional windows. Moreover, the surface of a dialog box always contains several additional windows called "child windows." These child windows take the form of push buttons, radio buttons, check boxes, text entry fields, list boxes, and scroll bars.

The user sees these windows as objects on the screen and interacts directly with these objects by pushing a button or scrolling a scroll bar. Interestingly enough, the programmer's perspective is analogous to the user's perspective. The window receives this user input in the form of "messages" to the window. A window also uses messages to communicate with other windows.

Understanding these messages is one of the hurdles you'll have to jump in becoming a Windows programmer.

Message-Driven Architecture

The first time I saw a graphical user interface in action, I was puzzled. The demonstration included a rudimentary word processor running in a window. The word processor would reformat its text when the program's window was resized.

It was obvious to me that the operating system was handling the details of the window-resizing logic, and that the program was capable of responding to this system function. How did the program *know* when its window was resized? What was the mechanism the operating system used to convey this information to the window? My previous programming experience was useless in understanding how this worked.

It turns out that the answer to this question is central to understanding the architecture used in graphical user interfaces. In Windows, when a user resizes a window, Windows sends a message to the program indicating the new window size. The program can then adjust the contents of its window to reflect the new size.

"Windows sends a message to the program." I hope you didn't read that statement without blinking. What on earth could it mean? We're talking about program code here, not an electronic mail system. How can an operating system send a message to a program?

When I say that "Windows sends a message to a program," I mean that Windows calls a function within the program. The parameters to this function describe the particular message. This function located in your Windows program is known as the "window procedure."

The Window Procedure

You are undoubtedly accustomed to the idea of a program making calls to the operating system. This is how a program opens a disk file, for example. What you may not be accustomed to is the idea of an operating system making calls to a program. Yet this is fundamental to Windows' object-oriented architecture.

Every window that a program creates has an associated window procedure. This window procedure is a function that could be either in the program itself or in a dynamic link library. Windows sends a message to a window by calling the window procedure. The window procedure does some processing based on the message and then returns control to Windows.

More precisely, a window is always created based on a "window class." The window class identifies the window procedure that processes messages to the window. The use of a window class allows multiple windows to be based on the same window class and hence use the same window procedure. For example, all buttons in all Windows programs are based on the same window class. This window class is associated with a window procedure (located in the Windows USER.EXE dynamic link library) that processes messages to all the button windows.

In object-oriented programming, an "object" is a combination of code and data. A window is an object. The code is the window procedure. The data is information retained by the window procedure and information retained by Windows for each window and window class that exists in the system.

A window procedure processes messages to the window. Very often these messages inform a window of user input from the keyboard or mouse. This is how a push-button window knows that it's being "pressed," for example. Other messages tell a window when it is being resized, or when the surface of the window needs to be repainted.

When a Windows program begins execution, Windows creates a "message queue" for the program. This message queue stores messages to all the various windows a program may create. The program includes a short chunk of code called the "message loop" to retrieve these messages from the queue and dispatch them to the appropriate window procedure. Other messages are sent directly to the window procedure without being placed in the message queue.

If your eyes are beginning to glaze over with this excessively abstract description of Windows architecture, maybe it will help to see how the window, the window class, the window procedure, the message queue, the message loop, and the window messages all fit together in the context of a real program.

YOUR FIRST WINDOWS PROGRAM

In their classic book *The C Programming Language* (2d ed., Prentice Hall, 1988), Brian Kernighan and Dennis Ritchie begin discussing C with the now-famous "Hello, world" program:

```
#include <stdio.h>

main ()
    {
    printf ("Hello, world\n") ;
    }
```

In the remainder of this chapter, I will show you the analogous program written for Microsoft Windows. The program is called HELLOWIN, and it creates a window that displays the text string "Hello, Windows!"

Lest you collapse from shock when you first look at the HELLOWIN code, I'll warn you now that there are three files involved, and that the HELLOWIN.C source code file is over 80 lines long. Most of these 80 lines are overhead. You'll have similar overhead in almost every Windows program you write.

Rather than ask why the "Hello, Windows" program is so long and complex, let's ask why the traditional "Hello, world" program is so short and simple.

What's Wrong with this Program?

The output model for the "Hello, world" program and other traditional C programs is an antique piece of hardware known as the teletype. The teletype resembles a typewriter with a continuous roll of paper. In the not too distant past, programmers would sit at a teletype and type in commands that were echoed to the paper. The computer responded by printing its output on the paper.

The teletype metaphor was extended to the video display in the early days of computers. The video display became a "glass teletype" that simply scrolled when text reached the bottom of the screen.

How can the traditional "Hello, world" program display text without telling the operating system the particular output device on which the text is to appear? Because there is only one output device—the video display used as if it were a teletype. If the user wishes the output to go elsewhere, it must be redirected from the command line.

How can the program display text without telling the system where on the output device the text is to appear? Because the text always appears where the cursor happens to be, probably on the next line after you execute the program. Suppose you want to display "Hello, world" in the center of the screen. You'd have to use some device-dependent control codes to first position the cursor at the desired location.

Let's say you want to run several "Hello, world" programs at one time and see their output on the screen. What a mess! The copies of the program would interfere with each other. There is nothing in the teletype metaphor to separate output from several programs running concurrently.

It's also interesting that you see the "Hello, world" output even after the program terminates. Rather than properly cleaning up after itself, the program is leaving remnants of its existence on the video display.

The "Hello, world" program is so simple because it is designed for a simpler age and simpler computers and simpler output devices. It's not in the same ballpark as what we think of today as modern software, and it's not even playing the same game.

The HELLOWIN Files

The three files necessary to create the "Hello, Windows" program are shown in Figure 1-5:

- HELLOWIN.MAK is a "make" file.
- HELLOWIN.C is the C source code file.
- HELLOWIN.DEF is a module definition file.

HELLOWIN.MAK

```
#---------------------------
# HELLOWIN.MAK make file
#---------------------------

hellowin.exe : hellowin.obj hellowin.def
     link hellowin, /align:16, NUL, /nod slibcew libw, hellowin
     rc hellowin.exe

hellowin.obj : hellowin.c
     cl -c -Gsw -Ow -W2 -Zp hellowin.c
```

Figure 1-5. *The HELLOWIN program.*

HELLOWIN.C

```c
/*-------------------------------------------------------------
   HELLOWIN.C -- Displays "Hello, Windows!" in client area
                 (c) Charles Petzold, 1990
   -------------------------------------------------------------*/

#include <windows.h>

long FAR PASCAL WndProc (HWND, WORD, WORD, LONG) ;

int PASCAL WinMain (HANDLE hInstance, HANDLE hPrevInstance,
                    LPSTR lpszCmdParam, int nCmdShow)
    {
    static char szAppName[] = "HelloWin" ;
    HWND        hwnd ;
    MSG         msg ;
    WNDCLASS    wndclass ;

    if (!hPrevInstance)
        {
        wndclass.style         = CS_HREDRAW | CS_VREDRAW ;
        wndclass.lpfnWndProc   = WndProc ;
        wndclass.cbClsExtra    = 0 ;
        wndclass.cbWndExtra    = 0 ;
        wndclass.hInstance     = hInstance ;
        wndclass.hIcon         = LoadIcon (NULL, IDI_APPLICATION) ;
        wndclass.hCursor       = LoadCursor (NULL, IDC_ARROW) ;
        wndclass.hbrBackground = GetStockObject (WHITE_BRUSH) ;
        wndclass.lpszMenuName  = NULL ;
        wndclass.lpszClassName = szAppName ;

        RegisterClass (&wndclass) ;
        }

    hwnd = CreateWindow (szAppName,             // window class name
                "The Hello Program",    // window caption
                WS_OVERLAPPEDWINDOW,    // window style
                CW_USEDEFAULT,          // initial x position
                CW_USEDEFAULT,          // initial y position
                CW_USEDEFAULT,          // initial x size
                CW_USEDEFAULT,          // initial y size
                NULL,                   // parent window handle
                NULL,                   // window menu handle
                hInstance,              // program instance handle
                NULL) ;                 // creation parameters

    ShowWindow (hwnd, nCmdShow) ;
    UpdateWindow (hwnd) ;
```

(continued)

17

```
      while (GetMessage (&msg, NULL, 0, 0))
           {
           TranslateMessage (&msg) ;
           DispatchMessage (&msg) ;
           }
      return msg.wParam ;
      }

long FAR PASCAL WndProc (HWND hwnd, WORD message, WORD wParam, LONG lParam)
      {
      HDC          hdc ;
      PAINTSTRUCT ps ;
      RECT         rect ;

      switch (message)
           {
           case WM_PAINT :
                hdc = BeginPaint (hwnd, &ps) ;

                GetClientRect (hwnd, &rect) ;

                DrawText (hdc, "Hello, Windows!", -1, &rect,
                          DT_SINGLELINE : DT_CENTER : DT_VCENTER) ;

                EndPaint (hwnd, &ps) ;
                return 0 ;

           case WM_DESTROY :
                PostQuitMessage (0) ;
                return 0 ;
           }

      return DefWindowProc (hwnd, message, wParam, lParam) ;
      }
```

HELLOWIN.DEF

```
;------------------------------------
; HELLOWIN.DEF module definition file
;------------------------------------

NAME            HELLOWIN

DESCRIPTION     'Hello Windows Program (c) Charles Petzold, 1990'
EXETYPE         WINDOWS
STUB            'WINSTUB.EXE'
CODE            PRELOAD MOVEABLE DISCARDABLE
```

(continued)

```
DATA        PRELOAD MOVEABLE MULTIPLE
HEAPSIZE    1024
STACKSIZE   8192
EXPORTS     WndProc
```

These are standard files that you'll create for every Windows program you write. Generally when you begin a new Windows program, you'll copy the standard files from an existing program and then make appropriate changes to them.

Most Windows programmers do all their program development and compiling outside of Windows under MS-DOS, and then load Windows to test the program. You can also create and compile a Windows program in the Microsoft C 6 Programmer's WorkBench. I'll be discussing the source code files as if you create them in a text editor of your choice and then compile the program from the MS-DOS command line outside of Windows.

If you have Windows, the Windows Software Development Kit, and the Microsoft C Professional Development System (the C 6 compiler) properly installed, you can create HELLOWIN.EXE from the three files shown in Figure 1-5 by executing:

    NMAKE HELLOWIN.MAK

on the MS-DOS command line. You can then run Windows and the HELLOWIN.EXE program by executing:

    WIN HELLOWIN

The program creates a normal application window as shown in Figure 1-6 on the following page. The window displays "Hello, Windows!" in the center of its client area.

When you think about it, this window has an amazing amount of functionality in its mere 80 lines of code. You can grab the title bar with the mouse pointer and move the window around the screen. You can grab the sizing borders and resize the window. When the window changes size, the program will automatically reposition the "Hello, Windows!" text string in the new center of the client area. You can press the maximize button and zoom HELLOWIN to fill the screen. You can press the minimize button and compress the program into an icon. You can invoke all these options from the system menu and, in addition, close the window to terminate the program.

While you may be pleased to see that HELLOWIN has all the functionality of a normal Windows program, you may not look so pleasant-faced when you see the source code required to create this program. But let's be brave while I proceed to dissect this program piece by piece and analyze it to death.

Figure 1-6. *HELLOWIN running under Windows.*

The Make File

To ease compilation of Windows programs, you can use the NMAKE utility included in the Microsoft C Professional Development System. Whenever you change something in one of the HELLOWIN source files, all you need do is run:

```
NMAKE HELLOWIN.MAK
```

to create the updated HELLOWIN.EXE executable.

A make file consists of one or more sections, each of which begins with a left-justified line that lists a target file, followed by a colon, followed by one or more dependent files. This line is followed by one or more indented command lines. These commands create the target file from the dependent files. If the last modification date and time of any of the dependent files is later than the last modification date and time of the target file, then NMAKE executes the indented command lines.

Normally, NMAKE will update only the target file in the first section of the make file. However, if one of the dependent files is itself a target file in another section of the make file, then NMAKE will update that target first.

The HELLOWIN.MAK make file contains two sections. The first runs the LINK.EXE linker if HELLOWIN.OBJ or HELLOWIN.DEF has been altered more recently than HELLOWIN.EXE:

```
hellowin.exe : hellowin.obj hellowin.def
    link hellowin, /align:16, NUL, /nod slibcew libw, hellowin
    rc hellowin.exe
```

The second section runs the CL.EXE C compiler if HELLOWIN.C has been changed more recently than HELLOWIN.OBJ:

```
hellowin.obj : hellowin.c
    cl -c -Gsw -Ow -W2 -Zp hellowin.c
```

Because HELLOWIN.OBJ is a dependent file in the first section of the make file and a target file in the second section, NMAKE will check whether HELLOWIN.OBJ needs updating before re-creating HELLOWIN.EXE. Thus, the make file should be analyzed from the bottom up.

Running the CL.EXE C compiler creates the HELLOWIN.OBJ object module from the HELLOWIN.C source code file:

```
cl -c -Gsw -Ow -W2 -Zp hellowin.c
```

Several compiler switches are required (or recommended) for compiling Windows programs:

- The -c switch indicates that the program should be compiled only and not yet linked. The link is a separate step.

- The -Gsw switch is actually two switches: -Gs and -Gw. The -Gs switch disables checks for stack overflow. Because stack overflow messages are written to standard error output (and are hence ignored by Windows), it's best simply to be sure that you are using a sufficient stack. (Four kilobytes is recommended.)

- The -Gw switch is a special Windows switch that inserts special prolog and epilog code in all *far* functions in the program. This code (which I'll discuss in Chapter 7) aids Windows in moving code and data segments in memory.

- The -Ow switch concerns optimization. With this switch the compiler will avoid some optimizations that may cause problems specifically with Windows programs.

- The -W2 switch enables warning level 2 for displaying warning messages. You should make an effort to write programs that show no warning messages when you compile with this switch. Windows will not tolerate sloppy programming, which can lead to nasty bugs.

- The -Zp switch packs structure fields on byte boundaries. This is required for some of the structures defined in WINDOWS.H that programs use to communicate with Windows. Windows assumes that all structures are packed.

The first section of the make file runs two commands if HELLOWIN.OBJ or HELLOWIN.DEF has been altered more recently than HELLOWIN.EXE. The first indented command runs LINK:

```
link hellowin, /align:16, NUL, /nod slibcew libw, hellowin
```

The first field indicates the HELLOWIN.OBJ object file. The .OBJ extension is assumed. The second field would normally list the name of the executable file, but I'm letting it default to HELLOWIN.EXE. The *align:16* switch tells LINK to align code and data segments on 16-byte boundaries in the HELLOWIN.EXE file for better space efficiency. (The default is 512-byte boundaries.)

The third field is the name of an optional map file. This is set to NUL to create no map file. The fourth field lists the libraries followed by the */nod* (no default libraries) switch. SLIBCEW.LIB is the small model Windows C run time library created during installation of the Windows Software Development Kit.

LIBW.LIB is an import library that contains information LINK uses to set up a table in the .EXE file so that Windows can dynamically link the program's calls to Windows functions with the Windows dynamic link libraries that contain those functions.

The fifth field indicates the name of the program's module definition file, HELLOWIN.DEF. The .DEF extension is assumed. (I'll discuss this file later in this chapter.) It contains information that LINK uses to construct HELLOWIN.EXE.

The second indented command runs the Windows resource compiler, RC.EXE:

```
rc hellowin.exe
```

The resource compiler sets a couple flags in the HELLOWIN.EXE file to indicate that this is a Windows 3–compatible application. Primarily, this avoids a Windows 3 message that warns the user that the program may crash because it has not been modified for protected-mode operation. Later on, we'll use the resource compiler to add menus and dialog boxes to our Windows programs.

The C Source Code File

The second file in Figure 1-5 is HELLOWIN.C, the C source code file. It may take awhile before you recognize that this program is indeed written in C!

Let's first take a global look at HELLOWIN.C before getting into details. The file contains only two functions: *WinMain* and *WndProc*. *WinMain* is the entry point to the program. It is the equivalent of the standard C *main* function. Every Windows program has a *WinMain* function.

WndProc is the window procedure for HELLOWIN's window. This function processes messages to the window. No code in HELLOWIN.C calls *WndProc* directly: *WndProc* is called only from Windows. However, there is a reference to *WndProc* in *WinMain*, which is why the function is declared near the top of the program before *WinMain*.

The Windows Function Calls

HELLOWIN makes calls to no less than 16 Windows functions. In the order they occur in HELLOWIN, these functions (with a brief description) are:

- *LoadIcon*—Loads an icon for use by a program
- *LoadCursor*—Loads a cursor for use by a program
- *GetStockObject*—Obtains a graphics object (in this case a brush used for painting the window's background)
- *RegisterClass*—Registers a window class for the program's window
- *CreateWindow*—Creates a window based on a window class
- *ShowWindow*—Displays the window on the screen
- *UpdateWindow*—Directs the window to paint itself
- *GetMessage*—Obtains a message from the message queue
- *TranslateMessage*—Translates some keyboard messages
- *DispatchMessage*—Sends a message to a window procedure
- *BeginPaint*—Initiates the beginning of window painting
- *GetClientRect*—Obtains the dimensions of the window's client area
- *DrawText*—Displays a text string
- *EndPaint*—Ends window painting
- *PostQuitMessage*—Inserts a "quit" message into the message queue
- *DefWindowProc*—Performs default processing of messages

These functions are documented in the Windows Programmer's Reference and declared in WINDOWS.H. I'll discuss each of them as we encounter them while dissecting the program.

Uppercase Identifiers

You'll notice the use of quite a few uppercase identifiers in HELLOWIN.C. These identifiers are defined in WINDOWS.H.

Several of these identifiers contain a two-letter or three-letter prefix followed by an underscore:

CS_HREDRAW	DT_SINGLELINE	WM_DESTROY
IDI_APPLICATION	CS_VREDRAW	DT_CENTER
WS_OVERLAPPEDWINDOW	IDC_ARROW	DT_VCENTER
WM_PAINT	CW_USEDEFAULT	

These are simply numeric constants. The prefix indicates a general category to which the constant belongs, as indicated in this table:

Prefix	Category
CS	class style
IDI	ID for an icon
IDC	ID for a cursor
WS	window style
CW	create window
WM	window message
DT	draw text

You almost never need to remember numeric constants when programming for Windows. Virtually every numeric constant used in Windows has an identifier defined in WINDOWS.H.

New Data Types

Other identifiers used in HELLOWIN.C are new data types, also defined in WINDOWS.H. The ones used in the program are:

Data Type	Meaning
FAR	same as *far*
PASCAL	same as *pascal*
WORD	unsigned integer (16 bits)
DWORD	unsigned long integer (32 bits)
LONG	signed long integer (32 bits)
LPSTR	far (or long) pointer to a character string

These are fairly self-explanatory. The people who originally developed Windows thought that it would someday be ported to other microprocessors. These new data types were defined to ease the porting of Windows applications to other architectures. Rather than use machine-specific data sizes (such as the size of C integer), the new data types were devised to keep programs consistent regardless of the processor on which they run.

Of course, Windows will probably never be ported to other architectures, but the Windows functions are still defined using these new data types, and Windows programmers continue to use them.

HELLOWIN also uses four data structures (which I'll discuss later in this chapter) defined in WINDOWS.H:

Structure	*Meaning*
MSG	The message structure
WNDCLASS	The window class structure
PAINTSTRUCT	The paint structure
RECT	The rectangle structure

The first two data structures are used in *WinMain* to define two structures named *msg* and *wndclass*. The second two are used in *WndProc* to define two structures named *ps* and *rect*.

Getting a Handle on Handles

Finally, there are three uppercase identifiers for various types of "handles":

Identifier	*Meaning*
HANDLE	Generic handle
HWND	Handle to a window
HDC	Handle to a device context

Handles are used quite frequently in Windows. Before the chapter is over, you also encounter HICON (a handle to an icon), HCURSOR (a handle to a mouse cursor), and HBRUSH (a handle to a graphics brush).

A handle is simply a 16-bit number that refers to an object. The handles in Windows are similar to file handles used in conventional C or MS-DOS programming. A program almost always obtains a handle by calling a Windows function. The program uses the handle in other Windows functions to refer to the object. The actual value of the handle is unimportant to your program, but the Windows module that gives your program the handle knows how to use it to reference the object.

Hungarian Notation

You may also notice that some of the variables in HELLOWIN.C have peculiar-looking names. One example is *lpszCmdParam*, passed as a parameter to *WinMain*.

Many Windows programmers use a variable-naming convention known as Hungarian notation, in honor of the legendary Microsoft programmer Charles Simonyi. Very simply, the variable name begins with a lowercase letter or letters that denote the data type of the variable. For example, the *lpsz* prefix in *lpszCmdParam* stands for "long pointer to a string terminated by zero."

The *h* prefix in *hInstance* and *hPrevInstance* stands for "handle"; the *n* prefix in *nCmdShow* stands for "number," and usually specifies an integer. Two of the parameters to *WndProc* also use Hungarian notation: *wParam* is a WORD and *lParam* is a LONG.

When naming structure variables, you can use the structure name (or an abbreviation of the structure name) in lowercase as either a prefix to the variable name or as the entire variable name. For example, in the *WinMain* function in HELLOWIN.C, the *msg* variable is a structure of the MSG type; *wndclass* is a structure of the WNDCLASS type. In the *WndProc* function, *ps* is a PAINTSTRUCT structure and *rect* is a RECT structure.

Hungarian notation helps you avoid errors in your code before they turn into bugs. Because the name of a variable describes both the use of a variable and its data type, you are much less inclined to make coding errors involving mismatched data types.

The variable name prefixes I'll be using in this book are shown in the following table:

Prefix	Data Type
c	char
by	BYTE (unsigned char)
n	short or int
i	int
x, y	short (used as *x*-coordinate or *y*-coordinate)
cx, cy	short (used as *x* or *y* length; the c stands for "count")
b	BOOL (int)
w	WORD (unsigned int)
l	LONG (long)
dw	DWORD (unsigned long)
fn	function
s	string
sz	string terminated by 0 byte

The Program Entry Point

With this global look at HELLOWIN.C out of the way, we can now begin the line-by-line dissection of the program. The code begins with an *#include* statement to include the WINDOWS.H header file:

```
#include <windows.h>
```

WINDOWS.H contains declarations of the Windows functions, the Windows structures, the new data types, and numeric constants.

This is followed by a forward declaration of the *WndProc* function:

```
long FAR PASCAL WndProc (HWND, WORD, WORD, LONG) ;
```

The declaration is required because *WndProc* is referenced by some code in the *WinMain* function.

In a C program written for a conventional environment, the entry point is a function called *main*. This is where the program begins execution. (Actually, the *main* function is the entry point to the part of the program written by the programmer. Usually the C compiler will insert some start-up code in the executable file. The start-up code then calls *main*.) The entry point of a Windows program is a function called *WinMain*. (As is the case with *main*, *WinMain* is actually called from some start-up code inserted into the executable file.) *WinMain* is always defined like this:

```
int PASCAL WinMain (HANDLE hInstance, HANDLE hPrevInstance,
                    LPSTR lpszCmdParam, int nCmdShow)
```

This function uses the PASCAL calling sequence and returns an integer to the start-up code. The function must be named *WinMain*. It has four parameters.

The *hInstance* parameter is called the "instance handle." This is a number that uniquely identifies the program when it is running under Windows. It could be that the user is running multiple copies of the same program under Windows. (For example, most Windows users at one time or another have loaded multiple versions of the CLOCK program to see what happens.) Each copy is called an "instance," and each has a different *hInstance* value. The instance handle is comparable to a "task ID" or "process ID" number common in mulitasking operating systems.

The *hPrevInstance* ("previous instance") parameter is the instance handle of the most recent previous instance of the same program that is still active. If no other copies of the program are currently loaded, then *hPrevInstance* will be 0 or NULL.

The *lpszCmdParam* parameter is a long (or far) pointer to a 0-terminated string that contains any command-line parameters passed to the program. It is possible to run a Windows program with a command-line parameter by typing the program name and the parameter into the Run dialog box invoked from either the Program Manager or the File Manager.

The *nCmdShow* parameter is a number indicating how the window is to be initially displayed in Windows. This number is assigned by whatever program executes the program to run under Windows. Programs do not often need to examine this number, but they can if they want. In most cases the number is either a 1 or a 7. But it's best not to think of the value as a 1 or a 7. Rather, think of the value as SW_SHOWNORMAL (defined in WINDOWS.H as 1) or SW_SHOWMINNOACTIVE (defined as 7). The SW prefix in these identifiers stands for "show window." This indicates whether the user launched the program to be displayed as a normal window or to be initially minimized.

Registering the Window Class

A window is always created based on a window class. The window class identifies the window procedure that processes messages to the window. This is important, so I'll repeat it: A window is always created based on a window class. The window class identifies the window procedure that processes messages to the window.

More than one window can be created based on a single window class. For example, all button windows in Windows are created based on the same window class. The window class defines the window procedure and some other characteristics of the windows that are created based on that class. When you create a window you define additional characteristics of the window that are unique to that window.

Before you create a window for your program, you must register a window class by calling *RegisterClass*. The *RegisterClass* function requires a single parameter: a pointer to a structure of type WNDCLASS. The WNDCLASS structure is defined in WINDOWS.H like this:

```
typedef struct tagWNDCLASS
    {
    WORD    style ;
    LONG    (FAR PASCAL *lpfnWndProc) () ;
    int     cbClsExtra ;
    int     cbWndExtra ;
    HANDLE  hInstance ;
    HICON   hIcon ;
    HCURSOR hCursor ;
    HBRUSH  hbrBackground ;
    LPSTR   lpszMenuName ;
    LPSTR   lpszClassName ;
    }
    WNDCLASS ;
```

In *WinMain*, you must define a structure of type WNDCLASS, generally like this:

```
WNDCLASS wndclass ;
```

You then define the 10 fields of the structure and call *RegisterClass*:

```
RegisterClass (&wndclass) ;
```

Only the first instance of a program needs to register the window class. The window class then becomes available to all subsequent instances of the program. For this reason, HELLOWIN initializes the fields of the WNDCLASS structure and calls *RegisterClass* only if *hPrevInstance* equals NULL.

The WNDCLASS structure has 10 fields. The two most important fields are the last and the second. The last field is the name of the window class (which is generally the same as the name of the program). The second field (*lpfnWndProc*) is the address of the window procedure used for all windows created based on this class (which is the function *WndProc* in HELLOWIN.C). All the other fields describe characteristics of all windows based on this window class.

The statement:

```
wndclass.style = CS_HREDRAW : CS_VREDRAW ;
```

combines two "class style" identifiers with a C bitwise OR operator. In WINDOWS.H, the various identifiers beginning with the CS prefix are defined as 16-bit constants with one bit set. For example, CS_VREDRAW is defined as 0x0001, and CS_HREDRAW is defined as 0x0002. Identifiers defined in this way are sometimes called "bit flags." You combine the bit-flag identifiers with the C OR operator.

These two class-style identifiers indicate that all windows created based on this class are to be completely repainted whenever the horizontal window size (CS_HREDRAW) or the vertical window size (CS_VREDRAW) changes. If you resize HELLOWIN's window, you'll see that the text string is redrawn to be in the new center of the window. These two identifiers ensure that this happens.

The second field of the WNDCLASS structure is initialized by the statement:

```
wndclass.lpfnWndProc = WndProc ;
```

This sets the window procedure for this window class to *WndProc*, which is the second function in HELLOWIN.C. This window procedure will process all messages to all windows created based on this window class. The *lpfn* prefix in the field name is Hungarian notation for "long pointer to a function."

The next two statements:

```
wndclass.cbClsExtra = 0 ;
wndclass.cbWndExtra = 0 ;
```

reserve some extra space in the class structure and the window structure that Windows maintains internally. A program can use this extra space for its own purpose. HELLOWIN does not use this feature, so zero is specified. The *cb* prefix in the field names stands for a "count of bytes."

The next field is simply the instance handle of the program (which is one of the parameters to *WinMain*):

```
wndclass.hInstance = hInstance ;
```

The statement:

```
wndclass.hIcon = LoadIcon (NULL, IDI_APPLICATION) ;
```

sets an icon for all windows created based on this window class. The icon is a small bitmap picture that appears when the program is minimized. Later in this book you'll learn how to create customized icons for your Windows programs. Right now, we'll take an easy approach and use a predefined icon.

To obtain a handle to a predefined icon, you call *LoadIcon* with a first parameter set to NULL. (When loading your own customized icon, this parameter would be set to the instance handle of the program.) The second parameter is an identifier beginning with the IDI ("ID for an icon") defined in WINDOWS.H. The IDI_APPLICATION icon is simply a white square with a black outline. The *LoadIcon* function returns a handle to this icon. We don't really care about the value of this handle. It's simply used to set the value of the *hIcon* field. The *hIcon* field is defined in the WNDCLASS structure to be of type HICON, which stands for "handle to an icon."

The statement:

```
wndclass.hCursor = LoadCursor (NULL, IDC_ARROW) ;
```

is very similar to the previous statement. The *LoadCursor* function loads a predefined mouse cursor known as IDC_ARROW and returns a handle to the cursor. This handle is assigned to the *hCursor* field of the WNDCLASS structure. When the mouse cursor appears over the client area of a window that is created based on this class, the cursor becomes a small arrow.

The next field specifies the background color of the client area of windows created based on this class. The *hbr* prefix of the *hbrBackground* field name stands for "handle to a brush." A brush is a graphics term that refers to a colored pattern of pixels used to fill an area. Windows has several standard, or "stock," brushes. The *GetObject* call shown here returns a handle to a white brush:

```
wndclass.hbrBackground = GetStockObject (WHITE_BRUSH) ;
```

This means the background of the client area of the window will be solid white, which is a common choice.

The next field specifies the window class menu. HELLOWIN has no application menu, so the field is set to NULL:

```
wndclass.lpszMenuName  = NULL ;
```

Finally the class must be given a name. This is the same as the name of the program, which is the "HelloWin" string stored in the *szAppName* variable:

```
wndclass.lpszClassName = szAppName ;
```

When all 10 fields of the structure have been initialized, HELLOWIN registers the window class by calling *RegisterClass*. The only parameter to the function is a pointer to the WNDCLASS structure:

```
RegisterClass (&wndclass) ;
```

Creating the Window

The window class defines general characteristics of a window, thus allowing the same window class to be used for creating many different windows. When you actually create a window by calling *CreateWindow*, you specify more detailed information about the window. Rather than using a data structure as *RegisterClass* does, the *CreateWindow* call requires all the information to be passed as parameters to the function. Here's the *CreateWindow* call in HELLOWIN.C:

```
hwnd = CreateWindow (szAppName,         // window class name
                "The Hello Program",    // window caption
                WS_OVERLAPPEDWINDOW,    // window style
                CW_USEDEFAULT,          // initial x position
                CW_USEDEFAULT,          // initial y position
                CW_USEDEFAULT,          // initial x size
                CW_USEDEFAULT,          // initial y size
                NULL,                   // parent window handle
                NULL,                   // window menu handle
                hInstance,              // program instance handle
                NULL) ;                 // creation parameters
```

The Microsoft C compiler recognizes the // symbol for single-line comments. The comments describe the parameters to the *CreateWindow* function.

Although you need to register a window class only for the first instance of a program, you must create a window separately for each instance. Each instance has its own window, and all the windows are based on the same window class.

The parameter marked "window class name" is *szAppName*, which contains the string "HelloWin"—the name of the window class we just registered. This is how the window is associated with the window class.

The window created by this program is a normal overlapped window with a caption bar, a system menu box to the left of the caption bar, minimize and maximize icons to the right of the caption bar, and a thick window-sizing border. That's a standard style of windows, and it has the WINDOWS.H name WS_OVERLAPPEDWINDOW, which appears as the "window style" parameter. The "window caption" is the text that will appear in the caption bar.

The parameters marked "initial x position" and "initial y position" specify the initial position of the upper left corner of the window relative to the upper left corner of the screen. By using the identifier CW_USEDEFAULT for these parameters, we're indicating we want Windows to use the default position for an overlapped window. (CW_USEDEFAULT is defined as 0x8000.) By default, Windows positions successive overlapped windows at stepped horizontal and vertical offsets from the upper left corner of the display.

Similarly, the "initial x size" and "initial y size" parameters specify the width and height of the window. The CW_USEDEFAULT identifier again indicates that we want Windows to use a default size for the window. The default size extends to the right side of the display and above the icon area at the bottom of the screen.

The parameter marked "parent window handle" is set to NULL because this window has no parent window. (When a parent-child relationship exists between two windows, the child window always appears on the surface of its parent.) The "window menu handle" is also set to NULL because the window has no menu. The "program instance handle" is set to the instance handle passed to the program as a parameter of *WinMain*. Finally, a "creation parameters" pointer is set to NULL. You could use this pointer to access some data that you might later want to reference in the program.

The *CreateWindow* call returns a handle to the created window. This handle is saved in the variable *hwnd*, which is defined to be of type HWND (handle to a window). Every window in Windows has a handle. Your program uses the handle to refer to the window. Many Windows functions require *hwnd* as a parameter so that Windows knows to which window the function applies. If a program creates many windows, each has a different handle. The handle to a window is one of the most important handles a Windows program (pardon the expression) handles.

Displaying the Window

After the *CreateWindow* call returns, the window has been created internally in Windows. However, the window does not yet appear on the video display. Two more calls are needed. The first is:

```
ShowWindow (hwnd, nCmdShow) ;
```

The first parameter is the handle to the window just created by *CreateWindow*. The second parameter is the *nCmdShow* value passed as a parameter to *WinMain*. This determines how the window is to be initially displayed on the screen. If *nCmdShow* is SW_SHOW-NORMAL (equal to 1), the window is displayed normally. If *nCmdShow* is SW_SHOWMIN-NOACTIVE (equal to 7), then the window is initially displayed as an icon.

The *ShowWindow* function puts the window (or icon) on the display. If the second parameter to *ShowWindow* is SW_SHOWNORMAL, the client area of the window is erased with the background brush specified in the window class. The function call:

```
UpdateWindow (hwnd) ;
```

then causes the client area to be painted. It accomplishes this by sending the window procedure (the *WndProc* function in HELLOWIN.C) a WM_PAINT message. We'll examine shortly how *WndProc* deals with this message.

The Message Loop

After the *UpdateWindow* call, the window is fully visible on the video display. The program must now make itself ready to read keyboard and mouse input from the user. Windows maintains a "message queue" for each Windows program currently running under Windows. When an input event occurs, Windows translates the event into a "message" that it places in the program's message queue.

A program retrieves these messages from the message queue by executing a block of code known as the "message loop":

```
while (GetMessage (&msg, NULL, 0, 0))
     {
     TranslateMessage (&msg) ;
     DispatchMessage (&msg) ;
     }
return msg.wParam ;
```

The *msg* variable is a structure of type MSG, which is defined in WINDOWS.H as follows:

```
typedef struct tagMSG
     {
     HWND   hwnd ;
     WORD   message ;
     WORD   wParam ;
     LONG   lParam ;
     DWORD time ;
     POINT pt ;
     }
     MSG ;
```

The POINT data type is yet another structure, defined like this:

```
typedef struct tagPOINT
     {
     int x ;
     int y ;
     }
     POINT ;
```

The *GetMessage* call that begins the message loop retrieves a message from the message queue:

```
GetMessage (&msg, NULL, 0, 0) ;
```

This call passes to Windows a far pointer to the MSG structure called *msg*. The second, third, and fourth parameters are set to NULL or 0 to indicate that the program wants all messages for all windows created by the program. Windows fills in the fields of the message structure with the next message from the message queue. The fields of this structure are:

- *hwnd*—the handle to the window to which the message is directed. In the HELLOWIN program, this is the same as the *hwnd* value returned from *CreateWindow*, because that's the only window this program has.

- *message*—the message identifier. This is a number that identifies the message. For each message, there is a corresponding identifier defined in WINDOWS.H that begins with the prefix WM ("window message"). For example, if you position the mouse pointer over HELLOWIN's client area and press the left mouse button, Windows will put a message in the message queue with a *message* field equal to WM_LBUTTONDOWN, which is the value 0x0201.

- *wParam*—a 16-bit "message parameter," the meaning and value of which depend on the particular message.

- *lParam*—a 32-bit message parameter dependent on the message.

- *time*—the time the message was placed in the message queue.

- *pt*—the mouse coordinates at the time the message was placed in the message queue.

If the *message* field of the message retrieved from the message queue is anything except WM_QUIT (which equals 0x0012), then *GetMessage* returns a nonzero value. A WM_QUIT message causes the program to fall out of the message loop. The program then terminates, returning the *wParam* member of the *msg* structure.

The statement:

```
TranslateMessage (&msg) ;
```

passes the MSG structure back to Windows for some keyboard translation. (I'll discuss this more in Chapter 3.) The statement:

```
DispatchMessage (&msg) ;
```

again passes the MSG structure back to Windows. Windows then sends the message to the appropriate window procedure for processing. That window procedure is the *WndProc* function in HELLOWIN. After *WndProc* processes the message, it then returns to Windows, which is still servicing the *DispatchMessage* call. When Windows returns to HELLOWIN following the *DispatchMessage* call, the message loop continues with the next *GetMessage* call.

The Window Procedure

All that I've described so far is really just overhead. The window class has been registered, the window has been created, the window has been displayed on the screen, and the program has entered a message loop to retrieve messages from the message queue.

The real action occurs in the window procedure, which Windows programmers commonly call a "window proc" (pronounced "prock"). The window procedure determines what the window displays in its client area and how the window responds to user input.

In HELLOWIN, the window procedure is the function called *WndProc*. A window procedure can have any name. A Windows program can contain more than one window procedure. A window procedure is always associated with a particular window class that you register by calling *RegisterClass*. The *CreateWindow* function creates a window based on a particular window class. More than one window can be created based on the same window class.

A window procedure is always defined like this:

```
long FAR PASCAL WndProc (HWND hwnd, WORD message, WORD wParam, LONG lParam)
```

Note that the four parameters to the window procedure are identical to the first four fields of the MSG structure.

The first parameter is *hwnd*, the handle to the window receiving the message. This is the same handle returned from the *CreateWindow* function. For a program like HELLOWIN, which creates only one window, this is the only window handle the program knows about. If a program creates multiple windows based on the same window class (and hence the same window procedure), then *hwnd* identifies the particular window receiving the message.

The second parameter is a number (specifically, a 16-bit unsigned integer or WORD) that identifies the message. The last two parameters (a WORD called *wParam* and a 32-bit signed long integer or LONG called *lParam*) provide more information about the message. These are called "message parameters." What these parameters contain is specific to each type of message.

Processing the Messages

Each message that a window procedure receives is identified by a number, which is the *message* parameter to the window procedure. The WINDOWS.H header file defines identifiers beginning with the prefix WM ("window message") for each message parameter.

Generally, Windows programmers use a *switch* and *case* construction to determine what message the window procedure is receiving and how to process it accordingly. When a window procedure processes a message, it should return 0 from the window procedure. All messages that a window procedure chooses not to process must be passed to a Windows function named *DefWindowProc*. The value returned from *DefWindowProc* must be returned from the window procedure.

In HELLOWIN, *WndProc* chooses to process only two messages: WM_PAINT and WM_DESTROY. The window procedure is structured like this:

```
switch (message)
    {
    case WM_PAINT :
    [ process WM_PAINT message ]
        return 0 ;

    case WM_DESTROY :
    [ process WM_DESTROY message ]
        return 0 ;
    }

    return DefWindowProc (hwnd, message, wParam, lParam) ;
```

It is essential to call *DefWindowProc* for all messages that your window procedure does not process.

The WM_PAINT Message

The first message that *WndProc* processes is WM_PAINT. This message is extremely important in Windows programming. It informs a program when part or all of the window's client area is "invalid" and must be repainted.

How does a client area become invalid? When the window is first created, the entire client area is invalid because the program has not yet drawn anything on the window. The first WM_PAINT message (which normally occurs when the program calls *UpdateWindow* in *WinMain*) directs the window procedure to draw something on the client area.

When you resize HELLOWIN's window, the client area also becomes invalid. You'll recall that the *style* parameter of HELLOWIN's *wndclass* structure was set to the flags CS_HREDRAW and CS_VREDRAW. This directs Windows to invalidate the whole window when the size changes. The window procedure receives a WM_PAINT message.

When you minimize HELLOWIN to be displayed as an icon and then restore the window again to its previous size, Windows does not save the contents of the client area. Under a graphical environment, this would be too much data. Instead, Windows invalidates the window. The window procedure receives a WM_PAINT message and itself restores the contents of its window.

When you move windows around so they overlap, Windows does not save the area of a window covered by another window. When that area of the window is later uncovered, it is flagged as invalid. The window procedure receives a WM_PAINT message to repaint the contents of the window.

Before sending the window procedure a WM_PAINT message, Windows erases the background of the invalid area using the brush specified in the *hbrBackground* field of the

WNDCLASS structure used to register the window class. In the case of HELLOWIN, this is a stock white brush, which means that Windows erases the background of the window by coloring it white.

WM_PAINT processing almost always begins with a call to *BeginPaint*:

```
hdc = BeginPaint (hwnd, &ps) ;
```

and ends with a call to *EndPaint*:

```
EndPaint (hwnd, &ps) ;
```

In both cases, the first parameter is a handle to the program's window and the second parameter is a pointer to a structure of type PAINTSTRUCT. PAINTSTRUCT contains some information that a window procedure can use for painting the client area. (I'll discuss the fields of this structure in the next chapter.)

BeginPaint returns a "handle to a device context." A device context refers to a physical output device (such as a video display) and its device driver. You need the device context handle to display text and graphics in the client area of a window. Using the device context handle returned from *BeginPaint*, you cannot draw outside the client area, even if you try. *EndPaint* releases the device context handle so that it is no longer valid. *EndPaint* also validates the entire client area.

If a window procedure does not process WM_PAINT messages (which is very rare), they must be passed on to *DefWindowProc*. *DefWindowProc* simply calls *BeginPaint* and *EndPaint* in succession so that the client area is validated.

After *WndProc* calls *BeginPaint*, it calls *GetClientRect*:

```
GetClientRect (hwnd, &rect) ;
```

The first parameter is the handle to the program's window. The second parameter is a pointer to a variable named *rect* defined as type RECT in *WndProc*.

RECT is a "rectangle" structure defined in WINDOWS.H. It has four *int* fields named *left*, *top*, *right*, and *bottom*. *GetClientRect* sets these four fields to the dimensions of the client area of the window. The *left* and *top* fields are always set to 0. The *right* and *bottom* fields are set to the width and height of the client area in pixels.

WndProc doesn't do anything with this RECT structure except pass a pointer to it as the fourth parameter of *DrawText*:

```
DrawText (hdc, "Hello, Windows!", -1, &rect,
          DT_SINGLELINE : DT_CENTER : DT_VCENTER) ;
```

DrawText (as the name implies) draws text. Because this function draws something, the first parameter is a handle to the device context returned from *BeginPaint*. The second parameter is the text to draw, and the third parameter is set to −1 to indicate that the text string is terminated with a 0 byte.

The last parameter is a series of bit flags defined in WINDOWS.H. The flags indicate that the text should be displayed as a single line centered horizontally and vertically within the rectangle specified by the fourth parameter. This function call thus causes the string "Hello, Windows!" to be displayed centered in the client area.

Whenever the client area becomes invalid (as it does when you change the size of the window), Windows erases the background of the window and *WndProc* receives a new WM_PAINT message. *WndProc* obtains the updated window size by calling *GetClientRect* and again displays the text in the new center of the window.

The WM_DESTROY Message

The WM_DESTROY message is another important message. This message indicates that Windows is in the process of destroying a window based on a command from the user. The message is a result of the user selecting Close from the program's system menu or pressing Alt-F4.

HELLOWIN responds to this message in a standard way by calling:

```
PostQuitMessage (0) ;
```

This function inserts a WM_QUIT message in the program's message queue. I mentioned earlier that *GetMessage* returns nonzero for any message other than WM_QUIT that it retrieves from the message queue. When *GetMessage* retrieves a WM_QUIT message, *GetMessage* returns 0. This causes *WinMain* to drop out of the message loop and exit, terminating the program.

The Module Definition File

In addition to the C source code, another file is required for Windows programs. It is called a "module definition file" and has the extension .DEF. The module definition file aids the LINK linker in creating the .EXE file by telling it the characteristics of the program's code and data segments, the size of the program's local data heap (from which the program can allocate memory), and the size of the program's stack. This information becomes part of the header section of the New Executable file format. The HELLOWIN.DEF file is shown in Figure 1-5 on page 16.

The NAME line defines HELLOWIN as a program (rather than a dynamic link library) and gives it a module name, which is usually the name of the program's .EXE file. The DESCRIPTION line simply inserts some text into the .EXE file. This is an excellent place for a copyright notice or version information. The EXETYPE line identifies the program as a Windows program. (OS/2 programs also use module definition files and the New Executable file format.)

The STUB is a program that is inserted into the .EXE file to be executed when anyone attempts to run HELLOWIN.EXE from the MS-DOS command line. The

WINSTUB.EXE program included with the Windows Software Development Kit simply displays the message "This program requires Microsoft Windows" and terminates.

The CODE statement indicates that the program's code segment is flagged as PRELOAD (which means that Windows will load the segment into memory immediately) and MOVEABLE (which means that Windows can move the code segment to another location in memory if it needs to consolidate blocks of free memory). The DISCARDABLE option makes the code "discardable" (which means that Windows can discard the code segment from memory and later reload it from the .EXE file). These are the normal options for Windows programs. If you follow proper Windows programming practice, you will not (in theory) encounter any problems when Windows moves your code.

The DATA statement indicates that we want the data segment to be PRELOAD, MOVEABLE, and MULTIPLE. Again, we are giving Windows permission to move the data segment in memory if necessary. The MULTIPLE keyword requests that each instance of the program gets its own separate data segment. This is necessary because the data segment contains the program's stack and other data items that must be separate for each instance. The code segment, on the other hand, is shared by all instances of the program.

The HEAPSIZE line specifies the amount of extra local memory (memory in the program's own data segment) that will be available for allocation. The value depends on what the program needs. HELLOWIN doesn't need to allocate any local memory, but we'll throw in a small value nonetheless. Windows can expand a program's local heap if necessary.

The STACKSIZE line specifies the size of the stack. The value 8192 bytes is a minimum recommended value. You'll want a bigger stack size if your program has recursive functions or large non-*static* variables.

Finally, the EXPORTS line lists the window procedure *WndProc*. For reasons I'll discuss in Chapter 7, all window procedures that a program contains must be listed in the EXPORTS section of the module definition file.

THE WINDOWS PROGRAMMING HURDLES

Even with my explanation of HELLOWIN, the structure and workings of the program are probably still somewhat mysterious. In a short C program written for a conventional environment, the entire program may be contained in the *main* function. In HELLOWIN, *WinMain* contains only program overhead necessary to register the window class, create the window, and retrieve and dispatch messages from the message queue.

All the real action of the program occurs in the window procedure. In HELLOWIN, this action is not much—it simply displays a text string in its window. But in later chapters you'll find that almost everything a Windows program does it does in response to a message to a window procedure. This is one of the major conceptual hurdles that you must leap to begin writing Windows programs.

Don't Call Me, I'll Call You

As I mentioned earlier, programmers are familiar with the idea of calling on the operating system to do something. For instance, C programmers use the *open* or *fopen* function to open a file. The library functions provided with the compiler have code that eventually calls the operating system to open the file. No problem.

But Windows is different. Although Windows has more than 550 functions that your program can call, Windows also makes calls to *your* program, specifically to the window procedure we have called *WndProc*. The window procedure is associated with a window class that the program registers by calling *RegisterClass*. A window that is created based on this class uses this window procedure for processing all messages to the window. Windows sends a message to the window by calling the window procedure.

Windows calls *WndProc* when a window is first being created. Windows calls *WndProc* when the window is later destroyed. Windows calls *WndProc* when the window has been resized or moved or made into an icon. Windows calls *WndProc* when an item has been selected from a menu. Windows calls *WndProc* when a scroll bar is being moved or clicked with the mouse. Windows calls *WndProc* to tell it when it must repaint its client area.

All these calls are in the form of messages. In most Windows programs, the bulk of the program is dedicated to handling these messages. The 130 or so different messages that Windows can send to a window procedure are all identified with names that begin with the letters WM and defined in WINDOWS.H.

Actually, the idea of a routine within a program that is called from outside the program is not unheard of in normal programming. The *signal* function in C can trap a Ctrl-Break. You may have experience with intercepting hardware interrupts in assembly language or using one of the ON constructions in Microsoft BASIC. The Microsoft Mouse driver has a method that non-Windows programs can use to be notified of mouse activity.

In Windows, this concept is extended to cover everything. Everything that happens to a window is relayed to the window procedure in the form of a message. The window procedure then responds to this message in some way or passes the message to *DefWin-dowProc* for default processing.

The *wParam* and *lParam* parameters to the window procedure are not used in HELLOWIN except as parameters to *DefWindowProc*. These parameters give the window additional information about the message. The meaning of the parameters is message-dependent.

Let's look at an example. Whenever the client area of a window changes in size, Windows calls that window's window procedure. The *hwnd* parameter to the window procedure is the handle of the window changing in size. The *message* parameter is WM_SIZE. The *wParam* parameter for a WM_SIZE message is the value SIZENORMAL, SIZEICONIC, SIZEFULLSCREEN, SIZEZOOMSHOW, or SIZEZOOMHIDE (defined in WINDOWS.H as the numbers 0 through 4). The *wParam* parameter indicates whether the window is being minimized, maximized, or hidden (as a result of another window being maximized). The *lParam* parameter contains the new size of the window. The new width (a 16-bit value) and the new height (a 16-bit value) have been stuck together in the 32-byte *lParam*. WINDOWS.H includes macros to help you extract these two values from *lParam*. We'll do this in the next chapter.

Sometimes messages generate other messages as a result of *DefWindowProc* processing. For example, suppose you run HELLOWIN and select Close from the system menu using either the keyboard or the mouse. *DefWindowProc* processes this keyboard and mouse input. When it detects that you have selected the Close option, it sends a WM_SYSCOMMAND message to the window procedure. *WndProc* passes this message to *DefWindowProc*. *DefWindowProc* responds by sending a WM_CLOSE message to the window procedure. *WndProc* again passes this message to *DefWindowProc*. *DefWindowProc* responds to the WM_CLOSE message by calling *DestroyWindow*. *DestroyWindow* causes Windows to send a WM_DESTROY message to the window procedure. *WndProc* finally responds to this message by calling *PostQuitMessage* to put a WM_QUIT message in the message queue. This message causes the message loop in *WinMain* to terminate and the program to end.

Queued and Nonqueued Messages

I've talked about Windows sending messages to a window, which means that Windows calls the window procedure. But a Windows program also has a message loop that retrieves messages from a message queue by calling *GetMessage* and dispatches them to the window procedure by calling *DispatchMessage*.

So, does a Windows program poll for messages (exactly as a normal program polls for keyboard data) and then route these messages to some location? Or does it receive messages directly from outside the program? Well, both.

Messages can be either "queued" or "nonqueued." The queued messages are those that are placed in a program's message queue by Windows and retrieved and dispatched in the message loop. The nonqueued messages are sent to the window directly when Windows calls the window procedure. The result is that the window procedure gets all the messages—both queued and nonqueued—for the window. Structurally, Windows programs are very clean, because they have one central point of message processing. It is said that queued messages are *posted* to a message queue while nonqueued messages are *sent* to the window procedure.

The queued messages are primarily those that result from user input in the form of keystrokes (such as WM_KEYDOWN and WM_KEYUP), characters that result from keystrokes (WM_CHAR), mouse movement (WM_MOUSEMOVE), and mouse button clicks (WM_LBUTTONDOWN). Queued messages also include the timer message (WM_TIMER), the repaint message (WM_PAINT), and the quit message (WM_QUIT). The nonqueued messages are everything else. In many cases the nonqueued messages result from queued messages. When you pass a nonqueued message to *DefWindowProc* within the window procedure, Windows often processes the message by sending the window procedure other messages.

This process is obviously complex, but fortunately most of the complexity is Windows' problem rather than our program's. From the perspective of the window procedure, these messages come through in an orderly, synchronized manner. The window procedure can do something with these messages or ignore them. For this reason, the window procedure has been called the "ultimate hook." Messages notify the window procedure of almost everything that affects the window.

The nonqueued messages often result from calling certain Windows function calls or by explicitly sending a message by calling *SendMessage*. (Messages can also be placed in a message queue by calling *PostMessage*.)

For example, when *WinMain* calls *CreateWindow*, Windows creates the window and in the process sends the window procedure a WM_CREATE message. When *WinMain* calls *ShowWindow*, Windows sends the window procedure WM_SIZE and WM_SHOW-WINDOW messages. When *WinMain* calls *UpdateWindow*, Windows sends the window procedure a WM_PAINT message.

Messages are not like hardware interrupts. While processing one message in a window procedure the program will not be interrupted by another message. Only when the window procedure calls a function that generates a new message will the message procedure process the message before the function returns.

The message loop and the window procedure do not run concurrently. When the window procedure is processing a queued message, it is the result of a call to *DispatchMessage* in *WinMain*. *DispatchMessage* does not return until the window procedure has processed the message.

But notice that the window procedure must be reentrant. That is, Windows often calls *WndProc* with a new message as a result of *WndProc* calling *DefWindowProc* with a previous message. This is one reason that a Windows program requires a 8-KB stack, as indicated in the module definition (.DEF) file. In most cases the reentrancy of the window procedure presents no problem, but you should be aware of it.

In many cases, the window procedure must retain information it obtains in one message and use it while processing another message. This information must be saved in variables defined as *static* in the window procedure or in global variables.

Of course, you'll get a much better feel for all this in later chapters as the window procedures are expanded to process more messages.

Nonpreemptive Multitasking

The *GetMessage* call within the message loop is important for another reason. Except for some device drivers that must process hardware interrupts (such as the timer, keyboard, mouse, and serial port), Windows usually treats HELLOWIN as if it were the only program running under the system. Windows will not arbitrarily switch away from HELLOWIN and run some other program. The exception is during the *GetMessage* call. If HELLOWIN's message queue has no waiting messages and another program has some messages in its message queue, then Windows switches from HELLOWIN to the other program. That makes sense, does it not?

You can think of it this way: In most cases, when your program calls a function in Windows, you can expect that the function will be processed and return control to your program within a reasonable period of time. When you call *GetMessage*, however, it may be some time before Windows returns with a message if the program's message queue does not contain any messages and another program's message queue does. Windows can take advantage of the delay caused by an empty message queue during a *GetMessage* call to switch to another program that has messages waiting. As a result, Windows has a "jumpy" type of multitasking. Sometimes a program has a long job to do, and all other programs running under Windows seem to stop running during this time.

Rather than "jumpy multitasking," this characteristic is usually called "nonpreemptive multitasking." Windows is multitasking between programs by switching between them. But Windows is not doing this as it is done within a traditional multitasking system, based on the tick of a hardware clock and allocating each program a tiny time-slice to do its stuff. It's multitasking at the point where programs check the message queue for messages.

The process is actually a little more complex than that: Windows also switches between programs during *PeekMessage* and *WaitMessage* calls, but these are less common than *GetMessage*. Furthermore, the WM_PAINT and WM_TIMER messages are treated as low-priority messages, so Windows can switch from a program if only WM_PAINT and WM_TIMER messages are present in the queue.

The Learning Curve

Yes, as you've undoubtedly determined from this chapter, Windows programming is certainly different from programming for a conventional environment like MS-DOS. Nobody will claim that Windows programming is easy.

When I first started learning Windows programming, I decided to do what I had always done when learning a new operating system or a new language—to write a simple "hex dump" program to display the contents of a file. In the conventional MS-DOS environment, such a program involves command-line processing, rudimentary file I/O, and screen output formatting. However, my Windows hex-dump program turned into a monster. It required that I learn about menus, dialog boxes, scroll bars, and the like. As a first Windows program, it was definitely a mistake, demanding that I absorb too much all at once.

Yet when this program was finished, it was quite unlike any hex-dump program I had written. Rather than obtain the filename from a command line, WINDUMP (as I called it) presented a list box showing all the files in the current directory. Rather than write its output to the screen in a simple teletype fashion, WINDUMP had scroll bars so I could move to any part of the file. As an extra bonus, I could even run two copies of WINDUMP to compare two files side by side. In short, WINDUMP was the first hex-dump program I wrote that I was actually proud of.

What you have to ask yourself is this: Do I want my programs to use a more modern and productive user interface, one that includes menus, dialog boxes, scroll bars, and graphics? If you answer yes, then the question becomes: Do I want to write all this menu, dialog box, scroll bar, and graphics code myself? Or would I rather take advantage of all the code already inside Windows for this? In other words, is it easier to learn how to use 550 function calls or to write them yourself? Is it easier to orient your programming mind to the message-driven architecture of Windows or struggle with using several different sources of user input in a traditional model?

If you're going to write your own user interface logic, you had better close this book and get to work right away. Meanwhile, the rest of us are going to learn how to display and scroll text in a window.

Chapter 2

Painting
with Text

In the previous chapter you saw a simple Windows program that displayed a single line of text in the center of its client area. The client area occupies all the space of the window that is not taken up by the caption bar, the window-sizing border, the menu bar (if any), and scroll bars (if any). The client area is the part of the window on which a program is free to draw. You can do almost anything you want with that client area—anything, that is, except assume that it will be a particular size or that the size will remain constant while your program is running. If you are accustomed to writing programs for the IBM PC, this exception may come as a bit of a shock. You can no longer think in terms of 25 lines and 80 columns of text. Your program shares the video display with other Windows programs. The user controls how the programs are arranged on the screen. Your program must accept the size it's given and do something reasonable with it. (A program could create a window of a specific fixed size, but it isn't very common.)

This works both ways. Just as your program may find itself with a client area barely large enough in which to say "Hello," it may also someday be run on a big-screen high-resolution video system and discover a client area big enough for two entire pages of text and plenty of closet space besides. Dealing intelligently with both these eventualities is an important part of Windows programming.

Although Windows has extensive Graphics Device Interface (GDI) functions for displaying graphics, in this chapter I'll stick to displaying simple lines of text. I'll also ignore the various fonts (typefaces) and font sizes that Windows makes available and use only Windows' default "system font." This may seem limiting, but it really isn't. The problems we encounter—and solve—in this chapter apply to all Windows programming. When you display a combination of text and graphics (as, for instance, the Windows CALENDAR, CARDFILE, and CALCULATOR programs do), the character dimensions of Windows' default system font often determine the dimensions of the graphics.

This chapter is ostensibly about learning how to paint, but it's really about learning the basics of device-independent programming. Windows programs can assume little about their environment. Instead, they must use the facilities that Windows provides to obtain information about the environment.

PAINTING AND REPAINTING

Under MS-DOS, a program using the display in a full-screen mode can write to any part of the display. What the program puts on the display will stay there and will not mysteriously disappear. The program can then discard information needed to re-create the screen display. If another program (such as a RAM-resident popup) overlays part of the display, then the popup is responsible for restoring the display when it leaves.

In Windows, you can display only to the client area of your window, and you cannot be assured that what you display to the client area will remain there until your program specifically writes over it. For instance, the dialog box from another application may overlay part of your client area. Although Windows will attempt to save and restore the area of the display underneath the dialog box, it sometimes cannot do so. When the dialog box is removed from the screen, Windows will request that your program repaint this portion of your client area.

Windows is a message-driven system. Windows informs applications of various events by posting messages in the application's message queue or sending messages to the appropriate window procedure. Windows informs a window procedure that part of the window's client area needs updating by posting a WM_PAINT message.

The WM_PAINT Message

Most Windows programs call the function *UpdateWindow* during initialization in *Win-Main* shortly before entering the message loop. Windows takes this opportunity to send the window procedure its first WM_PAINT message. That message informs your window procedure that the client area is ready to be painted. Thereafter, that window procedure should be ready at any time to process additional WM_PAINT messages and even repaint the entire client area of the window if necessary. A window procedure receives a WM_PAINT message whenever one of the following occurs:

- A previously hidden area of the window is brought into view when a user moves a window or uncovers a window.

- The user resizes the window (if the window class style has the CS-_HREDRAW and CS_VREDRAW bits set).

- The program uses the *ScrollWindow* function to scroll part of its client area.

- The program uses the *InvalidateRect* or *InvalidateRgn* function to explicitly generate a WM_PAINT message.

In some cases in which part of the client area is temporarily written over, Windows attempts to save an area of the display and restore it later. This is not always successful. Windows may sometimes post a WM_PAINT message when:

- Windows removes a dialog box or message box that was overlaying part of the window.

- A menu is pulled down and then released.

In a few cases, Windows always saves the area of the display it overwrites and then restores it. This is the case whenever:

- The cursor is moved across the client area.

- An icon is dragged across the client area.

Dealing with WM_PAINT messages requires that you alter your thinking about how you write to the display. Your program should be structured so that it accumulates all the information necessary to paint the client area but paints only "on demand"—when Windows sends the window procedure a WM_PAINT message. If your program needs to update its client area, it can force Windows to generate this WM_PAINT message. This may seem a roundabout method of displaying something on the screen, but the structure of your programs will benefit from it.

Valid and Invalid Rectangles

Although a window procedure should be prepared to update the entire client area whenever it receives a WM_PAINT message, it often needs to update only a smaller rectangular area. This is most obvious when part of the client area is overlaid by a dialog box. Repainting is required only for the rectangular area uncovered when the dialog box is removed.

That rectangular area is known as an "invalid rectangle." The presence of an invalid rectangle in a client area is what prompts Windows to place a WM_PAINT message in the application's message queue. Your window procedure receives a WM_PAINT message only if part of your client area is invalid.

Windows internally maintains a "paint information structure" for each window. This structure contains (among other information) the coordinates of the invalid rectangle. If another rectangular area of the client area becomes invalid before the window procedure processes the WM_PAINT message, Windows calculates a new invalid rectangle that encompasses both areas and stores this updated information in the paint information structure. Windows does not place multiple WM_PAINT messages in the message queue.

A window procedure can invalidate a rectangle in its own client area by calling *InvalidateRect*. If the message queue already contains a WM_PAINT message, Windows calculates a new invalid rectangle. Otherwise, it places a WM_PAINT message in the message queue. A window procedure can obtain the coordinates of the invalid rectangle when it receives a WM_PAINT message (as we'll see shortly). It can also obtain these coordinates at any other time by calling *GetUpdateRect*.

After the window procedure calls *EndPaint* during the WM_PAINT message, the entire client area is validated. A program can also validate any rectangular region in the client area by calling the *ValidateRect* function. If this call has the effect of validating the entire invalid area, then any WM_PAINT message currently in the queue is deleted.

AN INTRODUCTION TO GDI

To paint the client area of your window, you use Windows' Graphics Device Interface (GDI) functions. (A full discussion of GDI is in Chapters 11–15.) Windows provides five GDI functions for writing text strings to the client area of the window. We've already encountered the *DrawText* function in Chapter 1, but the most popular text output function by far is *TextOut*. This function has the following format:

```
TextOut (hdc, x, y, lpsString, nLength) ;
```

TextOut writes a character string to the display. The *lpsString* parameter is a long (or far) pointer to the character string, and *nLength* is the length of the string. The *x* and *y* parameters define the starting position, in "logical coordinates," of the character string in the client area. The *hdc* parameter is a "handle to a device context," and it is an important part of GDI. Virtually every GDI function requires this handle as the first parameter to the function.

The Device Context

A handle, you'll recall, is simply a number that Windows uses for internal reference to an object. You obtain the handle from Windows and then use the handle in other functions. The device context handle is your window's passport to the GDI functions. With that device context handle you are free to paint your client area and make it as beautiful or as ugly as you like.

The device context (also called the "DC") is really a data structure maintained by GDI. A device context is associated with a particular display device, such as a printer, plotter, or video display. For a video display, a device context is usually associated with a particular window on the display.

Windows uses the values in the device context structure (also called "attributes" of the device context) in conjunction with the GDI functions. With *TextOut*, for instance, the attributes of the device context determine the color of the text, the color of the text background, how the *x*-coordinate and *y*-coordinate are mapped to the client area of the window, and what font Windows uses when displaying the text.

When a program needs to paint, it must first obtain a handle to a device context. After it has finished painting, the program should release the handle. When a program releases the handle, the handle is no longer valid and must not be used. The program should obtain the handle and release the handle during processing of a single message. Except for a device context created with a call to *CreateDC*, you should not keep a device context handle around from one message to another.

Windows applications generally use two methods for getting the handle to the device context in preparation for painting the screen.

Getting a Device Context Handle: Method One

You use this method when you process WM_PAINT messages. Two functions are involved: *BeginPaint* and *EndPaint*. These two functions require the handle to the window (passed to the window procedure as a parameter) and the address of a structure variable of type PAINTSTRUCT. Windows programmers usually name this structure variable *ps* and define it within the window procedure, like so:

```
PAINTSTRUCT ps ;
```

While processing a WM_PAINT message, a Windows function first calls *BeginPaint* to fill in the fields of the *ps* structure. The value returned from *BeginPaint* is the device context handle. This is commonly saved in a variable named *hdc*. You define this variable in your window procedure like this:

```
HDC hdc ;
```

The HDC data type is defined in WINDOWS.H as a HANDLE. The program may then use GDI functions such as *TextOut*. A call to *EndPaint* releases the device context handle and validates the window.

Typically, processing of the WM_PAINT message looks like this:

```
case WM_PAINT :
     hdc = BeginPaint (hwnd,&ps) ;
     [use GDI functions]
     EndPaint (hwnd, &ps) ;
     return 0 ;
```

The window procedure must call *BeginPaint* and *EndPaint* as a pair while processing the WM_PAINT message. If a window procedure does not process WM_PAINT messages, then it must pass the WM_PAINT message to *DefWindowProc* (the default window procedure) located in Windows.

DefWindowProc processes WM_PAINT messages with the following code:

```
case WM_PAINT :
     BeginPaint (hwnd, &ps) ;
     EndPaint (hwnd, &ps) ;
     return 0 ;
```

This sequence of *BeginPaint* and *EndPaint* with nothing in between simply validates the previously invalid rectangle. But don't do this:

```
case WM_PAINT :
     return 0 ;    // WRONG !!!
```

Windows places a WM_PAINT message in the message queue because part of the client area is invalid. Unless you call *BeginPaint* and *EndPaint* (or *ValidateRect*), Windows will not validate that area. Instead, Windows will send you another WM_PAINT message. And another, and another, and another…

The Paint Information Structure

Earlier I mentioned a "paint information structure" that Windows maintains for each window. That's what PAINTSTRUCT is. The structure is defined in WINDOWS.H as follows:

```
typedef struct tagPAINTSTRUCT
   {
   HDC       hdc ;
   BOOL      fErase ;
   RECT      rcPaint ;
   BOOL      fRestore ;
   BOOL      fIncUpdate ;
   BYTE      rgbReserved[16] ;
   } PAINTSTRUCT ;
```

Windows fills in the fields of this structure when your program calls *BeginPaint*. Your program may use only the first three fields. The others are used internally by Windows.

The *hdc* field is the handle to the device context. In a redundancy typical of Windows, the value returned from *BeginPaint* is also this device context handle.

In most cases, *fErase* will be flagged TRUE (nonzero), meaning that Windows has erased the background of the invalid rectangle. Windows erases the background using the brush specified in the *hbrBackground* field of the WNDCLASS structure that you use when registering the window class during *WinMain* initialization. Many Windows programs use a white brush:

```
wndclass.hbrBackground = GetStockObject (WHITE_BRUSH) ;
```

However, if your program invalidates a rectangle of the client area by calling the Windows function *InvalidateRect*, one of the parameters to this function specifies whether you want the background erased. If this parameter is FALSE (or 0), then Windows will not erase the background, and the *fErase* field will also be FALSE.

The *rcPaint* field of the PAINTSTRUCT structure is a structure of type RECT. As you learned in Chapter 1, the RECT structure defines a rectangle. The four fields are *left*, *top*, *right*, and *bottom*. The *rcPaint* field in the PAINTSTRUCT structure defines the boundaries of the invalid rectangle, as shown in Figure 2-1. The values are in units of pixels relative to the upper left corner of the client area. The invalid rectangle is the area that you should repaint. Although a Windows program can simply repaint the entire client area of the window whenever it receives a WM_PAINT message, repainting only the area of the window defined by that rectangle saves time.

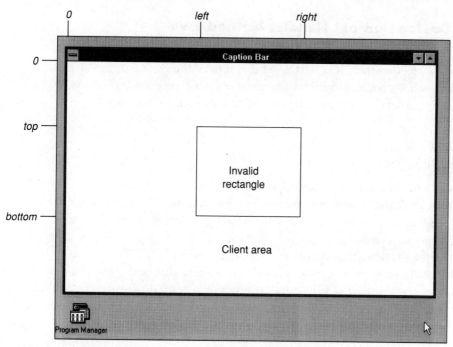

Figure 2-1. *The boundaries of the invalid rectangle.*

The *rcPaint* rectangle in PAINTSTRUCT is not only the invalid rectangle; it is also a "clipping" rectangle. This means that Windows restricts painting to within the clipping rectangle. When you use the device context handle from the PAINTSTRUCT structure, Windows will not paint outside the *rcPaint* rectangle.

To paint outside this *rcPaint* rectangle while processing WM_PAINT messages, you can make this call:

```
InvalidateRect (hWnd, NULL, TRUE) ;
```

before calling *BeginPaint*. This invalidates the entire client area and erases the background. A FALSE value in the last parameter will not erase the background, however. Whatever was there will stay.

In the HELLOWIN program in Chapter 1, we didn't care about invalid rectangles or clipping rectangles when processing the WM_PAINT message. If the area where the text was displayed happened to be within the invalid rectangle, then *DrawText* restored it. If not, then at some point during processing of the *DrawText* call, Windows determined it didn't have to write anything to the display. But this determination takes time. A programmer concerned about performance and speed will want to use the invalid-rectangle dimensions during processing of WM_PAINT to avoid unnecessary GDI calls.

Getting a Device Context Handle: Method Two

You can also obtain a handle to a device context if you want to paint the client area when processing messages other then WM_PAINT or if you need the device context handle for other purposes, such as obtaining information about the device context. Call *GetDC* to obtain the handle to the device context, and *ReleaseDC* after you're done with it:

```
hdc = GetDC (hwnd) ;
    [use GDI functions]
ReleaseDC (hwnd, hdc) ;
```

Like *BeginPaint* and *EndPaint*, the *GetDC* and *ReleaseDC* functions should be called in pairs. When you call *GetDC* while processing a message, you should call *ReleaseDC* before you exit the window procedure. Do not call *GetDC* in response to one message and *ReleaseDC* in response to another.

Unlike the device context handle obtained from the PAINTSTRUCT structure, the device context handle returned from *GetDC* has a clipping rectangle equal to the entire client area. You can paint on any part of the client area, not merely on the invalid rectangle (if indeed there is an invalid rectangle). Unlike *EndPaint*, *ReleaseDC* does not validate any invalid rectangles.

TextOut: The Details

When you obtain the handle to the device context, Windows fills the device context structure with default values. As you'll see in later chapters, you can change these defaults with GDI functions. The GDI function we're interested in right now is *TextOut*:

```
TextOut (hdc, x, y, lpsString, nLength) ;
```

Let's examine this function in more detail.

The first parameter is the handle to the device context—either the *hdc* value returned from *GetDC* or the *hdc* value returned from *BeginPaint* during processing of a WM_PAINT message.

The attributes of the device context control the characteristics of this displayed text. For instance, one attribute of the device context specifies the text color. The default color is black. The default device context also defines a background color of white. When a program writes text to the display, Windows uses this background color to fill in the space surrounding the characters.

This text background color is not the same background you set when defining the window class. The background in the window class is a brush—which is a pattern that may or may not be a pure color—that Windows uses to erase the client area. It is not part of the device context structure. When defining the window class structure, most Windows applications use WHITE_BRUSH so that the background color in the default device context is the same color as the brush Windows uses to erase the background of the client area.

The *lpsString* parameter is a long pointer to a character string, and *nLength* is the length of the string. The string should not contain any ASCII control characters such as carriage returns, linefeeds, tabs, or backspaces. Windows displays these control characters as solid blocks. *TextOut* does not recognize a 0 as denoting the end of the string and requires the *nLength* parameter for the length.

The *x* and *y* values in *TextOut* define the starting point of the character string within the client area. The *x* value is the horizontal position; the *y* value is the vertical position. The upper left corner of the first character in the string is positioned at *x* and *y*. In the default device context, the origin (the point where *x* and *y* both equal 0) is the upper left corner of the client area. If you use 0 values for *x* and *y* in *TextOut*, the character string starts flush against the upper left corner of the client area.

GDI coordinates are "logical coordinates." Windows has a variety of "mapping modes" that govern how the logical coordinates specified in GDI functions are translated to the physical pixel coordinates of the display. The mapping mode is defined in the device context. The default mapping mode is called MM_TEXT (using the WINDOWS.H identifier). Under the MM_TEXT mapping mode, logical units are the same as physical units, which are pixels. Values of *x* increase as you move to the right in the client area and values of *y* increase as you move down in the client area. (See Figure 2-2 on the following page.) The MM_TEXT coordinate system is identical to the coordinate system that Windows uses to define the invalid rectangle in the PAINTSTRUCT structure. Very convenient. (This is not the case with other mapping modes, however.)

The device context also defines a clipping region. As you've seen, the default clipping region is the entire client area for a device context handle obtained from *GetDC* and the invalid rectangle for the device context handle obtained from *BeginPaint*. Windows will not display any part of the character string that lies outside the clipping rectangle. If a character is partly within the clipping rectangle, Windows displays only the portion of the character inside the rectangle. Writing outside the client area of your window isn't easy to do, so don't worry about doing it inadvertently.

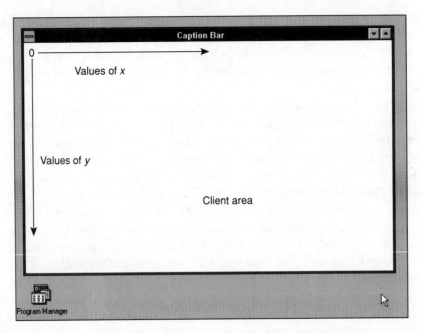

Figure 2-2. *The x-coordinate and y-coordinate in the MM_TEXT mapping mode.*

The System Font

The device context also defines the font that Windows uses when writing text to the client area. The default is a font called the "system font" or (using the WINDOWS.H identifier) SYSTEM_FONT. The system font is the font that Windows uses for text in caption bars, menus, and dialog boxes.

Under Windows 3, the system font is a variable-width font, which means that different characters have different widths. A "W" is wider than an "i." In earlier versions of Windows, the system font was a fixed-pitch font in which all the characters had the same width.

The system font is a "raster font," which means that the characters are defined as blocks of pixels. The floppy disks for the Windows installation include several system fonts in various sizes for use with different video display adapters.

When manufacturers of a new video board develop a new Windows display driver, they are also responsible for developing a new system font appropriate for the resolution of the display. Alternatively, the manufacturer might specify that one of the system font files supplied with the retail version of Windows be used. The system font must be designed so that at least 25 lines of 80-character text can fit on the display. That is the only guarantee you have about the relationship between screen size and font size in Windows.

The Size of a Character

To display multiple lines of text using the *TextOut* function, you need to determine the dimensions of font characters. You can space successive lines of text based on the height of a character, and you can space columns of text across the client area based on the width of a character.

You can obtain character dimensions with the *GetTextMetrics* call. *GetTextMetrics* requires a handle to the device context because it returns information about the font currently selected in the device context. Windows copies the various values of text metrics into a structure of type TEXTMETRIC. The values are in units that depend on the mapping mode selected in the device context. In the default device context, this mapping mode is MM_TEXT, so the dimensions are in units of pixels.

To use the *GetTextMetrics* function, you first need to define a structure variable (commonly called *tm*):

```
TEXTMETRIC tm ;
```

Next, get a handle to the device context and call *GetTextMetrics*:

```
hdc = GetDC (hwnd) ;
GetTextMetrics (hdc, &tm) ;
```

After you examine the values in the text metric structure (and probably save a few of them for future use), you release the device context:

```
ReleaseDC (hwnd, hdc) ;
```

Text Metrics: The Details

The TEXTMETRIC structure provides a wealth of information about the current font selected in the device context. However, the vertical size of a font is defined by only five values, as shown in Figure 2-3 on the following page.

These are fairly self-explanatory. The *tmInternalLeading* value is the amount of space allowed for an accent mark above a character. If the value is set to 0, accented capital letters are made a little shorter so that the accent fits within the ascent of the character. The *tmExternalLeading* value is the amount of space that the designer of the font is suggesting be added between character rows. You can accept or reject the font designer's suggestion for including external leading when spacing lines of text.

The TEXTMETRIC structure has two fields that describe character width: *tmAveCharWidth* (a weighted average width of lowercase characters) and *tmMaxChar-Width* (the width of the widest character in the font). For a fixed-pitch font, these two values are the same.

The sample programs in this chapter will require another character width—the average width of uppercase letters. This can be calculated as 150% of *tmAveCharWidth*.

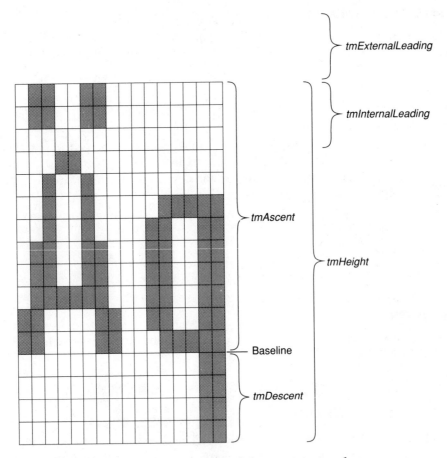

Figure 2-3. *The five values defining vertical character size in a font.*

It's important to realize that the dimensions of the system font are dependent on the resolution of the video display on which Windows runs. Windows provides a device-independent graphics interface, but you have to help. Don't write your Windows program so that it guesses at character dimensions. Don't hard code any values. Use the *GetText-Metrics* function to obtain this information.

Formatting Text

Because the dimensions of the system font do not change during a Windows session, you need to call *GetTextMetrics* only once when your program executes. A good place to make this call is while processing the WM_CREATE message in the window procedure. The WM_CREATE message is the first message the window procedure receives. Windows calls your window procedure with a WM_CREATE message when you call *CreateWindow* in *WinMain*.

Suppose you're writing a Windows program that displays several lines of text running down the client area. You'll want to obtain values for the character width and height. Within the window procedure you can define two variables to save the average character width (*cxChar*) and the total height (*cyChar*):

```
static short cxChar, cyChar ;
```

The prefix *c* added to the variable names stands for "count," and in combination with *x* or *y* refers to a width or a height. These variables are defined as *static* because they must be valid when the window procedure processes other messages (such as WM_PAINT). If the variables are defined outside any functions, they need not be defined as *static*.

Here's the WM_CREATE code:

```
case WM_CREATE :
     hdc = GetDC  (hwnd) ;

     GetTextMetrics (hdc, &tm) ;
     cxChar = tm.tmAveCharWidth ;
     cyChar = tm.tmHeight + tm.tmExternalLeading ;

     ReleaseDC (hwnd, hdc) ;
     return 0 ;
```

If you do not want to include external leading to space lines of text, you can use:

```
cyChar = tm.tmHeight ;
```

How you use this character size to calculate display coordinates is up to you. A simple method is to leave a *cyChar* margin at the top of the client area and a *cxChar* margin at the left. To display several lines of left-justified text, use the following *x*-coordinate values when calling the *TextOut* function:

```
cxChar
```

The *y*-coordinate values in *TextOut* are:

```
cyChar * (1 + i)
```

where *i* is the line number starting at 0.

You'll often find it necessary to display formatted numbers as well as simple character strings. If you were programming in MS-DOS using standard C library functions, you would probably use *printf* for this formatting. You cannot use *printf* in Windows, because *printf* writes to the standard output device, and that concept makes no sense under Windows.

Instead, you can use *sprintf*. The *sprintf* function works just like *printf* except that it puts the formatted string into a character array. You can then use *TextOut* to write the string to the display. Very conveniently, the value returned from *sprintf* is the length of the string—you can pass this value to *TextOut* as the *nLength* parameter. This code shows a typical *sprintf* and *TextOut* combination:

```
short nLength ;
char  szBuffer [40] ;
     [other program lines]
nLength = sprintf (szBuffer, "The sum of %d and %d is %d",
                    nA, nB, nA + nB) ;
TextOut (hdc, x, y, szBuffer, nLength) ;
```

For something as simple as this you could dispense with the *nLength* definition and combine the two statements into one:

```
TextOut (hdc, x, y, szBuffer,
     sprintf (szBuffer, "The sum of %d and %d is %d",
                    nA, nB, nA + nB)) ;
```

It's not pretty, but it works.

If you don't need to display floating-point numbers, you can use *wsprintf* rather than *sprintf*. The *wsprintf* function has the same syntax as *sprintf*, but it's included in Windows, so using it won't increase the size of your .EXE file.

Putting It All Together

Now we seem to have everything we need to write a simple program that displays multiple lines of text on the screen. We know how to get a handle to a device context, how to use the *TextOut* function, and how to space text based on the size of a single character. The only thing left to do is to display something interesting.

The information available in the Windows *GetSystemMetrics* call looks interesting enough. This function returns information about the size of various graphical items in Windows, such as icons, cursors, caption bars, and scroll bars. These sizes vary with the display adapter and driver. *GetSystemMetrics* requires a single parameter called an "index." This index is 1 of 37 integer identifiers defined in WINDOWS.H. *GetSystemMetrics* returns an integer, usually the size of the item specified in the parameter.

Let's write a program that displays all the information available from the *GetSystem-Metrics* call in a simple one-line-per-item format. Working with this information is easier if we create a header file that defines an array of structures containing both the WIN-DOWS.H identifiers for the *GetSystemMetrics* index and the text we want to display for each value returned from the call. This header file is called SYSMETS.H and is shown in Figure 2-4.

SYSMETS.H

```
/*-------------------------------------------------
   SYSMETS.H -- System metrics display structure
   ----------------------------------------------*/

#define NUMLINES (sizeof sysmetrics / sizeof sysmetrics [0])

struct
    {
    int  nIndex ;
    char *szLabel ;
    char *szDesc ;
    }
    sysmetrics [] =
    {
    SM_CXSCREEN,        "SM_CXSCREEN",        "Screen width in pixels",
    SM_CYSCREEN,        "SM_CYSCREEN",        "Screen height in pixels",
    SM_CXVSCROLL,       "SM_CXVSCROLL",       "Vertical scroll arrow width",
    SM_CYHSCROLL,       "SM_CYHSCROLL",       "Horizontal scroll arrow height",
    SM_CYCAPTION,       "SM_CYCAPTION",       "Caption bar height",
    SM_CXBORDER,        "SM_CXBORDER",        "Border width",
    SM_CYBORDER,        "SM_CYBORDER",        "Border height",
    SM_CXDLGFRAME,      "SM_CXDLGFRAME",      "Dialog window frame width",
    SM_CYDLGFRAME,      "SM_CYDLGFRAME",      "Dialog window frame height",
    SM_CYVTHUMB,        "SM_CYVTHUMB",        "Vertical scroll thumb height",
    SM_CXHTHUMB,        "SM_CXHTHUMB",        "Horizontal scroll thumb width",
    SM_CXICON,          "SM_CXICON",          "Icon width",
    SM_CYICON,          "SM_CYICON",          "Icon height",
    SM_CXCURSOR,        "SM_CXCURSOR",        "Cursor width",
    SM_CYCURSOR,        "SM_CYCURSOR",        "Cursor height",
    SM_CYMENU,          "SM_CYMENU",          "Menu bar height",
    SM_CXFULLSCREEN,    "SM_CXFULLSCREEN",    "Full-screen client window width",
    SM_CYFULLSCREEN,    "SM_CYFULLSCREEN",    "Full-screen client window height",
    SM_CYKANJIWINDOW,   "SM_CYKANJIWINDOW",   "Kanji window height",
    SM_MOUSEPRESENT,    "SM_MOUSEPRESENT",    "Mouse present flag",
    SM_CYVSCROLL,       "SM_CYVSCROLL",       "Vertical scroll arrow height",
    SM_CXHSCROLL,       "SM_CXHSCROLL",       "Horizontal scroll arrow width",
    SM_DEBUG,           "SM_DEBUG",           "Debug version flag",
    SM_SWAPBUTTON,      "SM_SWAPBUTTON",      "Mouse buttons swapped flag",
    SM_RESERVED1,       "SM_RESERVED1",       "Reserved",
    SM_RESERVED2,       "SM_RESERVED2",       "Reserved",
    SM_RESERVED3,       "SM_RESERVED3",       "Reserved",
    SM_RESERVED4,       "SM_RESERVED4",       "Reserved",
    SM_CXMIN,           "SM_CXMIN",           "Minimum window width",
    SM_CYMIN,           "SM_CYMIN",           "Minimum window height",
    SM_CXSIZE,          "SM_CXSIZE",          "Minimize/Maximize icon width",
    SM_CYSIZE,          "SM_CYSIZE",          "Minimize/Maximize icon height",
```

Figure 2-4. *SYSMETS.H.*   *(continued)*

```
SM_CXFRAME,        "SM_CXFRAME",        "Window frame width",
SM_CYFRAME,        "SM_CYFRAME",        "Window frame height",
SM_CXMINTRACK,     "SM_CXMINTRACK",     "Minimum tracking width of window",
SM_CYMINTRACK,     "SM_CYMINTRACK",     "Minimum tracking height of window",
SM_CMETRICS,       "SM_CMETRICS",       "Number of system metrics"
} ;
```

The program that displays this information is called SYSMETS1. The files required to create SYSMETS1.EXE (make file, C source code, and module definition file) are shown in Figure 2-5. Most of the code should look familiar by now. With the exception of the program name, the make file, resource script, and DEF file are identical to those for HELLOWIN. In SYSMETS1.C, *WinMain* is virtually identical to HELLOWIN.

SYSMETS1.MAK

```
#-----------------------
# SYSMETS1.MAK make file
#-----------------------

sysmets1.exe : sysmets1.obj sysmets1.def
    link sysmets1, /align:16, NUL, /nod slibcew libw, sysmets1
    rc sysmets1.exe

sysmets1.obj : sysmets1.c sysmets.h
    cl -c -Gsw -Ow -W2 -Zp sysmets1.c
```

SYSMETS1.C

```
/*-------------------------------------------------------
   SYSMETS1.C -- System Metrics Display Program No. 1
                 (c) Charles Petzold, 1990
   -------------------------------------------------------*/

#include <windows.h>
#include "sysmets.h"

long FAR PASCAL WndProc (HWND, WORD, WORD, LONG) ;

int PASCAL WinMain (HANDLE hInstance, HANDLE hPrevInstance,
                    LPSTR lpszCmdLine, int nCmdShow)
```

Figure 2-5. *The SYSMETS1 program.*   *(continued)*

```
        {
        static char szAppName[] = "SysMets1" ;
        HWND        hwnd ;
        MSG         msg ;
        WNDCLASS    wndclass ;

        if (!hPrevInstance)
             {
             wndclass.style         = CS_HREDRAW : CS_VREDRAW ;
             wndclass.lpfnWndProc   = WndProc ;
             wndclass.cbClsExtra    = 0 ;
             wndclass.cbWndExtra    = 0 ;
             wndclass.hInstance     = hInstance ;
             wndclass.hIcon         = LoadIcon (NULL, IDI_APPLICATION) ;
             wndclass.hCursor       = LoadCursor (NULL, IDC_ARROW) ;
             wndclass.hbrBackground = GetStockObject (WHITE_BRUSH) ;
             wndclass.lpszMenuName  = NULL ;
             wndclass.lpszClassName = szAppName ;

             RegisterClass (&wndclass) ;
             }

        hwnd = CreateWindow (szAppName, "Get System Metrics No. 1",
                             WS_OVERLAPPEDWINDOW,
                             CW_USEDEFAULT, CW_USEDEFAULT,
                             CW_USEDEFAULT, CW_USEDEFAULT,
                             NULL, NULL, hInstance, NULL) ;

        ShowWindow (hwnd, nCmdShow) ;
        UpdateWindow (hwnd) ;

        while (GetMessage (&msg, NULL, 0, 0))
             {
             TranslateMessage (&msg) ;
             DispatchMessage (&msg) ;
             }
        return msg.wParam ;
        }

long FAR PASCAL WndProc (HWND hwnd, WORD message, WORD wParam, LONG lParam)
        {
        static short cxChar, cxCaps, cyChar ;
        char        szBuffer[10] ;
        HDC         hdc ;
        short       i ;
        PAINTSTRUCT ps ;
        TEXTMETRIC  tm ;
```

(continued)

61

```
    switch (message)
        {
    case WM_CREATE :
         hdc = GetDC (hwnd) ;

         GetTextMetrics (hdc, &tm) ;
         cxChar = tm.tmAveCharWidth ;
         cxCaps = (tm.tmPitchAndFamily & 1 ? 3 : 2) * cxChar / 2 ;
         cyChar = tm.tmHeight + tm.tmExternalLeading ;

         ReleaseDC (hwnd, hdc) ;
         return 0 ;

    case WM_PAINT :
         hdc = BeginPaint (hwnd, &ps) ;

         for (i = 0 ; i < NUMLINES ; i++)
              {
              TextOut (hdc, cxChar, cyChar * (1 + i),
                       sysmetrics[i].szLabel,
                       lstrlen (sysmetrics[i].szLabel)) ;

              TextOut (hdc, cxChar + 18 * cxCaps, cyChar * (1 + i),
                       sysmetrics[i].szDesc,
                       lstrlen (sysmetrics[i].szDesc)) ;

              SetTextAlign (hdc, TA_RIGHT : TA_TOP) ;

              TextOut (hdc, cxChar + 18 * cxCaps + 40 * cxChar,
                       cyChar * (1 + i), szBuffer,
                       wsprintf (szBuffer, "%5d",
                            GetSystemMetrics (sysmetrics[i].nIndex))) ;

              SetTextAlign (hdc, TA_LEFT : TA_TOP) ;
              }

         EndPaint (hwnd, &ps) ;
         return 0 ;

    case WM_DESTROY :
         PostQuitMessage (0) ;
         return 0 ;
        }

    return DefWindowProc (hwnd, message, wParam, lParam) ;
    }
```

SYSMETS1.DEF

```
;------------------------------------------
; SYSMETS1.DEF module definition file
;------------------------------------------

NAME            SYSMETS1

DESCRIPTION     'System Metrics Display No. 1 (c) Charles Petzold, 1990'
EXETYPE         WINDOWS
STUB            'WINSTUB.EXE'
CODE            PRELOAD MOVEABLE DISCARDABLE
DATA            PRELOAD MOVEABLE MULTIPLE
HEAPSIZE        1024
STACKSIZE       8192
EXPORTS         WndProc
```

Figure 2-6 shows SYSMETS1 running on a VGA. As you can see from the program's window, the screen width is 640 pixels and the screen height is 480 pixels. These two values, as well as many of the other values shown by the program, will be different for different types of video displays.

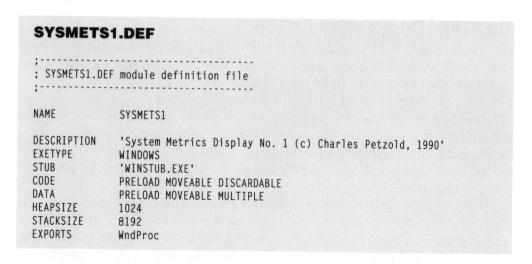

	Get System Metrics No. 1	
SM_CXSCREEN	Screen width in pixels	640
SM_CYSCREEN	Screen height in pixels	480
SM_CXVSCROLL	Vertical scroll arrow width	17
SM_CYHSCROLL	Horizontal scroll arrow height	17
SM_CYCAPTION	Caption bar height	20
SM_CXBORDER	Border width	1
SM_CYBORDER	Border height	1
SM_CXDLGFRAME	Dialog window frame width	4
SM_CYDLGFRAME	Dialog window frame height	4
SM_CYVTHUMB	Vertical scroll thumb height	17
SM_CXHTHUMB	Horizontal scroll thumb width	17
SM_CXICON	Icon width	32
SM_CYICON	Icon height	32
SM_CXCURSOR	Cursor width	32
SM_CYCURSOR	Cursor height	32
SM_CYMENU	Menu bar height	18
SM_CXFULLSCREEN	Full screen client window width	640
SM_CYFULLSCREEN	Full screen client window height	460
SM_CYKANJIWINDOW	Kanji window height	0
SM_MOUSEPRESENT	Mouse present flag	1
SM_CYVSCROLL	Vertical scroll arrow height	17
SM_CXHSCROLL	Horizontal scroll arrow width	17

Program Manager

Figure 2-6. *The SYSMETS1 display.*

The SYSMETS1.C Window Procedure

The *WndProc* window procedure in the SYSMETS1.C program processes three messages: WM_CREATE, WM_PAINT, and WM_DESTROY. The WM_DESTROY message is processed in the same way as the HELLOWIN program in Chapter 1.

The WM_CREATE message is the first message the window procedure receives. It is generated by Windows when the *CreateWindow* function creates the window. During the WM_CREATE message, SYSMETS1 obtains a device context for the window by calling *GetDC*, and gets the text metrics for the default system font by calling *GetTextMetrics*. SYSMETS1 saves the average character width in *cxChar* and the total height of the characters including external leading in *cyChar*.

SYSMETS1 also saves an average width of uppercase letters in the static variable *cxCaps*. For a fixed-pitch font, *cxCaps* would equal *cxChar*. For a variable-width font, *cxCaps* is about 150% of *cxChar*. The low bit of the *tmPitchAndFamily* field of the TEXTMETRIC structure is 1 for a variable-width font and 0 for a fixed-pitch font. SYSMETS1 uses this bit value to calculate *cxCaps* from *cxChar*:

```
cxCaps = (tm.tmPitchAndFamily & 1 ? 3 : 2) * cxChar / 2 ;
```

SYSMETS1 does all window painting during the WM_PAINT message. As normal, the window procedure first obtains a handle to the device context by calling *BeginPaint*. A *for* statement loops through all the lines of the *sysmetrics* structure defined in SYSMETS.H. The three columns of text are displayed with three *TextOut* functions. In each case, the third parameter to *TextOut* is set to:

```
cyChar * (1 + i)
```

This parameter indicates the pixel position of the top of the character string relative to the top of the client area. Thus, the program leaves a margin at the top equal to *cyChar*. The first line of text (when *i* equals 0) begins *cyChar* pixels below the top of the client area.

The first *TextOut* statement displays the uppercase identifiers in the first of the three columns. The second parameter to *TextOut* is *cxChar*. This leaves a one-character margin between the left edge of the client area and the text string. The text is obtained from the *szLabel* field of the *sysmetrics* structure. I use the Windows function *lstrlen* (which is similar to *strlen*) to obtain the length of the string, which is required as the last parameter to *TextOut*.

The second *TextOut* statement displays the description of the system metrics value. These descriptions are stored in the *szDesc* field of the *sysmetrics* structure. In this case, the second parameter to *TextOut* is set to:

```
cxChar + 18 * cxCaps
```

The longest uppercase identifier displayed in the first column is 16 characters, so the second column must begin at least 16 × *cxCaps* to the right of the beginning of the first column of text.

The third *TextOut* statement displays the numeric values obtained from the *Get-SystemMetrics* function. The variable-width font makes formatting a column of right-justified numbers a little tricky. All the digits from 0 through 9 have the same width, but this width is greater than the width of a space. Numbers can be one or more digits wide, so different numbers can begin at different horizontal positions.

Wouldn't it be easier if we could display a column of right-justified numbers by specifying the pixel position where the number ends rather than where it begins? This is what the *SetTextAlign* function lets us do. After SYSMETS1 calls

```
SetTextAlign (hdc, TA_RIGHT | TA_TOP) ;
```

then the coordinates passed to subsequent *TextOut* functions will specify the top-right corner of the text string rather than the top-left corner.

The *TextOut* function to display the column of numbers has a second parameter set to:

```
cxChar + 18 * cxCaps + 40 * cxChar
```

The 40 × *cxChar* value accommodates the width of the second column and the width of the third column. Following the *TextOut* function, another call to *SetTextAlign* sets things back to normal for the next time through the loop.

Not Enough Room!

One little nasty problem exists with the SYSMETS1 program: Unless you have a big-screen high-resolution video adapter, you can't see the last few lines of the system metrics list. If you make the window narrower, you can't see even the values.

SYSMETS1 doesn't know how large its client area is. It begins the text at the top of the window and relies on Windows to clip everything that drifts beyond the edges of the client area. Our first job is to determine how much of the program's output can actually fit within the client area.

The Size of the Client Area

If you experiment with existing Windows applications, you'll find that window sizes can vary widely. At the most (assuming the window does not have a menu or scroll bars), the window can be maximized, and the client area will occupy the entire screen except for the caption bar. The minimum size of the window can be quite small, sometimes almost non-existent, eliminating the client area.

One common method for determining the size of a window's client area is to process the WM_SIZE message within your window procedure. Windows sends a WM_SIZE message to a window procedure whenever the size of the window changes. The *lParam* variable passed to the window procedure contains the width of the client area in the low word and the height in the high word. The code to process this message looks like this:

```
static short cxClient, cyClient ;
    [other program lines]
case WM_SIZE :
    cxClient = LOWORD (lParam) ;
    cyClient = HIWORD (lParam) ;
    break ;
```

The LOWORD and HIWORD macros are defined in WINDOWS.H. Like *cxChar* and *cyChar*, the *cxClient* and *cyClient* variables are defined as static inside the window procedure because they are used later when processing other messages.

The WM_SIZE message will eventually be followed by a WM_PAINT message. Why? Because when we define the window class, we specify that the class style is:

```
CS_HREDRAW | CS_VREDRAW
```

This class style tells Windows to force a repaint if either the horizontal or vertical size changes.

You can calculate the number of full lines of text displayable within the client area with the formula:

```
cyClient / cyChar
```

This may be 0 if the height of the client area is too small to display a full character. Similarly, the approximate number of lowercase characters you can display horizontally within the client area is equal to:

```
cxClient / cxChar
```

If you determine *cxChar* and *cyChar* during a WM_CREATE message, don't worry about dividing by 0 in these calculations. Your window procedure receives a WM_CREATE message when *WinMain* calls *CreateWindow*. The first WM_SIZE message comes a little later when *WinMain* calls *ShowWindow*, at which point *cxChar* and *cyChar* have already been assigned positive values.

Knowing the size of the window's client area is the first step in providing a way for the user to move the text within the client area if the client area is not large enough to hold everything. If you're familiar with other Windows applications that have similar requirements, you probably know what we need: This is a job for scroll bars.

SCROLL BARS

Scroll bars are one of the best features of a graphics and mouse interface. They are easy to use and provide good visual feedback. You can use scroll bars whenever you need to display anything—text, graphics, a spreadsheet, database records, pictures—that requires more space than the available client area of the window.

Scroll bars are positioned either vertically (for up and down movement) or horizontally (for left and right movement). You can click with the mouse on the arrows at each end of a scroll bar or on the area between the arrows. A "scroll box," or "thumb," travels the length of the scroll bar to indicate the approximate location of the material shown on the display in relation to the entire document. You can also drag the thumb with the mouse to move to a particular location. Figure 2-7 shows the recommended use of a vertical scroll bar for text.

Programmers sometimes have problems with scrolling terminology because their perspective is different from the user's: A user who scrolls down wants to bring a lower part of the document into view. However, the program actually moves the document up in relation to the display window. The Windows documentation and the WINDOWS.H identifiers are based on the user's perspective: Scrolling up means moving toward the beginning of the document; scrolling down means moving toward the end.

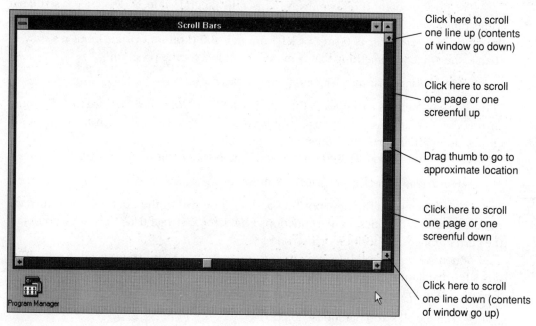

Click here to scroll one line up (contents of window go down)

Click here to scroll one page or one screenful up

Drag thumb to go to approximate location

Click here to scroll one page or one screenful down

Click here to scroll one line down (contents of window go up)

Figure 2-7. *The vertical scroll bar.*

It is very easy to include a horizontal or vertical scroll bar in your application window. All you need to do is include the identifier WS_VSCROLL (vertical scroll) or WS_HSCROLL (horizontal scroll) or both to the window style in the *CreateWindow* statement. These scroll bars are always placed against the right side or bottom of the window and extend for the full length or width of the client area. The client area does not include the space occupied by the scroll bar. The width of a vertical window scroll bar and the height of a horizontal window scroll bar are constant for a particular display driver. If you need these values, you can obtain them (as you may have observed) from the *GetSystemMetrics* call.

Windows takes care of all mouse logic for the scroll bars. However, window scroll bars do not have an automatic keyboard interface. If you want the cursor keys to duplicate some of the window scroll bars' functions, you must explicitly provide logic for that (as we'll do in the next chapter).

Scroll Bar Range and Position

Scroll bars have a "range" and a current "position." The range is defined by minimum and maximum integer values. When the thumb is at the top (or left) of the scroll bar, the position of the thumb is the minimum value of the range. At the bottom (or right) of the scroll bar, the thumb position is the maximum value of the range.

The position of the thumb is always a discrete integral value. For instance, a scroll bar with a range from 0 through 4 has five thumb positions, as shown in Figure 2-8. By default, the range of a scroll bar is 0 (top or left) through 100 (bottom or right), but it's easy to change the range to something that is more convenient for the program:

```
SetScrollRange (hwnd, nBar, nMin, nMax, bRedraw) ;
```

The *nBar* parameter is either SB_VERT or SB_HORZ, *nMin* and *nMax* are the minimum and maximum positions of the range, and *bRedraw* is set to TRUE if you want Windows to redraw the scroll bar based on the new range.

You can use *SetScrollPos* to set a new thumb position within the range:

```
SetScrollPos (hwnd, nBar, nPos, nRedraw) ;
```

The *nPos* parameter is the new position and must be within the range of *nMin* through *nMax*. Windows provides similar functions (*GetScrollRange* and *GetScrollPos*) to obtain the current range and position of a scroll bar.

When you use scroll bars within your program, you share responsibility with Windows for maintaining the scroll bars and updating the position of the scroll bar thumb. These are Windows' responsibilities for scroll bars:

- Handle all scroll bar mouse logic
- Provide a "reverse video" flash when the user clicks on the scroll bar

- Display a "ghost" box when the user drags the thumb within the scroll bar
- Send scroll bar messages to the window procedure for the window containing the scroll bar

These are your program's responsibilities:

- Initialize the range of the scroll bar
- Process the scroll bar messages
- Update the position of the scroll bar thumb

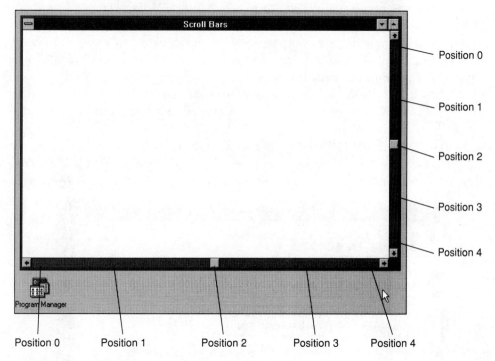

Figure 2-8. *Scroll bars with five thumb positions.*

Scroll Bar Messages

Windows sends the window procedure WM_VSCROLL and WM_HSCROLL messages when the scroll bar is clicked with the mouse or the thumb is dragged. Each mouse action on the scroll bar generates at least two messages, one when the mouse button is pressed and another when it is released.

The value of *wParam* that accompanies the WM_VSCROLL and WM_HSCROLL messages describes what the mouse is doing to the scroll bar. These values of *wParam* have WINDOWS.H identifiers that begin with SB, which stands for "scroll bar." Although some of these identifiers use the words "UP" and "DOWN," they apply to horizontal as well as vertical scroll bars, as you see in Figure 2-9. Your window procedure can receive multiple SB_LINEUP, SB_PAGEUP, SB_LINEDOWN, or SB_PAGEDOWN messages if the mouse button is held down while positioned on the scroll bar. The SB_ENDSCROLL message signals that the mouse button has been released. You can generally ignore SB_ENDSCROLL messages.

When *wParam* is SB_THUMBTRACK or SB_THUMBPOSITION, the low word of *lParam* is the current position of the dragged scroll bar. This position is within the minimum and maximum values of the scroll bar range. For other values of *wParam*, the low word of *lParam* should be ignored. You can also ignore the high word of *lParam*.

The Windows documentation indicates that the *wParam* value can also be SB_TOP and SB_BOTTOM, indicating that the scroll bar has been moved to its minimum or maximum position. However, you will never receive these values for a scroll bar created as part of your application window.

Handling the SB_THUMBTRACK and SB_THUMBPOSITION messages is problematic. If you set a large scroll bar range and the user quickly drags the thumb inside the scroll bar, Windows sends your window function a barrage of SB_THUMBTRACK messages.

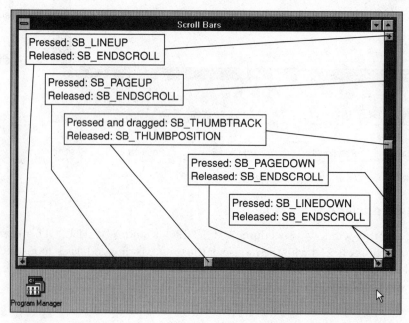

Figure 2-9. *WINDOWS.H identifiers for the* wParam *values of scroll bar messages.*

Your program may have problems keeping up with these messages. For this reason, most Windows applications ignore these messages and take action only on receipt of SB_THUMBPOSITION, which means that the thumb is again at rest.

However, if you can update your display quickly, you may want to include SB_THUMBTRACK processing in your program. But be aware that users who discover that your program scrolls as they move the scroll bar thumb will undoubtedly try to move it as quickly as possible to see if your program can keep up. They will get an inordinate amount of satisfaction if it cannot.

Scrolling SYSMETS

Enough explanation. It's time to put this stuff into practice. But let's start simply. We'll begin with vertical scrolling because that's what we desperately need. The horizontal scrolling can wait. SYSMETS2 is shown in Figure 2-10.

The new *CreateWindow* call adds a vertical scroll bar to the window; the scroll bar has this window style:

```
WS_OVERLAPPEDWINDOW : WS_VSCROLL
```

SYSMETS2.MAK

```
#----------------------
# SYSMETS2.MAK make file
#----------------------

sysmets2.exe : sysmets2.obj sysmets2.def
    link sysmets2, /align:16, NUL, /nod slibcew libw, sysmets2
    rc sysmets2.exe

sysmets2.obj : sysmets2.c sysmets.h
    cl -c -Gsw -Ow -W2 -Zp sysmets2.c
```

SYSMETS2.C

```
/*------------------------------------------------------
   SYSMETS2.C -- System Metrics Display Program No. 2
                 (c) Charles Petzold, 1990
   ------------------------------------------------------*/

#include <windows.h>
#include "sysmets.h"

long FAR PASCAL WndProc (HWND, WORD, WORD, LONG) ;
```

Figure 2-10. *The SYSMETS2 program.* *(continued)*

```
int PASCAL WinMain (HANDLE hInstance, HANDLE hPrevInstance,
                    LPSTR lpszCmdLine, int nCmdShow)
     {
     static char szAppName[] = "SysMets2" ;
     HWND         hwnd ;
     MSG          msg ;
     WNDCLASS     wndclass ;

     if (!hPrevInstance)
          {
          wndclass.style         = CS_HREDRAW : CS_VREDRAW ;
          wndclass.lpfnWndProc   = WndProc ;
          wndclass.cbClsExtra    = 0 ;
          wndclass.cbWndExtra    = 0 ;
          wndclass.hInstance     = hInstance ;
          wndclass.hIcon         = LoadIcon (NULL, IDI_APPLICATION) ;
          wndclass.hCursor       = LoadCursor (NULL, IDC_ARROW) ;
          wndclass.hbrBackground = GetStockObject (WHITE_BRUSH) ;
          wndclass.lpszMenuName  = NULL ;
          wndclass.lpszClassName = szAppName ;

          RegisterClass (&wndclass) ;
          }

     hwnd = CreateWindow (szAppName, "Get System Metrics No. 2",
                          WS_OVERLAPPEDWINDOW : WS_VSCROLL,
                          CW_USEDEFAULT, CW_USEDEFAULT,
                          CW_USEDEFAULT, CW_USEDEFAULT,
                          NULL, NULL, hInstance, NULL) ;

     ShowWindow (hwnd, nCmdShow) ;
     UpdateWindow (hwnd) ;

     while (GetMessage (&msg, NULL, 0, 0))
          {
          TranslateMessage (&msg) ;
          DispatchMessage (&msg) ;
          }
     return msg.wParam ;
     }

long FAR PASCAL WndProc (HWND hwnd, WORD message, WORD wParam, LONG lParam)
     {
     static short cxChar, cxCaps, cyChar, cxClient, cyClient, nVscrollPos ;
     char         szBuffer[10] ;
     HDC          hdc ;
     short        i, y ;
     PAINTSTRUCT  ps ;
     TEXTMETRIC   tm ;
```

(continued)

```
switch (message)
     {
     case WM_CREATE :
          hdc = GetDC (hwnd) ;

          GetTextMetrics (hdc, &tm) ;
          cxChar = tm.tmAveCharWidth ;
          cxCaps = (tm.tmPitchAndFamily & 1 ? 3 : 2) * cxChar / 2 ;
          cyChar = tm.tmHeight + tm.tmExternalLeading ;

          ReleaseDC (hwnd, hdc) ;

          SetScrollRange (hwnd, SB_VERT, 0, NUMLINES, FALSE) ;
          SetScrollPos   (hwnd, SB_VERT, nVscrollPos, TRUE) ;
          return 0 ;

     case WM_SIZE :
          cyClient = HIWORD (lParam) ;
          cxClient = LOWORD (lParam) ;
          return 0 ;

     case WM_VSCROLL :
          switch (wParam)
               {
               case SB_LINEUP :
                    nVscrollPos -= 1 ;
                    break ;

               case SB_LINEDOWN :
                    nVscrollPos += 1 ;
                    break ;

               case SB_PAGEUP :
                    nVscrollPos -= cyClient / cyChar ;
                    break ;

               case SB_PAGEDOWN :
                    nVscrollPos += cyClient / cyChar ;
                    break ;

               case SB_THUMBPOSITION :
                    nVscrollPos = LOWORD (lParam) ;
                    break ;

               default :
                    break ;
               }
          nVscrollPos = max (0, min (nVscrollPos, NUMLINES)) ;

          if (nVscrollPos != GetScrollPos (hwnd, SB_VERT))
```

(continued)

```
                    {
                    SetScrollPos (hwnd, SB_VERT, nVscrollPos, TRUE) ;
                    InvalidateRect (hwnd, NULL, TRUE) ;
                    }
               return 0 ;

          case WM_PAINT :
               hdc = BeginPaint (hwnd, &ps) ;

               for (i = 0 ; i < NUMLINES ; i++)
                    {
                    y = cyChar * (1 - nVscrollPos + i) ;

                    TextOut (hdc, cxChar, y,
                              sysmetrics[i].szLabel,
                              lstrlen (sysmetrics[i].szLabel)) ;

                    TextOut (hdc, cxChar + 18 * cxCaps, y,
                              sysmetrics[i].szDesc,
                              lstrlen (sysmetrics[i].szDesc)) ;

                    SetTextAlign (hdc, TA_RIGHT | TA_TOP) ;

                    TextOut (hdc, cxChar + 18 * cxCaps + 40 * cxChar, y,
                              szBuffer,
                              wsprintf (szBuffer, "%5d",
                                   GetSystemMetrics (sysmetrics[i].nIndex))) ;

                    SetTextAlign (hdc, TA_LEFT | TA_TOP) ;
                    }

               EndPaint (hwnd, &ps) ;
               return 0 ;

          case WM_DESTROY :
               PostQuitMessage (0) ;
               return 0 ;
          }

     return DefWindowProc (hwnd, message, wParam, lParam) ;
     }
```

SYSMET2.DEF

```
;--------------------------------------
; SYSMETS2.DEF module definition file
;--------------------------------------

NAME            SYSMETS2

DESCRIPTION     'System Metrics Display No. 2 (c) Charles Petzold, 1990'
EXETYPE         WINDOWS
STUB            'WINSTUB.EXE'
CODE            PRELOAD MOVEABLE DISCARDABLE
DATA            PRELOAD MOVEABLE MULTIPLE
HEAPSIZE        1024
STACKSIZE       8192
EXPORTS         WndProc
```

The *WndProc* window procedure has two additional lines to set the range and position of the vertical scroll bar during processing of the WM_CREATE message:

```
SetScrollRange (hwnd, SB_VERT, 0, NUMLINES, FALSE) ;
SetScrollPos   (hwnd, SB_VERT, nVscrollPos, TRUE) ;
```

The *sysmetrics* structure has NUMLINES lines of text, so the scroll bar range is set from 0 through NUMLINES. Each position of the scroll bar corresponds to a line of text displayed at the top of the client area. If the scroll bar thumb is at position 0, a blank line is left at the top of the screen for a margin. As you increase the position of the scroll bar by scrolling down, the text should move up. When the scroll bar position is at the bottom, the last line of the structure is at the top.

To help with processing of the WM_VSCROLL messages, a static variable called *nVscrollPos* is defined within the *WndProc* window procedure. This variable is the current position of the scroll bar thumb. For SB_LINEUP and SB_LINEDOWN, all we need to do is adjust the scroll position by 1. For SB_PAGEUP and SB_PAGEDOWN, we want to move the text by the contents of one screen, or *cyClient* divided by *cyChar*. For SB_THUMBPOSITION, the new thumb position is the low word of *lParam*. SB_ENDSCROLL and SB_THUMBTRACK messages are ignored.

The *nVscrollPos* is then adjusted using the *min* and *max* macros (defined in WINDOWS.H) to ensure that it is between the minimum and maximum range values. If the scroll position has changed, then it is updated using *SetScrollPos*, and the entire window is invalidated by an *InvalidateRect* call.

The *InvalidateRect* call generates a WM_PAINT message. When the original SYSMETS1 processed WM_PAINT messages, the *y*-coordinate of each line was calculated as:

```
cyChar * (1 + i)
```

In SYSMETS2, the formula is:

```
cyChar * (1 - nVscrollPos + i)
```

The loop still displays NUMLINES lines of text, but for values of *nVscrollPos* of 2 and above, the loop begins displaying lines above the client area. Windows merely ignores these lines.

I told you we'd start simply. This is rather wasteful and inefficient code. We'll fix it shortly, but first consider how we update the client area after a WM_VSCROLL message.

Structuring Your Program for Painting

The window procedure in SYSMETS2 does not repaint the client area after processing a scroll bar message. Instead, it calls *InvalidateRect* to invalidate the client area. This causes Windows to place a WM_PAINT message in the message queue.

It is best to structure your Windows programs so that you do all client-area painting in response to a WM_PAINT message. Because your program should be able to repaint the entire client area of the window at any time on receipt of a WM_PAINT message, you will probably duplicate code if you also paint in other parts of the program.

At first, you may rebel at this dictum because it is so different from normal PC programming. I won't deny that, on occasion, painting in response to messages other than WM_PAINT is much more convenient. (The KEYLOOK program in the next chapter is an example of such a program.) But in many cases it's simply unnecessary, and after you master the discipline of accumulating all the information you need to paint in response to a WM_PAINT message, you'll be pleased with the results. However, your program will often determine that it must repaint a particular area of the display when processing a message other than WM_PAINT. This is where *InvalidateRect* comes in handy. You can use it to invalidate specific rectangles of the client area or the entire client area.

Simply marking areas of the window as invalid to generate WM_PAINT messages may not be entirely satisfactory in some applications. After you make an *InvalidateRect* call, Windows places a WM_PAINT message in the message queue, and the window procedure eventually processes it. However, Windows treats WM_PAINT messages as low priority. If your message queue contains only a WM_PAINT message and another application has other messages waiting, Windows switches to the other application when you make a *GetMessage* call.

If you prefer to update the invalid area immediately, you can call *UpdateWindow* after you call *InvalidateRect*:

```
UpdateWindow (hwnd) ;
```

UpdateWindow causes the window procedure to be called immediately with a WM_PAINT message if any part of the client area is invalid. (It will not call the window procedure if the entire client area is valid.) This WM_PAINT message bypasses the message queue. The window procedure is called directly from Windows. When the window procedure has finished repainting, it exits and Windows returns control to the program at the statement following the *UpdateWindow* call.

You'll note that *UpdateWindow* is the same function used in *WinMain* to generate the first WM_PAINT message. When a window is first created, the entire client area is invalid. *UpdateWindow* directs the window procedure to paint it.

Building a Better Scroll

Because SYSMETS2 is too inefficient a model to be imitated in other programs, let's clean it up. SYSMETS3—our final version of the SYSMETS program in this chapter—is shown in Figure 2-11. This version adds a horizontal scroll bar for left and right scrolling and repaints the client area more efficiently.

SYSMETS3.MAK

```
#------------------------
# SYSMETS3.MAK make file
#------------------------

sysmets3.exe : sysmets3.obj sysmets3.def
     link sysmets3, /align:16, NUL, /nod slibcew libw, sysmets3
     rc sysmets3.exe

sysmets3.obj : sysmets3.c sysmets.h
     cl -c -Gsw -Ow -W2 -Zp sysmets3.c
```

SYSMETS3.C

```
/*------------------------------------------------------------
   SYSMETS3.C -- System Metrics Display Program No. 3
                 (c) Charles Petzold, 1990
   ------------------------------------------------------------*/

#include <windows.h>
#include "sysmets.h"

long FAR PASCAL WndProc (HWND, WORD, WORD, LONG) ;

int PASCAL WinMain (HANDLE hInstance, HANDLE hPrevInstance,
                    LPSTR lpszCmdLine, int nCmdShow)
```

Figure 2-11. *The SYSMETS3 program.*

(continued)

```
      {
      static char szAppName[] = "SysMets3" ;
      HWND        hwnd ;
      MSG         msg ;
      WNDCLASS    wndclass ;

      if (!hPrevInstance)
           {
           wndclass.style         = CS_HREDRAW : CS_VREDRAW ;
           wndclass.lpfnWndProc   = WndProc ;
           wndclass.cbClsExtra    = 0 ;
           wndclass.cbWndExtra    = 0 ;
           wndclass.hInstance     = hInstance ;
           wndclass.hIcon         = LoadIcon (NULL, IDI_APPLICATION) ;
           wndclass.hCursor       = LoadCursor (NULL, IDC_ARROW) ;
           wndclass.hbrBackground = GetStockObject (WHITE_BRUSH) ;
           wndclass.lpszMenuName  = NULL ;
           wndclass.lpszClassName = szAppName ;

           RegisterClass (&wndclass) ;
           }

      hwnd = CreateWindow (szAppName, "Get System Metrics No. 3",
                           WS_OVERLAPPEDWINDOW : WS_VSCROLL : WS_HSCROLL,
                           CW_USEDEFAULT, CW_USEDEFAULT,
                           CW_USEDEFAULT, CW_USEDEFAULT,
                           NULL, NULL, hInstance, NULL) ;

      ShowWindow (hwnd, nCmdShow) ;
      UpdateWindow (hwnd) ;

      while (GetMessage (&msg, NULL, 0, 0))
           {
           TranslateMessage (&msg) ;
           DispatchMessage (&msg) ;
           }
      return msg.wParam ;
      }

long FAR PASCAL WndProc (HWND hwnd, WORD message, WORD wParam, LONG lParam)
      {
      static short cxChar, cxCaps, cyChar, cxClient, cyClient, nMaxWidth,
                   nVscrollPos, nVscrollMax, nHscrollPos, nHscrollMax ;
      char         szBuffer[10] ;
      HDC          hdc ;
      short        i, x, y, nPaintBeg, nPaintEnd, nVscrollInc, nHscrollInc ;
      PAINTSTRUCT  ps ;
      TEXTMETRIC   tm ;

      switch (message)
```

(continued)

```
    {
case WM_CREATE :
     hdc = GetDC (hwnd) ;

     GetTextMetrics (hdc, &tm) ;
     cxChar = tm.tmAveCharWidth ;
     cxCaps = (tm.tmPitchAndFamily & 1 ? 3 : 2) * cxChar / 2 ;
     cyChar = tm.tmHeight + tm.tmExternalLeading ;

     ReleaseDC (hwnd, hdc) ;

     nMaxWidth = 40 * cxChar + 18 * cxCaps ;
     return 0 ;

case WM_SIZE :
     cyClient = HIWORD (lParam) ;
     cxClient = LOWORD (lParam) ;

     nVscrollMax = max (0, NUMLINES + 2 - cyClient / cyChar) ;
     nVscrollPos = min (nVscrollPos, nVscrollMax) ;

     SetScrollRange (hwnd, SB_VERT, 0, nVscrollMax, FALSE) ;
     SetScrollPos   (hwnd, SB_VERT, nVscrollPos, TRUE) ;

     nHscrollMax = max (0, 2 + (nMaxWidth - cxClient) / cxChar) ;
     nHscrollPos = min (nHscrollPos, nHscrollMax) ;

     SetScrollRange (hwnd, SB_HORZ, 0, nHscrollMax, FALSE) ;
     SetScrollPos   (hwnd, SB_HORZ, nHscrollPos, TRUE) ;
     return 0 ;

case WM_VSCROLL :
     switch (wParam)
          {
          case SB_TOP :
               nVscrollInc = -nVscrollPos ;
               break ;

          case SB_BOTTOM :
               nVscrollInc = nVscrollMax - nVscrollPos ;
               break ;

          case SB_LINEUP :
               nVscrollInc = -1 ;
               break ;

          case SB_LINEDOWN :
               nVscrollInc = 1 ;
               break ;
```

(continued)

```
          case SB_PAGEUP :
               nVscrollInc = min (-1, -cyClient / cyChar) ;
               break ;

          case SB_PAGEDOWN :
               nVscrollInc = max (1, cyClient / cyChar) ;
               break ;

          case SB_THUMBTRACK :
               nVscrollInc = LOWORD (lParam) - nVscrollPos ;
               break ;

          default :
               nVscrollInc = 0 ;
          }
     if (nVscrollInc = max (-nVscrollPos,
               min (nVscrollInc, nVscrollMax - nVscrollPos)))
          {
          nVscrollPos += nVscrollInc ;
          ScrollWindow (hwnd, 0, -cyChar * nVscrollInc, NULL, NULL) ;
          SetScrollPos (hwnd, SB_VERT, nVscrollPos, TRUE) ;
          UpdateWindow (hwnd) ;
          }
     return 0 ;

case WM_HSCROLL :
     switch (wParam)
          {
          case SB_LINEUP :
               nHscrollInc = -1 ;
               break ;

          case SB_LINEDOWN :
               nHscrollInc = 1 ;
               break ;

          case SB_PAGEUP :
               nHscrollInc = -8 ;
               break ;

          case SB_PAGEDOWN :
               nHscrollInc = 8 ;
               break ;

          case SB_THUMBPOSITION :
               nHscrollInc = LOWORD (lParam) - nHscrollPos ;
               break ;

          default :
               nHscrollInc = 0 ;
          }
```

(continued)

```
          if (nHscrollInc = max (-nHscrollPos,
                  min (nHscrollInc, nHscrollMax - nHscrollPos)))
              {
              nHscrollPos += nHscrollInc ;
              ScrollWindow (hwnd, -cxChar * nHscrollInc, 0, NULL, NULL) ;
              SetScrollPos (hwnd, SB_HORZ, nHscrollPos, TRUE) ;
              }
          return 0 ;

     case WM_PAINT :
          hdc = BeginPaint (hwnd, &ps) ;

          nPaintBeg = max (0, nVscrollPos + ps.rcPaint.top / cyChar - 1) ;
          nPaintEnd = min (NUMLINES,
                        nVscrollPos + ps.rcPaint.bottom / cyChar) ;

          for (i = nPaintBeg ; i < nPaintEnd ; i++)
              {
              x = cxChar * (1 - nHscrollPos) ;
              y = cyChar * (1 - nVscrollPos + i) ;

              TextOut (hdc, x, y,
                       sysmetrics[i].szLabel,
                       lstrlen (sysmetrics[i].szLabel)) ;

              TextOut (hdc, x + 18 * cxCaps, y,
                       sysmetrics[i].szDesc,
                       lstrlen (sysmetrics[i].szDesc)) ;

              SetTextAlign (hdc, TA_RIGHT | TA_TOP) ;

              TextOut (hdc, x + 18 * cxCaps + 40 * cxChar, y,
                       szBuffer,
                       wsprintf (szBuffer, "%5d",
                            GetSystemMetrics (sysmetrics[i].nIndex))) ;

              SetTextAlign (hdc, TA_LEFT | TA_TOP) ;
              }

          EndPaint (hwnd, &ps) ;
          return 0 ;

     case WM_DESTROY :
          PostQuitMessage (0) ;
          return 0 ;
     }

return DefWindowProc (hwnd, message, wParam, lParam) ;
}
```

SYSMETS3.DEF

```
;-------------------------------------
; SYSMETS3.DEF module definition file
;-------------------------------------

NAME            SYSMETS3

DESCRIPTION     'System Metrics Display No. 3 (c) Charles Petzold, 1990'
EXETYPE         WINDOWS
STUB            'WINSTUB.EXE'
CODE            PRELOAD MOVEABLE DISCARDABLE
DATA            PRELOAD MOVEABLE MULTIPLE
HEAPSIZE        1024
STACKSIZE       8192
EXPORTS         WndProc
```

These are the improvements in SYSMETS3 and how they are implemented in the program:

- You can no longer scroll the display so that the last line appears at the top of the client area. You can scroll only far enough to see the last line at the bottom of the client area. This requires that the program calculate a new scroll bar range (and possibly a new thumb position) when it processes a WM_SIZE message. The WM_SIZE logic calculates the scroll bar range based on the number of lines of text, the width of the text, and the size of the client area. This approach results in a smaller range—only that necessary to bring into view the text that falls outside the client area.

    This offers an interesting dividend. Suppose that the client area of the window is large enough to display the entire text with top and bottom margins. In this case, both the minimum position and maximum position of the scroll bar range will equal zero. What will Windows do with this information? It will remove the scroll bar from the window! It's no longer needed. Similarly, if the client area is wide enough to show the full 60-column width of the text, no horizontal scroll bar is displayed in the window.

- The WM_VSCROLL and WM_HSCROLL messages are processed by first calculating an increment of the scroll bar position for each value of *wParam*. This value is then used to scroll the existing contents of the window using the Windows *ScrollWindow* call. This function has the following format:

```
ScrollWindow (hwnd, xInc, yInc, lpRect, lpClipRect) ;
```

The *xInc* and *yInc* values specify an amount to scroll in pixels. In SYSMETS3, the *lpRect* and *lpClipRect* values are set to NULL to specify that the entire client area should be scrolled. Windows invalidates the rectangle in the client area "uncovered" by the scrolling operation. This generates a WM_PAINT message. *InvalidateRect* is no longer needed. (Note that *ScrollWindow* is *not* a GDI procedure because it does not require a handle to a device context. It is one of the few non-GDI Windows functions that changes the appearance of the client area of a window.)

■ The WM_PAINT processing now determines which lines are within the invalid rectangle and rewrites only those lines. It does this by analyzing the top and bottom coordinates of the invalid rectangle stored in the PAINTSTRUCT structure. The program paints only those text lines within the invalid rectangle. The code is more complex, but it is much faster.

■ Because WM_PAINT was speeded up, I decided to let SYSMETS3 process SB_THUMBTRACK operations for WM_VSCROLL messages. Previously, the program would ignore SB_THUMBTRACK messages (which occur as the user drags the scroll bar thumb) and would act only on SB-_THUMBPOSITION messages, which occur when the user stops dragging the thumb. The WM_VSCROLL code also calls *UpdateWindow* to update the client area immediately. When you move the thumb on the vertical scroll bar, SYSMETS3 will continually scroll and update the client area. I'll let you decide whether SYSMETS3 (and Windows) is fast enough to justify this change.

But I Don't Like to Use the Mouse

If you don't have a mouse on your PC, you can't scroll SYSMETS3 at all. Scroll bars created as part of your application window do not have an automatic keyboard interface. Because Windows can be installed without a mouse, it is highly recommended that you write programs that do not require the mouse.

In the next chapter you'll learn how to use the keyboard and how to add a keyboard interface to SYSMETS. You'll notice that SYSMETS3 seems to process WM_VSCROLL messages where *wParam* equals SB_TOP and SB_BOTTOM. I mentioned earlier that a window procedure doesn't receive these messages for scroll bars, so right now this is superfluous code. When we come back to this program in the next chapter, you'll see the reason for including this code.

SECTION II
READING
INPUT

Chapter 3

The Keyboard

Like most interactive programs that run on personal computers, Windows applications rely heavily on the keyboard for user input. Although Windows also supports a mouse as an input device, you can't depend on a mouse being present in an installed version of Windows. For this reason, program developers should attempt to allow complete program functionality from the keyboard. (Of course, in some cases, such as drawing programs or desktop publishing programs, this is simply not practical and a mouse will be required.)

The keyboard cannot be treated solely as an input device in isolation from other program functions. For example, a program almost always echoes the keyboard input by displaying typed characters in the client area of a window. Handling keyboard input and displaying text must be treated together. Sometimes the keystrokes result in a document being created that is eventually saved in a disk file. Sometimes a program requires that the user enter an MS-DOS filename. These apparently straightforward chores raise issues related to the support of the ASCII extended character set (codes of 128 and above) and of international characters. For this reason, topics such as the character sets supported by Windows and multibyte character codes are also covered in this chapter.

KEYBOARD BASICS

As the user presses and releases keys, the keyboard driver passes the keystrokes to Windows. Windows saves the keystrokes in the system message queue and then transfers them to the message queue of the program with the "input focus." These messages are processed in the program's window procedure. In most cases, the keyboard information encoded in these messages is probably more than your program needs. Part of the job of handling the keyboard is knowing which messages are important and which are not.

The Keyboard Driver

Windows is shipped with several keyboard drivers for the support of various keyboard hardware and dynamic link libraries that support international keyboard configurations. Keyboards for European languages must include additional characters (such as letters with diacritics) and symbols (such as the British pound sign). When you install Windows, the SETUP program copies the keyboard driver for the keyboard and country you request into the SYSTEM subdirectory of your Windows directory.

KEYBOARD.DRV is a relatively small and simple driver. When Windows starts up, it enables the keyboard driver, which responds by saving the original interrupt vector addresses for Interrupt 09H (the hardware keyboard interrupt) and setting this interrupt vector to routines within the driver.

Pressing or releasing a key generates an Interrupt 09H. This is sometimes called an "asynchronous" interrupt because it can occur at any time. The interrupt suspends the program currently running and passes control to the Interrupt 09H keyboard handler. When the keyboard handler is finished, it passes control back to the interrupted program. The Interrupt 09H keyboard handler within KEYBOARD.DRV decodes the key and calls a routine within the Windows USER module, which stores them as queued messages. The Windows program then obtains the keyboard messages when the program calls *GetMessage*.

Because a Windows program effectively polls for keyboard input by calling *GetMessage*, Windows programs are not very different from PC programs that obtain keystrokes by polling through the software Interrupts 16H and 21H. However, the quantity of information that Windows encodes in the keyboard messages is much greater than that available from Interrupts 16H and 21H.

Some application programs written for the IBM PC intercept Interrupt 09H and do their own hardware keyboard processing. This allows the program to use all possible combinations of keystrokes, not only those defined by the PC BIOS. Windows programs are not very different from these programs either, because the window procedure is a message handler that receives messages about all keyboard events. The only real difference between message handling and interrupt handling is that the Windows messages are not asynchronous. A Windows program is never interrupted to be notified of a keystroke; the program receives a new keyboard message only from the message queue. In short, Windows provides programs with all the benefits of intercepting the hardware Interrupt 09H but with none of the hassles.

When a user types on the keyboard faster than a program can process the keys, Windows stores the extra keystrokes in a system message queue rather than in an individual program's message queue. One of these extra keystrokes (Alt-Tab, for instance) may have the effect of switching to another program. The keys following Alt-Tab should then go to the other program. Windows correctly synchronizes such keyboard messages.

Windows sends eight different messages to programs to indicate various keyboard events. That may seem like a lot, but your program can safely ignore many of them.

Ignoring the Keyboard

Although the keyboard is the primary source of user input to Windows programs, your program does not need to act on every keyboard message it receives. Windows handles many keyboard functions itself. For instance, you can ignore keystrokes that pertain to system functions. These keystrokes generally involve the Alt key.

A program need not monitor these keystrokes itself because Windows notifies a program of the effect of the keystrokes. (A program can monitor the keystrokes if it wants to, however.) For instance, if the Windows user selects a menu item with the keyboard, Windows sends the program a message that the menu item has been selected, regardless of whether it was selected by using the mouse or by using the keyboard. (Menus are covered in Chapter 9.)

Some Windows programs use "keyboard accelerators" to invoke common menu items. The accelerators generally involve the function keys, special noncharacter keys such as Insert or Delete, or a letter in combination with the Ctrl key. These keyboard accelerators are defined in a program's resource script. (Chapter 9 shows how Windows translates the accelerators into menu command messages. You don't have to do the translation yourself.)

Dialog boxes (covered in Chapter 10) also have a keyboard interface, but programs usually do not need to monitor the keyboard when a dialog box is active. The keyboard interface is handled by Windows, and Windows sends messages to your program about the effects of the keystrokes. Dialog boxes can contain "edit" controls for text input. These are generally small boxes in which the user types a character string. Windows handles all the edit control logic and gives your program the final contents of the edit control when the user is done.

Even within your main window you can define child windows that function as edit controls. An extreme example of this is the Windows NOTEPAD program, which is little more than a large multiline edit control. NOTEPAD does little keyboard processing on its own and relies on Windows to handle all the dirty work. (Chapter 6 discusses how this works.)

Focus, Focus, Who's Got the Focus?

The keyboard must be shared by all applications running under Windows. Some applications may have more than one window, and the keyboard must be shared by these windows within the same application. When a key on the keyboard is pressed, only one window procedure can receive a message that the key has been pressed. The window that receives this keyboard message is the window with the "input focus."

The concept of input focus is closely related to the concept of "active window." The window with the input focus is either the active window or a child window of the active window. The active window is usually easy to identify. If the active window has a caption bar, Windows highlights the caption bar. If the active window has a dialog frame (a form most commonly seen in dialog boxes) instead of a caption bar, Windows highlights the frame. If the active window is an icon, Windows highlights the window's caption bar text below the icon.

The most common child windows are controls such as push buttons, radio buttons, check boxes, scroll bars, edit boxes, and list boxes that usually appear in a dialog box. Child windows are never themselves active windows. If a child window has the input focus, then the active window is its parent. Child window controls indicate that they have the input focus generally by using a flashing cursor or caret.

If the active window is an icon, then no window has the input focus. Windows continues to send keyboard messages to the icon, but these messages are in a different form from keyboard messages sent to active windows that are not icons.

A window procedure can determine when it has the input focus by trapping WM_SETFOCUS and WM_KILLFOCUS messages. WM_SETFOCUS indicates that the window is receiving the input focus, and WM_KILLFOCUS signals that the window is losing the input focus.

Keystrokes and Characters

The messages that an application receives from Windows about keyboard events distinguish between "keystrokes" and "characters." This is in accordance with the two ways you can view the keyboard. First, you can think of the keyboard as a collection of keys. The keyboard has only one A key. Pressing that key is a keystroke. Releasing that key is a keystroke. But the keyboard is also an input device that generates displayable characters. The A key can generate several characters depending on the status of the Ctrl, Shift, and Caps Lock keys. Normally, the character is a lowercase a. If the Shift key is down or Caps Lock is toggled on, the character is an uppercase A. If Ctrl is down, the character is a Ctrl-A. On a foreign-language keyboard, the A keystroke may be preceded by a "dead-character key" or by Shift, Ctrl, or Alt in various combinations. The combinations could generate a lowercase a or an uppercase A with an accent mark.

For keystroke combinations that result in displayable characters, Windows sends a program both keystroke messages and character messages. Some keys do not generate characters. These include the shift keys, the function keys, the cursor movement keys, and special keys such as Insert and Delete. For these keys, Windows generates only keystroke messages.

KEYSTROKE MESSAGES

When you press a key, Windows places either a WM_KEYDOWN or WM_SYSKEYDOWN message in the message queue of the window with the input focus. When you release a key, Windows places either a WM_KEYUP or WM_SYSKEYUP message in the message queue.

	Key Pressed	*Key Released*
Nonsystem Keystroke:	WM_KEYDOWN	WM_KEYUP
System Keystroke:	WM_SYSKEYDOWN	WM_SYSKEYUP

Usually the "down" and "up" messages occur in pairs. However, if you hold down a key so that the typematic (autorepeat) action takes over, Windows sends the window procedure a series of WM_KEYDOWN (or WM_SYSKEYDOWN) messages and a single WM_KEYUP (or WM_SYSKEYUP) message when the key is finally released. Like all messages, keystroke messages are time-stamped. You can obtain the relative time a key was pressed or released by calling *GetMessageTime*.

System and Nonsystem Keystrokes

The "SYS" in WM_SYSKEYDOWN and WM_SYSKEYUP stands for "system" and refers to keystrokes that are more important to Windows than to the Windows application. The WM_SYSKEYDOWN and WM_SYSKEYUP messages are usually generated for keys typed in combination with the Alt key. These keystrokes invoke options on the program's menu or system menu, or they are used for system functions such as switching the active window (Alt-Tab or Alt-Esc) or for system menu accelerators (Alt in combination with a function key). Programs usually ignore the WM_SYSKEYUP and WM_SYSKEYDOWN messages and pass them to *DefWindowProc*. Because Windows takes care of all the Alt-key logic, you really have no need to trap these messages. Your window procedure will eventually receive other messages concerning the result of these keystrokes (such as a menu selection). If you want to include code in your window procedure to trap the system keystroke messages (as we will do in the KEYLOOK program later in this chapter), pass the messages to *DefWindowProc* after you process them so that Windows can still use them for their normal purposes.

But think about this for a moment. Almost everything that affects your program's window passes through your window procedure first. Windows does something with the message only if you pass the message to *DefWindowProc*. For instance, if you add the lines:

```
case WM_SYSKEYDOWN :
case WM_SYSKEYUP :
case WM_SYSCHAR :
    return 0 ;
```

to a window procedure, then you effectively disable all Alt-key operations (menu commands, Alt-Tab, Alt-Esc, and so on) when your program has the input focus. Although I doubt you would want to do this, I trust you're beginning to sense the power in your window procedure.

The WM_KEYDOWN and WM_KEYUP messages are usually generated for keys that are pressed and released without the Alt key. Your program may use or discard these keystroke messages. Windows itself doesn't care about them.

The *lParam* Variable

For all four keystroke messages, the 32-bit *lParam* variable passed to the window procedure is divided into six fields: Repeat Count, OEM Scan Code, Extended Key Flag, Context Code, Previous Key State, and Transition State. (See Figure 3-1.)

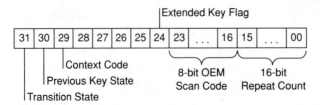

Figure 3-1. *The six keystroke-message fields of the* lParam *variable.*

Repeat Count

The Repeat Count is the number of keystrokes represented by the message. In most cases the Repeat Count is set to 1. However, if a key is held down and your window procedure is not fast enough to process key-down messages at the typematic rate (approximately a 10-character-per-second default), Windows combines several WM_KEYDOWN or WM_SYSKEYDOWN messages into a single message and increases Repeat Count accordingly. The Repeat Count is always 1 for a WM_KEYUP or WM_SYSKEYUP message.

Because a Repeat Count greater than 1 indicates that typematic keystrokes are occurring faster than your program can process them, you may want to ignore the Repeat Count when processing the keyboard messages. Almost everyone has had the experience of "overscrolling" a word-processing document or spreadsheet because extra keystrokes have stacked up in the keyboard buffer. Ignoring the Repeat Count in your program will significantly reduce the possibilities for overscrolling. However, in other cases you will want to use the Repeat Count. You should probably try your programs both ways and see which approach feels the most natural.

OEM Scan Code

The OEM Scan Code is the keyboard scan code generated by the hardware of the computer. For the IBM PC, this scan code is the same as the value passed back to a program in register AH during a BIOS Interrupt 16H call. Windows applications generally ignore the OEM Scan Code because there are better ways to decode keyboard information.

Extended Key Flag

The Extended Key Flag is 1 if the keystroke results from one of the additional keys on the IBM Enhanced Keyboard. (The IBM Enhanced Keyboard has function keys across the top and a separate [combined] keypad for cursor keys and number keys.) This flag is set to 1 for the Alt and Ctrl keys at the right of the keyboard, the cursor movement keys (including Insert and Delete) that are not part of the numeric keypad, the Slash (/) and Enter keys on the numeric keypad, and the Num Lock key. Windows programs generally ignore the Extended Key Flag.

Context Code

The Context Code is 1 if the Alt key is pressed. This bit will always be 1 for the WM_SYSKEYUP and WM_SYSKEYDOWN messages and 0 for the WM_KEYUP and WM_KEYDOWN messages with two exceptions:

- If the active window is an icon, it does not have the input focus. All keystrokes generate WM_SYSKEYUP and WM_SYSKEYDOWN messages. If the Alt key is not pressed, the Context Code field is set to 0. (Windows uses SYS keyboard messages so that the active window that is an icon doesn't process these keystrokes.)

- On some foreign-language keyboards, certain characters are generated by combining Shift, Ctrl, or Alt with another key. In these cases the *lParam* variable that accompanies WM_KEYUP and WM_KEYDOWN messages has a 1 in the Context Code field, but the messages are not system keystroke messages.

Previous Key State

The Previous Key State is 0 if the key was previously up and 1 if the key was previously down. It is always set to 1 for a WM_KEYUP or WM_SYSKEYUP message, but it can be 0 or 1 for a WM_KEYDOWN or WM_SYSKEYDOWN message. A 1 indicates second and subsequent messages for keys that are the result of typematic action.

Transition State

The Transition State is 0 if the key is being pressed and 1 if the key is being released. The field is set to 0 for a WM_KEYDOWN or WM_SYSKEYDOWN message and to 1 for a WM_KEYUP or WM_SYSKEYUP.

Virtual Key Codes

Although some information in *lParam* might be useful for processing WM_KEYUP, WM_KEYDOWN, WM_SYSKEYUP, and WM_SYSKEYDOWN messages, the *wParam* parameter is much more important. This parameter contains the "virtual key code" that identifies the key that was pressed or released. The developers of Windows have attempted to

VIRTUAL KEY CODES

Decimal	Hex	WINDOWS.H Identifier	Required	IBM Keyboard
1	01	VK_LBUTTON		
2	02	VK_RBUTTON		
3	03	VK_CANCEL	*	Ctrl-Break
4	04	VK_MBUTTON		
8	08	VK_BACK	*	Backspace
9	09	VK_TAB	*	Tab
12	0C	VK_CLEAR		Numeric keypad 5 with Num Lock OFF
13	0D	VK_RETURN	*	Enter
16	10	VK_SHIFT	*	Shift
17	11	VK_CONTROL	*	Ctrl
18	12	VK_MENU	*	Alt
19	13	VK_PAUSE		Pause
20	14	VK_CAPITAL	*	Caps Lock
27	1B	VK_ESCAPE	*	Esc
32	20	VK_SPACE	*	Spacebar
33	21	VK_PRIOR	*	Page Up
34	22	VK_NEXT	*	Page Down
35	23	VK_END		End
36	24	VK_HOME	*	Home
37	25	VK_LEFT	*	Left Arrow
38	26	VK_UP	*	Up Arrow
39	27	VK_RIGHT	*	Right Arrow
40	28	VK_DOWN	*	Down Arrow
41	29	VK_SELECT		
42	2A	VK_PRINT		
43	2B	VK_EXECUTE		
44	2C	VK_SNAPSHOT		Print Screen
45	2D	VK_INSERT	*	Insert
46	2E	VK_DELETE	*	Delete
47	2F	VK_HELP		
48–57	30–39		*	0 through 9 on main keyboard
65–90	41–5A		*	A through Z
96	60	VK_NUMPAD0		Numeric keypad 0 with Num Lock ON

(continued)

VIRTUAL KEY CODES *continued*

Decimal	Hex	WINDOWS.H Identifier	Required	IBM Keyboard
97	61	VK_NUMPAD1		Numeric keypad 1 with Num Lock ON
98	62	VK_NUMPAD2		Numeric keypad 2 with Num Lock ON
99	63	VK_NUMPAD3		Numeric keypad 3 with Num Lock ON
100	64	VK_NUMPAD4		Numeric keypad 4 with Num Lock ON
101	65	VK_NUMPAD5		Numeric keypad 5 with Num Lock ON
102	66	VK_NUMPAD6		Numeric keypad 6 with Num Lock ON
103	67	VK_NUMPAD7		Numeric keypad 7 with Num Lock ON
104	68	VK_NUMPAD8		Numeric keypad 8 with Num Lock ON
105	69	VK_NUMPAD9		Numeric keypad 9 with Num Lock ON
106	6A	VK_MULTIPY		Numeric keypad * (enhanced keyboard)
107	6B	VK_ADD		Numeric keypad + (enhanced keyboard)
108	6C	VK_SEPARATOR		
109	6D	VK_SUBTRACT		Numeric keypad – (enhanced keyboard)
110	6E	VK_DECIMAL		Numeric keypad
111	6F	VK_DIVIDE		Numeric keypad /(enhanced keyboard)
112	70	VK_F1	*	Function key F1
113	71	VK_F2	*	Function key F2
114	72	VK_F3	*	Function key F3
115	73	VK_F4	*	Function key F4
116	74	VK_F5	*	Function key F5
117	75	VK_F6	*	Function key F6
118	76	VK_F7	*	Function key F7
119	77	VK_F8	*	Function key F8
120	78	VK_F9	*	Function key F9
121	79	VK_F10	*	Function key F10
122	7A	VK_F11		Function key F11 (enhanced keyboard)
123	7B	VK_F12		Function Key F12 (enhanced keyboard)
124	7C	VK_F13		

(continued)

VIRTUAL KEY CODES *continued*

Decimal	Hex	WINDOWS.H Identifier	Required	IBM Keyboard
125	7D	VK_F14		
126	7E	VK_F15		
127	7F	VK_F16		
144	90	VK_NUMLOCK		Num Lock

define virtual keys in a device-independent manner. For this reason, some virtual key codes cannot be generated on the IBM PC and strict compatibles but may be found on other manufacturer's keyboards.

The virtual key codes you use most often have names defined in WINDOWS.H. The table above shows these names along with the numeric key codes and the IBM PC key that corresponds to the virtual key. Although all keys cause keystroke messages, the table does not include any symbol keys (such as the key with the / and ? symbols). These keys have virtual key codes of 128 and above, and they are often defined differently for international keyboards. You can determine the values of these virtual key codes using the KEYLOOK program that is shown later in this chapter, but normally you should not process keystroke messages for these keys.

An asterisk (∗) in the column labeled "Required" indicates that the key is mandatory for any Windows implementation. Windows also requires that a keyboard and keyboard driver allow the Shift, Ctrl, and Shift and Ctrl keys together to be combined with all letter keys, all required cursor keys, and all required function keys. The VK_LBUTTON, VK_MBUTTON, and VK_RBUTTON virtual key codes refer to the left, middle, and right buttons of a mouse. However, you will never receive keystroke messages with *wParam* set to these values. The mouse generates its own messages.

Shift States

The *wParam* and *lParam* parameters that accompany WM_KEYDOWN, WM_KEYUP, WM_SYSKEYDOWN, and WM_SYSKEYUP messages do not tell your program about the state of the shift keys. You can obtain the current state of any virtual key using the *GetKeyState* function. This function generally is used to obtain the state of shift keys (Shift, Ctrl, and Alt) and toggle keys (Caps Lock and Num Lock). For instance:

```
GetKeyState (VK_SHIFT) ;
```

returns a negative value (that is, the high bit is set) if the Shift key is down. The value returned from:

```
GetKeyState (VK_CAPITAL) ;
```

has the low bit set if the Caps Lock key is toggled on. You can also obtain the state of the mouse buttons using the virtual key codes VK_LBUTTON, VK_RBUTTON, and VK_MBUTTON. However, most Windows programs that need to monitor a combination of mouse buttons and keystrokes usually do it the other way around—by checking keystrokes when they receive a mouse message. In fact, shift-state information is included in the mouse messages (as you'll see in the next chapter).

Be careful with *GetKeyState*. It is not a real-time keyboard status check. Rather, it is a check of the keyboard status up to and including the current message being processed. *GetKeyState* does not let you retrieve keyboard information independent of normal keyboard messages. For instance, you may want to hold up processing in your window procedure until the user presses the F1 function key:

```
while (GetKeyState (VK_F1) >= 0) ;  // WRONG !!!
```

This statement will execute for a very long time—until you reset your machine with Ctrl-Alt-Delete. Your program must retrieve the keyboard message from the queue before *GetKeyState* can retrieve the state of the key. This synchronization actually works to your advantage, because if you need to know the shift state for a particular keystroke message, *GetKeyState* is guaranteed to be accurate, even if you are processing the message after the shift key has been released. If you really need the current state of the key, you can use *GetAsyncKeyState*.

Using Keystroke Messages

The idea of a program getting information about every keystroke is certainly nice, but most Windows programs ignore all but a few keystroke messages. The WM_SYSKEYDOWN and WM_SYSKEYUP messages are for Windows system functions, and you don't need to look at them. If you process WM_KEYDOWN messages, you can also ignore WM_KEYUP messages.

Windows programs generally use WM_KEYDOWN messages for keystrokes that do not generate characters. Although you may think that it's possible to use keystroke messages in combination with shift-state information to translate keystroke messages into character messages, don't do it. You'll have problems with international keyboard differences. For instance, if you get a WM_KEYDOWN message with *wParam* equal to 33H, you know the user pressed the 3 key. So far, so good. If you use *GetKeyState* and find out that the Shift key is down, you might assume that the user is typing a pound sign (#). Not necessarily so. A British user is typing a £. So the WM_KEYDOWN messages are most useful for the cursor movement keys, the function keys, and special keys such as Insert and Delete. However, Insert, Delete, and the function keys often appear as menu accelerators. Because Windows translates menu accelerators into menu command messages, you don't have to process the keystrokes themselves. Some non-Windows programs for the PC use function keys extensively in combination with the Shift, Ctrl, and Alt keys. You can do something similar in your Windows programs, but it's not recommended. If you want to use the function keys, they should duplicate menu commands. One objective in Windows is to provide a user interface that doesn't require memorizing or using complex command charts.

We've managed to eliminate everything except one final case: Most of the time, you will process WM_KEYDOWN messages only for cursor movement keys. When you use the cursor keys, you can check the Shift-key and Ctrl-key states through *GetKeyState*. Windows functions often use the Shift key in combination with the cursor keys to extend a selection in (for instance) a word-processing document. The Ctrl key is often used to alter the meaning of the cursor key. (For example, Ctrl in combination with the Right Arrow key might mean to move the cursor one word to the right.)

The Common User Access: Advanced Interface Design Guide contains a list of recommended keyboard definitions. (The guide, hereinafter referred to as the CUA Advanced Interface Design Guide, is included in the Windows Software Development Kit and is part of the IBM Systems Application Architecture Library.) You can also examine how the keyboard is used in existing Windows programs. If you don't like those definitions, you are free to do something different. But keep in mind that doing so may be detrimental to a user's ability to quickly learn your program.

ENHANCING SYSMETS: ADDING A KEYBOARD INTERFACE

When we wrote the three versions of the SYSMETS program in Chapter 2, we didn't know anything about the keyboard. We were able to scroll the text only by using the mouse on the scroll bars. Now that we know how to process keystroke messages, let's add a keyboard interface to SYSMETS. This is obviously a job for cursor movement keys. We'll use most of the cursor movement keys (Home, End, Page Up, Page Down, Up Arrow, and Down Arrow) for vertical scrolling. The Left Arrow key and the Right Arrow key can take care of the less-important horizontal scrolling.

Adding WM_KEYDOWN Logic

One obvious way to create a keyboard interface is to add some WM_KEYDOWN logic to the window procedure that parallels the WM_VSCROLL and WM_HSCROLL logic:

```
case WM_KEYDOWN :
     nVscrollInc = nHscrollInc = 0 ;

     switch (wParam)
         {
         case VK_HOME :        // same as WM_VSCROLL, SB_TOP
              nVscrollInc = -nVscrollPos ;
              break ;

         case VK_END :         // same as WM_VSCROLL, SB_BOTTOM
              nVscrollInc = nVscrollMax - nVscrollPos ;
              break ;
```

```
          case VK_UP :              // same as WM_VSCROLL, SB_LINEUP
               nVscrollInc = -1 ;
               break ;

          case VK_DOWN :            // same as WM_VSCROLL, SB_LINEDOWN
               nVscrollInc = 1 ;
               break ;

          case VK_PRIOR :           // same as WM_VSCROLL, SB_PAGEUP
               nVscrollInc = min (-1, -cyClient / cyChar) ;
               break ;

          case VK_NEXT :            // same as WM_VSCROLL, SB_PAGEDOWN
               nVscrollInc = max (1, cyClient / cyChar) ;
               break ;

          case VK_LEFT :            // same as WM_HSCROLL, SB_PAGEUP
               nHscrollInc = -8 ;
               break ;

          case VK_RIGHT :           // same as WM_HSCROLL, SB_PAGEDOWN
               nHscrollInc = 8 ;
               break ;

          default :
               break ;
          }

     if (nVscrollInc = max (-nVscrollPos,
               min (nVscrollInc, nVscrollMax - nVscrollPos)))
          {
          nVscrollPos += nVscrollInc ;
          ScrollWindow (hwnd, 0, -cyChar * nVscrollInc, NULL, NULL) ;
          SetScrollPos (hwnd, SB_VERT, nVscrollPos, TRUE) ;
          UpdateWindow (hwnd) ;
          }

     if (nHscrollInc = max (-nHscrollPos,
               min (nHscrollInc, nHscrollMax - nHscrollPos)))
          {
          nHscrollPos += nHscrollInc ;
          ScrollWindow (hwnd, -cxChar * nHscrollInc, 0, NULL, NULL) ;
          SetScrollPos (hwnd, SB_HORZ, nHscrollPos, TRUE) ;
          }

     return 0 ;
```

Do you dislike this code as much as I do? Simply duplicating all the scroll bar code is unwise, because if we ever wanted to change the scroll bar logic, we'd have to make parallel changes in WM_KEYDOWN. There has to be a better way. And there is.

Sending Messages

Wouldn't it be better to simply translate each of these WM_KEYDOWN messages into an equivalent WM_VSCROLL and WM_HSCROLL message and then perhaps fool *WndProc* into thinking that it's getting a WM_VSCROLL or WM_HSCROLL message, perhaps by sending a phony scroll bar message to the window procedure? Windows lets you do this. The function is called *SendMessage*, and it takes the same parameters as those passed to the window procedure:

```
SendMessage (hwnd, message, wParam, lParam) ;
```

When you call *SendMessage*, Windows calls the window procedure whose window handle is *hwnd*, passing to it these four parameters. When the window procedure has completed processing the message, Windows returns control to the next statement following the *SendMessage* call. The window procedure to which you send the message could be the same window procedure, another window procedure in the same program, or a window procedure in another application.

Here's how we might use *SendMessage* for processing WM_KEYDOWN codes in the SYSMETS program:

```
case WM_KEYDOWN :
    switch (wParam)
        {
        case VK_HOME :
            SendMessage (hwnd, WM_VSCROLL, SB_TOP, OL) ;
            break ;

        case VK_END :
            SendMessage (hwnd, WM_VSCROLL, SB_BOTTOM, OL) ;
            break ;

        case VK_PRIOR :
            SendMessage (hwnd, WM_VSCROLL, SB_PAGEUP, OL) ;
            break ;
    [other program lines]
```

OK, you get the general idea. Our goal was to add a keyboard interface to the scroll bars, and that's exactly what we've done. We've made the cursor movement keys duplicate scroll bar logic by actually sending the window procedure a scroll bar message. Now you see why I included SB_TOP and SB_BOTTOM processing for WM_VSCROLL messages in the SYSMETS3 program. It wasn't used then, but it's used now for processing the Home and End keys. The final SYSMETS program, shown in Figure 3-2, incorporates these changes. You'll also need the SYSMETS.H file from Chapter 2 (Figure 2-4) to compile this program.

Remember: To send a message to a window procedure, use the *SendMessage* function. Do not try to call the window procedure directly like this:

```
WndProc (hwnd, WM_VSCROLL, SB_PAGEUP, OL) ; // WRONG !!!
```

This statement will cause "unpredictable results" (if you call a system crash "unpredictable"). You may define and call other subroutines within a Windows program, but you must not call a window procedure directly. You'll find out why in Chapter 7.

SYSMETS.MAK

```
#----------------------
# SYSMETS.MAK make file
#----------------------

sysmets.exe : sysmets.obj sysmets.def
     link sysmets, /align:16, NUL, /nod slibcew libw, sysmets
     rc sysmets.exe

sysmets.obj : sysmets.c sysmets.h
     cl -c -Gsw -Ow -W2 -Zp sysmets.c
```

SYSMETS.C

```
/*-------------------------------------------------------
   SYSMETS.C -- System Metrics Display Program (Final)
                (c) Charles Petzold, 1990
   -------------------------------------------------------*/

#include <windows.h>
#include "sysmets.h"

long FAR PASCAL WndProc (HWND, WORD, WORD, LONG) ;

int PASCAL WinMain (HANDLE hInstance, HANDLE hPrevInstance,
                    LPSTR lpszCmdLine, int nCmdShow)
     {
     static char szAppName[] = "SysMets" ;
     HWND        hwnd ;
     MSG         msg ;
     WNDCLASS    wndclass ;

     if (!hPrevInstance)
         {
         wndclass.style         = CS_HREDRAW | CS_VREDRAW ;
         wndclass.lpfnWndProc   = WndProc ;
         wndclass.cbClsExtra    = 0 ;
         wndclass.cbWndExtra    = 0 ;
         wndclass.hInstance     = hInstance ;
         wndclass.hIcon         = LoadIcon (NULL, IDI_APPLICATION) ;
         wndclass.hCursor       = LoadCursor (NULL, IDC_ARROW) ;
```

Figure 3-2. *The SYSMETS program.*   *(continued)*

```
        wndclass.hbrBackground = GetStockObject (WHITE_BRUSH) ;
        wndclass.lpszMenuName  = NULL ;
        wndclass.lpszClassName = szAppName ;

        RegisterClass (&wndclass) ;
        }

    hwnd = CreateWindow (szAppName, "System Metrics",
                    WS_OVERLAPPEDWINDOW : WS_VSCROLL : WS_HSCROLL,
                    CW_USEDEFAULT, CW_USEDEFAULT,
                    CW_USEDEFAULT, CW_USEDEFAULT,
                    NULL, NULL, hInstance, NULL) ;

    ShowWindow (hwnd, nCmdShow) ;
    UpdateWindow (hwnd) ;

    while (GetMessage (&msg, NULL, 0, 0))
        {
        TranslateMessage (&msg) ;
        DispatchMessage (&msg) ;
        }
    return msg.wParam ;
    }

long FAR PASCAL WndProc (HWND hwnd, WORD message, WORD wParam, LONG lParam)
    {
    static short  cxChar, cxCaps, cyChar, cxClient, cyClient, nMaxWidth,
                  nVscrollPos, nVscrollMax, nHscrollPos, nHscrollMax ;
    char          szBuffer[10] ;
    HDC           hdc ;
    short         i, x, y, nPaintBeg, nPaintEnd, nVscrollInc, nHscrollInc ;
    PAINTSTRUCT   ps ;
    TEXTMETRIC    tm ;

    switch (message)
        {
        case WM_CREATE :
            hdc = GetDC (hwnd) ;

            GetTextMetrics (hdc, &tm) ;
            cxChar = tm.tmAveCharWidth ;
            cxCaps = (tm.tmPitchAndFamily & 1 ? 3 : 2) * cxChar / 2 ;
            cyChar = tm.tmHeight + tm.tmExternalLeading ;

            ReleaseDC (hwnd, hdc) ;

            nMaxWidth = 40 * cxChar + 18 * cxCaps ;
            return 0 ;

        case WM_SIZE :
            cyClient = HIWORD (lParam) ;
            cxClient = LOWORD (lParam) ;
```

(continued)

```
            nVscrollMax = max (0, NUMLINES + 2 - cyClient / cyChar) ;
            nVscrollPos = min (nVscrollPos, nVscrollMax) ;

            SetScrollRange (hwnd, SB_VERT, 0, nVscrollMax, FALSE) ;
            SetScrollPos   (hwnd, SB_VERT, nVscrollPos, TRUE) ;

            nHscrollMax = max (0, 2 + (nMaxWidth - cxClient) / cxChar) ;
            nHscrollPos = min (nHscrollPos, nHscrollMax) ;

            SetScrollRange (hwnd, SB_HORZ, 0, nHscrollMax, FALSE) ;
            SetScrollPos   (hwnd, SB_HORZ, nHscrollPos, TRUE) ;
            return 0 ;

case WM_VSCROLL :
     switch (wParam)
          {
          case SB_TOP :
               nVscrollInc = -nVscrollPos ;
               break ;

          case SB_BOTTOM :
               nVscrollInc = nVscrollMax - nVscrollPos ;
               break ;

          case SB_LINEUP :
               nVscrollInc = -1 ;
               break ;

          case SB_LINEDOWN :
               nVscrollInc = 1 ;
               break ;

          case SB_PAGEUP :
               nVscrollInc = min (-1, -cyClient / cyChar) ;
               break ;

          case SB_PAGEDOWN :
               nVscrollInc = max (1, cyClient / cyChar) ;
               break ;

          case SB_THUMBTRACK :
               nVscrollInc = LOWORD (lParam) - nVscrollPos ;
               break ;

          default :
               nVscrollInc = 0 ;
          }
     if (nVscrollInc = max (-nVscrollPos,
             min (nVscrollInc, nVscrollMax - nVscrollPos)))
```

(continued)

103

```
                    {
               nVscrollPos += nVscrollInc ;
               ScrollWindow (hwnd, 0, -cyChar * nVscrollInc, NULL, NULL) ;
               SetScrollPos (hwnd, SB_VERT, nVscrollPos, TRUE) ;
               UpdateWindow (hwnd) ;
               }
          return 0 ;

     case WM_HSCROLL :
          switch (wParam)
               {
               case SB_LINEUP :
                    nHscrollInc = -1 ;
                    break ;

               case SB_LINEDOWN :
                    nHscrollInc = 1 ;
                    break ;

               case SB_PAGEUP :
                    nHscrollInc = -8 ;
                    break ;

               case SB_PAGEDOWN :
                    nHscrollInc = 8 ;
                    break ;

               case SB_THUMBPOSITION :
                    nHscrollInc = LOWORD (lParam) - nHscrollPos ;
                    break ;

               default :
                    nHscrollInc = 0 ;
               }
          if (nHscrollInc = max (-nHscrollPos,
                    min (nHscrollInc, nHscrollMax - nHscrollPos)))
               {
               nHscrollPos += nHscrollInc ;
               ScrollWindow (hwnd, -cxChar * nHscrollInc, 0, NULL, NULL) ;
               SetScrollPos (hwnd, SB_HORZ, nHscrollPos, TRUE) ;
               }
          return 0 ;

     case WM_KEYDOWN :
          switch (wParam)
               {
               case VK_HOME :
                    SendMessage (hwnd, WM_VSCROLL, SB_TOP, 0L) ;
                    break ;
```

(continued)

```
            case VK_END :
                SendMessage (hwnd, WM_VSCROLL, SB_BOTTOM, OL) ;
                break ;

            case VK_PRIOR :
                SendMessage (hwnd, WM_VSCROLL, SB_PAGEUP, OL) ;
                break ;

            case VK_NEXT :
                SendMessage (hwnd, WM_VSCROLL, SB_PAGEDOWN, OL) ;
                break ;

            case VK_UP :
                SendMessage (hwnd, WM_VSCROLL, SB_LINEUP, OL) ;
                break ;

            case VK_DOWN :
                SendMessage (hwnd, WM_VSCROLL, SB_LINEDOWN, OL) ;
                break ;

            case VK_LEFT :
                SendMessage (hwnd, WM_HSCROLL, SB_PAGEUP, OL) ;
                break ;

            case VK_RIGHT :
                SendMessage (hwnd, WM_HSCROLL, SB_PAGEDOWN, OL) ;
                break ;
            }
        return 0 ;

case WM_PAINT :
    hdc = BeginPaint (hwnd, &ps) ;

    nPaintBeg = max (0, nVscrollPos + ps.rcPaint.top / cyChar - 1) ;
    nPaintEnd = min (NUMLINES,
                    nVscrollPos + ps.rcPaint.bottom / cyChar) ;

    for (i = nPaintBeg ; i < nPaintEnd ; i++)
        {
        x = cxChar * (1 - nHscrollPos) ;
        y = cyChar * (1 - nVscrollPos + i) ;

        TextOut (hdc, x, y,
                    sysmetrics[i].szLabel,
            lstrlen (sysmetrics[i].szLabel)) ;

        TextOut (hdc, x + 18 * cxCaps, y,
                    sysmetrics[i].szDesc,
            lstrlen (sysmetrics[i].szDesc)) ;
```

(continued)

105

```
                              SetTextAlign (hdc, TA_RIGHT | TA_TOP) ;

                              TextOut (hdc, x + 18 * cxCaps + 40 * cxChar, y,
                                       szBuffer,
                                       wsprintf (szBuffer, "%5d",
                              GetSystemMetrics (sysmetrics[i].nIndex))) ;

                              SetTextAlign (hdc, TA_LEFT | TA_TOP) ;
                              }

                    EndPaint (hwnd, &ps) ;
                    return 0 ;

          case WM_DESTROY :
               PostQuitMessage (0) ;
               return 0 ;
          }

     return DefWindowProc (hwnd, message, wParam, lParam) ;
     }
```

SYSMETS.DEF

```
;----------------------------------------
; SYSMETS.DEF module definition file
;----------------------------------------

NAME            SYSMETS

DESCRIPTION     'System Metrics Display (c) Charles Petzold, 1990'
EXETYPE         WINDOWS
STUB            'WINSTUB.EXE'
CODE            PRELOAD MOVEABLE DISCARDABLE
DATA            PRELOAD MOVEABLE MULTIPLE
HEAPSIZE        1024
STACKSIZE       8192
EXPORTS         WndProc
```

CHARACTER MESSAGES

Earlier I discussed the idea of translating keystroke messages into character messages by taking into account shift-state information, and I warned that shift-state information is not enough: You also need to know about country-dependent keyboard configurations. For this reason, you should not attempt to translate keystroke messages into character codes yourself.

Windows does it for you. You've seen this code before:

```
while (GetMessage (&msg, NULL, 0, 0))
      {
      TranslateMessage (&msg) ;
      DispatchMessage (&msg) ;
      }
```

This is a typical message loop that appears in *WinMain*. The *GetMessage* function fills in the *msg* structure fields with the next message from the queue. *DispatchMessage* calls the appropriate window procedure with this message.

Between these two functions is *TranslateMessage*, which translates keystroke messages into character messages. If the message is WM_KEYDOWN or WM_SYSKEYDOWN, and if the keystroke in combination with the shift states produces a character, then *TranslateMessage* places a character message in the message queue. This character message will be the next message that *GetMessage* retrieves from the queue after the keystroke message.

There are four character messages:

	Characters	*Dead Characters*
Nonsystem Characters:	WM_CHAR	WM_DEADCHAR
System Characters:	WM_SYSCHAR	WM_SYSDEADCHAR

The WM_CHAR and WM_DEADCHAR messages are derived from WM_KEYDOWN messages. The WM_SYSCHAR and WM_SYSDEADCHAR messages are derived from WM_SYSKEYDOWN messages. In most cases, your Windows program can ignore everything except WM_CHAR messages. The *lParam* parameter passed to the window procedure with the character code message is the same as the *lParam* parameter for the keystroke message that generated the character code message. The *wParam* parameter is the ASCII code for the character (yes, good old familiar ASCII).

The character messages are delivered to your window procedure sandwiched between keystroke messages. For instance, if Caps Lock is not toggled on and you press and release the A key, the window procedure receives the following three messages:

Message	*Key or Code*
WM_KEYDOWN	Virtual key A
WM_CHAR	ASCII code a
WM_KEYUP	Virtual key A

If you type an uppercase A by pressing the Shift key, pressing the A key, releasing the A key, and then releasing the Shift key, the window procedure receives five messages:

Message	Key or Code
WM_KEYDOWN	Virtual key VK_SHIFT
WM_KEYDOWN	Virtual key A
WM_CHAR	ASCII code A
WM_KEYUP	Virtual key A
WM_KEYUP	Virtual key VK_SHIFT

The Shift key by itself does not generate a character message.

If you hold down the A key so that the typematic action generates keystrokes, you'll get a character message for each WM_KEYDOWN message:

Message	Key or Code
WM_KEYDOWN	Virtual key A
WM_CHAR	ASCII code a
WM_KEYDOWN	Virtual key A
WM_CHAR	ASCII code a
WM_KEYDOWN	Virtual key A
WM_CHAR	ASCII code a
WM_KEYDOWN	Virtual key A
WM_CHAR	ASCII code a
WM_KEYUP	Virtual key A

If some of the WM_KEYDOWN messages have a Repeat Count greater than 1, the corresponding WM_CHAR messages will have the same Repeat Count.

The Ctrl key in combination with a letter key generates ASCII control codes from 01H (Ctrl-A) through 1AH (Ctrl-Z). You can also use other keys to generate these control codes. The following table shows the value of *wParam* in a WM_CHAR message for keys that generate control codes:

Key	ASCII Code	Duplicated by
Backspace	08H	Ctrl-H
Tab	09H	Ctrl-I
Ctrl-Enter	0Ah	Ctrl-J
Enter	0Dh	Ctrl-M
Esc	1BH	Ctrl-[

Windows programs sometimes use the Ctrl key in combination with letter keys for menu accelerators, in which case the letter keys are not translated into character messages.

WM_CHAR Messages

When your Windows program needs to process characters from the keyboard (for instance, in a word-processing or communications program), it will process WM_CHAR messages. You'll probably want some special processing for the Backspace, Tab, and Enter keys (and perhaps the Linefeed key), but you'll treat all other characters the same:

```
case WM_CHAR :

    switch (wParam)
        {
        case '\b' :     // backspace
        [other program lines]
            break ;

        case '\t' :     // tab
        [other program lines]
            break ;

        case '\n' :     // linefeed
        [other program lines]
            break ;

        case '\r' :     // carriage return
        [other program lines]
            break ;

        default :       // character code
        [other program lines]
            break ;
        }
    return 0 ;
```

This program fragment is virtually identical to keyboard character processing in regular MS-DOS programs.

Dead-Character Messages

Windows programs can usually ignore WM_DEADCHAR and WM_SYSDEADCHAR messages. On some non-U.S. keyboards, certain keys are defined to add a diacritic to a letter. These are called "dead keys" because they don't create characters by themselves. For instance, when the German keyboard is installed, the key that is in the same position as the +/= key on a U.S. keyboard is a dead key for the acute accent (´) when unshifted and the grave accent (`) when shifted.

When a user presses this dead key, your window procedure receives a WM_DEADCHAR message with *wParam* equal to the ASCII code for the diacritic by itself. When the user then presses a letter key (for instance, the A key), the window procedure receives a WM_CHAR message where *wParam* is the ASCII code for the letter a with the diacritic. Thus, your program does not have to process the WM_DEADCHAR message, because the WM_CHAR message gives the program all the information it needs. The Windows logic even has built-in error handling: If the dead key is followed by a letter that can't take a diacritic (such as the letter s), then the window procedure receives two WM_CHAR messages in a row—the first with *wParam* equal to the ASCII code for the diacritic by itself (the same *wParam* value delivered with the WM_DEADCHAR message) and the second with *wParam* equal to the ASCII code for the letter s.

LOOKING AT KEYBOARD MESSAGES

If you'd like to see how Windows sends keyboard messages to a program, KEYLOOK, shown in Figure 3-3, will help. This program displays in its client area all the information that Windows sends the window procedure for the eight different keyboard messages.

KEYLOOK.MAK

```
#------------------------
# KEYLOOK.MAK make file
#------------------------

keylook.exe : keylook.obj keylook.def
     link keylook, /align:16, NUL, /nod slibcew libw, keylook
     rc keylook.exe

keylook.obj : keylook.c
     cl -c -Gsw -Ow -W2 -Zp keylook.c
```

KEYLOOK.C

```
/*-------------------------------------------------------------
   KEYLOOK.C -- Displays Keyboard and Character Messages
               (c) Charles Petzold, 1990
  -------------------------------------------------------------*/

#include <windows.h>
#include <stdio.h>

long  FAR PASCAL WndProc (HWND, WORD, WORD, LONG) ;
```

Figure 3-3. *The KEYLOOK program.*

(continued)

```
RECT   rect ;
short cxChar, cyChar ;

int PASCAL WinMain (HANDLE hInstance, HANDLE hPrevInstance,
                    LPSTR lpszCmdLine, int nCmdShow)
     {
     static char szAppName[] = "KeyLook" ;
     HWND        hwnd ;
     MSG         msg ;
     WNDCLASS    wndclass ;

     if (!hPrevInstance)
         {
         wndclass.style         = CS_HREDRAW | CS_VREDRAW ;
         wndclass.lpfnWndProc   = WndProc ;
         wndclass.cbClsExtra    = 0 ;
         wndclass.cbWndExtra    = 0 ;
         wndclass.hInstance     = hInstance ;
         wndclass.hIcon         = LoadIcon (NULL, IDI_APPLICATION) ;
         wndclass.hCursor       = LoadCursor (NULL, IDC_ARROW) ;
         wndclass.hbrBackground = (HBRUSH) GetStockObject (WHITE_BRUSH) ;
         wndclass.lpszMenuName  = NULL ;
         wndclass.lpszClassName = szAppName ;

         RegisterClass (&wndclass) ;
         }

     hwnd = CreateWindow (szAppName, "Keyboard Message Looker",
                          WS_OVERLAPPEDWINDOW,
                          CW_USEDEFAULT, CW_USEDEFAULT,
                          CW_USEDEFAULT, CW_USEDEFAULT,
                          NULL, NULL, hInstance, NULL) ;

     ShowWindow (hwnd, nCmdShow) ;
     UpdateWindow (hwnd) ;

     while (GetMessage (&msg, NULL, 0, 0))
         {
         TranslateMessage (&msg) ;
         DispatchMessage (&msg) ;
         }
     return msg.wParam ;
     }

void ShowKey (HWND hwnd, int iType, char *szMessage, WORD wParam, LONG lParam)
     {
     static char *szFormat[2] = { "%-14s %3d    %c %6u %4d %3s %3s %4s %4s",
                                  "%-14s    %3d %c %6u %4d %3s %3s %4s %4s" } ;
     char        szBuffer[80] ;
     HDC         hdc ;
```

(continued)

111

```
        ScrollWindow (hwnd, 0, -cyChar, &rect, &rect) ;
        hdc = GetDC (hwnd) ;

        SelectObject (hdc, GetStockObject (SYSTEM_FIXED_FONT)) ;

        TextOut (hdc, cxChar, rect.bottom - cyChar, szBuffer,
                  wsprintf (szBuffer, szFormat [iType],
                             (LPSTR) szMessage, wParam,
                             (BYTE) (iType ? wParam : ' '),
                             LOWORD (lParam),
                             HIWORD (lParam) & 0xFF,
                             (LPSTR) (0x01000000 & lParam ? "Yes"  : "No"),
                             (LPSTR) (0x20000000 & lParam ? "Yes"  : "No"),
                             (LPSTR) (0x40000000 & lParam ? "Down" : "Up"),
                             (LPSTR) (0x80000000 & lParam ? "Up"   : "Down"))) ;

        ReleaseDC (hwnd, hdc) ;
        ValidateRect (hwnd, NULL) ;
        }

long FAR PASCAL WndProc (HWND hwnd, WORD message, WORD wParam, LONG lParam)
     {
     static char szTop[] =
                    "Message          Key Char Repeat Scan Ext ALT Prev Tran";
     static char szUnd[]=
                    "_____          ___ ____ _____ ____ ___ ___ ____ ____";
     HDC         hdc ;
     PAINTSTRUCT ps ;
     TEXTMETRIC  tm ;

     switch (message)
          {
          case WM_CREATE :
               hdc = GetDC (hwnd) ;

               SelectObject (hdc, GetStockObject (SYSTEM_FIXED_FONT)) ;

               GetTextMetrics (hdc, &tm) ;
               cxChar = tm.tmAveCharWidth ;
               cyChar = tm.tmHeight ;

               ReleaseDC (hwnd, hdc) ;

               rect.top = 3 * cyChar / 2 ;
               return 0 ;

          case WM_SIZE :
               rect.right  = LOWORD (lParam) ;
               rect.bottom = HIWORD (lParam) ;
               UpdateWindow (hwnd) ;
               return 0 ;
```

(continued)

112

```
        case WM_PAINT :
             InvalidateRect (hwnd, NULL, TRUE) ;
             hdc = BeginPaint (hwnd, &ps) ;

             SelectObject (hdc, GetStockObject (SYSTEM_FIXED_FONT)) ;

             SetBkMode (hdc, TRANSPARENT) ;
             TextOut (hdc, cxChar, cyChar / 2, szTop, (sizeof szTop) - 1) ;
             TextOut (hdc, cxChar, cyChar / 2, szUnd, (sizeof szUnd) - 1) ;
             EndPaint (hwnd, &ps) ;
             return 0 ;

        case WM_KEYDOWN :
             ShowKey (hwnd, 0, "WM_KEYDOWN", wParam, lParam) ;
             return 0 ;

        case WM_KEYUP :
             ShowKey (hwnd, 0, "WM_KEYUP", wParam, lParam) ;
             return 0 ;

        case WM_CHAR :
             ShowKey (hwnd, 1, "WM_CHAR", wParam, lParam) ;
             return 0 ;

        case WM_DEADCHAR :
             ShowKey (hwnd, 1, "WM_DEADCHAR", wParam, lParam) ;
             return 0 ;

        case WM_SYSKEYDOWN :
             ShowKey (hwnd, 0, "WM_SYSKEYDOWN", wParam, lParam) ;
             break ;        // i.e., call DefWindowProc

        case WM_SYSKEYUP :
             ShowKey (hwnd, 0, "WM_SYSKEYUP", wParam, lParam) ;
             break ;        // i.e., call DefWindowProc

        case WM_SYSCHAR :
             ShowKey (hwnd, 1, "WM_SYSCHAR", wParam, lParam) ;
             break ;        // i.e., call DefWindowProc

        case WM_SYSDEADCHAR :
             ShowKey (hwnd, 1, "WM_SYSDEADCHAR", wParam, lParam) ;
             break ;        // i.e., call DefWindowProc

        case WM_DESTROY :
             PostQuitMessage (0) ;
             return 0 ;
        }
   return DefWindowProc (hwnd, message, wParam, lParam) ;
   }
```

KEYLOOK.DEF

```
;------------------------------------------
; KEYLOOK.DEF module definition file
;------------------------------------------

NAME            KEYLOOK

DESCRIPTION     'Key Look Program (c) Charles Petzold, 1990'
EXETYPE         WINDOWS
STUB            'WINSTUB.EXE'
CODE            PRELOAD MOVEABLE DISCARDABLE
DATA            PRELOAD MOVEABLE MULTIPLE
HEAPSIZE        1024
STACKSIZE       8192
EXPORTS         WndProc
```

KEYLOOK uses the display like an old-fashioned teletype output device. When KEYLOOK receives a keystroke message, it calls *ScrollWindow* to scroll the contents of the entire client area of the window so that the contents move up the height of one character. *TextOut* is used to display the line of new information beginning one character height from the bottom. This is about as simple as a teletype output can get. Figure 3-4 shows what the KEYLOOK display looks like when you type the word "Windows." The first column shows the keyboard message, the second shows the virtual key code for keystroke messages, the

```
┌──────────────────────────── Keyboard Message Looker ────────────────────────┐
│                                                                              │
│ Message        Key Char Repeat Scan Ext ALT Prev Tran                        │
│                                                                              │
│ WM_KEYDOWN      16          1   54   No  No   Up Down                         │
│ WM_KEYDOWN      87          1   17   No  No   Up Down                         │
│ WM_CHAR            87 W     1   17   No  No   Up Down                         │
│ WM_KEYUP        87          1   17   No Down      Up                          │
│ WM_KEYUP        16          1   54   No  No Down   Up                         │
│ WM_KEYDOWN      73          1   23   No  No   Up Down                         │
│ WM_CHAR           105 i     1   23   No  No   Up Down                         │
│ WM_KEYUP        73          1   23   No  No Down   Up                         │
│ WM_KEYDOWN      78          1   49   No  No   Up Down                         │
│ WM_CHAR           110 n     1   49   No  No   Up Down                         │
│ WM_KEYUP        78          1   49   No  No Down   Up                         │
│ WM_KEYDOWN      68          1   32   No  No   Up Down                         │
│ WM_CHAR           100 d     1   32   No  No   Up Down                         │
│ WM_KEYUP        68          1   32   No  No Down   Up                         │
│ WM_KEYDOWN      79          1   24   No  No   Up Down                         │
│ WM_CHAR           111 o     1   24   No  No   Up Down                         │
│ WM_KEYUP        79          1   24   No  No Down   Up                         │
│ WM_KEYDOWN      87          1   17   No  No   Up Down                         │
│ WM_CHAR           119 w     1   17   No  No   Up Down                         │
│ WM_KEYUP        87          1   17   No  No Down   Up                         │
│ WM_KEYDOWN      83          1   31   No  No   Up Down                         │
│ WM_CHAR           115 s     1   31   No  No   Up Down                         │
│ WM_KEYUP        83          1   31   No  No Down   Up                         │
│                                                                              │
└──────────────────────────────────────────────────────────────────────────────┘
```

Program Manager

Figure 3-4. *The KEYLOOK display.*

third shows the character code (and the character itself) for character messages, and the other six columns show the states of the six fields in the *lParam* message parameter.

Most of KEYLOOK.C uses features of Windows that have already been covered in the various SYSMETS programs, but a few new functions are used here.

The column formatting of KEYLOOK would be difficult with the default proportional font. The code to display each line would need to be broken into nine sections to get everything lined up. For something like this, a much easier approach is to simply switch to a fixed-pitch font. This requires two functions in a single statement:

```
SelectObject (hdc, GetStockObject (SYSTEM_FIXED_FONT)) ;
```

KEYLOOK calls these two functions whenever it obtains a device context. This occurs in three places: the *ShowKey* function, while processing the WM_CREATE message in *WndProc*, and while processing the WM_PAINT message. The *GetStockObject* function obtains a handle to a "stock" graphics object, which is a predefined graphics object that Windows makes available to programs. In this case, *GetStockObject* obtains a handle to a font known as SYSTEM_FIXED_FONT, which is the fixed-pitch font that was used in versions of Windows prior to Windows 3. The *SelectObject* call places that object into the device context. Following this call, all text that is displayed will use the fixed-pitch font. It is possible to switch back to the default proportional font by calling:

```
SelectObject (hdc, GetStockObject (SYSTEM_FONT)) ;
```

I'll discuss these functions in more depth in Chapter 12.

The *ShowKey* function calls *ScrollWindow* to scroll the previous lines of keystrokes up before displaying a new line. Normally this would cause part of the window to become invalid and hence generate a WM_PAINT message. The *ShowKey* function concludes with a call to *ValidateRect* to prevent this.

Notice the use of the Windows *wsprintf* function in the *ShowKey* function. The character strings must be explicitly cast to far pointers using the LPSTR data type (defined in WINDOWS.H as a far pointer to a character string). The *wsprintf* function is one of the very few functions in Windows that explicitly requires casting of its parameters.

KEYLOOK does not save the keystrokes it receives, so on receipt of a WM_PAINT message it cannot re-create the window. For this reason, KEYLOOK simply displays the header at the top of the client area during the WM_PAINT message. Before calling *Begin-Paint* during the WM_PAINT message, KEYLOOK invalidates the entire window. This allows the whole window to be erased rather than just the invalid rectangle.

(That KEYLOOK does not save the keystrokes and hence cannot redraw the window during a WM_PAINT message is certainly a flaw. The TYPE program shown later in this chapter corrects this flaw.)

KEYLOOK draws a header at the top of the client area identifying the nine columns. Although it's possible to create an underlined font, I took a slightly different approach here. I defined two character string variables named *szTop* (which has the text) and *szUnd* (which has the underlining) and displayed both of them at the same position at the top of the window during the WM_PAINT message. Normally, Windows displays text in an "opaque" mode, meaning that Windows erases the character background area while displaying a character. This would cause the second character string (*szUnd*) to erase the first (*szTop*). To prevent this, switch the device context into the "transparent" mode:

```
SetBkMode (hdc, TRANSPARENT) ;
```

THE CARET (NOT THE CURSOR)

When you type text into a program, generally a little underline or box shows you where the next character you type will appear on the screen. You may know this as a "cursor," but you'll have to get out of that habit when programming for Windows. In Windows, it's called the "caret." The word "cursor" is used for the bitmap image that represents the mouse position.

The Caret Functions

There are five essential caret functions:

- *CreateCaret* creates a caret associated with a window.
- *SetCaretPos* sets the position of the caret on the window.
- *ShowCaret* shows the caret.
- *HideCaret* hides the caret.
- *DestroyCaret* destroys the caret.

There are also functions to get the caret position (*GetCaretPos*) and to get and set the caret blink time (*GetCaretBlinkTime* and *SetCaretBlinkTime*).

The caret is customarily a horizontal line, or a box that is the size of a character, or a vertical line. The vertical line is recommended when you use a proportional font such as the Windows default system font. Because the characters in a proportional font are not a fixed size, the horizontal line and box can't be set to the size of a character.

You cannot simply create a caret during the WM_CREATE message and destroy it during the WM_DESTROY message. The caret is what is known as a "systemwide resource." What this means is that there is only one caret in the system. In effect, a program "borrows" the caret from the system when it needs to display a caret in its window.

Does this sound bizarrely restrictive? It's really not. Think about it: The display of a caret in a window makes sense only when the window has the input focus. This indicates to the user that he or she may enter text in the program. Only one window has the input focus at any time so only one caret is needed in the whole system.

A program can determine if it has the input focus by processing the WM_SETFOCUS and WM_KILLFOCUS messages. A window procedure receives a WM_SETFOCUS message when it receives the input focus, and a WM_KILLFOCUS message when it loses the input focus. These messages occur in pairs: A window procedure will always receive a WM_SETFOCUS message before it receives a WM_KILLFOCUS message, and it always receives an equal number of WM_SETFOCUS and WM_KILLFOCUS messages over the course of the window's lifetime.

The main rule for using the caret is simple: A window procedure calls *CreateCaret* during the WM_SETFOCUS message and *DestroyCaret* during the WM_KILLFOCUS message.

There are a few other rules: The caret is created hidden. After calling *CreateCaret*, the window procedure must call *ShowCaret* for the caret to be visible. In addition, the window procedure must hide the caret by calling *HideCaret* whenever it draws something on its window during a message other than WM_PAINT. After it finishes drawing on the window, it calls *ShowCaret* to display the caret again. The effect of *HideCaret* is additive: If you call *HideCaret* several times without calling *ShowCaret*, you must call *ShowCaret* the same number of times before the caret becomes visible again.

The TYPE Program

The TYPE program shown in Figure 3-5 (beginning on the following page) brings together much of what we've learned in this chapter. You can think of TYPE as an extremely rudimentary text editor. You can type in the window, move the cursor (I mean caret) around with the cursor movement (or are they caret movement?) keys, and erase the contents of the window by pressing Escape. The contents of the window are also erased when you resize the window. There's no scrolling, no search and replace, no way to save files, and no spell checker, but it's a start.

To make things easy for myself, TYPE uses SYSTEM_FIXED_FONT. Writing a text editor for a proportional font is, as you might imagine, much more difficult. The program obtains a device context in several places: during the WM_CREATE message, the WM_KEYDOWN message, the WM_CHAR message, and the WM_PAINT message. Each time, calls to *GetStockObject* and *SelectObject* select the fixed-pitch font.

During the WM_SIZE message, TYPE calculates the character width and height of the window and saves these values in the variables *cxBuffer* and *cyBuffer*. It then uses *malloc* to allocate a buffer to hold all the characters that can be typed in the window. The *xCaret* and *yCaret* variables store the character position of the caret.

During the WM_SETFOCUS message, TYPE calls *CreateCursor* to create a cursor that is the width and height of a character, *SetCaretPos* to set the caret position, and *ShowCaret* to make the caret visible. During the WM_KILLFOCUS message, TYPE calls *HideCaret* and *DestroyCaret*.

TYPE.MAK

```
#--------------------
# TYPE.MAK make file
#--------------------

type.exe : type.obj type.def
    link type, /align:16, NUL, /nod slibcew libw, type
    rc type.exe

type.obj : type.c
    cl -c -Gsw -Ow -W2 -Zp type.c
```

TYPE.C

```c
/*-----------------------------------------
   TYPE.C -- Typing Program
            (c) Charles Petzold, 1990
   -----------------------------------------*/

#include <windows.h>
#include <stdlib.h>

#define BUFFER(x, y) *(pBuffer + y * cxBuffer + x)

long FAR PASCAL WndProc (HWND, WORD, WORD, LONG) ;

int PASCAL WinMain (HANDLE hInstance, HANDLE hPrevInstance,
                LPSTR lpszCmdLine, int nCmdShow)
    {
    static char szAppName[] = "Type" ;
    HWND        hwnd ;
    MSG         msg ;
    WNDCLASS    wndclass ;

    if (!hPrevInstance)
        {
        wndclass.style         = CS_HREDRAW | CS_VREDRAW ;
        wndclass.lpfnWndProc   = WndProc ;
        wndclass.cbClsExtra    = 0 ;
        wndclass.cbWndExtra    = 0 ;
        wndclass.hInstance     = hInstance ;
        wndclass.hIcon         = LoadIcon (NULL, IDI_APPLICATION) ;
        wndclass.hCursor       = LoadCursor (NULL, IDC_ARROW) ;
        wndclass.hbrBackground = (HBRUSH) GetStockObject (WHITE_BRUSH) ;
```

Figure 3-5. *The TYPE program.*   *(continued)*

```
            wndclass.lpszMenuName  = NULL ;
            wndclass.lpszClassName = szAppName ;

            RegisterClass (&wndclass) ;
            }

     hwnd = CreateWindow (szAppName, "Typing Program",
                         WS_OVERLAPPEDWINDOW,
                         CW_USEDEFAULT, CW_USEDEFAULT,
                         CW_USEDEFAULT, CW_USEDEFAULT,
                         NULL, NULL, hInstance, NULL) ;

     ShowWindow (hwnd, nCmdShow) ;
     UpdateWindow (hwnd) ;

     while (GetMessage (&msg, NULL, 0, 0))
          {
          TranslateMessage (&msg) ;
          DispatchMessage (&msg) ;
          }
     return msg.wParam ;
     }

long FAR PASCAL WndProc (HWND hwnd, WORD message, WORD wParam, LONG lParam)
     {
     static char *pBuffer = NULL ;
     static int  cxChar, cyChar, cxClient, cyClient, cxBuffer, cyBuffer,
                 xCaret, yCaret ;
     HDC         hdc ;
     int         x, y, i ;
     PAINTSTRUCT ps ;
     TEXTMETRIC  tm ;

     switch (message)
          {
          case WM_CREATE :
               hdc = GetDC (hwnd) ;

               SelectObject (hdc, GetStockObject (SYSTEM_FIXED_FONT)) ;
               GetTextMetrics (hdc, &tm) ;
               cxChar = tm.tmAveCharWidth ;
               cyChar = tm.tmHeight ;

               ReleaseDC (hwnd, hdc) ;
               return 0 ;

          case WM_SIZE :
                              // obtain window size in pixels
```

(continued)

```
                    cxClient = LOWORD (lParam) ;
                    cyClient = HIWORD (lParam) ;

                                  // calculate window size in characters

                    cxBuffer = max (1, cxClient / cxChar) ;
                    cyBuffer = max (1, cyClient / cyChar) ;

                                  // allocate memory for buffer and clear it

               if (pBuffer != NULL)
                    free (pBuffer) ;

               if ((LONG) cxBuffer * cyBuffer > 65535L ::
                         (pBuffer = malloc (cxBuffer * cyBuffer)) == NULL)

                    MessageBox (hwnd, "Window too large.  Cannot "
                                  "allocate enough memory.", "Type",
                              MB_ICONEXCLAMATION : MB_OK) ;

               else
                    for (y = 0 ; y < cyBuffer ; y++)
                         for (x = 0 ; x < cxBuffer ; x++)
                              BUFFER(x, y) = ' ' ;

                                  // set caret to upper left corner
               xCaret = 0 ;
               yCaret = 0 ;

               if (hwnd == GetFocus ())
                    SetCaretPos (xCaret * cxChar, yCaret * cyChar) ;

               return 0 ;

          case WM_SETFOCUS :
                                  // create and show the caret

               CreateCaret (hwnd, NULL, cxChar, cyChar) ;
               SetCaretPos (xCaret * cxChar, yCaret * cyChar) ;
               ShowCaret (hwnd) ;
               return 0 ;

          case WM_KILLFOCUS :
                                  // hide and destroy the caret
               HideCaret (hwnd) ;
               DestroyCaret () ;
               return 0 ;
```

(continued)

```
    case WM_KEYDOWN :
         switch (wParam)
              {
              case VK_HOME :
                   xCaret = 0 ;
                   break ;

              case VK_END :
                   xCaret = cxBuffer - 1 ;
                   break ;

              case VK_PRIOR :
                   yCaret = 0 ;
                   break ;

              case VK_NEXT :
                   yCaret = cyBuffer - 1 ;
                   break ;

              case VK_LEFT :
                   xCaret = max (xCaret - 1, 0) ;
                   break ;

              case VK_RIGHT :
                   xCaret = min (xCaret + 1, cxBuffer - 1) ;
                   break ;

              case VK_UP :
                   yCaret = max (yCaret - 1, 0) ;
                   break ;

              case VK_DOWN :
                   yCaret = min (yCaret + 1, cyBuffer - 1) ;
                   break ;

              case VK_DELETE :
                   for (x = xCaret ; x < cxBuffer - 1 ; x++)
                        BUFFER (x, yCaret) = BUFFER (x + 1, yCaret) ;

                   BUFFER (cxBuffer - 1, yCaret) = ' ' ;

                   HideCaret (hwnd) ;
                   hdc = GetDC (hwnd) ;

                   SelectObject (hdc,
                        GetStockObject (SYSTEM_FIXED_FONT)) ;

                   TextOut (hdc, xCaret * cxChar, yCaret * cyChar,
                             & BUFFER (xCaret, yCaret),
                             cxBuffer - xCaret) ;
```

(continued)

```
                    ShowCaret (hwnd) ;
                    ReleaseDC (hwnd, hdc) ;
                    break ;
               }

          SetCaretPos (xCaret * cxChar, yCaret * cyChar) ;
          return 0 ;

     case WM_CHAR :
          for (i = 0 ; i < LOWORD (lParam) ; i++)
               {
               switch (wParam)
                    {
                    case '\b' :                      // backspace
                         if (xCaret > 0)
                              {
                              xCaret-- ;
                              SendMessage (hwnd, WM_KEYDOWN,
                                        VK_DELETE, 1L) ;
                              }
                         break ;

                    case '\t' :                      // tab
                         do
                              {
                              SendMessage (hwnd, WM_CHAR, ' ', 1L) ;
                              }
                         while (xCaret % 8 != 0) ;
                         break ;

                    case '\n' :                      // linefeed
                         if (++yCaret == cyBuffer)
                              yCaret = 0 ;
                         break ;

                    case '\r' :                      // carriage return
                         xCaret = 0 ;

                         if (++yCaret == cyBuffer)
                              yCaret = 0 ;
                         break ;

                    case '\x1B' :                    // escape
                         for (y = 0 ; y < cyBuffer ; y++)
                              for (x = 0 ; x < cxBuffer ; x++)
                                   BUFFER (x, y) = ' ' ;

                         xCaret = 0 ;
                         yCaret = 0 ;
```

(continued)

122

```
                              InvalidateRect (hwnd, NULL, FALSE) ;
                              break ;

                    default :                        // character codes
                         BUFFER (xCaret, yCaret) = (char) wParam ;

                         HideCaret (hwnd) ;
                         hdc = GetDC (hwnd) ;

                         SelectObject (hdc,
                              GetStockObject (SYSTEM_FIXED_FONT)) ;

                         TextOut (hdc, xCaret * cxChar, yCaret * cyChar,
                                   & BUFFER (xCaret, yCaret), 1) ;

                         ShowCaret (hwnd) ;
                         ReleaseDC (hwnd, hdc) ;

                         if (++xCaret == cxBuffer)
                              {
                              xCaret = 0 ;

                              if (++yCaret == cyBuffer)
                                   yCaret = 0 ;
                              }
                         break ;
                    }
               }

          SetCaretPos (xCaret * cxChar, yCaret * cyChar) ;
          return 0 ;

     case WM_PAINT :
          hdc = BeginPaint (hwnd, &ps) ;
          SelectObject (hdc, GetStockObject (SYSTEM_FIXED_FONT)) ;

          for (y = 0 ; y < cyBuffer ; y++)
               TextOut (hdc, 0, y * cyChar, & BUFFER(0, y), cxBuffer) ;

          EndPaint (hwnd, &ps) ;
          return 0 ;

     case WM_DESTROY :
          PostQuitMessage (0) ;
          return 0 ;
     }
return DefWindowProc (hwnd, message, wParam, lParam) ;
}
```

TYPE.DEF

```
;------------------------------------
; TYPE.DEF module definition file
;------------------------------------

NAME            TYPE

DESCRIPTION     'Typing Program (c) Charles Petzold, 1990'
EXETYPE         WINDOWS
STUB            'WINSTUB.EXE'
CODE            PRELOAD MOVEABLE DISCARDABLE
DATA            PRELOAD MOVEABLE MULTIPLE
HEAPSIZE        1024
STACKSIZE       8192
EXPORTS         WndProc
```

The processing of the WM_KEYDOWN and WM_CHAR messages is more extensive. The WM_KEYDOWN processing mostly involves the cursor movement keys. Home and End send the caret to the beginning and end of a line respectively, and Page Up and Page Down send the caret to the top and bottom of the window. The arrow keys work as you would expect. For the Delete key, TYPE must move everything left in the buffer from the next caret position to the end of the line and then display a blank at the end of the line.

The WM_CHAR processing handles the Backspace, Tab, Linefeed (Ctrl-Enter), Enter, Escape, and character keys. Notice I've used Repeat Count in *lParam* when processing the WM_CHAR message (under the assumption that every character the user types is important) but not during the WM_KEYDOWN message (to prevent inadvertent overscrolling). The Backspace and Tab processing is simplified somewhat by the use of the *SendMessage* function. Backspace is emulated by the Delete logic, and Tab is emulated by a series of spaces.

As I mentioned earlier, you should hide the cursor when drawing on the window during messages other then WM_PAINT. The program does this when processing the WM_KEYDOWN message for the Delete key and the WM_CHAR message for character keys. In both these cases, TYPE alters the contents of the buffer and then draws the new character or characters on the window.

I use TYPE when working on speeches, as shown in Figure 3-6.

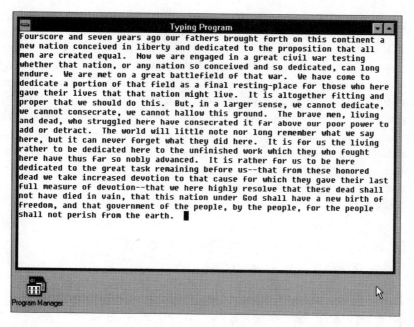

Figure 3-6. *The TYPE display.*

THE WINDOWS CHARACTER SETS

I mentioned earlier that letter keys preceded by dead-character keys generate WM_CHAR messages where *wParam* is the ASCII code for a character with a diacritic. This may be a little puzzling because the ASCII character set doesn't include any codes for characters with diacritics. What exactly is the value of *wParam* in this case? The answer to this question requires that we tackle the subject of character sets, a topic that may at first seem more appropriate for a later discussion about character fonts. However, it is also of vital importance in keyboard handling.

The standard 7-bit ASCII character set defines codes from 0 through 31 (1FH) and 127 (7FH) as control characters, and it defines codes from 32 (20H) through 126 (7EH) as displayable characters. None of these characters have diacritics. Because personal computers use 8-bit bytes, computer manufacturers often define character sets that use 256 codes rather than the 128 ASCII codes. The additional codes may be assigned characters with diacritics. The resultant "extended character set" then includes the ASCII character set and up to 128 other characters.

If Windows supported such an extended character set, displaying characters with diacritics would be easy. But Windows doesn't support a simple extended character set. Windows supports two extended character sets. Unfortunately, the presence of these two character sets doesn't make things twice as easy.

The OEM Character Set

First, let's go back to the hardware that Windows runs on—the IBM PC and compatibles. In the early 1980s the developers of the IBM PC decided to extend the ASCII character set as shown in Figure 3-7. The codes from 20H through 7EH are displayable characters from the ASCII character set. The rest are nonstandard—or at least were at the time.

This character set cannot be ignored. It is encoded in millions of ROM chips in IBM video adapters, printers, and system board BIOS's. It has been duplicated in the hardware of numerous manufacturers of IBM-compatible computers and peripherals. This character set is part of what is meant by the phrase "the IBM standard." Many programs written for the IBM PC require this extended character set because they use the block-drawing and line-drawing characters (codes B0H through DFH) in their screen output.

Figure 3-7. *The IBM extended character set arranged by character code.*

The only problem is this: The IBM extended character set is inappropriate for Windows. First, the block-drawing and line-drawing characters commonly used by PC programs in text-mode applications are not needed in Windows because Windows does real graphics. If you want to draw a horizontal line in Windows, it's easier to draw a line than to display a string of C4H characters. Second, the Greek alphabet and mathematical symbols are less important in Windows than are the accented letters used in most European languages. A program that needs to display mathematical symbols can best draw them using graphics functions.

In short, Windows supports the IBM character set, but it is relegated to secondary importance, mostly for old applications that run in a window. Windows applications do not normally use the IBM character set. In Windows documentation, the IBM character set is referred to as the "OEM character set." The OEM character set is more precisely defined as the character set that is native to the machine currently running Windows.

International Support under DOS

There are a number of variants on the IBM PC character set, called "code pages." The variant used in the United States and in most European countries is called Code Page 437. Systems sold in Norway, Denmark, Portugal, and a few other European countries use different, special, code pages, which contain more of the special characters required by the languages of those countries. Recently, a number of these countries began to use Code Page 850, which contains fewer graphics symbols and more accented letters and other special characters.

Windows 3.0 supports code pages by installing OEM fonts (used for running DOS applications in windows and in the clipboard viewer), which correspond to the system's code page, and by installing appropriate translation tables for the *AnsiToOem* and *OemToAnsi* functions (discussed later). If the system is running DOS version 3.3 or later, the Windows Setup program will use the current DOS code page. For earlier versions of DOS, Setup will select a code page based on the localized (national) version of Windows.

The ANSI Character Set

The extended character set that Windows and Windows programs use for most purposes is called the "ANSI character set." When your program receives a WM_CHAR message, the *wParam* parameter is the ANSI character code. The ANSI character set is shown in Figure 3-8. As you can see, the codes from 20H through 7EH represent the same characters that appear in the OEM character set and the ASCII character set. The characters displayed as solid blocks are undefined characters. They may appear differently on other output devices (such as a printer).

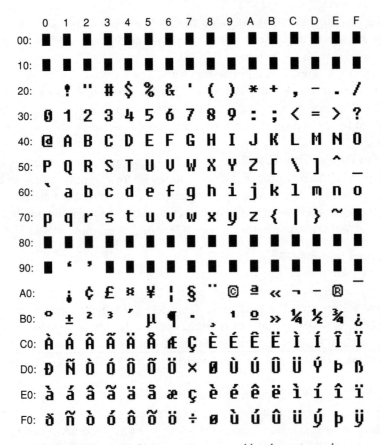

Figure 3-8. *The ANSI character set arranged by character code.*

OEM, ANSI, and Fonts

Windows has different fonts for displaying the ANSI and OEM character sets. When you first obtain a handle to a device context, one of the attributes in the device context is a font.

By default this is the SYSTEM_FONT or "system font," which uses the ANSI character set. If you want to display characters from the OEM character set, you can select the OEM_FIXED_FONT (also called the "terminal font") in the device context by using the following code:

```
SelectObject (hdc, GetStockObject (OEM_FIXED_FONT)) ;
```

This is the only font in Windows guaranteed to support the OEM character set.

INTERNATIONALIZATION CONCERNS

Here's why we have to talk about fonts in the middle of the keyboard chapter. We've established that when a Windows user on a non-U.S. keyboard types a character with a diacritic, the *wParam* parameter of the WM_CHAR message is the code for that character in the ANSI character set.

So, if you need to echo that character to the display, you had better be using a font with the ANSI character set (such as the SYSTEM_FONT or SYSTEM_FIXED_FONT). If you instead use the OEM_FIXED_FONT, the character you write to the display will be incorrect and will surprise the user. A few other simple rules will allow the keyboard logic in your Windows programs to survive intact when you convert your programs for a European market.

Working with the Character Set

When you get a WM_CHAR message, keep in mind that *wParam* may legitimately have values above 128. Don't assume that anything above 127 is an invalid character.

You may want to convert a character to uppercase. Don't use your own algorithm:

```
if (ch >= 'a' && ch <= 'z')
    ch -= 32 ;              // WRONG !!!
```

That's a poor practice even when writing non-Windows C. But don't use the standard C function either:

```
ch = toupper (ch) ;        // WRONG !!!
```

Both these functions work only for the lower half of the ANSI character set. They will not convert a C0H to an E0H.

Instead, you should use the Windows functions *AnsiUpper* and *AnsiLower*. If *str* is a zero-terminated character string, you can convert it to uppercase using *AnsiUpper*:

```
AnsiUpper (pString) ;
```

or using the *AnsiUpperBuff* function for character strings that are not zero-terminated:

```
AnsiUpperBuff (pString, nLength) ;
```

You can also use *AnsiUpper* to convert a single character, but some casting is required because the high-order word of the parameter must be zero:

```
ch = AnsiUpper ((LPSTR) (LONG) (BYTE) ch) ;
```

If *ch* is defined as an unsigned character, the initial BYTE cast is not required. Windows also includes *AnsiLower* and *AnsiLowerBuff* functions for converting to lowercase.

If you are really serious about writing Windows programs that can be easily converted to foreign languages, you should also investigate the *AnsiNext* and *AnsiPrev* functions. These functions facilitate handling of multibyte character sets. The Japanese character set requires more than 256 characters, some of which use 2 bytes. If you use normal C pointer arithmetic to scan a string (perhaps searching for a backslash character in a directory path string), you may think you've found the character when you've really found the second byte of a 2-byte character code. *AnsiNext* and *AnsiPrev* take a far pointer to a character string and return a far pointer that has been correctly incremented or decremented past 2-byte character codes.

Talking with MS-DOS

If Windows were the only operating environment running on a machine, then you could forget about the OEM character set and use only the ANSI character set. However, users can create files in the MS-DOS environment and use them in Windows; they can also create files in Windows and use them when back in MS-DOS. Unfortunately, MS-DOS uses the OEM character set.

Here's an example of the communications problems that can occur. Suppose that a German-speaking PC user creates a file named ÜBUNGEN.TXT ("practice exercises") in an MS-DOS program such as EDLIN. On the IBM PC, the Ü is part of the IBM (that is, OEM) character set and has a code of 154 or 9AH. (When using MS-DOS with a U.S. keyboard on an IBM PC, you can also create this letter by typing Alt-154 using the numeric keypad.) MS-DOS uses that character code in the directory entry of the file.

If a Windows program uses MS-DOS function calls to obtain a directory of files and then writes them directly to the display using an ANSI character set font, the first letter of ÜBUNGEN will show up as a solid block, because the code 154 is one of the undefined characters in the ANSI character set. The Windows program needs to convert the IBM extended character set code of 154 (9AH) to an ANSI character set code of 220 (or DCH), which is the letter Ü in the ANSI character set. That's what the Windows function *OemToAnsi* does for you. It requires two far pointers to strings. The OEM characters in the first string are converted to ANSI characters and stored in the second string:

```
OemToAnsi (lpszOemStr, lpszAnsiStr) ;
```

Now let's take the opposite example. The German-speaking user wants your Windows program to create a file named ÜBUNGEN.TXT. The filename entered by the user has a 220 (DCH) as the first character. If you use an MS-DOS function call to open the file, MS-DOS uses that character in the filename. When the user later looks at the file under MS-DOS, the first character shows up as a block. Before you use the MS-DOS function calls, you must convert the filename to the OEM character set:

```
AnsiToOem (lpszAnsiStr, lpszOemStr) ;
```

This converts a 220 (DCH) to a 154 (9AH). Windows also includes two functions named *AnsiToOemBuff* and *OemToAnsiBuff* that do not require a zero-terminated string.

Windows has an *OpenFile* call that will convert this for you. If you use *OpenFile*, don't do your own *AnsiToOem* conversion. If you use MS-DOS function calls to obtain lists of filenames (as the Windows File Manager program does), then these filenames should be passed through *OemToAnsi* before being displayed.

Converting the contents of files is another problem that arises when files are used in both Windows and MS-DOS. If your Windows program uses files that you are certain have been created in an MS-DOS program, then you may need to pass the text contents of the file through the *OemToAnsi* function. (For instance, Windows WRITE does this when converting Microsoft Word files to WRITE format.) Similarly, if your Windows program is preparing a file for use in an MS-DOS program, you may want to use *AnsiToOem* to convert the text.

The *OemToAnsi* and *AnsiToOem* functions are located in the keyboard driver. They incorporate very simple lookup tables. The *OemToAnsi* routine converts an OEM code from 80H through FFH to a character code in the ANSI set that most closely resembles the OEM character. In some cases, this conversion is only grossly approximate. For instance, most of the line-drawing characters in the IBM character set are translated as plus signs, dashes, and vertical lines. Most of the OEM codes from 00H through 1FH are not translated to ANSI codes.

The *AnsiToOem* routine converts ANSI codes from A0H through FFH into codes in the OEM set. The accented characters in the ANSI character set that do not appear in the OEM character set are translated into regular ASCII codes for the characters without the diacritics.

Using the Numeric Keypad

As you probably know, the IBM PC keyboard and BIOS let you enter codes for the IBM extended character set by pressing and holding down the Alt key, typing on the numeric keypad the three-digit decimal code representing the OEM character, and releasing the Alt key. This facility is duplicated in Windows in two ways:

First, when you type Alt-[*OEM code*] on the numeric keypad, Windows gives to you the ANSI character code in the *wParam* parameter of the WM_CHAR message that most closely approximates the OEM character represented by the OEM code. That is, Windows passes the code through the *OemToAnsi* function before generating the WM_CHAR message. This facility is for the user's convenience: If you do not have a foreign-language keyboard and you are accustomed to typing a Ü by typing Alt-154, you can do the same thing in a Windows program. You don't need to relearn the ANSI character codes.

Second, if you want to generate ANSI extended character codes from the U.S. keyboard, type Alt-0[*OEM code*] on the numeric keypad. The *wParam* parameter of the WM_CHAR message is that OEM code. Thus, Alt-0220 is also a Ü. You can try this out in the TYPE program.

Chapter 4

The Mouse

The mouse is a pointing device with one or more buttons. Although a mouse is considered an important part of Windows' user interface, it is an optional accessory. You can install Windows without a mouse, and you can control most Windows programs entirely from the keyboard. Often, the most difficult aspect of using the mouse in your program is adding a keyboard interface to duplicate the mouse functions.

MOUSE BASICS

Windows can support a one-button, two-button, or three-button mouse or use a joystick or light pen to mimic a one-button mouse. The support of a second and third mouse button is rarely exploited, however. Unless you know your Windows program will run only on machines equipped with a two-button or three-button mouse, you must write programs for the lowest common denominator and use only a single button.

You can determine if a mouse is present by using the *GetSystemMetrics* function:

```
fMouse = GetSystemMetrics (SM_MOUSEPRESENT) ;
```

The value of *fMouse* will be TRUE (nonzero) if a mouse is installed. No method is documented for determining the number of buttons on the installed mouse.

Some Quick Definitions

When the Windows user moves the mouse, Windows moves a small bit-mapped picture on the display called the "mouse cursor." The mouse cursor has a single-pixel "hot spot" that points to a precise location on the display.

The display driver contains several predefined mouse cursors that programs may use. The most common is the slanted arrow called IDC_ARROW in WINDOWS.H. The hot spot is the tip of the arrow. The IDC_CROSS cursor (used in the BLOWUP1 program shown in this chapter) has a hot spot in the center of a cross-hair pattern. The IDC_WAIT cursor is an hourglass generally used by programs to indicate they are busy. Programmers can also design their own cursors (as we'll do in Chapter 8). The default cursor for a particular window is specified when defining the window class structure, for instance:

```
wndclass.hCursor = LoadCursor (NULL, IDC_ARROW) ;
```

The following terms describe the actions you take with mouse buttons:

- Clicking—Pressing and releasing a mouse button
- Double-clicking—Pressing and releasing a mouse button twice in quick succession
- Dragging—Moving the mouse while holding down a button

On a three-button mouse, the buttons are called the left button, middle button, and right button. Mouse-related identifiers defined in WINDOWS.H use the abbreviations LBUTTON, MBUTTON, and RBUTTON. A two-button mouse has only a left button and a right button. The single button on a one-button mouse is a left button.

CLIENT-AREA MOUSE MESSAGES

In the previous chapter you saw how Windows sends keyboard messages only to the window with the input focus. Mouse messages are different: A window procedure receives mouse messages whenever the mouse passes over the window or is clicked within the window, even if the window is not active or does not have the input focus.

Windows defines 21 messages for the mouse. However, 11 of these messages do not relate to the client area (hereinafter, "nonclient-area" messages), and Windows programs usually ignore them. Of the 10 "client-area" mouse messages, 6 pertain to the right and middle buttons. Windows programs usually ignore these messages also.

When the mouse is moved over the client area of a window, the window procedure receives the message WM_MOUSEMOVE. When a mouse button is pressed or released within the client area of a window, the window procedure receives these messages:

Button	Pressed	Released	Pressed (2d Click)
Left	WM_LBUTTONDOWN	WM_LBUTTONUP	WM_LBUTTONDBLCLK
Middle	WM_MBUTTONDOWN	WM_MBUTTONUP	WM_MBUTTONDBLCLK
Right	WM_RBUTTONDOWN	WM_RBUTTONUP	WM_RBUTTONDBLCLK

Your window procedure receives "MBUTTON" messages only for a three-button mouse and "RBUTTON" messages only for a two-button or three-button mouse. The window procedure receives "DBLCLK" (double-click) messages only if the window class has been defined to receive them (as described below).

For all these messages, the value of *lParam* contains the position of the mouse. The low word is the *x*-coordinate, and the high word is the *y*-coordinate relative to the upper left corner of the client area of the window. You can extract the *x*-coordinate and *y*-coordinate from *lParam* using the *LOWORD* and *HIWORD* macros defined in WINDOWS.H. The value of *wParam* indicates the state of the mouse buttons and the Shift and Ctrl keys. You can test *wParam* using the bit masks defined in WINDOWS.H. The MK prefix stands for "mouse key."

MK_LBUTTON	Left button is down
MK_MBUTTON	Middle button is down
MK_RBUTTON	Right button is down
MK_SHIFT	Shift key is down
MK_CONTROL	Ctrl key is down

As you move the mouse over the client area of a window, Windows does *not* generate a WM_MOUSEMOVE message for every possible pixel position of the mouse. The number of WM_MOUSEMOVE messages your program receives depends on the mouse hardware and on the speed at which your window procedure can process the mouse movement messages. You'll get a good idea of the rate of WM_MOUSEMOVE messages when you experiment with the CONNECT program described below.

If you click the left mouse button in the client area of an inactive window, Windows changes the active window to the window that is being clicked and then passes the WM_LBUTTONDOWN message to the window procedure. When your window procedure gets a WM_LBUTTONDOWN message, your program can safely assume the window is active. However, your window procedure can receive a WM_LBUTTONUP message without first receiving a WM_LBUTTONDOWN message. This can happen if the mouse button is pressed in one window, moved to your window, and released. Similarly, the window procedure can receive a WM_LBUTTONDOWN without a corresponding WM_LBUTTONUP message if the mouse button is released while positioned over another window.

There are two exceptions to these rules:

- A window procedure can "capture the mouse" and continue to receive mouse messages even when the mouse is outside the window's client area. You'll learn how to capture the mouse later in this chapter.

- If a system-modal message box or a system-modal dialog box is on the display, no other program can receive mouse messages. System-modal message boxes and dialog boxes prohibit switching to another window or program while the box is active. (An example of a system-modal message box is the one that says "This will end your Windows session" when you close the Program Manager.)

Simple Mouse Processing: An Example

The CONNECT program, shown in Figure 4-1, does some simple mouse processing to let you get a good feel for how Windows sends your program mouse messages.

CONNECT.MAK

```
#----------------------
# CONNECT.MAK make file
#----------------------

connect.exe : connect.obj connect.def
    link connect, /align:16, NUL, /nod slibcew libw, connect
    rc connect.exe

connect.obj : connect.c
    cl -c -Gsw -Ow -W2 -Zp connect.c
```

CONNECT.C

```
/*-----------------------------------------------------
    CONNECT.C -- Connect-the-Dots Mouse Demo Program
                 (c) Charles Petzold, 1990
   -----------------------------------------------------*/

#include <windows.h>
#define MAXPOINTS 1000

long FAR PASCAL WndProc (HWND, WORD, WORD, LONG) ;

int PASCAL WinMain (HANDLE hInstance, HANDLE hPrevInstance,
                    LPSTR lpszCmdLine, int nCmdShow)
    {
    static char szAppName[] = "Connect" ;
    HWND        hwnd ;
    MSG         msg ;
    WNDCLASS    wndclass ;
```

Figure 4-1. *The CONNECT program.*   *(continued)*

```
        if (!hPrevInstance)
            {
            wndclass.style         = CS_HREDRAW : CS_VREDRAW ;
            wndclass.lpfnWndProc   = WndProc ;
            wndclass.cbClsExtra    = 0 ;
            wndclass.cbWndExtra    = 0 ;
            wndclass.hInstance     = hInstance ;
            wndclass.hIcon         = LoadIcon (NULL, IDI_APPLICATION) ;
            wndclass.hCursor       = LoadCursor (NULL, IDC_ARROW) ;
            wndclass.hbrBackground = GetStockObject (WHITE_BRUSH) ;
            wndclass.lpszMenuName  = NULL ;
            wndclass.lpszClassName = szAppName ;

            RegisterClass (&wndclass) ;
            }

    hwnd = CreateWindow (szAppName, "Connect-the-Dots Mouse Demo",
                        WS_OVERLAPPEDWINDOW,
                        CW_USEDEFAULT, CW_USEDEFAULT,
                        CW_USEDEFAULT, CW_USEDEFAULT,
                        NULL, NULL, hInstance, NULL) ;

    ShowWindow (hwnd, nCmdShow) ;
    UpdateWindow (hwnd) ;

    while (GetMessage (&msg, NULL, 0, 0))
        {
        TranslateMessage (&msg) ;
        DispatchMessage (&msg) ;
        }
    return msg.wParam ;
    }

long FAR PASCAL WndProc (HWND hwnd, WORD message, WORD wParam, LONG lParam)
    {
    static POINT points[MAXPOINTS] ;
    static short nCount ;
    HDC         hdc ;
    PAINTSTRUCT ps ;
    short       i, j ;

    switch (message)
        {
        case WM_LBUTTONDOWN :
            nCount = 0 ;
            InvalidateRect (hwnd, NULL, TRUE) ;
            return 0 ;
```

(continued)

```
        case WM_MOUSEMOVE :
             if (wParam & MK_LBUTTON && nCount < MAXPOINTS)
                 {
                 points [nCount++] = MAKEPOINT (lParam) ;
                 hdc = GetDC (hwnd) ;
                 SetPixel (hdc, LOWORD (lParam), HIWORD (lParam), OL) ;
                 ReleaseDC (hwnd, hdc) ;
                 }
             return 0 ;

        case WM_LBUTTONUP :
             InvalidateRect (hwnd, NULL, FALSE) ;
             return 0 ;

        case WM_PAINT :
             hdc = BeginPaint (hwnd, &ps) ;

             for (i = 0 ; i < nCount - 1 ; i++)
                  for (j = i ; j < nCount ; j++)
                      {
                      MoveTo (hdc, points[i].x, points[i].y) ;
                      LineTo (hdc, points[j].x, points[j].y) ;
                      }

             EndPaint (hwnd, &ps) ;
             return 0 ;

        case WM_DESTROY :
             PostQuitMessage (0) ;
             return 0 ;
        }
   return DefWindowProc (hwnd, message, wParam, lParam) ;
   }
```

CONNECT.DEF

```
;------------------------------------
; CONNECT.DEF module definition file
;------------------------------------

NAME            CONNECT

DESCRIPTION     'Mouse Connect Program (c) Charles Petzold, 1990'
EXETYPE         WINDOWS
STUB            'WINSTUB.EXE'
CODE            PRELOAD MOVEABLE DISCARDABLE
DATA            PRELOAD MOVEABLE MULTIPLE
HEAPSIZE        1024
STACKSIZE       8192
EXPORTS         WndProc
```

CONNECT processes three mouse messages:

- WM_LBUTTONDOWN—CONNECT clears the client area.

- WM_MOUSEMOVE—If the left button is down, CONNECT draws a black dot on the client area at the mouse position.

- WM_LBUTTONUP—CONNECT connects every dot drawn in the client area to every other dot. Sometimes this results in a pretty design; sometimes in a dense blob. (See Figure 4-2.)

To use CONNECT, bring the mouse cursor into the client area, press the left button, move the mouse around a little, and release the left button. CONNECT works best for a curved pattern of a few dots, which you can draw by moving the mouse quickly while the left button is depressed. CONNECT uses several simple Graphics Device Interface (GDI) functions. *SetPixel* draws a one-pixel dot of a particular color, in this case black. (On high-resolution displays, the pixel may be nearly invisible.) Drawing the lines requires two functions: *MoveTo* marks the *x*-coordinate and *y*-coordinate of the beginning of the line, and *LineTo* draws the line.

If you move the mouse cursor out of the client area before releasing the button, CONNECT does not connect the dots, because it doesn't receive the WM_LBUTTONUP message. If you move the mouse back into the client area and press the left button again, CONNECT clears the client area. (If you want to continue a design after releasing the

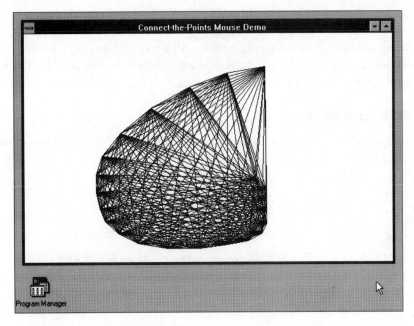

Figure 4-2. *The CONNECT display.*

button outside the client area, press the left button again while the mouse is outside the client area and then move the mouse back inside.)

CONNECT stores a maximum of 1000 points. The number of lines it draws is equal to:

$$\frac{(P) \times (P - 1)}{2}$$

where P is the number of points. With 1000 points, this involves almost 500,000 lines, which can take several minutes to draw. For anything but a demonstration program, this is too long for a Windows program to hog system resources.

If CONNECT is busy drawing lines, you can press the mouse button, move the mouse around, and release the mouse button, but nothing will happen. CONNECT does not receive these messages because it is busy and not making any *GetMessage* calls. After CONNECT finishes drawing the lines, it does not receive these messages because the mouse button has been released already. In this respect, the mouse is not like the keyboard. Windows treats every keystroke as if it were important. However, if a mouse button is pressed and released in the client area while a program is busy, the mouse clicks are discarded.

Now try this: While CONNECT is engaged in a lengthy drawing routine, hold down the mouse button and move the mouse around. After CONNECT is finished drawing, it will retrieve the WM_LBUTTONDOWN message from the queue (and clear the client area) because the button is currently down. However, it receives only the WM_MOUSEMOVE messages that occur after it receives the WM_LBUTTONDOWN message.

Sometimes the word "tracking" is used to refer to the way that programs process mouse movement. Tracking does not mean, however, that your program sits in a loop in its window procedure attempting to follow the mouse's movements on the display. The window procedure instead processes each mouse message as it comes and then quickly exits.

POINT, RECT, and *lParam*

CONNECT uses an array of POINT structures for saving points. The POINT structure is defined in WINDOWS.H and has two fields named x and y:

```
typedef struct tagPOINT
  {
    int x ;
    int y ;
  } POINT ;
```

Some Windows functions require a POINT structure (or a pointer to a POINT structure) as a parameter. You can define a POINT structure variable (named *point*, for instance) in your program with this definition:

```
POINT point ;
```

If you need to convert an *lParam* value—the x and y mouse coordinates—to a POINT structure, you can use the MAKEPOINT macro:

```
point = MAKEPOINT (lParam) ;
```

In WINDOWS.H, MAKEPOINT is defined like this:

```
#define MAKEPOINT(l) (*((POINT *)&l))
```

Despite the apparent complexity of this macro, it compiles very efficiently because all it does is store *lParam* at the address of *point.* WINDOWS.H defines the type PPOINT as a pointer to a POINT structure, so perhaps this statement (without using the macro) makes the conversion a little clearer:

```
point = * (PPOINT) &lParam ;
```

(Remember that standard C order-of-evaluation rules cause address, indirection, and type cast operators to be evaluated from right to left.)

The RECT structure defines a rectangle. Here's the WINDOWS.H definition:

```
typedef struct tagRECT
    {
    int left ;
    int top ;
    int right ;
    int bottom ;
    } RECT ;
```

This structure really contains two points side by side: *left* and *right* are x-coordinates, and *top* and *bottom* are y-coordinates. You can define a structure variable (named *rect*, for instance) with the statement:

```
RECT rect ;
```

Transferring coordinates from a RECT structure to a POINT structure is also straightforward. This statement sets *point* to the upper left corner of the rectangle:

```
point = * (PPOINT) &rect.left ;
```

This does the same for the lower right corner:

```
point = * (PPOINT) &rect.right ;
```

You can also define an array of two points:

```
POINT points [2] ;
```

and transfer these two points into a RECT structure:

```
rect = * (PRECT) points ;
```

PRECT is defined in WINDOWS.H as a pointer to a RECT structure. You don't need the & (address) operator before *points* because *points* is an array. In C, an array name is the address of the first element of the array.

Processing Shift Keys

When CONNECT receives a WM_MOUSEMOVE message, it performs a bitwise AND operation on the value of *wParam* and MK_LBUTTON to determine if the left button is depressed. You can also use *wParam* to determine the state of the Shift keys. For instance, if processing must be dependent on the status of the Shift and Ctrl keys, you might use logic that looks like this:

```
if (MK_SHIFT & wParam)
     if (MK_CONTROL & wParam)
          {
          [Shift and Ctrl keys are down]
          }
     else
          {
          [Shift key is down]
          }
else if (MK_CONTROL & wParam)
          {
          [Ctrl key is down]
          }
     else
          {
          [neither Shift nor Ctrl key is down]
          }
```

The Windows function *GetKeyState* (described in Chapter 3) can also return the state of the mouse buttons or shift keys using the virtual-key codes VK_LBUTTON, VK_RBUTTON, VK_MBUTTON, VK_SHIFT, and VK_CONTROL. The button or key is down if the value returned from *GetKeyState* is negative. Because *GetKeyState* returns mouse or key states as of the message currently being processed, the status information is properly synchronized with the messages. But just as you cannot use *GetKeyState* for a key that has yet to be pressed, so you cannot use it for a mouse button that has yet to be pressed. Don't do this:

```
while (GetKeyState (VK_LBUTTON) >= 0) ;   // WRONG !!!
```

The *GetKeyState* function will report that the left button is depressed only if the button is already depressed when you process the message during which you call *GetKeyState*.

Mouse Double-Clicks

A mouse double-click is two clicks in quick succession. To qualify as a double-click, the two clicks must occur within a specific interval called the "double-click time." If you want your window procedure to receive double-click mouse messages, you must include the identifier CS_DBLCLKS when initializing the window style in the window class structure before calling *RegisterClass*:

```
wndclass.style = CS_HREDRAW ¦ CS_VREDRAW ¦ CS_DBLCLKS ;
```

If you do *not* include CS_DBLCLKS in the window style and the user clicks the left mouse button twice in quick succession, your window procedure receives these messages: WM_LBUTTONDOWN, WM_LBUTTONUP, WM_LBUTTONDOWN, and WM_LBUT-TONUP. (The window procedure might also receive other messages between these button messages.) If you want to implement your own double-click logic, you can use the Windows function *GetMessageTime* to obtain the relative times of the WM_LBUTTONDOWN messages. This function is discussed in more detail in Chapter 5.

If you include CS_DBLCLKS in your window class, the window procedure receives these messages for a double-click: WM_LBUTTONDOWN, WM_LBUTTONUP, WM-_LBUTTONDBLCLK, and WM_LBUTTONUP. The WM_LBUTTONDBLCLK message simply replaces the second WM_LBUTTONDOWN message.

Double-click messages are much easier to process if the first click of a double-click performs the same action as a single click. The second click (the WM_LBUTTONDBLCLK message) then does something in addition to the first click. For example, look at how the mouse works with the file list in the File Manager program. A single click selects the file. The File Manager highlights the file with a reverse-video bar. A double-click performs two actions: The first click selects the file, just as a single click does; the second click (which is a WM_LBUTTONDBLCLK message) directs the File Manager to run the file. That's fairly easy logic.

Mouse-handling logic could get more complex if the first click of a double-click does not perform the same action as a single click.

NONCLIENT-AREA MOUSE MESSAGES

The 10 mouse messages discussed so far occur when the mouse is moved or clicked within the client area of a window. If the mouse is outside a window's client area but still within the window, Windows sends the window procedure a "nonclient-area" mouse message. The nonclient area includes the caption bar, the menu, and window scroll bars.

You do not usually need to process nonclient-area mouse messages. Instead, you simply pass them on to *DefWindowProc* so Windows can perform system functions. In this respect, the nonclient-area mouse messages are similar to the system keyboard messages WM_SYSKEYDOWN, WM_SYSKEYUP, and WM_SYSCHAR.

The nonclient-area mouse messages parallel almost exactly the client-area mouse messages. The messages include the letters "NC" to indicate "nonclient." If the mouse is moved within a nonclient area of a window, then the window procedure receives the message WM_NCMOUSEMOVE. The mouse buttons generate these messages:

Button	Pressed	Released	Pressed (2d Click)
Left	WM_NCLBUTTONDOWN	WM_NCLBUTTONUP	WM_NCLBUTTONDBLCLK
Middle	WM_NCMBUTTONDOWN	WM_NCMBUTTONUP	WM_NCMBUTTONDBLCLK
Right	WM_NCRBUTTONDOWN	WM_NCRBUTTONUP	WM_NCRBUTTONDBLCLK

However, the *wParam* and *lParam* parameters for nonclient-area mouse messages are different from those for client-area mouse messages. The *wParam* parameter indicates the nonclient area where the mouse was moved or clicked. It is set to one of the identifiers beginning with HT that are defined in WINDOWS.H (such as HTCAPTION and HTSYSMENU).

The *lParam* variable contains an x-coordinate in the low word and a y-coordinate in the high word. However, these are screen coordinates, not client-area coordinates as they are for client-area mouse messages. For screen coordinates, the upper left corner of the display area has x and y values of 0. Values of x increase as you move to the right, and values of y increase as you move down. (See Figure 4-3.)

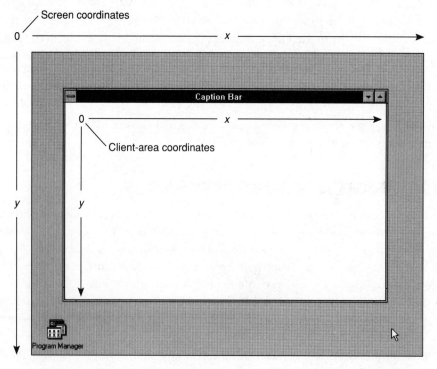

Figure 4-3. *Screen coordinates and client-area coordinates.*

You can convert screen coordinates to client-area coordinates and vice versa with two Windows functions:

```
ScreenToClient (hwnd, lpPoint) ;
ClientToScreen (hwnd, lpPoint) ;
```

The *lpPoint* parameter is a far (or long) pointer to a structure of type POINT. These two functions convert the values stored in the structure without preserving the old values. Note that if a screen-coordinate point is above the window's client area, then the converted client-area *y*-coordinate will be negative. Similarly, a screen coordinate to the left of a client area is a negative *x* value when expressed as a client-area coordinate.

The Hit-Test Message

If you've been keeping count, you know that we've covered 20 of the 21 mouse messages. The last message is WM_NCHITTEST, which stands for "nonclient hit test." This message precedes all other client-area and nonclient-area mouse messages. The *lParam* parameter contains the *x* and *y* screen coordinates of the mouse position. The *wParam* parameter is not used.

Windows applications usually pass this message to *DefWindowProc*. Windows then uses the WM_NCHITTEST message to generate all other mouse messages based on the position of the mouse. For nonclient-area mouse messages, the value returned from *DefWindowProc* when processing WM_NCHITTEST becomes the *wParam* parameter in the mouse message. This value can be any of the *wParam* values that accompany the nonclient-area mouse messages plus the following:

HTCLIENT	Client area
HTNOWHERE	Not on any window
HTTRANSPARENT	A window covered by another window
HTERROR	Causes *DefWindowProc* to produce a beep

If *DefWindowProc* returns HTCLIENT after it processes a WM_NCHITTEST message, then Windows converts the screen coordinates to client-area coordinates and generates a client-area mouse message.

If you remember how we disabled all system keyboard functions by trapping the WM_SYSKEYDOWN message, you may wonder if you can do something similar by trapping mouse messages. Sure. If you include the lines:

```
case WM_NCHITTEST :
     return (long) HTNOWHERE ;
```

in your window procedure, you will effectively disable all client-area and nonclient-area mouse messages to your window. The mouse buttons will simply not work while the mouse is anywhere within your window, including the system menu box and size box.

Messages Beget Messages

Windows uses the WM_NCHITTEST message to generate all other mouse messages. The idea of messages giving birth to other messages is common in Windows. Let's take an example. As you know, if you double-click the system menu box of a Windows program, the program will be terminated. The double-click generates a series of WM_NCHITTEST messages. Because the mouse is positioned over the system menu box, *DefWindowProc* returns a value of HTSYSMENU and Windows puts a WM_NCLBUTTONDBLCLK message in the message queue with *wParam* equal to HTSYSMENU.

The window procedure usually passes that mouse message to *DefWindowProc.* When *DefWindowProc* receives the WM_NCLBUTTONDBLCLK message with *wParam* equal to HTSYSMENU, it puts a WM_SYSCOMMAND message with *wParam* equal to SC_CLOSE in the message queue. (This WM_SYSCOMMAND message is also generated when a user selects Close from the system menu box.) Again, the window procedure usually passes that message to *DefWindowProc. DefWindowProc* processes the message by sending a WM_CLOSE message to the window procedure.

If a program wants to require confirmation from a user before terminating, the window procedure can trap WM_CLOSE. Otherwise, *DefWindowProc* processes WM_CLOSE by calling the *DestroyWindow* function. Among other actions, *DestroyWindow* sends a WM_DESTROY message to the window procedure. Normally, a window procedure processes WM_DESTROY with the code:

```
case WM_DESTROY :
     PostQuitMessage (0) ;
     return 0 ;
```

The *PostQuitMessage* causes Windows to place a WM_QUIT message in the message queue. This message never reaches the window procedure because it causes *GetMessage* to return 0, which terminates the message loop and the program.

HIT-TESTING IN YOUR PROGRAMS

Earlier I discussed how the File Manager responded to mouse clicks and double-clicks. Obviously, the program must determine which file the user is pointing at with the mouse. This is called "hit-testing." Just as *DefWindowProc* must do some hit-testing when processing WM_NCHITTEST messages, very often a window procedure must do some hit-testing within the client area. In general, hit-testing involves calculations using the *x*- and *y*-coordinates passed to your window procedure in the *lParam* parameter of the mouse message.

A Hypothetical Example

Here's an example. Your program displays several columns of alphabetically sorted files similar to the File Manager file windows. The file list starts at the top of the client area, which is *cxClient* pixels wide and *cyClient* pixels high; each character is *cyChar* pixels high. The filenames are stored in a sorted array of pointers to character strings called *szFileNames*.

Let's assume that the columns are *cxColWidth* pixels wide. The number of files you can fit in each column is:

```
nNumInCol = cyClient / cyChar ;
```

You receive a mouse click message with the coordinates *cxMouse* and *cyMouse* derived from *lParam*. You can determine which column of filenames the user is pointing to by using the formula:

```
nColumn = cxMouse / cxColWidth ;
```

The position of the filename in relation to the top of the column is:

```
nFromTop = cyMouse / cyChar ;
```

Now you can calculate an index to the *szFileNames* array:

```
nIndex = nColumn * nNumInCol + nFromTop ;
```

Obviously, if *nIndex* exceeds the number of files in the array, the user is clicking on a blank area of the display.

In many cases, hit-testing is more complex than this example suggests. For instance, it can become very messy in a word processing program that uses variable font sizes (such as WRITE). When you display something to the client area, you must determine the coordinates for each item you display. In hit-testing calculations, you must go backward from the coordinates to the object. However, if the objects you display are strings, then going backward involves finding the character position within the string.

A Sample Program

The CHECKER1 program, shown in Figure 4-4, demonstrates some simple hit-testing. The program divides the client area into a 5-by-5 array of 25 rectangles. If you click the mouse on one of the rectangles, the rectangle is filled with an X. If you click there again, the X is removed.

CHECKER1.MAK

```
#------------------------
# CHECKER1.MAK make file
#------------------------

checker1.exe : checker1.obj checker1.def
     link checker1, /align:16, NUL, /nod slibcew libw, checker1
     rc checker1.exe
```

Figure 4-4. *The CHECKER1 program.*   *(continued)*

```
checker1.obj : checker1.c
    cl -c -Gsw -Ow -W2 -Zp checker1.c
```

CHECKER1.C

```
/*---------------------------------------------------
   CHECKER1.C -- Mouse Hit-Test Demo Program No. 1
                 (c) Charles Petzold, 1990
   -----------------------------------------------*/

#include <windows.h>
#define DIVISIONS 5

long FAR PASCAL WndProc (HWND, WORD, WORD, LONG) ;

int PASCAL WinMain (HANDLE hInstance, HANDLE hPrevInstance,
                    LPSTR  lpszCmdLine, int nCmdShow)
     {
     static char szAppName[] = "Checker1" ;
     HWND        hwnd ;
     MSG         msg ;
     WNDCLASS    wndclass ;

     if (!hPrevInstance)
         {
         wndclass.style         = CS_HREDRAW : CS_VREDRAW ;
         wndclass.lpfnWndProc   = WndProc ;
         wndclass.cbClsExtra    = 0 ;
         wndclass.cbWndExtra    = 0 ;
         wndclass.hInstance     = hInstance ;
         wndclass.hIcon         = NULL ;
         wndclass.hCursor       = LoadCursor (NULL, IDC_ARROW) ;
         wndclass.hbrBackground = GetStockObject (WHITE_BRUSH) ;
         wndclass.lpszMenuName  = NULL ;
         wndclass.lpszClassName = szAppName ;

         RegisterClass (&wndclass) ;
         }

     hwnd = CreateWindow (szAppName, "Checker1 Mouse Hit-Test Demo",
                    WS_OVERLAPPEDWINDOW,
                    CW_USEDEFAULT, CW_USEDEFAULT,
                    CW_USEDEFAULT, CW_USEDEFAULT,
                    NULL, NULL, hInstance, NULL) ;

     ShowWindow (hwnd, nCmdShow) ;
     UpdateWindow (hwnd) ;
```

(continued)

```
    while (GetMessage (&msg, NULL, 0, 0))
        {
        TranslateMessage (&msg) ;
        DispatchMessage (&msg) ;
        }
    return msg.wParam ;
    }

long FAR PASCAL WndProc (HWND hwnd, WORD message, WORD wParam, LONG lParam)
    {
    static BOOL  fState[DIVISIONS][DIVISIONS] ;
    static short cxBlock, cyBlock ;
    HDC          hdc ;
    PAINTSTRUCT  ps ;
    RECT         rect ;
    short        x, y ;

    switch (message)
        {
        case WM_SIZE :
            cxBlock = LOWORD (lParam) / DIVISIONS ;
            cyBlock = HIWORD (lParam) / DIVISIONS ;
            return 0 ;

        case WM_LBUTTONDOWN :
            x = LOWORD (lParam) / cxBlock ;
            y = HIWORD (lParam) / cyBlock ;

            if (x < DIVISIONS && y < DIVISIONS)
                {
                fState [x][y] ^= 1 ;
                rect.left   = x * cxBlock ;
                rect.top    = y * cyBlock ;
                rect.right  = (x + 1) * cxBlock ;
                rect.bottom = (y + 1) * cyBlock ;

                InvalidateRect (hwnd, &rect, FALSE) ;
                }
            else
                MessageBeep (0) ;
            return 0 ;

        case WM_PAINT :
            hdc = BeginPaint (hwnd, &ps) ;

            for (x = 0 ; x < DIVISIONS ; x++)
                for (y = 0 ; y < DIVISIONS ; y++)
                    {
                    Rectangle (hdc, x * cxBlock, y * cyBlock,
                               (x + 1) * cxBlock, (y + 1) * cyBlock) ;
```

(continued)

149

```
                        if (fState [x][y])
                             {
                             MoveTo (hdc,  x    * cxBlock,  y    * cyBlock) ;
                             LineTo (hdc, (x+1) * cxBlock, (y+1) * cyBlock) ;
                             MoveTo (hdc,  x    * cxBlock, (y+1) * cyBlock) ;
                             LineTo (hdc, (x+1) * cxBlock,  y    * cyBlock) ;
                             }
                         }
             EndPaint (hwnd, &ps) ;
             return 0 ;

        case WM_DESTROY :
             PostQuitMessage (0) ;
             return 0 ;
        }
     return DefWindowProc (hwnd, message, wParam, lParam) ;
     }
```

CHECKER1.DEF

```
;------------------------------------------------
; CHECKER1.DEF module definition file
;------------------------------------------------

NAME            CHECKER1

DESCRIPTION     'Mouse Hit-Test Demo Program No. 1 (c) Charles Petzold, 1990'
EXETYPE         WINDOWS
STUB            'WINSTUB.EXE'
CODE            PRELOAD MOVEABLE DISCARDABLE
DATA            PRELOAD MOVEABLE MULTIPLE
HEAPSIZE        1024
STACKSIZE       8192
EXPORTS         WndProc
```

Figure 4-5 shows the CHECKER1 display. All 25 rectangles have the same width and height. These width and height values are stored in *cxBlock* and *cyBlock* and are recalculated when the size of the client area changes. The WM_LBUTTONDOWN logic uses the mouse coordinates to determine which rectangle has been clicked. It flags the current state of the rectangle in the array *fState* and invalidates the rectangle to generate a WM_PAINT message. If the width or height of the client area is not evenly divisible by five, a small strip of client area at the left or bottom will not be covered by a rectangle. For error processing, CHECKER1 responds to a mouse click in this area by calling *MessageBeep*.

When CHECKER1 receives a WM_PAINT message, it repaints the entire client area by drawing rectangles using the GDI *Rectangle* function. If the *fState* value is set,

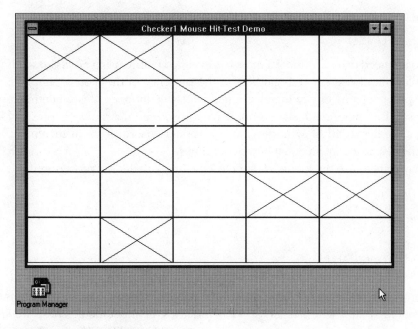

Figure 4-5. *The CHECKER1 display.*

CHECKER1 draws two lines using the *MoveTo* and *LineTo* functions. During WM_PAINT processing, CHECKER1 does not check the validity of each rectangular section before repainting it, but it could. One method for checking validity involves building a RECT structure for each rectangular block within the loop (using the same formulas as in the WM_LBUTTONDOWN logic) and checking whether it intersects the invalid rectangle (*ps.rcPaint*) by using the function *IntersectRect*. Another method is to use *PtInRect* to determine if any of the four corners of the rectangular block are within the invalid rectangle.

Emulating the Mouse with the Keyboard

CHECKER1 works only if you have a mouse. We'll be adding a keyboard interface to the program shortly, as we did for the SYSMETS program in Chapter 3. However, adding a keyboard interface to a program that uses the mouse cursor for pointing purposes requires that we also must worry about displaying and moving the mouse cursor.

Even if a mouse device is not installed, Windows can still display a mouse cursor. Windows maintains a "display count" for this cursor. If a mouse is installed, the display count is initially 0; if not, the display count is initially −1. The mouse cursor is displayed only if the display count is 0 or positive. You can increment the display count by calling:

```
ShowCursor (TRUE) ;
```

and decrement it by calling:

```
ShowCursor (FALSE) ;
```

You do not need to determine if a mouse is installed before using *ShowCursor*. If you want to display the mouse cursor regardless of the presence of the mouse, simply increment the display count. After you increment the display count once, decrementing it will hide the cursor if no mouse is installed but leave it displayed if a mouse is present. The display count applies to all of Windows, so you should ensure that you increment and decrement the display count an equal number of times.

You may want to use the following simple logic in your window procedure:

```
WM_SETFOCUS :
      ShowCursor (TRUE) ;
      return 0 ;

WM_KILLFOCUS :
      ShowCursor (FALSE) ;
      return 0 ;
```

A window procedure receives the WM_SETFOCUS message when the window obtains the keyboard input focus and WM_KILLFOCUS when it loses the input focus. These are ideal times to display and hide the mouse cursor. First, the WM_SETFOCUS and WM_KILL-FOCUS calls are balanced—that is, the window procedure will increment and decrement the mouse cursor display count an equal number of times. Second, for versions of Windows installed without a mouse, using the WM_SETFOCUS and WM_KILLFOCUS messages causes the cursor to be visible only when the window has the input focus. That is also the only time the user can move the cursor using the keyboard interface that you'll design.

Windows maintains a current mouse cursor position even if a mouse is not installed. If a mouse is not installed, and you display the mouse cursor, it may appear in any part of the display, and will remain in that position until you explicitly move it. You can obtain the cursor position by using:

```
GetCursorPos (lpPoint) ;
```

where *lpPoint* is a far pointer to a POINT structure. The function fills in the POINT fields with the *x*- and *y*-coordinates of the mouse. You can set the cursor position by using:

```
SetCursorPos (x, y) ;
```

In both cases, the x and y values are screen coordinates, not client-area coordinates. (This should be evident because the functions do not require a *hwnd* parameter.) As noted earlier, you can convert screen coordinates to client-area coordinates and vice versa by using *ScreenToClient* and *ClientToScreen*.

If you call *GetCursorPos* while processing a mouse message and convert to client-area coordinates, the coordinates may still be slightly different from those in *lParam* of the mouse message. The coordinates returned from *GetCursorPos* indicate the current position of the mouse. The coordinates in *lParam* of a mouse message are the coordinates of the mouse when the message was generated.

You'll probably want to write keyboard logic to move the mouse cursor with the keyboard arrow keys and simulate the mouse button with the Spacebar or Enter key. What you *don't* want to do is move the mouse cursor one pixel per keystroke. That forces a user to hold down an arrow key for more than a minute to move the mouse cursor from one side of the display to the other.

If you need to implement a keyboard interface to the mouse cursor but still maintain the ability to position the cursor at precise pixel locations, take a look at Windows' PAINT-BRUSH program. When you hold down an arrow key, the mouse cursor starts moving slowly but then speeds up. You'll recall that the *lParam* parameter in WM_KEYDOWN messages indicates if the keystroke messages are the result of typematic action. This is an excellent application of that information.

Adding a Keyboard Interface to CHECKER

The CHECKER2 program, shown in Figure 4-6, is the same as CHECKER1 except that it includes a keyboard interface. You can use the Left, Right, Up, and Down arrow keys to move the cursor among the 25 rectangles. The Home key sends the cursor to the upper left rectangle; the End key drops it down to the lower right rectangle. Both the Spacebar and Enter keys toggle the X mark.

CHECKER2.MAK

```
#------------------------
# CHECKER2.MAK make file
#------------------------

checker2.exe : checker2.obj checker2.def
    link checker2, /align:16, NUL, /nod slibcew libw, checker2
    rc checker2.exe

checker2.obj : checker2.c
    cl -c -Gsw -Ow -W2 -Zp checker2.c
```

CHECKER2.C

```
/*-----------------------------------------------------
    CHECKER2.C -- Mouse Hit-Test Demo Program No. 2
                  (c) Charles Petzold, 1990
   -----------------------------------------------------*/
```

Figure 4-6. *The CHECKER2 program.*   *(continued)*

```
#include <windows.h>
#define DIVISIONS 5

long FAR PASCAL WndProc (HWND, WORD, WORD, LONG) ;

int PASCAL WinMain (HANDLE hInstance, HANDLE hPrevInstance,
                    LPSTR lpszCmdLine, int nCmdShow)

     {
     static char szAppName[] = "Checker2" ;
     HWND        hwnd ;
     MSG         msg ;
     WNDCLASS    wndclass ;

     if (!hPrevInstance)
          {
          wndclass.style         = CS_HREDRAW | CS_VREDRAW ;
          wndclass.lpfnWndProc   = WndProc ;
          wndclass.cbClsExtra    = 0 ;
          wndclass.cbWndExtra    = 0 ;
          wndclass.hInstance     = hInstance ;
          wndclass.hIcon         = NULL ;
          wndclass.hCursor       = LoadCursor (NULL, IDC_ARROW) ;
          wndclass.hbrBackground = GetStockObject (WHITE_BRUSH) ;
          wndclass.lpszMenuName  = NULL ;
          wndclass.lpszClassName = szAppName ;

          RegisterClass (&wndclass) ;
          }

     hwnd = CreateWindow (szAppName, "Checker2 Mouse Hit-Test Demo",
                     WS_OVERLAPPEDWINDOW,
                     CW_USEDEFAULT, CW_USEDEFAULT,
                     CW_USEDEFAULT, CW_USEDEFAULT,
                     NULL, NULL, hInstance, NULL) ;

     ShowWindow (hwnd, nCmdShow) ;
     UpdateWindow (hwnd) ;

     while (GetMessage (&msg, NULL, 0, 0))
          {
          TranslateMessage (&msg) ;
          DispatchMessage (&msg) ;
          }
     return msg.wParam ;
     }

long FAR PASCAL WndProc (HWND hwnd, WORD message, WORD wParam, LONG lParam)
     {
     static BOOL  fState[DIVISIONS][DIVISIONS] ;
```

(continued)

```
static short cxBlock, cyBlock ;
HDC         hdc ;
PAINTSTRUCT ps ;
POINT       point ; ⌐
RECT        rect ;
short       x, y ;

switch (message)
    {
    case WM_SIZE :
        cxBlock = LOWORD (lParam) / DIVISIONS ;
        cyBlock = HIWORD (lParam) / DIVISIONS ;
        return 0 ;

    case WM_SETFOCUS :
        ShowCursor (TRUE) ;
        return 0 ;

    case WM_KILLFOCUS :
        ShowCursor (FALSE) ;

        return 0 ;

    case WM_KEYDOWN :
        GetCursorPos (&point) ;
        ScreenToClient (hwnd, &point) ;

        x = max (0, min (DIVISIONS - 1, point.x / cxBlock)) ;
        y = max (0, min (DIVISIONS - 1, point.y / cyBlock)) ;

        switch (wParam)
            {
            case VK_UP :
                y-- ;
                break ;

            case VK_DOWN :
                y++ ;
                break ;

            case VK_LEFT :
                x-- ;
                break ;

            case VK_RIGHT :
                x++ ;
                break ;

            case VK_HOME :
                x = y = 0 ;
                break ;
```

(continued)

```
                    case VK_END :
                        x = y = DIVISIONS - 1 ;
                        break ;

                    case VK_RETURN :
                    case VK_SPACE :
                        SendMessage (hwnd, WM_LBUTTONDOWN, MK_LBUTTON,
                                MAKELONG (x * cxBlock, y * cyBlock)) ;
                        break ;
                    }
               x = (x + DIVISIONS) % DIVISIONS ;
               y = (y + DIVISIONS) % DIVISIONS ;

               point.x = x * cxBlock + cxBlock / 2 ;
               point.y = y * cyBlock + cyBlock / 2 ;

               ClientToScreen (hwnd, &point) ;
               SetCursorPos (point.x, point.y) ;
               return 0 ;

          case WM_LBUTTONDOWN :
               x = LOWORD (lParam) / cxBlock ;
               y = HIWORD (lParam) / cyBlock ;

               if (x < DIVISIONS && y < DIVISIONS)
                    {
                    fState[x][y] ^= 1 ;

                    rect.left   = x * cxBlock ;
                    rect.top    = y * cyBlock ;
                    rect.right  = (x + 1) * cxBlock ;
                    rect.bottom = (y + 1) * cyBlock ;

                    InvalidateRect (hwnd, &rect, FALSE) ;
                    }
               else
                    MessageBeep (0) ;
               return 0 ;

          case WM_PAINT :
               hdc = BeginPaint (hwnd, &ps) ;

               for (x = 0 ; x < DIVISIONS ; x++)
                    for (y = 0 ; y < DIVISIONS ; y++)
                         {
                         Rectangle (hdc, x * cxBlock, y * cyBlock,
                                 (x + 1) * cxBlock, (y + 1) * cyBlock) ;

                         if (fState [x][y])
                              {
                              MoveTo (hdc, x     * cxBlock, y     * cyBlock) ;
```

(continued)

```
                              LineTo (hdc, (x+1) * cxBlock, (y+1) * cyBlock) ;
                              MoveTo (hdc, x     * cxBlock, (y+1) * cyBlock) ;
                              LineTo (hdc, (x+1) * cxBlock, y     * cyBlock) ;
                              }
                    }
          EndPaint (hwnd, &ps) ;
          return 0 ;

     case WM_DESTROY :
          PostQuitMessage (0) ;
          return 0 ;
     }
     return DefWindowProc (hwnd, message, wParam, lParam) ;
}
```

CHECKER2.DEF

```
;-------------------------------------------
; CHECKER2.DEF module definition file
;-------------------------------------------

NAME            CHECKER2

DESCRIPTION     'Mouse Hit-Test Demo Program No. 2 (c) Charles Petzold, 1990'
EXETYPE         WINDOWS
STUB            'WINSTUB.EXE'
CODE            PRELOAD MOVEABLE DISCARDABLE
DATA            PRELOAD MOVEABLE MULTIPLE
HEAPSIZE        1024
STACKSIZE       8192
EXPORTS         WndProc
```

The WM_KEYDOWN logic in CHECKER2 determines the position of the cursor (*Get-CursorPos*), converts the screen coordinates to client-area coordinates (*ScreenToClient*), and divides the coordinates by the width and height of the rectangular block. This produces x and y values that indicate the position of the rectangle in the 5-by-5 array. The mouse cursor may or may not be in the client area when a key is pressed, so x and y must be passed through the WINDOWS.H *min* and *max* macros to ensure that they range from 0 through 4.

For arrow keys, CHECKER2 increments or decrements x and y appropriately. If the key is the Enter key (VK_RETURN) or Spacebar (VK_SPACE), CHECKER2 uses *SendMessage* to send a WM_LBUTTONDOWN message to itself. This technique is similar to the method used in the SYSMETS program in Chapter 3 to add a keyboard interface to the window scroll bar. The WM_KEYDOWN logic finishes by calculating client-area coordinates that point to the center of the rectangle, converting to screen coordinates (*Client-ToScreen*), and setting the cursor position (*SetCursorPos*).

Using Child Windows for Hit-Testing

Some programs, like the Windows PAINTBRUSH program, divide the client area into several smaller logical areas. The PAINTBRUSH program, shown in Figure 4-7, has an area at the left for its icon-based menu and an area at the bottom for the color menu. PAINTBRUSH, when hit-testing on these two menus, must take into account the location of the menu within the client area before determining the menu item being selected by the user.

Or maybe not. In reality, PAINTBRUSH simplifies the menu drawing and hit-testing through the use of "child windows." The child windows divide the entire client area into several smaller rectangular regions. Each child window has its own window handle, window procedure, and client area. Each window procedure receives mouse messages that apply only to its child window. The *lParam* parameter in the mouse message contains coordinates relative to the upper left corner of the client area of the child window, not of the parent window.

Child windows used in this way can help you structure and modularize your programs. If the child windows use different window classes, each child window can have its

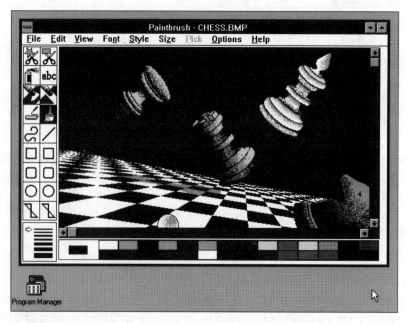

Figure 4-7. *The Windows PAINTBRUSH program.*

own window procedure. The different window classes can also define different background colors and different default cursors. In Chapter 6, we'll look at "child window controls"—predefined child windows that take the form of scroll bars, buttons, and edit boxes. Right now, let's see how we can use child windows in the CHECKER program.

Child Windows in CHECKER

Figure 4-8 shows CHECKER3. This version of the program creates 25 child windows to process mouse clicks. It does not have a keyboard interface, but one could be easily added.

CHECKER3 has two window procedures called *WndProc* and *ChildWndProc*. *WndProc* is still the window procedure for the main (or parent) window. *ChildWndProc* is the window procedure for the 25 child windows. The names of both window procedures must appear as EXPORTS in the CHECKER3.DEF file because both procedures are called from Windows.

Because the window procedure is defined by the window class structure that you register with Windows using the *RegisterClass* call, the two window procedures in CHECKER3.C require two window classes. The first window class is for the main window and has the name "Checker3". The second window class is given the name "Checker3_Child".

Most of the fields of the *wndclass* structure variable are simply reused when "Checker3_Child" is registered in *WinMain*. The *lpszClassName* field is set to "Checker3_Child"—the name of the class. The *lpfnWndProc* field is set to *ChildWndProc*, the window procedure for this window class, and the *hIcon* field is set to NULL, because icons are not used with child windows. For the "Checker3_Child" window class, the *cbWndExtra* field in the *wndclass* structure variable is set to 2 bytes, or more precisely, *sizeof*(WORD). This field tells Windows to reserve 2 bytes of extra space in a structure that Windows maintains for each window based on this window class. You can use this space to store information that may be different for each window.

CHECKER3.MAK

```
#-----------------------
# CHECKER3.MAK make file
#-----------------------

checker3.exe : checker3.obj checker3.def
    link checker3, /align:16, NUL, /nod slibcew libw, checker3
    rc checker3.exe

checker3.obj : checker3.c
    cl -c -Gsw -Ow -W2 -Zp checker3.c
```

Figure 4-8. *The CHECKER3 program.*

CHECKER3.C

```
/*-------------------------------------------------
   CHECKER3.C -- Mouse Hit-Test Demo Program No. 3
                 (c) Charles Petzold, 1990
   -------------------------------------------------*/

#include <windows.h>
#define DIVISIONS 5

long FAR PASCAL WndProc      (HWND, WORD, WORD, LONG) ;
long FAR PASCAL ChildWndProc (HWND, WORD, WORD, LONG) ;

char szChildClass[] = "Checker3_Child" ;

int PASCAL WinMain (HANDLE hInstance, HANDLE hPrevInstance,
                    LPSTR lpszCmdLine, int nCmdShow)
     {
     static char szAppName[] = "Checker3" ;
     HWND        hwnd ;
     MSG         msg ;
     WNDCLASS    wndclass ;

     if (!hPrevInstance)
          {
          wndclass.style         = CS_HREDRAW : CS_VREDRAW ;
          wndclass.lpfnWndProc   = WndProc ;
          wndclass.cbClsExtra    = 0 ;
          wndclass.cbWndExtra    = 0 ;
          wndclass.hInstance     = hInstance ;
          wndclass.hIcon         = LoadIcon (NULL, IDI_APPLICATION) ;
          wndclass.hCursor       = LoadCursor (NULL, IDC_ARROW) ;
          wndclass.hbrBackground = GetStockObject (WHITE_BRUSH) ;
          wndclass.lpszMenuName  = NULL ;
          wndclass.lpszClassName = szAppName ;

          RegisterClass (&wndclass) ;

          wndclass.lpfnWndProc   = ChildWndProc ;
          wndclass.cbWndExtra    = sizeof (WORD) ;
          wndclass.hIcon         = NULL ;
          wndclass.lpszClassName = szChildClass ;

          RegisterClass (&wndclass) ;
          }

     hwnd = CreateWindow (szAppName, "Checker3 Mouse Hit-Test Demo",
                    WS_OVERLAPPEDWINDOW,
                    CW_USEDEFAULT, CW_USEDEFAULT,
```

(continued)

```
                    CW_USEDEFAULT, CW_USEDEFAULT,
                    NULL, NULL, hInstance, NULL) ;

    ShowWindow (hwnd, nCmdShow) ;
    UpdateWindow (hwnd) ;

    while (GetMessage (&msg, NULL, 0, 0))
         {
         TranslateMessage (&msg) ;
         DispatchMessage (&msg) ;
         }
    return msg.wParam ;
    }

long FAR PASCAL WndProc (HWND hwnd, WORD message, WORD wParam, LONG lParam)
    {
    static HWND hwndChild [DIVISIONS] [DIVISIONS] ;
    short      cxBlock, cyBlock, x, y ;

    switch (message)
         {
         case WM_CREATE :
              for (x = 0 ; x < DIVISIONS ; x++)
                  for (y = 0 ; y < DIVISIONS ; y++)
                       {
                       hwndChild [x][y] = CreateWindow (szChildClass, NULL,
                           WS_CHILDWINDOW : WS_VISIBLE,
                           0, 0, 0, 0,
                           hwnd, y << 8 : x,
                           GetWindowWord (hwnd, GWW_HINSTANCE), NULL) ;
                       }
              return 0 ;

         case WM_SIZE :
              cxBlock = LOWORD (lParam) / DIVISIONS ;
              cyBlock = HIWORD (lParam) / DIVISIONS ;
              for (x = 0 ; x < DIVISIONS ; x++)
                  for (y = 0 ; y < DIVISIONS ; y++)
                       MoveWindow (hwndChild [x][y],
                           x * cxBlock, y * cyBlock,
                           cxBlock, cyBlock, TRUE) ;
              return 0 ;

         case WM_LBUTTONDOWN :
              MessageBeep (0) ;
              return 0 ;

         case WM_DESTROY :
              PostQuitMessage (0) ;
              return 0 ;
         }
```

(continued)

```
            return DefWindowProc (hwnd, message, wParam, lParam) ;
            }

long FAR PASCAL ChildWndProc (HWND hwnd, WORD message, WORD wParam, LONG lParam)
       {
       HDC         hdc ;
       PAINTSTRUCT ps ;
       RECT        rect ;

       switch (message)
            {
            case WM_CREATE :
                 SetWindowWord (hwnd, 0, 0) ;        // on/off flag
                 return 0 ;

            case WM_LBUTTONDOWN :
                 SetWindowWord (hwnd, 0, 1 ^ GetWindowWord (hwnd, 0)) ;
                 InvalidateRect (hwnd, NULL, FALSE) ;
                 return 0 ;

            case WM_PAINT :
                 hdc = BeginPaint (hwnd, &ps) ;

                 GetClientRect (hwnd, &rect) ;
                 Rectangle (hdc, 0, 0, rect.right, rect.bottom) ;

                 if (GetWindowWord (hwnd, 0))
                      {
                      MoveTo (hdc, 0,           0) ;
                      LineTo (hdc, rect.right, rect.bottom) ;
                      MoveTo (hdc, 0,           rect.bottom) ;
                      LineTo (hdc, rect.right, 0) ;
                      }

                 EndPaint (hwnd, &ps) ;
                 return 0 ;
            }
       return DefWindowProc (hwnd, message, wParam, lParam) ;
       }
```

CHECKER3.DEF

```
;------------------------------------
; CHECKER3.DEF module definition file
;------------------------------------
```

(continued)

```
NAME            CHECKER3

DESCRIPTION     'Mouse Hit-Test Demo Program No. 3 (c) Charles Petzold, 1990'
EXETYPE         WINDOWS
STUB            'WINSTUB.EXE'
CODE            PRELOAD MOVEABLE DISCARDABLE
DATA            PRELOAD MOVEABLE MULTIPLE
HEAPSIZE        1024
STACKSIZE       8192
EXPORTS         WndProc
                ChildWndProc
```

The *CreateWindow* call in *WinMain* creates the main window based on the "Checker3" class. This is normal. However, when *WndProc* receives a WM_CREATE message, it calls *CreateWindow* 25 times to create 25 child windows based on the "Checker3_Child" window class. Here's a comparison of the parameters to the *CreateWindow* call in *WinMain* that creates the main window and the *CreateWindow* call in *WndProc* that creates the 25 child windows:

Parameter	Main Window	Child Window
window class	"Checker3"	"Checker3_Child"
window caption	"Checker3..."	NULL
window style	WS_OVERLAPPEDWINDOW	WS_CHILDWINDOW ¦ WS_VISIBLE
horizontal position	CW_USEDEFAULT	0
vertical position	CW_USEDEFAULT	0
width	CW_USEDEFAULT	0
height	CW_USEDEFAULT	0
parent window handle	NULL	hwnd
menu handle / child ID	NULL	$y << 8$ ¦ x
instance handle	*hInstance*	*GetWindowWord* (*hwnd*, GWW_HINSTANCE)
extra parameters	NULL	NULL

Normally, the position, width, and height parameters are required for child windows, but in CHECKER3 the child windows are positioned and resized later in *WndProc*. The parent window handle is NULL for the main window because it is the parent. The parent window handle is required when using the *CreateWindow* call to create a child window.

The main window doesn't have a menu, so that parameter is NULL. For child windows, the same parameter position is called a "child ID." This is a number that uniquely identifies the child window. The child ID becomes much more important when working with child window controls because messages to the parent window are identified by this child ID. For CHECKER3, I've used the child ID to identify the position in the 5-by-5 array that each child window occupies within the main window.

The instance handle is *hInstance* in both cases. When the child window is created, the *hInstance* value is extracted using the function *GetWindowWord* from the structure that Windows maintains for the window. (Rather than use *GetWindowWord*, I could have saved the value of *hInstance* in a global variable and used it directly.)

Each child window has a different window handle that is stored in the *hwndChild* array. When *WndProc* receives a WM_SIZE message, it calls *MoveWindow* for each of the 25 child windows. The parameters indicate the upper left corner of the child window relative to the parent window client-area coordinates, the width and height of the child window, and whether the child window needs repainting.

Now let's take a look at *ChildWndProc*. This window procedure processes messages for all 25 child windows. The *hwnd* parameter to *ChildWndProc* is the handle to the child window receiving the message. When *ChildWndProc* processes a WM_CREATE message (which will happen 25 times because there are 25 child windows), it uses *SetWindowWord* to store a 0 in the extra area reserved within the window structure. (Recall that we reserved this space by using the *cbWndExtra* field when defining the window class structure.) *ChildWndProc* uses this value to store the current state (X or no X) of the rectangle. When the child window is clicked, the WM_LBUTTONDOWN logic simply flips the value of this word (from 0 to 1 or from 1 to 0) and invalidates the entire child window client area. This area is the single rectangle being clicked. The WM_PAINT processing is trivial, because the size of the rectangle it draws is the same size as the client window.

Because the C source code file and the .EXE file of CHECKER3 are larger than those for CHECKER1 (to say nothing of my explanation of the programs), I will not try to convince you that CHECKER3 is "simpler" than CHECKER1. But note that we no longer have to do any mouse hit-testing! If a child window in CHECKER3 gets a WM_LBUTTONDOWN message, the window has been hit, and that's all it needs to know.

If you want to add a keyboard interface to CHECKER3, be aware that the main window still gets keyboard messages because it has the input focus. We'll explore child windows more in Chapter 6.

CAPTURING THE MOUSE

A window procedure normally receives mouse messages only when the mouse cursor is positioned over the client or nonclient area of the window. A program that needs to receive mouse messages when the mouse is outside the window can "capture" the mouse.

Capturing the mouse is easier than baiting a mousetrap. You need only call:

```
SetCapture (hwnd) ;
```

After this function call, Windows sends all mouse messages to the window procedure for the window whose handle is *hwnd*. The mouse messages are always client-area messages, even when the mouse is in a nonclient area of the window. The *lParam* parameter still indicates the position of the mouse in client-area coordinates. These *x*- and *y*-coordinates, however, can be negative if the mouse is to the left of or above the client area.

During the time the mouse is captured, system keyboard functions are also disabled. When you want to release the mouse, call:

```
ReleaseCapture () ;
```

This returns processing to normal.

The BLOWUP1 Program

The BLOWUP1 program, shown in Figure 4-9, uses *SetCapture* and *ReleaseCapture* and a few other interesting techniques. The program lets you use the mouse to block out any rectangular area of the screen. BLOWUP1 then copies the contents of that rectangular area into its own client area, stretching or compressing the image as appropriate. (See Figure 4-10 on page 169.)

BLOWUP1.MAK

```
#----------------------
# BLOWUP1.MAK make file
#----------------------

blowup1.exe : blowup1.obj blowup1.def
     link blowup1, /align:16, NUL, /nod slibcew libw, blowup1
     rc blowup1.exe

blowup1.obj : blowup1.c
     cl -c -Gsw -Ow -W2 -Zp blowup1.c
```

BLOWUP1.C

```
/*-------------------------------------------------
   BLOWUP1.C -- Screen Capture Mouse Demo Program
                (c) Charles Petzold, 1990
   -------------------------------------------------*/

#include <windows.h>

long FAR PASCAL WndProc (HWND, WORD, WORD, LONG) ;

int PASCAL WinMain (HANDLE hInstance, HANDLE hPrevInstance,
                    LPSTR lpszCmdLine, int nCmdShow)
```

Figure 4-9. *The BLOWUP1 program.*   *(continued)*

```
     {
     static char szAppName[] = "BlowUp1" ;
     HWND       hwnd ;
     MSG        msg ;
     WNDCLASS   wndclass ;

     if (!hPrevInstance)
          {
          wndclass.style         = CS_HREDRAW : CS_VREDRAW ;
          wndclass.lpfnWndProc   = WndProc ;
          wndclass.cbClsExtra    = 0 ;
          wndclass.cbWndExtra    = 0 ;
          wndclass.hInstance     = hInstance ;
          wndclass.hIcon         = LoadIcon (NULL, IDI_APPLICATION) ;
          wndclass.hCursor       = LoadCursor (NULL, IDC_ARROW) ;
          wndclass.hbrBackground = GetStockObject (WHITE_BRUSH) ;
          wndclass.lpszMenuName  = NULL ;
          wndclass.lpszClassName = szAppName ;

          RegisterClass (&wndclass) ;
          }

     hwnd = CreateWindow (szAppName, "Blow-Up Mouse Demo",
                    WS_OVERLAPPEDWINDOW,
                    CW_USEDEFAULT, CW_USEDEFAULT,
                    CW_USEDEFAULT, CW_USEDEFAULT,
                    NULL, NULL, hInstance, NULL) ;

     ShowWindow (hwnd, nCmdShow) ;
     UpdateWindow (hwnd) ;

     while (GetMessage (&msg, NULL, 0, 0))
          {
          TranslateMessage (&msg) ;
          DispatchMessage (&msg) ;
          }
     return msg.wParam ;
     }

void InvertBlock (HWND hwnd, POINT ptBeg, POINT ptEnd)
     {
     HDC hdc ;

     hdc = CreateDC ("DISPLAY", NULL, NULL, NULL) ;
     ClientToScreen (hwnd, &ptBeg) ;
     ClientToScreen (hwnd, &ptEnd) ;
     PatBlt (hdc, ptBeg.x, ptBeg.y, ptEnd.x - ptBeg.x, ptEnd.y - ptBeg.y,
             DSTINVERT) ;
     DeleteDC (hdc) ;
     }
```

(continued)

166

```
long FAR PASCAL WndProc (HWND hwnd, WORD message, WORD wParam, LONG lParam)
    {
    static BOOL  fCapturing, fBlocking ;
    static POINT ptBeg, ptEnd ;
    HDC          hdc ;
    RECT         rect ;

    switch (message)
        {
        case WM_LBUTTONDOWN :
            if (!fCapturing)
                {
                fCapturing = TRUE ;
                SetCapture (hwnd) ;
                SetCursor (LoadCursor (NULL, IDC_CROSS)) ;
                }
            else if (!fBlocking)

                {
                fBlocking = TRUE ;
                ptBeg = MAKEPOINT (lParam) ;
                }
            return 0 ;

        case WM_MOUSEMOVE :
            if (fBlocking)
                {
                ptEnd = MAKEPOINT (lParam) ;
                InvertBlock (hwnd, ptBeg, ptEnd) ;
                InvertBlock (hwnd, ptBeg, ptEnd) ;
                }
            return 0 ;

        case WM_LBUTTONUP :
            if (fBlocking)
                {
                fCapturing = fBlocking = FALSE ;
                ptEnd = MAKEPOINT (lParam) ;
                SetCursor (LoadCursor (NULL, IDC_WAIT)) ;

                hdc = GetDC (hwnd) ;
                GetClientRect (hwnd, &rect) ;
                StretchBlt (hdc, 0, 0, rect.right, rect.bottom,
                            hdc, ptBeg.x, ptBeg.y,
                            ptEnd.x - ptBeg.x, ptEnd.y - ptBeg.y,
                            SRCCOPY) ;

                ReleaseDC (hwnd, hdc) ;
                SetCursor (LoadCursor (NULL, IDC_ARROW)) ;
```

(continued)

```
                            ReleaseCapture () ;
                        }
                    return 0 ;

            case WM_DESTROY :
                    PostQuitMessage (0) ;
                    return 0 ;
                }
            return DefWindowProc (hwnd, message, wParam, lParam) ;
            }
```

BLOWUP1.DEF

```
;------------------------------------
; BLOWUP1.DEF module definition file
;------------------------------------

NAME            BLOWUP1

DESCRIPTION     'Blow-Up Mouse Demo Program (c) Charles Petzold, 1990'
EXETYPE         WINDOWS
STUB            'WINSTUB.EXE'
CODE            PRELOAD MOVEABLE DISCARDABLE
DATA            PRELOAD MOVEABLE MULTIPLE
HEAPSIZE        1024
STACKSIZE       8192
EXPORTS         WndProc
```

The job of stretching and compressing bitmapped images may seem complex, but it's simplified for us by a Windows GDI function called *StretchBlt*. (The abbreviation *Blt* is pronounced "blit." The function is related to the Windows *BitBlt* function, which stands for "bit-block transfer." These functions are discussed in more detail in Chapter 13.)

Here's how to use BLOWUP1:

1. Click the mouse in BLOWUP1's client area. The mouse cursor changes to a cross hair.

2. Position the mouse cursor over the upper left corner of the area of the screen you want to transfer.

3. Press the mouse button, drag the mouse to the lower right corner, and release the mouse button. The mouse cursor changes to an hourglass.

4. In a few seconds (or perhaps a little longer), the area that you blocked out is copied to BLOWUP1's client area, compressed or expanded appropriately.

If you block out a rectangle by moving from the upper right corner to the lower left corner, BLOWUP1 displays a mirror image. If you move from the lower left to the upper right, BLOWUP1 displays an upside-down image. And if you move from lower right to upper left, the program combines the two effects.

BLOWUP1 does not retain the captured image, and doesn't process the WM_PAINT message. If you change the size of the window, the window will be erased.

Figure 4-10. *The BLOWUP1 client area.*

Changing the Mouse Cursor Shape

BLOWUP1 uses the *SetCursor* calls to change the cursor shape from an arrow to a cross hair, then to an hourglass, and back to an arrow. All these are stock cursors available in Windows. You obtain the handle to the cursor using the *LoadCursor* function. In Chapter 8 we'll use *LoadCursor* to display customized mouse cursors.

Many applications display an hourglass cursor (defined in WINDOWS.H as IDC-_WAIT) while doing processing that may take some time to complete. This is fairly simple to implement. You can save the handle to the original cursor by storing the return value from *SetCursor* and using it to reset the cursor later. First, you'll need a variable of type HCURSOR (defined in WINDOWS.H as a HANDLE, or 16-bit WORD) to store that value:

```
HCURSOR hCursor ;
```

Right before you start the lengthy processing, use the following two lines:

```
hCursor = SetCursor (LoadCursor (NULL, IDC_WAIT)) ;
ShowCursor (TRUE) ;
```

After you're done with the work, call:

```
ShowCursor (FALSE) ;
SetCursor (hCursor) ;
```

The two *ShowCursor* calls display and then hide the hourglass cursor if a mouse is not actually present.

Normally, Windows changes the mouse cursor to the cursor included in the window class structure whenever the window procedure receives a WM_MOUSEMOVE message. If you use *SetCursor* to change the mouse cursor and then exit the window procedure, the mouse cursor will be restored to the cursor in the window class structure the next time the mouse is moved. This does not happen in BLOWUP1, because the mouse is captured during the time the cross-hair cursor (IDC_CROSS) is displayed. Windows will not change the cursor to the window class cursor when the mouse is captured. Also, if you need to display an hourglass cursor when doing some lengthy work (as BLOWUP1 does when it calls *StretchBlt*), you don't have to worry about the problem, because you're not receiving any other messages during that time.

But if you want to use different mouse cursors for other purposes, you should define a NULL cursor handle in your window class:

```
wndclass.hCursor = NULL ;
```

In your window function, you then call *SetCursor* for each WM_MOUSEMOVE message. The *SetCursor* call is fast if the mouse cursor is not being changed.

The *StretchBlt* Call

BLOWUP1 calls the *StretchBlt* function during processing of the WM_LBUTTONUP message to transfer the blocked-out image to BLOWUP1's client area:

```
StretchBlt (hdc, 0, 0, rect.right, rect.bottom,
            hdc, ptBeg.x, ptBeg.y,
            ptEnd.x - ptBeg.x, ptEnd.y - ptBeg.y,
            SRCCOPY) ;
```

This function is discussed in more detail in Chapter 13, but let's take a quick look at it here.

StretchBlt transfers a bitmapped image from a source to a destination. The first five parameters are for the destination of the image, defining the device context handle, the *x*- and *y*-coordinates of the upper left corner, and the width and height. The next five parameters give the same information for the source of the image. The last parameter is the operation, which in this case is a simple copy from source to destination.

The source of the image involves two POINT structures named *ptBeg* (beginning of the block) and *ptEnd* (end of the block). These two points have negative coordinate values if you block out an image to the left of or above the client area. *StretchBlt* can read a bit-mapped image that falls outside the client area, but like all GDI functions it cannot write outside the client area.

Drawing the Capture Block

But wait. When you use BLOWUP1 to block out an image outside its client area, the program briefly displays the image in reverse video and then restores it to normal. BLOWUP1 is apparently writing outside its client area. Can that be so?

It certainly can. This little trick is carried off in BLOWUP1's *InvertBlock* function. Rather than obtain a device context handle from *GetDC*, *InvertBlock* uses *CreateDC*:

```
hdc = CreateDC ("DISPLAY", NULL, NULL, NULL) ;
```

This returns a device context handle for the entire display. Using this device context handle, you can write outside your client area.

InvertBlock uses the GDI *PatBlt* function (a "pattern bit-block transfer") to invert the blocked-out image. BLOWUP1 calls *InvertBlock* twice in succession. When called the second time, the block is restored to normal. This means that you can see the block briefly only when you move the mouse cursor.

Why do it like this? BLOWUP1 doesn't leave the block in an inverted state because other Windows programs can receive messages between BLOWUP1's WM_MOUSEMOVE messages. (For instance, the Windows CLOCK gets WM_TIMER messages every second.) If BLOWUP1 left the block inverted when it exited its window function, then the program with the altered client area could write over the inverted block. When BLOWUP1 then reinverted the block—that is, returned it to normal—the result would start looking like a mess. Keep considerations like this in mind when you start working with powerful functions like *CreateDC*. Windows gives you the power to do almost anything, but your programs must share resources such as the display with other programs. Try to exercise a little restraint.

Chapter 5

The Timer

The Windows timer is an input device that periodically notifies an application when a specified interval of time has elapsed. Your program tells Windows the interval, in effect saying, for example, "Give me a nudge every 10 seconds." Windows then sends your program recurrent WM_TIMER messages to signal the intervals.

At first, the Windows timer may seem a less important input device than the keyboard or mouse, and certainly it is for many applications. But the timer is more useful than you may think, and not only for programs (like the Windows CLOCK) that keep time. The CALENDAR, CONTROL, REVERSI, SPOOLER, TERMINAL, and WRITE programs supplied with Windows also use the timer. Here are some uses for the Windows timer, some obvious and some perhaps not so obvious:

- Keeping time—Both the CLOCK and CONTROL programs that come with Windows display the current time. The timer tells the programs when to update the clock. The DIGCLOCK program, described later in this chapter, uses the timer to display a digital clock.

- Maintaining an updated status report—The FREEMEM program, shown in this chapter, uses the timer to display available memory in Windows. The display is updated every second.

- Waking up—The Windows CALENDAR program uses the timer to trigger a preset alarm.

- Multitasking—Windows is a nonpreemptive multitasking environment, and it is important that programs return control to Windows as quickly as possible. If a program must do a large amount of processing, it can divide the job into smaller pieces and process each piece on receipt of a WM_TIMER message.

- Implementing an "autosave" feature—The timer can prompt a Windows program to save a user's work to disk whenever a specified amount of time has elapsed.

- Pacing movement—Graphical objects in a game or successive displays in a computer-assisted instruction program may need to proceed at a set rate. Using the timer eliminates the inconsistencies that might result from variations in microprocessor speed.

- Terminating demonstration versions of programs—Some demonstration versions of programs are designed to terminate, say, 30 minutes after they begin. The timer can signal such applications when the time is up.

- Using serial or parallel communications—Unlike most other input devices in Windows, serial or parallel communications ports do not generate messages. Rather, these programs must poll for input, and the timer can tell them when to do so. (An alternative to using the timer for polling involves a message loop built around the *PeekMessage* call. This technique is discussed in Chapter 15.)

This chapter also explores topics that extend beyond the timer to other areas of Windows programming. Foremost among these topics is that of "call-back" functions. To the uninitiated, these important functions might seem to work in mysterious ways, and the timer is not the only place you will encounter them. This chapter also discusses what to do when a program cannot gain access to a timer—a problem that occurs because Windows maintains only a limited number of timers. Solving this problem is fundamental to working with the Windows timer, but the method presented here can also be applied to error handling in other programs. Finally, the sample programs shown here deal with such decidedly nontimer issues as Windows' use of color, using a type of window known as a "popup," forcing an application to be loaded as an icon, obtaining the amount of free memory available in Windows, using floating-point mathematics in your Windows programs, and accessing the WIN.INI file to obtain information about international time and date formats.

TIMER BASICS

You can allocate a timer for your Windows program by calling the *SetTimer* function. *SetTimer* includes a parameter specifying an interval that can range (in theory) from 1 msec (millisecond) to 65,535 msec, or about 65.5 seconds. The value indicates the rate at which Windows sends your program WM_TIMER messages. For instance, an interval of 1000 msec causes Windows to send your program a WM_TIMER message every second.

When your program is done using the timer, it calls the *KillTimer* function to stop the timer messages. You can program a "one-shot" timer by calling *KillTimer* during the processing of the WM_TIMER message. The *KillTimer* call purges the message queue of any pending WM_TIMER messages. Your program will never receive a stray WM_TIMER message following a *KillTimer* call.

As you've undoubtedly learned from experimenting with loading multiple instances of CLOCK, Windows allows only 16 timers to be active at one time. If all 16 timers are already allocated, *SetTimer* returns NULL. Windows programs that use a timer must include some way to deal with this problem.

SYSTEM.DRV and the Windows Timer

The Windows timer is a relatively simple extension of the timer logic built into the IBM PC's hardware and ROM BIOS. The PC's ROM BIOS initializes an Intel 8259 timer chip to generate the hardware Interrupt 08H. This interrupt is sometimes called the "clock tick" or "timer tick" interrupt. An Interrupt 08H occurs every 54.925 msec, or about 18.2 times per second. Among other purposes, the BIOS uses Interrupt 08H to update a "time-of-day" value stored in the BIOS data area. MS-DOS uses this value to calculate the current time.

The SYSTEM.DRV driver located in the SYSTEM subdirectory of your Windows directories handles hardware timer interrupts. SYSTEM.DRV sets a new Interrupt 08H vector address during initialization and restores the original vector address before Windows terminates. The Interrupt 08H routine within SYSTEM.DRV calls the original Interrupt 08H handler before doing its own processing so that underlying system functions that require this interrupt will continue to work normally.

When SYSTEM.DRV receives an Interrupt 08H, it calls a routine within the USER module of Windows that decrements counters for each timer set by Windows applications. When a counter reaches 0, USER places a WM_TIMER message in that application's message queue and resets the counter to the original value.

Because a Windows application retrieves WM_TIMER messages from the normal message queue, you never have to worry about your program being "interrupted" by a sudden WM_TIMER message while doing other processing. In this way, the timer is similar to the keyboard and mouse: The driver handles the asynchronous hardware interrupt events, and Windows translates these events into orderly, structured, serialized messages.

SYSTEM.DRV does not attempt to reprogram the 8259 timer chip in the IBM PC. The Windows timer has the same 54.925-msec resolution as the underlying PC timer. This fact has two important implications:

- A Windows application cannot receive WM_TIMER messages at a rate faster than about 18.2 times per second when using a single timer.

- The time interval you specify in the *SetTimer* call is always rounded down to an integral multiple of clock ticks. For instance, a 1000-msec interval divided by 54.925 msec is 18.207 clock ticks, which is rounded down to 18 clock ticks, which is really a 989-msec interval. For intervals less than 55 msec, each clock tick generates a single WM_TIMER message.

Do not attempt to intercept the ROM BIOS timer interrupt in your Windows programs. Use the Windows timer instead.

Timer Messages Are Not Asynchronous

Non-Windows programs written for the IBM PC and compatibles can use the timer tick interrupt by intercepting Interrupt 08H or Interrupt 1CH (a software interrupt called by the BIOS Interrupt 08H handler). When the hardware interrupt occurs, the program currently running is suspended, and control passes to the interrupt handler. When the interrupt handler is done, it passes control back to the interrupted program.

Like the hardware keyboard and mouse interrupts, the hardware timer tick interrupt is sometimes called an asynchronous interrupt because it occurs randomly with respect to the program that it interrupts. (Actually, the term isochronous is more accurate than asynchronous for a timer interrupt because the interrupts occur at equal intervals. But the interrupts are still asynchronous with respect to other processing.)

Although the SYSTEM.DRV driver also handles asynchronous Interrupt 08H clock ticks, the WM_TIMER messages that Windows sends to applications are not asynchronous. The WM_TIMER messages are placed in the normal message queue and ordered with all the other messages. Therefore, if you specify 1000 msec in the *SetTimer* call, your program is not guaranteed to receive a WM_TIMER message every second or even (as I mentioned above) every 989 msec. If another application is busy for more than a second, your program will not get any WM_TIMER messages during that time. Only when the other application yields control to Windows (by calling *GetMessage*, *PeekMessage*, or *WaitMessage*) will your program retrieve its next WM_TIMER message from the queue.

You can easily demonstrate this to yourself with the CLOCK program included with Windows or with the sample programs shown in this chapter. If another program has a long paint job and does not immediately relinquish control, CLOCK will stop. When CLOCK regains control, it will jump ahead to the correct time. In fact, Windows handles WM_TIMER messages much like WM_PAINT messages. Both these messages are low priority. If a program's message queue contains only WM_PAINT or WM_TIMER messages, and another program's message queue contains messages other than WM_PAINT or WM_TIMER, Windows will pass control to the other application.

The WM_TIMER messages are similar to WM_PAINT messages in another respect: Windows does not keep loading up the message queue with multiple WM_TIMER messages. Instead, Windows combines several WM_TIMER messages in the message queue into a single message. Therefore, the application won't get a bunch of them all at once, although it may get two WM_TIMER messages in quick succession. An application cannot determine the number of "missing" WM_TIMER messages that result from this process.

When CLOCK regains control and jumps ahead to the correct time, it is not because it gets several WM_TIMER messages in a row. CLOCK must determine the actual time and then set itself. The WM_TIMER messages only inform CLOCK when it should be updated. A program can't keep time itself solely by counting WM_TIMER messages. (Later in this chapter we will write a clock application that updates every second, and we'll see precisely how this is accomplished.)

For convenience, I'll be talking about the timer in terms such as "getting a WM_TIMER message every second." But keep in mind that these messages are not precise clock tick interrupts.

USING THE TIMER: THREE METHODS

If you need a timer for the entire duration of your program, you'll probably call *SetTimer* from the *WinMain* function or while processing the WM_CREATE message, and *KillTimer* in response to a WM_DESTROY message. Setting the timer in *WinMain* provides the easiest error handling if a timer is unavailable. You can use a timer in one of three ways, depending on the parameters to the *SetTimer* call.

Method One

This method, the easiest, causes Windows to send WM_TIMER messages to the normal window procedure of the application. The *SetTimer* call looks like this:

```
SetTimer (hwnd, 1, wMsecInterval, NULL) ;
```

The first parameter is a handle to the window whose window procedure will receive the WM_TIMER messages. The second parameter is the timer ID, which should be a nonzero number. I have arbitrarily set it to 1 in this example. The third parameter is a WORD (16-bit unsigned integer) that specifies an interval in milliseconds. The largest value (65535) will deliver a WM_TIMER message about once a minute.

You can stop the WM_TIMER messages at any time (even while processing a WM_TIMER message) by calling:

```
KillTimer (hwnd, 1) ;
```

The second parameter is the same timer ID used in the *SetTimer* call. You should kill any active timers in response to a WM_DESTROY message before your program terminates.

When your window procedure receives a WM_TIMER message, *wParam* is equal to the timer ID (which in the above case is simply 1), and *lParam* is 0. If you need to set more than one timer, use a different timer ID for each timer. The value of *wParam* will differentiate the WM_TIMER messages passed to your window procedure. To make your program more readable, you may want to use *#define* statements for the different timer IDs:

```
#define TIMER_SEC  1
#define TIMER_MIN  2
```

You can then set the two timers with two *SetTimer* calls:

```
SetTimer (hwnd, TIMER_SEC, 1000, NULL) ;
SetTimer (hwnd, TIMER_MIN, 60000, NULL) ;
```

The WM_TIMER logic might look something like this:

```
case WM_TIMER :
    switch (wParam)
        {
        case TIMER_SEC :
            [once-per-second processing]
            break ;
        case TIMER_MIN :
            [once-per-minute processing]
            break ;
        }
    return 0 ;
```

If you want to set an existing timer to a different elapsed time, kill the timer and call *SetTimer* again. This code assumes that the timer ID is 1:

```
KillTimer (hwnd, 1) ;
SetTimer (hwnd, 1, wMsecInterval, NULL) ;
```

The *wMsecInterval* parameter is the new elapsed time in milliseconds. The Windows CLOCK application uses this method to change the timer from 1000 msec to 60,000 msec when it becomes an icon. As an icon, CLOCK needs to update the clock every minute rather than every second. When it is expanded from an icon to a window, CLOCK changes the timer back to 1000 msec.

What to do if no timer is available

Windows allows only 16 timers to be active at any time. If no timer is available, *SetTimer* returns NULL. Your program might be able to function reasonably well without the timer, but if you need the timer (as CLOCK certainly does), the application has no choice but to terminate if it can't get one. If you call *SetTimer* in *WinMain*, you can terminate the program simply by returning FALSE from WinMain.

Let's assume you want a 1000-msec timer. Following the *CreateWindow* call but before the message loop, you might have a statement like this:

```
if (!SetTimer (hwnd, 1, 1000, NULL))
    return FALSE ;
```

This is the unfriendly way to terminate. The user is left wondering why the application will not load. (Surely the 16 clocks sitting down in the icon area have nothing to do with it!) It's much friendlier—and fairly easy—to use a Windows message box for displaying a message. A complete discussion of message boxes awaits you in Chapter 10, but this will get you started.

A message box is a popup window that always appears in the center of the display. Message boxes have a caption bar but no size box. The caption bar usually contains the name of the application. The message box encloses a message and one, two, or three buttons (some combination of OK, Retry, Cancel, Yes, No, and others). The message box can also contain a predefined icon: a lowercase "i" (which stands for "information"), an exclamation point, a question mark, or a stop sign. You have probably seen plenty of message boxes when working with Windows.

This code creates an informatory message box that you can use when *SetTimer* fails to allocate a timer:

```
if (!SetTimer (hwnd, 1, 1000, NULL))
    {
    MessageBox (hwnd,
        "Too many clocks or timers!",
        "Program Name",
        MB_ICONEXCLAMATION : MB_OK) ;
    return FALSE ;
    }
```

The message box is shown in Figure 5-1. When the user presses Enter or clicks the OK button, *WinMain* terminates by returning FALSE.

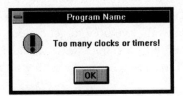

Figure 5-1. *A message box for "friendly termination."*

By default, message boxes are "application modal" windows. This means that a user must respond to the message box before the application will continue. However, the user can switch to other applications by pressing Alt-Tab or Alt-Esc or by clicking the mouse in the window of another program.

Why not give the user the opportunity to close one of those 16 minimized clocks at the bottom of the display and successfully load your application? That's what this code does:

```
while (!SetTimer (hwnd, 1, 1000, NULL))

    if (IDCANCEL == MessageBox (hwnd,
            "Too many clocks or timers!",
            "Program Name",
            MB_ICONEXCLAMATION : MB_RETRYCANCEL))
        return FALSE ;
```

This message box, shown in Figure 5-2, has two buttons, labeled Retry and Cancel. If the user selects Cancel, the *MessageBox* function returns a value equal to IDCANCEL, and the program terminates. If the user selects Retry, *SetTimer* is called again.

Figure 5-2. *A message box that offers a choice.*

A sample program

Figure 5-3 shows a sample program that uses the timer. This program, called BEEPER1, sets a timer for 1-second intervals. When it receives a WM_TIMER message, it alternates coloring the client area blue and red, and it beeps by calling the function *MessageBeep*. (Although *MessageBeep* is documented as a companion to *MessageBox*, it's really an all-purpose beep function. The WORD parameter to *MessageBeep* can be any value.) BEEPER1 sets the timer in the *WinMain* function and processes the WM_TIMER messages in the *WndProc* window procedure. During the WM_TIMER message, BEEPER1 calls *MessageBeep*, inverts the value of *bFlipFlop* and invalidates the window to generate a WM_PAINT message. During the WM_PAINT message, BEEPER1 obtains a RECT structure for the size of the window by calling *GetClientRect* and colors the window by calling *FillRect*.

BEEPER1.MAK

```
#-----------------------
# BEEPER1.MAK make file
#-----------------------

beeper1.exe : beeper1.obj beeper1.def
    link beeper1, /align:16, NUL, /nod slibcew libw, beeper1
    rc beeper1.exe

beeper1.obj : beeper1.c
    cl -c -Gsw -Ow -W2 -Zp beeper1.c
```

Figure 5-3. *The BEEPER1 program.*

BEEPER1.C

```
/*-------------------------------------------
   BEEPER1.C  -- Timer Demo Program No. 1
                (c) Charles Petzold, 1990
   -------------------------------------------*/

#include <windows.h>
#define ID_TIMER    1

long FAR PASCAL WndProc (HWND, WORD, WORD, LONG) ;

int PASCAL WinMain (HANDLE hInstance, HANDLE hPrevInstance,
                    LPSTR lpszCmdLine, int nCmdShow)
     {
     static char szAppName[] = "Beeper1" ;
     HWND        hwnd ;
     MSG         msg ;
     WNDCLASS    wndclass ;

     if (!hPrevInstance)
          {
          wndclass.style         = CS_HREDRAW : CS_VREDRAW ;
          wndclass.lpfnWndProc   = WndProc ;
          wndclass.cbClsExtra    = 0 ;
          wndclass.cbWndExtra    = 0 ;
          wndclass.hInstance     = hInstance ;
          wndclass.hIcon         = LoadIcon (NULL, IDI_APPLICATION) ;
          wndclass.hCursor       = LoadCursor (NULL, IDC_ARROW) ;
          wndclass.hbrBackground = GetStockObject (WHITE_BRUSH) ;
          wndclass.lpszMenuName  = NULL ;
          wndclass.lpszClassName = szAppName ;

          RegisterClass (&wndclass) ;
          }

     hwnd = CreateWindow (szAppName, "Beeper1 Timer Demo",
                     WS_OVERLAPPEDWINDOW,
                     CW_USEDEFAULT, CW_USEDEFAULT,
                     CW_USEDEFAULT, CW_USEDEFAULT,
                     NULL, NULL, hInstance, NULL) ;
     while (!SetTimer (hwnd, ID_TIMER, 1000, NULL))
          if (IDCANCEL == MessageBox (hwnd,
                         "Too many clocks or timers!", szAppName,
                         MB_ICONEXCLAMATION : MB_RETRYCANCEL))
               return FALSE ;
```

(continued)

```
        ShowWindow (hwnd, nCmdShow) ;
        UpdateWindow (hwnd) ;

        while (GetMessage (&msg, NULL, 0, 0))
                {
                TranslateMessage (&msg) ;
                DispatchMessage (&msg) ;
                }
        return msg.wParam ;
        }

long FAR PASCAL WndProc (HWND hwnd, WORD message, WORD wParam, LONG lParam)
        {
        static BOOL fFlipFlop = FALSE ;
        HBRUSH      hBrush ;
        HDC         hdc ;
        PAINTSTRUCT ps ;
        RECT        rc ;

        switch (message)
                {
                case WM_TIMER :
                        MessageBeep (0) ;

                        fFlipFlop = !fFlipFlop ;
                        InvalidateRect (hwnd, NULL, FALSE) ;

                        return 0 ;

                case WM_PAINT :
                        hdc = BeginPaint (hwnd, &ps) ;

                        GetClientRect (hwnd, &rc) ;

                        hBrush = CreateSolidBrush (fFlipFlop ? RGB(255,0,0) :
                                                              RGB(0,0,255)) ;
                        FillRect (hdc, &rc, hBrush) ;
                        EndPaint (hwnd, &ps) ;
                        DeleteObject (hBrush) ;
                        return 0 ;

                case WM_DESTROY :
                        KillTimer (hwnd, ID_TIMER) ;
                        PostQuitMessage (0) ;
                        return 0 ;
                }
        return DefWindowProc (hwnd, message, wParam, lParam) ;
        }
```

BEEPER1.DEF

```
;------------------------------------
; BEEPER1.DEF module definition file
;------------------------------------

NAME            BEEPER1

DESCRIPTION     'Timer Demo Program No. 1 (c) Charles Petzold, 1990'
EXETYPE         WINDOWS
STUB            'WINSTUB.EXE'
CODE            PRELOAD MOVEABLE DISCARDABLE
DATA            PRELOAD MOVEABLE MULTIPLE
HEAPSIZE        1024
STACKSIZE       8192
EXPORTS         WndProc
```

Because BEEPER1 audibly indicates every WM_TIMER message it receives, you can get a good idea of the erratic nature of WM_TIMER messages by loading BEEPER1 and performing some other actions within Windows. For instance, try moving or resizing a window. This stops all messages, and BEEPER1 stops beeping. When you complete the move or resize, you'll note that BEEPER1 doesn't get all the WM_TIMER messages it has missed, although the first two messages may be less than a second apart.

This is our first encounter with a Windows program that uses color, so a brief look at how Windows handles color is worthwhile here.

Windows' use of color

Windows uses an unsigned long (32-bit) integer value to represent a color. The lowest three bytes specify red, green, and blue values that range from 0 through 255, as illustrated by Figure 5-4. This results in a potential 2^{24} (or about 16 million) colors.

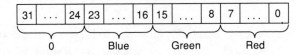

Figure 5-4. *The 32-bit color value.*

This unsigned long is often referred to as an "RGB color." The WINDOWS.H header file provides several macros for working with RGB color values. The RGB macro in WINDOWS.H takes three arguments representing red, green, and blue values and combines them into an unsigned long:

```
#define RGB(r,g,b) ((DWORD)(((BYTE)(r) ¦ \
                   ((WORD)(g) << 8)) ¦ \
                   (((DWORD)(BYTE)(b)) << 16)))
```

Thus, the value:

```
RGB (255, 0, 255)
```

is really 0x00FF00FF, an RGB color value for magenta. When all three arguments are set to 0, the color is black; when the arguments are set to 255, the color is white. The *GetRValue*, *GetGValue*, and *GetBValue* macros extract the unsigned character primary-color values from an unsigned long RGB color value. These macros are sometimes handy when you're using Windows functions that return RGB color values to your program.

The most common video display adapters used for Windows are the Enhanced Graphics Adapter (EGA) and Video Graphics Array (VGA). In the display resolutions that Windows uses, both these adapters can display 16 different colors. (Some "Super VGA" boards can display 256 different colors under Windows.) Windows can display additional colors by "dithering," which is creating a pixel pattern that combines pixels of different pure colors.

Not all unique combinations of red, green, and blue bytes produce different dithering patterns. For instance, on a color EGA or VGA, a red, green, or blue value must generally be incremented by 4 to produce a different dithering pattern. So for these adapters, you have 2^{18} (or 262,144) dithered colors.

BEEPER1 uses the *FillRect* function to color its client area. The first parameter to *FillRect* is the device context handle, the second is a pointer to the RECT structure, and the third is a handle to a "brush." A brush is a graphics object that Windows uses to fill an area. Brushes can be solid colors or composed of various hatchmarks or patterns.

BEEPER1 creates a brush of a solid color by calling *CreateSolidBrush*. The only parameter is an RGB color value. Depending on the value of *fFlipFlop*, BEEPER sets this parameter to RGB(255,0,0), which is red, or RGB(0,0,255), which is blue.

A brush is a graphics object. If you create a brush, you must also delete it when you're finished. After calling *FillRect*, BEEPER1 deletes the brush by calling *DeleteObject*.

Method Two

The first method for setting the timer causes WM_TIMER messages to be sent to the normal window procedure. With this second method, you can direct Windows to send the timer messages to another function within your program.

The function that will receive these timer messages is termed a "call-back" function. This is a function within your program that is called by Windows. You tell Windows the address of this function (well, not really the address of the function, but we'll get to that), and Windows later calls the function. This should sound familiar because a program's window procedure is really a type of call-back function. You tell Windows the address of the function when registering the window class, and Windows calls the function when sending messages to the program. However, call-back functions that are not window procedures must be handled a little differently.

SetTimer is not the only Windows function that uses a call-back function. The *CreateDialog* and *DialogBox* functions (discussed in Chapter 10) use call-back functions to process messages in a dialog box; several Windows functions (*EnumChildWindows*, *EnumFonts*, *EnumObjects*, *EnumProps*, and *EnumWindows*) pass enumerated information to call-back functions; and several less commonly used functions (*GrayString*, *LineDDA*, *SetResourceHandler*, and *SetWindowsHook*) also require call-back functions. Call-back functions are often a major hang-up for beginning Windows programmers. Some strange things are involved. I'm first going to tell you how to use call-back functions, and then I'll tell you the reasons for what you're doing.

Like a window procedure, a call-back function must be defined as FAR PASCAL because it is called by Windows from outside the code segment of the program. The parameters to the call-back function and the value returned from the call-back function depend on the purpose of the call-back function. In the case of the call-back function associated with the timer, the input parameters are the same as the input parameters to a window procedure. The timer call-back function returns a WORD value to Windows.

Let's name the call-back function *TimerProc*. (You can name it anything you like.) It will process only WM_TIMER messages.

```
WORD FAR PASCAL TimerProc (HWND hwnd, WORD message, WORD wParam, LONG lParam)
    {
    [process WM_TIMER messages]
    return 0 ;
    }
```

The *hwnd* input parameter is the handle to the window specified when you call *SetTimer*. Windows will send only WM_TIMER messages to *TimerProc*, so a message will always equal WM_TIMER. The *wParam* value is the timer ID, and the *lParam* value can be ignored. (It is set to the address of the function.)

Just as you must include your regular window procedure in the EXPORTS section of the module definition (.DEF) file, you must also include the names of any call-back functions within your program. When using a call-back function named *TimerProc*, your module definition file contains the following lines:

```
EXPORTS WndProc
        TimerProc
```

As I noted earlier, the first method for setting a timer requires a *SetTimer* call that looks like this:

```
SetTimer (hwnd, 1, wMsecInterval, NULL) ;
```

When you use a call-back function to process WM_TIMER messages, the fourth parameter to *SetTimer* is instead the far address of the call-back function.

But not really.

Now listen carefully: The far address that you must pass to Windows as the fourth parameter of the *SetTimer* call is not the address of the function within the program. It is instead a far address obtained from the Windows function *MakeProcInstance*. To use *MakeProcInstance*, first define a variable that is a far pointer to a function. You can use the WINDOWS.H identifier FARPROC for this definition:

```
FARPROC lpfnTimerProc ;
```

In *WinMain* (or any other section of your program that is executed only once for each instance), call *MakeProcInstance*. The parameters to *MakeProcInstance* are the address of *TimerProc* and the value of *hInstance*. *MakeProcInstance* returns a far pointer that you save in *lpfnTimerProc*:

```
lpfnTimerProc = MakeProcInstance (TimerProc, hInstance) ;
```

You can now use this *lpfnTimerProc* value when you call *SetTimer*:

```
SetTimer (hwnd, 1, wMsecInterval, lpfnTimerProc) ;
```

You're done. Now that's not too bad, is it?

Well, you may say, "This is so weird that I'll never use this method for setting a timer. I'll use the first method, where I don't have to bother with call-back functions." That's fine. But you're going to be forced to deal with call-back functions, EXPORTS, and *Make-ProcInstance* when we start discussing dialog boxes. You can't do a dialog box without them. So you can pay your dues now, or you can pay them later.

A sample program

Let's look at some sample code so you can see how this stuff fits together. Then we'll explore *MakeProcInstance* some more. The BEEPER2 program, shown in Figure 5-5, is functionally the same as BEEPER1 except that Windows sends the timer messages to *TimerProc* rather than *WndProc*. To tell the C compiler that *TimerProc* is a function so that we can use the name of the function when calling *MakeProcInstance*, we declare *TimerProc* at the top of the program along with *WndProc*. Notice that the program calls *MakeProcInstance* for each instance.

I mentioned above that the *lParam* value passed to *TimerProc* is the address of the *TimerProc* function. Not exactly. It is actually the value of *lpfnTimerProc* returned from *MakeProcInstance*, if you ever need to use it.

BEEPER2.MAK

```
#----------------------
# BEEPER2.MAK make file
#----------------------
```

Figure 5-5. *The BEEPER2 program.*   *(continued)*

```
beeper2.exe : beeper2.obj beeper2.def
    link beeper2, /align:16, NUL, /nod slibcew libw, beeper2
    rc beeper2.exe

beeper2.obj : beeper2.c
    cl -c -Gsw -Ow -W2 -Zp beeper2.c
```

BEEPER2.C

```
/*-------------------------------------------
   BEEPER2.C -- Timer Demo Program No. 2
                (c) Charles Petzold, 1990
   -----------------------------------------*/

#include <windows.h>
#define ID_TIMER    1

long FAR PASCAL WndProc   (HWND, WORD, WORD, LONG) ;
WORD FAR PASCAL TimerProc (HWND, WORD, WORD, LONG) ;

int PASCAL WinMain (HANDLE hInstance, HANDLE hPrevInstance,
                    LPSTR lpszCmdLine, int nCmdShow)
    {
    static char szAppName[] = "Beeper2" ;
    FARPROC     lpfnTimerProc ;
    HWND        hwnd ;
    MSG         msg ;
    WNDCLASS    wndclass ;

    if (!hPrevInstance)
        {
        wndclass.style         = CS_HREDRAW | CS_VREDRAW ;
        wndclass.lpfnWndProc   = WndProc ;
        wndclass.cbClsExtra    = 0 ;
        wndclass.cbWndExtra    = 0 ;
        wndclass.hInstance     = hInstance ;
        wndclass.hIcon         = LoadIcon (NULL, IDI_APPLICATION) ;
        wndclass.hCursor       = LoadCursor (NULL, IDC_ARROW) ;
        wndclass.hbrBackground = GetStockObject (WHITE_BRUSH) ;
        wndclass.lpszMenuName  = NULL ;
        wndclass.lpszClassName = szAppName ;

        RegisterClass (&wndclass) ;
        }
```

(continued)

```
        hwnd = CreateWindow (szAppName, "Beeper2 Timer Demo",
                        WS_OVERLAPPEDWINDOW,
                        CW_USEDEFAULT, CW_USEDEFAULT,
                        CW_USEDEFAULT, CW_USEDEFAULT,
                        NULL, NULL, hInstance, NULL) ;

        lpfnTimerProc = MakeProcInstance (TimerProc, hInstance) ;

        while (!SetTimer (hwnd, ID_TIMER, 1000, lpfnTimerProc))
            if (IDCANCEL == MessageBox (hwnd,
                        "Too many clocks or timers!", szAppName,
                        MB_ICONEXCLAMATION | MB_RETRYCANCEL))
                return FALSE ;

        ShowWindow (hwnd, nCmdShow) ;
        UpdateWindow (hwnd) ;

        while (GetMessage (&msg, NULL, 0, 0))
            {
            TranslateMessage (&msg) ;
            DispatchMessage (&msg) ;
            }
        return msg.wParam ;
        }

long FAR PASCAL WndProc (HWND hwnd, WORD message, WORD wParam, LONG lParam)
        {
        switch (message)
            {
            case WM_DESTROY :
                KillTimer (hwnd, ID_TIMER) ;
                PostQuitMessage (0) ;
                return 0 ;
            }
        return DefWindowProc (hwnd, message, wParam, lParam) ;
        }

WORD FAR PASCAL TimerProc (HWND hwnd, WORD message, WORD wParam, LONG lParam)
        {
        static BOOL fFlipFlop = FALSE ;
        HBRUSH      hBrush ;
        HDC         hdc ;
        RECT        rc ;
        MessageBeep (0) ;
        fFlipFlop = !fFlipFlop ;

        GetClientRect (hwnd, &rc) ;
```

(continued)

```
    hdc = GetDC (hwnd) ;
    hBrush = CreateSolidBrush (fFlipFlop ? RGB(255,0,0) : RGB(0,0,255)) ;

    FillRect (hdc, &rc, hBrush) ;
    ReleaseDC (hwnd, hdc) ;
    DeleteObject (hBrush) ;

    return 0 ;
    }
```

BEEPER2.DEF

```
;-------------------------------------
; BEEPER2.DEF module definition file
;-------------------------------------

NAME            BEEPER2

DESCRIPTION     'Timer Demo Program No. 2 (c) Charles Petzold, 1990'
EXETYPE         WINDOWS
STUB            'WINSTUB.EXE'
CODE            PRELOAD MOVEABLE DISCARDABLE
DATA            PRELOAD MOVEABLE MULTIPLE
HEAPSIZE        1024
STACKSIZE       8192
EXPORTS         WndProc
                TimerProc
```

Proper handling of call-back functions

Let's summarize the three requirements for call-back functions. Any function within your program that is called by Windows must be handled as follows:

1. The function must be defined as FAR PASCAL.

2. The function must be included in the EXPORTS section of the module definition (.DEF) file.

3. The address of the function that you give to Windows must be the return value from a *MakeProcInstance* call. (This third rule does not apply to window procedures that are passed to Windows as part of a window's class structure in a *RegisterClass* call. Windows itself handles the *MakeProcInstance* requirement in this case.)

As you'll discover in Chapter 7, "Memory Management," these three requirements are closely related to each other. They are part of the overhead necessary for Windows to run several instances of the same program using the same code segment, where each instance must have its own data segment. Windows also requires this overhead to move the code segment and the data segments around in memory. Here are the practical results of the three requirements:

1. When you define a function as FAR and you compile with the -Gw (Windows) flag, the compiler inserts special prolog and epilog code in the function. In assembly language, the prolog code sets the value of the AX register equal to the DS (data segment) register by using the PUSH DS and POP AX instructions. It then saves the value of DS (with PUSH DS) and sets DS equal to AX by using a MOV DS, AX instruction. The epilog code at the end of the function pops the original value of DS off the stack.

2. If the FAR function is also exported (that is, if the function is listed in the EXPORTS section of the module definition file), Windows replaces the PUSH DS and POP AX instructions at the top of the function prolog with NOP (no operation) instructions when the code segment is loaded into memory. With this change the function sets DS from the value of AX. But what is the value of AX on entry to the function? Well, if you didn't do anything else, the value of AX would be indeterminate. So would the operation of your program.

3. *MakeProcInstance* creates a small piece of code elsewhere in Windows called a "thunk." The far address returned from *MakeProcInstance* is the address of this thunk. The thunk loads the segment address of the data segment in AX and branches to the function. The function prolog then loads DS from AX. Perfect.

Note that *MakeProcInstance* requires *hInstance* as a parameter. You must use *MakeProcInstance* to create a different thunk for each instance because each instance has its own data segment. For a particular call-back function, the thunks for each instance all branch to the same function address (because all instances use the same code segment), but each thunk sets AX to a different data segment—the data segment for that instance. When Windows moves a data segment in memory, it must change the thunk for that instance so that the thunk sets AX to the new data segment address. The thunk itself is always in an unmoveable area of memory.

(To further complicate this matter, any reference in your program to a FAR function—such as the address passed to the *MakeProcInstance* call and the address that the thunk branches to—is not even the address of the function within your program. Another small routine sits between the thunk and the actual function. This routine loads the code segment into memory if it has not yet been loaded or if it has been discarded from memory. But let's forget about this for now and come back to it in Chapter 7. The last thing I want to do here is make this subject sound as complex as it actually is.)

These requirements imply that you should never call exported far functions directly from within your program. For instance, you might want to simulate a timer message with the following statement:

```
TimerProc (hwnd, WM_TIMER, 1, 0L) ;  // WRONG !!!
```

It looks OK, but don't do it! The prolog of *TimerProc* will set DS equal to AX, but the value of AX could be anything, and it very likely is not the segment address of the program's data segment. If you need to directly call an exported function from within your program, use the far pointer returned from *MakeProcInstance*:

```
(*lpfnTimerProc) (hwnd, WM_TIMER, 1, 0L) ;  // RIGHT
```

This code calls the thunk, and the thunk sets AX equal to the correct data segment before branching to the function.

Method Three

The third method of setting the timer is similar to the second method. It requires a far pointer created from *MakeProcInstance* to a function that processes the WM_TIMER messages. However, the *hwnd* parameter to *SetTimer* is set to NULL, and the second parameter (normally the timer ID) is ignored. Instead, the function returns a timer ID:

```
nTimerID = SetTimer (NULL, 0, wMsecInterval, lpfnTimerProc) ;
```

The *nTimerID* returned from *SetTimer* will be NULL if no timer is available.

The first parameter to *KillTimer* (usually the window handle) must also be NULL. The timer ID must be the value returned from *SetTimer*:

```
KillTimer (NULL, nTimerID) ;
```

The *hwnd* parameter passed to the *TimerProc* timer function will also be NULL. The *wParam* parameter is the timer ID, and *lParam* is *lpfnTimerProc*, the same as in the second method.

This method for setting a timer is rarely used. It might come in handy if you do a lot of *SetTimer* calls at different times in your program and don't want to keep track of which timer IDs you've already used.

Now that you know how to use the Windows timer, you're ready for a couple of useful timer programs.

USING THE TIMER FOR A STATUS REPORT

One use of a Windows timer is to periodically update a status report displayed on the screen. The program can relinquish control until the next WM_TIMER message and thus not hog precious processing time. The FREEMEM program, shown in Figure 5-6 on the following pages, displays the amount of free memory available in Windows in megabytes. The free memory value is updated every second and is consistent with the figure shown in the Program Manager's and File Manager's About box. FREEMEM can let you know how close Windows is to running out of memory. While testing a new Windows program, you may want to keep an eye on FREEMEM for a rough indication of how your program is allocating and freeing memory.

FREEMEM.MAK

```
#----------------------
# FREEMEM.MAK make file
#----------------------

freemem.exe : freemem.obj freemem.def
     link freemem, /align:16, NUL, /nod slibcew win87em libw, freemem
     rc freemem.exe

freemem.obj : freemem.c
     cl -c -Gsw -Ow -W2 -Zp freemem.c
```

FREEMEM.C

```
/*---------------------------------------------
    FREEMEM.C -- Free Memory Display Program
              (c) Charles Petzold, 1990
    ---------------------------------------------*/

#include <windows.h>
#include <stdio.h>
#define ID_TIMER    1

long FAR PASCAL WndProc (HWND, WORD, WORD, LONG) ;

int PASCAL WinMain (HANDLE hInstance, HANDLE hPrevInstance,
                    LPSTR lpszCmdLine, int nCmdShow)
     {
     static char szAppName[] = "FreeMem" ;
     HDC          hdc ;
     HWND         hwnd ;

     MSG          msg ;
     TEXTMETRIC   tm ;
     WNDCLASS     wndclass ;
```

Figure 5-6. *The FREEMEM program.*   *(continued)*

```
    if (hPrevInstance)
         return FALSE ;

    wndclass.style         = CS_HREDRAW : CS_VREDRAW ;
    wndclass.lpfnWndProc   = WndProc ;
    wndclass.cbClsExtra    = 0 ;
    wndclass.cbWndExtra    = 0 ;
    wndclass.hInstance     = hInstance ;
    wndclass.hIcon         = NULL ;
    wndclass.hCursor       = LoadCursor (NULL, IDC_ARROW) ;
    wndclass.hbrBackground = GetStockObject (WHITE_BRUSH) ;
    wndclass.lpszMenuName  = NULL ;
    wndclass.lpszClassName = szAppName ;

    RegisterClass (&wndclass) ;

    hwnd = CreateWindow (szAppName, "Free Memory",
                        WS_OVERLAPPEDWINDOW,
                        CW_USEDEFAULT, CW_USEDEFAULT,
                        CW_USEDEFAULT, CW_USEDEFAULT,
                        NULL, NULL, hInstance, NULL) ;

    hdc = GetDC (hwnd) ;
    GetTextMetrics (hdc, &tm) ;
    ReleaseDC (hwnd, hdc) ;

    if (4 * tm.tmAveCharWidth > GetSystemMetrics (SM_CXICON) ::
            2 * tm.tmHeight > GetSystemMetrics (SM_CYICON))
        {
        MessageBox (hwnd, "Icon size too small for display!",
                    szAppName, MB_ICONEXCLAMATION : MB_OK) ;
        return FALSE ;
        }

    if (!SetTimer (hwnd, ID_TIMER, 1000, NULL))
        {
        MessageBox (hwnd, "Too many clocks or timers!",
                    szAppName, MB_ICONEXCLAMATION : MB_OK) ;
        return FALSE ;
        }

    ShowWindow (hwnd, SW_SHOWMINNOACTIVE) ;
    UpdateWindow (hwnd) ;

    while (GetMessage (&msg, NULL, 0, 0))
        {
        TranslateMessage (&msg) ;
        DispatchMessage (&msg) ;
        }
```

(continued)

```
        return msg.wParam ;
        }

long FAR PASCAL WndProc (HWND hwnd, WORD message, WORD wParam, LONG lParam)
        {
        static DWORD   dwFreeMem, dwPrevMem ;
        static RECT    rect ;
        char           cBuffer [20] ;
        HDC            hdc ;
        PAINTSTRUCT    ps ;

        switch (message)
             {
             case WM_TIMER :
                  dwFreeMem = GetFreeSpace (0) ;

                  if (dwFreeMem != dwPrevMem)
                       InvalidateRect (hwnd, NULL, TRUE) ;

                  dwPrevMem = dwFreeMem ;
                  return 0 ;

             case WM_SIZE :
                  GetClientRect (hwnd, &rect) ;
                  return 0 ;

             case WM_PAINT :
                  hdc = BeginPaint (hwnd, &ps) ;

                  DrawText (hdc, cBuffer,
                            sprintf (cBuffer, "%.2f megs",
                                     dwFreeMem / 1024.0 / 1024.0),
                            &rect, DT_WORDBREAK) ;

                  EndPaint (hwnd, &ps) ;
                  return 0 ;

             case WM_QUERYOPEN :
                  return 0 ;

             case WM_DESTROY :
                  KillTimer (hwnd, ID_TIMER) ;
                  PostQuitMessage (0) ;
                  return 0 ;
             }
        return DefWindowProc (hwnd, message, wParam, lParam) ;
        }
```

FREEMEM.DEF

```
;-------------------------------------------
; FREEMEM.DEF module definition file
;-------------------------------------------

NAME            FREEMEM

DESCRIPTION     'Free Memory Display (c) Charles Petzold, 1990'
EXETYPE         WINDOWS
STUB            'WINSTUB.EXE'
CODE            PRELOAD MOVEABLE DISCARDABLE
DATA            PRELOAD MOVEABLE MULTIPLE
HEAPSIZE        1024
STACKSIZE       8192
EXPORTS         WndProc
```

Because FREEMEM doesn't need much display space, I've written it to appear as an icon at the bottom of the Windows screen. (See Figure 5-7.) This is about as unobtrusive a window as you can create in Windows.

Figure 5-7. *The FREEMEM icon.*

Although FREEMEM's use of the timer is simple enough, the program illustrates some interesting tricks that admittedly have nothing to do with the timer.

Creative Use of Icons

Unlike most Windows programs, FREEMEM starts out life as an icon, displays everything it needs to display within the icon, and cannot be opened into a regular window. Most Windows applications have static pictorial icons that you specify in the windows class structure. These icons are usually created with the ICONEDIT utility supplied with the Windows Software Development Kit (as you'll see in Chapter 8). So far, we've been using predefined Windows icons in our programs. Alternatively, you can specify a NULL icon in the window class structure with the statement:

```
wndclass.hIcon = NULL ;
```

A NULL icon means that the application is responsible for drawing the icon. Windows sends the application WM_PAINT messages when the icon needs to be painted. Thus, a program can change the appearance of the icon while the program is running. The CLOCK application included with Windows uses this technique to display the clock even when the window is an icon. A NULL icon is really just a tiny window that you can draw on in the same way that you draw on the client area of a normal window. If you need to know when your application is becoming an icon, you can get the information from the *wParam* parameter of a WM_SIZE message. For instance, when CLOCK becomes an icon, it eliminates the second hand from the clock and changes the timer from a 1-second interval to a 1-minute interval.

FREEMEM displays two lines of text within its icon. This will work fine on the most common displays used for Windows, but it may not work for some high-resolution boards that may use a larger system font. Because FREEMEM cannot display correctly on these video boards, it checks the size of the system font against the icon size and uses a message box to inform the user if the icon size is too small.

Forcing the Icon

Shortly before entering the message loop in *WinMain*, most Windows applications execute the function:

```
ShowWindow (hwnd, nCmdShow) ;
```

The *nCmdShow* variable is passed to the program as a parameter to *WinMain*.

If you run a program from the File Manager (by selecting Run from the File menu, pressing Enter when the cursor is on the program name, or double-clicking the program), *nCmdShow* is set equal to SW_SHOWNORMAL. If you load an application as an icon (by selecting Load from the File menu or pressing Shift-Enter with the cursor on the program name), *nCmdShow* is set equal to SW_SHOWMINNOACTIVE. Your application usually doesn't have to figure this out but simply passes this parameter to *ShowWindow*.

However, you aren't required to use the *nCmdShow* variable with *ShowWindow*. Instead, FREEMEM uses the line:

```
ShowWindow (hwnd, SW_SHOWMINNOACTIVE) ;
```

This forces the window to appear as an icon regardless of the value of *nCmdShow*. The active program remains active.

You can perform other tricks with this technique. If you always want a particular application to appear first as a maximized full-screen display, you can use:

```
ShowWindow (hwnd, SW_SHOWMAXIMIZED) ;
```

You can even force FREEMEM to occupy a particular icon position at the bottom of the display. If you replace the existing *ShowWindow* call in FREEMEM with:

```
ShowWindow (hwnd, (int) 0xFF8F) ;
```

the icon will be positioned in icon slot 15. This syntax is a little obscure but is documented in the Programmer's Reference.

Keeping the Icon an Icon

FREEMEM does not allow itself to be opened into a regular window. Would you believe this trick requires merely two simple lines in the *WndProc* function? Here they are:

```
case WM_QUERYOPEN :
    return 0 ;
```

These two lines don't seem to be doing very much, but let's take a closer look.

Windows sends a WM_QUERYOPEN message to a program when it wants to open an icon into a window. Normally, WM_QUERYOPEN is passed on to the *DefWindowProc* function, which returns a nonzero value; Windows then opens the icon. With the two lines . shown above, however, *WndProc* returns a value of 0 for a WM_QUERYOPEN message. So when Windows asks, "Do you want to be opened?" *WndProc* answers "Zero," which in this case means "No thanks."

Calculating Free Memory

When Windows sends FREEMEM a WM_TIMER message, FREEMEM must determine the amount of free memory. Like the About box in the Program Manager and File Manager, FREEMEM gets a free memory value by calling *GetFreeSpace* with a parameter of 0. The *GetFreeSpace* function is new in Windows 3. Prior to Windows 3, Windows programs used *GlobalCompact* with a parameter of 0 to obtain the largest block of contiguous free memory in the system, which is not nearly as useful as the total amount of free memory. (Windows memory management is covered in detail in Chapter 7.)

If the free memory value has changed since the last *GetFreeSpace* call, FREEMEM invalidates the client area to generate a WM_PAINT message. FREEMEM processes WM-_PAINT messages by calling *DrawText*, a convenient function for simple word-wrapped text. FREEMEM converts the free memory in bytes to a floating-point value in megabytes, and *sprintf* stores it formatted to two decimal places.

Using Floating-Point Math

When a Windows program uses floating-point math (as FREEMEM does) and you link with the floating-point emulator library (SLIBCEW.LIB for small model), you must also include the WIN87LIB.LIB import library in the library field of the LINK command.

Alternatively, you can compile with the -FPa switch and link with the "alternate math library" (SLIBCAW.LIB for small library). This library does not use the math coprocessor chip, even if one is present.

USING THE TIMER FOR A CLOCK

A clock is the most obvious application for the timer. Although digital clocks were once in fashion, the pendulum has swung back (so to speak) to analog clocks. But you already have an analog clock with Windows. Although the CLOCK program has a digital-clock setting, I'm going to write a good old digital-clock program—because it provides an interesting example of the use of the timer. The DIGCLOCK program, shown in Figure 5-8, creates a popup window that positions itself in the lower right corner of the display in the icon area. The program displays the day of the week, the time, and the date. (See Figure 5-9 on page 202.)

DIGCLOCK.MAK

```
#------------------------
# DIGCLOCK.MAK make file
#------------------------

digclock.exe : digclock.obj digclock.def
     link digclock, /align:16, NUL, /nod slibcew libw, digclock
     rc digclock.exe

digclock.obj : digclock.c
     cl -c -Gsw -Ow -W2 -Zp digclock.c
```

DIGCLOCK.C

```
/*---------------------------------------------
    DIGCLOCK.C -- Digital Clock Program
               (c) Charles Petzold, 1990
   ---------------------------------------------*/

#include <windows.h>
#include <time.h>
#define ID_TIMER    1

#define YEAR  (datetime->tm_year % 100)
#define MONTH (datetime->tm_mon  + 1)
#define MDAY  (datetime->tm_mday)
#define WDAY  (datetime->tm_wday)
#define HOUR  (datetime->tm_hour)
#define MIN   (datetime->tm_min)
#define SEC   (datetime->tm_sec)
```

Figure 5-8. *The DIGCLOCK program.*

(continued)

```
long FAR PASCAL WndProc (HWND, WORD, WORD, LONG);
void SizeTheWindow (short *, short *, short *, short *) ;

char   sDate [2], sTime [2], sAMPM [2][5] ;
int    iDate, iTime ;

int PASCAL WinMain (HANDLE hInstance, HANDLE hPrevInstance,
                    LPSTR lpszCmdLine, int nCmdShow)
    {
    static char szAppName[] = "DigClock" ;
    HWND        hwnd;
    MSG         msg;
    short       xStart, yStart, xClient, yClient ;
    WNDCLASS    wndclass ;

    if (!hPrevInstance)
        {
        wndclass.style         = CS_HREDRAW ! CS_VREDRAW ;
        wndclass.lpfnWndProc   = WndProc ;
        wndclass.cbClsExtra    = 0 ;
        wndclass.cbWndExtra    = 0 ;
        wndclass.hInstance     = hInstance ;
        wndclass.hIcon         = NULL ;
        wndclass.hCursor       = LoadCursor (NULL, IDC_ARROW) ;
        wndclass.hbrBackground = GetStockObject (WHITE_BRUSH) ;
        wndclass.lpszMenuName  = NULL ;
        wndclass.lpszClassName = szAppName ;

        RegisterClass (&wndclass) ;
        }

    SizeTheWindow (&xStart, &yStart, &xClient, &yClient) ;

    hwnd = CreateWindow (szAppName, szAppName,
                         WS_POPUP ! WS_DLGFRAME ! WS_SYSMENU,
                         xStart, yStart,
                         xClient, yClient,
                         NULL, NULL, hInstance, NULL) ;

    if (!SetTimer (hwnd, ID_TIMER, 1000, NULL))
        {
        MessageBox (hwnd, "Too many clocks or timers!", szAppName,
                    MB_ICONEXCLAMATION ! MB_OK) ;
        return FALSE ;
        }

    ShowWindow (hwnd, SW_SHOWNOACTIVATE) ;
    UpdateWindow (hwnd) ;
```

(continued)

```
        while (GetMessage (&msg, NULL, 0, 0))
             {
             TranslateMessage (&msg) ;
             DispatchMessage (&msg) ;
             }
        return msg.wParam ;
        }

void SizeTheWindow (short *pxStart,  short *pyStart,
                    short *pxClient, short *pyClient)
        {
        HDC        hdc ;
        TEXTMETRIC tm ;

        hdc = CreateIC ("DISPLAY", NULL, NULL, NULL) ;
        GetTextMetrics (hdc, &tm) ;
        DeleteDC (hdc) ;

        *pxClient = 2 * GetSystemMetrics (SM_CXDLGFRAME) + 16*tm.tmAveCharWidth ;
        *pxStart  =     GetSystemMetrics (SM_CXSCREEN)   - *pxClient ;
        *pyClient = 2 * GetSystemMetrics (SM_CYDLGFRAME) + 2*tm.tmHeight ;
        *pyStart  =     GetSystemMetrics (SM_CYSCREEN)   - *pyClient ;
        }

void SetInternational (void)
        {
        static char cName [] = "intl" ;

        iDate = GetProfileInt (cName, "iDate", 0) ;
        iTime = GetProfileInt (cName, "iTime", 0) ;

        GetProfileString (cName, "sDate",  "/", sDate,    2) ;
        GetProfileString (cName, "sTime",  ":", sTime,    2) ;
        GetProfileString (cName, "s1159", "AM", sAMPM [0], 5) ;
        GetProfileString (cName, "s2359", "PM", sAMPM [1], 5) ;
        }

void WndPaint (HWND hwnd, HDC hdc)
        {
        static char szWday[] = "Sun\0Mon\0Tue\0Wed\0Thu\0Fri\0Sat" ;
        char        cBuffer[40] ;
        long        lTime ;
        RECT        rect ;
        short       nLength ;
        struct tm   *datetime ;

        time (&lTime) ;
        datetime = localtime (&lTime) ;
```

(continued)

200

```
       nLength = wsprintf (cBuffer, "  %s  %d%s%02d%s%02d  \r\n",
              (LPSTR) szWday +.4 * WDAY,
              iDate == 1 ? MDAY  : iDate == 2 ? YEAR  : MONTH, (LPSTR) sDate,
              iDate == 1 ? MONTH : iDate == 2 ? MONTH : MDAY,  (LPSTR) sDate,
              iDate == 1 ? YEAR  : iDate == 2 ? MDAY  : YEAR) ;

    if (iTime == 1)
        nLength += wsprintf (cBuffer + nLength, "  %02d%s%02d%s%02d  ",
                            HOUR, (LPSTR) sTime, MIN, (LPSTR) sTime, SEC) ;
    else
        nLength += wsprintf (cBuffer + nLength, "  %d%s%02d%s%02d %s  ",
                            (HOUR % 12) ? (HOUR % 12) : 12,
                            (LPSTR) sTime, MIN, (LPSTR) sTime, SEC,
                            (LPSTR) sAMPM [HOUR / 12]) ;

    GetClientRect (hwnd, &rect) ;
    DrawText (hdc, cBuffer, -1, &rect, DT_CENTER | DT_NOCLIP) ;
    }

long FAR PASCAL WndProc (HWND hwnd, WORD message, WORD wParam, LONG lParam)
    {
    HDC        hdc ;
    PAINTSTRUCT ps ;

    switch (message)
        {
        case WM_CREATE :
            SetInternational () ;
            return 0 ;

        case WM_TIMER :
            InvalidateRect (hwnd, NULL, FALSE) ;
            return 0 ;

        case WM_PAINT :
            hdc = BeginPaint (hwnd, &ps) ;
            WndPaint (hwnd, hdc) ;
            EndPaint (hwnd, &ps) ;
            return 0 ;

        case WM_WININICHANGE :
            SetInternational () ;
            InvalidateRect (hwnd, NULL, TRUE) ;
            return 0 ;

        case WM_DESTROY :
            KillTimer (hwnd, ID_TIMER) ;
            PostQuitMessage (0) ;
            return 0 ;
        }
    return DefWindowProc (hwnd, message, wParam, lParam) ;
    }
```

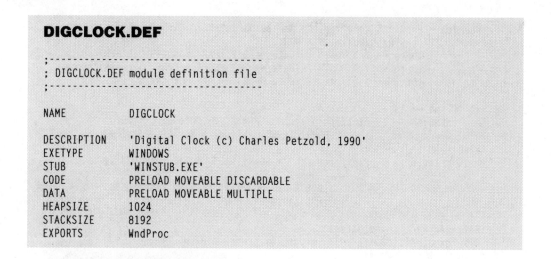

DIGCLOCK.DEF

```
;------------------------------------------
; DIGCLOCK.DEF module definition file
;------------------------------------------

NAME            DIGCLOCK

DESCRIPTION     'Digital Clock (c) Charles Petzold, 1990'
EXETYPE         WINDOWS
STUB            'WINSTUB.EXE'
CODE            PRELOAD MOVEABLE DISCARDABLE
DATA            PRELOAD MOVEABLE MULTIPLE
HEAPSIZE        1024
STACKSIZE       8192
EXPORTS         WndProc
```

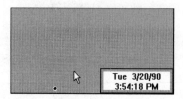

Figure 5-9. *The DIGCLOCK window.*

All the programs shown so far have used the window style WS_OVERLAPPEDWINDOW as the third parameter to the *CreateWindow* function. DIGCLOCK uses the window style:

```
WS_POPUP : WS_DLGFRAME : WS_SYSMENU
```

This creates a style of window known as "popup," with a dialog box frame and a system menu. The popup style is most commonly used for dialog boxes and message boxes, and only rarely for applications. DIGCLOCK also uses yet another variation of the *Show-Window* call:

```
ShowWindow (hwnd, SW_SHOWNOACTIVATE) ;
```

Normally, a program becomes the active window when you run it. SW_SHOWNOACTI-VATE tells Windows that the program that loaded DIGCLOCK should remain the active window. You can make DIGCLOCK active, however, by clicking on its window with the mouse or by pressing Alt-Tab or Alt-Esc. Although DIGCLOCK has no system menu box, you can still access the system menu when DIGCLOCK is active by pressing Alt-Spacebar. If you select Move, you can move the window with the keyboard.

Positioning and Sizing the Popup

The DIGCLOCK popup window is positioned at the lower right corner of the display. The window must be large enough to accommodate two lines of text of 16 characters each. The *SizeTheWindow* procedure in DIGCLOCK.C determines the correct parameters to use in the *CreateWindow* call. Normally, a program cannot obtain a text size without first creating a window, because it needs the window handle to obtain a device context handle. DIGCLOCK gets around this problem by obtaining an information device context handle for the screen using *CreateIC*. This function is similar to *CreateDC* (used in the BLOWUP program in Chapter 4) but is used to obtain information from the device context. The text size in combination with information available from *GetSystemMetrics* is enough to derive an initial starting position and window size.

Getting the Date and Time

In its *WndPaint* function, DIGCLOCK uses the *time* and *localtime* C functions available in the Microsoft C Compiler library to determine the current date and time. The *localtime* function puts all the information we need into a structure; several macro definitions near the top of the program help make the *wsprintf* calls more readable. (You should avoid making MS-DOS or ROM BIOS function calls in your Windows programs; use Windows functions or the C run time library instead.)

Going International

Windows includes international support. The WIN.INI file created during installation of Windows contains a section headed *[intl]*. This lists information concerning formats of dates, time, currency, and numbers. You can display dates in one of three different formats: month-day-year, year-month-day, or day-month-year. The separator between these three numbers can be a slash, a dash, a period, or, in fact, any character you like. You can display the time in either 12-hour or 24-hour format; a semicolon or a period is commonly used to separate hours, minutes, and seconds.

The *SetInternational* function in DIGCLOCK retrieves this formatting information from the WIN.INI file by using the Windows *GetProfileInt* (for integers) and *GetProfileString* (for strings). These calls must include default values if Windows cannot find the values in WIN.INI. *SetInternational* stores the values in global variables that have the same names as the text strings that identify them in WIN.INI. The *WndPaint* function uses the values obtained from WIN.INI to format the date and time displays and then calls *DrawText* to center the two lines of text within the window.

As you would expect, whenever DIGCLOCK's window procedure receives a WM_TIMER message, it invalidates the window to generate a WM_PAINT message. But *WndProc* also invalidates the window when it receives a WM_WININICHANGE message.

Any application that changes WIN.INI sends the WM_WININICHANGE message to all active Windows applications. If the *[intl]* section of WIN.INI is changed, DIGCLOCK will know and will obtain the new international information. To see how this works, load DIGCLOCK, load the CONTROL PANEL program included with Windows, select Country Settings from the Preferences menu, and change either the date format, the date separator, the time format, or the time separator. Now press Enter. The Control Panel updates the WIN.INI file, and DIGCLOCK's display reflects that change—Windows' message magic at work.

When the window procedure receives a WM_WININICHANGE message, it invalidates the window using:

```
InvalidateRect (hwnd, NULL, TRUE) ;
```

When DIGCLOCK receives a WM_TIMER message, it invalidates the window using:

```
InvalidateRect (hwnd, NULL, FALSE) ;
```

A value of TRUE in the last parameter tells Windows to erase the background before drawing the window. A value of FALSE tells Windows simply to draw over the existing background. We use FALSE when processing WM_TIMER messages because this approach reduces flickering of the display. You may be wondering why we need to use the TRUE value at all.

A TRUE value is necessary when processing WM_WININICHANGE messages because the length of the displayed strings can change by several characters if you switch the time format from 12 hours to 24 hours. However, the largest change that occurs as a result of a WM_TIMER message is two characters—for instance, when the date advances from 12/31/87 to 1/1/88—and the formatted string that *WndPaint* uses for the display has a couple of blanks on each end to account for this change in length and the proportional font.

We could also have DIGCLOCK process WM_TIMECHANGE messages, which notify applications of changes to the system date or time. Because DIGCLOCK is updated every second by WM_TIMER messages this is unnecessary. Processing WM_TIMECHANGE messages would make more sense for a clock that was updated every minute.

WINDOWS STANDARD TIME

If you've been scouting around the Programmer's Reference of the Windows Software Development Kit, you may be wondering why the Windows *GetCurrentTime* function is not used in DIGCLOCK. The answer is that *GetCurrentTime* tells you about "Windows time" rather than real time. This is the time (in milliseconds) since the beginning of the current Windows session. *GetCurrentTime* is used mostly for calculating a difference from the time returned from *GetMessageTime*. You can use these two calls while processing a message to determine how long the message was in the message queue before you retrieved it for processing.

Chapter 6

Child Window Controls

Chapter 4 showed programs in the CHECKER series that display a grid of rectangles. When you click the mouse in a rectangle, the program draws an X. When you click again, the X disappears. As you played with the program, you may have thought that the rectangle with the X inside looked vaguely familiar. If the rectangle were reduced in size, it would resemble a "check box" that Windows programs use in dialog boxes to allow the selection of options.

Although the CHECKER1 and CHECKER2 versions of this program use only one main window, the CHECKER3 version uses a child window for each rectangle. The rectangles are maintained by a separate window procedure called *ChildWndProc*. If we wanted to, we could add a facility to *ChildWndProc* to send a message to its parent window procedure (*WndProc*) whenever a rectangle is checked or unchecked.

Here's how: The child window procedure can determine the window handle of its parent by calling *GetParent*:

```
hwndParent = GetParent (hwnd) ;
```

where *hwnd* is the window handle of the child window. It can then send a message to the parent window procedure:

```
SendMessage (hwndParent, message, wParam, lParam) ;
```

Perhaps for this message the child window could set *wParam* to its child window ID. The *lParam* could be set to a 1 if the child window were being checked and a 0 if it were being unchecked.

This in effect creates a "child window control." The child window processes mouse and keyboard messages and notifies the parent window when the child window's state has changed. In this way, the child window becomes an input device for the parent window.

Although you can create your own child window controls, you can also take advantage of several predefined window classes (and window procedures) that your program can use to create child window controls. These controls take the form of buttons, check boxes, edit boxes, list boxes, combo boxes, text strings, and scroll bars. For instance, if you want to put a button labeled "Recalculate" in a corner of your spreadsheet program, you can create it with a single *CreateWindow* call. You don't have to worry about the mouse logic or button painting logic or about making the button "flash" when it's clicked. That's all done in Windows. All you have to do is trap WM_COMMAND messages—that's how the button informs your window procedure when it has been triggered.

Is it really that simple? Well, almost.

Child window controls are used most often in dialog boxes. As you'll see in Chapter 10, the position and size of the child window controls are defined in a dialog box template contained in the program's resource script. However, you can also use predefined child window controls on the surface of a normal overlapped window's client area. You create each child window with a *CreateWindow* call and adjust the position and size of the child windows with calls to *MoveWindow*. The parent window procedure sends messages to the child window controls, and the child window controls send messages back to the parent window procedure.

When you bring up your normal window, you first define a window class and register it with Windows using *RegisterClass*. You then create the window based on that class using *CreateWindow*. When you use one of the predefined controls, however, you do not register a window class for the child window. The class already exists within Windows and has one of these names: "button," "static," "scrollbar," "edit," "listbox," or "combobox." You simply use the name as the window class parameter in *CreateWindow*. The window style parameter to *CreateWindow* defines more precisely the appearance and functionality of the child window control. Windows contains the window procedures that process messages to the child windows based on these classes.

Using child window controls directly on the surface of your window involves tasks of a lower level than are required for using child window controls in dialog boxes, where the dialog box manager adds a layer of insulation between your program and the controls themselves. In particular, you'll discover that the child window controls you create on the surface of your window have no built-in facility to move the input focus from one control to another using the Tab or cursor movement keys. A child window control can obtain the input focus, but once it does, it won't relinquish the input focus back to the parent window. This is a problem we'll struggle with throughout this chapter.

THE BUTTON CLASS

We'll begin our exploration of the button window class with a program called BTNLOOK ("button look"), which is shown in Figure 6-1. BTNLOOK creates 11 child window button controls, one for each of the 11 styles of buttons.

BTNLOOK.MAK

```
#---------------------
# BTNLOOK.MAK make file
#---------------------

btnlook.exe : btnlook.obj btnlook.def
      link btnlook, /align:16, NULL, /nod slibcew libw, btnlook
      rc btnlook.exe

btnlook.obj : btnlook.c
      cl -c -Gsw -Ow -W2 -Zp btnlook.c
```

BTNLOOK.C

```
/*-----------------------------------------
     BTNLOOK.C -- Button Look Program
                (c) Charles Petzold, 1990
     -----------------------------------------*/

#include <windows.h>
#include <stdio.h>

struct
     {
     long style ;
     char *text ;
     }
     button[] =
     {
     BS_PUSHBUTTON,       "PUSHBUTTON",
     BS_DEFPUSHBUTTON,    "DEFPUSHBUTTON",
     BS_CHECKBOX,         "CHECKBOX",
     BS_AUTOCHECKBOX,     "AUTOCHECKBOX",
     BS_RADIOBUTTON,      "RADIOBUTTON",
     BS_3STATE,           "3STATE",
     BS_AUTO3STATE,       "AUTO3STATE",
     BS_GROUPBOX,         "GROUPBOX",
```

Figure 6-1. *The BTNLOOK program.*

(continued)

```
      BS_USERBUTTON,      "USERBUTTON",
      BS_AUTORADIOBUTTON, "AUTORADIO",
      BS_PUSHBOX,         "PUSHBOX"
      } ;

#define NUM (sizeof button / sizeof button [0])

long FAR PASCAL WndProc (HWND, WORD, WORD, LONG) ;

int PASCAL WinMain (HANDLE hInstance, HANDLE hPrevInstance,
                    LPSTR lpszCmdLine, int nCmdShow)
      {
      static char szAppName[] = "BtnLook" ;
      HWND        hwnd ;
      MSG         msg ;
      WNDCLASS    wndclass ;

      if (!hPrevInstance)
          {
          wndclass.style         = CS_HREDRAW : CS_VREDRAW ;
          wndclass.lpfnWndProc   = WndProc ;
          wndclass.cbClsExtra    = 0 ;
          wndclass.cbWndExtra    = 0 ;
          wndclass.hInstance     = hInstance ;
          wndclass.hIcon         = LoadIcon (NULL, IDI_APPLICATION) ;
          wndclass.hCursor       = LoadCursor (NULL, IDC_ARROW) ;
          wndclass.hbrBackground = GetStockObject (WHITE_BRUSH) ;
          wndclass.lpszMenuName  = NULL ;
          wndclass.lpszClassName = szAppName ;

          RegisterClass (&wndclass) ;
          }

      hwnd = CreateWindow (szAppName, "Button Look",
                        WS_OVERLAPPEDWINDOW,
                        CW_USEDEFAULT, CW_USEDEFAULT,
                        CW_USEDEFAULT, CW_USEDEFAULT,
                        NULL, NULL, hInstance, NULL) ;

      ShowWindow (hwnd, nCmdShow) ;
      UpdateWindow (hwnd) ;

      while (GetMessage (&msg, NULL, 0, 0))
          {
          TranslateMessage (&msg) ;
          DispatchMessage (&msg) ;
          }
      return msg.wParam ;
      }
```

(continued)

```
long FAR PASCAL WndProc (HWND hwnd, WORD message, WORD wParam, LONG lParam)
    {
    static char   szPrm []    = "wParam      LOWORD(lParam)  HIWORD(lParam)",
                  szTop []    = "Control ID  Window Handle   Notification",
                  szUnd []    = " _____   _____   _____",
                  szFormat [] = " %5u          %4X            %5u",
                  szBuffer [50] ;
    static HWND   hwndButton [NUM] ;
    static RECT   rect ;
    static int    cxChar, cyChar ;
    HDC           hdc ;
    PAINTSTRUCT   ps ;
    int           i ;
    TEXTMETRIC    tm ;

    switch (message)
        {
        case WM_CREATE :
            hdc = GetDC (hwnd) ;
            SelectObject (hdc, GetStockObject (SYSTEM_FIXED_FONT)) ;
            GetTextMetrics (hdc, &tm) ;
            cxChar = tm.tmAveCharWidth ;
            cyChar = tm.tmHeight + tm.tmExternalLeading ;
            ReleaseDC (hwnd, hdc) ;

            for (i = 0 ; i < NUM ; i++)
                hwndButton [i] = CreateWindow ("button", button[i].text,
                        WS_CHILD | WS_VISIBLE | button[i].style,
                        cxChar, cyChar * (1 + 2 * i),
                        20 * cxChar, 7 * cyChar / 4,
                        hwnd, i,
                        ((LPCREATESTRUCT) lParam) -> hInstance, NULL) ;
            return 0 ;

        case WM_SIZE :
            rect.left   = 24 * cxChar ;
            rect.top    =  3 * cyChar ;
            rect.right  = LOWORD (lParam) ;
            rect.bottom = HIWORD (lParam) ;
            return 0 ;

        case WM_PAINT :
            InvalidateRect (hwnd, &rect, TRUE) ;

            hdc = BeginPaint (hwnd, &ps) ;
            SelectObject (hdc, GetStockObject (SYSTEM_FIXED_FONT)) ;
            SetBkMode (hdc, TRANSPARENT) ;
```

(continued)

209

```
                    TextOut (hdc, 24 * cxChar, 1 * cyChar, szPrm, sizeof szPrm - 1) ;
                    TextOut (hdc, 24 * cxChar, 2 * cyChar, szTop, sizeof szTop - 1) ;
                    TextOut (hdc, 24 * cxChar, 2 * cyChar, szUnd, sizeof szUnd - 1) ;

                    EndPaint (hwnd, &ps) ;
                    return 0 ;

          case WM_COMMAND :
                    ScrollWindow (hwnd, 0, -cyChar, &rect, &rect) ;
                    hdc = GetDC (hwnd) ;
                    SelectObject (hdc, GetStockObject (SYSTEM_FIXED_FONT)) ;

                    TextOut (hdc, 24 * cxChar, cyChar * (rect.bottom / cyChar - 1),
                             szBuffer, sprintf (szBuffer, szFormat, wParam,
                             LOWORD (lParam), HIWORD (lParam))) ;

                    ReleaseDC (hwnd, hdc) ;
                    ValidateRect (hwnd, NULL) ;
                    return 0 ;

          case WM_DESTROY :
                    PostQuitMessage (0) ;
                    return 0 ;
          }
     return DefWindowProc (hwnd, message, wParam, lParam) ;
     }
```

BTNLOOK.DEF

```
;------------------------------------
; BTNLOOK.DEF module definition file
;------------------------------------

NAME            BTNLOOK

DESCRIPTION     'Button Look Program (c) Charles Petzold, 1990'
EXETYPE         WINDOWS
STUB            'WINSTUB.EXE'
CODE            PRELOAD MOVEABLE DISCARDABLE
DATA            PRELOAD MOVEABLE MULTIPLE
HEAPSIZE        1024
STACKSIZE       8192
EXPORTS         WndProc
```

As you click on each button, it sends a WM_COMMAND message to the parent window procedure, which is the familiar *WndProc*. BTNLOOK's *WndProc* displays the *wParam* and *lParam* parameters of this message on the right half of the client area, as shown in Figure 6-2.

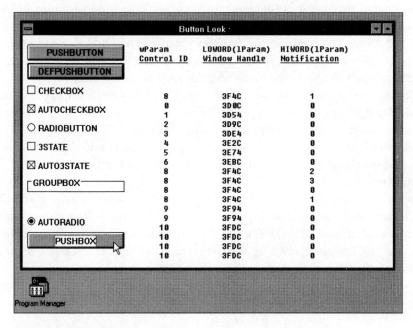

Figure 6-2. *The BTNLOOK display.*

Creating the Child Windows

BTNLOOK defines a structure called *button* that contains button window styles and descriptive text strings for each of the 11 types of buttons. The button window styles all begin with the letters BS, which stand for "button style."

The 11 button child windows are created in a *for* loop during WM_CREATE message processing in *WndProc*. The *CreateWindow* call uses the following parameters:

Class name	"button"
Window text	button[i].text
Window style	WS_CHILD ¦ WS_VISIBLE ¦ button[i].style
x position	cxChar
y position	cyChar * (1 + 2 * i)
Width	20 * xChar
Height	7 * yChar / 4
Parent window	hwnd

Child window ID	i
Instance handle	((LPCREATESTRUCT) lParam) -> hInstance
Extra parameters	NULL

The class name parameter is the predefined name. The window style uses WS-_CHILD, WS_VISIBLE, and one of the eleven button styles (BS_PUSHBUTTON, BS-_DEFPUSHBUTTON, and so forth) in the *button* structure. The window text parameter (which for a normal window is the text that appears in the caption bar) is text that will be displayed with each button. I've simply used text that identifies the button style.

The *x* position and *y* position parameters indicate the placement of the upper left corner of the child window relative to the upper left corner of the parent window's client area. The width and height parameters specify the width and height of each child window.

The child window ID parameter should be unique for each child window. This ID helps your window procedure identify the child window when processing WM_COM-MAND messages from it.

The instance handle parameter of the *CreateWindow* call looks a little strange, but we're taking advantage of the fact that during a WM_CREATE message *lParam* is actually a pointer to a structure of type CREATESTRUCT ("creation structure") that has a member *hInstance*. So we cast *lParam* into a long (or far) pointer to a CREATESTRUCT structure and get *hInstance* out.

(Some Window programs use a global variable named *hInst* to give window procedures access to the instance handle available in *WinMain*. In *WinMain*, you need simply set:

```
hInst = hInstance ;
```

before creating the main window. In Chapter 4 we used *GetWindowWord* to obtain the instance handle:

```
GetWindowWord (hwnd, GWW_HINSTANCE)
```

Any of these methods is fine.)

After the *CreateWindow* call, we don't have to do anything more with these child windows. The button window procedure within Windows maintains them for us and handles all repainting jobs. (The exception is the button with the BS_USERBUTTON style; as I'll discuss shortly, this button style requires the program to draw the button.) At the program's termination, Windows destroys these child windows when the parent window is destroyed.

The Child Talks to Its Parent

When you run BTNLOOK, you see the different button types displayed on the left side of the client area. (The BS_USERBUTTON button is not visible.) As I mentioned earlier, when you click a button with the mouse, the child window control sends a WM_COMMAND message to its parent window. BTNLOOK traps the WM_COMMAND message and displays the values of *wParam* and *lParam*. Here's what they mean:

wParam	Child window ID
LOWORD (*lParam*)	Child window handle
HIWORD (*lParam*)	Notification code

The child window ID is the value passed to *CreateWindow* when the child window is created. In BTNLOOK these IDs are 0 through 10 for the 11 buttons displayed in the client area. The child window handle is the value that Windows returns from the *CreateWindow* call.

The notification code is a submessage code that the child window uses to tell the parent window in more detail what the message means. The possible values of button notification codes are defined in WINDOWS.H:

Button Notification Code Identifier	*Value*
BN_CLICKED	0
BN_PAINT	1
BN_HILITE	2
BN_UNHILITE	3
BN_DISABLE	4
BN_DOUBLECLICKED	5

For all button styles except BS_USERBUTTON, this notification code is always BN_CLICKED, which simply tells the parent window that the button has been clicked. The other notification codes are used for the BS_USERBUTTON style.

You'll notice that when you click a button with the mouse, a dashed line surrounds the text of the button. This indicates that the button has the input focus. All keyboard input now goes to the child window button control rather than to the main window. However, when the button control has the input focus, it ignores all keystrokes except the Spacebar, which now has the same effect as a mouse click.

The Parent Talks to Its Child

Although BTNLOOK does not demonstrate this fact, a window procedure can also send messages to the child window control. Five button-specific messages are defined in WINDOWS.H; each begins with the letters "BM," which stand for "button message." These messages are defined in WINDOWS.H in terms of the WM_USER identifier:

```
#define BM_GETCHECK  (WM_USER+0)
#define BM_SETCHECK  (WM_USER+1)
#define BM_GETSTATE  (WM_USER+2)
#define BM_SETSTATE  (WM_USER+3)
#define BM_SETSTYLE  (WM_USER+4)
```

The WM_USER identifier is available for programs to define their own messages beyond the predefined messages. Each window class can have its own separate set of messages unique to that class. The other classes of predefined child window controls also can have their own messages defined in terms of WM_USER.

The BM_GETCHECK and BM_SETCHECK messages are sent by a parent window to a child window control to get and set the check mark of check boxes and radio buttons. The BM_GETSTATE and BM_SETSTATE messages refer to the normal or "pushed" state of a window when you click it with the mouse or press it with the Spacebar. We'll see how these messages work when we look at each type of button. The BM_SETSTYLE message lets you change the button style after the button is created.

Push Buttons

The first two buttons shown in BTNLOOK are "push" buttons. A push button is a rectangle enclosing text specified in the window text parameter of the *CreateWindow* call. The rectangle takes up the full height and width of the dimensions given in the *CreateWindow* or *MoveWindow* call. The text is centered within the rectangle.

Push-button controls are used mostly to trigger an immediate action without retaining any type of on/off indication. The two types of push-button controls have window styles called BS_PUSHBUTTON and BS_DEFPUSHBUTTON. The "DEF" in BS_DEFPUSH-BUTTON stands for "default." When used to design dialog boxes, BS_PUSHBUTTON controls and BS_DEFPUSHBUTTON controls function differently from one another. When used as child window controls, however, the two types of push buttons function the same way, although BS_DEFPUSHBUTTON has a heavier outline.

A push button looks best when its height is 7/4 times the height of a SYSTEM_FONT character, which is what BTNLOOK uses. The push button's width must accommodate at least the width of the text plus two additional characters.

When the mouse cursor is inside the push button, pressing the mouse button causes the button to repaint itself using 3D-style shading to appear as if it's been depressed. Releasing the mouse button restores the original appearance and sends a WM_COM-MAND message to the parent window with notification code BN_CLICKED. As with the other button types, when a push button has the input focus, a dashed line surrounds the text, and pressing and releasing the Spacebar has the same effect as pressing and releasing the mouse button.

You can simulate a push-button flash by sending the window a BM_SETSTATE message. This causes the button to be depressed:

```
SendMessage (hwndButton, BM_SETSTATE, 1, 0L) ;
```

This call causes the button to return to normal:

```
SendMessage (hwndButton, BM_SETSTATE, 0, 0L) ;
```

The *hwndButton* window handle is the value returned from the *CreateWindow* call.

You can also send a BM_GETSTATE message to a push button. The child window control returns the current state of the button—TRUE if the button is depressed and FALSE (or 0) if normal. Most applications do not require this information, however. And because push buttons do not retain any on/off information, the BM_SETCHECK and BM_GET-CHECK messages are not used.

Buttons created with the BS_PUSHBOX style are displayed only when the button has the input focus. This style of button is rarely used by Windows applications.

Check Boxes

A check box is a square box with text; the text usually appears to the right of the check box. (If you include the BS_LEFTTEXT style when creating the button, the text appears to the left.) Check boxes are usually incorporated in an application to allow a user to select options. The check box commonly functions as a toggle switch: Clicking the box once causes an X to appear; clicking again toggles the X off.

The two most common styles for a check box are BS_CHECKBOX and BS_AUTO-CHECKBOX. When you use the BS_CHECKBOX style, you must set the X mark yourself by sending the control a BM_SETCHECK message. The *wParam* parameter is set to 1 to create an X and to 0 to remove it. You can obtain the current check state of the box by sending the control a BM_GETCHECK message. You might use code like this to toggle the X mark when processing a WM_COMMAND message from the control:

```
SendMessage (LOWORD (lParam), BM_SETCHECK, (WORD)
        !SendMessage (LOWORD (lParam), BM_GETCHECK, 0, 0L), 0L) ;
```

Note the *!* operator in front of the second *SendMessage* call. The low word of *lParam* is the child window handle passed to your window procedure in the WM_COMMAND message. When you later need to know the state of the button, send it another BM_GETCHECK message. Or you can retain the current check state in a static variable in your window procedure. You can also initialize a BS_CHECKBOX check box with an X by sending it a BM_SETCHECK message:

```
SendMessage (hwndButton, BM_SETCHECK, 1, 0L) ;
```

For the BS_AUTOCHECKBOX style, the button control itself toggles the X on and off. Your window procedure can ignore WM_COMMAND messages. When you need the current state of the button, send the control a BM_GETCHECK message:

```
nCheck = (WORD) SendMessage (hwndButton, BM_GETCHECK, 0, 0L) ;
```

The value of *nCheck* is TRUE or nonzero if the button is checked, FALSE or zero if not.

The other two check box styles are BS_3STATE and BS_AUTO3STATE. As their names indicate, these styles can display a third state as well—a gray color within the check box—which occurs when you send the control a WM_SETCHECK message with *wParam* equal to 2. The gray color indicates to the user that the box cannot be checked—that is, that it's disabled. However, the check box control continues to send messages to the parent when the box is clicked. Better methods for disabling a check box are described later.

The check box is aligned with the rectangle's left edge and is centered within the top and bottom dimensions of the rectangle that were specified during the *CreateWindow* call. Clicking anywhere within the rectangle causes a WM_COMMAND message to be sent to the parent. The minimum height for a check box is one character height. The minimum width is the number of characters in the text plus two.

Radio Buttons

A radio button looks very much like a check box except that it is shaped like a circle rather than a box. A heavy dot within the circle indicates that the radio button has been checked. The radio button has the window style BS_RADIOBUTTON or BS_AUTORADIOBUT-TON, but the latter is used only in dialog boxes.

In dialog boxes, groups of radio buttons are conventionally used to indicate mutually exclusive options. (For instance, look at the dialog box in the Windows Terminal program that appears when you select Communications from the Settings menu.) Unlike check boxes, radio buttons do not work as toggles—that is, when you click a radio button a second time, its state remains unchanged.

When you receive a WM_COMMAND message from a radio button, you should display its check by sending it a BM_SETCHECK message with *wParam* equal to 1:

```
SendMessage (hwndButton, BM_SETCHECK, 1, 0L) ;
```

For all other radio buttons in the same group, you can turn off the checks by sending them BM_SETCHECK messages with *wParam* equal to 0:

```
SendMessage (hwndButton, BM_SETCHECK, 0, 0L) ;
```

Group Boxes

The group box, style BS_GROUPBOX, is an oddity in the button class. It neither processes mouse or keyboard input nor sends WM_COMMAND messages to its parent. The group box is a rectangular outline with its window text at the top. Group boxes are often used to enclose other button controls.

User-Defined Buttons

The user-defined button, which has the style BS_USERBUTTON, is the only button that sends WM_COMMAND messages to its parent with these notification codes:

BN_PAINT	Button is normal
BN_HILITE	Button is being clicked
BN_UNHILITE	Clicking is finished
BN_DISABLE	Button is disabled

These notification codes indicate that the window must be painted. The parent window is responsible for this painting. It can use the low word of *lParam* to obtain the window handle of the button, *GetClientRect* to determine the button's dimensions, and *GetDC* to get the button's device context in preparation for painting. BTNLOOK doesn't process these notification codes, so only a dotted outline appears when the button has the input focus.

Changing the Button Text

You can change the text in a button (or in any other window) by calling *SetWindowText*:

```
SetWindowText (hwnd, lpszString) ;
```

where *hwnd* is a handle to the window whose text is being changed and *lpszString* is a long (or far) pointer to a null-terminated string. For a normal window, this text is the text of the caption bar. For a button control, it's the text displayed with the button.

You can also obtain the current text of a window:

```
nLength = GetWindowText (hwnd, lpszBuffer, nMaxLength) ;
```

The *nMaxLength* parameter specifies the maximum number of characters to copy into the buffer pointed to by *lpszBuffer*. The function returns the string length copied. You can prepare your program for a particular text length by first calling:

```
nLength = GetWindowTextLength (hwnd) ;
```

Visible and Enabled Buttons

To receive mouse and keyboard input, a child window must be both visible (displayed) and enabled. When a child window is visible but not enabled, Windows displays it in gray rather than black.

If you do not include WS_VISIBLE in the window class when creating the child window, the child window will not be displayed until you make a call to *ShowWindow*:

```
ShowWindow (hwndChild, SW_SHOWNORMAL) ;
```

If you include WS_VISIBLE in the window class, you do not need to call *ShowWindow*. However, you can hide the child window by a call to *ShowWindow*:

```
ShowWindow (hwndChild, SW_HIDE) ;
```

You can determine if a child window is visible by a call to:

```
IsWindowVisible (hwndChild) ;
```

You can also enable and disable a child window. By default, a window is enabled. You can disable it by calling:

```
EnableWindow (hwndChild, FALSE) ;
```

For button controls, this has the effect of graying the button text string. The button no longer responds to mouse or keyboard input. This is the best method for indicating that a button option is currently unavailable.

You can reenable a child window by calling:

```
EnableWindow (hwndChild, TRUE) ;
```

You can determine whether a child window is enabled by calling:

```
IsWindowEnabled (hwndChild) ;
```

Buttons and Input Focus

As I noted earlier in this chapter, push buttons, check boxes, radio buttons, and user-defined buttons receive the input focus when they are clicked with the mouse. The control indicates it has the input focus by a dashed line surrounding the text. When the child window control gets the input focus, the parent window loses it; all keyboard input then goes to the control rather than to the parent window. However, the child window control responds only to the Spacebar, which now functions like the mouse. This situation presents an obvious problem: Your program has lost control of keyboard processing. Let's see what we can do about it.

When Windows switches the input focus from one window (such as a parent) to another (such as a child window control), it first sends a WM_KILLFOCUS message to the window losing the input focus. The *wParam* parameter is the handle of the window that is to receive the input focus. Windows then sends a WM_SETFOCUS message to the window receiving the input focus, with *wParam* the handle of the window losing the input focus. (In both cases, *wParam* may be NULL, which indicates that no window has or is receiving the input focus.)

A parent window can prevent a child window control from getting the input focus by processing WM_KILLFOCUS messages. Assume that the array *hwndChild* contains the window handles of all child windows. (These were saved in the array during the *CreateWindow* calls that created the windows.) NUM is the number of child windows:

```
case WM_KILLFOCUS :
     for (i = 0 ; i < NUM ; i++)
          if (hwndChild [i] == wParam)
               {
               SetFocus (hwnd) ;
               break ;
               }
     return 0 ;
```

In this code, when the parent window detects that it's losing the input focus to one of its child window controls, it calls *SetFocus* to restore the input focus to itself.

Here's a simpler (but less obvious) way of doing it:

```
case WM_KILLFOCUS :
     if (hwnd == GetParent (wParam))
          SetFocus (hwnd) ;
     return 0 ;
```

Both these methods have a shortcoming, however: They prevent the button from responding to the Spacebar, because the button never gets the input focus. A better approach would be to let the button get the input focus but also to include the facility for the user to move from button to button using the Tab key. At first this sounds impossible, but I'll show you how to accomplish it with a technique called "window subclassing" in the COLORS1 program shown later in this chapter.

CONTROLS AND COLORS

I deliberately put a little "gotcha" into BTNLOOK. There is something wrong with the program. It may not be immediately apparent, but here's how to see it: Run BTNLOOK and bring up the Control Panel program included with Windows. Select the Colors icon; this brings up a dialog box that lets you change system colors. Select Color Palette and change the colors of Window Background and Window Text, and save the new settings by clicking the OK button: The background and text of the buttons (with the exception of the push buttons) in BTNLOOK changes to reflect the new colors, but the background color and text color of the rest of BTNLOOK's client area remain the same—black text on a white background. It looks dreadful.

What happened? Simple—the button colors change because they are based on the system colors you set in Control Panel, but BTNLOOK's client-area background remains white because white is specified in the window class:

```
wndclass.hbrBackground = GetStockObject (WHITE_BRUSH) ;
```

When BTNLOOK writes text to the display, it uses the text color and background color defined in the default device context. These are always black and white, regardless of the system colors set with Control Panel.

Let's fix this problem. I discussed Windows' use of color in Chapter 5, but this problem involves Windows "system colors."

System Colors

Windows maintains 19 system colors for painting various parts of the display. You can obtain and set these colors using *GetSysColor* and *SetSysColor*. Identifiers defined in WINDOWS.H specify the system color. Setting a system color with *SetSysColor* changes it only for the current Windows session.

You can set system colors for future Windows sessions using the Windows Control Panel program. You can also modify the *[colors]* section in the WIN.INI file. The *[colors]* section uses keywords for the 19 system colors (different from the *GetSysColor* and *SetSysColor* identifiers) followed by red, green, and blue values that can range from 0 to 255. The following table shows how the 19 system colors are identified using the WINDOWS.H identifiers for *GetSysColor* and *SetSysColor*, the WIN.INI keywords, and the Control Panel terms:

GetSysColor & SetSysColor	*WIN.INI*	*Control Panel*
COLOR_SCROLLBAR	Scrollbar	Scroll Bars
COLOR_BACKGROUND	Background	Desktop Background
COLOR_ACTIVECAPTION	ActiveTitle	Active Title Bar
COLOR_INACTIVECAPTION	InactiveTitle	Inactive Title Bar
COLOR_MENU	Menu	Menu Bar
COLOR_WINDOW	Window	Window Background
COLOR_WINDOWFRAME	WindowFrame	Window Frame
COLOR_MENUTEXT	MenuText	Menu Text
COLOR_WINDOWTEXT	WindowText	Window Text
COLOR_CAPTIONTEXT	TitleText	Title Bar Text
COLOR_ACTIVEBORDER	ActiveBorder	Active Border
COLOR_INACTIVEBORDER	InactiveBorder	Inactive Border
COLOR_APPWORKSPACE	AppWorkspace	Application Workspace
COLOR_HIGHLIGHT	Highlight	
COLOR_HIGHLIGHTTEXT	HighlightText	
COLOR_BTNFACE	ButtonFace	
COLOR_BTNSHADOW	ButtonShadow	
COLOR_GRAYTEXT	GrayText	
COLOR_BTNTEXT	ButtonText	

Most of these are self-explanatory. COLOR_BACKGROUND is the color of the desktop area behind all the windows. The COLOR_WINDOWFRAME color is the color used for lines drawn between many of the sections of the display, such as between a menu and a client area. The last six system colors cannot be changed from the Control Panel: The two "Highlight" colors involve selected options in menus and list boxes. The last four system colors determine the colors used in push buttons.

Default values for these 19 colors are provided by the display driver. Windows uses these default values unless they are overriden by the *[colors]* section of WIN.INI.

The Button Colors

COLOR_WINDOW and COLOR_WINDOWTEXT are used by many windows to color themselves. The button controls (with the exception of push buttons) use COLOR_WINDOW to color the background behind the button. (For a group box, COLOR_WINDOW is used only for the background behind the text.) The button controls use COLOR_WINDOWTEXT for text, for the box in a check box control, and for the round button in a radio-button control. The outline of push buttons and group boxes is defined by using COLOR_WINDOWFRAME.

You can use one of two methods to make your main window and the child window control consistent in their use of colors. The first method is to use system colors for your main window. To begin, you use COLOR_WINDOW for the background of your client area when defining the window class:

```
wndclass.hbrBackground = COLOR_WINDOW + 1 ;
```

(Windows requires that you add 1 when you use these identifiers in your *wndclass* structure, but doing so has no profound purpose other than to prevent the value from being 0.) But that causes another problem. When you display text using *TextOut*, Windows uses values defined in the device context for the text background color (which erases the background behind the text) and the text color. The default values are white (background) and black (text) regardless of both the system colors and the *hbrBackground* field of the window class structure. So you need to use *SetTextColor* and *SetBkColor* to change your text and text background colors to the system colors. You do this after you obtain the handle to a device context:

```
SetBkColor (hdc, GetSysColor (COLOR_WINDOW)) ;
SetTextColor (hdc, GetSysColor (COLOR_WINDOWTEXT)) ;
```

Now the client-area background, text background, and text color are all consistent with button colors. That's the first method.

The second method is to force the child window controls to use the colors you want to use. This method is a little more involved; it requires processing WM_CTLCOLOR messages.

The WM_CTLCOLOR Messages

WM_CTLCOLOR is a message that a predefined child window control sends to its parent window procedure when the child window is about to paint its client area. The parent window can use this opportunity to alter the colors that the child window procedure will use for painting.

When the parent window procedure receives a WM_CTLCOLOR message, the *wParam* and *lParam* parameters have the following meaning:

wParam	Handle to child window's device context
LOWORD (*lParam*)	Handle to child window
HIWORD (*lParam*)	Type of window

The high word of *lParam* can be one of the following:

HIWORD (lParam)	**Type of Window**
CTLCOLOR_MSGBOX	Message box
CTLCOLOR_EDIT	Edit control
CTLCOLOR_LISTBOX	List box control
CTLCOLOR_BTN	Button control
CTLCOLOR_DLG	Dialog box
CTLCOLOR_SCROLLBAR	Scroll bar control
CTLCOLOR_STATIC	Static control

Right now, we're interested in CTLCOLOR_BTN, the WM_CTLCOLOR message from a button control. When the parent window procedure gets this message, the child window control has already obtained its device context. The handle to this device context is in *wParam*. Any GDI (Graphics Device Interface) calls you make using this device context will affect the painting that the child window does when you pass control back to the child window.

You must perform three actions when processing a WM_CTLCOLOR message:

- Set a text color using *SetTextColor*.

- Set a background color using *SetBkColor*.

- Return a handle to a brush to the child window.

A "brush" is a GDI object that defines a bitmapped pattern of pixels. Windows uses brushes to fill areas with color. You can get a handle to a brush using *GetStockObject*, *CreateSolidBrush*, *CreateHatchBrush*, or *CreatePatternBrush*. For processing the WM_CTLCOLOR message, you'll probably use *CreateSolidBrush*. Before your program terminates, you must explicitly delete any brushes you create. A good time to do this is while processing the WM_DESTROY message.

For most child window controls, the color you set in *SetBkColor* should be the same as the color of the brush you return from the WM_CTLCOLOR message. For instance, button controls use the brush to color the background of the entire child window client area. The text background color is used only for the background behind the text. These two colors should be the same. To see how this works, let's take an example of processing a WM_CTLCOLOR message for button controls where the window procedure simply sets the normal default colors. During initialization (probably when processing a WM_CREATE message), you can create a brush:

```
hBrush = CreateSolidBrush (GetSysColor (COLOR_WINDOW)) ;
```

The *hBrush* brush handle should be stored in a static variable. Here's what the WM_CTLCOLOR processing looks like:

```
case WM_CTLCOLOR :
     if (HIWORD (lParam) == CTLCOLOR_BTN)
          {
          SetBkColor (wParam, GetSysColor (COLOR_WINDOW)) ;
          SetTextColor (wParam, GetSysColor (COLOR_WINDOWTEXT)) ;

          UnrealizeObject (hBrush) ;
          point.x = point.y = 0 ;
          ClientToScreen (hwnd, &point) ;
          SetBrushOrg (wParam, point.x, point.y) ;

          return ((DWORD) hBrush) ;
          }
     break ;
```

Note that *wParam* is the device context handle of the button control. The four statements that culminate in the *SetBrushOrg* call require some further explanation.

As noted earlier, a brush defines a bitmapped pattern of pixels. When Windows uses this brush to fill an area with color, the pattern of the brush is repeated horizontally and vertically until the area is filled. The origin of this brush—the place where Windows assumes the repeating pattern begins—is the upper left corner of the client area associated with the device context.

But if you color both the client area of a parent window and the client area of a child window with this same brush, the pattern won't merge correctly at the edge of the child window because Windows is using two different origins for the same brush. To avoid this problem, you call *UnrealizeObject*. This function causes Windows to reset the origin of the brush the next time it is selected into a device context (which will follow the return from the WM_CTLCOLOR processing). The origin Windows will use is the one you set with *SetBrushOrg*; in this example, the function sets the brush origin to the screen origin of the parent window. (Don't use *UnrealizeObject* for a stock brush handle that you obtain from *GetStockObject*, and don't worry if this sounds a bit obscure right now. We'll cover the issues in more depth in Chapter 12.)

The brush we created in our example is based on the system color COLOR_WIN-DOW. If this color changes while the program is running, the window procedure receives a WM_SYSCOLORCHANGE message. The program deletes the brush and creates a new one:

```
case WM_SYSCOLORCHANGE :
     DeleteObject (hBrush) ;
     hBrush = CreateSolidBrush (GetSysColor (COLOR_WINDOW)) ;
     return 0 ;
```

Finally, when the program is about to terminate, the brush should be deleted:

```
case WM_DESTROY :
     DeleteObject (hBrush) ;
     PostQuitMessage (0) ;
     return 0 ;
```

I've shown here how you can reproduce the default processing of WM_CTLCOLOR messages for button controls. Using your own colors is much the same. You would not need to trap WM_SYSCOLORCHANGE messages unless you wanted to base the brush on a system color. We'll come back to WM_CTLCOLOR messages later in this chapter, when we use the COLORS1 program. For now, let's explore another class of child window controls.

THE STATIC CLASS

You create a static child window control using "static" as the window class in the *CreateWindow* function. These are fairly benign child windows. They do not accept mouse or keyboard input, and they do not send WM_COMMAND messages back to the parent window. (When you move or click the mouse over a static child window, the child window traps the WM_NCHITTEST message and returns a value of HTTRANSPARENT to Windows. This causes Windows to send the same WM_NCHITTEST message to the underlying window, which is usually the parent. The parent usually passes the message to *DefWindowProc*, where it is converted into a client-area mouse message.)

The first six static window styles simply draw a rectangle or a frame in the client area of the child window. The three "RECT" static styles (left column below) are filled-in rectangles; the three "FRAME" styles (right column) are rectangular outlines that are not filled in:

SS_BLACKRECT	SS_BLACKFRAME
SS_GRAYRECT	SS_GRAYFRAME
SS_WHITERECT	SS_WHITEFRAME

"BLACK," "GRAY," and "WHITE" do not mean the colors are black, gray, and white. Rather, the colors are based on system colors as shown here:

Static Control	System Color
BLACK	COLOR_WINDOWFRAME
GRAY	COLOR_BACKGROUND
WHITE	COLOR_WINDOW

Most display drivers define default settings of black for COLOR_WINDOWFRAME and white for COLOR_WINDOW. (Of course, a user can change any of these colors using the Control Panel program in Windows.) The colors used in the "RECT" and "FRAME" static styles cannot be changed by trapping WM_CTLCOLOR messages. The window text field of the *CreateWindow* call is ignored for these styles. The upper left corner of the rectangle begins at the *x* position and *y* position coordinates relative to the parent window.

The static class also includes three text styles: SS_LEFT, SS_RIGHT, and SS_CENTER. These create left-justified, right-justified, and centered text. The text is given in the window text parameter of the *CreateWindow* call, and it can be changed later using *SetWindowText*. When the window procedure for static controls displays this text, it uses the *DrawText* function with DT_WORDBREAK, DT_NOCLIP, and DT_EXPANDTABS parameters. The text is wordwrapped within the rectangle of the child window. The background of these three text-style child windows is normally COLOR_WINDOW, and the text itself is COLOR_WINDOWTEXT. When you intercept WM_CTLCOLOR messages, you can change the text color by calling *SetTextColor* and the background color by calling *SetBkColor* and by returning the handle to the background brush.

Finally, the static class also includes the window styles SS_ICON and SS_USERITEM. However, these have no meaning when used as child window controls. We'll look at them again when discussing dialog boxes.

THE SCROLLBAR CLASS

When the subject of scroll bars first came up in Chapter 2 while I was designing the SYSMETS series of programs, I discussed some of the differences between "window scroll bars" and "scroll bar controls." SYSMETS uses window scroll bars, which appear at the right and bottom of the window. You add window scroll bars to a window by including the identifier WS_VSCROLL or WS_HSCROLL or both in the window style when creating the window. Now we're ready to make some scroll bar controls, which are child windows that can appear anywhere in the client area of the parent window. You create child window scroll bar controls by using the predefined window class "scrollbar" and one of the two scroll bar styles SBS_VERT and SBS_HORZ.

Unlike the button controls (and the edit and list box controls to be discussed later), scroll bar controls do not send WM_COMMAND messages to the parent window. Instead, they send WM_VSCROLL and WM_HSCROLL messages, just like window scroll bars. When processing the scroll bar messages, you can differentiate between window scroll bars and scroll bar controls by the high word of the *lParam* parameter:

Scroll Bar Type	HIWORD (lParam)
Window scroll bar	0
Scroll bar control	Window handle of control

The *wParam* parameter and the low word of *lParam* have the same meaning for window scroll bars and scroll bar controls.

Although window scroll bars have a fixed width, Windows uses the full rectangle dimensions given in the *CreateWindow* call (or later in the *MoveWindow* call) to size scroll bar controls. You can make long, thin scroll bar controls or short, pudgy scroll bar controls. If you want to create scroll bar controls that have the same dimensions as window scroll bars, you can use *GetSystemMetrics* to obtain the height of a horizontal scroll bar:

```
GetSystemMetrics (SM_CYHSCROLL) ;
```

or the width of a vertical scroll bar:

```
GetSystemMetrics (SM_CXVSCROLL) ;
```

(The scroll bar window style identifiers SBS_LEFTALIGN, SBS_RIGHTALIGN, SBS_TOP-ALIGN, and SBS_BOTTOMALIGN are documented to give standard dimensions to scroll bars. However, these styles work only for scroll bars in dialog boxes.)

You can set the range and position of a scroll bar control with the same calls used for window scroll bars:

```
SetScrollRange (hwndScroll, SB_CTL, nMin, nMax, bRedraw) ;
SetScrollPos (hwndScroll, SB_CTL, nPos, bRedraw) ;
```

The difference is that window scroll bars use a handle to the parent window as the first parameter and SB_VERT or SB_HORZ as the second parameter.

The interior bar of the scroll bar is COLOR_SCROLLBAR. The thumb and arrow colors are based on the push button colors. If you trap WM_CTLCOLOR messages, you can return a brush from the message to override this color. Let's do it.

The COLORS1 Program

To see some uses of scroll bars and static child windows—and also to explore color in more depth—we'll use the COLORS1 program, shown in Figure 6-3. COLORS1 displays three scroll bars in the left half of the client area labeled "Red," "Green," and "Blue." As you scroll the scroll bars, the right half of the client area changes to the composite color indicated by the mix of the three primary colors. The numeric values of the three primary colors are displayed under the three scroll bars.

COLORS1.MAK

```
#----------------------
# COLORS1.MAK make file
#----------------------

colors1.exe : colors1.obj colors1.def
     link colors1, /align:16, NUL, /nod slibcew libw, colors1
     rc colors1.exe

colors1.obj : colors1.c
     cl -c -Gsw -Ow -W2 -Zp colors1.c
```

COLORS1.C

```
/*-------------------------------------------
   COLORS1.C -- Colors Using Scroll Bars
                (c) Charles Petzold, 1990
   -------------------------------------------*/

#include <windows.h>
#include <stdlib.h>

long FAR PASCAL WndProc    (HWND, WORD, WORD, LONG) ;
long FAR PASCAL ScrollProc (HWND, WORD, WORD, LONG) ;

FARPROC lpfnOldScr[3] ;
HWND    hwndScrol[3], hwndLabel[3], hwndValue[3], hwndRect ;
short   color[3], nFocus ;

int PASCAL WinMain (HANDLE hInstance, HANDLE hPrevInstance,
                    LPSTR lpszCmdLine, int nCmdShow)
     {
     static char szAppName[] = "Colors1" ;
     static char *szColorLabel[] = { "Red", "Green", "Blue" } ;
     FARPROC     lpfnScrollProc ;
     HWND        hwnd ;
     MSG         msg ;
     short       n ;
     WNDCLASS    wndclass ;

     if (hPrevInstance)
          return FALSE ;
```

Figure 6-3. *The COLORS1 program.*   *(continued)*

```
wndclass.style        = CS_HREDRAW : CS_VREDRAW ;
wndclass.lpfnWndProc  = WndProc ;
wndclass.cbClsExtra   = 0 ;
wndclass.cbWndExtra   = 0 ;
wndclass.hInstance    = hInstance ;
wndclass.hIcon        = NULL ;
wndclass.hCursor      = LoadCursor (NULL, IDC_ARROW) ;
wndclass.hbrBackground = CreateSolidBrush (0L) ;
wndclass.lpszMenuName = NULL ;
wndclass.lpszClassName = szAppName ;

RegisterClass (&wndclass) ;

hwnd = CreateWindow (szAppName, "Color Scroll",
                     WS_OVERLAPPEDWINDOW : WS_CLIPCHILDREN,
                     CW_USEDEFAULT, CW_USEDEFAULT,
                     CW_USEDEFAULT, CW_USEDEFAULT,
                     NULL, NULL, hInstance, NULL) ;

hwndRect = CreateWindow ("static", NULL,
                     WS_CHILD : WS_VISIBLE : SS_WHITERECT,
                     0, 0, 0, 0,
                     hwnd, 9, hInstance, NULL) ;

lpfnScrollProc = MakeProcInstance ((FARPROC) ScrollProc, hInstance) ;

for (n = 0 ; n < 3 ; n++)
    {
    hwndScrol[n] = CreateWindow ("scrollbar", NULL,
                     WS_CHILD : WS_VISIBLE : WS_TABSTOP : SBS_VERT,
                     0, 0, 0, 0,
                     hwnd, n, hInstance, NULL) ;

    hwndLabel[n] = CreateWindow ("static", szColorLabel[n],
                     WS_CHILD : WS_VISIBLE : SS_CENTER,
                     0, 0, 0, 0,
                     hwnd, n + 3, hInstance, NULL) ;

    hwndValue[n] = CreateWindow ("static", "0",
                     WS_CHILD : WS_VISIBLE : SS_CENTER,
                     0, 0, 0, 0,
                     hwnd, n + 6, hInstance, NULL) ;

    lpfnOldScr[n] = (FARPROC) GetWindowLong (hwndScrol[n], GWL_WNDPROC) ;
    SetWindowLong (hwndScrol[n], GWL_WNDPROC, (LONG) lpfnScrollProc) ;
```

(continued)

```
          SetScrollRange (hwndScrol[n], SB_CTL, 0, 255, FALSE) ;
          SetScrollPos   (hwndScrol[n], SB_CTL, 0, FALSE) ;
          }

     ShowWindow (hwnd, nCmdShow) ;
     UpdateWindow (hwnd);

     while (GetMessage (&msg, NULL, 0, 0))
          {
          TranslateMessage (&msg) ;
          DispatchMessage  (&msg) ;
          }
     return msg.wParam ;
     }

long FAR PASCAL WndProc (HWND hwnd, WORD message, WORD wParam, LONG lParam)
     {
     static HBRUSH hBrush[3] ;
     char          szbuffer[10] ;
     HDC           hdc ;
     POINT         point ;
     short         n, cxClient, cyClient, cyChar ;
     TEXTMETRIC    tm ;

     switch (message)
          {
          case WM_CREATE :
               hBrush[0] = CreateSolidBrush (RGB (255, 0, 0)) ;
               hBrush[1] = CreateSolidBrush (RGB (0, 255, 0)) ;
               hBrush[2] = CreateSolidBrush (RGB (0, 0, 255)) ;
               return 0 ;

          case WM_SIZE :
               cxClient = LOWORD (lParam) ;
               cyClient = HIWORD (lParam) ;

               hdc = GetDC (hwnd) ;
               GetTextMetrics (hdc, &tm) ;
               cyChar = tm.tmHeight ;
               ReleaseDC (hwnd, hdc) ;

               MoveWindow (hwndRect, 0, 0, cxClient / 2, cyClient, TRUE) ;

               for (n = 0 ; n < 3 ; n++)
                    {
                    MoveWindow (hwndScrol[n],
                         (2 * n + 1) * cxClient / 14, 2 * cyChar,
                         cxClient / 14, cyClient - 4 * cyChar, TRUE) ;
```

(continued)

```
                    MoveWindow (hwndLabel[n],
                         (4 * n + 1) * cxClient / 28, cyChar / 2,
                         cxClient / 7, cyChar, TRUE) ;

                    MoveWindow (hwndValue[n],
                         (4 * n + 1) * cxClient / 28, cyClient - 3 * cyChar / 2,
                         cxClient / 7, cyChar, TRUE) ;
               }
          SetFocus (hwnd) ;
          return 0 ;

     case WM_SETFOCUS :
          SetFocus (hwndScrol[nFocus]) ;
          return 0 ;

     case WM_VSCROLL :
          n = GetWindowWord (HIWORD (lParam), GWW_ID) ;

          switch (wParam)
               {
               case SB_PAGEDOWN :
                    color[n] += 15 ;            /* fall through */
               case SB_LINEDOWN :
                    color[n] = min (255, color[n] + 1) ;
                    break ;
               case SB_PAGEUP :
                    color[n] -= 15 ;            /* fall through */
               case SB_LINEUP :
                    color[n] = max (0, color[n] - 1) ;
                    break ;
               case SB_TOP :
                    color[n] = 0 ;
                    break ;
               case SB_BOTTOM :
                    color[n] = 255 ;
                    break ;
               case SB_THUMBPOSITION :
               case SB_THUMBTRACK :
                    color[n] = LOWORD (lParam) ;
                    break ;
               default :
                    break ;
               }
          SetScrollPos (hwndScrol[n], SB_CTL, color[n], TRUE) ;
          SetWindowText (hwndValue[n], itoa (color[n], szbuffer, 10)) ;
```

(continued)

```
                    DeleteObject (GetClassWord (hwnd, GCW_HBRBACKGROUND)) ;
                    SetClassWord (hwnd, GCW_HBRBACKGROUND,
                         CreateSolidBrush (RGB (color[0], color[1], color[2]))) ;

                    InvalidateRect (hwnd, NULL, TRUE) ;
                    return 0 ;

          case WM_CTLCOLOR :
                    if (HIWORD (lParam) == CTLCOLOR_SCROLLBAR)
                         {
                         SetBkColor (wParam, GetSysColor (COLOR_CAPTIONTEXT)) ;
                         SetTextColor (wParam, GetSysColor (COLOR_WINDOWFRAME)) ;

                         n = GetWindowWord (LOWORD (lParam), GWW_ID) ;
                         point.x = point.y = 0 ;
                         ClientToScreen (hwnd, &point) ;
                         UnrealizeObject (hBrush[n]) ;
                         SetBrushOrg (wParam, point.x, point.y) ;
                         return ((DWORD) hBrush[n]) ;
                         }
                    break ;

          case WM_DESTROY :
                    DeleteObject (GetClassWord (hwnd, GCW_HBRBACKGROUND)) ;
                    for (n = 0 ; n < 3 ; DeleteObject (hBrush [n++])) ;
                    PostQuitMessage (0) ;
                    return 0 ;
          }
     return DefWindowProc (hwnd, message, wParam, lParam) ;
     }

long FAR PASCAL ScrollProc (HWND hwnd, WORD message, WORD wParam, LONG lParam)
     {
     short n = GetWindowWord (hwnd, GWW_ID) ;

     switch (message)
          {
          case WM_KEYDOWN :
                    if (wParam == VK_TAB)
                         SetFocus (hwndScroll[(n +
                              (GetKeyState (VK_SHIFT) < 0 ? 2 : 1)) % 3]) ;
                    break ;

          case WM_SETFOCUS :
                    nFocus = n ;
                    break ;
          }
     return CallWindowProc (lpfnOldScr[n], hwnd, message, wParam, lParam) ;
     }
```

COLORS1.DEF

```
;------------------------------------
; COLORS1.DEF module definition file
;------------------------------------

NAME            COLORS1

DESCRIPTION     'Colors Using Scroll Bars (c) Charles Petzold, 1990'
EXETYPE         WINDOWS
STUB            'WINSTUB.EXE'
CODE            PRELOAD MOVEABLE DISCARDABLE
DATA            PRELOAD MOVEABLE MULTIPLE
HEAPSIZE        1024
STACKSIZE       8192
EXPORTS         WndProc
                ScrollProc
```

COLORS1 puts its children to work. The program uses 10 child window controls: 3 scroll bars, 6 windows of static text, and 1 static rectangle. COLORS1 traps WM_CTLCOLOR messages to color the interior sections of the three scroll bars red, green, and blue. You can scroll the scroll bars using either the mouse or the keyboard. You can use COLORS1 as a development tool in experimenting with color and choosing attractive (or, if you prefer, ugly) colors for your own Windows programs. A monochrome version of the COLORS1 display is shown in Figure 6-4; obviously, to take advantage of the program's manipulation of color, you'll need to use a color monitor.

COLORS1 doesn't process WM_PAINT messages, and the program obtains a device context handle only for determining the height of a character. Most of the work in COLORS1 is done by the child windows.

The color shown on the right half of the client area is actually the background color of the parent window. A static child window with style SS_WHITERECT blocks out the left half of the client area. The three scroll bars are child window controls with the style SBS_VERT placed on top of the SS_WHITERECT child. Six more static child windows of style SS_CENTER (centered text) provide the labels and the color values. COLORS1 creates its normal overlapped window and the ten child windows within the *WinMain* function using *CreateWindow*. The SS_WHITERECT and SS_CENTER static windows use the window class "static," and the three scroll bars use the window class "scrollbar."

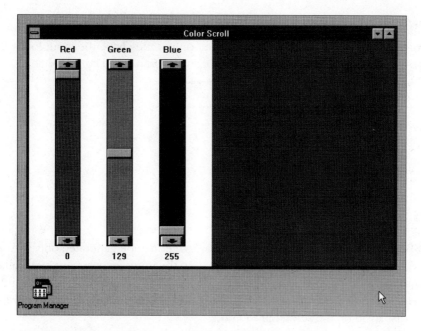

Figure 6-4. *A monochrome version of the COLORS1 display.*

The *x* position, *y* position, width, and height parameters of the *CreateWindow* call are initially set to 0 because the position and sizing depend on the size of the client area, which is not yet known. COLORS1's window procedure resizes all ten child windows using *MoveWindow* when it receives a WM_SIZE message. So whenever you resize the COLORS1 window, the size of the scroll bars changes proportionally.

When the *WndProc* window procedure receives a WM_VSCROLL message, the high word of the *lParam* parameter is the handle to the child window. We can use *GetWindow-Word* to get the window ID number:

```
n = GetWindowWord (HIWORD (1Param), GWW_ID) ;
```

For the three scroll bars, we have conveniently set the ID numbers to 0, 1, and 2, so *WndProc* can tell which scroll bar is generating the message.

Because the handles to the child windows were saved in arrays when the windows were created, *WndProc* can process the scroll bar message and set the new value of the appropriate scroll bar using the *SetScrollPos* call:

```
SetScrollPos (hwndScrol[n], SB_CTL, color[n], TRUE) ;
```

WndProc also changes the text of the child window at the bottom of the scroll bar:

```
SetWindowText (hwndValue[n], itoa (color[n], szbuffer, 10)) ;
```

The Automatic Keyboard Interface

Scroll bar controls can also process keystrokes, but only if they have the input focus. The following table shows how keyboard cursor keys translate into scroll bar messages:

Cursor Key	Scroll Bar Message wParam Value
Home	SB_TOP
End	SB_BOTTOM
Page Up	SB_PAGEUP
Page Down	SB_PAGEDOWN
Left or Up	SB_LINEUP
Right or Down	SB_LINEDOWN

In fact, the SB_TOP and SB_BOTTOM scroll bar messages can be generated only by using the keyboard. If you want a scroll bar control to obtain the input focus when the scroll bar is clicked with the mouse, you must include the WS_TABSTOP identifier in the window class parameter of the *CreateWindow* call. When a scroll bar has the input focus, a blinking gray block is displayed on the scroll bar thumb.

To provide a full keyboard interface to the scroll bars, however, some more work is necessary. First, the *WndProc* window procedure must specifically give a scroll bar the input focus. It does this by processing the WM_SETFOCUS message, which the parent window receives when it obtains the input focus. *WndProc* simply sets the input focus to one of the scroll bars:

```
SetFocus (hwndScroll[nFocus]) ;
```

But you also need some way to get from one scroll bar to another by using the keyboard, preferably by using the Tab key. This is more difficult, because once a scroll bar has the input focus, it processes all keystrokes. But the scroll bar cares only about the cursor keys; it ignores the Tab key. The way out of this dilemma lies in a technique called "window subclassing." We'll use it to add a facility to COLORS1 to jump from one scroll bar to another using the Tab key.

Window Subclassing

The window procedure for the scroll bar controls is somewhere inside Windows. However, you can obtain the address of this window procedure by a call to *GetWindowLong* using the GWL_WNDPROC identifier as a parameter. Moreover, you can set a new window procedure for the scroll bars by calling *SetWindowLong*. This technique, called "window subclassing," is very powerful. It lets you hook into existing window procedures, process some messages within your own program, and pass all other messages to the old window procedure.

The window procedure that does preliminary scroll bar message processing in COLORS1 is called *ScrollProc*; it is toward the end of the COLORS1.C listing. Because *ScrollProc* is a function within COLORS1 that is called by Windows, it must be defined as FAR PASCAL and must be listed under EXPORTS in the COLORS1.DEF module definition file.

First, to ensure that *ScrollProc* accesses the proper data segment, COLORS1 must obtain a far address for the function using *MakeProcInstance*:

```
lpfnScrollProc = MakeProcInstance ((FARPROC) ScrollProc, hInstance);
```

For each of the three scroll bars, COLORS1 uses *GetWindowLong* to obtain and save the address of the existing scroll bar window procedure:

```
lpfnOldScr[n] = (FARPROC) GetWindowLong (hwndScrol[n], GWL_WNDPROC) ;
```

Next, the program sets the new scroll bar window procedure:

```
SetWindowLong (hwndScrol[n], GWL_WNDPROC, (LONG) lpfnScrollProc) ;
```

Now the function *ScrollProc* gets all messages that Windows sends to the scroll bar window procedure for the three scroll bars in COLORS1 (but not, of course, for scroll bars in other programs). The *ScrollProc* window procedure simply changes the input focus to the next (or previous) scroll bar when it receives a Tab or Shift-Tab keystroke. It calls the old scroll bar window procedure using *CallWindowProc*.

Coloring the Background

When COLORS1 defines its window class, it gives the background of its client area a solid black brush:

```
wndclass.hbrBackground = CreateSolidBrush (0L) ;
```

When you change the settings of COLORS1's scroll bars, the program must create a new brush and put the new brush handle in the window class structure. Just as we were able to get and set the scroll bar window procedure using *GetWindowLong* and *SetWindowLong*, we can get and set the handle to this brush using *GetClassWord* and *SetClassWord*.

First you must delete the existing brush:

```
DeleteObject (GetClassWord (hwnd, GCW_HBRBACKGROUND)) ;
```

Then you can create the new brush and insert the handle in the window class structure:

```
SetClassWord (hwnd, GCW_HBRBACKGROUND,
    CreateSolidBrush (RGB (color[0], color[1], color[2]))) ;
```

The next time Windows recolors the background of the window, Windows will use this new brush. To force Windows to erase the background, we invalidate the entire client area:

```
InvalidateRect (hwnd, NULL, TRUE) ;
```

The TRUE (nonzero) value as the third parameter indicates that we want the background erased before repainting.

InvalidateRect causes Windows to put a WM_PAINT message in the message queue of the window procedure. Because WM_PAINT messages are low priority, this message will not be processed immediately if you are still moving the scroll bar with the mouse or the cursor keys. Alternatively, if you want the window to be updated immediately after the color is changed, you can add the statement:

```
UpdateWindow (hwnd) ;
```

after the *InvalidateRect* call. But this slows down keyboard and mouse processing.

COLORS1's *WndProc* function doesn't process the WM_PAINT message but passes it to *DefWindowProc*. Window's default processing of WM_PAINT messages simply involves calling *BeginPaint* and *EndPaint* to validate the window. Because we specified in the *InvalidateRect* call that the background should be erased, the *BeginPaint* call causes Windows to generate a WM_ERASEBKGND (erase background) message. *WndProc* ignores this message also. Windows processes it by erasing the background of the client area using the brush specified in the window class.

Normally, Windows would erase the entire client area using the window class brush. Doing so would erase the 10 child windows, however, and Windows would then have to send WM_PAINT messages to all the child windows so they could repaint themselves — very annoying. We avoid the problem by using the WS_CLIPCHILDREN style value when first creating the parent window using *CreateWindow*; this style prevents the parent window from painting over its children. Take the WS_CLIPCHILDREN style out of *CreateWindow*, and you'll see a big difference in how COLORS1 works.

Like all GDI objects, the brushes created by a program using *CreateSolidBrush* are not automatically deleted by Windows when the program terminates. We've been good about deleting each brush before creating a new one, but when the program is about to terminate, one last brush in the window class still should be discarded. Thus, during processing of the WM_DESTROY message, *DeleteObject* is called once more:

```
DeleteObject (GetClassWord (hwnd, GCW_HBRBACKGROUND)) ;
```

Coloring the Scroll Bars

On a color display, the interiors of the three scroll bars in COLORS1 are red, green, and blue. This coloring is accomplished by processing WM_CTLCOLOR messages.

In *WndProc* we define a static array of three handles to brushes:

```
static HBRUSH hBrush [3] ;
```

During processing of WM_CREATE, we create the three brushes:

```
hBrush[0] = CreateSolidBrush (RGB (255, 0, 0)) ;
hBrush[1] = CreateSolidBrush (RGB (0, 255, 0)) ;
hBrush[2] = CreateSolidBrush (RGB (0, 0, 255)) ;
```

During the WM_CTLCOLOR processing, the text and text background colors are set to the normal values for scroll bars. The brush that's returned from this message is one of the three brushes created earlier:

```
case WM_CTLCOLOR :
     if (HIWORD (lParam) == CTLCOLOR_SCROLLBAR)
          {
          SetBkColor (wParam, GetSysColor (COLOR_CAPTIONTEXT)) ;
          SetTextColor (wParam, GetSysColor (COLOR_WINDOWFRAME)) ;

          n = GetWindowWord (LOWORD (lParam), GWW_ID) ;
          point.x = point.y = 0 ;
          ClientToScreen (hwnd, &point) ;
          UnrealizeObject (hBrush[n]) ;
          SetBrushOrg (wParam, point.x, point.y) ;

          return ((DWORD) hBrush[n]) ;
          }
     break ;
```

These brushes must be destroyed during processing of the WM_DESTROY message:

```
for (n = 0 ; n < 3 ; DeleteObject (hBrush [n++])) ;
```

Dealing with Multiple Instances

Normally, Windows programs reuse the same window class when you load multiple instances of the program. The window class is registered only if the previous instance is NULL:

```
if (!hPrevInstance)
     {
     wndclass.style = CS_HREDRAW ¦ CS_VREDRAW ;
     [more program lines]
```

But COLORS1 can't do this, because the background color is specified in the window class. If all instances of COLORS1 used the same window class, then each instance would use (and change) the same background color. We can avoid this problem entirely by allowing only one instance of COLORS1 to run:

```
if (hPrevInstance)
     return FALSE ;
```

COLORS1 as an Icon

When you make COLORS1 into an icon, the entire surface of the icon—rather than only the right half—is the color of the parent window's background. Yet COLORS1 doesn't seem to have any separate icon logic.

You'll note that COLORS1 specifies a NULL icon in the window class:

```
wndclass.hIcon = NULL ;
```

This indicates that COLORS1 is responsible for painting its icon. The entire icon appears as the background color because Windows hides child windows when a program becomes an icon, and thus the colored background is completely uncovered.

THE EDIT CLASS

The edit class is in some ways the simplest predefined window class and in other ways the most complex. When you create a child window using the class name "edit," you define a rectangle based on the x position, y position, width, and height parameters of the *CreateWindow* call. This rectangle contains editable text. When the child window control has the input focus, you can type text, move the cursor around, select portions of text using either the mouse or the Shift key and a cursor key, delete selected text to the clipboard by pressing Shift-Del, or insert text from the clipboard by pressing Shift-Ins.

One of the simplest uses of edit controls is for single-line entry fields. For instance, the Windows PIF Editor program uses edit controls in this way on its main window. But edit controls are not limited to single lines. For example, the Windows Notepad program uses a multiline edit control. The file size of the Notepad program is surprisingly small—less than 32 KB. Most of the editing logic is not in Notepad at all; it's in the edit control logic within Windows.

To give you an idea of the power of edit controls, we'll write a "Notepad clone" program called POPPAD1. We'll begin the program in this chapter and continue it in Chapters 9 (when we'll add a menu) and 10 (when we'll use dialog boxes to load and save files). POPPAD1 is shown in Figure 6-5.

POPPAD1.MAK

```
#---------------------
# POPPAD1.MAK make file
#---------------------

poppad1.exe : poppad1.obj poppad1.def
    link poppad1, /align:16, NUL, /nod slibcew libw, poppad1.def
    rc poppad1.exe

poppad1.obj : poppad1.c
    cl -c -Gsw -Ow -W2 -Zp poppad1.c
```

Figure 6-5. *The POPPAD1 program.*

POPPAD1.C

```
/*------------------------------------------------------------
    POPPAD1.C -- Popup Editor Using Child Window Edit Box
                 (c) Charles Petzold, 1990
   ---------------------------------------------------------*/

#include <windows.h>

long FAR PASCAL WndProc (HWND, WORD, WORD, LONG);

char szAppName[] = "PopPad1" ;

int PASCAL WinMain (HANDLE hInstance, HANDLE hPrevInstance,
                    LPSTR lpszCmdLine, int nCmdShow)
     {
     HWND     hwnd ;
     MSG      msg;
     WNDCLASS wndclass ;

     if (!hPrevInstance)
          {
          wndclass.style         = CS_HREDRAW : CS_VREDRAW ;
          wndclass.lpfnWndProc    = WndProc ;
          wndclass.cbClsExtra     = 0 ;
          wndclass.cbWndExtra     = 0 ;
          wndclass.hInstance      = hInstance ;
          wndclass.hIcon          = LoadIcon (NULL, IDI_APPLICATION) ;
          wndclass.hCursor        = LoadCursor (NULL, IDC_ARROW) ;
          wndclass.hbrBackground  = GetStockObject (WHITE_BRUSH) ;
          wndclass.lpszMenuName   = NULL ;
          wndclass.lpszClassName  = szAppName ;

          RegisterClass (&wndclass) ;
          }

     hwnd = CreateWindow (szAppName, szAppName,
                          WS_OVERLAPPEDWINDOW,
                          CW_USEDEFAULT, CW_USEDEFAULT,
                          GetSystemMetrics (SM_CXSCREEN) / 2,
                          GetSystemMetrics (SM_CYSCREEN) / 2,
                          NULL, NULL, hInstance, NULL) ;

     ShowWindow (hwnd, nCmdShow) ;
     UpdateWindow (hwnd) ;
```

(continued)

```
      while (GetMessage (&msg, NULL, 0, 0))
          {
          TranslateMessage (&msg) ;
          DispatchMessage (&msg) ;
          }
      return msg.wParam ;
      }

long FAR PASCAL WndProc (HWND hwnd, WORD message, WORD wParam, LONG lParam)
      {
      static HWND hwndEdit ;

      switch (message)
          {
          case WM_CREATE :
              hwndEdit = CreateWindow ("edit", NULL,
                          WS_CHILD : WS_VISIBLE : WS_HSCROLL : WS_VSCROLL :
                            WS_BORDER : ES_LEFT : ES_MULTILINE :
                            ES_AUTOHSCROLL : ES_AUTOVSCROLL,
                          0, 0, 0, 0,
                          hwnd, 1,
                          ((LPCREATESTRUCT) lParam) -> hInstance, NULL) ;
              return 0 ;

          case WM_SETFOCUS :
              SetFocus (hwndEdit) ;
              return 0 ;

          case WM_SIZE :
              MoveWindow (hwndEdit, 0, 0, LOWORD (lParam),
                                          HIWORD (lParam), TRUE) ;
              return 0 ;

          case WM_COMMAND :
              if (wParam == 1 && HIWORD (lParam) == EN_ERRSPACE)
                  MessageBox (hwnd, "Edit control out of space.",
                              szAppName, MB_OK : MB_ICONSTOP) ;
              return 0 ;

          case WM_DESTROY :
              PostQuitMessage (0) ;
              return 0 ;
          }
      return DefWindowProc (hwnd, message, wParam, lParam) ;
      }
```

POPPAD1.DEF

```
;-----------------------------------------
; POPPAD1.DEF module definition file
;-----------------------------------------

NAME            POPPAD1

DESCRIPTION     'Popup Editor Version 1 (c) Charles Petzold, 1990'
EXETYPE         WINDOWS
STUB            'WINSTUB.EXE'
CODE            PRELOAD MOVEABLE DISCARDABLE
DATA            PRELOAD MOVEABLE MULTIPLE
HEAPSIZE        1024
STACKSIZE       8192
EXPORTS         WndProc
```

POPPAD1 is a multiline editor (without any file I/O just yet) in less than 100 lines of C. As you can see, POPPAD1 itself doesn't do very much. The predefined edit control is doing quite a lot. In this form, the program lets you explore what edit controls can do without any help from a program.

The Edit Class Styles

As noted earlier, you create an edit control using "edit" as the window class in the *CreateWindow* call. The window style is WS_CHILD plus several options. As in static child window controls, the text in edit controls can be either left-justified, right-justified, or centered. You specify this formatting with the window styles ES_LEFT, ES_RIGHT, and ES_CENTER.

By default, an edit control has a single line. You can create a multiline edit control with the window style ES_MULTILINE. For a single-line edit control, you can normally enter text only to the end of the edit control rectangle. To create an edit control that automatically scrolls horizontally, you use the style ES_AUTOHSCROLL. For a multiline edit control, text wordwraps unless you use the ES_AUTOHSCROLL style, in which case you must press the Enter key to start a new line. You can also include vertical scrolling in a multiline edit control by using the style ES_AUTOVSCROLL.

When you include these scrolling styles in multiline edit controls, you might also want to add scroll bars to the edit control. You do so by using the same window style identifiers as for nonchild windows: WS_HSCROLL and WS_VSCROLL.

By default, an edit control has no border. You can add one by using the style WS_BORDER.

When you select text in an edit control, Windows displays it in reverse video. When the edit control loses the input focus, however, the selected text is no longer highlighted. If you want the selection to be highlighted even when the edit control does not have the input focus, you can use the style ES_NOHIDESEL.

When POPPAD1 creates its edit control, the style is given in the *CreateWindow* call as:

```
WS_CHILD | WS_VISIBLE | WS_HSCROLL | WS_VSCROLL |
    WS_BORDER | ES_LEFT | ES_MULTILINE |
    ES_AUTOHSCROLL | ES_AUTOVSCROLL
```

In POPPAD1 the dimensions of the edit control are later defined by a call to *MoveWindow* when *WndProc* receives a WM_SIZE message. The size of the edit control is simply set to the size of the main window:

```
MoveWindow (hwndEdit, 0, 0, LOWORD (lParam),
                          HIWORD (lParam), TRUE) ;
```

For a single-line edit control, the height of the control must accommodate the height of a character. If the edit control has a border (as most do), use 1½ times the height of a character (including external leading).

Edit Control Notification

Edit controls send WM_COMMAND messages to the parent window procedure. The meanings of the *wParam* and *lParam* variables are the same as for button controls:

Parameter	Description
wParam	Child window ID
LOWORD (*lParam*)	Child window handle
HIWORD (*lParam*)	Notification code

The notification codes are shown below:

EN_SETFOCUS	Edit control has gained the input focus
EN_KILLFOCUS	Edit control has lost the input focus
EN_CHANGE	Edit control's contents will change
EN_UPDATE	Edit control's contents have changed
EN_ERRSPACE	Edit control has run out of space
EN_MAXTEXT	Edit control has run out of space on insertion
EN_HSCROLL	Edit control's horizontal scroll bar has been clicked
EN_VSCROLL	Edit control's vertical scroll bar has been clicked

POPPAD1 traps only EN_ERRSPACE notification codes and displays a message box.

The edit control stores text in the local heap of its parent window's program. The contents of an edit control are limited to about 32 KB. You'll note that POPPAD1 reserves only 1 KB of space for its local heap in the module definition file. As we'll see in Chapter 7, this is not a problem. Windows will expand the program's local heap if an edit control needs more space.

Using the Edit Controls

If you use several single-line edit controls on the surface of your main window (as PIFEDIT does), you'll need to use window subclassing to move the input focus from one control to another. You can accomplish this much as COLORS1 does, by intercepting Tab and Shift-Tab keystrokes. (Another example of window subclassing is shown later in this chapter in the HEAD program.) How you handle the Enter key is up to you. You can use it the same way as the Tab key or as a signal to your program that all the edit fields are ready.

If you want to insert text into an edit field, you can do so using *SetWindowText*. Getting text out of an edit control involves *GetWindowTextLength* and *GetWindowText*. We'll see examples of these facilities in our later revisions to the POPPAD1 program.

Messages to an Edit Control

We won't cover all the messages you can send to an edit control using *SendMessage*, because there are quite a few of them, and several will be used in the later POPPAD1 revisions. Here's a broad overview.

These messages let you cut, copy, or clear the current selection. A user selects the text to be acted upon by using the mouse or the Shift key and a cursor key, thus highlighting the selected text in the edit control.

```
SendMessage (hwndEdit, WM_CUT, 0, 0L) ;
SendMessage (hwndEdit, WM_COPY, 0, 0L) ;
SendMessage (hwndEdit, WM_CLEAR, 0, 0L) ;
```

WM_CUT removes the current selection from the edit control and sends it to the clipboard. WM_COPY copies the selection to the clipboard but leaves it intact in the edit control. WM_CLEAR deletes the selection from the edit control without passing it to the clipboard.

You can also insert clipboard text into the edit control at the cursor position:

```
SendMessage (hwndEdit, WM_PASTE, 0, 0L) ;
```

You can obtain the starting and ending positions of the current selection:

```
lSelect = SendMessage (hwndEdit, EM_GETSEL, 0, 0L) ;
```

The low word of *lSelect* has the starting position. The high word has the end position plus 1.

You can select text:

```
SendMessage (hwndEdit, EM_SETSEL, 0, MAKELONG (wBegin, wEnd)) ;
```

You can also replace a current selection with other text:

```
SendMessage (hwndEdit, EM_REPLACESEL, 0, (LONG) lpszString) ;
```

For multiline edit controls, you can obtain the number of lines:

```
nCount = SendMessage (hwndEdit, EM_GETLINECOUNT, 0, 0L) ;
```

For any particular line, you can obtain an offset from the beginning of the edit buffer text:

```
nOffset = SendMessage (hwndEdit, EM_LINEINDEX, wLine, 0L) ;
```

Lines are numbered starting at 0. A *wLine* value of −1 returns the offset of the line containing the cursor. You obtain the length of the line from:

```
nOffset = SendMessage (hwndEdit, EM_LINELENGTH, wLine, 0L) ;
```

and copy the line itself into a buffer using:

```
nLength = SendMessage (hwndEdit, EM_GETLINE, wLine, lpszBuffer) ;
```

THE LISTBOX CLASS

The final predefined child window control I'll discuss in this chapter is the list box. (The combo box is a combination of a list box and an edit field.) A list box is a collection of text strings displayed as a scrollable columnar list within a rectangle. A program can add or remove strings in the list by sending messages to the list box window procedure. The list box control sends WM_COMMAND messages to its parent window when an item in the list is selected. The parent window can then determine which item has been selected.

List boxes are most commonly used in dialog boxes called up by selecting Open from the File menu. The list box displays files in the current directory and can also display other subdirectories and disk drives. List boxes are also used in the CONTROL program for changing colors and in WRITE for selecting fonts. A list box can be either single selection or multiple selection. The latter allows the user to select more than one item from the list box. When a list box has the input focus, it displays a dashed line surrounding an item in the list box. This cursor does not indicate the selected item in the list box. The selected item is indicated by highlighting, which displays the item in reverse video.

In a single-selection list box, the user can select the item that the cursor is positioned on by pressing the Spacebar. The arrow keys move both the cursor and the current selection and can scroll contents of the list box. The Page Up and Page Down keys also scroll the list box by moving the cursor but not the selection. Pressing a letter key moves the cursor and the selection to the first (or next) item that begins with that letter. An item can also be selected by clicking or double-clicking the mouse on the item.

In a multiple-selection list box, the Spacebar toggles the selection state of the item where the cursor is positioned. (If the item is already selected, it is deselected.) The arrow keys deselect all previously selected items and move the cursor and selection just as in single-selection list boxes. However, the Ctrl key and the arrow keys can move the cursor without moving the selection. The Shift key and arrow keys can extend a selection.

Clicking or double-clicking an item in a multiple-selection list box deselects all previously selected items and selects the clicked item. However, clicking an item while pressing the Shift key toggles the selection state of the item without changing the selection state of any other item.

List Box Styles

You create a list box child window control with *CreateWindow* using "listbox" as the window class and WS_CHILD as the window style. However, this default list box style does not send WM_COMMAND messages to its parent, meaning that a program would have to interrogate the list box (via messages to the list box controls) regarding the selection of items within the list box. Therefore, list box controls almost always include the list box style identifier LBS_NOTIFY, which allows the parent window to receive WM_COMMAND messages from the list box. If you want the list box control to sort the items in the list box, you can also use LBS_SORT, another common style.

By default, list boxes are single selection. Multiple-selection list boxes are relatively rare. If you want to create one, you use the style LBS_MULTIPLESEL.

Normally, a list box updates itself when a new item is added to the scroll box list. You can prevent this by including the style LBS_NOREDRAW. You will probably not want to use this style, however. Instead, you can temporarily prevent repainting of a list box control by using the WM_SETREDRAW message that I'll describe a little later.

By default, the list box window procedure displays only the list of items without any border around it. You can add a border with the window style identifier WS_BORDER. And to add a vertical scroll bar for scrolling through the list with the mouse, you use the window style identifier WS_VSCROLL.

WINDOWS.H defines a list box style called LBS_STANDARD that includes the most commonly used styles. It is defined as:

```
(LBS_NOTIFY ¦ LBS_SORT ¦ WS_VSCROLL ¦ WS_BORDER)
```

You can also use the WS_SIZEBOX and WS_CAPTION identifiers, but these will allow the user to resize the list box and to move it around its parent's client area.

The width of a list box should accommodate the width of the longest string plus the width of the scroll bar. You can get the width of the vertical scroll bar using:

```
GetSystemMetrics (SM_CXVSCROLL) ;
```

You can calculate the height of the list box by multiplying the height of a character by the number of items you want to appear in view. A list box does not use *tmExternalLeading* when spacing lines of text.

Putting Strings in the List Box

After you've created the list box, the next step is to put text strings in it. You do this by sending messages to the list box window procedure using the *SendMessage* call. The text strings are generally referenced by an index number that starts at 0 for the topmost item. In the examples that follow, *hwndList* is the handle to the child window list box control, and *wIndex* is the index value.

In cases where you pass a text string in the *SendMessage* call, the *lParam* parameter is a far pointer to a null-terminated string. To avoid error messages during compilation, cast this pointer to a LONG. Note that when you cast a near pointer to a LONG, the C compiler will first cast the near pointer to a far pointer.

In most of these examples, the *SendMessage* call returns LB_ERRSPACE (defined as −2) if the window procedure runs out of available memory space to store the contents of the list box. *SendMessage* returns LB_ERR (−1) if an error occurs for other reasons and LB_OKAY (0) if the operation is successful. You can test *SendMessage* for a nonzero value to detect either of the two errors. The list box allocates global memory (outside your program's data segment) for the list box contents.

If you use the LBS_SORT style (or if you are placing strings in the list box in the order that you want them to appear), then the easiest way to fill up a list box is with the LB-_ADDSTRING message:

```
SendMessage (hwndList, LB_ADDSTRING, 0, (LONG) szString) ;
```

If you do not use LBS_SORT, you can insert strings into your list box by specifying an index value with LB_INSERTSTRING:

```
SendMessage (hwndList, LB_INSERTSTRING, wIndex, (LONG) szString) ;
```

For instance, if *wIndex* is equal to 4, *szString* becomes the new string with an index value of 4—the fifth string from the top because counting starts at 0. Any strings below this point are pushed down. A *wIndex* value of −1 adds the string to the bottom. You can use LB_INSERTSTRING with list boxes that have the LBS_SORT style, but the list box contents will not be re-sorted. (You can also insert strings into a list box using the LB_DIR message, which is discussed in detail toward the end of this chapter.)

You can delete a string from the list box by specifying the index value with the LB_DELETESTRING message:

```
SendMessage (hwndList, LB_DELETESTRING, wIndex, 0L) ;
```

You can clear out the list box using LB_RESETCONTENT:

```
SendMessage (hwndList, LB_RESETCONTENT, 0, 0L) ;
```

The list box window procedure updates the display when an item is added to or deleted from the list box. If you have a number of strings to add or delete, you may want to temporarily inhibit this action by turning off the control's redraw flag:

```
SendMessage (hwndList, WM_SETREDRAW, FALSE, OL) ;
```

After you've finished, you can turn the redraw flag back on:

```
SendMessage (hwndList, WM_SETREDRAW, TRUE, OL) ;
```

A list box created with the LBS_NOREDRAW style begins with the redraw flag turned off.

Selecting and Extracting Entries

The *SendMessage* calls that carry out the tasks shown below usually return a value. If an error occurs, this value is set to LB_ERR (defined as −1). Note that the return value from *SendMessage* is normally a signed long (LONG), but the values are unsigned integers (WORD), so some casting is necessary.

After you've put some items into a list box, you can find out how many items are in the list box:

```
nCount = (WORD) SendMessage (hwndList, LB_GETCOUNT, 0, OL) ;
```

Some of the other calls are different for single-selection and multiple-selection list boxes. Let's first look at single-selection list boxes.

Normally, you'll let a user select from a list box. But if you want to highlight a default selection, you can use:

```
SendMessage (hwndList, LB_SETCURSEL, nIndex, OL) ;
```

Setting *lParam* to −1 in this call deselects all items.

You can also select an item based on its initial characters:

```
nIndex = (WORD) SendMessage (hwndList, LB_SELECTSTRING, wIndex,
                             (LONG) szSearchString) ;
```

The *wIndex* given as the *wParam* parameter to the *SendMessage* call is the index following which the search begins for an item with initial characters that match *szSearchString*. A *wIndex* value of −1 starts the search from the top. *SendMessage* returns the index of the selected item, or LB_ERR if no initial characters match *szSearchString*.

When you get a WM_COMMAND message from the list box (or at any other time), you can determine the index of the current selection using LB_GETCURSEL:

```
nIndex = (WORD) SendMessage (hwndList, LB_GETCURSEL, 0, OL) ;
```

The *nIndex* value returned from the call is LB_ERR if no item is selected.

You can determine the length of any string in the list box:

```
nLength = (WORD) SendMessage (hwndList, LB_GETTEXTLEN, nIndex, OL) ;
```

247

and copy the item into the text buffer:

```
nLength = (WORD) SendMessage (hwndList, LB_GETTEXT, nIndex,
                              (LONG) szBuffer) ;
```

In both cases, the *nLength* value returned from the call is the length of the string. The *szBuffer* array must be large enough for the length of the string and a terminating NULL. You may want to use LB_GETTEXTLEN to first allocate some local memory to hold the string (which you'll learn how to do in Chapter 8).

For a multiple-selection list box, you cannot use LB_SETCURSEL, LB_GETCURSEL, or LB_SELECTSTRING. Instead, you use LB_SETSEL to set the selection state of a particular item without affecting other items that may also be selected:

```
SendMessage (hwndList, LB_SETSEL, wParam, (LONG) wIndex) ;
```

The *wParam* parameter is nonzero to select and highlight the item and 0 to deselect it. If the *lParam* parameter is –1, all items are either selected or deselected. You can also determine the selection state of a particular item using:

```
wSelect = (WORD) SendMessage (hwndList, LB_GETSEL, wIndex, 0L) ;
```

where *wSelect* is set to nonzero if the item indexed by *wIndex* is selected and 0 if it is not.

Receiving Messages from List Boxes

When a user clicks on a list box with the mouse, the list box receives the input focus. A parent window can give the input focus to a list box control by using:

```
SetFocus (hwndList) ;
```

When a list box has the input focus, the cursor movement keys, letter keys, and Spacebar can also be used to select items from the list box.

A list box control sends WM_COMMAND messages to its parent. The meanings of the *wParam* and *lParam* variables are the same as for the button and edit controls:

wParam	Child window ID
LOWORD (*lParam*)	Child window handle
HIWORD (*lParam*)	Notification code

The notification codes and their values are as follows:

LBN_ERRSPACE	−2
LBN_SELCHANGE	1
LBN_DBLCLK	2
LBN_SELCANCEL	3
LBN_SETFOCUS	4
LBN_KILLFOCUS	5

The list box control sends the parent window LBN_SELCHANGE and LBN_DBLCLK codes only if the list box window style includes LBS_NOTIFY.

The LBN_ERRSPACE code indicates that the list box control has run out of space. The LBN_SELCHANGE code indicates that the current selection has changed; these messages occur as the user moves the highlight through the list box, toggles the selection state with the Spacebar, or clicks an item with the mouse. The LBN_DBLCLK code indicates that a list box item has been double-clicked with the mouse. (The notification code values for LBN_SELCHANGE and LBN_DBLCLK refer to the number of mouse clicks.)

Depending on your application, you may want to use either LBN_SELCHANGE or LBN_DBLCLK messages or both. Your program will get many LBN_SELCHANGE messages, but LBN_DBLCLK messages occur only when the user double-clicks with the mouse. If your program uses double-clicks, you'll need to provide a keyboard interface that duplicates LBN_DBLCLK.

A Simple List Box Application

Now that you know how to create a list box, fill it with text items, receive messages from the list box, and extract strings, it's time to program an application. The ENVIRON program, shown in Figure 6-6, uses a list box in its client area to display the name of your current MS-DOS environment variables (such as PATH, COMSPEC, and PROMPT). As you select a variable, the name and the environment string are displayed across the top of the client area.

ENVIRON.MAK

```
#----------------------
# ENVIRON.MAK make file
#----------------------

environ.exe : environ.obj environ.def
    link environ, /align:16, NUL, /nod slibcew libw, environ
    rc environ.exe

environ.obj : environ.c
    cl -c -Gsw -Ow -W2 -Zp environ.c
```

ENVIRON.C

```
/*-----------------------------------------
   ENVIRON.C -- Environment List Box
               (c) Charles Petzold, 1990
   -----------------------------------------*/
```

Figure 6-6. *The ENVIRON program.*

(continued)

```
#include <windows.h>
#include <stdlib.h>
#include <string.h>
#define  MAXENV  4096

long FAR PASCAL WndProc (HWND, WORD, WORD, LONG) ;

int PASCAL WinMain (HANDLE hInstance, HANDLE hPrevInstance,
                    LPSTR lpszCmdLine, int nCmdShow)
    {
    static char szAppName[] = "Environ" ;
    HWND        hwnd ;
    MSG         msg ;
    WNDCLASS    wndclass ;

    if (!hPrevInstance)
        {
        wndclass.style         = CS_HREDRAW | CS_VREDRAW ;
        wndclass.lpfnWndProc   = WndProc ;
        wndclass.cbClsExtra    = 0 ;
        wndclass.cbWndExtra    = 0 ;
        wndclass.hInstance     = hInstance ;
        wndclass.hIcon         = LoadIcon (NULL, IDI_APPLICATION) ;
        wndclass.hCursor       = LoadCursor (NULL, IDC_ARROW) ;
        wndclass.hbrBackground = COLOR_WINDOW + 1 ;
        wndclass.lpszMenuName  = NULL ;
        wndclass.lpszClassName = szAppName ;

        RegisterClass (&wndclass) ;
        }

    hwnd = CreateWindow (szAppName, "Environment List Box",
                        WS_OVERLAPPEDWINDOW,
                        CW_USEDEFAULT, CW_USEDEFAULT,
                        CW_USEDEFAULT, CW_USEDEFAULT,
                        NULL, NULL, hInstance, NULL) ;

    ShowWindow (hwnd, nCmdShow) ;
    UpdateWindow (hwnd) ;

    while (GetMessage (&msg, NULL, 0, 0))
        {
        TranslateMessage (&msg) ;
        DispatchMessage (&msg) ;
        }
    return msg.wParam ;
    }
```

(continued)

```
long FAR PASCAL WndProc (HWND hwnd, WORD message, WORD wParam, LONG lParam)
    {
    static char szBuffer [MAXENV + 1] ;
    static HWND hwndList, hwndText ;
    HDC        hdc ;
    TEXTMETRIC tm ;
    WORD       n ;

    switch (message)
        {
        case WM_CREATE :
            hdc = GetDC (hwnd) ;
            GetTextMetrics (hdc, &tm) ;
            ReleaseDC (hwnd, hdc) ;

            hwndList = CreateWindow ("listbox", NULL,
                        WS_CHILD | WS_VISIBLE | LBS_STANDARD,
                        tm.tmAveCharWidth, tm.tmHeight * 3,
                        tm.tmAveCharWidth * 16 +
                            GetSystemMetrics (SM_CXVSCROLL),
                        tm.tmHeight * 5,
                        hwnd, 1,
                        GetWindowWord (hwnd, GWW_HINSTANCE), NULL) ;

            hwndText = CreateWindow ("static", NULL,
                        WS_CHILD | WS_VISIBLE | SS_LEFT,
                        tm.tmAveCharWidth,              tm.tmHeight,
                        tm.tmAveCharWidth * MAXENV, tm.tmHeight,
                        hwnd, 2,
                        GetWindowWord (hwnd, GWW_HINSTANCE), NULL) ;

            for (n = 0 ; environ[n] ; n++)
                {
                if (strlen (environ [n]) > MAXENV)
                    continue ;
                *strchr (strcpy (szBuffer, environ [n]), '=') = '\0' ;
                SendMessage (hwndList, LB_ADDSTRING, 0,
                            (LONG) (LPSTR) szBuffer) ;
                }
            return 0 ;

        case WM_SETFOCUS :
            SetFocus (hwndList) ;
            return 0 ;
```

(continued)

```
        case WM_COMMAND :
             if (wParam == 1 && HIWORD (lParam) == LBN_SELCHANGE)
                  {
                  n = (WORD) SendMessage (hwndList, LB_GETCURSEL, 0, 0L) ;
                  n = (WORD) SendMessage (hwndList, LB_GETTEXT, n,
                                                (LONG) (LPSTR) szBuffer) ;

                  strcpy (szBuffer + n + 1, getenv (szBuffer)) ;
                  *(szBuffer + n) = '=' ;

                  SetWindowText (hwndText, szBuffer) ;
                  }
             return 0 ;

        case WM_DESTROY :
             PostQuitMessage (0) ;
             return 0 ;
        }
    return DefWindowProc (hwnd, message, wParam, lParam) ;
    }
```

ENVIRON.DEF

```
;-------------------------------------
; ENVIRON.DEF module definition file
;-------------------------------------

NAME            ENVIRON

DESCRIPTION     'Environment List Box Program (c) Charles Petzold, 1990'
EXETYPE         WINDOWS
STUB            'WINSTUB.EXE'
CODE            PRELOAD MOVEABLE DISCARDABLE
DATA            PRELOAD MOVEABLE MULTIPLE
HEAPSIZE        1024
STACKSIZE       8192
EXPORTS         WndProc
```

ENVIRON creates two child windows: a list box with the style LBS_STANDARD and a static window with the style SS_LEFT (left-justified text). ENVIRON uses the *environ* variable (declared external in STDLIB.H) to obtain the list of environment strings, and it uses the message LB_ADDSTRING to direct the list box window procedure to place each string in the list box.

When you run ENVIRON, you can select an environment variable using the mouse or the keyboard. Each time you change the selection, the list box sends a WM_COMMAND message to the parent window, which is *WndProc*. When *WndProc* receives a WM_COM-MAND message, it checks to see if *wParam* is 1 (the child ID of the list box) and if the high word of *lParam* (the notification code) is equal to LBN_SELCHANGE. If so, it obtains the index of the selection using the LB_GETCURSEL message and the text itself—the environment variable name—using LB_GETTEXT. ENVIRON uses the C function *getenv* to obtain the environment string corresponding to that variable and *SetWindowText* to pass this string to the static child window control, which displays the text.

Note that ENVIRON cannot use the index returned from LB_GETCURSEL to index the *environ* variable and obtain the environment string. Because the list box has an LBS_SORT style (included in LBS_STANDARD), the indices no longer match.

Listing Files

I've been saving the best for last: LB_DIR, the most powerful list box message. This fills the list box with a file directory list, optionally including subdirectories and valid disk drives:

```
SendMessage (hwndList, LB_DIR, wAttr, (LONG) lpszFileSpec) ;
```

Using file attribute codes

The *wAttr* parameter is a file attribute code. The least significant byte is the normal file attribute code when making MS-DOS function calls:

wAttr	*Attribute*
0x0000	Normal file
0x0001	Read-only file
0x0002	Hidden file
0x0004	System file
0x0010	Subdirectory
0x0020	File with archive bit set

The high byte provides some additional control over the items desired:

wAttr	*Option*
0x4000	Include drive letters
0x8000	Exclusive search only

When the *wAttr* value of the LB_DIR message is 0x0000, the list box lists normal files, read-only files, and files with the archive bit set. This is consistent with the logic used by MS-DOS function calls to find files. When the value is 0x0010, the list includes child subdirectories in addition to these files; this list is the equivalent of that displayed by the Directory command or by Windows' File Manager. A value of 0x4010 expands the 0x0010 list to include all valid drives; for many Windows programs, this is the list in the dialog box called up by selecting Open from the program's File menu. To list all files, child subdirectories, and drives, you set the *wAttr* value to 0x4037.

Setting the topmost bit of *wAttr* lists the files with the indicated flag while excluding normal files. For a Windows file backup program, for instance, you might want to list only files that have been modified since the last backup. Such files have their archive bits set, so you would use 0x8020. A value of 0x8010 lists only subdirectories; 0xC000, only valid disk drives; and 0xC010, subdirectories and valid disk drives but no files.

Ordering file lists

The *lParam* parameter is a far pointer to a file specification string such as "*.*". This file specification does not affect the subdirectories that the list box includes.

You'll want to use the LBS_SORT message for list boxes with file lists. The list box will first list files satisfying the file specification and then (optionally) list valid disk drives in the form:

    [-A-]

and (also optionally) subdirectory names. The first subdirectory listing will take the form:

    [..]

This "double-dot" subdirectory entry lets the user back up one level toward the root directory. (The entry will not appear if you're listing files in the root directory.) Finally, the specific subdirectory names are listed in the form:

    [SUBDIR]

If you do not use LBS_SORT, the filenames and subdirectory names are intermixed and the drive letters appear at the bottom of the list box.

A *head* for Windows

A well-known UNIX utility called *head* displays the beginning lines of a file. Let's use a list box to write a similar program for Windows. HEAD, shown in Figure 6-7, lists all files and child subdirectories in the list box. You can choose a file to display by double-clicking on the filename with the mouse or by pressing the Enter key when the filename is selected. You can also change the subdirectory using either of these methods. The program displays up to 2 KB of the beginning of the file in the right side of the client area of HEAD's window.

HEAD.MAK

```
#-------------------
# HEAD.MAK make file
#-------------------

head.exe : head.obj head.def
    link head, /align:16, NUL, /nod slibcew libw, head
    rc head.exe

head.obj : head.c
    cl -c -Gsw -Ow -W2 -Zp head.c
```

HEAD.C

```
/*-----------------------------------------------
   HEAD.C -- Displays Beginning (Head) of File
             (c) Charles Petzold, 1990
   -----------------------------------------------*/

#include <windows.h>
#include <io.h>
#include <string.h>
#include <direct.h>

#define  MAXPATH    100
#define  MAXREAD     2048

long FAR PASCAL WndProc  (HWND, WORD, WORD, LONG) ;
long FAR PASCAL ListProc (HWND, WORD, WORD, LONG) ;

char    sReadBuffer [MAXREAD] ;
FARPROC lpfnOldList ;

int PASCAL WinMain (HANDLE hInstance, HANDLE hPrevInstance,
                    LPSTR lpszCmdLine, int nCmdShow)
    {
    static char szAppName [] = "Head" ;
    HWND        hwnd ;
    MSG         msg ;
    WNDCLASS    wndclass ;

    if (!hPrevInstance)
        {
        wndclass.style          = CS_HREDRAW : CS_VREDRAW ;
        wndclass.lpfnWndProc    = WndProc ;
```

Figure 6-7. *The HEAD program.*   *(continued)*

```
        wndclass.cbClsExtra    = 0 ;
        wndclass.cbWndExtra    = 0 ;
        wndclass.hInstance     = hInstance ;
        wndclass.hIcon         = LoadIcon (NULL, IDI_APPLICATION) ;
        wndclass.hCursor       = LoadCursor (NULL, IDC_ARROW) ;
        wndclass.hbrBackground = COLOR_WINDOW + 1 ;
        wndclass.lpszMenuName  = NULL ;
        wndclass.lpszClassName = szAppName ;

        RegisterClass (&wndclass) ;
        }

    hwnd = CreateWindow (szAppName, "File Head",
                    WS_OVERLAPPEDWINDOW : WS_CLIPCHILDREN,
                    CW_USEDEFAULT, CW_USEDEFAULT,
                    CW_USEDEFAULT, CW_USEDEFAULT,
                    NULL, NULL, hInstance, NULL) ;

    ShowWindow (hwnd, nCmdShow) ;
    UpdateWindow (hwnd) ;

    while (GetMessage (&msg, NULL, 0, 0))
        {
        TranslateMessage (&msg) ;
        DispatchMessage (&msg) ;
        }
    return msg.wParam ;
    }

long FAR PASCAL WndProc (HWND hwnd, WORD message, WORD wParam, LONG lParam)
    {
    static BOOL      bValidFile ;
    static char      szFile [16] ;
    static HWND      hwndList, hwndText ;
    static OFSTRUCT  ofs ;
    static RECT      rect ;
    char             szBuffer [MAXPATH + 1] ;
    HDC              hdc ;
    int              iHandle, i, iCount ;
    PAINTSTRUCT      ps ;
    TEXTMETRIC       tm ;

    switch (message)
        {
        case WM_CREATE :
            hdc = GetDC (hwnd) ;
            SelectObject (hdc, GetStockObject (SYSTEM_FIXED_FONT)) ;
            GetTextMetrics (hdc, &tm) ;
            ReleaseDC (hwnd, hdc) ;
```

(continued)

```
                    rect.left = 20 * tm.tmAveCharWidth ;
                    rect.top  =  3 * tm.tmHeight ;

                    hwndList = CreateWindow ("listbox", NULL,
                                WS_CHILDWINDOW | WS_VISIBLE | LBS_STANDARD,
                                tm.tmAveCharWidth, tm.tmHeight * 3,
                                tm.tmAveCharWidth * 13 +
                                     GetSystemMetrics (SM_CXVSCROLL),
                                tm.tmHeight * 10,
                                hwnd, 1,
                                GetWindowWord (hwnd, GWW_HINSTANCE), NULL) ;

                    hwndText = CreateWindow ("static", getcwd (szBuffer, MAXPATH),
                                WS_CHILDWINDOW | WS_VISIBLE | SS_LEFT,
                                tm.tmAveCharWidth,            tm.tmHeight,
                                tm.tmAveCharWidth * MAXPATH, tm.tmHeight,
                                hwnd, 2,
                                GetWindowWord (hwnd, GWW_HINSTANCE), NULL) ;

                    lpfnOldList = (FARPROC) GetWindowLong (hwndList, GWL_WNDPROC) ;

                    SetWindowLong (hwndList, GWL_WNDPROC,
                         (LONG) MakeProcInstance ((FARPROC) ListProc,
                                   GetWindowWord (hwnd, GWW_HINSTANCE))) ;

                    SendMessage (hwndList, LB_DIR, 0x37, (LONG) (LPSTR) "*.*") ;
                    return 0 ;

               case WM_SIZE :
                    rect.right  = LOWORD (lParam) ;
                    rect.bottom = HIWORD (lParam) ;
                    return 0 ;

               case WM_SETFOCUS :
                    SetFocus (hwndList) ;
                    return 0 ;

               case WM_COMMAND :
                    if (wParam == 1 && HIWORD (lParam) == LBN_DBLCLK)
                         {
                         if (LB_ERR == (i = (WORD) SendMessage (hwndList,
                                                  LB_GETCURSEL, 0, 0L)))
                              break ;

                         SendMessage (hwndList, LB_GETTEXT, i,
                                          (LONG) (char far *) szBuffer) ;
```

(continued)

```
                    if (-1 != OpenFile (szBuffer, &ofs, OF_EXIST : OF_READ))
                         {
                         bValidFile = TRUE ;
                         strcpy (szFile, szBuffer) ;
                         getcwd (szBuffer, MAXPATH) ;
                         if (szBuffer [strlen (szBuffer) - 1] != '\\')
                              strcat (szBuffer, "\\") ;
                         SetWindowText (hwndText, strcat (szBuffer, szFile)) ;
                         }
                    else
                         {
                         bValidFile = FALSE ;
                         szBuffer [strlen (szBuffer) - 1] = '\0' ;
                         chdir (szBuffer + 1) ;
                         getcwd (szBuffer, MAXPATH) ;
                         SetWindowText (hwndText, szBuffer) ;
                         SendMessage (hwndList, LB_RESETCONTENT, 0, 0L) ;
                         SendMessage (hwndList, LB_DIR, 0x37,
                                   (LONG) (LPSTR) "*.*") ;
                         }
                    InvalidateRect (hwnd, NULL, TRUE) ;
                    }
          return 0 ;

     case WM_PAINT :
          hdc = BeginPaint (hwnd, &ps) ;
          SelectObject (hdc, GetStockObject (SYSTEM_FIXED_FONT)) ;
          SetTextColor (hdc, GetSysColor (COLOR_WINDOWTEXT)) ;
          SetBkColor   (hdc, GetSysColor (COLOR_WINDOW)) ;

          if (bValidFile && -1 != (iHandle =
                    OpenFile (szFile, &ofs, OF_REOPEN : OF_READ)))
                {
                i = read (iHandle, sReadBuffer, MAXREAD) ;
                close (iHandle) ;
                DrawText (hdc, sReadBuffer, i, &rect, DT_WORDBREAK :
                         DT_EXPANDTABS : DT_NOCLIP : DT_NOPREFIX) ;
                }
          else
                bValidFile = FALSE ;

          EndPaint (hwnd, &ps) ;
          return 0 ;

     case WM_DESTROY :
          PostQuitMessage (0) ;
          return 0 ;
     }
```

(continued)

```
        return DefWindowProc (hwnd, message, wParam, lParam) ;
        }

long FAR PASCAL ListProc (HWND hwnd, WORD message, WORD wParam, LONG lParam)
        {
        if (message == WM_KEYDOWN && wParam == VK_RETURN)

                SendMessage (GetParent (hwnd), WM_COMMAND, 1,
                                MAKELONG (hwnd, LBN_DBLCLK)) ;

        return CallWindowProc (lpfnOldList, hwnd, message, wParam, lParam) ;
        }
```

HEAD.DEF

```
;-----------------------------------
; HEAD.DEF module definition file
;-----------------------------------

NAME            HEAD

DESCRIPTION     'File Head Program (c) Charles Petzold, 1990'
EXETYPE         WINDOWS
STUB            'WINSTUB.EXE'
CODE            PRELOAD MOVEABLE DISCARDABLE
DATA            PRELOAD MOVEABLE MULTIPLE
HEAPSIZE        1024
STACKSIZE       8192
EXPORTS         WndProc
                ListProc
```

In ENVIRON, when we selected an environment variable—either with a mouse click or with the keyboard—the program displayed an environment string. If we used this select-display approach in HEAD, however, the program would be too slow because it would continually need to open and close files as you moved the selection through the list box. Instead, HEAD requires that the file or subdirectory be double-clicked. This presents a bit of a problem because list box controls have no automatic keyboard interface that corresponds to a mouse double-click. As we know, we shouldn't write Windows programs that require a mouse.

The solution? Window subclassing, of course. The list box subclass function in HEAD is called *ListProc*. It simply looks for a WM_KEYDOWN message with *wParam* equal to VK_RETURN and sends a WM_COMMAND message with an LBN_DBLCLK notification code back to the parent. The WM_COMMAND processing in *WndProc* uses the Windows function *OpenFile* to check for the selection from the list. If OpenFile returns an error, the selection is not a file, so it's probably a subdirectory. HEAD then uses *chdir* to change the subdirectory. It sends a LB_RESETCONTENT message to the list box to clear out the contents and a LB_DIR message to fill the list box with files from the new subdirectory.

The WM_PAINT message processing in *WndProc* opens the file using the Windows *OpenFile* function. This returns an MS-DOS handle to the file that can be passed to the normal C functions *read* and *close*. The contents of the file are displayed using *DrawText*.

2 KB of Wasted Space

HEAD includes a 2-KB array called *sReadBuffer* that is needed only briefly, when the contents of the file are read and passed to *DrawText*. But this array remains in the program's data segment during the entire time this program is running. Wouldn't it make more sense to allocate that memory before the read call and free it up after *DrawText*?

Yes, it would. For that reason we can no longer avoid the subject of Windows memory management. It's not an easy subject, but let's begin.

SECTION III
USING RESOURCES

Chapter 7

Memory Management

Multitasking without memory management is like having a party in a closet: You may be able to accommodate some of the earlier arrivals, but once everybody starts mingling, some toes are going to get smashed.

Memory management has always been one of the most remarkable aspects of Windows. Even Windows 1 included a sophisticated memory management scheme that implemented in software some of the memory management features you might expect to find in a protected-mode operating system. Here are some examples of Windows 1 memory management:

- When Windows runs multiple instances of the same program, it uses the same code segments and the same resources for each instance. (Resources include icons, cursors, menu templates, and dialog box templates, all of which are covered in the next three chapters.) In most cases, Windows requires only that data segments be unique for each instance of a program.

- Much of the memory allocated within Windows is moveable, including (in most cases) the memory allocated for a program's code segments, data segments, and resources.

- Code segments and resources are often "demand-loaded": Windows does not load them into memory until a program specifically needs them.

- Code segments and resources are often discardable: When Windows needs to free some memory, it discards the segments from memory and later reloads them from the program's .EXE file as the program requires.

These memory management features allowed Windows 1 to run several large programs in a memory space that might not be large enough for even one of the programs under a less ambitious memory management scheme. The problem is that this memory management scheme requires that Windows often reload code segments and resources from the hard disk, hurting program performance. For this reason, support of the Expanded Memory Specification (EMS) 4.0 was added to Windows 2, and protected-mode support was added to Windows 3.

Windows 3 can run in three distinct modes:

- On a machine based around the Intel 8086 processor (or an 80286 or 80386 processor with less than 1 MB of memory), Windows 3 runs in "real mode." This is essentially compatible with the memory configuration of Windows 2.1. Windows and its applications occupy an upper area of the 640 KB of conventional memory above MS-DOS and any device drivers and RAM-resident programs that may be loaded.

     In this mode, Windows can take advantage of any expanded memory under the Lotus-Intel-Microsoft Expanded Memory Specification 4.0 (LIM EMS 4.0). This configuration requires an EMS memory board and an EMS 4 device driver.

- On a machine based around the Intel 80286 processor with at least 1 MB of memory (or an 80386 processor with less than 2 MB of memory), Windows 3 runs in "standard mode." This is 286-compatible protected mode. Windows can use up to 16 MB of conventional memory and extended memory.

- On a machine based around the Intel 80386 processor with at least 2 MB of memory, Windows 3 runs in "386 enhanced mode." This is essentially standard mode with two additional features: Windows uses the paging registers of the 386 processor to implement virtual memory. The 386 pages are 4 KB in length. Windows can swap pages to disk and reload them when necessary. (This is the only form of virtual memory supported for Windows applications.) The page swapping is something you normally don't have to think about when coding for Windows. The second feature of 386 enhanced mode uses the Virtual-86 mode of the 386 processor to support multiple virtual DOS machines. This does not impact Windows programming.

You can override the default configuration by running Windows from the command line with a /R (real mode), /2 (standard mode), or /3 (386 enhanced mode) parameter. A Windows program can obtain information about the mode in which it is running by calling *GetWinFlags*.

Much of this chapter discusses the real mode memory configuration because this is the least common denominator of all the modes in which Windows can run. (Another reason for this is that the techniques Windows uses to manage memory in real mode are quite interesting!) If you initially feel a little queasy when thinking about Windows moving your program around in memory in real mode, that's good. It means that you're already aware that this is not an easy feat. You must keep this fact in mind in order to write programs that run without problems. You must cooperate with Windows' memory management. That's what we'll look at in this chapter.

SEGMENTED MEMORY, INTEL STYLE

Windows organizes memory in "segments"—so before we proceed, let's quickly review the segmented memory architecture of the Intel 8086 family of microprocessors. This family includes the 8088 found in the PC and PC/XT, the 8086 and the 186 found in some compatibles, the 286 found in the PC/AT, and the 386 and 486.

When these processors run in real mode, a memory address consists of two parts, a 16-bit segment address and a 16-bit offset address. The 16-bit segment address is shifted 4 bits to the left and added to the offset address. The resultant 20-bit physical address can access 1 MB of data:

16-bit offset address	xxxxxxxxxxxxxxxx
16-bit segment address	+ xxxxxxxxxxxxxxxx0000
20-bit physical address	xxxxxxxxxxxxxxxxxxxx

Four internal registers of the microprocessor hold segment addresses. These segment registers are called CS (code segment), DS (data segment), SS (stack segment), and ES (extra segment). The 386 and 486 have two additional segment registers: FS and GS.

Software for the 8086 family runs most efficiently when the segment addresses are held constant and all addressing is done by varying the offset addresses. The offset addresses generated by the microprocessor include the instruction pointer (IP), which accesses code in combination with the CS register; the stack pointer (SP) and base pointer (BP), which access the stack in combination with the SS register; and the BX (base), SI (source index), and DI (destination index) registers, which access data, most often in combination with the DS or ES register. An address that uses only the offset address with an implied segment address (the current segment address) is called a "near pointer" or sometimes a "short pointer." An address that uses both the segment and offset addresses is called a "far pointer" or a "long pointer."

For any particular segment address, the offset address can vary within a 64-KB range, from 0000H through FFFFH. A block of memory that is based on a particular segment address is called (appropriately enough) a "segment." People used to think of segments as 64-KB blocks of memory, but this definition is becoming less common. Now we say that segments can be any size up to 64 KB. Sometimes the size of a segment (or the size of an area of memory larger than 64 KB) is given in terms of "paragraphs." A paragraph is 16 bytes. Memory allocated for a segment is often a multiple of 16 bytes, because a segment must begin on a 16-byte boundary of physical memory. (When the segment register is shifted left 4 bits, the bottom 4 bits are 0.)

When the 286, 386, and 486 processors run in 286-compatible protected mode, the segment does not refer to a physical memory address. Instead, the segment is an offset into a "descriptor table" that provides a 24-bit base address in physical memory. The offset address is then added to this base address to generate a 24-bit physical address that can access up to 16 megabytes of memory.

The use of segments is central to Windows' memory organization. The entire memory space controlled by Windows is divided into segments of various lengths. Some of these segments contain code, and others contain data.

MEMORY ORGANIZATION IN WINDOWS

The entire memory area that Windows controls is called "global memory" or the "global heap." This area begins at the location where MS-DOS first loads Windows into memory and ends at the top of available memory, which most often is the top of physical memory. (In C programming, the word *global* usually refers to variables or functions in one source code file that can be referenced from functions in another source code file of the same program. That is not the meaning of global here. In this discussion of Windows' memory organization, the word *global* instead means "everything.") Every block of memory allocated from the global heap is a segment. Global memory not currently allocated is called "free memory."

A Windows program can have one or more code segments and one or more data segments. (The example programs shown in this book have only one of each.) When Windows loads a program into memory, it allocates at least one segment from the global heap for code and one segment for data. When the program begins to execute, the microprocessor's CS register is set to the segment address of the code segment that contains the entry point of the program. The DS and SS registers are set to the segment address of the program's automatic, or default, data segment, which is the data segment that contains the stack. (The combination of the data and the stack into one segment referenced by both DS and SS is normal for C compilers. DS is used to reference data declared as static; SS is used to reference data on the stack, which includes local nonstatic data and arguments passed to functions. This approach allows near pointers to be used for function parameters. The function doesn't have to know whether it's dealing with static data or stack data. Problems related to unequal DS and SS segment registers are discussed in Chapter 19, "Dynamic Link Libraries.")

When loading a program, Windows also allocates two other segments from the global heap for program overhead. One of these segments contains the header portion of the program's .EXE file. This segment is used for all instances of a program, so it is allocated only for the first instance. The other segment contains information unique to each instance, such as the program's command-line string and the program's current subdirectory. When a program loads resources (such as icons, cursors, or menu templates) into memory, each resource gets its own segment in the global heap. A program may itself also allocate some memory from the global heap.

If a program has only one code segment, then any calls it makes to functions within the program are compiled as near calls. The CS code segment register remains the same. However, when a program calls a Windows function, the Windows function is in a different code segment. This situation requires that the program generate a far call, which is the reason that all Windows functions (and all functions within your program that are called by Windows) must be declared as far.

A Windows program that has one data segment can use near pointers to access memory within that data segment. However, when a Windows program passes a pointer to a Windows function, the pointer must be a far (or long) pointer; otherwise, the code that contains the Windows function will use its own data segment. The far pointer is required for the Windows function to access the data within your program's data segment.

Fixed and Moveable Segments

Every segment in Windows' total memory space is marked with certain attributes that tell Windows how to manage the segment. First and foremost, segments are marked as either "fixed" or "moveable." Windows can move moveable segments in memory if necessary to make room for other memory allocations. When Windows moves a segment in memory, all existing near pointers to that segment continue to be valid, because near pointers reference an offset from the beginning of a segment. However, far pointers become invalid when the segment they reference is moved. A fixed segment cannot be moved in memory. Segments must be marked as fixed if Windows is incapable of modifying an existing far pointer to the segment.

In protected mode, all program segments are moveable because Windows can move the segment without changing the segment address. Windows need only change the physical base address in the descriptor table.

Most segments—including the segments allocated for your program's code and data—are moveable, but some exceptions exist. Whenever Windows gives your program a far pointer, the pointer references a fixed data segment. For instance, when your Windows program begins executing, Windows passes a parameter to *WinMain* that we call *lpszCmdLine.* This is a far pointer to an area of memory that contains a command-line argument for the program. I mentioned above that this command-line string is stored in a program overhead segment that Windows creates for each instance of a program. This program overhead segment must be fixed. If Windows moves it, the command-line pointer passed to your program becomes invalid.

Here's one way Windows deals with moveable segments: You've seen how Windows and your programs use numbers called "handles." In many cases, the handles are really near pointers. Windows maintains a segment called BURGERMASTER (named after a favorite restaurant of the early Windows developers) that contains a master handle-to-memory table. The handle points to a small area of memory within BURGERMASTER that contains the segment address of the item that the handle references. When Windows moves the segment that contains the item, it can adjust the address in BURGERMASTER without invalidating the handle. BURGERMASTER is itself a moveable segment.

All non-Windows MS-DOS programs are assigned fixed segments when they run under Windows. Windows cannot determine how these programs reference memory, so Windows has no choice but to make them fixed. However, you should try very hard to ensure that the code and data segments of your Windows programs (as well as any additional segments your programs allocate) are moveable segments. Fixed segments stand like brick walls in memory space and clog up Windows' memory management. Users quickly learn which programs seem to use little memory (because they use moveable segments) and which seem to use a lot of memory (because they use fixed segments). Users have a name for programs that use a lot of memory. They say, "This program is a real pig." Your goal should be to write programs that are not pigs.

Discardable Memory

Moveable segments can also be marked as discardable. This means that when Windows needs additional memory space, it can free up the area occupied by the segment. Windows uses a "least recently used" (LRU) algorithm to determine which segments to discard when attempting to free up memory.

Discardable segments are almost always those that do not change after they are loaded. Code segments of Windows programs are discardable because (in most cases) programs do not modify their code segments. Indeed, code segments cannot be modified in protected mode. When Windows discards a code segment, it can later reload the code segment by accessing the .EXE file. Most of Windows' own code in the USER and GDI modules and various driver libraries is also discardable. (The KERNEL module is fixed. This is the module responsible for Windows' memory management.) Resources—such as dialog box templates, cursors, and icons—also are often marked as discardable. Again, Windows can simply reload the resource into memory by accessing the .EXE file that contains the resource.

Sometimes you'll see that a disk is being accessed when you move the mouse from the client area of one program to the client area of another. Why is this? Windows has to send mouse movement messages to the second application. If the program's code to process this message is not currently in memory, Windows must reload it from the disk file. If you have several large Windows programs loaded simultaneously, you may witness some "thrashing" (an inordinate amount of disk activity) as you move from program to program. Windows is reloading previously discarded segments.

Discardable segments must also be moveable segments, because discardable segments can be reloaded in a different area of memory than the area they occupied earlier. However, moveable segments are not always discardable segments. This is usually the case with data segments. Windows cannot discard a program's automatic data segment, because the segment always contains read-write data and the stack.

Many people are under the impression that Windows also swaps memory—that is, that when Windows needs additional memory, it saves some portion of memory on the disk and reloads it at a later time. For Windows programs, this is true only when Windows is running in 386 enhanced mode. Windows swaps memory to disk only when running non-Windows programs (otherwise known as "old applications"). When Windows loads these old applications from disk back into memory, it must load them at the same memory address they occupied previously.

The Global Memory Layout

As I noted before, global memory ranges from the spot where MS-DOS first loads Windows to the top of available memory. At the bottom of global memory (the area with the lowest memory address), Windows allocates fixed segments. Fixed segments are allocated from the bottom up. At the top of global memory, Windows allocates discardable code segments. (Remember that discardable segments are also moveable segments.) Discardable segments are allocated from the top down.

Between fixed segments and discardable segments, Windows allocates moveable segments and nondiscardable data segments. The largest block of free memory is usually located below the discardable segments. The memory layout looks something like that shown in Figure 7-1 on the following page, with arrows indicating the direction in which the areas expand. When Windows needs to allocate a fixed segment, it starts searching from the bottom up for a sufficiently large free block below the area of moveable segments. If it can't find one, it starts moving moveable segments up in memory to make room. If that doesn't work, Windows begins discarding discardable segments, based on an LRU (least recently used) algorithm, again moving moveable segments. To allocate moveable but non-discardable segments, Windows searches the free memory area below the discardable segments. If it doesn't find enough room, Windows moves other moveable segments down in memory and eventually starts discarding discardable segments.

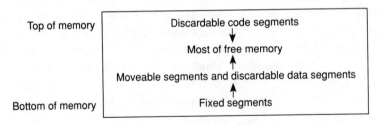

Figure 7-1. *The organization of global memory.*

Within the area of discardable memory, Windows maintains a space large enough to accommodate the largest code segment of every currently running program. Windows never runs out of memory space when reloading code segments. However, Windows can run out of memory space when a program attempts to allocate global memory or load a resource. Sometimes it can be a little tricky to deal with this problem—you may need a text string or icon not currently in memory to display an error message. If your program needs to report that it is low on memory, you can use a message box. Windows keeps in memory all the code necessary to create a message box. You'll want to use the MB_SYSTEMMODAL flag to prevent the user from switching to another application. MB_ICONHAND (which is supposed to accompany messages about severe problems) is also always in memory. The text message in the message box should either be in your default data segment or be a string resource that has previously been copied into your data segment.

Local Memory

Every Windows program has at least one data segment called the default, or automatic, data segment. A program's DS and SS segment registers both point to this segment. In contrast to the "global memory" that Windows manages, this automatic data segment is called your program's "local memory." Within Windows' global memory organization, your program's automatic data segment is most often a moveable but nondiscardable segment. The segment is called DGROUP.

In both regular MS-DOS C programs and Windows programs, the memory within DGROUP is organized into four areas, as shown in Figure 7-2. These four areas are described below:

- Initialized static data—This area contains initialized variables defined outside of functions, initialized static variables within functions, and explicit strings and floating-point numbers.

- Uninitialized static data—This area has uninitialized variables that are defined outside of functions and uninitialized variables defined as static within functions. In accordance with C standards, all uninitialized static variables are initialized to 0 when the data segment is created in memory.

■ Stack—This area is used for "automatic" data items defined within functions (variables not defined as static), for data passed to functions, and for return addresses during function calls.

■ Local heap—This is free memory available for dynamic allocation by the program.

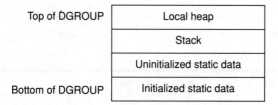

Figure 7-2. *The organization of memory in DGROUP.*

The module definition (.DEF) file specifies your program's stack and local heap size:

```
HEAPSIZE  1024
STACKSIZE 8192
```

In a regular C program, you can allocate memory from the local heap using the *malloc* and *calloc* functions. In Windows programs, you can also allocate memory from the local heap, but you'll want to use the Windows memory allocation functions rather than the C functions. When you use Windows functions to allocate local memory, Windows organizes the local heap just like global memory, as shown in Figure 7-3. Although the stack is fixed in size, Windows can dynamically expand the local heap if you attempt to allocate more local memory than is specified in your module definition file. Windows can even move your data segment if that is necessary to expand the local heap.

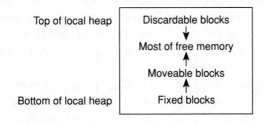

Figure 7-3. *The organization of the local heap.*

CODE AND DATA SEGMENTS

All the Windows programs shown so far have one code segment and one data segment. Windows programs can also have multiple code and data segments. For larger programs, using multiple code segments is highly recommended because it helps relieve memory congestion in Windows. Using multiple data segments, on the other hand, is a real problem. Let's take a look at this interesting subject.

Memory Models: Small, Medium, Compact, Large, and Huge

When we speak about a program having one code or data segment or multiple code or data segments, we're referring to "memory models." Microsoft C 6 supports five memory models that you can use for Windows programs:

Model	Code Segments	Data Segments
Small	1	1
Medium	Multiple	1
Compact	1	Multiple
Large	Multiple	Multiple
Huge	Multiple	Multiple

Command-line switches of the compiler determine the memory model you use. The small memory model is the default, but programs that have more than 64 KB of code must contain two or more code segments, and programs that have more than 64 KB of data must contain two or more data segments. In medium-model and large-model programs, all functions (unless explicitly declared as near) are far, and the compiler generates far calls for them. In compact-model and large-model programs, all data references use far pointers.

The small, compact, medium, and large models all have their own C libraries. The medium-model and large-model libraries contain functions that assume they have been called from another segment. The functions in the compact-model and large-model libraries always assume they have been passed long pointers to data. The huge model is essentially the same as the large model, except that individual data items may be greater than 64 KB. The huge model has limited library support.

Most small Windows programs are compiled as small-model programs, with one code segment and one data segment. Strictly speaking, however, Windows programs are really "mixed-model" programs, because they extensively use the near and far keywords. Windows programs make far calls to Windows functions, and Windows makes far calls to functions within a program, such as window procedures or call-back functions. All data pointers passed between a program and Windows (with one oddball exception—the *GetInstanceData* function) are far pointers.

Windows programs can also be compiled as medium-model programs. You can try this out on any of the programs shown so far. You need to make two changes to the make file:

- Add the -AM switch to the compile step. This compiles for the medium model.

- Change SLIBCEW to MLIBCEW in the link step. This is the library that contains the Windows-specific C run time library functions.

Delete the .OBJ file and run NMAKE. You'll find that the .EXE file is somewhat larger than before because all the functions within your program—not only the window procedure and call-back functions—now require far calls.

Multiple Code Segments

The medium model doesn't make sense for a small program, and it comes into play only when you have more than one source code module. But then it starts making a lot of sense. In the medium model, each source code module becomes a different code segment. Each of these code segments can be moveable and discardable. The amount of space required to fit your code into memory is the size of the largest code segment.

For instance, the approximately 160 KB of code in Windows WRITE is distributed among 78 separate moveable and discardable code segments. The largest code segment in WRITE is about 8 KB. Thus, when memory is limited, WRITE can continue to run with only an 8-KB code space. As program logic within WRITE moves from segment to segment, the code segment currently in memory can be discarded and a new one can be loaded in.

If you like, you can think of the medium model as a simplified overlay manager: You split your program into multiple source code modules and compile for the medium model. Windows does the rest. In order to work efficiently, the medium-model approach requires some planning. The functions in each of your source modules should be organized in functional groups. When your program is dealing with such routine matters as processing mouse messages, for example, it should not have to load several code segments to get from the top of the window procedure to the bottom.

While using the medium model is certainly the easiest approach to take with a large program, it is not the most efficient. As you'll see shortly, when you run the Microsoft C Compiler with the -Gw switch (the Windows switch), the compiler adds some extra prolog code to all far functions. Only those functions actually called by Windows (such as window procedures or call-back functions) need this prolog code, however. When all the functions in your program are far functions (as they are in the medium model), this extra code can add up to a significant waste of space.

There are several solutions to this problem. The first is fairly simple. When compiling a module that does not include any functions that are called from Windows (such as window procedures, dialog procedures, or call-back functions), compile with the -GW switch rather than the -Gw switch. This reduces the prolog code on far functions.

Another approach to reduce wasted space in a medium-model program is to define all functions used only within a module as near functions. Another solution is to use a mixed model with a small model as a base. Let's assume you have five source code modules:

- Module 1 contains *WinMain*, the message loop, your window procedure, and most message processing.

- Module 2 contains one function that has all initialization code. This function is called by *WinMain* from Module 1 before entering the message loop.

- Module 3 contains one function called from your window procedure and several other functions called only within this module.

- Module 4 also contains a function called from your window procedure and several other functions called only within this module. This module also calls a function in Module 5.

- Module 5 contains a function called from Module 4 and several other functions called only within this module.

You can organize this program into four segments, with Modules 4 and 5 in a single segment. Within each module, you explicitly define as far any function called from outside the segment. This involves one function each in Modules 2, 3, and 4. In the modules that call these functions, the functions must be declared as far using the function name prefaced by FAR near the top of the program.

You compile each module for the small model, except that you assign one code segment name to Module 2, another to Module 3, and yet another to Modules 4 and 5. These names are assigned by including the -NT ("name the text segment") switch when compiling. Each module with the same code segment name is in the same segment. Now you have far functions only where you need them—for functions that are called from another segment.

As you can see, this mixed-model approach is more of a headache than the medium-model approach. It requires that you figure out which functions must be declared far and which can be near. It also has an additional problem: You can call normal C library routines from only one segment—the segment that gets the default segment name _TEXT when you compile without the -NT switch.

What About the Compact and Large Models?

Windows programmers who require more than 64 KB of data in their programs might be feeling a little nervous at this point. They have a right to be, because the compact and large models are not recommended for Windows programs. This doesn't mean they can't be used, however. The Windows Software Development Kit allows you to install compact-model and large-model Windows libraries, so obviously these models are legal. However, compact-model and large-model programs are subject to a very strict penalty: The data segments must be fixed in memory. They cannot be flagged as moveable.

Why this restriction? There are various reasons; here's an easy example that illustrates one of them. Suppose that somewhere within your program you define a static pointer that looks like this:

```
char *pointer ;
```

Because you're compiling for a compact model or large model, this is a far pointer. During your program's execution, you assign a value to that pointer. If the pointer references a moveable data segment, then the value of the pointer must be adjusted when Windows moves the data segment it references. But the compiler and linker will not even generate a relocation address for that pointer because it's not initialized.

Program developers who cry "but I need the large model" should consider the alternatives made evident by existing Windows applications. Take a look at some large Windows programs such as Microsoft Excel and Aldus PageMaker. These programs use many code segments but only one data segment. And if these programs don't need the large model, then you probably don't either. If your program needs more than 64 KB of data, you have alternatives to using the compact model or large model. Here they are:

- If your program uses large blocks of uninitialized data, do not define these data as variables within the program. Instead, use the Windows *GlobalAlloc* function (discussed later in this chapter) to allocate a block of moveable memory outside your program.

- If your program uses large blocks of initialized read-only data (the most obvious example is "help" text), make the data a discardable "user-defined resource" (discussed in Chapter 8) to be loaded from the disk only when necessary. This keeps the data out of memory when not needed.

- If your program uses large blocks of initialized read-write data, put the initialized data in a discardable "user-defined resource" and transfer the data to a global memory block allocated with *GlobalAlloc*.

Avoiding Movement Problems

We have been creating small Windows programs for several chapters now and have not run into problems when Windows has moved the code and data segments in memory. Here are some general rules for continuing to avoid problems:

- Use the small model or medium model.

- Don't declare any variables as far. For instance, don't do something like this:

```
int far array [10][1000] ;    // Bad!!!!!
```

   This code creates a second data segment in your program. Unless you mark this segment as fixed, Windows does not properly handle references to this array.

- Don't store any far pointers to data except those that Windows gives you. The *lpszCmdLine* parameter passed to *WinMain* is OK. The far addresses returned from *GlobalLock* (discussed later in this chapter) and *LockResource* (discussed in Chapter 8) point to fixed data until you specifically unlock the data, so these are legitimate also. Some window messages (WM_CREATE, for instance) have *lParam* values that are far pointers. Use these pointers only for the duration of the message.

- When you call Windows functions, you must often pass far pointers to data that are within your data segment. But don't declare far pointers and assign them far addresses to local data items and then later use the far pointers when calling Windows functions. Instead, cast the near pointers into far pointers when you call the functions, or let the compiler do this casting for you.

- Don't store or use any far pointers to code, except for pointers to functions that are specifically declared as far or far pointers returned from *MakeProcInstance*. (Pointers to functions in medium-model programs are also OK.)

- When you need to give Windows a far pointer to a function for a call-back function (as discussed in Chapter 5), a window subclassing function (as discussed in Chapter 6), or a dialog box function (as discussed in Chapter 10), obtain the pointer from *MakeProcInstance*. The function must be declared as FAR PASCAL and included in the EXPORTS section of your module definition file.

Although these rules are numerous and important, don't let them drive you to paranoia. Keep in mind that Windows is nonpreemptive. Windows will not pull the rug out from under you by interrupting your code. Windows will move or discard your code segments only when you make a Windows call. Windows will not move your data segment except when you make a few select Windows calls. If you have a long stretch of code between two Windows calls, you can be as carefree as you like in that code without worrying about sudden movements.

Program Segment Attributes

I have been talking about program segments that are fixed, moveable, and discardable. These characteristics are called "segment attributes." To tell Windows the attributes you want in your program segments, you use the CODE, DATA, and SEGMENTS statements in the module definition file. During linking, LINK encodes the attributes for each program segment into a 16-bit flag and stores this flag in the segment table of the .EXE file. Windows has access to these segment attributes when loading your code and data segments. The sample programs presented so far contain these two lines in their module definition files:

```
CODE PRELOAD MOVEABLE DISCARDABLE
DATA PRELOAD MOVEABLE MULTIPLE
```

We have not yet encountered the SEGMENTS statement.

The CODE statement applies to all code segments within your program that are not explicitly listed in the SEGMENTS statement. Similarly, the DATA statement applies to all data segments except those listed in the SEGMENTS statement.

There are four standard attributes: "load," "memory," "discardable," and "instance."

The "load" attribute can be either PRELOAD or LOADONCALL. This attribute tells Windows when to load the segment. The default is PRELOAD, which means that the code segment (or segments) should be loaded at the time the program begins execution. A LOADONCALL segment will be loaded into memory the first time it is needed. For a program with a single code module, it really doesn't matter which attribute you use. For programs with multiple code modules, you should use PRELOAD for segments that are required when the program first starts up (for instance, those that do initialization from *WinMain*) and LOADONCALL for the other code segments. To specify different attributes for multiple code segments, you must use the SEGMENTS statement, discussed later.

The "memory" attribute can be either FIXED or MOVEABLE. The default is FIXED. If you're writing normal Windows programs, you should have no problem specifying MOVEABLE. (Device drivers that must process hardware interrupts are another matter. These usually require one fixed code segment.)

The "discardable" attribute is indicated by the DISCARDABLE keyword. This indicates that Windows can discard the segment from memory and reload it from the .EXE file when necessary. Code segments in normal Windows programs should be flagged as DISCARDABLE. The default data segment cannot be flagged as DISCARDABLE.

The "instance" attribute is relevant only for data segments. It should be set to MULTIPLE for Windows programs, indicating that each instance gets its own data segments.

The NONE and INSTANCE options are for Windows dynamic link libraries (discussed in Chapter 19), because Windows libraries can have only one instance. If the Windows library has a data segment, INSTANCE (or SINGLE) is used. If not, NONE is used.

The SEGMENTS statement lets you assign different segment attributes to other code and data segments within your program. The general form of the SEGMENTS statement is:

```
SEGMENTS segment-name [CLASS 'class-name'] [allocate] [attributes]
```

You'll probably use this statement most often if you create a medium-model program or a small-model program with multiple code segments. For a medium-model program, the C library functions and start-up code are in a code segment named _TEXT. Each source code module is assigned a different code segment name that by default is the filename of the source code file followed by _TEXT. For instance, if you have three source code modules called PROGRAM.C, MODULE1.C, and MODULE2.C, the PROGRAM.EXE file has four code segments: _TEXT, PROGRAM_TEXT, MODULE1_TEXT, and MODULE2_TEXT.

If you do not include a SEGMENTS statement, all four code modules take on the attributes from the CODE statements. If you do include a SEGMENTS statement, however, your results might look something like this:

```
CODE       PRELOAD MOVEABLE DISCARDABLE
DATA       PRELOAD MOVEABLE MULTIPLE
SEGMENTS   MODULE1_TEXT LOADONCALL MOVEABLE DISCARDABLE
           MODULE2_TEXT LOADONCALL MOVEABLE DISCARDABLE
```

Now the _TEXT and PROGRAM_TEXT segments are PRELOAD and are loaded when the program first begins execution. MODULE1_TEXT and MODULE2_TEXT are LOADONCALL. Windows loads them only when they are needed.

If you use the SEGMENTS statement for data segments, you must include:

```
CLASS 'DATA'
```

By default, the class is CODE. You can also add a minimum allocation size to increase the size of the data segment when it's loaded into memory.

HOW WINDOWS MOVES AND RELOADS PROGRAM SEGMENTS

In this section, I want to give you some insights into how Windows is able to move your program's code and data segments and (in the case of code segments) discard and later reload the segments in real mode. If you'd rather not know (or if the assembly language in the pages ahead looks like Greek to you), that's fine. But you're likely to see some of this code when debugging Windows programs, so it's better that you see it here first and understand what's going on.

I'll be discussing the most general recommended case—a program that contains multiple moveable and discardable code segments and a single moveable data segment. Everything works a little differently (and more simply) when the segments are fixed and nondiscardable.

When a program has a single data segment, neither the code nor the data have to contain any explicit references to the segment address of the data. When a Windows program begins running, Windows has already set the DS and SS registers to the data segment. All pointers are near pointers. When the program needs the data segment address (for instance, for casting near pointers into far pointers when calling Windows functions), it simply uses the value of DS. (In contrast to this, when you run a regular .EXE program outside Windows, MS-DOS does not set DS to the program's data segment on entry to the program. The program must begin by executing code like this:

```
MOV AX, DGROUP
MOV DS, AX
```

You'll never see code like this in a compiled Windows program.) If you cast a near data pointer into a far pointer and store the far pointer in a variable, you're storing the current value of the data segment address. If Windows moves the data segment, that far pointer will no longer be valid. That's why it is recommended that you not do this.

Windows moves a program's data segment only during certain Windows calls. Most often, movement of a data segment occurs during a *GetMessage* or *PeekMessage* call. Windows always returns the new values of DS and SS to the program when it returns from one of these calls.

Windows programs use the same segment for data and the stack. However, Windows libraries (including the USER, KERNEL, and GDI modules, as well as the drivers) have their own data segments but not their own stacks. They use the stack of the program calling the Windows function. Thus, the stack segment address is always that of the currently running program, even if the program is calling a Windows function. When switching from one program to another, Windows must also switch the stack.

When Windows calls a function in your program (such as a window procedure, a window subclassing function, a call-back function, or a dialog box function), the stack segment address is set to your program's stack segment, but the data segment address is still the one used by the Windows library calling your function. For this reason, Windows must also include a facility so that programs retrieve their own data segments during one of these calls.

All these aspects of Windows' memory management—supporting multiple instances, moving code and data segments, and discarding and reloading code segments—are tied together.

Special Treatment of Far Functions

When you compile a C program, the compiler inserts prolog and epilog code in each function. This code sets up a "stack frame" for the function. The function uses the stack frame
to retrieve parameters passed to the function on the stack and to temporarily store the
function's own local variables. For a normal MS-DOS program, the prolog and epilog can
be as simple as this:

```
PUSH BP
MOV  BP, SP
SUB  SP, x
[other program lines]
MOV  SP, BP
POP  BP
RET  y
```

I'm assuming here that stack overflow checking has been disabled. The value of x that the
prolog subtracts from SP is the total size of the function's local nonstatic data (increased to
the next even number).

After the three prolog instructions have been executed, the stack is organized as
shown in Figure 7-4 (from higher addresses to lower). The function uses the BP register to
reference both data passed to the function on the stack (which have positive offsets to BP)
and local data declared within the function (which have negative offsets to BP). If the function uses the SI and DI registers, these registers will also be saved on the stack because
they can be used by the caller for register variables. The DS register must also be preserved
during a function call.

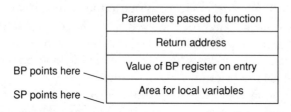

Parameters passed to function
Return address
Value of BP register on entry
Area for local variables

BP points here — (Value of BP register on entry)
SP points here — (Area for local variables)

Figure 7-4. *The stack after execution of the three prolog instructions.*

For a function declared as near, the return address is only one word—the offset address.
For a far function, the return address is two words. A function declared as near or far normally has the same prolog and epilog, but the compiled function must take into account the
size of the return address—one word or two—when accessing the parameters passed to
the function.

At the end of the function, the value of SP is set equal to BP, and BP is popped off the
stack to restore it to its original value. The function is now ready to return to the caller. This

involves a near RET or a far RET, depending on whether the function is near or far. If the function is also declared as *pascal*, the *y* value in the code above is the total size of parameters passed to the function. Otherwise, *y* is not used, and the caller adjusts the stack pointer when the function returns.

That's a normal compilation. When you compile a Windows program with the -Gw switch (the Windows switch), every far function gets special prolog and epilog code that looks like this:

```
PUSH DS
POP  AX        ; set AX to DS
NOP
INC  BP
PUSH BP        ; save incremented BP on stack
MOV  BP, SP
PUSH DS        ; save DS on stack
MOV  DS, AX    ; set DS to AX
SUB  SP, x

[other program lines]

DEC  BP
DEC  BP
MOV  SP, BP    ; reset SP to point to DS on stack
POP  DS        ; get back DS
POP  BP        ; get back incremented BP
DEC  BP        ; restore BP to normal
RET  y
```

Functions that are declared as near get the normal prolog and epilog even with the -Gw switch. Notice two points here: First, the prolog sets the value of AX equal to DS, saves the DS register on the stack, and then sets DS from AX. On exiting, DS is retrieved from the stack. That code is not doing anything (or anything harmful) except taking up unnecessary space. Second, the previous value of the BP register is incremented before being saved on the stack and decremented after it is retrieved from the stack. This certainly looks mystifying right now. Figure 7-5 shows what the stack frame looks like for far functions compiled with the -Gw compiler switch after the prolog code is executed.

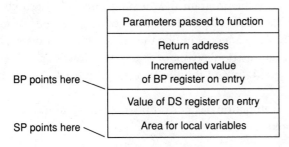

Figure 7-5. *The stack after execution of the special Windows prolog.*

When LINK creates the program's .EXE file, it treats every far function in a moveable code segment as a "moveable entry point." In the .EXE header, LINK builds an entry table that contains 6 bytes of information for every moveable entry point in the program. This information includes the segment ordinal number of the function—simply a sequential numbering of the program's segments—and the offset of the function within that segment. The entry table also includes the 2 bytes CDH and 3FH for every moveable entry point. These 2 bytes are actually the instruction INT 3FH. This same software interrupt shows up in non-Windows programs, where it is used for overlay management. In Windows, the interrupt performs a similar function in that it loads a program's code segment from disk into memory.

A flag in the entry table indicates whether the far function was listed in the EXPORTS section of the module definition (.DEF) file. As I've discussed, the EXPORTS section of the .DEF file must list all far functions in your program that are called by Windows. These include window procedures (such as the function I've been calling *WndProc*), call-back functions, window subclassing functions, and dialog box functions.

When your program's code contains references to the addresses of far functions, LINK has to leave the instruction incomplete. For example, if you call a far function, the compiler generates a far CALL instruction, but the address is not yet known because LINK doesn't know where the segment containing the function will be loaded in memory. LINK builds a relocation table in the .EXE file at the end of each code segment. This table lists all the references to far functions within your program as well as all references to Windows functions.

Now that the compiler and LINK have done all these strange things to your program, it's time for Windows to run the program and do its magic.

When Windows Runs the Program

When Windows runs the first instance of a program, it loads the data segment and also loads one or more code segments. Windows also builds two fixed segments for program overhead. One segment contains information unique to each instance of the program, such as the command-line argument passed to the program and the program's current subdirectory. The other overhead segment, which is used for all instances of the program, contains a large chunk of the program's .EXE file header, including the entry table. The entry table already has 6 bytes of data for every far function in your program. Windows expands each entry into 8 bytes. These entries, called "reload thunks," are small pieces of code that handle segment loading.

If the segment containing the far function has not yet been loaded into memory, the reload thunk for that far function looks like this:

```
SAR BY CS:[xxxx], 1
INT 3F 01 yyyy
```

The first statement is part of Windows' mechanism to determine whether a segment is a candidate for discarding. The second statement calls Interrupt 3FH, the software interrupt that loads into memory the appropriate segment containing the function.

If the segment containing the far function is present in memory, the reload thunk looks like this:

```
SAR BY CS:[xxxx], 1
JMP ssss:0000
```

The second instruction is a far jump instruction. The *ssss:0000* segment and offset address points to the beginning of the far function in the loaded code segment.

The references in your program's code to far functions are listed in the segment's relocation table. Windows must insert the addresses of the far functions into your code. The addresses that Windows uses for this are not the actual addresses of the far functions but rather the addresses of the reload thunks for the far functions. Because the reload thunk is in fixed memory, Windows doesn't need to make other changes to the code when moving the code segment that contains the far call or moving the code segment that the far call references. Windows needs to change only the *ssss:0000* address in the reload thunk.

When the program calls a far function, it's actually calling the reload thunk. If the segment containing the far function is not currently in memory, the reload thunk executes the Interrupt 3FH loader that loads the segment into memory. Windows then alters the reload thunk to contain a JMP instruction to the function. Windows jumps back to the reload thunk, which then jumps to the actual function. When Windows discards a segment from memory, it changes the reload thunk from the JMP instruction back to the INT 3FH instruction. The next time a function in that segment is needed, the segment is reloaded.

The calls in your program to Windows functions are translated into far CALL instructions and are also listed in the segment's relocation tables. When Windows loads your code segment into memory, it also resolves the calls to Windows functions. For Windows functions in fixed code segments, Windows simply inserts the address of the Windows function into your code. Windows functions in moveable segments have their own reload thunks, and Windows inserts the addresses of these thunks into your code.

Windows also does something special with functions that have been listed in the EXPORTS section of the program's module definition file. Windows modifies the function prolog of these functions when loading the segment into memory. It replaces the first 2 bytes of every exported far function with NOP (no operation) instructions. The prolog now looks like this in memory:

```
NOP
NOP
NOP
INC  BP
PUSH BP          ; save incremented BP on stack
MOV  BP, SP
PUSH DS          ; save DS on stack
MOV  DS, AX      ; set DS to AX
SUB  SP, x
```

Those two NOPs make a big difference. Now the prolog saves the original value of DS and sets DS to AX. When this function is called, AX must already be set to the data segment that the function must use. This change makes the exported function unusable for normal calls to the function. This is why you cannot call your window procedure (or any other exported function) directly from within your program.

What *MakeProcInstance* Does

You've just seen that far functions listed in the EXPORTS section of your .DEF file become unsuitable for normal use when Windows loads them into memory. These functions require that the value of AX on entry be the program's data segment. This data segment is different for every instance of your program. You can do only one of two things with an exported far function:

- If the function is a window procedure, you can give Windows the address of the function in the window class structure when registering the window class with *RegisterClass*:

```
wndclass.lpfnWndProc = WndProc ;
```

- If the function is a call-back function, a window subclassing function, or a dialog box function, you must give Windows an address returned from *MakeProcInstance*. For instance, if *CallBackProc* is the name of a call-back function, you must first make a call like this:

```
lpfnCallBack = MakeProcInstance (CallBackProc, hInstance)
```

Because *CallBackProc* is a far function, the address you pass to *MakeProcInstance* is actually the address of the reload thunk. The *lpfnCallBack* address you get back from *MakeProcInstance* can now be used as a parameter to a Windows function such as *SetTimer*.

MakeProcInstance and *RegisterClass* both deal with the exported far function in the same way. They create an "instance thunk" for the function. The address that *MakeProcInstance* returns is the address of the instance thunk. Instance thunks are in a fixed area of memory, and they look like this:

```
MOV AX, xxxx
JMP ssss:0000
```

The *xxxx* value is the data segment address for this instance of your program. The instance thunks are different for each instance because each instance uses a different data segment. The *ssss:0000* address in the instance thunk is the segment and offset address of the reload thunk that reloads (or jumps to) the function. The same reload thunks are used for all instances of a program because they jump to the same shareable code.

When Windows needs to call a function in your program (such as a window procedure), it actually calls the instance thunk. The instance thunk sets AX equal to the data segment address for that instance and jumps to the reload thunk. The reload thunk loads the segment if it is not currently present in memory and branches to the function. The function then saves the previous value of DS and sets DS from the value of AX—the data segment address for the instance. When the function ends, it retrieves the original value of DS from the stack and returns control to Windows. When Windows moves the data segment for a particular instance, Windows must also change the *xxxx* values in all the instance thunks for that instance.

The Difference for Dynamic Libraries

You've seen that the far function prolog inserted by the compiler is modified by Windows if the function is exported. When far functions are in memory, they can have one of three possible prologs. If the prolog starts off like this:

```
MOV AX, DS
NOP
```

then the far function is called only from within the same program and is not called by Windows. If the prolog starts off like this:

```
NOP
NOP
NOP
```

then the far function has been exported. It is not called from within the program but instead is called only by Windows. A program's window procedure starts off in this way.

What's the purpose of the extra NOP that shows up in both prologs? The extra NOP disappears in the third form of the prolog:

```
MOV AX, xxxx
```

You'll find this form at the beginning of many Windows functions in the Windows library modules (USER, KERNEL, and GDI) and drivers (MOUSE, KEYBOARD, SYSTEM, and so forth). Unlike Windows programs, Windows libraries cannot have multiple instances, so they do not need instance thunks. The far function itself can contain code that sets AX equal to the segment address of the library's data segment (the value *xxxx*). The rest of the prolog then saves DS and sets DS equal to AX.

When Windows moves a library's data segment in memory, it must change the prologs of the library functions that use that data segment. And when your program calls a Windows function, the address it calls is either the address of the function's reload thunk (if the function is in a moveable segment) or the function itself (if the function is in a fixed segment).

Note that Windows library functions use their own data segments but continue to use the stack of the caller. If the library function were to use its own stack, it would need to copy function parameters from the caller's stack. Windows switches the stack only when switching between tasks; calling a library function does not constitute a task switch.

Walking the Stack

One little mystery remains. You'll recall that the far function prolog includes the statements:

```
INC  BP
PUSH BP
```

The epilog then returns BP to normal:

```
POP  BP
DEC  BP
```

What is this for?

Think about this problem: Free memory is very low. A function in one of your program's code segments calls a far function in another of your program's code segments. This function then calls a Windows function. The code segment containing this Windows function is not currently present in memory. To load it into memory, Windows has to move your data segment and discard both your code segments. This sounds like a serious problem, because when the Windows function returns to your program, your program will be gone.

When Windows must discard code segments, it first goes through a little exercise called "walking the stack." Within any function, the value of SS:[BP] is the value of BP from the previous function. If this previous value of BP is even, the previous function is a near function; if it's odd, the previous function is a far function. By using successive values of BP stored on the stack, Windows can trace through the stack until it reaches the top, which is the stack pointer address originally given to your program when the program began executing. Windows can determine the segment addresses and the saved DS register values of all the functions involved in making the current Windows function call.

If Windows has to move your program's data segment (which also requires moving the stack), it can adjust the DS register on the stack to the new segment address. If Windows has to move a code segment containing functions that have been involved in the current Windows function call, it changes the return address on the stack. If Windows has to discard a code segment, it replaces the return address with an address that points to code, which reloads the segment and which then branches to the appropriate return address.

As I mentioned at the onset of this discussion, you may prefer not to think about all this activity going on in the innards of Windows.

Expanded Memory

So far, I've been discussing how Windows manages memory in simple 640-KB systems. Windows also supports bank-switched memory that follows the Lotus-Intel-Microsoft Expanded Memory Specification 4.0 (LIM EMS 4.0).

In a bank-switched memory scheme such as EMS, special memory boards provide multiple banks of memory that can occupy a single same address space. Only one of these multiple banks occupies the address space at any time. By manipulating registers on the memory board, the EMS device driver can switch out one bank of memory and switch in another bank.

Expanded memory under EMS 4.0 is supported in Windows 3 in two configurations:

In the first configuration (called "small frame"), the bank-switched memory resides in an unused area above the 640-KB level of conventional memory and below the 1-MB level addressable by the 8086 family running in real mode. This 384-KB area contains the ROM BIOS, some BIOS device drivers, and video adapter buffers, but at least 64 KB are usually available for expanded memory.

In the second configuration (called "large frame"), the bank-switched memory also occupies an area of the 640-KB address space containing conventional memory. The bank-switched memory can usually occupy as much as 384 KB of conventional memory, from the 256-KB level to the 640-KB level. The level above which memory is bank-switched is called the "bankline."

The *GetWinFlags* function includes the flags WF_SMALLFRAME and WF_LARGE-FRAME if you need to determine the configuration under which your program is running.

Windows 3 uses bank-switched memory on a per process basis. When switching between Windows programs (which normally occurs during calls to the *GetMessage, PeekMessage*, and *WaitMessage* functions), Windows 3 will switch out the banks of memory associated with the first process and switch in the banks of memory associated with the second process.

The chapter entitled "More Memory Management" in the Windows Guide to Programming discusses which memory objects are stored below the bankline and above the bankline in the small-frame and large-frame configurations. Generally, this is transparent to the Windows application. The only problem arises when two Windows programs share memory using a technique other than the clipboard, dynamic data exchange, or dynamic link libraries. Such sharing is not recommended because it may not work in future versions of Windows.

Protected Mode

When running on a 286 or 386 processor with at least 1 MB of memory, Windows runs in 286-compatible protected mode. In this mode, Windows can use the 640 KB of conventional memory and memory allocated from extended memory using the XMS (Extended Memory) driver included in the retail release of Windows 3.

In this mode, segment addresses do not correspond to physical memory. Instead, the segment addresses are called "selectors," which reference physical memory through a descriptor table. Protected mode is called "protected" because the hardware of the 286 and 386 microprocessors ensures that programs do not load invalid segment addresses or attempt to access a segment beyond the segment's size. The processor generates a protection exception that the operating system (or in this case, Windows) traps. Windows responds by terminating the offending application.

For this reason, several rules are associated with protected mode:

- Do not perform segment arithmetic.

- Do not load far pointers with invalid addresses.

- Do not attempt to address a segment beyond its allocated length.

- Do not store data in code segments.

If you follow the memory allocation guidelines I discuss below, you should have no problem running your program in protected mode. You should do your development work in protected mode to more easily catch bugs; if you can't, you should definitely test your code in protected mode, because it can reveal bugs in your code that are not so evident when running in real mode.

ALLOCATING MEMORY WITHIN A PROGRAM

Programs often need to dynamically allocate blocks of memory for internal use. Windows programs can allocate memory either from the program's private local heap or from Windows' global heap. Windows includes two sets of memory allocation functions, one set for using the local heap and one for the global heap.

There are certain trade-offs between local and global memory allocations. Local memory allocations are generally faster and require less overhead, but the memory in the local heap is limited to 64 KB less the combined size of the program's initialized static variables, the program's uninitialized static variables, and the stack. Global memory allocations are not limited to 64 KB, either in the size of single blocks or in the total memory you can allocate. However, pointers to global memory blocks are far pointers, which can be awkward to work with in your program. (You cannot pass a far pointer to small-model and medium-model C library functions, for instance.)

This chart summarizes the differences between memory allocations from the local heap and the global heap:

	Local Heap	Global Heap
Size of block:	Less than 64 KB	Any size
Total memory:	Less than 64 KB	Free global memory
Pointer:	Near	Far

You'll probably find local heap allocations convenient for small, short-lived blocks of memory and global heap allocations for large, long-lived blocks.

The memory blocks you allocate can be fixed, moveable, or discardable. You specify the attributes you want when you allocate the memory block. When you write polite, well-mannered Windows programs, you'll probably want to use moveable blocks when allocating global memory, but you can use either fixed or moveable blocks for local memory. How do you deal with a moveable memory block in your program? Very carefully.

Lock Your Blocks

At first, it seems impossible for Windows to support moveable memory blocks in real mode. When a program allocates some local or global memory, Windows has to give the program a pointer so that the program can access the memory. If Windows later moves the memory block, then that pointer will be invalid. It will no longer point to the right place.

How does Windows do it? The catch here is that the memory allocation functions do not directly return pointers that the program may use. Instead, these functions return—as you can probably guess by now—handles. WINDOWS.H defines two data types called LOCALHANDLE and GLOBALHANDLE. These are defined as type HANDLE (which is a WORD, or unsigned 16-bit short integer). Before your program can use the allocated memory block, it must pass that handle back to Windows in another function that locks the memory block and returns a pointer. When a memory block is locked, Windows will not move it. The pointer will continue to be valid until you call another function to unlock the block. After that, Windows is free to move the memory again.

More precisely, the functions that lock a block of memory increment a "lock count" for the memory block. The unlocking functions decrement the lock count. When you first allocate moveable memory, the lock count is 0, meaning that Windows can move it if necessary. When the lock count is positive, Windows cannot move the block. (A lock count is preferable to a simple flag that denotes whether a block is locked, because different parts of your program can independently lock a block, use it, and unlock it. If Windows used a flag instead of a lock count, the memory block could become unlocked when another section of the program still needed it.)

When you use moveable memory in your Windows program, you should keep it locked only when your program has control. You should unlock it before you leave your window procedure. When you are entirely done with the memory block, you can then free the block.

A Quick Example

Before going into details, let's look at a quick example to get the feel of this process. Let's say that your program needs a 48-KB chunk of global memory during the entire time the program is running. During initialization (for instance, when processing the WM_CREATE message), the program uses *GlobalAlloc* to allocate a 48-KB segment of moveable memory:

```
hGlobalMemory = GlobalAlloc (GMEM_MOVEABLE, 0xC000L) ;
```

The value returned from *GlobalAlloc* is a handle to a 48-KB global memory segment. Store the handle in a static variable (here called *hGlobalMemory*).

While processing other messages, you might need to read from or write to this memory segment. At that time you lock the block of memory using *GlobalLock* and save the far pointer returned from that function:

```
lpGlobalMemory = GlobalLock (hGlobalMemory) ;
```

You can now use the *lpGlobalMemory* pointer as a normal far pointer. When you are finished using the memory or processing the message, unlock the segment so that Windows can move it around in memory again:

```
GlobalUnlock (hGlobalMemory) ;
```

When your program cleans up in preparing to terminate (probably when processing the WM_DESTROY message), it can free up the memory segment by using:

```
GlobalFree (hGlobalMemory) ;
```

This procedure shows how a polite, well-behaved Windows program uses global memory. (I've ignored some details for now but will cover them shortly.) Good Windows programmers keep in mind that their programs share resources with other Windows programs. Good Windows programmers structure their programs to allow Windows to move the global segments around in memory if necessary. Good Windows programmers lock their segments only when they need to use the memory and unlock the segments when they are done.

An impolite, bad Windows program uses initialization code like this:

```
lpGlobalMemory = GlobalLock (GlobalAlloc (GMEM_FIXED, 0xC000L)) ;
```

The GMEM_FIXED flag in *GlobalAlloc* specifies that the segment is fixed in memory. Windows can't move it; therefore, the *lpGlobalMemory* value returned from *GlobalLock* will be valid until the segment is freed up. More convenient, yes. But don't do it.

Global Memory Functions

Now for the details. This is the general syntax of the *GlobalAlloc* call:

```
hGlobalMemory = GlobalAlloc (wFlags, dwBytes) ;
```

The *dwBytes* parameter is a double word (unsigned long). This value can be greater than 65,536, but there are special considerations in using global memory blocks larger than 64 KB. (These will be discussed later.)

The *wFlags* parameter can be a combination of several identifiers that are combined with the C bitwise OR operator. You first have a choice of three identifiers to define the attribute of the allocated memory block:

- GMEM_FIXED—Memory is fixed. (This is the default if *wFlags* is 0.)

- GMEM_MOVEABLE—Memory is moveable.

- GMEM_DISCARDABLE—Memory is discardable. This option should be used only with GMEM_MOVEABLE. I'll discuss later how you can manage discardable global memory in your programs.

With any of the above three flags, you can use the GMEM_ZEROINIT flag for convenience; this flag tells Windows to initialize memory contents to 0.

You can use two more flags to tell Windows what to do if not enough free memory exists in the global heap. When Windows attempts to allocate the block requested by *GlobalAlloc*, it first searches to see if a large enough free block exists already. If not, Windows begins moving blocks of memory that are moveable and not currently locked. If that still doesn't generate enough space, Windows begins discarding blocks that are marked as discardable and not currently locked, again moving moveable unlocked segments. You can inhibit this action by using one of two flags:

- GMEM_NOCOMPACT—Windows will neither compact memory nor discard memory when attempting to allocate the block.

- GMEM_NODISCARD—Windows will not discard discardable global memory when attempting to allocate the block. Windows may still compact memory by moving moveable blocks.

If your program implements Dynamic Data Exchange (DDE), you'll need to use the GMEM_DDESHARE flag to allocate blocks of memory that are shareable among multiple programs. I'll discuss this in Chapter 17.

WINDOWS.H includes two shorthand flags for the most common global memory allocations. The flag GHND (which stands for "global handle") is defined as:

```
GMEM_MOVEABLE | GMEM_ZEROINIT
```

The flag GPTR ("global pointer") is defined as:

```
GMEM_FIXED | GMEM_ZEROINIT
```

The name of this flag seems odd. Why is a fixed global block referred to as a "global pointer"? The answer is given later in this chapter, in the section entitled "Memory Allocation Shortcuts."

The *hGlobalMemory* value returned from *GlobalAlloc* is a handle to the global memory block. It is NULL if *GlobalAlloc* could not allocate the requested memory. You should definitely check the return value from *GlobalAlloc* when allocating global memory.

The function *GlobalLock* locks the segment in memory by incrementing the lock count and returns a far pointer to type *char*. You should have a variable declared for this pointer:

```
LPSTR lpGlobalMemory ;
      [other program lines]
lpGlobalMemory = GlobalLock (hGlobalMemory) ;
```

If *hGlobalMemory* is valid, *GlobalLock* can return NULL only if you flagged the memory block with GMEM_DISCARDABLE. The NULL return value indicates that the block has been discarded.

Because *GlobalLock* is declared as returning a far pointer to type *char*, you should use casting if you need something different:

```
DWORD FAR *lpdwGlobalMemory ;
      [other program lines]
lpdwGlobalMemory = (DWORD FAR *) GlobalLock (hGlobalMemory) ;
```

The far pointer returned from *GlobalLock* points to the beginning of a segment. The offset address is 0. If you need to save pointers to areas within a moveable block, do not save them as far pointers. These far pointers may be invalid the next time you lock the segment. Instead, store an offset from the beginning of the block. For a global block less than 64 KB, for instance, you need save only the offset address (the lower 16 bits) of the pointer.

The *GlobalUnlock* function decrements the lock count for the *hGlobalMemory* handle:

```
GlobalUnlock (hGlobalMemory) ;
```

Calling *GlobalUnlock* invalidates the *lpGlobalMemory* pointer returned from *GlobalLock*. When the lock count is 0, Windows can move the block in memory.

GlobalLock and *GlobalUnlock* are fairly fast, so you don't suffer a real performance penalty if you use the two functions liberally. You should definitely not keep a block locked from one message to another. Remember that Windows performs best when memory is moveable. When you make a call to a Windows function, Windows may need to load code into memory. If you have a locked memory block sitting around, Windows may have to discard other segments to make room.

When you are entirely finished with the memory block, you can call:

```
GlobalFree (hGlobalMemory) ;
```

Following this call, the *hGlobalMemory* handle is no longer valid, and the block is freed.

More Global Memory Functions

Although the four global memory functions shown above are the ones you'll use most often, Windows also provides several others. Before using *GlobalAlloc*, you may want to determine the amount of global memory currently available:

```
dwAvailable = GlobalCompact (dwRequested) ;
```

GlobalCompact causes Windows to move moveable blocks and to calculate the area of free memory that could be obtained by also discarding discardable blocks. If the function cannot generate *dwRequested* bytes, it returns the largest block of free memory available. Discarding doesn't take place until you call *GlobalAlloc* using the size returned from *GlobalCompact*.

After you allocate a memory block, you can determine its size using:

```
dwBytes = GlobalSize (hGlobalMemory) ;
```

You can also change the size of the memory block or change its attributes using *GlobalReAlloc*. This function is a little tricky, because it can be used in one of three ways. Here's the general syntax:

```
hGlobalMemory = GlobalReAlloc (hGlobalMemory, dwBytes, wFlags) ;
```

First, you can change the size of a global memory block (either increasing or decreasing it) using:

```
GlobalReAlloc (hGlobalMemory, dwNewBytes, wFlags) ;
```

The data already stored in the block are preserved. The function returns NULL if it cannot increase the block to the requested size.

The *wFlags* parameter is used in the same way as the *wFlags* parameter for *GlobalAlloc*: GMEM_NODISCARD and GMEM_NOCOMPACT place restrictions on what Windows will do to satisfy the allocation request. GMEM_ZEROINIT zeroes out additional bytes if you are expanding the block. When calling *GlobalReAlloc*, you don't have to include the GMEM_FIXED, GMEM_MOVEABLE, or GMEM_DISCARDABLE flags. Windows preserves the attribute specified when the block was allocated. However, you may want to use the GMEM_MOVEABLE flag for reallocating a fixed block. Doing so gives Windows permission to move the block in memory to satisfy the allocation request. In this case, *GlobalReAlloc* returns a new global memory handle to the fixed block:

```
hGlobalMemoryNew = GlobalReAlloc (hGlobalMemoryOld, dwNewBytes,
                                  GMEM_MOVEABLE) ;
```

If *GlobalReAlloc* returns NULL, the request for memory was refused, and the original *hGlobalMemoryOld* value passed to *GlobalReAlloc* is still valid for the fixed block.

The second way to use *GlobalReAlloc* is to change the discardable attribute of moveable blocks. The *dwNewBytes* value is ignored. You can change a moveable block to a discardable one:

```
GlobalReAlloc (hGlobalMemory, OL, GMEM_MODIFY | GMEM_DISCARDABLE) ;
```

or change a discardable block to a moveable (but nondiscardable) one:

```
GlobalReAlloc (hGlobalMemory, OL, GMEM_MODIFY | GMEM_MOVEABLE) ;
```

The third use of *GlobalReAlloc* is to discard a discardable memory block. This requires *dwNewBytes* to be 0 and the *wFlags* parameter to be GMEM_MOVEABLE:

```
GlobalReAlloc (hGlobalMemory, OL, GMEM_MOVEABLE) ;
```

You can do the same thing using:

```
GlobalDiscard (hGlobalMemory) ;
```

In fact, *GlobalDiscard* is a macro defined in terms of *GlobalReAlloc*.

Using Discardable Global Memory

Discardable memory segments are generally used for data that can be easily regenerated. For example, suppose you decide to use a separate file for "help" text that your program displays when the user requests it. You could allocate a moveable block, lock it, read some data from the file, display it on the screen, unlock the block, and free it. However, this approach requires that your program allocate a new block of memory and access this file every time help information is requested.

Alternatively, you could keep a moveable block for this file buffer in memory all the time. When the user requests some help information, you check to see that the information is already in the buffer, and then you use that information rather than access the disk again. The performance of your program improves, but it does so at the cost of having a block of global memory allocated for the duration of your program.

How about using a discardable block instead? This keeps the buffer in memory but also gives Windows permission to discard it if necessary. When you lock the block:

```
lpGlobalMemory = GlobalLock (hGlobalMemory) ;
```

the *lpGlobalMemory* return value will be NULL if the block has been discarded. In that case, you use *GlobalReAlloc* to reallocate the segment. Windows never discards a discardable block when the lock count is nonzero.

If you have obtained a valid far pointer from *GlobalLock*, that pointer is valid until you call *GlobalUnlock*. Even after the block is discarded, the handle is still valid. (This avoids problems when you pass the handle to *GlobalLock*.)

You can also determine that a block is discardable or has been discarded by using the *GlobalFlags* function:

```
wFlags = GlobalFlags (hGlobalMemory) ;
```

WINDOWS.H has identifiers you can use in combination with *wFlags*. This value is nonzero if the block is discardable:

```
(GMEM_DISCARDABLE & wFlags)
```

This value is nonzero if the block has been discarded:

```
(GMEM_DISCARDED & wFlags)
```

Another approach is to include the GLOBAL_NOTIFY flag when allocating a discardable segment. In this case, Windows will call a call-back function in your program that has been registered with the *GlobalNotify* function when it is about to discard a discardable segment.

Huge Global Memory Blocks

The *dwSize* parameter in *GlobalAlloc* is a 32-bit DWORD (double word), large enough in theory to allocate a 4-gigabyte block of memory. Although you obviously won't be able to get a block quite that large, it appears that you can still allocate a block of memory larger than 64 KB. Yes, you can, but you have to be careful. Beginning with version 4 of the Microsoft C Compiler, the *huge* keyword was implemented for defining variables that are larger than 64 KB. A huge pointer is 32 bits, just like a far pointer. However, the Microsoft C Compiler assumes that a far pointer addresses only a 64-KB range and will never run past the end of the segment. With a huge pointer, the compiler generates code that checks for segment overrun and does appropriate segment arithmetic on the pointer.

The phrase "segment arithmetic" should have triggered a bell in your head! I mentioned earlier that you should not perform segment arithmetic in your Windows programs because it violates rules of protected mode. Fortunately, the Microsoft C 6 compiler and Windows work together to perform different segment arithmetic depending on whether the program is running in real mode or protected mode. In real mode, jumping from the end of one 64-KB segment to the beginning of another segment requires adding 0x1000. In protected mode, the selectors are allocated so that 8 is added for the segment jump. (Note: Don't rely on this number; it may change under future versions.)

When you use *GlobalAlloc* to allocate memory greater than 64 KB, you must cast the pointer returned from *GlobalLock* into a huge pointer and save it as a huge pointer. For instance, this code allocates a 128-KB memory block and locks it:

```
GLOBALHANDLE hGlobalMemory ;
char huge    *lpGlobalMemory ;
    [other program lines]
hGlobalMemory = GlobalAlloc (GMEM_MOVEABLE, 0x20000L) ;
    [other program lines]
lpGlobalMemory = (char huge *) GlobalLock (hGlobalMemory) ;
```

Every function that manipulates this huge pointer must be aware that the pointer is huge. If a function that is passed a huge pointer believes that the pointer is a simple far pointer, the Microsoft C Compiler will not generate any segment arithmetic when you manipulate the pointer. For this reason, you should not pass a huge pointer to most of the standard C library functions (the C 6 manuals list functions that support huge arrays) or to any of the Windows functions unless you know that the function will not be referencing the pointer past the end of a segment.

That's one problem with huge pointers. Another problem is the possibility that a single data item referenced by the pointer may straddle two segments. With a huge pointer to character data, this is never a problem, because each character is a byte. The offset address that *GlobalLock* returns is always 0, so the huge pointer can also safely reference arrays of all the standard data types (char, int, short, long, float, and double).

If you use a huge pointer to an array of structures, you will have no problems if the size of the structure is a power of 2 (such as 2, 4, 8, 16, and so forth). That guarantees that no single structure will straddle two segments. If the size of the structure is not a power of 2, then you are bound by two restrictions:

■ The data block allocated with *GlobalAlloc* cannot be larger than 128 KB.

■ The offset address returned from *GlobalLock* must be adjusted so that a structure does not straddle two segments.

The first rule is actually implied by the second rule. If the initial offset address is adjusted so that an element of the structure does not straddle the first and second segments, it will straddle the second and third segments.

This explanation requires an example. Let's say you want a huge memory block to hold an array of 15,000 structures, where each structure requires 6 bytes. You can use *typedef* statements for this structure and a far pointer to the structure:

```
#typedef struct
        {
        int  element1 ;
        long element2 ;
        }
        MYSTRUCT ;

#typedef MYSTRUCT huge *LPMYSTRUCT ;
```

In your program you can define a variable for the far pointer to the structure:

```
GLOBALHANDLE    hGlobalMemory ;
LPMYSTRUCT      lpMyStruct ;
        [other program lines]
hGlobalMemory = GlobalAlloc (GHND, 15001 * sizeof (MYSTRUCT)) ;

lpMyStruct = (LPMYSTRUCT) ((65536L % sizeof (MYSTRUCT)) +
                        GlobalLock (hMem)) ;
```

The pointer returned from *GlobalLock* will have an offset address of 0. You must increase that so that a single structure does not straddle the two segments. The adjustment value is the remainder of 65,536 divided by the size of the structure. (In this case, the adjustment value is 4.) Because you have a little waste here, *GlobalAlloc* allocates one more structure than is really needed.

Allocating Local Memory

I've been stressing the importance of using moveable (and, if possible, discardable) global memory blocks. With local memory you have the same options, but the guidelines are more relaxed. Whether you use fixed or moveable memory blocks within your local heap is up to you. Because your entire data segment is moveable (as it will be if you use the small or medium model), what you do inside your data segment doesn't affect other applications.

In fact, Windows makes it easier to use local memory if the blocks are fixed. The question to ask is: Can my local heap be smaller if I use moveable blocks instead of fixed blocks? If you use local memory a lot, and the life spans of the memory blocks overlap each other, then the answer to that question may be yes. If you use local memory allocations solely for short-lived memory, there's no reason to make the blocks moveable.

The local memory functions are similar to the global memory functions. Instead of *GlobalAlloc*, *GlobalLock*, *GlobalUnlock*, and *GlobalFree*, you use *LocalAlloc*, *LocalLock*, *LocalUnlock*, and *LocalFree*. Instead of identifiers that begin with GMEM, you use identifiers that begin with LMEM. The only real differences are these: The memory size passed to *LocalAlloc* is a WORD (unsigned integer) rather than a DWORD, and the pointer returned from *LocalLock* is a near pointer rather than a far pointer.

This is the syntax of *LocalAlloc*:

```
hLocalMemory = LocalAlloc (wFlags, wSize) ;
```

The *wSize* parameter is large enough to accommodate a requested size of 65,536 bytes, but you won't get a local block that large, because the data segment also includes your program's stack and static variables.

The *wFlags* parameter can first specify the attributes of the block:

- LMEM_FIXED—Memory is fixed. (This is the default if *wFlags* is 0.)

- LMEM_MOVEABLE—Memory is moveable.

- LMEM_DISCARDABLE—Memory is discardable. This option should be used only with LMEM_MOVEABLE.

The LMEM_ZEROINIT flag zeroes out the memory block.

These two flags are equivalent to the similar flags for *GlobalAlloc*:

- LMEM_NOCOMPACT—Windows will neither compact nor discard memory in the local heap when attempting to allocate the block.

- LMEM_NODISCARD—Windows will not discard discardable memory in the local heap when attempting to allocate the block. Windows may still compact memory by moving moveable blocks.

WINDOWS.H also includes two shorthand flags for local memory allocations. The flag LHND (which stands for "local handle") is defined as:

```
LMEM_MOVEABLE : LMEM_ZEROINIT
```

The flag LPTR ("local pointer") is defined as:

```
LMEM_FIXED : LMEM_ZEROINIT
```

If Windows cannot find enough memory in the local heap to allocate the block, it will attempt to expand the local heap by enlarging the size of the entire data segment. (Remember that the local heap is always at the top of the automatic data segment.) Windows may even move the data segment to another location in memory if that will provide the space it needs to expand the local heap. When *LocalAlloc* returns, your data segment may have been moved. (If this makes you nervous, check the section below entitled "Locking Your Own Data Segment.") The HEAPSIZE specification in the module definition (.DEF) file is really a minimum value for the heap.

If, after all this, Windows still cannot find enough memory in the local heap to allocate the memory block, the handle returned from *LocalAlloc* will be NULL. If you use local memory allocation only for small, short-lived memory blocks, you probably don't need to check the handle for a NULL value. (Alternatively, you might want to check the value during program development but not in the final version of the program.) If you do a lot of random local memory allocation with blocks of various sizes and different life spans, then you'll have to implement some kind of error processing.

LocalLock turns the local memory handle into a near pointer and then locks the block. *LocalUnlock* unlocks the block and invalidates the pointer. *LocalFree* frees the memory block and invalidates the handle.

Here's an example of using local memory to define the window class structure during program initialization:

```
LOCALHANDLE     hLocalMemory ;
NPWNDCLASS      npwndclass ;
     [other program lines]
if (!hPrevInstance)
     {
     hLocalMemory = LocalAlloc (LHND, sizeof (WNDCLASS)) ;
     npwndclass = (NPWNDCLASS) LocalLock (hLocalMemory) ;

     npwndclass->style          = CS_HREDRAW | CS_VREDRAW ;
     npwndclass->lpfnWndProc     = WndProc ;
     npwndclass->cbClsExtra      = 0 ;
     npwndclass->cbWndExtra      = 0 ;
     npwndclass->hInstance       = hInstance ;
     npwndclass->hIcon           = LoadIcon (NULL, IDI_APPLICATION) ;
     npwndclass->hCursor         = LoadCursor (NULL, IDC_ARROW) ;
     npwndclass->hbrBackground   = GetStockObject (WHITE_BRUSH) ;
     npwndclass->lpszMenuName    = NULL ;
     npwndclass->lpszClassName   = szAppName ;

     RegisterClass (npwndclass) ;

     LocalUnlock (hLocalMemory) ;
     LocalFree (hLocalMemory) ;
     }
```

The size of the memory block passed to *LocalAlloc* is the size of the WNDCLASS structure. *LocalLock* always returns a near pointer regardless of the memory model, because it allocates memory from the local heap in the program's automatic data segment. In this example, the pointer to type *char* that *LocalLock* returns is cast into a pointer to a WNDCLASS structure. The -> notation is used to reference the elements of a structure based on a pointer to the structure. In the *RegisterClass* call, we don't use the address (&) operator because *npwndclass* is already a pointer. Note also that the use of LHND initializes the block of memory to 0. All variables in the structure that take a 0 or NULL value need not be explicitly assigned.

Other Local Memory Functions

Some other local memory functions parallel those for global memory allocations, except that sizes are in terms of *wBytes* rather than *dwBytes*. You can get the current size of a local memory block by calling:

```
wBytes = LocalSize (hLocalMemory) ;
```

The function *LocalReAlloc* can change the size of an allocated memory block, change a moveable block to discardable, change a discardable block to nondiscardable, and discard a discardable block, just like *GlobalReAlloc*. During a *LocalReAlloc* call, Windows may expand the size of the local heap by expanding the size of the entire data segment, possibly moving it to another location in memory. *LocalCompact* can determine the amount of free local memory available in the heap, *LocalDiscard* discards a discardable memory block, and *LocalFlags* provides the current status of discardable blocks.

Two other local memory functions do not have counterparts in the global memory functions. You can prevent your local heap from being compacted by calling:

```
LocalFreeze (0) ;
```

When you later want to allow compacting, you can call:

```
LocalMelt (0) ;
```

Locking Your Own Data Segment

Now that you are thoroughly paranoid about locking and unlocking memory blocks, you may start to wonder about the automatic data segment of the program itself. When the program begins executing, your automatic data segment has a lock count of 1, and the data segment cannot be moved in memory. Windows decrements that lock count when the program makes one of the following calls: *GetMessage*, *PeekMessage*, *WaitMessage*, *LocalAlloc*, or *LocalReAlloc*.

The *GetMessage*, *PeekMessage*, and *WaitMessage* calls can cause a switch from your program to another program. When your program gets control again, your data segment may have been moved. A *LocalAlloc* or *LocalReAlloc* call can cause Windows to expand the size of your local heap, in the process moving the data segment to another location in memory. Windows increments the lock count when it returns from these calls to your program. So in most cases, your program's data segment is locked when your program has control. This means that you can construct (through casting) far pointers to data in your data segment, and they will remain valid until you make one of these five calls or exit the window procedure.

If you want to prevent the movement of your data segment during a *LocalAlloc* or *LocalReAlloc* call, you can increase the lock count by 1 before calling the function:

```
LockData (0) ;
```

Following the *LockData* call, the lock count of your data segment will be 2. When Windows decrements the count during a *LocalAlloc* or *LocalReAlloc* call, it will still be positive and your data segment will still be locked. You can decrement the lock count by calling:

```
UnlockData (0) ;
```

If you're brave, you might also want to take the opposite approach. You might be willing to keep your data segment unlocked while making Windows calls. You would do this by calling *UnlockData* to decrement the lock count to 0 and then *LockData* to increment it to 1 again before exiting the window procedure. When your data segment is unlocked, Windows has more flexibility in moving segments in memory because Windows can move your data segment as well. However, when your data segment is unlocked, you should not make any Windows calls that require a far pointer to your data segment. Depending on what happens during that call, the pointer may become invalid by the time Windows needs to use it.

Memory Allocation Shortcuts

We have been treating handles as abstract numbers. But sometimes handles are actually pointers. If you use LMEM_FIXED in *LocalAlloc*, the handle returned from the call is a near pointer that you can use directly. You do not need to call *LocalLock*. (If you do, it simply returns the same value you pass as a parameter—the handle that is actually a valid near pointer.) In fact, WINDOWS.H defines a special flag for calling *LocalAlloc* with an LMEM-_FIXED parameter. The flag is LPTR ("local pointer") and is defined as:

```
LMEM_FIXED : LMEM_ZEROINIT
```

When you use this flag, you need only cast the return value from *LocalAlloc* into a near pointer of the type you want:

```
npString = (char NEAR *) LocalAlloc (LPTR, wSize) ;
```

You free it up by casting the near pointer back to a handle and calling *LocalFree*:

```
LocalFree ((LOCALHANDLE) npString) ;
```

This technique is handy for allocating small chunks of local memory. For instance, here's the example shown above for allocating memory for the window class structure. It now uses a fixed block of local memory:

```
NPWNDCLASS      npwndclass ;
     [other program lines]
if (!hPrevInstance)
     {
     npwndclass = (NPWNDCLASS) LocalAlloc (LPTR, sizeof (WNDCLASS)) ;

     npwndclass->style         = CS_HREDRAW : CS_VREDRAW ;
     npwndclass->lpfnWndProc    = WndProc ;
     npwndclass->cbClsExtra     = 0 ;
```

```
npwndclass->cbWndExtra      = 0 ;
npwndclass->hInstance       = hInstance ;
npwndclass->hIcon           = LoadIcon (NULL, IDI_APPLICATION) ;
npwndclass->hCursor         = LoadCursor (NULL, IDC_ARROW) ;
npwndclass->hbrBackground   = GetStockObject (WHITE_BRUSH) ;
npwndclass->lpszMenuName    = NULL ;
npwndclass->lpszClassName   = szAppName ;

RegisterClass (npwndclass) ;

LocalFree ((LOCALHANDLE) npwndclass) ;
}
```

We've eliminated two lines of code (*LocalLock* and *LocalUnlock*) and one variable (the local memory handle). Note the casting in the *LocalAlloc* and *LocalFree* calls.

The same technique is even applicable for *GlobalAlloc* when the GMEM_FIXED (or GPTR) flag is used. The "handle" returned from *GlobalAlloc* is the segment address of the segment. It's a little more clumsy to convert that into a far pointer, but here's how to do it:

```
lpString = (LPSTR) MAKELONG (0, GlobalAlloc (GPTR, dwSize)) ;
```

The MAKELONG macro combines the segment address returned from *GlobalAlloc* and an offset address of 0 to make a long integer, which is then cast into a long pointer to type *char*. To free this block, you have to extract the segment address from the pointer and pass it to *GlobalFree*:

```
GlobalFree ((GLOBALHANDLE) LOWORD ((LONG) lpString))) ;
```

I don't like the memory allocation shortcuts, and I don't think they should be used. I've included them only because many sample Windows programs use them, particularly when allocating local memory.

Using C Memory Allocation Functions

The start-up code that LINK attaches to C programs running under Windows contains functions for many of the memory allocation functions in Microsoft C 6, such as *calloc*, *malloc*, *realloc*, and *free*. The routines in the start-up code convert the normal C memory allocation functions into equivalent Windows memory allocation functions. For instance, the function:

```
malloc (wSize) ;
```

is translated into:

```
LocalAlloc (LMEM_FIXED | LMEM_NOCOMPACT, min (1, wSize)) ;
```

These functions are included in the Windows start-up code not for your benefit, but because several other C functions from the standard library make calls to these C memory allocation functions. These other C functions cannot work properly without using the

Windows memory allocation calls. Although it's not intended that you use these functions, you can use them. Be aware, however, that in compact-memory and large-memory models (which you shouldn't be using for Windows programs anyway), the Windows *malloc* returns a far pointer to your program's automatic data segment—as opposed to the non-Windows *malloc*, which returns a far pointer to a block of memory outside the automatic data segment. Also be aware that *_fmalloc* and *halloc* are translated into *GlobalAlloc* calls with a flag that is equal to (GMEM_FIXED | GMEM_NODISCARD), and as you know, you should not use fixed global memory blocks. Moreover, the pointer returned from the Windows *halloc* is not properly aligned for an array of elements that are not multiples of 2, and the memory is not initialized to 0. The point is clear: Unless you feel deprived doing C programming without *malloc*, use the Windows functions for all memory allocations.

If You Know You're Running in Protected Mode

In this chapter, I have tried to present guidelines for memory management that are valid in all modes in which Windows 3 can run. However, if your program is so large that it can (realistically) run only in protected mode, then you can simplify your memory management. Such a program should use *GetWinFlags* and terminate if it's running in real mode.

When allocating moveable global memory, you can lock the memory block immediately to obtain the pointer. Even though the block is locked, Windows can still move it in memory—and the pointer will remain valid. You don't even have to save the global memory handle. To free the block, you can use *GlobalHandle* to obtain the handle from the pointer. Then unlock the block and free it as normal.

You can compile with the -G2 flag to generate 286 code.

Chapter 8

Icons, Cursors, Bitmaps, and Strings

Most Windows programs include a customized icon that Windows displays when the program is minimized. Some programs (such as the Windows PAINTBRUSH program) also use customized cursors to represent different operations of the program. Most Windows programs also use menus and dialog boxes.

Icons, cursors, menus, and dialog boxes are all examples of "resources." Resources are data and are included in a program's .EXE file, but they do not reside in a program's normal data segment. When Windows loads a program into memory for execution, it usually leaves the resources on disk. Only when Windows needs a particular resource does it load the resource into memory. (You've probably noticed dynamic loading of resources when working with Windows programs. When you invoke a program's dialog box for the first time, Windows usually accesses the disk to copy the dialog box resource from the program's .EXE file into memory.)

Most resources are read-only data and are marked as discardable. When Windows needs more memory, segments occupied by discardable resources can be freed up. If the resource is required again later, Windows reloads it from the .EXE file. Just as multiple instances of the same program share the same code, multiple instances also usually share resources. I'll be discussing these resources:

- Icons
- Cursors
- Bitmaps
- Character strings
- User-defined resources
- Menus
- Keyboard accelerators
- Dialog boxes
- Fonts

The first five resources in the list are discussed in this chapter. Menus and keyboard accelerators are covered in Chapter 9, dialog boxes in Chapter 10, and fonts in Chapter 14.

COMPILING RESOURCES

During program development, resources are defined in a "resource script," which is an ASCII text file with the extension .RC. The resource script can contain ASCII representations of resources and can also reference other files (either ASCII or binary files) that contain resources. The resource compiler (RC.EXE) compiles the resource script into a binary form, adds the resources to the end of the .EXE file that LINK generates, and creates a "resource table" in the .EXE header.

You can use the resource compiler included in the Windows Software Development Kit in one of three ways:

- You can compile resources and add them to the linked .EXE file in one step by executing the command:

  ```
  RC filename
  ```

  where *filename.RC* is the name of the resource script (the .RC extension is assumed) and *filename.EXE* is the name of the linked .EXE file. You can also use:

  ```
  RC resource-name exe-name
  ```

  if the name of your .RC resource script and the name of your .EXE executable are different. (This is usually not the case.)

- You can compile a .RC resource script into a binary compiled form with the extension .RES by executing:

```
RC -r filename
```

   This uses the ASCII *filename.RC* file to create a binary file called *filename.RES*. You can then add the resources to the linked file by executing:

```
RC filename.RES
```

   The .RES extension is required here to differentiate this command from the command shown earlier that both compiles the resource script and adds the resources to the .EXE file.

- If your program has no resources, you should run *rc.exe* on the linked file:

```
RC filename.EXE
```

   This flags the program as being "Windows 3 aware."

This second method is the one most commonly used when the resource script contains resources. Although it requires that the RC.EXE resource compiler be run twice—once to compile the resource script and again to add the resources to the .EXE file—it actually results in a faster edit-make-run cycle when developing Windows programs. The reason is that compiling the resources generally takes much longer than adding them to the .EXE file. During program development, you will probably modify your C source code much more frequently than the resource script, so you have no need to recompile the resources each time.

The procedure of compiling resources is reflected in a different make file. Up until now we have been using a make file that looks something like this:

```
progname.exe : progname.obj progname.def
    link progname, /align:16, NUL, /nod slibcew libw, progname
    rc progname.exe

progname.obj : progname.c
    cl -c -Gsw -Ow -W2 -Zp progname.c
```

When we start using resources, we'll use an expanded make file that looks like this:

```
progname.exe : progname.obj progname.def progname.res
    link progname, /align:16, NUL, /nod slibcew libw, progname
    rc progname.res

progname.obj : progname.c [progname.h]
    cl -c -Gsw -Ow -W2 -Zp progname.c

progname.res : progname.rc [progname.h] [and other files]
    rc -r progname.rc
```

In the second and third sections I've indicated that a .H header file can be used in both the C source code and the resource script. This header file usually defines identifiers used by the program to reference resources. I've also indicated in the third section that the dependent file list possibly includes "other files." These are files referenced from within the resource script. Generally they are binary files that contain icons, cursors, or bitmaps.

The RC.EXE resource compiler uses a preprocessor called RCPP.EXE. This preprocessor folds added or subtracted constants, recognizes /*and */ as comment delimiters, and recognizes the C preprocessor directives *#define, #undef, #ifdef, #ifndef, #include, #if, #elif, #else,* and *#endif.* The *#include* directive works a little differently than in normal C programs. We'll examine this in greater detail in Chapter 10.

In the first section of the make file, the .OBJ and .RES files are dependent files for the .EXE target. NMAKE checks the rest of the make file to determine if these dependent files must be updated. The second section compiles the C source code as usual. The third section compiles the .RC resource script into a binary .RES file.

The first section is then executed if either the .OBJ, .DEF, or .RES file has changed since the last .EXE file was created. This section links the program as usual and runs .RC again to add the resources to the .EXE file. If you change only the .RC resource script file, you still need to relink to produce a new .EXE file without the previous resources. The resource compiler cannot remove old resources from a .EXE file when adding new ones.

ICONS AND CURSORS

Let's begin by looking at a sample program that uses two resources—an icon and a cursor. RESOURC1, shown in Figure 8-1, displays a customized icon when the program is minimized and uses a customized cursor when the mouse is in RESOURC1's client area. RESOURC1 also draws its icon in several rows and columns within the client area.

RESOURC1.MAK

```
#----------------------
# RESOURC1.MAK make file
#----------------------

resourc1.exe : resourc1.obj resourc1.def resourc1.res
    link resourc1, /align:16, NUL, /nod slibcew libw, resourc1
    rc resourc1.res

resourc1.obj : resourc1.c
    cl -c -Gsw -Ow -W2 -Zp resourc1.c

resourc1.res : resourc1.rc resourc1.ico resourc1.cur
    rc -r resourc1.rc
```

Figure 8-1. *The RESOURC1 program, including an icon and a cursor.*

306

RESOURC1.C

```
/*-----------------------------------------------------------
   RESOURC1.C -- Icon and Cursor Demonstration Program No. 1
                 (c) Charles Petzold, 1990
   -----------------------------------------------------------*/

#include <windows.h>

long FAR PASCAL WndProc (HWND, WORD, WORD, LONG) ;

char    szAppName [] = "Resourc1" ;
HANDLE hInst ;

int PASCAL WinMain (HANDLE hInstance, HANDLE hPrevInstance,
                    LPSTR lpszCmdLine, int nCmdShow)
     {
     HWND     hwnd ;
     MSG      msg ;
     WNDCLASS wndclass ;

     if (!hPrevInstance)
          {
          wndclass.style         = CS_HREDRAW : CS_VREDRAW ;
          wndclass.lpfnWndProc    = WndProc ;
          wndclass.cbClsExtra     = 0 ;
          wndclass.cbWndExtra     = 0 ;
          wndclass.hInstance      = hInstance ;
          wndclass.hIcon          = LoadIcon (hInstance, szAppName) ;
          wndclass.hCursor        = LoadCursor (hInstance, szAppName) ;
          wndclass.hbrBackground  = COLOR_WINDOW + 1 ;
          wndclass.lpszMenuName   = NULL ;
          wndclass.lpszClassName  = szAppName ;

          RegisterClass (&wndclass) ;
          }

     hInst = hInstance ;

     hwnd = CreateWindow (szAppName, "Icon and Cursor Demo",
                          WS_OVERLAPPEDWINDOW,
                          CW_USEDEFAULT, CW_USEDEFAULT,
                          CW_USEDEFAULT, CW_USEDEFAULT,
                          NULL, NULL, hInstance, NULL) ;

     ShowWindow (hwnd, nCmdShow) ;
     UpdateWindow (hwnd) ;
```

(continued)

```
      while (GetMessage (&msg, NULL, 0, 0))
           {
           TranslateMessage (&msg) ;
           DispatchMessage (&msg) ;
           }
      return msg.wParam ;
      }

long FAR PASCAL WndProc (HWND hwnd, WORD message, WORD wParam, LONG lParam)
      {
      static HICON  hIcon ;
      static short  cxIcon, cyIcon, cxClient, cyClient ;
      HDC           hdc ;
      RECT          rect ;
      PAINTSTRUCT   ps ;
      short         x, y ;

      switch (message)
           {
           case WM_CREATE :
                hIcon = LoadIcon (hInst, szAppName) ;
                cxIcon = GetSystemMetrics (SM_CXICON) ;
                cyIcon = GetSystemMetrics (SM_CYICON) ;
                return 0 ;

           case WM_SIZE :
                cxClient = LOWORD (lParam) ;
                cyClient = HIWORD (lParam) ;
                return 0 ;

           case WM_PAINT :
                hdc = BeginPaint (hwnd, &ps) ;

                for (y = cyIcon ; y < cyClient ; y += 2 * cyIcon)
                    for (x = cxIcon ; x < cxClient ; x += 2 * cxIcon)
                         DrawIcon (hdc, x, y, hIcon) ;

                EndPaint (hwnd, &ps) ;
                return 0 ;

           case WM_DESTROY :
                PostQuitMessage (0) ;
                return 0 ;
           }
      return DefWindowProc (hwnd, message, wParam, lParam) ;
      }
```

RESOURC1.RC

```
/*-----------------------------
   RESOURC1.RC resource script
-----------------------------*/

resourc1   ICON     resourc1.ico
resourc1   CURSOR   resourc1.cur
```

RESOURC1.ICO

RESOURC1.CUR

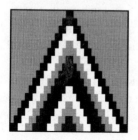

RESOURC1.DEF

```
;-------------------------------------
; RESOURC1.DEF module definition file
;-------------------------------------

NAME            RESOURC1
DESCRIPTION     'Icon and Cursor Demo Program No. 1 (c) Charles Petzold, 1990'
EXETYPE         WINDOWS
STUB            'WINSTUB.EXE'
```

(continued)

```
CODE         PRELOAD MOVEABLE DISCARDABLE
DATA         PRELOAD MOVEABLE MULTIPLE
HEAPSIZE     1024
STACKSIZE    8192
EXPORTS      WndProc
```

Both the icon and the cursor were created using the SDKPAINT program supplied with the Windows Software Development Kit. They are shown in Figure 8-1 against a light gray background. SDKPAINT is a Windows application, and it requires a mouse. Icons are saved from SDKPAINT with a .ICO extension; cursors have a .CUR extension. These files are referred to in the RESOURC1.RC resource script.

The SDKPAINT Tool

SDKPAINT is one of the most important development tools in the Windows Software Development Kit. The program allows you to create bitmaps, icons, and cursors for use in your Windows programs. Icons and cursors are both variations of bitmaps, so it will be helpful to examine bitmaps first.

A bitmap is an array of bits where one or more bits corresponds to each display pixel. In a monochrome bitmap, one bit corresponds to one pixel. (In the simplest case, a 1 bit represents white and a 0 bit represents black. However, bitmaps are often used in logical operations rather than merely to create simple drawings.) In a color bitmap, multiple bits correspond to each pixel to represent color. SDKPAINT supports the creation of monochrome bitmaps and 16-color bitmaps. In a 16-color bitmap, 4 bits are required for each pixel.

A bitmap may have any number of rows and columns. (However, the bitmaps you create in SDKPAINT are limited to 72 rows and 72 columns. You can create larger bitmaps in PAINTBRUSH.) Bitmaps are stored in files with a .BMP extension. (I'll discuss the format of the bitmap file in Chapter 13.)

You can also create icons and cursors in SDKPAINT. Icons and cursors are very similar, and they are both variations of bitmaps.

Windows displays icons and cursors on the screen in a pixel size that depends on the resolution of the video display. This ensures that the icons and cursors are neither too large nor too small. A program can obtain these pixel dimensions using the *GetSystem-Metrics* function with parameters of SM_CXICON, SM_CYICON, SM_CXCURSOR, and SM_CYCURSOR. On most video displays, the dimensions of icons and cursors are identical. To keep it simple in the following discussion, I'll refer only to icons, but keep in mind that everything I say applies to cursors also.

On an IBM Color Graphics Adapter (CGA), the width of an icon is 32 pixels and the height is 16 pixels. On an Enhanced Graphics Adapter (EGA), Video Graphics Array (VGA), and the IBM 8514/A video adapter, the icons are 32 pixels wide and 32 pixels high. For higher-resolution adapters, icons could be displayed as 64 pixels by 64 pixels.

Each .ICO file can contain multiple icon images, each one designed for particular resolutions and color capabilities of the various video adapters on which your Windows program can run. SDKPAINT supports four different image formats. When you create a new icon file (by selecting New from SDKPAINT's File menu), you select one of these four formats. After creating an icon in this format, you can then select another of the four formats from the New option on the Image menu. These four formats are:

- 32 pixels by 16 pixels with 2 colors (monochrome)

- 32 pixels by 32 pixels with 2 colors (monochrome)

- 32 pixels by 32 pixels with 8 colors

- 32 pixels by 32 pixels with 16 colors

The first format is for the CGA, and the second is for other video adapters (EGA, VGA, and 8514/A) running in a monochrome mode. The third and fourth are for non-CGA adapters running in color modes. The 8-color format is of limited use: SDKPAINT actually uses a 16-color format internally and when saving the image to the file, but allows you to color it with only 8 colors. The EGA, VGA, and 8514/A are all capable of 16 colors.

You don't need to create icon images in all four formats. When a program contains an icon resource, Windows will choose the format that most closely approximates the size and color capabilities appropriate to the video adapter. For example, if you create only 32-by-32-pixel icons and your program is run on a CGA, Windows will display the icon using every other row of pixels, effectively compressing the height of the icon.

If you create only a 32-by-32 icon with 16 colors, use color sparingly because the colors can be approximated only with gray shades (or converted to black or white) when running with a monochrome display. All the icons and cursors in the programs in this chapter were created in the 32-by-32 monochrome format.

When you create an icon image in one of the four formats, SDKPAINT actually stores it as two bitmaps—a monochrome bitmap "mask" and a monochrome or color bitmap image. Icons are always rectangular, but this mask allows the icon to appear to be nonrectangular. That is, part of the icon allows the background against which the icon is displayed to be visible. The icon can also contain areas that invert the background color.

These two options are indicated in SDKPAINT by radio buttons labeled "Screen" and "Inverse." After selecting "Screen," anything you draw in the icon will be transparent, and after selecting "Inverse," anything you draw in the icon will invert the background. You can select different background colors to see how this looks. The icons and cursor in Figure 8-1 are shown against a light gray background. The light gray areas were colored using the "Screen" option, and the dark gray areas were colored using the "Inverse" option.

For a monochrome icon, the following table shows how SDKPAINT constructs the two bitmaps that describe the icon:

Color:	Black	White	Screen	Inverse Screen
Mask Bitmap:	0	0	1	1
Image Bitmap:	0	1	0	1

When displaying the icon, Windows first uses a bitwise AND operation of the display and the first bitmap. The display pixels corresponding to 0 bits from the first bitmap all become 0's, which are black. The display pixels corresponding to 1 bit remain the same. This is shown in the following logic table.

	Display Pixel	
Mask Bit	0	1
0	0	0
1	0	1

Next, Windows performs a bitwise exclusive OR operation of the image bitmap and the display. A 0 in the second bitmap leaves the display pixel the same; a 1 in the second bitmap inverts the display pixel. Here's the logic table:

	Display Pixel	
Image Bit	0	1
0	0	1
1	1	0

Using C notation for the operations, the display is altered by the following formula:

Display = (Display & Mask) ^ Image

For a 16-color icon, the mask bitmap is still monochrome and constructed as shown above. The image bitmap contains 4 bits per pixel to represent 16 colors. All four bits are set to 1 for areas of the icon that invert the background.

Earlier I said that when talking about bitmaps, 0 does not necessarily mean black, and 1 does not necessarily mean white. As you can see here, it depends on how Windows uses the bitmaps. (I'll discuss this more in Chapter 13.)

In RESOURC1, I've defined the window class to make the background of the client area be COLOR_WINDOW. You may want to bring up the Windows Control Panel program and change the window color to see how the icon and cursor invert colors.

Getting a Handle on Icons

A resource script references the icon file with a statement that looks like this:

```
myicon ICON iconfile.ico
```

where ICONFILE.ICO is the name of the icon file. This statement assigns the name "myicon" to the icon. In your C program, you use the *LoadIcon* function to obtain a handle to the icon. *LoadIcon* requires two parameters. The first is the instance handle of your program, generally called *hInstance* in *WinMain*. Windows needs this handle to determine which .EXE file contains the icon resource. The second parameter is the icon name from the resource script, in the form of a pointer to a null-terminated string. *LoadIcon* returns a value of type HICON, which is defined in WINDOWS.H.

This diagram shows the relationship between the icon name in the resource script and the LoadIcon statement in your C program:

Resource script:	*myicon ICON iconfile.ico*
Program source:	*hIcon = LoadIcon (hInstance, "**myicon** ") ;*

Don't worry about uppercase and lowercase here. The resource compiler converts the name in the resource script file to uppercase and inserts the name in the resource table of the program's .EXE file header. The first time you call *LoadIcon*, Windows converts the string from the second parameter to uppercase and searches the resource table of the .EXE file for a matching name.

You can speed up this search by using a number (an unsigned integer) instead of a name. This number is called an ID number for the icon. Here's how it's done:

Resource script:	*125 ICON iconfile.ico*
Program source:	*hIcon = LoadIcon (hInstance, MAKEINTRESOURCE**(125)**) ;*

MAKEINTRESOURCE ("make an integer into a resource string") is a macro defined in WINDOWS.H that converts a number into a far pointer. The offset address is set to the number, and the segment address is set to 0. Here's how MAKINTRESOURCE is defined in WINDOWS.H:

```
#define MAKEINTRESOURCE(i) (LPSTR)((DWORD)((WORD)(i)))
```

Windows knows that the second parameter is a number rather than a pointer to a character string because the segment address is 0.

Sample programs presented earlier in this book use predefined icons:

```
LoadIcon (NULL, IDI_APPLICATION) ;
```

Windows knows that this is a predefined icon because the *hInstance* parameter is set to NULL. IDI_APPLICATION happens also to be defined in WINDOWS.H in terms of MAKEINTRESOURCE:

```
#define IDI_APPLICATION MAKEINTRESOURCE(32512)
```

The predefined icons and cursors are part of the display driver file.

You can also reference the icon name using a third method that combines the string method and the number method:

Resource script: ***125*** *ICON iconfile.ico*

Program source: *hIcon = LoadIcon (hInstance, "**#125**") ;*

Windows recognizes the initial # character as prefacing a number in ASCII form.

How about a fourth method? This one uses a macro definition in a header file that is included (using the *#include* directive) in both the resource script and your program:

Header file: *#define myicon 125*

Resource script: ***myicon*** *ICON iconfile.ico*

Program source: *hIcon = LoadIcon (hInstance, MAKEINTRESOURCE(**myicon**)) ;*

Be careful when you use this method! Although case does not matter when the icon name is a character string, case does make a difference for identifiers that are generated from *#define* statements.

Using ID numbers rather than names for icons reduces the .EXE file size and speeds up the *LoadIcon* call. Moreover, if your program uses many icons, you'll find it easier to store the ID numbers in an array.

Using Icons in Your Program

Icons have only a couple of purposes. Most Windows programs use an icon only for displaying the program in the icon area. This is accomplished when defining the window class:

```
wndclass.hIcon = LoadIcon (hInstance, "myicon") ;
```

If you later want to change the program's icon, you can do so using *SetClassWord*. Let's assume you had a second icon in your resource script:

```
anothericon ICON iconfil2.ico
```

You can substitute this icon for "myicon" with the statement:

```
SetClassWord (hwnd, GCW_HICON, LoadIcon (hInstance,"anothericon")) ;
```

If you save the icon handle from a *LoadIcon* call, you can also draw the icon on the client area of your window:

```
DrawIcon (hdc, x, y, hIcon) ;
```

Windows itself uses the *DrawIcon* function when displaying your program's icon in the icon area. Windows obtains the handle to the icon from the window class structure. You can obtain the handle in the same way:

```
DrawIcon (hdc, x, y, GetClassWord (hwnd, GGW_HICON)) ;
```

314

The RESOURC1 sample program uses the same icon for the window class and for displaying in its client area. In the resource script the icon is given the same name as the program:

```
resourc1  ICON  resourc1.ico
```

Because the character string "Resourc1" is stored in the array *szAppName* and is already used in the program for the window class name, the *LoadIcon* call is simply:

```
LoadIcon (hInstance, szAppName) ;
```

You'll notice that *LoadIcon* is called twice in RESOURC1 for the same icon, once when defining the window class in *WinMain* and again when obtaining a handle to the icon while processing the WM_CREATE message in *WndProc*. Calling *LoadIcon* twice presents no problem: Both calls return the same handle. Windows actually loads the icon only once from the .EXE file and then uses it for all instances of the RESOURC1 program.

Using Alternate Cursors

The statements that you use to specify a cursor in your resource script and to obtain a handle to a cursor in your program are very similar to the icon statements shown above:

Resource script: ***mycursor*** *CURSOR cursfile.cur*

Program source: *hCursor = LoadCursor (hInstance, "**mycursor**") ;*

The other methods shown for icons (using ID numbers and MAKEINTRESOURCE) work with cursors also. WINDOWS.H includes a *typedef* definition for HCURSOR that you can use for storing the cursor handle. (Both HICON and HCURSOR are defined as HANDLE.)

You can use the cursor handle obtained from *LoadCursor* when setting the *hCursor* member of the window class structure:

```
wndclass.hCursor = LoadCursor (hInstance, "mycursor") ;
```

This causes the mouse cursor to be displayed as your customized cursor when the mouse is within the client area of your window.

If you use child windows, you may want the cursor to appear differently, depending on the child window below the cursor. If your program defines the window class for these child windows, you can use different cursors for each class by appropriately setting the *hCursor* field in each window class. And if you use predefined child window controls, you can alter the *hCursor* field of the window class using:

```
SetClassWord (hwndChild, GCW_HCURSOR,
              LoadCursor (hInstance, "childcursor") ;
```

If you separate your client area into smaller logical areas without using child windows, you can use *SetCursor* to change the mouse cursor:

```
SetCursor (hCursor) ;
```

You should call *SetCursor* during processing of the WM_MOUSEMOVE message. Otherwise, Windows uses the cursor specified in the window class to redraw the cursor when it is moved.

RESOURC1 uses the name of the program for the name of the cursor:

```
resourc1 CURSOR resourc1.cur
```

When RESOURC1.C defines the window class, this *szAppName* variable is used for *LoadCursor*:

```
wndclass.hCursor = LoadCursor (hInstance, szAppName) ;
```

RESOURCES AND MEMORY

The *LoadIcon* and *LoadCursor* functions certainly sound as if they load the icon or cursor from the .EXE file into memory. They do not. Windows doesn't load the icon or cursor until it needs the object for drawing. During loading, Windows may alter the object to fit the dimensions and color capabilities of the display.

Icons and cursors (as well as all other resources except bitmaps) are "owned" by the program. Multiple instances of the same program share the same cursors and icons loaded into memory. When the last instance terminates, Windows frees up the memory occupied by the resource. And for most resources, Windows can discard the resource from memory to generate free space and then load it back into memory when needed.

You can override some of these characteristics, however. For all resources except the keyboard accelerators (covered in Chapter 9), you can specify "load" and "memory" options in the resource script file. These options are similar to the module definition file options for code and data segments discussed in Chapter 7. In the resource script, the load and memory options follow the resource type. This is the generalized form of the ICON statement in a resource script file:

```
iconID ICON [load-option] [memory-option] iconfile.ico
```

The load option can be either PRELOAD or LOADONCALL. A resource defined as PRELOAD will be loaded into memory when the program is loaded. LOADONCALL means that the resource will not be loaded until Windows needs it. LOADONCALL is the default for all resources. You will probably want to use PRELOAD only when you know that your program will need the resource immediately after beginning to execute.

The memory options are FIXED, MOVEABLE, and DISCARDABLE. DISCARDABLE resources must also be MOVEABLE. For the resources discussed in this chapter, the icon, cursor, and character string resources have default memory options of MOVEABLE and DISCARDABLE. The bitmap and user-defined resources are MOVEABLE only. Why the difference? Icon, cursor, and character string resources are read-only, so Windows can safely discard them from memory. Windows allows bitmaps and user-defined resources to be modified from within a program—and modified resources cannot be discarded.

Bitmaps: Pictures in Pixels

We've already talked about the use of bitmaps in icons and cursors. Windows also includes a resource type called BITMAP.

Bitmaps are used for two major purposes. The first is to draw pictures on the display. For instance, the Windows display driver files contain lots of tiny bitmaps used for drawing the arrows in scroll bars, the check mark in pull-down menus, the system menu box, the size box, check boxes, and radio buttons. Programs such as PAINTBRUSH use bitmaps to display a graphics menu.

The second major use of bitmaps is to create brushes. Brushes, you'll recall, are patterns of pixels that Windows uses to fill an area of the display. (Chapter 9 discusses a third and less common use of bitmaps, as selection items in menus.)

Using Bitmaps and Brushes

The RESOURC2 program, shown in Figure 8-2, is an upgraded version of RESOURC1 that includes a monochrome bitmap resource used to create a brush for the background of the client area. The bitmap was created in SDKPAINT with dimensions of 8 by 8, which is the minimum size for a brush.

RESOURC2.MAK

```
#------------------------
# RESOURC2.MAK make file
#------------------------

resourc2.exe : resourc2.obj resourc2.def resourc2.res
    link resourc2, /align:16, NUL, /nod slibcew libw, resourc2
    rc resourc2.res

resourc2.obj : resourc2.c
    cl -c -Gsw -Ow -W2 -Zp resourc2.c

resourc2.res : resourc2.rc resourc2.ico resourc2.cur resourc2.bmp
    rc -r resourc2.rc
```

RESOURC2.C

```
/*-------------------------------------------------------------
   RESOURC2.C -- Icon and Cursor Demonstration Program No. 2
                 (c) Charles Petzold, 1990
   -----------------------------------------------------------*/
```

Figure 8-2. *The RESOURC2 program, including an icon, a cursor, and a bitmap.*   (continued)

```
#include <windows.h>

long FAR PASCAL WndProc  (HWND, WORD, WORD, LONG) ;

char    szAppName[] = "Resourc2" ;
HANDLE hInst ;

int PASCAL WinMain (HANDLE hInstance, HANDLE hPrevInstance,
                    LPSTR lpszCmdLine, int nCmdShow)
     {
     HBITMAP  hBitmap ;
     HBRUSH   hBrush ;
     HWND     hwnd ;
     MSG      msg ;
     WNDCLASS wndclass ;

     hBitmap = LoadBitmap (hInstance, szAppName) ;
     hBrush = CreatePatternBrush (hBitmap) ;

     if (!hPrevInstance)
          {
          wndclass.style         = CS_HREDRAW | CS_VREDRAW ;
          wndclass.lpfnWndProc   = WndProc ;
          wndclass.cbClsExtra    = 0 ;
          wndclass.cbWndExtra    = 0 ;
          wndclass.hInstance     = hInstance ;
          wndclass.hIcon         = LoadIcon (hInstance, szAppName) ;
          wndclass.hCursor       = LoadCursor (hInstance, szAppName) ;
          wndclass.hbrBackground = hBrush ;
          wndclass.lpszMenuName  = NULL ;
          wndclass.lpszClassName = szAppName ;

          RegisterClass (&wndclass) ;
          }

     hInst = hInstance ;

     hwnd = CreateWindow (szAppName, "Icon and Cursor Demo",
                     WS_OVERLAPPEDWINDOW,
                     CW_USEDEFAULT, CW_USEDEFAULT,
                     CW_USEDEFAULT, CW_USEDEFAULT,
                     NULL, NULL, hInstance, NULL) ;

     ShowWindow (hwnd, nCmdShow) ;
     UpdateWindow (hwnd) ;
```

(continued)

```
        while (GetMessage (&msg, NULL, 0, 0))
            {
            TranslateMessage (&msg) ;
            DispatchMessage (&msg) ;
            }

        DeleteObject (hBrush) ;        // clean up
        DeleteObject (hBitmap) ;

        return msg.wParam ;
        }

long FAR PASCAL WndProc (HWND hwnd, WORD message, WORD wParam, LONG lParam)
        {
        static HICON  hIcon ;
        static short  cxIcon, cyIcon, cxClient, cyClient ;
        HDC           hdc ;
        PAINTSTRUCT   ps ;
        RECT          rect ;
        short         x, y ;

        switch (message)
            {
            case WM_CREATE :
                    hIcon = LoadIcon (hInst, szAppName) ;
                    cxIcon = GetSystemMetrics (SM_CXICON) ;
                    cyIcon = GetSystemMetrics (SM_CYICON) ;
                    return 0 ;

            case WM_SIZE :
                    cxClient = LOWORD (lParam) ;
                    cyClient = HIWORD (lParam) ;
                    return 0 ;

            case WM_PAINT :
                    hdc = BeginPaint (hwnd, &ps) ;

                    for (y = cyIcon ; y < cyClient ; y += 2 * cyIcon)
                        for (x = cxIcon ; x < cxClient ; x += 2 * cxIcon)
                            DrawIcon (hdc, x, y, hIcon) ;

                    EndPaint (hwnd, &ps) ;
                    return 0 ;

            case WM_DESTROY :
                    PostQuitMessage (0) ;
                    return 0 ;
            }
        return DefWindowProc (hwnd, message, wParam, lParam) ;
        }
```

RESOURC2.RC

```
/*----------------------------
   RESOURC2.RC resource script
   --------------------------*/

resourc2   ICON     resourc2.ico
resourc2   CURSOR   resourc2.cur
resourc2   BITMAP   resourc2.bmp
```

RESOURC2.ICO

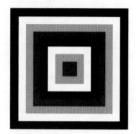

RESOURC2.CUR

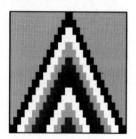

RESOURC2.BMP

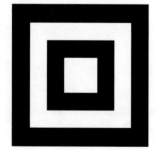

RESOURC2.DEF

```
;------------------------------------
; RESOURC2.DEF module definition file
;------------------------------------

NAME            RESOURC2

DESCRIPTION     'Icon and Cursor Demo Program No. 2 (c) Charles Petzold, 1990'
EXETYPE         WINDOWS
STUB            'WINSTUB.EXE'
CODE            PRELOAD MOVEABLE DISCARDABLE
DATA            PRELOAD MOVEABLE MULTIPLE
HEAPSIZE        1024
STACKSIZE       8192
EXPORTS         WndProc
```

The bitmap resource is included in the resource script in the same format as the icon and cursor:

```
resourc2 BITMAP resourc2.bmp
```

The *LoadBitmap* function used in *WinMain* is similar to the *LoadIcon* and *Load-Cursor* calls. It returns a handle to a bitmap:

```
hBitmap = LoadBitmap (hInstance, szAppName) ;
```

This handle is then used to create a pattern brush. The brush is based on the bitmap:

```
hBrush = CreatePatternBrush (hBitmap) ;
```

When Windows fills an area of the display with this brush, the bitmap is repeated horizontally and vertically every eight pixels. We want to use this brush to color the background of the client area, which we accomplish when defining the window class:

```
wndclass.hbrBackground = hBrush ;
```

The major difference between bitmaps and other resources is of practical significance and can be simply stated: Bitmaps are GDI objects. They are not shared among instances of your program, and they are not automatically deleted from memory when your program terminates. Because bitmaps and brushes are GDI objects, they must be deleted before the program terminates. In RESOURC2 this is done at the end of *WinMain*:

```
DeleteObject (hBrush) ;
DeleteObject (hBitmap) ;
```

CHARACTER STRINGS

Having a resource for character strings may seem odd at first. Certainly we haven't had any problem using regular old character strings defined as variables right in our source code.

Character string resources are primarily for easing the translation of your program to other languages. As you'll discover in the next two chapters, menus and dialog boxes are also part of the resource script. If you use character string resources rather than put strings directly into your source code, then all text that your program uses will be in one file—the resource script. If the text in this resource script is translated, all you need do to create a foreign-language version of your program is relink the program and add the translated resources to the .EXE file. This method is much safer than messing around with your source code. (Of course, you could also choose to define all your character strings as macros and store them in a header file. This method also avoids altering source code during language translations.)

A second reason for using character string resources is to reduce memory space. This reason is less obvious—in fact, if you use character string resources inefficiently, you might not reduce memory space at all. We'll examine this problem after we get through the basics.

Using Character String Resources

The character string resources are defined in your resource script using the keyword STRINGTABLE:

```
STRINGTABLE [load option] [memory option]
    {
        nID1, "character string 1"
        nID2, "character string 2"
        [other string definitions]
    }
```

The resource script can contain only one string table. LOADONCALL is the default load option; MOVEABLE and DISCARDABLE are the default memory options. Each string can be only one line long with a maximum of 255 characters. The strings cannot contain any C-style control characters except for \t (tab). However, the strings *can* contain octal constants:

Tab	\011
Linefeed	\012
Carriage return	\015

These control characters are recognized by the *DrawText* and *MessageBox* functions.

Your program can use the *LoadString* call to copy a string resource into a buffer in the program's data segment:

```
LoadString (hInstance, nID, lpszBuffer, nMaxLength) ;
```

The *nID* parameter refers to the ID number that precedes each string in the resource script; *lpszBuffer* is a far (or long) pointer to a character array that receives the character string; and *nMaxLength* is the maximum number of characters to transfer into the *lpszBuffer*. The string ID numbers that precede each string are generally macro identifiers defined in a header file. Many Windows programmers use the prefix *IDS_* to denote an ID number for a string. Sometimes a filename or other information must be embedded in the string when the string is displayed. In this case you put C formatting characters in the string and use it as a formatting string in *sprintf* or *wsprintf*.

Using Strings with *MessageBox*

Let's look at an example of a program that uses three character strings to display three error messages in a message box. A header file that we'll call PROGRAM.H defines three identifiers for these messages:

```
#define IDS_FILENOTFOUND 1
#define IDS_FILETOOBIG   2
#define IDS_FILEREADONLY 3
```

The resource script looks like this:

```
#include "program.h"
      [other resource script]
STRINGTABLE
    {
        IDS_FILENOTFOUND,   "File %s not found."
        IDS_FILETOOBIG,     "File %s too large to edit."
        IDS_FILEREADONLY,   "File %s is read-only."
    }
```

The C source code file also includes this header file and defines a function to display a message box. (I'm assuming that *szAppName* is a global variable that contains the program name.)

```
#include "program.h"
      [other program lines]
OkMessage (HWND hwnd, WORD wErrorNumber, char *szFileName)
    {
    char szFormat [40] ;
    char szBuffer [60] ;
```

```
LoadString (hInst, wErrorNumber, szFormat, 40) ;

sprintf (szBuffer, szFormat, szFilename) ;

return MessageBox (hwnd, szBuffer, szAppName,
                   MB_OK ¦ MB_ICONEXCLAMATION) ;
}
```

To display a message box containing the "file not found" message, the program calls:

```
OkMessage (hwnd, IDS_FILENOTFOUND, szFileName) ;
```

Character Strings and Memory Space

Character string resources usually save memory space, but the amount of space saved depends on how efficiently they're used. When the RC.EXE resource compiler adds strings to the .EXE file, the strings are grouped into different segments depending on the ID numbers of the strings. Each segment contains a maximum of 16 strings. Strings with ID numbers from 0 to 15 are stored in one segment, from 16 to 31 are in another, and so forth. Because of this grouping into segments, your .EXE file will be shorter if you use consecutive numbers for your string IDs.

When you use *LoadString* to copy a string resource into memory, however, Windows loads the entire segment (containing up to 16 strings) into memory as a resource. Windows then also copies the content of the string specified in the *LoadString* call to a buffer in your program's data segment. So when string resources are loaded into memory, they initially occupy less memory if you do not use consecutive numbers for the string IDs. Probably the worst way to use string resources is to load all the strings into separate global static arrays during program initialization in *WinMain*. If you do that, you don't use any less space than if you had included the strings in your C source code. In fact, you'll use more space, because you'll set the size of these arrays somewhat larger than the actual string lengths. Here are some general rules for using string resources:

- Assign string ID numbers according to logical groupings. For instance, if five strings are involved in one section of your program and six strings are involved in another section, you might use ID numbers 0 to 4 for the first group of strings and 16 to 21 for the second group.

- Whenever possible, load the strings into automatic local variables within functions, thus freeing up the space when the function is exited. (The *OkMessage* function shown above uses this approach.)

- Alternatively, reuse a single static array for loading strings.

Here's an example of the last approach. Let's assume that your program never requires more than one string at a time. You can define a function that loads the string and returns a pointer to a static variable containing the string:

```
char *String (WORD wID)
    {
    static szBuffer [256] ;

    LoadString (hInst, wID, szBuffer, 255) ;
    return buffer ;
    }
```

If you want to use *DrawText* to display the string with ID number 45, you use this statement:

```
DrawText (hdc, String (45), -1, &rect, DT_LEFT) ;
```

Each call to *String* destroys the contents of the static buffer. If you require access to (for example) three strings at one time, you can modify *String* as follows:

```
char *String (WORD wID, short n)
    {
    static szBuffer [3][256] ;

    LoadString (hInst, wID, szBuffer [n], 255) ;
    return szBuffer [n] ;
    }
```

When you call *String* now, you pass an ID number and a second parameter that is either 0, 1, or 2.

USER-DEFINED RESOURCES

The "user-defined resource" is convenient for attaching miscellaneous data to your .EXE file and obtaining access to that data within the program. The data can be in any format you want. The Windows functions used to access user-defined resources return a far pointer to the data when Windows loads the data into memory. You can do whatever you want with that data. For instance, suppose you have a file called PROGHELP.TXT that contains "help" text for your program. This file needn't be a pure ASCII file: It can also contain binary data, such as pointers that would aid your program in referencing various sections of this file. Reference this file with a statement in your resource script that looks like this:

```
helptext TEXT proghelp.txt
```

For *helptext* (the name of the resource) and TEXT (the type of the resource), you can use any names you want. I've capitalized TEXT simply to make it look like the ICON, CURSOR, and BITMAP statements. What we're doing here is making up our own type of resource, called TEXT.

During program initialization (for example, during processing of the WM_CREATE message), you can obtain a handle to this resource:

```
hResource = LoadResource (hInstance,
                FindResource (hInstance, "TEXT", "helptext")) ;
```

The variable *hResource* is defined with type HANDLE. Despite its name, *LoadResource* does not actually load the resource into memory just yet. The *LoadResource* and *FindResource* functions used together like this are essentially equivalent to the *LoadIcon* and *LoadCursor* functions. In fact, *LoadIcon* and *LoadCursor* use the *LoadResource* and *FindResource* functions.

You can use numbers rather than names for the resource name and resource type. The numbers can be converted to far pointers in the *FindResource* call using *MakeInt-Resource*. The numbers used for the resource type must be greater than 255. (Windows uses numbers between 1 and 9 when calling *FindResource* for existing resource types.)

When you need access to the text, call *LockResource*:

```
lpHelpText = LockResource (hResource) ;
```

LockResource loads the resource into memory (if it has not already been loaded), locks it using the *GlobalLock* function, and returns a far pointer to it. When you are finished accessing the memory, unlock the segment:

```
UnlockResource (hResource) ;
```

This allows Windows to move the segment in memory. When you're finished with the resource, you can free it from memory:

```
FreeResource (hResource) ;
```

The resource will be freed when your program terminates, even if you don't call *FreeResource*.

Normally, user-defined resources are not discardable unless you include the DIS-CARDABLE keyword before the filename in the resource script. But if you use the pointer returned from *LockResource* to alter as well as read the data, don't make the resource DISCARDABLE. Note also that the same resource is shared among all instances of the program. If each instance needs its own copy of the resource, you should make the resource discardable, use *LockResource* to obtain a pointer to the resource, use *GlobalAlloc* to obtain a global memory block of the same size, use *GlobalLock* to lock that block, and then copy the contents of the resource into the global memory block.

Let's look at a sample program that uses three resources—an icon, a string table, and a user-defined resource. The POEPOEM program, shown in Figure 8-3, displays the text of Edgar Allan Poe's "Annabel Lee" in its client area. The user-defined resource is the file POEPOEM.ASC, which contains the text of the poem. The text file is terminated with a backslash (\).

POEPOEM.MAK

```
#----------------------
# POEPOEM.MAK make file
#----------------------

poepoem.exe : poepoem.obj poepoem.def poepoem.res
     link poepoem, /align:16, NUL, /nod slibcew libw, poepoem
     rc poepoem.res

poepoem.obj : poepoem.c poepoem.h
     cl -c -Gsw -Ow -W2 -Zp poepoem.c

poepoem.res : poepoem.rc poepoem.ico poepoem.asc poepoem.h
     rc -r poepoem.rc
```

POEPOEM.C

```
/*----------------------------------------------------
   POEPOEM.C -- Demonstrates User-Defined Resource
               (c) Charles Petzold, 1990
   ----------------------------------------------------*/

#include <windows.h>
#include "poepoem.h"

long FAR PASCAL WndProc  (HWND, WORD, WORD, LONG) ;

char    szAppName [10] ;
char    szCaption [35] ;
HANDLE hInst ;

int PASCAL WinMain (HANDLE hInstance, HANDLE hPrevInstance,
                    LPSTR lpszCmdLine, int nCmdShow)
     {
     HWND     hwnd ;
     MSG      msg ;
     WNDCLASS wndclass ;

     if (!hPrevInstance)
         {
         LoadString (hInstance, IDS_APPNAME, szAppName, sizeof szAppName) ;
         LoadString (hInstance, IDS_CAPTION, szCaption, sizeof szCaption) ;
```

Figure 8-3. *The POEPOEM program, including an icon and a user-defined resource.*   *(continued)*

```
        wndclass.style         = CS_HREDRAW ! CS_VREDRAW ;
        wndclass.lpfnWndProc    = WndProc ;
        wndclass.cbClsExtra     = 0 ;
        wndclass.cbWndExtra     = 0 ;
        wndclass.hInstance      = hInstance ;
        wndclass.hIcon          = LoadIcon (hInstance, szAppName) ;
        wndclass.hCursor        = LoadCursor (NULL, IDC_ARROW) ;
        wndclass.hbrBackground  = GetStockObject (WHITE_BRUSH) ;
        wndclass.lpszMenuName   = NULL ;
        wndclass.lpszClassName  = szAppName ;

        RegisterClass (&wndclass) ;
        }
    else
        {
        GetInstanceData (hPrevInstance, szAppName, sizeof szAppName) ;
        GetInstanceData (hPrevInstance, szCaption, sizeof szCaption) ;
        }

    hInst = hInstance ;

    hwnd = CreateWindow (szAppName, szCaption,
                    WS_OVERLAPPEDWINDOW ! WS_CLIPCHILDREN,
                    CW_USEDEFAULT, CW_USEDEFAULT,
                    CW_USEDEFAULT, CW_USEDEFAULT,
                    NULL, NULL, hInstance, NULL) ;

    ShowWindow (hwnd, nCmdShow) ;
    UpdateWindow (hwnd) ;

    while (GetMessage (&msg, NULL, 0, 0))
        {
        TranslateMessage (&msg) ;
        DispatchMessage (&msg) ;
        }
    return msg.wParam ;
    }

long FAR PASCAL WndProc (HWND hwnd, WORD message, WORD wParam, LONG lParam)
    {
    static HANDLE hResource ;
    static HWND   hScroll ;
    static short  nPosition, cxChar, cyChar, cyClient, nNumLines, xScroll ;
    char          szPoemRes [15] ;
    char far      *lpText ;

    HDC           hdc ;
    PAINTSTRUCT   ps ;
    RECT          rect ;
    TEXTMETRIC    tm ;
```

(continued)

```
switch (message)
     {
     case WM_CREATE :
          hdc = GetDC (hwnd) ;
          GetTextMetrics (hdc, &tm) ;
          cxChar = tm.tmAveCharWidth ;
          cyChar = tm.tmHeight + tm.tmExternalLeading ;
          ReleaseDC (hwnd, hdc) ;

          xScroll = GetSystemMetrics (SM_CXVSCROLL) ;

          hScroll = CreateWindow ("scrollbar", NULL,
                        WS_CHILD | WS_VISIBLE | SBS_VERT,
                        0, 0, 0, 0,
                        hwnd, 1, hInst, NULL) ;

          LoadString (hInst, IDS_POEMRES, szPoemRes, sizeof szPoemRes) ;
          hResource = LoadResource (hInst,
                        FindResource (hInst, szPoemRes, "TEXT")) ;

          lpText = LockResource (hResource) ;

          nNumLines = 0 ;

          while (*lpText != '\\' && *lpText != '\0')
               {
               if (*lpText == '\n')
                    nNumLines ++ ;
               lpText = AnsiNext (lpText) ;
               }
          *lpText = '\0' ;

          GlobalUnlock (hResource) ;

          SetScrollRange (hScroll, SB_CTL, 0, nNumLines, FALSE) ;
          SetScrollPos   (hScroll, SB_CTL, 0, FALSE) ;
          return 0 ;

     case WM_SIZE :
          MoveWindow (hScroll, LOWORD (lParam) - xScroll, 0,
               xScroll, cyClient = HIWORD (lParam), TRUE) ;
          SetFocus (hwnd) ;
          return 0 ;

     case WM_SETFOCUS :
          SetFocus (hScroll) ;
          return 0 ;
```

(continued)

```
    case WM_VSCROLL :
         switch (wParam)
              {
              case SB_TOP :
                   nPosition = 0 ;
                   break ;
              case SB_BOTTOM :
                   nPosition = nNumLines ;
                   break ;
              case SB_LINEUP :
                   nPosition -= 1 ;
                   break ;
              case SB_LINEDOWN :
                   nPosition += 1 ;
                   break ;
              case SB_PAGEUP :
                   nPosition -= cyClient / cyChar ;
                   break ;
              case SB_PAGEDOWN :
                   nPosition += cyClient / cyChar ;
                   break ;
              case SB_THUMBPOSITION :
                   nPosition = LOWORD (lParam) ;
                   break ;
              }
         nPosition = max (0, min (nPosition, nNumLines)) ;

         if (nPosition != GetScrollPos (hScroll, SB_CTL))
              {
              SetScrollPos (hScroll, SB_CTL, nPosition, TRUE) ;
              InvalidateRect (hwnd, NULL, TRUE) ;
              }
         return 0 ;

    case WM_PAINT :
         hdc = BeginPaint (hwnd, &ps) ;

         lpText = LockResource (hResource) ;

         GetClientRect (hwnd, &rect) ;
         rect.left += cxChar ;
         rect.top  += cyChar * (1 - nPosition) ;
         DrawText (hdc, lpText, -1, &rect, DT_EXTERNALLEADING) ;

         GlobalUnlock (hResource) ;

         EndPaint (hwnd, &ps) ;
         return 0 ;
```

(continued)

```
         case WM_DESTROY :
              FreeResource (hResource) ;
              PostQuitMessage (0) ;
              return 0 ;
         }
    return DefWindowProc (hwnd, message, wParam, lParam) ;
    }
```

POEPOEM.RC

```
/*---------------------------
   POEPOEM.RC resource script
---------------------------*/

#include "poepoem.h"

poepoem      ICON  poepoem.ico
AnnabelLee   TEXT  poepoem.asc

STRINGTABLE
    {
    IDS_APPNAME, "poepoem"
    IDS_CAPTION, """Annabel Lee"" by Edgar Allen Poe"
    IDS_POEMRES, "AnnabelLee"
    }
```

POEPOEM.ICO

POEPOEM.H

```
/*----------------------
    POEPOEM.H header file
  ---------------------*/

#define IDS_APPNAME 0
#define IDS_CAPTION 1
#define IDS_POEMRES 2
```

POEPOEM.ASC

```
It was many and many a year ago,
    In a kingdom by the sea,
That a maiden there lived whom you may know
    By the name of Annabel Lee;
And this maiden she lived with no other thought
    Than to love and be loved by me.

I was a child and she was a child
    In this kingdom by the sea,
But we loved with a love that was more than love --
    I and my Annabel Lee --
With a love that the wingèd seraphs of Heaven
    Coveted her and me.

And this was the reason that, long ago,
    In this kingdom by the sea,
A wind blew out of a cloud, chilling
    My beautiful Annabel Lee;
So that her highborn kinsmen came
    And bore her away from me,
To shut her up in a sepulchre
    In this kingdom by the sea.

The angels, not half so happy in Heaven,
    Went envying her and me --
Yes! that was the reason (as all men know,
    In this kingdom by the sea)
That the wind came out of the cloud by night,
    Chilling and killing my Annabel Lee.
```

(continued)

332

```
But our love it was stronger by far than the love
    Of those who were older than we --
    Of many far wiser than we --
And neither the angels in Heaven above
    Nor the demons down under the sea
Can ever dissever my soul from the soul
    Of the beautiful Annabel Lee:

For the moon never beams, without bringing me dreams
    Of the beautiful Annabel Lee;
And the stars never rise, but I feel the bright eyes
    Of the beautiful Annabel Lee:
And so, all the night-tide, I lie down by the side
Of my darling -- my darling -- my life and my bride,
    In her sepulchre there by the sea --
    In her tomb by the sounding sea.


                              [May 1849]

\
```

POEPOEM.DEF

```
;------------------------------------
; POEPOEM.DEF module definition file
;------------------------------------

NAME            POEPOEM

DESCRIPTION     'Demo of User-Defined Resource (c) Charles Petzold, 1990'
EXETYPE         WINDOWS
STUB            'WINSTUB.EXE'
CODE            PRELOAD MOVEABLE DISCARDABLE
DATA            PRELOAD MOVEABLE MULTIPLE
HEAPSIZE        1024
STACKSIZE       8192
EXPORTS         WndProc
```

In the POEPOEM.RC resource script, the user-defined resource is given the type TEXT and the name *AnnabelLee*:

```
AnnabelLee  TEXT  poepoem.asc
```

During WM_CREATE processing in *WndProc*, a handle to the resource is obtained using *FindResource* and *LoadResource*. The resource is locked using *LockResource*, and a small routine replaces the backslash (\) at the end of the file with a 0. (This is for the benefit of the *DrawText* function used later.) In most cases it's not a good idea to write on a user-defined resource directly, because the same resource is shared among all instances of the program. However, later instances of POEPOEM will not encounter problems with the change we've made. The resource is then unlocked using *GlobalUnlock*.

The resource is also locked and unlocked during processing of WM_PAINT to write the text to the display using *DrawText*. Note the use of a child window scroll bar control rather than a window scroll bar. The child window scroll bar control has an automatic keyboard interface, so no WM_KEYDOWN processing is required in POEPOEM.

POEPOEM also uses three character strings, the IDs of which are defined in the POEPOEM.H header file. For the first instance of the program, the IDS_APPNAME and IDS_CAPTION strings are loaded into global static variables using *LoadString*:

```
LoadString (hInstance, IDS_APPNAME, szAppName, sizeof szAppName) ;
LoadString (hInstance, IDS_CAPTION, szCaption, sizeof szCaption) ;
```

However, for subsequent instances of POEPOEM, the strings are copied from the previous instance:

```
GetInstanceData (hPrevInstance, szAppName, sizeof szAppName) ;
GetInstanceData (hPrevInstance, szCaption, sizeof szCaption) ;
```

GetInstanceData is faster than *LoadString* if the string resource has been discarded from memory. The pointers (*szAppName* and *szCaption*) are near pointers to static global variables. Windows uses these pointers in combination with the data segment address of the previous instance and the data segment address of the current instance to copy the contents of the variables.

Now that we've defined all the character strings used in POEPOEM as resources, we've made it easier for translators to convert the program into a foreign-language version. Of course, they'd also have to translate the text of "Annabel Lee"—which would, I suspect, be a somewhat more difficult task.

Chapter 9

Menus and Accelerators

Menus are an important part of the consistent user interface that Windows programs offer. Adding a menu to your program is a relatively easy part of Windows programming: You simply define the structure of the menu in your resource script and assign a unique ID number to each menu item. You specify the name of the menu in the window class structure. When the user chooses a menu item, Windows sends your program a WM_COMMAND message containing that ID. But we won't stop with that simple example. One of the more interesting things you can do with menus is display bitmaps in the menu rather than character strings, so we'll take a detailed look at how that is done.

This chapter also covers "keyboard accelerators." These are key combinations that are used primarily to duplicate menu functions.

MENUS

A window's menu bar is displayed immediately below the caption bar. This menu bar is sometimes called a program's "main menu" or the "top-level menu." Items listed in the top-level menu almost always invoke a drop-down menu, which is called either a "popup menu" or a "submenu." Beginning with Windows 3, you can define multiple nestings of popups: that is, an item on a popup menu can invoke another popup menu. Sometimes items in popup menus invoke a dialog box for more information. (Dialog boxes are covered in Chapter 10.) Most parent windows have, to the far left of the caption bar, a box containing a single line. This box invokes the system menu, which is really another popup menu.

Menu items in popups can be "checked," which means that Windows draws a small check mark to the left of the menu text. The use of check marks lets the user choose different program options from the menu. These options can be mutually exclusive, but they don't have to be. Top-level menu items cannot be checked.

Menu items in the top-level menu or in popup menus can be "enabled," "disabled," or "grayed." The words "active" and "inactive" are sometimes used synonymously with "enabled" and "disabled." Menu items flagged as enabled or disabled look the same to the user, but a grayed menu item is displayed in gray text.

From the perspective of the user, enabled, disabled, and grayed menu items can all be "selected" (highlighted). That is, the user can click the mouse on a disabled menu item, or move the reverse-video cursor bar to a disabled menu item, or trigger the menu item using the item's key letter. However, from the perspective of your program, enabled, disabled, and grayed menu items function differently. Windows sends your program a WM_COMMAND message only for enabled menu items. You use disabled and grayed menu items for options that are not currently valid. If you want to let the user know the option is not valid, make it grayed.

Menu Structure

When you create or change menus in a program, it's useful to think of the top-level menu and each popup menu as being separate menus. The top-level menu has a menu handle, each popup menu within a top-level menu has its own menu handle, and the system menu (which is also a popup) has a menu handle.

Each item in a menu is defined by three characteristics: The first characteristic is what appears in the menu. This is either a text string or a bitmap. The second characteristic is either an ID number that Windows sends to your program in a WM_COMMAND message or a popup menu that Windows displays when the user chooses that menu item. The third characteristic describes the attribute of the menu item, including whether the item is disabled, grayed, or checked.

The Menu Template

You can create a menu in three different ways. The most common (and the easiest) is to define the menu in your resource script in the form of a menu template. This example shows all the different options you can use in this template.

```
MyMenu MENU [load option] [memory option]
     {
     MENUITEM "&One",    1
     POPUP "&Two"
          {
          MENUITEM "&Ten",        10, CHECKED
          MENUITEM "&Eleven",     11
          MENUITEM SEPARATOR
          MENUITEM "T&welve",     12, INACTIVE
          MENUITEM "T&hirteen",   13
          MENUITEM "&Fourteen",   14, MENUBREAK
          MENUITEM "F&ifteen",    15,
          MENUITEM "&Sixteen",    16, MENUBARBREAK
          POPUP     "Se&venteen", 17,
               {
               MENUITEM "&Twenty",      20
               MENUITEM "T&wenty-One",  21
               MENUITEM "Tw&enty-Two",  22
               }
          MENUITEM "Ei&ghteen",  18, GRAYED
          }
     MENUITEM "Th&ree",  3
     MENUITEM "&Four",   4, INACTIVE
     MENUITEM "Fi&ve",   5
     MENUITEM "Si&x",    6, MENUBREAK
     MENUITEM "&Seven",  7,
     MENUITEM "&Eight",  8, GRAYED
     MENUITEM "\a&Help", 9, HELP
     }
```

This particular menu template defines a top-level menu that displays the labels "One" through "Eight" and "Help," as shown in Figure 9-1 on the following page. Only the second item invokes a popup menu. The popup menu displays the labels "Ten" through "Eighteen," as shown in Figure 9-2 on the following page. The little arrow to the right of the "Seventeen" option indicates that it invokes yet another popup menu.

MyMenu is the name of the menu. This name performs the same function as the names of icon, cursor, and bitmap resources discussed in Chapter 8. As with other resources, the load option on the MENU statement can be either PRELOAD (in which case Windows loads the resource into memory when the program is executed) or LOADON-CALL (in which case Windows loads the resource into memory only when it is needed). The default is LOADONCALL. The memory options are FIXED, MOVEABLE, and DIS-CARDABLE. The default is MOVEABLE and DISCARDABLE. Discardable menus must also be moveable. Although we'll change menus in some of the programs shown later, don't worry that the menu resource is discardable. Windows makes a copy of the menu for your program to use and change.

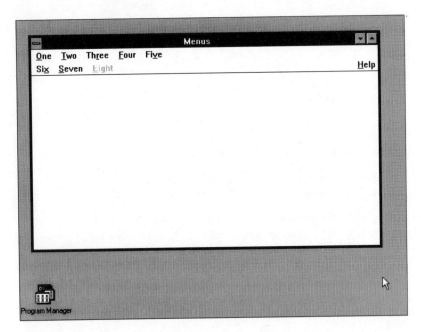

Figure 9-1. *A top-level menu.*

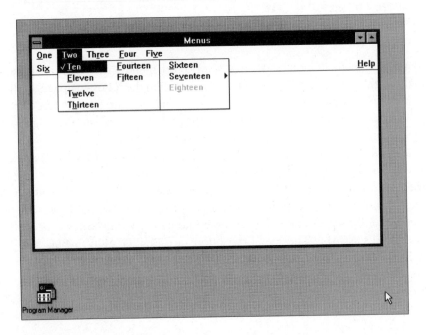

Figure 9-2. *A popup menu.*

The top-level menu is enclosed in left and right brackets. (You can use BEGIN and END statements instead if you wish.) The two types of statements allowed within these brackets are:

```
MENUITEM "text", wID, options
```

and:

```
POPUP "text", options
```

The text displayed for each menu must be enclosed in double quotation marks. An ampersand (&) causes the character that follows it to be underlined when Windows displays the menu. This is also the character Windows searches for when you select a menu item using the Alt key. If you don't include an ampersand in the text, no underline will appear, and Windows will use instead the first letter of the text for Alt-key searches.

The options on the MENUITEM and POPUP statements that appear in the top-level menu list are as follows:

- GRAYED—The menu item is inactive, and it does not generate a WM_COMMAND message. The text is grayed.

- INACTIVE—The menu item is inactive, and it does not generate a WM_COMMAND message. The text is displayed normally.

- MENUBREAK—This item and following items appear on a new line of the menu.

- HELP—When used in combination with \a before the text, this item is right-justified.

Options can be combined using the C bitwise OR symbol (¦), but GRAYED and INACTIVE cannot be used together. MENUBREAK is uncommon in a top-level menu, because Windows automatically separates a top-level menu into multiple lines if the window is too narrow to fit the entire menu.

Following a POPUP statement in the main menu, the left and right brackets (or the BEGIN and END keywords) block off a list of items in the popup. The following statements are allowed in a popup definition:

```
MENUITEM "text", wID, options
```

and:

```
MENUITEM SEPARATOR
```

and:

```
POPUP  "text", options
```

MENUITEM SEPARATOR draws a horizontal line in the popup menu. This line is often used to separate groups of related options.

For items in popup menus, you can use the columnar tab character \t in the text string. Text following the \t is placed in a new column spaced far enough to the right to accommodate the longest text string in the first column of the popup. We'll see how this works when discussing keyboard accelerators toward the end of this chapter. A \a right-justifies the text that follows it. The options for MENUITEM in a popup are as follows:

- CHECKED—A check mark appears to the left of the text.

- GRAYED—The menu item is inactive and does not generate a WM_COMMAND message. The text is grayed.

- INACTIVE—The menu item is inactive and does not generate a WM_COMMAND message. The text is displayed normally.

- MENUBREAK—This item and the following items appear in a new column of the menu.

- MENUBARBREAK—This item and the following items appear in a new column of the menu. A vertical line separates the columns.

GRAYED and INACTIVE cannot be used together. MENUBREAK and MENUBARBREAK cannot be used together. You should use either MENUBREAK or MENUBARBREAK when the number of items in a popup is too long to be displayed in a single column.

The *wID* values in the MENUITEM statements are the numbers that Windows sends to the window procedure in menu messages. The *wID* values should be unique within a menu. Instead of using numbers, you'll probably want to use identifiers defined in a header file. By convention, these identifiers begin with the letters IDM ("ID for a menu").

Referencing the Menu in Your Program

Most Windows applications have only one menu in the resource script. The program makes reference to this menu in the definition of the window class:

```
wndclass.lpszMenuName = "MyMenu" ;
```

Programmers often use the name of the program as the name of the menu so that the same text string can also be used for the window class, the name of the program's icon, and the name of the menu. However, you can also use a number (or a macro identifier) for the menu rather than a name. The resource script would look like this:

```
45 MENU
    {
    [menu definition]
    }
```

In this case, the assignment statement for the *lpszMenuName* field of the window class structure can be either:

```
wndclass.lpszMenuName = MAKEINTRESOURCE (45) ;
```

or:

```
wndclass.lpszMenuName = "#45" ;
```

Although specifying the menu in the window class is the most common way to reference a menu resource, you have alternatives. A Windows application can load a menu resource into memory with the *LoadMenu* function, which is similar to the *LoadIcon* and *LoadCursor* functions described in Chapter 8. If you use a name for the menu in the resource script, *LoadMenu* returns a handle to the menu:

```
hMenu = LoadMenu (hInstance, "MyMenu") ;
```

If you use a number, the *LoadMenu* call takes either this form:

```
hMenu = LoadMenu (hInstance, MAKEINTRESOURCE (45)) ;
```

or this form:

```
hMenu = LoadMenu (hInstance, "#45") ;
```

You can then specify this menu handle as the ninth parameter to *CreateWindow*:

```
hwnd = CreateWindow ("MyClass", "Window Caption",
            WS_OVERLAPPEDWINDOW,
            CW_USEDEFAULT,CW_USEDEFAULT,
            CW_USEDEFAULT,CW_USEDEFAULT,
            NULL,
            hMenu,
            hInstance,
            NULL) ;
```

In this case, the menu specified in the *CreateWindow* call overrides any menu specified in the window class. You can think of the menu in the window class as being a default menu for the windows based on the window class if the ninth parameter to *CreateWindow* is NULL. Therefore, you can use different menus for several windows based on the same window class.

You can also have a NULL menu in the window class and a NULL menu in the *CreateWindow* call and assign a menu to a window after the window has been created:

```
SetMenu (hwnd, hMenu) ;
```

This form lets you dynamically change a window's menu. We'll see an example of this in the NOPOPUPS program shown later in this chapter.

Menus and Messages

Windows usually sends a window procedure several different messages when the user selects a menu item. In most cases your program can ignore many of these messages and simply pass them to *DefWindowProc*. Let's take a look at them anyway.

The first message your program receives when the user selects a menu item with the keyboard or mouse is a WM_SYSCOMMAND message. The values of *wParam* and *lParam* are shown below:

	wParam	*lParam*
Mouse:	F09x	0
Keyboard:	F10x	0

The WINDOWS.H identifier SC_MOUSEMENU is equal to F090H; SC_KEYMENU is F100H, but the last digit in *wParam* (indicated by an x in the table above) can be anything. Use:

```
(wParam & 0xFFF0)
```

if you need to check this value. Most programs pass these messages to *DefWindowProc*.

The second message your program receives is a WM_INITMENU message with the following parameters:

wParam	*LOWORD (lParam)*	*HIWORD (lParam)*
Handle to main menu	0	0

The value of *wParam* is the handle to your main menu even if the user is selecting an item from the system menu. Windows programs generally ignore the WM_INITMENU message. Although the message exists to give you the opportunity to change the menu before an item is chosen, I suspect any changes to the top-level menu at this time would be very disconcerting to the user.

The next message your program receives is WM_MENUSELECT. A program can receive many WM_MENUSELECT messages as the user moves the cursor or mouse among the menu items. The parameters that accompany WM_SELECT are as follows:

wParam	*LOWORD (lParam)*	*HIWORD (lParam)*
Selected item: Menu ID or popup menu handle	Selection flags	Handle to menu containing selected item

WM_MENUSELECT is a menu-tracking message. The value of *wParam* tells you what item of the menu is currently selected (highlighted). The "selection flags" in the low word of *lParam* can be a combination of the following: MF_GRAYED, MF_DISABLED, MF_CHECKED, MF_BITMAP, MF_POPUP, MF_HELP, MF_SYSMENU, and MF_MOUSE-SELECT. You may want to use WM_MENUSELECT if you need to change something in the client area of your window based on the movement of the highlight among the menu items. Most programs pass this message to *DefWindowProc*.

When Windows is ready to display a popup menu, it sends the window procedure a WM_INITMENUPOPUP message with the following parameters:

wParam	*LOWORD (lParam)*	*HIWORD (lParam)*
Popup menu handle	Popup index	1 for system menu, 0 otherwise

This message is important if you need to enable or disable items in a popup menu before it is displayed. For instance, suppose your program can copy text from the clipboard using the Paste command on a popup menu. When you receive a WM_INITMENUPOPUP message for that popup, you should determine if the clipboard has text in it. If it doesn't, you should gray the Paste menu item. We'll see an example of this in the revised POPPAD program shown toward the end of this chapter.

The most important menu message is WM_COMMAND. This message indicates that the user has chosen an enabled menu item from your window's menu. You'll recall from Chapter 6 that WM_COMMAND messages also result from child window controls. If you happen to use the same ID codes for menus and child window controls, you can differentiate between them by the low word of *lParam*, which will be 0 for a menu item:

	wParam	*LOWORD (lParam)*	*HIWORD (lParam)*
Menu:	Menu ID	0	0
Control:	Control ID	Child window handle	Notification code

The WM_SYSCOMMAND message is similar to the WM_COMMAND message except that WM_SYSCOMMAND signals that the user has chosen an enabled menu item from the system menu:

	wParam	*LOWORD (lParam)*	*HIWORD (lParam)*
System menu:	Menu ID	0	0

The menu ID indicates which item on the system menu has been chosen. For the predefined system menu items, the bottom four bits should be masked out. The resultant value will be one of the following: SC_SIZE, SC_MOVE, SC_MINIMIZE, SC_MAXIMIZE, SC_NEXTWINDOW, SC_PREVWINDOW, SC_CLOSE, SC_VSCROLL, SC_HSCROLL, SC_-_ARRANGE, SC_RESTORE, and SC_TASKLIST. In addition, *wParam* can be SC_MOUSE-MENU or SC_KEYMENU, as indicated earlier.

If you add menu items to the system menu, *wParam* will be the menu ID that you define. To avoid conflicts with the predefined menu IDs, use values below F000H. It is important that you pass normal WM_SYSCOMMAND messages to *DefWindowProc*. If you do not, you'll effectively disable the normal system menu commands.

The final message we'll discuss is WM_MENUCHAR, which isn't really a menu message at all. Windows sends this message to your window procedure in one of two circumstances: if the user presses Alt and a character key that does not correspond to a menu item, or, when a popup is displayed, if the user presses a character key that does not correspond to an item in the popup. The parameters that accompany the WM_MENUCHAR message are as follows:

wParam	*LOWORD (lParam)*	*HIWORD (lParam)*
ASCII code	Selection code	Handle to menu

The selection code is:

- 0—No popup is displayed.

- MF_POPUP—Popup is displayed.

- MF_SYSMENU—System menu popup is displayed.

Windows programs usually pass this message to *DefWindowProc*, which normally returns a 0 to Windows, which causes Windows to beep. We'll see a use for the WM_MENUCHAR message in the GRAFMENU program shown later in this chapter.

A Sample Program

Let's look at a simple example. The MENUDEMO program, shown in Figure 9-3, has five items in the main menu—File, Edit, Background, Timer, and Help. Each of these items has a popup. MENUDEMO does the simplest and most common type of menu processing, which involves trapping WM_COMMAND messages and checking the value of *wParam*.

MENUDEMO.MAK

```
#------------------------
# MENUDEMO.MAK make file
#------------------------

menudemo.exe : menudemo.obj menudemo.def menudemo.res
     link menudemo, /align:16, NUL, /nod slibcew libw, menudemo
     rc menudemo.res
```

Figure 9-3. *The MENUDEMO program.* *(continued)*

```
menudemo.obj : menudemo.c menudemo.h
    cl -c -Gsw -Ow -W2 -Zp menudemo.c

menudemo.res : menudemo.rc menudemo.h
    rc -r menudemo.rc
```

MENUDEMO.C

```c
/*-------------------------------------------
   MENUDEMO.C -- Menu Demonstration
                 (c) Charles Petzold, 1990
   -------------------------------------------*/

#include <windows.h>
#include "menudemo.h"

long FAR PASCAL WndProc (HWND, WORD, WORD, LONG) ;

char szAppName [] = "MenuDemo" ;

int PASCAL WinMain (HANDLE hInstance, HANDLE hPrevInstance,
                    LPSTR lpszCmdLine, int nCmdShow)
    {
    HWND     hwnd ;
    MSG      msg ;
    WNDCLASS wndclass ;

    if (!hPrevInstance)
        {
        wndclass.style         = CS_HREDRAW | CS_VREDRAW ;
        wndclass.lpfnWndProc   = WndProc ;
        wndclass.cbClsExtra    = 0 ;
        wndclass.cbWndExtra    = 0 ;
        wndclass.hInstance     = hInstance ;
        wndclass.hIcon         = LoadIcon (NULL, IDI_APPLICATION) ;
        wndclass.hCursor       = LoadCursor (NULL, IDC_ARROW) ;
        wndclass.hbrBackground = GetStockObject (WHITE_BRUSH) ;
        wndclass.lpszMenuName  = szAppName ;
        wndclass.lpszClassName = szAppName ;

        RegisterClass (&wndclass) ;
        }

    hwnd = CreateWindow (szAppName, "Menu Demonstration",
                        WS_OVERLAPPEDWINDOW,
                        CW_USEDEFAULT, CW_USEDEFAULT,
                        CW_USEDEFAULT, CW_USEDEFAULT,
                        NULL, NULL, hInstance, NULL) ;
```

(continued)

345

```
    ShowWindow (hwnd, nCmdShow) ;
    UpdateWindow (hwnd) ;

    while (GetMessage (&msg, NULL, 0, 0))
         {
         TranslateMessage (&msg) ;
         DispatchMessage (&msg) ;
         }
    return msg.wParam ;
    }

long FAR PASCAL WndProc (HWND hwnd, WORD message, WORD wParam, LONG lParam)
    {
    static int   wColorID [5] = { WHITE_BRUSH,  LTGRAY_BRUSH, GRAY_BRUSH,
                                  DKGRAY_BRUSH, BLACK_BRUSH } ;
    static WORD wSelection = IDM_WHITE ;
    HMENU       hMenu ;

    switch (message)
         {
         case WM_COMMAND :
              hMenu = GetMenu (hwnd) ;

              switch (wParam)
                   {
                   case IDM_NEW :
                   case IDM_OPEN :
                   case IDM_SAVE :
                   case IDM_SAVEAS :
                        MessageBeep (0) ;
                        return 0 ;

                   case IDM_EXIT :
                        SendMessage (hwnd, WM_CLOSE, 0, 0L) ;
                        return 0 ;

                   case IDM_UNDO :
                   case IDM_CUT :
                   case IDM_COPY :
                   case IDM_PASTE :
                   case IDM_CLEAR :
                        MessageBeep (0) ;
                        return 0 ;

                   case IDM_WHITE :          // Note: Logic below
                   case IDM_LTGRAY :         //    assumes that IDM_WHITE
                   case IDM_GRAY :           //    through IDM_BLACK are
                   case IDM_DKGRAY :         //    consecutive numbers in
                   case IDM_BLACK :          //    the order shown here.
```

(continued)

```
                    CheckMenuItem (hMenu, wSelection, MF_UNCHECKED) ;
                    wSelection = wParam ;
                    CheckMenuItem (hMenu, wSelection, MF_CHECKED) ;

                    SetClassWord (hwnd, GCW_HBRBACKGROUND,
                         GetStockObject (wColorID [wParam - IDM_WHITE])) ;

                    InvalidateRect (hwnd, NULL, TRUE) ;
                    return 0 ;

               case IDM_START :
                    if (SetTimer (hwnd, 1, 1000, NULL))
                         {
                         EnableMenuItem (hMenu, IDM_START, MF_GRAYED) ;
                         EnableMenuItem (hMenu, IDM_STOP,  MF_ENABLED) ;
                         }
                    return 0 ;

               case IDM_STOP :
                    KillTimer (hwnd, 1) ;
                    EnableMenuItem (hMenu, IDM_START, MF_ENABLED) ;
                    EnableMenuItem (hMenu, IDM_STOP,  MF_GRAYED) ;
                    return 0 ;

               case IDM_HELP :
                    MessageBox (hwnd, "Help not yet implemented.",
                              szAppName, MB_ICONINFORMATION | MB_OK) ;
                    return 0 ;

               case IDM_ABOUT :
                    MessageBox (hwnd, "Menu Demonstration Program.",
                              szAppName, MB_ICONINFORMATION | MB_OK) ;
                    return 0 ;
               }
          break ;

     case WM_TIMER :
          MessageBeep (0) ;
          return 0 ;

     case WM_DESTROY :
          PostQuitMessage (0) ;
          return 0 ;
     }
return DefWindowProc (hwnd, message, wParam, lParam) ;
}
```

MENUDEMO.RC

```
/*----------------------------
    MENUDEMO.RC resource script
    -------------------------*/

#include "menudemo.h"

MenuDemo MENU
    {
    POPUP "&File"
        {
        MENUITEM "&New",                    IDM_NEW
        MENUITEM "&Open...",                IDM_OPEN
        MENUITEM "&Save",                   IDM_SAVE
        MENUITEM "Save &As...",             IDM_SAVEAS
        MENUITEM SEPARATOR
        MENUITEM "E&xit",                   IDM_EXIT
        }
    POPUP "&Edit"
        {
        MENUITEM "&Undo",                   IDM_UNDO
        MENUITEM SEPARATOR
        MENUITEM "Cu&t",                    IDM_CUT
        MENUITEM "&Copy",                   IDM_COPY
        MENUITEM "&Paste",                  IDM_PASTE
        MENUITEM "C&lear",                  IDM_CLEAR
        }
    POPUP "&Background"
        {
        MENUITEM "&White",                  IDM_WHITE, CHECKED
        MENUITEM "&Lt Gray",                IDM_LTGRAY
        MENUITEM "&Gray",                   IDM_GRAY
        MENUITEM "&Dk Gray",                IDM_DKGRAY
        MENUITEM "&Black",                  IDM_BLACK
        }
    POPUP "&Timer"
        {
        MENUITEM "&Start"                   IDM_START
        MENUITEM "S&top"                    IDM_STOP,  GRAYED
        }
    POPUP "&Help"
        {
        MENUITEM "&Help",                   IDM_HELP
        MENUITEM "&About MenuDemo...",      IDM_ABOUT
        }
    }
```

MENUDEMO.H

```
/*------------------------
   MENUDEMO.H header file
   ------------------------*/

#define IDM_NEW       1
#define IDM_OPEN      2
#define IDM_SAVE      3
#define IDM_SAVEAS    4
#define IDM_EXIT      5

#define IDM_UNDO      10
#define IDM_CUT       11
#define IDM_COPY      12
#define IDM_PASTE     13
#define IDM_CLEAR     14

#define IDM_WHITE     20
#define IDM_LTGRAY    21
#define IDM_GRAY      22
#define IDM_DKGRAY    23
#define IDM_BLACK     24

#define IDM_START     30
#define IDM_STOP      31

#define IDM_HELP      40
#define IDM_ABOUT     41
```

MENUDEMO.DEF

```
;----------------------------------------
; MENUDEMO.DEF module definition file
;----------------------------------------

NAME           MENUDEMO

DESCRIPTION    'Menu Demonstration Program (c) Charles Petzold, 1990'
EXETYPE        WINDOWS
STUB           'WINSTUB.EXE'
CODE           PRELOAD MOVEABLE DISCARDABLE
DATA           PRELOAD MOVEABLE MULTIPLE
HEAPSIZE       1024
STACKSIZE      8192
EXPORTS        WndProc
```

Identifiers for all menu IDs are defined in MENUDEMO.H. This file must be specified (using a *#include* statement) in both the resource script file and the C source code file. The identifiers begin with IDM. (The ID numbers defined for the menu items need not be consecutive. However, if you process these IDs in your program using switch and case statements, keep in mind that the C compiler can best optimize this code using jump tables if you use consecutive menu ID numbers.)

The MENUDEMO program simply beeps when it receives a WM_COMMAND message for most items in the File and Edit popups. The Background popup lists five stock brushes that MENUDEMO can use to color the background. In the MENUDEMO.RC resource script the White menu item (with a menu ID of IDM_WHITE) is flagged as CHECKED, which places a check mark next to the item. In MENUDEMO.C, the value of *wSelection* is initially set to IDM_WHITE.

The five brushes on the Background popup are mutually exclusive. When MENUDEMO.C receives a WM_COMMAND message where *wParam* is one of these five items on the Background popup, it must remove the check mark from the previously chosen background color and add a check mark to the new background color. To do this, it first gets a handle to its menu:

```
hMenu = GetMenu (hwnd) ;
```

The *CheckMenuItem* function is used to uncheck the currently checked item:

```
CheckMenuItem (hMenu, wSelection, MF_UNCHECKED) ;
```

The *wSelection* value is set to the value of *wParam*, and the new background color is checked:

```
wSelection = wParam ;
CheckMenuItem (hMenu, wSelection, MF_CHECKED) ;
```

The background color in the window class is then replaced with the new background color, and the window client area is invalidated. Windows erases the window using the new background color.

The Timer popup lists two options—Start and Stop. Initially, the Stop option is grayed (as indicated in the menu definition for the resource script). When you choose the Start option, MENUDEMO tries to start a timer and, if successful, grays the Start option and makes the Stop option active:

```
EnableMenuItem (hMenu, IDM_START, MF_GRAYED) ;
EnableMenuItem (hMenu, IDM_STOP,  MF_ENABLED) ;
```

On receipt of a WM_COMMAND message with *wParam* equal to IDM_STOP, MENUDEMO kills the timer, activates the Start option, and grays the Stop option:

```
EnableMenuItem (hMenu, IDM_START, MF_ENABLED) ;
EnableMenuItem (hMenu, IDM_STOP,  MF_GRAYED) ;
```

Notice that it's impossible for MENUDEMO to receive a WM_COMMAND message with *wParam* equal to IDM_START when the timer is going. Similarly, it's impossible to receive a WM_COMMAND with *wParam* equal to IDM_STOP when the timer is not going.

When MENUDEMO receives a WM_COMMAND message with the *wParam* parameter equal to IDM_ABOUT or IDM_HELP, it displays a message box. (In Chapter 10 we'll change this to a dialog box.)

When MENUDEMO receives a WM_COMMAND message with *wParam* equal to IDM_EXIT, it sends itself a WM_CLOSE message. This is the same message that *DefWindowProc* sends the window procedure when it receives a WM_SYSCOMMAND message with *wParam* equal to SC_CLOSE. We'll examine this more in the POPPAD2 program shown toward the end of this chapter.

Menu Etiquette

The format of the File and Edit popups in MENUDEMO follows the recommendations of the CUA Advanced Interface Design Guide. Many Windows programs have File and Edit popups. One of the objectives of Windows is to provide a user with a recognizable interface that does not require relearning basic concepts for each program. It certainly helps if the File and Edit menus look the same in every Windows program and use the same letters for selection with the Alt key.

Beyond the File and Edit popups, the menus of most Windows programs will be different. When designing a menu you should look at existing Windows programs and aim for some consistency. Of course, if you think these other programs are wrong and you know the right way to do it, nobody's going to stop you. Also keep in mind that revising a menu usually requires revising only the resource script and not your program code. You can move menu items around at a later time without many problems.

At the beginning of this chapter, I showed you a menu with nine top-level items but with only one popup that is invoked from the top-level menu. This menu is certainly atypical. Most often, each top-level item has a popup, even if the popup has only one option. Top-level items without popups can be too easily chosen by mistake.

Defining a Menu the Hard Way

Defining a menu in a program's resource script is usually the easiest way to add a menu in your window, but it's not the only way. You can dispense with the resource script and create a menu entirely within your program using two functions called *CreateMenu* and *AppendMenu*. After you finish defining the menu, you can pass the menu handle to *CreateWindow* or use *SetMenu* to set the window's menu.

Here's how it's done. *CreateMenu* simply returns a handle to a new menu:

```
hMenu = CreateMenu () ;
```

The menu is initially empty. *AppendMenu* inserts items into the menu. You must obtain a different menu handle for the top-level menu item and for each popup. The popups are constructed separately; the popup menu handles are then inserted into the top-level menu. The code shown in Figure 9-4 creates a menu in this fashion; in fact, it is the same menu as in the MENUDEMO program.

```
hMenu = CreateMenu () ;

hMenuPopup = CreateMenu () ;

AppendMenu (hMenuPopup, MF_STRING,    IDM_NEW,    "&New") ;
AppendMenu (hMenuPopup, MF_STRING,    IDM_OPEN,   "&Open...") ;
AppendMenu (hMenuPopup, MF_STRING,    IDM_SAVE,   "&Save") ;
AppendMenu (hMenuPopup, MF_STRING,    IDM_SAVEAS, "Save &As...") ;
AppendMenu (hMenuPopup, MF_SEPARATOR, 0,          NULL) ;
AppendMenu (hMenuPopup, MF_STRING,    IDM_EXIT,   "E&xit") ;

AppendMenu (hMenu, MF_POPUP, hMenuPopup, "&File") ;

hMenuPopup = CreateMenu () ;

AppendMenu (hMenuPopup, MF_STRING,    IDM_UNDO, "&Undo") ;
AppendMenu (hMenuPopup, MF_SEPARATOR, 0,        NULL) ;
AppendMenu (hMenuPopup, MF_STRING,    IDM_CUT,   "Cu&t") ;
AppendMenu (hMenuPopup, MF_STRING,    IDM_COPY,  "&Copy") ;
AppendMenu (hMenuPopup, MF_STRING,    IDM_PASTE, "&Paste") ;
AppendMenu (hMenuPopup, MF_STRING,    IDM_CLEAR, "C&lear") ;

AppendMenu (hMenu, MF_POPUP, hMenuPopup, "&Edit") ;

hMenuPopup = CreateMenu () ;

AppendMenu (hMenuPopup, MF_STRING | MF_CHECKED, IDM_WHITE,  "&White") ;
AppendMenu (hMenuPopup, MF_STRING,              IDM_LTGRAY, "&Lt Gray") ;
AppendMenu (hMenuPopup, MF_STRING,              IDM_GRAY,   "&Gray") ;
AppendMenu (hMenuPopup, MF_STRING,              IDM_DKGRAY, "&Dk Gray") ;
AppendMenu (hMenuPopup, MF_STRING,              IDM_BLACK,  "&Black") ;

AppendMenu (hMenu, MF_POPUP, hMenuPopup, "&Background") ;

hMenuPopup = CreateMenu () ;

AppendMenu (hMenuPopup, MF_STRING,             IDM_START, "&Start") ;
AppendMenu (hMenuPopup, MF_STRING | MF_GRAYED, IDM_STOP,  "S&top") ;
```

Figure 9-4. *C code that creates the same menu used in the MENUDEMO program*   *(continued)*
but without requiring a resource script file.

```
AppendMenu (hMenu, MF_POPUP, hMenuPopup, "&Timer") ;

hMenuPopup = CreateMenu () ;

AppendMenu (hMenuPopup, MF_STRING, IDM_HELP,  "&Help") ;
AppendMenu (hMenuPopup, MF_STRING, IDM_ABOUT, "&About MenuDemo...") ;

AppendMenu (hMenu, MF_POPUP, hMenuPopup, "&Help") ;
```

I think you'll agree that the resource script menu template is easier and clearer. I'm not recommending that you define a menu in this way, only showing that it can be done. Certainly you can cut down on the code size substantially by using some arrays of structures containing all the menu item character strings, IDs, and flags. But if you do that, you might as well take advantage of the third method Windows provides for defining a menu.

A Third Approach to Defining Menus

The *LoadMenuIndirect* function accepts a pointer to a structure of type MENUITEM-TEMPLATE and returns a handle to a menu. This function is used within Windows to construct a menu after loading the normal menu template from a resource script. If you're brave, you can try using it yourself.

Be forewarned, however: The MENUITEMTEMPLATE structure has a field defined as LPSTR that is set to a far pointer to a character string, a handle to a popup, or a handle to a bitmap. But you can't simply define a MENUITEMTEMPLATE structure in your program and initialize the field to a character string. During compilation, the pointer to the character string is converted to a far pointer. This violates one of the most important rules discussed in Chapter 7: Don't store far pointers to your data segment. Instead, immediately before calling *LoadMenuIndirect*, you use a series of assignment statements to set this field to the character string pointers. Between these assignment statements and the *LoadMenuIndirect* call, you can't make any Windows calls that can result in your data segment being moved (such as *GetMessage*).

Floating Popup Menus

Beginning with Windows 3, you can make use of menus without having a top-level menu bar. You can instead cause a popup menu to appear on top of any part of the screen. One approach is to invoke this popup menu in response to a click of the right mouse button. However, menu items must still be selected with the left mouse button. The POPMENU program in Figure 9-5 (beginning on the following page) shows how this is done.

POPMENU.MAK

```
#---------------------
# POPMENU.MAK make file
#---------------------

popmenu.exe : popmenu.obj popmenu.def popmenu.res
     link popmenu, /align:16, NUL, /nod slibcew libw, popmenu
     rc popmenu.res

popmenu.obj : popmenu.c popmenu.h
     cl -c -Gsw -Ow -W2 -Zp popmenu.c

popmenu.res : popmenu.rc popmenu.h
     rc -r popmenu.rc
```

POPMENU.C

```c
/*-------------------------------------------
   POPMENU.C -- Popup Menu Demonstration
              (c) Charles Petzold, 1990
   -------------------------------------------*/

#include <windows.h>
#include "popmenu.h"

long FAR PASCAL WndProc (HWND, WORD, WORD, LONG) ;

char   szAppName [] = "PopMenu" ;
HANDLE hInst ;

int PASCAL WinMain (HANDLE hInstance, HANDLE hPrevInstance,
                    LPSTR lpszCmdLine, int nCmdShow)
     {
     HWND      hwnd ;
     MSG       msg ;
     WNDCLASS wndclass ;

     if (!hPrevInstance)
          {
          wndclass.style         = CS_HREDRAW ! CS_VREDRAW ;
          wndclass.lpfnWndProc   = WndProc ;
          wndclass.cbClsExtra    = 0 ;
          wndclass.cbWndExtra    = 0 ;
          wndclass.hInstance     = hInstance ;
          wndclass.hIcon         = LoadIcon (NULL, IDI_APPLICATION) ;
          wndclass.hCursor       = LoadCursor (NULL, IDC_ARROW) ;
```

Figure 9-5. *The POPMENU program.*   *(continued)*

354

```
        wndclass.hbrBackground = GetStockObject (WHITE_BRUSH) ;
        wndclass.lpszMenuName  = NULL ;
        wndclass.lpszClassName = szAppName ;

        RegisterClass (&wndclass) ;
        }

    hInst = hInstance ;

    hwnd = CreateWindow (szAppName, "Popup Menu Demonstration",
                    WS_OVERLAPPEDWINDOW,
                    CW_USEDEFAULT, CW_USEDEFAULT,
                    CW_USEDEFAULT, CW_USEDEFAULT,
                    NULL, NULL, hInstance, NULL) ;

    ShowWindow (hwnd, nCmdShow) ;
    UpdateWindow (hwnd) ;

    while (GetMessage (&msg, NULL, 0, 0))
        {
        TranslateMessage (&msg) ;
        DispatchMessage (&msg) ;
        }
    return msg.wParam ;
    }

long FAR PASCAL WndProc (HWND hwnd, WORD message, WORD wParam, LONG lParam)
    {
    static HMENU hMenu ;
    static int   wColorID [5] = { WHITE_BRUSH,  LTGRAY_BRUSH, GRAY_BRUSH,
                                  DKGRAY_BRUSH, BLACK_BRUSH } ;
    static WORD  wSelection = IDM_WHITE ;
    POINT        point ;

    switch (message)
        {
        case WM_CREATE :
            hMenu = LoadMenu (hInst, szAppName) ;
            hMenu = GetSubMenu (hMenu, 0) ;
            return 0 ;

        case WM_RBUTTONDOWN :
            point = MAKEPOINT (lParam) ;
            ClientToScreen (hwnd, &point) ;

            TrackPopupMenu (hMenu, 0, point.x, point.y, 0, hwnd, NULL) ;
            return 0 ;

        case WM_COMMAND :
            switch (wParam)
                {
```

(continued)

```
               case IDM_NEW :
               case IDM_OPEN :
               case IDM_SAVE :
               case IDM_SAVEAS :
               case IDM_UNDO :
               case IDM_CUT :
               case IDM_COPY :
               case IDM_PASTE :
               case IDM_CLEAR :
                    MessageBeep (0) ;
                    return 0 ;

               case IDM_WHITE :          // Note: Logic below
               case IDM_LTGRAY :         //    assumes that IDM_WHITE
               case IDM_GRAY :           //    through IDM_BLACK are
               case IDM_DKGRAY :         //    consecutive numbers in
               case IDM_BLACK :          //    the order shown here.

                    CheckMenuItem (hMenu, wSelection, MF_UNCHECKED) ;
                    wSelection = wParam ;
                    CheckMenuItem (hMenu, wSelection, MF_CHECKED) ;

                    SetClassWord (hwnd, GCW_HBRBACKGROUND,
                         GetStockObject (wColorID [wParam - IDM_WHITE])) ;

                    InvalidateRect (hwnd, NULL, TRUE) ;
                    return 0 ;

               case IDM_ABOUT :
                    MessageBox (hwnd, "Popup Menu Demonstration Program.",
                              szAppName, MB_ICONINFORMATION | MB_OK) ;
                    return 0 ;

               case IDM_EXIT :
                    SendMessage (hwnd, WM_CLOSE, 0, 0L) ;
                    return 0 ;

               case IDM_HELP :
                    MessageBox (hwnd, "Help not yet implemented.",
                              szAppName, MB_ICONINFORMATION | MB_OK) ;
                    return 0 ;
               }
          break ;

     case WM_DESTROY :
          PostQuitMessage (0) ;
          return 0 ;
     }
return DefWindowProc (hwnd, message, wParam, lParam) ;
}
```

POPMENU.RC

```
/*--------------------------
   POPMENU.RC resource script
  --------------------------*/

#include "popmenu.h"

PopMenu MENU
    {
    POPUP ""
        {
        POPUP "&File"
            {
            MENUITEM "&New",            IDM_NEW
            MENUITEM "&Open...",        IDM_OPEN
            MENUITEM "&Save",           IDM_SAVE
            MENUITEM "Save &As...",     IDM_SAVEAS
            MENUITEM SEPARATOR
            MENUITEM "E&xit",           IDM_EXIT
            }
        POPUP "&Edit"
            {
            MENUITEM "&Undo",           IDM_UNDO
            MENUITEM SEPARATOR
            MENUITEM "Cu&t",            IDM_CUT
            MENUITEM "&Copy",           IDM_COPY
            MENUITEM "&Paste",          IDM_PASTE
            MENUITEM "C&lear",          IDM_CLEAR
            }
        POPUP "&Background"
            {
            MENUITEM "&White",          IDM_WHITE, CHECKED
            MENUITEM "&Lt Gray",        IDM_LTGRAY
            MENUITEM "&Gray",           IDM_GRAY
            MENUITEM "&Dk Gray",        IDM_DKGRAY
            MENUITEM "&Black",          IDM_BLACK
            }
        POPUP "&Help"
            {
            MENUITEM "&Help",           IDM_HELP
            MENUITEM "&About PopMenu...", IDM_ABOUT
            }
        }
    }
```

POPMENU.H

```
/*---------------------
   POPMENU.H header file
---------------------*/

#define IDM_NEW       1
#define IDM_OPEN      2
#define IDM_SAVE      3
#define IDM_SAVEAS    4
#define IDM_EXIT      5

#define IDM_UNDO     10
#define IDM_CUT      11
#define IDM_COPY     12
#define IDM_PASTE    13
#define IDM_CLEAR    14

#define IDM_WHITE    20
#define IDM_LTGRAY   21
#define IDM_GRAY     22
#define IDM_DKGRAY   23
#define IDM_BLACK    24

#define IDM_HELP     30
#define IDM_ABOUT    31
```

POPMENU.DEF

```
;------------------------------------
; POPMENU.DEF module definition file
;------------------------------------

NAME            POPMENU

DESCRIPTION     'Popup Menu Demonstration Program (c) Charles Petzold, 1990'
EXETYPE         WINDOWS
STUB            'WINSTUB.EXE'
CODE            PRELOAD MOVEABLE DISCARDABLE
DATA            PRELOAD MOVEABLE MULTIPLE
HEAPSIZE        1024
STACKSIZE       8192
EXPORTS         WndProc
```

The POPMENU.RC resource script defines a menu very similar to the one in MENU-DEMO.RC. The difference is that the top-level menu contains only one item—a popup that invokes the File, Edit, Background, and Help options.

During the WM_CREATE message in *WndProc*, POPMENU obtains a handle to this popup menu:

```
hMenu = LoadMenu (hInst, szAppName) ;
hMenu = GetSubMenu (hMenu, 0) ;
```

During the WM_RBUTTONDOWN message, POPMENU obtains the position of the mouse point, coverts the position to screen coordinates, and passes the coordinates to *TrackPopupMenu*:

```
point = MAKEPOINT (lParam) ;
ClientToScreen (hwnd, &point) ;

TrackPopupMenu (hMenu, 0, point.x, point.y, 0, hwnd, NULL) ;
```

Windows then displays the popup menu with the items File, Edit, Background, and Help. Selecting any of these options causes the nested popup menus to appear to the right. The menu functions the same as a normal menu.

Using the System Menu

Parent windows created with a style that includes WS_SYSMENU have a system menu box at the left of the caption bar. If you like, you can modify this menu. For instance, you can add your own menu commands to the system menu. While this is not recommended, modifying the system menu is often a quick-and-dirty way to add a menu to a short program without defining it in the resource script. The only restriction is this: The ID numbers you use to add commands to the system menu must be lower than F000H. Otherwise, they will conflict with the IDs that Windows uses for the normal system menu commands. And remember: When you process WM_SYSCOMMAND messages in your window procedure for these new menu items, you must pass the other WM_SYSCOMMAND messages to *DefWindowProc*. If you don't, you'll effectively disable all normal options on the system menu.

The program POORMENU ("poor person's menu"), shown in Figure 9-6 beginning on the following page, adds a separator bar and three commands to the system menu. The last of these commands removes the additions.

POORMENU.MAK

```
#-----------------------
# POORMENU.MAK make file
#-----------------------

poormenu.exe : poormenu.obj poormenu.def
    link poormenu, /align:16, NUL, /nod slibcew libw, poormenu
    rc poormenu.exe

poormenu.obj : poormenu.c
    cl -c -Gsw -Ow -W2 -Zp poormenu.c
```

POORMENU.C

```
/*-------------------------------------------
   POORMENU.C -- The Poor Person's Menu
                 (c) Charles Petzold, 1990
   -------------------------------------------*/

#include <windows.h>

#define IDM_ABOUT   1
#define IDM_HELP    2
#define IDM_REMOVE  3

long FAR PASCAL WndProc (HWND, WORD, WORD, LONG) ;

static char szAppName [] = "PoorMenu" ;

int PASCAL WinMain (HANDLE hInstance, HANDLE hPrevInstance,
                    LPSTR lpszCmdLine, int nCmdShow)
    {
    HMENU     hMenu ;
    HWND      hwnd ;
    MSG       msg ;
    WNDCLASS wndclass ;

    if (!hPrevInstance)
        {
        wndclass.style        = CS_HREDRAW | CS_VREDRAW ;
        wndclass.lpfnWndProc  = WndProc ;
        wndclass.cbClsExtra   = 0 ;
        wndclass.cbWndExtra   = 0 ;
        wndclass.hInstance    = hInstance ;
        wndclass.hIcon        = LoadIcon (NULL, IDI_APPLICATION) ;
```

Figure 9-6. *The POORMENU program.*

(continued)

```
        wndclass.hCursor        = LoadCursor (NULL, IDC_ARROW) ;
        wndclass.hbrBackground = GetStockObject (WHITE_BRUSH) ;
        wndclass.lpszMenuName  = NULL ;
        wndclass.lpszClassName = szAppName ;

        RegisterClass (&wndclass) ;
        }

    hwnd = CreateWindow (szAppName, "The Poor Person's Menu",
                        WS_OVERLAPPEDWINDOW,
                        CW_USEDEFAULT, CW_USEDEFAULT,
                        CW_USEDEFAULT, CW_USEDEFAULT,
                        NULL, NULL, hInstance, NULL) ;

    hMenu = GetSystemMenu (hwnd, FALSE) ;

    AppendMenu (hMenu, MF_SEPARATOR, 0,         NULL) ;
    AppendMenu (hMenu, MF_STRING,   IDM_ABOUT,  "About...") ;
    AppendMenu (hMenu, MF_STRING,   IDM_HELP,   "Help...") ;
    AppendMenu (hMenu, MF_STRING,   IDM_REMOVE, "Remove Additions") ;

    ShowWindow (hwnd, nCmdShow) ;
    UpdateWindow (hwnd) ;

    while (GetMessage (&msg, NULL, 0, 0))
        {
        TranslateMessage (&msg) ;
        DispatchMessage (&msg) ;
        }
    return msg.wParam ;
    }

long FAR PASCAL WndProc (HWND hwnd, WORD message, WORD wParam, LONG lParam)
    {
    switch (message)
        {
        case WM_SYSCOMMAND :
            switch (wParam)
                {
                case IDM_ABOUT :
                    MessageBox (hwnd, "The Poor Person's Menu Program.",
                                szAppName, MB_OK | MB_ICONEXCLAMATION) ;
                    return 0 ;

                case IDM_HELP :
                    MessageBox (hwnd, "Help not yet implemented.",
                                szAppName, MB_OK | MB_ICONEXCLAMATION) ;
                    return 0 ;
```

(continued)

```
                         case IDM_REMOVE :
                              GetSystemMenu (hwnd, TRUE) ;
                              return 0 ;
                         }
                    break ;

               case WM_DESTROY :
                    PostQuitMessage (0) ;
                    return 0 ;
               }
          return DefWindowProc (hwnd, message, wParam, lParam) ;
          }
```

POORMENU.DEF

```
;--------------------------------------------
; POORMENU.DEF module definition file
;--------------------------------------------

NAME             POORMENU

DESCRIPTION      'The Poor Person's Menu (c) Charles Petzold, 1990'
EXETYPE          WINDOWS
STUB             'WINSTUB.EXE'
CODE             PRELOAD MOVEABLE DISCARDABLE
DATA             PRELOAD MOVEABLE MULTIPLE
HEAPSIZE         1024
STACKSIZE        8192
EXPORTS          WndProc
```

The three menu IDs are defined near the top of POORMENU.C:

```
#define IDM_ABOUT    1
#define IDM_HELP     2
#define IDM_REMOVE   3
```

After the program's window has been created, POORMENU obtains a handle to the system menu:

```
hMenu = GetSystemMenu (hwnd, FALSE) ;
```

When you first call *GetSystemMenu*, you should set the second parameter to FALSE in preparation for modifying the menu.

The menu is altered with four *AppendMenu* calls:

```
AppendMenu (hMenu, MF_SEPARATOR, 0,          NULL) ;
AppendMenu (hMenu, MF_STRING,    IDM_ABOUT,  "About...") ;
AppendMenu (hMenu, MF_STRING,    IDM_HELP,   "Help...") ;
AppendMenu (hMenu, MF_STRING,    IDM_REMOVE, "Remove Additions") ;
```

The first *AppendMenu* call adds the separator bar. Choosing the Remove Additions menu item causes POORMENU to remove these additions, which it accomplishes simply by calling *GetSystemMenu* again with the second parameter set to TRUE:

```
GetSystemMenu (hwnd, TRUE) ;
```

The standard system menu has the options Restore, Move, Size, Minimize, Maximize, Close, and Switch To. These generate WM_SYSCOMMAND messages with *wParam* equal to SC_RESTORE, SC_MOVE, SC_SIZE, SC_MINIMUM, SC_MAXIMUM, SC_CLOSE, and SC_TASKLIST. Although Windows programs do not normally do so, you can process these messages yourself rather than pass them on to *DefWindowProc*. You can also disable or remove some of these standard options from the system menu using methods described below. The Windows documentation also includes some standard additions to the system menu. These use the identifiers SC_NEXTWINDOW, SC_PREVWINDOW, SC_VSCROLL, SC_HSCROLL, and SC_ARRANGE. You might find it appropriate to add these commands to the system menu in some applications.

Changing the Menu

We've already seen how the *AppendMenu* function can be used to define a menu entirely within a program and to add menu items to the system menu. Prior to Windows 3, you would have been forced to use the *ChangeMenu* function for this job. *ChangeMenu* was so versatile that it was one of the most complex functions in all of Windows. In Windows 3, *ChangeMenu* is still available, but its functionality has been divided among five new functions:

- *AppendMenu* adds a new item to the end of a menu.

- *DeleteMenu* deletes an existing item from a menu and destroys the item.

- *InsertMenu* inserts a new item into a menu.

- *ModifyMenu* changes an existing menu item.

- *RemoveMenu* removes an existing item from a menu.

The difference between *DeleteMenu* and *RemoveMenu* is important if the item is a popup menu. *DeleteMenu* destroys the popup menu—but *RemoveMenu* does not.

Other Menu Commands

Here are some more functions useful for working with menus:

When you change a top-level menu item, the change is not shown until Windows redraws the menu bar. You can force this redrawing by calling:

```
DrawMenuBar (hwnd) ;
```

Note that the parameter to *DrawMenuBar* is a handle to the window rather than a handle to the menu.

You can obtain the handle of a popup menu using:

```
hMenuPopup = GetSubMenu (hMenu, nPos) ;
```

where *nPos* is the index (starting at 0) of the popup within the top-level menu indicated by *hMenu*. You can then use the popup menu handle with other functions (such as *AppendMenu*).

You can obtain the current number of items in a top-level or popup menu using:

```
nCount = GetMenuItemCount (hMenu) ;
```

You can obtain the menu ID for an item in a popup menu from:

```
wID = GetMenuItemID (hMenuPopup, nPosition) ;
```

where *nPosition* is the position (starting at 0) of the item within the popup.

In MENUDEMO you saw how to check or uncheck an item in a popup menu using:

```
CheckMenuItem (hMenu, wID, wCheck) ;
```

In MENUDEMO, *hMenu* was the handle to the top-level menu, *wID* was the menu ID, and the value of wCheck was either MF_CHECKED or MF_UNCHECKED. If *hMenu* is a handle to a popup menu, then the *wID* parameter can be a positional index rather than a menu ID. If an index is more convenient, you include MF_BYPOSITION in the third parameter. For instance:

```
CheckMenuItem (hMenu, nPosition, MF_CHECKED | MF_BYPOSITION) ;
```

The *EnableMenuItem* function works similarly to *CheckMenuItem* except the third parameter is MF_ENABLED, MF_DISABLED, or MF_GRAYED. If you use *EnableMenuItem* on a top-level menu item that has a popup, you must also use the MF_BYPOSITION identifier in the third parameter because the menu item has no menu ID. We'll see an example of *EnableMenuItem* in the POPPAD program shown later in this chapter. *HiliteMenuItem* is similar to *CheckMenuItem* and *EnableMenuItem* but uses MF_HILITE and MF_UNHILITE. This highlighting is the reverse video that Windows uses when you move among menu items. You do not normally need to use *HiliteMenuItem*.

What else do you need to do with your menu? Have you forgotten what character string you used in a menu? You can refresh your memory by calling:

```
nByteCount = GetMenuString (hMenu, wID, lpString, nMaxCount, wFlag) ;
```

The *wFlag* is either MF_BYCOMMAND (where *wID* is a menu ID) or MF_BYPOSITION (*wID* is a positional index). The function copies up to *nMaxCount* bytes of the text string into *lpString* and returns the number of bytes copied.

Or perhaps you'd like to know what the current flags of a menu item are:

```
wFlags = GetMenuState (hMenu, wID, wFlag) ;
```

Again, *wFlag* is either MF_BYCOMMAND or MF_BYPOSITION. The *wFlags* parameter is a combination of all the current flags. You can determine them by testing against the MF_DISABLED, MF_GRAYED, MF_CHECKED, MF_MENUBREAK, MF_MENUBAR-BREAK, and MF_SEPARATOR identifiers.

Or maybe by this time you're a little fed up with menus. In that case you'll be pleased to know that if you no longer need a menu in your program, you can destroy it:

```
DestroyMenu (hMenu) ;
```

This invalidates the menu handle.

An Unorthodox Approach to Menus

Now let's step a little off the beaten path. Instead of having drop-down menus in your program, how about creating multiple top-level menus without any popups and switching between the top-level menus using the *SetMenu* call? The NOPOPUPS program, shown in Figure 9-7, demonstrates how to do it. This program includes similar File and Edit items that MENUDEMO uses but displays them as alternate top-level menus.

NOPOPUPS.MAK

```
#------------------------
# NOPOPUPS.MAK make file
#------------------------

nopopups.exe : nopopups.obj nopopups.def nopopups.res
     link nopopups, /align:16, NUL, /nod slibcew libw, nopopups
     rc nopopups.res

nopopups.obj : nopopups.c nopopups.h
     cl -c -Gsw -Ow -W2 -Zp nopopups.c

nopopups.res : nopopups.rc nopopups.h
     rc -r nopopups.rc
```

Figure 9-7. *The NOPOPUPS program.*

NOPOPUPS.C

```
/*-------------------------------------------------------
   NOPOPUPS.C -- Demonstrates No-Popup Nested Menu
                   (c) Charles Petzold, 1990
   ----------------------------------------------------*/

#include <windows.h>
#include "nopopups.h"

long FAR PASCAL WndProc (HWND, WORD, WORD, LONG) ;

int PASCAL WinMain (HANDLE hInstance, HANDLE hPrevInstance,
                    LPSTR lpszCmdLine, int nCmdShow)
     {
     static char szAppName [] = "NoPopUps" ;
     HWND        hwnd ;
     MSG         msg ;
     WNDCLASS    wndclass ;

     if (!hPrevInstance)
          {
          wndclass.style         = CS_HREDRAW | CS_VREDRAW ;
          wndclass.lpfnWndProc   = WndProc ;
          wndclass.cbClsExtra    = 0 ;
          wndclass.cbWndExtra    = 0 ;
          wndclass.hInstance     = hInstance ;
          wndclass.hIcon         = LoadIcon (NULL, IDI_APPLICATION) ;
          wndclass.hCursor       = LoadCursor (NULL, IDC_ARROW) ;
          wndclass.hbrBackground = GetStockObject (WHITE_BRUSH) ;
          wndclass.lpszMenuName  = NULL ;
          wndclass.lpszClassName = szAppName ;

          RegisterClass (&wndclass) ;
          }

     hwnd = CreateWindow (szAppName, "No-Popup Nested Menu Demonstration",
                    WS_OVERLAPPEDWINDOW,
                    CW_USEDEFAULT, CW_USEDEFAULT,
                    CW_USEDEFAULT, CW_USEDEFAULT,
                    NULL, NULL, hInstance, NULL) ;

     ShowWindow (hwnd, nCmdShow) ;
     UpdateWindow (hwnd) ;

     while (GetMessage (&msg, NULL, 0, 0))
          {
          TranslateMessage (&msg) ;
```

(continued)

```
            DispatchMessage (&msg) ;
            }
      return msg.wParam ;
      }

long FAR PASCAL WndProc (HWND hwnd, WORD message, WORD wParam, LONG lParam)
      {
      static HMENU hMenuMain, hMenuEdit, hMenuFile ;
      HANDLE      hInstance ;

      switch (message)
            {
            case WM_CREATE :
                  hInstance = GetWindowWord (hwnd, GWW_HINSTANCE) ;

                  hMenuMain = LoadMenu (hInstance, "MenuMain") ;
                  hMenuFile = LoadMenu (hInstance, "MenuFile") ;
                  hMenuEdit = LoadMenu (hInstance, "MenuEdit") ;

                  SetMenu (hwnd, hMenuMain) ;
                  return 0 ;

            case WM_COMMAND :
                  switch (wParam)
                        {
                        case IDM_MAIN :
                              SetMenu (hwnd, hMenuMain) ;
                              return 0 ;

                        case IDM_FILE :
                              SetMenu (hwnd, hMenuFile) ;
                              return 0 ;

                        case IDM_EDIT :
                              SetMenu (hwnd, hMenuEdit) ;
                              return 0 ;

                        case IDM_NEW :
                        case IDM_OPEN :
                        case IDM_SAVE :
                        case IDM_SAVEAS :
                        case IDM_UNDO :
                        case IDM_CUT :
                        case IDM_COPY :
                        case IDM_PASTE :
                        case IDM_CLEAR :
                              MessageBeep (0) ;
                              return 0 ;
                        }
                  break ;
```

(continued)

367

```
        case WM_DESTROY :
             PostQuitMessage (0) ;
             return 0 ;
        }
     return DefWindowProc (hwnd, message, wParam, lParam) ;
     }
```

NOPOPUPS.RC

```
/*-------------------------------
   NOPOPUPS.RC resource script
   ----------------------------*/

#include "nopopups.h"

MenuMain MENU
     {
     MENUITEM "MAIN:",        0,          INACTIVE
     MENUITEM "&File...",     IDM_FILE
     MENUITEM "&Edit...",     IDM_EDIT
     }

MenuFile MENU
     {
     MENUITEM "FILE:",        0,          INACTIVE
     MENUITEM "&New",         IDM_NEW
     MENUITEM "&Open...",     IDM_OPEN
     MENUITEM "&Save",        IDM_SAVE
     MENUITEM "Save &As...",  IDM_SAVEAS
     MENUITEM "(&Main)",      IDM_MAIN
     }

MenuEdit MENU
     {
     MENUITEM "EDIT:",        0,          INACTIVE
     MENUITEM "&Undo",        IDM_UNDO
     MENUITEM "Cu&t",         IDM_CUT
     MENUITEM "&Copy",        IDM_COPY
     MENUITEM "&Paste",       IDM_PASTE
     MENUITEM "C&lear",       IDM_CLEAR
     MENUITEM "(&Main)",      IDM_MAIN
     }
```

NOPOPUPS.H

```
/*------------------------
   NOPOPUPS.H header file
------------------------*/

#define IDM_NEW      1
#define IDM_OPEN     2
#define IDM_SAVE     3
#define IDM_SAVEAS   4

#define IDM_UNDO     5
#define IDM_CUT      6
#define IDM_COPY     7
#define IDM_PASTE    8
#define IDM_CLEAR    9

#define IDM_MAIN    10
#define IDM_EDIT    11
#define IDM_FILE    12
```

NOPOPUPS.DEF

```
;------------------------------------
; NOPOPUPS.DEF module definition file
;------------------------------------

NAME          NOPOPUPS

DESCRIPTION   'Demonstration of No-Popup Menu (c) Charles Petzold, 1990'
EXETYPE       WINDOWS
STUB          'WINSTUB.EXE'
CODE          PRELOAD MOVEABLE DISCARDABLE
DATA          PRELOAD MOVEABLE MULTIPLE
HEAPSIZE      1024
STACKSIZE     8192
EXPORTS       WndProc
```

The resource script has three menus rather than one. When the window procedure processes the WM_CREATE message, Windows loads each of the menu resources into memory:

```
hMenuMain = LoadMenu (hInstance, "MenuMain") ;
hMenuFile = LoadMenu (hInstance, "MenuFile") ;
hMenuEdit = LoadMenu (hInstance, "MenuEdit") ;
```

Initially, the program displays the main menu:

```
SetMenu (hwnd, hMenuMain) ;
```

The main menu lists the three options using the character strings "MAIN:", "File…", and "Edit…" However, "MAIN:" is disabled, so it doesn't cause WM_COMMAND messages to be sent to the window procedure. The File and Edit menus begin "FILE:" and "EDIT:" to identify these as submenus. The last item in each menu is the character string "(Main)"; this option indicates a return to the main menu. Switching among these three menus is simple:

```
case WM_COMMAND :

    switch (wParam)
        {
        case IDM_MAIN :
               SetMenu (hwnd, hMenuMain) ;
               return 0 ;

        case IDM_FILE :
               SetMenu (hwnd, hMenuFile) ;
               return 0 ;

        case IDM_EDIT :
               SetMenu (hwnd, hMenuEdit) ;
               return 0 ;
        [other program lines]
        }
    break ;
```

USING BITMAPS IN MENUS

Character strings are not the only way to display a menu item. You can also use a bitmap. If you immediately recoiled at the thought of pictures of file folders, paste jars, and trash cans in a menu, don't think of pictures. Think instead of how useful menu bitmaps might be for a drawing program. Think of using different fonts and font sizes, line widths, hatch patterns, and colors in your menus.

The program we're going to examine is called GRAFMENU ("graphics menu"). The top-level menu is shown in Figure 9-8. The enlarged block letters are obtained from 40-by-16-pixel monochrome bitmap files created in SDKPAINT and saved as .BMP files; they could be pictures instead. Choosing FONT from the menu invokes a popup containing three options—Courier, Helvetica, and Times Roman—each displayed in its respective font (Figure 9-9). These bitmaps were created in the program using a technique involving a "memory device context."

Figure 9-8. *The GRAFMENU program's top-level menu.*

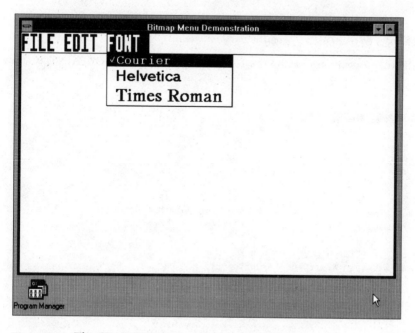

Figure 9-9. *The GRAFMENU program's popup FONT menu.*

Finally, when you pull down the system menu, you see that you have access to some "help" information, with the word "Help" perhaps mirroring the desperation of a new user (Figure 9-10). This 64-by-64-pixel monochrome bitmap was created in SDKPAINT.

Figure 9-10. *The GRAFMENU program's system menu.*

The GRAFMENU program, including the four bitmaps created in SDKPAINT, is shown in Figure 9-11.

GRAFMENU.MAK

```
#-----------------------
# GRAFMENU.MAK make file
#-----------------------

grafmenu.exe : grafmenu.obj grafmenu.def grafmenu.res
     link grafmenu, /align:16, NUL, /nod slibcew libw, grafmenu
     rc grafmenu.res

grafmenu.obj : grafmenu.c grafmenu.h
     cl -c -Gsw -Ow -W2 -Zp grafmenu.c

grafmenu.res : grafmenu.rc grafmenu.h \
               editlabl.bmp filelabl.bmp fontlabl.bmp bighelp.bmp
     rc -r grafmenu.rc
```

Figure 9-11. *The GRAFMENU program.*

GRAFMENU.C

```
/*-----------------------------------------------
   GRAFMENU.C -- Demonstrates Bitmap Menu Items
                 (c) Charles Petzold, 1990
   -----------------------------------------------*/

#include <windows.h>
#include <string.h>
#include "grafmenu.h"

long FAR PASCAL WndProc  (HWND, WORD, WORD, LONG) ;
HBITMAP StretchBitmap (HBITMAP) ;
HBITMAP GetBitmapFont (int) ;

char szAppName [] = "GrafMenu" ;

int PASCAL WinMain (HANDLE hInstance, HANDLE hPrevInstance,
                    LPSTR lpszCmdLine, int nCmdShow)
    {
    HBITMAP  hBitmapHelp, hBitmapFile, hBitmapEdit,
             hBitmapFont, hBitmapPopFont [3] ;
    HMENU    hMenu, hMenuPopup ;
    HWND     hwnd ;
    int      i ;
    MSG      msg ;
    WNDCLASS wndclass ;

    if (!hPrevInstance)
        {
        wndclass.style         = CS_HREDRAW : CS_VREDRAW ;
        wndclass.lpfnWndProc   = WndProc ;
        wndclass.cbClsExtra    = 0 ;
        wndclass.cbWndExtra    = 0 ;
        wndclass.hInstance     = hInstance ;
        wndclass.hIcon         = LoadIcon (NULL, IDI_APPLICATION) ;
        wndclass.hCursor       = LoadCursor (NULL, IDC_ARROW) ;
        wndclass.hbrBackground = GetStockObject (WHITE_BRUSH) ;
        wndclass.lpszMenuName  = NULL ;
        wndclass.lpszClassName = szAppName ;

        RegisterClass (&wndclass) ;
        }

    hMenu = CreateMenu () ;

    hMenuPopup = LoadMenu (hInstance, "MenuFile") ;
    hBitmapFile = StretchBitmap (LoadBitmap (hInstance, "BitmapFile")) ;
    AppendMenu (hMenu, MF_BITMAP : MF_POPUP, hMenuPopup,
                (LPSTR) (LONG) hBitmapFile) ;
```

(continued)

```
    hMenuPopup = LoadMenu (hInstance, "MenuEdit") ;
    hBitmapEdit = StretchBitmap (LoadBitmap (hInstance, "BitmapEdit")) ;
    AppendMenu (hMenu, MF_BITMAP | MF_POPUP, hMenuPopup,
                (LPSTR) (LONG) hBitmapEdit) ;

    hMenuPopup = CreateMenu () ;

    for (i = 0 ; i < 3 ; i++)
         {
         hBitmapPopFont [i] = GetBitmapFont (i) ;
         AppendMenu (hMenuPopup, MF_BITMAP, IDM_COUR + i,
                     (LPSTR) (LONG) hBitmapPopFont [i]) ;
         }

    hBitmapFont = StretchBitmap (LoadBitmap (hInstance, "BitmapFont")) ;
    AppendMenu (hMenu, MF_BITMAP | MF_POPUP, hMenuPopup,
                (LPSTR) (LONG) hBitmapFont) ;

    hwnd = CreateWindow (szAppName, "Bitmap Menu Demonstration",
                     WS_OVERLAPPEDWINDOW,
                     CW_USEDEFAULT, CW_USEDEFAULT,
                     CW_USEDEFAULT, CW_USEDEFAULT,
                     NULL, hMenu, hInstance, NULL) ;

    hMenu = GetSystemMenu (hwnd, FALSE) ;
    hBitmapHelp = StretchBitmap (LoadBitmap (hInstance, "BitmapHelp")) ;
    AppendMenu (hMenu, MF_SEPARATOR, NULL,      NULL) ;
    AppendMenu (hMenu, MF_BITMAP,    IDM_HELP, (LPSTR) (LONG) hBitmapHelp) ;

    ShowWindow (hwnd, nCmdShow) ;
    UpdateWindow (hwnd) ;

    while (GetMessage (&msg, NULL, 0, 0))
         {
         TranslateMessage (&msg) ;
         DispatchMessage (&msg) ;
         }

    DeleteObject (hBitmapHelp) ;
    DeleteObject (hBitmapEdit) ;
    DeleteObject (hBitmapFile) ;
    DeleteObject (hBitmapFont) ;

    for (i = 0 ; i < 3 ; i++)
         DeleteObject (hBitmapPopFont [i]) ;

    return msg.wParam ;
    }

HBITMAP StretchBitmap (HBITMAP hBitmap1)
    {
    BITMAP     bm1, bm2 ;
    HBITMAP    hBitmap2 ;
```

(continued)

```
    HDC        hdc, hdcMem1, hdcMem2 ;
    TEXTMETRIC tm ;

    hdc = CreateIC ("DISPLAY", NULL, NULL, NULL) ;
    GetTextMetrics (hdc, &tm) ;
    hdcMem1 = CreateCompatibleDC (hdc) ;
    hdcMem2 = CreateCompatibleDC (hdc) ;
    DeleteDC (hdc) ;

    GetObject (hBitmap1, sizeof (BITMAP), (LPSTR) &bm1) ;

    bm2 = bm1 ;
    bm2.bmWidth      = (tm.tmAveCharWidth * bm2.bmWidth)  / 4 ;
    bm2.bmHeight     = (tm.tmHeight       * bm2.bmHeight) / 8 ;
    bm2.bmWidthBytes = ((bm2.bmWidth + 15) / 16) * 2 ;

    hBitmap2 = CreateBitmapIndirect (&bm2) ;

    SelectObject (hdcMem1, hBitmap1) ;
    SelectObject (hdcMem2, hBitmap2) ;

    StretchBlt (hdcMem2, 0, 0, bm2.bmWidth, bm2.bmHeight,
                hdcMem1, 0, 0, bm1.bmWidth, bm1.bmHeight, SRCCOPY) ;

    DeleteDC (hdcMem1) ;
    DeleteDC (hdcMem2) ;
    DeleteObject (hBitmap1) ;

    return hBitmap2 ;
    }

HBITMAP GetBitmapFont (int i)
    {
    static  struct
        {
        BYTE lfPitchAndFamily ;
        BYTE lfFaceName [LF_FACESIZE] ;
        char *szMenuText ;
        }
        lfSet [3] =
        {
        FIXED_PITCH    : FF_MODERN, "Courier",   "Courier",
        VARIABLE_PITCH : FF_SWISS,  "Helvetica", "Helvetica",
        VARIABLE_PITCH : FF_ROMAN,  "Tms Rmn",   "Times Roman"
        } ;
    DWORD   dwSize ;
    HBITMAP hBitmap ;
    HDC     hdc, hdcMem ;
    HFONT   hFont ;
    LOGFONT lf ;
```

(continued)

```
        hFont = GetStockObject (SYSTEM_FONT) ;
        GetObject (hFont, sizeof (LOGFONT), (LPSTR) &lf) ;

        lf.lfHeight *= 2 ;
        lf.lfWidth  *= 2 ;
        lf.lfPitchAndFamily = lfSet[i].lfPitchAndFamily ;
        strcpy (lf.lfFaceName, lfSet[i].lfFaceName) ;

        hdc = CreateIC ("DISPLAY", NULL, NULL, NULL) ;
        hdcMem = CreateCompatibleDC (hdc) ;
        SelectObject (hdcMem, CreateFontIndirect (&lf)) ;
        dwSize = GetTextExtent (hdcMem, lfSet[i].szMenuText,
                            strlen (lfSet[i].szMenuText)) ;

        hBitmap = CreateBitmap (LOWORD (dwSize)-1, HIWORD (dwSize), 1, 1, NULL) ;
        SelectObject (hdcMem, hBitmap) ;


        TextOut (hdcMem, 0, 0, lfSet[i].szMenuText,
                            strlen (lfSet[i].szMenuText)) ;

        DeleteObject (SelectObject (hdcMem, hFont)) ;
        DeleteDC (hdcMem) ;
        DeleteDC (hdc) ;

        return hBitmap ;
        }

long FAR PASCAL WndProc (HWND hwnd, WORD message, WORD wParam, LONG lParam)
        {
        HMENU   hMenu ;
        static short nCurrentFont = IDM_COUR ;

        switch (message)
            {
            case WM_CREATE :
                    CheckMenuItem (GetMenu (hwnd), nCurrentFont, MF_CHECKED) ;
                    return 0 ;

            case WM_SYSCOMMAND :
                    switch (wParam)
                        {
                        case IDM_HELP :
                            MessageBox (hwnd, "Help not yet implemented.",
                                    szAppName, MB_OK ; MB_ICONEXCLAMATION) ;
                            return 0 ;
                        }
                    break ;
```

(continued)

```
        case WM_COMMAND :
             switch (wParam)
                  {
                  case IDM_NEW :
                  case IDM_OPEN :
                  case IDM_SAVE :
                  case IDM_SAVEAS :
                  case IDM_UNDO :
                  case IDM_CUT :
                  case IDM_COPY :
                  case IDM_PASTE :
                  case IDM_CLEAR :
                       MessageBeep (0) ;
                       return 0 ;

                  case IDM_COUR :
                  case IDM_HELV :
                  case IDM_TMSRMN :
                       hMenu = GetMenu (hwnd) ;
                       CheckMenuItem (hMenu, nCurrentFont, MF_UNCHECKED) ;
                       nCurrentFont = wParam ;
                       CheckMenuItem (hMenu, nCurrentFont, MF_CHECKED) ;
                       return 0 ;
                  }
             break ;

        case WM_DESTROY :
             PostQuitMessage (0) ;
             return 0 ;
        }
   return DefWindowProc (hwnd, message, wParam, lParam) ;
   }
```

GRAFMENU.RC

```
/*----------------------------
   GRAFMENU.RC resource script
   ----------------------------*/

#include "grafmenu.h"

BitmapEdit BITMAP editlabl.bmp
BitmapFile BITMAP filelabl.bmp
BitmapFont BITMAP fontlabl.bmp
BitmapHelp BITMAP bighelp.bmp
```

(continued)

377

```
MenuFile MENU
    {
    MENUITEM "&New",        IDM_NEW
    MENUITEM "&Open...",    IDM_OPEN
    MENUITEM "&Save",       IDM_SAVE
    MENUITEM "Save &As...", IDM_SAVEAS
    }

MenuEdit MENU
    {
    MENUITEM "&Undo",       IDM_UNDO
    MENUITEM SEPARATOR
    MENUITEM "Cu&t",        IDM_CUT
    MENUITEM "&Copy",       IDM_COPY
    MENUITEM "&Paste",      IDM_PASTE
    MENUITEM "C&lear",      IDM_CLEAR
    }
```

GRAFMENU.H

```
/*-------------------------
    GRAFMENU.H header file
    ---------------------*/

#define IDM_NEW      1
#define IDM_OPEN     2
#define IDM_SAVE     3
#define IDM_SAVEAS   4

#define IDM_UNDO     5
#define IDM_CUT      6
#define IDM_COPY     7
#define IDM_PASTE    8
#define IDM_CLEAR    9

#define IDM_COUR     10
#define IDM_HELV     11
#define IDM_TMSRMN   12

#define IDM_HELP     13
```

EDITLABL.BMP

378

FILELABL.BMP

FONTLABL.BMP

BIGHELP.BMP

GRAFMENU.DEF

```
;------------------------------------
; GRAFMENU.DEF module definition file
;------------------------------------

NAME            GRAFMENU

DESCRIPTION     'Demo of Bitmapped Menu Items (c) Charles Petzold, 1990'
EXETYPE         WINDOWS
STUB            'WINSTUB.EXE'
CODE            PRELOAD MOVEABLE DISCARDABLE
DATA            PRELOAD MOVEABLE MULTIPLE
HEAPSIZE        1024
STACKSIZE       8192
EXPORTS         WndProc
```

To examine the subject of bitmaps and menus in the detail it deserves, we'll need to cross the border into GDI territory—a full exploration of which awaits us in the next section of this book. The discussion here will serve as a preview of topics that we'll return to again in Chapter 11.

Two Methods of Creating Bitmaps for Menus

To insert a bitmap into a menu, you use *AppendMenu* or *InsertMenu*. Where does this bitmap come from? It can come from one of two places. First, you can create a bitmap using SDKPAINT and include the bitmap file in your resource script. Within the program, you can use *LoadBitmap* to load the bitmap resource into memory and use *AppendMenu* or *InsertMenu* to attach it to the menu. There's a problem with this approach, however. The bitmap will not be suitable for all types of video resolutions and aspect ratios; you have to stretch the loaded bitmap to account for this. Alternatively, you can create the bitmap right in the program and attach it to the menu.

Both of these methods sound a lot more difficult than they actually are. We don't have to mess around with the actual bits themselves. Windows provides functions that let us manipulate bitmaps cleanly using something called the "memory device context."

The Memory Device Context

When you use GDI calls (such as *TextOut*) to write on the client area of your window, you're actually writing to a block of memory (the video display memory) that is organized much like a giant bitmap. The width and height of this bitmap are equal to the resolution of the video adapter. The manner in which multiple bits define color is also defined by the video adapter. Windows should also be able to pretend that a block of regular memory is video display memory. It should be able to write on this memory the same way it writes on the screen. We should then be able to use this block of memory as a bitmap.

That's exactly what a memory device context is. It helps us fill up and manipulate bitmaps in a Windows program. Here are the steps involved:

1. Create a memory device context using the *CreateCompatibleDC* call. Initially, the display surface of this memory device context contains one monochrome pixel. You can think of this device context as being 1 pixel high and 1 pixel wide, with two colors (black and white).

2. Create an uninitialized bitmap using *CreateBitmap*, *CreateBitmapIndirect*, or *CreateCompatibleBitmap*. When you create the bitmap, you specify the height and width and the color organization. However, the pixels of the bitmap need not actually represent anything yet. Save the handle to the bitmap.

3. Select the bitmap into the memory device context using *SelectObject*. Now the memory device context has a display surface that is the size of the bitmap with the same number of colors as defined by the bitmap.

4. Use GDI functions to draw on the memory device context the same way you use GDI functions to draw on a normal device context. Anything you draw within the display surface of the memory device context is actually drawn on the bitmap selected into the device context.

5. Delete the memory device context. You are left with a handle to a bitmap that contains a pixel representation of what you drew on the memory device context.

Creating a Bitmap with Text

The *GetBitmapFont* function in GRAFMENU takes a parameter of 0, 1, or 2 and returns a handle to a bitmap. This bitmap contains the string "Courier," "Helvetica," or "Times Roman" in the appropriate font and about twice the size of the normal system font. Let's see how *GetBitmapFont* does it. (The code that follows is not the same as that in the GRAFMENU.C file. For purposes of clarity, I've replaced references to the *lfSet* structure with the values appropriate for Times Roman.)

The first step is to get a handle to the system font and use *GetObject* to copy characteristics of that font into the structure *lf* that has type LOGFONT ("logical font"):

```
hFont = GetStockObject (SYSTEM_FONT) ;
GetObject (hFont, sizeof (LOGFONT), (LPSTR) &lf) ;
```

Certain fields of this logical font structure must be modified to make it describe a larger Times Roman font:

```
lf.lfHeight *= 2 ;
lf.lfWidth  *= 2 ;
lf.lfPitchAndFamily = VARIABLE_PITCH | FF_ROMAN ;
strcpy (lf.lfFaceName, "Tms Rmn") ;
```

The next step is to get a device context for the screen and create a memory device context compatible with the screen:

```
hdc = CreateIC ("DISPLAY", NULL, NULL, NULL) ;
hdcMem = CreateCompatibleDC (hdc) ;
```

The handle to the memory device context is *hdcMem*. Next, we create a font based on the modified *lf* structure and select that font into the memory device context:

```
SelectObject (hdcMem, CreateFontIndirect (&lf)) ;
```

Now when we write some text to the memory device context, Windows will use the Times Roman font selected into the device context.

But this memory device context still has a one-pixel monochrome device surface. We have to create a bitmap large enough for the text we want to display on it. You can obtain the dimensions of the text through *GetTextExtent* and create a bitmap based on these dimensions with *CreateBitmap*:

```
dwSize = GetTextExtent (hdcMem, "Times Roman", 11) ;
hBitmap = CreateBitmap (LOWORD (dwSize), HIWORD (dwSize), 1, 1, NULL) ;
SelectObject (hdcMem, hBitmap) ;
```

This device context now has a monochrome display surface exactly the size of the text. Now all we have to do is write the text to it. You've seen this function before:

```
TextOut (hdcMem, 0, 0, "Times Roman", 11) ;
```

We're finished except for cleaning up. To do so, we select the system font (with handle *hFont*) back into the device context using *SelectObject*, and we delete the previous font handle that *SelectObject* returns, which is the handle to the Times Roman font:

```
DeleteObject (SelectObject (hdcMem, hFont)) ;
```

Now we can also delete the two device contexts:

```
DeleteDC (hdcMem) ;
DeleteDC (hdc) ;
```

We're left with a bitmap that has the text "Times Roman" in a Times Roman font.

Scaling Bitmaps

The memory device context also comes to the rescue when we need to scale fonts to a different display resolution or aspect ratio. I created the four bitmaps used in GRAFMENU to be the correct size for a display that has a system font height of 8 pixels and width of 4 pixels. For other system font dimensions, the bitmap has to be stretched. This is done in GRAFMENU's *StretchBitmap* function.

The first step is to get the device context for the screen, obtain the text metrics for the system font, and create two memory device contexts:

```
hdc = CreateIC ("DISPLAY", NULL, NULL, NULL) ;
GetTextMetrics (hdc, &tm) ;
hdcMem1 = CreateCompatibleDC (hdc) ;
hdcMem2 = CreateCompatibleDC (hdc) ;
DeleteDC (hdc) ;
```

The bitmap handle passed to the function is *hBitmap1*. The program can obtain the dimensions of this bitmap using *GetObject*:

```
GetObject (hBitmap1, sizeof (BITMAP), (LPSTR) &bm1) ;
```

This copies the dimensions into a structure *bm1* of type BITMAP. The structure *bm2* is set equal to *bm1*, and then certain fields are modified based on the system font dimensions:

```
bm2 = bm1 ;
bm2.bmWidth      = (tm.tmAveCharWidth * bm2.bmWidth)  / 4 ;
bm2.bmHeight     = (tm.tmHeight       * bm2.bmHeight) / 8 ;
bm2.bmWidthBytes = ((bm2.bmWidth + 15) / 16) * 2 ;
```

Then a new bitmap with handle *hBitmap2* can be created based on the altered dimensions:

```
hBitmap2 = CreateBitmapIndirect (&bm2) ;
```

You can then select these two bitmaps into the two memory display contexts:

```
SelectObject (hdcMem1, hBitmap1) ;
SelectObject (hdcMem2, hBitmap2) ;
```

We want to copy the first bitmap to the second bitmap and stretch it in the process. This involves the *StretchBlt* call:

```
StretchBlt (hdcMem2, 0, 0, bm2.bmWidth, bm2.bmHeight,
            hdcMem1, 0, 0, bm1.bmWidth, bm1.bmHeight, SRCCOPY) ;
```

Now the second bitmap has the properly scaled bitmap. We'll use that one in the menu. Cleanup is simple:

```
DeleteDC (hdcMem1) ;
DeleteDC (hdcMem2) ;
DeleteObject (hBitmap1) ;
```

Putting the Menu Together

GRAFMENU's *WinMain* function uses the *StretchBitmap* and *GetBitmapFont* functions when constructing the menu. GRAFMENU has two menus already defined in the resource script. These will become popups for the File and Edit options.

GRAFMENU begins by obtaining a handle to an empty menu:

```
hMenu = CreateMenu () ;
```

The popup menu for File (containing the four options New, Open, Save, and Save As) is loaded from the resource script:

```
hMenuPopup = LoadMenu (hInstance, "MenuFile") ;
```

The bitmap containing the word "FILE" is also loaded from the resource script and stretched using *StretchBitmap*:

```
hBitmapFile = StretchBitmap (LoadBitmap (hInstance, "BitmapFile")) ;
```

The bitmap handle and popup menu handle become parameters in the *ChangeMenu* call:

```
AppendMenu (hMenu, MF_BITMAP : MF_POPUP, hMenuPopup, (LPSTR) (LONG) hBitmapFile) ;
```

The same procedure is followed for the Edit menu:

```
hMenuPopup = LoadMenu (hInstance, "MenuEdit") ;
hBitmapEdit = StretchBitmap (LoadBitmap (hInstance, "BitmapEdit")) ;
AppendMenu (hMenu, MF_BITMAP | MF_POPUP, hMenuPopup, (LPSTR) (LONG) hBitmapEdit) ;
```

The popup menu for the three fonts is constructed from calls to the *GetBitmapFont* function:

```
hMenuPopup = CreateMenu () ;
for (i = 0 ; i < 3 ; i++)
     {
     hBitmapPopFont [i] = GetBitmapFont (i) ;
     AppendMenu (hMenuPopup, MF_BITMAP,IDM_COUR + i,
              (LPSTR) (LONG) hMenuPopupFont [i]) ;
```

The popup is then added to the menu:

```
hBitmapFont = StretchBitmap (LoadBitmap (hInstance, "BitmapFont")) ;
AppendMenu (hMenu, MF_BITMAP | MF_POPUP, hBitmapFont,
         (LONG) (LPSTR) hBitmapFont) ;
```

The window menu is complete. Now you can include *hMenu* in the *CreateWindow* call:

```
hwnd = CreateWindow (szAppName, "Bitmap Menu Demonstration",
              WS_OVERLAPPED,
              CW_USEDEFAULT, CW_USEDEFAULT,
              CW_USEDEFAULT, CW_USEDEFAULT,
              NULL, hMenu, hInstance, NULL) ;
```

After *hwnd* is available, GRAFMENU can alter the system menu. GRAFMENU first obtains a handle to it:

```
hMenu = GetSystemMenu (hwnd, FALSE) ;
```

This loads the "Help" bitmap and stretches it to an appropriate size:

```
hBitmapHelp = StretchBitmap (LoadBitmap (hInstance, "BitmapHelp")) ;
```

This adds a separator bar and the stretched bitmap to the system menu:

```
AppendMenu (hMenu, MF_SEPARATOR, 0, NULL) ;
AppendMenu (hMenu, MF_BITMAP, IDM_HELP, (LPSTR) (LONG) hBitmapHelp) ;
```

Remember that bitmaps are GDI objects and must be explicitly deleted before your program terminates. You accomplish this after GRAFMENU exits from its message loop:

```
DeleteObject (hBitmapHelp) ;
DeleteObject (hBitmapEdit) ;
DeleteObject (hBitmapFile) ;
DeleteObject (hBitmapFont) ;

for (i = 0 ; i < 3 ; i++)
     DeleteObject (hBitmapPopFont [i]) ;
```

I'll conclude this section with a couple of miscellaneous notes:

- In a top-level menu, Windows adjusts the menu bar height to accommodate the tallest bitmap. Other bitmaps (or character strings) are aligned at the top of the menu bar. The size of the menu bar obtained from:

  GetSystemMetrics (SM_CYMENU)

  is no longer valid after you put bitmaps in a top-level window.

- As you can see from playing with GRAFMENU, you can use check marks with bitmapped menu items in popups, but the check mark is of normal size. If that bothers you, you can create a customized check mark and use *SetMenuItemBitmaps.*

- Another approach to using non-text (or text in a font other than the system font) on a menu is the "owner-draw" item. The Windows Guide to Programming discusses this approach.

Adding a Keyboard Interface

Now we have another problem. When the menu contains text, Windows automatically adds a keyboard interface. You can select a menu item using the Alt key in combination with a letter of the character string. But once you put a bitmap in a menu, you've eliminated that keyboard interface. Even if the bitmap says something, Windows doesn't know about it.

This is where the WM_MENUCHAR message comes in handy. Windows sends a WM_MENUCHAR message to your window procedure when you press Alt with a character key that does not correspond to a menu item. We need to intercept WM_MENUCHAR messages and check the value of *wParam* (the ASCII character of the pressed key). If this corresponds to a menu item, we have to return a long integer back to Windows where the high word is set to 2 and the low word is set to the index of the menu item we want associated with that key. Windows does the rest.

KEYBOARD ACCELERATORS

Described as simply as possible, keyboard accelerators are key combinations that generate WM_COMMAND (or in some cases WM_SYSCOMMAND) messages. Most often, programs use keyboard accelerators to duplicate the action of common menu options. (However, keyboard accelerators can also perform nonmenu functions.) For instance, many Windows programs have an Edit menu that includes a Cut option; these programs conventionally assign the Del key as a keyboard accelerator for this option. The user can choose the Cut option from the menu by pressing an Alt-key combination or can use the keyboard accelerator by simply pressing the Del key. When the window procedure gets a

WM_COMMAND message, it does not have to determine whether the menu or the keyboard accelerator was used.

Why You Should Use Keyboard Accelerators

You may ask: Why should I use keyboard accelerators? Why can't I simply trap WM_KEYDOWN or WM_CHAR messages and duplicate the menu functions myself? What's the advantage? For a single-window application, you can certainly trap keyboard messages, but you get certain advantages from using keyboard accelerators: You don't need to duplicate the menu and keyboard accelerator logic. If the keyboard accelerator duplicates a menu function, Windows flashes the top-level item on the menu when a keyboard accelerator is used, thus providing some visual feedback to the user.

For applications with multiple windows and multiple window procedures, keyboard accelerators become very important. As we've seen, Windows sends keyboard messages to the window procedure for the window that currently has the input focus. For keyboard accelerators, however, Windows sends the WM_COMMAND message to the window procedure whose handle is specified in the Windows function *TranslateAccelerator*. Generally, this will be your main window, the same window that has the menu, which means that the logic for acting upon keyboard accelerators does not have to be duplicated in every window procedure.

This advantage becomes particularly important if you use modeless dialog boxes (discussed in Chapter 10) or child windows on your main window's client area. If a particular keyboard accelerator is defined to move among windows, then only one window procedure has to include this logic. The child windows do not receive WM_COMMAND messages from the keyboard accelerators.

Some Rules on Assigning Accelerators

In theory, you can define a keyboard accelerator for any virtual key or any character key in combination with the Shift key, the Ctrl key, or both. However, the CUA Advanced Interface Design Guide offers several recommendations that are intended to achieve some consistency among applications and to avoid interfering with Windows' use of the keyboard. For programs that have an Edit menu, the CUA Advanced Interface Design Guide highly recommends use of the following accelerators:

Key(s)	Function
Alt+Backspace	Undo
Del	Clear
Ctrl+Ins	Copy
Shift+Ins	Paste
Shift+Del	Cut

You should avoid using Tab, Enter, Esc, and the Spacebar in keyboard accelerators, because these are often used for system functions.

Although some older Windows programs use alphabetic keys in combination with the Ctrl key for keyboard accelerators, more recent Windows programs use function keys, sometimes in combination with the Shift key, the Ctrl key, or both. These function-key assignments are common in some applications:

Key(s)	Function
F1	Help
F3	Save
F6	Next window
Shift+F6	Previous window
Ctrl+F6	Next section
Shift+Ctrl+F6	Previous section

The Accelerator Table

Keyboard accelerator tables are defined in your .RC resource script. The general form is shown here:

```
MyAccelerators ACCELERATORS
    {
    [accelerator definitions]
    }
```

This accelerator table name is *MyAccelerators*. The ACCELERATORS table does not include load and memory options. You can have multiple ACCELERATORS tables in your resource script.

Each keyboard accelerator you define requires a different line in the table. There are four types of accelerator definitions:

```
"char",  wID        [,NOINVERT] [,SHIFT] [,CONTROL]

"^char", wID        [,NOINVERT] [,SHIFT] [,CONTROL]

nCode,   wID, ASCII   [,NOINVERT] [,SHIFT] [,CONTROL]

nCode,   wID, VIRTKEY [,NOINVERT] [,SHIFT] [,CONTROL]
```

In these examples, *"char"* means a single character enclosed in double quotation marks, and *"^char"* is the character ^ and a single character in double quotation marks. The *wID* number performs a function similar to the menu ID in a menu definition. It is the value that Windows sends to your window procedure in the WM_COMMAND message to identify the accelerator. These are usually identifiers defined in a header file. When the keyboard accelerator duplicates a menu command, use the same ID for both the menu and the accelerator. When the keyboard accelerator does not duplicate a menu command, use a unique ID.

Keyboard accelerators almost always select options in popup menus. Windows automatically flashes a top-level menu item when you press an accelerator key that duplicates an option in a popup. (For example, the Edit text flashes if you press the Del key.) If you don't want the menu to flash, include the option NOINVERT.

In the first type of accelerator definition, the keyboard accelerator is a case-sensitive match of the character in double quotes:

```
"char",  wID          [,NOINVERT] [,SHIFT] [,CONTROL]
```

If you want to define a keyboard accelerator for that key in combination with the Shift or Ctrl key or both, simply add SHIFT or CONTROL or both.

In the second type of definition, the keyboard accelerator is the character in combination with the Ctrl key:

```
"^char", wID          [,NOINVERT] [,SHIFT] [,CONTROL]
```

This type is the same as the first type when the CONTROL keyword is used with the character alone.

The third and fourth types use a number (*nCode*) rather than a character in quotes:

```
nCode,   wID, ASCII   [,NOINVERT] [,SHIFT] [,CONTROL]
nCode,   wID, VIRTKEY [,NOINVERT] [,SHIFT] [,CONTROL]
```

This number is interpreted as either case-sensitive ASCII code or a virtual key code, depending on the ASCII or VIRTKEY keyword.

The most common keyboard accelerators are the second and fourth types. You use the second type for character keys in combination with Ctrl. For example, this defines an accelerator for Ctrl-A:

```
"^A", wID
```

Use the fourth type for virtual key codes such as function keys. This defines an accelerator for the Ctrl-F9 combination:

```
VK_F9, wID, VIRTKEY, CONTROL
```

The identifier VK_F9 is defined in WINDOWS.H as the virtual key code for the F9 key, so you have to include the statement:

```
#include <windows.h>
```

near the top of the resource script. The resource compiler defines an identifier named RC_INVOKED that causes much of WINDOWS.H to be ignored.

The first and third types of definition shown above are rarely used. If you want to use them, watch out for case-sensitivity. Windows does a case-sensitive match on the *"char"* or *nCode* based on the character you press. When you add the SHIFT keyword, Windows checks to see if the Shift key is depressed. This situation sometimes causes results you may not anticipate. For instance, if *"char"* is *"A"*, the keyboard accelerator is invoked when you press the A key with the Shift key down or Caps Lock on, but not both. If you use *"A"* with SHIFT, the A key must be pressed with Shift down, but the accelerator can't be invoked at all when Caps Lock is on. Similarly, *"a"* by itself is a keyboard accelerator for the unshifted A key or for the A key with both Shift down and Caps Lock on. But *"a"* with SHIFT invokes the accelerator only when Shift is down and Caps Lock is on.

When you define keyboard accelerators for a menu item, you should include the key combination in the menu item text. The tab (\t) character separates the text from the accelerator so that the accelerators align in a second column. To notate accelerator keys in a menu, the CUA Advanced Interface Design Guide recommends the text Ctrl or Shift followed by a plus sign and the key—for instance:

- F6

- Shift+F6

- Ctrl+F6

Loading the Accelerator Table

Within your program, you use the *LoadAccelerators* function to load the accelerator table into memory and obtain a handle to it. The *LoadAccelerators* statement is very similar to the *LoadIcon*, *LoadCursor*, *LoadBitmap*, and *LoadMenu* statements.

First, define a handle to an accelerator table as type HANDLE:

```
HANDLE hAccel ;
```

Then load the accelerator table:

```
hAccel = LoadAccelerators (hInstance, "MyAccelerators") ;
```

As with icons, cursors, bitmaps, and menus, you can use a number for the accelerator table name and then use that number in the *LoadAccelerators* statement with the MAKE-INTRESOURCE macro or in quotations preceded by a # character.

Translating the Keystrokes

We will now tamper with three lines of code that are common to all the Windows programs that we've created so far in this book. The code is the standard message loop:

```
while (GetMessage (&msg, NULL, 0, 0))
     {
     TranslateMessage (&msg) ;
     DispatchMessage (&msg) ;
     }
```

Here's how we change it to use the keyboard accelerator table:

```
while (GetMessage (&msg, NULL, 0, 0))
     {
     if (!TranslateAccelerator (hwnd, hAccel, &msg))
        {
        TranslateMessage (&msg) ;
        DispatchMessage (&msg) ;
        }
     }
```

The *TranslateAccelerator* function determines if the message stored in the *msg* message structure is a keyboard message. If it is, the function searches for a match in the accelerator table whose handle is *hAccel*. If it finds a match, it calls the window procedure for the window whose handle is *hwnd*. If the keyboard accelerator ID corresponds to a menu item in the system menu, then the message is WM_SYSCOMMAND. Otherwise, the message is WM_COMMAND.

When *TranslateAccelerator* returns, the return value is nonzero if the message has been translated (and already sent to the window procedure) and 0 if not. If *TranslateAccelerator* returns a nonzero value, you should not call *TranslateMessage* and *DispatchMessage* but rather loop back to the *GetMessage* call.

The *hwnd* parameter in *TranslateMessage* looks a little out of place because it's not required in the other three functions in the message loop. Moreover, the message structure itself (the structure variable *msg*) has a member named *hwnd*, which is also a handle to a window.

The fields of the *msg* structure are filled in by the *GetMessage* call. When the second parameter of *GetMessage* is NULL, the function retrieves messages for all windows belonging to the application. When *GetMessage* returns, the *hwnd* member of the *msg* structure is the window handle of the window that will get the message. However, when *TranslateAccelerator* translates a keyboard message into a WM_COMMAND or WM_SYSCOMMAND message, it replaces the *msg.hwnd* window handle with the window handle *hwnd* specified as the first parameter to the function. That is how Windows sends all keyboard accelerator messages to the same window procedure even if another window in the application currently has the input focus. *TranslateAccelerator* does not translate keyboard messages when a modal dialog box or message box has the input focus, because messages for these windows do not come through the program's message loop.

In some cases in which another window in your program (such as a modeless dialog box) has the input focus, you may not want keyboard accelerators to be translated. You'll see how to handle this in Chapter 10.

Receiving the Accelerator Messages

When a keyboard accelerator corresponds to a menu item in the system menu, *TranslateAccelerator* sends the window procedure a WM_SYSCOMMAND message. If you need to, you can differentiate between a direct system menu selection and a keyboard accelerator for that system menu item by the high word of *lParam*:

	wParam	*LOWORD (lParam)*	*HIWORD (lParam)*
Accelerator:	Accelerator ID	0	1
Menu:	Menu ID	0	0

If the accelerator ID corresponds to a menu item (or does not correspond to any item on the menu or system menu), *TranslateAccelerator* sends the window procedure a WM_COMMAND message. The following table shows the types of WM_COMMAND messages you can receive for keyboard accelerators, menu commands, and child window controls:

	wParam	*LOWORD (lParam)*	*HIWORD (lParam)*
Accelerator:	Accelerator ID	0	1
Menu:	Menu ID	0	0
Control:	Control ID	Child window handle	Notification code

If the keyboard accelerator corresponds to a menu item, the window procedure also receives WM_INITMENU, WM_INITMENUPOPUP, and WM_MENUSELECT messages, just as if the menu option had been chosen. Programs usually enable and disable items in a popup menu when processing WM_INITMENUPOPUP, so you still have that facility when using keyboard accelerators. If the keyboard accelerator corresponds to a disabled or grayed menu item, however, *TranslateAccelerator* does not send the window procedure a WM_COMMAND or WM_SYSCOMMAND message.

If the active window is minimized, *TranslateAccelerator* sends the window procedure WM_SYSCOMMAND messages—but not WM_COMMAND messages—for keyboard accelerators that correspond to enabled system menu items. *TranslateAccelerator* also sends that window procedure WM_COMMAND messages for accelerators that do not correspond to any menu items.

POPPAD with a Menu and Accelerators

In Chapter 6 we created a program called POPPAD1 that uses a child window edit control to mimic some of the workings of Windows' Note Pad program. In this chapter we'll add a File and Edit menu and call it POPPAD2. The Edit items will all be functional; we'll finish the File functions in Chapter 10 and the Print function in Chapter 15. POPPAD2 is shown in Figure 9-12 beginning on the following page.

POPPAD2.MAK

```
#----------------------
# POPPAD2.MAK make file
#----------------------

poppad2.exe : poppad2.obj poppad2.def poppad2.res
     link poppad2, /align:16, NUL, /nod slibcew libw, poppad2.def
     rc poppad2.res

poppad2.obj : poppad2.c poppad2.h
     cl -c -Gsw -Ow -W2 -Zp poppad2.c

poppad2.res : poppad2.rc poppad2.h poppad2.ico
     rc -r poppad2.rc
```

POPPAD2.C

```
/*------------------------------------------------------
   POPPAD2.C -- Popup Editor Version 2 (includes menu)
                (c) Charles Petzold, 1990
   ------------------------------------------------------*/

#include <windows.h>
#include "poppad2.h"
long FAR PASCAL WndProc (HWND, WORD, WORD, LONG) ;

char szAppName [] = "PopPad2" ;

int PASCAL WinMain (HANDLE hInstance, HANDLE hPrevInstance,
                    LPSTR lpszCmdLine, int nCmdShow)
     {
     HANDLE   hAccel ;
     HWND     hwnd ;
     MSG      msg ;
     WNDCLASS wndclass ;

     if (!hPrevInstance)
          {
          wndclass.style        = CS_HREDRAW ; CS_VREDRAW ;
          wndclass.lpfnWndProc  = WndProc ;
          wndclass.cbClsExtra   = 0 ;
          wndclass.cbWndExtra   = 0 ;
```

Figure 9-12. *The POPPAD2 program.*   *(continued)*

```
        wndclass.hInstance      = hInstance ;
        wndclass.hIcon          = LoadIcon (hInstance, szAppName) ;
        wndclass.hCursor        = LoadCursor (NULL, IDC_ARROW) ;
        wndclass.hbrBackground  = GetStockObject (WHITE_BRUSH) ;
        wndclass.lpszMenuName   = szAppName ;
        wndclass.lpszClassName  = szAppName ;

        RegisterClass (&wndclass) ;
        }

   hwnd = CreateWindow (szAppName, szAppName,
                    WS_OVERLAPPEDWINDOW,
                    GetSystemMetrics (SM_CXSCREEN) / 4,
                    GetSystemMetrics (SM_CYSCREEN) / 4,
                    GetSystemMetrics (SM_CXSCREEN) / 2,
                    GetSystemMetrics (SM_CYSCREEN) / 2,
                    NULL, NULL, hInstance, NULL) ;

   ShowWindow (hwnd, nCmdShow) ;
   UpdateWindow (hwnd) ;

   hAccel = LoadAccelerators (hInstance, szAppName) ;

   while (GetMessage (&msg, NULL, 0, 0))
        {
        if (!TranslateAccelerator (hwnd, hAccel, &msg))
            {
            TranslateMessage (&msg) ;
            DispatchMessage (&msg) ;
            }
        }

   return msg.wParam ;
   }

AskConfirmation (HWND hwnd)
   {
   return MessageBox (hwnd, "Really want to close PopPad2?",
                    szAppName, MB_YESNO | MB_ICONQUESTION) ;
   }

long FAR PASCAL WndProc (HWND hwnd, WORD message, WORD wParam, LONG lParam)
   {
   static HWND  hwndEdit ;
   LONG         lSelect ;
   WORD         wEnable ;
```

(continued)

```
switch (message)
    {
    case WM_CREATE :
        hwndEdit = CreateWindow ("edit", NULL,
                    WS_CHILD : WS_VISIBLE : WS_HSCROLL : WS_VSCROLL :
                        WS_BORDER : ES_LEFT : ES_MULTILINE :
                        ES_AUTOHSCROLL : ES_AUTOVSCROLL,
                    0, 0, 0, 0,
                    hwnd, 1, ((LPCREATESTRUCT) lParam)->hInstance, NULL) ;
        return 0 ;

    case WM_SETFOCUS :
        SetFocus (hwndEdit) ;
        return 0 ;

    case WM_SIZE :
        MoveWindow (hwndEdit, 0, 0, LOWORD (lParam),
                                        HIWORD (lParam), TRUE) ;
        return 0 ;

    case WM_INITMENUPOPUP :
        if (lParam == 1)
            {
            EnableMenuItem (wParam, IDM_UNDO,
                SendMessage (hwndEdit, EM_CANUNDO, 0, 0L) ?
                    MF_ENABLED : MF_GRAYED) ;

            EnableMenuItem (wParam, IDM_PASTE,
                IsClipboardFormatAvailable (CF_TEXT) ?
                    MF_ENABLED : MF_GRAYED) ;

            lSelect = SendMessage (hwndEdit, EM_GETSEL, 0, 0L) ;

            if (HIWORD (lSelect) == LOWORD (lSelect))
                wEnable = MF_GRAYED ;
            else
                wEnable = MF_ENABLED ;

            EnableMenuItem (wParam, IDM_CUT,   wEnable) ;
            EnableMenuItem (wParam, IDM_COPY,  wEnable) ;
            EnableMenuItem (wParam, IDM_CLEAR, wEnable) ;

            return 0 ;
            }
        break ;
```

(continued)

```
case WM_COMMAND :
     if (LOWORD (lParam))
          {
          if (wParam == 1 && HIWORD (lParam) == EN_ERRSPACE)
               MessageBox (hwnd, "Edit control out of space.",
                          szAppName, MB_OK | MB_ICONSTOP) ;

          return 0 ;
          }

     else switch (wParam)
               {
               case IDM_NEW :
               case IDM_OPEN :
               case IDM_SAVE :
               case IDM_SAVEAS :
               case IDM_PRINT :
                    MessageBeep (0) ;
                    return 0 ;

               case IDM_EXIT :
                    SendMessage (hwnd, WM_CLOSE, 0, 0L) ;
                    return 0 ;

               case IDM_ABOUT :
                    MessageBox (hwnd,
                         "POPPAD2 (c) Charles Petzold, 1990",
                         szAppName, MB_OK | MB_ICONINFORMATION) ;
                    return 0 ;

               case IDM_UNDO :
                    SendMessage (hwndEdit, WM_UNDO, 0, 0L) ;
                    return 0 ;

               case IDM_CUT :
                    SendMessage (hwndEdit, WM_CUT, 0, 0L) ;
                    return 0 ;

               case IDM_COPY :
                    SendMessage (hwndEdit, WM_COPY, 0, 0L) ;
                    return 0 ;

               case IDM_PASTE :
                    SendMessage (hwndEdit, WM_PASTE, 0, 0L) ;
                    return 0 ;

               case IDM_CLEAR :
                    SendMessage (hwndEdit, WM_CLEAR, 0, 0L) ;
                    return 0 ;
```

(continued)

```
                    case IDM_SELALL :
                         SendMessage (hwndEdit, EM_SETSEL, 0,
                                      MAKELONG (0, 32767)) ;

                         return 0 ;
                    }
          break ;

     case WM_CLOSE :
          if (IDYES == AskConfirmation (hwnd))
               DestroyWindow (hwnd) ;
          return 0 ;

     case WM_QUERYENDSESSION :
          if (IDYES == AskConfirmation (hwnd))
               return 1L ;
          else
               return 0 ;

     case WM_DESTROY :
          PostQuitMessage (0) ;
          return 0 ;
     }
return DefWindowProc (hwnd, message, wParam, lParam) ;
}
```

POPPAD2.RC

```
/*------------------------------
   POPPAD2.RC resource script
----------------------------*/

#include <windows.h>
#include "poppad2.h"

PopPad2 ICON poppad2.ico

PopPad2 MENU
    {
    POPUP "&File"
        {
        MENUITEM "&New",          IDM_NEW
        MENUITEM "&Open...",      IDM_OPEN
        MENUITEM "&Save",         IDM_SAVE
        MENUITEM "Save &As...",   IDM_SAVEAS
        MENUITEM SEPARATOR
```

(continued)

```
            MENUITEM "&Print",            IDM_PRINT
            MENUITEM SEPARATOR
            MENUITEM "E&xit",             IDM_EXIT
            MENUITEM "&About PopPad2...", IDM_ABOUT
            }
        POPUP "&Edit"
            {
            MENUITEM "&Undo\tAlt+BkSp",    IDM_UNDO
            MENUITEM SEPARATOR
            MENUITEM "Cu&t\tShift+Del",    IDM_CUT
            MENUITEM "&Copy\tCtrl+Ins",    IDM_COPY
            MENUITEM "&Paste\tShift+Ins",  IDM_PASTE
            MENUITEM "C&lear\tDel",        IDM_CLEAR
            MENUITEM SEPARATOR
            MENUITEM "&Select All",        IDM_SELALL
            }
        }

PopPad2 ACCELERATORS
    {
    VK_DELETE, IDM_CUT,    VIRTKEY, SHIFT
    VK_INSERT, IDM_COPY,   VIRTKEY, CONTROL
    VK_INSERT, IDM_PASTE,  VIRTKEY, SHIFT
    VK_DELETE, IDM_CLEAR,  VIRTKEY
    }
```

POPPAD2.H

```
/*-----------------------
   POPPAD2.H header file
   ---------------------*/

#define IDM_NEW      1
#define IDM_OPEN     2
#define IDM_SAVE     3
#define IDM_SAVEAS   4
#define IDM_PRINT    5

#define IDM_EXIT     6
#define IDM_ABOUT    7

#define IDM_UNDO     8
#define IDM_CUT      9
#define IDM_COPY     10
#define IDM_PASTE    11
#define IDM_CLEAR    12
#define IDM_SELALL   13
```

POPPAD2.ICO

POPPAD2.DEF

```
;------------------------------------------
; POPPAD2.DEF module definition file
;------------------------------------------

NAME            POPPAD2

DESCRIPTION     'Popup Editor Version 2 (c) Charles Petzold, 1990'
EXETYPE         WINDOWS
STUB            'WINSTUB.EXE'
CODE            PRELOAD MOVEABLE DISCARDABLE
DATA            PRELOAD MOVEABLE MULTIPLE
HEAPSIZE        1024
STACKSIZE       8192
EXPORTS         WndProc
```

The POPPAD2.RC resource script file contains the menu and accelerator table. You'll notice that the accelerators are all indicated within the text strings of the Edit popup menu following the tab (\t) character.

Enabling Menu Items

The major job in the window procedure now involves enabling and graying the options in the Edit menu, which is done when processing the WM_INITMENUPOPUP. First, the program checks to see if the Edit popup is about to be displayed. Because the position index of Edit in the menu (starting with File at 0) is 1, *lParam* equals 1 if the Edit popup is about to be displayed.

To determine if the Undo option can be enabled, POPPAD2 sends an EM_CAN-UNDO message to the edit control. The *SendMessage* call returns nonzero if the edit control can perform an Undo action, in which case the option is enabled; otherwise, it is grayed:

```
EnableMenuItem (wParam, IDM_UNDO,
    SendMessage (hwndEdit, EM_CANUNDO, 0, 0L) ?
                    MF_ENABLED : MF_GRAYED) ;
```

The Paste option should be enabled only if the clipboard currently contains text. We can determine this through the *IsClipboardFormatAvailable* call with the CF_TEXT identifier:

```
EnableMenuItem (wParam, IDM_PASTE,
    IsClipboardFormatAvailable (CF_TEXT) ?
                    MF_ENABLED : MF_GRAYED) ;
```

The Cut, Copy, and Clear options should be enabled only if text in the edit control has been selected. Sending the edit control an EM_GETSEL message returns a long integer containing this information:

```
lSelect = SendMessage (hwndEdit, EM_GETSEL, 0, 0L) ;
```

The low word of *lSelect* is the position of the first selected character; the high word of *lSelect* is the position of the character following the selection. If these two words are equal, no text has been selected:

```
if (HIWORD (lSelect) == LOWORD (lSelect))
    wEnable = MF_GRAYED ;
else
    wEnable = MF_ENABLED ;
```

The value of *wEnable* is then used for the Cut, Copy, and Clear options:

```
EnableMenuItem (wParam, IDM_CUT,   wEnable) ;
EnableMenuItem (wParam, IDM_COPY,  wEnable) ;
EnableMenuItem (wParam, IDM_CLEAR, wEnable) ;
```

Processing the Menu Options

Of course, if we were not using a child window edit control for POPPAD2, we would now be faced with the problems involved with actually implementing the Undo, Cut, Copy, Paste, Clear, and Select All options from the Edit menu. But the edit control makes this process easy, because we merely send the edit control a message for each of these options:

```
case IDM_UNDO :
    SendMessage (hwndEdit, WM_UNDO, 0, 0L) ;
    return 0 ;

case IDM_CUT :
    SendMessage (hwndEdit, WM_CUT, 0, 0L) ;
    return 0 ;

case IDM_COPY :
    SendMessage (hwndEdit, WM_COPY, 0, 0L) ;
    return 0 ;
```

```
       case IDM_PASTE :
            SendMessage (hwndEdit, WM_PASTE, 0, 0L) ;
            return 0 ;

       case IDM_CLEAR :
            SendMessage (hwndEdit, WM_CLEAR, 0, 0L) ;
            return 0 ;

       case IDM_SELALL :
            SendMessage (hwndEdit, EM_SETSEL, 0,
                                   MAKELONG (0, 32767)) ;
            return 0 ;
```

Notice that we could have simplified this even further by making the values of IDM_UNDO, IDM_CUT, and so forth equal to the values of the corresponding window messages WM_UNDO, WM_CUT, and so forth.

The About option for the File popup invokes a simple message box:

```
       case IDM_ABOUT :
            MessageBox (hwnd,
                 "POPPAD2 (c) Charles Petzold, 1990",
                 szAppName, MB_OK | MB_ICONINFORMATION) ;
            break ;
```

In Chapter 10 we'll make this a dialog box.

The Exit option sends the window procedure a WM_CLOSE message:

```
       case IDM_EXIT :
            SendMessage (hwnd, WM_CLOSE, 0, 0L) ;
            return 0 ;
```

That is precisely what *DefWindowProc* does when it receives a WM_SYSCOMMAND message with *wParam* equal to SC_CLOSE.

In previous programs we have not processed the WM_CLOSE messages in our window procedure but have simply passed them to *DefWindowProc*. *DefWindowProc* does something very simple with WM_CLOSE: It calls the *DestroyWindow* function. Rather than send WM_CLOSE messages to *DefWindowProc*, however, POPPAD2 processes them. This fact is not so important now, but it will become very important in Chapter 10 when POPPAD can actually edit files:

```
       case WM_CLOSE :
            if (IDYES == AskConfirmation (hwnd))
                 DestroyWindow (hwnd) ;
            return 0 ;
```

AskConfirmation is a function in POPPAD2 that displays a message box asking for confirmation to close the program:

```
AskConfirmation (HWND hwnd)
    {
    return MessageBox (hwnd, "Really want to close POPPAD2?",
                       szAppName, MB_YESNO | MB_ICONQUESTION) ;
    }
```

The message box (as well as the *AskConfirmation* function) returns IDYES if the Yes button is selected. Only then does POPPAD2 call *DestroyWindow*. Otherwise, the program is not terminated.

If you want confirmation before terminating a program, you must also process WM-_QUERYENDSESSION messages. Windows begins sending every window procedure a WM_QUERYENDSESSION message when the user chooses Close from the MS-DOS Executive system menu. If any window procedure returns 0 from this message, the Windows session is not terminated. Here's how we handle WM_QUERYENDSESSION:

```
case WM_QUERYENDSESSION :
    if (IDYES == AskConfirmation (hwnd))
         return 1L ;
    else
         return 0 ;
```

The WM_CLOSE and WM_QUERYENDSESSION messages are the only two messages you have to process if you want to ask for user confirmation before ending a program. That's why we made the Exit menu option in POPPAD2 send the window procedure a WM_CLOSE message—by doing so, we avoided having to ask for confirmation at yet a third point.

If you process WM_QUERYENDSESSION messages, you may also be interested in the WM_ENDSESSION message. Windows sends this message to every window procedure that has previously received a WM_QUERYENDSESSION message. The *wParam* parameter is 0 if the session fails to terminate because another program has returned 0 from WM_QUERYENDSESSION. The WM_ENDSESSION message essentially answers the question: I told Windows it was OK to terminate me, but did I really get terminated?

Although I've included the normal New, Open, Save, and Save As options in POP-PAD2's File menu, they are currently nonfunctional. To process these commands, we need to use dialog boxes. You're now ready to learn about them.

Chapter 10

Dialog Boxes

Dialog boxes are most often used for obtaining additional input from the user beyond what can be easily managed through a menu. The programmer indicates that a menu item invokes a dialog box by adding an ellipsis (...) to the menu item.

A dialog box generally takes the form of a popup window containing various child window controls. The size and placement of these controls are specified in a "dialog box template" in the program's resource script file. Windows is responsible for creating the dialog box popup window and the child window controls and for providing a window procedure to process dialog box messages (including all keyboard and mouse input). The code within Windows that does all this is sometimes referred to as the "dialog box manager."

Many of the messages that are processed by the dialog box window procedure within Windows are also passed to a function within your own program, called a "dialog box procedure" or "dialog procedure." This function is similar to a normal window procedure, but with some important differences. Generally, you will not be doing very much within the dialog procedure except initializing the child window controls when the dialog box is created, processing messages from the child window controls, and ending the dialog box.

The subject of dialog boxes would normally be a big one, because it involves the use of child window controls. However, we have already explored child window controls in Chapter 6. When you use child window controls in dialog boxes, the Windows dialog box manager picks up many of the responsibilities that we assumed in Chapter 6. In particular, the problems we encountered with passing the input focus between the scroll bars in the COLORS1 program do not occur with dialog boxes. Windows handles all the logic necessary to shift input focus between controls in a dialog box.

However, adding a dialog box to a program is not a trivial undertaking. It involves changes to several files—the dialog box template goes in the resource script file, the dialog box procedure goes in the source code file, the name of the dialog box procedure goes in the module definition file, and identifiers used in the dialog box often go in the program's header file. We'll begin with a simple dialog box so that you get a feel for the interconnections between these various pieces.

MODAL DIALOG BOXES

Dialog boxes are either "modal" or "modeless." The modal dialog box is the most common. When your program displays a modal dialog box, the user cannot switch between the dialog box and another window in your program. The user must explicitly end the dialog box, usually by clicking a push button marked either OK or Cancel. The user can, however, generally switch to another program while the dialog box is still displayed. Some dialog boxes (called "system modal") do not allow even this. System modal dialog boxes must be ended before the user does anything else in Windows.

Creating an "About" Dialog Box

Even if a Windows program requires no user input, it will often have a dialog box that is invoked by an About option on the menu. This dialog box displays the name and icon of the program, a copyright notice, a push button labeled OK, and perhaps other information. The first program we'll look at does nothing except display an About dialog box. The ABOUT1 program is shown in Figure 10-1.

ABOUT1.MAK

```
#---------------------
# ABOUT1.MAK make file
#---------------------

about1.exe : about1.obj about1.def about1.res
     link about1, /align:16, NUL, /nod slibcew libw, about1
     rc about1.res

about1.obj : about1.c about1.h
     cl -c -Gsw -Ow -W2 -Zp about1.c

about1.res : about1.rc about1.h about1.ico
     rc -r about1.rc
```

Figure 10-1. *The ABOUT1 program.*

ABOUT1.C

```
/*-------------------------------------------
   ABOUT1.C -- About Box Demo Program No. 1
              (c) Charles Petzold, 1990
   -------------------------------------------*/

#include <windows.h>
#include "about1.h"

long FAR PASCAL WndProc (HWND, WORD, WORD, LONG) ;

int PASCAL WinMain (HANDLE hInstance, HANDLE hPrevInstance,
                    LPSTR lpszCmdLine, int nCmdShow)
     {
     static char szAppName [] = "About1" ;
     MSG         msg ;
     HWND        hwnd ;
     WNDCLASS    wndclass ;

     if (!hPrevInstance)
          {
          wndclass.style         = CS_HREDRAW | CS_VREDRAW ;
          wndclass.lpfnWndProc   = WndProc ;
          wndclass.cbClsExtra    = 0 ;
          wndclass.cbWndExtra    = 0 ;
          wndclass.hInstance     = hInstance ;
          wndclass.hIcon         = LoadIcon (hInstance, szAppName) ;
          wndclass.hCursor       = LoadCursor (NULL, IDC_ARROW) ;
          wndclass.hbrBackground = GetStockObject (WHITE_BRUSH) ;
          wndclass.lpszMenuName  = szAppName ;
          wndclass.lpszClassName = szAppName ;

          RegisterClass (&wndclass) ;
          }

     hwnd = CreateWindow (szAppName, "About Box Demo Program",
                         WS_OVERLAPPEDWINDOW,
                         CW_USEDEFAULT, CW_USEDEFAULT,
                         CW_USEDEFAULT, CW_USEDEFAULT,
                         NULL, NULL, hInstance, NULL) ;

     ShowWindow (hwnd, nCmdShow) ;
     UpdateWindow (hwnd) ;

     while (GetMessage (&msg, NULL, 0, 0))
          {
          TranslateMessage (&msg) ;
```

(continued)

```
            DispatchMessage (&msg) ;
            }
      return msg.wParam ;
      }

BOOL FAR PASCAL AboutDlgProc (HWND hDlg, WORD message, WORD wParam, LONG lParam)
      {
      switch (message)
            {
            case WM_INITDIALOG :
                  return TRUE ;

            case WM_COMMAND :
                  switch (wParam)
                        {
                        case IDOK :
                        case IDCANCEL :
                              EndDialog (hDlg, 0) ;
                              return TRUE ;
                        }
                  break ;
            }
      return FALSE ;
      }

long FAR PASCAL WndProc (HWND hwnd, WORD message, WORD wParam, LONG lParam)
      {
      static FARPROC lpfnAboutDlgProc ;
      static HANDLE  hInstance ;

      switch (message)
            {
            case WM_CREATE :
                  hInstance = ((LPCREATESTRUCT) lParam)->hInstance ;

                  lpfnAboutDlgProc = MakeProcInstance (AboutDlgProc, hInstance) ;
                  return 0 ;

            case WM_COMMAND :
                  switch (wParam)
                        {
                        case IDM_ABOUT :
                              DialogBox (hInstance, "AboutBox", hwnd,
                                          lpfnAboutDlgProc) ;
                              return 0 ;
                        }
                  break ;
```

(continued)

```
        case WM_DESTROY :
             PostQuitMessage (0) ;
             return 0 ;
        }
    return DefWindowProc (hwnd, message, wParam, lParam) ;
    }
```

ABOUT1.RC

```
/*---------------------------
   ABOUT1.RC resource script
---------------------------*/

#include <windows.h>
#include "about1.h"

About1 ICON about1.ico

About1 MENU
    {
    POPUP "&Help"
        {
        MENUITEM "&About About1...",      IDM_ABOUT
        }
    }

AboutBox DIALOG  20, 20, 160, 80
    STYLE WS_POPUP : WS_DLGFRAME
    {
    CTEXT "About1"                    -1,  0, 12, 160,  8
    ICON  "About1"                    -1,  8,  8,  0,  0
    CTEXT "About Box Demo Program"    -1,  0, 36, 160,  8
    CTEXT "(c) Charles Petzold, 1990" -1,  0, 48, 160,  8
    DEFPUSHBUTTON "OK"               IDOK, 64, 60, 32, 14, WS_GROUP
    }
```

ABOUT1.H

```
/*---------------------
   ABOUT1.H header file
---------------------*/

#define IDM_ABOUT      1
```

ABOUT1.ICO

ABOUT1.DEF

```
;-----------------------------------
; ABOUT1.DEF module definition file
;-----------------------------------

NAME          ABOUT1

DESCRIPTION   'About Box Demo No. 1 (c) Charles Petzold, 1990'
EXETYPE       WINDOWS
STUB          'WINSTUB.EXE'
CODE          PRELOAD MOVEABLE DISCARDABLE
DATA          PRELOAD MOVEABLE MULTIPLE
HEAPSIZE      1024
STACKSIZE     8192
EXPORTS       WndProc
              AboutDlgProc
```

The Dialog Box Template

The first job involved in adding a dialog box to a program is designing the dialog box template. This template can go directly in the resource script file, or it can be in a separate file that by convention uses the extension .DLG (for "dialog"). If you put the template in a separate file, you include the line:

```
rcinclude filename.dlg
```

in the resource script file.

You can create the dialog box template by hand in a text editor, or you can use the DIALOG program included with the Windows Software Development Kit. Because the output from DIALOG is virtually unreadable, I'll be showing dialog box templates that look as if they were created by hand. A discussion of DIALOG concludes this chapter.

The dialog box template for ABOUT1 looks like this:

```
AboutBox DIALOG  20, 20, 160, 80
        STYLE WS_POPUP : WS_DLGFRAME
        {
        CTEXT "About1"                  -1,   0, 12, 160,  8
        ICON  "About1"                  -1,   8,  8,   0,  0
        CTEXT "About Box Demo Program"  -1,   0, 36, 160,  8
        CTEXT "(c) Charles Petzold, 1990" -1,  0, 48, 160,  8
        DEFPUSHBUTTON "OK"              IDOK, 64, 60,  32, 14, WS_GROUP
        }
```

The first line gives the dialog box a name (in this case, *AboutBox*). As is the case for other resources, you can use a number instead. The name is followed by the keyword DIALOG and four numbers. The first two numbers are the *x*- and *y*-coordinates of the upper left corner of the dialog box, relative to the client area of its parent when the dialog box is invoked by the program. The second two numbers are the width and height of the dialog box.

These coordinates and sizes are not in units of pixels. They are instead based on a special coordinate system used only for dialog box templates. The numbers are based on the size of a system font character: *x*-coordinates and width are expressed in units of ¼ of an average character width; *y*-coordinates and height are expressed in units of ⅛ of a character height. Thus for this particular dialog box, the upper left corner of the dialog box is 5 characters from the left of the main window's client area and 2½ characters from the top. It is 40 characters wide and 10 characters high.

This coordinate system allows you to use coordinates and sizes that will retain the general dimensions and look of the dialog box regardless of the resolution of the video display. Because system font characters are often approximately twice as high as they are wide, the units on both the *x*- and *y*-axes are about the same.

The DIALOG statement can also include load options (PRELOAD and LOADON-CALL) and memory options (FIXED, MOVEABLE, and DISCARDABLE) immediately following the word DIALOG. The defaults are LOADONCALL and MOVEABLE. The STYLE statement in the template is similar to the style field of a *CreateWindow* call. Using WS_POPUP and WS_DLGFRAME is normal for modal dialog boxes, but we'll explore some alternatives later on.

Within the left and right brackets, you define the child window controls that will appear in the dialog box. This dialog box uses three types of child window controls: CTEXT (centered text), ICON (an icon), and DEFPUSHBUTTON (a default push button). The format of these statements is:

```
control-type "text" nID, xPos, yPos, xWidth, yHeight, dwStyle
```

The *dwStyle* value at the end is optional; it specifies additional window styles using identifiers defined in WINDOWS.H.

These CTEXT, ICON, and DEFPUSHBUTTON identifiers are used only in dialog boxes. They are shorthand for a particular window class and window style. For example, CTEXT indicates that the class of the child window control is "static" and that the style is:

```
WS_CHILD ! SS_CENTER ! WS_VISIBLE ! WS_GROUP
```

Although this is the first time we've encountered the WS_GROUP identifier, we used the WS_CHILD, SS_CENTER, and WS_VISIBLE window styles when creating static child window text controls in the COLORS1 program in Chapter 6.

For the icon, the text field is the name of the program's icon resource, which is also defined in the ABOUT1 resource script. For the push button, the text field is the text that appears inside the push button. This text is equivalent to the text specified as the second parameter to a *CreateWindow* call when you create a child window control in a program.

The *nID* field is a value that the child window uses to identify itself when sending messages (usually WM_COMMMAND messages) to its parent. The parent window of these child window controls is the dialog box window itself, which sends these messages to a window procedure in Windows. However, this window procedure also sends these messages to the dialog box procedure that you'll include in your program. The *nID* values are equivalent to the child window IDs used in the *CreateWindow* function when we created child windows in Chapter 6. Because the text and icon controls do not send messages back to the parent window, these values are set to −1. The *nID* value for the push button is IDOK, which is defined in WINDOWS.H as 1.

The next four numbers set the position of the child window control (relative to the upper left corner of the dialog box's client area) and the size. The position and size are expressed in units of ¼ the average width and ⅛ the height of a system font character. The width and height values are ignored for the ICON statement.

The DEFPUSHBUTTON statement in the dialog box template includes the window style WS_GROUP in addition to the window style implied by the DEFPUSHBUTTON keyword. I'll have more to say about WS_GROUP (and the related WS_TABSTOP style) when discussing the second version of this program, ABOUT2, a bit later.

The Dialog Box Procedure

The dialog box procedure within your program handles messages to the dialog box. Although it looks very much like a window procedure, it is not a true window procedure. The window procedure for the dialog box is within Windows. That window procedure calls your dialog box procedure with many of the messages that it receives. Here's the dialog box procedure for ABOUT1:

```
BOOL FAR PASCAL AboutDlgProc (HWND hDlg, WORD message,
                                WORD wParam, LONG lParam)
    {
    switch (message)
        {
        case WM_INITDIALOG :
            return TRUE ;

        case WM_COMMAND :
            switch (wParam)
                {
                case IDOK :
                case IDCANCEL :
                    EndDialog (hDlg, 0) ;
                    return TRUE ;
                }
            break ;
        }
    return FALSE ;
    }
```

The parameters to this function are the same as those for a normal window procedure. (Although I've used *hDlg* for the handle to the dialog box window, you can use *hwnd* instead if you like.) Let's note first the differences between this function and a window procedure:

- A window procedure returns a long; a dialog box procedure returns a BOOL (which is defined in WINDOWS.H as an *int*).

- A window procedure calls *DefWindowProc* if it does not process a particular message; a dialog box procedure returns TRUE (nonzero) if it processes a message and FALSE (0) if it does not.

- A dialog box procedure does not need to process WM_PAINT or WM_DESTROY messages. A dialog box procedure will not receive a WM_CREATE message; instead, the dialog box procedure performs initialization during the special WM_INITDIALOG message.

The WM_INITDIALOG message is the first message the dialog box procedure receives. This message is sent only to dialog box procedures. If the dialog box procedure returns TRUE, then Windows sets the input focus to the first child window control in the dialog box that has a WS_TABSTOP style (which I'll explain in the discussion of ABOUT2). In this dialog box, the first child window control that has a WS_TABSTOP style is the push button. Alternatively, during processing of WM_INITDIALOG the dialog box procedure can use *SetFocus* to set the focus to one of the child window controls in the dialog box and then return FALSE.

The only other message this dialog box processes is WM_COMMAND. This is the message the push-button control sends to its parent window either when the button is clicked with the mouse or when the Spacebar is pressed while the button has the input focus. The ID of the control (which we set to IDOK in the dialog box template) is in *wParam*. For this message, the dialog box procedure calls *EndDialog*, which tells Windows to destroy the dialog box. For all other messages, the dialog box procedure returns FALSE to tell the dialog box window procedure within Windows that our dialog box procedure did not process the message.

The messages for a modal dialog box don't go through your program's message queue, so you needn't worry about the effect of keyboard accelerators within the dialog box.

Exporting the Dialog Box Procedure

Because this dialog box procedure is called from outside the program, it must be included in the EXPORTS section of the module definition file:

```
EXPORTS   WndProc
          AboutDlgProc
```

This is the easiest part of the job but also the easiest to forget. I forget to export the dialog box procedure about one time in four. Often the function will seem to work (more or less), but because it's not using the program's data segment, it could be altering data inside Windows' data segment. Our simple dialog box procedure doesn't reference anything in ABOUT1's data segment, so strictly speaking, exporting the function is not required. But get into the habit of exporting the function; I hope you achieve a better track record than mine.

Invoking the Dialog Box

During processing of WM_CREATE, the program's instance handle is obtained (and stored in a static variable) and *MakeProcInstance* is called to create an instance thunk for the dialog procedure. The pointer to the instance thunk is also stored in a static variable:

```
hInstance = ((LPCREATESTRUCT) lParam)->hInstance ;
lpfnAboutDlgProc = MakeProcInstance (AboutDlgProc, hInstance) ;
```

The *MakeProcInstance* function assures that *AboutDlgProc* obtains the correct data segment address for this instance of ABOUT1.

The program checks for WM_COMMAND messages where *wParam* is equal to IDM_ABOUT. When it gets one, the program calls *DialogBox*:

```
DialogBox (hInstance, "AboutBox", hwnd, lpfnAboutDlgProc) ;
```

This function requires the instance handle (saved during WM_CREATE), the name of the dialog box (as defined in the resource script), the parent of the dialog box (which is the program's main window), and the address of the instance thunk return from *MakeProcInstance*. If you use a number rather than a name for the dialog box template, you can convert it to a string using the MAKEINTRESOURCE macro.

Selecting "About About1..." from the menu displays the dialog box, as shown in Figure 10-2. You can end this dialog box by clicking the OK button with the mouse, by pressing the Spacebar, or by pressing Enter. For any dialog box that contains a default push button, Windows sends a WM_COMMAND message to the dialog box, with *wParam* equal to the ID of the default push button when Enter or the Spacebar is pressed.

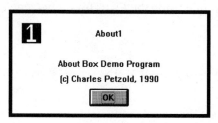

Figure 10-2. *The ABOUT1 program's dialog box.*

The *DialogBox* function you call to display the dialog box will not return control to *WndProc* until the dialog box is ended. The value returned from *DialogBox* is the second parameter to the *EndDialog* function called within the dialog box procedure. (This value is not used in ABOUT1 but is used in ABOUT2.) *WndProc* can then return control to Windows.

Even when the dialog box is displayed, *WndProc* can continue to receive messages. In fact, you can send messages to *WndProc* from within the dialog box procedure. ABOUT1's main window is the parent of the dialog box popup window, so the *Send-Message* call in *AboutDlgProc* would start off like this:

```
SendMessage (GetParent (hDlg), . . . ) ;
```

If you have a lot of dialog boxes within your program, you may not want to create and save instance thunks for all of them. You can instead create instance thunks as needed and free them after *DialogBox* returns:

```
lpfnDlgProc = MakeProcInstance (AboutDlgProc, hInstance) ;
DialogBox (hInstance, "AboutBox", hwnd, lpfnDlgProc) ;
FreeProcInstance (lpfnDlgProc) ;
```

More on the Dialog Box Style

The window style of the dialog box is specified in the STYLE line of the dialog box template. For ABOUT1, we used a style that is most common for modal dialog boxes:

```
STYLE WS_POPUP ¦ WS_DLGFRAME
```

However, you can also experiment with other styles. For example, you can try:

```
STYLE WS_POPUP ¦ WS_CAPTION
```

This creates a dialog box with a caption bar and a normal window border. The caption bar allows the user to move the dialog box around the display by using the mouse. When you use WS_CAPTION, the *x*- and *y*-coordinates specified in the DIALOG statement are the coordinates of the dialog box's client area, relative to the upper left corner of the parent window's client area. The caption bar will be shown above the *y*-coordinate.

If you have a caption bar, you can put text in it using the CAPTION statement in the dialog box template:

```
CAPTION "Dialog Box Caption"
```

following the STYLE statement. Or while processing the WM_INITDIALOG message in the dialog procedure, you can use:

```
SetWindowText (hDlg, "Dialog Box Caption") ;
```

If you use the WS_CAPTION style, you can also add a system menu box with the WS_SYSMENU style:

```
STYLE WS_POPUP ¦ WS_CAPTION ¦ WS_SYSMENU
```

This style allows the user to select Move or Close from the system menu.

Adding WS_THICKFRAME to the style allows the user to resize the dialog box, although resizing is unusual for a dialog box. If you don't mind being a little unusual, you can also try adding WS_MAXIMIZEBOX to the STYLE statement.

The STYLE statement is not required. If you do not include a STYLE or CAPTION statement in the template, the default style is:

```
WS_POPUP ¦ WS_BORDER
```

But this is rather dull looking. WS_DLGFRAME produces much more attractive results. If you include a CAPTION statement with a STYLE statement, the default style is:

```
WS_POPUP ¦ WS_CAPTION ¦ WS_SYSMENU
```

You can also add a menu to a dialog box by specifying:

```
MENU menu-name
```

in the dialog box template. The argument is either the name or number of a menu in the resource script. Menus are highly uncommon for modal dialog boxes. If you use one, be sure that all the ID numbers in the menu and the dialog box controls are unique.

Although the dialog box window procedure is normally within Windows, you can use one of your own window procedures to process dialog box messages. To do so, you specify a window class name in the dialog box template:

```
CLASS "class-name"
```

This approach is rare, but we'll use it in the HEXCALC program shown later in this chapter.

When you call *DialogBox* specifying the name of a dialog box template, Windows has almost everything it needs to create a popup window by calling the normal *CreateWindow* function. Windows obtains the coordinates and size of the window, the window style, the caption, and the menu from the dialog box template. Windows gets the instance handle and the parent window handle from the parameters to *DialogBox*. The only other piece of information it needs is a window class (assuming the dialog box template does not specify one). Windows registers a special window class for dialog boxes. The window procedure for this window class has access to the pointer to your dialog box procedure (which you provide in the *DialogBox* call), so it can keep your program informed of messages that this popup window receives. Of course, you can create and maintain your own dialog box by creating the popup window yourself. Using *DialogBox* is simply an easier approach.

More on Defining Controls

In the dialog box template in ABOUT1.RC, we used the shorthand notation CTEXT, ICON, and DEFPUSHBUTTON to define the 3 types of child window controls we wanted in the dialog box. There are 10 others you can use. Each type implies a particular predefined window class and a window style. The following table shows the equivalent window class and window style for each of the 13 control types:

Control Type	*Window Class*	*Window Style*
PUSHBUTTON	button	BS_PUSHBUTTON ¦ WS_TABSTOP
DEFPUSHBUTTON	button	BS_DEFPUSHBUTTON ¦ WS_TABSTOP
CHECKBOX	button	BS_CHECKBOX ¦ WS_TABSTOP
RADIOBUTTON	button	BS_RADIOBUTTON ¦ WS_TABSTOP
GROUPBOX	button	BS_GROUPBOX ¦ WS_TABSTOP
LTEXT	static	SS_LEFT ¦ WS_GROUP
CTEXT	static	SS_CENTER ¦ WS_GROUP
RTEXT	static	SS_RIGHT ¦ WS_GROUP
ICON	static	SS_ICON
EDITTEXT	edit	ES_LEFT ¦ WS_BORDER ¦ WS_TABSTOP
SCROLLBAR	scrollbar	SBS_HORZ
LISTBOX	listbox	LBS_NOTIFY ¦ WS_BORDER ¦ WS_VSCROLL
COMBOBOX	combobox	CBS_SIMPLE ¦ WS_TABSTOP

The RC resource compiler is the only program that understands this shorthand notation. In addition to the window styles shown above, each of these controls has the style:

```
WS_CHILD : WS_VISIBLE
```

For all these control types except EDITTEXT, SCROLLBAR, LISTBOX, and COMBO-BOX, the format of the control statement is:

```
control-type "text", nID, xPos, yPos, xWidth, yHeight, dwStyle
```

For EDITTEXT, SCROLLBAR, LISTBOX, and COMBOBOX, the format is:

```
control-type nID, xPos, yPos, xWidth, yHeight, dwStyle
```

which excludes the text field. In both statements, the *dwStyle* parameter is optional.

In Chapter 6, I discussed rules for determining the width and height of predefined child window controls. You might want to refer back to that chapter for these rules, keeping in mind that sizes specified in dialog box templates are always in terms of ¼ the average character width and ⅛ the character height.

The "style" field of the control statements is optional. It allows you to include other window style identifiers. For instance, if you wanted to create a check box consisting of text to the left of a square box, you could use:

```
CHECKBOX "text", nID, xPos, yPos, xWidth, yHeight, BS_LEFTTEXT
```

While the shorthand notation for child window controls is convenient, it is also incomplete. You can't create a child window edit control without a border, for example. For this reason, the RC resource compiler also recognizes a generalized control statement that looks like this:

```
CONTROL "text", nID, "class", dwStyle, xPos, yPos, xWidth, yHeight
```

This statement allows you to create any type of child window control by specifying the window class and the complete window style. For example, instead of using:

```
PUSHBUTTON "OK", IDOK, 10, 20, 32, 14
```

you can use:

```
CONTROL "OK", IDOK, "button", WS_CHILD : WS_VISIBLE :
        BS_PUSHBUTTON : WS_TABSTOP, 10, 20, 32, 14
```

When the resource script is compiled, these two statements are encoded identically in the .RES file and the .EXE file.

When you use CONTROL statements in a dialog box template, you don't need to include the WS_CHILD and WS_VISIBLE styles. Windows includes these in the window style when creating the child windows. The format of the CONTROL statement also clarifies what the Windows dialog manager does when it creates a dialog box. First, as I described earlier, it creates a popup window whose parent is the window handle that was provided in the *DialogBox* function. Then for each control in the dialog template, the dialog box manager creates a child window. The parent of each of these controls is the popup dialog box. The CONTROL statement shown above is translated into a *CreateWindow* call that looks like this:

```
CreateWindow ("button", "OK",
    WS_CHILD : WS_VISIBLE : WS_TABSTOP : BS_PUSHBUTTON,
    10 * cxChar / 4, 20 * cyChar / 8,
    32 * cxChar / 4, 14 * cyChar / 8,
    hDlg, nID, hInstance, NULL) ;
```

where *cxChar* and *cyChar* are the width and height of a system font character in pixels. The *hDlg* parameter is returned from the *CreateWindow* call that creates the dialog box window. The *hInstance* parameter is obtained from the original *DialogBox* call.

A More Complex Dialog Box

The simple dialog box in ABOUT1 demonstrates the basics of getting a dialog box up and running; now let's try something a little more complex. The ABOUT2 program, shown in Figure 10-3, demonstrates how to manage controls (in this case, radio buttons) within a dialog box procedure and also how to paint on the client area of the dialog box.

ABOUT2.MAK

```
#----------------------
# ABOUT2.MAK make file
#----------------------

about2.exe : about2.obj about2.def about2.res
    link about2, /align:16, NUL, /nod slibcew libw, about2
    rc about2.res

about2.obj : about2.c about2.h
    cl -c -Gsw -Ow -W2 -Zp about2.c

about2.res : about2.rc about2.h about2.ico
    rc -r about2.rc
```

ABOUT2.C

```
/*----------------------------------------------
    ABOUT2.C -- About Box Demo Program No. 2
            (c) Charles Petzold, 1990
    ----------------------------------------------*/
```

Figure 10-3. *The ABOUT2 program.*   *(continued)*

```
#include <windows.h>
#include "about2.h"

long FAR PASCAL WndProc (HWND, WORD, WORD, LONG) ;

short nCurrentColor  = IDD_BLACK,
      nCurrentFigure = IDD_RECT ;

int PASCAL WinMain (HANDLE hInstance, HANDLE hPrevInstance,
                    LPSTR lpszCmdLine, int nCmdShow)
     {
     static char szAppName [] = "About2" ;
     MSG        msg ;
     HWND       hwnd ;
     WNDCLASS   wndclass ;

     if (!hPrevInstance)
          {
          wndclass.style         = CS_HREDRAW | CS_VREDRAW ;
          wndclass.lpfnWndProc   = WndProc ;
          wndclass.cbClsExtra    = 0 ;
          wndclass.cbWndExtra    = 0 ;
          wndclass.hInstance     = hInstance ;
          wndclass.hIcon         = LoadIcon (hInstance, szAppName) ;
          wndclass.hCursor       = LoadCursor (NULL, IDC_ARROW) ;
          wndclass.hbrBackground = GetStockObject (WHITE_BRUSH) ;
          wndclass.lpszMenuName  = szAppName ;
          wndclass.lpszClassName = szAppName ;

          RegisterClass (&wndclass) ;
          }

     hwnd = CreateWindow (szAppName, "About Box Demo Program",
                          WS_OVERLAPPEDWINDOW,
                          CW_USEDEFAULT, CW_USEDEFAULT,
                          CW_USEDEFAULT, CW_USEDEFAULT,
                          NULL, NULL, hInstance, NULL) ;

     ShowWindow (hwnd, nCmdShow) ;
     UpdateWindow (hwnd) ;

     while (GetMessage (&msg, NULL, 0, 0))
          {
          TranslateMessage (&msg) ;
          DispatchMessage (&msg) ;
          }
     return msg.wParam ;
     }
```

(continued)

```
void PaintWindow (HWND hwnd, short nColor, short nFigure)
     {
     static DWORD dwColor [8] = { RGB (0,     0, 0), RGB ( 0,   0, 255),
                                  RGB (0,   255, 0), RGB ( 0, 255, 255),
                                  RGB (255,   0, 0), RGB (255,   0, 255),
                                  RGB (255, 255, 0), RGB (255, 255, 255) } ;
     HBRUSH       hBrush ;
     HDC          hdc ;
     RECT         rect ;

     hdc = GetDC (hwnd) ;
     GetClientRect (hwnd, &rect) ;
     hBrush = CreateSolidBrush (dwColor [nColor - IDD_BLACK]) ;
     hBrush = SelectObject (hdc, hBrush) ;

     if (nFigure == IDD_RECT)
          Rectangle (hdc, rect.left, rect.top, rect.right, rect.bottom) ;
     else
          Ellipse   (hdc, rect.left, rect.top, rect.right, rect.bottom) ;

     DeleteObject (SelectObject (hdc, hBrush)) ;
     ReleaseDC (hwnd, hdc) ;
     }

void PaintTheBlock (HWND hCtrl, short nColor, short nFigure)
     {
     InvalidateRect (hCtrl, NULL, TRUE) ;
     UpdateWindow (hCtrl) ;
     PaintWindow (hCtrl, nColor, nFigure) ;
     }

BOOL FAR PASCAL AboutDlgProc (HWND hDlg, WORD message, WORD wParam, LONG lParam)
     {
     static HWND   hCtrlBlock ;
     static short  nColor, nFigure ;

     switch (message)
          {
          case WM_INITDIALOG :
               nColor  = nCurrentColor ;
               nFigure = nCurrentFigure ;

               CheckRadioButton (hDlg, IDD_BLACK, IDD_WHITE, nColor) ;
               CheckRadioButton (hDlg, IDD_RECT,  IDD_ELL,   nFigure) ;

               hCtrlBlock = GetDlgItem (hDlg, IDD_PAINT) ;
               SetFocus (GetDlgItem (hDlg, nColor)) ;
               return FALSE ;
```

(continued)

```
          case WM_COMMAND :
              switch (wParam)
                  {
                  case IDOK :
                          nCurrentColor  = nColor ;
                          nCurrentFigure = nFigure ;
                          EndDialog (hDlg, TRUE) ;
                          return TRUE ;

                  case IDCANCEL :
                          EndDialog (hDlg, FALSE) ;
                          return TRUE ;

                  case IDD_BLACK :
                  case IDD_RED :
                  case IDD_GREEN :
                  case IDD_YELLOW :
                  case IDD_BLUE :
                  case IDD_MAGENTA :
                  case IDD_CYAN :
                  case IDD_WHITE :
                          nColor = wParam ;
                          CheckRadioButton (hDlg, IDD_BLACK, IDD_WHITE, wParam) ;
                          PaintTheBlock (hCtrlBlock, nColor, nFigure) ;
                          return TRUE ;

                  case IDD_RECT :
                  case IDD_ELL :
                          nFigure = wParam ;
                          CheckRadioButton (hDlg, IDD_RECT, IDD_ELL, wParam) ;
                          PaintTheBlock (hCtrlBlock, nColor, nFigure) ;
                          return TRUE ;
                  }
              break ;
          case WM_PAINT :
              PaintTheBlock (hCtrlBlock, nColor, nFigure) ;
              break ;
          }
     return FALSE ;
     }

long FAR PASCAL WndProc (HWND hwnd, WORD message, WORD wParam, LONG lParam)
     {
     static FARPROC  lpfnAboutDlgProc ;
     static HANDLE   hInstance ;
     PAINTSTRUCT     ps ;
```

(continued)

```
    switch (message)
        {
        case WM_CREATE :
            hInstance = ((LPCREATESTRUCT) lParam)->hInstance ;

            lpfnAboutDlgProc = MakeProcInstance (AboutDlgProc, hInstance) ;
            return 0 ;

        case WM_COMMAND :
            switch (wParam)
                {
                case IDM_ABOUT :
                    if (DialogBox (hInstance, "AboutBox", hwnd,
                                       lpfnAboutDlgProc))
                        InvalidateRect (hwnd, NULL, TRUE) ;
                    return 0 ;
                }
            break ;

        case WM_PAINT :
            BeginPaint (hwnd, &ps) ;
            EndPaint (hwnd, &ps) ;
            PaintWindow (hwnd, nCurrentColor, nCurrentFigure) ;
            return 0 ;

        case WM_DESTROY :
            PostQuitMessage (0) ;
            return 0 ;
        }
    return DefWindowProc (hwnd, message, wParam, lParam) ;
    }
```

ABOUT2.RC

```
/*---------------------------
   ABOUT2.RC resource script
   ---------------------------*/

#include <windows.h>
#include "about2.h"

about2 ICON about2.ico

About2 MENU
    {
    POPUP "&Help"
```

(continued)

```
          {
          MENUITEM "&About About2...",        IDM_ABOUT
          }
     }

#define TABGRP (WS_TABSTOP | WS_GROUP)

AboutBox DIALOG 20, 20, 140, 188
     STYLE WS_POPUP | WS_DLGFRAME
     {
     CTEXT       "About2"              -1,         0,  12, 140,   8
     ICON        "About2"              -1,         8,   8,   0,   0
     CTEXT       "About Box Demo Program" -1, 4,  36, 130,   8
     CTEXT       ""                    IDD_PAINT,  68,  54,  60,  60
     GROUPBOX    "&Color"              -1,         4,  50,  54, 112
     RADIOBUTTON "&Black"              IDD_BLACK,   8,  60,  40,  12, TABGRP
     RADIOBUTTON "B&lue"               IDD_BLUE,    8,  72,  40,  12
     RADIOBUTTON "&Green"              IDD_GREEN,   8,  84,  40,  12
     RADIOBUTTON "Cya&n"               IDD_CYAN,    8,  96,  40,  12
     RADIOBUTTON "&Red"                IDD_RED,     8, 108,  40,  12
     RADIOBUTTON "&Magenta"            IDD_MAGENTA, 8, 120,  40,  12
     RADIOBUTTON "&Yellow"             IDD_YELLOW,  8, 132,  40,  12
     RADIOBUTTON "&White"              IDD_WHITE,   8, 144,  40,  12
     GROUPBOX     "&Figure"            -1,         68, 120,  60,  40, WS_GROUP
     RADIOBUTTON "Rec&tangle"          IDD_RECT,   72, 134,  50,  12, TABGRP
     RADIOBUTTON "&Ellipse"            IDD_ELL,    72, 146,  50,  12
     DEFPUSHBUTTON "OK"                IDOK,       20, 168,  40,  14, WS_GROUP
     PUSHBUTTON   "Cancel"             IDCANCEL,   80, 168,  40,  14, WS_GROUP
     }
```

ABOUT2.H

```
/*---------------------
   ABOUT2.H header file
---------------------*/

#define IDM_ABOUT     1

#define IDD_BLACK    10
#define IDD_BLUE     11
#define IDD_GREEN    12
#define IDD_CYAN     13
#define IDD_RED      14
#define IDD_MAGENTA  15
#define IDD_YELLOW   16
#define IDD_WHITE    17
```

(continued)

422

```
#define IDD_RECT      20
#define IDD_ELL       21

#define IDD_PAINT     30
```

ABOUT2.ICO

ABOUT2.DEF

```
;-----------------------------------------
; ABOUT2.DEF module definition file
;-----------------------------------------

NAME           ABOUT2

DESCRIPTION    'About Box Demo No. 2 (c) Charles Petzold, 1990'
EXETYPE        WINDOWS
STUB           'WINSTUB.EXE'
CODE           PRELOAD MOVEABLE DISCARDABLE
DATA           PRELOAD MOVEABLE MULTIPLE
HEAPSIZE       1024
STACKSIZE      8192
EXPORTS        WndProc
               AboutDlgProc
```

The About box in ABOUT2 has two groups of radio buttons. One group is used to select a color, and the other group is used to select either a rectangle or an ellipse. The rectangle or ellipse is shown in the dialog box with the interior colored with the current color selection. If you press the OK button, the dialog box is ended, and the program's window procedure draws the selected figure on its own client area. If you press Cancel, the client area of the main window remains the same. The dialog box is shown in Figure 10-4 on the following page. Although the ABOUT2 dialog box uses the predefined identifiers IDOK and IDCANCEL for the two push buttons, each of the radio buttons has its own identifier beginning with the letters IDD ("ID for dialog box control"). These identifiers are defined in ABOUT2.H.

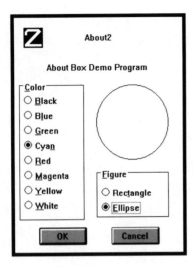

Figure 10-4. *The ABOUT2 program's dialog box.*

Working with Dialog Box Controls

In Chapter 6, you discovered that most child window controls send WM_COMMAND messages to the parent window. (The exception is scroll bar controls.) You also saw that the parent window can alter child window controls (for instance, checking or unchecking radio buttons or check boxes) by sending messages to the controls. You can similarly alter controls in a dialog box procedure. If you have a series of radio buttons, for example, you can check and uncheck the buttons by sending them messages. However, Windows also provides several shortcuts when working with controls in dialog boxes. Let's look at the way in which the dialog box procedure and the child window controls communicate.

The dialog box template for ABOUT2 is shown in the ABOUT2.RC resource script in Figure 10-3. The GROUPBOX control is simply a frame with a title (either Color or Figure) that surrounds each of the two groups of radio buttons. The eight radio buttons in the first group are mutually exclusive, as are the two radio buttons in the second group.

When one of the radio buttons is clicked with the mouse (or when the Spacebar is pressed while the radio button has the input focus), the child window sends its parent a WM_COMMAND message with *wParam* set to the ID of the control. The low word of *lParam* is the window handle of the control, and the high word of *lParam* is a notification code. For a radio button, this notification code is BN_CLICKED, or 0. The dialog box window procedure in Windows then passes this WM_COMMAND message to the dialog box procedure within ABOUT2.C. When the dialog box procedure receives a WM_COMMAND message for one of the radio buttons, it turns on the check mark for that button and turns off the check marks for all the other buttons in the group.

You may recall from Chapter 6 that checking and unchecking a button requires that you send the child window control a BM_CHECK message. To turn on a button check, you use:

```
SendMessage (hwndCtrl, BM_SETCHECK, 1, 0L) ;
```

To turn off the check, you use:

```
SendMessage (hwndCtrl, BM_SETCHECK, 0, 0L) ;
```

The *hwndCtrl* parameter is the window handle of the child window button control.

But this method presents a little problem in the dialog box procedure, because you don't know the window handles of all radio buttons. You know only the one you're getting the message from. Fortunately, Windows provides you with a function to obtain the window handle of a dialog box control using the dialog box window handle and the control ID:

```
hwndCtrl = GetDlgItem (hDlg, nID) ;
```

(You can also obtain the ID value of a control from the window handle by using this function:

```
nID = GetWindowWord (hwndCtrl, GWW_ID) ;
```

but this is rarely necessary.)

You'll notice in the ABOUT2.H header file shown in Figure 10-3 that the ID values for the eight colors are sequential from IDD_BLACK to IDD_WHITE. This arrangement helps in processing the WM_COMMAND messages from the radio buttons. For a first attempt at checking and unchecking the radio buttons, you might try something like the following in the dialog box procedure:

```
static short nColor ;
      [other program lines]
case WM_COMMAND :
     switch (wParam)
          {
          [other program lines]
          case IDD_BLACK :
          case IDD_RED :
          case IDD_GREEN :
          case IDD_YELLOW :
          case IDD_BLUE :
          case IDD_MAGENTA :
          case IDD_CYAN :
          case IDD_WHITE :
               nColor = wParam ;
```

```
                for (n = IDD_BLACK, n <= IDD_WHITE, n++)
                    SendMessage (GetDlgItem (hDlg, n),
                        BM_SETCHECK, n == wParam, OL) ;
                return TRUE ;
```
                [other program lines]

This approach works satisfactorily. You've saved the new color value in *nColor*, and you've also set up a loop that cycles through all the ID values for the eight colors. You obtain the window handle of each of these eight radio button controls and use *SendMessage* to send each handle a BM_SETCHECK message. The *wParam* value of this message is set to 1 only for the button that sent the WM_COMMAND message to the dialog box window procedure.

The first shortcut is the special dialog box procedure *SendDlgItemMessage*:

```
SendDlgItemMessage (hDlg, nCtrlID, message, wParam, lParam) ;
```

It is equivalent to:

```
SendMessage (GetDlgItem (hDlg, nCtrlID), message, wParam, lParam) ;
```

Now the loop would look like this:

```
for (n = IDD_BLACK, n <= IDD_WHITE, n++)
    SendDlgItemMessage (hDlg, n, BM_SETCHECK, n == wParam, OL) ;
```

That's a little better. But the real breakthrough comes when you discover the *CheckRadioButton* function:

```
CheckRadioButton (hDlg, nIDFirst, nIDLast, nIDCheck) ;
```

This function turns off the checks on all radio button controls with IDs from *nIDFirst* to *nIDLast* except for the radio button with an ID of *nIDCheck*, which is checked. The IDs must be sequential. So we can get rid of the loop entirely and use:

```
CheckRadioButton (hDlg, IDD_BLACK, IDD_WHITE, wParam) ;
```

That's how it's done in the dialog box procedure in ABOUT2.

A similar shortcut function is provided for working with check boxes. If you create a CHECKBOX dialog window control, you can turn the check mark on and off using the function:

```
CheckDlgButton (hDlg, nIDCheckbox, wCheck) ;
```

If *wCheck* is set to 1, the button is checked; if it's set to 0, the button is unchecked. You can obtain the status of a check box in a dialog box using:

```
wCheck = IsDlgButtonChecked (hDlg, nIDCheckbox) ;
```

You can either retain the current status of the check mark as a static variable within the dialog box procedure, or you can do something like this to toggle the button on a WM__COMMAND message:

```
CheckDlgButton (hDlg, nIDCheckbox,
    !IsDlgButtonChecked (hDlg, nIDCheckbox)) ;
```

If you define a BS_AUTOCHECKBOX control, then you don't need to process the WM_COMMAND message at all. You can simply obtain the current status of the button using *IsDlgButtonChecked* before terminating the dialog box.

The OK and Cancel Buttons

ABOUT2 has two push buttons, labeled OK and Cancel. In the dialog box template in ABOUT2.RC, the OK button has an ID of IDOK (defined in WINDOWS.H as 1) and the Cancel button an ID of IDCANCEL (defined in WINDOWS.H as 2). The OK button is the default:

```
DEFPUSHBUTTON "OK"      IDOK,     20, 168, 40, 14, WS_GROUP
PUSHBUTTON    "Cancel" IDCANCEL, 80, 168, 40, 14, WS_GROUP
```

This arrangement is normal for OK and Cancel buttons in dialog boxes; having the OK button as the default helps out with the keyboard interface. Here's how: Normally, you would end the dialog box by clicking one of these buttons with the mouse or pressing the Spacebar when the desired button has the input focus. However, the dialog box window procedure also generates a WM_COMMAND message when the user presses Enter, regardless of which control has the input focus. The value of *wParam* is set to the ID value of the default push button in the dialog box unless another push button has the input focus. In that case, *wParam* is set to the ID of the push button with the input focus. If no push button in the dialog box is a default push button, then Windows sends the dialog box procedure a WM_COMMAND message with *wParam* equal to IDOK. If the user presses the Esc key or Ctrl-Break, Windows sends the dialog box procedure a WM_COMMAND message with *wParam* equal to IDCANCEL. So you don't have to add separate keyboard logic to the dialog box procedure, because the keystrokes that normally terminate a dialog box are translated by Windows into WM_COMMAND messages for these two push buttons.

The *AboutDlgProc* function handles these two WM_COMMAND messages by calling *EndDialog*:

```
switch (wParam)
    {
    case IDOK :
        nCurrentColor  = nColor ;
        nCurrentFigure = nFigure ;
        EndDialog (hDlg, TRUE) ;
        return TRUE ;

    case IDCANCEL :
        EndDialog (hDlg, FALSE) ;
        return TRUE ;
```

ABOUT2's window procedure uses the global variables *nCurrentColor* and *nCurrentFigure* when drawing the rectangle or ellipse in the program's client area. *AboutDlgProc* uses the static local variables *nColor* and *nFigure* when drawing the figure within the dialog box.

Notice the different values in the second parameter of *EndDialog*. This is the value that is passed back as the return value from the original *DialogBox* function in *WndProc*:

```
case IDM_ABOUT :
    if (DialogBox (hInstance, "AboutBox", hwnd, lpfnAboutDlgProc))
        InvalidateRect (hwnd, NULL, TRUE) ;
    return 0 ;
```

If *DialogBox* returns TRUE (nonzero), meaning that the OK button was pressed, then the *WndProc* client area needs to be updated with the new figure and color. These were saved in the global variables *nCurrentColor* and *nCurrentFigure* by *AboutDlgProc* when it received a WM_COMMAND message with *wParam* equal to IDOK. If *DialogBox* returns FALSE, the main window continues to use the original settings of *nCurrentColor* and *nCurrentFigure*.

TRUE and FALSE are commonly used in *EndDialog* calls to signal to the main window procedure whether the user ended the dialog box with OK or Cancel. However, the parameter to *EndDialog* is actually an *int*, and *DialogBox* returns an *int*, so it's possible to return more information in this way than simply TRUE or FALSE.

Tab Stops and Groups

In Chapter 6, we used window subclassing to add a facility to COLORS1 that let us move from one scroll bar to another by pressing the Tab key. In a dialog box, window subclassing is unnecessary: Windows does all the logic for moving the input focus from one control to another. However, you have to help out by using the WS_TABSTOP and WS_GROUP window styles in the dialog box template. For all controls that you want to access using the Tab key, specify WS_TABSTOP in the window style. If you refer back to the table on page 415, you'll notice that many of the controls include WS_TABSTOP as a default, while others do not. Generally the controls that do not include WS_TABSTOP style (particularly the static controls) should not get the input focus because they can't do anything with it. Unless you set the input focus to a specific control in a dialog box during processing of the WM_INIT-DIALOG message and return FALSE from the message, Windows sets the input focus to the first control in the dialog box that has the WS_TABSTOP style.

The second keyboard interface that Windows adds to a dialog box involves the cursor movement keys. This interface is of particular importance with radio buttons. After you use the Tab key to move to the currently checked radio button within a group, you need to use the cursor movement keys to change the input focus from that radio button to other radio buttons within the group. You accomplish this by using the WS_GROUP window style. For a particular series of controls in the dialog box template, Windows will use the cursor movement keys to shift the input focus from the first control that has the WS_GROUP style up to (but not including) the next control that has the WS_GROUP style. Windows will cycle from the last control in a dialog box to the first control if necessary to find the end of the group.

By default, the controls LTEXT, CTEXT, RTEXT, and ICON include the WS_GROUP style, which conveniently marks the end of a group. You often have to add WS_GROUP styles to other types of controls.

Let's look at the dialog box template in ABOUT2.RC:

```
AboutBox DIALOG 20, 20, 140, 188
    STYLE WS_POPUP ¦ WS_DLGFRAME
    {
    CTEXT       "About2"        -1,         0,  12, 140,   8
    ICON        "About2"        -1,         8,   8,   0,   0
    CTEXT       "About Box Demo Program" -1, 4,  36, 130,   8
    CTEXT       ""              IDD_PAINT, 68,  54,  60,  60
    GROUPBOX    "&Color"        -1,         4,  50,  54, 112
    RADIOBUTTON "&Black"        IDD_BLACK,  8,  60,  40,  12, TABGRP
    RADIOBUTTON "B&lue"         IDD_BLUE,   8,  72,  40,  12
    RADIOBUTTON "&Green"        IDD_GREEN,  8,  84,  40,  12
    RADIOBUTTON "Cya&n"         IDD_CYAN,   8,  96,  40,  12
    RADIOBUTTON "&Red"          IDD_RED,    8, 108,  40,  12
    RADIOBUTTON "&Magenta"      IDD_MAGENTA, 8, 120, 40,  12
    RADIOBUTTON "&Yellow"       IDD_YELLOW, 8, 132,  40,  12
    RADIOBUTTON "&White"        IDD_WHITE,  8, 144,  40,  12
    GROUPBOX    "&Figure"       -1,        68, 120,  60,  40, WS_GROUP
    RADIOBUTTON "Rec&tangle"    IDD_RECT,  72, 134,  50,  12, TABGRP
    RADIOBUTTON "&Ellipse"      IDD_ELL,   72, 146,  50,  12
    DEFPUSHBUTTON "OK"          IDOK,      20, 168,  40,  14, WS_GROUP
    PUSHBUTTON  "Cancel"        IDCANCEL,  80, 168,  40,  14, WS_GROUP
    }
```

To simplify the appearance of the template, an identifier is defined in ABOUT2.RC that combines WS_TABSTOP and WS_GROUP:

```
#define TABGRP (WS_TABSTOP ¦ WS_GROUP)
```

The four controls that have the WS_TABSTOP style are the first radio buttons of each group (explicitly included) and the two push buttons (by default). When you first invoke the dialog box, these are the four controls you can move among using the Tab key.

Within each group of radio buttons, you use the cursor movement keys to change the input focus and the check mark. For example, the first radio button of the Color group (Black) and the group box labeled Figure have the WS_GROUP style. This means that you can use the cursor movement keys to move the focus from the Black radio button up to (but not including) the Figure group box. Similarly, the first radio button of the Figure group (Rectangle) and DEFPUSHBUTTON have the WS_GROUP style, so you can use the cursor movement keys to move between the two radio buttons in this group: Rectangle and

Ellipse. Both push buttons get a WS_GROUP style to prevent the cursor movement keys from doing anything when the push buttons have the input focus.

You'll notice when using ABOUT2 that the dialog box manager in Windows performs some magic in the two groups of radio buttons. As expected, the cursor movement keys within a group of radio buttons shift the input focus and send a WM_COMMAND message to the dialog box procedure. But when you change the checked radio button within the group, Windows also assigns the newly checked radio button the WS_TABSTOP style. The next time you tab to that group, Windows will set the input focus to the checked radio button.

An ampersand (&) causes the letter that follows to be underlined and adds another keyboard interface. You can move the input focus to any of the radio buttons by pressing the underlined letter. By pressing C (for the Color group box) or F (for the Figure group box), you can move the input focus to the currently checked radio button in that group.

Although programmers normally let the dialog box manager take care of all this, Windows includes two functions that let you search for the next or previous tab stop or group item. These functions are:

```
hwndCtrl = GetNextDlgTabItem (hDlg, hwndCtrl, bPrevious) ;
```

and:

```
hwndCtrl = GetNextDlgGroupItem (hDlg, hwndCtrl, bPrevious) ;
```

If *bPrevious* is TRUE, the functions return the previous tab stop or group item; if FALSE, they return the next tab stop or group item.

Painting on the Dialog Box

ABOUT2 also does something relatively unusual: It paints on the dialog box. Let's see how this works. Within the dialog box template in ABOUT2.RC, a blank text control is defined with a position and size for the area we want to paint:

```
CTEXT   ""  IDD_PAINT, 68, 54, 60, 60
```

This area is 15 characters wide and 7½ characters high. Because this control has no text, all that the window procedure for the "static" class does is erase the background when the child window control has to be repainted.

When the current color or figure selection changes or when the dialog box itself gets a WM_PAINT message, the dialog box procedure calls *PaintTheBlock*, which is a function in ABOUT2.C:

```
PaintTheBlock (hCtrlBlock, nColor, nFigure) ;
```

The window handle *hCtrlBlock* had been set during processing of the WM_INITDIALOG message:

```
hCtrlBlock = GetDlgItem (hDlg, IDD_PAINT) ;
```

Here's the *PaintTheBlock* function:

```
void PaintTheBlock (HWND hCtrl, short nColor, short nFigure)
    {
    InvalidateRect (hCtrl, NULL, TRUE) ;
    UpdateWindow (hCtrl) ;
    PaintWindow (hCtrl, nColor, nFigure) ;
    }
```

This invalidates the child window control, updates it, and then calls another function in ABOUT2 called *PaintWindow*.

The *PaintWindow* function obtains a device context handle for *hCtrl* and draws the selected figure, filling it with a colored brush based on the selected color. The size of the child window control is obtained from *GetClientRect*. Although the dialog box template defines the size of the control in terms of characters, *GetClientRect* obtains the dimensions in pixels. You can also use the function *MapDialogRect* to convert the character coordinates in the dialog box to pixel coordinates in the client area.

We're not really painting the dialog box's client area—we're actually painting the client area of the child window control. Whenever the dialog box gets a WM_PAINT message, the child window control is invalidated and then updated to make it believe that its client area is now valid. We then paint on top of it.

Using Other Functions with Dialog Boxes

Most functions that you can use with child windows you can also use with controls in a dialog box. For instance, if you're feeling devious, you can use *MoveWindow* to move the controls around the dialog box and have the user chase them around with the mouse.

Sometimes you need to dynamically enable or disable certain controls in a dialog box, depending on the settings of other controls. This call:

```
EnableWindow (hwndCtrl, bEnable) ;
```

enables the control where *bEnable* is TRUE (nonzero) and disables it where *bEnable* is FALSE (0). When a control is disabled, it receives no keyboard or mouse input. Don't disable a control that has the input focus.

Defining Your Own Controls

Although Windows assumes much of the responsibility for maintaining the dialog box and child window controls, various methods let you slip some of your own code into this process. We've already seen a method that allows you to paint on the surface of a dialog box. You can also use window subclassing (discussed in Chapter 6) to alter the operation of child window controls.

You can also define your own child window controls and use them in a dialog box. For example, suppose you don't particularly care for the normal rectangular push buttons and would prefer to create elliptical push buttons. You can do this by registering a window class and using your own window procedure to process messages for your customized child window. You then specify this window class in a CONTROL statement in the dialog box template. The ABOUT3 program, shown in Figure 10-5, does exactly that.

ABOUT3.MAK

```
#----------------------
# ABOUT3.MAK make file
#----------------------

about3.exe : about3.obj about3.def about3.res
     link about3, /align:16, NUL, /nod slibcew libw, about3
     rc about3.res

about3.obj : about3.c about3.h
     cl -c -Gsw -Ow -W2 -Zp about3.c

about3.res : about3.rc about3.h about3.ico
     rc -r about3.rc
```

ABOUT3.C

```
/*-----------------------------------------------
   ABOUT3.C -- About Box Demo Program No. 3
              (c) Charles Petzold, 1990
   -----------------------------------------------*/

#include <windows.h>
#include "about3.h"

long FAR PASCAL WndProc (HWND, WORD, WORD, LONG) ;
long FAR PASCAL EllipPushWndProc (HWND, WORD, WORD, LONG) ;

int PASCAL WinMain (HANDLE hInstance, HANDLE hPrevInstance,
                    LPSTR lpszCmdLine, int nCmdShow)
     {
     static char szAppName [] = "About3" ;
     MSG          msg ;
     HWND         hwnd ;
     WNDCLASS     wndclass ;

     if (!hPrevInstance)
          {
          wndclass.style        = CS_HREDRAW : CS_VREDRAW ;
          wndclass.lpfnWndProc  = WndProc ;
          wndclass.cbClsExtra   = 0 ;
```

Figure 10-5. *The ABOUT3 program.*   *(continued)*

432

```
            wndclass.cbWndExtra      = 0 ;
            wndclass.hInstance       = hInstance ;
            wndclass.hIcon           = LoadIcon (hInstance, szAppName) ;
            wndclass.hCursor         = LoadCursor (NULL, IDC_ARROW) ;
            wndclass.hbrBackground   = GetStockObject (WHITE_BRUSH) ;
            wndclass.lpszMenuName    = szAppName ;
            wndclass.lpszClassName   = szAppName ;

            RegisterClass (&wndclass) ;

            wndclass.style           = CS_HREDRAW | CS_VREDRAW ;
            wndclass.lpfnWndProc     = EllipPushWndProc ;
            wndclass.cbClsExtra      = 0 ;
            wndclass.cbWndExtra      = 0 ;
            wndclass.hInstance       = hInstance ;
            wndclass.hIcon           = NULL ;
            wndclass.hCursor         = LoadCursor (NULL, IDC_ARROW) ;
            wndclass.hbrBackground   = COLOR_WINDOW + 1 ;
            wndclass.lpszMenuName    = NULL ;
            wndclass.lpszClassName   = "EllipPush" ;

            RegisterClass (&wndclass) ;
            }

     hwnd = CreateWindow (szAppName, "About Box Demo Program",
                          WS_OVERLAPPEDWINDOW,
                          CW_USEDEFAULT, CW_USEDEFAULT,
                          CW_USEDEFAULT, CW_USEDEFAULT,
                          NULL, NULL, hInstance, NULL) ;

     ShowWindow (hwnd, nCmdShow) ;
     UpdateWindow (hwnd) ;

     while (GetMessage (&msg, NULL, 0, 0))
          {
          TranslateMessage (&msg) ;
          DispatchMessage (&msg) ;
          }
     return msg.wParam ;
     }

BOOL FAR PASCAL AboutDlgProc (HWND hDlg, WORD message, WORD wParam, LONG lParam)
     {
     switch (message)
          {
          case WM_INITDIALOG :
               return TRUE ;
```

(continued)

```
            case WM_COMMAND :
                switch (wParam)
                    {
                    case IDOK :
                            EndDialog (hDlg, 0) ;
                            return TRUE ;
                    }
                break ;
            }
        return FALSE ;
        }

long FAR PASCAL WndProc (HWND hwnd, WORD message, WORD wParam, LONG lParam)
        {
        static FARPROC lpfnAboutDlgProc ;
        static HANDLE  hInstance ;

        switch (message)
            {
            case WM_CREATE :
                hInstance = ((LPCREATESTRUCT) lParam)->hInstance ;

                lpfnAboutDlgProc = MakeProcInstance (AboutDlgProc, hInstance) ;
                return 0 ;

            case WM_COMMAND :
                switch (wParam)
                    {
                    case IDM_ABOUT :
                        DialogBox (hInstance, "AboutBox", hwnd,
                                    lpfnAboutDlgProc) ;

                        return 0 ;
                    }
                break ;

            case WM_DESTROY :
                . PostQuitMessage (0) ;
                return 0 ;
            }
        return DefWindowProc (hwnd, message, wParam, lParam) ;
        }

long FAR PASCAL EllipPushwndProc (HWND hwnd, WORD message,
                                    WORD wParam, LONG lParam)

        {
        char        szText [40] ;
        HBRUSH      hBrush ;
        HDC         hdc ;
        PAINTSTRUCT ps ;
        RECT        rect ;
```

(continued)

```
    switch (message)
         {
    case WM_PAINT :
         GetClientRect (hwnd, &rect) ;
         GetWindowText (hwnd, szText, sizeof szText) ;

         hdc = BeginPaint (hwnd, &ps) ;

         hBrush = CreateSolidBrush (GetSysColor (COLOR_WINDOW)) ;
         hBrush = SelectObject (hdc, hBrush) ;
         SetBkColor (hdc, GetSysColor (COLOR_WINDOW)) ;
         SetTextColor (hdc, GetSysColor (COLOR_WINDOWTEXT)) ;

         Ellipse (hdc, rect.left, rect.top, rect.right, rect.bottom) ;
         DrawText (hdc, szText, -1, &rect,
                        DT_SINGLELINE | DT_CENTER | DT_VCENTER) ;

         DeleteObject (SelectObject (hdc, hBrush)) ;

         EndPaint (hwnd, &ps) ;
         return 0 ;

    case WM_KEYUP :
         if (wParam != VK_SPACE)
              break ;
                                   // fall through
    case WM_LBUTTONUP :
         SendMessage (GetParent (hwnd), WM_COMMAND,
              GetWindowWord (hwnd, GWW_ID), (LONG) hwnd) ;
         return 0 ;
         }
    return DefWindowProc (hwnd, message, wParam, lParam) ;
    }
```

ABOUT3.RC

```
/*---------------------------
   ABOUT3.RC resource script
   ---------------------------*/

#include <windows.h>
#include "about3.h"

about3 ICON about3.ico
```

(continued)

```
About3 MENU
    {
    POPUP "&Help"
        {
        MENUITEM "&About About3...",        IDM_ABOUT
        }
    }

#define TABGRP (WS_TABSTOP : WS_GROUP)

AboutBox DIALOG  20, 20, 160, 80
    STYLE WS_POPUP : WS_DLGFRAME
    {
    CTEXT    "About3"                       -1,  0, 12, 160,  8
    ICON     "About3"                       -1,  8,  8,   0,  0
    CTEXT    "About Box Demo Program"       -1,  0, 36, 160,  8
    CTEXT    "(c) Charles Petzold, 1990"    -1,  0, 48, 160,  8
    CONTROL "OK" IDOK, "EllipPush", TABGRP,     64, 60,  32, 14
    }
```

ABOUT3.H

```
/*----------------------
   ABOUT3.H header file
   --------------------*/

#define IDM_ABOUT        1
```

ABOUT3.ICO

ABOUT3.DEF

```
;------------------------------------
; ABOUT3.DEF module definition file
;------------------------------------

NAME            ABOUT3

DESCRIPTION     'About Box Demo No. 3 (c) Charles Petzold, 1990'
EXETYPE         WINDOWS
STUB            'WINSTUB.EXE'
CODE            PRELOAD MOVEABLE DISCARDABLE
DATA            PRELOAD MOVEABLE MULTIPLE
HEAPSIZE        1024
STACKSIZE       8192
EXPORTS         WndProc
                AboutDlgProc
                EllipPushWndProc
```

The window class we'll be registering is called "EllipPush" ("elliptical push button"). Rather than use a DEFPUSHBUTTON statement in the dialog box template, we use a CONTROL statement that specifies this window class:

```
CONTROL "OK" IDOK, "EllipPush", TABGRP, 64, 60, 32, 14
```

The dialog box manager uses this window class in a *CreateWindow* call when creating the child window control in the dialog box.

The ABOUT3.C program registers the "EllipPush" window class in *WinMain*:

```
wndclass.style         = CS_HREDRAW : CS_VREDRAW ;
wndclass.lpfnWndProc   = EllipPushWndProc ;
wndclass.cbClsExtra    = 0 ;
wndclass.cbWndExtra    = 0 ;
wndclass.hInstance     = hInstance ;
wndclass.hIcon         = NULL ;
wndclass.hCursor       = LoadCursor (NULL, IDC_ARROW) ;
wndclass.hbrBackground = COLOR_WINDOW + 1 ;
wndclass.lpszMenuName  = NULL ;
wndclass.lpszClassName = "EllipPush" ;

RegisterClass (&wndclass) ;
```

The window class specifies that the window procedure is *EllipPushWndProc*, which is also in ABOUT3.C.

The *EllipPushWndProc* window procedure processes only three messages: WM_PAINT, WM_KEYUP, and WM_LBUTTONUP. During the WM_PAINT message, it obtains the size of its window from *GetClientRect* and obtains the text that appears in the push button from *GetWindowText*. It uses the Windows functions *Ellipse* and *DrawText* to draw the ellipse and the text.

The processing of the WM_KEYUP and WM_LBUTTONUP messages is very simple:

```
case WM_KEYUP :
     if (wParam != VK_SPACE)
         break ;
                              // fall through
case WM_LBUTTONUP :
     SendMessage (GetParent (hwnd), WM_COMMAND,
         GetWindowWord (hwnd, GWW_ID), (LONG) hwnd) ;
     return 0 ;
```

The window procedure obtains the handle of its parent window (the dialog box) using *GetParent* and sends a WM_COMMAND message with *wParam* equal to the control's ID. The ID is obtained using *GetWindowWord*. The dialog box window procedure then passes this message on to the dialog box procedure within ABOUT3. The result is a customized push button, as shown in Figure 10-6. You can use this same method to create other customized controls for dialog boxes.

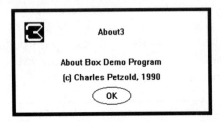

Figure 10-6. *A customized push button created by ABOUT3.*

Is that all there is to it? Well, not really. *EllipPushWndProc* is a bare-bones version of the logic generally involved in maintaining a child window control. For instance, the button doesn't flash like normal push buttons. To invert the colors on the interior of the push button, the window procedure would have to process WM_KEYDOWN (from the Spacebar) and WM_LBUTTONDOWN messages. The window procedure should also capture the mouse on a WM_LBUTTONDOWN message and release the mouse capture (and return the button's interior color to normal) if the mouse is moved outside the child window's client area while the button is still depressed. Only if the button is released while the mouse is captured should the child window send a WM_COMMAND message back to its parent.

EllipPushWndProc also does not process WM_ENABLE messages. As mentioned above, a dialog box procedure can disable a window using the *EnableWindow* function. The child window would then display gray rather than black text to indicate that it has been disabled and cannot receive messages.

If the window procedure for a child window control needs to store data that are different for each created window, then it can do so by using a positive value of *cbWndExtra* in the window class structure. This reserves space in the internal window structure that can be accessed by using *SetWindowWord*, *SetWindowLong*, *GetWindowWord*, and *GetWindowLong*.

THE MESSAGE BOX

Let's take a breather here. We've been looking at ways to customize dialog boxes. Now let's look at an alternative to dialog boxes, which is the message box. We began using message boxes way back in Chapter 5, but we haven't yet examined them in detail.

The message box is an appropriate and easy-to-use alternative to a dialog box when you need a simple response from the user. The general syntax is:

```
nItem = MessageBox (hwndParent, lpszText, lpszCaption, nType) ;
```

The message box has a caption (the character string *lpszCaption*), one or more lines of text (*lpszText*), one or more buttons, and (optionally) a predefined icon. One of the buttons is a default. The *nItem* value returned from *MessageBox* indicates the button that was pressed.

The *hwndParent* parameter is generally the handle to the window that creates the message box. The input focus will be set to this window when the message box is destroyed. If you don't have a window handle available or you don't want the input focus to go to one of your windows, you can use NULL for the handle. If you use a message box within a dialog box, use the dialog box window handle (which we've been calling *hDlg*) for this parameter.

The *lpszText* parameter is a long pointer to NULL-terminated text that appears in the body of the message box. Windows breaks this text into several lines if necessary. You can also include tab characters in the text, and you can define your own line breaks using carriage returns or linefeeds or both. The *lpszCaption* string is generally the name of the application.

The *nType* parameter is a collection of flags joined by the C bitwise OR operator. The first group of flags specifies the push buttons to appear at the bottom of the message box: MB_OK (the default), MB_OKCANCEL, MB_YESNO, MB_YESNOCANCEL, MB_RETRY-CANCEL, and MB_ABORTRETRYIGNORE. As you can see, these flags allow for a maximum of three buttons. The second group of flags specifies which of the buttons is the default: MB_DEFBUTTON1 (the default), MB_DEFBUTTON2, and MB_DEFBUTTON3.

The third group of flags specifies an icon to appear in the message box: MB_ICONINFORMATION, MB_ICONEXCLAMATION, MB_ICONSTOP, and MB_ICON-QUESTION. There is no default. If you omit one of these flags, the message box has no icon. You should use the information icon for a status message, the exclamation point for a reminder, the question mark for a warning of the consequences of an action, and the stop icon for a signal of serious problems.

The fourth set of flags governs whether the message box is application modal, in which case the user can switch to another application without ending the message box, or system modal, which requires the user to end the message box before doing anything else. The flags are MB_APPLMODAL (the default) and MB_SYSTEMMODAL. Finally, you can use a fifth flag, MB_NOFOCUS, which displays the message box but does not give it the input focus.

Depending on which button is pressed, the message box returns one of the following identifiers: IDOK, IDCANCEL, IDYES, IDNO, IDRETRY, and IDABORT.

The Assertion Message Box

Although message boxes are customarily used to convey messages and ask questions in finished programs, they are also helpful in debugging. For instance, you may be familiar with the *assert* macro included in the ASSERT.H header file with the Microsoft C Compiler. This macro is used for testing various conditions during a program's execution. If the condition does not hold, the macro displays the current source code filename and line number and terminates the program. You can create a similar macro for Windows:

```
#ifndef NDEBUG

#define WinAssert(exp)\
            {\
            if (!(exp))\
                {\
                char szBuffer [40] ;\
                sprintf (szBuffer, "File %s, Line %d",\
                    __FILE__, __LINE__) ;\
                MessageBox (NULL, szBuffer,\
                    "Assertion Error",\
                    MB_OK ¦ MB_ICONSTOP) ;\
                }\
            }

#else

#define WinAssert(exp)

#endif
```

You can then make various assertions in your code. For instance, to be sure that the value of *hwnd* in a certain section of your program is never NULL, you can do this:

```
WinAssert (hwnd != NULL) ;
```

If *hwnd* is NULL when this statement is executed, the message box will be displayed to alert you to the problem. A macro is used rather than a function, because the predefined identifiers __FILE__ and __LINE__ must equal the source code filename and line number where the assertion failed. If you used a function, these identifiers would always be set to the filename and line number where the function was located.

Unlike *assert*, the *WinAssert* macro shown above doesn't terminate the program if the assertion fails. If you use a debugging terminal, you can use a different version of this macro shown below. When you select the Abort button, the *FatalExit* function is called to display a stack trace on the debugging terminal.

```
if (IDABORT == MessageBox (NULL, szBuffer,
                    "Assertion Error",
                    MB_ABORTRETRYIGNORE | MB_ICONSTOP))
        FatalExit (-1) ;
```

Once you've finished debugging the program, you can compile with the identifier NDEBUG, defined by using the compiler switch -D NDEBUG. The *WinAssert* macro will then be defined as nothing.

Popup Information

Another handy use of a message box during program development is to provide information to you while the program is executing. It would be ideal if you could use a message box much as you use *printf* in C programs for MS-DOS, with a formatting string and a variable number of arguments. And in fact, you can create a function that lets you do this:

```
void OkMsgBox (char *szCaption, char *szFormat, ...)
        {
        char szBuffer [256] ;
        char *pArguments ;

        pArguments = (char *) &szFormat + sizeof szFormat ;
        vsprintf (szBuffer, szFormat, pArguments) ;
        MessageBox (NULL, szBuffer, szCaption, MB_OK) ;
        }
```

The *vsprintf* function is similar to *sprintf* except that it uses a pointer to a series of arguments (*pArguments*) rather than the arguments themselves. *OkMsgBox* sets *pArguments* to the arguments on the stack when *OkMsgBox* is called. The first parameter to *OkMsgBox* is the message box caption, the second parameter is a format string, and the third and subsequent parameters are values to be displayed. Let's say you want a message box to appear every time the window procedure gets a WM_SIZE message. Your code might look like this:

```
case WM_SIZE :
        OkMsgBox ("WM_SIZE Message",
                "wParam = %04X, lParam = %04X-%04X",
                wParam, HIWORD (lParam), LOWORD (lParam)) ;
                [other program lines]
        return 0 ;
```

This displays the values of *wParam* and *lParam* within the message box.

WORKING WITH FILES: POPPAD REVISITED

When we added a menu to POPPAD in Chapter 9, several menu options were left unimplemented. We are now almost ready to add logic to POPPAD to open files, read them in, and save the edited files to disk.

Working with files in Windows is no great joy. Although the standard dialog box template to open a file is fairly simple, the dialog box procedure itself is one of the most difficult you'll encounter. Before tackling that function, let's investigate methods of file I/O in Windows programs.

The *OpenFile* Function Call

Windows includes a function to open a file and return an MS-DOS file handle:

```
hFile = OpenFile (lpszFileName, &of, wFunction) ;
```

The *OpenFile* funtion call returns a −1 if an error is encountered. For most uses of *OpenFile*, a return value other than −1 will be an MS-DOS file handle that you can use to read from and write to the file.

The *lpszFileName* parameter is a long (or far) pointer to the filename. A disk drive and subdirectory are optional. The *wFunction* parameter tells Windows what to do with this file (open it, create it, delete it, and so forth). I'll describe this parameter in more detail shortly.

The *&of* parameter is a far pointer to a structure of type OFSTRUCT ("open file structure"). You don't need to set any of the fields of this structure before calling *OpenFile*: They are filled in by the first *OpenFile* function call you make and are then used in subsequent *OpenFile* calls for the same file. The OFSTRUCT fields are shown below:

Field	Data Type	Description
cBytes	BYTE	Length of structure in bytes
fFixedDisk	BYTE	Nonzero for fixed-disk file
nErrCode	WORD	MS-DOS error code
reserved[4]	BYTE	File date and time
szPathName[128]	BYTE	Fully qualified pathname and filename

If the *OpenFile* call is successful, the *szPathName* field is filled with the fully qualified filename, including the current disk drive and subdirectory path. Under current versions of MS-DOS, the 128 characters allowed for this name are about 40 more than needed. A fully qualified filename has 2 bytes for the drive letter and colon, up to 64 bytes for the directory path starting with the initial backslash, another byte for the backslash following the path, up to 12 bytes for the filename (8-character name, period, and 3-character extension), and a terminating 0.

The *OpenFile* function has three advantages over opening a file by other means:

- The *lpszFileName* parameter is assumed to contain characters from the ANSI character set. *OpenFile* does an *AnsiToOem* conversion on the name before trying to open the file. You would have to convert the filename yourself if you opened the file by other means.

- If the file is not found in the current directory, *OpenFile* searches for the file on all directories listed in the MS-DOS environment PATH string.

- Windows determines the fully qualified filename and inserts it in the *szPathName* field of the structure.

This last item is the most important feature of *OpenFile*. Generally, the *lpszFileName* parameter you pass to *OpenFile* when first opening or creating a file is only a filename. When you use *OpenFile* subsequently to open the same file, Windows uses the fully qualified *szPathName* field of the OFSTRUCT structure.

Here's why that's important: Although each program instance in Windows has a current disk drive and subdirectory associated with it, the *DlgDirList* function (which we'll use later in this chapter) can change the current drive and subdirectory associated with a program instance. Let's say you use some means other than *OpenFile* to obtain a filename (without a drive or directory path) located in the current directory and that you successfully open and close the file. The user then uses the dialog box to get a new file. In the process, the dialog box calls *DlgDirList* to change the current drive or subdirectory. The user then cancels the dialog box, and your program tries to open the original file again. It's gone! Well, it's not gone, but the current drive or subdirectory is different, so your program can't find the file. You avoid this problem by using *OpenFile*.

The *wFunction* parameter of the *OpenFile* call comprises one or more flags joined by the C bitwise OR operator. First, you use one of the following four flags to open an existing file or create a new file:

OF_READ	Opens an existing file for reading only
OF_WRITE	Opens an existing file for writing only
OF_READWRITE	Opens an existing file for reading and writing
OF_CREATE	Creates a new file, or opens an existing file and truncates the size of the file to 0

Following the *OpenFile* call, the file is open and ready for reading and writing. The value returned from *OpenFile* is the MS-DOS file handle (unless this value is −1, in which case the file could not be opened or created).

If you prefer that the file be closed following the *OpenFile* call, you can add the flag OF_EXIST. This flag is generally used with OF_READ, OF_WRITE, or OF_READWRITE to see if the specified file exists. You can also use this flag with OF_CREATE to create the file and immediately close it. The file can be reopened later. When you use OF_EXIST, the value returned from *OpenFile* is −1 if the file does not exist or (with OF_CREATE) if the file could not be created. Any file handle returned from *OpenFile* with an OF_EXIST flag should be ignored, because the file has been closed.

With OF_READ, OF_WRITE, or OF_READWRITE, you can also use the flag OF_PROMPT. If Windows can't find the file in the current directory or in one of the directories in the MS-DOS environment PATH string, this flag causes Windows to display the infamous "Insert [filename] disk in drive A:" message box. Windows users appreciate this message box about as much as MS-DOS users like the "Abort, Retry, Ignore" message, so use this flag with discretion. Also keep in mind that the OF_PROMPT message box has only an OK button, which means that fixed-disk users must scrounge up a disk to put in drive A before proceeding. If you must use the OF_PROMPT flag, also use the OF_CANCEL flag, which adds a Cancel button to the message box. If the user selects Cancel, the *OpenFile* function returns −1.

That's it for the flags to open a file for the first time. The file is open when the *OpenFile* function returns, unless you've included the OF_EXIST flag (in which case the file has been closed) or *OpenFile* returns −1 (in which case an error occurred). You can now read from or write to this file and then close it. How you perform these actions is discussed in the next section.

When you want to reopen the file, you use the OF_READ, OF_WRITE, OF_READWRITE, or OF_CREATE flag in combination with the OF_REOPEN flag. The OF_REOPEN flag causes Windows to use the *szPathName* field in the OFSTRUCT structure to obtain the original disk drive, subdirectory, and filename of the file. Even if the current drive or subdirectory has changed since the file was first opened, this flag ensures that Windows will use the same drive and subdirectory as in the first *OpenFile* call. If you use OF_REOPEN with OF_CREATE, the size of the file will be truncated to 0.

When you use the OF_READ flag to open a file for reading only, you can also use the OF_VERIFY flag. This flag causes Windows to use the reserved field in the OFSTRUCT structure to verify that the date and time of the file being reopened are the same as those stored during the original *OpenFile* call. This works only for files opened with OF_READ, because the value for the file date and time is updated when a write-only or read-write file is closed.

Also available are two *OpenFile* flags that do not open files. The OF_DELETE flag deletes a file. If the file cannot be found in the current subdirectory, *OpenFile* uses the MS-DOS environment PATH string to search for a file to delete. Perhaps you're feeling cruel, in which case you can use the OF_PROMPT flag with OF_DELETE so that Windows also gets the chance to delete the file on the disk in drive A. *OpenFile* returns −1 if no file was deleted. If the file has previously been opened with *OpenFile* and then closed, you can use OF_DELETE in combination with OF_REOPEN.

The OF_PARSE flag does not open a file or even check for a file's existence. This flag is used by itself to parse the filename and fill in the *szPathName* field of the OFSTRUCT structure. *OpenFile* returns −1 if the filename is invalid—say, if it uses illegal characters.

Two Methods of File I/O

The main rule of file I/O in Windows is this: Do not keep files open for long periods of time. More specifically, that means you should not keep a file open between messages. You should open or create a file, read it or write to it in several large gulps, and then close it— all in the course of processing a single message.

You have two options for using files that have been opened with the *OpenFile* call:

- Use normal C functions for file I/O. The file handle returned from *OpenFile* can be used directly with the "low-level" file I/O functions. The most important of these functions are *open, read, lseek, close, create, write*, and *tell*. We used the *read* and *close* functions in the HEAD program in Chapter 5.

    The problem with these functions is that you can't use far pointers with them unless your program is compact model or large model. As you know, compact model and large model are not recommended for Windows programs because their data segments must be fixed in memory. If you want to read part of a file into a global memory segment, you must first read the file into a local memory block and then transfer it to the global memory block.

    You can also use the normal C buffered file I/O functions such as *fopen, fread, fwrite*, and *fclose*. The MS-DOS file handle returned from *OpenFile* can be converted to a structure of type FILE using *fdopen*. The buffered file I/O functions are of less value in Windows than in other environments, because you need to read and write in large chunks, and buffering doesn't help unless you're reading small parts of a file.

- Use file I/O functions included in Windows. These go by the names of *_lopen, _lclose, _lcreat, _llseek, _lread*, and *_lwrite*. The "l" prefix indicates that these functions accept far pointers for read and write buffers, thus allowing you to use them with global memory blocks. (These functions existed in Windows since version 1 but have only been documented beginning in Windows 3.)

This third method turns out to be the easiest when the file must be read into or written from buffer areas accessible only with far pointers. (The normal C low-level file I/O calls are preferable when you can use near pointers.) Do not write your own assembly-language routines for interfacing with the MS-DOS file I/O functions.

You'll probably use *OpenFile* to open and create files, but you can also use *_lopen* and *_lcreat*. The syntax is:

```
hFile = _lopen (lpszPathName, iReadWrite) ;
```

The *lpszPathName* parameter is a filename with an optional drive and subdirectory path. The *iReadWrite* parameter should be set to one of the identifiers OF_READ, OF_WRITE, or OF_READWRITE. The *hFile* value returned from *_lopen* is an MS-DOS file handle if the file is opened or −1 if the file cannot be opened.

The *_lcreat* function looks similar to the *_lopen* call:

```
hFile = _lcreat (lpszPathName, iAttribute) ;
```

However, the second parameter is an MS-DOS file attribute. Use 0 for a normal (nonhidden, nonsystem, read-write) file. If the file already exists, the size is truncated to 0 and opened; if it doesn't exist, it is created and opened. Like the *_lopen* call, *_lcreat* returns an MS-DOS file handle if the function is successful or −1 if an error occurs.

After an *_lopen* or *_lcreat* call, the file pointer is set initially to the beginning of the file. Normally, all reading and writing is sequential. The file pointer is updated after each read or write. However, you can use *_llseek* (MS-DOS Function 42H) to change the file pointer:

```
lPosition = _llseek (hFile, lPosition, iMethod) ;
```

The *iMethod* parameter should be set to one of the following values:

Value	Purpose
0	Move the file pointer *lPosition* bytes from the beginning of the file
1	Move the file pointer *lPosition* bytes from the current position in the file
2	Move the file pointer *lPosition* bytes from the end of the file

The value of *lPosition* returned from *_llseek* is the new position of the file pointer if the function is successful or −1L if an error occurs.

If you want to open an existing file and add data to it, you call:

```
_llseek (hFile, 0L, 2) ;
```

This moves the file pointer to the end of the file. You can also use *_llseek* to determine the size of a file. You might want to define a function called *FileLength* to do this:

```
long FileLength (int hFile)
     {
     long    lCurrentPos = _llseek (hFile, 0L, 1) ;
     long    lFileLength = _llseek (hFile, 0L, 2) ;

     _llseek (hFile, lCurrentPos, 0) ;

     return lFileLength ;
     }
```

FileLength saves the current position of the file pointer, moves the file pointer to the end of the file, and then restores the file pointer to its original position.

To write to a file, use:

```
wBytesWritten = _lwrite (hFile, lpBuffer, wBytes) ;
```

The *lpBuffer* parameter is a far pointer to the data you want to write to the file, and *wBytes* is the number of bytes to write. The file buffer cannot extend past the end of a segment. The *wBytesWritten* value returned from the function is the number of bytes that are actually written. This can be less than *wBytes* if not enough disk space is available to write the entire buffer. Normally, MS-DOS function calls allow you to write up to 65,535 bytes to a file, but *_lwrite* returns –1 to signal an error, so you'll want to restrict yourself to 65,534 bytes or less.

The function to read from a file is similar:

```
wBytesRead = _lread (hFile, lpBuffer, wBytes) ;
```

The *lpBuffer* parameter is a far pointer to an area that receives the data read from the file, and *wBytes* is the number of bytes to read. The *wBytesRead* value returned can be less than *wBytes* if the end of the file is encountered before *wBytes* are read. A return value of –1 signals an error.

Finally, to close a file, use:

```
_lclose (hFile) ;
```

· When working with files and global memory blocks, you may also need to make use of string functions that work with far pointers. Windows includes functions called *lstrlen, lstrcpy, lstrcat,* and *lstrcmp* that are equivalent to the normal C string functions *strlen, strcpy, strcat,* and *strcmp,* except that they use far pointers. These functions are useful for moving data between two global memory blocks or between a global memory block and a local memory block. They are coded in assembly language and are thus much faster than equivalent C code. The *lstrcmp* function is a "Windows version" of the *strcmp* function: It is case sensitive for both the normal ASCII character codes and the ANSI character codes, and it can accommodate strings with multibyte character codes.

Dialog Boxes for Open and Save

With these preliminaries out of the way, we are now ready to create dialog box templates and dialog box procedures to assist our Windows programs in opening and saving files. The FILEDLG.C source code file, FILEDLG.H header file, and FILEDLG.DLG dialog box template file, shown in Figure 10-7 on the following pages, will be used in the POPPAD3 program in this chapter. You can use these routines (or similar ones) in your own programs.

FILEDLG.C

```
/*-----------------------------------------------
   FILEDLG.C -- Open and Close File Dialog Boxes
   -------------------------------------------*/

#include <windows.h>
#include "filedlg.h"

BOOL FAR PASCAL FileOpenDlgProc (HWND, WORD, WORD, LONG) ;
BOOL FAR PASCAL FileSaveDlgProc (HWND, WORD, WORD, LONG) ;

LPSTR lstrchr  (LPSTR str, char ch) ;
LPSTR lstrrchr (LPSTR str, char ch) ;

static char     szDefExt   [5] ;
static char     szFileName [96] ;
static char     szFileSpec [16] ;
static POFSTRUCT pof ;
static WORD     wFileAttr, wStatus ;

int DoFileOpenDlg (HANDLE hInst, HWND hwnd, char *szFileSpecIn,
                   char *szDefExtIn, WORD wFileAttrIn,
                   char *szFileNameOut, POFSTRUCT pofIn)
    {
    FARPROC lpfnFileOpenDlgProc ;
    int     iReturn ;

    lstrcpy (szFileSpec, szFileSpecIn) ;
    lstrcpy (szDefExt,   szDefExtIn) ;
    wFileAttr = wFileAttrIn ;
    pof = pofIn ;

    lpfnFileOpenDlgProc = MakeProcInstance (FileOpenDlgProc, hInst) ;

    iReturn = DialogBox (hInst, "FileOpen", hwnd, lpfnFileOpenDlgProc) ;

    FreeProcInstance (lpfnFileOpenDlgProc) ;

    lstrcpy (szFileNameOut, szFileName) ;
    return iReturn ;
    }

int DoFileSaveDlg (HANDLE hInst, HWND hwnd, char *szFileSpecIn,
                   char *szDefExtIn, WORD *pwStatusOut,
                   char *szFileNameOut, POFSTRUCT pofIn)
    {
    FARPROC lpfnFileSaveDlgProc ;
    int     iReturn ;
```

Figure 10-7. *The FILEDLG files for the file I/O dialog boxes.*   *(continued)*

```
        lstrcpy (szFileSpec, szFileSpecIn) ;
        lstrcpy (szDefExt,   szDefExtIn) ;
        pof = pofIn ;

        lpfnFileSaveDlgProc = MakeProcInstance (FileSaveDlgProc, hInst) ;

        iReturn = DialogBox (hInst, "FileSave", hwnd, lpfnFileSaveDlgProc) ;

        FreeProcInstance (lpfnFileSaveDlgProc) ;

        lstrcpy (szFileNameOut, szFileName) ;
        *pwStatusOut = wStatus ;
        return iReturn ;
        }

BOOL FAR PASCAL FileOpenDlgProc (HWND hDlg, WORD message,
                                 WORD wParam, LONG lParam)
        {
        char  cLastChar ;
        short nEditLen ;

        switch (message)
            {
            case WM_INITDIALOG :
                SendDlgItemMessage (hDlg, IDD_FNAME, EM_LIMITTEXT, 80, OL) ;
                DlgDirList (hDlg, szFileSpec, IDD_FLIST, IDD_FPATH, wFileAttr) ;
                SetDlgItemText (hDlg, IDD_FNAME, szFileSpec) ;
                return TRUE ;

            case WM_COMMAND :
                switch (wParam)
                    {
                    case IDD_FLIST :
                        switch (HIWORD (lParam))
                            {
                            case LBN_SELCHANGE :
                                if (DlgDirSelect (hDlg, szFileName, IDD_FLIST))
                                    lstrcat (szFileName, szFileSpec) ;
                                SetDlgItemText (hDlg, IDD_FNAME, szFileName) ;
                                return TRUE ;

                            case LBN_DBLCLK :
                                if (DlgDirSelect (hDlg, szFileName, IDD_FLIST))
                                    {
                                    lstrcat (szFileName, szFileSpec) ;
                                    DlgDirList (hDlg, szFileName, IDD_FLIST, IDD_FPATH,
                                                                    wFileAttr) ;
                                    SetDlgItemText (hDlg, IDD_FNAME, szFileSpec) ;
                                    }
```

(continued)

```
               else
                  {
                  SetDlgItemText (hDlg, IDD_FNAME, szFileName) ;
                  SendMessage (hDlg, WM_COMMAND, IDOK, OL) ;
                  }
               return TRUE ;
            }
      break ;

   case IDD_FNAME :
      if (HIWORD (lParam) == EN_CHANGE)
         EnableWindow (GetDlgItem (hDlg, IDOK),
            (BOOL) SendMessage (LOWORD (lParam),
                                  WM_GETTEXTLENGTH, 0, OL)) ;
      return TRUE ;

   case IDOK :
      GetDlgItemText (hDlg, IDD_FNAME, szFileName, 80) ;

      nEditLen  = lstrlen (szFileName) ;
      cLastChar = *AnsiPrev (szFileName, szFileName + nEditLen) ;

      if (cLastChar == '\\' || cLastChar == ':')
         lstrcat (szFileName, szFileSpec) ;

      if (lstrchr (szFileName, '*') || lstrchr (szFileName, '?'))
         {
         if (DlgDirList (hDlg, szFileName, IDD_FLIST,
                            IDD_FPATH, wFileAttr))
            {
            lstrcpy (szFileSpec, szFileName) ;
            SetDlgItemText (hDlg, IDD_FNAME, szFileSpec) ;
            }
         else
            MessageBeep (0) ;

         return TRUE ;
         }

      lstrcat (lstrcat (szFileName, "\\"), szFileSpec) ;

      if (DlgDirList (hDlg, szFileName, IDD_FLIST,
                                         IDD_FPATH, wFileAttr))
         {
         lstrcpy (szFileSpec, szFileName) ;
         SetDlgItemText (hDlg, IDD_FNAME, szFileSpec) ;
         return TRUE ;
         }

      szFileName [nEditLen] = '\0' ;
```

(continued)

```
                if (-1 == OpenFile (szFileName, pof, OF_READ ¦ OF_EXIST))
                    {
                    lstrcat (szFileName, szDefExt) ;
                    if (-1 == OpenFile (szFileName, pof, OF_READ ¦ OF_EXIST))
                        {
                        MessageBeep (0) ;
                        return TRUE ;
                        }
                    }
                lstrcpy (szFileName,
                         AnsiNext (lstrrchr (pof->szPathName, '\\'))) ;

                OemToAnsi (szFileName, szFileName) ;
                EndDialog (hDlg, TRUE) ;
                return TRUE ;

            case IDCANCEL :
                EndDialog (hDlg, FALSE) ;
                return TRUE ;
            }
        }
    return FALSE ;
    }

BOOL FAR PASCAL FileSaveDlgProc (HWND hDlg, WORD message,
                                 WORD wParam, LONG lParam)
    {
    switch (message)
        {
        case WM_INITDIALOG :
            SendDlgItemMessage (hDlg, IDD_FNAME, EM_LIMITTEXT, 80, 0L) ;
            DlgDirList (hDlg, szFileSpec, 0, IDD_FPATH, 0) ;
            SetDlgItemText (hDlg, IDD_FNAME, szFileSpec) ;
            return TRUE ;

        case WM_COMMAND :
            switch (wParam)
                {
                case IDD_FNAME :
                    if (HIWORD (lParam) == EN_CHANGE)
                        EnableWindow (GetDlgItem (hDlg, IDOK),
                            (BOOL) SendMessage (LOWORD (lParam),
                                                WM_GETTEXTLENGTH, 0, 0L)) ;
                    return TRUE ;
                case IDOK :
                    GetDlgItemText (hDlg, IDD_FNAME, szFileName, 80) ;
```

(continued)

```
                    if (-1 == OpenFile (szFileName, pof, OF_PARSE))
                        {
                        MessageBeep (0) ;
                        return TRUE ;
                        }

                    if (!lstrchr (AnsiNext (lstrrchr (pof->szPathName, '\\')),
                                '.'))
                        lstrcat (szFileName, szDefExt) ;

                    if (-1 != OpenFile (szFileName, pof, OF_WRITE | OF_EXIST))
                        wStatus = 1 ;

                    else if (-1 != OpenFile (szFileName, pof,
                                                OF_CREATE | OF_EXIST))

                        wStatus = 0 ;

                    else
                        {
                        MessageBeep (0) ;
                        return TRUE ;
                        }

                    lstrcpy (szFileName,
                            AnsiNext (lstrrchr (pof->szPathName, '\\'))) ;

                    OemToAnsi (szFileName, szFileName) ;
                    EndDialog (hDlg, TRUE) ;
                    return TRUE ;

               case IDCANCEL :
                    EndDialog (hDlg, FALSE) ;
                    return TRUE ;
               }
          }
     return FALSE ;
     }

LPSTR lstrchr (LPSTR str, char ch)
     {
     while (*str)
          {
          if (ch == *str)
               return str ;

          str = AnsiNext (str) ;
          }
     return NULL ;
     }
```

(continued)

452

```
LPSTR lstrrchr (LPSTR str, char ch)
     {
     LPSTR str1 = str + lstrlen (str) ;

     do
          {
          if (ch == *str1)
               return str1 ;

          str1 = AnsiPrev (str, str1) ;
          }
     while (str1 > str) ;

     return NULL ;
     }
```

FILEDLG.H

```
/*----------------------
   FILEDLG.H header file
   ---------------------*/

#define IDD_FNAME   0x10
#define IDD_FPATH   0x11
#define IDD_FLIST   0x12
```

FILEDLG.DLG

```
/*---------------------------------
   FILEDLG.DLG dialog definitions
   --------------------------------*/

FileOpen DIALOG 10, 10, 148, 116
     STYLE WS_POPUP | WS_DLGFRAME
     {
     LTEXT    "Open File &Name:", -1,      2,  4,  76, 10
     EDITTEXT               IDD_FNAME,   2, 18, 100, 12, ES_AUTOHSCROLL
     LTEXT          "&Files in", -1,       2, 40,  38, 10
     LTEXT          "",    IDD_FPATH,    44, 40,  98, 12
     LISTBOX               IDD_FLIST,    2, 54,  70, 58, WS_TABSTOP | WS_VSCROLL
     DEFPUSHBUTTON "&Open",   IDOK,      88, 62,  50, 14, WS_GROUP
     PUSHBUTTON    "Cancel", IDCANCEL,   88, 86,  50, 14, WS_GROUP
     }
```

(continued)

453

```
FileSave DIALOG 10, 10, 180, 54
    STYLE WS_POPUP ; WS_DLGFRAME
    {
    LTEXT "Save File &Name As:", -1,        6,  4,  84, 12
    LTEXT           "",         IDD_FPATH,  90,  4,  78, 12
    EDITTEXT                    IDD_FNAME,   6, 20, 104, 12, ES_AUTOHSCROLL
    DEFPUSHBUTTON   "OK",       IDOK,       124, 20,  50, 14, WS_GROUP
    PUSHBUTTON      "Cancel",   IDCANCEL,   124, 36,  50, 14, WS_GROUP
    }
```

FILEDLG.DLG contains two dialog box templates named "FileOpen" and "FileSave." When displayed, these look very much like the dialog boxes used in the programs that come with Windows, so the operation of the two dialog boxes will be familiar to Windows users. *FileOpen* contains Open and Cancel push buttons, and *FileSave* contains OK and Cancel push buttons. The static text field with an ID of IDD_FPATH is used to display the current disk drive and directory path. The edit field with the ID of IDD_FNAME allows a user to type in a filename. The *FileOpen* dialog box also contains a list box that displays all the files matching a particular file specification (we'll use "*.TXT" with POPPAD3), all valid disk drive letters, and all child subdirectories of the current drive and directory.

The FILEDLG.C file contains two functions named *DoFileOpenDlg* and *DoFile-SaveDlg* that a program can call to invoke the dialog boxes. These functions are responsible for copying input parameters to variables within FILEDLG.C, calling *DialogBox*, and returning information obtained from the dialog box procedure to the program that called the FILEDLG.C functions. The parameters to the *DoFileOpenDlg* and *DoFileSaveDlg* functions include a default file specification (*szFileSpecIn*), a default filename extension (*szDefExtIn*), and a pointer to a structure of type OFSTRUCT (*pofIn*). The *DoFileOpen-DlgProc* also requires a file attribute (*wFileAttrIn*) to be used when listing files in the list box.

The *DoFileOpenDlg* and *DoFileSaveDlg* functions return a 1 if the user ends the dialog box with Open or OK, and a 0 if the user ends with Cancel. If the user ends with Open or OK, the OFSTRUCT structure passed to the functions will contain the fully qualified filename of the selected file in the *szPathName* field. The filename only (without a drive or directory) is copied to the *szFileNameOut* character array. For *DoFileSaveDlg*, the *pwStatusOut* parameter points to a word that is set to 1 if the file does exist and to 0 if it does not.

The actual dialog box procedures are *FileOpenDlgProc* and *FileSaveDlgProc*. These are relatively complex because they must deal with the interaction between the list box and the edit control and with the checking that must be performed on filenames and subdirectories entered by the user. To help with these areas, the dialog box procedures extensively use the Windows functions *DlgDirList* and *DlgDirSelect*.

The *DlgDirList* and *DlgDirSelect* Functions

You'll recall from working with list boxes in Chapter 6 that you can fill a list box with a list of files, subdirectories, and disk drives by sending the list box a message:

```
SendMessage (hwndList, LB_DIR, wAttr, (LONG) lpszFileSpec) ;
```

The *wAttr* parameter is an MS-DOS file attribute (with some additional bits to indicate the listing of subdirectories and disk drives), and *lpszFileSpec* is a far pointer to a filename specification such as "*.*".

Although this list box message is quite convenient, within a dialog box you can use an even more sophisticated function:

```
iStatus = DlgDirList (hDlg, lpszFileSpec, nIDList, nIDStatic, wAttr) ;
```

The *nIDList* parameter is the ID of the list box, and *nIDStatic* is the ID of a static text field. *DlgDirList* parses the string pointed to by *lpszFileSpec* to extract any disk drive or subdirectory information from it. It then changes the current disk drive or subdirectory using MS-DOS function calls.

DlgDirList sends an LB_DIR message to the list box indicated by *nIDList* to fill it with filenames meeting the file specification and the file attribute word. The current disk drive and subdirectory path are then displayed in the static text field whose ID is *nIDStatic*. When *DlgDirList* returns, the string pointed to by *lpszFileSpec* contains only the file specification without any drive or subdirectory. The function returns nonzero if it is successful and 0 otherwise. A 0 value usually indicates that the string pointed to by *lpszFileSpec* does not contain a valid drive or subdirectory.

For example, suppose that drive C has a directory named WINDOWS and that your dialog box procedure contains this code:

```
char szFileSpec [] = "C:\\WINDOWS\\*.TXT" ;
     [other program lines]
DlgDirList (hDlg, szFileSpec, IDD_FLIST, IDD_FPATH, 0x4010) ;
```

When *DlgDirList* returns, the current disk drive and subdirectory for the instance of the program will have been changed to C:\WINDOWS. The list box whose ID is IDD_FLIST will list files with the extension .TXT, all subdirectories of the directory WINDOWS, and all valid disk drives. The static text field whose ID is IDD_FPATH will display the text C:\WINDOWS. The *szFileSpec* string array will contain "*.TXT". If either the *nIDList* or *nIDStatic* parameter is 0, however, *DlgDirList* will assume that the list box or static text field does not exist.

Both *FileOpenDlgProc* and *FileSaveDlgProc* use *DlgDirList* while processing the WM_INITDIALOG message. (In *FileSaveDlgProc*, *DlgDirList* is called with the *nIDList* parameter set to 0 because the dialog box does not contain a list box.)

SetDlgItemText is used to set the text of the edit control to the text file specification:

```
SetDlgItemText (hDlg, IDD_FNAME, szFileSpec) ;
```

This function does the same thing as the *SetWindowText* function or the WM_SETTEXT message. You can use the companion function *GetDlgItemText* to obtain the contents of the edit control.

FileOpenDlgProc also uses *DlgDirSelect* extensively. This function returns the currently selected string from a list box:

```
bDirectory = DlgDirSelect (hDlg, lpszString, nIDList) ;
```

The *nIDList* parameter is the ID of the list box. The currently selected string is copied to the character array pointed to by *lpszString*. If the return value is TRUE (nonzero), meaning that the string is either a disk drive or subdirectory name, *DlgDirSelect* removes the hyphens and brackets that appear when disk-drive letters and the subdirectory names are displayed in a list box. The function appends a colon to disk-drive letters and a backslash to subdirectory names when copying them to the *lpszString* array.

If *DlgDirSelect* returns a disk drive or directory, you can then append the default file specification ("*.TXT", for instance) to the string and use that as the *lpszFileSpec* parameter to *DlgDirList*. *DlgDirList* will then change the drive or directory and update the static text field. The file specification pointed to by *lpszFileSpec* on return from *DlgDirList* can then be transferred to the edit control. If *DlgDirSelect* returns FALSE (0), meaning that *lpszString* contains a filename from the list box, then this filename can be transferred to the edit field directly.

Getting Valid Filenames

The dialog box to open a file would be much simpler if it did not contain an edit control. The edit control forces the dialog box procedure into doing some filename parsing. Much of this logic occurs when *FileOpenDlgProc* processes the WM_COMMAND message with *wParam* equal to IDOK. (When the user double-clicks a list box filename, the dialog procedure transfers the name to the edit box and then generates a WM_COMMAND message with *wParam* equal to IDOK. This avoids repeating the parsing logic for a list box double-click message.)

The dialog box procedure uses *GetDlgItemText* to obtain the string in the edit control. The parsing logic begins with a check to determine if the last character in this string is a backslash or colon. If it is, the user is requesting that the drive or directory be changed, so the current file specification must be appended to the string the user entered. If the resultant filename string contains a global character (* or ?), the dialog box procedure calls *DlgDirList* with the new specification, and the dialog box procedure exits to wait for the next message.

If the character string entered by the user neither terminates with a backslash or colon nor contains a global character, it could be either a directory name or a filename.

FileOpenDlgProc appends a backslash and the current file specification to it. If *DlgDirList* doesn't report an error, processing of the message is over. Otherwise, the entered text string is probably a filename, in which case *FileOpenDlgProc* strips off the previously appended file specification and calls *OpenFile*. If *OpenFile* does not find the file, then the default extension is added, and *OpenFile* tries again. If either one of these *OpenFile* calls is successful in opening the file for reading, then the *szPathName* field of the OFSTRUCT structure is used to obtain the filename without any drive or subdirectory, and the dialog box is terminated. Otherwise, the dialog procedure beeps to indicate an error in the filename.

The FILEDLG.C file contains alternate *strchr* and *strrchr* functions that search for characters when parsing filename strings. These alternate functions use *AnsiNext* and *AnsiPrev* to allow multibyte characters in the filename strings.

The New Version of POPPAD

The new version of POPPAD that uses these two dialog boxes (called POPPAD3) is shown in Figure 10-8.

POPPAD3.MAK

```
#----------------------
# POPPAD3.MAK make file
#----------------------

poppad3.exe : poppad.obj  poppadf.obj poppadp0.obj \
             filedlg.obj poppad3.def poppad.res
    link poppad poppadf poppadp0 filedlg, poppad3.exe /align:16, \
         NUL, /nod slibcew libw, poppad3
    rc poppad.res  poppad3.exe

poppad.obj : poppad.c poppad.h
    cl -c -Gsw -Ow -W2 -Zp poppad.c

poppadf.obj : poppadf.c
    cl -c -Gsw -Ow -W2 -Zp poppadf.c

poppadp0.obj : poppadp0.c
    cl -c -Gsw -Ow -W2 -Zp poppadp0.c

filedlg.obj : filedlg.c filedlg.h
    cl -c -Gsw -Ow -W2 -Zp filedlg.c

poppad.res : poppad.rc poppad.h poppad.ico filedlg.dlg filedlg.h
    rc -r poppad.rc
```

Figure 10-8. *The POPPAD program.*

POPPAD.C

```
/*-----------------------------------------
   POPPAD.C -- Popup Editor
              (c) Charles Petzold, 1990
   -----------------------------------------*/

#include <windows.h>
#include "poppad.h"
#define  EDITID 1

long FAR PASCAL WndProc (HWND, WORD, WORD, LONG) ;

BOOL ReadFile  (HANDLE, HWND, HWND, POFSTRUCT, char *, BOOL) ;
BOOL WriteFile (HANDLE, HWND, HWND, POFSTRUCT, char *, BOOL) ;
BOOL PrintFile (HANDLE, HWND, HWND, char *) ;

LPSTR lstrrchr (LPSTR, char) ;

char szAppName  [] = "PopPad" ;
char szFileSpec [] = "*.TXT"  ;
char szUntitled [] = "(untitled)" ;

int PASCAL WinMain (HANDLE hInstance, HANDLE hPrevInstance,
                    LPSTR lpszCmdLine, int nCmdShow)
     {
     MSG      msg ;
     HWND     hwnd ;
     HANDLE   hAccel ;
     WNDCLASS wndclass ;

     if (!hPrevInstance)
         {
         wndclass.style         = CS_HREDRAW : CS_VREDRAW ;
         wndclass.lpfnWndProc    = WndProc ;
         wndclass.cbClsExtra     = 0 ;
         wndclass.cbWndExtra     = 0 ;
         wndclass.hInstance      = hInstance ;
         wndclass.hIcon          = LoadIcon (hInstance, szAppName) ;
         wndclass.hCursor        = LoadCursor (NULL, IDC_ARROW) ;
         wndclass.hbrBackground  = GetStockObject (WHITE_BRUSH) ;
         wndclass.lpszMenuName   = szAppName ;
         wndclass.lpszClassName  = szAppName ;

         RegisterClass (&wndclass) ;
         }

     hwnd = CreateWindow (szAppName, NULL,
                          WS_OVERLAPPEDWINDOW,
                          GetSystemMetrics (SM_CXSCREEN) / 4,
```

(continued)

458

```
                          GetSystemMetrics (SM_CYSCREEN) / 4,
                          GetSystemMetrics (SM_CXSCREEN) / 2,
                          GetSystemMetrics (SM_CYSCREEN) / 2,
                          NULL, NULL, hInstance, lpszCmdLine) ;

     ShowWindow (hwnd, nCmdShow) ;

     UpdateWindow (hwnd) ;

     hAccel = LoadAccelerators (hInstance, szAppName) ;

     while (GetMessage (&msg, NULL, 0, 0))
          {
          if (!TranslateAccelerator (hwnd, hAccel, &msg))
               {
               TranslateMessage (&msg) ;
               DispatchMessage (&msg) ;
               }
          }
     return msg.wParam ;
     }

BOOL FAR PASCAL AboutDlgProc (HWND hDlg, WORD message, WORD wParam, LONG lParam)
     {
     switch (message)
          {
          case WM_INITDIALOG :
               return TRUE ;

          case WM_COMMAND :
               switch (wParam)
                    {
                    case IDOK :
                         EndDialog (hDlg, 0) ;
                         return TRUE ;
                    }
               break ;
          }
     return FALSE ;
     }

void DoCaption (HWND hwnd, char *szFileName)
     {
     char szCaption [40] ;

     wsprintf (szCaption, "%s - %s", (LPSTR) szAppName,
               (LPSTR) (szFileName [0] ? szFileName : szUntitled)) ;

     SetWindowText (hwnd, szCaption) ;
     }
```

(continued)

```
short AskAboutSave (HWND hwnd, char *szFileName)
     {
     char  szBuffer [40] ;
     short nReturn ;

     wsprintf (szBuffer, "Save current changes: %s",
               (LPSTR) (szFileName [0] ? szFileName : szUntitled)) ;

     if (IDYES == (nReturn = MessageBox (hwnd, szBuffer, szAppName,
                                   MB_YESNOCANCEL : MB_ICONQUESTION)))

          if (!SendMessage (hwnd, WM_COMMAND, IDM_SAVE, OL))
               return IDCANCEL ;

     return nReturn ;
     }

long FAR PASCAL WndProc (HWND hwnd, WORD message, WORD wParam, LONG lParam)
     {
     static BOOL     bNeedSave = FALSE ;
     static char     szRealFileName [16] ;
     static FARPROC  lpfnAboutDlgProc ;
     static HANDLE   hInst ;
     static HWND     hwndEdit ;
     char            szFileName [16] ;
     LONG            lSelect ;
     OFSTRUCT        of ;
     WORD            wEnable ;

     switch (message)
          {
          case WM_CREATE :
               hInst = ((LPCREATESTRUCT) lParam)->hInstance ;
               lpfnAboutDlgProc = MakeProcInstance (AboutDlgProc, hInst) ;

               hwndEdit = CreateWindow ("edit", NULL,
                     WS_CHILD : WS_VISIBLE : WS_HSCROLL : WS_VSCROLL :
                          WS_BORDER : ES_LEFT : ES_MULTILINE :
                          ES_AUTOHSCROLL : ES_AUTOVSCROLL,
                     0, 0, 0, 0,
                     hwnd, EDITID, hInst, NULL) ;

               SendMessage (hwndEdit, EM_LIMITTEXT, 32000, OL) ;

               if (lstrlen (((LPCREATESTRUCT) lParam)->lpCreateParams))
                    {
                    OpenFile ((((LPCREATESTRUCT) lParam)->lpCreateParams,
                                   &of, OF_PARSE) ;
                    lstrcpy (szFileName,
                              AnsiNext (lstrrchr (of.szPathName, '\\'))) ;
```

(continued)

```
                 if (ReadFile (hInst, hwnd, hwndEdit, &of,
                           szFileName, FALSE))
                    lstrcpy (szRealFileName, szFileName) ;
               }
          DoCaption (hwnd, szRealFileName) ;
          return 0 ;

     case WM_SETFOCUS :
          SetFocus (hwndEdit) ;
          return 0 ;

     case WM_SIZE :
          MoveWindow (hwndEdit, 0, 0, LOWORD (lParam),
                                    HIWORD (lParam), TRUE) ;
          return 0 ;

     case WM_INITMENUPOPUP :
          if (lParam == 1)
               {
               EnableMenuItem (wParam, IDM_UNDO,
                    SendMessage (hwndEdit, EM_CANUNDO, 0, 0L) ?
                         MF_ENABLED : MF_GRAYED) ;

               EnableMenuItem (wParam, IDM_PASTE,
                    IsClipboardFormatAvailable (CF_TEXT) ?
                         MF_ENABLED : MF_GRAYED) ;

               lSelect = SendMessage (hwndEdit, EM_GETSEL, 0, 0L) ;

               if (HIWORD (lSelect) == LOWORD (lSelect))
                    wEnable = MF_GRAYED ;
               else
                    wEnable = MF_ENABLED ;

               EnableMenuItem (wParam, IDM_CUT,   wEnable) ;
               EnableMenuItem (wParam, IDM_COPY,  wEnable) ;
               EnableMenuItem (wParam, IDM_CLEAR, wEnable) ;
               }
          return 0 ;

     case WM_COMMAND :
          if (LOWORD (lParam) && wParam == EDITID)
               {
               switch (HIWORD (lParam))
                    {
                    case EN_UPDATE :
                         bNeedSave = TRUE ;
                         return 0 ;
```

(continued)

```
                    case EN_ERRSPACE :
                        MessageBox (hwnd, "Edit control out of space.",
                                szAppName, MB_OK : MB_ICONSTOP) ;
                        return 0 ;
                    }
            break ;
            }

        switch (wParam)
            {
            case IDM_NEW :
                if (bNeedSave && IDCANCEL ==
                        AskAboutSave (hwnd, szRealFileName))
                    return 0 ;

                SetWindowText (hwndEdit, "\0") ;
                szRealFileName [0] = '\0' ;
                DoCaption (hwnd, szRealFileName) ;
                bNeedSave = FALSE ;
                return 0 ;

            case IDM_OPEN :
                if (bNeedSave && IDCANCEL ==
                        AskAboutSave (hwnd, szRealFileName))
                    return 0 ;

                if (ReadFile (hInst, hwnd, hwndEdit, &of,
                        szFileName, TRUE))
                    {
                    lstrcpy (szRealFileName, szFileName) ;
                    DoCaption (hwnd, szRealFileName) ;
                    bNeedSave = FALSE ;
                    }

                return 0 ;

            case IDM_SAVE :
                if (szRealFileName [0])
                    {
                    if (WriteFile (hInst, hwnd, hwndEdit, &of,
                            szRealFileName, FALSE))
                        {
                        bNeedSave = FALSE ;
                        return 1 ;
                        }
                    return 0 ;
                    }
                                        // fall through
            case IDM_SAVEAS :
                if (WriteFile (hInst, hwnd, hwndEdit, &of,
                        szFileName, TRUE))
```

(continued)

```
                         {
                         lstrcpy (szRealFileName, szFileName) ;
                         DoCaption (hwnd, szFileName) ;
                         bNeedSave = FALSE ;
                         return 1 ;
                         }
               return 0 ;

          case IDM_PRINT :
               PrintFile (hInst, hwnd, hwndEdit,
                    szRealFileName [0] ? szRealFileName :
                                        szUntitled) ;
               return 0 ;

          case IDM_EXIT :
               SendMessage (hwnd, WM_CLOSE, 0, 0L) ;
               return 0 ;

          case IDM_ABOUT :
               DialogBox (hInst, "AboutBox", hwnd,
                         lpfnAboutDlgProc) ;
               return 0 ;

          case IDM_UNDO :
               SendMessage (hwndEdit, WM_UNDO, 0, 0L) ;
               return 0 ;

          case IDM_CUT :
               SendMessage (hwndEdit, WM_CUT, 0, 0L) ;
               return 0 ;

          case IDM_COPY :
               SendMessage (hwndEdit, WM_COPY, 0, 0L) ;
               return 0 ;

          case IDM_PASTE :
               SendMessage (hwndEdit, WM_PASTE, 0, 0L) ;
               return 0 ;

          case IDM_CLEAR :
               SendMessage (hwndEdit, WM_CLEAR, 0, 0L) ;
               return 0 ;

          case IDM_SELALL :
               SendMessage (hwndEdit, EM_SETSEL, 0,
                            MAKELONG (0, 32767)) ;
               return 0 ;
          }
     break ;
```

(continued)

463

```
          case WM_CLOSE :
               if (!bNeedSave !! IDCANCEL !=
                         AskAboutSave (hwnd, szRealFileName))
                    DestroyWindow (hwnd) ;

               return 0 ;

          case WM_QUERYENDSESSION :
               if (!bNeedSave !! IDCANCEL !=
                         AskAboutSave (hwnd, szRealFileName))
                    return 1L ;

               return 0 ;

          case WM_DESTROY :
               PostQuitMessage (0) ;
               return 0 ;
          }
     return DefWindowProc (hwnd, message, wParam, lParam) ;
     }
```

POPPADF.C

```
/*-------------------------------------
   POPPADF -- Popup Notepad File I/O
 -------------------------------------*/

#include <windows.h>
                                        // in FILEDLG.C

int DoFileOpenDlg (HANDLE, WORD, char *, char *, WORD,   char *, POFSTRUCT) ;
int DoFileSaveDlg (HANDLE, WORD, char *, char *, WORD *, char *, POFSTRUCT) ;

extern char szAppName [] ;              // in POPPAD.C
extern char szFileSpec [] ;

long FileLength (HANDLE hFile)
     {
     long   lCurrentPos = _llseek (hFile, 0L, 1) ;
     long   lFileLength = _llseek (hFile, 0L, 2) ;

     _llseek (hFile, lCurrentPos, 0) ;

     return lFileLength ;
     }
```

(continued)

```
void OkMessageBox (HWND hwnd, char *szString, char *szFileName)
     {
     char szBuffer [40] ;

     wsprintf (szBuffer, szString, (LPSTR) szFileName) ;

     MessageBox (hwnd, szBuffer, szAppName, MB_OK | MB_ICONEXCLAMATION) ;
     }

BOOL ReadFile (HANDLE hInstance, HWND hwnd, HWND hwndEdit, POFSTRUCT pof,
               char *szFileName, BOOL bAskName)
     {
     DWORD  dwLength ;
     HANDLE hFile, hTextBuffer ;
     LPSTR  lpTextBuffer ;

     if (bAskName)
          {
          if (!DoFileOpenDlg (hInstance, hwnd, szFileSpec, szFileSpec + 1,
                                         0x4010, szFileName, pof))
               return FALSE ;
          }

     if (-1 == (hFile = OpenFile (szFileName, pof, OF_READ | OF_REOPEN)))
          {
          OkMessageBox (hwnd, "Cannot open file %s", szFileName) ;
          return FALSE ;
          }

     if ((dwLength = FileLength (hFile)) >= 32000)
          {
          _lclose (hFile) ;
          OkMessageBox (hwnd, "File %s too large", szFileName) ;
          return FALSE ;
          }

     if (NULL == (hTextBuffer = GlobalAlloc (GHND, (DWORD) dwLength + 1)))
          {
          _lclose (hFile) ;
          OkMessageBox (hwnd, "Cannot allocate memory for %s", szFileName) ;
          return FALSE ;
          }

     lpTextBuffer = GlobalLock (hTextBuffer) ;
     _lread (hFile, lpTextBuffer, (WORD) dwLength) ;
     _lclose (hFile) ;
     lpTextBuffer [(WORD) dwLength] = '\0' ;

     SetWindowText (hwndEdit, lpTextBuffer) ;
     GlobalUnlock (hTextBuffer) ;
     GlobalFree (hTextBuffer) ;
```

(continued)

```
        return TRUE ;
        }

BOOL WriteFile (HANDLE hInstance, HWND hwnd, HWND hwndEdit, POFSTRUCT pof,
                char *szFileName, BOOL bAskName)
        {
        char    szBuffer [40] ;
        HANDLE  hFile, hTextBuffer ;
        NPSTR   npTextBuffer ;
        WORD    wStatus, wLength ;

        if (bAskName)
            {
            if (!DoFileSaveDlg (hInstance, hwnd, szFileSpec, szFileSpec + 1,
                                &wStatus, szFileName, pof))
                return FALSE ;

            if (wStatus == 1)
                {
                wsprintf (szBuffer, "Replace existing %s", (LPSTR) szFileName) ;
                if (IDNO == MessageBox (hwnd, szBuffer, szAppName,
                                        MB_YESNO : MB_ICONQUESTION))
                    return FALSE ;
                }
            }
        else
            OpenFile (szFileName, pof, OF_PARSE) ;

        if (-1 == (hFile = OpenFile (szFileName, pof, OF_CREATE : OF_REOPEN)))
            {
            OkMessageBox (hwnd, "Cannot create file %s", szFileName) ;
            return FALSE ;
            }

        wLength = GetWindowTextLength (hwndEdit) ;
        hTextBuffer = (HANDLE) SendMessage (hwndEdit, EM_GETHANDLE, 0, 0L) ;
        npTextBuffer = LocalLock (hTextBuffer) ;

        if (wLength != _lwrite (hFile, npTextBuffer, wLength))
            {
            _lclose (hFile) ;
            OkMessageBox (hwnd, "Cannot write file %s to disk", szFileName) ;
            return FALSE ;
            }

        _lclose (hFile) ;
        LocalUnlock (hTextBuffer) ;

        return TRUE ;
        }
```

POPPADP0.C

```
/*------------------------------------------------------------
   POPPADP0.C -- Popup Notepad Printing -- dummy functions
   ------------------------------------------------------------*/

#include <windows.h>

extern char szAppName [] ;                  // in POPPAD.C

BOOL FAR PASCAL PrintDlgProc (HWND hDlg, WORD message,
                             WORD wParam, LONG lParam)
    {
    return FALSE ;
    }

BOOL FAR PASCAL AbortProc (HDC hPrinterDC, short nCode)
    {
    return FALSE ;
    }

BOOL PrintFile (HANDLE hInstance, HWND hwnd, HWND hwndEdit, char *szFileName)
    {
    MessageBox (hwnd, "Printing not yet implemented", szAppName,
                MB_OK ! MB_ICONEXCLAMATION) ;
    return FALSE ;
    }
```

POPPAD.RC

```
/*---------------------------
   POPPAD.RC resource script
   ---------------------------*/

#include <windows.h>
#include "poppad.h"
#include "filedlg.h"

PopPad ICON "poppad.ico"

PopPad MENU
    {
    POPUP "&File"
        {
        MENUITEM "&New",            IDM_NEW
        MENUITEM "&Open...",        IDM_OPEN
        MENUITEM "&Save",           IDM_SAVE
```

(continued)

```
            MENUITEM "Save &As...",         IDM_SAVEAS
            MENUITEM SEPARATOR
            MENUITEM "&Print...",           IDM_PRINT
            MENUITEM SEPARATOR
            MENUITEM "E&xit",               IDM_EXIT
            }
        POPUP "&Edit"
            {
            MENUITEM "&Undo\tAlt+BkSp",     IDM_UNDO
            MENUITEM SEPARATOR
            MENUITEM "Cu&t\tShift+Del",     IDM_CUT
            MENUITEM "&Copy\tCtrl+Ins",     IDM_COPY
            MENUITEM "&Paste\tShift+Ins",   IDM_PASTE
            MENUITEM "C&lear\tDel",         IDM_CLEAR
            MENUITEM SEPARATOR
            MENUITEM "&Select All",         IDM_SELALL
            }
        POPUP "&Help"
            {
            MENUITEM "&About PopPad...",    IDM_ABOUT
            }
        }

PopPad ACCELERATORS
    {
    VK_DELETE, IDM_CUT,   VIRTKEY, SHIFT
    VK_INSERT, IDM_COPY,  VIRTKEY, CONTROL
    VK_INSERT, IDM_PASTE, VIRTKEY, SHIFT
    VK_DELETE, IDM_CLEAR, VIRTKEY
    }

AboutBox DIALOG  20, 20, 160, 80
    STYLE WS_POPUP : WS_DLGFRAME
    {
    CTEXT "PopPad"                              -1,  0, 12, 160,  8
    ICON  "PopPad"                              -1,  8,  8,  0,  0
    CTEXT "Popup Editor for Microsoft Windows" -1,  0, 36, 160,  8
    CTEXT "Copyright (c) Charles Petzold, 1990" -1,  0, 48, 160,  8
    DEFPUSHBUTTON "Ok"                          IDOK, 64, 60,  32, 14, WS_GROUP
    }

PrintDlgBox DIALOG 20, 20, 100, 76
    STYLE WS_POPUP : WS_CAPTION : WS_SYSMENU : WS_VISIBLE
    CAPTION "PopPad"
    {
    CTEXT "Sending",                -1,  0, 10, 100,  8
    CTEXT "",                   IDD_FNAME,  0, 20, 100,  8
    CTEXT "to print spooler.",      -1,  0, 30, 100,  8
    DEFPUSHBUTTON  "Cancel",    IDCANCEL, 34, 50,  32, 14, WS_GROUP
    }

rcinclude filedlg.dlg
```

POPPAD.H

```
/*---------------------
    POPPAD.H header file
---------------------*/

#define IDM_NEW      1
#define IDM_OPEN     2
#define IDM_SAVE     3
#define IDM_SAVEAS   4

#define IDM_PRINT    5

#define IDM_EXIT     6
#define IDM_ABOUT    7

#define IDM_UNDO     8
#define IDM_CUT      9
#define IDM_COPY    10
#define IDM_PASTE   11
#define IDM_CLEAR   12
#define IDM_SELALL  13
```

POPPAD.ICO

POPPAD3.DEF

```
;------------------------------------
; POPPAD3.DEF module definition file
;------------------------------------

NAME            POPPAD3

DESCRIPTION     'Popup Editor Version 3 (c) Charles Petzold, 1990'
EXETYPE         WINDOWS
STUB            'WINSTUB.EXE'
```

(continued)

```
CODE          PRELOAD MOVEABLE DISCARDABLE
DATA          PRELOAD MOVEABLE MULTIPLE
HEAPSIZE      1024
STACKSIZE     8192
EXPORTS       WndProc
              AboutDlgProc
              FileOpenDlgProc
              FileSaveDlgProc
              PrintDlgProc
              AbortProc
```

As you'll recall, the POPPAD series of programs uses a multiline edit control to do all the editing. The POPPADF.C file serves as an intermediary between the main POPPAD.C program and the functions in FILEDLG.C. The *ReadFile* function in POPPADF.C calls *DoFile-OpenDlgProc* and reads the file into a global memory block. *ReadFile* is responsible for reporting if the file is too large or if memory can't be allocated for the file. When the file is read into a global memory block, it's transferred to the edit window using *SetWindowText*.

WriteFile calls *DoFileSaveDlgProc* to obtain the name of the file. This function is responsible for asking the user if it's acceptable to replace an existing file by that name. *WriteFile* obtains the handle to the edit control's buffer, locks it, and writes the file to the disk directly from that buffer.

This doesn't leave the POPPAD.C module much to do in the way of file I/O. But note these facts:

- In *WinMain*, the *lpszCmdLine* address is used as the last field of the *CreateWindow* call. This string might contain a filename that was entered as a parameter to POPPAD3 when the program was executed. During processing of the WM_CREATE message in *WndProc*, this filename is passed to *ReadFile* with the *bAskName* parameter set to FALSE so that *ReadFile* won't call *DoFileOpenDlgProc*.

- Much of the new logic in *WndProc* involves keeping track of changes to the text in the edit control. Whenever this text changes, the control sends an EN_UPDATE notification message to *WndProc*, which then sets *bNeedSave* to TRUE. When the user wants to open a new file or end the program, *WndProc* must check the *bNeedSave* variable. If it is TRUE, then the program calls *AskAboutSave*, which displays a message box that asks whether the user wants to save the current changes. When a file is saved, *bNeedSave* is set to FALSE.

- POPPAD3's caption displays the name of the currently loaded file. If no filename is available (for instance, when the program is first executed), then the *DoCaption* function in POPPAD3 causes the character string "(untitled)" to be displayed.

We are not yet finished with the POPPAD programs. In Chapter 15 some of these files (POPPAD.C, POPPADF.C, POPPAD.RC, POPPAD.H, and POPPAD.ICO) will be used in the final POPPAD program. At that time a new file (POPPADP.C) will be substituted for POPPADP0.C to add logic to print files.

MODELESS DIALOG BOXES

At the beginning of this chapter, I explained that dialog boxes can be either "modal" or "modeless." So far we've been looking at modal dialog boxes, the more common of the two types. Modal dialog boxes (except for system modal dialog boxes) allow the user to switch between the dialog box and other programs. However, the user cannot switch to another window in the program until the modal dialog box is destroyed. Modeless dialog boxes allow the user to switch between the dialog box and the window that created it as well as between the dialog box and other programs. The modeless dialog box is thus more akin to the regular popup windows that your program might create.

Modeless dialog boxes are preferred when the user would find it convenient to keep the dialog box displayed for a while. For instance, the Windows WRITE program uses modeless dialog boxes for the Find and Change dialogs. If the Find dialog box were modal, the user would have to choose Find from the menu, enter the string to be found, end the dialog box to return to the document, and then repeat the entire process to search for another occurrence of the same string. Allowing the user to switch between the document and the dialog box is much more convenient.

As you've seen, modal dialog boxes are created using *DialogBox*. The function returns only after the dialog box is destroyed. It returns the value specified in the second parameter of the *EndDialog* call that was used within the dialog box procedure to terminate the dialog box. Modeless dialog boxes are created using *CreateDialog*. This function takes the same parameters as *DialogBox*:

```
hDlgModeless = CreateDialog (hInstance, lpszTemplate, hwndParent,
                                lpfnDialogProc) ;
```

The difference is that the *CreateDialog* function returns immediately with the window handle of the dialog box. Normally, you store this window handle in a global variable.

Although the use of the names *DialogBox* with modal dialog boxes and *CreateDialog* with modeless dialog boxes may seem arbitrary, you can remember which is which by keeping in mind that modeless dialog boxes are similar to normal windows. *CreateDialog* should remind you of the *CreateWindow* function, which creates normal windows.

Differences Between Modal and Modeless Dialog Boxes

Working with modeless dialog boxes is similar to working with modal dialog boxes, but there are several important differences:

- Modeless dialog boxes usually include a caption bar and a system menu box. The STYLE statement in the dialog box template for a modeless dialog box will look something like this:

```
STYLE WS_POPUP : WS_CAPTION : WS_SYSMENU : WS_VISIBLE
```

The caption bar and system menu allow the user to move the modeless dialog box to another area of the display using either the mouse or the keyboard. You don't normally provide a caption bar and system menu with a modal dialog box, because the user can't do anything in the underlying window anyway.

- Note that the WS_VISIBLE style is included in our sample STYLE statement. If you omit WS_VISIBLE, you must call *ShowWindow* after the *CreateDialog* call:

```
hDlgModeless = CreateDialog ( . . . ) ;
ShowWindow (hDlgModeless, SW_SHOW) ;
```

If you neither include WS_VISIBLE nor call *ShowWindow*, the modeless dialog box will not be displayed. In overlooking this fact, programmers who have mastered modal dialog boxes often experience difficulties when they first try to create a modeless dialog box.

- Unlike messages to modal dialog boxes and message boxes, messages to modeless dialog boxes come through your program's message queue. The message queue must be altered to pass these messages to the dialog box window procedure. Here's how you do it: When you use *CreateDialog* to create a modeless dialog box, you should save the dialog box handle returned from the call in a global variable (for instance, *hDlgModeless*). Change your message loop to look like this:

```
while (GetMessage (&msg, NULL, 0, 0))
    {
    if (hDlgModeless == 0 :: !IsDialogMessage (hDlgModeless, &msg))
        {
        TranslateMessage (&msg) ;
        DispatchMessage  (&msg) ;
        }
    }
```

If the message is intended for the modeless dialog box, then *IsDialogMessage* sends it to the dialog box window procedure and returns TRUE (nonzero); otherwise, it returns FALSE (0). The *TranslateMessage* and *DispatchMessage* functions should be called only if *hDlgModeless* is 0 or if the message is not for the dialog box.

If you use keyboard accelerators for your program's window, then the message loop looks like this:

```
while (GetMessage (&msg, NULL, 0, 0))
     {
     if (hDlgModeless == 0 || !IsDialogMessage (hDlgModeless, &msg))
          {
          if (!TranslateAccelerator (hwnd, hAccel, &msg))
               {
               TranslateMessage (&msg) ;
               DispatchMessage  (&msg) ;
               }
          }
     }
```

Because global variables are initialized to 0, *hDlgModeless* will be 0 until the dialog box is created, thus ensuring that *IsDialogMessage* is not called with an invalid window handle. You must take the same precaution when you destroy the modeless dialog box as explained below.

The *hDlgModeless* variable can also be used by other parts of the program as a test of the existence of the modeless dialog box. Other windows in the program can send messages to the dialog box while *hDlgModeless* is not equal to 0.

■ Use *DestroyWindow* rather than *EndDialog* to end a modeless dialog box. When you call *DestroyWindow*, set the *hDlgModeless* global variable to 0.

The user customarily terminates a modeless dialog box by choosing Close from the system menu. Although the Close option is enabled, the dialog box window procedure within Windows does not process the WM_CLOSE message. You must do this yourself in the dialog box procedure:

```
case WM_CLOSE :
     DestroyWindow (hDlg) ;
     hDlgModeless = 0 ;
     break ;
```

Note the difference between these two window handles: The *hDlg* parameter to *Destroy-Window* is the parameter passed to the dialog box procedure; *hDlgModeless* is the global variable returned from *CreateDialog* that you test within the message loop.

You can also allow a user to close a modeless dialog box using push buttons. Use the same logic as for the WM_CLOSE message. Any information that the dialog box must "return" to the window that created it can be stored in global variables.

The New COLORS Program

The COLORS1 program described in Chapter 6 created nine child windows to display three scroll bars and six text items. At that time, the program was one of the more complex we

had developed. Converting COLORS1 to use a modeless dialog box makes the program—
and particularly its *WndProc* function—almost ridiculously simple. The revised COLORS2
program is shown in Figure 10-9.

COLORS2.MAK

```
#----------------------
# COLORS2.MAK make file
#----------------------

colors2.exe : colors2.obj colors2.def colors2.res
     link colors2, /align:16, NUL, /nod slibcew libw, colors2
     rc colors2.res

colors2.obj : colors2.c
     cl -c -Gsw -Ow -W2 -Zp colors2.c

colors2.res : colors2.rc
     rc -r colors2.rc
```

COLORS2.C

```
/*----------------------------------------------------------
   COLORS2.C -- Version using Modeless Dialog Box Version
                 (c) Charles Petzold, 1990
   ----------------------------------------------------------*/

#include <windows.h>

long FAR PASCAL WndProc     (HWND, WORD, WORD, LONG) ;
BOOL FAR PASCAL ColorScrDlg (HWND, WORD, WORD, LONG) ;

HWND hDlgModeless ;

int PASCAL WinMain (HANDLE hInstance, HANDLE hPrevInstance,
                LPSTR lpszCmdLine, int nCmdShow)
     {
     static char szAppName[] = "Colors2" ;
     HWND        hwnd ;
     MSG         msg ;
     WNDCLASS    wndclass ;

     if (hPrevInstance)
          return FALSE ;

     wndclass.style        = CS_HREDRAW | CS_VREDRAW ;
     wndclass.lpfnWndProc  = WndProc ;
```

Figure 10-9. *The COLORS2 program.*   *(continued)*

```
        wndclass.cbClsExtra    = 0 ;
        wndclass.cbWndExtra    = 0 ;
        wndclass.hInstance     = hInstance ;
        wndclass.hIcon         = NULL ;
        wndclass.hCursor       = LoadCursor (NULL, IDC_ARROW) ;
        wndclass.hbrBackground = CreateSolidBrush (OL) ;
        wndclass.lpszMenuName  = NULL ;
        wndclass.lpszClassName = szAppName ;

        RegisterClass (&wndclass) ;

        hwnd = CreateWindow (szAppName, "Color Scroll",
                        WS_OVERLAPPEDWINDOW | WS_CLIPCHILDREN,
                        CW_USEDEFAULT, CW_USEDEFAULT,
                        CW_USEDEFAULT, CW_USEDEFAULT,
                        NULL, NULL, hInstance, NULL) ;

        ShowWindow (hwnd, nCmdShow) ;
        UpdateWindow (hwnd) ;

        hDlgModeless = CreateDialog (hInstance, "ColorScrDlg", hwnd,
                        MakeProcInstance (ColorScrDlg, hInstance)) ;

        while (GetMessage (&msg, NULL, 0, 0))
            {
            if (hDlgModeless == 0 || !IsDialogMessage (hDlgModeless, &msg))
                {
                TranslateMessage (&msg) ;
                DispatchMessage  (&msg) ;
                }
            }
        return msg.wParam ;
        }

BOOL FAR PASCAL ColorScrDlg (HWND hDlg, WORD message, WORD wParam, LONG lParam)
        {
        static short color [3] ;
        HWND          hwndParent, hCtrl ;
        short         nCtrlID, nIndex ;

        switch (message)
            {
            case WM_INITDIALOG :
                for (nCtrlID = 10 ; nCtrlID < 13 ; nCtrlID++)
                    {
                    hCtrl = GetDlgItem (hDlg, nCtrlID) ;
                    SetScrollRange (hCtrl, SB_CTL, 0, 255, FALSE) ;
                    SetScrollPos   (hCtrl, SB_CTL, 0, FALSE) ;
                    }
                return TRUE ;
```

(continued)

```
        case WM_VSCROLL :
            hCtrl  = HIWORD (lParam) ;
            nCtrlID = GetWindowWord (hCtrl, GWW_ID) ;
            nIndex = nCtrlID - 10 ;
            hwndParent = GetParent (hDlg) ;

            switch (wParam)
                {
                case SB_PAGEDOWN :
                    color [nIndex] += 15 ;          // fall through
                case SB_LINEDOWN :
                    color [nIndex] = min (255, color [nIndex] + 1) ;

                    break ;
                case SB_PAGEUP :
                    color [nIndex] -= 15 ;          // fall through
                case SB_LINEUP :
                    color [nIndex] = max (0, color [nIndex] - 1) ;
                    break ;
                case SB_TOP :
                    color [nIndex] = 0 ;
                    break ;
                case SB_BOTTOM :
                    color [nIndex] = 255 ;
                    break ;
                case SB_THUMBPOSITION :
                case SB_THUMBTRACK :
                    color [nIndex] = LOWORD (lParam) ;
                    break ;
                default :
                    return FALSE ;
                }
            SetScrollPos  (hCtrl, SB_CTL,      color [nIndex], TRUE) ;
            SetDlgItemInt (hDlg,  nCtrlID + 3, color [nIndex], FALSE) ;

            DeleteObject (GetClassWord (hwndParent, GCW_HBRBACKGROUND)) ;
            SetClassWord (hwndParent, GCW_HBRBACKGROUND,
                CreateSolidBrush (RGB (color [0], color [1], color [2]))) ;

            InvalidateRect (hwndParent, NULL, TRUE) ;
            return TRUE ;
        }
    return FALSE ;
    }

long FAR PASCAL WndProc (HWND hwnd, WORD message, WORD wParam, LONG lParam)
    {
    switch (message)
        {
        case WM_DESTROY :
            DeleteObject (GetClassWord (hwnd, GCW_HBRBACKGROUND)) ;
```

(continued)

```
                    PostQuitMessage (0) ;
                    return 0 ;
            }
     return DefWindowProc (hwnd, message, wParam, lParam) ;
     }
```

COLORS2.RC

```
/*----------------------------
   COLORS2.RC resource script
  ---------------------------*/

#include <windows.h>

#define SBS_VERT_TAB (SBS_VERT ! WS_TABSTOP)

ColorScrDlg DIALOG  8, 16, 124, 132
     STYLE WS_POPUP ! WS_CAPTION ! WS_SYSMENU ! WS_VISIBLE
     CAPTION "Color Scroll Scrollbars"
     {
     CONTROL "&Red",   -1, "static",    SS_CENTER,     10,   4, 24,   8
     CONTROL "",       10, "scrollbar", SBS_VERT_TAB, 10,  16, 24, 100
     CONTROL "0",      13, "static",    SS_CENTER,     10, 120, 24,   8
     CONTROL "&Green", -1, "static",    SS_CENTER,     50,   4, 24,   8
     CONTROL "",       11, "scrollbar", SBS_VERT_TAB, 50,  16, 24, 100
     CONTROL "0",      14, "static",    SS_CENTER,     50, 120, 24,   8
     CONTROL "&Blue",  -1, "static",    SS_CENTER,     90,   4, 24,   8
     CONTROL "",       12, "scrollbar", SBS_VERT_TAB, 90,  16, 24, 100
     CONTROL "0",      15, "static",    SS_CENTER,     90, 120, 24,   8
     }
```

COLORS2.DEF

```
;-------------------------------------
; COLORS2.DEF module definition file
;-------------------------------------

NAME            COLORS2

DESCRIPTION     'Color Scroll with Dialog Box (c) Charles Petzold, 1990'
EXETYPE         WINDOWS
STUB            'WINSTUB.EXE'
CODE            PRELOAD MOVEABLE DISCARDABLE
DATA            PRELOAD MOVEABLE MULTIPLE
HEAPSIZE        1024
STACKSIZE       8192
EXPORTS         WndProc
                ColorScrDlg
```

Although the original COLORS1 program displayed scroll bars that were based on the size of the window, the new version keeps them at a constant size within the modeless dialog box, as shown in Figure 10-10.

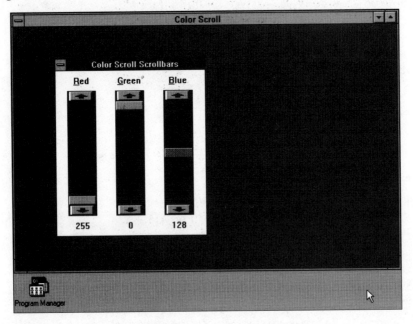

Figure 10-10. *The COLORS2 display.*

The dialog box template in COLORS2.RC uses CONTROL statements for all nine child windows in the dialog box. The modeless dialog box is created in COLORS2's *WinMain* function following the *ShowWindow* call for the program's main window. Note that the window style for the main window includes WS_CLIPCHILDREN, which allows the program to repaint the main window without erasing the dialog box.

The dialog box window handle returned from *CreateDialog* is stored in the global variable *hDlgModeless* and tested during the message loop, as described above. In this program, however, it isn't necessary to store the handle in a global variable or to test the value before calling *IsDialogMessage*. The message loop could have been written like this:

```
while (GetMessage (&msg, NULL, 0, 0))
     {
     if (!IsDialogMessage (hDlgModeless, &msg))
          {
          TranslateMessage (&msg) ;
          DispatchMessage  (&msg) ;
          }
     }
```

478

Because the dialog box is created before the program enters the message loop and the dialog box is not destroyed until the program terminates, the value of *hDlgModeless* will always be valid. I included the logic in case you want to add some code to the dialog box window procedure to destroy the dialog box:

```
case WM_CLOSE :
     DestroyWindow (hDlg) ;
     hDlgModeless = 0 ;
     break ;
```

In the original COLORS1 program, *SetWindowText* set the values of the three numeric labels after converting the integers to text with *itoa*. The code looked like this:

```
SetWindowText (hwndValue[n], itoa (color[n], szBuffer, 10)) ;
```

The value of *n* was the ID number of the current scroll bar being processed, and *hChValue* was an array containing the window handles of the three static text child windows for the numeric values of the colors.

The new version uses *SetDlgItemInt* to set each text field of each child window to a number:

```
SetDlgItemInt (hDlg, nCtrlID + 3, color [nCtrlID], FALSE) ;
```

(Although *SetDlgItemInt* and its companion, *GetDlgItemInt*, are most often used with edit controls, they can also be used to set the text field of other controls, such as static text controls.) The *nCtrlID* variable is the ID number of the scroll bar; adding 3 to the number converts it to the ID for the corresponding numeric label. The third parameter is the color value. Normally, the fourth parameter would be set to TRUE to indicate that numbers greater than 32,767 should be displayed as negatives. For this program, however, the values range from 0 to 255, so the fourth parameter has no effect.

In the process of converting COLORS1 to COLORS2, we passed more and more of the work to Windows. The earlier version called *CreateWindow* 10 times; the new version calls *CreateWindow* once and *CreateDialog* once. But if you think that we've reduced our *CreateWindow* calls to a minimum, get a load of this next program.

HEXCALC: Window or Dialog Box?

Perhaps the epitome of lazy programming is the HEXCALC program, shown in Figure 10-11 beginning on the following page. This program doesn't call *CreateWindow* at all, never processes WM_PAINT messages, never obtains a device context, and never processes mouse messages. Yet it manages to incorporate a 10-function hexadecimal calculator with a full keyboard and mouse interface in fewer than 150 lines of source code. The calculator is shown in Figure 10-12 on page 485.

HEXCALC.MAK

```
#----------------------
# HEXCALC.MAK make file
#----------------------

hexcalc.exe: hexcalc.obj hexcalc.def hexcalc.res
     link hexcalc, /align:16, NUL, /nod slibcew libw, hexcalc
     rc hexcalc.res

hexcalc.obj: hexcalc.c
     cl -c -Gsw -Ow -W2 -Zp hexcalc.c

hexcalc.res : hexcalc.rc hexcalc.ico
     rc -r hexcalc.rc
```

HEXCALC.C

```c
/*------------------------------------------
   HEXCALC.C -- Hexadecimal Calculator
                (c) Charles Petzold, 1990
   ----------------------------------------*/

#include <windows.h>
#include <limits.h>
#include <stdlib.h>
#include <string.h>
#include <ctype.h>

long FAR PASCAL WndProc (HWND, WORD, WORD, LONG) ;

int PASCAL WinMain (HANDLE hInstance, HANDLE hPrevInstance,
                    LPSTR lpszCmdLine, int nCmdShow)
     {
     static char szAppName [] = "HexCalc" ;
     HWND        hwnd ;
     MSG         msg ;
     WNDCLASS    wndclass ;

     if (!hPrevInstance)
          {
          wndclass.style          = CS_HREDRAW : CS_VREDRAW ;
          wndclass.lpfnWndProc     = WndProc ;
          wndclass.cbClsExtra      = 0 ;
          wndclass.cbWndExtra      = DLGWINDOWEXTRA ;
          wndclass.hInstance       = hInstance ;
          wndclass.hIcon           = LoadIcon (hInstance, szAppName) ;
```

Figure 10-11. *The HEXCALC program.*   *(continued)*

```
            wndclass.hCursor        = LoadCursor (NULL, IDC_ARROW) ;
            wndclass.hbrBackground  = COLOR_WINDOW + 1 ;
            wndclass.lpszMenuName   = NULL ;
            wndclass.lpszClassName  = szAppName ;

            RegisterClass (&wndclass) ;
            }

      hwnd = CreateDialog (hInstance, szAppName, 0, NULL) ;

      ShowWindow (hwnd, nCmdShow) ;

      while (GetMessage (&msg, NULL, 0, 0))
            {
            TranslateMessage (&msg) ;
            DispatchMessage (&msg) ;
            }
      return msg.wParam ;
      }

void ShowNumber (HWND hwnd, DWORD dwNumber)
      {
      char szBuffer [20] ;

      SetDlgItemText (hwnd, VK_ESCAPE, strupr (ltoa (dwNumber, szBuffer, 16))) ;
      }

DWORD CalcIt (DWORD dwFirstNum, short nOperation, DWORD dwNum)
      {
      switch (nOperation)
          {
          case '=' : return dwNum ;
          case '+' : return dwFirstNum +  dwNum ;
          case '-' : return dwFirstNum -  dwNum ;
          case '*' : return dwFirstNum *  dwNum ;
          case '&' : return dwFirstNum &  dwNum ;
          case '!' : return dwFirstNum !  dwNum ;
          case '^' : return dwFirstNum ^  dwNum ;
          case '<' : return dwFirstNum << dwNum ;
          case '>' : return dwFirstNum >> dwNum ;
          case '/' : return dwNum ? dwFirstNum / dwNum : ULONG_MAX ;
          case '%' : return dwNum ? dwFirstNum % dwNum : ULONG_MAX ;
          default  : return 0L ;
          }
      }

long FAR PASCAL WndProc (HWND hwnd, WORD message, WORD wParam, LONG lParam)
      {
      static BOOL  bNewNumber = TRUE ;
      static DWORD dwNumber, dwFirstNum ;
```

(continued)

```
        static short nOperation = '=' ;
        HWND        hButton ;

        switch (message)
            {
            case WM_KEYDOWN :                       // left arrow --> backspace
                if (wParam != VK_LEFT)
                    break ;
                wParam = VK_BACK ;
                                                    // fall through
            case WM_CHAR :
                if ((wParam = toupper (wParam)) == VK_RETURN)
                    wParam = '=' ;

                if (hButton = GetDlgItem (hwnd, wParam))
                    {
                    SendMessage (hButton, BM_SETSTATE, 1, 0L) ;
                    SendMessage (hButton, BM_SETSTATE, 0, 0L) ;
                    }
                else
                    {
                    MessageBeep (0) ;
                    break ;
                    }
                                                    // fall through
            case WM_COMMAND :
                SetFocus (hwnd) ;

                if (wParam == VK_BACK)                          // backspace
                    ShowNumber (hwnd, dwNumber /= 16) ;

                else if (wParam == VK_ESCAPE)                   // escape
                    ShowNumber (hwnd, dwNumber = 0L) ;

                else if (isxdigit (wParam))            // hex digit
                    {
                    if (bNewNumber)
                        {
                        dwFirstNum = dwNumber ;
                        dwNumber = 0L ;
                        }
                    bNewNumber = FALSE ;

                    if (dwNumber <= ULONG_MAX >> 4)
                        ShowNumber (hwnd, dwNumber = 16 * dwNumber + wParam -
                            (isdigit (wParam) ? '0' : 'A' - 10)) ;
                    else
                        MessageBeep (0) ;
                    }
                else                                           // operation
```

(continued)

```
                    {
                    if (!bNewNumber)
                         ShowNumber (hwnd, dwNumber =
                              CalcIt (dwFirstNum, nOperation, dwNumber)) ;
                    bNewNumber = TRUE ;
                    nOperation = wParam ;
                    }
               return 0 ;

          case WM_DESTROY :
               PostQuitMessage (0) ;
               return 0 ;
          }
     return DefWindowProc (hwnd, message, wParam, lParam) ;
     }
```

HEXCALC.RC

```
/*---------------------------
   HEXCALC.RC resource script
   ---------------------------*/

#include <windows.h>

HexCalc ICON hexcalc.ico

HexCalc DIALOG 32768, 0, 102, 122
     STYLE WS_OVERLAPPED : WS_CAPTION : WS_SYSMENU : WS_MINIMIZEBOX
     CLASS "HexCalc"
     CAPTION "Hex Calculator"
     {
     PUSHBUTTON "D",      68,  8,  24, 14, 14
     PUSHBUTTON "A",      65,  8,  40, 14, 14
     PUSHBUTTON "7",      55,  8,  56, 14, 14
     PUSHBUTTON "4",      52,  8,  72, 14, 14
     PUSHBUTTON "1",      49,  8,  88, 14, 14
     PUSHBUTTON "0",      48,  8, 104, 14, 14
     PUSHBUTTON "0",      27, 26,   4, 50, 14
     PUSHBUTTON "E",      69, 26,  24, 14, 14
     PUSHBUTTON "B",      66, 26,  40, 14, 14
     PUSHBUTTON "8",      56, 26,  56, 14, 14
     PUSHBUTTON "5",      53, 26,  72, 14, 14
     PUSHBUTTON "2",      50, 26,  88, 14, 14
     PUSHBUTTON "Back",    8, 26, 104, 32, 14
     PUSHBUTTON "C",      67, 44,  40, 14, 14
     PUSHBUTTON "F",      70, 44,  24, 14, 14
     PUSHBUTTON "9",      57, 44,  56, 14, 14
```

(continued)

```
PUSHBUTTON "6",      54, 44,  72, 14, 14
PUSHBUTTON "3",      51, 44,  88, 14, 14
PUSHBUTTON "+",      43, 62,  24, 14, 14
PUSHBUTTON "-",      45, 62,  40, 14, 14
PUSHBUTTON "*",      42, 62,  56, 14, 14
PUSHBUTTON "/",      47, 62,  72, 14, 14
PUSHBUTTON "%",      37, 62,  88, 14, 14
PUSHBUTTON "Equals", 61, 62, 104, 32, 14
PUSHBUTTON "&&",     38, 80,  24, 14, 14
PUSHBUTTON "|",     124, 80,  40, 14, 14
PUSHBUTTON "^",      94, 80,  56, 14, 14
PUSHBUTTON "<",      60, 80,  72, 14, 14
PUSHBUTTON ">",      62, 80,  88, 14, 14
}
```

HEXCALC.ICO

HEXCALC.DEF

```
;-------------------------------------
; HEXCALC.DEF module definition file
;-------------------------------------

NAME          HEXCALC

DESCRIPTION   'Hexadecimal Calculator (c) Charles Petzold, 1990'
EXETYPE       WINDOWS
STUB          'WINSTUB.EXE'
CODE          PRELOAD MOVEABLE DISCARDABLE
DATA          PRELOAD MOVEABLE MULTIPLE
HEAPSIZE      1024
STACKSIZE     8192
EXPORTS       WndProc
```

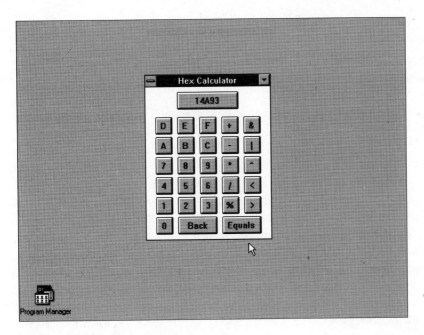

Figure 10-12. *The HEXCALC display.*

HEXCALC is a normal infix notation calculator that uses C notation for the operations. It works with unsigned 32-bit integers and does addition, subtraction, multiplication, division, and remainders; bitwise AND, OR, and exclusive OR operations; and left and right bit shifts. Division by 0 causes the result to be set to FFFFFFFF.

You can use either the mouse or keyboard with HEXCALC. You begin by "clicking in" or typing the first number (up to eight hexadecimal digits), then the operation, and then the second number. You can then show the result by clicking the Equals button or by pressing either the Equals key or Enter key. To correct your entries, you use the Back button or the Backspace or Left Arrow key. Click the "display" box or press the Esc key to clear the current entry.

What's so strange about HEXCALC is that the window displayed on the screen seems to be a hybrid of a normal overlapped window and a modeless dialog box. On the one hand, all the messages to HEXCALC are processed in a function called *WndProc* that appears to be a normal window procedure. The function returns a long, it processes the WM_DESTROY message, and it calls *DefWindowProc* just like a normal window procedure. On the other hand, the window is created in *WinMain* with a call to *CreateDialog* using a dialog box template from HEXCALC.RC. So is HEXCALC a normal overlapped window or a modeless dialog box?

The simple answer is that a dialog box *is* a window. Normally, Windows uses its own internal window procedure to process messages to a dialog box popup window. Windows then passes these messages to a dialog box procedure within the program that creates the dialog box. In HEXCALC we are forcing Windows to use the dialog box template to create a popup window, but we're processing messages to that window ourselves.

A closer look at HEXCALC.RC will reveal how this is done. The top of the dialog box template looks like this:

```
HexCalc DIALOG 32768, 0, 102, 122
        STYLE WS_OVERLAPPED ¦ WS_CAPTION ¦ WS_SYSMENU ¦ WS_MINIMIZEBOX
        CLASS "HexCalc"
        CAPTION "Hex Calculator"
```

Notice the identifiers such as WS_OVERLAPPED and WS_MINIMIZEBOX, which we might use to create a normal window using a *CreateWindow* call. The CLASS statement is the crucial difference between this dialog box and the others we've created so far. When we omitted this statement in previous dialog box templates, Windows registered a window class for the dialog box and used its own window procedure to process the dialog box messages. The inclusion of a CLASS statement here tells Windows to send the messages elsewhere—specifically, to the window procedure specified in the "HexCalc" window class.

The "HexCalc" window class is registered in the *WinMain* function of HEXCALC, just like a window class for a normal window. However, note this very important difference: The *cbWndExtra* field of the WNDCLASS structure is set to DLGWINDOWEXTRA. This is essential for dialog procedures that you register yourself.

After registering the window class, *WinMain* calls *CreateDialog*:

```
hwnd = CreateDialog (hInstance, szAppName, 0, NULL) ;
```

The second parameter (the string "HexCalc") is the name of the dialog box template. The third parameter, which is normally the window handle of the parent window, is set to 0 because the window has no parent. The last parameter, which is normally the address of the dialog procedure, isn't required because Windows won't be processing the messages and hence can't send them to a dialog procedure.

This *CreateDialog* call in conjunction with the dialog box template is effectively translated by Windows into a *CreateWindow* call that does the equivalent of this:

```
hwnd = CreateWindow ("HexCalc", "Hex Calculator",
        WS_OVERLAPPED ¦ WS_CAPTION ¦ WS_SYSMENU ¦ WS_MINIMIZEBOX
        CW_USEDEFAULT, CW_USEDEFAULT,
        102 * 4 / cxChar, 122 * 8 / cyChar,
        NULL, NULL, hInstance, NULL) ;
```

The *xChar* and *yChar* variables are the width and height of a system font character.

We reap an enormous benefit from letting Windows make this *CreateWindow* call: Windows will not stop at creating the 1 popup window but will also call *CreateWindow* for all 29 child window push-button controls defined in the dialog box template. All these controls send WM_COMMAND messages to the window procedure of the parent window, which is none other than *WndProc*. This is an excellent technique for creating a window that must contain a collection of child windows.

Creatively Using Control IDs

HEXCALC contains no header file with identifiers for all the ID numbers of the child window controls in the dialog box template. We can dispense with this file because the ID number for each of the push-button controls is set to the ASCII code of the text that appears in the control. This means that *WndProc* can treat WM_COMMAND messages and WM_CHAR messages in much the same way. In each case, *wParam* is the ASCII code of the button.

Of course, a little massaging of the keyboard messages is necessary. *WndProc* traps WM_KEYDOWN messages to translate the Left Arrow key to a Backspace key. During processing of WM_CHAR messages, *WndProc* converts the character code to uppercase and the Enter key to the ASCII code for the Equals key.

The validity of a WM_CHAR message is checked by calling *GetDlgItem*. If the *GetDlgItem* function returns 0, then the keyboard character is not one of the ID numbers defined in the dialog box template. If the character is one of the IDs, however, the appropriate button is flashed by sending it a couple of BM_SETSTATE messages:

```
if (hButton = GetDlgItem (hwnd, wParam))
    {
    SendMessage (hButton, BM_SETSTATE, 1, 0L) ;
    SendMessage (hButton, BM_SETSTATE, 0, 0L) ;
    }
```

This adds a nice touch to HEXCALC's keyboard interface, and with a minimum of effort.

When *WndProc* processes WM_COMMAND messages, it always sets the input focus to the parent window:

```
case WM_COMMAND :
    SetFocus (hwnd) ;
```

Otherwise, the input focus would be shifted to one of the buttons whenever it was clicked with the mouse.

USING THE DIALOG UTILITY

When you sit down to create a dialog box template, you'll discover that it's not quite as easy as it looks. Dialog boxes are an important part of your program, and the controls should be clearly and logically organized. But the process of placing and sizing these controls is mostly a matter of trial and error. You'll save yourself a lot of time and frustration by using the DIALOG program included with the Windows Software Development Kit. This program allows you to use the mouse to place controls within a dialog box frame, to move and resize them, and to give them various attributes.

Before you start haphazardly designing your dialog box in DIALOG, you should spend a little time in preparation. Although you can create a header file containing identifiers for the dialog box IDs, it's easier to create and edit the header file in a normal text editor. You should also have a general idea of how the controls will be arranged in the dialog box.

DIALOG can read .RES files (the binary compiled resource file, not the ASCII .RC resource script) and header files. DIALOG will prompt for the name of both a .RES file and a .H file when you choose Open from the File menu. Alternatively, you can read in a header file by using Open from the Include menu.

The names of all the dialog boxes currently stored in the .RES file are displayed when you choose View Dialog from the File menu. You can then pick one to edit. Thus, even if you begin by attempting to manually create a dialog box template in a .RC file and then give up in frustration, you can switch to DIALOG to get all the coordinates and sizes correct. Remember to compile the resource script before running DIALOG, however; as noted above, DIALOG cannot read .RC files, only compiled .RES files. Alternatively, you can begin a new dialog box by choosing New Dialog from the Edit menu.

You can fill up the dialog box with controls by choosing from the Control menu, which lists 13 basic types of controls such as Check Box, Radio Button, and Push Button. You then click the mouse where you want the control to be placed. If the control uses text, it will initially show only the string "Text." You can select the control for editing merely by clicking on it. You can stretch or size it by hooking the little boxes on the sides or corners, and you can move it around by hooking the center.

The process of placing and sizing controls becomes a little easier if you first choose Grid from the Options menu and change both numbers to 2, thus forcing all dialog box coordinates and sizes to be in even numbers of units. Otherwise, you'll continually be wondering whether a particular control in a group is really one pixel or two pixels off or whether you've merely been looking at the screen too long. Also, try to create the controls in the order that you'll want them to appear in the dialog box template, because this in turn governs the order of tab stops and groups. Don't worry inordinately about getting it precisely right the first time through; as you'll see below, you can always change the order later.

One by one, select each control in the dialog box, choose Styles from the Edit menu, and enter the text of the control and the ID number in the Styles dialog box. If you've read in a header file, you can use the defined names rather than numbers for the IDs. You can also use the Styles dialog box to change the window style of the control. For instance, if you created a push-button control by choosing Push Button from the Control menu, you can make it a default push button by checking the Def Push Button box.

The dialog box you're creating is initially shown with a simple frame. To add a caption bar and a system menu box, select the dialog box itself with the mouse, and then choose Styles from the Edit menu. As you've seen, controls in a Windows dialog box are organized by "groups" and "tab stops." You use the Tab key to move between controls marked as tab stops, and the arrow keys to move between controls within a group.

You can reorder the controls and select groups and tab stops through the Groups option of the Dialog menu, which displays a list of all the controls you've created. You can move a control by selecting it with the mouse and placing the horizontal black bar cursor in a new location. To define a group, you mark the first and last control of the group. You would also usually flag the first control of the group as a tab stop, but you can pick another control as the tab stop if you would like the cursor to jump to the middle of a group.

The best part of DIALOG is that you can try out these tab stops and groups to see if they work right. Simply choose Test from the Dialog menu. You can use both the keyboard and mouse to test how the input focus shifts between controls. (Don't expect radio buttons to work, however; they require some cooperation from a dialog box procedure.)

After you're done, you can save the file. DIALOG will actually save two files: a new .RES binary file containing the new dialog boxes and any changes to existing dialog boxes, and an ASCII file with the extension .DLG. The .DLG file contains the human-readable (well, almost readable) dialog box templates. All the controls will be expressed as CONTROL statements that include window style identifiers from WINDOWS.H. If you used names from a header file for the IDs, these names will be used in the .DLG file.

If you've changed the header file, you'll want to save that also. But beware: DIALOG will strip comments from it. For that reason, it's better to maintain the header file outside DIALOG and read it into DIALOG, rather than to save it from DIALOG.

DIALOG can't read or alter the ASCII .RC resource script file; it can't read .DLG files, either. DIALOG can read only the binary .RES file, which it saves in both the .RES and .DLG formats. If you create a dialog box in DIALOG and save it as MYPROG.RES and MYPROG.DLG (for instance), you should later edit the MYPROG.RC resource script and include the line:

```
rcinclude myprog.dlg
```

This allows the RC.EXE resource compiler to add the contents of the MYPROG.DLG file to the other resources included in MYPROG.RC. Do not use *#include* for the .DLG file. The RC.EXE resource compiler interprets only *#define* statements in any file included with *#include*. And if you started out by creating a dialog box in the MYPROG.RC resource script file and then edited it in DIALOG, you must also delete the original dialog box template from MYPROG.RC. Otherwise, you'll have two definitions for the same dialog box.

I have a confession to make. Although none of the dialog box templates in this chapter appear to be output from DIALOG, I originally created all of them in DIALOG. I later edited the .DLG files (and in many cases merged them into the .RC files) for the sole purpose of making them readable and presentable. DIALOG is almost essential when creating dialog boxes. Don't waste your time doing it any other way.

THE GRAPHICS DEVICE INTERFACE

Chapter 11

An Introduction to GDI

We have been using Graphics Device Interface (GDI) functions since Chapter 1, when we first started writing to the client area of our windows. Now it's time for a more formal coverage of the subject. This chapter discusses the preliminaries of GDI but stops short of drawing graphics, which is the subject of Chapter 12. Chapter 13 covers bitmaps and metafiles, which are means of storing graphical information; Chapter 14 discusses text and fonts; and Chapter 15 deals with printing.

THE GDI PHILOSOPHY

Graphics in Windows are handled primarily by functions exported from the GDI.EXE module (although some drawing functions actually have entry points in the USER.EXE file). The GDI.EXE module calls routines in the various driver files—a .DRV for the video display screen and possibly one or more other .DRV driver files that control printers or plotters. The video driver accesses the hardware of the video display. Different video display adapters and printers require different driver files.

The GDI system is constructed so that Windows can determine from the driver what the driver can handle itself and what it needs assistance with. For instance, if the video hardware includes a graphics coprocessor that can draw ellipses, then GDI can take advantage of that; otherwise, the GDI module must itself calculate the points of the ellipse and pass the points to the driver.

Because a large number of different display devices can be attached to the IBM PC and compatibles, one of the primary goals of GDI is to support device-independent graphics on output devices such as video displays, printers, and plotters. Windows programs should be able to run without problems on any graphics output device that Windows supports. GDI accomplishes this goal by providing facilities to insulate your programs from the particular characteristics of different output devices. In this way it is like other device-independent graphics programming languages. But where Windows GDI is different is in its strong support of pixel-level manipulation.

The world of graphics output devices is divided into two broad groups: raster devices and vector devices. Most PC output devices are raster devices, which means that they represent images as a pattern of dots. This category includes video display adapters, dot-matrix printers, and laser printers. Vector devices, which draw images using lines, are generally limited to plotters.

Although most video display adapters and printers are raster devices, most graphics interface languages are based solely on vectors. This means that a program using one of these graphics languages is a level of abstraction away from the hardware. The output device is using pixels for a graphics representation, but the program is not talking to the interface in terms of pixels. While you can certainly use Windows GDI as a high-level vector drawing system, you can also use it for relatively low-level pixel manipulation.

In this respect, Windows GDI is to other graphics interface languages what C is to other programming languages. C is well known for its high degree of portability among different operating systems and environments. Yet C is also well known for allowing a programmer to perform low-level system functions that are often impossible in other high-level languages. Just as C is sometimes thought of as a "high-level assembly language," you can think of GDI as a high-level interface to the hardware of the graphics device.

As you've seen, by default Windows uses a coordinate system based on pixels. Most other graphics languages use a "virtual" coordinate system with horizontal and vertical axes that range (for instance) from 0 to 32,767. Although some graphics languages don't let you use pixel coordinates, Windows GDI lets you use either system (as well as additional coordinate systems based on physical measurements). You can use a virtual coordinate system and keep your program distanced from the hardware, or you can use the device coordinate system and snuggle right up to the hardware.

Some programmers think that after you start working in terms of pixels, you've abandoned device independence. We've already seen that this is not necessarily true. The trick is to use the pixels in a device-independent fashion. This requires that the graphics interface language provide facilities for a program to determine the hardware characteristics of the device and make appropriate adjustments. For instance, we've frequently used the pixel size of a standard system font character to space text on the screen. This approach allows our programs to adjust to different display adapters' with different resolutions, text sizes, and aspect ratios. You'll see other methods in this chapter for determining display sizes.

Windows can run on either a monochrome display or a color display. If you choose, you can write a program without worrying very much about color. If you use color in your program and the program later runs on a monochrome display adapter, Windows will use a shade of gray to represent the color. However, you can also determine from your program how many colors are available on the particular display device and take best advantage of the hardware.

Of course, just as you can write C programs that have subtle portability problems when they run on other computers, you can also inadvertently let device dependencies creep into your Windows programs. That's part of the price of not being fully insulated from the hardware. We'll examine many of the device-dependent traps in the next few chapters.

You should also be aware of the limitations of Windows GDI. GDI is not (at this time) capable of doing everything you may want a graphics interface to do. Although you can move graphics objects around the display, GDI is generally a static display system with no real animation support. GDI provides no direct support for three-dimensional representations or for rotations of objects. For instance, when you draw an ellipse, the ellipse axes must be parallel to the horizontal and vertical coordinates. Although some graphics languages use floating-point numbers for virtual coordinates, Windows—for performance reasons—always uses 16-bit signed integers.

THE DEVICE CONTEXT

When you want to draw on a graphics output device (such as the screen or a printer), you must first obtain a handle to a device context (or DC). In giving your program this handle, Windows is giving you permission to use the device. You then include the handle as a parameter in the GDI functions to identify to Windows the device you want to draw on.

The device context contains many current "attributes" that determine how the GDI functions work on the device. These attributes allow the parameters to the GDI functions to include only starting coordinates or sizes and not everything else that Windows needs to display the object on the device. For example, when you call *TextOut*, you need specify in the function only the device context handle, the starting coordinates, the text, and the length of the text. You don't need to specify the font, the color of the text, the color of the background behind the text, and the intercharacter spacing, because these attributes are part of the device context. When you want to change one of these attributes, you call a function that changes the attribute in the device context. Subsequent *TextOut* calls use the changed attribute.

Getting the Handle to the Device Context

Windows provides several methods for obtaining a device context handle. If you obtain a device context handle while processing a message, you should release it (or delete it) before exiting the window function. After you release the handle, it is no longer valid.

The most common method for obtaining and then releasing a device context handle involves using the *BeginPaint* and *EndPaint* calls when processing the WM_PAINT message:

```
hdc = BeginPaint (hwnd, &ps) ;
        [other program lines]
EndPaint (hwnd, &ps) ;
```

The variable *ps* is a structure of type PAINTSTRUCT. The *hdc* field of this structure is the handle to the device context that *BeginPaint* returns. The PAINTSTRUCT structure also contains a RECT (rectangle) structure named *rcPaint* that contains a clipping rectangle indicating the invalid region of the window's client area. With the device context handle obtained from *BeginPaint*, you can draw only within this rectangle. The *EndPaint* call validates this region.

Windows programs can also obtain a handle to a device context during processing of messages other than WM_PAINT:

```
hdc = GetDC (hwnd) ;
        [other program lines]
ReleaseDC (hwnd, hdc) ;
```

This device context applies to the client area of the window whose handle is *hwnd*. The primary difference between the use of these calls and of the *BeginPaint* and *EndPaint* combination is that you can draw on your entire client area with the handle returned from *GetDC*. However, *ReleaseDC* doesn't validate any possibly invalid regions of the client area.

A Windows program can also obtain a handle to a device context that applies to the entire window and not only to the window's client area:

```
hdc = GetWindowDC (hwnd) ;
        [other program lines]
ReleaseDC (hwnd, hdc) ;
```

This device context includes the window caption bar, menu, scroll bars, and frame in addition to the client area. The *GetWindowDC* function is rarely used. If you want to experiment with it, you should trap WM_NCPAINT ("nonclient paint") messages, which prevent Windows from drawing on the nonclient area of the window.

The *BeginPaint, GetDC,* and *GetWindowDC* calls obtain a device context associated with a particular window. You can also obtain a device context for the entire display by calling *CreateDC:*

```
hdc = CreateDC (lpszDriver, lpszDevice, lpszOutput, lpData) ;
    [other program lines]
DeleteDC (hdc) ;
```

In the BLOWUP1 program in Chapter 4 we used this function to obtain a device context handle that allowed us to write outside our window's client area:

```
hdc = CreateDC ("DISPLAY", NULL, NULL, NULL) ;
```

Writing outside your windows is generally impolite, but it's convenient for some unusual applications. (Although this fact is undocumented, you can also retrieve a device context for the entire screen by calling *GetDC* with a NULL parameter.)

In Chapter 15 we'll use the *CreateDC* function to obtain a handle to a printer device context:

```
hdcPrinter = CreateDC ("IBMGRX", "IBM Graphics", "LPT1:", NULL) ;
```

Of course, we won't include the names of specific printers in our programs. Programs can instead obtain this information from WIN.INI.

Sometimes you need only to obtain some information about a device context and not to do any drawing. In these cases, you can obtain a handle to an "information context" using *CreateIC.* The parameters are the same as for the *CreateDC* function:

```
hdcInfo = CreateIC (lpszDriver, lpszDevice, lpszOutput, lpData) ;
    [other program lines]
DeleteDC (hdcInfo) ;
```

You can't write to the device using this information context handle. We'll use this function in the DEVCAPS1 program shown later in this chapter to obtain an information context for the display and the printer.

In the GRAFMENU program in Chapter 9, we obtained a memory device context to manipulate some bitmaps. A memory device context is always created to be compatible with an existing device context:

```
hdcMem = CreateCompatibleDC (hdc) ;
    [other program lines]
DeleteDC (hdcMem) ;
```

When you first obtain a memory device context, the display surface that it represents contains exactly 1 pixel. We'll work more with memory device contexts in Chapter 13.

In Chapter 13 we'll also work with "metafiles." A metafile is a collection of GDI calls encoded in binary form. You can create a metafile by obtaining a metafile device context:

```
hdcMeta = CreateMetaFile (lpszFilename) ;
     [other program lines]
hmf = CloseMetaFile (hdcMeta) ;
```

During the time that the metafile device context is valid, any GDI calls you make using *hdcMeta* become part of the metafile. When you call *CloseMetaFile*, the device context handle becomes invalid. The function returns a handle to the metafile (*hmf*).

Getting Device Context Information

A device context usually refers to a physical display device such as a video display or a printer. Often, you need to obtain information about this device, including the size of the display (in terms of both pixels and physical dimensions) and its color capabilities. You can get this information by calling the *GetDeviceCaps* ("get device capabilities") function:

```
nValue = GetDeviceCaps (hdc, nIndex) ;
```

The *nIndex* parameter is 1 of 28 identifiers defined in WINDOWS.H. For instance, the *nIndex* HORZRES causes *GetDeviceCaps* to return the width of the device in pixels; a VERTRES parameter returns the height of the device in pixels. If *hdc* is a handle to a screen device context, that's the same information you can get from *GetSystemMetrics*. If *hdc* is a handle to a printer device context, then *GetDeviceCaps* returns the height and width of the printer display area in pixels.

You can also use *GetDeviceCaps* to determine the device's capabilities of processing various types of graphics. This is unimportant for the video display, but it becomes very important when working with printers. For instance, most plotters can't draw bitmapped images—and *GetDeviceCaps* can tell you that.

The DEVCAPS1 Program

The DEVCAPS1 program, shown in Figure 11-1, displays all the information available from the *GetDeviceCaps* function for either the video display or the selected printer. (A second version of this program, called DEVCAPS2, will be presented in Chapter 15.) If you change the current printer using the Windows Control Panel program, DEVCAPS1 updates the printer information.

DEVCAPS1.MAK

```
#------------------------
# DEVCAPS1.MAK make file
#------------------------

devcaps1.exe : devcaps1.obj devcaps.obj devcaps1.def devcaps1.res
    link devcaps1 devcaps, /align:16, NUL, /nod slibcew libw, devcaps1
    rc devcaps1.res

devcaps1.obj : devcaps1.c devcaps1.h
    cl -c -Gsw -Ow -W2 -Zp devcaps1.c

devcaps.obj : devcaps.c
    cl -c -Gsw -Ow -W2 -Zp devcaps.c

devcaps1.res : devcaps1.rc devcaps1.h
    rc -r devcaps1.rc
```

DEVCAPS1.C

```
/*------------------------------------------------------------
   DEVCAPS1.C -- Displays Device Capability Information
                 (c) Charles Petzold, 1990
   ------------------------------------------------------------*/

#include <windows.h>
#include <string.h>
#include "devcaps1.h"

void DoBasicInfo (HDC, HDC, short, short) ;         // in DEVCAPS.C
void DoOtherInfo (HDC, HDC, short, short) ;
void DoBitCodedCaps (HDC, HDC, short, short, short) ;

long FAR PASCAL WndProc (HWND, WORD, WORD, LONG) ;

int PASCAL WinMain (HANDLE hInstance, HANDLE hPrevInstance,
                    LPSTR lpszCmdLine, int nCmdShow)
    {
    static char szAppName[] = "DevCaps" ;
    HWND        hwnd ;
    MSG         msg ;
    WNDCLASS    wndclass ;
```

Figure 11-1. *The DEVCAPS1 program.*

(continued)

```
    if (!hPrevInstance)
        {
        wndclass.style          = CS_HREDRAW : CS_VREDRAW ;
        wndclass.lpfnWndProc    = WndProc ;
        wndclass.cbClsExtra     = 0 ;
        wndclass.cbWndExtra     = 0 ;
        wndclass.hInstance      = hInstance ;
        wndclass.hIcon          = LoadIcon (NULL, IDI_APPLICATION) ;
        wndclass.hCursor        = LoadCursor (NULL, IDC_ARROW) ;
        wndclass.hbrBackground  = GetStockObject (WHITE_BRUSH) ;
        wndclass.lpszMenuName   = szAppName ;
        wndclass.lpszClassName  = szAppName ;

        RegisterClass (&wndclass) ;
        }

    hwnd = CreateWindow (szAppName, "Device Capabilities",
                         WS_OVERLAPPEDWINDOW,
                         CW_USEDEFAULT, CW_USEDEFAULT,
                         CW_USEDEFAULT, CW_USEDEFAULT,
                         NULL, NULL, hInstance, NULL) ;

    ShowWindow (hwnd, nCmdShow) ;
    UpdateWindow (hwnd) ;

    while (GetMessage (&msg, NULL, 0, 0))
        {
        TranslateMessage (&msg) ;
        DispatchMessage (&msg) ;
        }
    return msg.wParam ;
    }

HDC GetPrinterIC ()
    {
    char szPrinter [64] ;
    char *szDevice, *szDriver, *szOutput ;

    GetProfileString ("windows", "device", "", szPrinter, 64) ;

    if ((szDevice = strtok (szPrinter, "," )) &&
        (szDriver = strtok (NULL,      ", ")) &&
        (szOutput = strtok (NULL,      ", ")))

            return CreateIC (szDriver, szDevice, szOutput, NULL) ;

    return NULL ;
    }
```

(continued)

```
long FAR PASCAL WndProc (HWND hwnd, WORD message, WORD wParam, LONG lParam)
    {
    static short cxChar, cyChar, nCurrentDevice = IDM_SCREEN,
                                 nCurrentInfo   = IDM_BASIC ;
    HDC         hdc, hdcInfo ;
    HMENU       hMenu ;
    PAINTSTRUCT ps ;
    TEXTMETRIC  tm ;

    switch (message)
         {
         case WM_CREATE :
              hdc = GetDC (hwnd) ;
              SelectObject (hdc, GetStockObject (SYSTEM_FIXED_FONT)) ;

              GetTextMetrics (hdc, &tm) ;
              cxChar = tm.tmAveCharWidth ;
              cyChar = tm.tmHeight + tm.tmExternalLeading ;
              ReleaseDC (hwnd, hdc) ;
              return 0 ;

         case WM_COMMAND :
              hMenu = GetMenu (hwnd) ;

              switch (wParam)
                   {
                   case IDM_SCREEN :
                   case IDM_PRINTER :
                        CheckMenuItem (hMenu, nCurrentDevice, MF_UNCHECKED) ;
                        nCurrentDevice = wParam ;
                        CheckMenuItem (hMenu, nCurrentDevice, MF_CHECKED) ;
                        InvalidateRect (hwnd, NULL, TRUE) ;
                        return 0 ;

                   case IDM_BASIC :
                   case IDM_OTHER :
                   case IDM_CURVE :
                   case IDM_LINE :
                   case IDM_POLY :
                   case IDM_TEXT :
                        CheckMenuItem (hMenu, nCurrentInfo, MF_UNCHECKED) ;
                        nCurrentInfo = wParam ;
                        CheckMenuItem (hMenu, nCurrentInfo, MF_CHECKED) ;
                        InvalidateRect (hwnd, NULL, TRUE) ;
                        return 0 ;
                   }
              break ;
```

(continued)

```
          case WM_DEVMODECHANGE :
               InvalidateRect (hwnd, NULL, TRUE) ;
               return 0 ;

          case WM_PAINT :
               hdc = BeginPaint (hwnd, &ps) ;
               SelectObject (hdc, GetStockObject (SYSTEM_FIXED_FONT)) ;

               if (nCurrentDevice == IDM_SCREEN)
                    hdcInfo = CreateIC ("DISPLAY", NULL, NULL, NULL) ;
               else
                    hdcInfo = GetPrinterIC () ;

               if (hdcInfo)
                    {
                    switch (nCurrentInfo)
                         {
                         case IDM_BASIC :
                              DoBasicInfo (hdc, hdcInfo, cxChar, cyChar) ;
                              break ;

                         case IDM_OTHER :
                              DoOtherInfo (hdc, hdcInfo, cxChar, cyChar) ;
                              break ;

                         case IDM_CURVE :
                         case IDM_LINE :
                         case IDM_POLY :
                         case IDM_TEXT :
                              DoBitCodedCaps (hdc, hdcInfo, cxChar, cyChar,
                                              nCurrentInfo - IDM_CURVE) ;
                              break ;
                         }

                    DeleteDC (hdcInfo) ;
                    }

               EndPaint (hwnd, &ps) ;
               return 0 ;

     case WM_DESTROY :
          PostQuitMessage (0) ;
          return 0 ;
     }
return DefWindowProc (hwnd, message, wParam, lParam) ;
}
```

DEVCAPS.C

```
/*-------------------------------------------------------------
   DEVCAPS.C -- Display routines for DEVCAPS1 and DEVCAPS2
                (c) Charles Petzold, 1990
   ----------------------------------------------------------*/

#include <windows.h>
#include <string.h>
#include <stdio.h>

typedef struct
     {
     short nMask ;
     char  *szMask ;
     char  *szDesc ;
     }
     BITS ;

void DoBasicInfo (HDC hdc, HDC hdcInfo, short cxChar, short cyChar)
     {
     static struct
          {
          short nIndex ;
          char  *szDesc ;
          }
          info [] =
          {
          HORZSIZE,      "HORZSIZE      Width in millimeters:",
          VERTSIZE,      "VERTSIZE      Height in millimeters:",
          HORZRES,       "HORZRES       Width in pixels:",
          VERTRES,       "VERTRES       Height in raster lines:",
          BITSPIXEL,     "BITSPIXEL     Color bits per pixel:",
          PLANES,        "PLANES        Number of color planes:",
          NUMBRUSHES,    "NUMBRUSHES    Number of device brushes:",
          NUMPENS,       "NUMPENS       Number of device pens:",
          NUMMARKERS,    "NUMMARKERS    Number of device markers:",
          NUMFONTS,      "NUMFONTS      Number of device fonts:",
          NUMCOLORS,     "NUMCOLORS     Number of device colors:",
          PDEVICESIZE,   "PDEVICESIZE   Size of device structure:",
          ASPECTX,       "ASPECTX       Relative width of pixel:",
          ASPECTY,       "ASPECTY       Relative height of pixel:",
          ASPECTXY,      "ASPECTXY      Relative diagonal of pixel:",
          LOGPIXELSX,    "LOGPIXELSX    Horizontal dots per inch:",
          LOGPIXELSY,    "LOGPIXELSY    Vertical dots per inch:",
          SIZEPALETTE,   "SIZEPALETTE   Number of palette entries:",
          NUMRESERVED,   "NUMRESERVED   Reserved palette entries:",
          COLORRES,      "COLORRES      Actual color resolution:"
          } ;
```

(continued)

```
          char    szBuffer [80] ;
          short   i, nLine ;

          for (i = 0 ; i < sizeof info / sizeof info [0] ; i++)
               TextOut (hdc, cxChar, (i + 1) * cyChar, szBuffer,
                    sprintf (szBuffer, "%-40s%8d", info[i].szDesc,
                         GetDeviceCaps (hdcInfo, info[i].nIndex))) ;
          }

     void DoOtherInfo (HDC hdc, HDC hdcInfo, short cxChar, short cyChar)
          {
          static BITS clip [] =
               {
               CP_RECTANGLE,  "CP_RECTANGLE",     "Can clip to rectangle:"
               } ;

          static BITS raster [] =
               {
               RC_BITBLT,       "RC_BITBLT",       "Capable of simple BitBlt:",
               RC_BANDING,      "RC_BANDING",      "Requires banding support:",
               RC_SCALING,      "RC_SCALING",      "Requires scaling support:",
               RC_BITMAP64,     "RC_BITMAP64",     "Supports bitmaps >64K:",
               RC_GDI20_OUTPUT, "RC_GDI20_OUTPUT", "Has 2.0 output calls:",
               RC_DI_BITMAP,    "RC_DI_BITMAP",    "Supports DIB to memory:",
               RC_PALETTE,      "RC_PALETTE",      "Supports a palette:",
               RC_DIBTODEV,     "RC_DIBTODEV",     "Supports bitmap conversion:",
               RC_BIGFONT,      "RC_BIGFONT",      "Supports fonts >64K:",
               RC_STRETCHBLT,   "RC_STRETCHBLT",   "Supports StretchBlt:",
               RC_FLOODFILL,    "RC_FLOODFILL",    "Supports FloodFill:"
               } ;

          static char *szTech [] = { "DT_PLOTTER (Vector plotter)",
                              "DT_RASDISPLAY (Raster display)",
                              "DT_RASPRINTER (Raster printer)",
                              "DT_RASCAMERA (Raster camera)",
                              "DT_CHARSTREAM (Character-stream, PLP)",
                              "DT_METAFILE (Metafile, VDM)",
                              "DT_DISPFILE (Display-file)" } ;
          char        szBuffer [80] ;
          short       i ;

          TextOut (hdc, cxChar, cyChar, szBuffer,
               sprintf (szBuffer, "%-24s%04XH",
                    "DRIVERVERSION:", GetDeviceCaps (hdcInfo, DRIVERVERSION))) ;

          TextOut (hdc, cxChar, 2 * cyChar, szBuffer,
               sprintf (szBuffer, "%-24s%-40s",
                    "TECHNOLOGY:", szTech [GetDeviceCaps (hdcInfo, TECHNOLOGY)])) ;
```

(continued)

504

```
    TextOut (hdc, cxChar, 4 * cyChar, szBuffer,
        sprintf (szBuffer, "CLIPCAPS (Clipping capabilities)")) ;

    for (i = 0 ; i < sizeof clip / sizeof clip [0] ; i++)
        TextOut (hdc, 9 * cxChar, (i + 6) * cyChar, szBuffer,
            sprintf (szBuffer, "%-16s%-28s %3s",
                clip[i].szMask, clip[i].szDesc,
                GetDeviceCaps (hdcInfo, CLIPCAPS) & clip[i].nMask ?
                    "Yes" : "No")) ;

    TextOut (hdc, cxChar, 8 * cyChar, szBuffer,
        sprintf (szBuffer, "RASTERCAPS (Raster capabilities)")) ;

    for (i = 0 ; i < sizeof raster / sizeof raster [0] ; i++)
        TextOut (hdc, 9 * cxChar, (i + 10) * cyChar, szBuffer,
            sprintf (szBuffer, "%-16s%-28s %3s",
                raster[i].szMask, raster[i].szDesc,
                GetDeviceCaps (hdcInfo, RASTERCAPS) & raster[i].nMask ?
                    "Yes" : "No")) ;
    }

void DoBitCodedCaps (HDC hdc, HDC hdcInfo, short cxChar, short cyChar,
                    short nType)
    {
    static BITS curves [] =
        {
        CC_CIRCLES,     "CC_CIRCLES",     "circles:",
        CC_PIE,         "CC_PIE",         "pie wedges:",
        CC_CHORD,       "CC_CHORD",       "chord arcs:",
        CC_ELLIPSES,    "CC_ELLIPSES",    "ellipses:",
        CC_WIDE,        "CC_WIDE",        "wide borders:",
        CC_STYLED,      "CC_STYLED",      "styled borders:",
        CC_WIDESTYLED,  "CC_WIDESTYLED",  "wide and styled borders:",
        CC_INTERIORS,   "CC_INTERIORS",   "interiors:"
        } ;

    static BITS lines [] =
        {
        LC_POLYLINE,    "LC_POLYLINE",    "polylines:",
        LC_MARKER,      "LC_MARKER",      "markers:",
        LC_POLYMARKER,  "LC_POLYMARKER",  "polymarkers",
        LC_WIDE,        "LC_WIDE",        "wide lines:",
        LC_STYLED,      "LC_STYLED",      "styled lines:",
        LC_WIDESTYLED,  "LC_WIDESTYLED",  "wide and styled lines:",
        LC_INTERIORS,   "LC_INTERIORS",   "interiors:"
        } ;
```

(continued)

```
static BITS poly [] =
    {
    PC_POLYGON,      "PC_POLYGON",     "alternate fill polygon:",
    PC_RECTANGLE,    "PC_RECTANGLE",   "rectangle:",
    PC_TRAPEZOID,    "PC_TRAPEZOID",   "winding number fill polygon:",
    PC_SCANLINE,     "PC_SCANLINE",    "scanlines:",
    PC_WIDE,         "PC_WIDE",        "wide borders:",
    PC_STYLED,       "PC_STYLED",      "styled borders:",
    PC_WIDESTYLED,   "PC_WIDESTYLED",  "wide and styled borders:",
    PC_INTERIORS,    "PC_INTERIORS",   "interiors:"
    } ;

static BITS text [] =
    {
    TC_OP_CHARACTER, "TC_OP_CHARACTER", "character output precision:",
    TC_OP_STROKE,    "TC_OP_STROKE",    "stroke output precision:",
    TC_CP_STROKE,    "TC_CP_STROKE",    "stroke clip precision:",
    TC_CR_90,        "TC_CP_90",        "90-degree character rotation:",
    TC_CR_ANY,       "TC_CR_ANY",       "any character rotation:",
    TC_SF_X_YINDEP,  "TC_SF_X_YINDEP",  "scaling independent of x and y:",
    TC_SA_DOUBLE,    "TC_SA_DOUBLE",    "doubled character for scaling:",
    TC_SA_INTEGER,   "TC_SA_INTEGER",   "integer multiples for scaling:",
    TC_SA_CONTIN,    "TC_SA_CONTIN",    "any multiples for exact scaling:",
    TC_EA_DOUBLE,    "TC_EA_DOUBLE",    "double-weight characters:",
    TC_IA_ABLE,      "TC_IA_ABLE",      "italicizing:",
    TC_UA_ABLE,      "TC_UA_ABLE",      "underlining:",
    TC_SO_ABLE,      "TC_SO_ABLE",      "strikeouts:",
    TC_RA_ABLE,      "TC_RA_ABLE",      "raster fonts:",
    TC_VA_ABLE,      "TC_VA_ABLE",      "vector fonts:"
    } ;

static struct
    {
    short nIndex ;
    char  *szTitle ;
    BITS  (*pbits) [] ;
    short nSize ;
    }
    bitinfo [] =
    {
    CURVECAPS,   "CURVCAPS (Curve capabilities)",
                 (BITS (*)[]) curves, sizeof curves / sizeof curves [0],
    LINECAPS,    "LINECAPS (Line capabilities)",
                 (BITS (*)[]) lines, sizeof lines / sizeof lines [0],
    POLYGONALCAPS, "POLYGONALCAPS (Polygonal capabilities)",
                 (BITS (*)[]) poly, sizeof poly / sizeof poly [0],
```

(continued)

506

```
          TEXTCAPS,    "TEXTCAPS (Text capabilities)",
                    (BITS (*)[]) text, sizeof text / sizeof text [0]
     } ;

   static char szBuffer [80] ;
   BITS       (*pbits) [] = bitinfo [nType].pbits ;
   short      nDevCaps = GetDeviceCaps (hdcInfo, bitinfo [nType].nIndex) ;
   short      i ;

   TextOut (hdc, cxChar, cyChar, bitinfo [nType].szTitle,
              strlen (bitinfo [nType].szTitle)) ;

   for (i = 0 ; i < bitinfo [nType].nSize ; i++)
        TextOut (hdc, cxChar, (i + 3) * cyChar, szBuffer,
            sprintf (szBuffer, "%-16s %s %-32s %3s",
                (*pbits)[i].szMask, "Can do", (*pbits)[i].szDesc,
                nDevCaps & (*pbits)[i].nMask ? "Yes" : "No")) ;
   }
```

DEVCAPS1.RC

```
/*-----------------------------
   DEVCAPS1.RC resource script
   -----------------------------*/

#include "devcaps1.h"

DevCaps MENU
    {
    POPUP "&Device"
        {
        MENUITEM "&Screen",                IDM_SCREEN, CHECKED
        MENUITEM "&Printer",               IDM_PRINTER
        }
    POPUP "&Capabilities"
        {
        MENUITEM "&Basic Information",     IDM_BASIC, CHECKED
        MENUITEM "&Other Information",     IDM_OTHER
        MENUITEM "&Curve Capabilities",    IDM_CURVE
        MENUITEM "&Line Capabilities",     IDM_LINE
        MENUITEM "&Polygonal Capabilities",IDM_POLY
        MENUITEM "&Text Capabilities",     IDM_TEXT
        }
    }
```

DEVCAPS1.H

```
/*--------------------------
   DEVCAPS1.H header file
---------------------------*/

#define IDM_SCREEN   1
#define IDM_PRINTER  2

#define IDM_BASIC    3
#define IDM_OTHER    4
#define IDM_CURVE    5
#define IDM_LINE     6
#define IDM_POLY     7
#define IDM_TEXT     8
```

DEVCAPS1.DEF

```
;--------------------------------------
; DEVCAPS1.DEF module definition file
;--------------------------------------

NAME            DEVCAPS1

DESCRIPTION     'Displays Device Capability Info (c) Charles Petzold, 1990'
EXETYPE         WINDOWS
STUB            'WINSTUB.EXE'
CODE            PRELOAD MOVEABLE DISCARDABLE
DATA            PRELOAD MOVEABLE MULTIPLE
HEAPSIZE        1024
STACKSIZE       8192
EXPORTS         WndProc
```

The DEVCAPS1 Device menu lets you select either the screen or the printer. Because DEV-CAPS1 needs only to obtain information about this device, it gets a handle to an information context (using the *CreateIC* function) rather than to a device context. Getting an information context handle for the video device is easy:

```
HIC = CreateIC ("DISPLAY", NULL, NULL, NULL) ;
```

However, an information context handle for the printer requires more complex code:

```
HDC GetPrinterIC ()
    {
    char szPrinter [64] ;
    char *szDevice, *szDriver, *szOutput ;

    GetProfileString ("windows", "device", "", szPrinter, 64) ;

    if ((szDevice = strtok (szPrinter, ",")) &&
        (szDriver = strtok (NULL,       ", ")) &&
        (szOutput = strtok (NULL,       ", ")))
            return CreateIC (szDriver, szDevice, szOutput, NULL) ;

    return NULL ;
    }
```

The selected printer is listed in the *[windows]* section of the WIN.INI file in the following format:

```
device=device name,driver filename,port
```

For an IBM Graphics printer connected to the LPT1 printer port, the WIN.INI line is:

```
device=IBM Graphics,IBMGRX,LPT1:
```

IBM Graphics is the name of the printer, and IBMGRX.DRV is the name of the driver file.

To get an information context (or device context) for the current printer, you must first obtain the character string following *device=* in WIN.INI by using the *GetProfileString* function. You must then parse this string into the three components: the device name, the driver filename, and the port. You can do this in various ways. I happened to use the C *strtok* function, which is designed for parsing character strings separated by delimiters such as commas and spaces. Note that the device name itself can have embedded blanks.

If you'd like to use DEVCAPS1 to examine the device capabilities of other printers, you can add printer driver files to your Windows subdirectory using the Control Panel program and then select each of these printers, one by one, as the current printer. Specify that the port the printer is connected to is "NONE." An advantage of *CreateIC* over *CreateDC* is that *CreateDC* returns a device context handle only if the printer is attached to a port, whereas *CreateIC* doesn't care whether the printer is attached. To get an idea of the range of devices you'll be dealing with, you might want to obtain the *GetDeviceCaps* information for a few different types of printers, such as a simple nongraphics printer (the "Generic/Text Only" printer), a sophisticated laser printer (the Apple LaserWriter Plus), and a plotter (the Hewlett-Packard ColorPro). DEVCAPS1 intercepts the WM_DEVMODECHANGE message that Control Panel sends to all applications to signal that the current printer has been changed.

The Capabilities menu in DEVCAPS1 lets you display one of six screens that show the *GetDeviceCaps* information. Much of the DEVCAPS1 code is dedicated to formatting this information. When you choose the Basic Information option from the Capabilities menu, the most important information is displayed, including the size of the display, the number of pure colors it can display, and the organization of display memory into color planes and color bits per pixel. Figure 11-2 shows this basic information for a VGA; Figure 11-3 shows the information for an Apple LaserWriter Plus.

When you choose the Other Information option from the Capabilities menu, the program displays the type of device (usually "Raster device," "Raster printer," or "Vector plotter") and gives some information that is crucial for using printers, as you'll discover when you come to Chapter 15. Figure 11-4 shows this display for an Apple LaserWriter Plus. The RC_BITBLT identifier indicates that this printer can accept bitmaps; text-only printers and plotters cannot, however, which means that some GDI functions won't work on them. The RC_BANDING identifier indicates that this IBM printer, like many printers, requires "banding" support, which means that the GDI module must print to the printer in segments, each occupying a small section of the page. Again, we'll explore these issues further in Chapter 16.

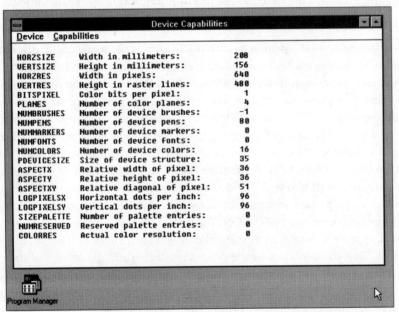

Figure 11-2. *The DEVCAPS1 display invoked by choosing Basic Information from the Capabilities menu when the specified device is an IBM VGA.*

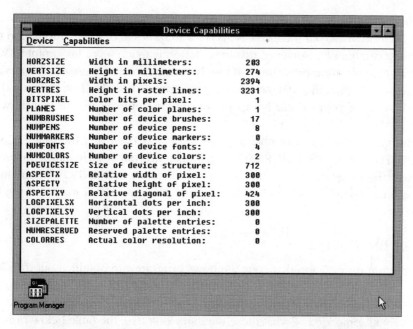

Figure 11-3. *The DEVCAPS1 display invoked by choosing Basic Information from the Capabilities menu when the specified device is an Apple LaserWriter Plus.*

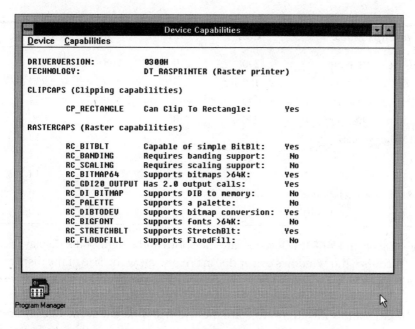

Figure 11-4. *The DEVCAPS1 display invoked by choosing Other Information from the Capabilities menu when the specified device is an Apple LaserWriter Plus.*

The other menu options in DEVCAPS display curve, line, polygon, and text capabilities. The information displayed indicates the type of graphics and text manipulation that the device driver can handle. However, this information is much more important to Windows itself than to application programs—if the driver lacks one of these capabilities and a program demands it, then the GDI module must assume the task. For instance, you don't have to check to see if your printer is capable of drawing ellipses before you draw an ellipse.

The information that you can obtain from *GetDeviceCaps* using the CURVECAPS, LINECAPS, POLYGONALCAPS, and TEXTCAPS parameters is encoded in bits in the return value. Although the Programmer's Reference doesn't indicate it, WINDOWS.H includes identifiers beginning with the letters CC, LC, PC, and TC to help you mask out the bits you want.

The Size of the Device

The most important information that your Windows program can obtain about the video device from *GetDeviceCaps* is the size of the display (in both millimeters and pixels) and the display's pixel aspect ratio. These dimensions can help in scaling images to be displayed. To give you some idea of what these numbers look like, the table below presents information from *GetDeviceCaps* for four common IBM video adapters: the Color/Graphics Adapter (CGA), Enhanced Graphics Adapter (EGA), the Video Graphics Array (VGA), and the 8514/A:

GetDeviceCaps Index	CGA	EGA	VGA	8514/A
HORZSIZE (width in mm)	240	240	208	280
VERTSIZE (height in mm)	180	175	156	210
HORZRES (pixel width)	640	640	640	1024
VERTRES (pixel height)	200	350	480	760
ASPECTX (horizontal)	5	38	36	10
ASPECTY (vertical)	12	48	36	14
ASPECTXY (diagonal)	13	61	51	14
LOGPIXELSX (x pixels/inch)	96	96	96	120
LOGPIXELSY (y pixels/inch)	48	72	96	120

The HORZSIZE and VERTSIZE values are the width and height of the display area in millimeters. Of course, the Windows driver doesn't really know the size of the display you have attached to your video adapter. These dimensions are based on standard display sizes for the adapters.

The HORZRES and VERTRES values are the width and height of the display area in pixels. For a device context for a video display, these are the same values as those returned from *GetSystemMetrics*.

The ASPECTX, ASPECTY, and ASPECTXY values are the relative width, height, and diagonal size of each pixel. ASPECTXY equals the square root of the sum of ASPECTX squared and ASPECTY squared.

The LOGPIXELSX and LOGPIXELSY values are the number of pixels per a horizontal and a vertical "logical inch." A logical inch is not a real inch (25.4 mm), as you can easily determine by performing a few calculations using the HORZSIZE, VERTSIZE, HORZRES, and VERTRES values. These LOGPIXELSX and LOGPIXELSY values require a little explanation. You may have noticed that the WRITE program and some other Windows programs display a ruler that isn't quite right: If you measure the ruler as displayed on an VGA, you'll find that what it declares as 1 inch is really more like 1½ inches. These programs are using the LOGPIXELSX and LOGPIXELSY values for the ruler. If WRITE used actual physical dimensions, normal 10-point or 12-point text would be so small as to be nearly illegible. These logical dimensions in effect blow up the display to allow an adequate size for displaying text. When we start working with text and fonts in Chapter 14, we'll wrestle again with this problem. It affects only video displays; for printers, all the dimensions returned from *GetDeviceCaps* are consistent.

Finding Out About Color

During the discussion of bitmaps in Chapter 8, I noted the two ways in which memory in a video display adapter can be organized for color. In some video adapters, memory is organized into a number of color planes. Within a plane, each bit corresponds to a single pixel and represents a particular primary color (such as red, green, or blue). Other video adapters have a single color plane, in which a number of adjacent bits represent the color of each pixel.

GetDeviceCaps lets you determine the organization of memory in the video adapter and the number of colors it can represent. This call returns the number of color planes:

```
nPlanes = GetDeviceCaps (hdc, PLANES) ;
```

This call returns the number of color bits per pixel:

```
nBitsPixel = GetDeviceCaps (hdc, BITSPIXEL) ;
```

Most graphics display devices that are capable of color use either multiple color planes or multiple color bits per pixel, but not both; in other words, one of these calls will return a value of 1. The number of colors that can be rendered on the video adapter can be calculated by the formula:

```
nColors = 1 << (nPlanes * nBitsPixel) ;
```

This value may or may not be the same as the number of colors obtainable with the NUMCOLORS parameter:

```
nColors = GetDeviceCaps (hdc, NUMCOLORS) ;
```

These two numbers will be different for most plotters. For a plotter, both the PLANES and BITSPIXEL values will equal 1, but the NUMCOLORS value will reflect the number of colored pens that the plotter has. For monochrome devices, *GetDeviceCaps* returns a 2 for the NUMCOLORS parameter.

The two values can also be different for video adapters that support loadable color palettes under Windows 3 (such as the IBM 8514/A adapter). The 8514/A has 1 plane and 8 bits per pixel, which means that 256 colors are possible. *GetDeviceCaps* with the NUMCOLORS parameter returns the number of colors reserved by Windows (20 in the case of the 8514/A). The remaining 236 colors can be set by a Windows program.

The number of colors returned from *GetDeviceCaps* is the number of pure colors that the device can display. Windows can use dithering (which involves a pixel pattern that combines pixels of different colors) to represent colors in addition to the pure colors.

A color is usually represented by an unsigned long integer with 3 bytes, one each for the intensity of red, green, and blue. (Chapters 5 and 6 discussed this subject in greater detail.) You can determine the closest pure color of a particular color value by calling *GetNearestColor*:

```
rgbPureColor = GetNearestColor (hdc, rgbColor) ;
```

The Device Context Attributes

As I noted above, Windows uses the device context to store "attributes" that govern how the GDI functions operate on the display. For instance, when you display some text using the *TextOut* function, you don't have to specify the color of the text or the font. Windows uses the device context to obtain this information.

When a program obtains a handle to a device context, Windows creates a device context with default values for all the attributes. The device context attributes are shown in the following table. A program can change or obtain any of the attributes.

Device Context Attribute	Default	Function(s) to Change	Function(s) to Get
Mapping mode	MM_TEXT	*SetMapMode*	*GetMapMode*
Window origin	(0, 0)	*SetWindowOrg*	*GetWindowOrg* *OffsetWindowOrg*
Viewport origin	(0, 0)	*SetViewportOrg*	*GetViewportOrg* *OffsetViewportOrg*
Window extents	(1, 1)	*SetWindowExt*	*GetWindowExt* *SetMapMode*

(continued)

continued

Device Context Attribute	Default	Function(s) to Change	Function(s) to Get
Viewport extents	(1, 1)	*SetViewportExt*	*GetViewportExt* *SetMapMode*
Pen	BLACK_PE	*SelectObject*	*SelectObject*
Brush	WHITE_BRUSH	*SelectObject*	*SelectObject*
Font	SYSTEM_FONT	*SelectObject*	*SelectObject*
Bitmap	None	*SelectObject*	*SelectObject*
Current pen position	(0, 0)	*MoveTo* *LineTo*	*GetCurrentPosition*
Background mode	OPAQUE	*SetBkMode*	*GetBkMode*
Background color	White	*SetBkColor*	*GetBkColor*
Text color	Black	*SetTextColor*	*GetTextColor*
Drawing mode	R2_COPYPEN	*SetROP2*	*GetROP2*
Stretching mode	BLACK-ONWHITE	*SetPolyFillMode*	*GetPolyFillMode*
Polygon filling mode	ALTERNATE	*SetPolyFillMode*	*GetPolyFillMode*
Intercharacter spacing	0	*SetTextCharacterExtra*	*GetTextCharacterExtra*
Brush origin	(0, 0) in screen coordinates	*SetBrushOrg*	*GetBrushOrg*
Clipping region	None	*SelectObject* *SelectClipRgn* *IntersectClipRect* *OffsetClipRgn* *ExcludeClipRect*	*SelectObject* *GetClipBox*

Saving Device Contexts

Throughout Section IV, you'll encounter various functions to change the device context attributes. Normally, Windows creates a new device context with default values when you call *GetDC* or *BeginPaint*. All changes you make to the attributes are lost when the device context is released with the *ReleaseDC* or the *EndPaint* call. If your program needs to use nondefault device context attributes, you'll have to initialize the device context every time you obtain a device context handle:

```
WM_PAINT :
     hdc = BeginPaint (hwnd, &ps) ;
```
     [initialize device context attributes]
     [paint client area of window]
```
     EndPaint (hwnd, &ps) ;
     return 0 ;
```

Although this approach is generally satisfactory, you might prefer that changes you make to the device context attributes be saved when you release the device context, so they will be in effect the next time you call *GetDC* or *BeginPaint*. You can accomplish this by including the CS_OWNDC flag as part of the window class when you register the window class:

```
wndclass.style = CS_HREDRAW | CS_VREDRAW | CS_OWNDC ;
```

Now each window that you create based on this window class will have its own private device context that exists until the window is destroyed. When you use the CS_OWNDC style, you need to initialize the device context attributes only once, perhaps during processing of the WM_CREATE message:

```
WM_CREATE :
     hdc = GetDC (hwnd) ;
```
     [initialize device context attributes]
```
     ReleaseDC (hwnd, hdc) ;
```

The attributes continue to be valid until you change them.

The CS_OWNDC style affects only the device contexts retrieved from *GetDC* and *BeginPaint* and not device contexts obtained from the other functions (such as *GetWindowDC*). The CS_OWNDC style is not without its cost: Windows requires about 800 bytes to store the device context for each window created with this style. Even if you use CS_OWNDC, you must still release the device context before exiting the window function.

You can also use the CS_CLASSDC style:

```
wndclass.style = CS_HREDRAW | CS_VREDRAW | CS_CLASSDC ;
```

This causes each window class to have its own device context that is shared by all windows created based on that class—even by windows created in other instances of the same program. Now you can initialize the device context attributes once in *WinMain* following creation of the first window based on that window class:

```
if (!hPrevInstance)
     {
     hdc = GetDC (hwnd) ;
```
     [initialize device context]
```
     ReleaseDC (hwnd, hdc) ;
     }
```

In general, the CS_CLASSDC type of device context is more difficult to use than the CS_OWNDC type, because any changes you make to the device context attributes affect all windows in all instances based on the same window class. This could have some strange effects, particularly if you use a customized mapping mode (a subject coming up shortly) based on the size of the window.

In some cases you might want to change certain device context attributes, do some painting using the changed attributes, and then revert to the original device context. To simplify this process, you save the state of a device context by calling:

```
nSavedID = SaveDC (hdc) ;
```

Now you change some attributes. When you want to return to the device context as it existed before the *SaveDC* call, you use:

```
RestoreDC (hdc, nSavedID) ;
```

You can call *SaveDC* any number of times before calling *RestoreDC*. If you want to revert to the device context as it existed before the last *SaveDC* call, you call:

```
RestoreDC (hdc, -1) ;
```

THE MAPPING MODE

One device context attribute that affects virtually all the drawing you do on the client area is the "mapping mode." Four other device context attributes—the window origin, the viewport origin, the window extents, and the viewport extents—are closely related to the mapping mode attribute.

Most of the GDI drawing functions require coordinate values or sizes. For instance, this is the *TextOut* function:

```
TextOut (hdc, x, y, szBuffer, nLength) ;
```

The x and y parameters indicate the starting position of the text. The x parameter is the position on the horizontal axis, and the y parameter is the position on the vertical axis. Often the notation (x, y) is used to indicate this point.

In *TextOut*, as in virtually all GDI functions, these coordinate values are in terms of "logical units." Windows must translate the logical units into "device units," or pixels. This translation is governed by the mapping mode, the window and viewport origins, and the window and viewport extents. The mapping mode also implies an origin and orientation of the x-axis and the y-axis; that is, it determines whether values of x increase as you move toward the left or right side of the display and whether values of y increase as you move up or down the display.

Windows defines eight mapping modes. These are listed in the table on the following page using the WINDOW.H identifiers.

Mapping Mode	Logical Unit	Increasing Values	
		x-axis	y-axis
MM_TEXT	Pixel	Right	Down
MM_LOMETRIC	0.1 mm	Right	Up
MM_HIMETRIC	0.01 mm	Right	Up
MM_LOENGLISH	0.01 in.	Right	Up
MM_HIENGLISH	0.001 in.	Right	Up
MM_TWIPS*	$\frac{1}{1440}$ in.	Right	Up
MM_ISOTROPIC	Arbitrary ($x = y$)	Selectable	Selectable
MM_ANISOTROPIC	Arbitrary ($x != y$)	Selectable	Selectable

*Twip is a fabricated word meaning "twentieth of a point." A point, which is a unit of measurement for type, is approximately $\frac{1}{72}$ inch but often assumed in graphics systems such as GDI to be exactly $\frac{1}{72}$ inch. A twip is $\frac{1}{20}$ point and hence $\frac{1}{1440}$ inch.

You can set the mapping mode by:

```
SetMapMode (hdc, nMapMode) ;
```

where *nMapMode* is one of the eight mapping mode identifiers. You can obtain the current mapping mode by calling:

```
nMapMode = GetMapMode (hdc) ;
```

The default mapping mode is MM_TEXT. In this mapping mode, logical units are the same as physical units, which allows us (or, depending on your perspective, forces us) to work directly in terms of pixels. In a *TextOut* call that looks like this:

```
TextOut (hdc, 8, 16, szBuffer, nLength) ;
```

the text begins 8 pixels from the left of the client area and 16 pixels from the top.

If the mapping mode is set to MM_LOENGLISH, then logical units are in terms of hundredths of an inch:

```
SetMapMode (hdc, MM_LOENGLISH) ;
```

Now the *TextOut* function call might look like this:

```
TextOut (hdc, 50, -100, szBuffer, nLength) ;
```

The text begins 0.5 inch from the left and 1 inch from the top of the client area. (The reason for the negative sign in front of the *y*-coordinate will become clear later when I discuss the mapping modes in more detail.) Other mapping modes allow programs to specify coordinates in terms of millimeters, a printer's point size, or an arbitrarily scaled axis.

If you feel comfortable working in terms of pixels, you don't need to use any mapping modes except the default MM_TEXT mode. If you need to display an image in actual inch or millimeter dimensions, you can obtain the information you need from *GetDeviceCaps* and do your own scaling. The other mapping modes are simply a convenient way to avoid doing your own scaling.

Regardless of the mapping mode, all coordinates you specify in Windows functions must be signed short integers in the range 32,767 through −32,768. Some Windows functions that use coordinates for the starting point and ending point of a rectangle also require that the width and height of the rectangle be 32,767 or less.

Device Coordinates and Logical Coordinates

You may ask: If I use the MM_LOENGLISH mapping mode, will I start getting WM_SIZE messages in terms of hundredths of an inch? Absolutely not. Windows continues to use device coordinates for all messages (such as WM_MOVE, WM_SIZE, and WM_-MOUSEMOVE), for all non-GDI functions, and even for some GDI functions. Think of it this way: The mapping mode is an attribute of the device context, so the only time the mapping mode comes into play is when you use GDI functions that require a handle to the device context as one of the parameters. *GetSystemMetrics* is not a GDI function, so it will continue to return sizes in terms of device units, which are pixels. And although *Get-DeviceCaps* is a GDI function that requires a handle to a device context, Windows continues to return device units for the HORZRES and VERTRES indexes, because one of the purposes of this function is to provide a program with the size of the device in pixels.

However, the values in the TEXTMETRIC structure that you obtain from the *GetText-Metrics* call are in terms of logical units. If the mapping mode is MM_LOENGLISH at the time the call is made, *GetTextMetrics* provides character widths and heights in terms of hundredths of an inch. When you call *GetTextMetrics* for information about the height and width of characters, the mapping mode should be set to the same mapping mode that you'll be using when you draw text based on these sizes. As I cover the various GDI functions in this and subsequent chapters, I'll note whether they use device coordinates or logical coordinates.

The Device Coordinate Systems

Windows maps logical coordinates specified in GDI functions to device coordinates. Before we discuss the logical coordinate systems used with the various mapping modes, let's examine the different device coordinate systems that Windows defines for the video display area. Although we have been working mostly within the client area of our window, Windows uses two other device coordinate areas at various times. In all device coordinate systems, units are in terms of pixels. Values on the horizontal, or *x*, axis increase from left to right, and values on the vertical, or *y*, axis increase from top to bottom.

When we use the entire screen, we are working in terms of "screen coordinates." The upper left corner of the screen is the point (0, 0). Screen coordinates are used in the

WM_MOVE message (for nonchild windows) and in the following Windows functions: *CreateWindow* and *MoveWindow* (both for nonchild windows), *GetMessagePos*, *GetCursorPos*, *SetCursorPos*, *GetWindowRect*, *WindowFromPoint*, and *SetBrushOrg*. These are generally either functions that don't have a window associated with them (such as the two cursor functions) or functions that must move (or find) a window based on a screen point. If you use *CreateDC* with a "DISPLAY" parameter to obtain a device context for the entire screen, then logical coordinates specified in GDI calls will be mapped to screen coordinates.

"Whole-window coordinates" refer to a program's entire window, including the caption bar, menu, scroll bars, and window frame. For a normal window, the point (0, 0) is the upper left corner of the sizing border. Whole-window coordinates are rare in Windows, but if you obtain a device context from *GetWindowDC*, logical coordinates in GDI functions will be mapped to whole-window coordinates.

The third device coordinate system—the one we've been working with the most—uses "client-area coordinates." The point (0, 0) is the upper left corner of the client area. When you obtain a device context using *GetDC* or *BeginPaint*, logical coordinates in GDI functions are translated to client-area coordinates.

You can convert client-area coordinates to screen coordinates and vice versa using the functions *ClientToScreen* and *ScreenToClient*. You can also obtain the position and size of the whole window in terms of screen coordinates using the *GetWindowRect* function. These three functions provide enough information to translate from any one device coordinate system to any other.

The Viewport and the Window

The mapping mode defines how Windows maps logical coordinates that are specified in GDI functions to device coordinates, where the particular device coordinate system depends on the function you use to obtain the device context. To continue our discussion of the mapping mode, we need some additional terminology: The mapping mode is said to define the mapping of the "window" (logical coordinates) to the "viewport" (device coordinates).

The use of the words *window* and *viewport* is unfortunate. In other graphics interface languages, *viewport* often implies a clipping region. We've been using the word *window* to talk about the area that a program occupies on the screen. We'll have to put aside our preconceptions about these words during this discussion.

The "viewport" is in terms of device coordinates (pixels). Most often, the viewport is the same as the client area, but it can also refer to whole-window coordinates or screen coordinates if you've obtained a device context from *GetWindowDC* or *CreateDC*. The point (0, 0) is the upper left corner of the client area (or the whole window or the screen). Values of *x* increase to the right, and values of *y* increase going down.

The "window" is in terms of logical coordinates, which may be pixels, millimeters, inches, or any other unit you want. You specify logical window coordinates in the GDI functions.

For all mapping modes, Windows translates window (logical) coordinates to viewport (device) coordinates by the use of two formulas:

$$xViewport = (xWindow - xWinOrg) * \frac{xViewExt}{xWinExt} + xViewOrg$$

$$yViewport = (yWindow - yWinOrg) * \frac{yViewExt}{yWinExt} + yViewOrg$$

where ($xWindow$, $yWindow$) is a logical point to be translated, and ($xViewport$, $yViewport$) is the translated point in device coordinates. If the device coordinates are client-area coordinates or whole-window coordinates, then Windows must also translate these device coordinates to screen coordinates before drawing an object.

These formulas use two points that specify an "origin" of the window and the viewport: ($xWinOrg$, $yWinOrg$) is the window origin in logical coordinates; ($xViewOrg$, $yViewOrg$) is the viewport origin in device coordinates. In the default device context, these two points are set to (0, 0), but they can be changed. The formulas imply that the logical point ($xWinOrg$, $yWinOrg$) is always mapped to the device point ($xViewOrg$, $yViewOrg$).

The formulas also use two points that specify "extents": ($xWinExt$, $yWinExt$) is the window extent in logical coordinates; ($xViewExt$, $yViewExt$) is the viewport extent in device coordinates. In most mapping modes, the extents are implied by the mapping mode and cannot be changed. Each extent means nothing by itself, but the ratio of the viewport extent to the window extent is a scaling factor for converting logical units to device units. The extents can be negative: This implies that values on the logical x-axis don't necessarily have to increase to the right and that values on the logical y-axis don't necessarily have to increase going down.

Windows can also translate from viewport (device) coordinates to window (logical) coordinates:

$$xWindow = (xViewport - xViewOrg) * \frac{xWinExt}{xViewExt} + xWinOrg$$

$$yWindow = (yViewport - yViewOrg) * \frac{yWinExt}{yViewExt} + yWinOrg$$

Windows provides two functions that let you convert device points to logical points and vice versa within a program. The following function converts device points to logical points:

```
DPtoLP (hdc, lpPoints, nNumber) ;
```

The variable *lpPoints* is a long pointer to an array of POINT structures, and *nNumber* is the number of points to be converted. You'll find this function useful for converting the size of the client area obtained from *GetClientRect* (which is always in terms of device units) to logical coordinates:

```
GetClientRect (hwnd, &rect) ;
DPtoLP (hdc, (LPPOINT) &rect, 2) ;
```

This function converts logical points to device points:

```
LPtoDP (hdc, lpPoints, nNumber) ;
```

Working with MM_TEXT

For the MM_TEXT mapping mode, the default origins and extents are shown below:

Window origin:	(0, 0)	Can be changed
Viewport origin:	(0, 0)	Can be changed
Window extent:	(1, 1)	Cannot be changed
Viewport extent:	(1, 1)	Cannot be changed

The ratio of the viewport extent to the window extent is 1, so no scaling is performed between logical coordinates and device coordinates. The formulas shown on the preceding page reduce to these:

$$xViewport = xWindow - xWinOrg + xViewOrg$$
$$yViewport = yWindow - yWinOrg + yViewOrg$$

This mapping mode is called a "text" mapping mode not because it's most suitable for text but because of the orientation of the axes. We read text from left to right and top to bottom, and MM_TEXT defines values on the axes to increase the same way:

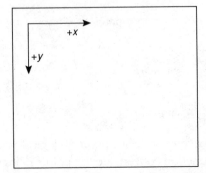

Windows provides the functions *SetViewportOrg* and *SetWindowOrg* for changing the viewport and window origins. These functions have the effect of shifting the axis so that the logical point (0, 0) no longer refers to the upper left corner. Generally, you'll use either *SetViewportOrg* or *SetWindowOrg* but not both.

Here's how these functions work: If you change the viewport origin to (*xViewOrg*, *yViewOrg*), then the logical point (0, 0) will be mapped to the device point (*xViewOrg*, *yViewOrg*). If you change the window origin to (*xWinOrg*, *yWinOrg*), then the logical point (*xWinOrg*, *yWinOrg*) will be mapped to the device point (0, 0), which is the upper left corner. Regardless of any changes you make to the window and viewport origins, the device point (0, 0) is always the upper left corner of the client area.

For instance, suppose your client area is *cxClient* pixels wide and *cyClient* pixels high. If you want to define the logical point (0, 0) to be the center of the client area, you can do so by calling:

```
SetViewportOrg (hdc, cxClient / 2, cyClient / 2) ;
```

The arguments to *SetViewportOrg* are always in terms of device units. The logical point (0, 0) will now be mapped to the device point (*cxClient / 2, cyClient / 2*). Now you use your client area as if it had the following coordinate system:

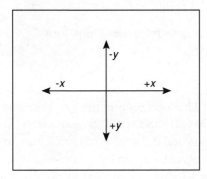

The logical *x*-axis ranges from −*cxClient / 2* to +*cxClient / 2*, and the logical *y*-axis ranges from −*cyClient / 2* to +*cyClient / 2*. The lower right corner of the client area is the logical point (*cxClient / 2, cyClient / 2*). If you want to display text starting at the upper left corner of the client area, which is the device point (0, 0), you need to use negative coordinates:

```
TextOut (hdc, -cxClient / 2, -cyClient / 2, "Hello", 5) ;
```

You can achieve the same result with *SetWindowOrg* as you did with *SetViewportOrg*:

```
SetWindowOrg (hdc, -cxClient / 2, -cyClient / 2) ;
```

The arguments to *SetWindowOrg* are always in terms of logical units. After this call, the logical point (−*cxClient / 2*, −*cyClient / 2*) is mapped to the device point (0, 0), the upper left corner of the client area.

What you probably don't want to do (unless you know what's going to happen) is to use both functions together:

```
SetViewportOrg (hdc, cxClient / 2, cyClient / 2) ;
SetWindowOrg (hdc, -cxClient / 2, -cyClient / 2) ;
```

This means that the logical point (*−cxClient / 2, −cyClient / 2*) is mapped to the device point (*cxClient / 2, cyClient / 2*), giving you a coordinate system that looks like this:

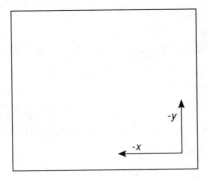

You can obtain the current viewport and window origins from these functions:

```
dwViewOrigin = GetViewportOrg (hdc) ;

dwWindowOrigin = GetWindowOrg (hdc) ;
```

Both functions return DWORDs (unsigned longs). The *x*-origin is in the low word and the *y*-origin is in the high word. You can use the LOWORD and HIWORD macros to extract these two values from the DWORD. The values returned from *GetViewportOrg* are in device coordinates; the values returned from *GetWindowOrg* are in logical coordinates.

You might want to change the viewport or window origin to shift display output within the client area of your window—for instance, in response to scroll bar input from the user. Changing the viewport or window origin doesn't shift the display output immediately, of course. You change the origin and then repaint the display. For instance, in the SYSMETS2 program in Chapter 2, we used the *nVscrollPos* value (the current position of the vertical scroll bar) to adjust the *y*-coordinates of the display output:

```
case WM_PAINT:
    BeginPaint (hwnd, &ps) ;

    for (i = 0 ; i < NUMLINES ; i++)
        {
        y = cyChar * (1 - nVscrollPos + i) ;
        [display text]
        }

    EndPaint (hwnd, &ps) ;
    return 0 ;
```

We can achieve the same result using *SetWindowOrg*:

```
case WM_PAINT:
     BeginPaint (hwnd, &ps) ;

     SetWindowOrg (ps.hdc, 0, cyChar * nVscrollPos) ;

     for (i = 0 ; i < NUMLINES ; i++)
          {
          y = cyChar * (1 + i) ;
          [display text]
          }

     EndPaint (hwnd, &ps) ;
     return 0 ;
```

Now the calculation of the *y*-coordinate for the *TextOut* functions doesn't require the *nVscrollPos* value. This means you can put the text output functions in a subroutine and not have to pass the *nVscrollPos* value to the subroutine, because we adjust the display of the text by changing the window origin.

If you have some experience working with rectangular (or Cartesian) coordinate systems, moving the logical point (0, 0) to the center of the client area as we did earlier may have seemed a reasonable action. However, there's a slight problem with the MM_TEXT mapping mode: A Cartesian coordinate system defines values on the *y*-axis to increase as you move up the axis, whereas MM_TEXT defines the values to increase as you move down. In this sense, MM_TEXT is an oddity, and these next five mapping modes do it correctly.

The "Metric" Mapping Modes

Windows includes five mapping modes that express logical coordinates in physical measurements. Because logical coordinates on the *x*-axis and *y*-axis are mapped to identical physical units, these mapping modes help you to draw round circles and square squares.

The five "metric" mapping modes are arranged below in order of lowest precision to highest precision. The two columns at the right show the size of the logical units in terms of inches (in.) and millimeters (mm) for comparison:

Mapping Mode	*Logical Unit*	*Inch*	*Millimeter*
MM_LOENGLISH	0.01 in.	0.01	0.254
MM_LOMETRIC	0.1 mm	0.00394	0.1
MM_HIENGLISH	0.001 in.	0.001	0.0254
MM_TWIPS*	$\frac{1}{1440}$ in.	0.000694	0.0176
MM_HIMETRIC	0.01 mm	0.000394	0.01

*A *twip* equals $\frac{1}{20}$ of a point, which itself equals $\frac{1}{72}$ inch.

To give you an idea of how the MM_TEXT mode fits in with these resolutions, on a standard EGA display each pixel is 0.375 mm wide and 0.5 mm tall, so EGA device coordinates are coarser than the logical coordinates for any of the metric mapping modes.

On a 300-dots-per-inch laser printer, each pixel is 0.0033 inch—a higher resolution than MM_LOENGLISH and MM_LOMETRIC but not as high as MM_HIENGLISH, MM_TWIPS, or MM_HIMETRIC.

The default origins and extents are shown below:

Window origin:	(0, 0)	Can be changed
Viewport origin:	(0, 0)	Can be changed
Window extent:	(?, ?)	Cannot be changed
Viewport extent:	(?, ?)	Cannot be changed

The window and viewport extents depend on the mapping mode and the aspect ratio of the device. As I mentioned earlier, the extents aren't important by themselves but take on meaning only when expressed as ratios. Here are the translation formulas again:

$$xViewport = (xWindow - xWinOrg) * \frac{xViewExt}{xWinExt} + xViewOrg$$

$$yViewport = (yWindow - yWinOrg) * \frac{yViewExt}{yWinExt} + yViewOrg$$

For MM_LOENGLISH, for instance, Windows calculates the extents to be the following:

$$\frac{xViewExt}{xWinExt} = number\ of\ horizontal\ pixels\ in\ 0.01\ in.$$

$$-\frac{yViewExt}{yWinExt} = number\ of\ vertical\ pixels\ in\ 0.01\ in.$$

For many display devices (such as the EGA), this ratio will be less than 1. Because Windows works entirely with integers, the use of a ratio rather than an absolute scaling factor is necessary to reduce loss of precision when converting logical and device coordinates.

Notice the negative sign in front of the ratio of extents for the vertical axis. This negative sign changes the orientation of the y-axis. For these five mapping modes, y values increase as you move up the device. The default window and viewport origins are (0, 0). This fact has an interesting implication. When you first change to one of these five mapping modes, the coordinate system looks like this:

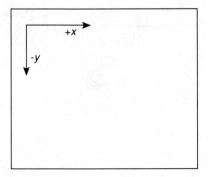

The only way you can display anything in the client area is to use negative values of *y*. For instance, this code:

```
SetMapMode (hdc, MM_LOENGLISH) ;
TextOut (hdc, 100, -100, "Hello", 5) ;
```

displays *Hello* 1 inch from the top and left edges of the client area.

To preserve your sanity, you'll probably want to avoid this. One solution is to set the logical (0, 0) point to be the lower left corner of the client area. Assuming that *cyClient* is the height of the client area in pixels, you can do this by calling *SetViewportOrg*:

```
SetViewportOrg (hdc, 0, cyClient) ;
```

Now the coordinate system looks like this:

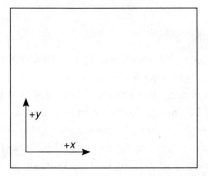

Alternatively, you can set the logical (0, 0) point to the center of the client area:

```
SetViewportOrg (hdc, cxClient / 2, cyClient / 2) ;
```

The coordinate system looks like this:

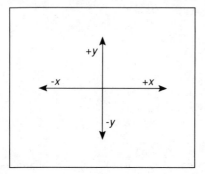

Now we have a real four-quadrant Cartesian coordinate system with equal logical units on the *x*-axis and *y*-axis in terms of inches, millimeters, or twips.

You can also use the *SetWindowOrg* function to change the logical (0, 0) point, but the task is a little more difficult because the parameters to *SetWindowOrg* have to be in logical coordinates. You would first need to convert *cyClient* to a logical coordinate using the *DPtoLP* function. Assuming that the variable *pt* is a structure of type POINT, this code changes the logical (0, 0) point to the center of the client area:

```
pt.x = cxClient ;
pt.y = cyClient ;
DPtoLP (hdc, &pt, 1) ;
SetWindowOrg (hdc, -pt.x, -pt.y) ;
```

The "Roll Your Own" Mapping Modes

The two remaining mapping modes are called MM_ISOTROPIC and MM_ANISOTROPIC. These are the only two mapping modes for which Windows lets you change the viewport and window extents, which means that you can change the scaling factor that Windows uses to translate logical and device coordinates. The word *isotropic* means "equal in all directions"; *anisotropic* is the opposite—"not equal." Like the metric mapping modes shown earlier, MM_ISOTROPIC uses equally scaled axes. Logical units on the *x*-axis have the same physical dimensions as logical units on the *y*-axis. This helps when you need to create images that retain the correct aspect ratio regardless of the aspect ratio of the display device.

The difference between MM_ISOTROPIC and the metric mapping modes is that with MM_ISOTROPIC you can control the physical size of the logical unit. If you want, you can adjust the physical size of the logical unit based on the size of the client area so that the images you draw are always contained within the client area, shrinking and expanding appropriately. For instance, the CLOCK and REVERSI programs included with Windows are examples of isotropic images. The clock is always round, and the Reversi playing board is always square. As you size the window, the image is resized appropriately. A Windows program can handle the resizing of an image entirely through adjusting the window and viewport extents. The program can then use the same logical units in the drawing functions regardless of the size of the window.

Sometimes the MM_TEXT and the "metric" mapping modes are called "fully constrained" mapping modes. This means that you cannot change the window and viewport extents and the way that Windows scales logical coordinates to device coordinates. MM_ISOTROPIC is a "partly constrained" mapping mode. Windows allows you to change the window and viewport extents, but it adjusts them so that x and y logical units represent the same physical dimensions. The MM_ANISOTROPIC mapping mode is "unconstrained." You can change the window and viewport extents, and Windows doesn't adjust the values.

The MM_ISOTROPIC mapping mode

The MM_ISOTROPIC mapping mode is ideal for using arbitrary axes while preserving equal logical units on the two axes. Rectangles with equal logical widths and heights are displayed as squares. Ellipses with equal logical widths and heights are displayed as circles.

When you first set the mapping mode to MM_ISOTROPIC, Windows uses the same window and viewport extents that it uses with MM_LOMETRIC. (Don't rely on this fact, however.) The difference is that you can now change the extents to suit your preferences by calling *SetWindowExt* and *SetViewportExt*. Windows will then adjust the extents so that the logical units on both axes represent equal physical distances.

Generally, you'll use parameters to *SetWindowExt* with the desired logical size of the logical window, and parameters to *SetViewportExt* with the actual height and width of the client area. When Windows adjusts these extents, it has to fit the logical window within the physical viewport, which can result in a section of the client area falling outside the logical window. You should call *SetWindowExt* before you call *SetViewportExt* to make the most efficient use of space in the client area.

For instance, suppose you want a "traditional" one-quadrant virtual coordinate system where (0, 0) is at the lower left corner of the client area and the width ranges from 0 to 32,767 and the height from 0 to 32,767. You want the x and y units to have the same physical dimensions. Here's what you need to do:

```
SetMapMode (hdc, MM_ISOTROPIC) ;
SetWindowExt (hdc, 32767, 32767) ;
SetViewportExt (hdc, cxClient, -cyClient) ;
SetViewportOrg (hdc, 0, cyClient) ;
```

If you then obtain the window and viewport extents using *GetWindowExt* and *GetViewportExt*, you'll find that they are not the values you specified. Windows adjusts the extents based on the aspect ratio of the display device so that logical units on the two axes represent the same physical dimensions.

If the client area is wider than it is high (in physical dimensions), Windows adjusts the *x* extents so that the logical window is narrower than the client-area viewport. The logical window will be positioned at the left of the client area:

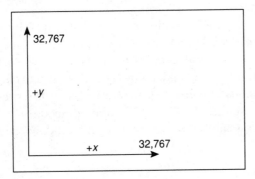

You can't display anything starting on the right side of the client area beyond the range of the *x*-axis, because that requires a logical *x*-coordinate greater than 32,767.

If the client area is higher than it is wide (in physical dimensions), Windows adjusts the *y* extents. The logical window will be positioned at the bottom of the client area:

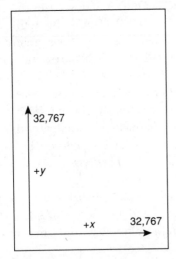

Now you can't display anything at the top of the client area, because you need a logical *y*-coordinate greater than 32,767.

If you prefer that the logical window always be positioned at the left and top of the client area, you can change the code on the preceding page to the following:

```
SetMapMode (hdc, MM_ISOTROPIC) ;
SetWindowExt (hdc, 32767, 32767) ;
SetViewportExt (hdc, cxClient, -cyClient) ;
SetWindowOrg (hdc, 0, 32767) ;
```

In the *SetWindowOrg* call we're saying that we want the logical point (0, 32,767) to be mapped to the device point (0, 0). Now if the client area is higher than it is wide, the coordinates are arranged like this:

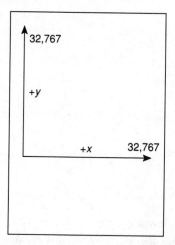

For a CLOCK-like image, you might want to use a four-quadrant Cartesian coordinate system with arbitrarily scaled axes in four directions where the logical point (0, 0) is in the center of the client area. If you want each axis to range from 0 to 1000 (for instance), you use this code:

```
SetMapMode (hdc, MM_ISOTROPIC) ;
SetWindowExt (hdc, 1000, 1000) ;
SetViewportExt (hdc, cxClient / 2, -cyClient / 2) ;
SetViewportOrg (hdc, cxClient / 2, cyClient / 2) ;
```

The logical coordinates look like this if the client area is wider than it is high:

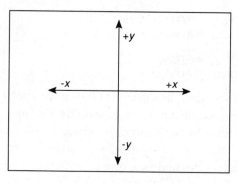

The logical coordinates are also centered if the client area is higher than it is wide:

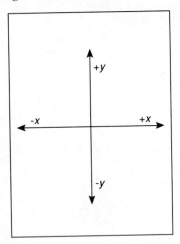

Keep in mind that no clipping is implied in window or viewport extents. When calling GDI functions, you are still free to use logical x and y values less than −1000 and greater than +1000. Depending on the shape of the client area, these points may or may not be visible.

With the MM_ISOTROPIC mapping mode, you can make logical units larger than pixels. For instance, suppose you want a mapping mode with the point (0,0) at the upper left corner of the display and values of y increasing as you move down (like MM_TEXT) but with logical coordinates in sixteenths of an inch. This mapping mode would let you draw a ruler starting at the top and left side of the client area with divisions of sixteenths of an inch:

```
SetMapMode (hdc, MM_ISOTROPIC) ;

SetWindowExt (hdc,
        (short) (160L * GetDeviceCaps (hdc, HORZSIZE) / 254),
        (short) (160L * GetDeviceCaps (hdc, VERTSIZE) / 254)) ;

SetViewportExt (hdc, GetDeviceCaps (hdc, HORZRES),
                     GetDeviceCaps (hdc, VERTRES)) ;
```

In this code, the viewport extents are set to the pixel dimensions of the entire screen. The window extents must be set to the dimensions of the entire screen in units of sixteenths of an inch. The HORZSIZE and VERTSIZE indexes to *GetDeviceCaps* return the dimensions of the device in millimeters. If we were working with floating-point numbers, we would convert the millimeters to inches by dividing by 25.4 and then convert inches to sixteenths of an inch by multiplying by 16. However, because we're working with integers, we must multiply by 160 and divide by 254. The calculation is done in long integers to prevent overflow.

For most output devices, this code makes the logical unit much larger than the physical unit. Everything you draw on the device will have coordinate values that map to an increment of $\frac{1}{16}$ inch. You cannot draw two horizontal lines that are $\frac{1}{32}$ inch apart, however, because that would require a fractional logical coordinate.

MM_ANISOTROPIC: Stretching the image to fit

When you set the viewport and window extents in the MM_ISOTROPIC mapping mode, Windows adjusts the values so that logical units on the two axes have the same physical dimensions. In the MM_ANISOTROPIC mapping mode, Windows makes no adjustments to the values you set. This means that MM_ANISOTROPIC does not necessarily maintain the correct aspect ratio.

One way you can use MM_ANISOTROPIC is to have arbitrary coordinates for the client area, as we did with MM_ISOTROPIC. This code sets the point (0, 0) at the lower left corner of the client area with both the x- and y-axes ranging from 0 to 32,767:

```
SetMapMode (hdc, MM_ANISOTROPIC) ;
SetWindowExt (hdc, 32767, 32767) ;
SetViewportExt (hdc, cxClient, -cyClient) ;
SetViewportOrg (hdc, 0, cyClient) ;
```

With MM_ISOTROPIC, similar code caused part of the client area to be beyond the range of the axes. With MM_ANISOTROPIC, the upper right corner of the client area is always the point (32767, 32767) regardless of its dimensions. If the client area is not square, then logical x and y units will be different physical dimensions.

In the previous section on the MM_ISOTROPIC mapping mode, I discussed drawing a CLOCK-like image in the client area where both the x- and y-axes ranged from −1000 to 1000. You can do something similar with MM_ANISOTROPIC:

```
SetMapMode (hdc, MM_ANISOTROPIC) ;
SetWindowExt (hdc, 1000, 1000) ;
SetViewportExt (hdc, cxClient / 2, -cyClient / 2) ;
SetViewportOrg (hdc, cxClient / 2, cyClient / 2) ;
```

The difference with MM_ANISOTROPIC is that in general the clock would be drawn as an ellipse rather than a circle.

Another way to use MM_ANISOTROPIC is to set x and y units to fixed but unequal values. For instance, if you have a program that displays only text, you may want to set coarse coordinates based on the height and width of a single character:

```
SetMapMode (hdc, MM_ANISOTROPIC) ;
SetWindowExt (hdc, 1, 1) ;
SetViewportExt (hdc, cxChar, cyChar) ;
```

(This assumes that *cxChar* and *cyChar* are the width and height of a character in pixels, for a fixed-pitch font.) Now you can specify character row and column coordinates in the

TextOut call rather than pixel coordinates. For instance, the following statement displays the text *Hello* three character spaces from the left and two character rows from the top:

```
TextOut (hdc, 3, 2, "Hello", 5) ;
```

This is almost like working in text mode in the non-Windows MS-DOS environment!

When you first set the MM_ANISOTROPIC mapping mode, it always inherits the extents of the previously set mapping mode, which can be very convenient. One way of thinking about MM_ANISOTROPIC is that it "unlocks" the extents; that is, it allows you to change the extents of an otherwise fully constrained mapping mode. For instance, suppose you want to use the MM_LOENGLISH mapping mode because you want logical units to be 0.01 inch. But you don't want the values along the *y*-axis to increase as you move up the screen—you prefer the MM_TEXT orientation, where *y* values increase moving down. Here's the code:

```
DWORD dwExtent ;
        [other program lines]
SetMapMode (hdc, MM_LOENGLISH) ;
SetMapMode (hdc, MM_ANISOTROPIC) ;

dwExtent = GetViewportExt (hdc) ;

SetViewportExt (hdc, LOWORD (dwExtent), -HIWORD (dwExtent)) ;
```

We first set the mapping mode to MM_LOENGLISH. Then we liberate the extents by setting the mapping mode to MM_ANISOTROPIC. The *GetViewportExt* obtains the viewport extents encoded in a DWORD variable. Then we call *SetViewportExt* with the extents extracted from the DWORD using the LOWORD and HIWORD macros, except that we make the *y* extent negative.

The WHATSIZE Program

We'll use various mapping modes as we explore the GDI functions in the next four chapters. Right now, let's simply look at the size of a client area in terms of inches and millimeters. The WHATSIZE program, shown in Figure 11-5, displays the size of the client area in terms of units associated with the six fully constrained mapping modes: MM_TEXT, MM_LOMETRIC, MM_HIMETRIC, MM_LOENGLISH, MM_HIENGLISH, and MM_TWIPS.

WHATSIZE.MAK

```
#------------------------
# WHATSIZE.MAK make file
#------------------------

whatsize.exe : whatsize.obj whatsize.def
     link whatsize, /align:16, NUL, /nod slibcew libw, whatsize
     rc whatsize.exe

whatsize.obj : whatsize.c
     cl -c -Gsw -Ow -W2 -Zp whatsize.c
```

WHATSIZE.C

```c
/*-------------------------------------------
   WHATSIZE.C -- What Size Is the Window?
                 (c) Charles Petzold, 1990
   -------------------------------------------*/

#include <windows.h>
#include <stdio.h>

long FAR PASCAL WndProc (HWND, WORD, WORD, LONG) ;

int PASCAL WinMain (HANDLE hInstance, HANDLE hPrevInstance,
                    LPSTR lpszCmdLine, int nCmdShow)
     {
     static char szAppName[] = "WhatSize" ;
     HWND        hwnd ;
     MSG         msg ;
     WNDCLASS    wndclass ;

     if (!hPrevInstance)
         {
         wndclass.style         = CS_HREDRAW : CS_VREDRAW;
         wndclass.lpfnWndProc   = WndProc ;
         wndclass.cbClsExtra    = 0 ;
         wndclass.cbWndExtra    = 0 ;
         wndclass.hInstance     = hInstance ;
         wndclass.hIcon         = LoadIcon (NULL, IDI_APPLICATION) ;
         wndclass.hCursor       = LoadCursor (NULL, IDC_ARROW) ;
         wndclass.hbrBackground = GetStockObject (WHITE_BRUSH) ;
         wndclass.lpszMenuName  = NULL ;
         wndclass.lpszClassName = szAppName ;
```

Figure 11-5. *The WHATSIZE program.*   *(continued)*

```
            RegisterClass (&wndclass) ;
            }

     hwnd = CreateWindow (szAppName, "What Size Is the Window?",
                          WS_OVERLAPPEDWINDOW,
                          CW_USEDEFAULT, CW_USEDEFAULT,
                          CW_USEDEFAULT, CW_USEDEFAULT,
                          NULL, NULL, hInstance, NULL) ;

     ShowWindow (hwnd, nCmdShow) ;
     UpdateWindow (hwnd) ;

     while (GetMessage (&msg, NULL, 0, 0))
          {
          TranslateMessage (&msg) ;
          DispatchMessage (&msg) ;
          }
     return msg.wParam ;
     }

void Show (HWND hwnd, HDC hdc, short xText, short yText, short nMapMode,
           char *szMapMode)
     {
     char szBuffer [60] ;
     RECT rect ;

     SaveDC (hdc) ;

     SetMapMode (hdc, nMapMode) ;
     GetClientRect (hwnd, &rect) ;
     DPtoLP (hdc, (LPPOINT) &rect, 2) ;

     RestoreDC (hdc, -1) ;

     TextOut (hdc, xText, yText, szBuffer,
              sprintf (szBuffer, "%-20s %7d %7d %7d %7d", szMapMode,
                       rect.left, rect.right, rect.top, rect.bottom)) ;
     }

long FAR PASCAL WndProc (HWND hwnd, WORD message, WORD wParam, LONG lParam)
     {
     static char  szHeading [] =
                    "Mapping Mode              Left   Right   Top  Bottom" ;
     static char  szUndLine [] =
                    "------------              ----   -----   ---  ------" ;
     static short cxChar, cyChar ;
     HDC          hdc ;
```

(continued)

536

```
PAINTSTRUCT  ps ;
TEXTMETRIC   tm ;

switch (message)
     {
     case WM_CREATE :
          hdc = GetDC (hwnd) ;
          SelectObject (hdc, GetStockObject (SYSTEM_FIXED_FONT)) ;

          GetTextMetrics (hdc, &tm) ;
          cxChar = tm.tmAveCharWidth ;
          cyChar = tm.tmHeight + tm.tmExternalLeading ;

          ReleaseDC (hwnd, hdc) ;
          return 0 ;

     case WM_PAINT :
          hdc = BeginPaint (hwnd, &ps) ;
          SelectObject (hdc, GetStockObject (SYSTEM_FIXED_FONT)) ;

          SetMapMode (hdc, MM_ANISOTROPIC) ;
          SetWindowExt (hdc, 1, 1) ;
          SetViewportExt (hdc, cxChar, cyChar) ;

          TextOut (hdc, 1, 1, szHeading, sizeof szHeading - 1) ;
          TextOut (hdc, 1, 2, szUndLine, sizeof szUndLine - 1) ;

          Show (hwnd, hdc, 1, 3, MM_TEXT,      "TEXT (pixels)") ;
          Show (hwnd, hdc, 1, 4, MM_LOMETRIC,  "LOMETRIC (.1 mm)") ;
          Show (hwnd, hdc, 1, 5, MM_HIMETRIC,  "HIMETRIC (.01 mm)") ;
          Show (hwnd, hdc, 1, 6, MM_LOENGLISH, "LOENGLISH (.01 in)") ;
          Show (hwnd, hdc, 1, 7, MM_HIENGLISH, "HIENGLISH (.001 in)") ;
          Show (hwnd, hdc, 1, 8, MM_TWIPS,     "TWIPS (1/1440 in)") ;

          EndPaint (hwnd, &ps) ;
          return 0 ;

     case WM_DESTROY :
          PostQuitMessage (0) ;
          return 0 ;
     }
return DefWindowProc (hwnd, message, wParam, lParam) ;
}
```

WHATSIZE.DEF

```
;------------------------------------
; WHATSIZE.DEF module definition file
;------------------------------------

NAME            WHATSIZE

DESCRIPTION     'What Size Is the Window? (c) Charles Petzold, 1990'
EXETYPE         WINDOWS
STUB            'WINSTUB.EXE'
CODE            PRELOAD MOVEABLE DISCARDABLE
DATA            PRELOAD MOVEABLE MULTIPLE
HEAPSIZE        1024
STACKSIZE       8192
EXPORTS         WndProc
```

For ease in displaying the information using the *TextOut* function, WHATSIZE uses the MM_ANISOTROPIC mapping mode with logical units set to character dimensions:

```
SetMapMode (hdc, MM_ANISOTROPIC) ;
SetWindowExt (hdc, 1, 1) ;
SetViewportExt (hdc, cxChar, cyChar) ;
```

The program can then specify logical coordinates to *TextOut* in character row and character column coordinates for a fixed-pitch font.

When WHATSIZE needs to obtain the size of the client area for one of the six mapping modes, it saves the current device context, sets a new mapping mode, obtains the client-area coordinates, converts them to logical coordinates, and then restores the original mapping mode before displaying the information. This code is in WHATSIZE's Show function:

```
SaveDC (hdc) ;

SetMapMode (hdc, nMapMode) ;
GetClientRect (hwnd, &rect) ;
DPtoLP (hdc, (LPPOINT) &rect, 2) ;

RestoreDC (hdc, -1) ;
```

Figure 11-6 shows a typical display from WHATSIZE.

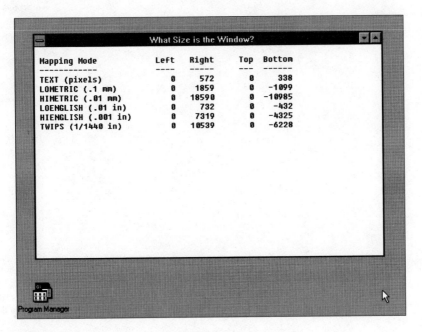

Figure 11-6. *A typical WHATSIZE display.*

Now that we have the preliminaries down, we're ready to start drawing.

Chapter 12

Drawing Graphics

Some theoretical discussions of computer graphics assume that you are supplied with only two graphics primitives—a "write pixel" routine and a "read pixel" routine. In theory, you can do anything you want with these two functions. Drawing a line, for instance, simply requires that you call the "write pixel" routine numerous times, adjusting the *x*- and *y*- coordinates appropriately.

In reality, you can indeed do anything you want with only "write pixel" and "read pixel" routines—if you don't mind waiting for the results. It is much more efficient for a graphics system to do line drawing and other complex graphics operations at the level of the device driver, which can have its own optimized code to perform the operations. Moreover, as video display technology becomes more sophisticated, the adapter boards will contain graphics coprocessors that allow the video hardware itself to draw the figures.

But of course, no graphics language would be complete without routines to draw one pixel at a time, and that's where we'll begin. From there we'll proceed to drawing lines, and then we'll tackle bounded areas.

DRAWING POINTS

You can draw a pixel of a particular color with the GDI *SetPixel* function:

```
rgbActualColor = SetPixel (hdc, x, y, rgbColor) ;
```

The *rgbColor* parameter is an unsigned long integer (32 bits) where the lowest 3 bytes represent the density of red, green, and blue. You can construct this color value using the RGB macro:

```
rgbColor = RGB (byRed, byGreen, byBlue) ;
```

(Chapters 5 and 6 contain a more extensive discussion of Windows' use of color.)

Although *x* and *y* are logical coordinates, *SetPixel* colors only a single physical pixel regardless of the mapping mode. Because *SetPixel* draws only a single pixel, the use of a dithered color (a color that combines pixels of various pure colors) is meaningless. For this reason, Windows translates the *rgbColor* parameter to a pure nondithered color and returns that color.

SetPixel is almost never used in Windows programs, but that didn't prevent us from using it in the CONNECT program in Chapter 4. You can obtain the color of a particular pixel this way:

```
rgbColor = GetPixel (hdc, x, y) ;
```

DRAWING LINES

After drawing points, the next step up is drawing lines. Windows can draw straight lines and elliptical lines. An elliptical line is a curved line on the circumference of an ellipse. The three functions that draw lines are *LineTo* (straight lines), *PolyLine* (series of connected lines), and *Arc* (elliptical lines). Five attributes of the device context affect the appearance of lines that you draw using these functions: current pen position (for *LineTo* only), pen, background mode (for nonsolid pens), background color (for the OPAQUE background mode), and drawing mode.

The *LineTo* function is one of the few GDI functions that does not include the full dimensions of the object to be drawn. Instead, *LineTo* draws a line from the current pen position defined in the device context up to (but not including) the logical point specified in the *LineTo* function. In the default device context, the current pen position is initially set at the logical point (0, 0). If you call *LineTo* without first setting the current pen position (or the viewport or window origin), it draws a line starting at the upper left corner of the client area.

To draw a line from the logical point (*xStart*, *yStart*) to the logical point (*xEnd*, *yEnd*), you first must use *MoveTo* to set the current pen position to the point (*xStart*, *yStart*):

```
MoveTo (hdc, xStart, yStart) ;
```

MoveTo doesn't draw anything. It simply changes the current pen position. You can then use *LineTo* to draw the line:

```
LineTo (hdc, xEnd, yEnd) ;
```

This draws the line up to (but not including) the point (*xEnd, yEnd*). Following the *LineTo* call, the current pen position is set to (*xEnd, yEnd*).

LineTo is the only Windows function that uses the current pen position. *MoveTo* and *LineTo* are the only functions that change it. You can obtain the current pen position by calling:

```
dwPoint = GetCurrentPosition (hdc) ;
```

The *dwPoint* return value is an unsigned long (or doubleword) that contains the *x*-coordinate in the low word and the *y*-coordinate in the high word. You can use the LOWORD and HIWORD macros to extract the two coordinates, or you can convert the value of *dwPoint* to a POINT structure using the MAKEPOINT macro:

```
point = MAKEPOINT (dwPoint) ;
```

The following code draws a grid in the client area of a window, spacing the lines 1 inch apart starting from the upper left corner. The variable *hwnd* is assumed to be a handle to the window, *hdc* is a handle to the device context, *rect* is a structure of type RECT, and *x* and *y* are short integers:

```
SetMapMode (hdc, MM_LOENGLISH) ;
GetClientRect (hwnd, &rect) ;
DPtoLP (hdc, (LPPOINT) &rect, 2) ;

for (x = 0 ; x < rect.right ; x += 100)
    {
    MoveTo (hdc, x, 0) ;
    LineTo (hdc, x, rect.bottom) ;
    }

for (y = 0 ; y > rect.bottom ; y -= 100)
    {
    MoveTo (hdc, 0, y) ;
    LineTo (hdc, rect.right, y) ;
    }
```

The dimensions of the client area are saved in the RECT structure called *rect* and converted to logical points with *DPtoLP*. After the *DPtoLP* conversion, *rect.right* is the width of the client area in units of 0.01 inch, and *rect.bottom* is the negative height of the client area. Notice that *y* is decremented rather than incremented in the second *for* loop because the MM_LOENGLISH mapping mode uses decreasing values of *y* as you move down the display.

Although it may seem like a nuisance to be forced to use two functions to draw a single line, the current pen position attribute comes in handy when you want to draw a series of connected lines. For instance, you might want to define an array of 5 points (10 values) that draw the outline of a rectangle:

```
POINT pt [5] = { 100, 100, 200, 100, 200, 200,
                 100, 200, 100, 100 } ;
```

Notice that the last point is the same as the first. Now you need only use *MoveTo* for the first point and *LineTo* for the successive points:

```
MoveTo (hdc, pt[0].x, pt[0].y) ;

for (i = 1 ; i < 5 ; i++)
    LineTo (hdc, pt[i].x, pt[i].y) ;
```

Because *LineTo* draws from the current point up to (but not including) the point in the *LineTo* function, no coordinate gets written twice by this code. While overwriting points is not a problem with a display, it might not look good on a plotter or with some drawing modes (to be covered shortly).

When you have an array of points that you want connected with lines, you can draw the lines more easily using the *PolyLine* function. This statement draws the same rectangle as in the code shown above:

```
PolyLine (hdc, &pt, 5) ;
```

The last parameter is the number of points. We could also have represented this value by (*sizeof pt* / *sizeof* (POINT)). *PolyLine* has the same effect as an initial *MoveTo* function followed by multiple *LineTo* functions. However, *PolyLine* doesn't use or change the current pen position.

The *Arc* function is a little more complex. Here's the general syntax:

```
Arc (hdc, xLeft, yTop, xRight, yBottom,
        xStart, yStart, xEnd, yEnd) ;
```

The *Arc* function draws a line on the circumference of an ellipse that is bounded by a rectangle with the upper left corner at (*xLeft, yTop*) and the lower right corner at (*xRight, yBottom*). The arc starts at the intersection of the ellipse and the line connecting (*xStart, yStart*) with the center of the ellipse. The arc is drawn counterclockwise around the circumference of the ellipse and ends at the intersection of the ellipse and the line connecting point (*xEnd, yEnd*) with the center of the ellipse. If you're having trouble visualizing this, don't worry about it: I'll discuss the *Arc* function in much more detail after we've covered rectangles and ellipses.

Using Stock Pens

When you call *LineTo, PolyLine,* or *Arc,* Windows uses the "pen" currently selected in the device context to draw the line. The pen determines the line's color, its width, and its style, which can be solid, dotted, or dashed. The pen in the default device context is called BLACK_PEN. This pen draws a solid black line with a width of one pixel regardless of the mapping mode. BLACK_PEN is one of three "stock pens" that Windows provides. The other two are WHITE_PEN and NULL_PEN. NULL_PEN is a pen that doesn't draw. You can also create your own customized pens.

In your Windows programs, you refer to pens with a handle. WINDOWS.H includes a type definition named HPEN, a handle to a pen. You can define a variable (for instance, *hPen*) using this type definition:

```
HPEN hPen ;
```

You obtain the handle to one of the stock pens by a call to *GetStockObject*. For instance, suppose you want to use the stock pen called WHITE_PEN. You get the pen handle like this:

```
hPen = GetStockObject (WHITE_PEN) ;
```

Now you must make that pen the currently selected pen in the device context, which requires a call to *SelectObject*:

```
SelectObject (hdc, hPen) ;
```

After this call, the lines you draw using *LineTo*, *PolyLine*, or *Arc* will use WHITE_PEN until you select another pen into the device context or release the device context.

Rather than explicitly defining an *hPen* variable, you can instead combine the *GetStockObject* and *SelectObject* calls in one statement:

```
SelectObject (hdc, GetStockObject (WHITE_PEN)) ;
```

If you then want to return to using BLACK_PEN, you can get the handle to that stock object and select it into the device context in one statement:

```
SelectObject (hdc, GetStockObject (BLACK_PEN)) ;
```

SelectObject returns the handle to the pen that had been previously selected into the device context. If you start off with a fresh device context and call:

```
hPen = SelectObject (hdc, GetStockObject (WHITE_PEN)) ;
```

then the current pen in the device context will be WHITE_PEN, and the variable *hPen* will be the handle to BLACK_PEN. You can then select BLACK_PEN into the device context by calling:

```
SelectObject (hdc, hPen) ;
```

Creating, Selecting, and Deleting Pens

Although the pens defined as stock objects are certainly convenient, you are limited to only a solid black pen, a solid white pen, or no pen at all. If you want to get fancier than that, you must create your own pens. Here's the general procedure: You create a "logical pen," which is merely the description of a pen, using the function *CreatePen* or *CreatePen-Indirect*. These functions return a handle to the logical pen. You select the pen into the device context by calling *SelectObject*. You can then draw lines with this new pen. Only one pen can be selected into the device context at any one time. After you release the device context (or after you select another pen into the device context), you can delete the logical pen you've created by calling *DeleteObject*. When you do so, the handle to the pen is no longer valid.

A logical pen is a "GDI object." You create and use the pen, but the pen doesn't belong to your program. The pen really belongs to the GDI module. A pen is one of six GDI objects that you can create. The other five are brushes, bitmaps, regions, fonts, and palettes.

This brings me to a very important point: Normally, Windows cleans up thoroughly when a program terminates. The one big exception is for GDI objects. When a program terminates, Windows doesn't automatically delete GDI objects that the program has created. The program itself is responsible for deleting GDI objects.

Three rules govern the use of GDI objects such as pens:

- Delete all GDI objects that you create.

- Don't delete GDI objects while they are selected in a valid device context.

- Don't delete stock objects.

These are not unreasonable rules, but they can be a little tricky sometimes. We'll run through some examples to get the hang of how the rules work.

The general syntax for the *CreatePen* function looks like this:

```
hPen = CreatePen (nPenStyle, nWidth, rgbColor) ;
```

The *nPenStyle* parameter determines whether the pen draws a solid line or a line made up of dots or dashes. The parameter can be one of the following identifiers defined in WINDOWS.H: PS_SOLID, PS_DASH, PS_DOT, PS_DASHDOT, PS_DASHDOTDOT, PS_NULL, and PS_INSIDEFRAME. Figure 12-1 shows the kind of line that each style produces.

```
PS_SOLID        ─────────
PS_DASH         ─ ── ──
PS_DOT          ··········
PS_DASHDOT      ─ · ─ · ─
PS_DASHDOTDOT   ─ ·· ─ ·· ─
PS_NULL
PS_INSIDEFRAME  ─────────
```

Figure 12-1. *The seven pen styles.*

For the PS_SOLID, PS_NULL, and PS_INSIDEFRAME styles, the *nWidth* parameter is the width of the pen in logical units. For instance, if the mapping mode is MM_LOENGLISH, a pen with an *nWidth* of 10 will be 0.1 inch wide. When you draw a line with a PS_SOLID or PS_NULL pen, the width of the pen will extend 0.05 inch on either side of the line. (The PS_INSIDEFRAME style is a little different.) For the MM_ANISOTROPIC mapping mode, Windows uses logical units on the *x*-axis to determine the physical width of the pen. An *nWidth* value of 0 directs Windows to use one physical unit (1 pixel) for the pen width. The stock pens are 1 pixel wide. If you specify a dotted or dashed pen style with a physical width greater than 1, Windows will use a solid pen instead.

The *rgbColor* parameter to *CreatePen* is an unsigned long integer specifying the color of the pen. For all the pen styles except PS_INSIDEFRAME, when you select the pen into the device context, Windows converts this parameter to the nearest pure color that the device can represent. The PS_INSIDEFRAME style is the only pen style that can use a dithered color, and then only when the width is greater than 1. (The PS_INSIDEFRAME style has another peculiarity, which I'll discuss later in this chapter in the section on the "bounding box.")

You can also create a pen by setting up a structure of type LOGPEN ("logical pen") and calling *CreatePenIndirect*. If your program uses a lot of different pens that you can initialize in your source code, this method is more efficient. First you define a structure variable of type LOGPEN—for instance, *logpen*:

```
LOGPEN logpen ;
```

This structure has three members: *lopnStyle* (WORD) is the pen style, *lopnWidth* (POINT) is the pen width in logical units, and *lopnColor* (DWORD) is the pen color. The *lopnWidth* member is a structure of type POINT, but Windows uses only the *lopnWidth.x* value for the pen width and ignores *lopnWidth.y*. Then you create the pen by passing the address of the structure to *CreatePenIndirect*:

```
hPen = CreatePenIndirect (&logpen) ;
```

You can also obtain the logical pen information for an existing pen. If you already have a handle to a pen, you can copy the data that defines the logical pen into a structure of type LOGPEN by using the *GetObject* call:

```
GetObject (hPen, sizeof (LOGPEN), (LPSTR) &logpen) ;
```

Note that the *CreatePen* and *CreatePenIndirect* functions do not require a handle to a device context. These functions create logical pens that have no connection with a device context until you call *SelectObject*. For instance, you can use the same logical pen for several different devices, such as the screen and a printer. Logical pens with a nonzero *nWidth* have a logical width; they have a physical width only when you select the pen into a device context, and then the physical width depends on the device context's mapping mode.

Here's one method for creating, selecting, and deleting pens. Suppose your program uses three pens—a black pen of width 1, a red pen of width 3, and a black dotted pen. You can first define variables for storing the handles to these pens:

```
static HPEN hPen1, hPen2, hPen3 ;
```

During processing of WM_CREATE, you can create the three pens:

```
hPen1 = CreatePen (PS_SOLID, 1, 0L) ;
hPen2 = CreatePen (PS_SOLID, 3, RGB (255, 0, 0)) ;
hPen3 = CreatePen (PS_DOT,   0, 0L) ;
```

During processing of WM_PAINT (or any other time you have a valid handle to a device context), you can select one of these pens into the device context and draw with it:

```
SelectObject (hdc, hPen2) ;
```
> [LineTo, PolyLine, or Arc calls]

```
SelectObject (hdc, hPen1) ;
```
> [other LineTo, PolyLine, or Arc calls]

During processing of WM_DESTROY, you can delete the three pens you created:

```
DeleteObject (hPen1) ;
DeleteObject (hPen2) ;
DeleteObject (hPen3) ;
```

This is the most straightforward method for creating, selecting, and deleting pens, but it requires that the logical pens take up memory space during the entire time your program is running. You might instead want to create the pens during each WM_PAINT message and delete them after you call *EndPaint*. (You can delete them before calling *EndPaint*, but you have to be careful not to delete the pen currently selected in the device context.)

You might also want to create pens on the fly and combine the *CreatePen* and the *SelectObject* calls in the same statement:

```
SelectObject (hdc, CreatePen (PS_DASH, 0, RGB (255, 0, 0))) ;
```

Now when you draw lines, you'll be using a red dashed pen. When you're finished drawing the red dashed lines, you can delete the pen. Whoops! How can you delete this pen when you haven't saved the pen handle? Recall that *SelectObject* returns the handle to the pen previously selected in the device context. So you can delete the pen by selecting the stock BLACK_PEN into the device context and deleting the value returned from *SelectObject*:

```
DeleteObject (SelectObject (hdc, GetStockObject (BLACK_PEN))) ;
```

Here's another method. When you select a newly created pen into the device context, save the handle to the pen that *SelectObject* returns:

```
hPen = SelectObject (hdc, CreatePen (PS_DASH, 0, RGB (255, 0, 0))) ;
```

What is *hPen*? If this is the first *SelectObject* call you've made since obtaining the device context, *hPen* is a handle to the BLACK_PEN stock object. You can now select that pen into the device context and delete the pen you created (the handle returned from this second *SelectObject* call) in one statement:

```
DeleteObject (SelectObject (hdc, hPen)) ;
```

If you delete a GDI object while it is selected in a device context and then try to draw lines, Windows will respond with a fatal error because the device context doesn't contain a valid pen. This is a fairly obvious bug to track down. Failing to delete GDI objects that you create can be a more difficult bug to discover, because the program will appear to work fine. If your program creates the same logical pen for every WM_PAINT message, you might want to cause the client area to be repainted over and over and check to see if free memory starts to drop. The FREEMEM program shown in Chapter 5 can identify problems related to dropping memory. If HEAPWALK shows a lot of small GDI segments after your program has terminated, some of them may be GDI objects you have failed to delete properly.

Avoiding Device Dependencies

Pen widths will vary according to the resolution of the display. The stock pens (and any pen created with a width of 0) are 1 pixel wide, which on a high-resolution display can result in very thin lines.

If you're working in MM_TEXT, you might want to obtain the width of the single-line window border by calling *GetSystemMetrics* with the SM_CXBORDER and SM_CYBORDER indexes. These values are appropriate for pen widths. You can also use one of the metric mapping modes and set specific physical widths for the pens your program needs to create.

Pen colors are also susceptible to device dependencies. If you develop a program on a color display and then run the program on a monochrome display, you can be in for some unpleasant surprises. Except for the PS_INSIDEFRAME style, Windows always uses pure colors for pens, and on a monochrome system, pens are either black or white. For instance, on your color EGA, you might be fond of magenta pens on a white background:

```
hPen = CreatePen (PS_SOLID, 1, RGB (255, 0, 255)) ;
```

But on a monochrome system, the pure color that is closest to magenta is white, so the pen will be invisible. If you want to use colored pens, be sure the sum of 2 times the red, 5 times the green, and 1 times the blue values is less than 1920 (half the maximum sum of the three primaries) for any pen that should default to black and greater than 1920 for any pen that should default to white.

Filling In the Gaps

The use of dotted pens and dashed pens raises an interesting question: What happens to the gaps between the dots and the dashes? The coloring of the gaps depends on both the background mode and the background color attributes defined in the device context. The default background mode is OPAQUE, which means that Windows fills in the gaps with the background color, which by default is white. This is consistent with the WHITE_BRUSH that many programs use in the window class for erasing the background of the window.

You can change the background color that Windows uses to fill in the gaps by calling:

```
SetBkColor (hdc, rgbColor) ;
```

As with the *rgbColor* value used for the pen color, Windows converts this background color to a pure color. You can obtain the current background color defined in the device context by calling *GetBkColor*.

You can also prevent Windows from filling in the gaps by changing the background mode to TRANSPARENT:

```
SetBkMode (hdc, TRANSPARENT) ;
```

Windows will ignore the background color and will not fill in the gaps. You can obtain the current background mode (either TRANSPARENT or OPAQUE) by calling *GetBkMode*.

Drawing Modes

The appearance of lines drawn on the display is also affected by the drawing mode defined in the device context. Imagine drawing a line that has a color based not only on the color of the pen but also on the original color of the display area where the line is drawn. Imagine a way in which you could use the same pen to draw a black line on a white surface and a white line on a black surface without knowing what color the surface is. Could such a facility be useful to you? It's made possible by the drawing mode.

When Windows uses a pen to draw a line, it actually performs a bitwise Boolean operation between the pixels of the pen and the pixels of the destination display surface. Performing a bitwise Boolean operation with pixels is called a "raster operation," or "ROP." Because drawing a line involves only two pixel patterns (the pen and the destination), the Boolean operation is called a "binary raster operation," or "ROP2." Windows defines 16 ROP2 codes that indicate how Windows combines the pen pixels and the destination pixels. In the default device context, the drawing mode is defined as R2_COPYPEN, which means that Windows simply copies the pixels of the pen to the destination, which is how we normally think about pens. There are 15 other ROP2 codes.

Where do these 16 different ROP2 codes come from? For illustration purposes, let's assume a monochrome system. The destination color (the color of the window's client area) can be either black (which we'll represent by a 0) or white (1). The pen also can be either black or white. There are four combinations of using a black or white pen to draw on a black or white destination: a white pen on a white destination, a white pen on a black destination, a black pen on a white destination, and a black pen on a black destination.

What happens to the destination after you draw with the pen? One possibility is that the line is always drawn as black regardless of the pen or destination color: This drawing mode is indicated by the ROP2 code R2_BLACK. Another possibility is that the line is drawn as black except when both the pen and destination are black, in which case the line is drawn as white. Although this might be a little strange, Windows has a name for it: The drawing mode is called R2_NOTMERGEPEN. Windows performs a bitwise OR operation on the destination pixels and the pen pixels and then inverts that result.

The table below shows all 16 ROP2 drawing modes. The table indicates how the original pen (P) and destination (D) colors are combined for the resultant destination color.

The column labeled "Boolean Operation" uses C notation to show how the destination pixels and pen pixels are combined.

| Pen (P): | 1 | 1 | 0 | 0 | Boolean | |
Destination (D):	1	0	1	0	Operation	Drawing Mode
Results:	0	0	0	0	0	R2_BLACK
	0	0	0	1	~(P ¦ D)	R2_NOTMERGEPEN
	0	0	1	0	~P & D	R2_MASKNOTPEN
	0	0	1	1	~P	R2_NOTCOPYPEN
	0	1	0	0	P & ~D	R2_MASKPENNOT
	0	1	0	1	~D	R2_NOT
	0	1	1	0	P ∧ D	R2_XORPEN
	0	1	1	1	~(P & D)	R2_NOTMASKPEN
	1	0	0	0	P & D	R2_MASKPEN
	1	0	0	1	~(P ∧ D)	R2_NOTXORPEN
	1	0	1	0	D	R2_NOP
	1	0	1	1	~P ¦ D	R2_MERGENOTPEN
	1	1	0	0	P	R2_COPYPEN (default)
	1	1	0	1	P ¦ ~D	R2_MERGEPENNOT
	1	1	1	0	P ¦ D	R2_MERGEPEN
	1	1	1	1	1	R2_WHITE

You can set a new drawing mode in the device context by:

```
SetROP2 (hdc, nDrawMode) ;
```

The *nDrawMode* parameter is one of the values listed in the "Drawing Mode" column of the table. You can obtain the current drawing mode using the function:

```
nDrawMode = GetROP2 (hdc) ;
```

The device context default is R2_COPYPEN, which simply transfers the pen color to the destination. The R2_NOTCOPYPEN mode draws white if the pen color is black and black if the pen color is white. The R2_BLACK mode always draws black, regardless of the color of the pen or the background. Likewise, the R2_WHITE mode always draws white. The R2_NOP mode is a "no operation": It leaves the destination unchanged.

We started out using an example of a pure monochrome system. In reality, on a monochrome display Windows can simulate various shades of gray by dithering black and white pixels. When drawing a pen on a dithered background, Windows simply performs the bitwise operation on a pixel-by-pixel basis. The R2_NOT mode always inverts the destination, again regardless of the color of the pen. This mode is useful when you don't know the color of the background, because it guarantees that the pen will be visible. (Well, *almost* guarantees—if the background is a 50 percent gray, then the pen will be virtually invisible.)

The ROP2LOOK Program

The ROP2LOOK program, shown in Figure 12-2, lets you experiment with these 16 ROP2 codes.

ROP2LOOK.MAK

```
#----------------------
# ROP2LOOK.MAK make file
#----------------------

rop2look.exe : rop2look.obj rop2look.def rop2look.res
    link rop2look, /align:16, NUL, /nod slibcew libw, rop2look
    rc rop2look.res

rop2look.obj : rop2look.c
    cl -c -Gsw -Ow -W2 -Zp rop2look.c

rop2look.res : rop2look.rc
    rc -r rop2look.rc
```

ROP2LOOK.C

```
/*----------------------------------------------
   ROP2LOOK.C -- ROP2 Demonstration Program
                 (c) Charles Petzold, 1990
   ------------------------------------------*/

#include <windows.h>

long FAR PASCAL WndProc (HWND, WORD, WORD, LONG) ;

int PASCAL WinMain (HANDLE hInstance, HANDLE hPrevInstance,
                    LPSTR lpszCmdLine, int nCmdShow)
```

Figure 12-2. *The ROP2LOOK program.*

(continued)

```
      {
      static char szAppName[] = "Rop2Look" ;
      HWND        hwnd ;
      MSG         msg ;
      WNDCLASS    wndclass ;

      if (!hPrevInstance)
            {
            wndclass.style         = CS_HREDRAW : CS_VREDRAW ;
            wndclass.lpfnWndProc   = WndProc ;
            wndclass.cbClsExtra    = 0 ;
            wndclass.cbWndExtra    = 0 ;
            wndclass.hInstance     = hInstance ;
            wndclass.hIcon         = NULL ;
            wndclass.hCursor       = LoadCursor (NULL, IDC_ARROW) ;
            wndclass.hbrBackground = GetStockObject (WHITE_BRUSH) ;
            wndclass.lpszMenuName  = szAppName ;
            wndclass.lpszClassName = szAppName ;

            RegisterClass (&wndclass) ;
            }


      hwnd = CreateWindow (szAppName, "ROP2 Demonstration Program",
                          WS_OVERLAPPEDWINDOW,
                          CW_USEDEFAULT, CW_USEDEFAULT,
                          CW_USEDEFAULT, CW_USEDEFAULT,
                          NULL, NULL, hInstance, NULL) ;

      ShowWindow (hwnd, nCmdShow) ;
      UpdateWindow (hwnd) ;

      while (GetMessage (&msg, NULL, 0, 0))
            {
            TranslateMessage (&msg) ;
            DispatchMessage (&msg) ;
            }
      return msg.wParam ;
      }

long FAR PASCAL WndProc (HWND hwnd, WORD message, WORD wParam, LONG lParam)
      {
      static LOGPEN lpBlack = { PS_SOLID, 1, 1, RGB (  0,   0,   0) },
                    lpWhite = { PS_SOLID, 1, 1, RGB (255, 255, 255) } ;
      static short  nDrawingMode = R2_COPYPEN ;
      HDC           hdc ;
      HMENU         hMenu ;
      HPEN          hPenBlack, hPenWhite ;
      PAINTSTRUCT   ps ;
```

(continued)

```
RECT        rect ;
short       i ;

switch (message)
     {
     case WM_COMMAND :
          hMenu = GetMenu (hwnd) ;
          CheckMenuItem (hMenu, nDrawingMode, MF_UNCHECKED) ;
          nDrawingMode = wParam ;
          CheckMenuItem (hMenu, nDrawingMode, MF_CHECKED) ;
          InvalidateRect (hwnd, NULL, FALSE) ;
          return 0 ;

     case WM_PAINT :
          hdc = BeginPaint (hwnd, &ps) ;

          hPenBlack = CreatePenIndirect (&lpBlack) ;
          hPenWhite = CreatePenIndirect (&lpWhite) ;

          SetMapMode (hdc, MM_ANISOTROPIC) ;
          GetClientRect (hwnd, &rect) ;
          SetViewportExt (hdc, rect.right, rect.bottom) ;
          SetWindowExt (hdc, 10, 4) ;

          for (i = 0 ; i < 10 ; i += 2)
                {
                SetRect (&rect, i, 0, i + 2, 4) ;
                FillRect (hdc, &rect, GetStockObject (i / 2)) ;
                }
          SetROP2 (hdc, nDrawingMode) ;

          SelectObject (hdc, hPenWhite) ;
          MoveTo (hdc, 1, 1) ;
          LineTo (hdc, 9, 1) ;

          SelectObject (hdc, hPenBlack) ;
          MoveTo (hdc, 1, 3) ;
          LineTo (hdc, 9, 3) ;

          EndPaint (hwnd, &ps) ;

          DeleteObject (hPenBlack) ;
          DeleteObject (hPenWhite) ;
          return 0 ;

     case WM_DESTROY :
          PostQuitMessage (0) ;
          return 0 ;
     }
 return DefWindowProc (hwnd, message, wParam, lParam) ;
 }
```

ROP2LOOK.RC

```
/*----------------------------
   ROP2LOOK.RC resource script
--------------------------*/

Rop2Look MENU
    {
    POPUP "&Drawing Mode"
        {
        MENUITEM "0\tR2_BLACK",        1
        MENUITEM "1\tR2_NOTMERGEPEN",  2
        MENUITEM "2\tR2_MASKNOTPEN",   3
        MENUITEM "3\tR2_NOTCOPYPEN",   4
        MENUITEM "4\tR2_MASKPENNOT",   5
        MENUITEM "5\tR2_NOT",          6
        MENUITEM "6\tR2_XORPEN",       7
        MENUITEM "7\tR2_NOTMASKPEN",   8
        MENUITEM "8\tR2_MASKPEN",      9
        MENUITEM "9\tR2_NOTXORPEN",    10
        MENUITEM "A\tR2_NOP",          11
        MENUITEM "B\tR2_MERGENOTPEN",  12
        MENUITEM "C\tR2_COPYPEN",      13, CHECKED
        MENUITEM "D\tR2_MERGEPENNOT",  14
        MENUITEM "E\tR2_MERGEPEN",     15
        MENUITEM "F\tR2_WHITE",        16
        }
    }
```

ROP2LOOK.DEF

```
;------------------------------------
; ROP2LOOK.DEF module definition file
;------------------------------------

NAME          ROP2LOOK

DESCRIPTION   'ROP2 Demonstration Program (c) Charles Petzold, 1990'
EXETYPE       WINDOWS
STUB          'WINSTUB.EXE'
CODE          PRELOAD MOVEABLE DISCARDABLE
DATA          PRELOAD MOVEABLE MULTIPLE
HEAPSIZE      1024
STACKSIZE     8192
EXPORTS       WndProc
```

The program draws a background divided into five sections colored with the white, light gray, gray, dark gray, and black stock brushes (a subject that we'll get to soon). It then draws two very thick pens: a white pen on the top and a black pen on the bottom. You can select one of the 16 ROP2 codes from the menu. Figure 12-3 shows the white pen on the top and the black pen on the bottom with the drawing mode set to R2_NOTMERGEPEN: The white pen always displays as black, and the black pen inverts the destination.

ROP2LOOK uses initialized logical pen structures for the white and black pens. You'll note that both these pens have a logical width of 1. Why do they appear so thick? The program uses the MM_ANISOTROPIC mapping mode and sets the width of the client area to 10 logical units and the height to 4 logical units. The pens are therefore one-tenth the width of the client area.

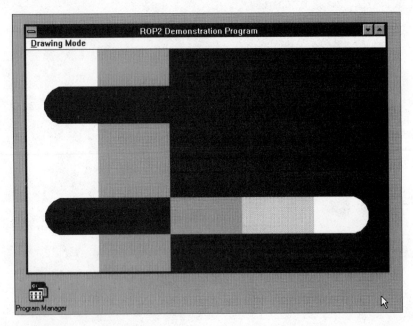

Figure 12-3. *The ROP2LOOK display with the drawing mode set to R2_NOTMERGEPEN.*

ROP2 and Color

The drawing mode gets more interesting—and much more complex—when color is introduced. Let's assume a display capable of eight pure colors (such as the EGA and VGA in versions of Windows prior to version 3). The pen can be any of these eight pure colors, and for simplicity's sake, let's restrict the background to these colors also. The eight colors are combinations of the bits in the red, green, and blue color planes, as shown in the following table—a 1 means the color is illuminated, and a 0 means the color is off.

Red	Green	Blue	Pure Color	Red	Green	Blue	Pure Color
0	0	0	Black	1	0	0	Red
0	0	1	Blue	1	0	1	Magenta
0	1	0	Green	1	1	0	Yellow
0	1	1	Cyan	1	1	1	White

Each of the three color planes is affected separately by the raster operation. For example, say you have a cyan background color and a magenta pen color, and your drawing mode is R2_NOTMERGEPEN. What color will the pen actually draw? For red, the pen is 1 (has red), and the destination is 0 (no red). Looking at the ROP2 table on page 551, you see that the result is 0 (no red). For green, the pen is 0 (no green), and the destination is 1 (has green), so the result is 0 (no green). For blue, the pen is 1 (has blue), and the destination is 1 (has blue), so the result is 0 (no blue). Thus the line has no red, no green, and no blue. The color will be black.

Let's take the R2_XORPEN drawing mode, which performs a bitwise exclusive OR operation on each of the possible combinations in the three color planes. The following table shows the resultant color for all combinations of the eight destination colors and the eight pen colors.

	PEN COLOR							
Destination	**Black**	**Blue**	**Green**	**Cyan**	**Red**	**Magenta**	**Yellow**	**White**
Black	Black	Blue	Green	Cyan	Red	Magenta	Yellow	White
Blue	Blue	Black	Cyan	Green	Magenta	Red	White	Yellow
Green	Green	Cyan	Black	Blue	Yellow	White	Red	Magenta
Cyan	Cyan	Green	Blue	Black	White	Yellow	Magenta	Red
Red	Red	Magenta	Yellow	White	Black	Blue	Green	Cyan
Magenta	Magenta	Red	White	Yellow	Blue	Black	Cyan	Green
Yellow	Yellow	White	Red	Magenta	Green	Cyan	Black	Blue
White	White	Yellow	Magenta	Red	Cyan	Green	Blue	Black

On certain devices (particularly on 256-color video boards), the bits that define each pixel may not correspond to color in a consistent manner, and the results of using some drawing modes are not well defined.

At the beginning of Chapter 11 I mentioned that Windows GDI is strong in the area of raster operations. The drawing mode is one example of that. And if you think that you'll probably never ever use some of these ROP2 codes, just wait until you see the regular raster operation codes in Chapter 13—there are more than 200 raster operations that you'll probably never use. But it's nice to know that they're available.

DRAWING FILLED AREAS

Now let's take the next step up, from drawing lines to drawing figures. Windows' six functions for drawing filled figures with borders are listed in the chart below:

Function	Figure
Rectangle	Rectangle with square corners
Ellipse	Ellipse
RoundRect	Rectangle with rounded corners
Chord	Arc on the circumference of an ellipse with endpoints connected by a chord
Pie	Pie wedge on the circumference of an ellipse
Polygon	Multisided figure
PolyPolygon	Multiple multisided figures

Windows draws the outline of the figure with the current pen selected in the device context. The current background mode, background color, and drawing mode are all used for this outline, just as if Windows were drawing a line. Everything we learned about lines also applies to the border around these figures.

The figure is filled with the current brush selected in the device context. By default, this is the stock object called WHITE_BRUSH, which means that the interior will be drawn as white. Windows defines six stock brushes: WHITE_BRUSH, LTGRAY_BRUSH, GRAY_BRUSH, DKGRAY_BRUSH, BLACK_BRUSH, and NULL_BRUSH (or HOLLOW_BRUSH). The first five of these brushes were used to color the client area of ROP2LOOK.

You can select one of the stock brushes into your device context the same way you select a stock pen. Windows defines HBRUSH to be a handle to a brush, so you can first define a variable for the brush handle:

```
HBRUSH hBrush ;
```

You can get the handle to GRAY_BRUSH by calling *GetStockObject*:

```
hBrush = GetStockObject (GRAY_BRUSH) ;
```

You can select it into the device context by calling *SelectObject*:

```
SelectObject (hdc, hBrush) ;
```

Now when you draw one of these figures, the interior will be gray.

If you want to draw a figure without a border, select the NULL_PEN into the device context:

```
SelectObject (hdc, GetStockObject (NULL_PEN)) ;
```

Or you can use the R2_NOP drawing mode:

```
SetROP2 (hdc, R2_NOP) ;
```

If you want to draw the outline of the figure but not fill in the interior, select the NULL_BRUSH into the device context:

```
SelectObject (hdc, GetStockObject (NULL_BRUSH)) ;
```

You can also create customized brushes just as you can create customized pens. We'll cover that topic shortly.

The Bounding Box

The *Rectangle, Ellipse, RoundRect, Chord,* and *Pie* functions (as well as the *Arc* line-drawing function) are all similar in that they are built up from a rectangular "bounding box." You define the coordinates of a box that encloses the object—a bounding box—and Windows draws the object within this box.

The simplest filled object is the rectangle:

```
Rectangle (hdc, xLeft, yTop, xRight, yBottom) ;
```

The point (*xLeft, yTop*) is the upper left corner of the rectangle, and (*xRight, yBottom*) is the lower right corner; both points are expressed in logical units. A figure drawn using the *Rectangle* function is shown in Figure 12-4. In the MM_TEXT mapping mode, *xRight* must be greater than *xLeft*, and *yBottom* must be greater than *yTop*. However, in all the other mapping modes (except possibly MM_ISOTROPIC and MM_ANISOTROPIC), the value of *yBottom* is less than that of *yTop* because the coordinates on the *y*-axis increase as you move up.

Programmers who have worked with graphics before are accustomed to the problem of being off by 1 pixel. Some graphics systems draw a figure to encompass the right and bottom coordinates, and some draw figures up to (but not including) the right and bottom coordinates. Windows uses the latter approach, but there's an easier way to think about it.

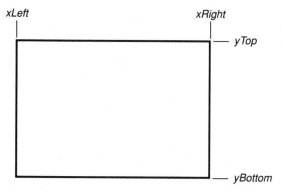

Figure 12-4. *A figure drawn using the* Rectangle *function.*

Consider the function call:

```
Rectangle (hdc, 1, 1, 5, 4) ;
```

I mentioned above that Windows draws the figure within a "bounding box." You can think of the display as a grid where each pixel is within a grid cell. The imaginary bounding box is drawn on the grid, and the rectangle is then drawn within this bounding box. Here's how the figure would be drawn in the MM_TEXT mapping mode:

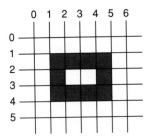

The area separating the rectangle from the top and left of the client area is 1 pixel wide. Windows uses the current brush to color the 2 pixels on the inside of the rectangle.

For all pen styles except PS_INSIDEFRAME, if the pen used to draw the outline is greater than 1 pixel wide, then the pen is centered on the border so that part of the line may be outside the bounding box. For the PS_INSIDEFRAME pen style, the entire line is drawn inside the bounding box.

Once you know how to draw a rectangle, then you also know how to draw an ellipse, because it uses the same parameters:

```
Ellipse (hdc, xLeft, yTop, xRight, yBottom) ;
```

A figure drawn using the *Ellipse* function is shown (with the imaginary bounding box) in Figure 12-5.

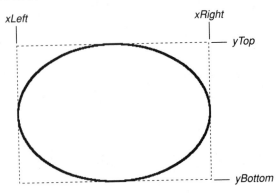

Figure 12-5. *A figure drawn using the* Ellipse *function.*

Windows does not include "square" or "circle" functions. In all mapping modes except MM_TEXT and MM_ANISOTROPIC, you can easily draw squares and circles using the *Rectangle* and *Ellipse* functions by making the difference between *xLeft* and *xRight* the same as the difference between *yTop* and *yBottom*. In MM_TEXT, squares and circles are a little more difficult. You have to call *GetDeviceCaps* with the ASPECTX and ASPECTY indexes and scale the dimensions based on the aspect ratio of the pixels. In MM_ANISOTROPIC, you also have to take into account the ratio of the window and viewport extents.

The function to draw rectangles with rounded corners uses the same bounding box as the *Rectangle* and *Ellipse* functions but includes two more parameters:

```
RoundRect (hdc, xLeft, yTop, xRight, yBottom,
            xCornerEllipse, yCornerEllipse) ;
```

A figure drawn using this function is shown in Figure 12-6.

Windows uses a small ellipse to draw the rounded corners. The width of this ellipse is *xCornerEllipse*, and the height is *yCornerEllipse*, with both points expressed in logical units. Imagine Windows splitting this small ellipse into four quadrants and using one quadrant for each of the four corners. The rounding of the corners is more pronounced for larger values of *xCornerEllipse* and *yCornerEllipse*. If *xCornerEllipse* is equal to the difference between *xLeft* and *xRight* and *yCornerEllipse* is equal to the difference between *yTop* and *yBottom*, then the *RoundRect* function will draw an ellipse.

The rounded rectangle shown in Figure 12-6 was drawn using the MM_TEXT mapping mode with the corner ellipse dimensions calculated with these formulas:

```
xCornerEllipse = (xRight - xLeft) / 4 ;
yCornerEllipse = (yBottom - yTop) / 4 ;
```

This is an easy approach, but the results admittedly don't look quite right, because the rounding of the corners is more pronounced along the larger rectangle dimension. To

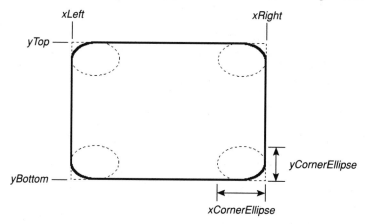

Figure 12-6. *A figure drawn using the* RoundRect *function.*

correct this problem, you'll probably want to make *xCornerEllipse* equal to *yCornerEllipse* in real dimensions.

The *Arc, Chord,* and *Pie* functions all take identical parameters:

```
Arc (hdc, xLeft, yTop, xRight, yBottom,
        xStart, yStart, xEnd, yEnd) ;

Chord (hdc, xLeft, yTop, xRight, yBottom,
        xStart, yStart, xEnd, yEnd) ;

Pie (hdc, xLeft, yTop, xRight, yBottom,
        xStart, yStart, xEnd, yEnd) ;
```

A line drawn using the *Arc* function is shown in Figure 12-7; figures drawn using the *Chord* and *Pie* functions are shown in Figures 12-8 and 12-9.

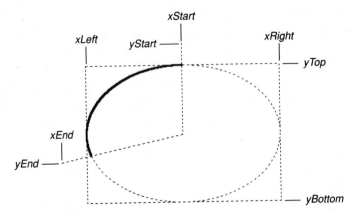

Figure 12-7. *A line drawn using the* Arc *function.*

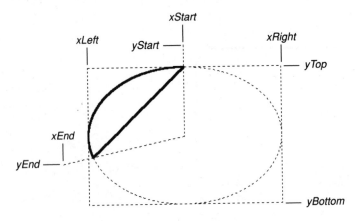

Figure 12-8. *A figure drawn using the* Chord *function.*

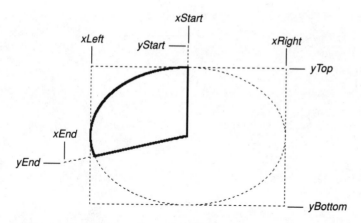

Figure 12-9. *A figure drawn using the* Pie *function.*

Windows uses an imaginary line to connect (*xStart, yStart*) with the center of the ellipse. At the point at which that line intersects the ellipse, Windows begins drawing an arc in a counterclockwise direction around the circumference of the ellipse. Windows also uses an imaginary line to connect (*xEnd, yEnd*) with the center of the ellipse. At the point at which that line intersects the ellipse, Windows stops drawing the arc.

For the *Arc* function, Windows is now finished, because the arc is an elliptical line rather than a filled area. For the *Chord* function, Windows connects the endpoints of the arc. For the *Pie* function, Windows connects each endpoint of the arc with the center of the ellipse. The interiors of the chord and pie-wedge figures are filled with the current brush.

The ARCS Program

You may wonder about this use of starting and ending positions in the *Arc, Chord,* and *Pie* functions. Why not simply specify starting and ending points on the circumference of the ellipse? Well, you can, but you would have to figure out what those points are. Windows' method gets the job done without requiring such precision.

You can experiment with arcs, chords, and pie wedges using the ARCS program, shown in Figure 12-10 on the following page. The program draws the bounding box and the ellipse using a dotted pen. Your menu choice determines whether the program draws an arc, a chord, or a pie wedge. The line or figure is drawn with a pen that is 3 pixels wide. The starting and ending points are connected to the center of the ellipse with a normal black pen.

ARCS.MAK

```
#--------------------
# ARCS.MAK make file
#--------------------

arcs.exe : arcs.obj arcs.def arcs.res
     link arcs, /align:16, NUL, /nod slibcew libw, arcs
     rc arcs.res

arcs.obj : arcs.c arcs.h
     cl -c -Gsw -Ow -W2 -Zp arcs.c

arcs.res : arcs.rc arcs.h
     rc -r arcs.rc
```

ARCS.C

```
/*--------------------------------------------------------
   ARCS.C -- Demonstrates Drawing Arcs, Chords, and Pies
             (c) Charles Petzold, 1990
   --------------------------------------------------------*/

#include <windows.h>
#include "arcs.h"

long FAR PASCAL WndProc (HWND, WORD, WORD, LONG) ;

int PASCAL WinMain (HANDLE hInstance, HANDLE hPrevInstance,
                    LPSTR lpszCmdLine, int nCmdShow)
     {
     static char szAppName[] = "Arcs" ;
     HWND         hwnd ;
     MSG          msg ;
     WNDCLASS     wndclass ;

     if (!hPrevInstance)
         {
         wndclass.style         = CS_HREDRAW | CS_VREDRAW ;
         wndclass.lpfnWndProc   = WndProc ;
         wndclass.cbClsExtra    = 0 ;
         wndclass.cbWndExtra    = 0 ;
         wndclass.hInstance     = hInstance ;
         wndclass.hIcon         = NULL ;
         wndclass.hCursor       = LoadCursor (NULL, IDC_ARROW) ;
         wndclass.hbrBackground = GetStockObject (WHITE_BRUSH) ;
         wndclass.lpszMenuName  = szAppName ;
         wndclass.lpszClassName = szAppName ;
```

Figure 12-10. *The ARCS program.*

(continued)

564

```
            RegisterClass (&wndclass) ;
            }

      hwnd = CreateWindow (szAppName, "Arcs, Chords, and Pies",
                        WS_OVERLAPPEDWINDOW,
                        CW_USEDEFAULT, CW_USEDEFAULT,
                        CW_USEDEFAULT, CW_USEDEFAULT,
                        NULL, NULL, hInstance, NULL) ;

      ShowWindow (hwnd, nCmdShow) ;
      UpdateWindow (hwnd) ;

      while (GetMessage (&msg, NULL, 0, 0))
            {
            TranslateMessage (&msg) ;
            DispatchMessage (&msg) ;
            }
      return msg.wParam ;
      }

long FAR PASCAL WndProc (HWND hwnd, WORD message, WORD wParam, LONG lParam)
      {
      static short cxClient, cyClient, x1, x2, x3, x4, y1, y2, y3, y4,
                  nFigure = IDM_ARC ;
      HDC         hdc ;
      HMENU       hMenu ;
      HPEN        hPen ;
      PAINTSTRUCT ps ;
      short       x, y ;

      switch (message)
            {
            case WM_SIZE :
                  x3 = y3 = 0 ;
                  x4 = cxClient = LOWORD (lParam) ;
                  y4 = cyClient = HIWORD (lParam) ;
                  x2 = 3 * (x1 = cxClient / 4) ;
                  y2 = 3 * (y1 = cyClient / 4) ;
                  return 0 ;

            case WM_COMMAND :
                  switch (wParam)
                        {
                        case IDM_ARC :
                        case IDM_CHORD :
                        case IDM_PIE :
                              hMenu = GetMenu (hwnd) ;
                              CheckMenuItem (hMenu, nFigure, MF_UNCHECKED) ;
```

(continued)

```
                    CheckMenuItem (hMenu, nFigure = wParam, MF_CHECKED) ;
                    InvalidateRect (hwnd, NULL, FALSE) ;
                    return 0 ;
               }
          break ;

     case WM_LBUTTONDOWN :
          if (!(wParam & MK_SHIFT))
               {
               x3 = LOWORD (lParam) ;
               y3 = HIWORD (lParam) ;
               InvalidateRect (hwnd, NULL, TRUE) ;
               return 0 ;
               }
                              // fall through for MK_SHIFT
     case WM_RBUTTONDOWN :
          x4 = LOWORD (lParam) ;
          y4 = HIWORD (lParam) ;
          InvalidateRect (hwnd, NULL, TRUE) ;
          return 0 ;

     case WM_PAINT :
          hdc = BeginPaint (hwnd, &ps) ;

          hPen = SelectObject (hdc, CreatePen (PS_DOT, 1, 0L)) ;
          Rectangle (hdc, x1, y1, x2, y2) ;
          Ellipse   (hdc, x1, y1, x2, y2) ;

          DeleteObject (SelectObject (hdc, CreatePen (PS_SOLID, 3, 0L))) ;

          switch (nFigure)
               {
               case IDM_ARC :
                    Arc (hdc, x1, y1, x2, y2, x3, y3, x4, y4) ;
                    break ;

               case IDM_CHORD :
                    Chord (hdc, x1, y1, x2, y2, x3, y3, x4, y4) ;
                    break ;

               case IDM_PIE :
                    Pie (hdc, x1, y1, x2, y2, x3, y3, x4, y4) ;
                    break ;
               }

          DeleteObject (SelectObject (hdc, hPen)) ;
```

(continued)

```
               MoveTo (hdc, x3, y3) ;
               LineTo (hdc, cxClient / 2, cyClient / 2) ;
               LineTo (hdc, x4, y4) ;

               EndPaint (hwnd, &ps) ;
               return 0 ;

          case WM_DESTROY :
               PostQuitMessage (0) ;
               return 0 ;
          }
     return DefWindowProc (hwnd, message, wParam, lParam) ;
     }
```

ARCS.RC

```
/*-------------------------
   ARCS.RC resource script
   ---------------------------*/

#include "arcs.h"

Arcs MENU
     {
     POPUP "&Options"
          {
          MENUITEM "&Arc",    IDM_ARC,  CHECKED
          MENUITEM "&Chord",  IDM_CHORD
          MENUITEM "&Pie",    IDM_PIE
          }
     }
```

ARCS.H

```
/*--------------------
   ARCS.H header file
   --------------------*/

#define IDM_ARC    1
#define IDM_CHORD  2
#define IDM_PIE    3
```

ARCS.DEF

```
;-----------------------------------
; ARCS.DEF module definition file
;-----------------------------------

NAME            ARCS

DESCRIPTION     'Arc, Chord, and Pie Drawing Program (c) Charles Petzold, 1990'
EXETYPE         WINDOWS
STUB            'WINSTUB.EXE'
CODE            PRELOAD MOVEABLE DISCARDABLE
DATA            PRELOADMOVEABLE MULTIPLE
HEAPSIZE        1024
STACKSIZE       8192
EXPORTS         WndProc
```

When you click on the client area using the left mouse button, ARCS uses that point as the starting point, which is the point $(x3, y3)$ in the program. Clicking on the client area with the right mouse button sets the ending point, the point $(x4, y4)$. Users with a one-button mouse can hold down the Shift key and click the mouse to set the ending point.

ARCS also shows some typical pen-handle manipulation. After the program gets the device context by calling *BeginPaint*, it creates a dotted pen and selects it into the device context:

```
hPen = SelectObject (hdc, CreatePen (PS_DOT, 1, 0L)) ;
```

The *hPen* handle returned from *SelectObject* is a handle to the stock BLACK_PEN.

When ARCS needs to draw the arc, chord, or pie wedge, it creates a 3-pixel-wide pen and selects that into the device context:

```
DeleteObject (SelectObject (hdc, CreatePen (PS_SOLID, 3, 0L))) ;
```

The pen handle returned from *SelectObject*, which is the handle to the dotted pen, is then deleted using *DeleteObject*.

When ARCS needs to draw the lines connecting the starting and ending points with the center of the ellipse, it selects *hPen*—the handle to the stock BLACK_PEN—into the device context and deletes the 3-pixel-wide pen returned from *SelectObject*:

```
DeleteObject (SelectObject (hdc, hPen)) ;
```

Now the two pens that were created have been deleted. The pen currently selected in the device context is a stock pen, and the device context can be released.

The Trigonometry of Pie Charts

If you use the *Pie* function to create pie charts, the size of each pie wedge will be based on the relative sizes of data items. This involves calculating starting and ending points of the pie figures that are derived from the internal angle of the pie wedge.

It's time for a trigonometry refresher. In a Cartesian coordinate system (with x increasing to the right and y increasing as it moves up), we can draw a triangle like this:

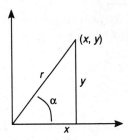

The relationship between each of the three sides of the triangle and the angle α is given by the formulas:

$sin\ (\alpha) = y/r$

$cos\ (\alpha) = x/r$

$tan\ (\alpha) = y/x$

If you know the angle α (which in a pie chart will be a fraction of a circle) and r (which will be the radius of the circle), you can determine that the point (x, y) is equal to:

$(r * cos\ (\alpha),\ r * sin\ (\alpha))$

In the C library functions *sin* and *cos*, angles are specified in terms of radians. There are 2 * PI radians in 360 degrees.

Let's try drawing a pie chart that uses five numbers. For convenience, we'll set this condition with a *#define* statement:

```
#define NUM 5
```

In a real program, that would be a variable.

You'll also find it convenient to define an identifier called TWO_PI that is the number of radians in a circle:

```
#define TWO_PI (2.0 * 3.14159)
```

Next you define some variables:

```
static short    nValues [NUM] = { 3, 5, 2, 7, 4 };
short           i, nSum [NUM + 1] ;
```

The initialized values in *nValues* are the data we'll be graphing. In a real program, these values would be variables. The *nSum* array is set to the accumulated sum of the data values where the first element of the array is set to 0:

```
nSum [0] = 0 ;
for (i = 0 ; i < NUM ; i++)
    nSum [i + 1] = nSum [i] + nValues [i] ;
```

The array element *nSum [NUM]* is the sum of the five values.

Now we are ready to start drawing the pie chart. Set the mapping mode to MM_ISOTROPIC, which is the mode in which you can most easily draw a circle:

```
SetMapMode (hdc, MM_ISOTROPIC) ;
SetWindowExt (hdc, 400, 400) ;
SetViewportExt (hdc, xClient, -yClient) ;
SetViewportOrg (hdc, xClient / 2, yClient / 2) ;
```

The logical point (0, 0) is the center of the client area, and the *x*- and *y*-coordinates define a normal Cartesian coordinate system.

Our pie has a radius of 100 logical units. Here's the code to paint the five pie segments:

```
for (i = 0 ; i < NUM ; i++)
    Pie (hdc, -100, 100, 100, -100,
        (short) (100.0 * cos (TWO_PI * nSum [i]     / nSum [NUM])),
        (short) (100.0 * sin (TWO_PI * nSum [i]     / nSum [NUM])),
        (short) (100.0 * cos (TWO_PI * nSum [i + 1] / nSum [NUM])),
        (short) (100.0 * sin (TWO_PI * nSum [i + 1] / nSum [NUM]))) ;
```

The pie chart produced from this code is shown in Figure 12-11. The first pie wedge is at the right of the pie chart, just above the *x*-axis. The other pie wedges are drawn in a counterclockwise direction.

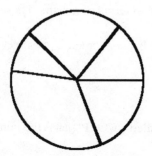

Figure 12-11. *A pie chart drawn using the* Pie *function.*

The values:

```
TWO_PI * nSum [i] / nSum [NUM]
```

and:

```
TWO_PI * nSum [i + 1] / nSum [NUM]
```

are ratios of the accumulated sum of the items to the total sum of the items converted to angles that are measured counterclockwise from the horizontal. The second formula includes the item that the particular pie wedge represents; the first does not. By taking the cosine and sine of these angles and multiplying by 100, we're calculating the starting and ending points on the circle.

The *Polygon* Function and the Polygon Filling Mode

Polygon is the sixth function for drawing a bordered and filled figure. The function call is similar to the *PolyLine* function:

```
Polygon (hdc, lpPoints, nCount) ;
```

The *lpPoints* parameter is a far pointer to an array of POINT structures (in logical coordinates), and *nCount* is the number of points. If the last point in this array is different from the first point, Windows adds another line that connects the last point with the first point. (This does not happen with the *PolyLine* function.)

Windows fills this bounded area with the current brush in one of two ways, depending on the current polygon filling mode defined in the device context. By default, the polygon filling mode is ALTERNATE, which means that Windows fills in only those interiors accessible from the outside of the polygon by crossing an odd number of lines (1, 3, 5, and so forth). The other interiors are not filled. You can also set the polygon filling mode to WINDING, in which case Windows fills in all the interior areas. The two polygon filling modes are most simply demonstrated with a five-pointed star. In Figure 12-12 on the following page, the star on the left was drawn with the ALTERNATE mode, and the star on the right was drawn with the WINDING mode. Both figures were drawn with an array of points defined like this:

```
static POINT pt [] =
        { -59, -81, 0, 100, 59, -81, -95, 31, 95, 31 } ;
```

The five points of the star were manually calculated from trigonometric tables. The WM_PAINT logic looks like this:

```
case WM_PAINT :
        hdc = BeginPaint (hwnd, &ps) ;

        hPen = CreatePen (PS_SOLID, 3, 0L) ;
        SelectObject (hdc, hPen) ;
        SelectObject (hdc, GetStockObject (LTGRAY_BRUSH)) ;
```

```
SetMapMode (hdc, MM_ISOTROPIC) ;
SetWindowExt (hdc, 440, -220) ;
SetViewportExt (hdc, xClient, yClient) ;
SetWindowOrg (hdc, -110, 110) ;

SetPolyFillMode (hdc, ALTERNATE) ;
Polygon (hdc, pt, sizeof (pt) / sizeof (POINT)) ;

SetWindowOrg (hdc, -330, 110) ;

SetPolyFillMode (hdc, WINDING) ;
Polygon (hdc, pt, sizeof (pt) / sizeof (POINT)) ;

EndPaint (hwnd, &ps) ;
DeleteObject (hPen) ;
break ;
```

The *PolyPolygon* function draws multiple polygons.

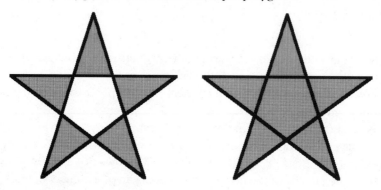

Figure 12-12. *Figures drawn with the two polygon filling modes: ALTERNATE (left) and WINDING (right).*

Brushing the Interior

The interiors of the *Rectangle, RoundRect, Ellipse, Chord, Pie, Polygon,* and *PolyPolygon* figures are filled in with the current brush (also sometimes called a "pattern") selected in the device context. A brush is an 8-by-8 bitmap that is repeated horizontally and vertically to fill the area.

When Windows uses dithering to display more colors than are normally available on a display, it actually uses a brush for the color. On a monochrome system, Windows can use dithering of black and white pixels to create 64 different shades of gray. More precisely, Windows can create 64 different monochrome brushes. For pure black, all bits in the 8-by-8 bitmap are 0. One bit out of the 64 is made 1 (that is, white) for the first gray shade, two bits are white for the second gray shade, and so on, until all bits in the 8-by-8 bitmap are 1 for pure white. On a color video system, dithered colors are also bitmaps, and a much wider range of color is available.

We've already used stock brushes. Windows also has four functions that let you create logical brushes. You select the brush into the device context with *SelectObject.* Like logical pens, logical brushes are GDI objects. Any brush that you create must be deleted, but it must not be deleted while it is selected in the device context.

Here's the first function to create a logical brush:

```
hBrush = CreateSolidBrush (rgbColor) ;
```

The word *Solid* in this function doesn't really mean that the brush is a pure color. When you select the brush into the device context, Windows creates an 8-by-8 bitmap for a dithered color and uses that bitmap for the brush. We used *CreateSolidBrush* in the COLORS1 program in Chapter 6. The brush was used as the background color defined in the window class structure.

You can also create a brush with "hatch marks" made up of horizontal, vertical, or diagonal lines. Brushes of this style are most commonly used for coloring the interiors of bar graphs and when drawing to plotters. The function for creating a hatch brush is:

```
hBrush = CreateHatchBrush (nHatchStyle, rgbColor) ;
```

The *nHatchStyle* parameter describes the appearance of the hatch marks. The parameter can be one of the following styles: HS_HORIZONTAL, HS_VERTICAL, HS_FDIAGONAL, HS_BDIAGONAL, HS_CROSS, and HS_DIAGCROSS. Figure 12-13 shows the kind of hatch marks that each of these styles produces.

HS_HORIZONTAL	HS_BDIAGONAL
HS_VERTICAL	HS_CROSS
HS_FDIAGONAL	HS_DIAGCROSS

Figure 12-13. *The six hatch brush styles.*

The *rgbColor* parameter of *CreateHatchBrush* is the color of the hatch lines. When you select the brush into a device context, Windows converts this color to the nearest pure color. The area between the hatch lines is colored based on the background mode and background color defined in the device context. If the background mode is OPAQUE, the background color (which is also converted to a pure color) is used to fill in the spaces between the lines. In this case, neither the hatch lines nor the fill color can be a dithered color. If the background mode is TRANSPARENT, Windows draws the hatch lines without filling in the area between them.

Earlier I discussed the problems that you can encounter with pen colors when you develop a program on a color display and later run the program on a monochrome display. You should beware of the same problems when you choose colors for hatch marks and the brush background. Colored hatch marks that look fine on a color display may disappear into the background when displayed in monochrome.

Because brushes are always 8-by-8 bitmaps, the appearance of hatch brushes will also vary according to the resolution of the device on which they are displayed. Each of the hatch marks shown in Figure 12-13 was drawn in a 32-by-16-pixel rectangle, which means that the 8-by-8 bitmap was repeated 4 times horizontally and 2 times vertically. On a 300-dots-per-inch laser printer, the same 32-by-16-pixel rectangle would occupy an area about $\frac{1}{9}$ inch wide and $\frac{1}{19}$ inch high.

You can also create your own brushes based on bitmaps using *CreatePatternBrush*:

```
hBrush = CreatePatternBrush (hBitmap) ;
```

This function was discussed in Chapter 9. The *hBitmap* parameter is a handle to an 8-by-8 bitmap. How you get this bitmap handle is covered in the next section of this chapter.

Windows also includes a function that encompasses the three other functions for creating brushes (*CreateSolidBrush*, *CreateHatchBrush*, and *CreatePatternBrush*):

```
hBrush = CreateBrushIndirect (&logbrush) ;
```

The variable *logbrush* is a structure of type LOGBRUSH ("logical brush"). The three fields of this structure are shown below. The value of the *lbStyle* field determines how Windows interprets the other two fields:

lbStyle (WORD)	*lbColor (DWORD)*	*lbHatch (short)*
BS_SOLID	Color of brush	Ignored
BS_HOLLOW	Ignored	Ignored
BS_HATCHED	Color of hatches	Hatch brush style
BS_PATTERN	Ignored	Handle to bitmap

Earlier we used *SelectObject* to select a logical pen into a device context, *DeleteObject* to delete a logical pen, and *GetObject* to get information about a logical pen. You can use these same three functions with brushes. Once you have a handle to a brush, you can select the brush into a device context using *SelectObject*:

```
SelectObject (hdc, hBrush) ;
```

You can later delete a created brush with the *DeleteObject* function:

```
DeleteObject (hBrush) ;
```

Do not delete a brush that is currently selected into a device context, however. If you need to obtain information about a brush, you can call *GetObject*:

```
GetObject (hBrush, sizeof (LOGBRUSH), (LPSTR) &logbrush) ;
```

where *logbrush* is a structure of type LOGBRUSH.

Brushes and Bitmaps

When you use the *CreatePatternBrush* or *CreateBrushIndirect* function with the *lbStyle* field set to BS_PATTERN, you first need a handle to a bitmap. The bitmap must be least 8 pixels wide and 8 pixels high. If it's larger, Windows uses only the upper left corner of the bitmap for the brush.

Because brushes and bitmaps are GDI objects, you must delete any that you create in your program before the program terminates. When you create a brush based on a bitmap, Windows makes a copy of the bitmap bits for use when drawing with the brush. You can delete the bitmap immediately after calling *CreatePatternBrush* (or *CreateBrushIndirect*) without affecting the brush. Similarly, you can delete the brush without affecting the bitmap.

One method of getting a handle to a bitmap was discussed in Chapter 8. You can use SDKPAINT to create a bitmap file (with the extension .BMP), include that filename in a BITMAP statement in the resource script, and then load the bitmap into your program. The *LoadBitmap* function returns a handle of type HBITMAP:

```
hBitmap = LoadBitmap (hInstance, lpszBitmap) ;
```

The variable *lpszBitmap* is the name of the bitmap in the resource script file.

The second method of getting a handle to a bitmap is to use this function:

```
hBitmap = CreateBitmap (nWidth, nHeight, nPlanes, nBitsPixel, lpBits) ;
```

To create a bitmap to use for a brush, *nWidth* and *nHeight* should both be set to 8. If you want a monochrome bitmap, *nPlanes* and *nBitsPixel* should both be set to 1. The variable *lpBits* is a long pointer to an array of bytes containing the pixel pattern of the bitmap. You can set this parameter to NULL if you want to create an uninitialized bitmap, in which case the bitmap will contain random data.

The third method of getting a handle to a bitmap is this:

```
hBitmap = CreateCompatibleBitmap (hdc, nWidth, nHeight) ;
```

This creates a bitmap with the same number of color planes and the same number of color bits per pixel as the device context indicated by *hdc*. (The only reason this function requires *hdc* is to get this color information.) The bitmap initially contains random data.

The final method for getting a handle to a bitmap requires a pointer to a structure (here named *bitmap*) of type BITMAP:

```
hBitmap = CreateBitmapIndirect (&bitmap) ;
```

Watch out for the difference between the types HBITMAP and BITMAP. HBITMAP is a handle to a bitmap. BITMAP is a structure that describes the bitmap. The BITMAP structure has seven fields, as described in the following list. Five of them are similar to the parameters of the *CreateBitmap* function.

bmType	Set to 0
bmWidth	Width of bitmap in pixels
bmHeight	Height of bitmap in pixels
bmWidthBytes	Number of bytes in each raster line
bmPlanes	Number of color planes
bmBitsPixel	Number of adjacent color bits per pixel
bmBits	Far pointer to an array of bytes containing the bitmap pattern

When you have a handle to a bitmap, you can use *GetObject* to obtain information about the bitmap:

```
GetObject (hBitmap, sizeof (BITMAP), (LPSTR) &bitmap) ;
```

where *bitmap* is a structure of type BITMAP. However, *GetObject* does not copy a valid far pointer into the *bmBits* field. To get the actual bits that make up the bitmap, you can call:

```
GetBitmapBits (hBitmap, dwCount, lpBits) ;
```

GetBitmapBits copies *dwCount* number of bytes into an array whose address is *lpBits*. You can also set the bits of a bitmap using the *SetBitmapBits* function:

```
SetBitmapBits (hBitmap, dwCount, lpBits) ;
```

The *bmBits* field of the BITMAP structure and the *lpBits* parameter of the *CreateBitmap*, *SetBitmapBits*, and *GetBitmapBits* functions are far pointers to an array of bytes that define the bitmap pattern. The array of bytes begins with the top scan line. Color bitmaps may be organized with multiple bits per pixel or multiple color planes per scan line. (I'll discuss this more in the next chapter.) If you wish to use a bitmap as a brush and be assured that it will work on all devices, use a monochrome bitmap.

The total size of this array of bytes is equal to (using the fields of the logical bitmap structure):

bmPlanes ∗ *bmHeight* ∗ *bmWidthBytes*

The *bmWidthBytes* field is the width of each scan line in bytes. This value must be the even number equal to or the next even number greater than:

bmWidth ∗ *bmBitsPixel* / 8

In other words, each scan line is padded with bytes if necessary to get an integral number of words. The scan line is padded at the right because the bytes are arranged from left to right. The most significant bit of the first byte is the leftmost pixel.

Creating and Using Bitmap Brushes

We've covered the background information you need to create and use brushes based on bitmaps. Now let's put that information to work. Let's say that you want to draw a rectangle filled in with a brush that looks like little bricks, as shown in Figure 12-14.

Figure 12-14. *A figure filled in with a customized brush.*

The bitmap you need has a pixel pattern that looks like this:

This is a monochrome bitmap with a height and width of 8. Here are three methods you can use to create a brush based on this bitmap.

Method one

Create an 8-by-8 monochrome bitmap in SDKPAINT that resembles the diagram shown above and save it under the name BRICK.BMP. In your resource script file, include a statement identifying this file as a bitmap and naming it "Brick":

```
Brick BITMAP brick.bmp
```

Within your program, define variables of type HBITMAP (handle to a bitmap) and HBRUSH (handle to a brush):

```
HBITMAP hBitmap ;
HBRUSH  hBrush ;
```

These two handles are set by the following statements:

```
hBitmap = LoadBitmap (hInstance, "Brick") ;
hBrush  = CreatePatternBrush (hBitmap) ;
```

When you have a valid device context, select the brush into the device context and display the rectangle:

```
SelectObject (hdc, hBrush) ;
Rectangle (hdc, xLeft, yTop, xRight, yBottom) ;
```

When you release the device context, delete the brush and bitmap:

```
DeleteObject (hBrush) ;
DeleteObject (hBitmap) ;
```

You don't have to wait until you release the device context to delete the bitmap—you can do so anytime after you create the brush based on the bitmap.

Method two

This method defines the bitmap pixels within the program as an array of eight unsigned integers. Each integer corresponds to a scan line in the bitmap pattern. A 1 bit is used for white and a 0 bit for black:

```
HBITMAP hBitmap ;
HBRUSH  hBrush ;
static  WORD wBrickBits [] =
     { 0xFF, 0x0C, 0x0C, 0x0C, 0xFF, 0xC0, 0xC0, 0xC0 } ;
```

The bitmap is created using *CreateBitmap* by referencing this array of integers:

```
hBitmap = CreateBitmap (8, 8, 1, 1, (LPSTR) wBrickBits) ;
hBrush = CreatePatternBrush (hBitmap) ;

SelectObject (hdc, hBrush) ;
Rectangle (hdc, xLeft, yTop, xRight, yBottom) ;
```

After you're finished with the brush and the bitmap (and the brush is no longer selected in a valid device context), you delete the bitmap and the brush:

```
DeleteObject (hBrush) ;
DeleteObject (hBitmap) ;
```

Rather than using an array of integers for the bitmap's bits, you can use instead an array of unsigned characters. Because each scan line must contain an even number of bytes, however, you have to insert a 0 after each byte:

```
static unsigned char cBrickBits [] =
         { 0xFF, 0, 0x0C, 0, 0x0C, 0, 0x0C, 0,
           0xFF, 0, 0xC0, 0, 0xC0, 0, 0xC0, 0 } ;
```

Method three

This method is similar to the second method except that you use the logical bitmap and logical brush structures to create the bitmap and the brush. Begin by defining these variables:

```
HBITMAP hBitmap ;
HBRUSH  hBrush ;
static  BITMAP   bitmap   = { 0, 8, 8, 2, 1, 1 } ;
static  LOGBRUSH logbrush = { BS_PATTERN, 0L } ;
static  WORD wBrickBits [] =
        { 0xFF, 0x0C, 0x0C, 0x0C, 0xFF, 0xC0, 0xC0, 0xC0 } ;
```

The last field of the logical bitmap structure remains uninitialized. This field must contain a far pointer to the array of bytes that define the bitmap pattern. Do not initialize the structure with this pointer, however. Instead use an assignment statement:

```
bitmap.bmBits = (LPSTR) wBrickBits ;
```

Watch out when you assign a far address of a local data item to the field of a structure. If the program's data segment is moved in memory (as it can be following a *GetMessage*, *LocalAlloc*, or *LocalReAlloc* call), that far address can become invalid. A good rule is to make this assignment immediately before using the structure. After the assignment, you use this structure to create the bitmap:

```
hBitmap = CreateBitmapIndirect (&bitmap) ;
```

Now that you have the handle to a bitmap, you can use the *CreateBrushIndirect* function to create the brush:

```
logbrush.lbHatch = hBitmap ;
hBrush = CreateBrushIndirect (&logbrush) ;

SelectObject (hdc, hBrush) ;
Rectangle (hdc, xLeft, yTop, xRight, yBottom) ;
```

Later on, delete both the brush and the bitmap:

```
DeleteObject (hBrush) ;
DeleteObject (hBitmap) ;
```

Brush Alignment

When Windows fills in an area with a brush, it repeats the 8-by-8 bitmap both horizontally and vertically. This brush's appearance can vary slightly, depending on how Windows aligns the upper left corner of the bitmap with the display surface. The attribute in the device context that determines this alignment is called the "brush origin." This attribute is always expressed in terms of screen coordinates. If you obtain a device context using *BeginPaint* or *GetDC*, the brush origin is initially set to the upper left corner of your window's client area. If the client area begins 30 pixels from the left of the screen and 20 pixels from the top of the screen, the brush origin is set to the point (30, 20).

Whenever Windows uses a brush within the client area, the upper left corner of the brush's bitmap coincides with those client-area device points where both *x* and *y* are multiples of 8. Let's take an example involving a hatch brush with style HS_FDIAGONAL, which looks like this:

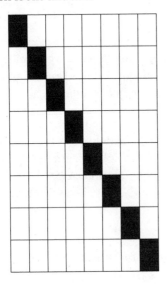

In MM_TEXT mode, when you draw a rectangle that is filled in with the HS_FDIAGONAL brush, the downward hatch line will intersect the upper left corner of the rectangle if this corner is at the logical point (8, 8). However, the hatch line will be aligned 4 pixels from the top of the corner if the rectangle begins at the logical point (8, 4).

In most cases, adjusting the brush origin is an unnecessary refinement to your drawing, but sometimes you'll want to do it. The process involves three steps:

1. Call *UnrealizeObject* for the brush. (Do not call *UnrealizeObject* for stock brushes.)

2. Set the brush origin with *SetBrushOrg*, remembering to use screen coordinates.

3. Select the brush into the device context using *SelectObject*.

One situation in which you'll need to change the brush origin is when you want the background of a child window to blend in with the background of its parent window. When you obtain a handle to the device context for the child window, the brush origin will be the upper left corner of the child window. You need to change the brush origin to be the upper left corner of the parent window. (We did this when coloring child window controls in Chapter 6.) In this case, you're changing the brush origin in one device context so that it coincides with the brush origin in another device context.

You'll also need to change brush origins when you draw several figures sharing the same device context but you don't want the brushes to coincide. For instance, suppose you want to use brushes to color the bars of a bar chart. If you didn't care about brush alignment, you might draw each of the bars using a function that looks like this:

```
void DrawBar1 (hdc, xLeft, yTop, xRight, yBottom, hBrush)
     HDC        hdc ;
     short      xLeft, yTop, xRight, yBottom ;
     HBRUSH     hBrush ;
     {
     HBRUSH     hBrushOriginal ;

     hBrushOriginal = SelectObject (hdc, hBrush) ;
     Rectangle (hdc, xLeft, yTop, xRight, yBottom) ;
     SelectObject (hdc, hBrushOriginal) ;
     }
```

This function simply selects the brush handle passed as a function parameter (saving the handle to the brush originally selected), draws a rectangle, and then selects the original brush back into the device context. If a program used this routine to draw several adjacent bars that it filled in with the HS_FDIAGONAL brush, the result would look like Figure 12-15. Notice that the hatch lines for all three bars align, which has the unfortunate effect of drawing the eye downward from left to right.

Figure 12-15. *Three bars that have the same device context and brush origin.*

To avoid this effect, you need to align the brush with each bar individually, which you can accomplish with the following function:

```
void DrawBar2 (hwnd, hdc, xLeft, yTop, xRight, yBottom, hBrush)
     HWND      hwnd ;
     HDC       hdc ;
     short     xLeft, yTop, xRight, yBottom ;
     HBRUSH    hBrush ;
     {
     HBRUSH    hBrushOriginal ;
     POINT     pt ;

     UnrealizeObject (hBrush) ;

     pt.x = xLeft ;
     pt.y = yTop ;
     LPtoDP (hdc, &pt, 1) ;
     ClientToScreen (hwnd, &pt) ;

     SetBrushOrg (hdc, pt.x, pt.y) ;

     hBrushOriginal = SelectObject (hdc, hBrush) ;
     Rectangle (hdc, xLeft, yTop, xRight, yBottom) ;
     SelectObject (hdc, hBrushOriginal) ;
     }
```

You "unrealize" the brush by calling *UnrealizeObject* and then set the brush origin to the upper left corner of the bar that's being drawn. This requires translating the upper left corner of the bar to client-area coordinates using *LPtoDP* and then to screen coordinates using *ClientToScreen*. The result is shown in Figure 12-16. Now the hatch lines begin in the upper left corner of each bar and do not align from one bar to the next.

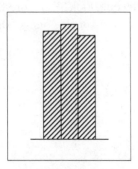

Figure 12-16. *Three bars that have the same device context but a different brush origin.*

RECTANGLES, REGIONS, AND CLIPPING

Windows includes several additional drawing functions that work with RECT (rectangle) structures and "regions." A region is an area of the screen that is a combination of rectangles, other polygons, and ellipses.

Working with Rectangles

These three drawing functions require a pointer to a rectangle structure:

```
FillRect (hdc, &rect, hBrush) ;
FrameRect (hdc, &rect, hBrush) ;
InvertRect (hdc, &rect) ;
```

In these functions, the *rect* parameter is a structure of type RECT with four fields: *left, top, right,* and *bottom.* The coordinates in this structure are treated as logical coordinates.

FillRect fills the rectangle (up to but not including the right and bottom coordinate) with the specified brush. This function doesn't require that you first select the brush into the device context. We used the *FillRect* function in the ROP2LOOK program earlier in this chapter to color the background with five stock brushes.

FrameRect uses the brush to draw a rectangular frame, but it does not fill in the rectangle. Using a brush to draw a frame may seem a little strange, because with the functions that you've seen so far (such as *Rectangle*), the border is drawn with the current pen. *FrameRect* allows you to draw a rectangular frame that isn't necessarily a pure color. This frame is one logical unit wide. If logical units are larger than device units, then the frame will be 2 or more pixels wide.

InvertRect inverts all the pixels in the rectangle, turning ones to zeros and zeros to ones. This function turns a white area to black, a black area to white, and a green area to magenta.

Windows also includes nine functions that allow you to manipulate RECT structures easily and cleanly. For instance, to set the four fields of a RECT structure to particular values, you would conventionally use code that looks like this:

```
rect.left   = xLeft ;
rect.top    = xTop ;
rect.right  = xRight ;
rect.bottom = xBottom ;
```

By calling the *SetRect* function, however, you can achieve the same result with a single line:

```
SetRect (&rect, xLeft, yTop, xRight, yBottom) ;
```

The other eight functions can also come in handy when you want to do one of the following:

- Move a rectangle a number of units along the x and y axes:

```
OffsetRect (&rect, x, y) ;
```

- Increase or decrease the size of a rectangle:

```
InflateRect (&rect, x, y) ;
```

- Set the fields of a rectangle equal to 0:

```
SetRectEmpty (&rect) ;
```

- Copy one rectangle to another:

```
CopyRect (&DestRect, &SrcRect) ;
```

- Obtain the intersection of two rectangles:

```
IntersectRect (&DestRect, &SrcRect1, &SrcRect2) ;
```

- Obtain the union of two rectangles:

```
UnionRect (&DestRect, &SrcRect1, &SrcRect2) ;
```

- Determine if a rectangle is empty:

```
bEmpty = IsRectEmpty (&rect) ;
```

- Determine if a point is in a rectangle:

```
bInRect = PtInRect (&rect, point) ;
```

In most cases, the equivalent code for these functions is simple. Sometimes, you'll find that using one of these functions actually increases the size of your .EXE file. In some instances, in fact, equivalent code even takes up less space in your source code file. For example, you can duplicate the *CopyRect* function call with:

```
DestRect = SrcRect ;
```

Creating and Painting Regions

A region is a description of an area of the display that is a combination of rectangles, other polygons, and ellipses. You can use regions for drawing or for clipping. You use a region for clipping by selecting the region into the device context.

Like pens, brushes, and bitmaps, regions are GDI objects. (The fifth and final type of GDI object is the logical font, which we'll look at in Chapter 15.) You must treat regions the same way you treat the other GDI objects: Delete any regions that you create, but don't delete a region while it is selected in the device context.

When you create a region, Windows returns a handle to the region of type HRGN. The simplest type of region describes a rectangle. You can create a rectangular region in one of two ways:

```
hRgn = CreateRectRgn (xLeft, yTop, xRight, yBottom) ;
```

or:

```
hRgn = CreateRectRgnIndirect (&rect) ;
```

Regions are always expressed in terms of device coordinates.

You can also create elliptical regions using:

```
hRgn = CreateEllipticRgn (xLeft, yTop, xRight, yBottom) ;
```

or:

```
hRgn = CreateEllipticRgnIndirect (&rect) ;
```

The *CreatRoundRectRgn* creates a rectangular region with rounded corners.

Creating a polygonal region is similar to using the *Polygon* function:

```
hRgn = CreatePolygonRgn (&point, nCount, nPolyFillMode) ;
```

The *point* parameter is an array of structures of type POINT, *nCount* is the number of points, and *nPolyFillMode* is either ALTERNATE or WINDING. You can also create multiple polygonal regions using *CreatePolyPolygonRgn*.

So what, you say? What makes these regions so special? Here's the function that unleashes the power of regions:

```
nRgnType = CombineRgn (hDestRgn, hSrcRgn1, hSrcRgn2, nCombine) ;
```

This combines two source regions (*hSrcRgn1* and *hSrcRgn2*) and causes the destination region handle (*hDestRgn*) to refer to that combined region. All three region handles must be valid, but the region previously described by *hDestRgn* is destroyed. (When you use this function, you might want to make *hDestRgn* refer initially to a small rectangular region.)

The *nCombine* parameter describes how the *hSrcRgn1* and *hSrcRgn2* regions are to be combined:

nCombine Value	New Region
RGN_AND	Overlapping area of the two source regions
RGN_OR	All the two source regions
RGN_XOR	All the two source regions excluding the overlapping area
RGN_DIFF	All of *hSrcRgn1* not in *hSrcRgn2*
RGN_COPY	The *hSrcRgn1* made the same as *hSrcRgn2*

The *nRgnType* value returned from *CombineRgn* is one of the following: NULLREGION, indicating an empty region; SIMPLEREGION, indicating a simple rectangle, ellipse, or polygon; COMPLEXREGION, indicating a combination of rectangles, ellipses, or polygons; and ERROR, meaning that an error has occurred.

Once you have a handle to a region, you can use it with four drawing functions:

```
FillRgn (hdc, hRgn, hBrush) ;
FrameRgn (hdc, hRgn, hBrush, xFrame, yFrame) ;
InvertRgn (hdc, hRgn) ;
PaintRgn (hdc, hRgn) ;
```

The *FillRgn*, *FrameRgn*, and *InvertRgn* functions are similar to the *FillRect*, *FrameRect*, and *InvertRect* functions. The *xFrame* and *yFrame* parameters to *FrameRgn* are the width and height of the frame to be painted around the region. Although regions always use device coordinates, these two parameters are specified in terms of logical units. The *PaintRgn* function fills in the region with the brush currently selected in the device context.

When you are finished with a region, you can delete it using the same function that deletes other GDI objects:

```
DeleteObject (hRgn) ;
```

Clipping with Rectangles and Regions

Regions can also play a role in clipping. (I discussed clipping in Chapter 2 when discussing the various SYSMETS programs.) The *InvalidateRect* function invalidates a rectangular area of the display and generates a WM_PAINT message. Often we use the *InvalidateRect* function to erase the client area and generate a WM_PAINT message:

```
InvalidateRect (hwnd, NULL, TRUE) ;
```

You can obtain the coordinates of the invalid rectangle by calling *GetUpdateRect*, and you can validate a rectangle of the client area using the *ValidateRect* function. When you receive a WM_PAINT message, the coordinates of the invalid rectangle are available from the PAINTSTRUCT structure that is filled in by the *BeginPaint* function. This invalid rectangle also defines a "clipping region." You cannot paint outside the clipping region.

Windows has two functions similar to *InvalidateRect* and *ValidateRect* that work with regions rather than rectangles:

```
InvalidateRgn (hwnd, hRgn, bErase) ;
```

and:

```
ValidateRgn (hwnd, hRgn) ;
```

However, when you receive a WM_PAINT message as a result of an invalid region, the clipping region will still be a rectangle that encompasses the invalid region.

If you want a nonrectangular clipping region, you can select a region into the device context using either:

```
SelectObject (hdc, hRgn) ;
```

or:

```
SelectClipRgn (hdc, hRgn) ;
```

SelectObject returns a handle to the previous clipping region selected in the device context, whereas *SelectClipRgn* returns an *nRgnType* value like *CombineRgn*. Windows also includes several functions to manipulate this clipping region, such as *ExcludeClipRect* to exclude a rectangle from the clipping region, *IntersectClipRect* to create a new clipping region that is the intersection of the previous clipping region and a rectangle, and *Off-setClipRgn* to move a clipping region to another part of the client area.

The CLOVER Program

The CLOVER program forms a region out of four ellipses, selects this region into the device context, and then draws a series of lines emanating from the center of the window's client area. The lines appear only in the area defined by the region. The resulting display is shown in Figure 12-17.

To draw this graphic by conventional methods, you would have to calculate the end point of each line based on formulas involving the circumference of an ellipse. By using a complex clipping region, you can draw the lines and let Windows determine the end points. The CLOVER program is shown in Figure 12-18, beginning on the following page.

Figure 12-17. *The CLOVER display, drawn using a complex clipping region.*

CLOVER.MAK

```
#---------------------
# CLOVER.MAK make file
#---------------------

clover.exe : clover.obj clover.def
     link clover, /align:16, NUL, /nod slibcew win87em libw, clover
     rc clover.exe

clover.obj : clover.c
     cl -c -Gsw -Ow -W2 -Zp clover.c
```

CLOVER.C

```
/*-------------------------------------------------
   CLOVER.C -- Clover Drawing Program Using Regions
               (c) Charles Petzold, 1990
   -------------------------------------------------*/

#include <windows.h>
#include <math.h>
#define TWO_PI (2.0 * 3.14159)

long FAR PASCAL WndProc (HWND, WORD, WORD, LONG) ;

int PASCAL WinMain (HANDLE hInstance, HANDLE hPrevInstance,
                    LPSTR lpszCmdLine, int nCmdShow)
     {
     static char szAppName[] = "Clover" ;
     HWND        hwnd ;
     MSG         msg ;
     WNDCLASS    wndclass ;

     if (!hPrevInstance)
          {
          wndclass.style         = CS_HREDRAW : CS_VREDRAW ;
          wndclass.lpfnWndProc   = WndProc ;
          wndclass.cbClsExtra    = 0 ;
          wndclass.cbWndExtra    = 0 ;
          wndclass.hInstance     = hInstance ;
          wndclass.hIcon         = NULL ;
          wndclass.hCursor       = LoadCursor (NULL, IDC_ARROW) ;
          wndclass.hbrBackground = GetStockObject (WHITE_BRUSH) ;
          wndclass.lpszMenuName  = NULL ;
          wndclass.lpszClassName = szAppName ;
```

Figure 12-18. *The CLOVER program.*

(continued)

```
            RegisterClass (&wndclass) ;
            }

    hwnd = CreateWindow (szAppName, "Draw a Clover",
                         WS_OVERLAPPEDWINDOW,
                         CW_USEDEFAULT, CW_USEDEFAULT,
                         CW_USEDEFAULT, CW_USEDEFAULT,
                         NULL, NULL, hInstance, NULL) ;

    ShowWindow (hwnd, nCmdShow) ;
    UpdateWindow (hwnd) ;

    while (GetMessage (&msg, NULL, 0, 0))
            {
            TranslateMessage (&msg) ;
            DispatchMessage (&msg) ;
            }
    return msg.wParam ;
    }

long FAR PASCAL WndProc (HWND hwnd, WORD message, WORD wParam, LONG lParam)
    {
    static HRGN    hRgnClip ;
    static short   cxClient, cyClient ;
    double         fAngle, fRadius ;
    HCURSOR        hCursor ;
    HDC            hdc ;
    HRGN           hRgnTemp [6] ;
    PAINTSTRUCT    ps ;
    short          i ;

    switch (message)
            {
            case WM_SIZE :
                    cxClient = LOWORD (lParam) ;
                    cyClient = HIWORD (lParam) ;

                    hCursor = SetCursor (LoadCursor (NULL, IDC_WAIT)) ;
                    ShowCursor (TRUE) ;

                    if (hRgnClip)
                            DeleteObject (hRgnClip) ;

                    hRgnTemp [0] = CreateEllipticRgn (0, cyClient / 3,
                                        cxClient / 2, 2 * cyClient / 3) ;
                    hRgnTemp [1] = CreateEllipticRgn (cxClient / 2, cyClient / 3,
                                        cxClient, 2 * cyClient / 3) ;
```

(continued)

```
            hRgnTemp [2] = CreateEllipticRgn (cxClient / 3, 0,
                                  2 * cxClient / 3, cyClient / 2) ;
            hRgnTemp [3] = CreateEllipticRgn (cxClient / 3, cyClient / 2,
                                  2 * cxClient / 3, cyClient) ;
            hRgnTemp [4] = CreateRectRgn (0, 0, 1, 1) ;
            hRgnTemp [5] = CreateRectRgn (0, 0, 1, 1) ;
            hRgnClip     = CreateRectRgn (0, 0, 1, 1) ;

            CombineRgn (hRgnTemp [4], hRgnTemp [0], hRgnTemp [1], RGN_OR) ;
            CombineRgn (hRgnTemp [5], hRgnTemp [2], hRgnTemp [3], RGN_OR) ;
            CombineRgn (hRgnClip,     hRgnTemp [4], hRgnTemp [5], RGN_XOR) ;

            for (i = 0 ; i < 6 ; i++)
                 DeleteObject (hRgnTemp [i]) ;

            SetCursor (hCursor) ;
            ShowCursor (FALSE) ;
            return 0 ;

       case WM_PAINT :
            hdc = BeginPaint (hwnd, &ps) ;

            SetViewportOrg (hdc, cxClient / 2, cyClient / 2) ;
            SelectClipRgn (hdc, hRgnClip) ;

            fRadius = hypot (cxClient / 2.0, cyClient / 2.0) ;

            for (fAngle = 0.0 ; fAngle < TWO_PI ; fAngle += TWO_PI / 360)
                 {
                 MoveTo (hdc, 0, 0) ;
                 LineTo (hdc, (short) ( fRadius * cos (fAngle) + 0.5),
                              (short) (-fRadius * sin (fAngle) + 0.5)) ;
                 }
            EndPaint (hwnd, &ps) ;
            return 0 ;

       case WM_DESTROY :
            DeleteObject (hRgnClip) ;
            PostQuitMessage (0) ;
            return 0 ;
       }
  return DefWindowProc (hwnd, message, wParam, lParam) ;
  }
```

CLOVER.DEF

```
;-------------------------------------------
; CLOVER.DEF module definition file
;-------------------------------------------

NAME            CLOVER

DESCRIPTION     'Clover Drawing Using Regions (c) Charles Petzold, 1990'
EXETYPE         WINDOWS
STUB            'WINSTUB.EXE'
CODE            PRELOAD MOVEABLE DISCARDABLE
DATA            PRELOAD MOVEABLE MULTIPLE
HEAPSIZE        1024
STACKSIZE       8192
EXPORTS         WndProc
```

Because regions always use device coordinates, the CLOVER program has to re-create the region every time it receives a WM_SIZE message. This takes several seconds. CLOVER begins by creating four elliptical regions that are stored as the first four elements of the *hRgnTemp* array. Then the program creates three "dummy" regions:

```
hRgnTemp [4] = CreateRectRgn (0, 0, 1, 1) ;
hRgnTemp [5] = CreateRectRgn (0, 0, 1, 1) ;
hRgnClip     = CreateRectRgn (0, 0, 1, 1) ;
```

The two elliptical regions at the left and right of the client area are combined:

```
CombineRgn (hRgnTemp [4], hRgnTemp [0], hRgnTemp [1], RGN_OR) ;
```

Similarly, the two elliptical regions at the top and bottom of the client area are combined:

```
CombineRgn (hRgnTemp [5], hRgnTemp [2], hRgnTemp [3], RGN_OR) ;
```

Finally, these two combined regions are in turn combined into *hRgnClip*:

```
CombineRgn (hRgnClip, hRgnTemp [4], hRgnTemp [5], RGN_XOR) ;
```

The RGN_XOR identifier is used to exclude overlapping areas from the resultant region. Finally, the six temporary regions are deleted:

```
for (i = 0 ; i < 6 ; i++)
    DeleteObject (hRgnTemp [i]) ;
```

The WM_PAINT processing is simple, considering the results. The viewport origin is set to the center of the client area (to make the line drawing easier), and the region created during the WM_SIZE message is selected as the device context's clipping region:

```
SetViewportOrg (hdc, xClient / 2, yClient / 2) ;
SelectClipRgn (hdc, hRgnClip) ;
```

Now all that's left is drawing the lines—360 of them, spaced 1 degree apart. The length of each line is the variable *fRadius*, which is the distance from the center to the corner of the client area:

```
fRadius = hypot (xClient / 2.0, yClient / 2.0) ;

for (fAngle = 0.0 ; fAngle < TWO_PI ; fAngle += TWO_PI / 360)
     {
     MoveTo (hdc, 0, 0) ;
     LineTo (hdc, (short) ( fRadius * cos (fAngle) + 0.5),
                  (short) (-fRadius * sin (fAngle) + 0.5)) ;
     }
```

During processing of WM_DESTROY, the region is deleted:

```
DeleteObject (hRgnClip) ;
```

SOME MISCELLANEOUS GDI FUNCTIONS

A few additional drawing functions don't fit into any convenient categories. These include *FloodFill, DrawIcon, ScrollWindow, ScrollDC, LineDDA,* and *LineProc.*

FloodFill fills in an area with the current brush. The syntax is:

```
FloodFill (hdc, xStart, yStart, rgbColor) ;
```

This is the function that the Windows PAINTBRUSH program calls when you use the "paint roller" icon. Starting at the logical point (*xStart, yStart*), the function fills in an area until it encounters a boundary of *rgbColor.*

FloodFill doesn't work if the point (*xStart, yStart*) is *rgbColor* itself or if the point is outside the clipping region. If you use *FloodFill* during normal repainting of your client area, you might want to invalidate the entire client area before calling *BeginPaint* to be sure that (*xStart, yStart*) is in the clipping region.

The *ExtFloodFill* function has the following syntax:

```
ExtFloodFill (hdc, xStart, yStart, rgbColor, wFill) ;
```

ExtFloodFill is an extended version of *FloodFill* that (depending on the last parameter) can fill to a boundary or over a surface the color of *rgbColor.*

DrawIcon draws an icon on the display:

```
DrawIcon (hdc, xStart, yStart, hIcon) ;
```

This function works only in the MM_TEXT mapping mode. (The *DrawIcon* function appears in Chapter 9.)

Both *ScrollWindow* and *ScrollDC* scroll part of the window's client area. We used *ScrollWindow* in the SYSMETS3 program in Chapter 2. It's not a GDI function, so it always uses device units. The general syntax is:

```
ScrollWindow (hwnd, xScroll, yScroll, &rectScroll, &rectClip) ;
```

Note that the first parameter is a handle to a window rather than to a device context. The section of the client area indicated by the *rectScroll* rectangle structure is shifted right *xScroll* pixels and down *yScroll* pixels. These two parameters can be negative if you use the function to scroll to the left or up.

Only the area within the *rectClip* rectangle is affected by this scrolling, so it makes sense to set *rectClip* only to be the same rectangle as *rectScroll*, a larger rectangle, or NULL. If you want the area within *rectScroll* to be scrolled without affecting anything outside the rectangle, set *rectClip* to equal *rectScroll*. If it is acceptable for the area within *rectScroll* to be shifted outside the rectangle, set *rectClip* to NULL. The area uncovered by the scrolling is invalidated and generates a WM_PAINT message. Because *ScrollWindow* is not a GDI function, it can't perform clipping and will also scroll dialog boxes or child windows that may be covering the surface of the client area.

ScrollDC is a GDI function and works differently. The syntax is:

```
ScrollDC (hdc, xScroll, yScroll, &rectScroll, &rectClip,
          hRgnUpdate, &rectUpdate) ;
```

When not set to NULL, the last two parameters return information to the program. If you pass a region handle to Windows in the sixth parameter, Windows sets the region to the invalid region uncovered by the scroll. If you pass a pointer to a RECT structure in the last parameter, Windows sets the structure to indicate the invalid rectangle uncovered by the scroll.

The *LineDDA* function calculates all the points on a straight line that connects two given points. (DDA stands for "digital differential analyzer.") The syntax is:

```
LineDDA (xStart, yStart, xEnd, yEnd, lpfnLineProc, lpData) ;
```

LineDDA requires a call-back function of the form:

```
void FAR PASCAL LineProc (x, y, lpData)
     short     x, y ;
     LPSTR     lpData ;
     {
     [other program lines]
     }
```

LineProc must be included in the EXPORTS section of your module definition (.DEF) file. The *lpfnLineProc* parameter you pass to *LineDDA* must be the result of a *MakeProc-Instance* call:

```
lpfnLineProc = MakeProcInstance (LineProc, hInstance) ;
```

When you call *LineDDA*, Windows calls *LineProc* once for each point on the line connecting (*xStart, yStart*) and (*xEnd, yEnd*). The point is indicated by the *x* and *y* parameters to *LineProc*. *LineProc* also receives the far pointer to programmer-defined data that you supply in the *LineDDA* call.

Note that *LineDDA* does not require a handle to a device context. The function is simply a line calculation algorithm that gives your program each point it calculates. What you do with these points is up to you. In the LINEDDA program, shown in Figure 12-19, I chose to draw a rectangle and connect the corners of the rectangle with the corners of the client area. Not satisfied with the mundane dotted and dashed line styles that Windows allows one to use with more ease, I chose to draw the lines as a series of tiny ellipses. The result is shown in Figure 12-20 on page 597.

LINEDDA.MAK

```
#-----------------------
# LINEDDA.MAK make file
#-----------------------

linedda.exe : linedda.obj linedda.def
     link linedda, /align:16, NUL, /nod slibcew libw, linedda
     rc linedda.exe

linedda.obj : linedda.c
     cl -c -Gsw -Ow -W2 -Zp linedda.c
```

Figure 12-19. *The LINEDDA program.*

LINEDDA.C

```
/*-------------------------------------------
    LINEDDA.C -- LineDDA Demonstration
                  (c) Charles Petzold, 1990
   -------------------------------------------*/

#include <windows.h>

long FAR PASCAL WndProc (HWND, WORD, WORD, LONG) ;
void FAR PASCAL LineProc (short, short, LPSTR) ;

HANDLE hInst ;

int PASCAL WinMain (HANDLE hInstance, HANDLE hPrevInstance,
                    LPSTR lpszCmdLine, int nCmdShow)
     {
     static char szAppName[] = "LineDDA" ;
     HWND        hwnd ;
     MSG         msg ;
     WNDCLASS    wndclass ;
```

(continued)

```
        if (!hPrevInstance)
            {
            wndclass.style          = CS_HREDRAW : CS_VREDRAW ;
            wndclass.lpfnWndProc    = WndProc ;
            wndclass.cbClsExtra     = 0 ;
            wndclass.cbWndExtra     = 0 ;
            wndclass.hInstance      = hInstance ;
            wndclass.hIcon          = NULL ;
            wndclass.hCursor        = LoadCursor (NULL, IDC_ARROW) ;
            wndclass.hbrBackground  = GetStockObject (WHITE_BRUSH) ;
            wndclass.lpszMenuName   = NULL ;
            wndclass.lpszClassName  = szAppName ;

            RegisterClass (&wndclass) ;
            }

    hInst = hInstance ;

    hwnd = CreateWindow (szAppName, "LineDDA Demonstration",
                        WS_OVERLAPPEDWINDOW,
                        CW_USEDEFAULT, CW_USEDEFAULT,
                        CW_USEDEFAULT, CW_USEDEFAULT,
                        NULL, NULL, hInstance, NULL) ;

    ShowWindow (hwnd, nCmdShow) ;
    UpdateWindow (hwnd) ;

    while (GetMessage (&msg, NULL, 0, 0))
        {
        TranslateMessage (&msg) ;
        DispatchMessage (&msg) ;
        }
    return msg.wParam ;
    }

long FAR PASCAL WndProc (HWND hwnd, WORD message, WORD wParam, LONG lParam)
    {
    static FARPROC  lpfnLineProc ;
    static short    cxClient, cyClient, xL, xR, yT, yB ;
    HDC             hdc ;
    PAINTSTRUCT     ps ;

    switch (message)
        {
        case WM_CREATE :
            lpfnLineProc = MakeProcInstance (LineProc, hInst) ;
            return 0 ;
```

```
        case WM_SIZE :
             xR = 3 * (xL = (cxClient = LOWORD (lParam)) / 4) ;
             yB = 3 * (yT = (cyClient = HIWORD (lParam)) / 4) ;
             return 0 ;

        case WM_PAINT :
             hdc = BeginPaint (hwnd, &ps) ;

             LineDDA (xL, yT, xR, yT, lpfnLineProc, (LPSTR) &hdc) ;
             LineDDA (xR, yT, xR, yB, lpfnLineProc, (LPSTR) &hdc) ;
             LineDDA (xR, yB, xL, yB, lpfnLineProc, (LPSTR) &hdc) ;
             LineDDA (xL, yB, xL, yT, lpfnLineProc, (LPSTR) &hdc) ;

             LineDDA (0,        0,        xL, yT, lpfnLineProc, (LPSTR) &hdc) ;
             LineDDA (cxClient, 0,        xR, yT, lpfnLineProc, (LPSTR) &hdc) ;
             LineDDA (cxClient, cyClient, xR, yB, lpfnLineProc, (LPSTR) &hdc) ;
             LineDDA (0,        cyClient, xL, yB, lpfnLineProc, (LPSTR) &hdc) ;

             EndPaint (hwnd, &ps) ;
             return 0 ;

        case WM_DESTROY :
             PostQuitMessage (0) ;
             return 0 ;
        }
     return DefWindowProc (hwnd, message, wParam, lParam) ;
     }

void FAR PASCAL LineProc (short x, short y, LPSTR lpData)
     {
     static short nCounter = 0 ;

     if (nCounter == 2)
          Ellipse (* (HDC far *) lpData, x - 2, y - 2, x + 3, y + 3) ;

     nCounter = (nCounter + 1) % 4 ;
     }
```

LINEDDA.DEF

```
;-----------------------------------
; LINEDDA.DEF module definition file
;-----------------------------------
```

(continued)

```
NAME            LINEDDA

DESCRIPTION     'LineDDA Demonstration (c) Charles Petzold, 1990'
EXETYPE         WINDOWS
STUB            'WINSTUB.EXE'
CODE            PRELOAD MOVEABLE DISCARDABLE
DATA            PRELOAD MOVEABLE MULTIPLE
HEAPSIZE        1024
STACKSIZE       8192
EXPORTS         WndProc
                LineProc
```

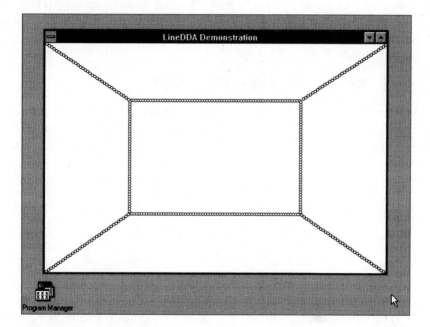

Figure 12-20. *The LINEDDA display.*

The *LineDDA* function is called eight times during processing of the WM_PAINT message, once for each of the eight lines. The *lpData* parameter is the address of the handle to the device context.

The *LineProc* function is short:

```
void FAR PASCAL LineProc (x, y, lpData)
     short        x, y ;
     LPSTR        lpData ;
     {
     static short nCounter = 0 ;

     if (nCounter == 2)
          Ellipse (* (HDC far *) lpData, x - 2, y - 2, x + 3, y + 3) ;

     nCounter = (nCounter + 1) % 4 ;
     }
```

Note that the *nCounter* variable is defined as static so that its value is preserved between *LineProc* calls. It cycles through the values 0, 1, 2, and 3. When the value is 2, *LineProc* draws an ellipse centered on the point.

PROGRAMS THAT DRAW FOREVER

A fun program in any graphics system is one that runs "forever," simply drawing a hypnotic series of rectangles with random sizes and colors. You can create such a program in Windows, but it's not quite as easy as it first seems. By now you should know that this is definitely not the way to do it:

```
case WM_PAINT :                 // Very, very bad code !!!

     hdc = BeginPaint (hwnd, &ps) ;

     while (TRUE)
          {
          xLeft   = rand () % xClient ;
          xRight  = rand () % xClient ;
          yTop    = rand () % yClient ;
          yBottom = rand () % yClient ;
          nRed    = rand () & 255 ;
          nGreen  = rand () & 255 ;
          nBlue   = rand () & 255 ;

          hdc = GetDC (hwnd) ;
          hBrush = CreateSolidBrush (RGB (nRed, nGreen, nBlue)) ;
          SelectObject (hdc, hBrush) ;

          Rectangle (hdc, min (xLeft, xRight), min (yTop, yBottom),
                          max (xLeft, xRight), max (yTop, yBottom)) ;
          }
     EndPaint (hwnd, &ps) ;
     return 0 ;
```

Sure, this will work, but nothing else will. Because Windows is a nonpreemptive multitasking environment, a program can't enter into an infinite loop like this. This loop will stop all other processing in the system.

One acceptable alternative is setting a Windows timer to send WM_TIMER messages to your window function. For each WM_TIMER message, you obtain a device context with *GetDC*, draw a random rectangle, and then release the device context with *ReleaseDC*. But that takes some of the fun out of the program, because the program can't draw the random rectangles as quickly as possible. It must wait for each WM_TIMER message.

There must be plenty of "dead time" in Windows, time during which all the message queues are empty and Windows is just sitting in a little loop waiting for keyboard or mouse input. Couldn't we somehow get control during that dead time and draw the rectangles, relinquishing control only when a message is added to a program's message queue? That's one of the purposes of the *PeekMessage* function. Here's one example of a *PeekMessage* call:

```
PeekMessage (&msg, NULL, 0, 0, PM_REMOVE) ;
```

The first four parameters (a pointer to a MSG structure, a window handle, and two values indicating a message range) are identical to those of *GetMessage*. Setting the second, third, and fourth parameters to NULL or 0 indicates that we want *PeekMessage* to return all messages for all windows in the program. Like *GetMessage*, *PeekMessage* effectively yields control to other programs if messages are waiting in the other programs' message queues. Like *GetMessage*, *PeekMessage* returns messages only for window functions in the program that makes the function call.

The last parameter to *PeekMessage* is set to PM_REMOVE if the message is to be removed from the message queue. You can set it to PM_NOREMOVE if the message isn't to be removed. This is why *PeekMessage* is a "peek" rather than a "get"—it allows a program to check the next message in the program's queue without actually removing it. *GetMessage* doesn't return control to a program unless it retrieves a message from the program's message queue. But *PeekMessage* will return under two conditions:

- When there's a message in the program's message queue, in which case the return value of *PeekMessage* is TRUE (nonzero).

- When there are no messages in the message queue of any program running under Windows, in which case the return value of *PeekMessage* is FALSE (0).

A message loop that uses *PeekMessage* rather than *GetMessage* essentially says to Windows, "Let other programs run for a little while, but once they've emptied their message queues, return control to me—I'm not finished with my work." If two or more programs are running that use a *PeekMessage* loop to retrieve messages, Windows uses a round-robin approach, returning control sequentially to each program waiting with a *PeekMessage* call.

This allows us to replace the normal message loop, which looks like this:

```
while (GetMessage (&msg, NULL, 0, 0))
     {
     TranslateMessage (&msg) ;
     DispatchMessage (&msg) ;
     }
return msg.wParam ;
```

with an alternative message loop like this:

```
while (TRUE)
     {
     if (PeekMessage (&msg, NULL, 0, 0, PM_REMOVE))
          {
          if (msg.message == WM_QUIT)
               break ;

          TranslateMessage (&msg) ;
          DispatchMessage (&msg) ;
          }
     else
          {
          [other program lines to do some work]
          }
     }
return msg.wParam ;
```

Notice that the WM_QUIT message is explicitly checked. You don't have to do this in a normal message loop, because the return value of *GetMessage* is 0 when it retrieves a WM_QUIT message. But *PeekMessage* uses its return value to indicate whether a message was retrieved, so the check of WM_QUIT is required.

If the return value of *PeekMessage* is TRUE, the message is processed normally. If the value is FALSE, the program can do some work (such as displaying yet another random rectangle) before returning control to Windows.

(Although the Windows documentation notes that you can't use *PeekMessage* to remove WM_PAINT messages from the message queue, this isn't really a problem. After all, *GetMessage* doesn't remove WM_PAINT messages from the queue either. The only way to remove a WM_PAINT message from the queue is to validate the invalid regions of the window's client area, which you can do with *ValidateRect*, *ValidateRgn*, or a *BeginPaint* and *EndPaint* pair. If you process a WM_PAINT message normally after retrieving it from the queue with *PeekMessage*, you'll have no problems. What you can't do is use code like this to empty your message queue of all messages:

```
while (PeekMessage (&msg, NULL, 0, 0, PM_REMOVE)) ;
```

This statement removes and discards all messages from your message queue except WM_PAINT. If a WM_PAINT message is in the queue, you'll be stuck inside the *while* loop forever.)

The Windows TERMINAL program uses a *PeekMessage* loop when it receives input from a communications line. This allows TERMINAL to check "continuously" for incoming data. The PRINT MANAGER program uses this technique to print on a printer or plotter and—as you'll see in Chapter 15—a Windows program that prints also includes a function with a *PeekMessage* loop. Armed with the *PeekMessage* function, we can now write a program that relentlessly displays random rectangles. The program, called RANDRECT, is shown in Figure 12-21.

RANDRECT.MAK

```
#------------------------
# RANDRECT.MAK make file
#------------------------

randrect.exe : randrect.obj randrect.def
    link randrect, /align:16, NUL, /nod slibcew libw, randrect
    rc randrect.exe

randrect.obj : randrect.c
    cl -c -Gsw -Ow -W2 -Zp randrect.c
```

RANDRECT.C

```
/*---------------------------------------------
    RANDRECT.C -- Displays Random Rectangles
                  (c) Charles Petzold, 1990
   ---------------------------------------------*/

#include <windows.h>
#include <stdlib.h>

long FAR PASCAL WndProc (HWND, WORD, WORD, LONG) ;
void DrawRectangle (HWND) ;

short cxClient, cyClient ;
```

Figure 12-21. *The RANDRECT program.*   *(continued)*

```
int PASCAL WinMain (HANDLE hInstance, HANDLE hPrevInstance,
                    LPSTR lpszCmdLine, int nCmdShow)
    {
    static char szAppName[] = "RandRect" ;
    HWND        hwnd ;
    MSG         msg ;
    WNDCLASS    wndclass ;

    if (!hPrevInstance)
        {
        wndclass.style         = CS_HREDRAW : CS_VREDRAW ;
        wndclass.lpfnWndProc   = WndProc ;
        wndclass.cbClsExtra    = 0 ;
        wndclass.cbWndExtra    = 0 ;
        wndclass.hInstance     = hInstance ;
        wndclass.hIcon         = NULL ;
        wndclass.hCursor       = LoadCursor (NULL, IDC_ARROW) ;
        wndclass.hbrBackground = GetStockObject (WHITE_BRUSH) ;
        wndclass.lpszMenuName  = NULL ;
        wndclass.lpszClassName = szAppName ;

        !RegisterClass (&wndclass) ;
        }

    hwnd = CreateWindow (szAppName, "Random Rectangles",
                         WS_OVERLAPPEDWINDOW,
                         CW_USEDEFAULT, CW_USEDEFAULT,
                         CW_USEDEFAULT, CW_USEDEFAULT,
                         NULL, NULL, hInstance, NULL) ;

    ShowWindow (hwnd, nCmdShow) ;
    UpdateWindow (hwnd) ;

    while (TRUE)
        {
        if (PeekMessage (&msg, NULL, 0, 0, PM_REMOVE))
            {
            if (msg.message == WM_QUIT)
                break ;

            TranslateMessage (&msg) ;
            DispatchMessage (&msg) ;
            }
        else
            DrawRectangle (hwnd) ;
        }
    return msg.wParam ;
    }
```

(continued)

```
long FAR PASCAL WndProc (HWND hwnd, WORD message, WORD wParam, LONG lParam)
     {
     switch (message)
          {
          case WM_SIZE :
               cxClient = LOWORD (lParam) ;
               cyClient = HIWORD (lParam) ;
               return 0 ;

          case WM_DESTROY :
               PostQuitMessage (0) ;
               return 0 ;
          }
     return DefWindowProc (hwnd, message, wParam, lParam) ;
     }

void DrawRectangle (HWND hwnd)
     {
     HBRUSH hBrush ;
     HDC    hdc ;
     short  xLeft, xRight, yTop, yBottom, nRed, nGreen, nBlue ;

     xLeft   = rand () % cxClient ;
     xRight  = rand () % cxClient ;
     yTop    = rand () % cyClient ;
     yBottom = rand () % cyClient ;
     nRed    = rand () & 255 ;
     nGreen  = rand () & 255 ;
     nBlue   = rand () & 255 ;

     hdc = GetDC (hwnd) ;
     hBrush = CreateSolidBrush (RGB (nRed, nGreen, nBlue)) ;
     SelectObject (hdc, hBrush) ;

     Rectangle (hdc, min (xLeft, xRight), min (yTop, yBottom),
                     max (xLeft, xRight), max (yTop, yBottom)) ;

     ReleaseDC (hwnd, hdc) ;
     DeleteObject (hBrush) ;
     }
```

RANDRECT.DEF

```
;----------------------------------------
; RANDRECT.DEF module definition file
;----------------------------------------

NAME            RANDRECT

DESCRIPTION     'Random Rectangle Drawing Program (c) Charles Petzold, 1990'
EXETYPE         WINDOWS
STUB            'WINSTUB.EXE'
CODE            PRELOAD MOVEABLE DISCARDABLE
DATA            PRELOAD MOVEABLE MULTIPLE
HEAPSIZE        1024
STACKSIZE       8192
EXPORTS         WndProc
```

Chapter 13

Bits, Blts, and Metafiles

Bitmaps and metafiles represent two very different ways of storing pictorial information. A bitmap is a complete digital representation of a picture. Each pixel in the image corresponds to one or more bits in the bitmap. Monochrome bitmaps require only one bit per pixel; color bitmaps require additional bits to indicate the color of each pixel.

A metafile, on the other hand, stores pictorial information as a series of records that correspond directly to GDI calls, such as *MoveTo*, *Rectangle*, *TextOut*, and others that you encountered in Chapter 12. A metafile is thus a description of a picture rather than a digital representation of it.

Both bitmaps and metafiles have their place in computer graphics. Bitmaps are very often used for very complex images originating from the real world, such as digitized photographs. Metafiles are more suitable for human- or machine-generated images, such as architectural drawings. Both bitmaps and metafiles can exist in memory or be stored on a disk as files, and both can be transferred among Windows applications using the clipboard.

You can construct a bitmap "manually" using the SDKPAINT program included with the Windows Software Development Kit. You can then include the bitmap as a resource in a resource script file and load it into a program using the *LoadBitmap* function. This was demonstrated in Chapter 8. In Chapter 9 we saw how bitmaps can substitute for text in a menu. In Chapter 12 we constructed small 8-by-8-pixel bitmaps to use for brushes.

Metafiles are more closely associated with Windows drawing programs (such as Micrografx's Designer) and other CAD (computer-aided design) programs. The user of these programs draws an image with lines, rectangles, ellipses, text, and other graphics primitives. Although these programs generally use a private format for storing the picture in a file, they can usually transfer the picture to the clipboard in the form of a metafile.

Windows 3 supports two different bitmap formats. The first format (sometimes called the "device-dependent" format) originated with Windows 1. (I'll be calling this the "old bitmap.") The second format is called the "device-independent bitmap" (DIB) and is new in Windows 3. The DIB is an extension of the bitmap format supported in the OS/2 1.1 Presentation Manager, and the WINDOWS.H header file contains some structures for working with OS/2 bitmaps.

Bitmaps have two major drawbacks. First, they are highly susceptible to problems involving device dependence. Even the device-independent bitmap is not entirely immune to these problems. The most obvious device dependency is color. Displaying a color bitmap on a monochrome device is often unsatisfactory. Another problem is that a bitmap implies a particular resolution and aspect ratio of an image. Although bitmaps can be stretched or compressed, this process generally involves duplicating or dropping rows or columns of pixels and can lead to distortion in the scaled image. A metafile can be scaled to any size without distortion.

The second major drawback of bitmaps is that they require a large amount of storage space. For instance, a bitmap representation of an entire 640-by-480, 16-color VGA screen requires over 150 KB. Metafiles usually require much less storage space than bitmaps. The storage space for a bitmap is governed by the size of the image and number of colors it contains, whereas the storage space for a metafile is governed by the complexity of the image and the number of individual GDI instructions it contains.

One advantage of bitmaps over metafiles, however, is speed. Copying a bitmap on a video display is usually much faster than rendering a metafile.

In the introduction to GDI in Chapter 11, I talked about two types of device contexts that don't refer to real devices: the memory device context and the metafile device context. We'll see how these work as we examine bitmaps and metafiles and explore the ways we can create, use, and manipulate them. The subject of bitmaps and metafiles will come up again in Chapter 16, "The Clipboard." Text, bitmaps, and metafiles are the three primary forms of data that can be shared by applications through the clipboard.

THE OLD BITMAP FORMAT

The old bitmap format that originated in Windows 1 is very limited and highly dependent on the output device for which the bitmap is created. You should use the DIB format rather than the old bitmap format for storing bitmap files on disk. However, when you need a bitmap solely for use within a program, working with the old bitmap format is much easier.

Creating Bitmaps in a Program

Windows includes four functions that let you create an old-style bitmap in your program. They are:

```
hBitmap = CreateBitmap (cxWidth, cyHeight, nPlanes, nBitsPixel, lpBits) ;
hBitmap = CreateBitmapIndirect (&bitmap) ;
hBitmap = CreateCompatibleBitmap (hdc, cxWidth, cyHeight) ;
hBitmap = CreateDiscardableBitmap (hdc, cxWidth, cyHeight) ;
```

The *cxWidth* and *cyHeight* parameters are the width and the height of the bitmap in pixels. In *CreateBitmap*, the *nPlanes* and *nBitsPixel* parameters are the number of color planes and the number of color bits per pixel in the bitmap. At least one of these parameters should be set to 1. If both parameters are 1, the function creates a monochrome bitmap. (I'll discuss how the color planes and color bits represent color shortly.)

In the *CreateBitmap* function, *lpBits* can be set to NULL if you are creating an uninitialized bitmap. The resultant bitmap contains random data. In the *CreateCompatibleBitmap* and *CreateDiscardableBitmap* functions, Windows uses the device context referenced by *hdc* to obtain the number of color planes and number of color bits per pixel. The bitmap created by these functions is uninitialized.

CreateBitmapIndirect is similar to *CreateBitmap* except that it uses the bitmap structure of type BITMAP to define the bitmap. The following table shows the fields of this structure:

Field	Type	Description
bmType	short	Set to 0
bmWidth	short	Width of bitmap in pixels
bmHeight	short	Height of bitmap in scan lines
bmWidthBytes	short	Width of bitmap in bytes (must be even)
bmPlanes	BYTE	Number of color planes
bmBitsPixel	BYTE	Number of color bits per pixel
bmBits	LPSTR	Far pointer to array of bits

The *bmWidthBytes* field must be an even number—the lowest even number of bytes required to store one scan line. The array of the bits referenced by *bmBits* must be organized based on the *bmWidthBytes* field. If *bm* is a structure variable of type BITMAP, you can calculate the *bmWidthBytes* field by the following statement:

```
bm.bmWidthBytes = (bm.bmWidth * bm.bmBitsPixel + 15) / 16 * 2 ;
```

If Windows cannot create the bitmap (generally because not enough memory is available), it will return a NULL. You should check the return value from the bitmap creation functions, particularly if you're creating large bitmaps.

The handle to the bitmap is not a handle to a global memory block, so don't try to use the *GlobalLock* function on it. The handle is instead a local handle to the GDI module's data segment. This handle references a small local memory block in GDI that contains a second handle to a global memory block containing the information in the BITMAP structure and the actual bits.

Once you create a bitmap, you cannot change the size, the number of color planes, or the number of color bits per pixel. You would have to create a new bitmap and transfer the bits from the original bitmap to this new bitmap. If you have a handle to a bitmap, you can get the size and color organization using:

```
GetObject (hBitmap, sizeof (BITMAP), (LPSTR) &bitmap) ;
```

This copies the information about the bitmap into a structure (called *bitmap* here) of type BITMAP. This function doesn't fill in the *bmBits* field. To get access to the actual bits of the bitmap, you must call:

```
GetBitmapBits (hBitmap, dwCount, lpBits) ;
```

This copies *dwCount* bits into a character array referenced by the far pointer *lpBits*. To ensure that all the bits of the bitmap are copied into this array, you can calculate the *dwCount* parameter based on the fields of the bitmap structure:

```
dwCount = (DWORD) bitmap.bmWidthBytes * bitmap.bmHeight *
                    bitmap.bmPlanes ;
```

You can also direct Windows to copy a character array containing the bitmap bits back into an existing bitmap using the function:

```
SetBitmapBits (hBitmap, dwCount, lpBits) ;
```

Because bitmaps are GDI objects, you should delete any bitmap you create:

```
DeleteObject (hBitmap) ;
```

The Monochrome Bitmap Format

For a monochrome bitmap, the format of the bits is relatively simple and can almost be derived directly from the image you want to create. For instance, suppose you want to create a bitmap that looks like this:

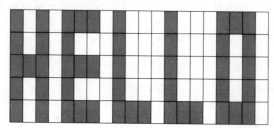

You can write down a series of bits (0 for black and 1 for white) that directly corresponds to this grid. Reading these bits from left to right, you can then assign each group of 8 bits a hexadecimal byte. If the width of the bitmap is not a multiple of 16, pad the bytes to the right with zeros to get an even number of bytes:

```
0 1 0 1 0 0 0 1 0 1 1 1 0 1 1 1 0 0 0 1 = 51 77 10 00
0 1 0 1 0 1 1 1 0 1 1 1 0 1 1 1 0 1 0 1 = 57 77 50 00
0 0 0 1 0 0 0 1 0 1 1 1 0 1 1 1 0 1 0 1 = 11 77 50 00
0 1 0 1 0 1 1 1 0 1 1 1 0 1 1 1 0 1 0 1 = 57 77 50 00
0 1 0 1 0 0 0 1 0 0 0 1 0 0 0 1 0 0 0 1 = 51 11 10 00
```

The width in pixels is 20, the height in scan lines is 5, and the width in bytes is 4. You can set up a BITMAP structure for this bitmap with the following statement:

```
static BITMAP bitmap    = { 0, 20, 5, 4, 1, 1 } ;
```

and you can store the bits in a BYTE array:

```
static BYTE   byBits [] = { 0x51, 0x77, 0x10, 0x00,
                            0x57, 0x77, 0x50, 0x00,
                            0x11, 0x77, 0x50, 0x00,
                            0x57, 0x77, 0x50, 0x00,
                            0x51, 0x11, 0x10, 0x00 } ;
```

Creating the bitmap with *CreateBitmapIndirect* requires two statements:

```
bitmap.bmBits = (LPSTR) byBits ;

hBitmap = CreateBitmapIndirect (&bitmap) ;
```

Be careful when working with the pointer to *byBits*. It's OK to call *CreateBitmapIndirect* right after you assign the far address to the *bmBits* field, but this field can become invalid if Windows moves your local data segment.

You may prefer the following statements, which avoid this problem:

```
hBitmap = CreateBitmapIndirect (&bitmap) ;

SetBitmapBits (hBitmap, (DWORD) sizeof byBits, byBits) ;
```

You can also avoid using the bitmap structure entirely and create the bitmap in one statement:

```
hBitmap = CreateBitmap (20, 5, 1, 1, byBits) ;
```

The Color Bitmap Format

An old-style color bitmap is a little more complex and extremely device dependent. A color bitmap is organized to facilitate the transfer of the bits to a particular output device. Whether the bitmap is organized as a series of color planes or as multiple color bits per pixel depends on the device for which the bitmap is suitable.

Let's look first at a bitmap that has a *bmBitsPixel* field of 1 (which means that it has 1 color bit per pixel) but a *bmPlanes* value greater than 1. A color bitmap for the EGA or VGA is a good example. Windows uses the 4 color planes of the EGA or VGA to display 16 colors, so *bmPlanes* is 4. The array of bits begins with the top scan line. The color planes for each scan line are stored sequentially—the red plane first, the green plane, the blue plane, and the intensity plane. The bitmap then continues with the second scan line.

A bitmap can also represent color as a multiple number of bits per pixel. Suppose a device (such as the IBM 8514/A) can represent 256 colors using 8 color bits (1 byte) per pixel. For each scan line, the first byte represents the color for the leftmost pixel, the second byte represents the color for the next pixel, and so forth. The *bmWidthBytes* value in the BITMAP structure reflects the increased byte width of each scan line, but the *bmWidth* value is still the number of pixels per scan line.

Here's the catch: Nothing in the bitmap specifies how these multiple color planes or multiple color bits correspond to actual display colors. A particular color bitmap is suitable only for an output device with display memory organized like the bitmap. For instance, suppose you have a device that stores color information using 8 bits per pixel, but the 256 values are interpreted by the device differently than on the 8514/A. This is perfectly legitimate, but a bitmap created for the 8514/A would have incorrect colors on this other device.

The device-independent bitmap solves this problem, as we'll see shortly.

The Dimensions of a Bitmap

Two other functions connected with bitmaps are the source of some confusion. These are:

    SetBitmapDimension (hBitmap, xDimension, yDimension) ;

and:

    dwDimension = GetBitmapDimension (hBitmap) ;

The *xDimension* and *yDimension* values (encoded as the low and high words in the *dwDimension* value returned from *GetBitmapDimension*) are the width and height of the bitmap in units of 0.1 mm, which correspond to logical units in the MM_LOMETRIC mapping mode. GDI itself doesn't use these dimensions. They are part of neither the BITMAP structure nor the bitmap file format. However, two cooperating applications could use these dimensions to aid in the scaling of bitmaps that are exchanged through the clipboard or other means.

THE DEVICE-INDEPENDENT BITMAP (DIB)

The device-independent bitmap (DIB) format is an extension of the bitmap format introduced in the OS/2 1.1 Presentation Manager. It solves some of the device dependencies of the old bitmap format by including a color table that defines an RGB value for each color in the bitmap.

The device-independent bitmap has several other differences from the old bitmap format: First, color is always represented by multiple color bits per pixel and never as multiple color planes, despite how buffer memory is organized on the output device. The number of color bits per pixel may be 1 (for monochrome bitmaps), 4 (16-color bitmaps), 8 (256 colors), or 24 (16 million colors). Second, the array of bits begins with the bottom row of pixels rather than the top. Third, additional information is included in the bitmap to indicate a resolution of the image. (This may help programs in scaling a bitmap to a proper size.) Fourth, the bitmap data may be compressed using a run-length-encoded (RLE) algorithm.

The DIB File

You can create a device-independent bitmap and save it to a disk file (with the extension .BMP) in either the SDKPAINT program included in the Windows Software Development Kit or the PAINTBRUSH program included in the retail Windows product. The file begins with a file header section defined by the BITMAPFILEHEADER structure. This structure has five fields:

Field	Size	Description
bfType	WORD	The bytes "BM" (for bitmap)
bfSize	DWORD	Total size of the file
bfReserved1	WORD	Set to 0
bfReserved2	WORD	Set to 0
bfOffBits	DWORD	Offset to the bitmap bits from the beginning of the file

This is followed by another header defined by the BITMAPINFOHEADER structure. This structure has 11 fields:

Field	Size	Description
biSize	DWORD	Size of the BITMAPINFOHEADER structure in bytes
biWidth	DWORD	Width of the bitmap in pixels
biHeight	DWORD	Height of the bitmap in pixels
biPlanes	WORD	Set to 1
biBitCount	WORD	Color bits per pixel (1, 4, 8, or 24)
biCompression	DWORD	Compression scheme (0 for none)
biSizeImage	DWORD	Size of bitmap bits in bytes (only required if compression is used)
biXPelsPerMeter	DWORD	Horizontal resolution in pixels per meter
biYPelsPerMeter	DWORD	Vertical resolution in pixels per meter
biClrUsed	DWORD	Number of colors used in image
biClrImportant	DWORD	Number of important colors in image

All fields following the *biBitCount* field may be set to 0 for default values.

If *biClrUsed* is set to 0 and the number of color bits per pixel is 1, 4, or 8, the BIT-MAPINFOHEADER structure is followed by a color table, which consists of two or more RGBQUAD structures. The RGBQUAD structure defines an RGB color value:

Field	Size	Description
rgbBlue	BYTE	Blue intensity
rgbGreen	BYTE	Green intensity
rgbRed	BYTE	Red intensity
rgbReserved	BYTE	Set to 0

The number of RGBQUAD structures is usually determined by the *biBitCount* field: 2 RGBQUAD structures are required for 1 color bit, 16 for 4 color bits, and 256 for 8 color bits. However, if the *biClrUsed* field is nonzero, then the *biClrUsed* field contains the number of RGBQUAD structures in the color table.

The color table is followed by the array of bits that define the bitmap image. This array begins with the bottom row of pixels. Each row begins with the leftmost pixels. Each pixel corresponds to 1, 4, 8, or 24 bits.

For a monochrome bitmap with 1 color bit per pixel, the first pixel in each row is represented by the most significant bit of the first byte in each row. If this bit is 0, the color of the pixel can be obtained from the first RGBQUAD structure in the color table. If the bit is 1, the color is given by the second RGBQUAD structure in the color table.

For a 16-color bitmap with 4 color bits per pixel, the first pixel in each row is represented by the most significant four bits of the first byte in each row. The color of each pixel is obtained by using the 4-bit value as an index into the 16 entries in the color table.

For a 256-color bitmap, each byte corresponds to one pixel. The color of the pixel is obtained by indexing the 256 entries in the color table by the byte.

If the bitmap image contains 24 color bits per pixel, each set of three bytes is an RGB value of the pixel. There is no color table (unless the *biClrUsed* field in the BITMAP-INFOHEADER structure is nonzero).

In each case, each row of the bitmap data contains a multiple of four bytes. The row is padded on the right to ensure this.

The bitmap format supported in OS/2 1.1 and above is very similar. It begins with a BITMAPFILEHEADER structure but is followed by a BITMAPCOREHEADER structure. (You can determine if a bitmap file uses this format or the Windows 3 format by examining the first field of this structure.) The color table consists of RGBTRIPLE structures rather than RGBQUAD structures.

Creating a DIB

The *CreateDIBitmap* function creates a device-independent bitmap. You can use this function in two different ways. The function call:

```
hBitmap = CreateDIBitmap (hdc, &bmih, OL, NULL, NULL, 0) ;
```

creates an uninitialized bitmap. The second parameter is a pointer to an initialized BIT-MAPINFOHEADER structure. The function call:

```
hBitmap = CreateDIBitmap (hdc, &bmih, CBM_INIT,
                          lpBits, &bmi, wUsage) ;
```

creates an initialized bitmap. The *lpBits* parameter is a pointer to the array of bits. The fifth parameter is a pointer to an initialized BITMAPINFO structure.

The BITMAPINFO structure is defined as follows:

```
typedef structure tagBITMAPINFO
    {
BITMAPINFOHEADER bmiHeader ;
    RGBQUAD          bmiColors[1] ;
    }
    BITMAPINFO ;
```

The first field is an initialized BITMAPINFOHEADER structure, and the second field is an array of initialized RGBQUAD structures that define the color table. Windows needs this color table when the bitmap is initialized to properly interpret the bitmap image data and to perform any color conversions required by the device.

Note that the RGBQUAD array contains only one element. To use this structure you must allocate a memory block equal in size to the BITMAPINFOHEADER structure plus enough RGBQUAD structures for the whole color table.

The *wUsage* parameter to *CreateDIBitmap* can be either DIB_RGB_COLORS (which means that the color table contains RGB color values) or DIB_PAL_COLORS (indicating that the color table is an array of 2-byte values that index a palette).

Two functions are available to set and obtain the bits of the bitmap. The first function sets the bits:

```
SetDIBits (hdc, hBitmap, nStart, nNum,
           lpBits, &bmi, wUsage) ;
```

The last three parameters are the same as in the *CreateDIBitmap* function. The *nStart* parameter indicates the beginning scan line addressed by *lpBits*. This can range from 0 (for the bottom scan line) to the height of the bitmap in pixels minus 1 (for the top scan line). The *nNum* parameter indicates the number of scan lines to set into the bitmap.

The *GetDIBits* function has identical parameters:

```
GetDIBits (hdc, hBitmap, nStart, nNum,
           lpBits, &bmi, wUsage) ;
```

But in this case *lpBits* points to a buffer to receive the bitmap bits. The function sets the fields of the BITMAPINFO structure to indicate the dimensions of the bitmap and the color table.

Like the old-style bitmap, a DIB can be deleted using *DeleteObject*.

THE MEMORY DEVICE CONTEXT

Two functions—*SetDIBitsToDevice* and *StretchDIBits*—allow you to render an array of bits on an output device. However, if you have a handle to a bitmap, there is no function to draw the bitmap on the display surface of a device context. You'll search in vain for a function that looks like this:

```
DrawBitmap (hdc, hBitmap, xStart, yStart) ; // No such function!!!
```

This function would copy a bitmap to the device context represented by *hdc* beginning at the logical point (*xStart, yStart*). We'll write our own *DrawBitmap* function later in this chapter. First, however, you need to become familiar with several concepts, starting with the memory device context.

A memory device context is a device context that has a "display surface" that exists only in memory. You can create a memory device context using the function:

```
hdcMem = CreateCompatibleDC (hdc) ;
```

The *hdc* handle is a handle to an existing valid device context. The function returns a handle to the memory device context. Upon creation of the memory device context, all the attributes are set to the normal default values. You can do almost anything you want with this memory device context. You can set the attributes to nondefault values, obtain the current settings of the attributes, and select pens, brushes, regions into it. And yes, you can even draw on it. But it doesn't make much sense to do so just yet. Here's why.

When you first create a memory device context, it has a "display surface" that contains exactly 1 monochrome pixel. That is a very small display surface. (Don't rely on *Get-DeviceCaps* to tell you this. The HORZSIZE, VERTSIZE, HORZRES, VERTRES, BITSPIXEL, and PLANES values for *hdcMem* will all be set to the values associated with the original *hdc*. If *GetDeviceCaps* really returned the correct values associated with the memory device context when it is first created, then the HORZRES, VERTRES, BITSPIXEL, and PLANES indexes would all return 1.) What you need to do is make the display surface of the memory device context larger. You do this by selecting a bitmap into the device context:

```
SelectObject (hdcMem, hBitmap) ;
```

Now the display surface of *hdcMem* has the same width, height, and color organization as the bitmap referenced by *hBitmap*. With the default window and viewport origins, the logical point (0, 0) of the memory device context corresponds to the upper left corner of the bitmap.

If the bitmap had some kind of picture on it, then that picture is now part of the memory device context's display surface. Any changes you make to that bitmap (for instance, by using *SetBitmapBits* to set a different array of bits to the bitmap) are reflected in this display surface. Anything you draw on the memory device context is actually drawn on the bitmap. In short, the bitmap is the display surface of the memory device context.

Earlier I discussed the various functions to create bitmaps. One of them is:

```
hBitmap = CreateCompatibleBitmap (hdc, xWidth, yHeight) ;
```

If *hdc* is the handle to the normal device context for a screen or a printer, then the number of color planes and number of bits per pixel of this bitmap are the same as for the device. However, if *hdc* is the handle to a memory device context (and no bitmap has yet been selected into the memory device context), then *CreateCompatibleBitmap* returns a monochrome bitmap that is *xWidth* pixels wide and *yHeight* pixels high.

A bitmap is one of six GDI objects. You saw in Chapter 12 how to use *SelectObject* to select a pen, brush, or region into a device context, and in Chapter 14 you'll learn how to use this function to select a font into a device context. You can use *SelectObject* to select these four GDI objects into a memory device context also. However, you cannot select a bitmap into a normal device context, only into a memory device context.

When you're finished with the memory device context, you must delete it:

```
DeleteDC (hdcMem) ;
```

Well, you may say, this is all very nice, but we haven't yet solved the problem of getting the bitmap on the display. All we've done is select it into a memory device context. Now what? Now we have to learn how to "blt" (pronounced "blit") the bits from one device context to another.

THE MIGHTY BLT

Graphics involves writing pixels to a display device. In Chapter 12 we looked at the more refined ways of doing this, but for power-pixel manipulation, nothing in Windows comes close to *BitBlt* and its two cousins, *PatBlt* and *StretchBlt*. *BitBlt* (pronounced "bit blit") stands for "bit-block transfer." *BitBlt* is a pixel-mover, or (more vividly) a raster-blaster. The simple word "transfer" doesn't really do justice to *BitBlt*. It does more than a transfer—it really does a logical combination of three sets of pixels using 1 of 256 different types of raster operations.

The *PatBlt* Function

PatBlt ("pattern block transfer") is the simplest of the three "blt" functions. It's really quite different from *BitBlt* and *StretchBlt* in that it uses only one device context. But *PatBlt* is nonetheless a reasonable place to begin.

In Chapter 12 you encountered the device context attribute called the drawing mode. This attribute can be set to 1 of 16 binary raster operation (ROP2) codes. When you draw a line, the drawing mode determines the type of logical operation that Windows performs on the pixels of the pen and the pixels of the device context destination. *PatBlt* is similar to the drawing mode except that it alters a rectangular area of the device context destination rather than merely a line. It performs a logical operation involving the pixels in this rectangle and a "pattern." This "pattern" is nothing new—*pattern* is simply another name for a brush. For this pattern, *PatBlt* uses the brush currently selected in the device context.

The syntax of *PatBlt* is:

```
PatBlt (hdc, xDest, yDest, xWidth, yHeight, dwROP) ;
```

The *xDest*, *yDest*, *xWidth*, and *yHeight* parameters are in logical units. The logical point (*xDest*, *yDest*) specifies the upper left corner of a rectangle. The rectangle is *xWidth* units wide and *yHeight* units high. (See the section entitled "Blt Coordinates," later in this chapter, for a more precise definition of these values.) This is the rectangular area that *PatBlt* alters. The logical operation that *PatBlt* performs on the brush and the destination device context is determined by the *dwROP* parameter, which is a doubleword (32-bit integer) ROP code—not one of the ROP2 codes used for the drawing mode.

Windows has 256 ROP codes. These define all possible logical combinations of a source display area, a destination display area, and a pattern (or brush). The device driver for the video display supports all 256 raster operations through the use of a "compiler" of sorts. This compiler uses the 32-bit ROP code to create a set of machine-language instructions on the stack that can carry out this logical operation on the pixels of the display; it then executes these instructions. The high word of the 32-bit ROP code is a number between 0 and 255. The low word is a number that assists the device driver "compiler" in constructing the machine code for the logical operation. Fifteen of the 256 ROP codes have names. If you want to use any of the others, you'll have to look up the number in the table in the Programmer's Reference included with the Windows Software Development Kit.

Because the *PatBlt* function uses only a destination device context and a pattern (and not a source device context), it can accept only a subset of these 256 ROP codes—that is, the 16 ROP codes that use only the destination device context and a pattern. The 16 raster operations supported by *PatBlt* are shown in the table below. You'll note that this is similar to the table showing ROP2 codes on page 551 of Chapter 12.

Pattern (P):	1	1	0	0	Boolean	ROP	
Destination (D):	1	0	1	0	Operation	Code	Name
Result:	0	0	0	0	0	000042	BLACKNESS
	0	0	0	1	~(P¦D)	0500A9	
	0	0	1	0	~P & D	0A0329	
	0	0	1	1	~P	0F0001	
	0	1	0	0	P & ~D	500325	
	0	1	0	1	~D	550009	DSTINVERT
	0	1	1	0	P ∧ D	5A0049	PATINVERT
	0	1	1	1	~(P & D)	5F00E9	
	1	0	0	0	P & D	A000C9	
	1	0	0	1	~(P ∧ D)	A50065	
	1	0	1	0	D	AA0029	
	1	0	1	1	~P¦D	AF0229	
	1	1	0	0	P	F00021	PATCOPY
	1	1	0	1	P¦~D	F50225	
	1	1	1	0	P¦D	FA0089	
	1	1	1	1	1	FF0062	WHITENESS

For a monochrome device context, a 1 bit corresponds to a white pixel and a 0 bit to a black pixel. Destinations and patterns that are either pure black or pure white are the easiest to consider when you start thinking about *PatBlt*. For instance, if you call:

```
PatBlt (hdc, xDest, yDest, xWidth, yHeight, 0x5F00E9L) ;
```

then the rectangular area that begins at the logical point (*xDest, yDest*) and that is *xWidth* pixels wide and *yHeight* pixels high will be colored black only if the destination was originally white and you had WHITE_BRUSH selected in the device context. Otherwise, the destination will be colored white. Of course, even in a monochrome device context, destinations and brushes can be dithered combinations of black and white pixels. In this case, Windows performs the logical combination on a pixel-by-pixel basis, which can lead to some odd results. For instance, if your destination has already been colored with GRAY-_BRUSH, and GRAY_BRUSH is also the current brush selected in the device context, then:

```
PatBlt (hdc, xDest, yDest, xWidth, yHeight, PATINVERT) ;
```

will set the destination to either pure white or pure black, depending on how the dithered pixels of the destination coincide with the dithered pixels of the brush.

Color introduces more complexities. Windows performs the logical operation for each color plane separately or each set of color bits separately, depending on how the memory of the device is organized.

Some of the more common uses of *PatBlt* are shown below. If you want to draw a black rectangle, you call:

```
PatBlt (hdc, xDest, yDest, xWidth, yHeight, BLACKNESS) ;
```

To draw a white rectangle, use:

```
PatBlt (hdc, xDest, yDest, xWidth, yHeight, WHITENESS) ;
```

The function:

```
PatBlt (hdc, xDest, yDest, xWidth, yHeight, DSTINVERT) ;
```

always inverts the colors of the rectangle. If WHITE_BRUSH is currently selected in the device context, then the function:

```
PatBlt (hdc, xDest, yDest, xWidth, yHeight, PATINVERT) ;
```

also inverts the rectangle.

You'll recall that the *FillRect* function fills in a rectangular area with a brush:

```
FillRect (hdc, &rect, hBrush) ;
```

The *FillRect* function is equivalent to the following code:

```
hBrush = SelectObject (hdc, hBrush) ;
PatBlt (hdc, rect.left, rect.top,
               rect.right - rect.left,
               rect.bottom - rect.top, PATCOPY) ;
SelectObject (hdc, hBrush) ;
```

In fact, this code (in more optimized assembly language) is what Windows uses to execute the *FillRect* function. When you call:

```
InvertRect (hdc, &rect) ;
```

Windows translates it into the function:

```
PatBlt (hdc, rect.left, rect.top,
               rect.right - rect.left,
               rect.bottom - rect.top, DSTINVERT) ;
```

Blt Coordinates

When I introduced the syntax of the *PatBlt* function, I said that the point (*xDest, yDest*) specifies the upper left corner of a rectangle and that this rectangle is *xWidth* units wide and *yHeight* units high. Actually, although that's also what the Windows documentation says, the statement is not entirely accurate. Before we proceed any further, I need to clear up some confusion concerning the *blt* functions and coordinates.

BitBlt, *PatBlt*, and *StretchBlt* are the only GDI drawing functions that specify logical rectangular coordinates in terms of a logical width and height measured from a single corner. All the other GDI drawing functions that use rectangular bounding boxes require that coordinates be specified in terms of an upper left corner and a lower right corner. For the MM_TEXT mapping mode, the above description of the *PatBlt* parameters is accurate. For the metric mapping modes, however, it's not. If you use positive values of *xWidth* and *yHeight*, then the point (*xDest, yDest*) will be the lower left corner of the rectangle. If you want (*xDest, yDest*) to be the upper left corner of the rectangle, the *yHeight* parameter must be set to the negative height of the rectangle.

To be more precise, the rectangle that *PatBlt* colors has a logical width given by the absolute value of *xWidth* and a logical height given by the absolute value of *yHeight*. These two parameters can be negative. The rectangle is defined by two corners given by the logical points (*xDest, yDest*) and (*xDest + xWidth, yDest + yHeight*). The upper left corner of the rectangle is always included in the area that *PatBlt* modifies. The lower right corner is outside the rectangle. Depending on the mapping mode and the signs of the *xWidth* and *yHeight* parameters, the upper left corner of this rectangle could be the point:

    (xDest, yDest)

or:

    (xDest, yDest + yHeight)

or:

    (xDest + xWidth, yDest)

or:

    (xDest + xWidth, yDest + yHeight)

If you've set the mapping mode to MM_LOENGLISH and you want to use *PatBlt* on the square inch at the upper left corner of the client area, you can use:

    PatBlt (hdc, 0, 0, 100, -100, dwROP) ;

or:

    PatBlt (hdc, 0, -100, 100, 100, dwROP) ;

or:

    PatBlt (hdc, 100, 0, -100, -100, dwROP) ;

or:

    PatBlt (hdc, 100, -100, -100, 100, dwROP) ;

The easiest way to set the correct parameters to *PatBlt* is to set *xDest* and *yDest* to the upper left corner of the rectangle. If your mapping mode defines *y*-coordinates as increasing as you move up the display, use a negative value for the *yHeight* parameter. If your mapping mode defines *x*-coordinates as increasing to the left (which is almost unheard of), use a negative value for the *xWidth* parameter.

Transferring Bits with *BitBlt*

In one sense, *BitBlt* is a superset of *PatBlt*. It does everything *PatBlt* does but also introduces a second device context into the logical operation. Here's the general syntax:

```
BitBlt (hdcDest, xDest, yDest, xWidth, yHeight,
        hdcSrc,  xSrc,  ySrc,  dwROP) ;
```

The *BitBlt* call modifies the destination device context (whose handle is *hdcDest*) within the rectangle defined by the logical point (*xDest, yDest*) and the *xWidth* and *yHeight* parameters, both of which are in logical units. These parameters define a rectangle as described in the previous section. *BitBlt* also uses a rectangle in a source device context (whose handle is *SrcDC*). This rectangle begins at the logical point (*xSrc, ySrc*) and is also *xWidth* logical units wide and *yHeight* logical units high.

    BitBlt performs a logical combination of three elements: the brush selected in the destination device context, the pixels in the source device context rectangle, and the pixels in the destination device context rectangle. The result is written to the destination device context rectangle. You can use any of the 256 ROP codes for the *dwROP* parameter to *BitBlt*. The 15 ROP codes that have names are shown in the table below. If you need to use any of the others, you can look them up in the Programmer's Reference.

Pattern (P):	1	1	1	1	0	0	0	0			
Source (S):	1	1	0	0	1	1	0	0	*Boolean*	*ROP*	
Destination (D):	1	0	1	0	1	0	1	0	*Operation*	*Code*	*Name*
Result:	0	0	0	0	0	0	0	0	0	000042	BLACKNESS
	0	0	0	1	0	0	0	1	~ (S!D)	1100A6	NOTSRCERASE
	0	0	1	1	0	0	1	1	~ S	330008	NOTSRCCOPY
	0	1	0	0	0	1	0	0	S & ~D	440328	SRCERASE
	0	1	0	1	0	1	0	1	~D	550009	DSTINVERT
	0	1	0	1	1	0	1	0	P ∧ D	5A0049	PATINVERT
	0	1	1	0	0	1	1	0	S ∧ D	660046	SRCINVERT
	1	0	0	0	1	0	0	0	S & D	8800C6	SRCAND
	1	0	1	1	1	0	1	1	~S!D	BB0226	MERGEPAINT
	1	1	0	0	0	0	0	0	P & S	C000CA	MERGECOPY
	1	1	0	0	1	1	0	0	S	CC0020	SRCCOPY
	1	1	1	0	1	1	1	0	S!D	EE0086	SRCPAINT
	1	1	1	1	0	0	0	0	P	F00021	PATCOPY
	1	1	1	1	1	0	1	1	P!~S!D	FB0A09	PATPAINT
	1	1	1	1	1	1	1	1	1	FF0062	WHITENESS

    Look at the eight 0's and 1's that show the result of the logical combination. The two-digit hexadecimal number that corresponds to these bits is the high word of the ROP code.

If we can create a table of the result we want from the pattern, source, and destination, we can easily determine the ROP code from the table of ROP codes in the Programmer's Reference. We'll be doing this a little later. If you use 1 of the 16 ROP codes shown in the table on page 617, then you can use *PatBlt* instead of *BitBlt*, because you're not referencing a source device context.

You can set *hdcSrc* and *hdcDest* to the same device context handle, in which case *BitBlt* will perform a logical combination of the destination rectangle, the source rectangle, and the current brush selected in the device context. However, it's a little risky to do this in your client-area device context. If part of the source rectangle is covered by another window, then Windows will use the pixels of this other window as the source. Windows doesn't know what's underneath that other window in your client area.

However, examples of the *BitBlt* function using the same device context for the source and destination are the easiest to grasp. The function:

```
BitBlt (hdc, 100, 0, 50, 100, hdc, 0, 0, SRCCOPY) ;
```

copies the rectangle beginning at logical point (0, 0) that is 50 logical units wide and 100 logical units high to the rectangular area beginning at the logical point (100, 0).

The *DrawBitmap* Function

BitBlt becomes most valuable in working with bitmaps that have been selected into a memory device context. When you perform a "bit-block transfer" from the memory device context to a device context for your client area, the bitmap selected in the memory device context is transferred to your client area.

Earlier I mentioned a hypothetical *DrawBitmap* function that would draw a bitmap on a display surface. Such a function would have the syntax:

```
DrawBitmap (hdc, hBitmap, xStart, yStart) ;
```

I promised we'd write a *DrawBitmap* function; here it is:

```
void DrawBitmap (HDC hdc, HBITMAP hBitmap,
                 short xStart, short yStart)
     {
     BITMAP    bm ;
     HDC       hdcMem ;
     DWORD     dwSize ;
     POINT     ptSize, ptOrg ;

     hdcMem = CreateCompatibleDC (hdc) ;
     SelectObject (hdcMem, hBitmap) ;
     SetMapMode (hdcMem, GetMapMode (hdc)) ;

     GetObject (hBitmap, sizeof (BITMAP), (LPSTR) &bm) ;
```

```
          ptSize.x = bm.bmWidth ;
          ptSize.y = bm.bmHeight ;
          DPtoLP (hdc, &ptSize, 1) ;

          ptOrg.x = 0 ;
          ptOrg.y = 0 ;
          DPtoLP (hdcMem, &ptOrg, 1) ;

          BitBlt (hdc, xStart, yStart, ptSize.x, ptSize.y,
                  hdcMem, ptOrg.x, ptOrg.y, SRCCOPY) ;

          DeleteDC (hdcMem) ;
          }
```

I'm assuming here that you don't want the height or width of the bitmap stretched or compressed in any way. That is, if your bitmap is 100 pixels wide, you want it to cover a 100-pixel-wide rectangle of your client area regardless of the mapping mode.

DrawBitmap first creates a memory device context using *CreateCompatibleDC* and then selects the bitmap into it with *SelectObject*. The mapping mode of the memory device context is set to the same mapping mode as the video device context. Because *BitBlt* works with logical coordinates and logical sizes and you don't want the bitmap stretched or compressed, the *xWidth* and *yHeight* parameters to *BitBlt* must be logical units that correspond to the physical pixel size of the bitmap. For this reason, *DrawBitmap* gets the dimensions of the bitmap using *GetObject* and makes a POINT structure out of the width and height. It then converts this point to logical coordinates. This is done similarly for the origin of the bitmap—the point (0, 0) in device coordinates.

Note that it doesn't matter what brush is currently selected in the destination device context (*hdc*), because SRCCOPY doesn't use the brush.

Using Different ROP Codes

SRCCOPY is definitely the most popular *dwROP* parameter to *BitBlt*, and you may be hard-pressed to find uses for the other 255 ROP codes. So I'll give you a couple of examples in which other ROP codes show their stuff.

In the first example, you have a monochrome bitmap that you want to transfer to the screen. However, you want to display the bitmap so that the black (0) bits don't affect anything currently on the client area. Moreover, you want all the white (1) bits to color the client area with a brush, perhaps a colored brush created from *CreateSolidBrush*. How do you do it? I'll assume that you're working in the MM_TEXT mapping mode and that you want to write the bitmap starting at the point (*xStart, yStart*) in your client area. You already have a handle to the monochrome bitmap (*hBitmap*) and a handle to the colored brush (*hBrush*). You know the width and height of the bitmap and have them stored in a BITMAP structure named *bm*. Here's the code:

```
hdcMem = CreateCompatibleDC (hdc) ;
SelectObject (hdcMem, hBitmap) ;
hBrush = SelectObject (hdc, hBrush) ;

BitBlt (hdc, xStart, yStart, bm.bmWidth, bm.bmHeight,
        hdcMem, 0, 0, 0xE20746L) ;

SelectObject (hdc, hBrush) ;
DeleteDC (hdcMem) ;
```

BitBlt performs a logical combination of a destination device context (*hdc*), a source device context (*hdcMem*), and the brush currently selected in the destination device context. So you create a memory device context, select the bitmap into it, select the colored brush into your client-area display context, and call *BitBlt*. Then you select the original brush into your display device context and delete the memory device context.

The only puzzling part of this code is the ROP code 0xE20746. This ROP code causes Windows to perform the logical operation:

$$((Destination \wedge Pattern)\ \&\ Source) \wedge Destination$$

Still not obvious? Try this approach: Copy this part of the table on page 620:

Pattern:	1	1	1	1	0	0	0	0
Source:	1	1	0	0	1	1	0	0
Destination:	1	0	1	0	1	0	1	0
Result:	?	?	?	?	?	?	?	?

For every black bit in the bitmap (which will be selected into the source memory device context), you want the destination device context to be unchanged. This means that everywhere the Source is a 0, you want the Result to be the same bit as the Destination:

Pattern:	1	1	1	1	0	0	0	0
Source:	1	1	0	0	1	1	0	0
Destination:	1	0	1	0	1	0	1	0
Result:	?	?	1	0	?	?	1	0

We're halfway there. For every white bit in the bitmap, you want the destination device context to be colored with the pattern. The brush you select in the destination device context is this pattern. So everywhere the Source is 1, you want the Result to be the Pattern:

Pattern:	1	1	1	1	0	0	0	0
Source:	1	1	0	0	1	1	0	0
Destination:	1	0	1	0	1	0	1	0
Result:	1	1	1	0	0	0	1	0

This means that the high word of the ROP code is 0xE2. You can look that up in the ROP table in Chapter 11 of the Programmer's Reference and find that the full ROP code is 0xE20746.

Perhaps at this point you discover that you mixed up the white and black bits when you created the bitmap in SDKPAINT. That's easy to fix. It's merely a different logical operation:

Pattern:	1	1	1	1	0	0	0	0
Source:	1	1	0	0	1	1	0	0
Destination:	1	0	1	0	1	0	1	0
Result:	1	0	1	1	1	0	0	0

Now the high word of the ROP code is 0xB8, and the entire ROP code is 0xB8074A, which performs the logical operation:

((Destination ∧ Pattern) & Source) ∧ Pattern

Here's the second example: Back in Chapter 8, I discussed the two bitmaps that make up icons and cursors. The use of two bitmaps allows these figures to be "transparent" in spots or to invert the display surface underneath. For a monochrome icon or cursor, the two bitmaps are coded as follows:

Bitmap 1:	0	0	1	1
Bitmap 2:	0	1	0	1
Result:	Black	White	Screen	Inverse Screen

Windows selects Bitmap 1 into a memory device context and uses *BitBlt* with a ROP code called SRCAND to transfer the bitmap to the display. This ROP code performs the logical operation:

Destination & Source

In Bitmap 1, the destination is left unchanged for 1 bits and set to 0 for 0 bits. Windows then selects Bitmap 2 into the device context and uses *BitBlt* with SRCINVERT. The logical operation is:

Destination ∧ Source

In Bitmap 2, this leaves the destination unchanged for all 0 bits and inverts the destination for all 1 bits.

Look at the first and second columns of the table: Bitmap 1 with SRCAND blacks out the bits, and Bitmap 2 with SRCINVERT turns selected bits to white by inverting the black bits. These operations set the black and white bits that make up the icon or cursor. Now look at the third and fourth columns of the table: Bitmap 1 with SRCAND leaves the display unchanged, and Bitmap 2 with SRCINVERT inverts the colors of selected bits. These operations let the icon or cursor be transparent or invert the underlying colors.

Another example of the creative use of ROP codes accompanies the description of the *GrayString* function in Chapter 14.

More Fun with Memory Device Contexts

We've been using memory device contexts to transfer an existing bitmap to the display. You can also use memory device contexts to draw on the surface of a bitmap. We did this in the GRAFMENU program in Chapter 9, when we used the *GetBitmapFont* function to make menu items using bitmaps. First, you create a memory device context:

```
hdcMem = CreateCompatibleDC (hdc) ;
```

Next, you create a bitmap of the desired size. If you want to create a monochrome bitmap, you can make it compatible with *hdcMem*:

```
hBitmap = CreateCompatibleBitmap (hdcMem, xWidth, yHeight) ;
```

Or to make the bitmap have the same color organization as the video display, you can make the bitmap compatible with *hdc*:

```
hBitmap = CreateCompatibleBitmap (hdc, xWidth, yHeight) ;
```

You can now select the bitmap into the memory device context:

```
SelectObject (hdcMem, hBitmap) ;
```

Now you can draw on this memory device context (and by extension, the bitmap) using all the GDI functions we discussed in Chapters 11 and 12 and more that you'll encounter in Chapter 14. When you first create the bitmap, it contains random bits, so you may want to begin by using the *PatBlt* function with a ROP code of WHITENESS or BLACKNESS to erase the background of the memory device context.

When you're finished drawing on the memory device context, simply delete it:

```
DeleteDC (hdcMem) ;
```

Now you're left with a bitmap containing everything you drew on it while it was selected in the memory device context. (We'll go through this process again in the BOUNCE program, shown later in this chapter.)

The SCRAMBLE program, shown in Figure 13-1, uses a memory device context as a temporary holding space for *BitBlt* operations that swap the contents of two rectangles of the display.

SCRAMBLE.MAK

```
#-----------------------
# SCRAMBLE.MAK make file
#-----------------------

scramble.exe : scramble.obj scramble.def
     link scramble, /align:16, NUL, /nod slibcew libw, scramble
     rc scramble.exe
```

Figure 13-1. *The SCRAMBLE program.*   *(continued)*

```
scramble.obj : scramble.c
     cl -c -Gsw -Ow -W2 -Zp scramble.c
```

SCRAMBLE.C

```
/*-------------------------------------------------
   SCRAMBLE.C -- Scramble (and Unscramble) Screen
                 (c) Charles Petzold, 1990
   -------------------------------------------------*/

#include <windows.h>
#include <stdlib.h>
#define   NUM 200

long FAR PASCAL WndProc (HWND, WORD, WORD, LONG) ;

int PASCAL WinMain (HANDLE hInstance, HANDLE hPrevInstance,
                    LPSTR lpszCmdLine, int nCmdShow)
     {
     static short nKeep [NUM][4] ;
     HDC        hdc    = CreateDC ("DISPLAY", NULL, NULL, NULL) ;
     HDC        hdcMem = CreateCompatibleDC (hdc) ;
     short      cxSize = GetSystemMetrics (SM_CXSCREEN) / 10 ;
     short      cySize = GetSystemMetrics (SM_CYSCREEN) / 10 ;
     HBITMAP    hBitmap = CreateCompatibleBitmap (hdc, cxSize, cySize) ;
     short      i, j, x1, y1, x2, y2 ;

     SelectObject (hdcMem, hBitmap) ;

     srand (LOWORD (GetCurrentTime ())) ;

     for (i = 0 ; i < 2 ; i++)
         for (j = 0 ; j < NUM ; j++)
             {
             if (i == 0)
                 {
                 nKeep [j] [0] = x1 = cxSize * (rand () % 10) ;
                 nKeep [j] [1] = y1 = cySize * (rand () % 10) ;
                 nKeep [j] [2] = x2 = cxSize * (rand () % 10) ;
                 nKeep [j] [3] = y2 = cySize * (rand () % 10) ;
                 }
             else
                 {
                 x1 = nKeep [NUM - 1 - j] [0] ;
                 y1 = nKeep [NUM - 1 - j] [1] ;
                 x2 = nKeep [NUM - 1 - j] [2] ;
                 y2 = nKeep [NUM - 1 - j] [3] ;
                 }
```

(continued)

```
              BitBlt (hdcMem, 0, 0, cxSize, cySize, hdc,  x1, y1, SRCCOPY) ;
              BitBlt (hdc,  x1, y1, cxSize, cySize, hdc,  x2, y2, SRCCOPY) ;
              BitBlt (hdc,  x2, y2, cxSize, cySize, hdcMem, 0, 0, SRCCOPY) ;
              }
     return FALSE ;
     }
```

SCRAMBLE.DEF

```
;------------------------------------
; SCRAMBLE.DEF module definition file
;------------------------------------

NAME          SCRAMBLE

DESCRIPTION   'Screen Scrambler (c) Charles Petzold, 1990'
EXETYPE       WINDOWS
STUB          'WINSTUB.EXE'
CODE          PRELOAD MOVEABLE DISCARDABLE
DATA          PRELOAD MOVEABLE MULTIPLE
HEAPSIZE      1024
STACKSIZE     8192
```

SCRAMBLE doesn't have a window function. In *WinMain*, it obtains a device context for the entire screen:

```
hdc = CreateDC ("DISPLAY", NULL, NULL, NULL) ;
```

and also a memory device context:

```
hdcMem = CreateCompatibleDC (hdc) ;
```

Then it determines the dimensions of the full screen and divides them by 10:

```
xSize = GetSystemMetrics (SM_CXSCREEN) / 10 ;
ySize = GetSystemMetrics (SM_CYSCREEN) / 10 ;
```

The program uses these dimensions to create a bitmap:

```
hBitmap = CreateCompatibleBitmap (hdc, xSize, ySize) ;
```

and selects it into the memory device context:

```
SelectObject (hdcMem, hBitmap) ;
```

Using the normal C *rand* ("random number generator") function, SCRAMBLE finds four random values that are multiples of the *xSize* and *ySize* values:

```
x1 = xSize * (rand () % 10) ;
y1 = ySize * (rand () % 10) ;
x2 = xSize * (rand () % 10) ;
y2 = ySize * (rand () % 10) ;
```

The program swaps two rectangular blocks of the display through the use of three *BitBlt* functions. The first copies the rectangle beginning at point (*x1, y1*) into the memory device context:

```
BitBlt (hdcMem, 0, 0, xSize, ySize, hdc, x1, y1, SRCCOPY) ;
```

The second copies the rectangle beginning at point (*x2, y2*) into the location beginning at (*x1, y1*):

```
BitBlt (hdc, x1, y1, xSize, ySize, hdc, x2, y2, SRCCOPY) ;
```

The third copies the rectangle in the memory device context to the area beginning at point (*x2, y2*):

```
BitBlt (hdc, x2, y2, xSize, ySize, hdcMem, 0, 0, SRCCOPY) ;
```

This process effectively swaps the contents of the two rectangles on the display. SCRAMBLE does this 200 times, after which the screen should be thoroughly scrambled. But do not fear, because SCRAMBLE keeps track of this mess and then unscrambles the screen, returning it to normal before exiting.

You can also use memory device contexts to copy the contents of one bitmap to another. For instance, suppose you want to create a bitmap that contains only the upper left quadrant of another bitmap. If the original bitmap has the handle *hBitmap*, you can copy the dimensions into a structure of type BITMAP:

```
GetObject (hBitmap, sizeof (BITMAP), (LPSTR) &bm) ;
```

and create a new uninitialized bitmap of one-quarter the size:

```
hBitmap2 = CreateBitmap (bm.bmWidth / 2, bm.bmHeight / 2,
            bm.bmPlanes, bm.bmBitsPixel, NULL) ;
```

Now create two memory device contexts and select the original bitmap and the new bitmap into them:

```
hdcMem1 = CreateCompatibleDC (hdc) ;
hdcMem2 = CreateCompatibleDC (hdc) ;

SelectObject (hdcMem1, hBitmap) ;
SelectObject (hdcMem2, hBitmap2) ;
```

Finally, copy the upper left quadrant of the first bitmap to the second:

```
BitBlt (hdcMem2, 0, 0, bm.bmWidth / 2, bm.bmHeight / 2,
        hdcMem1, 0, 0, SRCCOPY) ;
```

You're done except for cleaning up:

```
DeleteDC (hdcMem1) ;
DeleteDC (hdcMem2) ;
```

Color Conversions

If the destination and source device contexts in the *BitBlt* call have different color characteristics, Windows must convert the bitmap from one color format to another. The best
color conversion occurs when the source bitmap is monochrome. Windows uses the text
color and background color attributes in the destination device context for this conversion:

Monochrome DC (Source)	Color DC (Destination)
0 (Black)	Text color (default is black)
1 (White)	Background color (default is white)

The background color attribute, which you encountered in Chapter 12, is the color
Windows uses to fill in the gaps in dotted and dashed lines and between the hatches in
hatched brushes. You can change the background color with *SetBkColor*. The text color,
which you'll encounter in Chapter 14, determines the color of text. You can change this
with *SetTextColor*. With default settings, the monochrome bitmap simply turns into a
black-and-white bitmap on the color device context.

Translating a bitmap in a color source device context to a monochrome destination
device context is less satisfactory:

Color DC (Source)	Monochrome DC (Destination)
Pixel != Background color	0 (Black)
Pixel == Background color	1 (White)

In this case Windows uses the background color of the source device context to determine
what color is translated to white. Every other color is translated to black.

Here's another color-related problem: Windows needs to equate a particular combination of color bits in the bitmap (either in different planes or in the same plane) to the 24-
bit color value of the background color. This means that the color device context must refer
to a real device or be a memory device context based on a real device. For instance, suppose you have a monochrome device driver. You create a memory device context based on
the screen device context and select a color bitmap into that memory device context. You
now try to transfer that bitmap to a monochrome device context. It won't work, because
Windows doesn't know how the multiple planes or multiple bits per pixel in the memory
device context bitmap relate to real colors.

Mapping Mode Conversions

The *BitBlt* call requires different starting coordinates for the source and destination device contexts, but it needs only one width and one height:

```
BitBlt (hdcDest, xDest, yDest, xWidth, yHeight,
        hdcSrc, xSrc, ySrc, dwROP) ;
```

The *xWidth* and *yHeight* values are in logical units, and they apply to both the rectangle in the source device context and the rectangle in the destination device context. *BitBlt* must convert all coordinates and sizes to device coordinates before calling on the driver file to perform the actual operation. Because the *xWidth* and *yHeight* values are used for both the source and destination device contexts, the values must be converted to device units (pixels) separately for each device context.

When the source and destination device contexts are the same, or when both device contexts use the MM_TEXT mapping mode, then the size of this rectangle in device units will be the same in both device contexts. Windows can then do a simple pixel-to-pixel transfer. However, when the size of the rectangle in device units is different in the two device contexts, Windows turns the job over to the more versatile *StretchBlt* function.

Stretching Bitmaps with *StretchBlt*

StretchBlt adds two parameters to the *BitBlt* call:

```
StretchBlt (hdcDest, xDest, yDest, xDestWidth, yDestHeight,
            hdcSrc, xSrc, ySrc, xSrcWidth, ySrcHeight, dwROP) ;
```

Because *StretchBlt* accepts different width and height parameters for the source and destination rectangles, it allows you to stretch or compress a bitmap in the source device context to fit a larger or smaller area in the destination device context.

Just as *BitBlt* provides a superset of *PatBlt*'s functionality, *StretchBlt* expands on *BitBlt* by allowing you to specify the sizes of the source and destination rectangles separately. As with *PatBlt* and *BitBlt*, all coordinates and values in *StretchBlt* are in logical units. (We've already used *StretchBlt* in two programs: The BLOWUP1 program in Chapter 4 used the function to copy an area of the display into BLOWUP1's client area; the GRAFMENU program in Chapter 9 used *StretchBlt* to expand the size of a bitmap for use in a menu.)

StretchBlt also allows you to flip an image vertically or horizontally. If the signs of *xSrcWidth* and *xDestWidth* (when converted to device units) are different, then *StretchBlt* creates a mirror image: Left becomes right, and right becomes left. If *ySrcHeight* and *yDestHeight* are different, then *StretchBlt* turns the image upside down. You can verify this with the BLOWUP1 program by capturing the image starting at the upper right corner (a negative width), the lower left corner (a negative height), or the lower right corner (a negative height and width).

If you've experimented with BLOWUP1, you've probably discovered that *StretchBlt* can be slow, particularly when it works with a large bitmap. *StretchBlt* also has some problems related to the inherent difficulties of scaling bitmaps. When expanding a bitmap, *StretchBlt* must duplicate rows or columns of pixels. If the expansion is not an integral multiple, then the process can result in some distortion of the image.

When shrinking a bitmap, *StretchBlt* must combine two or more rows or columns of pixels into a single row or column. It does this in one of three ways, depending on the stretching mode attribute in the device context. You can use the *SetStretchBltMode* function to change this attribute:

```
SetStretchBltMode (hdc, nMode) ;
```

The value of *nMode* can be one of the following:

- BLACKONWHITE (default)—If two or more pixels have to be combined into one pixel, *StretchBlt* performs a logical AND operation on the pixels. The resulting pixel is white only if all the original pixels are white, which in practice means that black pixels predominate over white pixels.

- WHITEONBLACK—If two or more pixels have to be combined into one pixel, *StretchBlt* performs a logical OR operation. The resulting pixel is black only if all the original pixels are black, which means that white pixels predominate.

- COLORONCOLOR—*StretchBlt* simply eliminates rows or columns of pixels without doing any logical combination. This is often the best approach for color bitmaps, because the other two modes can cause color distortions.

Animation

I mentioned at the beginning of Chapter 11 that GDI supports only static pictures. Although it's true that Windows has no traditional animation support (such as the ability to flip video pages, check for vertical retrace of the video signal, or construct rotatable sprites), that doesn't mean that we can't move images around on the display. Yes, it's time for the bouncing ball program. The BOUNCE program, shown in Figure 13-2 beginning on the following page, constructs a ball that bounces around in the window's client area. The program uses the timer to pace the ball; it draws the ball with a simple "bit-block transfer" from a memory device context.

BOUNCE.MAK

```
#---------------------
# BOUNCE.MAK make file
#---------------------

bounce.exe : bounce.obj bounce.def
     link bounce, /align:16, NUL, /nod slibcew libw, bounce
     rc bounce.exe

bounce.obj : bounce.c
     cl -c -Gsw -Ow -W2 -Zp bounce.c
```

BOUNCE.C

```
/*-----------------------------------------
   BOUNCE.C -- Bouncing Ball Program
            (c) Charles Petzold, 1990
   -------------------------------------*/

#include <windows.h>

long FAR PASCAL WndProc (HWND, WORD, WORD, LONG) ;

int PASCAL WinMain (HANDLE hInstance, HANDLE hPrevInstance,
                    LPSTR lpszCmdLine, int nCmdShow)
     {
     static char szAppName [] = "Bounce" ;
     HWND       hwnd ;
     MSG        msg ;
     WNDCLASS   wndclass ;

     if (!hPrevInstance)
        {
        wndclass.style         = CS_HREDRAW | CS_VREDRAW ;
        wndclass.lpfnWndProc   = WndProc ;
        wndclass.cbClsExtra    = 0 ;
        wndclass.cbWndExtra    = 0 ;
        wndclass.hInstance     = hInstance ;
        wndclass.hIcon         = NULL ;
        wndclass.hCursor       = LoadCursor (NULL, IDC_ARROW) ;
        wndclass.hbrBackground = GetStockObject (WHITE_BRUSH) ;
        wndclass.lpszMenuName  = NULL ;
        wndclass.lpszClassName = szAppName ;

        RegisterClass (&wndclass) ;
        }
```

Figure 13-2. *The BOUNCE program.*   *(continued)*

```
        hwnd = CreateWindow (szAppName, "Bouncing Ball",
                             WS_OVERLAPPEDWINDOW,
                             CW_USEDEFAULT, CW_USEDEFAULT,
                             CW_USEDEFAULT, CW_USEDEFAULT,
                             NULL, NULL, hInstance, NULL) ;

        if (!SetTimer (hwnd, 1, 50, NULL))
             {
             MessageBox (hwnd, "Too many clocks or timers!",
                         szAppName, MB_ICONEXCLAMATION : MB_OK) ;
             return FALSE ;
             }

        ShowWindow (hwnd, nCmdShow) ;
        UpdateWindow (hwnd) ;

        while (GetMessage (&msg, NULL, 0, 0))
             {
             TranslateMessage (&msg) ;
             DispatchMessage (&msg) ;
             }
        return msg.wParam ;
        }

long FAR PASCAL WndProc (HWND hwnd, WORD message, WORD wParam, LONG lParam)
        {
        static HANDLE hBitmap ;
        static short  cxClient, cyClient, xCenter, yCenter, cxTotal, cyTotal,
                      cxRadius, cyRadius, cxMove, cyMove, xPixel, yPixel ;
        HBRUSH        hBrush ;
        HDC           hdc, hdcMem ;
        short         nScale ;

        switch (message)
             {
             case WM_CREATE :
                   hdc = GetDC (hwnd) ;
                   xPixel = GetDeviceCaps (hdc, ASPECTX) ;
                   yPixel = GetDeviceCaps (hdc, ASPECTY) ;
                   ReleaseDC (hwnd, hdc) ;
                   return 0 ;

             case WM_SIZE :
                   xCenter = (cxClient = LOWORD (lParam)) / 2 ;
                   yCenter = (cyClient = HIWORD (lParam)) / 2 ;

                   nScale = min (cxClient * xPixel, cyClient * yPixel) / 16 ;

                   cxRadius = nScale / xPixel ;
                   cyRadius = nScale / yPixel ;
```

(continued)

```
          cxMove = max (1, cxRadius / 4) ;
          cyMove = max (1, cyRadius / 4) ;

          cxTotal = 2 * (cxRadius + cxMove) ;
          cyTotal = 2 * (cyRadius + cyMove) ;

          if (hBitmap)
               DeleteObject (hBitmap) ;

          hdc = GetDC (hwnd) ;
          hdcMem = CreateCompatibleDC (hdc) ;
          hBitmap = CreateCompatibleBitmap (hdc, cxTotal, cyTotal) ;
          ReleaseDC (hwnd, hdc) ;

          SelectObject (hdcMem, hBitmap) ;
          Rectangle (hdcMem, -1, -1, cxTotal + 1, cyTotal + 1) ;

          hBrush = CreateHatchBrush (HS_DIAGCROSS, 0L) ;
          SelectObject (hdcMem, hBrush) ;
          SetBkColor (hdcMem, RGB (255, 0, 255)) ;
          Ellipse (hdcMem, cxMove, cyMove, cxTotal - cxMove,
                                           cyTotal - cyMove) ;
          DeleteDC (hdcMem) ;
          DeleteObject (hBrush) ;
          return 0 ;

     case WM_TIMER :
          if (!hBitmap)
               break ;

          hdc = GetDC (hwnd) ;
          hdcMem = CreateCompatibleDC (hdc) ;
          SelectObject (hdcMem, hBitmap) ;

          BitBlt (hdc, xCenter - cxTotal / 2,
                       yCenter - cyTotal / 2, cxTotal, cyTotal,
                  hdcMem, 0, 0, SRCCOPY) ;

          ReleaseDC (hwnd, hdc) ;
          DeleteDC (hdcMem) ;

          xCenter += cxMove ;
          yCenter += cyMove ;

          if ((xCenter + cxRadius >= cxClient) ||
              (xCenter - cxRadius <= 0))
                    cxMove = -cxMove ;
```

(continued)

```
                    if ((yCenter + cyRadius >= cyClient) ||
                        (yCenter - cyRadius <= 0))
                            cyMove = -cyMove ;
                    return 0 ;

            case WM_DESTROY :
                    if (hBitmap)
                        DeleteObject (hBitmap) ;

                    KillTimer (hwnd, 1) ;
                    PostQuitMessage (0) ;
                    return 0 ;
            }
        return DefWindowProc (hwnd, message, wParam, lParam) ;
        }
```

BOUNCE.DEF

```
;-----------------------------------------
; BOUNCE.DEF module definition file
;-----------------------------------------

NAME            BOUNCE

DESCRIPTION     'Bouncing Ball Program (c) Charles Petzold, 1990'
EXETYPE         WINDOWS
STUB            'WINSTUB.EXE'
CODE            PRELOAD MOVEABLE DISCARDABLE
DATA            PRELOAD MOVEABLE MULTIPLE
HEAPSIZE        1024
STACKSIZE       8192
EXPORTS         WndProc
```

BOUNCE reconstructs the ball whenever the program gets a WM_SIZE message, the diameter of the ball being one-sixteenth of either the height or the width of the client area, whichever is shorter. However, the program constructs a bitmap that is larger than the ball—on each of its four sides, the bitmap extends beyond the ball's dimensions by one quarter of the ball's radius.

After the bitmap is selected into a memory device context, it is colored white:

```
Rectangle (hdcMem, -1, -1, xTotal + 1, yTotal + 1) ;
```

A diagonally hatched brush is selected into the memory device context, and the ball is drawn in the center of the bitmap:

```
Ellipse (hdcMem, xMove, yMove, xTotal - xMove, yTotal - yMove) ;
```

The margins around the edges of the ball effectively erase the previous image of the ball when the ball is moved. Redrawing the ball at another position requires only a simple *BitBlt* call using the ROP code of SRCCOPY:

```
BitBlt (hdc, xCenter - xTotal / 2,
              yCenter - yTotal / 2, xTotal, yTotal,
              hdcMem, 0, 0, SRCCOPY) ;
```

BOUNCE demonstrates the simplest way to move an image around the display, but this approach isn't satisfactory for general purposes. If you're interested in animation, you'll want to explore some of the other ROP codes (such as SRCINVERT) that perform an exclusive OR operation on the source and destination.

METAFILES

A metafile is a collection of GDI functions that are encoded in a binary form. You create a metafile by first creating a metafile device context. You can then use most of the GDI drawing functions to draw on this metafile device context. These GDI calls don't really draw on anything, however. Instead, they are stored within the metafile. When you close the metafile device context, you get back a handle to the metafile. You can then "play" this metafile on a real device context and execute the GDI functions in the metafile.

Metafiles are used most often for sharing pictures between programs through the clipboard. Because metafiles describe a picture as a collection of GDI calls, they take up much less space and are more device independent than bitmaps. I'll begin the discussion of metafiles with some simple examples, and then I'll take up the more theoretical considerations.

Simple Use of Memory Metafiles

Suppose your company's logo consists of a rectangle with lines drawn between the opposing corners and a blue circle in the center. You need to draw this logo often on the client area of your programs' windows and on the printer. Let's make that logo a metafile.

We'll begin by defining a few necessary variables:

```
static HANDLE  hmf ;
HANDLE         hBrush ;
HDC            hdcMeta ;
```

During processing of the WM_CREATE message, you can create the metafile. You call *CreateMetaFile* to obtain a handle to a metafile device context:

```
hMetaDC = CreateMetaFile (NULL) ;
```

The NULL parameter indicates that this will be a "memory" metafile; that is, the metafile will be stored in memory rather than as a disk file.

You can now draw your logo on this metafile device context. You decide you want it to be 100 units high and 100 units wide:

```
Rectangle (hdcMeta, 0, 0, 100, 100) ;
MoveTo (hdcMeta, 0, 0) ;
LineTo (hdcMeta, 100, 100) ;
MoveTo (hdcMeta, 0, 100) ;
LineTo (hdcMeta, 100, 0) ;

hBrush = CreateSolidBrush (RGB (0, 0, 255)) ;
SelectObject (hdcMeta, hBrush) ;
Ellipse (hdcMeta, 20, 20, 80, 80) ;
```

When you're finished drawing, you close the metafile device context by calling *Close-MetaFile*, which returns a handle to the metafile:

```
hmf = CloseMetaFile (hdcMeta) ;
```

Now you can delete the brush you created:

```
DeleteObject (hBrush) ;
```

You're done creating the metafile. The *hmf* variable is defined as static, so it will remain in existence during other messages.

You drew the logo with a height and width of 100. Are these logical units or device units? At this point, they are neither: They are simply units. They will take on meaning only when you play the metafile. Let's do so. During processing of your WM_PAINT message, you may want to fill up the client area with 100 logos, and you don't care whether they get stretched out somewhat. We'll assume that you've obtained values of *cxClient* and *cyClient*, representing the width and height of the client area, and that you've defined some of the other variables used in this code.

You obtain a handle to the client-area device context and set a mapping mode of MM_ANISOTROPIC with 1000 logical units horizontally and vertically:

```
hdc = BeginPaint (hwnd, &ps) ;

SetMapMode (hdc, MM_ANISOTROPIC) ;
SetWindowExt (hdc, 1000, 1000) ;
SetViewportExt (hdc, cxClient, cyClient) ;
```

Now you can "play the metafile" 100 times by calling *PlayMetaFile*, each time changing the window origin to move the metafile to a new position:

```
for (x = 0 ; x < 10 ; x++)
    for (y = 0 ; y < 10 ; y++)
        {
        SetWindowOrg (hdc, -100 * x, -100 * y) ;
        PlayMetaFile (hdc, hmf) ;
        }
```

In calling *PlayMetaFile*, you're in effect repeating all the calls that you made between *CreateMetaFile* and *CloseMetaFile* when you originally created the metafile during the WM_CREATE message. The results are shown in Figure 13-3.

When you're finished processing the WM_PAINT message, you can end it normally:

```
EndPaint (hwnd, &ps) ;
```

One task remains. When you create a metafile, the handle is really the property of the GDI module, and you must explicitly delete it with *DeleteMetaFile* before you terminate the program. You can do this during processing of the WM_DESTROY message:

```
case WM_DESTROY :
    DeleteMetaFile (hmf) ;
    PostQuitMessage (0) ;
    return 0 ;
```

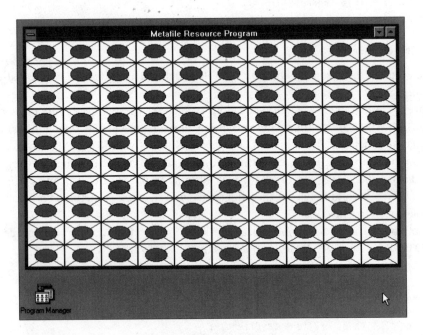

Figure 13-3. *Multiple figures drawn using the* PlayMetaFile *function.*

Storing Metafiles on Disk

In the above example, the NULL parameter to *CreateMetaFile* meant that we wanted to create a metafile stored in memory. We can also create a metafile stored on the disk as a normal file. This method is preferred for large metafiles because it uses less memory space. Windows has to maintain a relatively small area in memory to store the name of the file containing the metafile. On the other hand, a metafile stored on disk requires a disk access every time you play it.

Let's use the example of the company logo again. In addition to the variables shown above, you'll need a variable to store the filename of the metafile:

```
static char szFileName [80] ;
```

In this example, we'll use a temporary file. During processing of the WM_CREATE message, you can create a filename for a temporary file using the Windows *GetTempFileName* function:

```
GetTempFileName (0, MF, 0, szFileName) ;
```

Windows first checks the TEMP variable in the MS-DOS environment to select a disk and subdirectory for this file. If there is no TEMP variable in the MS-DOS environment, Windows uses the root directory of the first fixed disk. The filename begins with a tilde (~) followed by the characters we've specified in the *GetTempFileName* function (MF) and a unique number; the extension is .TMP. On return from the call, the filename is stored in the *szFileName* array.

We create the metafile device context using this filename:

```
hMetaDC = CreateMetaFile (szFileName) ;
```

We can write to this device context just as we did in the original example and then close the metafile device context to get the metafile handle:

```
hmf = CloseMetaFile (hdcMeta) ;
```

The processing of the WM_PAINT message is the same as in the original example. However, during processing of the WM_DESTROY message, you'll have to add something. The statement:

```
DeleteMetaFile (hmf) ;
```

deletes the area of memory that references the metafile handle to the disk file, but the disk file still exists. You should also delete that file using the normal C function:

```
unlink (szFileName) ;
```

Here's another way to use disk-based metafiles. This method doesn't require that you maintain *hmf* as a static variable. First, you get a temporary filename and create the metafile device context as before:

```
GetTempFileName (0, MF, 0, szFileName) ;
hdcMeta = CreateMetaFile (szFileName) ;
```

Now you draw on the metafile device context. When you're finished, you can close the device context and get a handle to the metafile:

```
hmf = CloseMetaFile (hdcMeta) ;
```

But now you also delete the metafile:

```
DeleteMetaFile (hmf) ;
```

Do we really want to do this? We might. Deleting a disk-based metafile invalidates the metafile handle, freeing the memory required for the metafile but leaving the disk file intact. During processing of the WM_PAINT message, you can get a metafile handle to this disk file by calling *GetMetaFile*:

```
hmf = GetMetaFile (szFileName) ;
```

Now you can play this metafile just as before. When processing of the WM_PAINT message is over, you can delete the metafile handle:

```
DeleteMetaFile (hmf) ;
```

When it comes time to process the WM_DESTROY message, you don't have to delete the metafile, because it was deleted at the end of the WM_CREATE message and at the end of each WM_PAINT message. But you still should delete the disk file:

```
unlink (szFileName) ;
```

Using Preexisting Metafiles

What we've done in the last example above seems to imply that we can create a disk-based metafile in one program and then use it in another program by calling *GetMetaFile*. We can. The MFCREATE ("metafile create") program, shown in Figure 13-4, is the shortest Windows program in this book. All it does is create a disk-based metafile with the name MYLOGO.WMF. The .WMF extension stands for "Windows metafile" and is the customary extension for a metafile stored as a disk file.

MFCREATE.MAK

```
#------------------------
# MFCREATE.MAK make file
#------------------------

mfcreate.exe : mfcreate.obj mfcreate.def
     link mfcreate, /align:16, NUL, /nod slibcew libw, mfcreate
     rc mfcreate.exe

mfcreate.obj : mfcreate.c
     cl -c -Gsw -Ow -W2 -Zp mfcreate.c
```

Figure 13-4. *The MFCREATE program.*

MFCREATE.C

```
/*-------------------------------------------
   MFCREATE.C -- Metafile Creation Program
                   (c) Charles Petzold, 1990
   -----------------------------------------*/

#include <windows.h>

int PASCAL WinMain (HANDLE hInstance, HANDLE hPrevInstance,
                    LPSTR lpszCmdLine, int nCmdShow)
     {
     HBRUSH hBrush  = CreateSolidBrush (RGB (0, 0, 255)) ;
     HDC    hdcMeta = CreateMetaFile ("MYLOGO.WMF") ;

     Rectangle (hdcMeta, 0, 0, 100, 100) ;
     MoveTo (hdcMeta, 0, 0) ;
     LineTo (hdcMeta, 100, 100) ;
     MoveTo (hdcMeta, 0, 100) ;
     LineTo (hdcMeta, 100, 0) ;
     SelectObject (hdcMeta, hBrush) ;
     Ellipse (hdcMeta, 20, 20, 80, 80) ;

     DeleteMetaFile (CloseMetaFile (hdcMeta)) ;
     DeleteObject (hBrush) ;

     MessageBeep (0) ;

     return FALSE ;
     }
```

MFCREATE.DEF

```
;-----------------------------------------
; MFCREATE.DEF module definition file
;-----------------------------------------

NAME            MFCREATE

DESCRIPTION     'Metafile Creation Program (c) Charles Petzold, 1990'
EXETYPE         WINDOWS
STUB            'WINSTUB.EXE'
CODE            PRELOAD MOVEABLE DISCARDABLE
DATA            PRELOAD MOVEABLE MULTIPLE
HEAPSIZE        1024
STACKSIZE       8192
```

In the *WinMain* function, MFCREATE creates a metafile device context using the filename MYLOGO.WMF:

```
hMetaDC = CreateMetaFile ("MYLOGO.WMF") ;
```

It then draws on this device context. When it's finished, it closes the metafile device context and deletes the metafile handle in one statement:

```
DeleteMetaFile (CloseMetaFile (hdcMeta)) ;
```

The program beeps to indicate that it's finished and then exits *WinMain*.

Now you can use this metafile in another program. Here's the entire WM_PAINT logic. All you need to obtain the handle to the disk-based metafile is *GetMetaFile*. When you're done with the metafile, you call *DeleteMetaFile*:

```
hdc = BeginPaint (hwnd, &ps) ;

SetMapMode (hdc, MM_ANISOTROPIC) ;
SetWindowExt (hdc, 1000, 1000) ;
SetViewportExt (hdc, xClient, yClient) ;

hmf = GetMetaFile ("MYLOGO.WMF") ;

for (x = 0 ; x < 10 ; x++)
    for (y = 0 ; y < 10 ; y++)
        {
        SetWindowOrg (hdc, -100 * x, -100 * y) ;
        PlayMetaFile (hdc, hmf) ;
        }

DeleteMetaFile (hmf) ;
EndPaint (hwnd, &ps) ;
```

Alternatively, you can define *hmf* as a static variable and call *GetMetaFile* once during processing of WM_CREATE and call *DeleteMetaFile* during processing of WM_DESTROY. Of course, this approach has some problems. The code assumes that MYLOGO.WMF is in the current directory or a directory listed in the PATH environment variable. If the file isn't in the current directory when you call *GetMetaFile*, Windows will display a message box asking the user to insert the MYLOGO.WMF disk in drive A. (The usual response of a user to a message box of this sort is "Huh?") You should search for the file before you call *GetMetaFile*.

Now let's try another approach.

Using Metafiles as Resources

In Chapter 8 you encountered a "user-defined resource," which in that case was a block of text. Now let's transform a metafile into a user-defined resource. MYLOGO.WMF will then become part of the .EXE file for the program that needs it. The program MFRESORC ("metafile resource"), shown in Figure 13-5, accomplishes this using the MYLOGO.WMF metafile created by MFCREATE.

MFRESORC.MAK

```
#------------------------
# MFRESORC.MAK make file
#------------------------

mfresorc.exe : mfresorc.obj mfresorc.def mfresorc.res
     link mfresorc, /align:16, NUL, /nod slibcew libw, mfresorc
     rc mfresorc.res

mfresorc.obj : mfresorc.c
     cl -c -Gsw -Ow -W2 -Zp mfresorc.c

mfresorc.res : mfresorc.rc mylogo.wmf
     rc -r mfresorc.rc
```

MFRESORC.C

```
/*-------------------------------------------
   MFRESORC.C -- Metafile Resource Program
                 (c) Charles Petzold, 1990
   -------------------------------------------*/

#include <windows.h>

long FAR PASCAL WndProc (HWND, WORD, WORD, LONG) ;

int PASCAL WinMain (HANDLE hInstance, HANDLE hPrevInstance,
                    LPSTR lpszCmdLine, int nCmdShow)
     {
     static char szAppName [] = "MFResorc" ;
     HWND        hwnd ;
     MSG         msg ;
     WNDCLASS    wndclass ;

     if (!hPrevInstance)
         {
         wndclass.style        = CS_HREDRAW | CS_VREDRAW ;
         wndclass.lpfnWndProc  = WndProc ;
         wndclass.cbClsExtra   = 0 ;
         wndclass.cbWndExtra   = 0 ;
```

Figure 13-5. *The MFRESORC program.* (*continued*)

```
        wndclass.hInstance      = hInstance ;
        wndclass.hIcon          = NULL ;
        wndclass.hCursor        = LoadCursor (NULL, IDC_ARROW) ;
        wndclass.hbrBackground  = GetStockObject (WHITE_BRUSH) ;
        wndclass.lpszMenuName   = NULL ;
        wndclass.lpszClassName  = szAppName ;

        RegisterClass (&wndclass) ;
        }

    hwnd = CreateWindow (szAppName, "Metafile Resource Program",
                    WS_OVERLAPPEDWINDOW,
                    CW_USEDEFAULT, CW_USEDEFAULT,
                    CW_USEDEFAULT, CW_USEDEFAULT,
                    NULL, NULL, hInstance, NULL) ;

    ShowWindow (hwnd, nCmdShow) ;
    UpdateWindow (hwnd) ;

    while (GetMessage (&msg, NULL, 0, 0))
        {
        TranslateMessage (&msg) ;
        DispatchMessage (&msg) ;
        }
    return msg.wParam ;
    }

long FAR PASCAL WndProc (HWND hwnd, WORD message, WORD wParam, LONG lParam)
    {
    static HANDLE hmf ;
    static short  cxClient, cyClient ;
    HANDLE        hInstance, hResource ;
    HDC           hdc ;
    PAINTSTRUCT   ps ;
    short         x, y ;

    switch (message)
        {
        case WM_CREATE :
            hInstance = ((LPCREATESTRUCT) lParam) -> hInstance ;
            hResource = LoadResource (hInstance,
                        FindResource (hInstance, "MyLogo", "METAFILE")) ;

            LockResource (hResource) ;
            hmf = SetMetaFileBits (hResource) ;
            UnlockResource (hResource) ;
            return 0 ;
```

(continued)

644

```
          case WM_SIZE :
               cxClient = LOWORD (lParam) ;
               cyClient = HIWORD (lParam) ;
               return 0 ;

          case WM_PAINT :
               hdc = BeginPaint (hwnd, &ps) ;

               SetMapMode (hdc, MM_ANISOTROPIC) ;
               SetWindowExt (hdc, 1000, 1000) ;
               SetViewportExt (hdc, cxClient, cyClient) ;

               for (x = 0 ; x < 10 ; x++)
                    for (y = 0 ; y < 10 ; y++)
                         {
                         SetWindowOrg (hdc, -100 * x, -100 * y) ;
                         PlayMetaFile (hdc, hmf) ;
                         }

               EndPaint (hwnd, &ps) ;
               return 0 ;

          case WM_DESTROY :
               DeleteMetaFile (hmf) ;
               PostQuitMessage (0) ;
               return 0 ;
          }
     return DefWindowProc (hwnd, message, wParam, lParam) ;
     }
```

MFRESORC.RC

```
/*-----------------------------
   MFRESORC.RC resource script
-----------------------------*/

MyLogo METAFILE "mylogo.wmf"
```

The resource script is only one line. METAFILE may look like a normal resource script keyword such as MENU or DIALOG, but it isn't. We're defining this resource type. The name we give to this particular resource of the METAFILE type is "MyLogo."

MFRESORC.DEF

```
;------------------------------------------
; MFRESORC.DEF module definition file
;------------------------------------------

NAME            MFRESORC

DESCRIPTION     'Metafile Resource Program (c) Charles Petzold, 1990'
EXETYPE         WINDOWS
STUB            'WINSTUB.EXE'
CODE            PRELOAD MOVEABLE DISCARDABLE
DATA            PRELOAD MOVEABLE MULTIPLE
HEAPSIZE        1024
STACKSIZE       8192
EXPORTS         WndProc
```

During processing of the WM_CREATE message, MFRESORC must first call *Find-Resource* and *LoadResource* to obtain a handle to the resource:

```
hResource = LoadResource (hInstance,
                FindResource (hInstance, "MyLogo", "METAFILE")) ;
```

Then the resource is locked:

```
LockResource (hResource) ;
```

Normally, you would lock a resource to obtain a pointer to the memory block. However, *LockResource* also performs the chore of actually loading the resource into memory. That's all we need to do. Now we can convert this global memory block to a metafile using *SetMetaFileBits*, and the resource can be unlocked:

```
hmf = SetMetaFileBits (hResource) ;

GlobalUnlock (hResource) ;
```

SetMetaFileBits has a companion function, *GetMetaFileBits*, that converts a metafile handle to a global memory handle. *GetMetaFileBits* can be used only with a memory metafile.

The metafile that we loaded as a resource is a memory metafile. If you'd prefer to use a disk-based metafile, you can copy it. This is the code you would use following the *GlobalUnlock* statement:

```
GetTempFileName (0, MF, 0, szFileName) ;
hmf2 = CopyMetaFile (hmf, szFileName) ;
DeleteMetaFile (hmf) ;
hmf = hmf2 ;
```

The *hmf2* handle need not be defined as a static variable. The MFRESORC program shows the deletion of the metafile handle during processing of WM_DESTROY:

```
DeleteMetaFile (hmf) ;
```

You should also delete the temporary file:

```
unlink (szFileName) ;
```

The *CopyMetaFile* function can also be used to copy an existing metafile to a memory metafile:

```
hmf2 = CopyMetaFile (hmf, NULL) ;
```

Looking at Metafiles

You can get a good idea of what a metafile is and is not by dumping out the contents of MYLOGO.WMF. The metafile begins with an 18-byte header record. This is followed by a series of metafile records, each of which contains three or more 2-byte words. The first word is the number of words in the record, including the first; the second word is 0; the third word is a code that indicates the GDI call that the record represents.

These codes are documented in Chapter 9 of the Programmer's Reference and in WINDOWS.H with identifiers that begin with the word META. The low byte of this word identifies the particular GDI call; the high byte is generally the number of words that are parameters to the call. The words that follow this code are the actual parameters to the call in reverse order, excluding the *hdc* parameter. For instance, the GDI call:

```
Rectangle (hdcMeta, 0, 0, 100, 100) ;
```

shows up in the metafile as a seven-word record. In hexadecimal, these words are:

0007 0000 041B 0064 0064 0000 0000

The 041B word means that the call is *Rectangle* with four parameters, excluding the initial *hdc*. The parameters follow.

The only real exception to this rule is the *SelectObject* call. Windows must save the object that the function is selecting into the metafile device context. For instance, the call:

```
hBrush = CreateSolidBrush (RGB (0, 0, 255)) ;
```

doesn't affect the metafile device context at all. You can even make this call before you create the metafile device context with *CreateMetaFile*. When you select that brush into the metafile device context, however, two records must be generated. The first is a record for *CreateBrushIndirect*:

0007 0000 FC02 0000 0000 00FF 0000

The four words following the identifying code FC02 are the elements of the LOGBRUSH structure in the same order as the structure (*lbStyle* first).

The call:

```
SelectObject (hdcMeta, hBrush) ;
```

is coded in this record:

0004 0000 012D 0000

The single parameter 0000 indicates that it's a handle to the first object created in the metafile. Any following *SelectObject* calls with other GDI objects will have sequentially increasing parameters.

For a memory-based metafile, these records are stored in a global memory block. (You can obtain the records using the *EnumMetaFile* function.) For a disk-based metafile, the records are stored in a disk file. The handle to a disk-based metafile references a small global memory block that contains the drive, the directory, and the name of the file.

Metafile Dos and Don'ts

When you play the metafile, Windows breaks down the metafile into records and executes the appropriate functions using the parameters in each record. From the format of the metafile records, some facts should be fairly obvious (and some not so obvious).

The metafile device context is not a true device context. It doesn't correspond to an actual device or even to a block of memory like the memory device context. It's simply a repository for GDI calls you make using the *hdcMeta* device context handle.

The metafile device context doesn't have any default device context attributes. It uses whatever device context attributes are in effect when you play the metafile.

All parameters enter the metafile device context as numbers. For instance, if the width and height of your client area are stored in *xClient* and *yClient*, and you call:

```
Rectangle (hdcMeta, 0, 0, xClient / 2, yClient / 2) ;
```

then the actual calculated values of *xClient / 2* and *yClient / 2* will enter the metafile. If you later play back that metafile, it will draw a rectangle based on these calculated values regardless of the current size of the client area.

If you change the mapping mode of your screen device context before you play the metafile, the coordinates in the metafile will be interpreted based on the newly chosen mapping mode (unless the metafile itself changes the mapping mode).

The only calls that go into the metafile are those that take a handle to a device context as the first parameter. Many GDI calls are not allowed in a metafile. It's easier to say what functions cannot be used with a metafile device context, because they fall into several categories:

- Any function that begins with the word *Get*, including *GetDeviceCaps* and *GetTextMetrics*. The metafile can do nothing with the information that these functions return.

- Any other function designed to return information to the program: *RectVisible*, *PtVisible*, *EnumFonts*, *EnumObjects*, *DPtoLP*, and *LPtoDP*. The *Escape* function (which you'll encounter in Chapter 16) is supported only for calls that don't return data.

- Any function that treats the metafile device context as if it were an actual device context: *ReleaseDC*, *DeleteDC*, *CreateCompatibleDC*, *CreateCompatibleBitmap*, *CreateDiscardableBitmap*, and *PlayMetaFile*.

- Some of the more complex GDI functions: *GrayString*, *DrawIcon*, and *SetBrushOrg*.

- Two functions that require handles to brushes: *FillRect* and *FrameRect*.

As I indicated above, *SelectObject* works a little differently for metafile device contexts. First, it doesn't return the handle of the object previously selected in the device context. When you use *SelectObject* with a metafile device context, the function returns a nonzero if it is successful and 0 otherwise. You can't use the construction:

```
DeleteObject (SelectObject (hdcMeta, . . . )) ; // WRONG !!!
```

For *SelectObject*, the metafile also stores a description of the logical object that you are selecting into the device context. When you play the metafile, Windows starts with the pen, brush, font, and region currently selected in the device context. For *SelectObject* calls, it creates the indicated object and selects it into the device context but saves the original object. When it is done playing the metafile, Windows restores the original objects and deletes all the objects it created to play the metafile.

When you play a metafile, it uses the device context attributes currently in effect. The metafile can change any of these attributes, including the mapping mode, the text color, the drawing mode, and so forth. These changes remain in effect for the device context after the metafile has finished playing. If you want to retain your original device context attributes after the metafile has finished playing, call:

```
SaveDC (hdc) ;
```

before you play the metafile and:

```
RestoreDC (hdc, -1) ;
```

after the *PlayMetaFile* call. The metafile itself can also save and restore the device context while it is playing. Each *SaveDC* call must be balanced by a *RestoreDC* call with a −1 parameter.

One of the purposes of metafiles is to provide a format for device-independent pictures that can be shared by applications. There are some other considerations involved with using metafiles with the clipboard that will be discussed in Chapter 16.

Chapter 14

Text
and Fonts

Writing text to the display was one of the first jobs we tackled in programming for Windows. Now it's time to explore the use of different font sizes and learn how to justify text. This chapter is largely restricted to writing text on the video display. The subject becomes more complex when you need to write text using the printer. The printer may be capable of using a greater variety of fonts than the video display, and the characteristics of these fonts can be quite different from the characteristics of the video fonts. Therefore, the subject of text and fonts is continued in the next chapter, "Using the Printer."

SIMPLE TEXT OUTPUT

Let's begin by looking at the different functions Windows provides for text output, the device context attributes that affect text, and the use of "stock" fonts.

The Text Drawing Functions

The most common text output function is one we've used in almost all sample programs:

```
TextOut (hdc, xStart, yStart, lpString, nCount) ;
```

The *xStart* and *yStart* parameters are the starting position of the string in logical coordinates. Normally, this is the point at which Windows begins drawing the upper left corner of the first character. *TextOut* requires a far pointer to the character string and the length of the string. The function knows nothing about NULL-terminated character strings.

The meaning of the *xStart* and *yStart* parameters to *TextOut* can be altered by the *SetTextAlign* function. The TA_LEFT, TA_RIGHT, and TA_CENTER flags affect the horizontal positioning of the character string. For example, if you call *SetTextAlign* with the TA_CENTER flag, subsequent *TextOut* calls position the center of the string at *xStart*. Similarly, the TA_TOP, TA_BOTTOM, and TA_BASELINE flags affect the vertical positioning. If you call *SetTextAlign* with the TA_UPDATECP flag, then Windows ignores the *xStart* and *yStart* parameters to *TextOut* and instead uses the current position previously set by *MoveTo* or *LineTo*. The TA_UPDATECP flag also causes the *TextOut* function to update the current position to the end of the string (for TA_LEFT) or the beginning of the string (for TA_RIGHT). When the horizontal positioning is TA_CENTER, the current position remains the same after a *TextOut* call.

You'll recall that displaying columnar-aligned text in the series of SYSMETS programs in Chapter 2 required that one *TextOut* call be used for each column. An alternative is the *TabbedTextOut* function. If the text string contains embedded tab characters ('\t' or 0x09), *TabbedTextOut* will expand the tabs into spaces based on an array of integers you pass to the function.

The *ExtTextOut* function gives you much more control over the spacing of individual characters in the text string. The function also lets you specify a clipping rectangle.

A higher-level function for writing text is *DrawText*, which we first encountered in the HELLOWIN program in Chapter 1. Rather than specifying a coordinate starting position, you provide a structure of type RECT that defines a rectangle in which you want the text to appear:

```
DrawText (hdc, lpString, nCount, &rect, wFormat) ;
```

DrawText also requires a far pointer to the character string and the length of the string. If you use *DrawText* with NULL-terminated strings, however, you can set *nCount* to –1, and Windows will calculate the length of the string.

When *wFormat* is set to 0, Windows interprets the text as a series of lines that are separated by carriage-return characters (ASCII number 13) or linefeed characters (ASCII number 10). The text begins at the upper left corner of the rectangle. A carriage return or linefeed is interpreted as a "newline" character; Windows breaks the current line and starts a new one. The new line begins at the left side of the rectangle, spaced one character height (without external leading) below the previous line. Any text (including parts of letters) that would be displayed to the right or below the bottom of the rectangle is clipped.

You can change the default operation of *DrawText* by including a *wFormat* parameter, which consists of one or more flags defined in WINDOWS.H and separated by the C bitwise OR operator. The DT_LEFT flag (the default) specifies a left-justified line, DT_RIGHT specifies a right-justified line, and DT_CENTER specifies a line centered between the left and right sides of the rectangle. Because the value of DT_LEFT is 0, you needn't include the identifier if you want text to be left-justified only.

If you don't want carriage returns or linefeeds to be interpreted as newline characters, you can include the identifier DT_SINGLELINE. Windows then interprets those ASCII numbers as displayable characters rather than as control characters. When using DT_SINGLELINE, you can also specify whether the line is to be placed at the top of the rectangle (DT_TOP, the default), at the bottom of the rectangle (DT_BOTTOM), or halfway between the top and bottom (DT_VCENTER). DT_TOP, like DT_LEFT, has a value of 0, so you don't need to explicitly include the flag.

When displaying multiple lines of text, Windows normally breaks the lines only at carriage returns or linefeeds. If the lines are too long to fit in the rectangle, however, you can use the DT_WORDBREAK flag, which causes Windows to make breaks at the ends of words within lines. For both single-line and multiple-line displays, Windows truncates any part of the text that falls outside the rectangle. You can override this by including the flag DT_NOCLIP, which also speeds up the operation of the function. When Windows spaces multiple lines of text, it uses the character height without external leading. If you prefer that external leading be included in the line spacing, use the flag DT_EXTERNALLEADING.

If your text contains tab characters (ASCII number 9), you need to include the flag DT_EXPANDTABS. By default, the tab stops are set at every eighth character position. You can specify a different tab setting by using the flag DT_TABSTOP, in which case the upper byte of *wFormat* contains the character-position number of the new tab stops. I recommend that you avoid using DT_TABSTOP, however, because the upper byte of *wFormat* is also used for some other flags.

Device Context Attributes for Text

Several device context attributes affect text. In the default device context, the text color is black, but you can change that:

```
SetTextColor (hdc, rgbColor) ;
```

As with pen colors and hatch brush colors, Windows converts the value of *rgbColor* to a pure color. You can obtain the current text color by calling *GetTextColor*.

The spaces between the character strokes are colored in, based on the setting of the background mode and the background color. You can change the background mode using:

```
SetBkMode (hdc, nMode) ;
```

where *nMode* is either OPAQUE or TRANSPARENT. The default background mode is OPAQUE, which means that Windows uses the background color to fill in the area between the character strokes. You can change the background color by using:

```
SetBkColor (hdc, rgbColor) ;
```

The value of *rgbColor* is converted to that of a pure color. The default background color is white. If the background mode is set to TRANSPARENT, Windows ignores the background color and doesn't color the area between the character strokes. Windows also uses the background mode and background color to color the spaces between dotted and dashed lines and the area between the hatches of hatched brushes, as you saw in Chapter 12.

Many Windows programs specify WHITE_BRUSH as the brush that Windows uses to erase the background of a window. The brush is specified in the window class structure. However, you may want to make the background of your program's window consistent with the "system colors" that a user can set in the CONTROL program. In that case, you would specify the background color this way:

```
wndclass.hbrBackground = COLOR_WINDOW + 1 ;
```

When you want to write text to the client area, you can set the text color and background color using the current system colors:

```
SetTextColor (hdc, GetSysColor (COLOR_WINDOWTEXT)) ;
SetBkColor (hdc, GetSysColor (COLOR_WINDOW)) ;
```

If you do this, then you'll want your program to be alerted if the system colors change:

```
case WM_SYSCOLORCHANGE:
     InvalidateRect (hwnd, NULL, TRUE) ;
     break ;
```

Another device context attribute that affects text is the intercharacter spacing. By default it's set to 0, which means that Windows doesn't add any space between characters. You can insert space by using the function:

```
SetTextCharacterExtra (hdc, nExtra) ;
```

The *nExtra* parameter is in logical units. Windows converts it to the nearest pixel, which can be 0. If you use a negative value for *nExtra* (perhaps in an attempt to squeeze characters closer together), Windows takes the absolute value of the number: You can't make the value less than 0. You can obtain the current intercharacter spacing by calling *GetTextCharacterExtra*. Windows converts the pixel spacing to logical units before returning the value.

Using Stock Fonts

When you call *TextOut, TabbedTextOut, ExtTextOut,* or *DrawText* to write text, Windows uses the font currently selected in the device context. The font defines a particular typeface and size. The easiest way to write text in a choice of fonts is to use the six stock fonts that Windows provides. You can first obtain a handle to a stock font by calling:

```
hFont = GetStockObject (nFont) ;
```

where *nFont* is one of the six identifiers discussed below. You can then select that font into the device context:

```
SelectObject (hdc, hFont) ;
```

Or you can do it in one step:

```
SelectObject (hdc, GetStockObject (nFont)) ;
```

GetStockObject is the same function that we used in Chapter 12 to obtain stock pens and brushes; SelectObject we used in Chapters 12 and 13 to select pens, brushes, bitmaps, and regions into the device context.

The font selected in the default device context is called the system font and is identified by the *GetStockObject* parameter SYSTEM_FONT. This is the proportional ANSI character set font that Windows uses for text in menus, dialog boxes, message boxes, and window caption bars. Specifying SYSTEM_FIXED_FONT in *GetStockObject* gives you a handle to a fixed-pitch ANSI font compatible with the system font used in versions of Windows prior to version 3. We've frequently encountered this font in sample programs in this book when using a fixed-pitch font seemed to be easier than using a proportional font. The OEM_FIXED_FONT identifier gives you a handle to a font that is often called the terminal font. This is the font that Windows uses for windowed DOS character-mode programs. On most devices, the terminal font is similar to the fixed-pitch system font but uses the OEM rather than the ANSI character set. (The ANSI and OEM character sets are discussed in Chapter 4.)

The identifier ANSI_FIXED_FONT gives you a handle to a Courier font that is usually smaller than the system or terminal font. You can obtain a handle to a font with variable character widths by using the identifier ANSI_VAR_FONT. This returns a handle to a Helvetica or Times Roman font, either of which is usually smaller than the system font.

Finally, the identifier DEVICE_DEFAULT_FONT is designed to return a handle to a font that is built into the output device and that is most suitable for the device. For most graphics-based video displays, no font meets this condition, so the identifier returns a handle to the system font. For a dot-matrix printer, however, this identifier returns a handle to a font that is specific to the printer and that in some cases does not require Windows to operate the printer in a graphics mode.

When you select a new font into a device context, you must calculate the font's character height and average character width using *GetTextMetrics*. If you've selected a proportional font, be aware that the average character width is really an average and that a given character can have a smaller or larger width. Later in this chapter you'll learn how to use *GetTextExtent* to calculate the full width of a string made up of variable-width characters.

Although *GetStockObject* certainly offers the easiest access to different fonts, you don't have much control over what font Windows gives you. You'll see shortly how you can be very specific about the typeface and type size that you want.

Graying Character Strings

Although *TextOut* and *DrawText* are the functions used most often to write character strings, Windows has another text output function called *GrayString* that exists for the express purpose of displaying grayed text. Windows uses grayed text most often to show disabled items in menus and dialog boxes. However, you might also want to use some grayed text within your client area. *GrayString* is complex and has some limitations. I'll begin by explaining how *GrayString* generally works and then show you an easier way to use it. Here's the general syntax:

```
GrayString (hdc, hBrush, lpfnOutputFunction, dwData,
    nCount, xStart, yStart, xWidth, yHeight) ;
```

GrayString uses a call-back function of the form:

```
BOOL FAR PASCAL OutputFunction (hdc, dwData, nCount)
    HDC       hdc ;
    DWORD     dwData ;
    short     nCount ;
    {
    [other program lines]
    return 1 ;
    }
```

The name of this function must be included in the EXPORTS section of your module definition (.DEF) file. You must obtain a far pointer to the function by calling *MakeProcInstance*:

```
lpfnOutputFunction = MakeProcInstance (hInstance, OutputFunction) ;
```

This far pointer is the third parameter to *GrayString*. The *dwData* and *nCount* parameters to *GrayString* are passed as parameters to this call-back function. Most often, *dwData* is a far pointer (converted to a doubleword) to the text you want to gray, and *nCount* is set to the number of characters.

Here's what happens when you call *GrayString*. Windows creates a memory device context and a monochrome bitmap using the *xWidth* and *yHeight* parameters to *Gray-String*. It selects the bitmap into the memory device context and passes to the call-back function the memory device context handle and the *dwData* and *nCount* parameters.

Within the call-back function, you draw on this memory device context. The text color has been set to black and the background color to white. The drawing you do is relative to the upper left corner of this memory device context rather than the upper left corner of your original device context. The output function returns a 1 if all goes well. Windows then uses the *PatBlt* function to perform a bitwise OR operation on this memory device context and the 50-percent gray brush. (The ROP code is 0xFA0089.) As a result, the white pixels in the memory device context are unchanged, and half the black pixels become white pixels.

Windows then performs a *BitBlt* operation on this memory device context and the device context you specified in the *GrayString* call (probably your client-area device context), starting at the point (*xStart, yStart*). The ROP code is 0xB8074A, which corresponds to a Boolean operation of:

((Destination ∧ Pattern) & Source) ∧ Pattern

You may recall this particular ROP code from Chapter 13. The pixels in your original device context (the destination) that correspond to white pixels in the memory device context (the source) are unchanged. The pixels in your original device context that correspond to black pixels in the memory device context are colored with the brush specified in the *GrayString* call. In other words, every other pixel that you color black in the memory device context is colored with the brush in your original device context.

The *GrayString* function has certain limitations. Here are the most important ones. *GrayString* requires the MM_TEXT mapping mode. This is because the *xWidth* and *yHeight* parameters to *GrayString* are treated as device units when Windows creates the bitmap, but they are treated as logical units when *PatBlt* and *BitBlt* are called.

The memory device context has default device context attributes when Windows calls the output function. Therefore, if you've selected a non–default font into your device context before calling *GrayString*, this font will not be selected in the memory device context. You can, however, select the same font into the memory device context within the output function.

Normally, the *dwData* parameter points to a character string, and *nCount* is the number of characters, but *dwData* and *nCount* can really be anything you want. Be aware of the following:

- If *nCount* is 0, then Windows assumes that *dwData* is a zero-terminated character string and calculates the number of characters. That calculated value is passed to the call-back function.

- If you specify an *xWidth* or *yHeight* value of 0, then Windows computes the height and width of the string pointed to by *dwData*. It uses the memory device context for this calculation, so these heights and widths are based on the height and width of the system font, regardless of the font you eventually use in the call-back function.

- If the output function returns 0, then Windows assumes that an error has occurred and doesn't draw anything on your original device context. However, if you set the *nCount* parameter to −1 and the output function returns 0, then Windows simply transfers the memory device context intact to your original device context without first graying it. In this case, you have to determine the number of characters in the character string yourself, within the call-back function.

If you have a good feel for bitmaps, memory device contexts, and the raster operations, you might want to sidestep these limitations by writing your own text-graying function. Or you might prefer to use the easy *GrayString* syntax presented below.

The Easy Use of *GrayString*

In the general syntax to *GrayString*, the parameter called *lpfnOutputFunction* is a long pointer to a call-back function. If you set that parameter to NULL, Windows uses the *Text-Out* function. You can also set the *nWidth* and *nHeight* parameters to 0. Here's the syntax you'll want to use for writing grayed text to the display:

```
GrayString (hdc, GetStockObject (BLACK_BRUSH), NULL,
            (DWORD) lpString, nCount, xStart, yStart, 0, 0) ;
```

If *lpString* is a pointer to a NULL-terminated text string, then *nCount* can also be set to 0, and Windows will calculate the length. *GrayString* uses the system font regardless of the font currently selected in the device context. The function ignores the device context settings for the text color, background mode, and background color, and it requires the MM_TEXT mapping mode.

On color displays, you can also pass to *GrayString* a brush handle from *CreateSolid-Brush*, if you've created a brush of a pure color. On monochrome displays, however, this brush would become a black-and-white dithered brush, and you would encounter the same problems as with a gray brush.

Gray Strings Without *GrayString*

In versions of Windows prior to 3, the display drivers for the EGA and VGA supported only eight pure colors (black, red, green, blue, yellow, magenta, cyan, and white) on color displays. Grays had to be simulated using a dithered pattern of black and white pixels.

Beginning in Windows 3, the EGA and VGA display drivers support 16 colors, including two shades of gray. This means that you can display gray text without using the *GrayString* function.

To do this, first call *GetSysColor* with a parameter of COLOR_GRAYTEXT:

```
rgbGrayText = GetSysColor (COLOR_GRAYTEXT) ;
```

If *rgbGrayText* is equal to 0L, then your program should use the *GrayString* function to draw a grayed string. Otherwise, you can simply set the text color to *rgbGrayText*:

```
SetTextColor (hdc, rgbGrayText) ;
```

BACKGROUND ON FONTS

Much of the remainder of this chapter concerns working with different fonts. Before you get involved with specific code, however, you'll benefit from having a firm grasp of the subject's basics.

The Types of Fonts

Windows supports two broad categories of fonts, called "GDI fonts" and "device fonts."

The GDI-based fonts are stored in files with the extension .FON. These files are sometimes called "font resource files," and they are stored in the SYSTEM subdirectory of your Windows directory. Each file contains one or more complete fonts. These files are in New Executable format, which you can verify by running EXEHDR on them. They are library modules, although somewhat unusual ones in that they contain no code or data. All they contain are two types of resources: a font directory and the fonts themselves.

Device fonts are internal to the graphics output device. For video display adapters, device fonts are currently rare. Windows uses the video adapter in graphics mode, so it must use the GDI fonts and write the pixels to the video display.

For printers, however, device-based fonts are common. For instance, Windows can write text to a dot-matrix printer using either the printer's normal text mode or the printer's graphics mode. With the text mode, Windows uses a device font and needs to send only the ASCII numbers of the characters out to the printer. With the graphics mode, Windows uses a GDI font and must send the pixel patterns to the printer. For laser printers, device fonts can be stored in ROM within the printer or in ROM cartridges. If the printer requires a downloadable font that originates from a disk file, this font is also classified as a device font, because it is specific to the particular device.

GDI fonts come in two flavors—"raster," or bitmap, fonts (the more common variety) and "stroke" fonts. In a raster font file, each character is stored as a bitmap pixel pattern. Figure 14-1 shows a character from a GDI raster font, blown up so that you can see the pixel formation.

Figure 14-1. *A GDI-based raster font character.*

Each raster font is designed for a specific aspect ratio and character size. Windows can create larger character sizes from GDI raster fonts by simply duplicating rows or columns of pixels. However, this can be done only in integral multiples and within certain limits. Right away, you can probably perceive one major difference between drawing graphics on the display and writing text to the display using the GDI raster fonts. Although you can draw a rectangle of virtually any size, GDI raster fonts are available only in discrete sizes. You can't write text using a font smaller than the smallest font. If you want a GDI raster font of a specific size, that size may not be available.

The GDI stroke fonts partly solve this problem. The stroke fonts are defined as a series of line segments in a "connect-the-dots" format. Stroke fonts are continuously scalable, which means that the same font can be used for all aspect ratios and can be increased or decreased to any size. In general, GDI raster fonts look better than stroke fonts at small sizes because raster font designs were based on small sizes. At very large sizes, however, the raster fonts look grainy—as you can see in Figure 14-1—because Windows has to start doubling rows or columns of pixels. Thus, the stroke fonts are usually preferable for large sizes, although the characters look somewhat weak because their strokes are single lines. Figure 14-2 shows a character from a blown-up GDI stroke font.

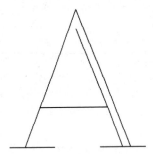

Figure 14-2. *A GDI-based stroke font character.*

For both GDI raster fonts and stroke fonts, Windows can "synthesize" boldface, italics, underlining, and strikethrough without storing separate fonts for each attribute. For italics, for instance, Windows simply shifts the upper part of the character to the right. Because device fonts are stored and used in a device-specific manner, it is impossible to discuss them in the same detail as GDI fonts. Sometimes the device can italicize or boldface a device font, and sometimes it can't. You can obtain such information from the *GetDeviceCaps* function using the TEXTCAPS index. If you want to obtain this information for particular printers, you can use the *GetDeviceCaps* function as illustrated in the DEVCAPS1 program in Chapter 11.

Type Talk I: Families and Faces

I've been using the word font rather loosely until now. The more rigorous definition of font that is preferred by typographers is this: A font is a complete collection of characters of a particular typeface and a particular size.

To a typographer, the term typeface denotes not only the style of type (such as Courier or Helvetica) but also whether the characters are italic or boldface, for example. When working with Windows, we'll use the word typeface to denote simply the style of the type. Common typefaces, in addition to Courier and Helvetica, are Times Roman, Gothic, and Palatino.

Windows groups typefaces into five "families," based on the general appearance of the type. These families are called Modern, Swiss, Roman, Script, and Decorative. The most common typefaces are categorized as Modern, Swiss, or Roman, depending on two characteristics. The first characteristic involves "stroke width"—the width of the lines that make up the characters—which can be constant or variable. Typefaces in the Modern family have constant stroke widths. Typefaces in the Swiss and Roman families have variable stroke widths. (Typefaces with variable stroke widths are generally of "variable pitch," which means that the characters have variable widths. However, it is the stroke width rather than the use of fixed or variable pitch that determines the family of a particular typeface.) The second characteristic involves "serifs," which are small lines that finish off the character strokes. The Swiss family comprises "sans serif" typefaces (typefaces with no serifs); the Roman family comprises serif typefaces.

The Script family comprises typefaces that resemble script handwriting. The Decorative family includes typefaces that comprise "symbols" (sometimes also called "ornaments" or "dingbats") and can also contain typefaces of elaborate design such as Old English.

The table below summarizes the grouping of typefaces into families and shows the identifiers (defined in WINDOWS.H) that programs can use to specify the font family:

Font Family	Stroke	Usual Pitch	Serifs	Typical Typefaces
FF_MODERN	Fixed	Fixed	—	Courier, Elite, Pica
FF_SWISS	Variable	Variable	No	Helvetica, Avant Garde
FF_ROMAN	Variable	Variable	Yes	Times Roman, Palatino, New Century Schoolbook
FF_SCRIPT	—	—	—	Cursive, Zapf Chancery
FF_DECORATIVE	—	—	—	Old Symbol, English, Zapf Dingbats

WINDOWS.H also includes a sixth font-family identifier, FF_DONTCARE, which a program can use when it wants to create a font but doesn't care what family it comes from.

The typeface names shown in this table are the common names by which these typefaces are known, but when a Windows program specifies a typeface, in most cases it uses an abbreviation (such as "Helv" for Helvetica and "Tms Rmn" for Times Roman) rather than the full name. (The reason for this is that the names Times Roman and Helvetica are copyrighted and cannot be used to identify fonts not licensed from the copyright holder.) As you'll see, Windows provides functions for programs to determine the names of the typefaces available on a particular device. These functions become particularly important when the device is a printer, because printers can include many device fonts with names that can be determined only when the program interrogates the device. Typefaces available for the video display are shown in Figure 14-3.

Courier
Modern
Helv
Tms Rmn
Roman
Script

Figure 14-3. *Windows typefaces for the video display.*

Courier, Helv, and Tms Rmn are the raster fonts; the stroke fonts (Modern, Roman, and Script) have typeface names that are the same as the names of three font families. The reason that the stroke fonts are not assigned true typeface names is that they are not really fonts in any traditional typographical sense.

The Font Resource Files

The SYSTEM subdirectory of the Windows directory contains several files with the extension .FON. Some of the filenames begin with the letters COUR (Courier), HELV (Helvetica), TMSR (Times Roman) and SYMBOL (Symbol) followed by another letter: A, B, C, D, E, or F; these are the font resource files containing the GDI raster fonts. Each font resource file contains one or more sizes of a particular typeface. The terminating letter indicates the resolution and aspect ratio for which the font was designed. The GDI stroke fonts are stored in the MODERN.FON, ROMAN.FON, and SCRIPT.FON files. Because the GDI stroke fonts are continuously scalable, they aren't based on a particular aspect ratio or device resolution.

The system and terminal fonts are stored in files that begin with the name of the device for which they have been designed (such as CGA, EGA, VGA, and 8514/A) and ending with the words SYS (proportional system font), FIX (fixed-pitch system font), and OEM (terminal font).

The following table lists the GDI font resource files, the font-family identifiers, the typefaces, and the character sets:

Filename	Type	Family	Typeface	Character Set
___SYS.FON	Raster	FF_SWISS	System	ANSI
___FIX.FON	Raster	FF_DONTCARE	System	ANSI
___OEM.FON	Raster	FF_MODERN	Terminal	OEM
COURx.FON	Raster	FF_MODERN	Courier	ANSI
HELVx.FON	Raster	FF_SWISS	Helv	ANSI
TMSRx.FON	Raster	FF_ROMAN	Tms Rmn	ANSI
SYMBOLx.FON	Raster	FF_DECORATIVE	Symbol	N/A
MODERN.FON	Stroke	FF_MODERN	Modern	OEM
ROMAN.FON	Stroke	FF_ROMAN	Roman	OEM
SCRIPT.FON	Stroke	FF_SCRIPT	Script	OEM

The GDI stroke font files are sometimes referred to as "Set #1." There are six other sets corresponding to the terminating letter of the COURx.FON, HELVx.FON, TMSRx.FON, and SYMBOLx.FONT filenames:

Set	Letter	Aspect Ratio	X (Horz)	Y (Vert)	Device
			Pixels per Logical Inch		
#2	A	200	96	48	CGA
#3	B	133	96	72	EGA
#4	C	83	60	72	Okidata printers
#5	D	167	120	72	IBM, Epson printers
#6	E	100	96	96	VGA
#7	F	100	120	120	8514/A

Depending on what printers you've installed and whether you've used the Windows Setup program to change the video display driver, some of these files may or may not be present on your hard disk. Also, some users may have other Windows font files present.

The aspect ratio in the above table is calculated as:

$$100 * \frac{horizontal\ pixels\ per\ logical\ inch}{vertical\ pixels\ per\ logical\ inch}$$

You might recall encountering this peculiar "logical inch" measurement in Chapter 11, when we explored the information available from *GetDeviceCaps* with the LOGPIXELSX and LOGPIXELSY parameters. We quickly established that a logical inch is different from a real inch.

For an EGA, *GetDeviceCaps* reports that the device has 96 pixels horizontally per logical inch and 72 pixels vertically per logical inch. This means that the raster fonts stored in the COURB.FON, HELVB.FON, TMSRB.FON, and SYMBOLB.FON files are appropriate for display on an EGA. The fonts in the Set #2 files are too short for the EGA because they are based on a lower vertical resolution, and the fonts in Set #4 are too wide because they are based on a lower horizontal resolution.

Type Talk II: Getting the Point

Type size is expressed in units called "points." A point is very close to $\frac{1}{72}$ inch, so close that it's often defined as exactly $\frac{1}{72}$ inch. The point size indicates the height of the characters. For instance, when we speak of 12-point type, we're referring to characters that are $\frac{12}{72}$ ($\frac{1}{6}$) inch high from the top of the ascenders to the bottom of the descenders.

In Windows, another convenient measurement is the "twip"; this fabricated word stands for "twentieth of a point," which equals $\frac{1}{1440}$ inch. Note that the pixels-per-logical-inch measurements associated with each of the five sets of GDI raster fonts are such that the size of each pixel is an integral number of twips. Or rather, each pixel is an integral number of a measurement we can call "logical twips":

Pixels per Logical Inch	Logical Twips per Pixel
48	30
60	24
72	20
96	15
120	12

If you run the EXEHDR utility on the COURx.FON, HELVx.FON, TMSRx.FON, and SYMBOL.FON font resource files, you'll see in the module description that the files contain fonts of particular point sizes. The COURx.FON files comprise 8-point, 10-point, and 12-point fonts. The HELVx.FON and TMSRx.FON files include those sizes and add 14-point, 18-point, and 24-point fonts. But here's the catch: These point sizes are dependent on the resolution given by the number of pixels per logical inch. For instance, the 24-point Times Roman font in the TMSRB.FON file has characters that are 24 pixels high. Only on a display that has 72 pixels per vertical inch will the 24 pixels correspond to a 24-point font.

Why Logical Inches?

The fact remains that the EGA actually displays 68 pixels per horizontal inch and 51 pixels per vertical inch. The logical inch is some 40 percent larger than the real inch. Why not simply base the fonts on the real dimensions of the EGA display and forget about this logical-inch business?

On paper, 8-point type with about 14 characters per horizontal inch is perfectly readable. If you were programming a word-processing or page-composition application for Windows, you would want to be able to show legible 8-point type on the display. But if you used the actual dimensions of the video display, each character would be about 6 pixels high and 5 pixels wide. Such characters would not be legible. Even if the display had sufficient resolution, you might still have problems reading actual 8-point type on a screen. When people read print on paper, the distance between the eyes and the paper is generally about a foot, but a video display is commonly viewed from a distance of 2 feet. The logical inch in effect provides a magnification of the screen, allowing the display of legible fonts in a size as small as 8-point. You can see this magnification effect in Windows WRITE when you display the ruler at the top of the client area.

Note also that having 96 pixels per logical inch horizontally makes the 640-pixel-wide display of the CGA and EGA equal to about 6.5 logical inches. This is precisely the width of text that you'll print on 8.5-inch-wide paper when you use margins of an inch on each side. So the logical inch also takes advantage of the width of the screen to allow text to be displayed as large as possible.

This whole subject of logical inches is relevant only for the video display. For printers, a logical inch is the same as a real inch.

Type Talk III: Leading and Spacing

When we wrote text to the display in Chapter 2, we obtained information from *GetText-Metrics* that allowed us to space the text properly. The five values from the TEXTMETRIC structure that describe the size of a character were shown in a diagram (Figure 2-3). Those five character-height values are shown again in Figure 14-4 on the following page.

The word *leading* (pronounced "ledding") is derived from the lead that typesetters insert between blocks of metal type to add white space between lines of text. The *tmInternalLeading* value is the space for diacritics. (For the terminal font, *tmInternalLeading* is 0, and characters with diacritics are simply reduced in size to make room for the diacritics.) The *tmExternalLeading* "suggests" an additional space to leave between lines of characters. Programmers can use or ignore the external leading value. The Courier, Helvetica, and Times Roman fonts usually have *tmExternalLeading* values of 0 and have positive *tmInternalLeading* values (except in the very smallest sizes) to more closely approximate how fonts are used in printed material.

When we refer to a font as being 8-point or 12-point, we're actually talking about the height of the font less the internal leading. The diacritics on certain capitals are considered to occupy the space that normally separates lines of type. The *tmHeight* value refers to the line spacing. In the case of the 24-point Times Roman font for the EGA (which conveniently has 72 pixels per logical inch vertically, or 1 pixel per logical point), the *tmHeight* value is 26 and the *tmInternalLeading* is 2. The line spacing is 28 points. The size of the font is 26 minus 2, or 24 points. We speak of this as a 24-point font on a 26-point line spacing, which is often abbreviated as 24/26 (and pronounced "twenty-four on twenty-six"). The 10-point Courier, Helvetica, and Times Roman fonts designed for the EGA all have a *tmHeight* value of 12 and a *tmInternalLeading* value of 2. The line spacing is 12 points, or ⅙ logical inch, which is the normal line spacing of a printer or typewriter.

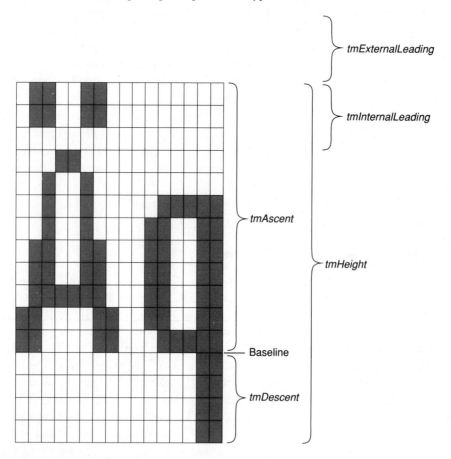

Figure 14-4. *The five values defining character height.*

The "Logical Twips" Mapping Mode

When I discussed mapping modes in Chapter 11, you might have thought the MM_TWIPS mapping mode would be used by programs that make heavy use of formatted text. In this mapping mode, logical units are in terms of ¹⁄₂₀ point. However, you probably won't want to use MM_TWIPS for the video display, because the mapping mode is based on real inches rather than logical inches. As a result, your program won't be able to equate the correct point sizes (8, 10, 12, 14, 18, and 24) of the available screen fonts to their heights in MM_TWIPS units.

You'll be better off if you define your mapping mode based on the logical-pixels-per-inch dimensions available from *GetDeviceCaps*. I call this the "Logical Twips" mapping mode; here's all you need to set it:

```
SetMapMode (hdc, MM_ANISOTROPIC) ;
SetWindowExt (hdc, 1440, 1440) ;
SetViewportExt (hdc, GetDeviceCaps (hdc, LOGPIXELSX),
                     GetDeviceCaps (hdc, LOGPIXELSY)) ;
```

Because the pixels-per-logical-inch values are always divisors of 1440, the scaling factor for this mapping mode is an integer. With this mapping mode set, if you want to request a font with 12-point line spacing (as we'll do shortly), you can specify the height of the font as 240 (12 times 20) logical units.

If you select a font into your device context and call *GetTextMetrics* to obtain the dimensions of the font, you can calculate the type size in points by using the formula:

(tm.tmHeight − tm.tmInternalLeading) / 20

The line spacing in points is equal to:

tm.tmHeight / 20

For some smaller fonts on low-resolution devices, the size and spacing of the type might actually involve a fraction of a point—for example, 8-point type with 8.5-point line spacing. To round to the nearest integer point size, you might instead want to use the formulas:

(tm.tmHeight − tm.tmInternalLeading + 10) / 20

and:

(tm.tmHeight + 10) / 20

We'll use the "Logical Twips" mapping mode in the JUSTIFY program toward the end of this chapter.

Once again, remember that the discrepancy between logical inches and real inches occurs only for the display. If you use the "Logical Twips" mapping mode with a printer, you'll simply duplicate the MM_TWIPS mapping mode.

CREATING, SELECTING, AND DELETING LOGICAL FONTS

Now that we've nailed down the concept of logical inches, it's time to talk about logical fonts. The logical font is the sixth and final type of GDI object.

A logical font is the description of a font. Like the logical pen and logical brush, it is an abstract item that becomes real only when it is selected into a device context. For logical pens (for instance), you can specify any color you want for the pen, but Windows converts that to a pure color when you select the pen into the device context. Only then does Windows know about the color capabilities of the device.

With fonts, this distinction between the logical font that you request and the real font that you get is much more important, because the logical font and the real font can be very different. For example, suppose you request a 32-point Zapf Chancery font. Windows returns to your program a handle to a logical font. Now you select that font into a device context. What happens? It depends. If the device context is a printer device context for an Apple LaserWriter Plus, you will indeed be able to write text to the printer using a 32-point Zapf Chancery font. But if you select this logical font into your screen device context, you'll get something that only approximates this font.

This is the process for creating, selecting, and deleting logical fonts:

1. Create a logical font by calling *CreateFont* or *CreateFontIndirect*. These functions return a handle to a font of type HFONT.

2. Select the logical font into the device context using *SelectObject*. Windows chooses a real font that matches most closely the logical font.

3. Determine the size and characteristics of the real font with *Get-TextMetrics*. (You can also get the name of the font with *GetTextFace*.) The information lets you properly space the text that you write when this font is selected into the device context.

4. Delete the logical font by calling *DeleteObject*. Don't delete the font while it is selected in a valid device context, however, and never delete stock fonts.

Windows has two functions for creating logical fonts. The first is:

```
hFont = CreateFont (nHeight  . . .  lpszFaceName) ;
```

The *CreateFont* function has more parameters than any other Windows function—14 of them. The 14 parameters to *CreateFont* correspond directly to the 14 fields of the LOG-FONT structure. You can also create a logical font using the LOGFONT structure and the *CreateFontIndirect* function:

```
LOGFONT logfont ;
     [other program lines]
hFont = CreateFontIndirect (&logfont) ;
```

In most cases, using *CreateFontIndirect* and the logical font structure is neater and more efficient than specifying the 14 parameters to *CreateFont*.

After you create a logical font, you select it into your device context with *SelectObject*:

```
hFontOld = SelectObject (hdc, hFont) ;
```

Windows then matches the logical font with a real font. You can determine the name of the typeface by using the function:

```
GetTextFace (hdc, sizeof szFaceName, szFaceName) ;
```

where *szFaceName* is a character array to receive the name. You can have Windows copy the various sizes of the font into a structure of type TEXTMETRIC using the familiar:

```
GetTextMetrics (hdc, &tm) ;
```

The *GetObject* function, which you can use to obtain information about a logical pen, brush, or bitmap, can also be used for logical fonts:

```
GetObject (hFont, sizeof (LOGFONT), &logfont) ;
```

But this function returns only the information that you put into *logfont* to create the font in the first place.   .

You can delete a logical font (but not while it is selected in a device context) with *DeleteObject*:

```
DeleteObject (hFont) ;
```

The PICKFONT Program

With the PICKFONT program, shown in Figure 14-5, you can create a logical font and see the characteristics of the real font after the logical font is selected into the screen device context.

```
PICKFONT.MAK

#-----------------------
# PICKFONT.MAK make file
#-----------------------

pickfont.exe : pickfont.obj pickfont.def pickfont.res
      link pickfont, /align:16, NUL, /nod slibcew libw, pickfont
      rc pickfont.res

pickfont.obj : pickfont.c pickfont.h
      cl -c -Gsw -Ow -W2 -Zp pickfont.c

pickfont.res : pickfont.rc pickfont.h
      rc -r pickfont.rc
```

Figure 14-5. *The PICKFONT program.*

PICKFONT.C

```
/*-------------------------------------------
   PICKFONT.C -- Font Picker Program
                 (c) Charles Petzold, 1990
   -----------------------------------------*/

#include <windows.h>
#include "pickfont.h"

long FAR PASCAL WndProc (HWND, WORD, WORD, LONG) ;
BOOL FAR PASCAL DlgProc (HWND, WORD, WORD, LONG) ;

char     szAppName [] = "PickFont" ;
DWORD    dwAspectMatch = 0L ;
HWND     hDlg ;
LOGFONT  lf ;
short    nMapMode = IDD_TEXT ;

int PASCAL WinMain (HANDLE hInstance, HANDLE hPrevInstance,
                    LPSTR lpszCmdLine, int nCmdShow)
     {
     HWND      hwnd ;
     MSG       msg ;
     WNDCLASS  wndclass ;

     if (!hPrevInstance)
         {
         wndclass.style         = CS_HREDRAW | CS_VREDRAW ;
         wndclass.lpfnWndProc   = WndProc ;
         wndclass.cbClsExtra    = 0 ;
         wndclass.cbWndExtra    = 0 ;
         wndclass.hInstance     = hInstance ;
         wndclass.hIcon         = LoadIcon (NULL, IDI_APPLICATION) ;
         wndclass.hCursor       = LoadCursor (NULL, IDC_ARROW) ;
         wndclass.hbrBackground = GetStockObject (WHITE_BRUSH) ;
         wndclass.lpszMenuName  = NULL ;
         wndclass.lpszClassName = szAppName ;

         RegisterClass (&wndclass) ;
         }

     hwnd = CreateWindow (szAppName, "Font Picker",
                     WS_OVERLAPPEDWINDOW | WS_CLIPCHILDREN,
                     CW_USEDEFAULT, CW_USEDEFAULT,
                     CW_USEDEFAULT, CW_USEDEFAULT,
                     NULL, NULL, hInstance, NULL) ;

     ShowWindow (hwnd, nCmdShow) ;
     UpdateWindow (hwnd) ;
```

(continued)

```
      while (GetMessage (&msg, NULL, 0, 0))
           {
           if (hDlg == 0 !! !IsDialogMessage (hDlg, &msg))
                {
                TranslateMessage (&msg) ;
                DispatchMessage  (&msg) ;
                }
           }
      return msg.wParam ;
      }

void MySetMapMode (HDC hdc)
      {
      if (nMapMode == IDD_LTWPS)
           {
           SetMapMode (hdc, MM_ANISOTROPIC) ;
           SetWindowExt (hdc, 1440, 1440) ;
           SetViewportExt (hdc, GetDeviceCaps (hdc, LOGPIXELSX),
                               GetDeviceCaps (hdc, LOGPIXELSY)) ;
           }
      else
           SetMapMode (hdc, MM_TEXT + nMapMode - IDD_TEXT) ;
      }

void ShowMetrics (HWND hDlg)
      {
      static TEXTMETRIC tm ;
      static struct
           {
           short nDlgID ;
           short *pData ;
           }
           shorts [] =
           {
           TM_HEIGHT,     &tm.tmHeight,
           TM_ASCENT,     &tm.tmAscent,
           TM_DESCENT,    &tm.tmDescent,
           TM_INTLEAD,    &tm.tmInternalLeading,
           TM_EXTLEAD,    &tm.tmExternalLeading,
           TM_AVEWIDTH,   &tm.tmAveCharWidth,
           TM_MAXWIDTH,   &tm.tmMaxCharWidth,
           TM_WEIGHT,     &tm.tmWeight,
           TM_OVER,       &tm.tmOverhang,
           TM_DIGX,       &tm.tmDigitizedAspectX,
           TM_DIGY,       &tm.tmDigitizedAspectY
           } ;
      static char    *szFamily [] = { "Don't Care", "Roman",  "Swiss",
                                    "Modern",      "Script", "Decorative" } ;
      BOOL           bTrans ;
      char           szFaceName [LF_FACESIZE] ;
```

(continued)

```
HDC          hdc ;
HFONT        hFont ;
short        i ;

lf.lfHeight    = GetDlgItemInt (hDlg, IDD_HEIGHT, &bTrans, TRUE) ;
lf.lfWidth     = GetDlgItemInt (hDlg, IDD_WIDTH,  &bTrans, FALSE) ;
lf.lfWeight    = GetDlgItemInt (hDlg, IDD_WEIGHT, &bTrans, FALSE) ;

lf.lfItalic    = (BYTE) (IsDlgButtonChecked (hDlg, IDD_ITALIC) ? 1 : 0) ;
lf.lfUnderline = (BYTE) (IsDlgButtonChecked (hDlg, IDD_UNDER)  ? 1 : 0) ;
lf.lfStrikeOut = (BYTE) (IsDlgButtonChecked (hDlg, IDD_STRIKE) ? 1 : 0) ;

GetDlgItemText (hDlg, IDD_FACE, lf.lfFaceName, LF_FACESIZE) ;

dwAspectMatch = IsDlgButtonChecked (hDlg, IDD_ASPECT) ? 1L : 0L ;

hdc = GetDC (hDlg) ;
MySetMapMode (hdc) ;
SetMapperFlags (hdc, dwAspectMatch) ;

hFont = SelectObject (hdc, CreateFontIndirect (&lf)) ;
GetTextMetrics (hdc, &tm) ;
GetTextFace (hdc, sizeof szFaceName, szFaceName) ;

DeleteObject (SelectObject (hdc, hFont)) ;
ReleaseDC (hDlg, hdc) ;

for (i = 0 ; i < sizeof shorts / sizeof shorts [0] ; i++)
     SetDlgItemInt (hDlg, shorts[i].nDlgID, *shorts[i].pData, TRUE) ;

SetDlgItemText (hDlg, TM_PITCH, tm.tmPitchAndFamily & 1 ?
                                        "VARIABLE":"FIXED") ;

SetDlgItemText (hDlg, TM_FAMILY, szFamily [tm.tmPitchAndFamily >> 4]) ;
SetDlgItemText (hDlg, TM_CHARSET, tm.tmCharSet ? "OEM" : "ANSI") ;
SetDlgItemText (hDlg, TF_NAME, szFaceName) ;
}

BOOL FAR PASCAL DlgProc (HWND hDlg, WORD message, WORD wParam, LONG lParam)
     {
     switch (message)
         {
         case WM_INITDIALOG :
             CheckRadioButton (hDlg, IDD_TEXT,   IDD_LTWPS,  IDD_TEXT) ;
             CheckRadioButton (hDlg, IDD_ANSI,   IDD_OEM,    IDD_ANSI) ;
             CheckRadioButton (hDlg, IDD_QDRAFT, IDD_QPROOF, IDD_QDRAFT) ;
             CheckRadioButton (hDlg, IDD_PDEF,   IDD_PVAR,   IDD_PDEF) ;
             CheckRadioButton (hDlg, IDD_DONT,   IDD_DEC,    IDD_DONT) ;

             lf.lfEscapement  = 0 ;
             lf.lfOrientation = 0 ;
```

(continued)

```
             lf.lfOutPrecision  = OUT_DEFAULT_PRECIS ;
             lf.lfClipPrecision = CLIP_DEFAULT_PRECIS ;

          ShowMetrics (hDlg) ;
                                   /* fall through */
     case WM_SETFOCUS :
          SetFocus (GetDlgItem (hDlg, IDD_HEIGHT)) ;
          return FALSE ;

     case WM_COMMAND :
          switch (wParam)
               {
               case IDD_TEXT :
               case IDD_LOMET :
               case IDD_HIMET :
               case IDD_LOENG :
               case IDD_HIENG :
               case IDD_TWIPS :
               case IDD_LTWPS :
                    CheckRadioButton (hDlg, IDD_TEXT, IDD_LTWPS, wParam) ;
                    nMapMode = wParam ;
                    break ;

               case IDD_ASPECT :
               case IDD_ITALIC :
               case IDD_UNDER :
               case IDD_STRIKE :
                    CheckDlgButton (hDlg, wParam,
                         IsDlgButtonChecked (hDlg, wParam) ? 0 : 1) ;
                    break ;

               case IDD_ANSI :
               case IDD_OEM :
                    CheckRadioButton (hDlg, IDD_ANSI, IDD_OEM, wParam) ;
                    lf.lfCharSet = (BYTE) (wParam == IDD_ANSI ? 0 : 255) ;
                    break ;

               case IDD_QDRAFT :
               case IDD_QDEF :
               case IDD_QPROOF :
                    CheckRadioButton (hDlg, IDD_QDRAFT, IDD_QPROOF,
                                                              wParam) ;
                    lf.lfQuality = (BYTE) (wParam - IDD_QDRAFT) ;
                    break ;

               case IDD_PDEF :
               case IDD_PFIXED :
               case IDD_PVAR :
                    CheckRadioButton (hDlg, IDD_PDEF, IDD_PVAR, wParam) ;
                    lf.lfPitchAndFamily &= 0xF0 ;
```

(continued)

673

```
                               lf.lfPitchAndFamily |= (BYTE) (wParam - IDD_PDEF) ;
                               break ;
                    case IDD_DONT :
                    case IDD_ROMAN :
                    case IDD_SWISS :
                    case IDD_MODERN :
                    case IDD_SCRIPT :
                    case IDD_DEC :
                         CheckRadioButton (hDlg, IDD_DONT, IDD_DEC, wParam) ;
                         lf.lfPitchAndFamily &= 0x0F ;
                         lf.lfPitchAndFamily |= (BYTE) (wParam-IDD_DONT << 4) ;
                         break ;

                    case IDD_OK :
                         ShowMetrics (hDlg) ;
                         InvalidateRect (GetParent (hDlg), NULL, TRUE) ;
                         break ;
                    }
               break ;

          default :
               return FALSE ;
          }
     return TRUE ;
     }

long FAR PASCAL WndProc (HWND hwnd, WORD message, WORD wParam, LONG lParam)
     {
     static char  szText [] =
                    "AaBbCcDdEeFfGgHhIiJjKkLlMmNnOoPqQqRrSsTtUuVvWwXxYyZz" ;
     static short cxClient, cyClient ;
     HANDLE       hInstance ;
     HDC          hdc ;
     HFONT        hFont ;
     FARPROC      lpfnDlgProc ;
     PAINTSTRUCT  ps ;
     RECT         rect ;

     switch (message)
          {
          case WM_CREATE :
               hInstance = ((LPCREATESTRUCT) lParam)->hInstance ;
               lpfnDlgProc = MakeProcInstance (DlgProc, hInstance) ;
               hDlg = CreateDialog (hInstance, szAppName, hwnd, lpfnDlgProc) ;
               return 0 ;

          case WM_SETFOCUS :
               SetFocus (hDlg) ;
               return 0 ;
```

(continued)

```
        case WM_PAINT :
            hdc = BeginPaint (hwnd, &ps) ;
            MySetMapMode (hdc) ;
            SetMapperFlags (hdc, dwAspectMatch) ;
            GetClientRect (hDlg, &rect) ;
            rect.bottom += 1 ;
            DPtoLP (hdc, (LPPOINT) &rect, 2) ;

            hFont = SelectObject (hdc, CreateFontIndirect (&lf)) ;

            TextOut (hdc, rect.left, rect.bottom, szText, 52) ;

            DeleteObject (SelectObject (hdc, hFont)) ;
            EndPaint (hwnd, &ps) ;
            return 0 ;

        case WM_DESTROY :
            PostQuitMessage (0) ;
            return 0 ;
        }
    return DefWindowProc (hwnd, message, wParam, lParam) ;
    }
```

PICKFONT.RC

```
/*-----------------------------
   PICKFONT.RC resource script
 -----------------------------*/

#include <windows.h>
#include "pickfont.h"

#define GT (WS_GROUP | WS_TABSTOP)
#define GR (WS_GROUP)
#define TA (WS_TABSTOP)

PickFont DIALOG 0, 0, 320, 170
    STYLE WS_CHILD | WS_BORDER | WS_VISIBLE | DS_ABSALIGN
    {
    LTEXT         "&Height"         -1,          6,   8,  30,  8
    EDITTEXT                        IDD_HEIGHT,  36,  6,  30, 12
    LTEXT         "&Width"          -1,          6,  24,  30,  8
    EDITTEXT                        IDD_WIDTH,   36, 22,  30, 12
    LTEXT         "Weigh&t"         -1,          6,  40,  30,  8
    EDITTEXT                        IDD_WEIGHT,  36, 38,  30, 12
    GROUPBOX      "&Mapping Mode"   -1,          70,  2, 116, 60
    RADIOBUTTON   "Text"            IDD_TEXT,    74, 12,  50, 12, GT
```

(continued)

```
RADIOBUTTON     "Lo Metric"        IDD_LOMET,     74,  24,  50,  12
RADIOBUTTON     "Hi Metric"        IDD_HIMET,     74,  36,  50,  12
RADIOBUTTON     "Lo English"       IDD_LOENG,    130,  12,  54,  12
RADIOBUTTON     "Hi English"       IDD_HIENG,    130,  24,  52,  12
RADIOBUTTON     "Twips"            IDD_TWIPS,    130,  36,  52,  12
RADIOBUTTON     "'Logical Twips'", IDD_LTWPS,     74,  48,  80,  12
CHECKBOX        "Match &Aspect"    IDD_ASPECT,     6,  52,  60,  12, GT
CHECKBOX        "&Italic"          IDD_ITALIC,     6,  64,  60,  12, GT
CHECKBOX        "&Underline"       IDD_UNDER,      6,  76,  60,  12, GT
CHECKBOX        "&Strike-Out"      IDD_STRIKE,     6,  88,  60,  12, GT
GROUPBOX        "&Char Set"        -1,            70,  66,  52,  36, GR
RADIOBUTTON     "ANSI"             IDD_ANSI,      74,  76,  28,  12, GT
RADIOBUTTON     "OEM"              IDD_OEM,       74,  88,  28,  12
GROUPBOX        "&Quality"         -1,             4, 102,  62,  48, GR
RADIOBUTTON     "Draft"            IDD_QDRAFT,     8, 112,  42,  12, GT
RADIOBUTTON     "Default"          IDD_QDEF,       8, 124,  40,  12
RADIOBUTTON     "Proof"            IDD_QPROOF,     8, 136,  42,  12
GROUPBOX        "&Pitch"           -1,            70, 102,  52,  48, GR
RADIOBUTTON     "Default"          IDD_PDEF,      74, 112,  46,  12, GT
RADIOBUTTON     "Fixed"            IDD_PFIXED,    74, 124,  46,  12
RADIOBUTTON     "Variable"         IDD_PVAR,      74, 136,  46,  12
GROUPBOX        "&Family"          -1,           126,  66,  60,  84, GR
RADIOBUTTON     "Don't Care"       IDD_DONT,     130,  76,  54,  12, GT
RADIOBUTTON     "Roman"            IDD_ROMAN,    130,  88,  54,  12
RADIOBUTTON     "Swiss"            IDD_SWISS,    130, 100,  54,  12
RADIOBUTTON     "Modern"           IDD_MODERN,   130, 112,  54,  12
RADIOBUTTON     "Script"           IDD_SCRIPT,   130, 124,  54,  12
RADIOBUTTON     "Decorative"       IDD_DEC,      130, 136,  52,  12
LTEXT           "Face &Name"       -1,             4, 154,  42,   8
EDITTEXT                           IDD_FACE,      48, 152,  74,  14
DEFPUSHBUTTON   "&Ok"              IDD_OK,       126, 152,  60,  14, GT
GROUPBOX        "Text Metrics"     -1,           192,   2, 110, 164, GR
LTEXT           "Height:"          -1,           200,  14,  44,   8
LTEXT           "Ascent:"          -1,           200,  24,  44,   8
LTEXT           "Descent:"         -1,           200,  34,  46,   8
LTEXT           "Int Lead:"        -1,           200,  44,  44,   8
LTEXT           "Ext Lead:"        -1,           200,  54,  44,   8
LTEXT           "Ave Width:"       -1,           200,  64,  44,   8
LTEXT           "Max Width:"       -1,           200,  74,  44,   8
LTEXT           "Weight:"          -1,           200,  84,  44,   8
LTEXT           "Pitch:"           -1,           200,  94,  44,   8
LTEXT           "Family:"          -1,           200, 104,  42,   8
LTEXT           "Char Set:"        -1,           200, 114,  44,   8
LTEXT           "Overhang:"        -1,           200, 124,  44,   8
LTEXT           "X Aspect:"        -1,           200, 134,  44,   8
LTEXT           "Y Aspect:"        -1,           200, 144,  44,   8
LTEXT           "Face Name:"       -1,           200, 154,  44,   8
RTEXT           "0"                TM_HEIGHT,    250,  14,  44,   8
RTEXT           "0"                TM_ASCENT,    250,  24,  44,   8
RTEXT           "0"                TM_DESCENT,   250,  34,  44,   8
```

(continued)

```
    RTEXT        "0"        TM_EXTLEAD,  250,  54,  44,   8
    RTEXT        "0"        TM_INTLEAD,  250,  44,  44,   8
    RTEXT        "0"        TM_AVEWIDTH, 250,  64,  44,   8
    RTEXT        "0"        TM_MAXWIDTH, 250,  74,  44,   8
    RTEXT        "0"        TM_WEIGHT,   250,  84,  44,   8
    RTEXT        ""         TM_PITCH,    250,  94,  44,   8
    RTEXT        ""         TM_FAMILY,   250, 104,  44,   8
    RTEXT        ""         TM_CHARSET,  250, 114,  44,   8
    RTEXT        "0"        TM_OVER,     250, 124,  44,   8
    RTEXT        "0"        TM_DIGX,     250, 134,  44,   8
    RTEXT        "0"        TM_DIGY,     250, 144,  44,   8
    RTEXT        ""         TF_NAME,     250, 154,  44,   8
    }
```

PICKFONT.H

```
/*-----------------------
    PICKFONT.H header file
   ------------------------*/

#define IDD_OK         1
#define IDD_HEIGHT    10
#define IDD_WIDTH     11
#define IDD_WEIGHT    12
#define IDD_ITALIC    13
#define IDD_UNDER     14
#define IDD_STRIKE    15
#define IDD_ASPECT    16
#define IDD_TEXT      17
#define IDD_LOMET     18
#define IDD_HIMET     19
#define IDD_LOENG     20
#define IDD_HIENG     21
#define IDD_TWIPS     22
#define IDD_LTWPS     23
#define IDD_ANSI      24
#define IDD_OEM       25
#define IDD_QDRAFT    26
#define IDD_QDEF      27
#define IDD_QPROOF    28
#define IDD_PDEF      29
#define IDD_PFIXED    30
#define IDD_PVAR      31
#define IDD_DONT      32
#define IDD_ROMAN     33
#define IDD_SWISS     34
#define IDD_MODERN    35
```

(continued)

```
#define IDD_SCRIPT      36
#define IDD_DEC         37
#define IDD_FACE        38
#define TM_HEIGHT       39
#define TM_ASCENT       40
#define TM_DESCENT      41
#define TM_INTLEAD      42
#define TM_EXTLEAD      43
#define TM_AVEWIDTH     44
#define TM_MAXWIDTH     45
#define TM_WEIGHT       46
#define TM_PITCH        47
#define TM_FAMILY       48
#define TM_CHARSET      49
#define TM_OVER         50
#define TM_DIGX         51
#define TM_DIGY         52
#define TF_NAME         53
```

PICKFONT.DEF

```
;------------------------------------
; PICKFONT.DEF module definition file
;------------------------------------

NAME            PICKFONT

DESCRIPTION     'Font Picker Program (c) Charles Petzold, 1990'
EXETYPE         WINDOWS
STUB            'WINSTUB.EXE'
CODE            PRELOAD MOVEABLE DISCARDABLE
DATA            PRELOAD MOVEABLE MULTIPLE
HEAPSIZE        1024
STACKSIZE       8192
EXPORTS         WndProc
                DlgProc
```

Figure 14-6 shows a typical PICKFONT screen. The left side of the PICKFONT display is a modeless dialog box that allows you to select most of the fields of the logical font structure. The right side shows the results of *GetTextMetrics* after the font is selected into the device context. A sample line of text using this font appears at the bottom of the screen.

The modeless dialog box also contains some options that are not part of the logical font structure. These are the mapping mode (including my "Logical Twips" mapping mode) and the "Match Aspect" option, which changes the way Windows matches a logical font to a real font.

Much of the PICKFONT program contains the logic necessary to maintain the dialog box, so I won't go into detail on the workings of the program. Instead, I'll explain what you're doing when you create and select a logical font.

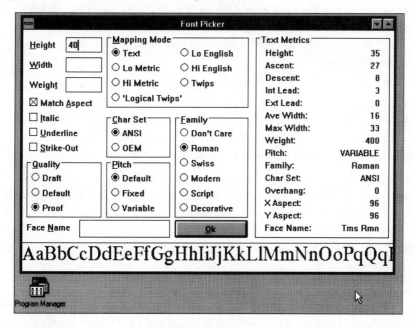

Figure 14-6. *A typical PICKFONT display.*

The Logical Font Structure

As I mentioned, the best way to create a logical font is to first define a structure of type LOGFONT:

```
LOGFONT logfont ;
```

When you call *CreateFontIndirect*, you give Windows a pointer to this structure:

```
hFont = CreateFontIndirect (&logfont) ;
```

The 14 fields of this structure are the same as the 14 parameters to *CreateFont*.

You don't need to set each and every field of the LOGFONT structure. If your logical font structure is defined as a static variable, it will be initialized to 0. The 0 values are defaults. You can use that structure directly without any changes, and *CreateFontIndirect* will return a handle to a font. When you select that font into the device context, you'll get a reasonable default font. You can be as specific or as vague as you want in the LOGFONT structure, and Windows will attempt to match your requests with a real font.

The first two fields of the LOGFONT structure are in logical units, so they depend on the current setting of the mapping mode:

- *lfHeight* (short integer)—This is the desired height of the characters (including internal leading but not external leading) in logical units. Because the point size of the font itself is the height of the font less internal leading, you're really specifying a line spacing here. You can set it to 0 for a default size. If you set *lfHeight* to a negative number, Windows treats the absolute value of that number as a desired ascent size rather than as a full height.

- *lfWidth* (short integer)—This is the desired width of the characters in logical units. In most cases you'll want to set this to 0 and let Windows choose a font based on the height. If you use a nonzero value, Windows might be forced to use a font designed for an aspect ratio different from that of the device context into which you later select the font.

The next two fields specify the "escapement" and "orientation" of the text. In theory, *lfEscapement* allows character strings to be written at an angle, and *lfOrientation* allows characters to be tilted. These two fields are not included in the PICKFONT program, however, because they currently don't work well on the screen. Before you try to use these on a device, you should use the TEXTCAPS index to *GetDeviceCaps* to check the device's ability to do character rotation.

- *lfEscapement* (short integer)—This is an angle in tenths of a degree, measured from the horizontal in a counterclockwise direction. It specifies the placement of the string when you write text with *TextOut*. Here are some examples:

Value	Placement of Characters
0	Run from left to right (default)
900	Go up
1800	Run from right to left
2700	Go down

- *lfOrientation* (short integer)—This is an angle in tenths of a degree, measured from the horizontal in a counterclockwise direction. It specifies the appearance of each character. Here are some examples:

Value	Character Appearance
0	Normal (default)
900	Tipped 90 degrees to the left
1800	Upside down
2700	Tipped 90 degrees to the right

The remaining 10 fields follow:

- *lfWeight* (short integer)—This field allows you to specify boldface. Currently, there are only two recommended values:

Value	Result
400	Normal
700	Boldface

In actuality, any value from 0 to 550 is normal, and any value greater than 550 is boldface. If you like to plan for the future, WINDOWS.H has a collection of font weight identifiers:

Value	Identifier
0	FW_DONTCARE
100	FW_THIN
200	FW_EXTRALIGHT or FW_ULTRALIGHT
300	FW_LIGHT
400	FW_NORMAL or FW_REGULAR
500	FW_MEDIUM
600	FW_SEMIBOLD or FW_DEMIBOLD
700	FW_BOLD
800	FW_EXTRABOLD or FW_ULTRABOLD
900	FW_HEAVY or FW_BLACK

- *lfItalic* (BYTE)—When nonzero, this specifies italics. Windows can synthesize italics on GDI fonts. To determine what a particular device can do with a device font, check the TC_IA_ABLE bit of the TEXTCAPS value returned from *GetDeviceCaps*.

- *lfUnderline* (BYTE)—When nonzero, this specifies underlining, which is synthesized on GDI fonts. For device fonts, check the TC_UA_ABLE bit from *GetDeviceCaps*.

- *lfStrikeOut* (BYTE)—When nonzero, this specifies that the font should have a line drawn through the characters. This also is synthesized on GDI fonts. For device fonts, check the TC_SO_ABLE bit.

- *lfCharSet* (BYTE)—This is the character set of the font. WINDOWS.H currently contains three identifiers for the character set:

Value	Identifier
0	ANSI_CHARSET
2	SYMBOL_CHARSET
128	SHIFTJIS_CHARSET (Japanese Kanji)
255	OEM_CHARSET

Note: The Kanji character sets are not, of course, included with American or Western European releases of Windows.

■ *lfOutPrecision* (BYTE)—This specifies how Windows should attempt to match the desired font sizes and characteristics with actual fonts. This field is not yet implemented and is not included in the PICKFONT program. WINDOWS.H contains four identifiers for the field:

Value	Identifier
0	OUT_DEFAULT_PRECIS
1	OUT_STRING_PRECIS
2	OUT_CHARACTER_PRECIS
3	OUT_STROKE_PRECIS

■ *lfClipPrecision* (BYTE)—This specifies how to clip characters that are partly outside the clipping region. The field is not included in the PICKFONTS program. WINDOWS.H contains three identifiers:

Value	Identifier
0	CLIP_DEFAULT_PRECIS
1	CLIP_CHARACTER_PRECIS
2	CLIP_STROKE_PRECIS

■ *lfQuality* (BYTE)—This is actually an instruction to Windows regarding the matching of a desired font with a real font. You can use three identifiers:

Value	Identifier
0	DEFAULT_QUALITY
1	DRAFT_QUALITY
2	PROOF_QUALITY

If you specify PROOF_QUALITY, you're telling Windows that you don't want a font to be increased to a larger size to match the character height or width that you request. The PROOF_QUALITY fonts are the most attractive, but they may be smaller than what you request.

- *lfPitchAndFamily* (BYTE)—This byte is composed of two parts. You can use the C OR operator to combine two identifiers for this field. The lowest two bits specify the pitch of the font:

Value	Identifier
0	DEFAULT_PITCH
1	FIXED_PITCH
2	VARIABLE_PITCH

If you specify FIXED_PITCH, Windows will pick a font that has a fixed pitch, because you're essentially telling Windows that your program can't deal with variable-pitch fonts.

The upper half of this byte specifies the font family:

Value	Identifier
0x00	FF_DONTCARE
0x10	FF_ROMAN
0x20	FF_SWISS
0x30	FF_MODERN
0x40	FF_SCRIPT
0x50	FF_DECORATIVE

- *lfFaceName* (BYTE array)—This is the name of a typeface (such as Courier, Helv, or Tms Rmn). WINDOWS.H includes a LF_FACESIZE identifier that equals 32, which is the maximum number of characters allowed for the typeface name.

The Font-Mapping Algorithm

After you set up the logical font structure, you call *CreateFontIndirect* to get a handle to the logical font. When you use *SelectObject* to select that logical font into a device context, Windows finds the real font that most closely matches the request. In doing so, it uses a "font-mapping algorithm." Certain fields of the structure are more important than other fields.

The best way to get a feel for font mapping is to spend an hour or so experimenting with PICKFONT. Here are some general guidelines:

■ The *lfCharSet* (character set) field is very important. For the display, if you specify OEM_CHARSET, you'll get either one of the stroke fonts or the terminal font, because these are the only fonts that do not use the ANSI character set. You have to use OEM_CHARSET if you want a GDI stroke font. A value of ANSI_CHARSET always gives you a raster font.

■ A pitch value of FIXED_PITCH (in the *lfPitchAndFamily* field) is important, because you are in effect telling Windows that you don't want to deal with a variable-pitch font.

■ The *lfFaceName* field is important, because you're being specific about the typeface of the font that you want. If you leave *lfFaceName* set to NULL and set the *lfFamily* field to a value other than FF_DONTCARE, then the latter field becomes important, because you're being specific about the font family.

■ Windows will attempt to match the *lfHeight* value even if it needs to increase the size of a smaller font. The height of the actual font will always be less than or equal to that of the requested font unless there is no font small enough to satisfy your request.

■ You can prevent Windows from scaling a font by setting *lfQuality* to PROOF_QUALITY. By doing so, you're telling Windows that the requested height of the font is less important than the appearance of the font.

■ If you specify *lfHeight* and *lfWidth* values that are out of line for the particular aspect ratio of the display, Windows can map to a font that is designed for a display or other device of a different aspect ratio. You can use this trick to get a particularly thin or fat font. In general, however, you'll probably want to avoid this situation, which you do in PICKFONT by clicking the check box marked Match Aspect. PICKFONT makes a call to *SetMapperFlags* with a flag set to 1:

```
SetMapperFlags (hdc, 1L) ;
```

This specifies that Windows should only match fonts that have the same aspect ratio as the display. You can get fonts of other aspect ratios by setting the mapper flag back to the default value:

```
SetMapperFlags (hdc, 0L) ;
```

If you don't like the way that Windows weights these various characteristics of the logical font to match a real font, you can change them all using the *SetFontMapperFlags* function.

Finding Out About the Font

At the right side of its client area, PICKFONT shows you the type of information you can obtain after you select the logical font into the device context. *GetTextMetrics* tells you the real characteristics of the font, and *GetTextFace* tells you the typeface name.

To obtain the typeface name, you first define a character array to receive the name:

```
char szFaceName [LF_FACESIZE] ;
```

The LF_FACESIZE identifier is the maximum number of characters in the typeface name. You then tell Windows to copy the typeface name into this array:

```
GetTextFace (hdc, sizeof szFaceName, szFaceName) ;
```

The *GetTextMetrics* function retrieves information on the size and other characteristics of the font currently selected in the device context:

```
TEXTMETRIC    tm ;
      [other program lines]
GetTextMetrics (hdc, &tm) ;
```

All the size values that Windows copies into the TEXTMETRIC structure are in logical units except for the digitized aspect ratios. The fields of the TEXTMETRIC structure are as follows:

- *tmHeight* (short integer)—The height of the character in logical units. This is the value that should approximate the *lfHeight* field specified in the LOGFONT structure. It is the sum of the *tmAscent* and *tmDescent* fields. Like the *lfHeight* field in the LOGFONT structure, it actually represents the line spacing of the font rather than the size, because it includes internal leading.

- *tmAscent* (short integer)—The height of the character above the baseline in logical units. This should approximate the absolute value of the *lfHeight* field in the LOGFONT structure if *lfHeight* is set to a negative value.

- *tmDescent* (short integer)—The height of the character below the baseline in logical units.

- *tmInternalLeading* (short integer)—The area used for diacritics on some capital letters. As noted above, the actual internal leading is included in the *tmHeight* value. You can calculate the point size of the font by subtracting the *tmInternalLeading* value from the *tmHeight* value.

- *tmExternalLeading* (short integer)—An additional amount of line spacing (beyond *tmHeight*) recommended by the designer of the font.

- *tmAveCharWidth* (short integer)—The average width of the characters in logical units.

- *tmMaxCharWidth* (short integer)—The width of the widest character in logical units. This value is the same as *tmAveCharWidth* for a fixed-pitch font.

- *tmWeight* (short integer)—The weight of the font, ranging from 0 to 999. Currently, it will be set to either 400 (normal) or 700 (boldface).

- *tmItalic* (BYTE)—Nonzero for an italic font.

- *tmUnderlined* (BYTE)—Nonzero for an underlined font.

- *tmStruckOut* (BYTE)—Nonzero for a strikethrough font.

- *tmPitchAndFamily* (BYTE)—A value comprising the pitch in the lower two bits and the family in the higher four bits. This field is coded in the same way as the *lfPitchAndFamily* field in the LOGFONT structure, and you can use the same identifiers to extract the information.

- *tmCharSet* (BYTE)—The character set. Under most circumstances, it will be either 0 (ANSI_CHARSET) or 255 (OEM_CHARSET).

- *tmOverhang* (short integer)—The amount of extra width (in logical units) that Windows adds to a character when synthesizing italic or boldface. When a font is italicized, the *tmAveCharWidth* value remains unchanged, because a string of italicized characters has the same overall width as the same string of normal characters. For boldfacing, Windows must slightly expand the width of each character. For a boldfaced font, the *tmAveCharWidth* value less the *tmOverhang* value equals the *tmAveCharWidth* value for the same font without boldfacing.

- *tmDigitizedAspectX* and *tmDigitizedAspectY* (short integers)—The aspect ratio for which the font is appropriate. If you specify Proof (under Quality) and check Match Aspect in PICKFONT, then for most devices these values will be equivalent to the pixels-per-logical-inch values returned from *GetDeviceCaps*. Note, however, that these two TEXTMETRIC fields are switched around in relation to the corresponding *GetDeviceCaps* parameters: *tmDigitizedAspectX* is equivalent to the *GetDeviceCaps* value for the LOGPIXELSY parameter, and *tmDigitizedAspectY* is equivalent to the value for LOGPIXELSX. If the font is scaled to a larger size, then the *tmDigitizedAspectX* and *tmDigitizedAspectY* values increase accordingly.

Because of space restrictions, the following four fields were not included in the display screen of the PICKFONTS program:

- *tmFirstChar* (BYTE)—The character code of the first character in the font. For ANSI_CHARSET fonts, this is normally 32, the space character.

- *tmLastChar* (BYTE)—The character code of the last character in the font. For ANSI_CHARSET fonts, this is normally 255.

- *tmDefaultChar* (BYTE)—The character that Windows uses to display characters that are not in the font. For ANSI_CHARSET fonts, this is normally 128.

- *tmBreakChar* (BYTE)—The character that Windows (and your programs) should use to determine word breaks when justifying text. For ANSI_CHARSET fonts, this is normally 32, the space character.

ENUMERATING THE FONTS

Earlier in the chapter, I covered the particular typefaces and sizes that are available when you're writing a program to display text on the screen. If you want to send this text to a printer, however, how do you know which fonts the printer has? The Windows WRITE program knows. When you change the current printer, Write often comes up with a different list of typeface names and sizes that you can choose from. The function that lets WRITE do this is *EnumFonts*. *EnumFonts* uses a call-back function that Windows calls once for each typeface or font that is available on the device.

You use *EnumFonts* in one of two ways. The first requires that the second parameter be NULL:

```
EnumFonts (hdc, NULL, lpfnEnumFunction, lpData) ;
```

The *lpfnEnumFunction* parameter is a pointer to the call-back function. *EnumFonts* calls this call-back function once for each typeface name available on the device indicated by the *hdc* parameter. Normally, you use *EnumFonts* this way first to get a list of all typefaces supported by the device.

After you have the list of typeface names, you can call *EnumFonts* once for each typeface:

```
EnumFonts (hdc, szTypeFace, lpfnEnumFunction, lpData) ;
```

For each call you make to *EnumFonts* in this format, Windows calls *EnumFunction* once for each available size of the particular typeface.

The call-back function has the format:

```
short FAR PASCAL EnumFunction (lplf, lptm, nFontType, lpData)
    LOGFONT    far *lf ;
    TEXTMETRIC far *lptm ;
    short          nFontType ;
    LPSTR          lpData ;
    {
         [other program lines]
    return 1 ;
    }
```

The function must be listed in the EXPORTS section of the module definition (.DEF) file, and you must obtain a pointer to the function with *MakeProcInstance*:

```
FARPROC    lpfnEnumFunction ;
    [other program lines]
lpfnEnumFunction = MakeProcInstance (EnumFunction, hInstance) ;
```

The call-back function receives a far pointer to the particular LOGFONT structure that you can use to create this particular font, a far pointer to the TEXTMETRIC structure that will be obtained when you select this font into the device context, a short integer that indicates the type (raster or stroke) of the font, and a pointer to programmer-supplied data specified in the *EnumFonts* call. (This last parameter simply provides a clean way of passing information to the call-back function without using global data.)

The lower two bits of the *nFontType* parameter to the *EnumFunction* call-back function indicate the type of the font:

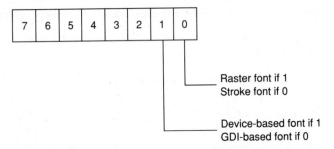

You can use the identifiers RASTER_FONTTYPE (which equals 1) to determine if the font is raster or stroke and DEVICE_FONTTYPE (which equals 2) to determine if the font is device or GDI. Windows will continue calling the call-back function until all the fonts are enumerated or until the function returns a 0.

The FONTLIST program, shown in Figure 14-7, uses *EnumFonts* to obtain the fonts available on either the display or the current printer. If no printer is available, then *Enum-Fonts* displays nothing when the Printer option is selected from the menu.

FONTLIST.MAK

```
#----------------------
# FONTLIST.MAK make file
#----------------------

fontlist.exe : fontlist.obj fontlist.def fontlist.res
    link fontlist, /align:16, NUL, /nod slibcew libw, fontlist
    rc fontlist.res

fontlist.obj : fontlist.c fontlist.h
    cl -c -Gsw -Ow -W2 -Zp fontlist.c

fontlist.res : fontlist.rc fontlist.h
    rc -r fontlist.rc
```

FONTLIST.C

```
/*--------------------------------------------
   FONTLIST.C -- Font Enumeration Program
                 (c) Charles Petzold, 1990
   --------------------------------------------*/

#include <windows.h>
#include <string.h>
#include "fontlist.h"

typedef struct
    {
    GLOBALHANDLE hGMem ;
    short        nCount ;
    }
    ENUMER ;

typedef struct
    {
    short       nFontType ;
    LOGFONT     lf ;
    TEXTMETRIC  tm ;
    }
    FONT ;
```

Figure 14-7. *The FONTLIST program.*

(continued)

```
long FAR PASCAL WndProc (HWND, WORD, WORD, LONG) ;
int  FAR PASCAL EnumAllFaces (LPLOGFONT, LPTEXTMETRIC, short, ENUMER FAR *) ;
int  FAR PASCAL EnumAllFonts (LPLOGFONT, LPTEXTMETRIC, short, ENUMER FAR *) ;

char szAppName[] = "FontList" ;

int PASCAL WinMain (HANDLE hInstance, HANDLE hPrevInstance,
                    LPSTR lpszCmdLine, int nCmdShow)
      {
      HWND     hwnd ;
      MSG      msg ;
      WNDCLASS wndclass ;

      if (!hPrevInstance)
          {
          wndclass.style         = CS_HREDRAW : CS_VREDRAW ;
          wndclass.lpfnWndProc   = WndProc ;
          wndclass.cbClsExtra    = 0 ;
          wndclass.cbWndExtra    = 0 ;
          wndclass.hInstance     = hInstance ;
          wndclass.hIcon         = LoadIcon (NULL, IDI_APPLICATION) ;
          wndclass.hCursor       = LoadCursor (NULL, IDC_ARROW) ;
          wndclass.hbrBackground = GetStockObject (WHITE_BRUSH) ;
          wndclass.lpszMenuName  = szAppName ;
          wndclass.lpszClassName = szAppName ;

          RegisterClass (&wndclass) ;
          }
      hwnd = CreateWindow (szAppName, "Font Enumeration",
                           WS_OVERLAPPEDWINDOW : WS_VSCROLL,
                           CW_USEDEFAULT, CW_USEDEFAULT,
                           CW_USEDEFAULT, CW_USEDEFAULT,
                           NULL, NULL, hInstance, NULL) ;

      ShowWindow (hwnd, nCmdShow) ;
      UpdateWindow (hwnd) ;

      while (GetMessage (&msg, NULL, 0, 0))
          {
          TranslateMessage (&msg) ;
          DispatchMessage  (&msg) ;
          }
      return msg.wParam ;
      }

int FAR PASCAL EnumAllFaces (LPLOGFONT lf, LPTEXTMETRIC tm,
                             short nFontType, ENUMER FAR *enumer)
      {
      LPSTR lpFaces ;
```

(continued)

```
         if (NULL == GlobalReAlloc (enumer->hGMem,
                          (DWORD) LF_FACESIZE * (1 + enumer->nCount),
                          GMEM_MOVEABLE))
              return 0 ;

         lpFaces = GlobalLock (enumer->hGMem) ;
         lstrcpy (lpFaces + enumer->nCount * LF_FACESIZE, lf->lfFaceName) ;
         GlobalUnlock (enumer->hGMem) ;
         enumer->nCount ++ ;
         return 1 ;
         }

int FAR PASCAL EnumAllFonts (LPLOGFONT lf, LPTEXTMETRIC tm,
                              short nFontType, ENUMER FAR *enumer)
         {
         FONT FAR *font ;

         if (NULL == GlobalReAlloc (enumer->hGMem,
                          (DWORD) sizeof (FONT) * (1 + enumer->nCount),
                          GMEM_MOVEABLE))
              return 0 ;

         font = (FONT FAR *) GlobalLock (enumer->hGMem) + enumer->nCount ;
         font->nFontType = nFontType ;
         font->lf = *lf ;
         font->tm = *tm ;

         GlobalUnlock (enumer->hGMem) ;
         enumer->nCount ++ ;
         return 1 ;
         }

void Display (HDC hdc, short cxChar, short cyChar, FONT FAR *font)
         {
         static FONT f ;
         static char *szYN [] = { "No",         "Yes" } ;
         static char *szCS [] = { "ANSI",       "?????",  "Kanji",    "OEM" } ;
         static char *szOP [] = { "Default",    "String", "Char",     "Stroke" } ;
         static char *szCP [] = { "Default",    "Char",   "Stroke",   "?????" } ;
         static char *szQU [] = { "Draft",      "Default","Proof",    "?????" } ;
         static char *szP1 [] = { "Default",    "Fixed",  "Variable", "?????" } ;
         static char *szP2 [] = { "Fixed",      "Variable" } ;
         static char *szFA [] = { "Don't Care", "Roman",       "Swiss", "Modern",
                                  "Script",     "Decorative", "?????", "?????" } ;
         static char *szVR [] = { "Stroke",     "Raster" } ;
         static char *szGD [] = { "GDI",        "Device" } ;
```

(continued)

```
static struct
     {
     short x ;
     short y ;
     char  *szFmt ;
     short *pData ;
     }
     shorts [] =
     {
      1,  1, "LOGFONT",              NULL,
      1,  2, "-------",              NULL,
      1,  3, "Height:       %10d",  &f.lf.lfHeight,
      1,  4, "Width:        %10d",  &f.lf.lfWidth,
      1,  5, "Escapement:   %10d",  &f.lf.lfEscapement,
      1,  6, "Orientation:  %10d",  &f.lf.lfOrientation,
      1,  7, "Weight:       %10d",  &f.lf.lfWeight,
     28,  1, "TEXTMETRIC",           NULL,
     28,  2, "----------",           NULL,
     28,  3, "Height:        %5d",  &f.tm.tmHeight,
     28,  4, "Ascent:        %5d",  &f.tm.tmAscent,
     28,  5, "Descent:       %5d",  &f.tm.tmDescent,
     28,  6, "Int. Leading: %5d",   &f.tm.tmInternalLeading,
     28,  7, "Ext. Leading: %5d",   &f.tm.tmExternalLeading,
     28,  8, "Ave. Width:    %5d",  &f.tm.tmAveCharWidth,
     28,  9, "Max. Width:    %5d",  &f.tm.tmMaxCharWidth,
     28, 10, "Weight:        %5d",  &f.tm.tmWeight,
     51, 10, "Overhang:     %10d",  &f.tm.tmOverhang,
     51, 11, "Digitized X:  %10d",  &f.tm.tmDigitizedAspectX,
     51, 12, "Digitized Y:  %10d",  &f.tm.tmDigitizedAspectY
     } ;

static struct
     {
     short x ;
     short y ;
     char  *szFmt ;
     BYTE  *pData ;
     }
     bytes [] =
     {
     51,  3, "First Char:   %10d",  &f.tm.tmFirstChar,
     51,  4, "Last Char:    %10d",  &f.tm.tmLastChar,
     51,  5, "Default Char: %10d",  &f.tm.tmDefaultChar,
     51,  6, "Break Char:   %10d",  &f.tm.tmBreakChar
     } ;

static struct
     {
     short x ;
     short y ;
```

(continued)

```
           char  *szFmt ;
           BYTE  *pData ;
           char  **szArray ;
           short sAnd ;
           short sShift ;
           }
       strings [] =
       {
         1,  8, "Italic:      %10s", &f.lf.lfItalic,          szYN, 1,    0,
         1,  9, "Underline:   %10s", &f.lf.lfUnderline,       szYN, 1,    0,
         1, 10, "Strike-Out:  %10s", &f.lf.lfStrikeOut,       szYN, 1,    0,
         1, 11, "Char Set:    %10s", &f.lf.lfCharSet,         szCS, 0xC0, 6,
         1, 12, "Out  Prec:   %10s", &f.lf.lfOutPrecision,    szOP, 3,    0,
         1, 13, "Clip Prec:   %10s", &f.lf.lfClipPrecision,   szCP, 3,    0,
         1, 14, "Quality:     %10s", &f.lf.lfQuality,         szQU, 3,    0,
         1, 15, "Pitch:       %10s", &f.lf.lfPitchAndFamily,  szP1, 3,    0,
         1, 16, "Family:      %10s", &f.lf.lfPitchAndFamily,  szFA, 0x70, 4,
        28, 11, "Italic:       %5s", &f.tm.tmItalic,          szYN, 1,    0,
        28, 12, "Underline:    %5s", &f.tm.tmUnderlined,      szYN, 1,    0,
        28, 13, "Strike-Out:   %5s", &f.tm.tmStruckOut,       szYN, 1,    0,
        51,  7, "Pitch:       %10s", &f.tm.tmPitchAndFamily,  szP2, 1,    0,
        51,  8, "Family:      %10s", &f.tm.tmPitchAndFamily,  szFA, 0x70, 4,
        51,  9, "Char Set:    %10s", &f.tm.tmCharSet,         szCS, 0xC0, 6,
        36, 15, "Font Type: %6s",    (BYTE *) &f.nFontType,   szVR, 1,    0,
        55, 15, "%s",                (BYTE *) &f.nFontType,   szGD, 2,    1
       } ;

   char szBuffer [80] ;
   int  i ;

   f = *font ;

   for (i = 0 ; i < sizeof shorts / sizeof shorts [0] ; i++)
       TextOut (hdc, cxChar * shorts[i].x, cyChar * shorts[i].y, szBuffer,
                wsprintf (szBuffer, shorts[i].szFmt,
                        *shorts[i].pData)) ;

   for (i = 0 ; i < sizeof bytes / sizeof bytes [0] ; i++)
       TextOut (hdc, cxChar * bytes[i].x, cyChar * bytes[i].y, szBuffer,
                wsprintf (szBuffer, bytes[i].szFmt,
                        *bytes[i].pData)) ;

   for (i = 0 ; i < sizeof strings / sizeof strings [0] ; i++)
       TextOut (hdc, cxChar * strings[i].x, cyChar * strings[i].y, szBuffer,
                wsprintf (szBuffer, strings[i].szFmt,
                        (LPSTR) ((strings[i].szArray)
                           [(*strings[i].pData & strings[i].sAnd) >>
                                strings[i].sShift]))) ;
```

(continued)

```
        TextOut (hdc, cxChar, cyChar * 17, szBuffer,
                wsprintf (szBuffer, "Face Name:   %10s",
                          (LPSTR) f.lf.lfFaceName)) ;
        }

HDC GetPrinterIC ()
    {
    char szPrinter [64] ;
    char *szDevice, *szDriver, *szOutput ;

    GetProfileString ("windows", "device", "", szPrinter, 64) ;

    if ((szDevice = strtok (szPrinter, "," )) &&
        (szDriver = strtok (NULL,      ", ")) &&
        (szOutput = strtok (NULL,      ", ")))

                return CreateIC (szDriver, szDevice, szOutput, NULL) ;

    return NULL ;
    }

long FAR PASCAL WndProc (HWND hwnd, WORD message, WORD wParam, LONG lParam)
    {
    static BOOL    bHaveInfo = FALSE ;
    static ENUMER  enumer1, enumer2 ;
    static FARPROC lpfnEnumAllFaces, lpfnEnumAllFonts ;
    static short   cxChar, cyChar, nCurrent ;
    static WORD    wCurrentDC = IDM_SCREEN ;
    HANDLE         hInstance ;
    HDC            hdc ;
    HFONT          hFont ;
    HMENU          hMenu ;
    FONT FAR       *font ;
    LPSTR          lpFaces ;
    PAINTSTRUCT    ps ;
    short          i ;
    TEXTMETRIC     tm ;

    switch (message)
        {
        case WM_CREATE :
            hInstance = ((LPCREATESTRUCT) lParam)-> hInstance ;
            lpfnEnumAllFaces = MakeProcInstance (EnumAllFaces, hInstance) ;
            lpfnEnumAllFonts = MakeProcInstance (EnumAllFonts, hInstance) ;

            hdc = GetDC (hwnd) ;
            SelectObject (hdc, GetStockObject (SYSTEM_FIXED_FONT)) ;
```

(continued)

694

```
            GetTextMetrics (hdc, (LPTEXTMETRIC) &tm) ;
            cxChar = tm.tmAveCharWidth ;
            cyChar = tm.tmHeight + tm.tmExternalLeading ;

            ReleaseDC (hwnd, hdc) ;
            return 0 ;

       case WM_COMMAND :
            if (wParam == IDM_EXIT)
                 {
                 SendMessage (hwnd, WM_CLOSE, 0, 0L) ;
                 return 0 ;
                 }
            else if (wParam == wCurrentDC)
                 return 0 ;

            hMenu = GetMenu (hwnd) ;
            CheckMenuItem (hMenu, wCurrentDC, MF_UNCHECKED) ;
            CheckMenuItem (hMenu, wCurrentDC = wParam, MF_CHECKED) ;

                                // fall through

       case WM_DEVMODECHANGE :
       case WM_FONTCHANGE :
            bHaveInfo = FALSE ;
            InvalidateRect (hwnd, NULL, TRUE) ;
            return 0 ;

       case WM_PAINT :
            if (!bHaveInfo)
                 {
                 if (enumer2.hGMem)
                      GlobalFree (enumer2.hGMem) ;

                 enumer1.hGMem  = GlobalAlloc (GHND, 1L) ;
                 enumer1.nCount = 0 ;

                 enumer2.hGMem  = GlobalAlloc (GHND, 1L) ;
                 enumer2.nCount = 0 ;

                 if (NULL == enumer1.hGMem || NULL == enumer2.hGMem)
                      goto MEMORY_ERROR ;

                 if (wCurrentDC == IDM_SCREEN)
                      hdc = CreateIC ("DISPLAY", NULL, NULL, NULL) ;
                 else
                      hdc = GetPrinterIC () ;
```

(continued)

695

```
            if (hdc)
                {
                if (0 == EnumFonts (hdc, NULL, lpfnEnumAllFaces,
                                           (LPSTR) &enumer1))
                    goto MEMORY_ERROR ;

                lpFaces = GlobalLock (enumer1.hGMem) ;

                for (i = 0 ; i < enumer1.nCount ; i++)
                    if (0 == EnumFonts (hdc,
                                    lpFaces + i * LF_FACESIZE,
                                    lpfnEnumAllFonts,
                                    (LPSTR) &enumer2))
                        goto MEMORY_ERROR ;

                GlobalUnlock (enumer1.hGMem) ;
                enumer2.nCount-- ;

                DeleteDC (hdc) ;
                bHaveInfo = TRUE ;
                }
            GlobalFree (enumer1.hGMem) ;
            SetScrollRange (hwnd, SB_VERT, 0, enumer2.nCount, FALSE) ;
            SetScrollPos   (hwnd, SB_VERT, nCurrent = 0, TRUE) ;
            }

    hdc = BeginPaint (hwnd, &ps) ;

    if (bHaveInfo)
        {
        SelectObject (hdc, GetStockObject (SYSTEM_FIXED_FONT)) ;

        font = (FONT FAR *) GlobalLock (enumer2.hGMem) + nCurrent ;
        Display (hdc, cxChar, cyChar, font) ;

        hFont = SelectObject (hdc, CreateFontIndirect (&font->lf)) ;

        TextOut (hdc, 1 * cxChar, 19 * cyChar,
            "AaBbCcDdEeFfGgHhIiJjKkLlMmNnOoPpQqRrSsTtUuVvWwXxYyZz",
            52) ;

        GlobalUnlock (enumer2.hGMem) ;
        DeleteObject (SelectObject (hdc, hFont)) ;
        }

    EndPaint (hwnd, &ps) ;
    return 0 ;
```

(continued)

696

```
          case WM_KEYDOWN :
               switch (wParam)
                    {
                    case VK_HOME :
                         SendMessage (hwnd, WM_VSCROLL, SB_TOP, 0L) ;
                         break ;
                    case VK_END :
                         SendMessage (hwnd, WM_VSCROLL, SB_BOTTOM, 0L) ;
                         break ;
                    case VK_LEFT :
                    case VK_UP :
                    case VK_PRIOR :
                         SendMessage (hwnd, WM_VSCROLL, SB_LINEUP, 0L) ;
                         break ;
                    case VK_RIGHT :
                    case VK_DOWN :
                    case VK_NEXT :
                         SendMessage (hwnd, WM_VSCROLL, SB_LINEDOWN, 0L) ;
                         break ;
                    default :
                         return 0 ;
                    }
               return 0 ;

          case WM_VSCROLL :
               switch (wParam)
                    {
                    case SB_TOP :
                         nCurrent = 0 ;
                         break ;
                    case SB_BOTTOM :
                         nCurrent = enumer2.nCount ;
                         break ;
                    case SB_LINEUP :
                    case SB_PAGEUP :
                         nCurrent -- ;
                         break ;
                    case SB_LINEDOWN :
                    case SB_PAGEDOWN :
                         nCurrent ++ ;
                         break ;
                    case SB_THUMBPOSITION :
                         nCurrent = LOWORD (lParam) ;
                         break ;
                    default :
                         return 0 ;
                    }
               nCurrent = min (max (0, nCurrent), enumer2.nCount) ;
               SetScrollPos (hwnd, SB_VERT, nCurrent, TRUE) ;
               InvalidateRect (hwnd, NULL, TRUE) ;
```

(continued)

697

```
                    return 0 ;

            MEMORY_ERROR :
                MessageBox (hwnd, "Cannot allocate memory, must end.",
                     szAppName, MB_OK : MB_ICONHAND : MB_SYSTEMMODAL) ;

                                        // fall through
            case WM_CLOSE :
                DestroyWindow (hwnd) ;
                return 0 ;

            case WM_DESTROY :
                PostQuitMessage (0) ;
                return 0 ;
            }
     return DefWindowProc (hwnd, message, wParam, lParam) ;
     }
```

FONTLIST.RC

```
/*-----------------------------
   FONTLIST.RC resource script
   ----------------------------*/

#include "fontlist.h"

FontList MENU
     {
     POPUP "&Device"
          {
          MENUITEM "&Screen",  IDM_SCREEN, CHECKED
          MENUITEM "&Printer", IDM_PRINTER
          MENUITEM SEPARATOR
          MENUITEM "E&xit",    IDM_EXIT
          }
     }
```

FONTLIST.H

```
/*-----------------------
   FONTLIST.H header file
   ----------------------*/

#define IDM_SCREEN  1
#define IDM_PRINTER 2
#define IDM_EXIT    3
```

FONTLIST.DEF

```
;------------------------------------
; FONTLIST.DEF module definition file
;------------------------------------

NAME            FONTLIST

DESCRIPTION     'Font Enumeration Program (c) Charles Petzold, 1990'
EXETYPE         WINDOWS
STUB            'WINSTUB.EXE'
CODE            PRELOAD MOVEABLE DISCARDABLE
DATA            PRELOAD MOVEABLE MULTIPLE
HEAPSIZE        1024
STACKSIZE       8192
EXPORTS         WndProc
                EnumAllFaces
                EnumAllFonts
```

FONTLIST uses two separate call-back functions to enumerate the fonts. The first, called *EnumAllFaces*, accumulates the typeface names. The second, *EnumAllFonts*, accumulates all the sizes for each typeface name. The program uses global memory blocks to store this information. If FONTLIST runs out of memory space, the program aborts after displaying a message box.

After FONTLIST is finished getting the fonts, it displays both the logical font structure and the text metrics structure for each font, one font per screen, with a sample line of text at the bottom of the screen. You can move through the fonts using the vertical scroll bar or the cursor keys. A large part of the program (the *Display* function) is devoted to formatting the information for display. Figure 14-8 on the following page shows a typical FONTLIST screen.

FONTLIST will list all the fonts in any COURx.FON, HELVx.FON, TMSRx.FON, and SYMBOLx.FON files in the SYSTEM subdirectory of your Windows directory. You'll note from the "Digitized X" and "Digitized Y" fields that some of these fonts may not match the aspect ratio of the video display and may look a little funny. When using the *EnumFonts* function in a real application to obtain screen fonts, you should first obtain the resolution of the device in logical pixels per inch by using the *GetDeviceCaps* function with the LOGPIXELSX and LOGPIXELSY parameters. You should then reject any font in which the *tmDigitizedAspectX* and *tmDigitizedAspectY* values of the TEXTMETRICS structure does not match these values. (The JUSTIFY program shown towards the end of this chapter does this.)

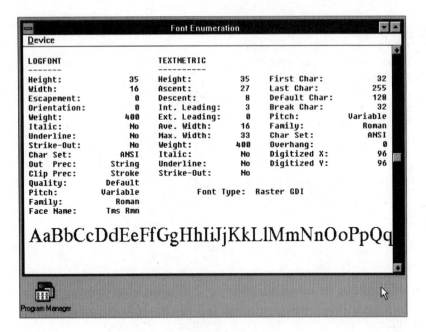

Figure 14-8. *A typical FONTLIST display.*

FONTLIST intercepts the WM_DEVMODECHANGE message (which indicates a change of the printer) and the WM_FONTCHANGE message (which indicates a change in the font resources). You can use FONTLIST to examine the fonts available on different printers by changing the current printer using the Control Panel. If you choose to list the fonts for the current printer, you may wonder how FONTLIST is able to display a device printer font at the bottom of the client area. Although FONTLIST shows the logical font and text metrics structures for device printer fonts, the sample text is a normal GDI font that Windows picks based on the logical font structure for the printer font. It's the closest approximation of the printer font that Windows can display on the screen.

FORMATTING TEXT

Now that you know how to determine the fonts available on a particular device, how to create a font and select it into the device context, and how to determine the sizes and characteristics of the fonts, it's time to try your hand at text formatting. The process involves placing each line of text within margins in one of four ways: aligned on the left margin, aligned on the right margin, centered between the margins, or justified—that is, running from one margin to the other, with equal spaces between the words. For the first three jobs, you can use the *DrawText* function with the DT_WORDBREAK parameter, but this approach has limitations. For instance, you can't determine what part of the text *DrawText* was able to fit within the rectangle. *DrawText* is convenient for some simple jobs, but for more complex formatting tasks, you'll probably want to employ *TextOut*.

One of the most useful functions for working with text is *GetTextExtent*. This function tells you the width and height of a character string based on the current font selected in the device context:

```
dwExtent = GetTextExtent (hdc, lpString, nCount) ;
```

The width of the text in logical units is in the low word of *dwExtent*, and the height of the text in logical units is in the high word. Although you can also obtain the text height from the *tmHeight* field of the TEXTMETRIC structure, the TEXTMETRIC width is inadequate when you're working with variable-pitch fonts or with italic or boldface text.

Breaking text into lines involves searching for break characters. In theory, you should determine the font's break character from the *tmBreakChar* field of the TEXTMETRIC structure, but you can also simply assume that it's the space character (ASCII number 32). In theory, you should also use the *AnsiNext* and *AnsiPrev* functions to step through the string, but you'll get better performance if you use normal C pointer arithmetic. (Of course, if you hope eventually to convert your programs to languages that use other character sets, which might have 2 or more bytes per character, then you had best follow these "in theory" rules right from the start.)

One-Line Text Alignment

I'll begin with an example using one line of text. Let's say that you have selected a font into your device context and now want to write the text:

```
char *szText [] = "Hello, how are you?" ;
```

You want the text to start at the vertical coordinate *yStart*, within margins set by the coordinates *xLeft* and *xRight*. Your job is to calculate the *xStart* value for the horizontal coordinate where the text begins. This job would be considerably easier if the text were displayed using a fixed-pitch font, but you can't assume a fixed-pitch font in general.

First, you get the text extents of the string:

```
dwExtent = GetTextExtent (hdc, szText, strlen (szText)) ;
```

If the low word of *dwExtent* is larger than (*xRight* − *xLeft*), then the line is too long to fit within the margins. Let's assume it can fit.

To align the text on the left margin, you simply set *xStart* equal to *xLeft* and then write the text:

```
TextOut (hdc, xStart, yStart, szText, strlen (szText)) ;
```

This is easy. You can now add the high word of *dwExtent* to *yStart*, and you're ready to write the next line of text.

To align the text on the right margin, you use this formula for *xStart*:

```
xStart = xRight - LOWORD (dwExtent) ;
```

To center the text between the left and right margins, use this formula:

```
xStart = (xLeft + xRight - LOWORD (dwExtent)) / 2 ;
```

Now here's the tough job—to justify the text within the left and right margins. The distance between the margins is (*xRight − xLeft*). Without justification, the text is *LOWORD* (*dwExtent*) wide. The difference between these two values, which is:

```
xRight - xLeft - LOWORD (dwExtent)
```

must be equally distributed among the three space characters in the character string. It sounds like a terrible job, but it's not too bad. To do it, you call:

```
SetTextJustification (hdc, xRight - xLeft - LOWORD (dwExtent), 3) ;
```

The second parameter is the amount of space that must be distributed among the space characters in the character string. The third parameter is the number of space characters—in this case, 3.

Now set *xStart* equal to *xLeft* and write the text with *TextOut*:

```
TextOut (hdc, xStart, yStart, szText, strlen (szText)) ;
```

The text will be justified between the *xLeft* and *xRight* margins.

Whenever you call *SetTextJustification*, it accumulates an error term if the amount of space doesn't distribute evenly among the space characters. This error term will affect subsequent *GetTextExtent* calls. Each time you start a new line, you should clear out the error term by calling:

```
SetTextJustification (hdc, 0, 0) ;
```

Working with Paragraphs

If you're working with a whole paragraph, you have to start at the beginning and scan through the string looking for blanks. Every time you encounter a blank, you call *GetText-Extent* to determine if the text still fits between the left and right margins. When the text exceeds the space allowed for it, then you backtrack to the previous blank. Now you have determined the character string for the line. If you want to justify the line, call *SetText-Justification* and *TextOut*, clear out the error term, and proceed to the next line.

The JUSTIFY program, shown in Figure 14-9, does this job for the first paragraph of Herman Melville's *Moby Dick*. You choose a screen font, and the Alignment menu lets you align the text on the left or right, center it, or justify it. Figure 14-10 on page 713 shows a typical JUSTIFY screen.

JUSTIFY.MAK

```
#----------------------
# JUSTIFY.MAK make file
#----------------------

justify.exe : justify.obj justify.def justify.res
     link justify, /align:16, NUL, /nod slibcew libw, justify
     rc justify.res

justify.obj : justify.c justify.h
     cl -c -Gsw -Ow -W2 -Zp justify.c

justify.res : justify.rc justify.asc justify.h
     rc -r justify.rc
```

JUSTIFY.C

```
/*----------------------------------------
   JUSTIFY.C -- Justified Type Program
                (c) Charles Petzold, 1990
   ----------------------------------------*/

#include <windows.h>
#include <string.h>
#include "justify.h"

typedef struct
     {
     short nNumFaces ;
     char  szFaceNames [MAX_FACES] [LF_FACESIZE] ;
     }
     ENUMFACE ;

typedef struct
     {
     short     nNumSizes ;
     short     xLogPixPerInch ;
     short     yLogPixPerInch ;
     LOGFONT   lf [MAX_SIZES] ;
     TEXTMETRIC tm [MAX_SIZES] ;
     }
     ENUMSIZE ;

long FAR PASCAL WndProc (HWND, WORD, WORD, LONG) ;
int  FAR PASCAL EnumAllFaces (LPLOGFONT, LPTEXTMETRIC, short, ENUMFACE FAR *) ;
int  FAR PASCAL EnumAllSizes (LPLOGFONT, LPTEXTMETRIC, short, ENUMSIZE FAR *) ;
```

Figure 14-9. *The JUSTIFY program.*   *(continued)*

```
int PASCAL WinMain (HANDLE hInstance, HANDLE hPrevInstance,
                    LPSTR lpszCmdLine, int nCmdShow)
     {
     static  char szAppName[] = "Justify" ;
     HWND     hwnd ;
     MSG      msg ;
     WNDCLASS wndclass ;

     if (!hPrevInstance)
          {
          wndclass.style         = CS_HREDRAW : CS_VREDRAW : CS_OWNDC ;
          wndclass.lpfnWndProc   = WndProc ;
          wndclass.cbClsExtra    = 0 ;
          wndclass.cbWndExtra    = 0 ;
          wndclass.hInstance     = hInstance ;
          wndclass.hIcon         = LoadIcon (NULL, IDI_APPLICATION) ;
          wndclass.hCursor       = LoadCursor (NULL, IDC_ARROW) ;
          wndclass.hbrBackground = GetStockObject (WHITE_BRUSH) ;
          wndclass.lpszMenuName  = szAppName ;
          wndclass.lpszClassName = szAppName ;

          RegisterClass (&wndclass) ;
          }
     hwnd = CreateWindow (szAppName, "Justified Type",
                          WS_OVERLAPPEDWINDOW,
                          CW_USEDEFAULT, CW_USEDEFAULT,
                          CW_USEDEFAULT, CW_USEDEFAULT,
                          NULL, NULL, hInstance, NULL) ;

     ShowWindow (hwnd, nCmdShow) ;
     UpdateWindow (hwnd) ;

     while (GetMessage (&msg, NULL, 0, 0))
          {
          TranslateMessage (&msg) ;
          DispatchMessage (&msg) ;
          }
     return msg.wParam ;
     }

int FAR PASCAL EnumAllFaces (LPLOGFONT lplf, LPTEXTMETRIC lptm,
                             short nFontType, ENUMFACE FAR *lpef)
     {
     if (nFontType & RASTER_FONTTYPE)
          {
          lstrcpy (lpef->szFaceNames[lpef->nNumFaces], lplf->lfFaceName) ;
          if (++lpef->nNumFaces == MAX_FACES)
               return 0 ;
          }
     return 1 ;
     }
```

(continued)

```
int FAR PASCAL EnumAllSizes (LPLOGFONT lplf, LPTEXTMETRIC lptm,
                             short nFontType, ENUMSIZE FAR *lpes)
    {
    if (lpes->xLogPixPerInch == lptm->tmDigitizedAspectX &&
        lpes->yLogPixPerInch == lptm->tmDigitizedAspectY)
        {
        lpes->lf [lpes->nNumSizes] = *lplf ;
        lpes->tm [lpes->nNumSizes] = *lptm ;
        if (++lpes->nNumSizes == MAX_SIZES)
            return 0 ;
        }
    return 1 ;
    }

short MakeSizeMenu (HWND hwnd, FARPROC lpfnEnumAllSizes,
                    ENUMSIZE *pes, char *szFaceName)
    {
    static LOGFONT lfBlank ;
    char           szBuffer[20] ;
    HDC            hdc ;
    HMENU          hPopup ;
    short          i ;

    hdc = GetDC (hwnd) ;
    hPopup = GetSubMenu (GetMenu (hwnd), SIZE_MENU) ;

    pes->nNumSizes = 0 ;
    EnumFonts (hdc, szFaceName, lpfnEnumAllSizes, (LPSTR) pes) ;
    ReleaseDC (hwnd, hdc) ;

    while (GetMenuItemCount (hPopup) > 0)
        DeleteMenu (hPopup, 0, MF_BYPOSITION) ;

    if (pes->nNumSizes)
        for (i = 0 ; i < pes->nNumSizes ; i++)
            {
            wsprintf (szBuffer, "%i  %2d / %2d", i + 1,
                (pes->tm[i].tmHeight - pes->tm[i].tmInternalLeading + 10)
                                                                    / 20,
                (pes->tm[i].tmHeight + 10) / 20) ;
            AppendMenu (hPopup, 0, IDM_ISIZE + i, szBuffer) ;
            }
    else        /* no fonts found that match aspect ratio of display */
        {
        pes->lf[0] = lfBlank ;
        strcpy (pes->lf[0].lfFaceName, szFaceName) ;
        AppendMenu (hPopup, 0, IDM_ISIZE, "Default") ;
        }
```

(continued)

```
        CheckMenuItem (hPopup, IDM_ISIZE, MF_CHECKED) ;
        return 0 ;
        }

void DrawRuler (HDC hdc, POINT ptClient)
        {
        static short nRuleSize [16] = { 360, 72, 144, 72, 216, 72, 144, 72,
                                        288, 72, 144, 72, 216, 72, 144, 72 } ;
        short        i, j ;

        MoveTo (hdc, 0,           -360) ;
        LineTo (hdc, ptClient.x, -360) ;
        MoveTo (hdc, -360,           0) ;
        LineTo (hdc, -360, ptClient.y) ;

        for (i = 0, j = 0 ; i <= ptClient.x ; i += 1440 / 16, j++)
            {
            MoveTo (hdc, i, -360) ;
            LineTo (hdc, i, -360 - nRuleSize [j % 16]) ;
            }
        for (i = 0, j = 0 ; i <= ptClient.y ; i += 1440 / 16, j++)
            {
            MoveTo (hdc, -360, i) ;
            LineTo (hdc, -360 - nRuleSize [j % 16], i) ;
            }
        }

void Justify (HDC hdc, HANDLE hResource, POINT ptClient, short nCurAlign)
        {
        DWORD  dwExtent ;
        LPSTR  lpText, lpBegin, lpEnd ;
        short  i, xStart, yStart, nBreakCount ;

        lpText = LockResource (hResource) ;

        yStart = 0 ;
        do                              // for each text line
            {
            nBreakCount = 0 ;
            while (*lpText == ' ')    // skip over leading blanks
                lpText++ ;
            lpBegin = lpText ;

            do                              // until the line is known
                {
                lpEnd = lpText ;

                while (*lpText != '\0' && *lpText++ != ' ') ;
                if (*lpText == '\0')
                    break ;
                                        // for each space, calculate extents
```

(continued)

```
                nBreakCount++ ;
                SetTextJustification (hdc, 0, 0) ;
                dwExtent = GetTextExtent (hdc, lpBegin, lpText - lpBegin - 1) ;
                }
           while (LOWORD (dwExtent) < ptClient.x) ;

           nBreakCount-- ;
           while (*(lpEnd - 1) == ' ')     // eliminate trailing blanks
                {
                lpEnd-- ;
                nBreakCount-- ;
                }

           if (*lpText == '\0' || nBreakCount <= 0)
                lpEnd = lpText ;

           SetTextJustification (hdc, 0, 0) ;
           dwExtent = GetTextExtent (hdc, lpBegin, lpEnd - lpBegin) ;

           if (nCurAlign == IDM_LEFT)            // use alignment for xStart
                xStart = 0 ;

           else if (nCurAlign == IDM_RIGHT)
                xStart = ptClient.x - LOWORD (dwExtent) ;

           else if (nCurAlign == IDM_CENTER)
                xStart = (ptClient.x - LOWORD (dwExtent)) / 2 ;

           else
                {
                if (*lpText != '\0' && nBreakCount > 0)
                     SetTextJustification (hdc, ptClient.x - LOWORD (dwExtent),
                                                    nBreakCount) ;
                xStart = 0 ;
                }

           TextOut (hdc, xStart, yStart, lpBegin, lpEnd - lpBegin) ;
           yStart += HIWORD (dwExtent) ;
           lpText = lpEnd ;
           }
      while (*lpText && yStart < ptClient.y) ;

      GlobalUnlock (hResource) ;
      }

long FAR PASCAL WndProc (HWND hwnd, WORD message, WORD wParam, LONG lParam)
      {
      static ENUMFACE ef ;
      static ENUMSIZE es ;
      static FARPROC  lpfnEnumAllFaces, lpfnEnumAllSizes ;
```

(continued)

```
     static HANDLE    hResource ;
     static POINT      ptClient ;
     static short      nCurSize, nCurFace, nCurAttr, nCurAlign = IDM_LEFT ;
     HANDLE            hInstance ;
     HDC               hdc ;
     HFONT             hFont ;
     HMENU             hMenu, hPopup ;
     PAINTSTRUCT       ps ;
     short             i ;

     switch (message)
          {
          case WM_CREATE :
               hdc = GetDC (hwnd) ;
               es.xLogPixPerInch = GetDeviceCaps (hdc, LOGPIXELSX) ;
               es.yLogPixPerInch = GetDeviceCaps (hdc, LOGPIXELSY) ;

                         // Set Map Mode

               SetMapMode (hdc, MM_ANISOTROPIC) ;
               SetWindowExt (hdc, 1440, 1440) ;
               SetViewportExt (hdc, es.xLogPixPerInch, es.yLogPixPerInch) ;
               SetWindowOrg (hdc, -720, -720) ;

                         // MakeProcInstance for 2 routines

               hInstance = ((LPCREATESTRUCT) lParam)-> hInstance ;
               lpfnEnumAllFaces = MakeProcInstance (EnumAllFaces, hInstance) ;
               lpfnEnumAllSizes = MakeProcInstance (EnumAllSizes, hInstance) ;

                         // Enumerate the Font Faces

               EnumFonts (hdc, NULL, lpfnEnumAllFaces, (LPSTR) &ef) ;
               ReleaseDC (hwnd, hdc) ;

                         // Initialize the Menus

               hMenu  = GetMenu (hwnd) ;
               hPopup = CreateMenu () ;

               for (i = 0 ; i < ef.nNumFaces ; i++)
                    AppendMenu (hPopup, 0, IDM_IFACE + i, ef.szFaceNames[i]) ;

               ModifyMenu (hMenu, IDM_FACE, MF_POPUP, hPopup, "&FaceName") ;
               CheckMenuItem (hMenu, IDM_IFACE, MF_CHECKED) ;

               nCurSize = MakeSizeMenu (hwnd, lpfnEnumAllSizes, &es,
                                   ef.szFaceNames [nCurFace]) ;

                         // Load the Text Resource
```

(continued)

```
        hResource = LoadResource (hInstance,
                    FindResource (hInstance, "Ishmael", "TEXT")) ;
        return 0 ;

case WM_SIZE :
        hdc = GetDC (hwnd) ;
        ptClient = MAKEPOINT (lParam) ;
        DPtoLP (hdc, &ptClient, 1) ;
        ptClient.x -= 360 ;
        ReleaseDC (hwnd, hdc) ;
        return 0 ;

case WM_COMMAND :
        hMenu = GetMenu (hwnd) ;

        if (wParam >= IDM_IFACE && wParam < IDM_IFACE + MAX_FACES)
            {
            CheckMenuItem (hMenu, nCurFace + IDM_IFACE, MF_UNCHECKED) ;
            CheckMenuItem (hMenu, wParam, MF_CHECKED) ;
            nCurFace = wParam - IDM_IFACE ;

            nCurSize = MakeSizeMenu (hwnd, lpfnEnumAllSizes, &es,
                            ef.szFaceNames [nCurFace]) ;
            }

        else if (wParam >= IDM_ISIZE && wParam < IDM_ISIZE + MAX_SIZES)
            {
            CheckMenuItem (hMenu, nCurSize + IDM_ISIZE, MF_UNCHECKED) ;
            CheckMenuItem (hMenu, wParam, MF_CHECKED) ;
            nCurSize = wParam - IDM_ISIZE ;
            }

        else switch (wParam)
            {
            case IDM_BOLD :
            case IDM_ITALIC :
            case IDM_STRIKE :
            case IDM_UNDER :
                    CheckMenuItem (hMenu, wParam, MF_CHECKED &
                        GetMenuState (hMenu, wParam, MF_BYCOMMAND) ?
                            MF_UNCHECKED : MF_CHECKED) ;
                    nCurAttr ^= wParam ;
                    break ;

            case IDM_NORM :
                    nCurAttr = 0 ;
                    CheckMenuItem (hMenu, IDM_BOLD,   MF_UNCHECKED) ;
                    CheckMenuItem (hMenu, IDM_ITALIC, MF_UNCHECKED) ;
                    CheckMenuItem (hMenu, IDM_STRIKE, MF_UNCHECKED) ;
                    CheckMenuItem (hMenu, IDM_UNDER,  MF_UNCHECKED) ;
                    break ;
```

(continued)

```
                        case IDM_LEFT :
                        case IDM_RIGHT :
                        case IDM_CENTER :
                        case IDM_JUST :
                                CheckMenuItem (hMenu, nCurAlign, MF_UNCHECKED) ;
                                nCurAlign = wParam ;
                                CheckMenuItem (hMenu, nCurAlign, MF_CHECKED) ;
                                break ;
                        }
                InvalidateRect (hwnd, NULL, TRUE) ;
                return 0 ;

        case WM_PAINT :
                hdc = BeginPaint (hwnd, &ps) ;

                es.lf[nCurSize].lfWeight    = nCurAttr & IDM_BOLD ? 700 : 400 ;
                es.lf[nCurSize].lfItalic    = (BYTE) (nCurAttr & IDM_ITALIC) ;
                es.lf[nCurSize].lfUnderline = (BYTE) (nCurAttr & IDM_UNDER) ;
                es.lf[nCurSize].lfStrikeOut = (BYTE) (nCurAttr & IDM_STRIKE) ;

                hFont = CreateFontIndirect (&es.lf[nCurSize]) ;
                hFont = SelectObject (hdc, hFont) ;

                DrawRuler (hdc, ptClient) ;
                Justify (hdc, hResource, ptClient, nCurAlign) ;

                DeleteObject (SelectObject (hdc, hFont)) ;
                EndPaint (hwnd, &ps) ;
                return 0 ;

        case WM_DESTROY :
                FreeResource (hResource) ;
                PostQuitMessage (0) ;
                return 0 ;
        }
    return DefWindowProc (hwnd, message, wParam, lParam) ;
    }
```

JUSTIFY.RC

```
/*---------------------------
   JUSTIFY.RC resource script
   ---------------------------*/

#include "justify.h"

Ishmael TEXT justify.asc
```

(continued)

```
Justify MENU
    {
    MENUITEM  "&FaceName",        IDM_FACE
    POPUP     "&PointSize"
        {
        MENUITEM "temp",          IDM_SIZE
        }
    POPUP      "&Attributes"
        {
        MENUITEM "&Bold",         IDM_BOLD
        MENUITEM "&Italic",       IDM_ITALIC
        MENUITEM "&StrikeOut",    IDM_STRIKE
        MENUITEM "&Underline",    IDM_UNDER
        MENUITEM SEPARATOR
        MENUITEM "&Normal",       IDM_NORM
        }
    POPUP      "A&lignment"
        {
        MENUITEM "&Left",         IDM_LEFT, CHECKED
        MENUITEM "&Right",        IDM_RIGHT
        MENUITEM "&Centered",     IDM_CENTER
        MENUITEM "&Justified",    IDM_JUST
        }
    }
```

JUSTIFY.ASC

Call me Ishmael. Some years ago -- never mind how long precisely -
- having little or no money in my purse, and nothing particular to
interest me on shore, I thought I would sail about a little and see
the watery part of the world. It is a way I have of driving off the
spleen, and regulating the circulation. Whenever I find myself
growing grim about the mouth; whenever it is a damp, drizzly November
in my soul; whenever I find myself involuntarily pausing before coffin
warehouses, and bringing up the rear of every funeral I meet; and
especially whenever my hypos get such an upper hand of me, that it
requires a strong moral principle to prevent me from deliberately
stepping into the street, and methodically knocking people's hats
off -- then, I account it high time to get to sea as soon as I can.
This is my substitute for pistol and ball. With a philosophical
flourish Cato throws himself upon his sword; I quietly take to the
ship. There is nothing surprising in this. If they but knew it,
almost all men in their degree, some time or other, cherish very
nearly the same feelings towards the ocean with me.

JUSTIFY.H

```
/*---------------------------
   JUSTIFY.H header file
   ---------------------*/

#define SIZE_MENU    1
#define MAX_FACES   16
#define MAX_SIZES   16

#define IDM_BOLD     1
#define IDM_ITALIC   2
#define IDM_STRIKE   4
#define IDM_UNDER    8

#define IDM_FACE    0x10
#define IDM_SIZE    0x11
#define IDM_NORM    0x12

#define IDM_LEFT    0x13
#define IDM_RIGHT   0x14
#define IDM_CENTER  0x15
#define IDM_JUST    0x16

#define IDM_IFACE   0x20
#define IDM_ISIZE   (IDM_IFACE + MAX_FACES)
```

JUSTIFY.DEF

```
;------------------------------------
; JUSTIFY.DEF module definition file
;------------------------------------

NAME            JUSTIFY

DESCRIPTION     'Demonstration of Justified Text (c) Charles Petzold, 1990'
EXETYPE         WINDOWS
STUB            'WINSTUB.EXE'
CODE            PRELOAD MOVEABLE DISCARDABLE
DATA            PRELOAD MOVEABLE MULTIPLE
HEAPSIZE        1024
STACKSIZE       8192
EXPORTS         WndProc
                EnumAllFaces
                EnumAllSizes
```

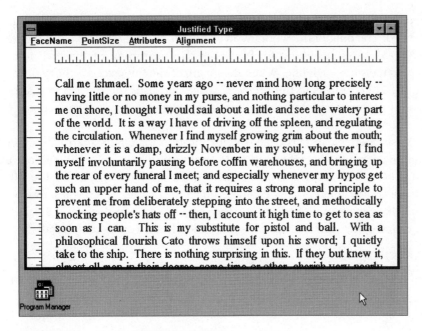

Figure 14-10. *A typical JUSTIFY display.*

Like the FONTLIST program, JUSTIFY uses the *EnumFonts* function to obtain the fonts available for the screen. The two call-back functions are called *EnumAllFaces* and *EnumAllSizes*. The program can store up to 16 typeface names and up to 16 font sizes for a particular typeface. During the WM_CREATE message, JUSTIFY calls *EnumFonts* with a NULL second parameter and puts the typeface names into the FaceName menu.

When you select a typeface from the FaceName menu, JUSTIFY calls *EnumFonts* again to get the available sizes of that typeface. JUSTIFY must then reconstruct the Point-Size menu, which displays the font sizes in this format:

24 / 28

which means a 24-point font on a 28-point line spacing. The Attributes menu offers the options Bold, Italic, StrikeOut, and Underline, and the aforementioned Alignment menu has the options Left, Right, Centered, and Justified.

JUSTIFY uses the "Logical Twips" mapping mode to facilitate the translation into point sizes of the information available from the TEXTMETRIC structure. To avoid setting this mapping mode every time it obtains a device context, JUSTIFY uses the CS_OWNDC class style.

JUSTIFY displays a ruler (in logical inches, of course) across the top and down the left side of the client area. The *DrawRuler* function draws the ruler. The window origin is adjusted to begin ½ inch from the left and top of the client area. JUSTIFY also leaves a ¼-inch margin at the right of the client area.

The text is a user-defined resource. It is in a one-line-per-paragraph format and is NULL-terminated. The bulk of the work involved with formatting this text is in the *Justify* function. JUSTIFY starts searching for blanks at the beginning of the text and uses *GetTextExtent* to measure each line. When the length of the line exceeds the width of the display area, JUSTIFY returns to the previous space and uses the line up to that point. Depending on the Alignment choice, the line is left aligned, right aligned, centered, or justified.

JUSTIFY isn't perfect. In particular, the justification logic falls apart when there is only one word in each line. Even if we solve this problem (which isn't a difficult one), the program still won't work properly when a single word is too long to fit within the left and right margins. Of course, matters can become even more complex when you start working with programs that can use multiple fonts on the same line (as Windows WRITE can). But nobody ever claimed this stuff was easy. It's just easier than if you were doing all the work yourself.

Chapter 15

Using the Printer

The concept of device independence may have seemed all well and good in the past four chapters, when we were using the video display for text and graphics, but how well does the concept hold up for printers and plotters? In general, the news is good. Under Windows, printers and plotters have a device-independent graphics interface. You can forget about printer control sequences and communications protocols when programming for the printer. Retail Windows programs conspicuously lack the disks of specialized printer drivers that have characterized recent word-processing software and graphics programs for MS-DOS. When a retail Windows program includes printer drivers, they are usually enhanced versions of existing printer drivers.

From a Windows program, you can print text and graphics on paper using the same GDI functions that we've been using for the video display. Many of the issues of device independence that we've explored in the past four chapters—mostly related to the size and resolution of the display surface and its color capabilities—can be approached and resolved in the same way. Yet a printer or plotter is not simply a display that uses paper rather than a cathode-ray tube. There are some very significant differences. For example, we have never had to consider the problem of a video display not being connected to the display adapter or of the display "running out of screen," but it is common for a printer to be off line or to run out of paper.

Nor have we worried about the video display adapter being incapable of performing certain graphics operations. Either the display adapter can handle graphics or it can't. And if it can't, then it can't be used with Windows at all. But some printers can't print graphics

715

(although they can still be used with Windows), and plotters can do vector graphics but have a real problem with bit-block transfers.

Here are some other issues to consider:

- Printers are slower than video displays. Although we have on occasion tried to tune our programs for best performance, we haven't worried about the time required for the video display to be refreshed. But nobody wants to wait for a printer to finish printing before getting back to work.

- Programs reuse the surface of the video display as they overwrite previous display output with new output. This can't be done on a printer. Instead, a printer must eject a completed page and go on to the next page.

- On the video display, different applications are windowed. On a printer, output from different applications must be separated into distinct documents or print jobs.

To add printer support to the rest of GDI, Windows includes only one new function, called *Escape*. Well, it's actually more than one. *Escape* has many subfunctions that are indicated by one of the *Escape* parameters. For example, the three most common *Escape* subfunctions are STARTDOC and ENDDOC (which begin and end a printing job) and NEWFRAME (which ends one page and goes on to the next).

PRINTING, SPOOLING, AND ESCAPE

When you use a printer in Windows, you're actually initiating a complex interaction involving the GDI library module, the printer device driver library module (which has a .DRV extension), and the Windows Print Manager program (PRINTMAN.EXE), as well as some other modules that get into the act. Before we start programming for the printer, let's examine how this process works.

When an application program wants to begin using a printer, it first obtains a handle to the printer device context using *CreateDC*. This causes the printer device driver library module to be loaded into memory (if it's not present already) and to initialize itself. The program then calls the *Escape* subfunction named STARTDOC, which signals the beginning of a new document. The *Escape* function is handled by the GDI module. The GDI module calls the *Control* function (which is equivalent to *Escape*) in the printer device driver. The device driver performs some initialization and calls *OpenJob*, which is in the GDI module. The GDI module then loads the Windows Print Manager program into memory.

Following the STARTDOC *Escape* call, the program can make the appropriate GDI calls for the first page of the document. For example, if the program wants to draw an ellipse on the page, it calls *Ellipse*, just as it does when drawing an ellipse on the screen.

The GDI module generally stores all these GDI calls in a disk-based metafile, which is located in the subdirectory indicated by the TEMP variable in the MS-DOS environment. (If no TEMP variable exists, Windows uses the root directory of the first fixed disk on the system.) The file begins with the characters ~MF and has a .TMP extension.

When the application program is finished with the GDI calls that define the first page, the program calls the NEWFRAME subfunction of *Escape*. Now the real work begins. The printer driver must translate the various drawing commands stored in the metafile into output for the printer. The printer output required to define a page of graphics can be very large, particularly if the printer has no high-level page-composition language. For example, a 300-dots-per-inch laser printer using 8½-by-11-inch paper might require more than a megabyte of data to define one page of graphics.

For this reason, printer drivers often implement a technique called "banding," which divides the page into rectangles called bands. (We'll examine banding later in this chapter.) The GDI module obtains the dimensions of each band from the printer driver. It then sets a clipping region equal to this band and calls the printer device driver *Output* function for each of the drawing functions contained in the metafile. This process is called "playing the metafile into the device driver." The GDI module must play the entire metafile into the device driver for each band that the device driver defines on the page. After the process is completed, the metafile can be deleted.

For each band, the device driver translates these drawing functions into the output necessary to realize them on the printer. The format of this output will be specific to the printer. For dot-matrix printers, it will be a collection of control sequences, including graphics sequences. (For some assistance with constructing this output, the printer driver can call various "helper" routines also located in the GDI module.) For laser printers with a high-level page-composition language (such as PostScript), the printer output will be in this language.

The printer driver uses the *WriteSpool* function to pass the printer output for each band to the GDI module, which then stores this printer output in a temporary file also located in the TEMP subdirectory. This file begins with the characters ~SPL and has a .TMP extension. When the entire page is finished, the GDI module uses the *SendMessage* function to send a message to the Print Manager indicating that a new print job is ready. The application program then goes on to the next page. When the application is finished with all the pages it must print, it makes the ENDDOC *Escape* call to signal that the print job is completed. Figure 15-1 on the following page shows the interaction of the program, the GDI module, and the printer driver.

The Windows Print Manager program is a print spooler that relieves application programs of some of the work involved with printing. The GDI module loads the Print Manager (if it is not already loaded) automatically when a program begins printing. The GDI module then creates the files that contain printer output. The Print Manager's job is to send these files out to the printer. It is notified of a new print job by a message from the GDI

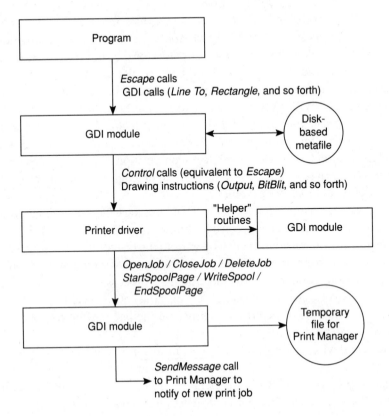

Figure 15-1. *The interaction of the application program, the GDI module, and the printer driver.*

module. It then begins reading the file and transferring it directly to the printer. To transfer the files, the Print Manager uses various communications functions (*OpenComm*, *Write-Comm*, and so forth included in the USER module) for the parallel or serial port that the printer is connected to. During the time that the Print Manager is writing the printer output to the output port, other Windows programs can function normally. When the Print Manager is done sending a file to a printer, it can delete the temporary file holding the output. This process is shown in Figure 15-2.

Most of this process is transparent to the application program. From the perspective of the program, "printing" occurs only during the time required for the GDI module to save all the printer output in disk files. After that, the program is freed up to do other things. The actual printing of the document becomes the Print Manager's responsibility rather than the program's. A user can direct the Print Manager to pause print jobs, to change their priority, or to cancel print jobs. This arrangement allows programs to "print" faster than would be possible if they were printing in real time and had to wait for the printer to finish one page before proceeding to the next.

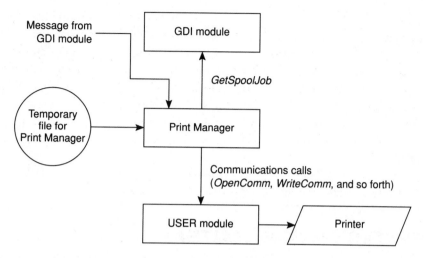

Figure 15-2. *The operation of the Print Manager program.*

Although I've described how printing works in general, there are some variations on this theme. One is that the Print Manager doesn't have to be present in order for Windows programs to use the printer. Normally, the *[windows]* section of WIN.INI contains this line:

```
Spooler=yes
```

But a user can change that to:

```
Spooler=no
```

If this line is present, the Print Manager doesn't allow itself to be executed.

Why would a user not want the Print Manager to be loaded? Well, perhaps the user has a hardware or software print spooler that works faster than the Print Manager. Or perhaps the printer is on a network that has its own spooler. The general rule is that one spooler is faster than two. Removing the Windows Print Manager would speed up printing, because the printer output doesn't have to be stored on disk. It can go right out to the printer and be intercepted by the external hardware or software print spooler.

If the Print Manager can't be loaded, the GDI module doesn't store the printer output from the device driver in a file. Instead, GDI itself sends the output directly to the parallel or serial printer port. Unlike the printing done by the Print Manager, the printing done by GDI has the potential of holding up the operation of application programs (particularly the program doing the printing) until the printing is completed.

Here's another variation on the general theme. Normally, the GDI module stores all the functions necessary to define a page in a metafile and then plays this metafile into the printer driver once for each band defined by the driver. If the printer driver doesn't require banding, however, the metafile isn't created; GDI simply passes the drawing functions directly to the driver. In a further variation, it is also possible for an application to assume responsibility for dividing printer output into bands. This makes the printing code in the application program more complex, but it relieves the GDI module of creating the metafile. Once again, GDI simply passes the functions for each band to the printer driver.

Now perhaps you're starting to see how printing from a Windows program might involve a bit more overhead than that required for using the video display. Several problems can occur—particularly if the GDI module runs out of disk space while creating the metafile or the printer output files. You can either get very involved in reporting these problems to the user and attempting to do something about them, or you can remain relatively aloof.

We'll examine several different approaches to printing in the pages that follow. But first things first—let's begin by obtaining a printer device context.

THE PRINTER DEVICE CONTEXT

Just as you must obtain a handle to a device context before you paint on the video display, you must obtain a printer device context handle before printing. Once you have this handle (and have made the *Escape* calls necessary to announce your intention of creating a new document), you can use this printer device context handle the same way you use the video display device context handle—as the first parameter to the various GDI calls we've covered in the last four chapters.

In Chapter 11, you learned that you can get a handle to a device context for the entire video display by calling:

```
hdc = CreateDC ("DISPLAY", NULL, NULL, NULL) ;
```

You obtain a printer device context handle using this same function. However, for a printer device context, the first three parameters are not fixed. The general syntax of *CreateDC* is:

```
hdc = CreateDC (lpszDriverName, lpszDeviceName, lpszOutputPort,
                          lpInitializationData) ;
```

Although *lpInitializationData* is generally set to NULL, the first three parameters must be far pointers to character strings that tell Windows the name of the printer driver, the name of the printer device, and the output port to which the device is connected. Before you can set these three parameters, you must do a little fishing in the WIN.INI file.

Getting the *CreateDC* Parameters

Printers are listed in two different sections of the WIN.INI file, reflecting the possibility that a system can have more than one printer attached to it. A single printer is listed in the *[windows]* section with the keyword device. The string that follows contains the device name, driver name, and output port required in the *CreateDC* call:

```
[windows]
    [other lines]
device=IBM Graphics,IBMGRX,LPT1:
```

In this case, the device name is IBM Graphics, the driver name is IBMGRX, and the output port is LPT1. The printer listed in this section of WIN.INI is the most recent printer that the user has selected using the Windows Control Panel. This printer is chosen from the dialog box invoked by the Printer option. It can be considered the "current printer" or the "default printer." Most small Windows programs use this printer for printing.

Here is one way to write a function to obtain this string from WIN.INI, parse it into the three components, and call *CreateDC* to obtain a printer device context handle:

```
HDC GetPrinterDC ()
    {
    char szPrinter [80] ;
    char *szDevice, *szDriver, *szOutput ;

    GetProfileString ("windows", "device", ",,,", szPrinter, 80) ;

    if ((szDevice = strtok (szPrinter, "," )) &&
        (szDriver = strtok (NULL,      ", ")) &&
        (szOutput = strtok (NULL,      ", ")))
                return CreateDC (szDriver, szDevice, szOutput, NULL) ;

    return 0 ;
    }
```

GetProfileString looks in the *[windows]* section for the keyword *device* and copies up to 80 characters following the equal sign into *szPrinter.* (The third parameter to *GetProfile-String* is a default string if Windows can't find the *[windows]* section or the device keyword in WIN.INI.) The string is parsed using the normal C *strtok* function, which breaks a string into tokens. Note that I use only a comma to find the end of the *szDevice* string, because the device name can include embedded blanks. Both a comma and space are used to separate the driver name and output port so that leading or trailing blanks are stripped from these strings. (Using *strtok* is not an entirely satisfactory method of parsing this string, because *strtok* doesn't take into account the multibyte character codes that can be used in versions of Windows for countries in the Far East. If this is of concern, you can write your own version of *strtok* that uses *AnsiNext* to advance through the string.)

The *CreateDC* function returns 0 if the printer device context could not be created. This can occur if the string in WIN.INI is malformed, if Windows can't find the printer driver, or if the output port name is "none" (which means the printer is not connected to an output port). You can, however, obtain an information context for a printer connected to "none" by using *CreateIC* rather than *CreateDC.*

The *[windows]* section of WIN.INI lists only one printer. But multiple printers can be listed in the *[devices]* section of WIN.INI. A printer is listed in this section when a user chooses the Add New Printer option from the Installation menu of CONTROL.EXE. The *[devices]* section looks something like this:

```
[devices]
IBM Graphics=IBMGRX,LPT1:
Generic / Text Only=TTY,output.prn
HP Plotter=HPPLOT,COM1:
Postscript Printer=PSCRIPT,COM2:
```

To the left of each equal sign is the device name; to the right is first the driver name and then the output port. Getting a device context handle using the printer specified in the *[windows]* section of WIN.INI is essentially the same as getting a device context handle using one of the printers from the *[devices]* section, except that the latter is more difficult because you have more than one choice.

Some larger Windows programs include a File menu option called Change Printer, which invokes a dialog box that lists all the printers from the *[devices]* section with the port each printer is connected to. This option allows the user to select a printer other than the one listed in the *[windows]* section of WIN.INI. A program that includes this option must first call *GetProfileString* with a NULL second parameter:

```
static char szAllDevices [4096] ;
    [other program lines]
GetProfileString ("devices", NULL, "", szAllDevices,
                                  sizeof szAllDevices) ;
```

On return, *szAllDevices* contains a list of the keywords (the device names) in the *[devices]* section. Each keyword is terminated by a NULL except for the final keyword, which is terminated by two NULLs. For the example list shown above, *szAllDevices* would contain (using C notation):

```
IBM Graphics\0Generic / Text Only\0HP Plotter\0Postscript Printer\0\0
```

You can then present these names to the user. (We'll do this shortly in the DEVCAPS2 program.)

Let's assume that a user selects one of these devices and that you've set the pointer *szDevice* to the beginning of that device name in *szAllDevices*. You can then obtain the rest of the string (the driver name and output port) by calling *GetProfileString* again:

```
GetProfileString ("devices", szDevice, "", szPrinter, 64) ;
```

You need to parse the *szPrinter* string to extract the driver name and the output port name:

```
szDriver = strtok (szPrinter, ", ") ;
szOutput = strtok (NULL     , ", ") ;
```

Now you have the *szDevice*, *szDriver*, and *szOutput* pointers necessary to call *CreateDC* or *CreateIC*.

The valid output ports on a particular system are listed in the *[ports]* section of WIN.INI. You don't need to access this section of WIN.INI to use the printer. You can assume that the user has identified a particular port for the printer using the Printer option in the Control Panel, and you can further assume that the user has properly defined the communications parameters for serial (COM) ports using the Ports option.

The *[ports]* section often looks something like this:

```
[ports]
LPT1:=
LPT2:=
LPT3:=
COM1:=9600,n,8,1
COM2:=1200,n,8,1
output.prn=
```

The OUTPUT.PRN file (or any file with a .PRN extension) can be listed here to direct printer output to a file. This filename can appear as the output port for a printer in the *[windows]* section or *[devices]* section of WIN.INI.

The Revised DEVCAPS Program

The original DEVCAPS1 program in Chapter 11 displays all the information available from the *GetDeviceCaps* function for the video display and the current printer. The new version, shown in Figure 15-3, displays a menu of all the printers from the *[devices]* section of WIN.INI and lets you choose one. In addition to the DEVCAPS2 files shown here, you'll also need the DEVCAPS.C file from Chapter 11 (Figure 11-1).

DEVCAPS2.MAK

```
#-----------------------
# DEVCAPS.MAK make file
#-----------------------

devcaps2.exe : devcaps2.obj devcaps.obj devcaps2.res devcaps2.def
    link devcaps2 devcaps, /align:16, NUL, /nod slibcew libw, devcaps2
    rc devcaps2.res

devcaps2.obj : devcaps2.c devcaps2.h
    cl -c -Gsw -Ow -W2 -Zp devcaps2.c

devcaps.obj : devcaps.c
    cl -c -Gsw -Ow -W2 -Zp devcaps.c

devcaps2.res : devcaps2.rc devcaps2.h
    rc -r devcaps2.rc
```

Figure 15-3. *The DEVCAPS2 program.*

DEVCAPS2.C

```
/*------------------------------------------------------------------
   DEVCAPS2.C -- Displays Device Capability Information (Version 2)
                 (c) Charles Petzold, 1990
   ----------------------------------------------------------------*/

#include <windows.h>
#include <string.h>
#include "devcaps2.h"

void DoBasicInfo (HDC, HDC, short, short) ;              // in DEVCAPS.C
void DoOtherInfo (HDC, HDC, short, short) ;
void DoBitCodedCaps (HDC, HDC, short, short, short) ;

typedef VOID (FAR PASCAL *DEVMODEPROC) (HWND, HANDLE, LPSTR, LPSTR) ;

long FAR PASCAL WndProc (HWND, WORD, WORD, LONG) ;

int PASCAL WinMain (HANDLE hInstance, HANDLE hPrevInstance,
                    LPSTR lpszCmdLine, int nCmdShow)
     {
     static char szAppName[] = "DevCaps2" ;
     HWND        hwnd ;
     MSG         msg ;
     WNDCLASS    wndclass ;

     if (!hPrevInstance)
          {
          wndclass.style         = CS_HREDRAW : CS_VREDRAW ;
          wndclass.lpfnWndProc   = WndProc ;
          wndclass.cbClsExtra    = 0 ;
          wndclass.cbWndExtra    = 0 ;
          wndclass.hInstance     = hInstance ;
          wndclass.hIcon         = LoadIcon (NULL, IDI_APPLICATION) ;
          wndclass.hCursor       = LoadCursor (NULL, IDC_ARROW) ;
          wndclass.hbrBackground = GetStockObject (WHITE_BRUSH) ;
          wndclass.lpszMenuName  = szAppName ;
          wndclass.lpszClassName = szAppName ;

          RegisterClass (&wndclass) ;
          }

     hwnd = CreateWindow (szAppName, NULL,
                          WS_OVERLAPPEDWINDOW,
                          CW_USEDEFAULT, CW_USEDEFAULT,
                          CW_USEDEFAULT, CW_USEDEFAULT,
                          NULL, NULL, hInstance, NULL) ;
```

(continued)

```
      ShowWindow (hwnd, nCmdShow) ;
      UpdateWindow (hwnd) ;

      while (GetMessage (&msg, NULL, 0, 0))
            {
            TranslateMessage (&msg) ;
            DispatchMessage (&msg) ;
            }
      return msg.wParam ;
      }

void DoEscSupport (HDC hdc, HDC hdcInfo, short cxChar, short cyChar)
      {
      static struct
            {
            char  *szEscCode ;
            short nEscCode ;
            }
            esc [] =
            {
            "NEWFRAME",          NEWFRAME,
            "ABORTDOC",          ABORTDOC,
            "NEXTBAND",          NEXTBAND,
            "SETCOLORTABLE",     SETCOLORTABLE,
            "GETCOLORTABLE",     GETCOLORTABLE,
            "FLUSHOUTPUT",       FLUSHOUTPUT,
            "DRAFTMODE",         DRAFTMODE,
            "QUERYESCSUPPORT",   QUERYESCSUPPORT,
            "SETABORTPROC",      SETABORTPROC,
            "STARTDOC",          STARTDOC,
            "ENDDOC",            ENDDOC,
            "GETPHYSPAGESIZE",   GETPHYSPAGESIZE,
            "GETPRINTINGOFFSET", GETPRINTINGOFFSET,
            "GETSCALINGFACTOR",  GETSCALINGFACTOR } ;

      static char *szYesNo [] = { "Yes", "No" } ;
      char        szBuffer [32] ;
      POINT       pt ;
      short       n, nReturn ;

      TextOut (hdc, cxChar, cyChar, "Escape Support", 14) ;

      for (n = 0 ; n < sizeof esc / sizeof esc [0] ; n++)
            {
            nReturn = Escape (hdcInfo, QUERYESCSUPPORT, 1,
                                 (LPSTR) & esc[n].nEscCode, NULL) ;
            TextOut (hdc, 6 * cxChar, (n + 3) * cyChar, szBuffer,
                  wsprintf (szBuffer, "%-24s %3s", (LPSTR) esc[n].szEscCode,
                        (LPSTR) szYesNo [nReturn > 0 ? 0 : 1])) ;
```

(continued)

725

```
                    if (nReturn > 0 && esc[n].nEscCode >= GETPHYSPAGESIZE
                              && esc[n].nEscCode <= GETSCALINGFACTOR)
                    {
                    Escape (hdcInfo, esc[n].nEscCode, 0, NULL, (LPSTR) &pt) ;
                    TextOut (hdc, 36 * cxChar, (n + 3) * cyChar, szBuffer,
                              wsprintf (szBuffer, "(%u,%u)", pt.x, pt.y)) ;
                    }
               }
          }

long FAR PASCAL WndProc (HWND hwnd, WORD message, WORD wParam, LONG lParam)
     {
     static char    szAllDevices [4096], szDevice [32], szDriver [16],
                    szDriverFile [16], szWindowText [64] ;
     static HANDLE hLibrary ;
     static short  n, cxChar, cyChar, nCurrentDevice = IDM_SCREEN,
                              nCurrentInfo   = IDM_BASIC ;
     char          *szOutput, *szPtr ;
     DEVMODEPROC   lpfnDM ;
     HDC           hdc, hdcInfo ;
     HMENU         hMenu ;
     PAINTSTRUCT   ps ;
     TEXTMETRIC    tm ;

     switch (message)
          {
          case WM_CREATE :
               hdc = GetDC (hwnd) ;
               SelectObject (hdc, GetStockObject (SYSTEM_FIXED_FONT)) ;
               GetTextMetrics (hdc, &tm) ;
               cxChar = tm.tmAveCharWidth ;
               cyChar = tm.tmHeight + tm.tmExternalLeading ;
               ReleaseDC (hwnd, hdc) ;

               lParam = NULL ;
                                             // fall through
          case WM_WININICHANGE :
               if (lParam != NULL && lstrcmp ((LPSTR) lParam, "devices") != 0)
                    return 0 ;

               hMenu = GetSubMenu (GetMenu (hwnd), 0) ;

               while (GetMenuItemCount (hMenu) > 1)
                    DeleteMenu (hMenu, 1, MF_BYPOSITION) ;

               GetProfileString ("devices", NULL, "", szAllDevices,
                         sizeof szAllDevices) ;

               n = IDM_SCREEN + 1 ;
               szPtr = szAllDevices ;
               while (*szPtr)
```

(continued)

726

```
                    {
                    AppendMenu (hMenu, n % 16 ? 0 : MF_MENUBARBREAK, n, szPtr) ;
                    n++ ;
                    szPtr += strlen (szPtr) + 1 ;
                    }
          AppendMenu (hMenu, MF_SEPARATOR, 0, NULL) ;
          AppendMenu (hMenu, 0, IDM_DEVMODE, "Device Mode") ;

          wParam = IDM_SCREEN ;
                                                 // fall through
     case WM_COMMAND :
          hMenu = GetMenu (hwnd) ;

          if (wParam < IDM_DEVMODE)             // IDM_SCREEN & Printers
               {
               CheckMenuItem (hMenu, nCurrentDevice, MF_UNCHECKED) ;
               nCurrentDevice = wParam ;
               CheckMenuItem (hMenu, nCurrentDevice, MF_CHECKED) ;
               }
          else if (wParam == IDM_DEVMODE)
               {
               GetMenuString (hMenu, nCurrentDevice, szDevice,
                              sizeof szDevice, MF_BYCOMMAND) ;

               GetProfileString ("devices", szDevice, "",
                                 szDriver, sizeof szDriver) ;

               szOutput = strtok (szDriver, ", ") ;
               strcat (strcpy (szDriverFile, szDriver), ".DRV") ;

               if (hLibrary >= 32)
                    FreeLibrary (hLibrary) ;

               hLibrary = LoadLibrary (szDriverFile) ;
               if (hLibrary >= 32)
                    {
                    lpfnDM = GetProcAddress (hLibrary, "DEVICEMODE") ;
                    (*lpfnDM) (hwnd, hLibrary, (LPSTR) szDevice,
                                             (LPSTR) szOutput) ;
                    }
               }
          else                                 // info menu items
               {
               CheckMenuItem (hMenu, nCurrentInfo, MF_UNCHECKED) ;
               nCurrentInfo = wParam ;
               CheckMenuItem (hMenu, nCurrentInfo, MF_CHECKED) ;
               }
          InvalidateRect (hwnd, NULL, TRUE) ;
          return 0 ;
```

(continued)

```
           case WM_INITMENUPOPUP :
                if (lParam == 0)
                     EnableMenuItem (GetMenu (hwnd), IDM_DEVMODE,
                          nCurrentDevice == IDM_SCREEN ?
                               MF_GRAYED : MF_ENABLED) ;
                return 0 ;

           case WM_PAINT :
                strcpy (szWindowText, "Device Capabilities: ") ;

                if (nCurrentDevice == IDM_SCREEN)
                     {
                     strcpy (szDriver, "DISPLAY") ;
                     strcat (szWindowText, szDriver) ;
                     hdcInfo = CreateIC (szDriver, NULL, NULL, NULL) ;
                     }
                else
                     {
                     hMenu = GetMenu (hwnd) ;

                     GetMenuString (hMenu, nCurrentDevice, szDevice,
                                    sizeof szDevice, MF_BYCOMMAND) ;

                     GetProfileString ("devices", szDevice, "", szDriver, 10) ;
                     szOutput = strtok (szDriver, ", ") ;
                     strcat (szWindowText, szDevice) ;

                     hdcInfo = CreateIC (szDriver, szDevice, szOutput, NULL) ;
                     }
                SetWindowText (hwnd, szWindowText) ;

                hdc = BeginPaint (hwnd, &ps) ;
                SelectObject (hdc, GetStockObject (SYSTEM_FIXED_FONT)) ;

                if (hdcInfo)
                     {
                     switch (nCurrentInfo)
                          {
                          case IDM_BASIC :
                               DoBasicInfo (hdc, hdcInfo, cxChar, cyChar) ;
                               break ;

                          case IDM_OTHER :
                               DoOtherInfo (hdc, hdcInfo, cxChar, cyChar) ;
                               break ;

                          case IDM_CURVE :
                          case IDM_LINE :
                          case IDM_POLY :
```

(continued)

```
                            case IDM_TEXT :
                                    DoBitCodedCaps (hdc, hdcInfo, cxChar, cyChar,
                                        nCurrentInfo - IDM_CURVE) ;
                                    break ;

                            case IDM_ESC :
                                    DoEscSupport (hdc, hdcInfo, cxChar, cyChar) ;
                                    break ;
                            }
                        DeleteDC (hdcInfo) ;
                        }

                EndPaint (hwnd, &ps) ;
                return 0 ;

        case WM_DESTROY :
                if (hLibrary >= 32)
                    FreeLibrary (hLibrary) ;

                PostQuitMessage (0) ;
                return 0 ;
            }
    return DefWindowProc (hwnd, message, wParam, lParam) ;
    }
```

DEVCAPS2.RC

```
/*-------------------------------
   DEVCAPS2.RC resource script
  ---------------------------*/

#include "devcaps2.h"

DevCaps2 MENU
    {
    POPUP "&Device"
        {
        MENUITEM "&Screen",                  IDM_SCREEN, CHECKED
        }
    POPUP "&Capabilities"
        {
        MENUITEM "&Basic Information",       IDM_BASIC, CHECKED
        MENUITEM "&Other Information",       IDM_OTHER
        MENUITEM "&Curve Capabilities",      IDM_CURVE
        MENUITEM "&Line Capabilities",       IDM_LINE
        MENUITEM "&Polygonal Capabilities",  IDM_POLY
        MENUITEM "&Text Capabilities",       IDM_TEXT
        MENUITEM SEPARATOR
        MENUITEM "&Escape Support",          IDM_ESC
        }
    }
```

DEVCAPS2.H

```
/*---------------------------
    DEVCAPS2.H header file
  ----------------------*/

#define IDM_SCREEN  1

#define IDM_DEVMODE 0x100

#define IDM_BASIC   0x101
#define IDM_OTHER   0x102
#define IDM_CURVE   0x103
#define IDM_LINE    0x104
#define IDM_POLY    0x105
#define IDM_TEXT    0x106
#define IDM_ESC     0x107
```

DEVCAPS2.DEF

```
;---------------------------------
; DEVCAPS2.DEF module definition file
;---------------------------------

NAME        DEVCAPS2

DESCRIPTION 'Displays Device Capability Info (c) Charles Petzold, 1990'
EXETYPE     WINDOWS
STUB        'WINSTUB.EXE'
CODE        PRELOAD MOVEABLE DISCARDABLE
DATA        PRELOAD MOVEABLE MULTIPLE
HEAPSIZE    1024
STACKSIZE   8192
EXPORTS     WndProc
```

Because DEVCAPS2 obtains only an information context for the printer, you can select printers from DEVCAPS2's menu, even though they may have an output port of "none." If you want to compare the capabilities of different printers, you can first use the Control Panel to add various printer drivers to WIN.INI.

DEVCAPS2 has an additional option on the Capabilities menu called Escape Support, which lets you see which of the more common *Escape* subfunctions are supported by the device driver. This information will become more meaningful a little later in this chapter, when we discuss the *Escape* function and its subfunctions.

The *DeviceMode* Call

The Device menu of the DEVCAPS2 program includes an option called Device Mode. To use it, first select a printer from the Device menu, and then select Device Mode: Up pops a dialog box. Where did the dialog box come from? It is invoked by the printer driver, and— at the very least—it requests that you make a choice of paper size. Most printer drivers also give you a choice of "portrait" or "landscape" mode. In portrait mode (often the default), the short side of the paper is the top; in landscape mode, the long side is the top. If you change this mode, the change is reflected in the information the DEVCAPS2 program obtains from the *GetDeviceCaps* function: The horizontal size and resolution are switched with the vertical size and resolution. Device Mode dialog boxes for color plotters can be quite extensive, requesting the colors of the pens installed in the plotter and the type of paper (or transparencies) being used.

All printer drivers contain an exported function called *DeviceMode* that invokes this dialog box and saves the information that the user enters. Some printer drivers store this information in their own section of the WIN.INI file, and some don't. Those that store the information have access to it during the next Windows session.

Windows programs that allow the user a choice of printers generally call the *DeviceMode* function of the printer driver so that the user can make changes in preparation for printing. Calling this function from a program requires a technique that we'll learn more about in Chapter 19. Here's how DEVCAPS2 does it.

The program first obtains the name of the printer currently selected in the Device menu and saves it in a character array named *szDevice*:

```
GetMenuString (hMenu, nCurrentDevice, szDevice,
                    sizeof szDevice, MF_BYCOMMAND) ;
```

Then it obtains the driver name and output port of this device using *GetProfileString*. This information is stored in *szDriver*:

```
GetProfileString ("devices", szDevice, "",
                    szDriver, sizeof szDriver) ;
```

The output port is separated from the *szDriver* string using *strtok*, and the pointer is saved in *szOutput*:

```
szOutput = strtok (szDriver, ", ") ;
```

The *szDriver* string contains the name of the driver, which is the driver's filename without the .DRV extension. This statement creates the full name of the driver file and saves it in *szDriverFile*:

```
strcat (strcpy (szDriverFile, szDriver), ".DRV") ;
```

This driver file is a dynamic link library module. (Library modules are the subject of Chapter 19.) We can obtain a handle to this module (which is actually the instance handle of the module) by calling *LoadLibrary*. If *LoadLibrary* returns a value greater than or equal to 32, the function was successful. Otherwise, the return value indicates an MS-DOS error code.

The library can be freed by a call to *FreeLibrary*. If no other program is using this library, then it can be deleted from memory. DEVCAPS2 holds the library handle (or whatever was returned from *LoadLibrary*) in a *static* variable, so before trying to load a new library, it first frees the old one if the handle was valid:

```
if (hLibrary >= 32)
     FreeLibrary (hLibrary) ;

hLibrary = LoadLibrary (szDriverFile) ;
```

Before proceeding, the program checks to see if this new handle is valid:

```
if (hLibrary >= 32)
```

It then calls *GetProcAddress* to obtain the address of the *DeviceMode* function:

```
lpfnDM = GetProcAddress (hLibrary, "DEVICEMODE") ;
```

The *DeviceMode* function can be called indirectly by prefacing it with an asterisk. The function is passed the window handle, library module handle, device name, and output port:

```
(*lpfnDM) (hwnd, hLibrary, (LPSTR) szDevice,
                           (LPSTR) szOutput) ;
```

This invokes the dialog box. Note that you must explicitly cast the strings into far pointers, because this function has no template in WINDOWS.H or anywhere else.

The currently loaded driver file is freed when the program terminates:

```
case WM_DESTROY :
     if (hLibrary >= 32)
          FreeLibrary (hLibrary) ;
```

The *LoadLibrary* call increments the library module's "reference count" (a number Windows maintains to indicate the number of programs using a module), and the *FreeLibrary* call decrements it. The library can be freed from memory when the reference count is 0. Calls to *CreateDC* and *CreateIC* for a printer driver also increment the reference count, and *DeleteDC* decrements it.

Checking for *BitBlt* Capability

You can use the *GetDeviceCaps* function to obtain the size and resolution of the printable area of the page. (In most cases, this area won't be the same as the entire size of the paper.) You can also obtain the relative pixel width and height, if you want to do your own scaling.

You can obtain another important printer characteristic from the RC_BITBLT bit of the value returned from *GetDeviceCaps* with a parameter of RASTERCAPS ("raster capabilities"). This bit indicates whether the device is capable of bit-block transfers. Most dot-matrix and laser printers are capable of bit-block transfers, but most plotters are not. Devices that can't handle bit-block transfers do not support the following GDI functions: *CreateCompatibleDC*, *CreateCompatibleBitmap*, *PatBlt*, *BitBlt*, *StretchBlt*, *GrayString*, *DrawIcon*, *SetPixel*, *GetPixel*, *FloodFill*, *ExtFloodFill*, *FillRgn*, *FrameRgn*, *InvertRgn*, *PaintRgn*, *FillRect*, *FrameRect*, and *InvertRect*. This is the single most important distinction between using GDI calls on a video display and using them on a printer.

PRINTING FUNDAMENTALS

We're now ready to print, and we're going to start as simply as possible. In fact, our first two printing programs will be so simple that they won't work unless the Print Manager program gets loaded when printing begins. (The Print Manager doesn't get loaded if a user specifies *Spooler=no* in the WIN.INI file or if Windows can't find the PRINTMAN.EXE file.)

The *Escape* Function

The Windows GDI module includes only one function—*Escape*—to support the additional requirements of printers. The name of this function implies that it is ignored by the GDI module and that it goes straight to the printer driver. In some cases, this is true, but often GDI also does some work during *Escape* calls.

The general syntax of *Escape* is:

```
nResult = Escape (hdcPrinter, nEscapeCode, nCount,
                    lpsDataIn, lpsDataOut) ;
```

The *nEscapeCode* parameter is a subfunction code that is specified using an identifier defined in WINDOWS.H. The last three parameters depend on the subfunction. Although the last two parameters are declared as far pointers to character strings, they are sometimes far pointers to structures. To cast the pointers into far pointers to strings, use (LPSTR).

Not all *Escape* subfunctions are implemented in all device drivers. In fact, *Escape* has been designed to be open-ended so that manufacturers of display devices can define their own *Escape* subfunctions to access certain unique facilities of the devices. The following *Escape* subfunctions are the ones I discuss in this chapter. They are implemented in all printer drivers:

nEscapeCode	Description	nEscapeCode	Description
STARTDOC	Starts a document	ABORTDOC	Aborts printing of a document
ENDDOC	Ends a document		
SETABORTPROC	Sets a pointer to the "abort procedure"	GETPHYSPAGESIZE	Gets the physical size of the paper
NEWFRAME	Ends the current page	QUERYESCSUPPORT	Finds out if the driver supports an *Escape* code
NEXTBAND	Gets rectangle coordinates for the next band		

DEVCAPS2 used the QUERYESCSUPPORT subfunction to list supported *Escape* functions. The GETPHYSPAGESIZE subfunction returns the size of the paper, which will generally be larger than the printable area obtained from *GetDeviceCaps*. We'll use other subfunctions in programs later in this chapter. *Escape* always returns 0 if the subfunction is not implemented and a negative value if an error occurs. A positive value indicates success.

The FORMFEED Program

Our first printing program does nothing but cause a printer formfeed to eject the page. The FORMFEED program, shown in Figure 15-4, demonstrates the absolute minimum requirements for printing.

FORMFEED.MAK

```
#---------------------
# FORMFEED.MAK make file
#---------------------

formfeed.exe: formfeed.obj formfeed.def
      link formfeed, /align:16, NUL, /nod slibcew libw, formfeed
      rc formfeed.exe

formfeed.obj: formfeed.c
      cl -c -Gsw -Ow -W2 -Zp formfeed.c
```

FORMFEED.C

```
/*---------------------------------------------------
   FORMFEED.C -- Advances printer to next page
                 (c) Charles Petzold, 1990
   ---------------------------------------------*/
```

Figure 15-4. *The FORMFEED program.*   (continued)

```
#include <windows.h>
#include <string.h>

HDC  GetPrinterDC (void) ;

int PASCAL WinMain (HANDLE hInstance, HANDLE hPrevInstance,
                    LPSTR lpszCmdLine, int nCmdShow)
    {
    static char szMsg [] = "FormFeed" ;
    HDC         hdcPrint ;

    if (hdcPrint = GetPrinterDC ())
        {
        if (Escape (hdcPrint, STARTDOC, sizeof szMsg - 1, szMsg, NULL) > 0)
            if (Escape (hdcPrint, NEWFRAME, 0, NULL, NULL) > 0)
                Escape (hdcPrint, ENDDOC, 0, NULL, NULL) ;

        DeleteDC (hdcPrint) ;
        }
    return FALSE ;
    }

HDC GetPrinterDC (void)
    {
    static char szPrinter [80] ;
    char        *szDevice, *szDriver, *szOutput ;

    GetProfileString ("windows", "device", ",,,", szPrinter, 80) ;

    if ((szDevice = strtok (szPrinter, "," )) &&
        (szDriver = strtok (NULL,       ", ")) &&
        (szOutput = strtok (NULL,       ", ")))

            return CreateDC (szDriver, szDevice, szOutput, NULL) ;

    return 0 ;
    }
```

FORMFEED.DEF

```
;----------------------------------------
; FORMFEED.DEF module definition file
;----------------------------------------

NAME            FORMFEED

DESCRIPTION     'Printer Form Feed Program (c) Charles Petzold, 1990'
```

(continued)

```
EXETYPE     WINDOWS
STUB        'WINSTUB.EXE'
CODE        PRELOAD MOVEABLE DISCARDABLE
DATA        PRELOAD MOVEABLE MULTIPLE
HEAPSIZE    1024
STACKSIZE   8192
```

FORMFEED includes the *GetPrinterDC* function shown earlier. Other than obtaining the printer device context (and later deleting it), the program makes only three *Escape* calls. The first uses the STARTDOC subfunction to start a new document. It tests the return value from *Escape* and proceeds only if the value is positive:

```
if (Escape (hdcPrint, STARTDOC, sizeof szMsg - 1, szMsg, NULL) > 0)
```

The fourth parameter is a far pointer to the string that the Print Manager will display in its client area to identify the document being printed. Generally, this string includes the name of the application doing the printing and the file being printed. In this case, it's simply the name "FormFeed." The third parameter is the length of this string.

If STARTDOC is successful (indicated by a positive return value), then FORMFEED calls the NEWFRAME *Escape* subfunction, which advances the printer to a new page. Once again, the return value is tested:

```
if (Escape (hdcPrint, NEWFRAME, 0, NULL, NULL) > 0)
```

The third, fourth, and fifth parameters are not used in this *Escape* call.

Finally, if everything has proceeded without error to this point, the document is ended:

```
Escape (hdcPrint, ENDDOC, 0, NULL, NULL) ;
```

Again, the last three parameters are not used. Note that the ENDDOC *Escape* function is called only if no printing errors have been reported. If one of the other *Escape* functions returns an error code, then GDI has already aborted the document. If the printer is not currently printing, such an error code often results in the printer being reset.

Simply testing the return values from the *Escape* calls is the easiest way to check for errors. However, WINDOWS.H includes identifiers for the error codes, which you can use if you want to report the particular error to the user. For example, the NEWFRAME *Escape* call could return the SP_OUTOFDISK error (−4), indicating insufficient disk space for GDI to store the printer output necessary to trigger the printer to do a formfeed. For most printers, this occurrence is extremely unlikely. For your own amusement, however, you might try specifying the PostScript printer driver as your current printer, with the output port OUTPUT.PRN. Run FORMFEED and check the size of the file. (It will be nearly 8 KB!)

If you've ever written a simple formfeed program for MS-DOS, you know that ASCII number 12 activates a formfeed for most printers. Why not simply open the printer port using the C library function *open* and then output an ASCII number 12 using *write*?

Well, nothing prevents you from doing this. You first have to determine the parallel port or the serial port the printer is attached to—that's available from WIN.INI. You then have to determine if another program (the Print Manager, for instance) is currently using the printer. You don't want the formfeed to be output in the middle of a document, do you? Finally, you have to determine if ASCII number 12 is a formfeed character for the connected printer. It's not universal, you know. In fact, the formfeed command in PostScript isn't a 12; it's the word *showpage*.

In short, don't even think about going around Windows; stick with the Windows functions for printing.

PRINTING GRAPHICS AND TEXT

Printing from a Windows program usually involves more overhead than shown in the FORMFEED program, as well as some GDI calls to actually print something. Let's write a program that prints one page of text and graphics. We'll start with the method shown in the FORMFEED program and then add some enhancements. We'll be looking at four versions of this program called PRINT1, PRINT2, PRINT3, and PRINT4. To avoid a lot of duplicated source code, each of these programs will use functions contained in the PRINT.C file, which is shown in Figure 15-5.

PRINT.C

```
/*-----------------------------------------------------------------
   PRINT.C -- Common Routines for Print1, Print2, Print3, and Print4
              (c) Charles Petzold, 1990
   -----------------------------------------------------------------*/

#include <windows.h>
#include <string.h>

long FAR PASCAL WndProc (HWND, WORD, WORD, LONG) ;
BOOL PrintMyPage (HWND) ;

extern HANDLE hInst ;
extern char szAppName [] ;
extern char szCaption [] ;

int PASCAL WinMain (HANDLE hInstance, HANDLE hPrevInstance,
                    LPSTR lpszCmdLine, int nCmdShow)
    {
    HWND      hwnd ;
    MSG       msg ;
    WNDCLASS  wndclass ;
```

Figure 15-5. *The PRINT.C file of the PRINT1, PRINT2, PRINT3, and PRINT4 programs.*   *(continued)*

```
      if (!hPrevInstance)
          {
          wndclass.style          = CS_HREDRAW : CS_VREDRAW ;
          wndclass.lpfnWndProc    = WndProc ;
          wndclass.cbClsExtra     = 0 ;
          wndclass.cbWndExtra     = 0 ;
          wndclass.hInstance      = hInstance ;
          wndclass.hIcon          = LoadIcon (NULL, IDI_APPLICATION) ;
          wndclass.hCursor        = LoadCursor (NULL, IDC_ARROW) ;
          wndclass.hbrBackground  = GetStockObject (WHITE_BRUSH) ;
          wndclass.lpszMenuName   = NULL ;
          wndclass.lpszClassName  = szAppName ;

          RegisterClass (&wndclass) ;
          }

      hInst = hInstance ;

      hwnd = CreateWindow (szAppName, szCaption,
                        WS_OVERLAPPEDWINDOW,
                        CW_USEDEFAULT, CW_USEDEFAULT,
                        CW_USEDEFAULT, CW_USEDEFAULT,
                        NULL, NULL, hInstance, NULL) ;

      ShowWindow (hwnd, nCmdShow) ;
      UpdateWindow (hwnd) ;

      while (GetMessage (&msg, NULL, 0, 0))
          {
          TranslateMessage (&msg) ;
          DispatchMessage (&msg) ;
          }
      return msg.wParam ;
      }

long FAR PASCAL WndProc (HWND hwnd, WORD message, WORD wParam, LONG lParam)
      {
      HMENU hMenu ;

      switch (message)
          {
          case WM_CREATE :
                hMenu = GetSystemMenu (hwnd, FALSE) ;
                AppendMenu (hMenu, MF_SEPARATOR, 0, NULL) ;
                AppendMenu (hMenu, 0, 1, "&Print") ;
                return 0 ;

          case WM_SYSCOMMAND :
                if (wParam == 1)
```

(continued)

```
                        {
                        if (PrintMyPage (hwnd))
                             MessageBox (hwnd, "Could not print page",
                                  szAppName, MB_OK : MB_ICONEXCLAMATION) ;
                        return 0 ;
                        }
                   break ;

              case WM_DESTROY :
                   PostQuitMessage (0) ;
                   return 0 ;
              }
         return DefWindowProc (hwnd, message, wParam, lParam) ;
         }

HDC GetPrinterDC (void)
     {
     static char szPrinter [80] ;
     char        *szDevice, *szDriver, *szOutput ;

     GetProfileString ("windows", "device", ",,,", szPrinter, 80) ;

     if ((szDevice = strtok (szPrinter, "," )) &&
         (szDriver = strtok (NULL,       ", ")) &&
         (szOutput = strtok (NULL,       ", ")))

              return CreateDC (szDriver, szDevice, szOutput, NULL) ;

     return 0 ;
     }

void PageGDICalls (HDC hdcPrn, short cxPage, short cyPage)
     {
     static char szTextStr [] = "Hello, Printer!" ;
     DWORD        dwExtent ;

     Rectangle (hdcPrn, 0, 0, cxPage, cyPage) ;

     MoveTo (hdcPrn, 0, 0) ;
     LineTo (hdcPrn, cxPage, cyPage) ;
     MoveTo (hdcPrn, cxPage, 0) ;
     LineTo (hdcPrn, 0, cyPage) ;

     SaveDC (hdcPrn) ;

     SetMapMode (hdcPrn, MM_ISOTROPIC) ;
     SetWindowExt    (hdcPrn, 1000, 1000) ;
     SetViewportExt (hdcPrn, cxPage / 2, -cyPage / 2) ;
     SetViewportOrg (hdcPrn, cxPage / 2,  cyPage / 2) ;
```

(continued)

```
    Ellipse (hdcPrn, -500, 500, 500, -500) ;

    dwExtent = GetTextExtent (hdcPrn, szTextStr, sizeof szTextStr - 1) ;
    TextOut (hdcPrn, LOWORD (dwExtent) / 2, HIWORD (dwExtent) / 2,
            szTextStr, sizeof szTextStr - 1) ;

    RestoreDC (hdcPrn, -1) ;
    }
```

PRINT.C contains the functions *WinMain*, *WndProc*, and *GetPrinterDC* and a function called *PageGDICalls*, which expects to receive a handle to the printer device context and two variables containing the width and height of the printer page. *PageGDICalls* draws a rectangle that encompasses the entire page, two lines between opposite corners of the page, a circle in the middle of the page (its diameter half the lesser of the printer height and width), and the text "Hello, Printer!" in the center of this ellipse.

During processing of the WM_CREATE message, *WndProc* adds a Print option to the system menu. Selecting this option causes a call to *PrintMyPage*, a function that we'll enhance over the course of the four versions of the program. *PrintMyPage* returns TRUE (nonzero) if it encounters an error during printing and returns FALSE otherwise. If *PrintMyPage* returns TRUE, *WndProc* displays a message box to inform you of the error.

Bare-Bones Printing

PRINT1, the first version of the printing program, is shown in Figure 15-6. After compiling PRINT1, you can execute it and then select Print from the system menu. If your WIN.INI file has the line *Spooler=yes* and if Windows can find PRINTMAN.EXE, you should see the Print Manager icon appear at the bottom of the screen. If the TEMP variable in your MS-DOS environment indicates a fixed disk (or if you have no TEMP variable), then you should see some disk activity as the GDI module saves the printer output to a temporary file. You won't be able to do anything in Windows during this time. After PRINT1 has finished, the Print Manager should display the text "Print1: Printing" in its client area and begin sending the disk file out to the printer. You'll be able to work normally in Windows again.

Let's look at the code in PRINT1.C. If *PrintMyPage* can't obtain a device context handle for the printer, it returns TRUE, and *WndProc* displays the message box indicating an error. If the function succeeds in obtaining the device context handle, it then determines the horizontal and vertical size of the page in pixels by calling *GetDeviceCaps*:

```
xPage = GetDeviceCaps (hdcPrn, HORZRES) ;
yPage = GetDeviceCaps (hdcPrn, VERTRES) ;
```

This is not the full size of the paper but rather its printable area. After that call, the code in PRINT1's *PrintMyPage* function is structurally the same as the code in FORMFEED, except that PRINT1 calls *PageGDICalls* between the STARTDOC and NEWFRAME *Escape* calls. Only if both the STARTDOC and NEWFRAME calls are successful does PRINT1 call END-DOC *Escape*.

PRINT1.MAK

```
#----------------------
# PRINT1.MAK make file
#----------------------

print1.exe : print.obj print1.obj print1.def
      link print1 print, /align:16, NUL, /nod slibcew libw, print1
      rc print1.exe

print.obj : print.c
      cl -c -Gsw -Ow -W2 -Zp print.c

print1.obj : print1.c
      cl -c -Gsw -Ow -W2 -Zp print1.c
```

PRINT1.C

```
/*------------------------------------------
    PRINT1.C -- Bare-Bones Printing
                (c) Charles Petzold, 1990
   ------------------------------------------*/

#include <windows.h>

HDC  GetPrinterDC (void) ;               // in PRINT.C
void PageGDICalls (HDC, short, short) ;

HANDLE hInst ;
char   szAppName [] = "Print1" ;
char   szCaption [] = "Print Program 1" ;

BOOL PrintMyPage (HWND hwnd)
     {
     static char szMessage [] = "Print1: Printing" ;
     BOOL        bError = FALSE ;
     HDC         hdcPrn ;
     short       xPage, yPage ;

     if (NULL == (hdcPrn = GetPrinterDC ()))
          return TRUE ;
```

Figure 15-6. *The PRINT1 program.*   (continued)

```
     xPage = GetDeviceCaps (hdcPrn, HORZRES) ;
     yPage = GetDeviceCaps (hdcPrn, VERTRES) ;

     if (Escape (hdcPrn, STARTDOC, sizeof szMessage - 1, szMessage, NULL) > 0)
          {
          PageGDICalls (hdcPrn, xPage, yPage) ;

          if (Escape (hdcPrn, NEWFRAME, 0, NULL, NULL) > 0)
               Escape (hdcPrn, ENDDOC, 0, NULL, NULL) ;
          else
               bError = TRUE ;
          }
     else
          bError = TRUE ;

     DeleteDC (hdcPrn) ;
     return bError ;
     }
```

PRINT1.DEF

```
;--------------------------------------
; PRINT1.DEF module definition file
;--------------------------------------

NAME            PRINT1

DESCRIPTION     'Printing Program No. 1 (c) Charles Petzold, 1990'
EXETYPE         WINDOWS
STUB            'WINSTUB.EXE'
CODE            PRELOAD MOVEABLE DISCARDABLE
DATA            PRELOAD MOVEABLE MULTIPLE
HEAPSIZE        1024
STACKSIZE       8192
EXPORTS         WndProc
```

Setting an Abort Procedure

The enhancement that we'll add in the PRINT2 version of our program prevents problems related to disk space. If you try to run PRINT1 when the drive containing the TEMP subdirectory lacks sufficient space to store the full page of graphics output, the NEWFRAME *Escape* call will return an SP_OUTOFDISK error. This error could result from the presence in the TEMP subdirectory of other temporary print files created by GDI for printing. If the Print Manager were given enough time to send these files to the printer, then the program currently printing could continue. It wouldn't be necessary for Windows to return an SP_OUTOFDISK error to the program. However, the Print Manager cannot transfer these files to the printer because—like all other Windows programs—it isn't receiving messages during the time your program is printing.

This problem is solved with something called an "abort procedure". The abort procedure is a small exported function in your program. You give Windows the address of this function using the *Escape* SETABORTPROC subfunction. If GDI runs out of disk space while creating temporary print files, and if enough space could eventually become available by having the Print Manager send existing print files to the printer, then the GDI module calls the program's abort procedure. The abort procedure then effectively yields control to allow the Print Manager to print.

Let's look first at what's required to add an abort procedure to the printing logic and then examine some of the ramifications. The abort procedure is commonly called *AbortProc*, and it takes the following form:

```
BOOL FAR PASCAL AbortProc (HDC hdcPrn, short nCode)
    {
    [other program lines]
    }
```

The function must be listed in the EXPORTS section of your module definition file. Before printing, you must obtain a pointer to this function from *MakeProcInstance*:

```
FARPROC   lpfnAbortProc ;
    [other program lines]
lpfnAbortProc = MakeProcInstance (AbortProc, hInstance) ;
```

You then set the abort procedure using the *Escape* SETABORTPROC subfunction. The *lpsDataIn* parameter is the pointer returned from *MakeProcInstance*:

```
Escape (hdcPrn, SETABORTPROC, 0, (LPSTR) lpfnAbortProc, NULL) ;
```

You make this call before the STARTDOC *Escape* call. You don't need to "unset" the abort procedure after you finish printing.

While processing the NEWFRAME *Escape* call (that is, while playing the metafile into the device driver and creating the temporary printer output files), GDI frequently calls the abort procedure. The *hdcPrn* parameter is the printer device context handle. The *nCode* parameter is 0 if all is going well or is SP_OUTOFDISK if the GDI module has run out of disk space because of the temporary printer output files.

AbortProc must return TRUE (nonzero) if the print job is to be continued and returns FALSE (0) if the print job is to be aborted. If *AbortProc* receives an *nCode* parameter of SP_OUTOFDISK and returns FALSE, then the NEWFRAME *Escape* call currently in progress returns an SP_APPABORT error code (equal to −2), and the print job is aborted.

The abort procedure can be as simple as this:

```
BOOL FAR PASCAL AbortProc (HDC hdcPrn, short nCode)
    {
    MSG    msg ;

    while (PeekMessage (&msg, NULL, 0, 0, PM_REMOVE))
        {
        TranslateMessage (&msg) ;
        DispatchMessage (&msg) ;
        }
    return TRUE ;
    }
```

This function may seem a little peculiar. In fact, it looks suspiciously like a message loop. What's a message loop doing here of all places? Well, it *is* a message loop. You'll note, however, that this message loop calls *PeekMessage* rather than *GetMessage*. I discussed *Peek-Message* in connection with the RANDRECT program at the end of Chapter 12. You'll recall that *PeekMessage* returns control to a program with a message from the program's message queue (just like *GetMessage*) but also returns control if there are no messages waiting in any program's message queue.

The message loop in the *AbortProc* function repeatedly calls *PeekMessage* while *PeekMessage* returns TRUE. This TRUE value means that *PeekMessage* has retrieved a message that can be sent to one of the program's window procedures using *TranslateMessage* and *DispatchMessage*. When there are no more messages in the program's message queue, Windows allows other programs to process messages from their queues. When there are no more messages in any program's message queue, Windows returns control to the program calling *PeekMessage* (that is, to the *AbortProc* function). The return value of *Peek-Message* is then FALSE, so *AbortProc* returns control to Windows.

The PRINT1 version of our program doesn't yield control during the entire time it is printing. Windows is essentially frozen during that time because no other program can process messages. As you've probably discovered by now, the *PrintMyPage* function in PRINT1 can take a while. Only when the function is finished can the Print Manager actually start to print. An abort procedure gives the Print Manager—and other programs running under Windows—a chance to run while a program is printing.

How Windows Uses *AbortProc*

When a program is printing, the bulk of the work takes place during the NEWFRAME *Escape* call. Before that call, the GDI module simply adds another record to the disk-based metafile every time the program calls a GDI drawing function. When GDI gets the NEWFRAME *Escape* call, it plays this metafile into the device driver once for each band the device driver defines on a page. GDI then stores the printer output created by the printer driver in a file. If the Print Manager isn't loaded, the GDI module itself must write this printer output to the printer.

During the NEWFRAME *Escape* call, the GDI module calls the abort procedure you've set. Normally, the *nCode* parameter is 0, but if GDI has run out of disk space because of the presence of other temporary files that haven't been printed yet, then the *nCode* parameter is SP_OUTOFDISK. (You wouldn't normally check this value, but you can if you want.) The abort procedure then goes into its *PeekMessage* loop. The loop first retrieves messages from the program's own message queue and then yields control so that other programs can retrieve and process their own messages. When no messages remain in any program's queue, control passes to another program currently waiting for its own *PeekMessage* call to return.

One of those programs is PRINTMAN.EXE, which also uses a *PeekMessage* call to retrieve messages. When the Print Manager returns from the *PeekMessage* call in its own message loop, it can transfer part of a disk file to the printer. The Print Manager then calls *PeekMessage* again in its own message loop. If there are still no messages in any program's message queue, control returns to *AbortProc*, and *PeekMessage* returns FALSE. The abort procedure then drops out of its message loop and returns a TRUE value to the GDI module to indicate that printing should continue. The GDI module then continues to process the NEWFRAME *Escape* call.

While the main purpose of the abort procedure is to allow the Print Manager the opportunity to transfer existing files to the printer to free up disk space, it also allows all other programs to run during the time a program is printing. This effect of the abort procedure is particularly important if the Print Manager isn't installed.

Implementing an Abort Procedure

Let's quickly review the mechanics of the abort procedure. You define an abort procedure that looks like this:

```
BOOL FAR PASCAL AbortProc (HDC hdcPrn, short nCode)
    {
    MSG  msg ;

    while (PeekMessage (&msg, NULL, 0, 0, PM_REMOVE))
        {
        TranslateMessage (&msg) ;
        DispatchMessage (&msg) ;
        }
    return TRUE ;
    }
```

You list *AbortProc* in the EXPORTS section of your module definition file. You obtain a pointer to the function using *MakeProcInstance*:

```
lpfnAbortProc = MakeProcInstance (AbortProc, hInstance) ;
```

When you want to print something, you give Windows this pointer with an *Escape* call:

```
Escape (hdcPrn, SETABORTPROC, 0, (LPSTR) lpfnAbortProc, NULL) ;
```

You make this *Escape* call before the *Escape* call for STARTDOC. And that's it.

Well, not quite. We've overlooked a problem with that *PeekMessage* loop in *AbortProc*—a big problem. *AbortProc* is called only while your program is in the midst of printing. Some very ugly things can happen if you retrieve a message in *AbortProc* and dispatch it to your own window procedure. A user could select Print from the menu again. But the program is already in the middle of the printing routine. A user could load a new file into the program while the program is trying to print the previous file. A user could even quit your program! If that happens, all your program's windows will be destroyed. You'll eventually return from the printing routine, but you'll have nowhere to go except to a window procedure that's no longer valid.

This stuff boggles the mind. Your program isn't prepared for it. For this reason, when you set an abort procedure, you should first disable your program's window so that it can't receive keyboard and mouse input. You do this with:

```
EnableWindow (hwnd, FALSE) ;
```

This prevents keyboard and mouse input from getting into the message queue. The user therefore can't do anything with your program during the time it's printing. When printing is finished, you reenable the window for input:

```
EnableWindow (hwnd, TRUE) ;
```

So why, you ask, do we even bother with the *TranslateMessage* and *DispatchMessage* calls in *AbortProc* when no keyboard or mouse messages will get into the message queue in the first place? It's true that the *TranslateMessage* call isn't strictly needed (although it's almost always included). But we must use *DispatchMessage* in case a WM_PAINT message gets in the message queue. If WM_PAINT isn't processed properly with a *BeginPaint* and *EndPaint* pair in the window procedure, the message will remain in the queue and clog up the works, because *PeekMessage* will never return a FALSE.

When you disable your window during the time you're printing, your program remains inert on the display. But a user can switch to another program and do some work there, and Print Manager can continue sending output files to the printer.

The PRINT2 program, shown in Figure 15-7, adds an abort procedure (and the necessary support) to the logic in PRINT1. More specifically, PRINT2 adds the abort procedure (including a listing in the EXPORTS section of PRINT2.DEF), a call to *MakeProcInstance* and *Escape* using the SETABORTPROC subfunction, a *FreeProcInstance* call at the end, and two calls to *EnableWindow*, the first to disable the window and the second to reenable it.

PRINT2.MAK

```
#--------------------
# PRINT2.MAK make file
#--------------------

print2.exe : print.obj print2.obj print2.def
    link print2 print, /align:16, NUL, /nod slibcew libw, print2
    rc print2.exe

print.obj : print.c
    cl -c -Gsw -Ow -W2 -Zp print.c

print2.obj : print2.c
    cl -c -Gsw -Ow -W2 -Zp print2.c
```

PRINT2.C

```c
/*---------------------------------------------
    PRINT2.C -- Printing with Abort Function
               (c) Charles Petzold, 1990
   ---------------------------------------------*/

#include <windows.h>

HDC  GetPrinterDC (void) ;                    // in PRINT.C
void PageGDICalls (HDC, short, short) ;

HANDLE hInst ;
char   szAppName [] = "Print2" ;
char   szCaption [] = "Print Program 2 (Abort Function)" ;

BOOL FAR PASCAL AbortProc (HDC hdcPrn, short nCode)
    {
    MSG   msg ;

    while (PeekMessage (&msg, NULL, 0, 0, PM_REMOVE))
        {
        TranslateMessage (&msg) ;
        DispatchMessage (&msg) ;
        }
    return TRUE ;
    }
```

Figure 15-7. *The PRINT2 program.*   *(continued)*

```
BOOL PrintMyPage (HWND hwnd)
    {
    static char szMessage [] = "Print2: Printing" ;
    BOOL        bError = FALSE ;
    FARPROC     lpfnAbortProc ;
    HDC         hdcPrn ;
    RECT        rect ;
    short       xPage, yPage ;

    if (NULL == (hdcPrn = GetPrinterDC ()))
        return TRUE ;

    xPage = GetDeviceCaps (hdcPrn, HORZRES) ;
    yPage = GetDeviceCaps (hdcPrn, VERTRES) ;

    EnableWindow (hwnd, FALSE) ;

    lpfnAbortProc = MakeProcInstance (AbortProc, hInst) ;
    Escape (hdcPrn, SETABORTPROC, 0, (LPSTR) lpfnAbortProc, NULL) ;

    if (Escape (hdcPrn, STARTDOC, sizeof szMessage - 1, szMessage, NULL) > 0)
        {
        PageGDICalls (hdcPrn, xPage, yPage) ;

        if (Escape (hdcPrn, NEWFRAME, 0, NULL, NULL) > 0)
            Escape (hdcPrn, ENDDOC, 0, NULL, NULL) ;
        else
            bError = TRUE ;
        }
    else
        bError = TRUE ;

    if (!bError)
        Escape (hdcPrn, ENDDOC, 0, NULL, NULL) ;

    FreeProcInstance (lpfnAbortProc) ;
    EnableWindow (hwnd, TRUE) ;
    DeleteDC (hdcPrn) ;
    return bError ;
    }
```

PRINT2.DEF

```
;-----------------------------------
; PRINT2.DEF module definition file
;-----------------------------------

NAME            PRINT2
```

(continued)

```
DESCRIPTION     'Printing Program No. 2 (c) Charles Petzold, 1990'
EXETYPE         WINDOWS
STUB            'WINSTUB.EXE'
CODE            PRELOAD MOVEABLE DISCARDABLE
DATA            PRELOAD MOVEABLE MULTIPLE
HEAPSIZE        1024
STACKSIZE       8192
EXPORTS         WndProc
                AbortProc
```

Adding a Printing Dialog Box

PRINT2 is not entirely satisfactory. First, the program doesn't directly indicate when it is printing and when it is finished with printing. Only when you poke at the program with the mouse and find that it doesn't respond can you determine that it must still be processing the *PrintMyPage* routine. Nor does PRINT2 give the user the opportunity to cancel the print job before it shows up in the Print Manager's client area.

You're probably aware that most Windows programs give users a chance to cancel a printing operation currently in progress. A small dialog box comes up on the screen; it contains some text and a push button labeled Cancel. The program displays this dialog box during the entire time that GDI is saving the printer output in a disk file or (if the Print Manager isn't loaded) while the printer is printing. This is a modeless dialog box, and you must supply the dialog procedure. As for all dialog boxes, you include the name of the dialog procedure in the EXPORTS section of the module definition file and use *MakeProcInstance* to obtain a pointer to the function.

This dialog box is often called the "abort dialog box," and the dialog procedure is often called the "abort dialog procedure." To distinguish it more clearly from the "abort procedure," I'll call this dialog procedure the "printing dialog procedure." The abort procedure (with the name *AbortProc*) and the printing dialog procedure (which I'll name *PrintDlgProc*) are two separate exported functions. If you want to print in a professional Windows-like manner, you must have both of these.

These two functions interact as follows. The *PeekMessage* loop in *AbortProc* must be modified to send messages for the modeless dialog box to the dialog box window procedure. *PrintDlgProc* must process WM_COMMAND messages to check the status of the Cancel button. If the Cancel button is pressed, it sets a variable called *bUserAbort* to TRUE. The value returned from *AbortProc* is the inverse of *bUserAbort*. You'll recall that *AbortProc* returns TRUE to continue printing and FALSE to abort printing. In PRINT2 we always returned TRUE. Now we'll return FALSE if the user clicks the Cancel button in the printing dialog box. This logic is implemented in the PRINT3 program, shown in Figure 15-8, beginning on the following page.

PRINT3.MAK

```
#---------------------
# PRINT3.MAK make file
#---------------------

print3.exe : print.obj print3.obj print3.def print.res
     link print3 print, /align:16, NUL, /nod slibcew libw, print3
     rc print.res print3.exe

print.obj : print.c
     cl -c -Gsw -Ow -W2 -Zp print.c

print3.obj : print3.c
     cl -c -Gsw -Ow -W2 -Zp print3.c

print.res : print.rc
     rc -r print.rc
```

PRINT3.C

```c
/*-----------------------------------------
   PRINT3.C -- Printing with Dialog Box
             (c) Charles Petzold, 1990
   -----------------------------------------*/

#include <windows.h>

HDC  GetPrinterDC (void) ;                // in PRINT.C
void PageGDICalls (HDC, short, short) ;

HANDLE hInst ;
char   szAppName [] = "Print3" ;
char   szCaption [] = "Print Program 3 (Dialog Box)" ;

BOOL   bUserAbort ;
HWND   hDlgPrint ;

BOOL FAR PASCAL PrintDlgProc (HWND hDlg, WORD message, WORD wParam, LONG lParam)
     {
     switch (message)
          {
          case WM_INITDIALOG :
               SetWindowText (hDlg, szAppName) ;
               EnableMenuItem (GetSystemMenu (hDlg, FALSE), SC_CLOSE,
                                                        MF_GRAYED) ;

               return TRUE ;
```

Figure 15-8. *The PRINT3 command.*   *(continued)*

```
            case WM_COMMAND :
                 bUserAbort = TRUE ;
                 EnableWindow (GetParent (hDlg), TRUE) ;
                 DestroyWindow (hDlg) ;
                 hDlgPrint = 0 ;
                 return TRUE ;
            }
      return FALSE ;
      }

BOOL FAR PASCAL AbortProc (HDC hdcPrn, short nCode)
      {
      MSG   msg ;

      while (!bUserAbort && PeekMessage (&msg, NULL, 0, 0, PM_REMOVE))
            {
            if (!hDlgPrint !! !IsDialogMessage (hDlgPrint, &msg))
                 {
                 TranslateMessage (&msg) ;
                 DispatchMessage (&msg) ;
                 }
            }
      return !bUserAbort ;
      }

BOOL PrintMyPage (HWND hwnd)
      {
      static char szMessage [] = "Print3: Printing" ;
      BOOL        bError = FALSE ;
      FARPROC     lpfnAbortProc, lpfnPrintDlgProc ;
      HDC         hdcPrn ;
      RECT        rect ;
      short       xPage, yPage ;

      if (NULL == (hdcPrn = GetPrinterDC ()))
            return TRUE ;

      xPage = GetDeviceCaps (hdcPrn, HORZRES) ;
      yPage = GetDeviceCaps (hdcPrn, VERTRES) ;

      EnableWindow (hwnd, FALSE) ;

      bUserAbort = FALSE ;
      lpfnPrintDlgProc = MakeProcInstance (PrintDlgProc, hInst) ;
      hDlgPrint = CreateDialog (hInst, "PrintDlgBox", hwnd, lpfnPrintDlgProc) ;

      lpfnAbortProc = MakeProcInstance (AbortProc, hInst) ;
      Escape (hdcPrn, SETABORTPROC, 0, (LPSTR) lpfnAbortProc, NULL) ;
```

(continued)

```
      if (Escape (hdcPrn, STARTDOC, sizeof szMessage - 1, szMessage, NULL) > 0)
            {
            PageGDICalls (hdcPrn, xPage, yPage) ;

            if (Escape (hdcPrn, NEWFRAME, 0, NULL, NULL) > 0)
                  Escape (hdcPrn, ENDDOC, 0, NULL, NULL) ;
            else
                  bError = TRUE ;
            }
      else
            bError = TRUE ;

      if (!bUserAbort)
            {
            EnableWindow (hwnd, TRUE) ;
            DestroyWindow (hDlgPrint) ;
            }

      FreeProcInstance (lpfnPrintDlgProc) ;
      FreeProcInstance (lpfnAbortProc) ;
      DeleteDC (hdcPrn) ;

      return bError || bUserAbort ;
      }
```

PRINT.RC

```
/*---------------------------
   PRINT.RC resource script
---------------------------*/

#include <windows.h>

PrintDlgBox DIALOG 40, 40, 120, 40
      STYLE WS_POPUP | WS_CAPTION | WS_SYSMENU | WS_VISIBLE
      {
      CTEXT           "Cancel Printing", -1,  4,  6, 120, 12
      DEFPUSHBUTTON   "Cancel",    IDCANCEL, 44, 22,  32, 14, WS_GROUP
      }
```

PRINT3.DEF

```
;-------------------------------------
; PRINT3.DEF module definition file
;-------------------------------------

NAME            PRINT3

DESCRIPTION     'Printing Program No. 3 (c) Charles Petzold, 1990'
EXETYPE         WINDOWS
STUB            'WINSTUB.EXE'
CODE            PRELOAD MOVEABLE DISCARDABLE
DATA            PRELOAD MOVEABLE MULTIPLE
HEAPSIZE        1024
STACKSIZE       8192
EXPORTS         WndProc
                AbortProc
                PrintDlgProc
```

Two global variables are added to PRINT3: a BOOL called *bUserAbort* and a handle to the dialog box window called *hDlgPrint*. The *PrintMyPage* function initializes *bUserAbort* to FALSE, and as in PRINT2, the program's main window is disabled. *PrintMyPage* then calls *MakeProcInstance* for both *AbortProc* and *PrintDlgProc*. The pointer to *AbortProc* is used in the SETABORTPROC *Escape* call, and the pointer to *PrintDlgProc* is used in a *Create-Dialog* call. The window handle returned from *CreateDialog* is saved in *hDlgPrint*.

The message loop in *AbortProc* now looks like this:

```
while (!bUserAbort && PeekMessage (&msg, NULL, 0, 0, PM_REMOVE))
    {
    if (!hDlgPrint !! !IsDialogMessage (hDlgPrint, &msg))
        {
        TranslateMessage (&msg) ;
        DispatchMessage (&msg) ;
        }
    }
return !bUserAbort ;
```

It calls *PeekMessage* only if *bUserAbort* is FALSE, that is, if the user hasn't yet aborted the printing operation. The *IsDialogMessage* function is required to send the message to the modeless dialog box. As is normal with modeless dialog boxes, the handle to the dialog box window is checked before this call is made. *AbortProc* returns the inverse of *bUserAbort*. Initially, *bUserAbort* is FALSE, so *AbortProc* returns TRUE, indicating that printing is to continue. But *bUserAbort* could be set to TRUE in the printing dialog procedure.

The *PrintDlgProc* function is fairly simple. While processing WM_INITDIALOG, the function sets the window caption to the name of the program and disables the Close option on the system menu. If the user clicks the Cancel button, *PrintDlgProc* receives a WM_COMMAND message:

```
case WM_COMMAND :
     bUserAbort = TRUE ;
     EnableWindow (GetParent (hDlg), TRUE) ;
     DestroyWindow (hDlg) ;
     hDlgPrint = 0 ;
     return TRUE ;
```

Setting *bUserAbort* to TRUE indicates that the user has decided to cancel the printing operation. The main window is enabled, and the dialog box is destroyed. (It is important that you perform these two actions in this order. Otherwise, some other program running under Windows will become the active program, and your program might disappear into the background.) As is normal, *hDlgPrint* is set to 0 to prevent *IsDialogMessage* from being called in the message loop.

The only time this dialog box receives messages is when *AbortProc* retrieves messages with *PeekMessage* and sends them to the dialog box window procedure with *IsDialogMessage*. The only time *AbortProc* is called is when the GDI module is processing the NEWFRAME *Escape* function. If GDI sees that the return value from *AbortProc* is FALSE, it returns control from the *Escape* call back to *PrintMyPage*. It doesn't return an error code. At that point, *PrintMyPage* thinks that the page is complete and calls the ENDDOC *Escape* function. Nothing is printed, however, because the GDI module didn't finish processing the NEWFRAME Escape call.

Some cleanup remains. If the user didn't cancel the print job from the dialog box, then the dialog box is still displayed. *PrintMyPage* reenables its main window and destroys the dialog box:

```
if (!bUserAbort)
     {
     EnableWindow (hwnd, TRUE) ;
     DestroyWindow (hDlgPrint) ;
     }
```

Two variables tell you what happened: *bUserAbort* tells you if the user aborted the print job, and *bError* tells you if an error occurred. You can do what you want with these variables. *PrintMyPage* simply performs a logical OR operation to return to *WndProc*:

```
return bError !! bUserAbort ;
```

Adding Printing to POPPAD

Now we're ready to add a printing facility to the POPPAD series of programs and declare POPPAD finished. You'll need the various POPPAD files from Chapter 10, plus the three new files in Figure 15-9.

POPPAD.MAK

```
#---------------------
# POPPAD.MAK make file
#---------------------

poppad.exe : poppad.obj  poppadf.obj poppadp.obj \
             filedlg.obj poppad.def  poppad.res
     link poppad poppadf poppadp filedlg, poppad.exe /align:16, \
          NUL, /nod slibcew libw, poppad
     rc poppad.res  poppad.exe

poppad.obj : poppad.c poppad.h
     cl -c -Gsw -Ow -W2 -Zp poppad.c

poppadf.obj : poppadf.c
     cl -c -Gsw -Ow -W2 -Zp poppadf.c

poppadp.obj : poppadp.c
     cl -c -Gsw -Ow -W2 -Zp poppadp.c

filedlg.obj : filedlg.c filedlg.h
     cl -c -Gsw -Ow -W2 -Zp filedlg.c

poppad.res : poppad.rc poppad.h poppad.ico filedlg.dlg filedlg.h
     rc -r poppad.rc
```

POPPADP.C

```
/*------------------------------------------------
   POPPADP.C -- Popup Editor Printing Functions
             (c) Charles Petzold, 1990
   ------------------------------------------------*/

#include <windows.h>
#include <string.h>
#include "filedlg.h"                 // for IDD_FNAME definition

extern char szAppName [] ;           // in POPPAD.C
```

Figure 15-9. *New POPPAD files to add printing capability.*   *(continued)*

```
BOOL bUserAbort ;
HWND hDlgPrint ;

BOOL FAR PASCAL PrintDlgProc (HWND hDlg, WORD message, WORD wParam, LONG lParam)
     {
     switch (message)
          {
          case WM_INITDIALOG :
                 EnableMenuItem (GetSystemMenu (hDlg, FALSE), SC_CLOSE,
                                                        MF_GRAYED) ;

                 return TRUE ;

          case WM_COMMAND :
                 bUserAbort = TRUE ;
                 EnableWindow (GetParent (hDlg), TRUE) ;
                 DestroyWindow (hDlg) ;
                 hDlgPrint = 0 ;
                 return TRUE ;
          }
     return FALSE ;
     }

BOOL FAR PASCAL AbortProc (HDC hPrinterDC, short nCode)
     {
     MSG   msg ;

     while (!bUserAbort && PeekMessage (&msg, NULL, 0, 0, PM_REMOVE))
          {
          if (!hDlgPrint !! !IsDialogMessage (hDlgPrint, &msg))
               {
               TranslateMessage (&msg) ;
               DispatchMessage (&msg) ;
               }
          }
     return !bUserAbort ;
     }

HDC GetPrinterDC (void)
     {
     static char szPrinter [80] ;
     char        *szDevice, *szDriver, *szOutput ;

     GetProfileString ("windows", "device", ",,,", szPrinter, 80) ;

     if ((szDevice = strtok (szPrinter, "," )) &&
         (szDriver = strtok (NULL,       ", ")) &&
         (szOutput = strtok (NULL,       ", ")))

               return CreateDC (szDriver, szDevice, szOutput, NULL) ;

     return 0 ;
     }
```

(continued)

```
BOOL PrintFile (HANDLE hInst, HWND hwnd, HWND hwndEdit, char *szFileName)
     {
     BOOL        bError = FALSE ;
     char        szMsg [40] ;
     FARPROC     lpfnAbortProc, lpfnPrintDlgProc ;
     HDC         hdcPrn ;
     NPSTR       psBuffer ;
     RECT        rect ;
     short       yChar, nCharsPerLine, nLinesPerPage,
                 nTotalLines, nTotalPages, nPage, nLine, nLineNum = 0 ;
     TEXTMETRIC tm ;

     if (0 == (nTotalLines = (short) SendMessage (hwndEdit,
                                         EM_GETLINECOUNT, 0, 0L)))
          return FALSE ;

     if (NULL == (hdcPrn = GetPrinterDC ()))
          return TRUE ;

     GetTextMetrics (hdcPrn, &tm) ;
     yChar = tm.tmHeight + tm.tmExternalLeading ;

     nCharsPerLine = GetDeviceCaps (hdcPrn, HORZRES) / tm.tmAveCharWidth ;
     nLinesPerPage = GetDeviceCaps (hdcPrn, VERTRES) / yChar ;
     nTotalPages   = (nTotalLines + nLinesPerPage - 1) / nLinesPerPage ;

     psBuffer = (NPSTR) LocalAlloc (LPTR, nCharsPerLine) ;

     EnableWindow (hwnd, FALSE) ;

     bUserAbort = FALSE ;
     lpfnPrintDlgProc = MakeProcInstance (PrintDlgProc, hInst) ;
     hDlgPrint = CreateDialog (hInst, "PrintDlgBox", hwnd, lpfnPrintDlgProc) ;
     SetDlgItemText (hDlgPrint, IDD_FNAME, szFileName) ;

     lpfnAbortProc = MakeProcInstance (AbortProc, hInst) ;
     Escape (hdcPrn, SETABORTPROC, 0, (LPSTR) lpfnAbortProc, NULL) ;

     strcat (strcat (strcpy (szMsg, szAppName), " - "), szFileName) ;

     if (Escape (hdcPrn, STARTDOC, strlen (szMsg), szMsg, NULL) > 0)
          {
          for (nPage = 0 ; nPage < nTotalPages ; nPage++)
               {
               for (nLine = 0 ; nLine < nLinesPerPage &&
                              nLineNum < nTotalLines ; nLine++, nLineNum++)
                    {
                    *(short *) psBuffer = nCharsPerLine ;
```

(continued)

```
                    TextOut (hdcPrn, 0, yChar * nLine, psBuffer,
                        (short) SendMessage (hwndEdit, EM_GETLINE,
                                    nLineNum, (LONG) (LPSTR) psBuffer)) ;
                    }

            if (Escape (hdcPrn, NEWFRAME, 0, NULL, (LPSTR) &rect) < 0)
                {
                bError = TRUE ;
                break ;
                }

            if (bUserAbort)
                break ;
            }
        }
    else
        bError = TRUE ;

    if (!bError)
        Escape (hdcPrn, ENDDOC, 0, NULL, NULL) ;

    if (!bUserAbort)
        {
        EnableWindow (hwnd, TRUE) ;
        DestroyWindow (hDlgPrint) ;
        }

    if (bError || bUserAbort)
        {
        strcat (strcpy (szMsg, "Could not print: "), szFileName) ;
        MessageBox (hwnd, szMsg, szAppName, MB_OK | MB_ICONEXCLAMATION) ;
        }

    LocalFree ((LOCALHANDLE) psBuffer) ;
    FreeProcInstance (lpfnPrintDlgProc) ;
    FreeProcInstance (lpfnAbortProc) ;
    DeleteDC (hdcPrn) ;

    return bError || bUserAbort ;
    }
```

POPPAD.DEF

```
;-----------------------------------
; POPPAD.DEF module definition file
;-----------------------------------

NAME            POPPAD
```

(continued)

```
DESCRIPTION    'Popup Editor (c) Charles Petzold, 1990'
EXETYPE        WINDOWS
STUB           'WINSTUB.EXE'
CODE           PRELOAD MOVEABLE DISCARDABLE
DATA           PRELOAD MOVEABLE MULTIPLE
HEAPSIZE       1024
STACKSIZE      8192
EXPORTS        WndProc
               AboutDlgProc
               FileOpenDlgProc
               FileSaveDlgProc
               PrintDlgProc
               AbortProc
```

POPPADP.C is structurally similar to PRINT3.C except that it is able to print multiple pages. The *PrintFile* routine performs some calculations to determine the number of characters it can fit on a line and the number of lines it can fit on a page. This process involves calls to *GetDeviceCaps* to determine the resolution of the page and to *GetTextMetrics* for the dimensions of a character.

The program obtains the total number of lines in the document (the variable *nTotalLines*) by sending an EM_GETLINECOUNT message to the edit control. A buffer for holding the contents of each line is allocated from local memory. For each line, the first word of this buffer is set to the number of characters in the line. Sending the edit control an EM_GETLINE message copies a line into the buffer; the line is then sent to the printer device context using *TextOut*.

The program breaks from the *for* loop incrementing the page number if the NEWFRAME *Escape* call returns an error or if *bUserAbort* is TRUE. Although the NEWFRAME call will return before GDI finishes the call if the return value of the abort procedure is FALSE, it doesn't return an error. For this reason, *bUserAbort* is tested explicitly before the next page is started. If no error is reported, the ENDDOC *Escape* call is made:

```
if (!bError)
    Escape (hdcPrn, ENDDOC, 0, NULL, NULL) ;
```

You might want to experiment with POPPAD by printing a multipage file. The file being printed first shows up in the Print Manager's client area after GDI has finished processing the first NEWFRAME *Escape* call. At that time, the Print Manager starts sending the file to the printer. If you then cancel the print job from POPPAD, the Print Manager aborts the printing also—that's a result of returning FALSE from the abort procedure. Once the file appears in the Print Manager's client area, you can also cancel the printing by selecting Terminate from the Queue menu. In that case, the NEWFRAME *Escape* call in progress in POPPAD returns an SP_USERABORT error (equal to −3).

Programmers new to Windows often become inordinately obsessed with the ABORTDOC *Escape* function. This function is rarely used in printing that also uses the NEWFRAME *Escape* function. As you can see in POPPAD, a user can cancel a print job at almost any time, either through POPPAD's printing dialog box or through the Print Manager. Neither requires that the program use the ABORTDOC *Escape* function. The only time that ABORTDOC would be allowed in POPPAD is between the STARTDOC *Escape* call and the first NEWFRAME *Escape* call, but that code goes so quickly that ABORTDOC isn't necessary.

Figure 15-10 shows the correct sequence of *Escape* calls for printing a multipage document. The best place to check for a *bUserAbort* value of TRUE is after each NEWFRAME *Escape* call. The ENDDOC *Escape* function is used only when the previous *Escape* calls have proceeded without error. In fact, once you get an error from any *Escape* call, the show is over, and you can go home.

Handling Error Codes

We have been handling the return value from the *Escape* function in a relatively simple manner: If *Escape* returns a negative value, then an error has occurred, and the printing operation is aborted. You can report more precise errors to the user by checking the *Escape* return value against five identifiers defined in WINDOWS.H. WINDOWS.H also includes an identifier called SP_NOTREPORTED, which is equal to 0x4000. If a bitwise AND of the return value from *Escape* with SP_NOTREPORTED is 0, then the error has already been reported to the user. A bitwise OR of the return value of *Escape* with SP_NOTREPORTED can be used to compare with the five error-code identifiers whether the error has been reported or not.

The following function shows one method of obtaining a text string identifying the error. The function returns NULL if no error has occurred or if the error has already been reported to the user:

```
char *GetErrorText (short nEscapeReturn)
    {
    static char *szErrorText [] = { "General Error",
                                    "Canceled from Program",
                                    "Canceled from Print Manager",
                                    "Out of disk space",
                                    "Out of memory space" } ;

    if (nEscapeReturn >= 0)
        return NULL ;

    if ((nEscapeReturn & SP_NOTREPORTED) == 0)
        return NULL ;

    return szErrorText [~nEscapeReturn] ;
    }
```

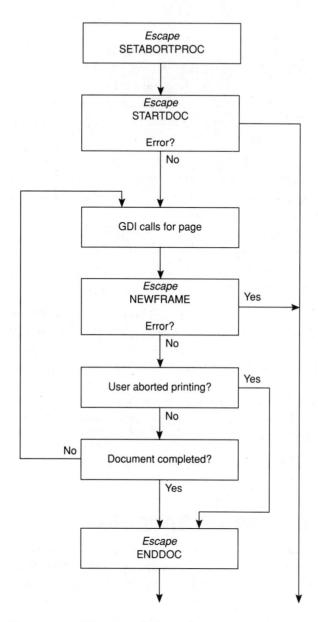

Figure 15-10. *The sequence of* Escape *calls for multipage printing.*

The five error codes (with some likely causes) are as follows:

- SP_ERROR (0xFFFF, or −1)—Defined as indicating a "general error," this is the only error code that can be returned from STARTDOC. It can occur if the GDI module or the printer device driver can't begin a document. If the Print Manager isn't loaded, you can also get this error from STARTDOC if another program is currently printing or if the printer is off line or has no paper.

- SP_APPABORT (0xFFFE, or −2)—This code is documented as indicating that the program's abort procedure has returned a FALSE value. However, this is the case only if the Print Manager isn't loaded. If the Print Manager is loaded and if the abort procedure is passed an *nCode* parameter of 0 and then returns a FALSE, the NEWFRAME *Escape* call will return a positive value, not an SP_APPABORT error.

- SP_USERABORT (0xFFFD, or −3)—This code indicates that the user canceled the printing job from the Print Manager.

- SP_OUTOFDISK (0xFFFC, or −4)—This code indicates that no more disk space is available. You'll encounter this error code if the disk drive containing the TEMP subdirectory can't accommodate any temporary metafiles or spooler files. If the TEMP subdirectory has some existing temporary spooler files, then the abort procedure is called during a NEWFRAME or NEXTBAND *Escape* call with an *nCode* parameter of SP_OUTOFDISK. If the abort procedure then returns FALSE, the *Escape* call returns SP_OUTOFDISK.

- SP_OUTOFMEMORY (0xFFFB, or −5)—This code indicates that insufficient memory is available for printing.

THE TECHNIQUE OF BANDING

Banding is the technique of defining a page of graphics as a series of separately constructed rectangles called bands. This approach relieves a printer driver of the necessity of constructing an entire bitmapped page image in memory. Banding is most important for raster printers that have no high-level page-composition control, such as dot-matrix printers and some laser printers.

Banding is one of the most misunderstood aspects of programming for the printer in Windows. Part of the problem lies in the documentation for the *GetDeviceCaps* function. The RC_BANDING bit of the value returned from *GetDeviceCaps* with the RASTERCAPS index is documented as "requires banding support." Programmers looking at this documentation assume that their applications must use banding with such printers. But this isn't so. Most of the information available from *GetDeviceCaps* is intended solely for the GDI module. This information allows GDI to determine what the device can do by itself and what it needs help with. The banding requirement falls into this category.

In general, an application program doesn't need to include its own banding logic. As you've seen, when you make GDI calls that define a page of graphics, the GDI module stores these calls in a metafile and then uses banding to set a clipping region before playing this metafile into the printer device driver. This is transparent to the application program. Under certain conditions, however, an application might want to take over the responsibility for doing banding. When an application uses banding, the GDI module doesn't create the intermediary metafile. Instead, the drawing commands for each band are passed to the printer device driver. There are two advantages to this approach:

- It can increase printing speed. The application needs to call only those GDI functions that draw something in each particular band, which is faster than having the GDI module play the entire metafile into the device driver for each band. Even if the program simply draws the entire page for each band, the process can still be faster than having the GDI module create and read the disk-based metafile, because the program doesn't have to access a disk.

- It can reduce the disk space normally required for printing. If the application is printing bitmaps but is not doing its own banding, then these bitmaps must be stored in the metafile that GDI creates. This situation can result in a metafile as large as the printer output file that the GDI module eventually creates.

- Banding is particularly important for printing bitmaps, because they occupy a large amount of space in the metafile. (Printing a bitmap requires selecting the bitmap into a memory device context and using *BitBlt* or *StretchBlt* to write it to the printer device context.)

But banding also further complicates the printing process, as you'll see when we create PRINT4, the final version of our printing program.

Strike Up the Bands

To have your program do its own banding, you first define a variable of type RECT:

```
RECT rect ;
```

You'll recall that the RECT structure has four fields named *left*, *top*, *right*, and *bottom*. For each page, you start by making an *Escape* call for the subfunction NEXTBAND, passing to it a pointer to *rect*. On return, *rect* contains the coordinates of the first band. The coordinates are always device coordinates (pixels) regardless of the current mapping mode of the printer device context. You make GDI calls to print in that band. You then call the NEXT-BAND *Escape* function again to obtain the coordinates of the next band, and you print in that band. When the RECT structure passed to *Escape* is returned empty (all fields set to 0), the page is done.

Here's what the code looks like to print a single page. For simplicity's sake, this code doesn't take into account errors that can be returned from the *Escape* functions or checks of the *bUserAbort* value:

```
Escape (hdcPrn, NEXTBAND, 0, NULL, (LPSTR) &rect) ;

while (!IsRectEmpty (&rect))
    {
    [call GDI functions to print in band]
    Escape (hdcPrn, NEXTBAND, 0, NULL, (LPSTR) &rect) ;
    }
```

Each NEXTBAND *Escape* call except the first performs a function similar to the NEWFRAME *Escape* call: It signals to the GDI module and to the printer device driver that the entire band has been defined and that it can now be saved in a disk file (or written to the printer if the Print Manager is not loaded). You don't want to call the NEWFRAME *Escape* function after this loop has run its course. If you do so, you'll get a blank page between each printed page. Nor can you terminate the loop before receiving an empty rectangle and then make a NEWFRAME *Escape* call to skip the rest of the page. In short, you use either NEWFRAME to print a page without banding or multiple NEXTBAND calls to print a page with banding. Don't mix NEWFRAME and NEXTBAND *Escape* functions for the same page.

It's easiest to visualize banding for a dot-matrix printer. Before illustrating the process, we need to make a distinction between the "top of the paper" (which is always the section of the paper printed first) and the "top of the page" (which depends on whether the printer driver is in portrait or landscape mode).

In portrait mode, the top of the page is the same as the top of the paper. The bands go down the page. The *rect.left* value in the RECT structure set by the NEXTBAND *Escape* call is always 0, and *rect.right* is always equal to the width of the printing area in pixels (the value obtained from *GetDeviceCaps* with a HORZRES parameter). For the first band, *rect.top* equals 0. For each successive band, *rect.top* equals the *rect.bottom* value of the previous band. For the last band, *rect.bottom* equals the height of the printing area in pixels. (See Figure 15-11.)

Thus in each band, you can print from the *rect.left* and *rect.top* coordinates up to (but not including) the *rect.right* and *rect.bottom* coordinates. If you call the function:

```
Rectangle (hdcPrn, rect.left, rect.top, rect.right, rect.bottom) ;
```

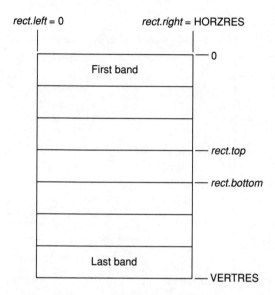

Figure 15-11. *Banding for a dot-matrix printer in portrait mode.*

the rectangle will be printed on the outermost edges of the band. (Recall that the right and bottom sides of the rectangle drawn by *Rectangle* are actually one pixel short of the points indicated by the last two parameters.)

In landscape mode, the dot-matrix printer must print the document sideways, starting from the left side of the page. The bands are in exactly the same area on the paper, but the rectangle coordinates are different, because the left side of the page is now the top of the paper. In landscape mode, *rect.top* is always 0, and *rect.bottom* is a constant equal to the height of the printing area in pixels (the value obtained from *GetDeviceCaps* using the VERTRES parameter). For the first band, *rect.left* equals 0. For the last band, *rect.right* is the width of the printing area in pixels. (See Figure 15-12 on the following page.)

A laser printer or a plotter might handle banding differently than a dot-matrix printer, because the printer output might not need to be sent to the printer sequentially from the top of the page to the bottom. Although Figures 15-11 and 15-12 represent the normal case, your program shouldn't assume that the banding rectangles will follow these patterns.

Separating your printer output into bands might seem like a major headache. But even if you use banding, you don't need to include a lot of banding logic. The band is a clipping region. You can make GDI calls that print outside the band, and Windows will ignore everything except what falls inside the band. This means that for each band, you can make all the GDI calls for the entire page.

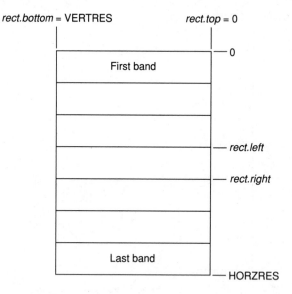

Figure 15-12. *Banding for a dot-matrix printer in landscape mode.*

You can determine whether a particular driver requires banding support by checking the RC_BANDING bit of the value returned from *GetDeviceCaps* using the RASTERCAPS parameter. As I mentioned before, this information is of concern only to GDI. Whether a driver requires banding support or not, the GDI module always supports the NEXTBAND *Escape* call. If the driver doesn't require banding support, the first NEXTBAND *Escape* call for a page returns a rectangle equal to the size of the printing area. The second NEXT-BAND call for a page returns an empty rectangle.

A Different Use of the Abort Procedure

When a program assumes responsibility for banding, the GDI module uses the abort procedure somewhat differently than it does otherwise. If the Print Manager isn't loaded, the GDI module frequently calls the abort procedure with an *nCode* parameter of 0 while processing the NEXTBAND *Escape* call, just as it does when processing NEWFRAME. However, if the Print Manager is loaded (the more normal case), the GDI module calls the abort procedure only if it runs out of disk space. The *nCode* parameter is SP_OUTOFDISK.

This arrangement presents a problem. Unless the GDI module runs out of disk space, the user can't switch to another program until the application currently printing is finished. Moreover, although the printing dialog box is displayed, the user can't cancel the print job, because the dialog box can't get messages until the abort procedure is called. The solution to this problem is fairly simple. Your printing routine can call the abort procedure itself between the GDI drawing functions that make up the page. Although the operation of Windows isn't as smooth as when the GDI module calls the abort procedure, this approach at least allows the user to cancel the print job or move on to another task.

Don't call the abort procedure directly. Instead, use the pointer returned from *MakeProcInstance*. For instance, if your abort procedure is called *AbortProc* and the pointer returned from *MakeProcInstance* is called *lpfnAbortProc*, you can call *AbortProc* using:

```
(*lpfnAbortProc) (hdcPrn, 0) ;
```

The PRINT4 program, shown in Figure 15-13, adds banding to the printing logic in PRINT3. PRINT4 also requires the PRINT.RC file in Figure 15-8 and—like all our PRINT programs—the PRINT.C file in Figure 15-5.

PRINT4.MAK

```
#---------------------
# PRINT4.MAK make file
#---------------------

print4.exe : print.obj print4.obj print4.def print.res
     link print4 print, /align:16, NUL, /nod slibcew libw, print4
     rc print.res print4.exe

print.obj : print.c
     cl -c -Gsw -Ow -W2 -Zp print.c

print4.obj : print4.c
     cl -c -Gsw -Ow -W2 -Zp print4.c

print.res : print.rc
     rc -r print.rc
```

PRINT4.C

```
/*-------------------------------------------
   PRINT4.C -- Printing with Banding
               (c) Charles Petzold, 1990
   -------------------------------------------*/

#include <windows.h>

HDC  GetPrinterDC (void) ;                // in PRINT.C

typedef BOOL (FAR PASCAL * ABORTPROC) (HDC, short) ;
```

Figure 15-13. *The PRINT4 program.*   *(continued)*

```
HANDLE hInst ;
char    szAppName [] = "Print4" ;
char    szCaption [] = "Print Program 4 (Banding)" ;

BOOL    bUserAbort ;
HWND    hDlgPrint ;

BOOL FAR PASCAL PrintDlgProc (HWND hDlg, WORD message, WORD wParam, LONG lParam)
    {
    switch (message)
        {
        case WM_INITDIALOG :
            SetWindowText (hDlg, szAppName) ;
            EnableMenuItem (GetSystemMenu (hDlg, FALSE), SC_CLOSE,
                                                     MF_GRAYED) ;
            return TRUE ;

        case WM_COMMAND :
            bUserAbort = TRUE ;
            EnableWindow (GetParent (hDlg), TRUE) ;
            DestroyWindow (hDlg) ;
            hDlgPrint = 0 ;
            return TRUE ;
        }
    return FALSE ;
    }

BOOL FAR PASCAL AbortProc (HDC hdcPrn, short nCode)
    {
    MSG   msg ;

    while (!bUserAbort && PeekMessage (&msg, NULL, 0, 0, PM_REMOVE))
        {
        if (!hDlgPrint !! !IsDialogMessage (hDlgPrint, &msg))
            {
            TranslateMessage (&msg) ;
            DispatchMessage (&msg) ;
            }
        }
    return !bUserAbort ;
    }

BOOL PrintMyPage (HWND hwnd)
    {
    static char szSpMsg [] = "Print4: Printing" ;
    static char szText  [] = "Hello, Printer!" ;
    ABORTPROC   lpfnAbortProc ;
    BOOL        bError = FALSE ;
```

(continued)

```
DWORD       dwExtent ;
FARPROC     lpfnPrintDlgProc ;
HDC         hdcPrn ;
POINT       ptExtent ;
RECT        rect ;
short       xPage, yPage ;

if (NULL == (hdcPrn = GetPrinterDC ()))
     return TRUE ;

xPage = GetDeviceCaps (hdcPrn, HORZRES) ;
yPage = GetDeviceCaps (hdcPrn, VERTRES) ;

EnableWindow (hwnd, FALSE) ;

bUserAbort = FALSE ;
lpfnPrintDlgProc = MakeProcInstance (PrintDlgProc, hInst) ;
hDlgPrint = CreateDialog (hInst, "PrintDlgBox", hwnd, lpfnPrintDlgProc) ;

lpfnAbortProc = MakeProcInstance (AbortProc, hInst) ;
Escape (hdcPrn, SETABORTPROC, 0, (LPSTR) lpfnAbortProc, NULL) ;

if (Escape (hdcPrn, STARTDOC, sizeof szSpMsg - 1, szSpMsg, NULL) > 0 &&
    Escape (hdcPrn, NEXTBAND, 0, NULL, (LPSTR) &rect) > 0)
     {
     while (!IsRectEmpty (&rect) && !bUserAbort)
          {
          (*lpfnAbortProc) (hdcPrn, 0) ;

          Rectangle (hdcPrn, rect.left, rect.top, rect.right,
                                               rect.bottom) ;
          (*lpfnAbortProc) (hdcPrn, 0) ;

          MoveTo (hdcPrn, 0, 0) ;
          LineTo (hdcPrn, xPage, yPage) ;

          (*lpfnAbortProc) (hdcPrn, 0) ;

          MoveTo (hdcPrn, xPage, 0) ;
          LineTo (hdcPrn, 0, yPage) ;

          SaveDC (hdcPrn) ;

          SetMapMode (hdcPrn, MM_ISOTROPIC) ;
          SetWindowExt   (hdcPrn, 1000, 1000) ;
          SetViewportExt (hdcPrn, xPage / 2, -yPage / 2) ;
          SetViewportOrg (hdcPrn, xPage / 2,  yPage / 2) ;

          (*lpfnAbortProc) (hdcPrn, 0) ;
```

(continued)

```
                    Ellipse (hdcPrn, -500, 500, 500, -500) ;

                    (*lpfnAbortProc) (hdcPrn, 0) ;

                    dwExtent = GetTextExtent (hdcPrn, szText, sizeof szText - 1) ;
                    ptExtent = MAKEPOINT (dwExtent) ;
                    TextOut (hdcPrn, -ptExtent.x / 2, ptExtent.y / 2, szText,
                                                      sizeof szText - 1) ;

                    RestoreDC (hdcPrn, -1) ;

                    (*lpfnAbortProc) (hdcPrn, 0) ;

                    if (Escape (hdcPrn, NEXTBAND, 0, NULL, (LPSTR) &rect) < 0)
                         {
                         bError = TRUE ;
                         break ;
                         }
                    }
               }
          else
               bError = TRUE ;

          if (!bError)
               {
               if (bUserAbort)
                    Escape (hdcPrn, ABORTDOC, 0, NULL, NULL) ;
               else
                    Escape (hdcPrn, ENDDOC, 0, NULL, NULL) ;
               }

          if (!bUserAbort)
               {
               EnableWindow (hwnd, TRUE) ;
               DestroyWindow (hDlgPrint) ;
               }

     FreeProcInstance (lpfnPrintDlgProc) ;
     FreeProcInstance (lpfnAbortProc) ;
     DeleteDC (hdcPrn) ;

     return bError !! bUserAbort ;
     }
```

PRINT4.DEF

```
;------------------------------------
; PRINT4.DEF module definition file
;------------------------------------

NAME            PRINT4

DESCRIPTION     'Printing Program No. 4 (c) Charles Petzold, 1990'
EXETYPE         WINDOWS
STUB            'WINSTUB.EXE'
CODE            PRELOAD MOVEABLE DISCARDABLE
DATA            PRELOAD MOVEABLE MULTIPLE
HEAPSIZE        1024
STACKSIZE       8192
EXPORTS         WndProc
                AbortProc
                PrintDlgProc
```

PRINT4 differs from PRINT3 in only a few particulars. In order for *AbortProc* to be called while the program is printing, the GDI drawing routines have been moved into *PrintMyPage*. You'll notice that the *Rectangle* function prints the rectangle for each band rather than a rectangle on the border of the entire page. This allows you to see where the bands are for a particular printer. The structure of the printing operation looks like this:

```
if (Escape (hdcPrn, STARTDOC, sizeof szSpMsg - 1, szSpMsg, NULL) > 0 &&
    Escape (hdcPrn, NEXTBAND, 0, NULL, (LPSTR) &rect) > 0)
    {
    while (!IsRectEmpty (&rect) && !bUserAbort)
        {
        [make GDI calls and call abort procedure]
        if (Escape (hdcPrn, NEXTBAND, 0, NULL, (LPSTR) &rect) < 0)
            {
            bError = TRUE ;
            break ;
            }
        }
    }
else
    bError = TRUE ;
```

The *while* loop for the band proceeds only if the rectangle isn't empty and if the user hasn't canceled the print job from the dialog box. PRINT4 has to check the return value from each NEXTBAND *Escape* call and set *bError* if *Escape* returns a negative value. If no *Escape* call returns an error, then the print job must either be ended with the ENDDOC *Escape* call or be aborted with the ABORTDOC *Escape* call. If the user cancels printing during the NEXTBAND loop, then the print job must be aborted using the ABORTDOC call. The code to do this is as follows:

```
if (!bError)
    {
    if (bUserAbort)
        Escape (hdcPrn, ABORTDOC, 0, NULL, NULL) ;
    else
        Escape (hdcPrn, ENDDOC, 0, NULL, NULL) ;
    }
```

THE PRINTER AND FONTS

Chapter 14 culminated in a program called JUSTIFY that uses GDI-based raster fonts to display formatted text. Programs that work with formatted text on the screen usually also need to print this text. In fact, word-processing and desktop publishing programs generally use the display solely to provide a preview of the printed output.

This is a difficult task: What you show on the display can only approximate what the printer will print. Even if the printer uses only GDI-based fonts (those fonts stored in .FON font resource files), it generally has a different resolution than the screen, meaning that the printed characters will be a slightly different size than on the display. And if the printer uses device-based fonts (fonts that are internal to the printer), the problem becomes even more complex. For example, in the case of a printer that offers a 15-point Zapf Chancery font, you'll be approximating that font on the display with a 14-point font of another typeface. Even if the user wants to print text in 14-point Times Roman, the various character widths of the printer's device-based font can differ from those of the display's GDI-based font. In short, if you're writing a program that must display formatted text destined for a printer, you can count on some work ahead. Here are some guidelines to get you started.

You'll want to let the user choose from a list of typeface names and sizes that are supported by the currently selected printer. That is, you need to enumerate the printer fonts (as we did in the FONTLIST program in Chapter 14), which requires using *EnumFonts* with a call-back function. This call-back function receives a pointer to a logical font (LOG-FONT) structure and a text metrics (TEXTMETRICS) structure describing each font. The call-back function also receives a short integer that indicates whether the font is a GDI-based or a device-based font. Another bit indicates whether the font is a raster font, in which case it is scalable (within limits) by integer multiples, or a vector font, in which case it is continuously scalable.

For device-based vector fonts, the call-back function will receive only one typeface size. You can check the value returned from *GetDeviceCaps* using the TEXTCAPS parameter to determine how the device can scale these vector fonts. If they can be scaled by any multiple, you might want to allow the user to specify a point size.

When you display formatted text on the screen, you want to space the text based on how it will be eventually printed. You can use *GetDeviceCaps* and the GETPHYSPAGESIZE *Escape* call to determine the size of the paper and the size of the printable area. For instance, if the paper is 8½ inches wide and the user selects left and right margins of 1 inch, then you want to display text on the screen using a width of 6½ inches. The "logical twips" mapping mode discussed in Chapter 14 is appropriate for this display. There's a catch, however. If the user selects a 15-point font that the printer supports, you'll have to approximate that font on the display with a 14-point font—but you can't use this 14-point display font to determine the amount of 15-point text that can fit in one printed line. You must determine this instead based on the printer font. Likewise, you must use the printer font to determine how many lines fit on a page.

To format the display text, you'll need both a handle to the screen device context (to display the text on the screen) and a handle to a printer information context. You don't need a printer device context handle until you actually want to print. Follow these steps:

1. Put together a logical font structure with the typeface name, the type size, and the attributes selected by the user, and select that logical font into the printer information context.

2. Call *GetTextMetrics* for the printer information context to determine the real size and characteristics of the selected printer font. Call *GetTextFace* to obtain the typeface name.

3. Use the information obtained in Step 2 to create another logical font structure based on the size and characteristics of the printer font, and select this logical font into the screen device context. The font now selected into the screen device context closely approximates the font selected into the printer information context.

4. When you write the text to the display, follow the general procedure used in the *Justify* function of the JUSTIFY program. However, go through the *GetTextExtent* and *SetTextJustification* logic using the printer information context, but stop short of *TextOut*. This approach allows you to determine the amount of text that fits on each line and the number of lines that fit on a page.

5. When you have established each line of text as appropriate for the printer, you can call *GetTextExtent* and (possibly) *SetTextJustification* using the screen display context. You then call *TextOut* to display the line.

To print the text, you'll probably use code structured like that in the POPPADP.C file combined with the logic in the *Justify* function of JUSTIFY.C. You obtain a printer device context and go through the *GetTextExtent* and *SetTextJustification* logic again, this time using *TextOut* to print each line.

SECTION V
DATA EXCHANGE AND LINKS

Chapter 16

The Clipboard

The Windows clipboard allows data to be transferred from one program to another. It is a relatively simple mechanism that doesn't require much overhead in either the program that places data in the clipboard or the program that later gets access to it.

Let's clear up one possible point of confusion right away: The CLIPBOARD program that comes with Windows is *not* the clipboard. It is instead a "clipboard viewer" that displays the current contents of the clipboard. (We'll write our own simple clipboard viewer later in this chapter.) The clipboard is simply a series of functions in Windows' USER module that facilitate the exchange of memory blocks between programs.

Many programs that deal with documents or other data include an Edit menu with the options Cut, Copy, and Paste. When a user selects Cut or Copy, the program transfers data from the program to the clipboard. This data is in a particular format, such as text, a bitmap, or a metafile. When a user selects Paste from the menu, the program determines if the clipboard contains data in a format that the program can use and, if so, transfers data from the clipboard to the program.

Programs should not transfer data into or out of the clipboard without an explicit instruction from the user. For example, a user who performs a Cut or a Copy operation in one program should be able to assume that the data will remain in the clipboard until the next Cut or Copy operation or until the user employs a program—such as the BLOWUP2 presented in this chapter—specifically designed to manipulate the clipboard.

SIMPLE USE OF THE CLIPBOARD

We'll begin by looking at the code involved for transferring data to the clipboard (Cut and Copy) and getting access to clipboard data (Paste).

The Standard Clipboard Data Formats

Windows supports various standard clipboard formats that have WINDOWS.H identifiers. These are:

- CF_TEXT—a NULL-terminated ANSI character-set character string containing a carriage return and a linefeed character at the end of each line. This is the simplest form of clipboard data. The data to be transferred to the clipboard is stored in a global memory block and is transferred using the handle to the block. The memory block becomes the property of the clipboard, and the program that creates the block should not continue to use it.

- CF_BITMAP—a Windows 2–compatible bitmap. The bitmap is transferred to the clipboard using the bitmap handle. Again, a program should not continue to use this bitmap after giving it to the clipboard.

- CF_METAFILEPICT—a "metafile picture." This isn't exactly the same as a metafile (described in Chapter 13). Rather, it's a metafile with some additional information in the form of a small structure of type METAFILEPICT. A program transfers a metafile picture to the clipboard using the handle to a global memory block containing this structure. The four fields of the METAFILEPICT structure are *mm* (int), the mapping mode for the metafile; *xExt* (int) and *yExt* (int), in simple terms, the width and height of the metafile image; and *hMF* (HANDLE), the handle to the metafile. (I'll discuss the *xExt* and *yExt* fields in detail later in this chapter.) After a program transfers a metafile picture to the clipboard, it should not continue to use either the global memory block containing the METAFILEPICT structure or the metafile handle, because both will be under the control of the USER module.

- CF_SYLK—a global memory block containing data in the Microsoft "Symbolic Link" format. This format is used for exchanging data between Microsoft Corporation's Multiplan, Chart, and Excel programs. It is an ASCII format with each line terminated with a carriage return and linefeed.

- CF_DIF—a global memory block containing data in the Data Interchange Format (DIF). This is a format devised by Software Arts for use with transferring data to the VisiCalc spreadsheet program. The format is now under the control of Lotus Corporation. This is also an ASCII format with lines terminated with carriage returns and linefeeds.

The CF_SYLK and CF_DIF formats are conceptually similar to the CF_TEXT format. However, character strings containing SYLK or DIF data are not necessarily NULL-terminated, because the formats define the end of the data. (For descriptions of these two formats, see Jeff Walden, *File Formats for Popular PC Software,* John Wiley & Sons, 1986.)

- CF_TIFF—a global memory block containing data in the Tag Image File Format (TIFF). This is a format devised by Microsoft, Aldus Corporation, and Hewlett-Packard Company in conjunction with some hardware manufacturers. The format (which describes bitmapped data) is available from Hewlett-Packard.

- CF_OEMTEXT—a global memory block containing text data (simple to CF_TEXT) but using the OEM character set.

- CF_DIB—a global memory block defining a device-independent bitmap. The global memory block begins with a BITMAPINFO structure followed by the bitmap bits.

- CF_PALETTE—a handle to a color palette. This is generally used in conjunction with CF_DIB for defining a color palette used by the bitmap.

Transferring Text to the Clipboard

Let's assume that you want to transfer a character string to the clipboard and that you have a pointer (called *pString*) to this string. This can be a near pointer if the text is stored in your program's local data segment or a far pointer if the text is stored in a global data segment. You want to transfer *wLength* bytes of this string.

First, allocate a moveable global memory block of *wLength* size. Include room for a terminating NULL:

```
hGlobalMemory = GlobalAlloc (GHND, (DWORD) wLength + 1) ;
```

The value of *hGlobalMemory* will be NULL if the block could not be allocated. If the allocation is successful, lock the block to get a far pointer to it:

```
lpGlobalMemory = GlobalLock (hGlobalMemory) ;
```

Copy the character string into the global memory block:

```
for (n = 0 ; n < wLength ; n++)
    *lpGlobalMemory++ = *pString++ ;
```

You don't need to add the terminating NULL, because the GHND flag for *GlobalAlloc* zeroes out the entire memory block during allocation. Unlock the block:

```
GlobalUnlock (hGlobalMemory) ;
```

Now you have a global memory handle that references a memory block containing the NULL-terminated text. To get this into the clipboard, open the clipboard and empty it:

```
OpenClipboard (hwnd) ;
EmptyClipboard () ;
```

Give the clipboard the global memory handle using the CF_TEXT identifier, and close the clipboard:

```
SetClipboardData (CF_TEXT, hGlobalMemory) ;
CloseClipboard () ;
```

You're done.

Here are some rules concerning this process:

- Call *OpenClipboard* and *CloseClipboard* while processing a single message. Don't leave the clipboard open when you exit the window procedure. Don't let control transfer to another program (perhaps by calling *SendMessage* or *PeekMessage*) while the clipboard is open.

- Don't give the clipboard a locked memory handle.

- After you call *SetClipboardData*, don't continue to use the global memory block. It no longer belongs to your program, and you should treat the handle as invalid. If you need to continue to access the data, make another copy of it or read it from the clipboard (as described in the next section). You can also continue to reference the block between the *SetClipboardData* call and the *CloseClipboard* call, but you must use the global handle that is returned from *SetClipboardData*. Unlock this handle before you call *CloseClipboard*.

Getting Text from the Clipboard

Getting text from the clipboard is only a little more complex than transferring text to the clipboard. You must first determine whether the clipboard does in fact contain data in the CF_TEXT format. One of the easiest methods is to use the call:

```
bAvailable = IsClipboardFormatAvailable (CF_TEXT) ;
```

This function returns TRUE (nonzero) if the clipboard contains CF_TEXT data. We used this function in the POPPAD2 program in Chapter 9 to determine whether the Paste item on the Edit menu should be enabled or grayed. *IsClipboardFormatAvailable* is one of the few clipboard functions that you can use without first opening the clipboard. However, if you later open the clipboard to get this text, you should also check again (using the same function or one of the other methods) to determine if the CF_TEXT data is still in the clipboard.

To transfer the text out, first open the clipboard:

```
OpenClipboard (hwnd) ;
```

Obtain the handle to the global memory block referencing the text:

```
hClipMemory = GetClipboardData (CF_TEXT) ;
```

This handle will be NULL if the clipboard doesn't contain data in the CF_TEXT format. This is another way to determine if the clipboard contains text. If *GetClipboardData* returns NULL, close the clipboard without doing anything else.

The handle you receive from *GetClipboardData* doesn't belong to your program—it belongs to the clipboard. The handle is valid only between the *GetClipboardData* and *CloseClipboard* calls. You can't free that handle or alter the data it references. If you need to have continued access to the data, you should make a copy of the memory block.

Here's one method for copying the data into a global memory segment that belongs to your program. First, allocate a global memory block of the same size as that referenced by *hClipMemory*:

```
hMyMemory = GlobalAlloc (GHND, GlobalSize (hClipMemory)) ;
```

Check for a NULL value from *GlobalAlloc* to determine if the block was really allocated. If it was allocated, lock both handles and get pointers to the beginning of the blocks:

```
lpClipMemory = GlobalLock (hClipMemory) ;
lpMyMemory = GlobalLock (hMyMemory) ;
```

Because the character string is NULL-terminated, you can transfer the data using Windows' *lstrcpy* function:

```
lstrcpy (lpMyMemory, lpClipMemory) ;
```

Or you can use some simple C code:

```
while (*lpMyMemory++ = *lpClipMemory++) ;
```

Unlock both blocks:

```
GlobalUnlock (hClipMemory) ;
GlobalUnlock (hMyMemory) ;
```

Finally, close the clipboard:

```
CloseClipboard () ;
```

Now you have a global handle called *hMyMemory* that you can later lock to access this data.

What the Clipboard Does

The clipboard works primarily by altering the memory allocation flags of global memory blocks. When a program allocates a global memory block using the GHND flag (a combination of the GMEM_MOVEABLE and GMEM_ZEROINIT flags), the memory block is marked as belonging to the program (more precisely, the particular instance of the program). Normally, Windows deletes this memory block when the instance terminates. When a program uses *SetClipboardData* to give the global handle to the clipboard, Windows must transfer ownership of the memory block from the program to itself. This action requires that Windows modify the memory allocation flags of the global memory block by calling:

```
GlobalReAlloc (hMem, OL, GMEM_MODIFY : GMEM_DDESHARE) ;
```

The USER module establishes ownership of the memory block. After the *SetClipboardData* call, the global memory handle no longer belongs to the program that allocated it, and the block won't be freed when the program terminates. The program that created the memory block can't continue to use it except when the clipboard gives the program access to the block. Now the USER module must explicitly free the memory block, which it does when a program calls *EmptyClipboard*.

When a program calls *GetClipboardData*, Windows gives the program making the call the handle to the global memory block and allows the program temporary access to the memory block. The program can then copy this data into another global memory block or a local memory block. Thus, the clipboard is really just a manager of shared memory segments. One program gives the clipboard a block of global memory. Other programs can get access to the block. The clipboard retains ownership of it.

Opening and Closing the Clipboard

Only one program can have the clipboard open at any time. The purpose of the *OpenClipboard* call is to prevent the clipboard contents from changing while a program is using the clipboard. *OpenClipboard* returns a BOOL value indicating whether the clipboard was successfully opened. It will not be opened if another application failed to close it. During the early stages of programming for the clipboard, you should probably check this value, but the check isn't crucial in a nonpreemptive multitasking environment. If every program politely opens and then closes the clipboard during a single message without giving control to other programs, then you'll never run into the problem of being unable to open the clipboard.

I've already mentioned avoiding the use of *SendMessage* or *PeekMessage* while the clipboard is open, but watch out for a more subtle problem involving message boxes: If you can't allocate a global memory segment to copy the contents of the clipboard, then you might want to display a message box. If this message box isn't system modal, however, the user can switch to another application while the message box is displayed. You should either make the message box system modal or close the clipboard before you display the message box.

You can also run into problems if you leave the clipboard open while you display a dialog box. Edit fields in a dialog box use the clipboard for cutting and pasting text.

Using the Clipboard with Bitmaps

In using the CF_BITMAP format, you give the clipboard a handle to a bitmap when calling *SetClipboardData*. The *GetClipboardData* function returns a handle to a bitmap.

You may recall the BLOWUP1 program from Chapter 4, which allowed you to block out any part of the display and copy it to BLOWUP1's client area. BLOWUP1 used *StretchBlt* to expand or compress the size of the blocked-out area so that it exactly fit the client area. The program had a problem, however: If part of BLOWUP1's client area was destroyed (perhaps by an overlapping window from another program), BLOWUP1 couldn't recreate it. We could have solved that problem by creating a bitmap based on the size of the area BLOWUP1 was copying. When BLOWUP1 needed to redisplay the bitmap in its client area, it could have selected the bitmap into a memory device context and used *StretchBlt* to copy it to the client area.

Let's go one step further and write a revised version of this program that uses the clipboard to hold onto this bitmap. This approach provides two advantages:

- Any part of the display can now be copied in bitmap format and stored in the clipboard.

- Any bitmap that is stored in the clipboard can be copied into and scaled to the size of the program's client area. You can then block out all or part of this display and copy that to the clipboard. This provides an easy manual approach to scaling or cropping bitmaps.

The Revised BLOWUP Program

The BLOWUP2 program is shown in Figure 16-1. You use it the same way as the BLOWUP1 program. First, click the mouse in BLOWUP1's client area. The cursor changes to a cross hair. Now place the cursor on one corner of the rectangle you want to capture, press the mouse button, drag the mouse to the opposite corner, and release the button.

BLOWUP2.MAK

```
#----------------------
# BLOWUP2.MAK make file
#----------------------

blowup2.exe : blowup2.obj blowup2.def
     link blowup2, /align:16, NUL, /nod slibcew libw, blowup2
     rc blowup2.exe

blowup2.obj : blowup2.c
     cl -c -Gsw -Ow -W2 -Zp blowup2.c
```

Figure 16-1. *The BLOWUP2 program.*

BLOWUP2.C

```
/*-----------------------------------------------
   BLOWUP2.C -- Capture Screen Image to Clipboard
                (c) Charles Petzold, 1990
   -----------------------------------------------*/

#include <windows.h>
#include <stdlib.h>

long FAR PASCAL WndProc (HWND, WORD, WORD, LONG) ;

int PASCAL WinMain (HANDLE hInstance, HANDLE hPrevInstance,
                    LPSTR lpszCmdLine, int nCmdShow)
     {
     static char szAppName [] = "Blowup2" ;
     HWND         hwnd ;
     MSG          msg ;
     WNDCLASS     wndclass ;

     if (!hPrevInstance)
          {
          wndclass.style         = CS_HREDRAW : CS_VREDRAW ;
          wndclass.lpfnWndProc   = WndProc ;
          wndclass.cbClsExtra    = 0 ;
          wndclass.cbWndExtra    = 0 ;
          wndclass.hInstance     = hInstance ;
          wndclass.hIcon         = NULL ;
          wndclass.hCursor       = LoadCursor (NULL, IDC_ARROW) ;
          wndclass.hbrBackground = GetStockObject (WHITE_BRUSH) ;
          wndclass.lpszMenuName  = NULL ;
          wndclass.lpszClassName = szAppName ;

          RegisterClass (&wndclass) ;
          }

     hwnd = CreateWindow (szAppName, szAppName,
                          WS_OVERLAPPEDWINDOW,
                          CW_USEDEFAULT, CW_USEDEFAULT,
                          CW_USEDEFAULT, CW_USEDEFAULT,
                          NULL, NULL, hInstance, NULL) ;

     ShowWindow (hwnd, nCmdShow) ;
     UpdateWindow (hwnd) ;

     while (GetMessage (&msg, NULL, 0, 0))
          {
          TranslateMessage (&msg) ;
          DispatchMessage (&msg) ;
          }
```

(continued)

```
          return msg.wParam ;
          }

void InvertBlock (HWND hwnd, POINT org, POINT len)
     {
     HDC    hdc ;

     hdc = CreateDC ("DISPLAY", NULL, NULL, NULL) ;
     ClientToScreen (hwnd, &org) ;
     PatBlt (hdc, org.x, org.y, len.x, len.y, DSTINVERT) ;
     DeleteDC (hdc) ;
     }

long FAR PASCAL WndProc (HWND hwnd, WORD message, WORD wParam, LONG lParam)
     {
     static BOOL  bCapturing, bBlocking ;
     static POINT org, len ;
     static short cxClient, cyClient ;
     BITMAP       bm ;
     HDC          hdc, hdcMem ;
     HBITMAP      hBitmap ;
     PAINTSTRUCT  ps ;
     switch (message)
          {
          case WM_SIZE :
               cxClient = LOWORD (lParam) ;
               cyClient = HIWORD (lParam) ;
               return 0 ;

          case WM_LBUTTONDOWN :
               if (!bCapturing)
                    {
                    bCapturing = TRUE ;
                    SetCapture (hwnd) ;
                    SetCursor (LoadCursor (NULL, IDC_CROSS)) ;
                    }
               else if (!bBlocking)
                    {
                    bBlocking = TRUE ;
                    org = MAKEPOINT (lParam) ;
                    }
               return 0 ;

          case WM_MOUSEMOVE :
               if (bCapturing)
                    SetCursor (LoadCursor (NULL, IDC_CROSS)) ;

               if (bBlocking)
                    {
                    len = MAKEPOINT (lParam) ;
```

(continued)

```
                    len.x -= org.x ;
                    len.y -= org.y ;

                    InvertBlock (hwnd, org, len) ;
                    InvertBlock (hwnd, org, len) ;
                    }
               return 0 ;

          case WM_LBUTTONUP :
               if (!bBlocking)
                    break ;

               bCapturing = bBlocking = FALSE ;
               SetCursor (LoadCursor (NULL, IDC_ARROW)) ;
               ReleaseCapture () ;

               if (len.x == 0 || len.y == 0)
                    break ;

               hdc = GetDC (hwnd) ;
               hdcMem = CreateCompatibleDC (hdc) ;
               hBitmap = CreateCompatibleBitmap (hdc,
                              abs (len.x), abs (len.y)) ;
               if (hBitmap)
                    {
                    SelectObject (hdcMem, hBitmap) ;
                    StretchBlt (hdcMem, 0, 0, abs (len.x), abs (len.y),
                         hdc, org.x, org.y, len.x, len.y, SRCCOPY) ;

                    OpenClipboard (hwnd) ;
                    EmptyClipboard () ;
                    SetClipboardData (CF_BITMAP, hBitmap) ;
                    CloseClipboard () ;

                    InvalidateRect (hwnd, NULL, TRUE) ;
                    }
               else
                    MessageBeep (0) ;

               DeleteDC (hdcMem) ;
               ReleaseDC (hwnd, hdc) ;
               return 0 ;

          case WM_PAINT :
               InvalidateRect (hwnd, NULL, TRUE) ;
               hdc = BeginPaint (hwnd, &ps) ;
               OpenClipboard (hwnd) ;

               if (hBitmap = GetClipboardData (CF_BITMAP))
                    {
                    SetCursor (LoadCursor (NULL, IDC_WAIT)) ;
```

(continued)

```
                hdcMem = CreateCompatibleDC (hdc) ;
                SelectObject (hdcMem, hBitmap) ;
                GetObject (hBitmap, sizeof (BITMAP), (LPSTR) &bm) ;

                SetStretchBltMode (hdc, COLORONCOLOR) ;
                StretchBlt (hdc, 0, 0, cxClient, cyClient,
                            hdcMem, 0, 0, bm.bmWidth, bm.bmHeight,
                                        SRCCOPY) ;

                SetCursor (LoadCursor (NULL, IDC_ARROW)) ;
                DeleteDC (hdcMem) ;
                }

           CloseClipboard () ;
           EndPaint (hwnd, &ps) ;
           return 0 ;

      case WM_DESTROY :
           PostQuitMessage (0) ;
           return 0 ;
      }
    return DefWindowProc (hwnd, message, wParam, lParam) ;
    }
```

BLOWUP2.DEF

```
;---------------------------------------
; BLOWUP2.DEF module definition file
;---------------------------------------

NAME          BLOWUP2

DESCRIPTION   'Capture Screen Image to Clipboard (c) Charles Petzold, 1990'
EXETYPE       WINDOWS
STUB          'WINSTUB.EXE'
CODE          PRELOAD MOVEABLE DISCARDABLE
DATA          PRELOAD MOVEABLE MULTIPLE
HEAPSIZE      1024
STACKSIZE     8192
EXPORTS       WndProc
```

In the earlier BLOWUP1 program, the blocked-out section of the display was copied to BLOWUP1's client area. In the new version, the area of the display is copied to a bitmap in a memory device context, and the bitmap is transferred to the clipboard.

When you're blocking out an area of the display with the mouse, BLOWUP2 retains two structures of type POINT with the initial corner (*org*, for "origin") and the width and height of the rectangle (*len*, for "length"). If the *org* point isn't the upper left corner of the rectangle, then one or both of the values in *len* will be negative. When the mouse button is released (signaling to the program that the user has finished blocking out the rectangle), BLOWUP2 creates a memory device context and a bitmap using the absolute values of the lengths in the *len* point structure:

```
hdc = GetDC (hwnd) ;
hdcMem = CreateCompatibleDC (hdc) ;
hBitmap = CreateCompatibleBitmap (hdc,
                     abs (len.x), abs (len.y)) ;
```

If BLOWUP2 succeeds in creating this bitmap, the program selects the bitmap into the memory device context and uses *StretchBlt* to copy the blocked-out area of the display:

```
if (hBitmap)
     {
     SelectObject (hdcMem, hBitmap) ;
     StretchBlt (hdcMem, 0, 0, abs (len.x), abs (len.y),
          hdc, org.x, org.y, len.x, len.y, SRCCOPY) ;
```

Although we're using *StretchBlt* here, the image is not being stretched or compressed. However, if you block out the rectangle from right to left, then *StretchBlt* is needed to flip the image around a vertical axis. Similarly, if you block it out from bottom to top, then *StretchBlt* turns it upside down.

The program then opens and empties the clipboard, transfers the bitmap to the clipboard, and closes the clipboard:

```
OpenClipboard (hwnd) ;
EmptyClipboard () ;
SetClipboardData (CF_BITMAP, hBitmap) ;
CloseClipboard () ;
```

The bitmap is now the responsibility of the clipboard. Do not delete it! The clipboard will delete the bitmap itself the next time it gets an *EmptyClipboard* call.

Because the clipboard contains a new bitmap, BLOWUP2 invalidates its own client area, as follows:

```
InvalidateRect (hwnd, NULL, TRUE) ;
     }
```

If BLOWUP2 wasn't successful in creating a bitmap, it beeps:

```
else
     MessageBeep (0) ;
```

Finally, the memory device context is deleted, and the window's device context is released:

```
DeleteDC (hdcMem) ;
ReleaseDC (hwnd, hdc) ;
```

When BLOWUP2 gets a WM_PAINT message, it opens the clipboard and checks to see if a bitmap is available:

```
OpenClipboard (hwnd) ;

if (hBitmap = GetClipboardData (CF_BITMAP))
    {
```

If the clipboard contains a bitmap, BLOWUP2 creates a memory device context and selects the bitmap from the clipboard into the device context:

```
hdcMem = CreateCompatibleDC (hdc) ;
SelectObject (hdcMem, hBitmap) ;
```

To copy the dimensions of this bitmap into a BITMAP structure, BLOWUP2 uses *GetObject*:

```
GetObject (hBitmap, sizeof (BITMAP), (LPSTR) &bm) ;
```

It can then copy the bitmap to the client area, stretching it to the larger or smaller dimensions:

```
SetStretchBltMode (hdc, COLORONCOLOR) ;
StretchBlt (hdc, 0, 0, xClient, yClient,
            hdcMem, 0, 0, bm.bmWidth, bm.bmHeight,
                    SRCCOPY) ;
```

The only cleanup involved is deleting the memory device context:

```
DeleteDC (hdcMem) ;
    }
```

and closing the clipboard:

```
CloseClipboard () ;
```

The bitmap isn't deleted, because it belongs to the clipboard.

If we wanted to make an exact copy of the bitmap, we could use *GetObject* to obtain the dimensions:

```
GetObject (hBitmap, sizeof (BITMAP), (LPSTR) &bm) ;
```

and create a new bitmap and another memory device context:

```
hBitmap2 = CreateBitmapIndirect (&bm) ;
hdcMem2 = CreateCompatibleDC (hdc) ;
SelectObject (hdcMem2, hBitmap2) ;
```

A simple *BitBlt* copies the bitmap:

```
BitBlt (hdcMem2, 0, 0, bm.bmWidth, bm.bmHeight,
        hdcMem, 0, 0, SRCCOPY) ;
```

You would then delete the two memory device contexts.

Although BLOWUP2 will display in its client area any bitmap that is currently in the clipboard, it checks the contents of the clipboard only when it gets a WM_PAINT message. For instance, if you draw something in the Windows PAINTBRUSH program, block it out, and copy it to the clipboard, BLOWUP2's client area won't show this new bitmap until BLOWUP2 gets a WM_PAINT message. For this reason, BLOWUP2 isn't a true clipboard viewer. We'll examine clipboard viewers later in this chapter.

The Metafile and the Metafile Picture

Using the clipboard to transfer metafiles from one program to another involves complexities not present when dealing with text and bitmaps. You can determine the length of a NULL-terminated string by simply searching for the NULL terminator. You can determine the dimensions of a bitmap using *GetObject*. But if you have a handle to a metafile, how can you determine how large the image will be when you play the metafile? Unless you start digging into the internals of the metafile itself, you can't.

Moreover, when a program obtains a metafile from the clipboard, it has the most flexibility in working with it if the metafile has been designed to be played in an MM_ISOTROPIC or MM_ANISOTROPIC mapping mode. The program that receives the metafile can then scale the image by simply setting viewport extents before playing the metafile. But if the mapping mode is set to MM_ISOTROPIC or MM_ANISOTROPIC within the metafile, then the program that receives the metafile is stuck. The program can make GDI calls only before or after the metafile is played. It can't make a GDI call in the middle of a metafile.

To solve these problems, metafile handles are not directly put into the clipboard and retrieved by other programs. Instead, the metafile handle is part of a "metafile picture," which is a structure of type METAFILEPICT. This structure allows the program that obtains the metafile picture from the clipboard to set the mapping mode and viewport extents itself before playing the metafile.

The METAFILEPICT structure is 8 bytes long and has four fields: *mm* (int), the mapping mode; *xExt* (int) and *yExt* (int), the width and height of the metafile image; and *hMF* (WORD), the handle to the metafile. For all the mapping modes except MM_ISOTROPIC and MM_ANISOTROPIC, the *xExt* and *yExt* values are the size of the image in units of the mapping mode given by *mm*. With this information, the program that copies the metafile picture structure from the clipboard can determine how much display space the metafile will encompass when it is played. The program that creates the metafile can set these values to the largest *x*- and *y*-coordinates it uses in the GDI drawing functions that enter the metafile.

For the MM_ISOTROPIC and MM_ANISOTROPIC mapping modes, the *xExt* and *yExt* fields function differently. You will recall from Chapter 11 that a program uses the MM_ISOTROPIC or MM_ANISOTROPIC mapping mode when it wants to use arbitrary logical units in GDI functions independent of the measurable size of the image. A program uses MM_ISOTROPIC when it wants to maintain an aspect ratio regardless of the size of the viewing surface and MM_ANISOTROPIC when it doesn't care about the aspect ratio. You will also recall from Chapter 11 that after a program sets the mapping mode to MM_ISOTROPIC or MM_ANISOTROPIC, it generally makes calls to *SetWindowExt* and *SetViewportExt*. The *SetWindowExt* call uses logical units to specify the units the program wants to use when drawing. The *SetViewportExt* call uses device units based on the size of the viewing surface (for instance, the size of the window's client area).

If a program creates an MM_ISOTROPIC or MM_ANISOTROPIC metafile for the clipboard, then the metafile should not itself contain a call to *SetViewportExt*, because the device units in that call would be based on the display surface of the program creating the metafile and not on the display surface of the program that reads the metafile from the clipboard and plays it. Instead, the *xExt* and *yExt* values should assist the program that obtains the metafile from the clipboard in setting appropriate viewport extents for playing the metafile. But the metafile itself contains a call to set the window extent when the mapping mode is MM_ISOTROPIC or MM_ANISOTROPIC. The coordinates of the GDI drawing functions within the metafile are based on these window extents.

The program that creates the metafile and metafile picture follows these rules:

- The *mm* field of the METAFILEPICT structure is set to specify the mapping mode.

- For mapping modes other than MM_ISOTROPIC and MM_ANISO-TROPIC, the *xExt* and *yExt* fields are set to the width and height of the image in units corresponding to the *mm* field. For metafiles to be played in an MM_ISOTROPIC or MM_ANISOTROPIC environment, matters get a little more complex. For MM_ANISOTROPIC, 0 values of *xExt* and *yExt* are used when the program is suggesting neither a size nor an aspect ratio for the image. For MM_ISOTROPIC or MM_ANISO-TROPIC, positive values of *xExt* and *yExt* indicate a suggested width and height of the image in units of 0.01 mm (MM_HIMETRIC units). For MM_ISOTROPIC, negative values of *xExt* and *yExt* indicate a suggested aspect ratio of the image but not a suggested size.

- For the MM_ISOTROPIC and MM_ANISOTROPIC mapping modes, the metafile itself contains calls to *SetWindowExt* and (possibly) *Set-WindowOrg*. That is, the program that creates the metafile calls these functions in the metafile device context. Generally, the metafile will not contain calls to *SetMapMode*, *SetViewportExt*, or *SetViewportOrg*.

- The metafile should be a memory-based metafile, not a disk-based metafile.

Here's some sample code for a program creating a metafile and copying it to the clipboard. If the metafile uses the MM_ISOTROPIC or MM_ANISOTROPIC mapping mode, the first calls in the metafile should be to set the window extent. (The window extent is fixed in the other mapping modes.) Regardless of the mapping mode, the window origin can also be set:

```
hdcMeta = CreateMetaFile (NULL) ;
SetWindowExt (hdcMeta, ...) ;
SetWindowOrg (hdcMeta, ...) ;
```

The coordinates in the drawing functions of the metafile are based on these window extents and the window origin. After the program uses GDI calls to draw on the metafile device context, the metafile is closed to get a handle to the metafile:

```
hmf = CloseMetaFile (hdcMeta) ;
```

The program also needs to define a far pointer to a structure of type METAFILEPICT and allocate a block of global memory for this structure:

```
GLOBALHANDLE   hGMem ;
LPMETAFILEPICT lpMFP ;

    [other program lines]

hGMem = GlobalAlloc (GHND, (DWORD) sizeof (METAFILEPICT)) ;

lpMFP = (LPMETAFILEPICT) GlobalLock (hGMem) ;
```

Next, the program sets the four fields of this structure.

```
lpMFP->mm   = MM_... ;
lpMFP->xExt = ... ;
lpMFP->yExt = ... ;
lpMFP->hMF  = hmf ;

GlobalUnlock (hGMem) ;
```

The program then transfers the global memory block containing the metafile picture structure to the clipboard:

```
OpenClipboard (hwnd) ;
EmptyClipboard () ;
SetClipboardData (CF_METAFILEPICT, hGMem) ;
CloseClipboard () ;
```

Following these calls, the *hGMem* handle (the memory block containing the metafile picture structure) and the *hmf* handle (the metafile itself) become invalid for the program that created them.

Now for the hard part. When a program obtains a metafile from the clipboard and plays this metafile, it must do the following:

1. The program uses the *mm* field of the metafile picture structure to set the mapping mode.

2. For mapping modes other than MM_ISOTROPIC or MM_ANISOTROPIC, the program uses the *xExt* and *yExt* values to set a clipping rectangle or simply to determine the size of the image. For the MM_ISOTROPIC and MM_ANISOTROPIC mapping modes, the program uses *xExt* and *yExt* to set the viewport extents.

3. The program then plays the metafile.

Here's the code. You first open the clipboard, get the handle to the metafile picture structure, and lock it:

```
OpenClipboard (hwnd) ;
hGMem = GetClipboardData (CF_METAFILEPICT) ;
lpMFP = (LPMETAFILEPICT) GlobalLock (hGMem) ;
```

You can then save the attributes of your current device context and set the mapping mode to the *mm* value of the structure:

```
SaveDC (hdc) ;
SetMappingMode (lpMFP->mm) ;
```

If the mapping mode isn't MM_ISOTROPIC or MM_ANISOTROPIC, you can set a clipping rectangle to the values of *xExt* and *yExt*. Because these values are in logical units, you have to use *LPtoDP* to convert the coordinates to device units for the clipping rectangle. Or you can simply save the values so you know how large the image is.

For the MM_ISOTROPIC or MM_ANISOTROPIC mapping mode, you use *xExt* and *yExt* to set the viewport extent. One possible function to perform this task is shown below. This function assumes that *cxClient* and *cyClient* represent the pixel height and width of the area in which you want the metafile to appear if no suggested size is implied by *xExt* and *yExt*.

```
void PrepareMetaFile (HDC hdc, LPMETAFILEPICT lpmfp,
                      SHORT cxClient, SHORT cyClient)
     {
     long xlScale, ylScale, lScale ;

     SetMapMode (hdc, lpmfp->mm) ;

     if (lpmfp->mm == MM_ISOTROPIC || lpmfp->mm == MM_ANISOTROPIC)
          {
          if (lpmfp->xExt == 0)
               SetViewportExt (hdc, cxClient, cyClient) ;
```

```
         else if (lpmfp->xExt > 0)
              SetViewportExt (hdc,
                  (short) ((long) lpmfp->xExt *
                            GetDeviceCaps (hdc, HORZRES) /
                            GetDeviceCaps (hdc, HORZSIZE) / 100),
                  (short) ((long) lpmfp->yExt *
                            GetDeviceCaps (hdc, VERTRES) /
                            GetDeviceCaps (hdc, VERTSIZE) / 100)) ;

         else if (lpmfp->xExt < 0)
              {
              xlScale = 100L * (long) cxClient *
                            GetDeviceCaps (hdc, HORZSIZE) /
                            GetDeviceCaps (hdc, HORZRES) /
                                      -lpmfp->xExt ;
              ylScale = 100L * (long) cyClient *
                            GetDeviceCaps (hdc, VERTSIZE) /
                            GetDeviceCaps (hdc, VERTRES) /
                                      -lpmfp->yExt ;
              lScale = min (xlScale, ylScale) ;

              SetViewportExt (hdc,
                  (short) ((long) -lpmfp->xExt * lScale *
                            GetDeviceCaps (hdc, HORZRES) /
                            GetDeviceCaps (hdc, HORZSIZE) / 100),
                  (short) ((long) -lpmfp->yExt * lScale *
                            GetDeviceCaps (hdc, VERTRES) /
                            GetDeviceCaps (hdc, VERTSIZE) / 100)) ;
              }
         }
    }
```

This code assumes that both *xExt* and *yExt* are 0, greater than 0, or less than 0, (which should be the case). If the extents are 0, no size or aspect ratio is suggested. The viewport extents are set to the area in which you want to display the metafile. Positive values of *xExt* and *yExt* are a suggested image size in units of 0.01 mm. The *GetDeviceCaps* function assists in determining the number of pixels per 0.01 mm, and this value is multiplied by the extent values in the metafile picture structure. Negative values of *xExt* and *yExt* indicate a suggested aspect ratio but not a suggested size. The value *lScale* is first calculated based on the aspect ratio of the size in millimeters corresponding to *cxClient* and *cyClient*. This scaling factor is then used to set a viewport extent in pixels.

With this job out of the way, you can set a viewport origin if you want, play the metafile, and return the device context to normal:

```
PlayMetaFile (lpMFP->hMF) ;
RestoreDC (hdc, -1) ;
```

794

Then you unlock the memory block and close the clipboard:

```
GlobalUnlock (hGMem) ;
CloseClipboard () ;
```

BEYOND SIMPLE CLIPBOARD USE

In using text and bitmaps, you've seen that transferring data to the clipboard requires four calls after the data has been prepared:

```
OpenClipboard (hwnd) ;
EmptyClipboard () ;
SetClipboardData (wFormat, hHandle) ;
CloseClipboard () ;
```

Getting access to this data requires three calls:

```
OpenClipboard (hwnd) ;
hHandle = GetClipboardData (wFormat) ;

     [other program lines]

CloseClipboard () ;
```

You can make a copy of the clipboard data or use it in some other manner between the *GetClipboardData* and *CloseClipboard* calls. That approach may be all you'll need for most purposes, but you can also use the clipboard in more sophisticated ways.

Using Multiple Data Items

When you open the clipboard to put data into it, you must call *EmptyClipboard* to signal Windows to free or delete the contents of the clipboard. You can't add something to the existing contents of the clipboard. So in this sense, the clipboard holds only one item at a time.

However, between the *EmptyClipboard* and the *CloseClipboard* calls, you can call *SetClipboardData* several times, each time using a different clipboard format. For instance, if you want to store a short string of text in the clipboard, you can create a metafile device context and write that text to the metafile. You can also create a bitmap large enough to hold the character string, select the bitmap into a memory device context, and write the string to the bitmap. In this way, you make that character string available not only to programs that can read text from the clipboard but also to programs that read bitmaps and metafiles from the clipboard. Moreover, if you select a different font into the metafile device context or memory device context before writing the text, programs that read bitmaps or metafiles will use the string with this different font. (Of course, these programs won't be able to recognize the metafile or bitmap as actually containing a character string.)

If you want to write several handles to the clipboard, you call *SetClipboardData* for each of them:

```
OpenClipboard (hwnd) ;
EmptyClipboard () ;
SetClipboardData (CF_TEXT, hGMemText) ;
SetClipboardData (CF_BITMAP, hBitmap) ;
SetClipboardData (CF_METAFILEPICT, hGMemMFP) ;
CloseClipboard () ;
```

While these three formats of data are in the clipboard, an *IsClipboardFormatAvailable* call with the CF_TEXT, CF_BITMAP, or CF_METAFILEPICT argument will return TRUE. A program can get access to these handles by calling:

```
hGMemText = GetClipboardData (CF_TEXT) ;
```

or:

```
hBitmap = GetClipboardData (CF_BITMAP) ;
```

or:

```
hGMemMFP = GetClipboardData (CF_METAFILEPICT) ;
```

The next time a program calls *EmptyClipboard*, Windows will free or delete all three of the handles retained by the clipboard as well as the metafile that is part of the METAFILEPICT structure.

A program can determine all the formats stored by the clipboard by first opening the clipboard and then calling *EnumClipboardFormats*. Start off by setting a variable *wFormat* to 0:

```
wFormat = 0 ;
OpenClipboard (hwnd) ;
```

Now make successive *EnumClipboardFormats* calls starting with the 0 value. The function will return a positive *wFormat* value for each format currently in the clipboard. When the function returns 0, you're done:

```
while (wFormat = EnumClipboardFormats (wFormat))
     {
     [logic for each wFormat value]

     }
CloseClipboard () ;
```

You can obtain the number of different formats currently in the clipboard by calling:

```
nCount = CountClipboardFormats () ;
```

Delayed Rendering

When you put data into the clipboard, you generally make a copy of the data and give the clipboard a handle to a global memory block that contains the copy. For very large data items, this approach can waste memory. If the user never pastes that data into another program, it will continue to occupy memory space until it is replaced by something else.

You can avoid this problem by using a technique called "delayed rendering," in which your program doesn't actually supply the data until another program needs it. Rather than give Windows a handle to the data, you simply use a NULL in the *SetClipboardData* call:

```
OpenClipboard (hwnd) ;
EmptyClipboard () ;
SetClipboardData (wFormat, NULL) ;
CloseClipboard () ;
```

You can have multiple *SetClipboardData* calls using different values of *wFormat*. You can use NULL parameters with some of them and real handles with others.

That's simple enough, but now the process gets a little more complex. When another program calls *GetClipboardData*, Windows will check to see if the handle for that format is NULL. If it is, Windows will send a message to the "clipboard owner" (your program) asking for a real handle to the data. Your program must then supply this handle.

More specifically, the "clipboard owner" is the last window that put data into the clipboard. Windows can identify the clipboard owner, because the *OpenClipboard* call requires a window handle. (Because programs can also call *OpenClipboard* when reading data from the clipboard or enumerating clipboard formats, it's really the *EmptyClipboard* call that establishes this window handle as the clipboard owner.)

A program that uses delayed rendering has to process three messages in its window procedure: WM_RENDERFORMAT, WM_RENDERALLFORMATS, and WM_DESTROY-CLIPBOARD. Windows sends your window procedure a WM_RENDERFORMAT message when another program calls *GetClipboardData*. The value of *wParam* is the format requested. When you process the WM_RENDERFORMAT message, don't open and empty the clipboard. Simply create a global memory block for the format given by *wParam*, transfer the data to it, and call *SetClipboardData* with the correct format and the global handle. Obviously, you'll need to retain information in your program in order to construct this data properly when processing WM_RENDERFORMAT. When another program calls *EmptyClipboard*, Windows sends your program a WM_DESTROYCLIPBOARD message. This tells you that the information to construct the clipboard data is no longer needed. You are no longer the clipboard owner.

If your program terminates while it is still the clipboard owner, and the clipboard still contains NULL data handles that your program set with *SetClipboardData*, you'll receive a WM_RENDERALLFORMATS message. You should open the clipboard, empty it, put the data in global memory blocks, and call *SetClipboardData* for each format. Then close the clipboard. The WM_RENDERALLFORMATS message is one of the last messages your window procedure receives. It is followed by a WM_DESTROYCLIPBOARD message (because you've rendered all the data) and then the normal WM_DESTROY.

If your program can transfer only one format of data to the clipboard (text, for instance), you can combine the WM_RENDERALLFORMATS and WM_RENDERFORMAT processing. The code will look something like this:

```
case WM_RENDERALLFORMATS :
     OpenClipboard (hwnd) ;
     EmptyClipboard () ;
                              // fall through
case WM_RENDERFORMAT :

     [put text into global memory block]

     SetClipboardData (CF_TEXT, hMem) ;

     if (iMessage == WM_RENDERALLFORMATS)
         CloseClipboard () ;
     return 0 ;
```

If your program uses several clipboard formats, then you will want to process the WM_RENDERFORMAT message only for the format requested by *wParam*. You don't need to process the WM_DESTROYCLIPBOARD message unless it is burdensome for your program to retain the information necessary to construct the data.

Private Data Formats

So far we've dealt with only the standard clipboard formats defined by Windows. However, you may want to use the clipboard to store a "private data format." The Windows WRITE program uses this technique to store text that contains font and formatting information.

At first, this concept may seem nonsensical. If the purpose of the clipboard is to transfer data between applications, why should the clipboard contain data that only one application understands? The answer is simple: The clipboard also exists to allow the transfer of data between different instances of the same program, and these instances obviously understand the same private formats.

There are several ways to use private data formats. The easiest involves data that is ostensibly in one of the standard clipboard formats (text, bitmap, or metafile) but that has meaning only to your program. In this case, you use one of the following *wFormat* values in your *SetClipboardData* and *GetClipboardData* calls: CF_DSPTEXT, CF_DSPBITMAP, or CF_DSPMETAFILEPICT. DSP stands for "display"—these formats allow CLIPBOARD to display the data as text, a bitmap, or a metafile. However, another program that calls *GetClipboardData* using the normal CF_TEXT, CF_BITMAP, or CF_METAFILEPICT format won't obtain this data.

If you use one of these formats to put data in the clipboard, you must also use the same format to get the data out. But how do you know if the data is from another instance of your program or from another program using one of these formats? Here's one way: You can first obtain the clipboard owner by calling:

```
hwndClipOwner = GetClipboardOwner () ;
```

You can then get the name of the window class of this window handle:

```
char szClassName [16] ;

    [other program lines]

GetClassName (hwndClipOwner, &szClassName, 16) ;
```

If the class name is the same as your program's, then the data was put into the clipboard by another instance of your program.

The second way to use private formats involves the CF_OWNERDISPLAY flag. The global memory handle to *SetClipboardData* is NULL:

```
SetClipboardData (CF_OWNERDISPLAY, NULL) ;
```

This is the method that WRITE uses to show formatted text in the client area of the CLIP-BOARD clipboard viewer. Obviously, CLIPBRD.EXE doesn't know how to display this formatted text. When WRITE specifies the CF_OWNERDISPLAY format, WRITE is taking responsibility for painting CLIPBOARD's client area.

Because the global memory handle is NULL, a program that calls *SetClipboardData* with the CF_OWNERDISPLAY format (the clipboard owner) must process the delayed rendering messages sent to the clipboard owner by Windows as well as five additional messages. These five messages are sent by the clipboard viewer to the clipboard owner:

■ WM_ASKCBFORMATNAME—The clipboard viewer sends this message to the clipboard owner to get a name for the format of the data. The *lParam* parameter is a pointer to a buffer, and *wParam* is the maximum number of characters for this buffer. The clipboard owner must copy the name of the clipboard format into this buffer.

■ WM_SIZECLIPBOARD—This message tells the clipboard owner that the size of the clipboard viewer's client area has changed. The *wParam* parameter is a handle to the clipboard viewer, and *lParam* is a pointer to a RECT structure containing the new size. If the RECT structure contains all zeros, the clipboard viewer is being destroyed or made an icon. Although CLIPBRD.EXE allows only one instance of itself to be running, other clipboard viewers can also send this message to the clipboard owner. Handling these multiple clipboard viewers isn't impossible for the clipboard owner (given that *wParam* identifies the particular viewer), but it isn't easy, either.

- WM_PAINTCLIPBOARD—This message tells the clipboard owner to update the clipboard viewer's client area. Again, *wParam* is a handle to the clipboard viewer's window. The *lParam* parameter is a pointer to a PAINTSTRUCT structure. The clipboard owner can obtain a handle to the clipboard viewer's device context from the *hdc* field of this structure.

- WM_HSCROLLCLIPBOARD and WM_VSCROLLCLIPBOARD—These messages inform the clipboard owner that a user has scrolled the clipboard viewer's scroll bars. The *wParam* parameter is a handle to the clipboard viewer's window, the low word of *lParam* is the scrolling request (the same as *wParam* in normal scroll bar messages), and the high word of *lParam* is the thumb position if the low word is SB_THUMB-POSITION. (This value is the same as the low word of *lParam* in a normal scroll bar message.)

Handling these messages may look like more trouble than it's worth. However, the process does provide a benefit to the user: When copying text from WRITE to the clipboard, the user will find it comforting to see the text still formatted in CLIPBOARD's client area.

The third way to use private clipboard data formats is to register your own clipboard format name. You supply a name for this format to Windows, and Windows gives your program a number to use as the format parameter in *SetClipboardData* and *GetClipboardData*. Programs that use this method generally also copy data to the clipboard in one of the standard formats. This approach allows CLIPBRD.EXE to display data in its client area (without the hassles involved with CF_OWNERDISPLAY) and permits other programs to copy data from the clipboard.

As an example, let's assume we've written a vector drawing program that copies data to the clipboard in a bitmap format, a metafile format, and its own registered clipboard format. CLIPBRD.EXE will display the metafile. Other programs that can read bitmaps or metafiles from the clipboard will obtain those formats. However, when the vector drawing program itself needs to read data from the clipboard, it will copy the data in its own registered format, because that format probably contains more information than the bitmap or metafile.

A program registers a new clipboard format by calling:

```
wFormat = RegisterClipboardFormat (lpszFormatName) ;
```

The *wFormat* value is between 0xC000 and 0xFFFF. A clipboard viewer (or a program that obtains all the current clipboard formats by calling *EnumClipboardFormats*) can obtain the ASCII name of this format by calling:

```
GetClipboardFormatName (wFormat, lpsBuffer, nMaxCount) ;
```

Windows copies up to *nMaxCount* characters into *lpsBuffer*.

Programmers who use this method for copying data to the clipboard might want to publicize the format name and the actual format of the data. If the program becomes popular, other programs can then copy data in this format from the clipboard.

BECOMING A CLIPBOARD VIEWER

A program that is notified of changes in the clipboard contents is called a "clipboard viewer." The CLIPBOARD program that comes with Windows is a clipboard viewer, but you can also write your own clipboard viewer program. Clipboard viewers are notified of changes to the clipboard through messages to the viewer's window procedure.

The Clipboard Viewer Chain

Any number of clipboard viewer applications can be running in Windows at the same time, and they can all be notified of changes to the clipboard. From Windows' perspective, however, there is only one clipboard viewer, which I'll call the "current clipboard viewer." Windows maintains only one window handle to identify the current clipboard viewer, and it sends messages only to that window when the contents of the clipboard change.

Clipboard viewer applications have the responsibility of participating in the "clipboard viewer chain" so that all running clipboard viewer programs receive the messages that Windows sends to the current clipboard viewer. When a program registers itself as a clipboard viewer, that program becomes the current clipboard viewer. Windows gives that program the window handle of the previous current clipboard viewer, and the program saves this handle. When the program receives a clipboard viewer message, it sends that message to the window procedure of the next program in the clipboard chain.

Clipboard Viewer Functions and Messages

A program can become part of the clipboard viewer chain by calling the *SetClipboardViewer* function. If the primary purpose of the program is to serve as a clipboard viewer, the program can call this function during processing of the WM_CREATE message. The function returns the window handle of the previous current clipboard viewer. The program should save that handle in a static variable:

```
static HWND hwndNextViewer ;
     [other program lines]
case WM_CREATE :
     [other program lines]
     hwndNextViewer = SetClipboardViewer (hwnd) ;
```

If your program is the first program to become a clipboard viewer during the Windows session, then *hwndNextViewer* will be NULL.

Windows sends a WM_DRAWCLIPBOARD message to the current clipboard viewer (the most recent window to register itself as a clipboard viewer) whenever the contents of the clipboard change. Each program in the clipboard viewer chain should use *SendMessage* to pass this message to the next clipboard viewer. The last program in the clipboard viewer chain (the first window to register itself as a clipboard viewer) will have stored a NULL *hwndNextViewer* value. If *hwndNextViewer* is NULL, the program simply returns without sending the message to another program. (Don't confuse the WM_DRAWCLIPBOARD and WM_PAINTCLIPBOARD messages. The WM_PAINTCLIPBOARD message is sent by a clipboard viewer to programs that use the CF_OWNERDISPLAY clipboard format. The WM_DRAWCLIPBOARD message is sent by Windows to the current clipboard viewer.)

The easiest way to process the WM_DRAWCLIPBOARD message is to send the message to the next clipboard viewer (unless *hwndNextViewer* is NULL) and invalidate the client area of your window:

```
case WM_DRAWCLIPBOARD :
     if (hwndNextViewer)
          SendMessage (hwndNextViewer, iMessage, wParam, lParam) ;

     InvalidateRect (hwnd, NULL, TRUE) ;
     return 0 ;
```

During processing of the WM_PAINT message, you can read the contents of the clipboard by using the normal *OpenClipboard*, *GetClipboardData*, and *CloseClipboard* calls.

When a program wishes to remove itself from the clipboard viewer chain, it must call *ChangeClipboardChain*. This function requires the window handle of the program leaving the viewer chain and the window handle of the next clipboard viewer:

```
ChangeClipboardChain (hwnd, hwndNextViewer) ;
```

When a program calls *ChangeClipboardChain*, Windows sends a WM_CHANGECLIP-BOARD message to the current clipboard viewer. The *wParam* parameter is the handle of the window removing itself from the chain (the first parameter to *ChangeClipboardChain*), and the low word of *lParam* is the window handle of the next clipboard viewer after the one removing itself from the chain (the second parameter to *ChangeClipboardChain*).

When your program receives a WM_CHANGECLIPBOARD message, you must therefore check to see if *wParam* is equal to the value of *hwndNextViewer* that you've saved. If it is, your program must set *hwndNextViewer* to the low word of *lParam*. This action ensures that any future WM_DRAWCLIPBOARD messages you get won't be sent to the window removing itself from the clipboard viewer chain. If *wParam* isn't equal to *hwndNext-Viewer*, and *hwndNextViewer* isn't NULL, send the message to the next clipboard viewer:

```
case WM_CHANGECBCHAIN :
     if (wParam == hwndNextViewer)
          hwndNextViewer = LOWORD (lParam) ;

     else if (hwndNextViewer)
          SendMessage (hwndNextViewer, iMessage, wParam, lParam) ;
     return 0 ;
```

You shouldn't need to include the else if statement, which checks *hwndNextViewer* for a
non-NULL value. A NULL *hwndNextViewer* value would indicate that the program executing this code is the last viewer on the chain, in which case the message should never have
gotten this far.

If your program is still in the clipboard viewer chain when it is about to terminate,
you must remove your program from the chain. You can do this during processing of the
WM_DESTROY message by calling *ChangeClipboardChain*.

```
case WM_DESTROY :
     ChangeClipboardChain (hwnd, hwndNextViewer) ;
     PostQuitMessage (0) ;
     return 0 ;
```

Windows also has a function that allows a program to obtain the window handle of
the first clipboard viewer:

```
hwndViewer = GetClipboardViewer () ;
```

This function isn't normally needed. The return value can be NULL if there is no current
clipboard viewer.

Here's an example to illustrate how the clipboard viewer chain works. When Windows first starts up, the current clipboard viewer is NULL:

Current clipboard viewer: NULL

A program with a window handle of *hwnd1* calls *SetClipboardViewer*. The function
returns NULL, which becomes the *hwndNextViewer* value in this program:

Current clipboard viewer: hwnd1
hwnd1's next viewer: NULL

A second program with a window handle of *hwnd2* now calls *SetClipboardViewer* and
gets back *hwnd1*:

Current clipboard viewer: hwnd2
hwnd2's next viewer: hwnd1
hwnd1's next viewer: NULL

A third program (*hwnd3*) and then a fourth (*hwnd4*) also call *SetClipboardViewer* and get back *hwnd2* and *hwnd3*:

Current clipboard viewer:	hwnd4
hwnd4's next viewer:	hwnd3
hwnd3's next viewer:	hwnd2
hwnd2's next viewer:	hwnd1
hwnd1's next viewer:	NULL

When the contents of the clipboard change, Windows sends a WM_DRAWCLIPBOARD message to *hwnd4*, *hwnd4* sends the message to *hwnd3*, *hwnd3* sends it to *hwnd2*, *hwnd2* sends it to *hwnd1*, and *hwnd1* returns.

Now *hwnd2* decides to remove itself from the chain by calling:

```
ChangeClipboardChain (hwnd2, hwnd1) ;
```

Windows sends *hwnd4* a WM_CHANGECBCHAIN message with *wParam* equal to *hwnd2* and the low word of *lParam* equal to *hwnd1*. Because *hwnd4*'s next viewer is *hwnd3*, *hwnd4* sends this message to *hwnd3*. Now *hwnd3* notes that *wParam* is equal to its next viewer (*hwnd2*), so it sets its next viewer equal to the low word of *lParam* (*hwnd1*) and returns. The mission is accomplished. The clipboard viewer chain now looks like this:

Current clipboard viewer:	hwnd4
hwnd4's next viewer:	hwnd3
hwnd3's next viewer:	hwnd1
hwnd1's next viewer:	NULL

A Simple Clipboard Viewer

Clipboard viewers don't have to be as sophisticated as CLIPBRD.EXE. A clipboard viewer can, for instance, display only one clipboard format. The CLIPVIEW program, shown in Figure 16-2, is a clipboard viewer that displays only the CF_TEXT format.

CLIPVIEW.MAK

```
#------------------------
# CLIPVIEW.MAK make file
#------------------------

clipview.exe : clipview.obj clipview.def
      link clipview, /align:16, NUL, /nod slibcew libw, clipview
      rc clipview.exe

clipview.obj : clipview.c
      cl -c -Gsw -Ow -W2 -Zp clipview.c
```

Figure 16-2. *The CLIPVIEW program.*

CLIPVIEW.C

```
/*-------------------------------------------
   CLIPVIEW.C -- Simple Clipboard Viewer
                 (c) Charles Petzold, 1990
   -----------------------------------------*/

#include <windows.h>

long FAR PASCAL WndProc (HWND, WORD, WORD, LONG) ;

int PASCAL WinMain (HANDLE hInstance, HANDLE hPrevInstance,
                    LPSTR lpszCmdLine, int nCmdShow)
     {
     static   char szAppName [] = "ClipView" ;
     HWND      hwnd ;
     MSG       msg ;
     WNDCLASS  wndclass ;

     if (!hPrevInstance)
          {
          wndclass.style         = CS_HREDRAW | CS_VREDRAW ;
          wndclass.lpfnWndProc   = WndProc ;
          wndclass.cbClsExtra    = 0 ;
          wndclass.cbWndExtra    = 0 ;
          wndclass.hInstance     = hInstance ;
          wndclass.hIcon         = NULL ;
          wndclass.hCursor       = LoadCursor (NULL, IDC_ARROW) ;
          wndclass.hbrBackground = GetStockObject (WHITE_BRUSH) ;
          wndclass.lpszMenuName  = NULL ;
          wndclass.lpszClassName = szAppName ;

          RegisterClass (&wndclass) ;
          }

     hwnd = CreateWindow (szAppName, "Simple Clipboard Viewer (Text Only)",
                          WS_OVERLAPPEDWINDOW,
                          CW_USEDEFAULT, CW_USEDEFAULT,
                          CW_USEDEFAULT, CW_USEDEFAULT,
                          NULL, NULL, hInstance, NULL) ;

     ShowWindow (hwnd, nCmdShow) ;
     UpdateWindow (hwnd) ;

     while (GetMessage (&msg, NULL, 0, 0))
          {
          TranslateMessage (&msg) ;
          DispatchMessage (&msg) ;
          }
```

(continued)

```
        return msg.wParam ;
        }

long FAR PASCAL WndProc (HWND hwnd, WORD message, WORD wParam, LONG lParam)
        {
        static HWND hwndNextViewer ;
        HANDLE      hGMem ;
        HDC         hdc ;
        LPSTR       lpGMem ;
        PAINTSTRUCT ps ;
        RECT        rect ;

        switch (message)
            {
            case WM_CREATE :
                hwndNextViewer = SetClipboardViewer (hwnd) ;
                return 0 ;

            case WM_CHANGECBCHAIN :
                if (wParam == hwndNextViewer)
                    hwndNextViewer = LOWORD (lParam) ;

                else if (hwndNextViewer)
                    SendMessage (hwndNextViewer, message, wParam, lParam) ;

                return 0 ;

            case WM_DRAWCLIPBOARD :
                if (hwndNextViewer)
                    SendMessage (hwndNextViewer, message, wParam, lParam) ;

                InvalidateRect (hwnd, NULL, TRUE) ;
                return 0 ;

            case WM_PAINT :
                hdc = BeginPaint (hwnd, &ps) ;
                GetClientRect (hwnd, &rect) ;
                OpenClipboard (hwnd) ;

                if (hGMem = GetClipboardData (CF_TEXT))
                    {
                    lpGMem = GlobalLock (hGMem) ;
                    DrawText (hdc, lpGMem, -1, &rect, DT_EXPANDTABS) ;
                    GlobalUnlock (hGMem) ;
                    }

                CloseClipboard () ;
                EndPaint (hwnd, &ps) ;
                return 0 ;
```

(continued)

```
        case WM_DESTROY :
                ChangeClipboardChain (hwnd, hwndNextViewer) ;
                PostQuitMessage (0) ;
                return 0 ;
        }
    return DefWindowProc (hwnd, message, wParam, lParam) ;
    }
```

CLIPVIEW.DEF

```
;-------------------------------------
; CLIPVIEW.DEF module definition file
;-------------------------------------

NAME            CLIPVIEW

DESCRIPTION     'Simple Clipboard Viewer (c) Charles Petzold, 1990'
EXETYPE         WINDOWS
STUB            'WINSTUB.EXE'
CODE            PRELOAD MOVEABLE DISCARDABLE
DATA            PRELOAD MOVEABLE MULTIPLE
HEAPSIZE        1024
STACKSIZE       8192
EXPORTS         WndProc
```

CLIPVIEW processes WM_CREATE, WM_CHANGECBCHAIN, WM_DRAWCLIP-BOARD, and WM_DESTROY messages as discussed above. The WM_PAINT message simply opens the clipboard and uses *GetClipboardData* with a format of CF_TEXT. If the function returns a global memory handle, CLIPVIEW locks it and uses *DrawText* to display the text in its client area.

A clipboard viewer that handles data formats beyond the five standard formats (as CLIPBRD.EXE does) has additional work to do, such as displaying the names of all the formats currently in the clipboard. You can do this by calling *EnumClipboardFormats* and obtaining the names of the nonstandard formats from *GetClipboardFormatName*. A clipboard viewer that uses the CF_OWNERDISPLAY format must send these four messages to the clipboard to display the data:

WM_PAINTCLIPBOARD	WM_VSCROLLCLIPBOARD
WM_SIZECLIPBOARD	WM_HSCROLLCLIPBOARD

If you want to write such a clipboard viewer, you have to obtain the window handle of the clipboard owner using *GetClipboardOwner* and send that window these messages when you need to update the clipboard viewer's client area.

Chapter 17

Dynamic Data Exchange (DDE)

Dynamic Data Exchange (DDE) is one of three mechanisms of interprocess communication supported under Windows. The other two are the Windows clipboard (which I discussed in Chapter 16) and shared memory in dynamic link libraries (Chapter 19).

DDE is based on the messaging system built into Windows. Two Windows programs carry on a DDE "conversation" by posting messages to each other. These two programs are known as the "server" and the "client." A DDE server is the program that has access to data that may be useful to other Windows programs. A DDE client is the program that obtains this data from the server.

A DDE conversation is initiated by the client program. The client broadcasts a message (called WM_DDE_INITIATE) to all currently running Windows programs. This message indicates a general category of data the client needs. A DDE server that has this data can respond to this broadcasted message. At that point, the conversation begins.

A single Windows program can be both a client to one program and a server to another, but this requires two different DDE conversations. A server can deliver data to multiple clients, and a client can obtain data from multiple servers, but again, this requires multiple DDE conversations. To keep these conversations unique and separate, each conversation (on both the client and server sides) uses a different window. Generally, a program that supports DDE will create a hidden child window for each conversation it maintains.

The programs involved in a DDE conversation need not be specifically coded to work with each other. As I'll discuss in the next section, generally the writer of a DDE server will publicly document how the data is identified. A user of a program that can act as a DDE client (such as Microsoft Excel) can use this information to establish a DDE conversation between the two programs.

If you write a family of two or more Windows programs that must communicate with each other but not with other Windows programs, you may consider defining your own messaging protocol. However, this is not recommended. While it may work in Windows 3, it is possible that future versions of Windows will not support any form of message-based interprocess communication except for DDE.

Because DDE uses the messaging system built into Windows, it fits very naturally in the environment. But this is not to say that DDE is easy to implement. The protocol has many options, and programs must be ready to deal with some rather tricky problems.

BASIC CONCEPTS

When a client asks a server for data, it must be able to identify the type of data it wants. This is done with three character strings, called the "application," the data "topic," and the data "item."

Application, Topic, and Item

The idea of the application, topic, and item is best approached with an example. In this chapter, I'll show you how to write a Windows DDE server program called DDEPOP. This program contains population data of the United States from the 1970 census and 1980 census. Based on a linear extrapolation, the program can calculate the instantaneous ("at this moment") population of any state or of the United States as a whole. (A linear extrapolation is not quite accurate, of course, but then again, this is only a sample program.)

Anybody who writes a DDE server program should document how this data is identified using three character strings:

- The server application name: In this example, this is simply "DDEPOP." Each server has only one application name, the name of the program.

- The topic name: All DDE servers support at least one topic. In the case of DDEPOP, only one topic is supported, which is identified by the string "US_Population." Conceivably, the DDEPOP program could be expanded to include data concerning the square-mile areas of the states, in which case the program would support a second topic named "US_Area."

■ The item name: Within each topic, a DDE server supports one or more data items. In DDEPOP, the item identifies the state using the standard two-character post-office abbreviation, such as "NY" for New York, "CA" for California, and "US" for the total. DDEPOP supports 52 items—the 50 states, the District of Columbia ("DC"), and the total.

This documentation is sufficient to use the DDEPOP server with another Windows program that can act as a client, for example, Microsoft Excel. To use DDEPOP with Microsoft Excel, you can type the following into a spreadsheet cell:

```
=DDEPOP!US_Population!US
```

These three strings indicate the application, topic, and item (in this case, the total United States population). If DDEPOP.EXE is not already running, Microsoft Excel will attempt to execute it. (DDEPOP must be in the current directory or in a directory listed in the PATH environment variable.) If successful, Excel will initiate a DDE conversation with DDEPOP, obtain the population data, and display the population as a number in the cell. These population figures can be formatted, graphed, or used in calculations.

What's most interesting is that the population figures will be periodically updated in the spreadsheet. This is known as a "hot link" or (in a slight variation) "warm link." Every 5 seconds, DDEPOP recalculates the population data and notifies a client when an item has changed. In the case of the total U.S. population, you'll see the figure increase by 1 about every 15 seconds.

The Types of Conversations

There are three basic types of DDE conversations—cold link, hot link, and warm link. These conversations use DDE messages defined in the DDE.H header file. The simplest of the three conversations is known as the cold link.

1. The Cold Link

A cold link conversation begins when a client broadcasts a WM_DDE_INITIATE message identifying the application and topic it requires. (The application and topic may be set to NULL to begin a conversation with any server application or any data topic.) A server application that supports the specified topic responds to the client with a WM_DDE_ACK ("acknowledge") message:

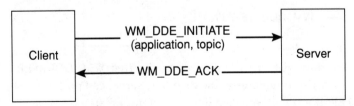

The client then requests a particular data item by posting a WM_DDE-
_REQUEST message. If the server can supply this data item, it responds
by posting a WM_DDE_DATA message to the client:

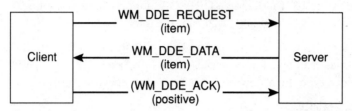

I've also indicated here that the client can acknowledge to the server that
it has received the WM_DDE_DATA message. This is optional (which I've
indicated by putting the WM_DDE_ACK message within parenthesis).
The server indicates whether it wants this acknowledgment in a flag
passed with the WM_DDE_DATA message. A flag passed with the
WM_DDE_ACK message indicates a "positive" acknowledgment.

If the client posts a WM_DDE_REQUEST message to the server, and
the server cannot supply the requested data item, then the server posts a
"negative" WM_DDE_ACK message to the client:

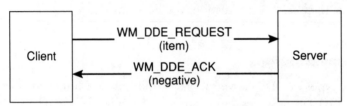

The DDE conversation continues with the client posting WM_DDE-
_REQUEST messages to the server—for the same data item or different
data items—and the server responding with WM_DDE_DATA or
WM_DDE_ACK messages. The conversation is terminated when the
client and server post each other WM_DDE_TERMINATE messages:

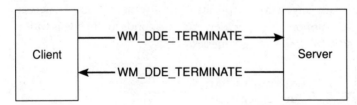

Although I've indicated that the client posts the first WM_DDE_TER-
MINATE message, this is not always the case. The server can post the first
WM_DDE_TERMINATE message, and the client must respond to that.

2. The Hot Link

One problem with the cold link is that the data the server has access to may change with the passing of time. (This is the case with DDEPOP, which calculates an instantaneous population that can change.) In the cold link, the client does not know when the data changes. The hot link solves this problem.

Again, the DDE conversation begins with a WM_DDE_INITIATE message and a WM_DDE_ACK message:

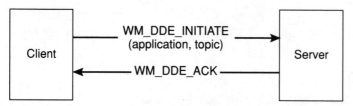

The client indicates the data item it requires by posting a WM_DDE-_ADVISE message to the server. The server responds by posting a WM_DDE_ACK message indicating if it has access to this item:

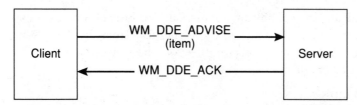

A positive acknowledgment indicates the server can supply the data; a negative acknowledgment indicates that it cannot.

At this point, the server is obligated to notify the client whenever the value of the data item changes. This notification uses a WM-_DDE_DATA message, to which the client (based on a flag set in the WM_DDE_DATA message) may or may not respond with a WM-_DDE_ACK message:

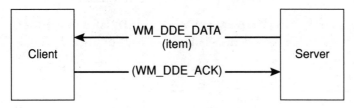

When the client no longer wishes to be advised of updates to the data item, it posts a WM_DDE_UNADVISE message to the server, and the server acknowledges:

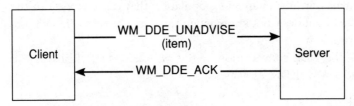

The conversation is terminated with the posting of WM_DDE_TER-MINATE messages:

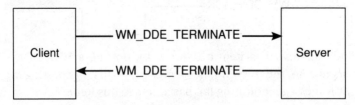

The cold link and the hot link are not mutually exclusive. During a single DDE conversation, a client may ask for some data items by using WM-_DDE_REQUEST (for a cold link) and ask for others by using WM_DDE-_ADVISE (for a hot link).

3. The Warm Link

The warm link combines elements of the cold link and hot link. The conversation begins as normal:

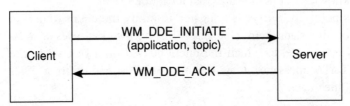

As with the hot link, the client posts a WM_DDE_ADVISE message to the server, and the server acknowledges either positively or negatively:

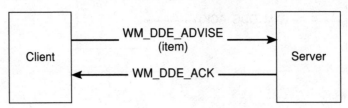

However, a flag passed with the WM_DDE_ADVISE message indicates that the client wishes only to be informed of changes in data without immediately receiving the new data item. So the server posts WM_DDE_DATA messages with NULL data:

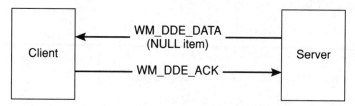

Now the client knows that a particular data item has changed. To obtain this item, the client uses a WM_DDE_REQUEST message, just as in the cold link:

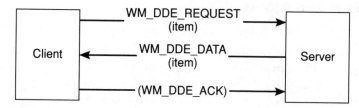

As in the hot link, a client can stop being advised of changes in data items by posting a WM_DDE_ADVISE message to the server:

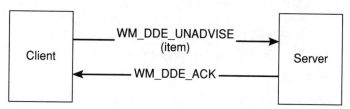

The conversation is terminated with the WM_DDE_TERMINATE messages:

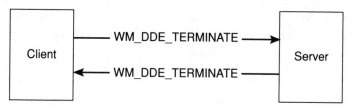

These three types of conversations use all the DDE messages except two: WM_DDE_POKE (in which a client gives a server unsolicited data) and WM_DDE_EXECUTE (in which a client sends a command string to a server). These messages are rarely used, and I won't be covering them in this chapter.

The DDE.H header file also defines four structures:

- DDEACK (used in the WM_DDE_ACK message)
- DDEADVISE (used in the WM_DDE_ADVISE message)
- DDEDATA (used in the WM_DDE_DATA message)
- DDEPOKE (used in the WM_DDE_POKE message)

I'll deal with the first three structures as I discuss the sample programs in this chapter.

Character Strings and Atoms

I've discussed how a DDE client and server identify data using three character strings—the application, topic, and item. But in the actual messages between the client and server, these character strings do not appear: "Atoms" are used instead.

Atoms are WORD values that refer to character strings in a case-insensitive manner. You can use atoms within your own program for working with character strings, in which case the atom table (the table that references the atom values with the strings) is stored in your program's default data segment.

You define an atom as follows:

```
ATOM aAtom ;
```

You can add a string to the atom table using the function:

```
aAtom = AddAtom (lpString) ;
```

If the character string does not already exist in the atom table, this function adds it and returns a unique value identifying the string. Each atom has a "reference count," which is the number of times *AddAtom* has been called for the same string. The reference count is initially set to 1. If the character string already exists in the atom table (that is, if this is the second or subsequent time that *AddAtom* has been called for the same string), the function returns the number identifying the character string and increments the reference count.

The function:

```
DeleteAtom (aAtom) ;
```

decrements the reference count. When the count is 0, the atom and character string are removed from the atom table.

The function:

```
aAtom = FindAtom (lpString) ;
```

will return the atom associated with the character string (or 0 if the string is not in the atom table). This function does not affect the reference count of the atom.

The function:

```
nBytes = GetAtomName (aAtom, lpBuffer, nBufferSize) ;
```

returns the character string for an atom. The last parameter indicates the size of the buffer pointed to by the second parameter. The function returns the number of bytes copied to the buffer and does not affect the reference count.

These four functions (there are several others of lesser importance) allow you to work with atoms within your own program. However, because the atom table is stored in your program's default data segment, the atoms are unique to your program. To use atoms with DDE, you must use another set of four functions, similar to the functions described above:

```
aAtom = GlobalAddAtom (lpString) ;
GlobalDeleteAtom (aAtom) ;
aAtom = GlobalFindAtom (lpString) ;
nBytes = GlobalGetAtomName (aAtom, lpBuffer, nBufferSize) ;
```

The atom table for these atoms is stored in a shared data segment in a dynamic link library within Windows and hence is common to all Windows programs. One program can use *GlobalAddAtom* to add a string to the atom table and pass the atom to another program. This other program can use *GlobalGetAtomName* to obtain the character string associated with the atom. This is how Windows programs identify the DDE application, topic, and item.

The rules regarding the use of atoms with DDE are described in the documentation of the DDE messages in Chapter 15 of the Microsoft Windows Programmer's Reference. These rules are extremely important: It is not good if an atom that is still required by one program is deleted from the atom table by another program. Neither is it good if atoms that are no longer required are not deleted from the atom table. For this reason, you must be careful about how your program handles atoms.

Atoms are used for the DDE application, topic, and item strings. The data structures that are transferred from one Windows program to another must be allocated using *GlobalAlloc* with the GMEM_DDESHARE option. This allows the global memory block to be shared among multiple Windows programs. The DDE rules that govern which program is responsible for allocating and freeing these global memory blocks are also quite strict.

A DDE SERVER PROGRAM

We are now ready to begin looking at DDEPOP, the DDE server program that can supply instantaneous state population data to a DDE client. This program is shown in Figure 17-1.

DDEPOP.MAK

```
#----------------------
# DDEPOP.MAK make file
#----------------------

ddepop.exe : ddepop.obj ddepop.def ddepop.res
     link ddepop, /align:16, NUL, /nod slibcew win87em libw, ddepop
     rc ddepop.res

ddepop.obj : ddepop.c
     cl -c -Gsw -Ow -W2 -Zp ddepop.c

ddepop.res : ddepop.rc ddepop.ico
     rc -r ddepop.rc
```

DDEPOP.C

```
/*---------------------------------------------
    DDEPOP.C -- DDE Server for Population Data
                (c) Charles Petzold, 1990
   ------------------------------------------*/

#include <windows.h>
#include <dde.h>
#include <string.h>
#include <time.h>

struct
     {
     char *szState ;
     long lPop70 ;
     long lPop80 ;
     long lPop ;
     }
     pop [] = {
          "AL",  3444354,  3894025, 0, "AK",   302583,   401851, 0,
          "AZ",  1775399,  2716598, 0, "AR",  1923322,  2286357, 0,
          "CA", 19971069, 23667764, 0, "CO",  2209596,  2889735, 0,
          "CT",  3032217,  3107564, 0, "DE",   548104,   594338, 0,
          "DC",   756668,   638432, 0, "FL",  6791418,  9746961, 0,
```

Figure 17-1. *The DDEPOP program.*   *(continued)*

818

```
          "GA",  4587930,  5462982, 0, "HI",    769913,    964691, 0,
          "ID",   713015,   944127, 0, "IL", 11110285, 11427409, 0,
          "IN",  5195392,  5490212, 0, "IA",  2825368,  2913808, 0,
          "KS",  2249071,  2364236, 0, "KY",  3220711,  3660324, 0,
          "LA",  3644637,  4206116, 0, "ME",   993722,  1125043, 0,
          "MD",  3923897,  4216933, 0, "MA",  5689170,  5737093, 0,
          "MI",  8881826,  9262044, 0, "MN",  3806103,  4075970, 0,
          "MS",  2216994,  2520770, 0, "MO",  4677623,  4916762, 0,
          "MT",   694409,   786690, 0, "NE",  1485333,  1569825, 0,
          "NV",   488738,   800508, 0, "NH",   737681,   920610, 0,
          "NJ",  7171112,  7365011, 0, "NM",  1017055,  1303302, 0,
          "NY", 18241391, 17558165, 0, "NC",  5084411,  5880415, 0,
          "ND",   617792,   652717, 0, "OH", 10657423, 10797603, 0,
          "OK",  2559463,  3025487, 0, "OR",  2091533,  2633156, 0,
          "PA", 11800766, 11864720, 0, "RI",   949723,   947154, 0,
          "SC",  2590713,  3120730, 0, "SD",   666257,   690768, 0,
          "TN",  3926018,  4591023, 0, "TX", 11198655, 14225513, 0,
          "UT",  1059273,  1461037, 0, "VT",   444732,   511456, 0,
          "VA",  4651448,  5346797, 0, "WA",  3413244,  4132353, 0,
          "WV",  1744237,  1950186, 0, "WI",  4417821,  4705642, 0,
          "WY",   332416,   469557, 0, "US", 203302031, 226542580, 0
          } ;

#define NUM_STATES (sizeof (pop) / sizeof (pop [0]))

typedef struct
     {
     unsigned int fAdvise:1 ;
     unsigned int fDeferUpd:1 ;
     unsigned int fAckReq:1 ;
     unsigned int dummy:13 ;
     long         lPopPrev ;
     }
     POPADVISE ;

#define ID_TIMER    1
#define DDE_TIMEOUT 3000

long FAR PASCAL WndProc         (HWND, WORD, WORD, LONG) ;
long FAR PASCAL ServerProc      (HWND, WORD, WORD, LONG) ;
BOOL FAR PASCAL TimerEnumProc   (HWND, LONG) ;
BOOL FAR PASCAL CloseEnumProc   (HWND, LONG) ;
BOOL           PostDataMessage (HWND, HWND, int, BOOL, BOOL, BOOL) ;

char   szAppName []     = "DdePop" ;
char   szServerClass [] = "DdePop.Server" ;
HANDLE hInst ;

int PASCAL WinMain (HANDLE hInstance, HANDLE hPrevInstance,
                    LPSTR lpszCmdLine, int nCmdShow)
```

(continued)

```
                {
                HWND      hwnd ;
                MSG       msg ;
                WNDCLASS wndclass ;

                if (hPrevInstance)
                     return FALSE ;

                hInst = hInstance ;

                          // Register window class

                wndclass.style         = 0 ;
                wndclass.lpfnWndProc   = WndProc ;
                wndclass.cbClsExtra    = 0 ;
                wndclass.cbWndExtra    = 0 ;
                wndclass.hInstance     = hInstance ;
                wndclass.hIcon         = LoadIcon (hInstance, szAppName) ;
                wndclass.hCursor       = LoadCursor (NULL, IDC_ARROW) ;
                wndclass.hbrBackground = GetStockObject (WHITE_BRUSH) ;
                wndclass.lpszMenuName  = NULL ;
                wndclass.lpszClassName = szAppName ;

                RegisterClass (&wndclass) ;

                          // Register window class for DDE Server

                wndclass.style         = 0 ;
                wndclass.lpfnWndProc   = ServerProc ;
                wndclass.cbClsExtra    = 0 ;
                wndclass.cbWndExtra    = 2 * sizeof (WORD) ;
                wndclass.hInstance     = hInstance ;
                wndclass.hIcon         = NULL ;
                wndclass.hCursor       = NULL ;
                wndclass.hbrBackground = NULL ;
                wndclass.lpszMenuName  = NULL ;
                wndclass.lpszClassName = szServerClass ;

                RegisterClass (&wndclass) ;

                hwnd = CreateWindow (szAppName, "DDE Population Server",
                               WS_OVERLAPPEDWINDOW,
                               CW_USEDEFAULT, CW_USEDEFAULT,
                               CW_USEDEFAULT, CW_USEDEFAULT,
                               NULL, NULL, hInstance, NULL) ;

                SendMessage (hwnd, WM_TIMER, 0, 0L) ;   // initialize 'pop' structure
```

(continued)

```
        if (!SetTimer (hwnd, ID_TIMER, 5000, NULL))
             {
             MessageBox (hwnd, "Too many clocks or timers!", szAppName,
                         MB_ICONEXCLAMATION : MB_OK) ;

             return FALSE ;
             }

        ShowWindow (hwnd, SW_SHOWMINNOACTIVE) ;
        UpdateWindow (hwnd) ;

        while (GetMessage (&msg, NULL, 0, 0))
             {
             TranslateMessage (&msg) ;
             DispatchMessage (&msg) ;
             }

        KillTimer (hwnd, ID_TIMER) ;

        return msg.wParam ;
        }

long FAR PASCAL WndProc (HWND hwnd, WORD message, WORD wParam, LONG lParam)
        {
        static FARPROC lpTimerEnumProc, lpCloseEnumProc ;
        static char    szTopic [] = "US_Population" ;
        ATOM           aApp, aTop ;
        HWND           hwndClient, hwndServer ;
        int            i ;
        long double    ldSecsInDecade, ldSecSince1970 ;
        time_t         lSecSince1970 ;

        switch (message)
             {
             case WM_CREATE :
                  lpTimerEnumProc = MakeProcInstance (TimerEnumProc, hInst) ;
                  lpCloseEnumProc = MakeProcInstance (CloseEnumProc, hInst) ;
                  return 0 ;

             case WM_DDE_INITIATE :

                          // wParam          -- sending window handle
                          // LOWORD (lParam) -- application atom
                          // HIWORD (lParam) -- topic atom

                     hwndClient = wParam ;

                     aApp = GlobalAddAtom (szAppName) ;
                     aTop = GlobalAddAtom (szTopic) ;
```

(continued)

```
                // Check for matching atoms, create window, and acknowledge

        if ((LOWORD (lParam) == NULL :: LOWORD (lParam) == aApp) &&
            (HIWORD (lParam) == NULL :: HIWORD (lParam) == aTop))
                {
                hwndServer = CreateWindow (szServerClass, NULL,
                                           WS_CHILD, 0, 0, 0, 0,
                                           hwnd, NULL, hInst, NULL) ;

                SetWindowWord (hwndServer, 0, hwndClient) ;
                SendMessage (wParam, WM_DDE_ACK, hwndServer,
                             MAKELONG (aApp, aTop)) ;
                }

                // Otherwise, delete the atoms just created

        else
                {
                GlobalDeleteAtom (aApp) ;
                GlobalDeleteAtom (aTop) ;
                }

        return 0 ;

case WM_TIMER :
case WM_TIMECHANGE :
        time (&lSecSince1970) ;

                // Calculate new current populations

        ldSecSince1970 = (long double) lSecSince1970 ;
        ldSecsInDecade = (long double) 3652 * 24 * 60 * 60 ;

        for (i = 0 ; i < NUM_STATES ; i++)
                {
                pop[i].lPop = (long)
                    (((ldSecsInDecade - ldSecSince1970) * pop[i].lPop70 +
                        ldSecSince1970 * pop[i].lPop80) / ldSecsInDecade
                            + .5) ;
                }

                // Notify all child windows

        EnumChildWindows (hwnd, lpTimerEnumProc, 0L) ;
        return 0 ;

case WM_QUERYOPEN :
        return 0 ;
```

(continued)

```
        case WM_CLOSE :

                // Notify all child windows

            EnumChildWindows (hwnd, lpCloseEnumProc, 0L) ;

            break ;                    // for default processing

        case WM_DESTROY :
            PostQuitMessage (0) ;
            return 0 ;
        }
    return DefWindowProc (hwnd, message, wParam, lParam) ;
    }

long FAR PASCAL ServerProc (HWND hwnd, WORD message, WORD wParam, LONG lParam)
    {
    ATOM          aItem ;
    char          szItem [10], szPopulation [10] ;
    DDEACK        DdeAck ;
    DDEADVISE     Advise ;
    DDEADVISE FAR *lpDdeAdvise ;
    DDEDATA FAR   *lpDdeData ;
    DWORD         dwTime ;
    GLOBALHANDLE  hPopAdvise, hDdeData, hDdeAdvise, hCommands, hDdePoke ;
    int           i ;
    HWND          hwndClient ;
    MSG           msg ;
    POPADVISE FAR *lpPopAdvise ;
    WORD          cfFormat, wStatus ;

    switch (message)
        {
        case WM_CREATE :

                // Allocate memory for POPADVISE structures

            hPopAdvise = GlobalAlloc (GHND, NUM_STATES * sizeof (POPADVISE));

            if (hPopAdvise == NULL)
                DestroyWindow (hwnd) ;
            else
                SetWindowWord (hwnd, 2, hPopAdvise) ;

            return 0 ;

        case WM_DDE_REQUEST :
```

(continued)

```
              // wParam          -- sending window handle
              // LOWORD (lParam) -- data format
              // HIWORD (lParam) -- item atom

         hwndClient = wParam ;
         cfFormat   = LOWORD (lParam) ;
         aItem      = HIWORD (lParam) ;

              // Check for matching format and data item

         if (cfFormat == CF_TEXT)
              {
              GlobalGetAtomName (aItem, szItem, sizeof (szItem)) ;

              for (i = 0 ; i < NUM_STATES ; i++)
                   if (strcmp (szItem, pop[i].szState) == 0)
                        break ;

              if (i < NUM_STATES)
                   {
                   GlobalDeleteAtom (aItem) ;
                   PostDataMessage (hwnd, hwndClient, i,
                                    FALSE, FALSE, TRUE) ;
                   return 0 ;
                   }
              }

              // Negative acknowledge if no match

         DdeAck.bAppReturnCode = 0 ;
         DdeAck.reserved       = 0 ;
         DdeAck.fBusy          = FALSE ;
         DdeAck.fAck           = FALSE ;

         wStatus = * (WORD *) & DdeAck ;

         if (!PostMessage (hwndClient, WM_DDE_ACK, hwnd,
                   MAKELONG (wStatus, aItem)))
              {
              GlobalDeleteAtom (aItem) ;
              }

         return 0 ;

    case WM_DDE_ADVISE :

              // wParam          -- sending window handle
              // LOWORD (lParam) -- DDEADVISE memory handle
              // HIWORD (lParam) -- item atom
```

(continued)

```
hwndClient = wParam ;
hDdeAdvise = LOWORD (lParam) ;
aItem      = HIWORD (lParam) ;

lpDdeAdvise = (DDEADVISE FAR *) GlobalLock (hDdeAdvise) ;

     // Check for matching format and data item

if (lpDdeAdvise->cfFormat == CF_TEXT)
     {
     GlobalGetAtomName (aItem, szItem, sizeof (szItem)) ;

     for (i = 0 ; i < NUM_STATES ; i++)
          if (strcmp (szItem, pop[i].szState) == 0)
               break ;

          // Fill in the POPADVISE structure and acknowledge

     if (i < NUM_STATES)
          {
          hPopAdvise = GetWindowWord (hwnd, 2) ;
          lpPopAdvise = (POPADVISE FAR *)
                              GlobalLock (hPopAdvise) ;

          lpPopAdvise[i].fAdvise   = TRUE ;
          lpPopAdvise[i].fDeferUpd = lpDdeAdvise->fDeferUpd ;
          lpPopAdvise[i].fAckReq   = lpDdeAdvise->fAckReq ;
          lpPopAdvise[i].lPopPrev  = pop[i].lPop ;

          GlobalUnlock (hDdeAdvise) ;
          GlobalFree (hDdeAdvise) ;

          DdeAck.bAppReturnCode = 0 ;
          DdeAck.reserved       = 0 ;
          DdeAck.fBusy          = FALSE ;
          DdeAck.fAck           = TRUE ;

          wStatus = * (WORD *) & DdeAck ;

          if (!PostMessage (hwndClient, WM_DDE_ACK, hwnd,
                         MAKELONG (wStatus, aItem)))
               {
               GlobalDeleteAtom (aItem) ;
               }
          else
               {
               PostDataMessage (hwnd, hwndClient, i,
                              lpPopAdvise[i].fDeferUpd,
                              lpPopAdvise[i].fAckReq,
                              FALSE) ;
```

(continued)

```
                                      }

                    GlobalUnlock (hPopAdvise) ;
                    return 0 ;
                    }
             }

                    // Otherwise post a negative WM_DDE_ACK

        GlobalUnlock (hDdeAdvise) ;

        DdeAck.bAppReturnCode = 0 ;
        DdeAck.reserved       = 0 ;
        DdeAck.fBusy          = FALSE ;
        DdeAck.fAck           = FALSE ;

        wStatus = * (WORD *) & DdeAck ;

        if (!PostMessage (hwndClient, WM_DDE_ACK, hwnd,
                      MAKELONG (wStatus, aItem)))
             {
             GlobalFree (hDdeAdvise) ;
             GlobalDeleteAtom (aItem) ;
             }

        return 0 ;

case WM_DDE_UNADVISE :

             // wParam          -- sending window handle
             // LOWORD (lParam) -- data format
             // HIWORD (lParam) -- item atom

        hwndClient = wParam ;
        cfFormat   = LOWORD (lParam) ;
        aItem      = HIWORD (lParam) ;

        DdeAck.bAppReturnCode = 0 ;
        DdeAck.reserved       = 0 ;
        DdeAck.fBusy          = FALSE ;
        DdeAck.fAck           = TRUE ;

        hPopAdvise  = GetWindowWord (hwnd, 2) ;
        lpPopAdvise = (POPADVISE FAR *) GlobalLock (hPopAdvise) ;

             // Check for matching format and data item

        if (cfFormat == CF_TEXT || cfFormat == 0)
             {
```

(continued)

```
                   if (aItem == NULL)
                       for (i = 0 ; i < NUM_STATES ; i++)
                           lpPopAdvise[i].fAdvise = FALSE ;
                   else
                       {
                       GlobalGetAtomName (aItem, szItem, sizeof (szItem)) ;

                       for (i = 0 ; i < NUM_STATES ; i++)
                           if (strcmp (szItem, pop[i].szState) == 0)
                               break ;

                       if (i < NUM_STATES)
                           lpPopAdvise[i].fAdvise = FALSE ;
                       else
                           DdeAck.fAck = FALSE ;
                       }
                   }
              else
                   DdeAck.fAck = FALSE ;

                   // Acknowledge either positively or negatively

              wStatus = * (WORD *) & DdeAck ;

              if (!PostMessage (hwndClient, WM_DDE_ACK, hwnd,
                            MAKELONG (wStatus, aItem)))
                   {
                   if (aItem != NULL)
                       GlobalDeleteAtom (aItem) ;
                   }

         GlobalUnlock (hPopAdvise) ;
         return 0 ;

    case WM_DDE_EXECUTE :

              // Post negative acknowledge

         hwndClient = wParam ;
         hCommands  = HIWORD (lParam) ;

         DdeAck.bAppReturnCode = 0 ;
         DdeAck.reserved       = 0 ;
         DdeAck.fBusy          = FALSE ;
         DdeAck.fAck           = FALSE ;

         wStatus = * (WORD *) & DdeAck ;
```

(continued)

```
          if (!PostMessage (hwndClient, WM_DDE_ACK, hwnd,
                         MAKELONG (wStatus, hCommands)))
             {
             GlobalFree (hCommands) ;
             }
          return 0 ;

     case WM_DDE_POKE :

               // Post negative acknowledge

          hwndClient = wParam ;
          hDdePoke   = LOWORD (lParam) ;
          aItem      = HIWORD (lParam) ;

          DdeAck.bAppReturnCode = 0 ;
          DdeAck.reserved       = 0 ;
          DdeAck.fBusy          = FALSE ;
          DdeAck.fAck           = FALSE ;

          wStatus = * (WORD *) & DdeAck ;

          if (!PostMessage (hwndClient, WM_DDE_ACK, hwnd,
                         MAKELONG (wStatus, aItem)))
             {
             GlobalFree (hDdePoke) ;
             GlobalDeleteAtom (aItem) ;

             }

          return 0 ;

     case WM_DDE_TERMINATE :

               // Respond with another WM_DDE_TERMINATE message

          hwndClient = wParam ;
          PostMessage (hwndClient, WM_DDE_TERMINATE, hwnd, 0L) ;
          DestroyWindow (hwnd) ;
          return 0 ;

     case WM_TIMER :

               // Post WM_DDE_DATA messages for changed populations

          hwndClient  = GetWindowWord (hwnd, 0) ;
          hPopAdvise  = GetWindowWord (hwnd, 2) ;
          lpPopAdvise = (POPADVISE FAR *) GlobalLock (hPopAdvise) ;
```

(continued)

```
                    for (i = 0 ; i < NUM_STATES ; i++)
                        if (lpPopAdvise[i].fAdvise)
                            if (lpPopAdvise[i].lPopPrev != pop[i].lPop)
                                {
                                if (!PostDataMessage (hwnd, hwndClient, i,
                                                      lpPopAdvise[i].fDeferUpd,
                                                      lpPopAdvise[i].fAckReq,
                                                      FALSE))
                                    break ;

                                lpPopAdvise[i].lPopPrev = pop[i].lPop ;
                                }

              GlobalUnlock (hPopAdvise) ;
              return 0 ;

         case WM_CLOSE :

                   // Post a WM_DDE_TERMINATE message to the client

              hwndClient = GetWindowWord (hwnd, 0) ;
              PostMessage (hwndClient, WM_DDE_TERMINATE, hwnd, 0L) ;

              dwTime = GetCurrentTime () ;

              while (GetCurrentTime () - dwTime < DDE_TIMEOUT)
                    if (PeekMessage (&msg, hwnd, WM_DDE_TERMINATE,
                                     WM_DDE_TERMINATE, PM_REMOVE))
                          break ;

              DestroyWindow (hwnd) ;
              return 0 ;

         case WM_DESTROY :
              hPopAdvise = GetWindowWord (hwnd, 2) ;
              GlobalFree (hPopAdvise) ;
              return 0 ;
         }
    return DefWindowProc (hwnd, message, wParam, lParam) ;
    }

BOOL FAR PASCAL TimerEnumProc (HWND hwnd, LONG lParam)
    {
    SendMessage (hwnd, WM_TIMER, 0, 0L) ;

    return TRUE ;
    }
```

(continued)

```
BOOL FAR PASCAL CloseEnumProc (HWND hwnd, LONG lParam)
     {
     SendMessage (hwnd, WM_CLOSE, 0, 0L) ;

     return TRUE ;
     }

BOOL PostDataMessage (HWND hwndServer, HWND hwndClient, int iState,
                      BOOL fDeferUpd, BOOL fAckReq, BOOL fResponse)
     {
     ATOM         aItem ;
     char         szPopulation [10] ;
     DDEACK       DdeAck ;
     DDEDATA FAR  *lpDdeData ;
     DWORD        dwTime ;
     GLOBALHANDLE hDdeData ;
     MSG          msg ;

     aItem = GlobalAddAtom (pop[iState].szState) ;

          // Allocate a DDEDATA structure if not defered update

     if (fDeferUpd)
          {
          hDdeData = NULL ;
          }
     else
          {
          wsprintf (szPopulation, "%ld\r\n", pop[iState].lPop) ;

          hDdeData = GlobalAlloc (GHND | GMEM_DDESHARE,
                                  sizeof (DDEDATA) + strlen (szPopulation)) ;

          lpDdeData = (DDEDATA FAR *) GlobalLock (hDdeData) ;

          lpDdeData->fResponse = fResponse ;
          lpDdeData->fRelease  = TRUE ;
          lpDdeData->fAckReq   = fAckReq ;
          lpDdeData->cfFormat  = CF_TEXT ;

          lstrcpy ((LPSTR) lpDdeData->Value, szPopulation) ;

          GlobalUnlock (hDdeData) ;
          }

          // Post the WM_DDE_DATA message

     if (!PostMessage (hwndClient, WM_DDE_DATA, hwndServer,
                       MAKELONG (hDdeData, aItem)))
```

(continued)

```
            {
       if (hDdeData != NULL)
            GlobalFree (hDdeData) ;

       GlobalDeleteAtom (aItem) ;
       return FALSE ;
       }

       // Wait for the acknowledge message if it's requested

  if (fAckReq)
       {
       DdeAck.fAck = FALSE ;

       dwTime = GetCurrentTime () ;

       while (GetCurrentTime () - dwTime < DDE_TIMEOUT)
            {
            if (PeekMessage (&msg, hwndServer, WM_DDE_ACK, WM_DDE_ACK,
                         PM_REMOVE))
                 {
                 DdeAck = * (DDEACK *) & LOWORD (msg.lParam) ;
                 aItem  = HIWORD (msg.lParam) ;
                 GlobalDeleteAtom (aItem) ;
                 break ;
                 }
            }

       if (DdeAck.fAck == FALSE)
            {
            if (hDdeData != NULL)
                 GlobalFree (hDdeData) ;

            return FALSE ;
            }
       }

  return TRUE ;
  }
```

DDEPOP.RC

```
/*-------------------------
   DDEPOP.RC resource script
   ----------------------*/

DdePop ICON ddepop.ico
```

DDEPOP.ICO

DDEPOP.DEF

```
;------------------------------------
; DDEPOP.DEF module definition file
;------------------------------------

NAME            DDEPOP

DESCRIPTION     'DDE Server for Population Data (c) Charles Petzold, 1990'
EXETYPE         WINDOWS
STUB            'WINSTUB.EXE'
CODE            PRELOAD MOVEABLE DISCARDABLE
DATA            PRELOAD MOVEABLE MULTIPLE
HEAPSIZE        1024
STACKSIZE       8192
EXPORTS         WndProc
                ServerProc
                TimerEnumProc
                CloseEnumProc
```

I described earlier how you can use this server with Microsoft Excel. Later in this chapter I'll show you a DDE client program (called SHOWPOP) that also uses DDEPOP as a server.

The DDEPOP Program

You'll notice that the top of the DDEPOP.C listing contains the line:

```
#include <dde.h>
```

This is the header file that includes the DDE messages and data structures.

This is followed in the DDEPOP.C listing by the structure called *pop* that contains all the two-character state codes, the 1970 population figures, the 1980 population figures, and a fourth field initialized with zeros that will contain the current population based on the system date and time.

The program also defines a second structure (called POPADVISE) using a *typedef* statement. I'll discuss later how this structure is used.

In *WinMain*, the program terminates if *hPrevInstance* is not equal to NULL. There is no reason for multiple copies of DDEPOP to be running under Windows. The program registers two window classes. The first has the class name "DdePop" used for the program's main window. The second has the class name "DdePop.Server." This second class is used for the child windows that are created to maintain multiple DDE conversations. Each conversation requires its own child window based on this window class.

In this second window class, the *cbWndExtra* field of the WNDCLASS structure is set to hold two words per window. As you'll see, the first will be used to store the window handle of the client that the server window is communicating with. The second will be a handle to a global memory block that contains NUM_STATE structures of type POPADVISE.

After DDEPOP creates its main window, it explicitly sends the window a WM_TIMER message. The sole purpose of this message is to allow *WndProc* an opportunity to initialize the *lPop* field of the *pop* structure with the current population based on the *lPop70* and *lPop80* fields and the system date and time. The program also calls *SetTimer* to set a 5-second timer to periodically update the *lPop* field.

You'll notice that *ShowWindow* is called with the SW_SHOWMINNOACTIVE parameter and that *WndProc* returns 0 from the WM_QUERYOPEN message. This keeps DDEPOP displayed as an icon (similar to the FREEMEM program from Chapter 5).

The WM_DDE_INITIATE Message

A DDE conversation is initiated by a client by broadcasting a WM_DDE_INITIATE message to all top-level windows. (As you'll see when I discuss the DDE client program later in this chapter, this is accomplished by calling *SendMessage* with a 0xFFFF window handle as the first parameter.)

The WM_DDE_INITIATE message is handled by a DDE server in its main window procedure. As in every DDE message, the *wParam* parameter is the handle to the window sending the message. This is the window handle of the client. *WndProc* stores this in the variable *hwndClient*.

For the WM_DDE_INITIATE message, the low word of *lParam* is the atom identifying the desired application. This could be NULL if the client wants a response from any server. The high word of *lParam* is the atom identifying the desired topic. Again, this could be NULL if the client wants a response from a server that can supply any topic.

WndProc processes the WM_DDE_INITIATE message by calling *GlobalAddAtom* to add atoms for its application name ("DdePop") and topic name ("US_Population"). It then checks if the atoms supplied in the low word and high word of *lParam* are NULL or match these atoms.

If the atoms match, then *WndProc* creates a hidden child window based on the "DdePop.Server" window class. This window (whose window procedure is *ServerProc*) will handle all subsequent DDE messages in the DDE conversation. The first of the two words reserved for the window is set to the handle of the client using *SetWindowWord*.

WndProc then acknowledges the WM_DDE_INITIATE message by sending a WM-_DDE_ACK message back to the client. The *wParam* parameter is the handle of the just-created server window, and *lParam* contains the atoms identifying the server application name and the topic name. (If the client requested all topics and the server supports multiple topics, then the server would send multiple WM_DDE_ACK messages back to the client, one for each topic it supports.)

A program that receives a WM_DDE_ACK message is responsible for deleting all atoms that accompany the message. *WndProc* calls *GlobalDeleteAtom* for the two atoms it created only if it does not send a WM_DDE_ACK message to the client.

The WM_DDE_INITIATE message and the WM_DDE_ACK message (in response to WM_DDE_INITIATE) are the only two DDE messages that are sent using *SendMessage* rather than posted using *PostMessage*. As we'll see later in this chapter, this means that a client sending a WM_DDE_INITIATE message receives the WM_DDE_ACK responses before the original *SendMessage* call has returned.

The *ServerProc* Window Procedure

With the sending of the WM_DDE_ACK message in response to the WM_DDE_INITIATE message, the DDE conversation has begun. As I mentioned, when *WndProc* sends the WM_DDE_ACK message back to the client, it sets the *wParam* parameter to the handle of the child window it creates for the conversation. This means that all subsequent DDE messages occur between the client and this child window, whose window procedure is *ServerProc*.

ServerProc processes its WM_CREATE message by allocating memory required to hold NUM_STATES structures of type POPADVISE. (I'll discuss how these are used shortly.) The handle to this global memory block is stored as the second reserved word using *SetWindowWord*. This memory block is freed when *ServerProc* receives a WM_DESTROY message.

The WM_DDE_REQUEST Message

A client posts a WM_DDE_REQUEST message to a server when it wants data that is associated with a particular item. This is the type of transaction known as the cold link. The server responds by posting a WM_DDE_DATA message to the client with the data or a WM_DDE_ACK message if it cannot satisfy the request. Let's look at how *ServerProc* handles the WM_DDE_REQUEST message.

As is usual with DDE messages, the *wParam* parameter accompanying WM_DDE-_REQUEST is the handle to the window posting the message, in this case the client. The low word of the *lParam* parameter is a requested data format. The high word of *lParam* is an atom identifying the requested data item.

The formats of DDE data are the same as clipboard formats, so this low word of *lParam* will most commonly be one of the identifiers beginning with the CF prefix. A client may send multiple WM_DDE_REQUEST messages to a server for the same item but with different formats. The server should respond with a WM_DDE_DATA message for only the formats it supports. Far and away the most common format for DDE data is CF_TEXT, and this is the only format that DDEPOP supports.

So, when processing the WM_DDE_REQUEST message, *ServerProc* first checks if the requested format is CF_TEXT. *ServerProc* then calls the *GlobalGetAtomName* function to get the character string associated with the atom passed in the high word of *lParam*. If the client knows what it's doing, this will be a two-character string identifying the state. A *for* loop goes through the states and attempts to match this with the *szState* field of the *pop* structure. If there's a match, *ServerProc* deletes the atom by calling *GlobalDeleteAtom* and then calls *PostDataMessage* (a function towards the end of DDEPOP that posts the WM_DDE_DATA message and which I'll describe shortly). *ServerProc* then returns.

If the requested format is not CF_TEXT, or if there was no match between the item atom and one of the state names, then *ServerProc* posts a negative WM_DDE_ACK message indicating that the data was not available. It does this by setting the *fAck* field of a DDEACK structure (defined in DDE.H) to FALSE. The DDEACK structure is converted to a word, which forms the low word of *lParam*. The high word of *lParam* is the atom for the requested item. *PostMessage* posts the WM_DDE_ACK message to the client.

Notice how the atom is handled here. The documentation for WM_DDE_REQUEST states: "When responding with either a WM_DDE_DATA or WM_DDE_ACK message, reuse the *aItem* atom or delete it and create a new one." What this means is that the state of the global atom table should not be altered by the server—that is, the reference count for the *item* atom should not be incremented or decremented.

There are three cases here:

- If the requested format is CF_TEXT and the atom matches one of the state names, then *ServerProc* calls *GlobalDeleteAtom* before calling the function in DDEPOP.C named *PostDataMessage*. This *PostDataMessage* function (as we'll see shortly) re-creates the atom when posting a WM_DDE_DATA message to the client.

- If the requested format is not CF_TEXT or if the atom does not match one of the state names, then *ServerProc* calls *PostMessage* to deliver a negative WM_DDE_ACK message to the client. The atom is simply reused in this message.

- However, if this *PostMessage* call fails (perhaps indicating that the client has been unexpectedly terminated), then *ServerProc* deletes the atom because the client cannot.

We are not yet finished with the WM_DDE_REQUEST message because we have not yet examined how DDEPOP's *PostDataMessage* responds with the WM_DDE_DATA message. That's next.

DDEPOP's *PostDataMessage* Function

The *PostDataMessage* function towards the end of DDEPOP.C is responsible for posting a WM_DDE_DATA message to a client. This function is set up to also handle WM_DDE_ADVISE messages (which I'll discuss shortly), so it's a little more complex than if it only had to handle WM_DDE_REQUEST messages.

PostDataMessage has six parameters:

- *hwndServer*—the window handle of the server

- *hwndClient*—the window handle of the client

- *i*—which is the index of the *pop* array identifying the state for which population data is requested

- *fDeferUpd*—which *ServerProc* sets to FALSE when responding to WM_DDE_REQUEST messages

- *fAckReq*—which *ServerProc* also sets to FALSE in this case

- *fResponse*—which *ServerProc* sets to TRUE to indicate a response from a WM_DDE_REQUEST message

(I'll discuss the *fDeferUpd* and *fAckReq* parameters shortly when we get to the WM_DDE_ADVISE message. For now, just ignore all parts of *PostDataMessage* when either of these two parameters is set to TRUE.)

PostDataMessage begins by calling *GlobalAddItem* to create an atom for the two-character state name. (You'll recall that *ServerProc* deleted the atom before calling *PostDataMessage*.) It then calls *wsprintf* to convert the population for the state (updated by *WndProc* within the past 5 seconds) to a character string terminated with a carriage return and line feed.

PostDataMessage then uses *GlobalAlloc* with the GMEM_DDESHARE option to allocate a block of memory large enough for a DDEDATA structure (defined in DDE.H) with the actual data (the character string *szPopulation*) appended to the end. In the case of *PostDataMessage* being used in response to a WM_DDE_REQUEST message, the fields of the DDEDATA structure are set as follows:

- The *fResponse* field of the DDEDATA structure is set to TRUE, indicating that the data is in response to a WM_DDE_DATA message.

- The *fRelease* field is also set to TRUE, indicating that the client should free the global memory block just allocated.

- The *fAckReq* field is set to FALSE, indicating that a WM_DDE_ACK message from the client is not required.

- The *cfFormat* field is set to CF_TEXT, indicating that the data is in a text format.

- The *szPopulation* array is copied into the area of the memory block beginning at the *Value* field of the structure.

PostDataMessage then uses *PostMessage* to post a WM_DDE_DATA message to the client. As usual, *wParam* is the handle of the window sending the message (the server). The low word of *lParam* is the handle of the memory block containing the DDEDATA structure, and the high word of *lParam* is the atom identifying the data item (the two-character state name).

If *PostMessage* is successful, then we're done. The client is responsible for freeing the memory block and deleting the atom. If *PostMessage* fails (perhaps because the client is no longer with us), *PostDataMessage* frees the memory block it allocated and deletes the atom.

The WM_DDE_ADVISE Message

You are, I trust, beginning to recognize some of the complexities involved in DDE. It gets a little more complex with WM_DDE_ADVISE and the hot link.

The WM_DDE_REQUEST message I've just discussed allows the client to obtain data from the server. But if this data changes (as the instantaneous population will), then the client has no way to know that. Allowing the client to know when data has been updated is the purpose of the WM_DDE_ADVISE message. On receipt of this message, a server is responsible for notifying the client when the data has changed. (This notification is accomplished by the server posting WM_DDE_DATA messages to the client.) This can be tricky because the server must "remember" which items the client has asked to be advised on. Moreover, the client will ask that this data be posted in particular ways.

In a WM_DDE_ADVISE message, the low word of *lParam* is a handle to a global memory block containing a DDEADVISE structure as defined in DDE.H. The high word of *lParam* is the atom identifying the data item.

When processing WM_DDE_ADVISE, *ServerProc* first checks that the *cfFormat* field of the DDEADVISE structure is CF_TEXT. It then obtains the text string referenced by the atom and checks it against the *szState* field of the *pop* structure.

If there's a match, then *ServerProc* gets a pointer to the array of POPADVISE structures that it allocated during the WM_CREATE message. This array has a POPADVISE structure for each state, and there is a different array for each window carrying on a DDE conversation. This array is used to store all information *ServerProc* will need to update items to the client.

The fields of the POPADVISE structure for the selected state are set as follows:

- The *fAdvise* field is set to TRUE. This is simply a flag that indicates that the client wants updated information on this state.

- The *fDeferUpd* ("deferred update") field is set to the value of the same field in the DDEADVISE structure. A FALSE value indicates that the client wants to establish a warm link rather than a hot link. The client will be advised of a change in data without getting the data immediately. (In this case, the server posts a WM_DDE_DATA message with a NULL value rather than a handle to the global memory block containing a DDEDATA structure. The client will later post a normal WM_DDE_REQUEST message to obtain the actual data.) A TRUE value indicates that the client wants the data in the WM_DDE_DATA message.

■ The *fAckReq* ("acknowledgment requested") field is set to the value of the same field in the DDEADVISE structure. This is a very tricky value. A TRUE value instructs the server to post the WM_DDE_DATA with the *fAckReq* field of the DDEDATA structure set to TRUE so that the client is required to acknowledge the WM_DDE_DATA message with a WM_DDE_ACK message. A TRUE value does *not* mean that the client is requesting a WM_DDE_ACK message from the server; it's requiring that the server require a WM_DDE_ACK message from the client when later posting the WM_DDE_DATA message.

■ The *lPopPrev* field is set to the current population of the state. *ServerProc* uses this field to determine if the client needs notification that the population has changed.

ServerProc is now finished with the DDEADVISE structure and frees the memory block as the documentation for WM_DDE_ADVISE instructs. *ServerProc* must now acknowledge the WM_DDE_ADVISE message by posting a positive WM_DDE_SBACK message. The *fAck* field of the DDEACK structure is set to TRUE. If *PostMessage* fails, then *ServerProc* deletes the atom.

If the data format was not CF_TEXT, or if there was no match for the state, then *ServerProc* posts a negative WM_DDE_BACK message. In this case, if the *PostMessage* call fails, *ServerProc* both deletes the atom and frees the DDEADVISE memory block.

In theory, handling of the WM_DDE_ADVISE message is now complete. However, the client has asked that it be notified whenever a data item changes. Given that the client doesn't know any value of the data item, it is necessary for *ServerProc* to post a WM_DDE_DATA message to the client.

It does this using the *PostDataMessage* function, but with the third parameter set to the *fDeferUpd* field of the POPADVISE structure, the fourth parameter set to the *fAckReq* field of the POPADVISE structure, and the last parameter set to FALSE (indicating a WM_DDE_DATA message posted in response to WM_DDE_ADVISE rather than WM_DDE_REQUEST).

It's time for another look at *PostDataMessage*. Toward the beginning of the function, note that if the *fDeferUpd* parameter is TRUE, then the function simply sets *hDdeData* to NULL rather than allocating memory for it.

If the *fAckReq* parameter is TRUE, then *PostDataMessage* waits for a WM_DDE_ACK message from the client after posting the WM_DDE_DATA message. It does this by calling

PeekMessage. PostDataMessage deletes the atom in the WM_DDE_ACK message. If the WM_DDE_ACK message does not arrive within three seconds—or if the message is a negative acknowledgment—then *PostDataMessage* frees the global data block containing the DDEDATA structure.

If you think that you can skip over part of this work by assuming that a client will never post a WM_DDE_ADVISE message with the deferred update or acknowledgment requested fields set to TRUE, guess again. Microsoft Excel does precisely that, establishing a warm link with acknowledgments to the WM_DDE_DATA messages.

Updating the Items

After processing a WM_DDE_ADVISE message, a server is required to notify the client when an item has changed. How this works depends on the server. In the case of DDEPOP, a timer is used to recalculate the populations every 5 seconds. This occurs while processing the WM_TIMER message in *WndProc*.

WndProc then calls *EnumChildWindows* with the *TimerEnumProc* function (located after *ServerProc* in DDEPOP.C). *TimerEnumProc* sends WM_TIMER messages to all the child windows, which will all be using the *ServerProc* window procedure.

ServerProc processes the WM_TIMER message by looping through all the states and checking if the POPADVISE structure field *fAdvise* is set to TRUE and the population has changed. If so, it calls *PostDataMessage* to post a WM_DDE_DATA message to the client.

The WM_DDE_UNADVISE Message

The WM_DDE_UNADVISE message instructs a server to stop posting WM_DDE_DATA messages when a data item has changed. The low word of *lParam* is either the data format or 0, indicating all data formats. The high word of *lParam* is either the item ATOM or NULL to indicate all items.

DDEPOP handles the WM_DDE_UNADVISE message by setting the appropriate *fAdvise* fields of the POPADVISE structure to FALSE, and then acknowledging with a positive or negative WM_DDE_ACK message.

The WM_DDE_TERMINATE Message

When a client wishes to terminate the conversation, it posts a WM_DDE_TERMINATE message to the server. The server simply responds with its own WM_DDE_TERMINATE message back to the client. *ServerProc* also destroys the child window on receipt of WM_DDE_TERMINATE because it is no longer needed, and the conversation that the window has maintained is terminated.

ServerProc also processes WM_DDE_POKE and WM_DDE_EXECUTE messages, but in both cases simply responds with a negative acknowledgment.

If DDEPOP is closed from its system menu, then it must terminate all DDE conversations with its clients. So, when *WndProc* receives a WM_CLOSE message, it calls

EnumChildWindows with the *CloseEnumProc* function. *CloseEnumProc* sends WM-_CLOSE messages to all the child windows.

ServerProc responds to WM_CLOSE by posting a WM_DDE_TERMINATE message to the client and then waiting for another WM_DDE_TERMINATE message back from the client.

A DDE CLIENT PROGRAM

Now that we've examined a DDE server program that you can use with Microsoft Excel, let's examine a DDE client program that uses DDEPOP as a server. This program is called SHOWPOP and is shown in Figure 17-2.

SHOWPOP.MAK

```
#----------------------
# SHOWPOP.MAK make file
#----------------------

showpop.exe : showpop.obj showpop.def
    link showpop, /align:16, NUL, /nod slibcew libw, showpop
    rc showpop.exe

showpop.obj : showpop.c
    cl -c -Gsw -Ow -W2 -Zp showpop.c
```

SHOWPOP.C

```
/*---------------------------------------------
   SHOWPOP.C -- DDE Client using DDEPOP
                (c) Charles Petzold, 1990
   ---------------------------------------------*/

#include <windows.h>
#include <dde.h>
#include <stdlib.h>
#include <string.h>

struct
    {
    char *szAbb ;
    char *szState ;
    long lPop ;
    }
```

Figure 17-2. *The SHOWPOP program.* (continued)

```
        pop [] = {
                "AL", "Alabama",              0, "AK", "Alaska",               0,
                "AZ", "Arizona",              0, "AR", "Arkansas",             0,
                "CA", "California",           0, "CO", "Colorado",             0,
                "CT", "Connecticut",          0, "DE", "Delaware",             0,
                "DC", "Dist. of Columbia",    0, "FL", "Florida",              0,
                "GA", "Georgia",              0, "HI", "Hawaii",               0,
                "ID", "Idaho",                0, "IL", "Illinois",             0,
                "IN", "Indiana",              0, "IA", "Iowa",                 0,
                "KS", "Kansas",               0, "KY", "Kentucky",             0,
                "LA", "Louisiana",            0, "ME", "Maine",                0,
                "MD", "Maryland",             0, "MA", "Massachusetts",        0,
                "MI", "Michigan",             0, "MN", "Minnesota",            0,
                "MS", "Mississippi",          0, "MO", "Missouri",             0,
                "MT", "Montana",              0, "NE", "Nebraska",             0,
                "NV", "Nevada",               0, "NH", "New Hampshire",        0,
                "NJ", "New Jersey",           0, "NM", "New Mexico",           0,
                "NY", "New York",             0, "NC", "North Carolina",       0,
                "ND", "North Dakota",         0, "OH", "Ohio",                 0,
                "OK", "Oklahoma",             0, "OR", "Oregon",               0,
                "PA", "Pennsylvania",         0, "RI", "Rhode Island",         0,
                "SC", "South Carolina",       0, "SD", "South Dakota",         0,
                "TN", "Tennessee",            0, "TX", "Texas",                0,
                "UT", "Utah",                 0, "VT", "Vermont",              0,
                "VA", "Virginia",             0, "WA", "Washington",           0,
                "WV", "West Virginia",        0, "WI", "Wisconsin",            0,
                "WY", "Wyoming",              0, "US", "United States Total",  0
                } ;

#define NUM_STATES        (sizeof (pop) / sizeof (pop [0]))
#define WM_USER_INITIATE  (WM_USER + 1)
#define DDE_TIMEOUT       3000

long FAR PASCAL WndProc (HWND, WORD, WORD, LONG) ;

char    szAppName [] = "ShowPop" ;

int PASCAL WinMain (HANDLE hInstance, HANDLE hPrevInstance,
                    LPSTR lpszCmdLine, int nCmdShow)
    {
    HWND    hwnd ;
    MSG     msg ;
    WNDCLASS wndclass ;

    if (!hPrevInstance)
        {
        wndclass.style        = CS_HREDRAW : CS_VREDRAW ;
        wndclass.lpfnWndProc  = WndProc ;
        wndclass.cbClsExtra   = 0 ;
        wndclass.cbWndExtra   = 0 ;
```

(continued)

```
        wndclass.hInstance     = hInstance ;
        wndclass.hIcon         = LoadIcon (hInstance, szAppName) ;
        wndclass.hCursor       = LoadCursor (NULL, IDC_ARROW) ;
        wndclass.hbrBackground = GetStockObject (WHITE_BRUSH) ;
        wndclass.lpszMenuName  = NULL ;
        wndclass.lpszClassName = szAppName ;

        RegisterClass (&wndclass) ;
        }

    hwnd = CreateWindow (szAppName, "DDE Client - US Population",
                    WS_OVERLAPPEDWINDOW,
                    CW_USEDEFAULT, CW_USEDEFAULT,
                    CW_USEDEFAULT, CW_USEDEFAULT,
                    NULL, NULL, hInstance, NULL) ;

    ShowWindow (hwnd, nCmdShow) ;
    UpdateWindow (hwnd) ;

    SendMessage (hwnd, WM_USER_INITIATE, 0, 0L) ;

    while (GetMessage (&msg, NULL, 0, 0))
        {
        TranslateMessage (&msg) ;
        DispatchMessage (&msg) ;
        }
    return msg.wParam ;
    }

long FAR PASCAL WndProc (HWND hwnd, WORD message, WORD wParam, LONG lParam)
    {
    static BOOL    fDoingInitiate = TRUE ;
    static char    szServerApp [] = "DdePop",
                   szTopic     [] = "US_Population" ;
    static HWND    hwndServer = NULL ;
    static short   cxChar, cyChar ;
    ATOM           aApp, aTop, aItem ;
    char           szBuffer [24], szPopulation [16], szItem [16] ;
    DDEACK         DdeAck ;
    DDEDATA FAR    *lpDdeData ;
    DDEADVISE FAR  *lpDdeAdvise ;
    DWORD          dwTime ;
    GLOBALHANDLE   hDdeAdvise, hDdeData ;
    HDC            hdc ;
    MSG            msg ;
    PAINTSTRUCT    ps ;
    short          i, x, y ;
    TEXTMETRIC     tm ;
    WORD           wStatus, cfFormat ;
```

(continued)

```
switch (message)
    {
    case WM_CREATE :
        hdc = GetDC (hwnd) ;
        GetTextMetrics (hdc, &tm) ;
        cxChar = tm.tmAveCharWidth ;
        cyChar = tm.tmHeight + tm.tmExternalLeading ;
        ReleaseDC (hwnd, hdc) ;
        return 0 ;

    case WM_USER_INITIATE :

            // Broadcast WM_DDE_INITIATE message

        aApp = GlobalAddAtom (szServerApp) ;
        aTop = GlobalAddAtom (szTopic) ;

        SendMessage (0xFFFF, WM_DDE_INITIATE, hwnd,
                    MAKELONG (aApp, aTop)) ;

            // If no response, try loading DDEPOP first

        if (hwndServer == NULL)
            {
            WinExec (szServerApp, SW_SHOWMINNOACTIVE) ;

            SendMessage (0xFFFF, WM_DDE_INITIATE, hwnd,
                        MAKELONG (aApp, aTop)) ;
            }

            // Delete the atoms

        GlobalDeleteAtom (aApp) ;
        GlobalDeleteAtom (aTop) ;
        fDoingInitiate = FALSE ;

            // If still no response, display message box

        if (hwndServer == NULL)
            {
            MessageBox (hwnd, "Cannot connect with DDEPOP.EXE!",
                        szAppName, MB_ICONEXCLAMATION | MB_OK) ;

            return 0 ;
            }

            // Post WM_DDE_ADVISE messages
```

(continued)

```
for (i = 0 ; i < NUM_STATES ; i++)
    {
    hDdeAdvise = GlobalAlloc (GHND : GMEM_DDESHARE,
                              sizeof (DDEADVISE)) ;

    lpDdeAdvise = (DDEADVISE FAR *) GlobalLock (hDdeAdvise) ;

    lpDdeAdvise->fAckReq   = TRUE ;
    lpDdeAdvise->fDeferUpd = FALSE ;
    lpDdeAdvise->cfFormat  = CF_TEXT ;

    GlobalUnlock (hDdeAdvise) ;

    aItem = GlobalAddAtom (pop[i].szAbb) ;

    if (!PostMessage (hwndServer, WM_DDE_ADVISE, hwnd,
                      MAKELONG (hDdeAdvise, aItem)))
        {
        GlobalFree (hDdeAdvise) ;
        GlobalDeleteAtom (aItem) ;
        break ;
        }

    DdeAck.fAck = FALSE ;

    dwTime = GetCurrentTime () ;

    while (GetCurrentTime () - dwTime < DDE_TIMEOUT)
        {
        if (PeekMessage (&msg, hwnd, WM_DDE_ACK,
                         WM_DDE_ACK, PM_REMOVE))
            {
            GlobalDeleteAtom (HIWORD (msg.lParam)) ;

            DdeAck = * (DDEACK *) & LOWORD (msg.lParam) ;

            if (DdeAck.fAck == FALSE)
                GlobalFree (hDdeAdvise) ;

            break ;
            }
        }

    if (DdeAck.fAck == FALSE)
        break ;

    while (PeekMessage (&msg, hwnd, WM_DDE_FIRST,
                        WM_DDE_LAST, PM_REMOVE))
```

(continued)

```
                          {
                          DispatchMessage (&msg) ;
                          }
                     }

          if (i < NUM_STATES)
               {
               MessageBox (hwnd, "Failure on WM_DDE_ADVISE!",
                          szAppName, MB_ICONEXCLAMATION : MB_OK) ;
               }
          return 0 ;

case WM_DDE_ACK :

               // In response to WM_DDE_INITIATE, save server window

          if (fDoingInitiate)
               {
               hwndServer = wParam ;
               GlobalDeleteAtom (LOWORD (lParam)) ;
               GlobalDeleteAtom (HIWORD (lParam)) ;
               }
          return 0 ;

case WM_DDE_DATA :

               // wParam          -- sending window handle
               // LOWORD (lParam) -- DDEDATA memory handle
               // HIWORD (lParam) -- item atom

          hDdeData  = LOWORD (lParam) ;
          lpDdeData = (DDEDATA FAR *) GlobalLock (hDdeData) ;
          aItem     = HIWORD (lParam) ;

               // Initialize DdeAck structure

          DdeAck.bAppReturnCode = 0 ;
          DdeAck.reserved       = 0 ;
          DdeAck.fBusy          = FALSE ;
          DdeAck.fAck           = FALSE ;

               // Check for matching format and data item

          if (lpDdeData->cfFormat == CF_TEXT)
               {
               GlobalGetAtomName (aItem, szItem, sizeof (szItem)) ;

               for (i = 0 ; i < NUM_STATES ; i++)
                    if (strcmp (szItem, pop[i].szAbb) == 0)
                         break ;
```

(continued)

```
                    if (i < NUM_STATES)
                        {
                        lstrcpy (szPopulation, lpDdeData->Value) ;
                        pop[i].lPop = atol (szPopulation) ;
                        InvalidateRect (hwnd, NULL, FALSE) ;

                        DdeAck.fAck = TRUE ;
                        }
                    }

                // Acknowledge if necessary

            if (lpDdeData->fAckReq == TRUE)
                {
                wStatus = * (WORD *) & DdeAck ;

                if (!PostMessage (wParam, WM_DDE_ACK, hwnd,
                            MAKELONG (wStatus, aItem)))
                    {
                    GlobalDeleteAtom (aItem) ;
                    GlobalUnlock (hDdeData) ;
                    GlobalFree (hDdeData) ;
                    return 0 ;
                    }
                }
            else
                {
                GlobalDeleteAtom (aItem) ;
                }

                // Clean up

            if (lpDdeData->fRelease == TRUE || DdeAck.fAck == FALSE)
                {
                GlobalUnlock (hDdeData) ;
                GlobalFree (hDdeData) ;
                }
            else
                {
                GlobalUnlock (hDdeData) ;
                }

            return 0 ;

        case WM_PAINT :
            hdc = BeginPaint (hwnd, &ps) ;

            for (i = 0 ; i < NUM_STATES ; i++)
                {
                if (i < (NUM_STATES + 1) / 2)
```

(continued)

```
                    {
                    x = cxChar ;
                    y = i * cyChar ;
                    }
               else
                    {
                    x = 44 * cxChar ;
                    y = (i - (NUM_STATES + 1) / 2) * cyChar ;
                    }

          TextOut (hdc, x, y, szBuffer,
                    wsprintf (szBuffer, "%-20s",
                              (LPSTR) pop[i].szState)) ;

          x += 36 * cxChar ;

          SetTextAlign (hdc, TA_RIGHT ¦ TA_TOP) ;

          TextOut (hdc, x, y, szBuffer,
                    wsprintf (szBuffer, "%10ld", pop[i].lPop)) ;

          SetTextAlign (hdc, TA_LEFT ¦ TA_TOP) ;
          }

     EndPaint (hwnd, &ps) ;
     return 0 ;

case WM_DDE_TERMINATE :

          // Respond with another WM_DDE_TERMINATE message

     PostMessage (hwndServer, WM_DDE_TERMINATE, hwnd, OL) ;
     hwndServer = NULL ;
     return 0 ;

case WM_CLOSE :
     if (hwndServer == NULL)
          break ;

          // Post WM_DDE_UNADVISE message

     PostMessage (hwndServer, WM_DDE_UNADVISE, hwnd,
               MAKELONG (CF_TEXT, NULL)) ;

     dwTime = GetCurrentTime () ;

     while (GetCurrentTime () - dwTime < DDE_TIMEOUT)
          {
          if (PeekMessage (&msg, hwnd, WM_DDE_ACK,
                         WM_DDE_ACK, PM_REMOVE))
```

(continued)

```
                    break ;
          }

          // Post WM_DDE_TERMINATE message

     PostMessage (hwndServer, WM_DDE_TERMINATE, hwnd, OL) ;

     dwTime = GetCurrentTime () ;

     while (GetCurrentTime () - dwTime < DDE_TIMEOUT)
          {
          if (PeekMessage (&msg, hwnd, WM_DDE_TERMINATE,
                          WM_DDE_TERMINATE, PM_REMOVE))
               break ;
          }

     break ;               // for default processing

case WM_DESTROY :
     PostQuitMessage (0) ;
     return 0 ;
     }
return DefWindowProc (hwnd, message, wParam, lParam) ;
}
```

SHOWPOP.DEF

```
;------------------------------------
; SHOWPOP.DEF module definition file
;------------------------------------

NAME            SHOWPOP

DESCRIPTION     'DDE Population Client (c) Charles Petzold, 1990'
EXETYPE         WINDOWS
STUB            'WINSTUB.EXE'
CODE            PRELOAD MOVEABLE DISCARDABLE
DATA            PRELOAD MOVEABLE MULTIPLE
HEAPSIZE        1024
STACKSIZE       8192
EXPORTS         WndProc
```

This program displays the names of the states in its window with the updated populations obtained from DDEPOP using the WM_DDE_ADVISE facility. You'll note that SHOWPOP contains a structure called *pop* just like DDEPOP, but this version contains the two-letter state abbreviations, the state names, and a field called *lPop* (initialized with zeros) that will contain the updated populations obtained from DDEPOP.

SHOWPOP carries on only one DDE conversation, so it only needs one window for this conversation, and it uses *WndProc* for this purpose.

Initiating the DDE Conversation

I've chosen to initiate the DDE conversation by sending *WndProc* a user-defined message (which I've called WM_USER_INITIATE) after the *UpdateWindow* call in *WinMain*. Normally a client would initiate the conversation in response to a menu command.

In response to this user-defined message, *WndProc* calls *GlobalAddAtom* to create atoms for the application name of the server ("DdePop") and the topic name ("US_Population"). *WndProc* broadcasts the WM_DDE_INITIATE message by calling *SendMessage* with a 0xFFFF window handle.

As we've seen, a server that scores a match with the application and topic atoms is required to send a WM_DDE_ACK message back to the client. Because this message is sent using *SendMessage* rather than posted, the client will receive the WM_DDE_ACK message before the original *SendMessage* call with the WM_DDE_INITIATE message has returned. *WndProc* handles the WM_DDE_ACK message by storing the window handle of the server in the variable *hwndServer* and deleting the atoms that accompany the message.

If a client broadcasts a WM_DDE_INITIATE message with NULL application or topic names, then it must be prepared to receive multiple WM_DDE_ACK messages from each of the servers that can satisfy the request. In this case, the client must decide which server to use. The others must be posted WM_DDE_TERMINATE messages to terminate the conversation.

It is possible that *hwndServer* will still be NULL after the WM_DDE_INITIATE *SendMessage* call. This means that DDEPOP is not running under Windows. In this case, *WndProc* attempts to execute DDEPOP by calling *WinExec*. The *WinExec* call searches the current directory and the PATH environment variable to load DDEPOP. *WndProc* then again broadcasts the WM_DDE_INITIATE message. If *hwndServer* is still NULL, then *WndProc* displays a message box notifying the user of the problem.

Next, for each of the states listed in the *pop* structure, *WndProc* allocates a DDE-ADVISE structure by calling *GlobalAlloc* with the GMEM_DDESHARE flag. The *fAckReq* ("acknowledgment requested") flag is set to TRUE (indicating that the server should post WM_DDE_DATA messages with the *fAckReq* field in the DDEDATA field set to NULL). The *fDeferUpd* flag is set to FALSE (indicating a hot link rather than a warm link), and the *cfFormat* field is set to CF_TEXT. *GlobalAddAtom* adds an atom for the two-letter state abbreviation.

This structure and the atom are passed to the server when SHOWPOP posts the WM_DDE_ADVISE message. If the *PostMessage* call fails (which might happen if DDEPOP is suddenly terminated), then SHOWPOP frees the memory block, deletes the atom, and exits the loop.

Otherwise, SHOWPOP waits for a WM_DDE_ACK message by calling *PeekMessage*. As the DDE documentation indicates, the client deletes the atom accompanying the message, and also frees the global memory block if the client responds with a negative acknowledgment.

It's quite likely that this WM_DDE_ACK message from the client will be followed by a WM_DDE_DATA message for the item. For this reason, SHOWPOP calls *PeekMessage* and *DispatchMessage* to extract any DDE messages from the message queue and dispatch them to *WndProc*.

The WM_DDE_DATA Message

Following the WM_DDE_ADVISE messages, *WndProc* will receive WM_DDE_DATA messages from the server containing updated population data. The low word of *lParam* is a memory handle to a global block containing a WM_DDE_DATA structure, and the high word of *lParam* is the atom identifying the data item.

SHOWPOP checks if the *cfFormat* field of the DDEDATA structure is CF_TEXT. (Of course, we know that DDEPOP uses CF_TEXT exclusively, but this is just for the sake of completeness.) It then obtains the text string associated with the item atom by calling *GlobalGetAtomName*. This text string is the two-letter state abbreviation.

Using a *for* loop, SHOWPOP scans through the states looking for a match. If it finds one, it copies the population data from the DDEDATA structure into the *szPopulation* array, converts it to a long integer using the C function *atol* ("ASCII to long"), stores it in the *pop* structure, and invalidates the window.

All that remains now is cleaning up. If the client requested an acknowledgment of the WM_DDE_DATA message, *WndProc* posts one. If no acknowledgment was requested (or if the *PostMessage* call fails), then the *item* atom is deleted. If the *PostMessage* call fails, or if there was no match on the state (indicating a negative acknowledgment), or if the *fRelease* flag in the DDEDATA structure is set to TRUE, then SHOWPOP frees the memory block.

I originally wrote SHOWPOP so that it posted WM_DDE_ADVISE messages with the *fAckReq* field of the DDEADVISE structure set to FALSE. This indicates to the server that the WM_DDE_DATA messages should be posted with the *fAckReq* field of the DDEDATA structure set to FALSE, which in turn indicates to the client that it should not post WM_DDE_ACK messages to the server acknowledging the WM_DDE_DATA messages. This worked fine for normal updates. However, if I changed the system time in Windows while SHOWPOP was running, then DDEPOP posted 52 WM_DDE_DATA messages to SHOWPOP without waiting for acknowledgment. This caused SHOWPOP's message queue to overflow, and it lost many of the updated populations.

The lesson is clear: If a client wishes to be advised of many data items that can change all at once, then it must set the *fAckReq* field of the DDEADVISE structure to TRUE. This is the only safe approach.

The WM_DDE_TERMINATE Message

Handling a WM_DDE_TERMINATE message posted by the server is simple: SHOWPOP simply posts another WM_DDE_TERMINATE message back to the client and sets the *hwndServer* variable to NULL (indicating the conversation is over).

If SHOWPOP is closed (indicated by a WM_CLOSE message), then the program first posts a WM_DDE_UNADVISE message to the server to prevent any future updates. This uses a NULL item atom to indicate all data items. SHOWPOP then posts a WM_DDE_TER-MINATE message to the server and waits for a WM_DDE_TERMINATE message to return back from the server.

WHEN THINGS GO WRONG

Programming can be comparatively easy when you can assume that nothing can go wrong. But as you've seen, even when everything in a DDE conversation proceeds as expected, complexities involving the creation and deletion of atoms and global memory blocks can be tricky.

DDE is further complicated by the potential for problems, and these problems are accentuated because there are two programs involved rather than just one. You've seen that whenever a *PostMessage* calls (indicating that the other program has unexpectedly terminated), you must clean up afterwards.

It is almost impossible to reach a point in DDE coding when you are absolutely certain that you've accounted for all possibilities of error—particularly when considering that the program your program is communicating with may have errant behavior. The only advice I can offer here is simply to do the best you can.

## Chapter 18

The Multiple Document Interface (MDI)

The Multiple Document Interface (MDI) is a specification for applications that handle documents in Microsoft Windows. The specification describes a window structure and user interface that allow the user to work with multiple documents within a single application (such as text documents in a word processing program or spreadsheets in a spreadsheet program). Simply put, just as Windows maintains multiple application windows within a single screen, an MDI application maintains multiple document windows within a single client area. The first MDI application for Windows was the first Windows version of Microsoft Excel. Both the Program Manager and File Manager in Windows 3 are MDI applications.

Although the MDI specificiation has been around since Windows 2, at that time MDI applications were difficult to write and required some very intricate programming work. With Windows 3, however, much of that work has already been done for you. Windows 3 includes one new window class, four new functions, two new data structures, and eleven new messages for the specific purpose of simplifying MDI applications.

THE ELEMENTS OF MDI

The Multiple Document Interface is described in the CUA Advanced Interface Design Guide. The main application window of an MDI program is conventional—it has a title bar, a menu, a sizing border, a system menu icon, and minimize/maximize icons. The client area, however, is often called a "workspace" and is not directly used to display program output. This workspace contains zero or more child windows, each of which displays a document.

These child windows look much like normal application windows. They have a title bar, a sizing border, a system menu icon, minimize/maximize icons, and possibly scroll bars. None of the document windows has a menu, however. The menu on the main application window applies to the document windows.

At any one time, only one document window is active (indicated by a highlighted title bar) and appears in front of all the other document windows. All the document child windows are clipped to the workspace area and never appear outside the application window.

At first, MDI seems a fairly straightforward job for the Windows programmer. All you need to do is create a WS_CHILD window for each document, making the program's main application window the parent of the document window. But with a little exploration of an MDI application such as the Windows 3 File Manager, you'll find some complications that require difficult code.

- An MDI document window can be minimized. Its icon appears at the bottom of the workspace. (Generally an MDI application will use different icons for the main application window and each type of document window.)

- An MDI document window can be maximized. In this case, the title bar of the document window (normally used to show the filename of the document in the window) disappears, and the filename appears appended to the application name in the application window's title bar. The system menu icon of the document window becomes the first item in the top-level menu of the application window. The icon to restore the size of the document window becomes the last item in the top-level menu and appears to the far right.

- The system keyboard accelerator to close a document window is the same as that to close the main window, except using the Ctrl key rather than Alt. That is, Alt-F4 closes the application window while Ctrl-F4 closes the document window. In addition, Ctrl-F6 switches among the child document windows within the active MDI application. Alt-Spacebar invokes the system menu of the main window, as usual. Alt-- (minus) invokes the system menu of the active child document window.

- When using the cursor keys to move among items on the menu, control normally passes from the system menu to the first item on the menu bar. In an MDI application, control passes from the application system menu to the active document system menu to the first item on the menu bar.

- If the application is capable of supporting several types of child windows (for example, the worksheet and chart documents in Microsoft Excel), then the menu should reflect the operations associated with that type of document. This requires that the program change the menu when a different document window becomes active. In addition, when no document window exists, the menu should be stripped down to only those operations involved in opening a new document.

- The top-level menu bar has an item called Window. By convention, this is the last item on the top-level menu bar except for Help. The Window submenu generally has options to arrange the document windows within the workspace. Document windows can be "cascaded" from the upper left or "tiled" so that each document window is fully visible. This submenu also has a list of all the document windows. Selecting one moves that document window to the foreground.

All of these aspects of MDI are supported in Windows 3. Some overhead is required of course (as will be shown in a sample program), but it's not anywhere close to the amount of code you'd have to write to support all these features directly.

WINDOWS 3 AND MDI

Some new terminology is necessary when approaching the Windows 3 MDI support. The main application window is called the "frame window." Just as in a conventional Windows program, this is a window of the WS_OVERLAPPEDWINDOW style.

An MDI application also creates a "client window" based on the predefined window class "MDICLIENT." The client window is created by a call to *CreateWindow* using this window class and the WS_CHILD style. The last parameter to *CreateWindow* is a pointer to a small structure of type CLIENTCREATESTRUCT. This client window covers the client area of the frame window and is responsible for much of the MDI support. The color of this client window is the system color COLOR_APPWORKSPACE.

The document windows are called "child windows." You create these windows by initializing a structure of type MDICREATESTRUCT and sending the client window a WM_MDICREATE message with a pointer to this structure.

The document windows are children of the client window, which in turn is a child of the frame window. The parent-child hierarchy is shown in Figure 18-1 on the following page.

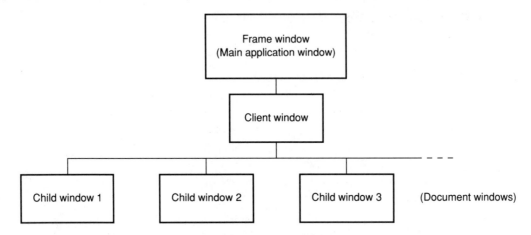

Figure 18-1. *The parent-child hierarchy of a Windows MDI application.*

You need a window class (and window procedure) for the frame window and for each type of child window supported by the application. You don't need a window procedure for the client window because the window class is preregistered.

I mentioned earlier that the MDI support of Windows 3 includes one new window class, four new functions, two new data structures, and eleven new messages. I've already mentioned the new window class, which is MDICLIENT, and the new data structures, CLIENTCREATESTRUCT and MDICREATESTRUCT. Two of the four new functions replace *DefWindowProc* in MDI applications: Rather than call *DefWindowProc* for all unprocessed messages, a frame window procedure calls *DefFrameProc* and a child window procedure calls *DefMDIChildProc*. Another new function, *TranslateMDISysAccel*, is used in the same way as *TranslateAccelerator*, which I discussed in Chapter 9. The fourth new function is *ArrangeIconicWindows*, but one of the special MDI messages makes this function unnecessary for MDI programs.

In the sample program coming up, I'll demonstrate nine of the eleven MDI messages. (The other two are not normally required.) These messages begin with the prefix WM_MDI. A frame window sends one of these messages to the client window to perform an operation on a child window or to obtain information about a child window. (For example, a frame window sends an WM_MDICREATE message to a client window to create a child window.) The WM_MDIACTIVATE message is an exception: While a frame window can send this message to the client window to activate one of the child windows, the client window also sends the message to the child windows being activated and deactivated to inform them of this change.

THE SAMPLE PROGRAM

The Windows 3 Software Development Kit (SDK) includes a sample program called MULTIPAD that demonstrates how to write an MDI program. However, MULTIPAD contains quite a bit of code that has nothing to do with MDI. It might be easier for you to get a better feel for MDI programming by examining a smaller program that does little except demonstrate the MDI features.

The components of this program, called MDIDEMO, are shown in Figure 18-2.

MDIDEMO.MAK

```
#----------------------
# MDIDEMO.MAK make file
#----------------------

mdidemo.exe : mdidemo.obj mdidemo.def mdidemo.res
     link mdidemo, /align:16, NUL, /nod slibcew libw, mdidemo
     rc mdidemo.res

mdidemo.obj : mdidemo.c mdidemo.h
     cl -c -Gsw -Ow -W2 -Zp mdidemo.c

mdidemo.res : mdidemo.rc mdidemo.h
     rc -r mdidemo.rc
```

MDIDEMO.C

```
/*------------------------------------------------------------
     MDIDEMO.C -- Multiple Document Interface Demonstration
                  (c) Charles Petzold, 1990
     ------------------------------------------------------*/

#include <windows.h>
#include <stdlib.h>
#include "mdidemo.h"

long FAR PASCAL FrameWndProc   (HWND, WORD, WORD, LONG) ;
BOOL FAR PASCAL CloseEnumProc  (HWND, LONG) ;
long FAR PASCAL HelloWndProc   (HWND, WORD, WORD, LONG) ;
long FAR PASCAL RectWndProc    (HWND, WORD, WORD, LONG) ;

          // structure for storing data unique to each Hello child window
```

Figure 18-2. *The MDIDEMO program.*   *(continued)*

```
typedef struct
    {
    short   nColor ;
    COLORREF clrText ;
    }
    HELLODATA ;

typedef HELLODATA NEAR *NPHELLODATA ;

        // structure for storing data unique to each Rect child window

typedef struct
    {
    short cxClient ;
    short cyClient ;
    }
    RECTDATA ;

typedef RECTDATA NEAR *NPRECTDATA ;

        // global variables

char   szFrameClass [] = "MdiFrame" ;
char   szHelloClass [] = "MdiHelloChild" ;
char   szRectClass  [] = "MdiRectChild" ;
HANDLE hInst ;
HMENU  hMenuInit, hMenuHello, hMenuRect ;
HMENU  hMenuInitWindow, hMenuHelloWindow, hMenuRectWindow ;

int PASCAL WinMain (HANDLE hInstance, HANDLE hPrevInstance,
                LPSTR lpszCmdLine, int nCmdShow)
    {
    HANDLE    hAccel ;
    HWND      hwndFrame, hwndClient ;
    MSG       msg ;
    WNDCLASS wndclass ;

    hInst = hInstance ;

    if (!hPrevInstance)
        {
                // Register the frame window class

        wndclass.style          = CS_HREDRAW : CS_VREDRAW ;
        wndclass.lpfnWndProc     = FrameWndProc ;
        wndclass.cbClsExtra      = 0 ;
        wndclass.cbWndExtra      = 0 ;
        wndclass.hInstance       = hInstance ;
        wndclass.hIcon           = LoadIcon (NULL, IDI_APPLICATION) ;
```

(continued)

```
          wndclass.hCursor        = LoadCursor (NULL, IDC_ARROW) ;
          wndclass.hbrBackground = COLOR_APPWORKSPACE + 1 ;
          wndclass.lpszMenuName  = NULL ;
          wndclass.lpszClassName = szFrameClass ;

          RegisterClass (&wndclass) ;

                  // Register the Hello child window class

          wndclass.style         = CS_HREDRAW | CS_VREDRAW ;
          wndclass.lpfnWndProc   = HelloWndProc ;
          wndclass.cbClsExtra    = 0 ;
          wndclass.cbWndExtra    = sizeof (LOCALHANDLE) ;
          wndclass.hInstance     = hInstance ;
          wndclass.hIcon         = LoadIcon (NULL, IDI_APPLICATION) ;
          wndclass.hCursor       = LoadCursor (NULL, IDC_ARROW) ;
          wndclass.hbrBackground = GetStockObject (WHITE_BRUSH) ;
          wndclass.lpszMenuName  = NULL ;
          wndclass.lpszClassName = szHelloClass ;

          RegisterClass (&wndclass) ;

                  // Register the Rect child window class

          wndclass.style         = CS_HREDRAW | CS_VREDRAW ;
          wndclass.lpfnWndProc   = RectWndProc ;
          wndclass.cbClsExtra    = 0 ;
          wndclass.cbWndExtra    = sizeof (LOCALHANDLE) ;
          wndclass.hInstance     = hInstance ;
          wndclass.hIcon         = NULL ;
          wndclass.hCursor       = LoadCursor (NULL, IDC_ARROW) ;
          wndclass.hbrBackground = GetStockObject (WHITE_BRUSH) ;
          wndclass.lpszMenuName  = NULL ;
          wndclass.lpszClassName = szRectClass ;

          RegisterClass (&wndclass) ;
          }
               // Obtain handles to three possible menus and submenus

hMenuInit  = LoadMenu (hInst, "MdiMenuInit") ;
hMenuHello = LoadMenu (hInst, "MdiMenuHello") ;
hMenuRect  = LoadMenu (hInst, "MdiMenuRect") ;


hMenuInitWindow  = GetSubMenu (hMenuInit,  INIT_MENU_POS) ;
hMenuHelloWindow = GetSubMenu (hMenuHello, HELLO_MENU_POS) ;
hMenuRectWindow  = GetSubMenu (hMenuRect,  RECT_MENU_POS) ;

          // Load accelerator table
```

(continued)

```
        hAccel = LoadAccelerators (hInst, "MdiAccel") ;

                // Create the frame window

        hwndFrame = CreateWindow (szFrameClass, "MDI Demonstration",
                            WS_OVERLAPPEDWINDOW : WS_CLIPCHILDREN,
                            CW_USEDEFAULT, CW_USEDEFAULT,
                            CW_USEDEFAULT, CW_USEDEFAULT,
                            NULL, hMenuInit, hInstance, NULL) ;

        hwndClient = GetWindow (hwndFrame, GW_CHILD) ;

        ShowWindow (hwndFrame, nCmdShow) ;
        UpdateWindow (hwndFrame) ;

                // Enter the modified message loop

        while (GetMessage (&msg, NULL, 0, 0))
             {
             if (!TranslateMDISysAccel (hwndClient, &msg) &&
                 !TranslateAccelerator (hwndFrame, hAccel, &msg))
                  {
                  TranslateMessage (&msg) ;
                  DispatchMessage (&msg) ;
                  }
             }
        return msg.wParam ;
        }

long FAR PASCAL FrameWndProc (HWND hwnd, WORD message, WORD wParam, LONG lParam)
        {
        static HWND        hwndClient ;
        CLIENTCREATESTRUCT clientcreate ;
        FARPROC            lpfnEnum ;
        HWND               hwndChild, hwndNext ;
        MDICREATESTRUCT    mdicreate ;

        switch (message)
             {
             case WM_CREATE :          // Create the client window

                  clientcreate.hWindowMenu  = hMenuInitWindow ;
                  clientcreate.idFirstChild = IDM_FIRSTCHILD ;

                  hwndClient = CreateWindow ("MDICLIENT", NULL,
                            WS_CHILD : WS_CLIPCHILDREN : WS_VISIBLE,
                            0, 0, 0, 0, hwnd, 1, hInst,
                            (LPSTR) &clientcreate) ;
                  return 0 ;
```

(continued)

```
case WM_COMMAND :
     switch (wParam)
         {
         case IDM_NEWHELLO :      // Create a Hello child window

              mdicreate.szClass = szHelloClass ;
              mdicreate.szTitle = "Hello" ;
              mdicreate.hOwner  = hInst ;
              mdicreate.x       = CW_USEDEFAULT ;
              mdicreate.y       = CW_USEDEFAULT ;
              mdicreate.cx      = CW_USEDEFAULT ;
              mdicreate.cy      = CW_USEDEFAULT ;
              mdicreate.style   = 0 ;
              mdicreate.lParam  = NULL ;

              hwndChild = SendMessage (hwndClient, WM_MDICREATE, 0,
                          (LONG) (LPMDICREATESTRUCT) &mdicreate) ;
              return 0 ;

         case IDM_NEWRECT :       // Create a Rect child window

              mdicreate.szClass = szRectClass ;
              mdicreate.szTitle = "Rectangles" ;
              mdicreate.hOwner  = hInst ;
              mdicreate.x       = CW_USEDEFAULT ;
              mdicreate.y       = CW_USEDEFAULT ;
              mdicreate.cx      = CW_USEDEFAULT ;
              mdicreate.cy      = CW_USEDEFAULT ;
              mdicreate.style   = 0 ;
              mdicreate.lParam  = NULL ;

              hwndChild = SendMessage (hwndClient,  WM_MDICREATE, 0,
                          (LONG) (LPMDICREATESTRUCT) &mdicreate) ;
              return 0 ;

         case IDM_CLOSE :          // Close the active window

              hwndChild = LOWORD (SendMessage (hwndClient,
                              WM_MDIGETACTIVE, 0, 0L)) ;

              if (SendMessage (hwndChild, WM_QUERYENDSESSION, 0, 0L))
                  SendMessage (hwndClient, WM_MDIDESTROY,
                               hwndChild, 0L) ;
              return 0 ;

         case IDM_EXIT :           // Exit the program

              SendMessage (hwnd, WM_CLOSE, 0, 0L) ;
              return 0 ;
```

(continued)

```
                              // Messages for arranging windows
            case IDM_TILE :
                SendMessage (hwndClient, WM_MDITILE, 0, 0L) ;
                return 0 ;

            case IDM_CASCADE :
                SendMessage (hwndClient, WM_MDICASCADE, 0, 0L) ;
                return 0 ;

            case IDM_ARRANGE :
                SendMessage (hwndClient, WM_MDIICONARRANGE, 0, 0L) ;
                return 0 ;

            case IDM_CLOSEALL :      // Attempt to close all children

                lpfnEnum = MakeProcInstance (CloseEnumProc, hInst) ;
                EnumChildWindows (hwndClient, lpfnEnum, 0L) ;
                FreeProcInstance (lpfnEnum) ;
                return 0 ;

            default :              // Pass to active child

                hwndChild = LOWORD (SendMessage (hwndClient,
                                       WM_MDIGETACTIVE, 0, 0L)) ;

                if (IsWindow (hwndChild))
                    SendMessage (hwndChild, WM_COMMAND,
                                 wParam, lParam) ;

                break ;            // and then to DefFrameProc
            }
        break ;

    case WM_QUERYENDSESSION :
    case WM_CLOSE :                          // Attempt to close all children

        SendMessage (hwnd, WM_COMMAND, IDM_CLOSEALL, 0L) ;

        if (NULL != GetWindow (hwndClient, GW_CHILD))
            return 0 ;

        break ;   // i.e., call DefFrameProc ;

    case WM_DESTROY :
        PostQuitMessage (0) ;
        return 0 ;
    }
        // Pass unprocessed messages to DefFrameProc (not DefWindowProc)
```

(continued)

```
          return DefFrameProc (hwnd, hwndClient, message, wParam, lParam) ;
          }

BOOL FAR PASCAL CloseEnumProc (HWND hwnd, LONG lParam)
     {
     if (GetWindow (hwnd, GW_OWNER))              // check for icon title
          return 1 ;

     SendMessage (GetParent (hwnd), WM_MDIRESTORE, hwnd, 0L) ;

     if (!SendMessage (hwnd, WM_QUERYENDSESSION, 0, 0L))
          return 1 ;

     SendMessage (GetParent (hwnd), WM_MDIDESTROY, hwnd, 0L) ;
          return 1 ;
     }

long FAR PASCAL HelloWndProc (HWND hwnd, WORD message, WORD wParam, LONG lParam)
     {
     static COLORREF clrTextArray [] = { RGB (0,   0, 0), RGB (255, 0,   0),
                                         RGB (0, 255, 0), RGB ( 0, 0, 255),
                                         RGB (255, 255, 255) } ;
     static HWND     hwndClient, hwndFrame ;
     HDC             hdc ;
     HMENU           hMenu ;
     LOCALHANDLE     hHelloData ;
     NPHELLODATA     npHelloData ;
     PAINTSTRUCT     ps ;
     RECT            rect ;

     switch (message)
          {
          case WM_CREATE :
                         // Allocate memory for window private data

               hHelloData = LocalAlloc (LMEM_MOVEABLE | LMEM_ZEROINIT,
                                   sizeof (HELLODATA)) ;

               npHelloData = (NPHELLODATA) LocalLock (hHelloData) ;
               npHelloData->nColor  = IDM_BLACK ;
               npHelloData->clrText = RGB (0, 0, 0) ;
               LocalUnlock (hHelloData) ;
               SetWindowWord (hwnd, 0, hHelloData) ;

                         // Save some window handles

               hwndClient = GetParent (hwnd) ;
               hwndFrame  = GetParent (hwndClient) ;
               return 0 ;
```

(continued)

```
    case WM_COMMAND :
         switch (wParam)
              {
              case IDM_BLACK :
              case IDM_RED :
              case IDM_GREEN :
              case IDM_BLUE :
              case IDM_WHITE :
                             // Change the text color

                   hHelloData  = GetWindowWord (hwnd, 0) ;
                   npHelloData = (NPHELLODATA) LocalLock (hHelloData) ;

                   hMenu = GetMenu (hwndFrame) ;

                   CheckMenuItem (hMenu, npHelloData->nColor,
                                        MF_UNCHECKED) ;
                   npHelloData->nColor = wParam ;
                   CheckMenuItem (hMenu, npHelloData->nColor,
                                        MF_CHECKED) ;

                   npHelloData->clrText =
                        clrTextArray [wParam - IDM_BLACK] ;

                   LocalUnlock (hHelloData) ;
                   InvalidateRect (hwnd, NULL, FALSE) ;
              }
         return 0 ;

    case WM_PAINT :
                    // Paint the window

         hdc = BeginPaint (hwnd, &ps) ;

         hHelloData  = GetWindowWord (hwnd, 0) ;
         npHelloData = (NPHELLODATA) LocalLock (hHelloData) ;
         SetTextColor (hdc, npHelloData->clrText) ;
         LocalUnlock (hHelloData) ;

         GetClientRect (hwnd, &rect) ;

         DrawText (hdc, "Hello, World!", -1, &rect,
                    DT_SINGLELINE | DT_CENTER | DT_VCENTER) ;

         EndPaint (hwnd, &ps) ;
         return 0 ;

    case WM_MDIACTIVATE :

                    // Set the Hello menu if gaining focus-
```

(continued)

```
               if (wParam == TRUE)
                    SendMessage (hwndClient, WM_MDISETMENU, 0,
                              MAKELONG (hMenuHello, hMenuHelloWindow)) ;

                         // check or uncheck menu item

               hHelloData  = GetWindowWord (hwnd, 0) ;
               npHelloData = (NPHELLODATA) LocalLock (hHelloData) ;
               CheckMenuItem (hMenuHello, npHelloData->nColor,
                              wParam ? MF_CHECKED : MF_UNCHECKED) ;
               LocalUnlock (hHelloData) ;

                         // Set the Init menu if losing focus

               if (wParam == FALSE)
                    SendMessage (hwndClient, WM_MDISETMENU, 0,
                              MAKELONG (hMenuInit, hMenuInitWindow)) ;

               DrawMenuBar (hwndFrame) ;
               return 0 ;

          case WM_QUERYENDSESSION :
          case WM_CLOSE :
               if (IDOK != MessageBox (hwnd, "OK to close window?", "Hello",
                              MB_ICONQUESTION | MB_OKCANCEL))

                    return 0 ;

               break ;   // i.e., call DefMDIChildProc

          case WM_DESTROY :
               hHelloData = GetWindowWord (hwnd, 0) ;
               LocalFree (hHelloData) ;
               return 0 ;
          }
               // Pass unprocessed message to DefMDIChildProc

     return DefMDIChildProc (hwnd, message, wParam, lParam) ;
     }

long FAR PASCAL RectWndProc (HWND hwnd, WORD message, WORD wParam, LONG lParam)
     {
     static HWND hwndClient, hwndFrame ;
     HPEN        hBrush ;
     HDC         hdc ;
     LOCALHANDLE hRectData ;
     NPRECTDATA  npRectData ;
     PAINTSTRUCT ps ;
     short       xLeft, xRight, yTop, yBottom, nRed, nGreen, nBlue ;
```

(continued)

```
    switch (message)
        {
      case WM_CREATE :
                        // Allocate memory for window private data

            hRectData = LocalAlloc (LMEM_MOVEABLE : LMEM_ZEROINIT,
                                    sizeof (RECTDATA)) ;

            SetWindowWord (hwnd, 0, hRectData) ;

                    // Start the timer going

            SetTimer (hwnd, 1, 250, NULL) ;

                    // Save some window handles

            hwndClient = GetParent (hwnd) ;
            hwndFrame  = GetParent (hwndClient) ;
            return 0 ;

      case WM_SIZE :           // Save the window size

            hRectData  = GetWindowWord (hwnd, 0) ;
            npRectData = (NPRECTDATA) LocalLock (hRectData) ;

            npRectData->cxClient = LOWORD (lParam) ;
            npRectData->cyClient = HIWORD (lParam) ;

            LocalUnlock (hRectData) ;

            break ;          // WM_SIZE must be processed by DefMDIChildProc

      case WM_TIMER :             // Display a random rectangle

            hRectData  = GetWindowWord (hwnd, 0) ;
            npRectData = (NPRECTDATA) LocalLock (hRectData) ;

            xLeft   = rand () % npRectData->cxClient ;
            xRight  = rand () % npRectData->cxClient ;
            yTop    = rand () % npRectData->cyClient ;
            yBottom = rand () % npRectData->cyClient ;
            nRed    = rand () & 255 ;
            nGreen  = rand () & 255 ;
            nBlue   = rand () & 255 ;

            hdc = GetDC (hwnd) ;
            hBrush = CreateSolidBrush (RGB (nRed, nGreen, nBlue)) ;
            SelectObject (hdc, hBrush) ;
```

(continued)

866

```
            Rectangle (hdc, min (xLeft, xRight), min (yTop, yBottom),
                       max (xLeft, xRight), max (yTop, yBottom)) ;

        ReleaseDC (hwnd, hdc) ;
        DeleteObject (hBrush) ;
        LocalUnlock (hRectData) ;
        return 0 ;

   case WM_PAINT :           // Clear the window

        InvalidateRect (hwnd, NULL, TRUE) ;
        hdc = BeginPaint (hwnd, &ps) ;
        EndPaint (hwnd, &ps) ;
        return 0 ;

   case WM_MDIACTIVATE :     // Set the appropriate menu
        if (wParam == TRUE)
             SendMessage (hwndClient, WM_MDISETMENU, 0,
                        MAKELONG (hMenuRect, hMenuRectWindow)) ;
        else
             SendMessage (hwndClient, WM_MDISETMENU, 0,
                        MAKELONG (hMenuInit, hMenuInitWindow)) ;

        DrawMenuBar (hwndFrame) ;
        return 0 ;

   case WM_DESTROY :
        hRectData = GetWindowWord (hwnd, 0) ;
        LocalFree (hRectData) ;
        KillTimer (hwnd, 1) ;
        return 0 ;
   }
        // Pass unprocessed message to DefMDIChildProc

   return DefMDIChildProc (hwnd, message, wParam, lParam) ;
   }
```

MDIDEMO.RC

```
/*-----------------------------
   MDIDEMO.RC resource script
   ------------------------------*/

#include <windows.h>
#include "mdidemo.h"
```

(continued)

```
MdiMenuInit MENU
     {
     POPUP "&File"
          {
          MENUITEM "New &Hello",            IDM_NEWHELLO
          MENUITEM "New &Rectangles",       IDM_NEWRECT
          MENUITEM SEPARATOR
          MENUITEM "E&xit",                 IDM_EXIT
          }
     }

MdiMenuHello MENU
     {
     POPUP "&File"
          {
          MENUITEM "New &Hello",            IDM_NEWHELLO
          MENUITEM "New &Rectangles",       IDM_NEWRECT
          MENUITEM "&Close",                IDM_CLOSE
          MENUITEM SEPARATOR
          MENUITEM "E&xit",                 IDM_EXIT
          }
     POPUP "&Color"
          {
          MENUITEM "&Black",                IDM_BLACK
          MENUITEM "&Red",                  IDM_RED
          MENUITEM "&Green",                IDM_GREEN
          MENUITEM "B&lue",                 IDM_BLUE
          MENUITEM "&White",                IDM_WHITE
          }
     POPUP "&Window"
          {
          MENUITEM "&Cascade\tShift+F5",    IDM_CASCADE
          MENUITEM "&Tile\tShift+F4",       IDM_TILE
          MENUITEM "Arrange &Icons",        IDM_ARRANGE
          MENUITEM "Close &All",            IDM_CLOSEALL
          }
     }

MdiMenuRect MENU
     {
     POPUP "&File"
          {
          MENUITEM "New &Hello",            IDM_NEWHELLO
          MENUITEM "New &Rectangles",       IDM_NEWRECT
          MENUITEM "&Close",                IDM_CLOSE
          MENUITEM SEPARATOR
          MENUITEM "E&xit",                 IDM_EXIT
          }
```

(continued)

```
      POPUP "&Window"
          {
          MENUITEM "&Cascade\tShift+F5",        IDM_CASCADE
          MENUITEM "&Tile\tShift+F4",           IDM_TILE
          MENUITEM "Arrange &Icons",            IDM_ARRANGE
          MENUITEM "Close &All",                IDM_CLOSEALL
          }
      }

MdiAccel ACCELERATORS
    {
    VK_F5, IDM_CASCADE, VIRTKEY, SHIFT
    VK_F4, IDM_TILE,    VIRTKEY, SHIFT
    }
```

MDIDEMO.H

```
/*-----------------------
    MDIDEMO.H header file
  -----------------------*/

#define INIT_MENU_POS      0
#define HELLO_MENU_POS     2
#define RECT_MENU_POS      1

#define IDM_NEWHELLO      10
#define IDM_NEWRECT       11
#define IDM_CLOSE         12
#define IDM_EXIT          13

#define IDM_BLACK         20
#define IDM_RED           21
#define IDM_GREEN         22
#define IDM_BLUE          23
#define IDM_WHITE         24

#define IDM_TILE          30
#define IDM_CASCADE       31
#define IDM_ARRANGE       32
#define IDM_CLOSEALL      33

#define IDM_FIRSTCHILD   100
```

MDIDEMO.DEF

```
;------------------------------------------
; MDIDEMO.DEF module definition file
;------------------------------------------

NAME           MDIDEMO

DESCRIPTION    'MDI Demonstration (c) Charles Petzold, 1990'
EXETYPE        WINDOWS
STUB           'WINSTUB.EXE'
CODE           PRELOAD MOVEABLE DISCARDABLE
DATA           PRELOAD MOVEABLE MULTIPLE
HEAPSIZE       1024
STACKSIZE      8192
EXPORTS        FrameWndProc
               CloseEnumProc
               HelloWndProc
               RectWndProc
```

MDIDEMO supports two types of extremely simple document windows: One displays
"Hello, World!" in the center of its client area, and the other displays a series of random
rectangles. (In the source code listings and identifier names, these are referred to as the
Hello document and the Rect document.) Different menus are associated with these two
types of document windows. The document window that displays "Hello, World!" has a
menu that allows you to change the color of the text.

Three Menus

Let's turn first to the MDIDEMO.RC resource script. The resource script defines three menu
templates used by the program.

The program displays the MdiMenuInit menu when no document windows are
present. This menu simply allows creating a new document or exiting the program.

The MdiMenuHello menu is associated with the document window that displays
"Hello, World!" The File submenu allows opening a new document of either type, closing
the active document, and exiting the program. The Color submenu lets you set the text
color. The Window submenu has options for arranging the document windows in a
cascaded or tiled fashion, arranging the document icons, and closing all the windows. This
submenu will also list all the document windows as they are created.

The MdiMenuRect menu is associated with the random rectangle document. This is
the same as the MdiMenuHello menu except that it does not include the Color submenu.

The MDIDEMO.H header file defines all the menu identifiers as well as three constants:

```
#define INIT_MENU_POS 0
#define HELLO_MENU_POS 2
#define RECT_MENU_POS 1
```

These identifiers indicate the position of the Window submenu in each of the three menu templates. This information is needed by the program to inform the client window where the document list is to appear. Of course, the MdiMenuInit menu doesn't have a Window submenu, so I've indicated that the list should be appended to the first submenu (position 0). The list will never actually be viewed there, however. (You'll see why this is needed when I discuss the program later.)

The IDM_FIRSTCHILD identifier doesn't correspond to a menu item. This is the identifier that will be associated with the first document window in the list that will appear in the Window submenu. You should choose this identifier to be greater than all the other menu IDs.

Program Initialization

In MDIDEMO.C, *WinMain* begins by registering window classes for the frame window and the two child windows. The window procedures are called *FrameWndProc*, *HelloWnd-Proc*, and *RectWndProc*. Normally, different icons should be associated with these window classes. For the purpose of simplicity, I've simply used the standard IDI_APPLICATION icon for the frame and child.

Note that I've defined the *hbrBackground* field of the WNDCLASS structure for the frame window class to be the COLOR_APPWORKSPACE system color. This is not entirely necessary because the client area of the frame window is covered up by the client window, and the client window has this color anyway. However, using this color looks a little better when the frame window is first displayed.

The *lpszMenuName* field is set to NULL for each of these three window classes. For the Hello and Rect child window classes, this is normal. For the frame window class I've chosen to indicate the menu handle in the *CreateWindow* function when creating the frame window.

The window classes for the Hello and Rect child windows allocate extra space for each window using a nonzero value as the *cbWndExtra* field of the WNDCLASS structure. This space will be used to store a local memory handle that will reference a block of memory (the size of the HELLODATA or RECTDATA structures defined near the top of MDIDEMO.C) used to store information unique to each document window.

Next, *WinMain* uses *LoadMenu* to load the three menus and save their handles in global variables. Three calls to the *GetSubMenu* function obtain handles to the Window submenu to which the document list will be appended. These are also saved in global variables. The *LoadAccelerators* function loads the accelerator table.

A call to *CreateWindow* in *WinMain* creates the frame window. During the WM-_CREATE processing in *FrameWndProc*, the frame window creates the client window. This involves another call to *CreateWindow*. The window class is set to MDICLIENT, which is the preregistered class for MDI client windows. The last parameter to *CreateWindow* must be set to a pointer to a structure of type CLIENTCREATESTRUCT. This structure has two fields:

- *hWindowMenu* is the handle of the submenu to which the document list will be appended. In MDIDEMO, this is *hMenuInitWindow*, which was obtained during *WinMain*. You'll see later how the menu is changed.

- *idFirstChild* is the menu ID to be associated with the first document window in the document list. This is simply IDM_FIRSTCHILD.

Back in *WinMain*, MDIDEMO displays the newly created frame window and enters the message loop. The message loop differs a little from a normal loop: After obtaining the message from the message queue with a call to *GetMessage*, an MDI program passes the message to *TranslateMDISysAccel* (and *TranslateAccelerator* if, like the MDIDEMO program, the program also has menu accelerators).

The *TranslateMDISysAccel* function translates any keystrokes that may correspond to the special MDI accelerators (Ctrl-F6, for example) into a WM_SYSCOMMAND message. If neither *TranslateMDISysAccel* nor *TranslateAccelerator* returns TRUE (indicating that a message was translated by one of these functions), do not call *TranslateMessage* and *DispatchMessage*.

Notice the two different window handles passed to *TranslateMDISysAccel* and *TranslateAccelerator*: *hwndClient* and *hwndFrame*, respectively. The *WinMain* function obtains the *hwndClient* window handle by calling *GetWindow* with the GW_CHILD parameter.

CREATING THE CHILDREN

The bulk of *FrameWndProc* is devoted to processing WM_COMMAND messages that signal menu selections. As usual, the *wParam* parameter to *FrameWndProc* contains the menu ID number.

For *wParam* values of IDM_NEWHELLO and IDM_NEWRECT, *FrameWndProc* must create a new document window. This involves initializing the fields of an MDICREATESTRUCT structure (most of which correspond to *CreateWindow* parameters) and sending the client window a WM_MDICREATE message with *lParam* set to a pointer to this structure. The client window then creates the child document window.

Normally, the *szTitle* field of the MDICREATESTRUCT structure would be the file-name corresponding to the document. The style field can be set to the window styles WS_HSCROLL or WS_VSCROLL or both to include scroll bars in the document window.

The style field can also include WS_MINIMIZE or WS_MAXIMIZE to initially display the document window in a minimized or maximized state.

(The *lParam* field of the MDICREATESTRUCT structure provides a way for the frame window and the child window to share some variables. This field could be set to a local or global memory handle that references a block of memory containing a structure. During the WM_CREATE message in the child document window, *lParam* is a pointer to a CREATESTRUCT structure, and the *lpCreateParams* field of this structure is a pointer to the MDICREATESTRUCT structure used to create the window.)

On receipt of the WM_MDICREATE message, the client window creates the child document window and adds the title of the window to the bottom of the submenu specified in the MDICLIENTSTRUCT structure used to create the client window. When the MDIDEMO program creates its first document window, this is the File submenu of the MdiMenuInit menu. We'll see later how this document list gets moved to the Window submenu of the MdiMenuHello and MdiMenuRect menus.

Up to nine documents can be listed on the menu, each preceded by an underlined number from 1 to 9. If more than nine document windows are created, this list is followed by a "More windows" item on the menu. This item invokes a dialog box with a list box that lists all the document windows. The maintenance of this document list is one of the nicest features of the Windows 3 MDI support.

MORE FRAME WINDOW MESSAGE PROCESSING

Let's continue with *FrameWndProc* message processing before turning our attention to the child document windows.

When you select Close from the File menu, MDIDEMO closes the active child window. It obtains the handle to the active child window by sending the client window a WM_MDIGETACTIVE message. If the child window responds affirmatively to a WM-_QUERYENDSESSION message, then MDIDEMO sends the client window a WM_MDI-DESTROY message to close the child window.

Processing the Exit option from the File menu requires only that the frame window procedure send itself a WM_CLOSE message.

Processing the Tile, Cascade, and Arrange Icons options from the Window submenu is a snap, requiring only that the WM_MDITILE, WM_MDICASCADE, and WM_MDI-ICONARRANGE messages be sent to the client window.

The Close All option is a little more complex. *FrameWndProc* calls *EnumChildWindows*, passing a pointer referencing the *CloseEnumProc* function. This function sends a WM_MDIRESTORE message to each child window, followed by a WM_QUERYENDSESSION and (possibly) a WM_MDIDESTROY message. This is not done for the icon title window, indicated by a non-NULL return of *GetWindow* with the GW_OWNER parameter.

You'll notice that *FrameWndProc* does not process any of the WM_COMMAND messages that signal one of the colors being selected from the Color menu. These messages are really the responsibility of the document window. For this reason, *FrameWndProc* sends all unprocessed WM_COMMAND messages to the active child window so that the child window can process those messages that pertain to its window.

All messages that the frame window procedure chooses not to process must be passed to *DefFrameProc*. This is one of the new MDI functions. It replaces *DefWindowProc* in the frame window procedure. Even if a frame window procedure traps the WM_MENUCHAR, WM_NEXTMENU, WM_SETFOCUS, or WM_SIZE messages, these also must be passed to *DefFrameProc*.

Unprocessed WM_COMMAND messages must be passed to *DefFrameProc*. In particular, *FrameWndProc* does not process any of the WM_COMMAND messages resulting from the user selecting one of the documents from the list in the Window submenu. (The *wParam* values for these options begin with IDM_FIRSTCHILD.) These messages are passed to *DefFrameProc* and processed there.

Notice that the frame window does not need to maintain a list of window handles of all document windows it creates. If ever these handles are needed (such as when processing the Close All option from the menu), they can be obtained using *EnumChildWindows*.

THE CHILD DOCUMENT WINDOWS

Now let's look at *HelloWndProc*, which is the window procedure used for the child document windows that display "Hello, World!"

As with any window class used for more than one window, static variables defined in the window procedure (or any function called from the window procedure) are shared by all windows created based on that window class.

Data that is unique to each window must be stored using a method other than static variables. One such technique involves window properties. Another approach (the one I used) uses memory space reserved by defining a nonzero value in the *cbWndExtra* field of the WNDCLASS structure used to register the window class.

In MDIDEMO, I use this space to store a local memory handle that references a block of memory the size of the HELLODATA structure. *HelloWndProc* allocates this memory during the WM_CREATE message, locks it, initializes the two fields (which indicate the currently checked menu item and the text color), unlocks the block, and stores the local memory handle using *SetWindowWord*.

When processing a WM_COMMAND message for changing the text colors (recall that these messages originate in the frame window procedure), *HelloWndProc* uses *GetWindowWord* to obtain a handle to the memory block containing the HELLODATA structure. Using this structure, *HelloWndProc* unchecks the checked menu item, checks the selected menu item, and saves the new color.

A document window procedure receives the WM_MDIACTIVATE message whenever the window becomes active or inactive (indicated by a TRUE or FALSE value in *wParam*). You'll recall that the MDIDEMO program has three different menus: MdiMenuInit for when no documents are present, MdiMenuHello for when a Hello document window is active, and MdiMenuRect for when a Rect document window is active.

The WM_MDIACTIVATE message provides an opportunity for the document window to change the menu. If *wParam* is TRUE (meaning the window is becoming active), *HelloWndProc* changes the menu to MdiMenuHello. If *wParam* is FALSE, *HelloWndProc* changes the menu to MdiMenuInit.

HelloWndProc changes the menu by sending a WM_MDISETMENU message to the client window. The client window processes this message by removing the document list from the current menu and appending it to the new menu. This is how the document list is transferred from the MdiMenuInit menu (which is in effect when the first document is created) to the MdiMenuHello menu. Do not use the *SetMenu* function to change a menu in an MDI application.

Another little chore involves the checkmarks on the Color submenu. Program options such as this should be unique to each document. For example, you should be able to set black text in one window and red text in another. The menu checkmarks should reflect the option chosen in the active window. For this reason, *HelloWndProc* unchecks the selected menu item when the window is becoming inactive and checks the appropriate item when the window is becoming active.

The window procedure gets the first WM_MDIACTIVATE message with *wParam* set to TRUE when the window is first created and gets the last message with *wParam* set to FALSE when the window is destroyed. When the user switches from one document to another, the first document window receives a WM_MDIACTIVATE message with *wParam* set to FALSE (at which time it sets the menu to MdiMenuInit) and the second document window receives a WM_MDIACTIVATE message with *wParam* set to TRUE (at which time it sets the menu to MdiMenuHello or MdiMenuRect as appropriate). If all the windows are closed, the menu is left as MdiMenuInit.

You'll recall that *FrameWndProc* sends the child window a WM_QUERYENDSESSION when the user selects Close or Close All from the menu. *HelloWndProc* processes the WM_QUERYENDSESSION and WM_CLOSE messages by displaying a message box and asking the user whether the window can be closed. (In a real program, this message box would ask whether a file needed to be saved.) If the user indicates that the window should not be closed, the window procedure returns 0.

During the WM_DESTROY message, *HelloWndProc* frees the local memory block allocated during the WM_CREATE message.

All unprocessed messages must be passed on to *DefMDIChildProc* (not *DefWindowProc*) for default processing. Several messages must be passed to *DefMDIChildProc* whether the child window procedure does something with them or not. These are:

WM_CHILDACTIVATE, WM_GETMINMAXINFO, WM_MENUCHAR, WM_MOVE, WM-_SETFOCUS, WM_SIZE, and WM_SYSCOMMAND.

RectWndProc is fairly similar to *HelloWndProc* in much of the overhead involved, but it's a little simpler (no menu options are involved and the window does not verify with the user whether it can be closed), so I needn't discuss it. But note that *RectWndProc* breaks after processing WM_SIZE so it is passed to *DefMDIChildProc*.

THE POWER OF WINDOW PROCEDURES

Much of the support in Windows 3 for the Multiple Document Interface is encapsulated in the MDICLIENT window class. I think this clearly illustrates the power of the object-oriented architecture of Windows. The client window procedure serves as an intermediary layer between the frame window and the various document windows.

Now let's look at another powerful feature of Windows—dynamic link libraries.

Chapter 19

Dynamic Link Libraries

Dynamic link libraries (also called DLLs, dynamic libraries, "dynalink" libraries, or library modules) are one of the most important structural elements of Windows. Most of the disk files associated with Windows are either program modules or dynamic link library modules. So far we've been writing Windows programs; now it's time to take a stab at writing dynamic link libraries. Many of the principles you've learned in writing programs are also applicable to writing these libraries, but there are some important differences.

LIBRARY BASICS

As you've seen, a Windows program is an executable file that generally creates one or more windows and uses a message loop to receive user input. Dynamic link libraries are generally not directly executable, and they do not receive messages. They are separate files containing functions that can be called by programs and other DLLs to perform certain jobs. A dynamic link library is brought into action only when another module calls one of the functions in the library.

The term *dynamic linking* refers to the process that Windows uses to link a function call in one module to the actual function in the library module. "Static linking" occurs when you run LINK to create a Windows .EXE file from various object (.OBJ) modules and run time library (.LIB) files. Dynamic linking occurs at run time.

TKERNEL.EXE, USER.EXE, and GDI.EXE files, the various driver files such as KEY-BOARD.DRV, SYSTEM.DRV, and SOUND.DRV, and the video and printer drivers are all dynamic link libraries. These are libraries that all Windows programs can use.

The various font resource files with the extension .FON are "resource-only" dynamic link libraries. They contain no code and no data but instead have fonts that all Windows programs can use. Thus, one purpose of dynamic link libraries is to provide functions and resources that can be used by many different programs. In a conventional operating system, only the operating system itself contains routines that other programs can call on to do a job. In Windows, the process of one module calling a function in another module is generalized. In effect, by writing a dynamic link library, you are writing an extension to Windows. Or you can think of dynamic link libraries (including those that make up Windows) as extensions to your program. The code, data, and resources in a dynamic link library module are shared among all programs using the module.

Although a dynamic link library module may have any extension (such as .EXE or .FON), the standard extension in Windows 3 is .DLL. Only dynamic link libraries with the extension .DLL will be loaded automatically by Windows. If the file has another extension, the program must explicitly load the module using the *LoadLibrary* function.

You'll generally find that dynamic libraries make most sense in the context of a large application. For instance, suppose you write a large accounting package for Windows that consists of several different programs. You'll probably find that these programs use many common routines. You could put these common routines in a normal object library (with the extension .LIB) and add them to each of the program modules during static linking with LINK. But this approach is wasteful, because each of the programs in this package contains identical code for the common routines. Moreover, if you change one of these routines in this library, you'll have to relink all the programs that use the changed routine. If, however, you put these common routines in a dynamic link library called (for instance) ACCOUNT.DLL, then you've solved both problems. Only the library module need contain the routines required by all the programs (thus requiring less disk space for the files and less memory space when running two or more of the applications), and you can make changes to the library module without relinking any of the individual programs.

Dynamic link libraries can themselves be viable products. For instance, suppose you write a collection of three-dimensional drawing routines and put them in a dynamic link library called GDI3.DLL. If you then interest other software developers in using your library, you can license it to be included with their graphics programs. A user who has several of these programs would need only one GDI3.DLL file.

Library: One Word, Many Meanings

Part of the confusion surrounding dynamic link libraries results from the appearance of the word library in several different contexts. Besides dynamic link libraries, we'll also be talking about "object libraries" and "import libraries."

An object library is a file with the extension .LIB containing code that is added to your program's .EXE file when you run the linker during static linking. For example, the normal Microsoft C object library that you link with small-model Windows programs is SLIBCEW.LIB.

An import library is a special form of an object library file. Like object libraries, import libraries have the extension .LIB and are used by the linker to resolve function calls in your source code. However, import libraries contain no code. Instead, they provide LINK with information necessary to set up relocation tables within the .EXE file for dynamic linking. The LIBW.LIB and WIN87EM.LIB files included with the Windows Software Development Kit are import libraries for Windows functions. If you call *Rectangle* in a program, LIBW.LIB tells LINK that this function is in the GDI.EXE library and has an "ordinal number" of 27. This information goes into the .EXE file so that Windows can perform dynamic linking with the GDI.EXE dynamic link library when your program is executed.

Object libraries and import libraries are used only during program development. Dynamic link libraries are used during run time. A dynamic library must be present on the disk when a program is run that uses the library. When Windows needs to load a dynamic link library module before running a program that requires it, the library file must be stored in either the current directory, a directory accessible through the PATH string in the MS-DOS environment, the Windows directory, or the SYSTEM subdirectory of the Windows directory.

Examining Libraries with EXEHDR

Both program files and dynamic link library files are in the New Executable format. You can get some sense of the workings of dynamic linking by running the EXEHDR program (included with Microsoft C 6) with the -v (verbose) parameter on the various files included with Windows and seeing what type of information the files contain. EXEHDR divides its output into five main sections, in this order:

- The old MS-DOS .EXE header information
- The New Executable format header information
- A list of the code and data segments in the module
- The exported functions of the module
- Relocation information for each segment

Some of this information won't be present for resource-only library modules (such as the .FON files). You'll notice that the first line of the second section begins with either "Module," indicating a program module, or "Library," indicating a dynamic link library.

If you run EXEHDR on KERNEL.EXE, USER.EXE, or GDI.EXE, you'll find that many of the names of the exported functions (the fourth section of the output) are familiar.

These are the functions that the library makes available for other modules to call. Each exported function has an "ordinal number" associated with it. This is simply a positive number in the "ord" column of the EXEHDR output.

Both program modules and library modules can call functions that are exported from other library modules. To the module that makes the call, the function is said to be "imported." These imported functions show up in the last section of the EXEHDR display as relocation items, generally in the form of the library module name followed by a period and the ordinal number of the function.

When Windows loads a program into memory for execution, it must resolve the calls that the program makes to imported functions. If the library module containing these functions has not yet been loaded into memory, Windows loads at least the data segment and one code segment into memory and calls a short initialization routine in the library module. Windows also creates "reload thunks" (a topic discussed in Chapter 7) for the exported functions in the library. The calls in the program to external functions can then be resolved by inserting the addresses of the reload thunks in the code segment of the program.

The second section of the EXEHDR output points up some differences between programs and libraries. Windows programs have a line that reads:

```
Data:     NOSHARED
```

This means that new data segments are created for each instance of the program. Because a single instance of a Windows library is shared by all programs that need it, this line is different for Windows libraries. It can be either:

```
Data:     SHARED
```

or:

```
Data:     NONE
```

depending on whether the library has one data segment or none.

A Windows program must have at least one data segment (called the automatic data segment), because this data segment contains the program's stack. In the EXEHDR output of a program file, you'll see an indication of the stack size ("Extra Stack Allocation"). However, a library module doesn't have its own stack, and thus EXEHDR won't show this line. A dynamic link library always uses the stack of the program that calls the functions in the library. The absence of a stack for the library module has some significant implications that I'll cover later in this chapter.

Because each Windows program has its own stack, Windows must switch between stacks when switching from one program to another. A stack's presence in a program identifies the program as a distinct process that can receive messages from Windows. A library module is not a process and does not receive messages. When a program calls a function in a library module, no task switch takes place. To Windows, the program making the call to the library is still running even though code in the library is being executed.

880

STRPROG AND STRLIB

We'll begin by writing a program with a dedicated dynamic link library and see how they work together. The program is called STRPROG ("string program"), and the dynamic link library is called STRLIB ("string library"). STRLIB has three exported functions that STRPROG calls. Just to make this interesting (and to force you to think about some of the implications), one of the functions in STRLIB uses a call-back function defined in STRPROG.

STRLIB is a dynamic link library module that stores and sorts up to 256 character strings. The strings are capitalized and stored in STRLIB's own data segment. STRPROG can use STRLIB's three functions to add strings, delete strings, and obtain all the current strings from STRLIB. The program has two menu items (Enter and Delete) that invoke dialog boxes to add and delete these strings. STRPROG lists all the current strings stored in STRLIB's data segment in STRPROG's client area.

This function defined in STRLIB adds a string to STRLIB's data segment:

```
BOOL FAR PASCAL AddString (lpStringIn)
```

The parameter *lpString* is a far pointer to the string. The string is capitalized within the *AddString* function. If an identical string already exists in STRLIB's data segment, this function adds another copy of the string. *AddString* returns TRUE (nonzero) if it is successful and FALSE (0) otherwise. A FALSE return value can result if the string has a length of 0, if memory could not be allocated to store the string, or if 256 strings are already stored.

This STRLIB function deletes a string from STRLIB's data segment:

```
BOOL FAR PASCAL DeleteString (lpStringIn)
```

Again, the parameter *lpString* is a far pointer to the string. If more than one string matches, only the first is removed. *DeleteString* returns TRUE (nonzero) if it is successful and FALSE (0) otherwise. A FALSE return value indicates that the length of the string is 0 or that a matching string could not be found.

This STRLIB function uses a call-back function located in the calling program to enumerate the strings currently stored in STRLIB's data segment:

```
short FAR PASCAL GetStrings (lpfnGetStrCallBack, lpParam)
```

The call-back function must be defined as follows:

```
BOOL FAR PASCAL GetStrCallBack (LPSTR lpString, LPSTR lpParam)
```

The *GetStrCallBack* function must be exported from the program that calls *GetStrings*. The *lpfnGetStrCallBack* parameter to *GetStrings* must be obtained from *MakeProcInstance*. *GetStrings* calls *GetStrCallBack* once for each string or until the call-back function returns FALSE (0). *GetStrings* returns the number of strings passed to the call-back function. The *lpParam* parameter is a far pointer to programmer-defined data. Note that all the pointers passed as function parameters are far pointers, because STRLIB must reference data in the caller's data segment.

The STRLIB Library

Figure 19-1 shows the three files necessary to create the STRLIB.DLL dynamic link library module. STRLIB has a lot in common with the Windows programs that we've been writing, but there are also some subtle (and some not-so-subtle) differences.

STRLIB.MAK

```
#---------------------
# STRLIB.MAK make file
#---------------------

strlib.dll : strlib.obj strlib.def
    link strlib libentry, strlib.dll /align:16, NUL, /nod sdllcew libw, strlib
    rc strlib.dll

strlib.obj : strlib.c
    cl -c -ASw -Gsw -Ow -W2 -Zp strlib.c
```

STRLIB.C

```
/*-------------------------------------------------
   STRLIB.C -- Library module for STRPROG program
               (c) Charles Petzold, 1990
   -------------------------------------------------*/

#include <windows.h>

typedef BOOL FAR PASCAL GETSTR (LPSTR, LPSTR) ;
HANDLE hStrings [256] ;
short  nTotal = 0 ;

int FAR PASCAL LibMain (HANDLE hInstance, WORD wDataSeg, WORD wHeapSize,
                        LPSTR lpszCmdLine)
     {
     if (wHeapSize > 0)
         UnlockData (0) ;

     return 1 ;
     }

BOOL FAR PASCAL AddString (LPSTR lpStringIn)
     {
     HANDLE hString ;
     NPSTR  npString ;
     short  i, nLength, nCompare ;
```

Figure 19-1. *The STRLIB library.*   *(continued)*

```
    if (nTotal == 255)
        return FALSE ;

    if (0 == (nLength = lstrlen (lpStringIn)))
        return FALSE ;

    if (NULL == (hString = LocalAlloc (LHND, 1 + nLength)))
        return FALSE ;

    npString = LocalLock (hString) ;
    lstrcpy (npString, lpStringIn) ;
    AnsiUpper (npString) ;
    LocalUnlock (hString) ;

    for (i = nTotal ; i > 0 ; i--)
        {
        npString = LocalLock (hStrings [i - 1]) ;
        nCompare = lstrcmpi (lpStringIn, npString) ;
        LocalUnlock (hStrings [i - 1]) ;

        if (nCompare > 0)
            {
            hStrings [i] = hString ;
            break ;
            }
        hStrings [i] = hStrings [i - 1] ;
        }

    if (i == 0)
        hStrings [0] = hString ;

    nTotal++ ;
    return TRUE ;
    }

BOOL FAR PASCAL DeleteString (LPSTR lpStringIn)
    {
    NPSTR npString ;
    short i, j, nCompare ;

    if (0 == lstrlen (lpStringIn))
        return FALSE ;

    for (i = 0 ; i < nTotal ; i++)
        {
        npString = LocalLock (hStrings [i]) ;
        nCompare = lstrcmpi (npString, lpStringIn) ;
        LocalUnlock (hStrings [i]) ;
```

(continued)

```
            if (nCompare == 0)
                break ;
            }

    if (i == nTotal)
        return FALSE ;

    for (j = i ; j < nTotal ; j++)
        hStrings [j] = hStrings [j + 1] ;

    nTotal-- ;
    return TRUE ;
    }

short FAR PASCAL GetStrings (GETSTR lpfnGetStrCallBack, LPSTR lpParam)
    {
    BOOL  bReturn ;
    NPSTR npString ;
    short i ;

    for (i = 0 ; i < nTotal ; i++)
        {
        npString = LocalLock (hStrings [i]) ;
        bReturn = (*lpfnGetStrCallBack) ((LPSTR) npString, lpParam) ;
        LocalUnlock (hStrings [i]) ;

        if (bReturn == FALSE)
            return i + 1 ;
        }
    return nTotal ;
    }
```

STRLIB.DEF

```
;-----------------------------------
; STRLIB.DEF module definition file
;-----------------------------------

LIBRARY        STRLIB

DESCRIPTION    'DLL for STRPROG Program (c) Charles Petzold, 1990'
EXETYPE        WINDOWS
CODE           PRELOAD MOVEABLE DISCARDABLE
DATA           PRELOAD MOVEABLE SINGLE
HEAPSIZE       1024
EXPORTS        AddString
               DeleteString
               GetStrings
```

In addition, you'll need the LIBENTRY.OBJ file included with the Windows Software Development Kit and stored in the library subdirectory of the SDK directory. (The assembly-language source code for this object module is also included in the SDK.)

Make File Differences

With a close look, you'll notice a couple differences between the STRLIB.MAK make file and previous make files used for creating Windows programs.

First, the compile line in STRLIB.MAK includes a compiler switch, -ASw, that isn't required when compiling Windows programs. The -A switch is the flag for a "customized memory model." The S indicates small model. The w means that the compiler is to assume that the data segment isn't equal to the stack segment. This isn't normal, but it's important that you use this for a library module. The implications of the -ASw switch are discussed in greater detail later in this chapter.

Second, the link section of the make file creates the STRLIB.DLL file using the following statement:

```
link strlib libentry, strlib.dll /align:16, NUL, /nod sdllcew libw, strlib
```

Note the inclusion of the LIBENTRY.OBJ file in the object module field. In the field that contains the nondefault libraries, I've listed SDLLCEW.LIB rather than SLIBCEW.LIB. SLIBCEW.LIB is the C run time library for Windows programs; SDLLCEW.LIB is the C run time library for dynamic link libraries. LIBW.LIB is the import library.

The Library Entry Point

The most obvious difference between STRLIB.C and our Windows programs is the absence of *WinMain*. Instead, there is a function called *LibMain*. *LibMain* is called from the LIBENTRY.OBJ module. This is required because of the different ways in which Windows programs and Windows dynamic link libraries are initialized during startup.

When you link a Windows program with LINK, a function called __astart__ is linked into the program. This is the entry point to the program. On entry to __astart__, the CPU registers contain the following information:

BX	Stack size
CX	Heap size
DI	Instance handle
SI	Previous instance
ES	Program segment prefix

The start-up code (which comes from SLIBCEW.LIB) performs some initialization and then calls the *WinMain* function, which is the perceived entry point when you program for Windows in C.

For dynamic link libraries, no start-up code is provided in SDLLCEW.LIB. That's why LIBENTRY.OBJ (or something similar) is required. Windows calls *LibEntry* once (when the first program that requires the dynamic link library is loaded) with the CPU registers set as follows:

DI	Instance handle
DS	Library's data segment
CX	Heap size
ES:SI	Command line

Note the differences between these registers and those for a Windows program. A register containing the stack size isn't required, because library modules don't have a stack. A register containing the previous instance handle isn't required, because library modules can't have multiple instances. For most uses of libraries, the command-line parameter in ES:SI isn't used. *LibEntry* must return nonzero if initialization is successful and 0 if errors are encountered. A failed initialization causes Windows to not run the program that requires the library.

LIBENTRY initializes the local heap by calling *LocalInit* and then calls *LibMain*, which is in STRLIB.C. The *LibMain* definition looks like this:

```
int FAR PASCAL LibMain (HANDLE hInstance, WORD wDataSeg, WORD wHeapSize,
                        LPSTR lpszCmdLine)
    {
    if (wHeapSize > 0)
        UnlockData (0) ;

    return 1 ;
    }
```

This simply unlocks the data segment of the library (which is locked by the *LocalInit* call in LIBENTRY) and returns 1. If you need to do additional initialization when the library is first loaded, you can do it here.

Note the differences implied here between programs and libraries. On entry to a program, the start-up code passes control to *WinMain*, which performs initialization and then enters a message loop. Multitasking takes place during *GetMessage* calls. The program exits the message loop (and *WinMain*) only when the program retrieves a WM_QUIT message from the message queue. On entry to a library, the start-up code must perform initialization and then return control to Windows with a nonzero value. The rest of the library sits dormant in memory until another module calls one of the exported functions.

You can also add a "de-initialization" routine to a library; the routine is called when a program using the library terminates. Information on this can be found in Chapter 20 of the Guide to Programming book, included in the Windows Software Development Kit.

The STRLIB Functions

Aside from the *LibMain* initialization function, STRLIB contains only the three functions that it will export to be used by other programs. All these functions are defined as FAR and PASCAL. They must be FAR because they will be called from the code segment of another module (STRPROG). You aren't required to define them as PASCAL, however: That's simply a convention used in other Windows libraries to save a few bytes of space. These three functions use Windows' local memory allocation functions to allocate space in the local heap for storing the character strings. Because the *AddString* function allocates moveable local blocks, we've essentially given Windows the job of reorganizing the local heap when necessary to allocate more memory.

The Library Module Definition File

The module definition file for a library looks somewhat similar to the .DEF file for a program, but there are also significant differences between the two. For program modules, the module definition file contains a NAME statement indicating that the module is a program. For libraries, the first line is a LIBRARY statement:

```
LIBRARY    STRLIB
```

This statement identifies the module as a library. The library CODE statement is the same as that used for programs:

```
CODE     PRELOAD MOVEABLE DISCARDABLE
```

You can also use LOADONCALL, but for a library with a single code segment, the segment must be loaded into memory so that the initialization routine can be executed.

For a Windows program, the DATA statement indicates that the data segment is MULTIPLE, which means that each instance of the program uses the same data segment. For the STRLIB library, the data segment is marked as SINGLE, because a library can have only one instance:

```
DATA     PRELOAD MOVEABLE SINGLE
```

If the library doesn't include a data segment, the DATA statement is:

```
DATA     NONE
```

Notice how these directives relate to the information obtained from EXEHDR.

Because we want STRLIB to use its local heap to store its character strings, we have to give it a local heap in the HEAPSIZE statement:

```
HEAPSIZE   1024
```

This is the initial size of the local heap. Windows can expand the data segment of the library to accommodate a larger heap if one is needed. Notice there's no STACKSIZE statement in the module definition file—a library module doesn't have its own stack.

For a Windows program, the EXPORTS section of the module definition file lists all far functions within the program that can be called by Windows. Generally, this list includes at least one window procedure. For a dynamic link library, the EXPORTS section lists all far functions that can be called by programs and other library modules. This is the EXPORTS section of STRLIB.DEF:

```
EXPORTS        AddString
               DeleteString
               GetStrings
```

The STRPROG Program

The STRPROG program, shown in Figure 19-2, is fairly straightforward. The two menu options (Enter and Delete) invoke dialog boxes that allow you to enter a string. STRPROG then calls *AddString* or *DeleteString*. When the program needs to update its client area, it calls *GetStrings* and uses the function *GetStrCallBack* to list the enumerated strings.

STRPROG.MAK

```
#----------------------
# STRPROG.MAK make file
#----------------------

strprog.exe : strprog.obj strprog.res strprog.def
     link strprog, /align:16, NUL, /nod slibcew libw, strprog
     rc strprog.res

strprog.obj : strprog.c strprog.h
     cl -c -Gsw -Ow -W2 -Zp strprog.c

strprog.res : strprog.rc strprog.h
     rc -r strprog.rc
```

STRPROG.C

```
/*---------------------------------------------------------------
     STRPROG.C -- Program using STRLIB dynamic link library
                  (c) Charles Petzold, 1990
     -----------------------------------------------------------*/

#include <windows.h>
#include <string.h>
#include "strprog.h"
```

Figure 19-2. *The STRPROG program.*

(continued)

888

```
#define MAXLEN 32
#define WM_DATACHANGE WM_USER

typedef struct
      {
      HDC    hdc ;
      short xText ;
      short yText ;
      short xStart ;
      short yStart ;
      short xIncr ;
      short yIncr ;
      short xMax ;
      short yMax ;
      }
      CBPARM ;

BOOL  FAR PASCAL AddString   (LPSTR) ;        // functions in STRLIB
BOOL  FAR PASCAL DeleteString (LPSTR) ;
short FAR PASCAL GetStrings  (FARPROC, CBPARM FAR *) ;

long  FAR PASCAL WndProc (HWND, WORD, WORD, LONG) ;

char  szAppName [] = "StrProg" ;
char  szString  [MAXLEN] ;

int PASCAL WinMain (HANDLE hInstance, HANDLE hPrevInstance,
                    LPSTR lpszCmdLine, int nCmdShow)
      {
      HWND    hwnd ;
      MSG     msg ;
      WNDCLASS wndclass ;

      if (!hPrevInstance)
           {
           wndclass.style        = CS_HREDRAW : CS_VREDRAW ;
           wndclass.lpfnWndProc  = WndProc ;
           wndclass.cbClsExtra   = 0 ;
           wndclass.cbWndExtra   = 0 ;
           wndclass.hInstance    = hInstance ;
           wndclass.hIcon        = LoadIcon (NULL, IDI_APPLICATION) ;
           wndclass.hCursor      = LoadCursor (NULL, IDC_ARROW) ;
           wndclass.hbrBackground = GetStockObject (WHITE_BRUSH) ;
           wndclass.lpszMenuName = szAppName ;
           wndclass.lpszClassName = szAppName ;

           RegisterClass (&wndclass) ;
           }
```

(continued)

```
        hwnd = CreateWindow (szAppName, "DLL Demonstration Program",
                            WS_OVERLAPPEDWINDOW,
                            CW_USEDEFAULT, CW_USEDEFAULT,
                            CW_USEDEFAULT, CW_USEDEFAULT,
                            NULL, NULL, hInstance, NULL) ;

     ShowWindow (hwnd, nCmdShow) ;
     UpdateWindow (hwnd) ;

     while (GetMessage (&msg, NULL, 0, 0))
          {
          TranslateMessage (&msg) ;
          DispatchMessage (&msg) ;
          }
     return msg.wParam ;
     }

BOOL FAR PASCAL DlgProc (HWND hDlg, WORD message, WORD wParam, LONG lParam)
     {
     switch (message)
          {
          case WM_INITDIALOG :
               SendDlgItemMessage (hDlg, IDD_STRING, EM_LIMITTEXT,
                                   MAXLEN - 1, 0L) ;
               return TRUE ;

          case WM_COMMAND :
               switch (wParam)
                    {
                    case IDOK :
                         GetDlgItemText (hDlg, IDD_STRING, szString, MAXLEN) ;
                         EndDialog (hDlg, TRUE) ;
                         return TRUE ;

                    case IDCANCEL :
                         EndDialog (hDlg, FALSE) ;
                         return TRUE ;
                    }
          }
     return FALSE ;
     }

BOOL FAR PASCAL EnumCallBack (HWND hwnd, LONG lParam)
     {
     char szClassName [16] ;

     GetClassName (hwnd, szClassName, sizeof szClassName) ;
```

(continued)

```
     if (0 == strcmp (szClassName, szAppName))
         SendMessage (hwnd, WM_DATACHANGE, 0, 0L) ;

     return TRUE ;
     }

BOOL FAR PASCAL GetStrCallBack (LPSTR lpString, CBPARM FAR *lpcbp)
     {
     TextOut (lpcbp->hdc, lpcbp->xText, lpcbp->yText,
              lpString, lstrlen (lpString)) ;

     if ((lpcbp->yText += lpcbp->yIncr) > lpcbp->yMax)
         {
         lpcbp->yText = lpcbp->yStart ;
         if ((lpcbp->xText += lpcbp->xIncr) > lpcbp->xMax)
             return FALSE ;
         }
     return TRUE ;
     }

long FAR PASCAL WndProc (HWND hwnd, WORD message, WORD wParam, LONG lParam)
     {
     static FARPROC lpfnDlgProc, lpfnGetStrCallBack, lpfnEnumCallBack ;
     static HANDLE  hInst ;
     static short   cxChar, cyChar, cxClient, cyClient ;
     CBPARM         cbparam ;
     HDC            hdc ;
     PAINTSTRUCT    ps ;
     TEXTMETRIC     tm ;

     switch (message)
         {
         case WM_CREATE :
             hInst = ((LPCREATESTRUCT) lParam)->hInstance ;

             lpfnDlgProc         = MakeProcInstance (DlgProc, hInst) ;
             lpfnGetStrCallBack  = MakeProcInstance (GetStrCallBack, hInst) ;
             lpfnEnumCallBack    = MakeProcInstance (EnumCallBack, hInst) ;

             hdc = GetDC (hwnd) ;
             GetTextMetrics (hdc, &tm) ;
             cxChar = tm.tmAveCharWidth ;
             cyChar = tm.tmHeight + tm.tmExternalLeading ;
             ReleaseDC (hwnd, hdc) ;

             return 0 ;

         case WM_COMMAND :
             switch (wParam)
```

(continued)

```
                      {
                 case IDM_ENTER :
                      if (DialogBox (hInst, "EnterDlg", hwnd, lpfnDlgProc))
                           {
                           if (AddString (szString))
                                EnumWindows (lpfnEnumCallBack, OL) ;
                           else
                                MessageBeep (0) ;
                           }
                      break ;

                 case IDM_DELETE :
                      if (DialogBox (hInst, "DeleteDlg", hwnd, lpfnDlgProc))
                           {
                           if (DeleteString (szString))
                                EnumWindows (lpfnEnumCallBack, OL) ;
                           else
                                MessageBeep (0) ;
                           }
                      break ;
                 }
            return 0 ;

       case WM_SIZE :
            cxClient = LOWORD (lParam) ;
            cyClient = HIWORD (lParam) ;
            return 0 ;

       case WM_DATACHANGE :
            InvalidateRect (hwnd, NULL, TRUE) ;
            return 0 ;

       case WM_PAINT :
            hdc = BeginPaint (hwnd, &ps) ;

            cbparam.hdc   = hdc ;
            cbparam.xText = cbparam.xStart = cxChar ;
            cbparam.yText = cbparam.yStart = cyChar ;
            cbparam.xIncr = cxChar * MAXLEN ;
            cbparam.yIncr = cyChar ;
            cbparam.xMax  = cbparam.xIncr * (1 + cxClient / cbparam.xIncr) ;
            cbparam.yMax  = cyChar * (cyClient / cyChar - 1) ;

            GetStrings (lpfnGetStrCallBack, &cbparam) ;

            EndPaint (hwnd, &ps) ;
            return 0 ;

       case WM_DESTROY :
            PostQuitMessage (0) ;
            return 0 ;
       }
```

(continued)

```
     return DefWindowProc (hwnd, message, wParam, lParam) ;
     }
```

STRPROG.RC

```
/*----------------------------
   STRPROG.RC resource script
   ------------------------*/

#include <windows.h>
#include "strprog.h"

StrProg MENU
     {
     MENUITEM  "&Enter!",  IDM_ENTER
     MENUITEM  "&Delete!", IDM_DELETE
     }

EnterDlg DIALOG 24, 24, 190, 44
     STYLE WS_POPUP | WS_DLGFRAME
     {
     LTEXT            "&Enter:", 0,               4,  8,  24,  8
     EDITTEXT                    IDD_STRING,  32,  6, 154, 12
     DEFPUSHBUTTON    "Ok",      IDOK,            44, 24,  32, 14
     PUSHBUTTON       "Cancel",  IDCANCEL,   114, 24,  32, 14
     }

DeleteDlg DIALOG 24, 24, 190, 44
     STYLE WS_POPUP | WS_DLGFRAME
     {
     LTEXT            "&Delete:", 0,              4,  8,  28,  8
     EDITTEXT                    IDD_STRING,  36,  6, 150, 12
     DEFPUSHBUTTON    "Ok",      IDOK,            44, 24,  32, 14
     PUSHBUTTON       "Cancel",  IDCANCEL,   114, 24,  32, 14
     }
```

STRPROG.H

```
/*----------------------
   STRPROG.H header file
   --------------------*/

#define IDM_ENTER    1
#define IDM_DELETE   2
#define IDD_STRING   0x10
```

STRPROG.DEF

```
;------------------------------------------
; STRPROG.DEF module definition file
;------------------------------------------

NAME            STRPROG

DESCRIPTION     'Program using STRLIB DLL (c) Charles Petzold, 1990'
EXETYPE         WINDOWS
STUB            'WINSTUB.EXE'
CODE            PRELOAD MOVEABLE DISCARDABLE
DATA            PRELOAD MOVEABLE MULTIPLE
HEAPSIZE        1024
STACKSIZE       8192
EXPORTS         WndProc
                DlgProc
                GetStrCallBack
                EnumCallBack
IMPORTS         STRLIB.AddString
                STRLIB.DeleteString
                STRLIB.GetStrings
```

Near the top of the STRPROG.C source code file are declarations of the three functions in STRLIB that STRPROG will call:

```
BOOL  FAR PASCAL AddString    (LPSTR) ;
BOOL  FAR PASCAL DeleteString (LPSTR) ;
short FAR PASCAL GetStrings   (FARPROC, CBPARM FAR *) ;
```

If you plan to use library functions in several different programs, you'll want to put the declarations in a header file. This header file will be similar to (although I hope not as long as) WINDOWS.H.

These three functions are also listed in the IMPORTS section of STRPROG's module definition file:

```
IMPORTS    STRLIB.AddString
           STRLIB.DeleteString
           STRLIB.GetStrings
```

These correspond to the three functions in the EXPORTS section of STRLIB.DEF. The IMPORTS section directs LINK to add information to STRPROG.EXE that allows Windows to dynamically link STRPROG's calls to these functions with the actual function routines in STRLIB.DLL. The EXPORTS section in STRLIB.DEF makes the functions in STRLIB.DLL available to other modules. The IMPORTS section in STRPROG.DEF indicates the module—STRLIB—and the functions in STRLIB that STRPROG requires.

Running STRPROG

Once you've created STRLIB.DLL and STRPROG.EXE, you're ready to run STRPROG. Before you do so, be sure that STRLIB.DLL is in the current directory or a directory that is listed in the PATH string of the MS-DOS environment. Windows must be able to load STRLIB.DLL when you execute STRPROG. If Windows can't find STRLIB.DLL, it will display a message box asking you to put the STRLIB.DLL disk in drive A.

When you execute STRPROG.EXE, Windows performs fixups to functions in external library modules. Many of these functions are in the normal KERNEL, USER, and GDI library modules. But Windows also sees that the program calls three functions from STRLIB, so Windows loads the STRLIB.DLL file into memory, creates reload thunks for the three functions, and calls STRLIB's initialization routine. The far calls within STRPROG to these three functions are dynamically linked with the reload thunks that branch to functions in STRLIB. You can then use STRPROG to add and delete strings from STRLIB's internal table. STRPROG's client area shows the strings currently in the table.

The calls from STRPROG to the *AddString*, *DeleteString*, and *GetStrings* functions in STRLIB are very efficient and have almost no overhead except for the reload thunk. In fact, the link between STRPROG and STRLIB is as efficient as if the three functions in STRLIB were simply in another moveable code segment in STRPROG. So what? you say. Why do I have to make this a dynamic link library? Can't I include these three routines in STRPROG.EXE?

Well, you could. In one sense, STRLIB is nothing more than an extension of STRPROG. However, you may be interested to see what happens when you execute a second instance of STRPROG. Because only one instance of STRLIB is loaded for both instances of the program, and because STRLIB uses its own local heap to store the character strings, all instances of STRPROG essentially share this data. (The *EnumCallBack* function in STRPROG serves to notify all STRPROG's instances that the contents of STRLIB's data segments have changed. *EnumWindows* causes Windows to call *EnumCallBack* with handles to all parent windows. *EnumCallBack* then checks to see if the class name of each window equals "StrProg"—if it does, the function sends the window a privately defined WM_DATACHANGE message.) And you can easily imagine an enhanced version of STRLIB managing a database that is shared by several instances of the same program or by single instances of different programs.

Far Function Prologs

In the discussion of memory management in Chapter 7, I went into great detail about how Windows moves code and data segments in memory and handles multiple instances of programs. Some of that discussion centered on the prolog that the compiler adds to far functions.

When Windows loads a code segment into memory, it alters the function prolog of all exported far functions in the segment. This table shows the results of that process:

Nonexported Far Function	Exported Function in a Program	Exported Function in a Library
PUSH DS	NOP	MOV AX, xxxx
POP AX	NOP	
NOP	NOP	
INC BP	INC BP	INC BP
PUSH BP	PUSH BP	PUSH BP
MOV BP, SP	MOV BP, SP	MOV BP, SP
PUSH DS	PUSH DS	PUSH DS
MOV DS, AX	MOV DS, AX	MOV DS, AX

These three prologs differ in the way that DS (the data segment address register) is set on entry to the function. In each case, the original value of DS is saved in the function prolog and restored in the function epilog.

The nonexported far function simply sets AX equal to DS and then DS equal to AX. This does nothing.

For an exported function in a program, Windows inserts NOPs in the first 2 bytes of the function. The resultant prolog then sets DS equal to AX. This prolog requires that AX be set to the data segment of the particular instance of the program. By itself, the function is incomplete. You must call *MakeProcInstance* for these exported functions so that Windows builds an "instance thunk" that sets AX equal to the data segment address of the instance. (The only case in which you don't need to call *MakeProcInstance* for an exported function is for a window procedure specified in a window class structure.)

The exported function in a library is somewhat simpler. Because the library can have only one instance, Windows can simply insert a 3-byte instruction that sets AX equal to the data segment address of the library. Thus, you don't need to use *MakeProcInstance* with exported far functions in library modules. When a program calls a far function exported from a library module, this prolog sets the data segment equal to the library's data segment. The library function can then use its own data segment. It continues to use the stack segment of the program that called it.

The Use of Call-Back Functions

Now that we know what these function prologs look like, let's examine what happens when STRPROG calls the *GetStrings* function. *GetStrings* requires a call-back function in STRPROG called *GetStrCallBack*.

Because *GetStrCallBack* is exported, Windows inserts NOPs in the first 2 bytes of the function when STRPROG's code segment is loaded into memory. While processing the WM_CREATE message, STRPROG calls *MakeProcInstance* for this function:

```
lpfnGetStrCallBack = MakeProcInstance (GetStrCallBack, hInst) ;
```

On return from *MakeProcInstance*, the variable *lpfnGetStrCallBack* points to code that looks like this:

```
MOV AX, yyyy
JMP GetStrCallBack
```

where *yyyy* is the data segment address of this instance of STRPROG.

STRPROG calls *GetStrings* to update its client area:

```
GetStrings (lpfnGetStrCallBack, &cbparam) ;
```

The *GetStrings* function is in STRLIB. The parameter *cbparam* is a structure containing information that *GetStrings* simply passes back to *GetStrCallBack*, which then uses the information to display the strings in the client area.

In STRLIB, the prolog to *GetStrings* sets AX equal to the data segment of the library, saves the current value of DS (the data segment of STRPROG), and sets DS equal to AX. Now the function can use its own data segment to obtain the strings currently stored. When it obtains a string, it calls the call-back function passed as a parameter to *GetStrings*:

```
bReturn = (*lpfnGetStrCallBack) ((LPSTR) npString, lpParam) ;
```

This actually calls the instance thunk for *GetStrCallBack* set up by *MakeProcInstance*. The instance thunk sets AX equal to STRPROG's data segment. The function prolog saves the current value of DS (the data segment of STRLIB) and sets DS equal to AX. Now *GetStrCallBack* is using STRPROG's own data segment and can process the string. When *GetStrCallBack* returns control to *GetStrings*, the function epilog restores the original value of DS, which is STRLIB's data segment. *GetStrings* is ready to find the next string.

When *GetStrings* is finished, the function epilog restores the value of DS to STRPROG's data segment. As you can see, although control bounces back and forth between STRPROG and STRLIB, each module is always using its own data segment. During this entire process, however, the stack segment never changes. It is always STRPROG's stack segment. For code in STRPROG, this situation is just fine. For code in STRLIB, it can pose some problems.

THE DS != SS ISSUE

The segmented architecture of the Intel 8086 family of microprocessors has been giving programmers grief for many years now. But nowhere does segmented architecture cause more problems than in Windows libraries. If you skipped the first half of Chapter 7, thinking that you'd never need to know about segmented architecture and the intricacies of near and far pointers, now is the time to read it. And even if you've read it carefully, you might still benefit from this quick review.

The Intel 8086 family of microprocessors operating in real mode can address 1 megabyte of memory. This memory is addressed by a combination of a 16-bit segment address and a 16-bit offset address. The 16-bit segment address marks the beginning of a 64-KB area of memory. The offset address is relative to the beginning of the segment. In protected mode, the segment address references a 24-bit base address in a descriptor table. The offset address is added to this.

The 8086-family microprocessors have four registers that contain segment addresses: the code segment register (CS), the data segment register (DS), the stack segment register (SS), and the extra segment register (ES). The instruction pointer (IP) always addresses code within the code segment. The stack pointer (SP) always addresses the stack within the stack segment. Registers that address data can do so relative to any of the four current segments. When programming in Microsoft C, 16-bit pointers that specify only an offset address are called near or short pointers, and 32-bit pointers that contain both a segment address and an offset address are called far or long pointers.

In C, all variables defined as outside functions (on the external level) and all variables defined as static within functions are stored in static memory. The compiler uses near pointers relative to the 8086 data segment (DS) to address variables stored in static memory.

All parameters to functions and all variables within functions that are not defined as static are stored on the stack. The compiler uses near pointers relative to the 8086 stack segment (SS) to address the stack.

When you use a near pointer in a C program, the pointer can reference a variable either in static memory or on the stack. The compiler has no way to determine whether the near pointer is an offset to DS or SS. For this reason, C programs are normally constructed to use the same segment for data and the stack. Simply put, DS == SS. This is almost required for a C implementation on 8086-family microprocessors, because C does not differentiate between pointers to static variables and pointers to stack variables.

Let's take an example. In a small-model or medium-model program, you can use the normal C *strlen* function to find the length of a string. The parameter to *strlen* is a near pointer to the string:

```
wLength = strlen (pString) ;
```

The string itself could be stored either in static memory or on the stack. You could define *pString* like this:

```
char *pString = "This is a string" ;
```

In this case, the string "This is a string" is stored in static memory, and the near pointer is relative to the beginning of the data segment. However, you could do something like this within a function:

```
char szString [20] ;
    [other program lines]
wLength = strlen (szString) ;
```

In this case, the *szString* array takes up 20 bytes on the stack. When you refer to *szString*, you're actually referring to a near pointer relative to the stack segment.

How does the *strlen* function know whether the near pointer is an offset in the stack segment or in the data segment? It doesn't. If you take a look at the assembly-language code for *strlen* in the SLIBCEW.LIB library, this is what you'll find:

```
_strlen   NEAR PROC

          PUSH BP          ; Prologue
          MOV  BP, SP
          MOV  DX, DI      ; Save DI

          MOV  AX, DS      ; Set ES equal to DS
          POP  ES, AX

          MOV  DI,[BP+4] ; Get DI ptr off stack
          XOR  AX, AX
          MOV  CX, -1
          REPNZ SCASB      ; Search for zero in ES:DI
          NOT  CX          ; Calculate length
          DEC  CX
          XCHG AX, CX

          MOV  DI, DX      ; Restore DI

          MOV  SP, BP      ; Epilogue
          POP  BP
          RET

_strlen   ENDP
```

The *strlen* function assumes that the near pointer is an offset in the data segment. It sets ES equal to DS using this code:

```
MOV  AX, DS
MOV  ES, AX
```

It then uses ES to scan the string for a terminating 0. To write a *strlen* function that would work with a near pointer in the stack segment, you would need to replace these lines with:

```
MOV  AX, SS
MOV  ES, AX
```

But you've never had to worry about this little problem in Windows programs, because DS equals SS.

Windows dynamic libraries are another story. The data segment is the library's own data segment, but the stack segment is the stack of the caller. That is, DS != SS. If you call *strlen* in a Windows library for a string that is stored on the stack, the function won't work correctly, because the *strlen* function assumes that the near pointer is relative to the data segment. When you first realize the implications of this, you're likely to assume that programming Windows dynamic libraries is very difficult. Let's just say that it's not quite as carefree a process as writing a Windows program, but the job certainly isn't impossible. After all, the bulk of Windows consists of dynamic libraries—the KERNEL, USER, and GDI modules.

At one time, the recommended practice was to use *no* normal C library functions within a dynamic library and to instead write your own functions. This restriction has now been loosened, and information is available to let you use C library functions intelligently. The conventions followed in the *strlen* function hold in most of the functions in the normal C library distributed with the Microsoft C Compiler: Most functions that accept pointers assume that the pointer is relative to the data segment; these functions do not assume that DS is equal to SS. Any C run time function that cannot be used in a dynamic link library is not included in SDLLCEW.LIB.

When you compile C source code for a small-model Windows library, include the switch -ASw, and for a medium-model Windows library, include the switch -AMw. These switches tell the compiler to assume that DS is not equal to SS. Nothing very magical happens here. The primary purpose of these switches is to alert you to possible problems in your code. For instance, within a function, you might define an array and a pointer:

```
int  array [3] ;
int  *ptr ;
```

If you say:

```
array [0] = array [1] + array [2] ;
```

the compiler uses SS to reference the elements of *array*, because the compiler knows that *array* is on the stack. However, you might have code like this:

```
ptr = array ;
*ptr = *(ptr + 1) + *(ptr + 2) ;
```

In the first statement, the compiler assigns the near address of *array* (which happens to be referenced from the stack segment) to the near pointer *ptr*. But when generating code for the second line, the compiler assumes that *ptr* references a variable in the data segment. That's wrong.

If you have a program with a construction like this and you compile with the -ASw switch and a warning level of 1 or 2, you'll get a warning message for the assignment of the *array* address to *ptr*:

```
warning C4058: address of automatic (local) variable taken, DS != SS
```

You can translate this message as: "You've assigned the address of a local variable on the stack to a near pointer. Future use of this near pointer will involve the data segment.

You've specified that you want the compiler to assume DS is not equal to SS. This assignment statement contradicts your intentions."

You can fix this by making *ptr* a far pointer, as follows:

```
int array [3] ;
int far *ptr ;

ptr = array ;
```

Now the compiler assigns the full 32-bit address of *array* (the stack segment and the offset) to *ptr*. You're safe in using *ptr*. Or you can make *array* a static variable:

```
static int array [3] ;
int *ptr ;

ptr = array ;
```

The compiler now assumes that *ptr* references data in the data segment; this is correct, because *array* is defined as static.

Don't assume that you'll always be alerted to problems like this. Here's another example. You have a function that sums up the first 100 elements of an integer array:

```
int sumup (int array [])
    {
    int i, n = 0 ;

    for (i = 0 ; i < 100 ; i++)
        n += array [i] ;
    return n ;
    }
```

If you call this function and the array happens to be on the stack, you're in trouble:

```
int array [100] ;
    [other program lines]
sumup (array) ;        /* A problem here */
```

This won't even generate a warning message, but it's obviously incorrect. How do you get around it? Use far pointers. Define the function like this:

```
int sumup (int far array [])
```

and call the function like this:

```
sumup ((int far *) array) ;
```

Or make *array* a static variable:

```
static int array [100] ;
    [other program lines]
sumup (array) ;        /* No problem here */
```

This is a better solution for an array of this size anyway, because it avoids putting 200 bytes on the calling program's stack.

You can avoid many of the DS != SS problems simply by not using stack variables and instead defining all your local variables as static. If you want to use stack variables for some items to save space in the data segment, you should avoid using the stack either for arrays or for any variables that require pointers. Finally, if you use pointers with stack variables, make them far pointers.

The parameters to a library function are always on the stack. If you need to use a pointer to reference a function parameter, use a far pointer.

OTHER LIBRARY RESTRICTIONS

The start-up code that is added to a Windows program during linking with LINK uses the registers passed to the program on entry, together with some DOS function calls, to set various global variables in the program's data segment. These variables allow programs access to the DOS environment and to other information. This start-up code isn't present in Windows libraries. For this reason, you can't use the *getenv* or *putenv* functions in libraries, nor can you use the following global variables defined in Microsoft C:

dosvermajor	_dosverminor_
osmajor	_osminor_
psp	environ
__argc_	__argv_

I mentioned earlier that a dynamic library module doesn't receive messages. However, a library module can call *GetMessage* and *PeekMessage*. The messages the library pulls from the queue with these functions are actually messages for the program that called the library function. In general, the library works on behalf of the program calling it, a rule that holds for most Windows functions that a library calls. The obvious exceptions are local memory allocation functions. As you saw with the STRLIB library, these functions use the library's local heap.

A library can allocate global memory for the program instance calling the library. The global memory blocks are automatically freed when the program instance terminates.

A dynamic library can load resources (such as icons, strings, and bitmaps) either from the library file or from the file of the program that calls the library. The functions that load resources require an instance handle. If the library uses its own instance handle (which is passed to the library during initialization), then the library can obtain resources from its own file. To load resources from the calling program's .EXE file, the library function requires the instance handle of the program calling the function.

Registering window classes and creating windows in a library can be a little tricky. Both the window class structure and the *CreateWindow* call require an instance handle. Although you can use the library module's instance handle in creating the window class and the window, the window messages still go through the message queue of the program calling the library when the library creates the window. If you must create window classes and windows within a library, then it's probably best to use the calling program's instance handle.

Because messages for modal dialog boxes are retrieved outside a program's message loop, you can create a modal dialog box in a library by calling *DialogBox*. The instance handle can be that of the library, and the *hwndParent* parameter to *DialogBox* can be set to NULL.

DIFFERENT METHODS FOR SPECIFYING LINKS

The module definition files for STRPROG and STRLIB show only one of several possible methods for listing functions to be exported from one module and imported in another. STRLIB's EXPORTS section looks like this:

```
EXPORTS    AddString
           DeleteString
           GetStrings
```

STRPROG's IMPORTS section refers to both the library module and the function names:

```
IMPORTS    STRLIB.AddString
           STRLIB.DeleteString
           STRLIB.GetStrings
```

Here's another method: The module definition file for STRLIB can assign "ordinals" to each of the functions. These are simply unique positive integers preceded by @:

```
EXPORTS    AddString      @1
           DeleteString   @2
           GetStrings     @3
```

STRPROG's IMPORTS section then references these numbers:

```
IMPORTS    AddString     = STRLIB.1
           DeleteString  = STRLIB.2
           GetStrings    = STRLIB.3
```

This method gives STRPROG a smaller .EXE file, because the file simply stores the ordinal numbers rather than the names of all the functions. For a large number of imported functions, this method provides a significant reduction in .EXE size. It's a little trickier to use than the first method, because you have to be sure you get the numbers right.

You can also use function names in the program that are different from those in the library. For instance, suppose that in STRPROG you use the names *AddStr*, *DelStr*, and

GetStr instead of *AddString*, *DeleteString*, and *GetStrings*. You can reference these aliases to the real function names in the IMPORTS section:

```
IMPORTS    AddStr = STRLIB.AddString
           DelStr = STRLIB.DeleteString
           GetStr = STRLIB.GetStrings
```

Or if the module definition file for STRLIB defines ordinals for each of the functions, the IMPORTS section will look like this:

```
IMPORTS    AddStr = STRLIB.1
           DelStr = STRLIB.2
           GetStr = STRLIB.3
```

Even if you don't explicitly specify ordinal numbers for the exported functions in the library module definition file, LINK assigns ordinal numbers to the functions. You can determine these ordinal numbers by running EXEHDR on the library module.

USING IMPORT LIBRARIES

I implied earlier that in writing your own library module, you're adding an extension to Windows—an extension that serves you in a manner similar to that of the standard KERNEL, USER, and GDI library modules. So, you ask, why do I have to list all the names of imported functions from my own dynamic libraries when I don't have to specifically import the KERNEL, USER, and GDI functions that I use? Well, in the early days of Windows programming (long before the introduction of the product), programmers had to do precisely that. They ended up with module definition files that looked like this:

```
IMPORTS    USER.RegisterClass
           USER.CreateWindow
```
        [etc, etc, etc.]

This process was simplified greatly by the use of "import libraries." Import libraries are much like object libraries in that LINK uses them to resolve function calls within a program. But the import library contains no (or very little) code, only a reference that reconciles the function name you use in your program with the library module containing this function and the actual function name. This is exactly what you do in the IMPORTS section of a .DEF file. An import library for STRLIB would allow LINK to know that a function call to *AddString* is really an imported function from STRLIB called *AddString* or an imported function from STRLIB with an ordinal number of 1.

When you link a Windows program or dynamic link library, the LIBW.LIB import library reconciles all the normal Windows functions you use in the program (mostly from KERNEL, USER, and GDI) and the ordinal numbers. That's why this import library must be specified in the library field of the LINK command line when linking. Think of it this way:

LINK has to resolve all calls that a program makes to external functions. It can do this in one of three ways: extract the function itself from an object library, get a reference to a library module name and function name (or ordinal) from an import library, or get a library module name and function name (or ordinal) from the IMPORTS section of the module definition file.

You can create an import library for a dynamic library module by running the IMPLIB program included with the Windows Software Development Kit. The syntax is:

```
IMPLIB libname.LIB libname.DEF
```

IMPLIB looks only at the EXPORTS section of the module definition file. It creates a file with the extension .LIB. After the import library is created, you can add normal object modules to the .LIB file using the LIB.EXE program included with the Microsoft C Compiler.

Figure 19-3 shows a revised make file and module definition file for STRLIB; Figure 19-4 on the following page shows a revised make file and module definition file for STRPROG. The new STRLIB make file creates an import library called STRLIB.LIB. In the STRPROG make file, this import library must be specified in the library field of the LINK command line. The new STRPROG.DEF file requires no IMPORTS section.

STRLIB.MAK

```
#----------------------
# STRLIB.MAK make file
#----------------------

strlib.dll : strlib.obj strlib.def
    link strlib libentry, strlib.dll /align:16, NUL, /nod sdllcew libw, strlib
    rc strlib.dll
    implib strlib.lib strlib.def

strlib.obj : strlib.c
    cl -c -ASw -Gsw -Ow -W2 -Zp strlib.c
```

STRLIB.DEF

```
;----------------------------------------
; STRLIB.DEF module definition file
;----------------------------------------

LIBRARY         STRLIB
```

Figure 19-3. *A revised make file and module definition file for the STRLIB library.* *(continued)*

```
DESCRIPTION    'DLL for STRPROG Program (c) Charles Petzold, 1990'
EXETYPE        WINDOWS
CODE           PRELOAD MOVEABLE DISCARDABLE
DATA           PRELOAD MOVEABLE SINGLE
HEAPSIZE       1024
EXPORTS        AddString      @1
               DeleteString   @2
               GetStrings     @3
```

STRPROG.MAK

```
#----------------------
# STRPROG.MAK make file
#----------------------

strprog.exe : strprog.obj strprog.res strprog.def
     link strprog, /align:16, NUL, /nod slibcew libw strlib, strprog
     rc strprog.res

strprog.obj : strprog.c strprog.h
     cl -c -Gsw -Ow -W2 -Zp strprog.c

strprog.res : strprog.rc strprog.h
     rc -r strprog.rc
```

STRPROG.DEF

```
;------------------------------------
; STRPROG.DEF module definition file
;------------------------------------

NAME           STRPROG

DESCRIPTION    'Program using STRLIB DLL (c) Charles Petzold, 1990'
EXETYPE        WINDOWS
STUB           'WINSTUB.EXE'
CODE           PRELOAD MOVEABLE DISCARDABLE
DATA           PRELOAD MOVEABLE MULTIPLE
HEAPSIZE       1024
STACKSIZE      8192
EXPORTS        WndProc
               DlgProc
               GetStrCallBack
               EnumCallBack
```

Figure 19-4. *A revised make file and module definition file for the STRPROG program.*

INTERCEPTING WINDOWS FUNCTION CALLS

One interesting use of dynamic libraries is in debugging. For instance, you might want to write a dynamic link library that extensively checks the parameters your program is passing to the normal Windows functions. Such a library for checking parameters to the GDI functions might be called CHECKGDI; a typical function in CHECKGDI.C would look something like this:

```
int xRectangle (hdc, xLeft, yTop, xRight, yBottom)
    HDC   hdc ;
    short xLeft, yTop, xRight, yBottom ;
    {
    BOOL  bError = FALSE ;
    int   iCode ;

        /* check parameters, set bError to FALSE and iCode
              to an error code if errors are encountered */

    if (bError)
        FatalExit (iCode) ;

    return Rectangle (hdc, xLeft, yTop, xRight, yBottom) ;
    }
```

You can give this function any name you want, as long as it isn't the same as the name of a real Windows function. (I've called it *xRectangle*.) The *FatalExit* function causes the debugging version of Windows to display a stack trace on a terminal attached to the COM1 port.

The EXPORTS section of CHECKGDI.DEF lists all these checking functions but gives each of them an external name that is the name of the actual Windows function:

```
EXPORTS   Rectangle = xRectangle @1
          Ellipse   = xEllipse   @2
          LineTo    = xLineTo     @3
```
        [and so forth]

You compile and link this CHECKGDI library in the same way as STRLIB. The creation of the CHECKGDI.LIB import library looks like this:

```
implib checkgdi.lib checkgdi.def
```

Now if you have a program in development that calls normal GDI functions, you can do parameter checks during run time by linking the program (I'll assume the program is called MYPROG) as shown below:

```
link myprog, /align:16, NUL, /nod /noe checkgdi slibcew libw, myprog
```

Because you have included the CHECKGDI.LIB library in the library field of LINK, any calls in your program to *Rectangle, Ellipse, LineTo,* and so forth will actually reference the *xRectangle, xEllipse,* and *xLineTo* functions in the CHECKGDI.EXE library. In CHECKGDI the functions perform the checks you want and then call the actual GDI functions.

Once you're done debugging, you can make the program call the regular Windows GDI functions simply by deleting MYPROG.EXE and relinking like this without the CHECKGDI.LIB import library:

```
link myprog, /align:16, NUL, slibcew libw, myprog
```

Now LINK will use LIBW.LIB to reconcile your GDI calls with the functions in the normal GDI module. Because this approach requires no changes to your program source code, it is a clean way of inserting debugging code between your calls to Windows functions and the actual functions.

DYNAMIC LINKING WITHOUT IMPORTS

Rather than have Windows perform dynamic linking when your program is first loaded into memory, you can link a program with a library module while the program is running. We used this technique in Chapter 15 when we had to call the *DeviceMode* function in a printer driver module.

For instance, you would normally call the *Rectangle* function like this:

```
Rectangle (hdc, xLeft, yTop, xRight, yBottom) ;
```

You can also call *Rectangle* by first defining two variables:

```
HANDLE  hLibrary ;
FARPROC lpfnRectangle ;
```

Now you set *hLibrary* to the handle of the library and *lpfnRectangle* to the address of the *Rectangle* function:

```
hLibrary = LoadLibrary ("GDI.EXE") ;
lpfnRectangle = GetProcAddress (hLibrary, MAKEINTRESOURCE (27)) ;
```

The *LoadLibrary* function returns an MS-DOS error code (less than 32) if the library file can't be found. In *GetProcAddress,* the second parameter is a number (27) that you convert to a far pointer to a string by setting the segment address equal to 0; 27 is the ordinal number of *Rectangle* obtained from the EXEHDR listing of GDI.EXE. Now you can call the function and then free the library:

```
(*lpfnRectangle) (hdc, xLeft, yTop, xRight, yBottom) ;
FreeLibrary (hLibrary) ;
```

For libraries in which the module definition file doesn't define ordinals for the exported functions, you can use the function name in the *GetProcAddress* call:

```
lpfnFunction = GetProcAddress (hLibrary, "FunctionName") ;
```

908

Don't use this method for linking to modules that use ordinal numbers for the exported functions. The names of the functions in a library remain resident in memory only if the module definition file doesn't include ordinals or if the keyword RESIDENTNAME is used with the functions in the EXPORTS statement.

Although this technique doesn't make much sense for the *Rectangle* function, it will definitely come in handy. You need to use it when you don't know the name of the library module until run time, as is the case with the *DeviceMode* function in the printer drivers.

The code above uses the *LoadLibrary* and *FreeLibrary* functions. Windows maintains "reference counts" for all library modules. *LoadLibrary* causes the reference count to be incremented. The reference count is also incremented when Windows loads any program that uses the library. *FreeLibrary* causes the reference count to be decremented, as does the termination of an instance of a program that uses this library. When the reference count is 0, Windows can discard the library from memory, because the library is no longer needed.

RESOURCE-ONLY LIBRARIES

Any function in a dynamic link library that Windows programs or other libraries can use must be exported. However, a dynamic link library need not contain any exported functions. What would such a DLL contain? The answer is resources.

Let's say you're working on a Windows application that requires a number of bitmaps. Normally, you would list these in the resource script of the program and load them into memory with the *LoadBitmap* function. But perhaps you want to create several sets of bitmaps, each set customized for one of the major display adapters used with Windows. It would make most sense to store these different sets of bitmaps in different files, because a user would need only one set of bitmaps on the fixed disk. These files are resource-only libraries.

Figure 19-5 shows how to create a resource-only library file called BITLIB.DLL that contains nine bitmaps. The BITLIB.RC file lists all the separate bitmap files and assigns each one a number. To create BITLIB.DLL, you need nine bitmaps named BITMAP1.BMP, BITMAP2.BMP, and so forth. You can create these bitmaps in SDK Paint.

BITLIB.MAK

```
#----------------------
# BITLIB.MAK make file
#----------------------

bitlib.dll : bitlib.obj bitlib.def bitlib.res
    link bitlib libentry, bitlib.dll /align:16, NUL, /nod sdllcew libw, bitlib
    rc bitlib.res bitlib.dll
```

Figure 19-5. *The BITLIB library.*

(continued)

```
bitlib.obj : bitlib.c
     cl -c -ASw -Gsw -Ow -W2 -Zp bitlib.c

bitlib.res : bitlib.rc
     rc -r bitlib.rc
```

BITLIB.C

```
/*-----------------------------------------------------------------
   BITLIB.C -- Code entry point for BITLIB dynamic link library
               (c) Charles Petzold,  1990
   -------------------------------------------------------------*/
#include <windows.h>

int FAR PASCAL LibMain (HANDLE hInstance, WORD wDataSeg, WORD wHeapSize,
                        LPSTR lpszCmdLine)
     {
     if (wHeapSize > 0)
          UnlockData (0) ;

     return 1 ;
     }
```

BITLIB.RC

```
/*---------------------------
   BITLIB.RC resource script
   ------------------------*/

1 BITMAP bitmap1.bmp
2 BITMAP bitmap2.bmp
3 BITMAP bitmap3.bmp
4 BITMAP bitmap4.bmp
5 BITMAP bitmap5.bmp
6 BITMAP bitmap6.bmp
7 BITMAP bitmap7.bmp
8 BITMAP bitmap8.bmp
9 BITMAP bitmap9.bmp
```

BITLIB.DEF

```
;------------------------------------
; BITLIB.DEF module definition file
;------------------------------------

LIBRARY         BITLIB

DESCRIPTION     'Bitmap DLL for SHOWBIT.EXE'
EXETYPE         WINDOWS
CODE            PRELOAD MOVEABLE DISCARDABLE
DATA            PRELOAD MOVEABLE SINGLE
```

The SHOWBIT program, shown in Figure 19-6, reads the bitmap resources from BITLIB and copies them to the clipboard. You can cycle through the bitmaps by pressing a key on the keyboard.

SHOWBIT.MAK

```
#----------------------
# SHOWBIT.MAK make file
#----------------------

showbit.exe : showbit.obj showbit.def
    link showbit, /align:16, NUL, /nod slibcew libw, showbit
    rc showbit.exe

showbit.obj : showbit.c
    cl -c -Gsw -Ow -W2 -Zp showbit.c
```

SHOWBIT.C

```
/*-------------------------------------------------------------
    SHOWBIT.C -- Shows bitmaps in BITLIB dynamic link library
                 (c) Charles Petzold, 1990
   -----------------------------------------------------------*/

#include <windows.h>

long FAR PASCAL WndProc (HWND, WORD, WORD, LONG) ;
```

Figure 19-6. *The SHOWBIT program.*   *(continued)*

```
int PASCAL WinMain (HANDLE hInstance, HANDLE hPrevInstance,
                    LPSTR lpszCmdLine, int nCmdShow)
     {
     static   char szAppName [] = "ShowBit" ;
     HWND      hwnd ;
     MSG       msg ;
     WNDCLASS wndclass ;

     if (!hPrevInstance)
          {
          wndclass.style         = CS_HREDRAW : CS_VREDRAW ;
          wndclass.lpfnWndProc   = WndProc ;
          wndclass.cbClsExtra    = 0 ;
          wndclass.cbWndExtra    = 0 ;
          wndclass.hInstance     = hInstance ;
          wndclass.hIcon         = NULL ;
          wndclass.hCursor       = LoadCursor (NULL, IDC_ARROW) ;
          wndclass.hbrBackground = GetStockObject (WHITE_BRUSH) ;
          wndclass.lpszMenuName  = NULL ;
          wndclass.lpszClassName = szAppName ;

          RegisterClass (&wndclass) ;
          }

     hwnd = CreateWindow (szAppName, "Show Bitmaps from BITLIB (Press Key)",
                          WS_OVERLAPPEDWINDOW,
                          CW_USEDEFAULT, CW_USEDEFAULT,
                          CW_USEDEFAULT, CW_USEDEFAULT,
                          NULL, NULL, hInstance, NULL) ;

     ShowWindow (hwnd, nCmdShow) ;
     UpdateWindow (hwnd) ;

     while (GetMessage (&msg, NULL, 0, 0))
          {
          TranslateMessage (&msg) ;
          DispatchMessage (&msg) ;
          }
     return msg.wParam ;
     }

void DrawBitmap (HDC hdc, short xStart, short yStart, HBITMAP hBitmap)
     {
     BITMAP bm ;
     DWORD  dwSize ;
     HDC    hMemDC ;
     POINT  pt ;
```

(continued)

912

```
      hMemDC = CreateCompatibleDC (hdc) ;
      SelectObject (hMemDC, hBitmap) ;
      GetObject (hBitmap, sizeof (BITMAP), (LPSTR) &bm) ;
      pt.x = bm.bmWidth ;
      pt.y = bm.bmHeight ;

      BitBlt (hdc, xStart, yStart, pt.x, pt.y, hMemDC, 0, 0, SRCCOPY) ;

      DeleteDC (hMemDC) ;
      }

long FAR PASCAL WndProc (HWND hwnd, WORD message, WORD wParam, LONG lParam)
      {
      static HANDLE hLibrary ;
      static short  nCurrent = 1 ;
      HANDLE        hBitmap ;
      HDC           hdc ;
      PAINTSTRUCT   ps ;

      switch (message)
          {
          case WM_CREATE :
              if ((hLibrary = LoadLibrary ("BITLIB.DLL")) < 32)
                  MessageBeep (0) ;

              return 0 ;

          case WM_CHAR :
              if (hLibrary >= 32)
                  {
                  nCurrent ++ ;
                  InvalidateRect (hwnd, NULL, TRUE) ;
                  }
              return 0 ;

          case WM_PAINT :
              hdc = BeginPaint (hwnd, &ps) ;

              if (hLibrary >= 32)
                  {
                  if (NULL == (hBitmap = LoadBitmap (hLibrary,
                                        MAKEINTRESOURCE (nCurrent))))
                      {
                      nCurrent = 1 ;
                      hBitmap = LoadBitmap (hLibrary,
                                        MAKEINTRESOURCE (nCurrent)) ;
                      }
```

(continued)

913

```
                    if (hBitmap)
                         DrawBitmap (hdc, 0, 0, hBitmap) ;
                    }

             EndPaint (hwnd, &ps) ;
             return 0 ;

        case WM_DESTROY :
             if (hLibrary >= 32)
                  FreeLibrary (hLibrary) ;

             PostQuitMessage (0) ;
             return 0 ;
        }
   return DefWindowProc (hwnd, message, wParam, lParam) ;
   }
```

SHOWBIT.DEF

```
;------------------------------------------
; SHOWBIT.DEF module definition file
;------------------------------------------

NAME          SHOWBIT

DESCRIPTION   'Program to show bitmaps from BITLIB (c) Charles Petzold, 1990'
EXETYPE       WINDOWS
STUB          'WINSTUB.EXE'
CODE          PRELOAD MOVEABLE DISCARDABLE
DATA          PRELOAD MOVEABLE MULTIPLE
HEAPSIZE      1024
STACKSIZE     8192
EXPORTS       WndProc
```

During processing of the WM_CREATE message, SHOWBIT gets a handle to BITLIB.DLL:

```
if ((hLibrary = LoadLibrary ("BITLIB.DLL")) < 32)
     MessageBeep (0) ;
```

If BITLIB.DLL isn't in the current directory or in a directory accessible through the PATH string in the MS-DOS environment, Windows displays a message box asking the user to insert the BITLIB.DLL disk in drive A. If the user presses Cancel, *LoadLibrary* returns an MS-DOS error code (less than 32), in which case SHOWBIT simply beeps.

SHOWBIT can obtain a handle to a bitmap by calling *LoadBitmap* with the library handle and the number of the bitmap:

```
hBitmap = LoadBitmap (hLibrary, MAKEINTRESOURCE (nCurrent)) ;
```

This returns an error if the bitmap corresponding to the number *nCurrent* isn't valid or if not enough memory exists to load the bitmap.

While processing the WM_DESTROY message, SHOWBIT frees the library:

```
FreeLibrary (hLibrary) ;
```

When the last instance of SHOWBIT terminates, the reference count of BITLIB.DLL drops to 0 and the memory it occupies is freed. As you can see, this is a simple method of implementing a "clip art" program that could load precreated bitmaps (or metafiles) into the clipboard for use by other programs.

Index

Note: Italicized page numbers refer to illustrations.

Special Characters

& (underlining) 339, 430

// (comments) 31

A

ABORTDOC 734

Abort procedure in printing 742–49

  banding and 766–67

  implementing 745

  operation of 744–45

  printing dialog box and 749, 753–54

ABOUT1 program 404–17

ABOUT2 program 417–31

ABOUT3 program 432–37

Accelerators. *See* Keyboard accelerator(s)

ACCELERATORS resource script statement 387

Active window 90, 135. *See also* Input focus

AddAtom 816

Address in memory 265

Alarm, preset 173

ALTERNATE polygon filling mode 571, *572*

Alt key

  character-set conversion using 131

  system keystrokes and 91–92, 93

Ami (software) 3

Animation 631–36

ANSI character set 127, *128*

  converting 129–31

  fonts and 128

ANSI_CHARSET character set 682, 686

ANSI_FIXED_FONT 655

AnsiLower 129

AnsiLowerBuff 129

AnsiNext 129

AnsiPrev 129

AnsiToOem 130, 131, 443

AnsiToOemBuff 130

AnsiUpper 129

AnsiUpperBuff 129

ANSI_VAR_FONT 655

AppendMenu 351–53, 363, 380

Apple Computer, Inc. 5

Apple LaserWriter Plus device *511*

Application modal windows 179

Application programs, interaction of GDI

  module, printer driver, and *718*

Application window, elements of 13

Arc 544, *562*

ARCS program 563–68

ArrangeIconicWindows 856

Arrow mouse cursor 134, 169

ASCII character set, standard vs. extended 125

ASCII code 107, 108

ASCII keyword option 388

Aspect ratio 660, 662, 686

  calculating 663

ASPECTX, ASPECTY, ASPECTXY 513

ASSERT.H 440

Assertion message box 440–41

assert macro 440

_astart 885

-ASw switch 885

Atoms 816–17, 835

Atom statement 816

Autosave feature 174

B

Background color 30, 53, 221

  in COLORS1 program 235–36, 237–38

  filling in line gaps and 549

  icons and 237–38, 311

  inverse 311

  multiple instances and 237

  OPAQUE mode 549, 573, 653

  setting 222, 653–54

  TRANSPARENT mode 573, 653

Banding technique 717, 762–71

  abort procedure and 766–67

  PRINT4 program illustrating 767–71

  RECT structures and 763–66

Bankline 287

Bank-switched memory 287

BEEPER1 program 180–83

BEEPER2 program 186–89

BeginPaint 37, 49, 496, 516, 520

Binary raster operation. *See* ROP2 codes for

  binary raster operations

Bit(s), transferring, with *BitBlt* 620–21

BitBlt 168, 615, 657

  color conversions of 629

  coordinates 618–19

  drawing bitmaps on display surface with

    621–22

  mapping mode conversions with 630

Charles Petzold

Charles Petzold is a freelance writer specializing in Windows and OS/2. He is a contributing editor to *PC Magazine,* where he writes about OS/2 programming in the "Environments" column. He has written articles about Windows and OS/2 for the *Microsoft Systems Journal* and is the author of *Programming the OS/2 Presentation Manager* (Microsoft Press). A new book, *The OS/2 Graphics Programming Interface,* is expected in 1991.

The manuscript for this book was prepared and submitted to Microsoft Press in electronic form. Text files were processed and formatted using Microsoft Word.

Principal word processors: Deb Kem and Judith Bloch
Principal proofreader: Shawn Peck
Principal typographer: Lisa G. Iversen
Interior text designer: Darcie S. Furlan
Principal illustrator: Rebecca Geisler-Johnson
Cover designer: Thomas A. Draper
Cover color separator: Rainier Color

Text composition by Microsoft Press in ITC Garamond Light with display type in Helvetica Black, using the Magna composition system and the Linotronic 300 laser imagesetter.

Printed on recycled paper stock.